29796

FOR REFERENCE

Do Not Take From This Room

Similes
Dictionary

Related Gale Titles

Allusions—Cultural, Literary, Biblical, and Historical: A Thematic Dictionary. 2nd edition. More than 8,700 literary, biblical, and cultural allusions and metaphors are identified by source in this dictionary. Entries are arranged alphabetically under more than 700 thematic headings.

Dictionary of Collective Nouns and Group Terms. 2nd edition. Furnishes definitions, usage examples, and source notes for 1,800 terms. Ancient phrases, general terms, modern punning terms, and terms of quantity and number are covered.

Idioms and Phrases Index. Contains over 400,000 entries identifying some 140,000 idioms, phrases, and expressions in the English language. Each entry guides users to one or more of 30 dictionaries that define the term.

Loanwords Dictionary. More than 6,500 words and phrases encountered in English contexts that are not fully assimilated into English and retain their foreign orthography, pronounciation, or flavor. Entries include the loanword, language of origin, and definition.

Modifiers. Presents some 16,000 English adjectives derived from, or relating to, over 4,000 selected common and technical nouns.

Mottoes. An extensive collection of more than 9,000 mottoes - familial, personal, institutional - from around the world and throughout history. Arranged under nearly 400 thematic categories with alphabetical indexes, each motto is identified as to source. Foreign mottoes are translated into English.

-Ologies and -Isms. A lexicon of more than 15,000 words containing such suffixes as -ologies, -isms, -ics, -cides, -phobias, -mancys, etc., that are not easily accessible in standard dictionaries. Words are arranged under thematic headings.

Picturesque Expressions: A Thematic Dictionary. 2nd edition. Explains 7,000 expressions. Entries give the expression, an explanation of its origin, its approximate date of appearance in written English, and, in most cases, usage notes and illustrative quotations.

Prefixes and Other Word-Initial Elements of English. For each of 3,000 common and technical prefixes, the dictionary gives examples of use, a description of its origin and meaning, and variant and related forms.

The Private Lives of English Words. Identifies and explains the etymologies of some 400 words that exemplify various processes of linguistic change. Most of these words have had their meanings drastically changed over the course of their history.

Slogans. This work collects more than 6,000 slogans, rallying cries, and other exhortations from such fields as advertising, politics, and everyday speech, and arranges them under appropriate thematic headings, along with a discussion of each slogan's origin and use.

Suffixes and Other Word-Final Elements of English. Provides definitions, usage notes, examples, and variant and related forms of 1,500 suffixes.

Similes
Dictionary

A Collection of More Than 16,000 Comparison
Phrases from Ancient Times to the Present
Compiled from Books, Folklore, Magazines,
Newspapers, Plays, Politics, Stage, Screen, and
Television and Arranged Under More Than
500 Thematic Categories

FIRST EDITION

Elyse Sommer, Editorial Director
Mike Sommer, Editor

Gale Research Company • Book Tower • Detroit, Michigan 48226

Elyse Sommer, Inc.

Editorial Director: Elyse Sommer

Editor: Mike Sommer

Consulting Editors: Dian Dincin Buchman, Ph.D.,
Paul S. Sommer, J.D., Esther Ratner, M.S.L.S.

Assistant Editors: Shirley Hass Fine, Michael Meyer, Ilse Vaughn

Gale Research Company Staff

Senior Editors: Annie M. Brewer, Linda Hubbard

Special thanks to Nancy Franklin, Marie Browne, Doris Lewandowski,
Prindle LaBarge, and the staffs of *Book Review Index* and *Library of Congress
Classification Catalogs*

Editorial Data Systems Director: Dennis LaBeau
PC Coordinator: Don Fuller

Production Manager: Mary Beth Trimper
Production Assistant: Patty Farley
Art Director: Arthur Chartow
Production Assistant: Linda A. Davis

Library of Congress Cataloging-in-Publication Data

Similes dictionary.

Bibliography: p.
1. Simile—Dictionaries.   I. Sommer, Elyse.
II. Sommer, Mike.
PN6084.S5S56   1988   082   87-36109
ISBN 0-8103-4361-4

The manuscript for this book was prepared on an IBM-XT with WordPerfect 4.2 and with
Productivity Plus and Electra-Find as enhancements.

Printed in the United States

Contents

Introduction

**The English language is like an enormous bank account
—Robert Claiborne**

Similes Dictionary brings together the similes from that vast and continually growing bank account into one comprehensive, timely, and easy-to-use inspirational guide and phrase finder.

Although used as a literary device and to lend color to daily conversation since time immemorial, the simile is not old in the sense associated with being old-fashioned. On the contrary, in an age that places a high premium on minimalism, the simile's effectiveness as a pithy and vivid word sketch makes it **as timely as tomorrow, as useful as a Swiss army knife.** It's more robust than a single word and more spontaneous than a formal quote.

Like a good picture, a good simile equals a thousand words when it comes to characterizing people, places, and ideas. Yet, its utility as a colorful language tool notwithstanding, the simile has not had an up-to-date book of its own, a lack which has caused many pithy examples to fall through the cracks unrecorded. Oliver Wendell Holmes, Sr. is a case in point. Only a few of the many similes that enlivened his medical lectures and conversations were put into a formal record. His biographer John T. Morse lamented this loss with a simile of his own: **They [the Holmes similes and other witticisms] have sunk away and disappeared like the raindrops which fall in the ocean.** This dictionary is a response to that lament and the formal outgrowth of a personal collecting habit.

To achieve comprehensive coverage, our selections span two millennia of more than 16,000 comparison phrases coined by more than 2000 famous and talented as well as little known and ordinary men and women. They include the simile in all its permutations—literary and colloquial, humorous and serious, original and derivative. Sources tapped include books; print, broadcast, and electronic media; stage and screen; plus, contributions from students, writers, friends, and colleagues.

In selecting similes from books, we tried to cover at least a representative number of titles. This highlighted the consistency or lack of it with which some authors use similes. For some a simile about similes by William H. Gass applies: **Similes dangle like baubles from me.** These consistent simile users include such writers from the past as William Shakespeare, Geoffrey Chaucer, Percy Bysshe Shelley, Algernon Charles Swinburne, and Edith Wharton; and contemporary authors like Norman Mailer, Truman Capote, T. Coraghessan Boyle, George Garrett, Flannery O'Connor, Eudora Welty, and Sharon Sheehe Stark.

Naturally, with such a large mass of material to choose from, it was necessary to cut down a few trees in order to more clearly see the forest. For a while we considered eliminating familiar expressions. However, while overuse has devalued many to cliches, they have a certain piquancy that lends itself to life-extending modifications ranging from extensions and perversions to unique new twists. Clearly, a book like this could not be considered comprehensive without including at least some of the more enduring colloquialisms, as well as their extensions and twists.

Comments from contributors and colleagues confirmed this decision; these include a writer who pointed out that familiar similes make great dialogue for certain characters and a crossword puzzle designer who needed easy access to cliches.

A question asked by many contributors, "must it contain the 'like' or 'as' to be acceptable?" also prompted the decision to include some entries illustrating a somewhat looser interpretation of the simile as a comparison than those made explicit with "like" or "as." Exceptions to the "like/as" rule include alternative introductory phrases such as:

> as if
> as though
> it was a bit like
> is comparable to
> akin to
> can be likened to
> not unlike
> is kind of like
> may be compared to
> similar to

Two other formats that depart from the traditional simile are sparingly represented: phrases in which "like" is implied and those in which "more" serves as a more emphatic substitute for "like."

The comprehensiveness criterion was also used to decide what information each entry should contain. This centered around context and attribution; to be specific:

1. Context. Because this is a phrase book, the sample similes tend to be more fragmentary than conventional quotes. To give the reader a better sense of how the simile was used, many entries include the descriptive frame of reference in parentheses or an explanation in brackets. In addition, comments were often added to explain the simile or show it in fuller context.

2. Attribution. Author attribution, though often difficult to pinpoint with absolute certainty, was considered a clear-cut must. On the other hand, the addition of sources for similes culled from books promised to detract from an uncluttered overview of the text as much as it might add. To offset this, whenever information about the source promised to add an extra dimension to an entry, an explanatory comment was added. Furthermore, there is a complete bibliography.

To achieve optimum timeliness, words in some examples from the past have been modernized, including some paraphrases to eliminate gender specific language. Such changes are always mentioned in a comment following the entry. As for selections from our era, these reflect the current trend towards more explicit language.

In applying the timeliness criterion to inclusion decisions, the selection process encompassed not only well-established writers but also newcomers and those with popular rather than literary reputations. An equally wide net was cast for selections from other sources, e.g. dialogue from popular television shows. Probably our most up-to-date sources included contributors on several computer bulletin boards.

In the final analysis, of course, the true criterion for a selection's timeliness depended on content and style. Some of the most poetic similes from the past now sound too flowery or dated. On the other hand, many a comparison made a century or more ago could have been made today.

To achieve easy accessibility to this dictionary's contents, the thematic category arrangement with extensive **See** and **See Also** cross references proved the ideal organizational approach. Because the simile is so frequently used to draw a graphic physical and character description, headings pertaining to these are significantly represented, often sub-divided into more specific headings. In addition to FACE(S), for example, readers will find categories for FACIAL COLOR; FACIAL DETAILS; FACIAL EXPRESSIONS, BLANK; FACIAL EXPRESSIONS, MISCELLANEOUS; and FACIAL EXPRESSIONS, SERIOUS. The simile maker's penchant for irony and disparaging remarks is also reflected in the headings. Besides a whole category of INSULTS, numerous synonyms lead the way to more. Many other headings encompass both positive and negative expressions, with the negative entries often outnumbering the positive ones.

A special feature, not found in other thematically organized reference works, are **See Also** cross references pertaining to individual entries rather than an entire category.

To satisfy our criterion for easy utility, the headings and cross references were thoroughly tested on potential users who were asked to search for a simile via a category heading. If the heading under which they looked was not the main heading or a **See/See Also** cross reference, we added their synonym to our list. When necessary, category headings were changed to more meaningful words.

Another utility feature, the Author Index, includes listings for the Bible, colloquialisms, proverbs, and also similes that do not have their own number but are part of a comment in another entry.

To sum up the editors' aims, we have tried to construct the most all-encompassing, useful, and interesting compendium of similes ever devised. We hope users will find the resulting book as helpful as we have tried to make it. Besides using it as an inspirational springboard for creating new similes or as a thesaurus, those who agree with George Orwell that you should never use a figure of speech you've seen in print, can use this book as an elimination guide. No matter how readers use the *Similes Dictionary,* we hope all will spend some time simply browsing through its pages for the casual pleasures it will yield. We would also remind all that the simile is just one device for language enrichment and should not be dragged into what is written or said indiscriminately. The key at all times is appropriateness to what is being described, as illustrated by this example from a review by *New York Times* drama critic Frank Rich:

> One long evening of evasions, as if the playwright were
> taking the Fifth Amendment on advice of counsel.

Rich, whose similes are unfailingly appropriate, used the above to describe a play about a blacklisted actor.

Finally, no book like this would be complete without acknowledging the collecting spirit of others. As the reference books listed in the Bibliography indicate, most have focused on proverbs and quotations that happen to include similes, as this dictionary happens to also include proverbs and quotations. This applies to books published before this century, as well as more contemporary references. Two notable exceptions are John Ray, whose simile-rich collection of proverbs was published in the seventeenth century, and Frank J. Wilstach, whose *Dictionary of Similes* was published in 1916.

The Wilstach book represents a serious and worthy effort to give the simile its just due. However, besides lacking the many fresh similes coined during the last seventy years, its key word organization makes it difficult to find anything unless you know exactly what you're looking for. Were Mr. Wilstach alive today, he would no doubt have a wonderful time perusing this updated and thematically organized dictionary, enjoying the many contemporary similes, looking through the older ones to see which have stood the test of time.

Many thanks are also due to the staff of the Hewlett-Woodmere Library and the New York State Library System through whom we were able to examine many out-of-print works that proved extremely fruitful, e.g.: Bohn's *Hand-book of Proverbs,* which encompassed Bohn's own collection as well as a complete reprint of the above-mentioned John Ray's proverbs; and the works of Josh Billings, Thomas Fuller, Jerome K. Jerome, and Walter Savage Landor.

Last, but by no means least, we thank the many friends, writers, and simile enthusiasts who learned about *Similes Dictionary* and contributed clippings, suggestions for authors with good simile potential, and similes from their own published and in-progress works:

> Alvin Boretz, John B. Drinks, John B. Drisko, Judith Clark-Reilly, Gerard Flynn, Dorothy Francis, Daniela Gioseffi, Larry Gottlieb, Ann Jasperson, Paul Kuttner, Dan P. Herod, Ruby E. McGreight, Newton E. Meltzer, Patterson Pepple, Harry Prince, Rochelle Ratner, Joe Sweet, and A. D. Winans.

Readers are invited to follow in their footsteps and send contributions and suggestions for the next edition to me, in care of Gale Research Company, Book Tower, Detroit, Michigan 48226.

Elyse Sommer

How To Use This Book

The *Similes Dictionary* is designed for the browser's enjoyment and inspiration and as a thesaurus for writers and speakers. Because many similes are complete little quotes, the book also serves as a quotation finder.

To best fulfill all these functions, the more than 16,000 entries have been grouped into 558 thematic categories, with 717 synonyms to ease and expedite access to them. The Table of Thematic Categories at the front of the book contains an alphabetical list that includes the subject categories, synonyms, and **See** and **See Also** cross references. All categories and synonyms with their cross references are also included in the text.

In keeping with the thematic principle, the entries within each category are arranged (and numbered) in alphabetical order. Alphabetizing is done letter-by-letter, except for articles (a, an, the) and text in parentheses or brackets. Cross references pertaining to the category in general appear after the thematic heading. Cross references specific to a single entry appear after that entry.

How to Locate Similes through the Subject Headings

Since this is a phrase book, most readers will be best served by searching through the thematic categories to find the phrases that interest them. Taking the thesaurus approach, turn first to the Table of Thematic Categories and go to a heading most likely to lead you to the similes that interest you. If you looked up ABILITY, you will find that it is a main heading and also a cross reference to a thematically related heading, ACCOMPLISHMENT. If you looked under ACCURACY, you would find it listed as a synonym, with a cross reference to the main heading, CORRECTNESS.

How to Locate Similes by Browsing

Taking the browser's approach, go right to the entries and let the thematic categories and cross references in the text guide you through your ramble.

How to Locate Similes by a Specific Author

If you're curious about who said what, turn to the Author Index and look up the categories and entry numbers for the author whose similes you want to see. If an author's listing includes many entries you can limit your search to just a few thematic categories.

How to Locate Familiar Similes

The search for a specific familiar phrase can often be narrowed down to similes from Shakespeare, the Bible, early writers and poets like Chaucer, Shelley, Swinburne, Tennyson and Longfellow. All can be tracked through the Author Index.

A second familiar simile category encompasses proverbs, proverbial comparisons and colloquialisms of unknown authorship. These too can be located through the Author Index which includes listings for Bohn's *Hand-book of Proverbs,* Bartlett's *Dictionary of Americanisms,* proverbs, and colloquialisms. Like the individual authors, they include the thematic categories and their numbers. Similes that appear in comment paragraphs have a (c) after the entry number.

Additional Source Information

The Bibliography lists the books and publications from which similes were culled. Entries are alphabetically arranged by author or editor. Anthologies without editors or with rotating editors are alphabetized by title.

Things to Bear in Mind When Reading the Entries

1. Spelling and punctuation in entries from printed sources are as they appeared there. The exception to this is words with spelling common only in England, e.g.: colour, favour, grey, honour, moustaches, odour which appear as color, favor, gray, honor, mustaches, odor.

2. Some similes contain modernized words and phrases but such changes are always called to the reader's attention, with the original form in a comment paragraph after the entry. The same holds true for dialectal words and phrases.

3. When the descriptive reference frame for a simile is not crucial to its meaning but would enhance reading or shed light on its use, a word or phrase preceding the simile is included in the entry. Such additional text is enclosed in parentheses. This keeps the focus on the simile and maintains the alphabetizing by simile system, e.g.:

(Gaze as) innocent as a teddy bear —Babs H. Deal

4. When additional text is in square brackets, the words are not the author's but were inserted for clarity by the editors, e.g.:

[School boys] frail, like thin-boned fledgling birds
clamoring for food —Sylvia Berkman

Words in parentheses or brackets may also appear in the middle or at the end
of an entry, e.g.:

> My efforts [to stir my husband out of a sense of doom] have
> been like so many waves, dashing against the Rock of Ages
> —Robert E. Sherwood

5. To enhance the browser's enjoyment and increase the book's utility, many
similes include brief comments. These can include any or all of the following:
information about the simile, its source, examples of variations, cross
references specific to that simile. The following comment appears after the
above simile: Sherwood wrote this simile for the character of Mary Todd
Lincoln in his play "Abe Lincoln in Illinois."

Table of Thematic Categories

In the following table, categories used throughout the text and synonyms that are cross-referenced to categories are combined in one alphabetic order.

ABANDONMENT
See Also: ALONENESS, BEARING, FRIENDSHIP, REJECTION

ABILITY
See Also: ACCOMPLISHMENT

ABSORBABILITY

ABSURDITY
See Also: DIFFICULTY, FOOLISHNESS, FUTILITY, IMPOSSIBILITY

ABUNDANCE
See Also: CLOSENESS, GROWTH, SPREADING

ABUSE
See: CRUELTY

ACCEPTABILITY
See: BELONGING

ACCESSIBILITY
See: AVAILABILITY

ACCIDENT
See: FATE

ACCOMPLISHMENT
See Also: ABILITY, CLEVERNESS, SUCCESS/FAILURE

ACCUMULATION
See: GROWTH, SPREADING

ACCURACY
See: CORRECTNESS

ACCUSATION
See: CRITICISM

ACTIONS
See Also: BEHAVIOR, CAUTION, LEAPING, JUMPING, MOVEMENT, VIOLENCE

ACTIVENESS
See Also: ALERTNESS, ENERGY, ENTHUSIASM, EXCITEMENT, MOVEMENT, PERSONALITY PROFILES

ACTORS
See: STAGE AND SCREEN

ADAPTABILITY
See: BELONGING, FLEXIBILITY/INFLEXIBILITY

ADJUSTMENT
See: HABIT, FLEXIBILITY/INFLEXIBILITY

ADMIRATION
See: FLATTERY, WORDS OF PRAISE

ADULTERY
See: MARRIAGE

ADVANCING
See Also: ENTRANCES/EXITS, MOVEMENT

ADVANTAGEOUSNESS
See Also: COST

ADVERSARY

ADVERSITY
See: FORTUNE/MISFORTUNE

ADVERTISING
See: BUSINESS

ADVICE
See Also: FRIENDSHIP, FUTILITY

AFFABILITY
See: AVAILABILITY, BEHAVIOR

AFFECTION
See Also: FRIENDSHIP, LOVE

AFFLICTION
See: HEALTH, PAIN

AFFLUENCE
See: RICHES

AGE
See Also: LIFE, MANKIND, YOUTH

AGGRESSION
See: PERSONAL TRAITS, VIOLENCE

AGILITY
See Also: MOVEMENT, SPEED, TURNING AND TWISTING, WALKING

AGITATION
See Also: EXCITEMENT, HEARTBEAT, NERVOUSNESS, TREMBLING

AGREEMENT/DISAGREEMENT
See Also: COMPATIBILITY, FIGHTING

AILMENTS
See: HEALTH, ILLNESS,

AIM
See: PURPOSEFULNESS

AIMLESSNESS
See Also: BELONGING, EMPTINESS

AIR
See Also: ATMOSPHERE

AIRPLANES
See: VEHICLES

ALCOHOL
See: DRINKING

ALERTNESS
See Also: ATTENTION, CLEVERNESS, SCRUTINY, WATCHFULNESS

ALIENATION
See Also: ALONENESS, REMOTENESS

ALIKENESS
See: SIMILARITY

ALIMONY
See: MARRIAGE

ALLURE
See: ATTRACTION

ALONENESS
See Also: ABANDONMENT

ALOOFNESS
See: PERSONAL TRAITS, REMOTENESS, RESERVE

AMAZEMENT
See: SURPRISE

AMBITION

ANGER
See Also: EMOTIONS, IRRITABLENESS

ANIMALS
See Also: BIRDS

ANIMATION
See: ACTIVENESS, ENERGY, ENTHUSIASM

ANNOYANCE
See Also: IRRITABLENESS

ANTICIPATION
See Also: HOPE

ANXIETY
See Also: EMOTIONS, NERVOUSNESS, TENSION

APATHY
See: REMOTENESS

APPAREL
See: CLOTHING

APPEARANCE
See: PHYSICAL APPEARANCE

APPETITE
See: HUNGER

APPRECIATION

APPROVAL
See Also: WORDS OF PRAISE

ARGUMENT
See Also: FIGHTING

ARITHMETIC
See: MATHEMATICS AND SCIENCE

ARM(S)
See Also: ARM MOVEMENTS, FINGERS, HAND(S)

ARM MOVEMENTS
See Also: HAND MOVEMENTS

ARMY

ART AND LITERATURE
See Also: BOOKS, POETS/POETRY, WRITERS/WRITING

ASTONISHMENT
See: SURPRISE

ATMOSPHERE
See Also: AIR

ATTENTION
See Also: ALERTNESS, SCRUTINY, WATCHFULNESS

ATTIRE
See: CLOTHING; CLOTHING ACCESSORIES; CLOTHING, ITS FIT

ATTRACTION

ATTRACTIVENESS
See Also: BEAUTY, DESIRABILITY, PHYSICAL APPEARANCE

AUTHENTICITY
See: REALNESS, TRUENESS/FALSENESS

AUTHORITY
See: POWER

AUTHORSHIP
See: POETS/POETRY, WRITERS/WRITING

AUTOMOBILES
See: VEHICLES

AVAILABILITY

AVARICE
See: GREED

AWARENESS
See: REALIZATION

AWKWARDNESS
See Also: MOVEMENT

BACHELOR
See: MEN AND WOMEN

BAD LUCK
See: FORTUNE/MISFORTUNE

BADNESS
See: CRUELTY, EVIL

BALANCE
See: REGULARITY/IRREGULARITY

BALDNESS
See Also: HAIR, PHYSICAL APPEARANCE

BARENESS

BARGAINS
See: ADVANTAGEOUSNESS

BARRENNESS
See: EMPTINESS

BASEBALL
See Also: SPORTS

BASKETBALL
See: SPORTS

BEACHES
See: OCEAN/OCEANFRONT

BEARDS
See Also: HAIR, PHYSICAL APPEARANCE

BEARING
See Also: FACIAL EXPRESSIONS, MISCELLANEOUS; LYING; PERSONALITY PROFILES; PHYSICAL APPEARANCE; POSTURE; SITTING; STANDING; WALKING

BEAUTY
See Also: BEAUTY, DEFINED; FACE; PHYSICAL APPEARANCE

BEAUTY, DEFINED

BEGINNINGS/ENDINGS
See Also: BIRTH, ENTRANCES/EXITS

BEHAVIOR
See Also: ACTION, LIFE, MANKIND, PROPRIETY/IMPROPRIETY

BELIEF
See Also: GOVERNMENT, MORALITY, POLITICS, RELIGION

BELIEVABILITY

BELONGING

BENDING/BENT

BENEFITS
See: ADVANTAGEOUSNESS

BEREAVEMENT
See: GRIEF, SADNESS

BEWILDERMENT
See Also: EMOTIONS,
STRANGENESS

BIBLE
See: BOOKS

BICYCLING
See: SPORTS

BIGNESS
See Also: FATNESS, PHYSICAL
APPEARANCE, TALLNESS

BIGOTRY
See: INTOLERANCE

BIOGRAPHY
See: BOOKS, WRITERS/WRITING

BIRDS
See Also: ANIMALS, INSECTS,
SINGING

BIRTH
See Also: BEGINNINGS/ENDINGS,
ENTRANCES/EXITS, DEATH, LIFE

BITTERNESS
See Also: ANGER, FRIENDSHIP,
LOVE

BLACK
See Also: COLORS; DEJECTION;
FACIAL EXPRESSIONS, SERIOUS;
GLOOM

BLESSEDNESS
See: FORTUNE/MISFORTUNE

BLINDNESS
See Also: EYE(S); EYE
EXPRESSIONS, BLANK

BLOOD
See Also: VIOLENCE

BLOOMING
See: GROWTH

BLUE
See Also: COLORS

BLUSHES
See Also: FACIAL COLOR, RED,
SHAME, SHYNESS

BOATS
See: SEASCAPES

BODY
See Also: AGILITY,
AWKWARDNESS, BODY ORGANS,
MUSCLES, FATNESS, PHYSICAL
APPEARANCE, SHOULDERS,
STOMACH, STRENGTH, THINNESS

BODY ORGANS
See Also: SEX, TONGUE

BOISTEROUSNESS
See: NOISE

BOLDNESS
See: COURAGE

BONDS
See: CONNECTIONS

BOOKS
See Also: READERS/READING

BOREDOM/BORING
See Also: DULLNESS, LIFE

BOUNCING
See: ROCKING AND ROLLING

BOUNDLESSNESS
See: CONTINUITY

BOXING AND WRESTLING
See Also: SPORTS

BRAIN
See: INTELLIGENCE, MIND

BRAVERY
See: COURAGE

BREASTS
See Also: BODY, BODY ORGANS

BREATHING

BREVITY
See Also: TIME

BRIGHTNESS
See Also: GLITTER AND GLOSS,
LIGHTING, SHINING

BRITTLENESS
See: FRAGILITY

BROWN
See Also: COLORS

BRUTALITY
See: CRUELTY, VIOLENCE

BUILDINGS
See: HOUSES

BURST
See Also: DISINTEGRATION, SUDDENNESS

BUSINESS
See Also: ADVERTISING, SUCCESS/FAILURE

BUSYNESS
See Also: ACTIVENESS, WORK

CALMNESS
See Also: PEACEFULNESS

CALUMNY
See: SLANDER

CANDOR
See Also: HONESTY

CAPABILITY
See: ABILITY

CAREFULNESS
See: ATTENTION, CAUTION, CORRECTNESS

CARELESSNESS

CARES
See: PROBLEMS/SOLUTIONS

CAUSE/EFFECT

CAUTION
See Also: BEHAVIOR

CELEBRITY
See: FAME

CENSORSHIP
See: CONTROL, CRITICISM

CERTAINTY

CESSATION
See: PAUSE

CHANGE
See Also: ENTRANCES/EXITS, PERMANENCE

CHAOS
See: ORDER/DISORDER

CHARACTER
See Also: PERSONAL TRAITS, REPUTATION

CHARACTERISTICS, NATIONAL

CHARITABLENESS
See: KINDNESS

CHARM
See: ATTRACTIVENESS

CHASTITY
See: VIRTUE

CHEAPNESS
See: COST, THRIFT

CHEEKS
See Also: BLUSHES, FACE(S), FACIAL COLOR, SKIN

CHEERFULNESS
See Also: BRIGHTNESS, GAIETY, HAPPINESS, SMILES

CHILDISHNESS
See: YOUTHFULNESS

CHILDREN
See Also: PARENTHOOD

CHIN
See Also: CHEEKS, FACE(S), MOUTH

CHOICES

CHURCHES
See: HOUSES

CITIES
See: CITY/STREETSCAPES, PLACES

CITY/STREETSCAPES
See Also: PLACES

CIVILIZATION
See: SOCIETY

CLARITY

CLEANLINESS
See Also: ORDER/DISORDER

CLEVERNESS
See Also: ALERTNESS

CLICHE
See: ORIGINALITY, MAXIMS AND SAYINGS

CLINGING
See Also: PERSISTENCE; PEOPLE, INTERACTION; RELATIONSHIPS

CLOSENESS
See Also: COMPATIBILITY, FRIENDSHIP

CLOTHING
See Also: CLOTHING ACCESSORIES; CLOTHING, ITS FIT

Thematic Categories

CLOTHING ACCESSORIES
See Also: JEWELRY

CLOTHING, ITS FIT
See Also: CLOTHING

CLOUD(S)
See Also: CLOUD MOVEMENTS, SKY

CLOUD MOVEMENTS
See Also: RAIN

CLUMSINESS
See: AWKWARDNESS

COLDNESS
See Also: RESERVE, REMOTENESS

COLLAPSE
See Also: DISINTEGRATION

COLORS
See Also: BLACK, BLUE, BRIGHTNESS, BROWN, GREEN, PINK, PALLOR, RED, WHITE

COMFORT

COMMONPLACE
See Also: FAMILIARITY

COMPASSION
See: KINDNESS, PITY

COMPATIBILITY
See Also: BELONGING

COMPETENCE
See: ABILITY, ACCOMPLISHMENT

COMPETITION
See Also: BUSINESS, SPORTS

COMPLACENCY
See: CONTENTMENT

COMPLAINTS
See: ANGER, CRITICISM

COMPLETENESS

COMPLEXION
See Also: SKIN, WRINKLES

COMPLEXITY
See Also: DIFFICULTY

COMPLIMENTS
See: FLATTERY, WORDS OF PRAISE

COMPOSITION
See: MUSIC

COMPREHENSIBLENESS
See: CLARITY

CONCEIT
See: VANITY

CONCENTRATION
See: ATTENTION, SCRUTINY

CONCISENESS
See: BREVITY

CONDEMNATION
See: CRITICISM

CONFIDENCE
See: SELF-CONFIDENCE, TRUST

CONFIDENTIALITY
See: SECRECY

CONFUSION
See: BEWILDERMENT

CONNECTIONS
See Also: CLINGING

CONSCIENCE
See Also: REGRET

CONSIDERATION
See: THOUGHT

CONSPICUOUSNESS
See: OBVIOUSNESS, VISIBILITY

CONSTANCY
See: LOYALTY/DISLOYALTY

CONTAGION
See: SPREADING

CONTEMPLATION
See: SCRUTINY, THOUGHT

CONTEMPT

CONTENTMENT
See Also: HAPPINESS, JOY

CONTINUITY
See Also: PERMANENCE

CONTROL

CONVERSATION

CONVICTION
See: BELIEFS

COOKERY
See: FOOD AND DRINK

COOLNESS
See: CALMNESS

COOPERATION
See: AGREEMENT

CORPORATIONS
See: BUSINESS

CORPULENCE
See: FATNESS

CORRECTNESS
See Also: TRUENESS/FALSENESS,
REPUTATION, MANNERS

CORRESPONDENCE
See Also: WRITERS/WRITING

COST
See Also: ADVANTAGEOUSNESS,
THRIFT

COUNSEL
See: ADVICE

COUNTENANCES
See: FACE(S)

COURAGE

COURTESY
See: BEHAVIOR, MANNERS

COURTSHIP
See: MEN AND WOMEN

COVERTNESS
See: SECRECY

COWARDICE
See: FEAR

COZINESS
See: COMFORT

CRAFTINESS
See: CLEVERNESS

CRAVING
See: DESIRE

CRAZINESS
See: MADNESS

CREDIBILITY
See: BELIEVABILITY

CREDIT

CRIME
See Also: DISHONESTY, EVIL

CRISPNESS
See: SHARPNESS

CRITICISM

**CRITICISM,
DRAMATIC/LITERARY**
See Also: WRITERS/WRITING,
POETS/POETRY

CROOKEDNESS
See: BENDING/BENT

CROWDEDNESS
See: CLOSENESS

CROWDS
See Also: CLOSENESS

CRUELTY
See Also: COLDNESS, EVIL

CRYING
See Also: GROANS AND
WHISPERS; SCREAMS

CUNNING
See: CLEVERNESS

CURIOSITY

CURSES
See Also: WORD(S)

CUSTOM
See: HABIT

DAMPNESS
See: DISCOMFORT

DANCING
See Also: AGILITY, INSULTS,
WORDS OF PRAISE

DANGER

DARING
See: COURAGE

DARKNESS

DAY
See Also: NIGHT, SLOWNESS,
TIME

DEATH
See Also: ADVANCING;
BEGINNINGS/ENDINGS; DEATH,
DEFINED; DEATH, FINALITY OF;
ENTRANCES/EXITS; SUDDENNESS;
TIMELINESS

DEATH, DEFINED

DEATH, FINALITY OF

DEBT
See: CREDIT

DECEPTION
See: TRUENESS/FALSENESS

DECISIONS
See: CHOICES

DECORATIVENESS
See: ATTRACTIVENESS

DECREASE

DEDICATION
See: ATTENTION

DEEDS
See: ACTIONS

DEJECTION
See Also: EMOTIONS, GLOOM

DELAY
See: LINGERING

DELIBERATENESS
See: PURPOSEFULNESS

DELIGHT
See: JOY

DEMOCRACY
See: FREEDOM, GOVERNMENT

DENIAL
See: BEHAVIOR

DENSITY
See: ABUNDANCE, THICKNESS

DEPARTURE
See: EXITS

DEPENDABILITY
See:
RELIABILITY/UNRELIABILITY

DEPLETION
See: DECREASE

DEPRESSION
See: DEJECTION, GLOOM

DESERTION
See: ABANDONMENT

DESIRABILITY
See Also: PLEASURE

DESIRE
See Also: SEX

DESOLATION
See: ABANDONMENT

DESTITUTION
See: POVERTY

DESTRUCTION/DESTRUCTIVENESS
See Also: DISINTEGRATION

DETACHMENT
See: REMOTENESS

DETERMINATION
See: PURPOSEFULNESS

DETIORATION
See: DISTINTEGRATION

DEVOTION
See: LOYALTY/DISLOYALTY

DEW
See: NATURE

DICTION
See: SPEECH PATTERNS

DICTIONARIES
See: BOOKS

DIETS
See: EATING AND DRINKING

DIFFERENCES

DIFFICULTY
See Also: FUTILITY,
IMPOSSIBILITY

DIGNITY
See: PRIDE

DILEMMAS
See: PROBLEMS/SOLUTIONS

DIPLOMACY
See: TACT

DIRECTNESS
See: CANDOR, STRAIGHTNESS

DISAGREEMENT
See:
AGREEMENT/DISAGREEMENT,
ARGUMENT

DISAPPEARANCE
See Also: BEGINNINGS/ENDINGS,
DISPERSAL, ELUSIVENESS

DISAPPOINTMENT
See Also: FACIAL EXPRESSIONS

DISAPPROVAL
See: CONTEMPT

DISASTER
See: FORTUNE/MISFORTUNE

DISCOMFORT
See Also: PAIN

DISCONTENT
See Also: DEJECTION, GLOOM

DISCORD
See:
AGREEMENT/DISAGREEMENT

DISCOURAGEMENT
See: DEJECTION
DISCRETION
See: CAUTION, TACT
DISCRIMINATION
See: STYLE
DISHONESTY
See Also: BELIEVABILITY,
CRIME, LIES/LIARS
DISILLUSIONMENT
See: DISAPPOINTMENT
DISINTEGRATION
See Also: DESTRUCTION
DISLOYALTY
See: LOYALTY/DISLOYALTY
DISORDER
See: ORDER/DISORDER
DISPERSAL
DISPOSABILITY
See: TRANSIENCE
DISSATISFACTION
See: DISCONTENT
DISSENSION
See:
AGREEMENT/DISAGREEMENT,
ARGUMENT FIGHTING
DISSIMILARITY
See: DIFFERENCES
DISTANCE
See: REMOTENESS
DISTINCTIVENESS
See: ORIGINALITY
DIVERSENESS
See Also: DIVERSENESS,
PERSONAL TRAITS
DIVORCE
See: MARRIAGE
DOCILITY
See: MEEKNESS
DOCTORS
See Also: PROFESSIONS
DOGS
See: ANIMALS
DOMINATION
See: POWER

DOUBT
See: TRUST/MISTRUST
DREAMS
See Also: AMBITION, HOPE,
SLEEP
DRINKING
See Also: EATING AND
DRINKING, FOOD AND DRINK
DRIVERS/DRIVING
See: VEHICLES
DRYNESS
DULLNESS
See Also: BOREDOM
DUMBNESS
See: STUPIDITY
DUTY
See:
RELIABILITY/UNRELIABILITY
EAGERNESS
See: ENTHUSIASM
EARS
See: FACIAL DETAILS
EARTH
See: NATURE
EASE
EASE (OPPOSITE MEANING)
See: DIFFICULTY
EATING AND DRINKING
See Also: FOOD AND DRINK
ECONOMICS
EDUCATION
See Also: KNOWLEDGE
EERINESS
See: STRANGENESS
EFFECT
See: CAUSE/EFFECT
EFFECTIVENESS
See: ABILITY, SUCCESS/FAILURE,
USEFULNESS/USELESSNESS
EFFORTLESSNESS
See: EASE
EGO
See: VANITY
ELASTICITY
See: FLEXIBILITY/INFLEXIBILITY

ELATION
See: JOY

ELEGANCE
See: CLOTHING, STYLE

ELOQUENCE
See: PERSUASIVENESS,
SPEECHMAKING

ELUSIVENESS
See Also: DIFFICULTY

EMBARRASSMENT
See: SHAME, SHYNESS

EMBRACES
See Also: KISSES, MEN AND
WOMEN, PEOPLE INTERACTIONS,
SEXUAL INTERACTION

EMINENCE
See: FAME

EMOTIONS
See Also: ANXIETY,
CHEERFULNESS,DEJECTION,
ENVY, FEAR, HAPPINESS, GLOOM,
HATE, JOY, LONELINESS, LOVE,
NERVOUSNESS, SADNESS, TENSION

EMPATHY
See: KINDNESS, PITY

EMPTINESS
See Also: ABANDONMENT,
ALONENESS

ENDURANCE
See: CONTINUITY, PERMANENCE

ENEMY
See: ADVERSARY

ENERGY
See Also: ACTIVENESS,
BUSYNESS, ENTHUSIASM

ENJOYMENT
See: PLEASURE

ENTHUSIASM
See Also: ENERGY, EXCITEMENT

ENTRANCES/EXITS
See Also: BEGINNINGS/ENDINGS,
DEATH, EXITS

ENTRAPMENT
See Also: ADVANCING; PEOPLE,
INTERACTION

ENVY

EPITAPHS
See: DEATH, PRIDE

EPITHETS
See: WORD(S)

ERECTNESS
See: POSTURE

ERRORS

ETERNITY
See: CONTINUITY

EVASIVENESS
See: ELUSIVENESS

EVENNESS
See: STRAIGHTNESS

EVIL
See Also: ACTION, CRUELTY

EXACTNESS
See: CORRECTNESS

EXAMINATION
See: SCRUTINY

EXCITEMENT
See Also:
AGITATION,ENERGY,ENTHUSIASM

EXERCISE
See: MOVEMENT, SPORTS

EXHAUSTION
See: WEARINESS

EXITS
See Also: BEGINNINGS/ENDINGS,
DISAPPEARANCE,
ENTRANCES/EXITS

EXPANSION
See: GROWTH

EXPECTATION
See: ANTICIPATION, HOPE

EXPENSIVENESS
See: COST

EXPERIENCE
See Also: KNOWLEDGE

EXPLOSION
See: BURST, SUDDENNESS

EYE(S)
See Also: EYES, BRIGHT;
EYEBROWS; EYE COLOR; EYE
EXPRESSIONS, MISCELLANEOUS;
EYELASHES; EYELIDS; EYE
MOVEMENTS

EYES, BRIGHT

EYEBROWS

EYE COLOR
See Also: BLACK, BLUE, BROWN,
EYE(S), GRAY, GREEN

**EYE EXPRESSIONS,
MISCELLANEOUS**

EYELASHES

EYELIDS

EYE MOVEMENTS

FACE(S)
See Also: CHEEKS; EYE(S);
FACIAL COLOR; FACIAL DETAILS;
FACIAL EXPRESSIONS, BLANK;
FACIAL EXPRESSIONS,
MISCELLANEOUS; FACIAL
EXPRESSIONS, SERIOUS; FACIAL
SHAPE; LIPS; MOUTH; PHYSICAL
APPEARANCE; SKIN; WRINKLES

FACIAL COLOR
See Also: BLUSHES,
COMPLEXION, COLORS, PALLOR,
RED, WHITE

FACIAL DETAILS

**FACIAL EXPRESSIONS,
BLANK**
See Also: EYE EXPRESSIONS,
MISCELLANEOUS

**FACIAL EXPRESSIONS,
MISCELLANEOUS**
See Also: EYE EXPRESSIONS,
MISCELLANEOUS

**FACIAL EXPRESSIONS,
SERIOUS**
See Also: EYE EXPRESSIONS,
MISCELLANEOUS

FACIAL SHAPE

FACTS
See Also: TRUTH

FAILURE
See: COLLAPSE,
DISINTEGRATION,
SUCCESS/FAILURE

FAITH
See: BELIEF, RELIGION

FAITHFULNESS/FAITHLESSNESS
See: LOYALTY/DISLOYALTY

FALL
See: SEASONS

FALLING
See: COLLAPSE

FALSENESS
See: TRUENESS/FALSENESS

FAME
See Also: GREATNESS

FAMILIARITY
See Also: COMMONPLACE

FAMILY
See: RELATIONSHIPS; PEOPLE,
INTERACTION

FASCINATION
See: ATTRACTIVENESS

FASHION
See: CLOTHING, STYLE

FATE
See Also: HELPLESSNESS, LIFE

FATIGUE
See: WEARINESS

FATNESS
See Also: BODY, INSULTS,
PHYSICAL APPEARANCE

FAULTFINDING
See: CRITICISM

FEAR
See Also: ANXIETY, EMOTIONS,
NERVOUSNESS

FEELINGS
See: EMOTIONS, PHYSICAL
FEELINGS

FEET
See: LEGS

FEROCITY
See Also: SCREAMS

FERTILITY
See: GROWTH

Thematic Categories

FERVOR
See: ENTHUSIASM

FICKLENESS
See: LOYALTY/DISLOYALTY

FICTION
See: STORIES

FIGHTING
See Also: ARGUMENTS

FIGURE
See: BODY

FINANCE
See: ECONOMICS

FINGERS
See Also: HAND(S)

FINISH
See: BEGINNINGS/ENDINGS

FIRE AND SMOKE
See Also: TOBACCO

FIRMNESS
See Also:
FLEXIBILITY/INFLEXIBILITY

FISHING
See: SPORTS

FITNESS
See: HEALTH

FLATNESS
See: SHAPE

FLATTERY
See Also: FRIENDSHIP, WORDS
OF PRAISE

FLAVOR
See: FOOD AND DRINK, TASTE

FLAWS
See: ERRORS

FLEXIBILITY/INFLEXIBILITY
See Also: HABIT

FLIGHT
See: DISAPPEARANCE, EXITS

FLIMSINESS
See: FRAGILITY

FLOWERS
See Also: NATURE

FOG
See Also: MIST

FOOD AND DRINK
See Also: EATING AND
DRINKING

FOOLISHNESS
See Also: ABSURDITY, FUTILITY,
STUPIDITY

FOOTBALL
See Also: SPORTS

FORCEFULNESS
See: POWER

FOREBODING
See: ANXIETY, FEAR

FOREHEAD
See Also: FACE(S)

FORGETFULNESS
See: MEMORY, MIND

FORGIVENESS

FORLORNNESS
See: ABANDONMENT, ALONENESS

FORMALITY
See Also: ORDER/DISORDER

FORTITUDE
See: COURAGE, PERSISTENCE

FORTUNE/MISFORTUNE
See Also: RICHES

FRAGILITY
See Also: WEAKNESS

FRANKNESS
See: CANDOR

FRAUD
See: CRIME, DISHONESTY

FRECKLES
See: FACIAL DETAILS, SKIN

FREEDOM

FRESHNESS

FRIENDLINESS
See: SOCIABILITY/UNSOCIABLITY

FRIENDSHIP
See Also: LOVE,
SOCIABILITY/UNSOCIABLITY

FRIENDSHIP, DEFINED

FROWNS
See Also: FACIAL EXPRESSIONS,
MISCELLANEOUS; LOOKS; STARES

FRUSTRATION
See Also: DEJECTION, EMOTIONS
FUN
See: PLEASURE
FURNITURE AND FURNISHINGS
See Also: HOUSES, ROOMS
FURTIVENESS
See: SECRECY
FURY
See: ANGER
FUTILITY
See Also: ABSURDITY, DIFFICULTY, IMPOSSIBILITY, USEFULNESS/USELESSNESS
FUTURE
See Also: ADVANCING, TIME
GAIETY
See Also: CHEERFULNESS, LAUGHTER
GAIT
See: WALKING
GARDEN SCENES
See: LANDSCAPES, FLOWERS, NATURE
GENEROSITY
See: KINDNESS
GENIUS
See: GREATNESS
GENTLENESS
See Also: KINDNESS
GESTURES
See: HAND MOVEMENTS
GIDDINESS
See: LIGHTNESS
GIFTS
See: KINDNESS
GLANCE
See: LOOKS
GLIMMER
See: GLITTER AND GLOSS
GLITTER
See: GLITTER AND GLOSS
GLITTER AND GLOSS
See Also: BRIGHTNESS, LIGHTING, SHINING

GLOOM
See Also: DEJECTION; FACIAL EXPRESSIONS, SERIOUS; SADNESS
GLORY
See: FAME, SUCCESS/FAILURE
GLOSSINESS
See: GLITTER AND GLOSS
GLUTTONY
See: GREED, EATING AND DRINKING
GOD
See: FORGIVENESS, RELIGION
GOLD
See: COLORS, MONEY
GOLF
See Also: SPORTS
GOOD HEALTH
See: HEALTH
GOODNESS
See: KINDNESS
GOSSIP
GOVERNMENT
See Also: LAW, POLITICS
GRACEFULNESS
See: AGILITY, BEAUTY
GRACIOUSNESS
See: BEHAVIOR, MANNERS
GRASS
See: NATURE
GRAVENESS
See: SERIOUSNESS
GRAY
See Also: COLORS, GLOOM, HAIR COLOR, SKY, WEATHER
GREATNESS
See Also: FAME, INTELLIGENCE, MIND
GREED
See Also: EATING AND DRINKING, ENVY
GREEN
See Also: COLORS, ENVY
GRIEF
See Also: SADNESS
GRINS
See Also: LAUGHTER, SMILES

GROANS AND WHISPERS
See Also: SIGHS

GROWTH
See Also: SPREADING

GRUMBLING
See: CRITICISM

GUILT
See Also: CONSCIENCE

HABIT
See Also: BEHAVIOR,
FLEXIBILITY/INFLEXIBILITY

HAIR
See Also: HAIR COLOR; HAIR,
CURLY; HAIR STYLES; HAIR
TEXTURE

HAIR COLOR
See Also: BLACK, BROWN, GRAY,
RED, WHITE

HAIR, CURLY
See Also: HAIR STYLES

HAIR STYLES

HAIR TEXTURE

HAND(S)
See Also: ARM(S), FINGERS,
HAND MOVEMENTS, HANDSHAKE

HAND MOVEMENTS
See Also: HANDSHAKE

HANDSHAKE

HANDWRITING

HAPPINESS
See Also: CONTENTMENT, JOY,
PLEASURE

HARDNESS
See: FIRMNESS, TOUGHNESS

HARD-HEARTEDNESS
See: CRUELTY

HARDSHIP
See: FORTUNE/MISFORTUNE

HARD WORK
See: AMBITION, WORK

HARMLESSNESS
See Also: INNOCENCE, KINDNESS

HARMONY
See: AGREEMENT,
COMPATIBILITY, PEACE

HARSHNESS
See Also: VOICE, HARSH

HASTE
See: SPEED

HASTINESS
See: CARELESSNESS

HATRED

HEAD(S)
See Also: HEAD MOVEMENTS

HEAD MOVEMENTS

HEALTH
See Also: PAIN

HEART(S)
See Also: AGITATION,
HEARTBEAT

HEARTBEAT
See Also: AGITATION

HEARTINESS
See: EMOTIONS

HEAT
See Also: WEATHER

HEAVINESS

HELPFULNESS
See: KINDNESS

HELPLESSNESS

HESITANCY
See: UNCERTAINTY

HILLS
See: MOUNTAINS

HISTORY
See Also: MEMORY, PAST, THE

HOCKEY
See: SPORTS

HOLLOWNESS
See: EMPTINESS

HOME
See: FURNITURE AND
FURNISHINGS, HOUSES, ROOMS

HONESTY
See Also:
RELIABILITY/UNRELIABILITY

HONOR
See: REPUTATION

HOPE
See Also: DREAMS

HORROR
See: FEAR
HOSPITALITY
HOSTILITY
See: ANGER
HOUSES
See Also: FURNITURE AND
FURNISHINGS, ROOMS
HOVERING
See: LINGERING
HOWLS
See: SCREAMS
HUMANITY
See: MANKIND
HUMILITY
See: MEEKNESS
HUMOR
See Also: CLEVERNESS,
LAUGHTER
HUNGER
See Also: EATING AND
DRINKING
HURRYING
See: SPEED, RUNNING
ICICLES
See: SNOW
IDEALS
See: BELIEFS
IDEAS
IDLENESS
See Also: SITTING
IGNORANCE
See Also: STUPIDITY
ILLNESS
See Also: HEALTH
ILL TEMPER
See: ANGER
ILLUSTRIOUSNESS
See: FAME
IMAGINATION
See: IDEAS
IMITATION
See: SIMILARITY
IMMEDIACY
See: SPEED

IMMOBILITY
See Also: DEATH, LYING,
POSTURE, SITTING, STANDING
IMPARTIALITY
IMPATIENCE
See: RESTLESSNESS
IMPERMANENCE
See: FRAGILITY, LIFE
IMPASSIVENESS
See: COLDNESS, REMOTENESS,
RESERVE
IMPOLITENESS
See: MANNERS
IMPORTANCE/UNIMPORTANCE
See Also: MEMORY, NECESSITY
IMPOSSIBILITY
See Also: ABSURDITY,
DIFFICULTY, FUTILITY,
OPPORTUNITY
IMPROBABILITY
See: IMPOSSIBILITY
IMPROPRIETY
See: PROPRIETY/IMPROPRIETY
INACCURACY
See: ERRORS
INACTIVITY
See: IDLENESS, IMMOBILITY
INAPPROPRIATENESS
See Also: BELONGING
INCISIVENESS
See: SHARPNESS
INCOMPLETENESS
INCONGRUITY
See: ABSURDITY
INCORRECTNESS
See: ERRORS
INCREASE
See: GROWTH
INDECISION
See: CHOICES
INDEPENDENCE
See: FREEDOM
INDIFFERENCE
See: REMOTENESS, RESERVE

INDIGNATION
See: ANGER
INDISTINCTNESS
See: VAGUENESS
INDIVIDUALITY
See: ORIGINALITY
INDOLENCE
See: IDLENESS
INDUSTRIOUSNESS
See: AMBITION, WORK
INEFFECTIVENESS
See: FUTILITY,
USEFULNESS/USELESSNESS
INEVITABILITY
See: CERTAINTY
INEXPENSIVENESS
See: COST
INEXORABILITY
See: STEADINESS
INFATUATION
See: LOVE
INFLATION
See: ECONOMICS
INFLUENCE
See: POWER
INFORMATION
See: KNOWLEDGE
INFREQUENCY
See: RARITY
INGRATITUDE
See: PARENTHOOD, SHARPNESS
INHERITANCE
See: PAST, THE
INJUSTICE
See: JUSTICE
INNOCENCE
See Also: HARMLESSNESS
INQUISITIVENESS
See: CURIOSITY,
QUESTIONS/ANSWERS
INSANITY
See: MADNESS
INSECTS
See Also: ANIMALS

INSEPARABILITY
See: CLOSENESS, FRIENDSHIP,
RELATIONSHIPS
INSIGHT
See: WISDOM
INSIGNIFICANCE
See: MEMORY,
IMPORTANCE/UNIMPORTANCE,
NECESSITY
INSTINCTIVENESS
See: NATURALNESS
INSULTS
INTANGIBILITY
See: ELUSIVENESS
INTELLIGENCE
See Also: MIND
INTEMPERANCE
See: DRINKING
INTENSITY
See Also: SHARPNESS, STARES
INTIMACY
See: CLOSENESS, RELATIONSHIPS
INTOLERANCE
IRONY
See: HUMOR
IRREGULARITY
See:
REGULARITY/IRREGULARITY
IRRITABLENESS
See Also: ANGER, NERVOUSNESS,
TENSION
ISOLATION
See: ALONENESS
JEALOUSY
See: ENVY
JEWELRY
See Also: CLOTHING
JOBS
See: WORK
JOKES
See: HUMOR
JOURNALISM
See: PROFESSIONS,
WRITERS/WRITING

JOY
  See Also: CONTENTMENT,
  HAPPINESS, PLEASURE
JUDGMENTS
  See: OPINIONS
JUMPING
  See Also: LEAPING; ROCKING
  AND ROLLING
JUSTICE
KINDNESS
  See Also: GENTLENESS,
  SWEETNESS
KISSES
  See Also: INSULTS
KNOWLEDGE
  See Also: EDUCATION, MIND
LANDSCAPES
  See Also: MOUNTAINS; NATURE;
  ROAD SCENES; SCENERY,
  MISCELLANEOUS; PONDS AND
  STREAMS; TREES
LANGUAGE
  See Also: SPEAKING, WORD(S)
LAUGHTER
  See Also: GAIETY, GRINS,
  HUMOR, SMILES
LAW
  See Also: LAWYERS
LAWBREAKING
  See: CRIME
LAWYERS
  See Also: LAW,PROFESSIONS
LAZINESS
  See: IDLENESS
LEAPING
  See Also: JUMPING, ROCKING
  AND ROLLING
LEARNING
  See: EDUCATION
LEAVES
  See Also: FLOWERS, NATURE,
  TREES
LEGS
  See Also: PAIN, PHYSICAL
  FEELING

LETTER-WRITING
  See: CORRESPONDENCE
LIBERTY
  See: FREEDOM
LIES/LIARS
  See Also: DISHONESTY
LIFE
  See Also: AGE; LIFE, DEFINED;
  MANKIND
LIFE, DEFINED
LIGHTING
  See Also: BRIGHTNESS, SHINING
LIGHTNESS
  See Also: SOFTNESS
LIGHTNING
  See: THUNDER AND LIGHTNING
LIKELIHOOD
  See: IMPOSSIBILITY
LIKENESS
  See: SIMILARITY
LIMBS
  See: ARMS(S), LEGS
LIMPNESS
  See: SOFTNESS, WEAKNESS
LINGERING
LIPS
  See Also: MOUTH
LITERATURE
  See: ART AND LITERATURE,
  BOOKS, WRITERS/WRITING
LIVELINESS
  See: ACTIVENESS, ENTHUSIASM,
  ENERGY
LOCALITIES
  See: PLACES
LOGIC
  See: SENSE
LONELINESS
  See: ABANDONMENT, ALONENESS
LONGING
  See: DESIRE
LONG-WINDEDNESS
  See: TALKATIVENESS

LOOKS
See Also: FROWNS, PHYSICAL
APPEARANCE, SCRUTINY, STARES

LOOSENESS

LOUDNESS
See: NOISE

LOVE
See Also: FRIENDSHIP; LOVE,
DEFINED; MEN AND WOMEN

LOVE, DEFINED

LOYALTY/DISLOYALTY
See: FRIENDSHIP, LOVE

LUCIDITY
See: CLARITY

LUCK
See: FORTUNE/MISFORTUNE

LUNACY
See: MADNESS

LUSHNESS
See: ABUNDANCE

LUST
See: DESIRE, SEX

LYING
See Also: BEARING,
BENDING/BENT, IMMOBILITY,
POSTURE, SITTING, SLEEP,
STANDING

MADNESS

MANIPULATION
See: POWER

MALICE
See: CRUELTY, EVIL, SLANDER

MANKIND
See Also: HELPLESSNESS, LIFE

MANNERS
See Also: BEHAVIOR,
PROPRIETY/IMPROPRIETY

MARRIAGE
See Also: MEN AND WOMEN,
RELATIONSHIPS

**MATHEMATICS AND
SCIENCE**

MATRIMONY
See: MARRIAGE

MAXIMS AND SAYINGS

MEANINGFULNESS
See Also: MEMORY,
IMPORTANCE/UNIMPORTANCE,
NECESSITY

MEANNESS
See: CRUELTY

MEEKNESS
See Also: MODESTY

MEETINGS
See Also: BEGINNINGS/ENDINGS;
PEOPLE, INTERACTION

MELANCHOLY
See: DEJECTION, GLOOM

MEMORY
See Also: PAST, THE

MEN AND WOMEN
See Also: LOVE, MARRIAGE,
SEXUAL INTERACTION

MERCY
See: KINDNESS

MERIT
See: VIRTUE

MERRIMENT
See: GAIETY, JOY

METHOD
See: PURPOSEFULNESS

MIDDLE AGE
See: AGE

MIND
See Also: ATTENTION; INSULTS;
MIND, DEFINED; THOUGHT

MIND, DEFINED

MIRTH
See: GAIETY

MISERLINESS
See: THRIFT

MISERY
See: DEJECTION, GLOOM

MISFORTUNE
See: FORTUNE/MISFORTUNE

MIST
See Also: FOG

MISTAKES
See: ERRORS

MISTRESS
See: MEN AND WOMEN

MIXTURE
See: CONNECTIONS

MOANS
See: GROANS AND WHISPERS

MODESTY
See Also: MEEKNESS, PERSONAL
TRAITS

MONARCHY
See: GOVERNMENT

MONEY
See Also: COST, GREED, RICHES

MONOTONY
See: DULLNESS, REPETITION

MONTHS
See: SEASONS

MOOD CHANGES
See: CHANGE

MOODINESS
See: GLOOM

MOON

MORALITY
See Also: BELIEFS, VIRTUE

MORTALITY
See: DEATH

MOTHERHOOD
See: CHILDREN, PARENTHOOD

MOTHERS-IN-LAW
See: PARENTHOOD

MOTIONLESSNESS
See: IMMOBILITY

MOTIVATION
See Also: AMBITION,
PURPOSEFULNESS

MOUNTAINS
See Also: LANDSCAPES, NATURE

MOURNING
See: GRIEF

MOUTH
See Also: CHIN; CHEEK; MOUTH,
OPEN/SHUT

MOUTH, OPEN/SHUT

MOVEMENT
See Also: ADVANCING, JUMPING,
LEAPING, ROCKING AND
ROLLING, RUNNING, TURNING
AND TWISTING, WALKING

MOVIES
See: STAGE AND SCREEN

MURDER
See: CRIME

MUSCLES
See Also: STRENGTH

MUSIC
See Also: SINGING

MUSTACHES
See Also: BEARDS, HAIR

MYSTERIOUSNESS
See: STRANGENESS

NAKEDNESS
See: BARENESS

NAMES
See Also: MEMORY

NARROWNESS
See: THINNESS

NATIONS
See: CHARACTERISTICS,
NATIONAL, GOVERNMENTS

NATURALNESS

NATURE
See Also: FLOWERS; LEAVES;
MOON; OCEAN/OCEANFRONT;
PONDS AND STREAMS; RAIN;
SEASCAPES; SKY; SNOW; STARS;
SUN; THUNDER AND LIGHTNING;
TREES; WEATHER

NEARNESS
See: CLOSENESS

NEATNESS
See: CLEANLINESS,
ORDER/DISORDER

NECESSITY
See Also:
IMPORTANCE/UNIMPORTANCE

NECK
See Also: CHIN, CHEEKS,
PHYSICAL APPEARANCE

NEED
See: DESIRE

NEGLECT
See: ABANDONMENT, REJECTION

NEGLIGENCE
See: CARELESSNESS

NERVE
See: COURAGE

NERVOUSNESS
See Also: ANXIETY, TENSION,
TREMBLING

NEUTRALITY
See: IMPARTIALITY

NEWNESS
See: FRESHNESS,
TIMELINESS/UNTIMELINESS

NEWS
See Also: GOSSIP, KNOWLEDGE

NIGHT
See Also: DARKNESS

NIGHTMARES
See: DREAMS

NOISE
See Also: IRRITABLENESS

NONSENSE
See: ABSURDITY, FOOLISHNESS,
IMPOSSIBILITY

NOSES
See Also: FACIAL DETAILS

NOSTALGIA
See: MEMORY, SENTIMENT

NOURISHMENT
See: FOOD AND DRINK

NOVELS
See: BOOKS

NUMBNESS
See: RESERVE

OATH
See: PROMISE

OBEDIENCE
See: MEEKNESS

OBESITY
See: FATNESS

OBJECTS, MISCELLANEOUS

OBLIVION
See: BLINDNESS, MEMORY

OBSCURITY
See: VAGUENESS

OBSERVATION
See: SCRUTINY

OBSOLESCENCE
See: TIMELINESS/UNTIMELINESS

OBSTINACY
See: PERSISTENCE

OBVIOUSNESS
See Also: CLARITY, VISIBILITY

OCEAN/OCEANFRONT
See Also: SEASCAPES

OCCUPATIONS
See: DOCTORS, LAWYERS,
PROFESSIONS

ODOR
See: SMELL

OLD
See: AGE

OPAQUENESS
See: VAGUENESS

OPEN/SHUT

OPENNESS
See: CANDOR

OPERA
See: MUSIC

OPINION
See Also: IDEAS

OPPORTUNENESS
See: TIMELINESS

OPPORTUNITY
See Also:
FORTUNE/MISFORTUNE,
IMPOSSIBILITY

OPTIMISM
See: CHEERFULNESS

ORANGE
See: COLORS

ORATORY
See: SPEECHMAKING

ORDER/DISORDER
See Also: CLEANLINESS

ORDINARINESS
See: COMMONPLACE

ORIGINALITY

OUT OF PLACE
See: BELONGING

OUTBURST
See: BURST

PAIN
See Also: HEALTH

PAINTINGS
See: ART AND LITERATURE

PALLOR
See Also: FACIAL COLOR, GRAY,
RED, WHITE

PARENTAL LOVE
See: PARENTHOOD

PARENTHOOD

PARTING
See: BEGINNINGS/ENDINGS

PASSION
See Also: DESIRE, LOVE, SEX

PAST, THE
See Also: HISTORY, MEMORY

PATIENCE

PATRIOTISM
See: BELIEFS

PAUNCHINESS
See: BODY, FATNESS, STOMACH

PAUSE
See Also: CAUTION

PEACEFULNESS
See Also: CALMNESS

PECULIARITY
See: STRANGENESS

PENETRATION
See: PERVASIVENESS

PENNANTS
See: OBJECTS, MISCELLANEOUS

PENSIVENESS
See: THOUGHT

PEOPLE, INTERACTION
See Also: CROWDS, FRIENDSHIP,
MEN AND WOMEN,
RELATIONSHIPS

PERCEPTIVENESS
See: ALERTNESS, SENSITIVENESS

PERMANENCE
See Also: CONTINUITY

PERPLEXITY
See: BEWILDERMENT

PERSISTENCE
See Also: CLINGING,
PURPOSEFULNESS

PERSONALITY PROFILES
See Also: PERSONAL TRAITS

PERSONAL TRAITS
See Also: DULLNESS

PERVASIVENESS
See Also: CLINGING

PHYSICAL APPEARANCE
See Also: ARM(S),
ATTRACTIVENESS, BEAUTY,
BODY, EYE(S), FACE(S), FATNESS,
HAIR, HAND(S), THINNESS,
UNATTRACTIVENESS

PHYSICAL FEELINGS
See Also: HEALTH, PAIN

PHYSICIANS
See: DOCTORS

PICTURES
See: ART AND LITERATURE

PINK
See Also: CHEEKS, COLORS,
FACIAL COLOR

PITY
See Also: KINDNESS

PLACES
See Also: CITY/STREETSCAPES,
INSULTS

PLAINNESS
See: SIMPLICITY

PLANNING
See: PURPOSEFULNESS

PLAYS
See: STAGE AND SCREEN

PLEASURE
See Also: GAIETY, HAPPINESS,
JOY

PLENTY
See: ABUNDANCE

POETS/POETRY
See Also: WRITERS/WRITING
POISE
See: BEARING
POLITENESS
See: MANNERS
POLITICS/POLITICIANS
PONDS AND STREAMS
See Also: NATURE, SEASCAPES
POPULARITY
POSSIBILITY
See: OPPORTUNITY
POSTURE
See Also: BEARING, BENT,
STRAIGHTNESS
POVERTY
See Also: ECONOMICS
POWER
POWERLESSNESS
See: HELPLESSNESS
PRAISE
See: FLATTERY, WORDS OF
PRAISE
PRAISEWORTHINESS
See: VIRTUE
PRAYER
See: RELIGION
PRECARIOUSNESS
See: DANGER
PRECISION
See: CORRECTNESS
PREDICAMENT
See: DANGER,
PROBLEMS/SOLUTIONS
PREDICTABILITY
See: CERTAINTY
PREJUDICE
See: INTOLERANCE
PREPAREDNESS
PRESENT, THE
PRESERVATION
See: PROTECTIVENESS
PRICE
See: COST

PRETTINESS
See: BEAUTY
PREVENTION
See: PROBLEMS/SOLUTIONS
PRIDE
PROBABILITY
See: CERTAINTY
PROBLEMS/SOLUTIONS
PROCRASTINATION
See: LINGERING
PROFANITY
See: CURSES
PROFESSIONS
See Also: DOCTORS, LAWYERS
PROFICIENCY
See: ABILITY
PROFUSION
See: ABUNDANCE
PROGRESS
See: GROWTH
PROLIFERATION
See: SPREADING
PROMISE
See Also:
RELIABILITY/UNRELIABILITY
PROMPTNESS
PRONUNCIATION
See: SPEECH PATTERNS
PROPRIETY/IMPROPRIETY
See Also: MANNERS
PROSE
See: POETS/POETRY,
WRITERS/WRITING
PROSPERITY
See: RICHES, SUCCESS/FAILURE
PROTECTIVENESS
See Also: WATCHFULNESS
PROTRUSION
See Also: BELONGING,
OBVIOUSNESS, VISIBILITY
PROVERBS
See: MAXIMS AND SAYINGS
PROXIMITY
See: CLOSENESS

PRUDENCE
See: CAUTION
PSYCHOLOGY
See: PROFESSIONS
PUBLIC OPINION
See: OPINION
PUBLIC, THE
See: POLITICS
PURITY
See Also: VIRTUE
PURPOSEFULNESS
PURSUIT
PUZZLEMENT
See: BEWILDERMENT
QUESTIONS/ANSWERS
See Also: PROBLEMS/SOLUTIONS
QUICKNESS
See: RUNNING, SPEED
QUIET
See: SILENCE
RAGE
See: ANGER
RAIN
See Also: WEATHER
RANTING
See: ANGER, SCREAMS
RAPIDITY
See: SPEED
RARITY
See Also: ORIGINALITY
RASHNESS
See: SPEED
READERS/READING
See Also: BOOKS
READINESS
See: PREPAREDNESS
REALIZATION
See Also: TRUTH
REALNESS/UNREALNESS
REAPPEARANCE
REASON
See: SENSE
RECOLLECTION
See: MEMORY

RED
See Also: BLUSHES, CHEEKS,
COLORS, HAIR, LIPS, MOUTH
REDUCTION
See: DECREASE, DISAPPEARANCE
REFLECTION
See: THOUGHT
REFORM
See: CHANGE
REGRET
See Also: CONSCIENCE
REGULARITY/IRREGULARITY
REJECTION
See Also: ABANDONMENT
RELATIONSHIPS
See Also: MARRIAGE; MEN AND
WOMEN; PARENTHOOD; PEOPLE,
INTERACTION
RELENTLESSNESS
See: PERSISTENCE
RELIABILITY/UNRELIABILITY
See Also: FIRMNESS, STEADINESS
RELIEF
See: EMOTIONS
RELIGION
See Also: BELIEFS
REMEDY
See: PROBLEMS/SOLUTIONS
REMEMBRANCE
See: MEMORY; PAST, THE
REMORSE
See: REGRET
REMOTENESS
See Also: RESERVE
RENOWN
See: FAME
REPETITION
See Also: CONTINUITY,
DULLNESS
REPUTATION
RESENTMENT
See: ANGER
RESERVE
See Also: EMOTIONS,
PERSONALITY TRAITS,
REMOTENESS

RESIGNATION
See: MEEKNESS
RESPONSE
See: QUESTIONS/ANSWERS,
WORD(S)
RESPONSIBILITY
See:
RELIABILITY/UNRELIABILITY
RESTLESSNESS
RESTRAINT
See: CONFINEMENT, EMOTIONS
RESULTS
See: CAUSE/EFFECT
RETREAT
See: DISAPPEARANCE, EXITS
RETURN
See: PAST, THE; REAPPEARANCE
REVELRY
See: GAIETY
REVENGE
See Also: BITTERNESS
REVOLUTIONS
See: POLITICS
RHETORIC
See: SPEECHMAKING, WORD(S)
RICHES
See Also: ABUNDANCE,
FORTUNE/MISFORTUNE, MONEY,
SUCCESS/FAILURE
RICHNESS
RIDICULE
See: INSULTS
RIDICULOUSNESS
See: ABSURDITY, FOOLISHNESS,
IMPOSSIBILITY
RIGHTEOUSNESS
See: JUSTICE, VIRTUE
RIGHTNESS
See: CORRECTNESS,
TRUENESS/FALSENESS
RISING
See Also: BEARING, STANDING
RISK
See Also: DANGER
RIVERS
See: PONDS AND STREAMS

ROAD SCENES
See Also: NOISE, VEHICLES
ROARS
See Also: NOISE, SCREAMS
ROBBERY
See: DISHONESTY
ROCKING AND ROLLING
See Also: MOVEMENT,
UNSTEADINESS, VIBRATION
ROMANCE
See: LOVE, MEN AND WOMEN
ROOMS
See Also: FURNITURE AND
FURNISHINGS, HOUSES
ROUNDNESS
See: SHAPE
ROWDINESS
See: NOISE
RUDENESS
See: MANNERS
RUMOR
See: GOSSIP
RUNNING
See Also: MOVEMENT, SPEED
RUTHLESSNESS
See: CRUELTY
SADNESS
See Also: DEJECTION, EMOTIONS,
GLOOM, GRIEF
SAFETY
See Also: DANGER, RISK
SALES
See: SUCCESS/FAILURE
SARCASM
See: HUMOR
SATISFACTION
See: CONTENTMENT
SAYINGS
See: MAXIMS AND SAYINGS
SCANDAL
See: REPUTATION, SHAME
SCARCITY
See: RARITY
SCARS
See: FACIAL DETAILS

SCATTERING
See: DISPERSAL

SCIENCE
See: MATHEMATICS AND
SCIENCE

SCOWLS
See: FROWNS

SCREAMS
See Also: NOISE, ROARS

SCRUPULOUSNESS
See: CORRECTNESS

SCRUTINY
See Also: INTENSITY

SEASCAPES
See Also: NATURE,
OCEAN/OCEANFRONT, PONDS
AND STREAMS

SEASONS

SECRECY

SEDATENESS
See: SERIOUSNESS

SELF-CONFIDENCE
See Also: PRIDE, VANITY

SELF-CONSCIOUSNESS
See: DISCOMFORT,NATURALNESS

SELFISHNESS

SELLING
See: BUSINESS

SENSATIONS
See: EMOTIONS

SENSE
See Also: INTELLIGENCE

SENSELESSNESS
See: ABSURDITY

SENSITIVENESS
See Also: KINDNESS

SENTIMENT

SEPARATION
See: BEGINNINGS/ENDINGS

SERENITY
See: PEACEFULNESS

SERIOUSNESS

SERMONS
See: SPEECHMAKING

SERVILITY
See: MEEKNESS

SEX
See Also: ATTRACTIVENESS, MEN
AND WOMEN, SEXUAL
INTERACTION

SEXUAL INTERACTION
See Also: INSULTS

SEXUALITY
See: SEX

SHADOW

SHALLOWNESS
See:
IMPORTANCE/UNIMPORTANCE

SHAME
See Also: BLUSHES

SHAPE

SHARPNESS
See Also: PAIN, PARENTHOOD

SHINING
See Also: BRIGHTNESS; GLITTER
AND GLOSS

SHOCK
See Also: CAUSE/EFFECT,
SURPRISE

SHOULDERS
See Also: BODY

SHOUTS
See: SCREAMS

SHREWDNESS
See: CLEVERNESS

SHRIEKS
See Also: SCREAMS

SHUT
See: OPEN/SHUT

SHYNESS
See Also: MEEKNESS, PERSONAL
TRAITS

SICKNESS
See: ILLNESS

SIDEBURNS
See: BEARDS

SIGHS
See Also: GROANS AND
WHISPERS

SIGNIFICANCE
See:
IMPORTANCE/UNIMPORTANCE
SILENCE
See Also: SECRECY
SILLINESS
See: ABSURDITY, FOOLISHNESS,
IMPOSSIBILITY, STUPIDITY
SIMILARITY
See Also: DISSIMILARITIES
SIMILES
See: MAXIMS AND SAYINGS
SIMPLICITY
See Also: EASE
SIN
See: EVIL
SINCERITY
See: CANDOR
SINGING
See Also: MUSIC
SITTING
See Also: BEARING, IMMOBILITY
SKEPTICISM
See: TRUST/MISTRUST
SKILLS
See: ABILITY, ACCOMPLISHMENT
SKIN
See Also: BALDNESS,
COMPLEXION, FACIAL COLOR,
FACIAL DETAILS, PALLOR,
WRINKLES
SKY
See Also: CLOUD(S), MOON, SKY
COLOR
SKY COLOR
SLANDER
SLEEP
See Also: DREAMS, SNORES
SLIGHTNESS
See: WEAKNESS
SLIMNESS
See: THINNESS
SLOPPINESS
See: CARELESSNESS,
ORDER/DISORDER

SLOWNESS
See Also: MOVEMENT
SMALLNESS
SMELL
See Also: AIR, SWEAT
SMILES
See Also: BRIGHTNESS, FACIAL
EXPRESSIONS, MISCELLANEOUS,
GRINS, LAUGHTER
SMOKE
See: FIRE AND SMOKE
SMOKING
See: TOBACCO
SMOOTHNESS
SNORES
See Also: SLEEP
SNOW
See Also: NATURE, WEATHER
SNOWFLAKES
See: SNOW, WEATHER
SOAP OPERA
See: STAGE AND SCREEN
SOCIABILITY/UNSOCIABILITY
See Also: BEHAVIOR
SOCIETY
SOFTNESS
SOLIDITY
See: FIRMNESS, STEADINESS,
STRENGTH
SOLITUDE
See: ALONENESS
SORROW
See: GRIEF
SOUL
SOUNDNESS
See: HEALTH
SOUNDS
See: NOISE
SPEAKING
See Also: CONVERSATION,
SPEECH PATTERNS,
TALKATIVENESS
SPEECHLESSNESS
See: SILENCE

SPEECHMAKING

SPEECH PATTERNS

SPEED
See Also: RUNNING

SPIRIT
See: COURAGE

SPOILAGE
See: DISINTEGRATION

SPONTANEITY
See: NATURALNESS

SPORTS
See Also: BASEBALL, BOXING
AND WRESTLING, FOOTBALL,
GOLF

SPREADING
See Also: GROWTH,
PERVASIVENESS

SPRIGHTLINESS
See: ACTIVENESS

SPRING
See: SEASONS

STAGE AND SCREEN

STALENESS
See Also:
TIMELINESS/UNTIMELINESS

STANDING
See Also: BEARING, IMMOBILITY,
PERSONAL PROFILES, POSTURE

STARES
See Also: FROWNS, LOOKS

STARS

STARTING AND STOPPING
See: BEGINNINGS/ENDINGS,
PAUSE

STATELINESS
See: BEARING

STATISTICS
See: FACTS

STEADINESS
See Also: FIRMNESS

STEALTH
See: SECRECY

STERILITY
See: EMPTINESS

STICKINESS
See: CLINGING

STIFFNESS
See: PAIN, PHYSICAL FEELINGS

STILLNESS
See: IMMOBILITY,
PEACEFULNESS, SILENCE

STINGINESS
See: THRIFT

STOMACH
See Also: BODY, FATNESS,
SHAPE, THINNESS

STOP
See: PAUSE

STORIES
See Also: BOOKS,
WRITERS/WRITING

STRAIGHTNESS
See Also: POSTURE

STRANGENESS

STREAMS
See: PONDS AND STREAMS

STREETSCAPES
See: CITY/STREETSCAPES

STRENGTH
See Also: BODY, COURAGE,
MUSCLES, TOUGHNESS

STRUGGLE
See Also: BEHAVIOR, FUTILITY,
LIFE

STUBBORNNESS
See: PERSISTENCE

STUDENTS
See: EDUCATION

STUPIDITY
See Also: ABSURDITY,
DULLNESS, FOOLISHNESS,
INSULTS, MIND

STURDINESS
See: FIRMNESS, STRENGTH

STYLE
See Also: CLOTHING

SUBSERVIENCE
See: MEEKNESS

SUBTLETY
See: TACT

Thematic Categories

SUCCESS/FAILURE
See Also: BUSINESS; GROWTH;
PAST, THE
SUDDENNESS
See Also: ENTRANCES/EXITS,
SHOCK, SURPRISE
SUMMER
See: SEASONS
SUN
See Also: MOON, SKY, SUNSET
SUNSET
SUPERFLUOUSNESS
See: NECESSITY
SURPRISE
See Also: SHOCK, SUDDENNESS
SURVIVAL
See: IMPOSSIBILITY,
SUCCESS/FAILURE
SUSPENSE
See: EXCITEMENT
SUSPICION
See: TRUST/MISTRUST
SWEARING
See: CURSES, WORD(S)
SWEAT
See Also: SMELLS
SWEETNESS
See Also: PLEASURE, TASTE
SWIMMING
See: SPORTS
SYMMETRY
See:
REGULARITY/IRREGULARITY
SYMPATHY
See: KINDNESS, PITY
TACT
See Also: INSULTS
TALENT
See: ABILITY, ACCOMPLISHMENT
TALKATIVENESS
See Also: CONVERSATION
TALLNESS
TASTE
TEACHING/TEACHERS
See: EDUCATION

TEARS
See Also: CRYING
TEDIUM
See: BOREDOM, DULLNESS,
REPETITION
TEETH
TEMPER
See: ANGER
TEMPERAMENT
See: PERSONAL TRAITS
TEMPTATION
See: ATTRACTION
TENACITY
See: PERSISTENCE
TENDERNESS
See: AFFECTION, GENTLENESS,
KINDNESS, LOVE
TENNIS
See: SPORTS
TENSION
See Also: ANXIETY,
NERVOUSNESS
TENTATIVENESS
See: UNCERTAINTY
TERROR
See: FEAR
THEATER
See: STAGE AND SCREEN
THEORIES
See: IDEAS
THICKNESS
See Also: ABUNDANCE
THIGHS
See: LEGS
THINNESS
See Also: BODY
THOUGHTS
See Also: IDEAS, INTELLIGENCE
THREATS
See: VIOLENCE
THRIFT
THROAT
See: NECK
THUNDER AND LIGHTNING
See Also: NATURE, WEATHER

TIDINESS
See: ORDER/DISORDER
TIGHTNESS
See: FIRMNESS, TENSION, THRIFT
TIME
See Also: DAY, DEATH, LIFE,
LIFE, NIGHTS, SLOWNESS, SPEED
TIMELESSNESS
See: TIMELINESS/UNTIMELINESS
TIMELINESS/UNTIMELINESS
See Also: STALENESS
TIREDNESS
See: WEARINESS
TOBACCO
See Also: SMELLS
TONGUE
See Also: MOUTH, SHARPNESS
TOUGHNESS
TRADING
See: ADVANTAGEOUSNESS,
SUCCESS/FAILURE
TRAFFIC
See: ROAD SCENES, VEHICLES
TRAIL
See: PURSUIT
TRANQUILITY
See: PEACEFULNESS
TRANSIENCE
See Also: BREVITY, DEATH, LIFE
TRANSPORTATION
See: VEHICLES
TRAVEL
TREES
See Also: LEAVES, NATURE
TREMBLING
See Also: ROCKING AND
ROLLING, VIBRATION
TRIUMPH
See: SUCCESS/FAILURE
TRITENESS
See: STALENESS
TROUBLES
See: PROBLEMS/SOLUTIONS
TROUBLESOMENESS
See: DIFFICULTY

TRUENESS/FALSENESS
TRUST/MISTRUST
See Also: UNCERTAINTY
TRUTH
See Also: CANDOR, HONESTY
TURNING AND TWISTING
TYRANNY
See: POWER
UMBRELLAS
See: OBJECTS, MISCELLANEOUS
UNATTRACTIVENESS
See Also: UNDESIRABILITY
UNAWARENESS
See: BLINDNESS
UNCERTAINTY
See Also: FATE
UNCOMFORTABLENESS
See: DISCOMFORT
UNCONSCIOUSNESS
See: NATURALNESS
UNDEMONSTRATIVENESS
See: COLDNESS, REMOTENESS,
RESERVE
UNDERSTANDABILITY
See: CLARITY
UNDERSTANDING
See: KNOWLEDGE
UNDESIRABILITY
UNEMPLOYMENT
See: WORK
UNEXPECTEDNESS
See: SUDDENNESS, SURPRISE
UNFAIRNESS
See: INTOLERANCE
UNFRIENDLINESS
See: SOCIABILITY
UNGRACIOUSNESS
See: MANNERS
UNHAPPINESS
See: DEJECTION, DISCONTENT,
GLOOM
UNHELPFULNESS
See: USEFULNESS/USELESSNESS
UNIQUENESS
See: ORIGINALITY

UNKINDNESS
See: CRUELTY

UNLIKELIHOOD
See: IMPOSSIBILITY

UNNATURALNESS
See: NATURALNESS

UNPLEASANTNESS
See: UNDESIRABLENESS

UNPREDICTABILITY
See: SURPRISES, UNCERTAINTY

UNPROFITABILITY
See: ADVANTAGEOUSNESS

UNREALITY
See: REALNESS/UNREALNESS

UNRELIABILITY
See:
RELIABILITY/UNRELIABILITY

UNRESPONSIVENESS
See: COLDNESS, REMOTENESS,
RESERVE

UNSTEADINESS
See Also: MOVEMENT

UNTIDINESS
See: ORDER/DISORDER

UNTIMELINESS
See: TIMELINESS/UNTIMELINESS

UNTRUSTWORTHINESS
See: TRUST/MISTRUST

UNTRUTH
See: LIES/LIARS

UNWELCOMENESS
See: UNDESIRABILITY

UPRIGHTNESS
See: POSTURE, STRAIGHTNESS

UP-TO-DATEDNESS
See: TIMELINESS/UNTIMELINESS

URGENCY
See:
IMPORTANCE/UNIMPORTANCE

USEFULNESS/USELESSNESS
See Also: NECESSITY

VAGUENESS

VALOR
See: COURAGE

VALUE
See:
IMPORTANCE/UNIMPORTANCE

VANITY
See Also: PRIDE

VARIETY
See: DIVERSENESS

VEHICLES
See Also: ROAD SCENES

VEHICLES, OPERATION OF

VERBOSENESS
See: TALKATIVENESS

VEXATION
See: ANGER, IRRITABLENESS

VIBRATION
See Also: TREMBLING

VICE
See: EVIL

VICTORY
See: SUCCESS/FAILURE

VIGILANCE
See: ALERTNESS,WATCHFULNESS

VIGOR
See: ENTHUSIASM, STRENGTH

VIOLENCE
See Also: ADVANCING,
BEHAVIOR

VIRTUE
See Also: ACCOMPLISHMENT,
MORALITY, PURITY

VISIBILITY
See Also: CLARITY,
OBVIOUSNESS, PROTRUSION

VIVIDNESS
See: BRIGHTNESS

VOCATION
See: PROFESSIONS

VOICE(S)
See Also: CRYING; GROANS AND
WHISPER; SINGING; VOICE,
EFFECT OF; VOICE, HARSH;
VOICE, MONOTONOUS; VOICE,
MUSIC-RELATED; VOICE, SOFT;
VOICE, WEAK

VOICE, EFFECT OF

VOICE, HARSH
See Also: HARSHNESS

VOICE, MONOTONOUS

VOICE, MUSIC-RELATED

VOICE, SOFT

VOICE, WEAK

VOTERS
See: POLITICS

VULGARITY
See: TASTE

VULNERABILITY
See: SENSITIVENESS

WALKING
See Also: AWKWARDNESS,
CAUTION, MOVEMENT, RUNNING

WAR
See Also: ARMY

WARMTH
See: COMFORT, HEAT

WASTE

WATCHFULNESS
See Also: ATTENTION,
PROTECTIVENESS, SCRUTINY

WATER
See: OCEAN/OCEANFRONT;
PONDS AND STREAMS;
SEASCAPES

WEAKNESS
See Also: HELPLESSNESS,
INSULTS, PERSONALITY TRAITS,
SOFTNESS

WEALTH
See: RICHES

WEARINESS

WEATHER
See Also: CLOUD(S), COLDNESS,
FOG, HEAT, MIST, RAIN, SUNS,
THUNDER AND LIGHTNING,
WIND

WEDDINGS
See: MARRIAGE

WEIGHT
See: HEAVINESS, LIGHTNESS

WELCOMENESS
See: DESIRABILITY

WELL-BEING
See: HEALTH

WHISPERS
See: GROANS AND WHISPERS

WHITE
See Also: COLORS, COMPLEXION,
PALLOR

WICKEDNESS
See: EVIL

WILDNESS
See: FEROCITY

WIND
See Also: WEATHER

WINNING
See: SPORTS, SUCCESS/FAILURE

WINTER
See: SEASONS

WISDOM
See Also: EDUCATION,
KNOWLEDGE

WISH
See: DESIRE

WIT
See Also: CLEVERNESS, HUMOR,
WISDOM

WIVES
See: MARRIAGE

WOMEN
See: HEART(S), MEN AND
WOMEN

WORD(S)
See Also: SPEAKING; WORDS,
DEFINED; WORDS, EFFECT OF;
WORDS OF PRAISE;
WRITERS/WRITING

WORDINESS
See: TALKATIVENESS

WORDS, DEFINED

WORDS, EFFECT OF

WORDS OF PRAISE

WORK
See Also: ATTENTION,
BOREDOM, DOCTORS, LAWYERS,
PROFESSIONS

WORLD
  See Also: LIFE

WORRY
  See: AGITATION, ANXIETY

WORTHINESS
  See: VIRTUE

WORTHLESSNESS
  See:
  IMPORTANCE/UNIMPORTANCE

WOUND
  See: PAIN

WRATH
  See: ANGER

WRINKLES
  See Also: COMPLEXION,
  FOREHEAD, SKIN

WRITERS/WRITING
  See Also: POETS/POETRY

YEARNING
  See: DESIRE

YELLS
  See: SCREAMS

YELLOW
  See Also: COLORS, HAIR

YOUTH
  See Also: AGE

ZEAL
  See: AMBITION, ENTHUSIASM

Similes
Dictionary

ABANDONMENT

See Also: ALONENESS, BEARING, FRIENDSHIP

1. Abandoned as a used Kleenex —Anon
2. Abandoned, like the waves we leave behind us —Donald G. Mitchell
3. Cast off friends, as a stripper her clothes —Anon
4. Cast off his friends, as a huntsman his pack —Oliver Goldsmith
5. (My youth has been) cast aside like a useless cigar stump —Anton Chekhov
6. Chuck me in the gutter like an empty purse —Edith Wharton
7. Deserted as a playwright after the first night of an unsuccessful play — W. Somerset Maugham
8. Deserted as a cemetery —Anon
9. Desolate . . . as the dark side of the moon —Pat Conroy
10. Discard like a withered leaf, since it has served its day —John Gould Fletcher
11. (What have we come to when people . . . could be) discarded . . . like an old beer can —May Sarton
12. Discarded . . . like used bandages —Louis MacNeice
13. Discard like a bad dream —Anon
14. Divest himself of his profoundest convictions and his beliefs as though they were a pair of old shoes whose soles had come loose and were flapping in the rain —Irving Stone
15. Feeling quite lost . . . like a fly that has had its head taken off —Luigi Pirandello
16. Felt stranded, as if some solid security has left him, as if he had, recklessly and ruthlessly, tossed away the compass which for years had kept him straight and true —Carolyn Slaughter
17. Leaving me alone like a shag on a rock —John Malcolm
18. Left like balloons with the air let out —Gloria Norris
19. Left high and dry like a shipwreck in a drained reservoir —Thomas McGuane

20. Neglected as the moon by day —Jonathan Swift

21. People had fallen away like veils —Susan Richards Shreve

22. Put off [as religious faith] quite simply, like a cloak that he no longer needed —W. Somerset Maugham

23. Shed [adult reality for past] like a snake sheds an old and worn skin — Guy Vanderhaeghe
    Vanderhaeghe used the snake comparison to describe someone shedding the reality of the present for the past.

24. Stood like a forgotten broom in the corner —Eudora Welty

ABILITY

See Also: ACCOMPLISHMENT

1. Able to absorb punishment as open buds absorb the dew —Grantland Rice

2. The abilities of man must fall short on one side or other, like too scanty a blanket —Sir William Temple

3. The ability to make a great individual fortune . . . is a sort of sublimated instinct in a way like the instinct of a rat-terrier for smelling out hidden rats —Irvin S. Cobb

4. Being creative without talent is a bit like being a perfectionist and not being able to do anything right —Jane Agner

5. Chose [people] with swift skill, like fruit tested for ripeness with a pinch —Paul Theroux

6. (My wife . . .) cooks like Escoffier on wheels —Moss Hart

7. Cuts like a saw through soft pine through the chatter of freeloaders, time-wasting delegations —Stephen Longstreet
    In Longstreet's novel, *Ambassador,* from which this is extracted, the efficiency tactics are diplomatic.

8. Efficient as a good deer rifle —Bruce DeSilva

9. Functioned as smoothly as a hospital kitchen —Laurie Colwin

10. Resourceful and energetic as a street dog —James Mills

11. Having communists draft the law for the most capitalist society on earth is like having a blind man guide you through the Louvre museum —Mark Faber, *Wall Street Journal,* June 19, 1986
    Faber's simile pertained to the basic law that will govern Hong Kong in future.

12. His [Brendan Sullivan's] management (of Oliver North) is like one of those pictures that museum directors settle for labeling "Workshop of Veronese" because the hand of the master is not there for certain but his touch and teaching inarguably are —Murray Kempton, *New York Post,* December 12, 1986

2

Kempton's simile describes the legal abilities of a member in the Edward Bennett Williams law firm, representing Colonel North during the Iran weapons scandal.

13. I can walk like an ox, run like a fox, swim like an eel . . . make love like a mad bull —David Crockett, speech to Congress

14. Instinct as sure as sight —Edgar Lee Masters

15. Native ability without education is like a tree without fruit —Aristippus

16. Natural abilities are like natural plants, that need pruning by study — Francis Bacon

17. Played bridge like an inspired card sharp —Marjory Stoneman Douglas

18. To see him [Chief Justice Hughes] preside was like witnessing Toscanini lead an orchestra —Justice Felix Frankfurter

19. Skilled . . . like a mischievous and thieving animal —Émile Zola

20. Skillful as jugglers —Daphne du Maurier

21. Talent is like a faucet. While it is open, one must write (paint, etc.) — Jean Anouilh, *New York Times,* October 2, 1960

22. Talent, like beauty, to be pardoned, must be obscure and unostentatious —Marguerite, Countess Blessington

23. You must work at the talent as a sculptor works at stone, chiselling, plotting, rounding, edging and making perfect —Dylan Thomas

ABSORBABILITY

1. Absorbed them [the influences of women around whom author grew up] as I would chloroform on a cloth laid against my face —Vivian Gornick

2. Absorbent as a sponge —Anon

3. Absorbent as blotting paper —Anon

4. Absorbent as cereal soaking up cream —Anon

5. It [a huge Christmas tree] soaked up baubles and tinsel like melting snow —Truman Capote

ABSURDITY

See Also: DIFFICULTY, FOOLISHNESS, FUTILITY, IMPOSSIBILITY, USELESSNESS

1. Absurd as a monkey in a dinner jacket —Anon

2. Absurd as an excuse —Anon

3. Absurd . . . as expecting a drowning man to laugh —German proverb
   Time and use often transform proverbs into similes. In this case, the original proverb was "A fool will laugh when he is drowning."

4. Absurd as hiring a street vendor to run a major corporation —Anon

5. Absurd as looking for hot water under the ice —Latin proverb

6. Absurd as mathematics without numbers —Anon

7. Absurd as to expect a harvest in the dead of winter —Robert South

8. Absurd as to instruct a rooster in the laying of eggs —H. L. Mencken

9. Absurd as . . . to put bread in a cold oven —Latin proverb

10. Absurd as . . . to put water in a basket —Danish proverb

11. Absurd as trying to drink from a colander —Latin proverb

12. Absurd . . . like baking snow in the oven —German proverb
    The simile has evolved from "He baked snow in the oven."

13. Absurd . . . like jumping into the water for fear of the rain —French proverb

14. Absurd, like using a guillotine to cure dandruff —Clare Booth Luce

15. Absurd . . . like vowing never to be sick again —Lynne Sharon Schwartz

16. As logical as trying to put out a fire with applications of kerosene — Tallulah Bankhead

17. Attending the Gerald R. Ford Symposium on Humor and the Presidency is sort of like attending the Ayatollah Khomeini Symposium on the sexual revolution —Pat Paulsen, at September 19, 1986 symposium in Grand Rapids, Michigan.

18. Bizarre and a little disconcerting, like finding out that the Mona Lisa was a WAC —Jonathan Valin

19. (His . . .) body so sleek with health, that his talk of death seemed ludicrous, like the description of a funeral by a painted clown — Christopher Isherwood

20. Comparing [Ronald] Reagan with [Franklin D.] Roosevelt is like comparing Charles Schulz ["Peanuts" cartoonist] to Rembrandt — Mike Sommer

21. Incongruous as a mouse dancing with an elephant —Anon

22. Incongruous as a priest going out with a prostitute —Anon

23. Looks as well as a diamond necklace about a sow's neck —H. G. Bohn's *Handbook of Proverbs*

24. Makes about as much sense . . . as it would to put army shoes on a . . . French poodle —William Diehl

25. Ridiculous as monkeys reading books —Delmore Schwartz

26. Stupid and awkward, like chimpanzees dressed up in formal gowns — Scott Spencer
    See Also: AWKWARDNESS

27. That's absurd, like Castro calling Tito a dictator —John Wainwright

28. You just can't go around thinking that McDonald's food is going to be steaming hot. It's like expecting the hamburger to be served on a French roll —Ann Beattie

ABUNDANCE
See Also: CLOSENESS; GROWTH, SPREADING

1. Abound like street vendors on a spring day —Anon

2. Abound like blades of grass —George Sandys

3. Abundant as the light of the sun —Thomas Carlyle

4. Abundant as the salt in the sea —Anon

5. Abundant as air —Anon
   Modern day life has added "Abundant as polluted air and water."

6. Abundant as June graduates in search of jobs —Anon

7. Abundant as poverty —Anon

8. Ample as the wants of man —Henry Wadsworth Longfellow

9. As full as a fruit tree in spring blossom —Janet Flanner
   The simile refers to a letter filled with good news.

10. As stuffed (with idle hopes and false illusions) as any Whitsun goose crammed with bread and spices —George Garrett

11. As stuffed with ideas as a quilt is with batting —Anon

12. Bountiful as April rains —William Cowper

13. Bountiful as the showers that fall into the Spring's green bosom — James Shirley

14. Bulging like a coin purse fallen on the ground —W. D. Snodgrass

15. [Dreams] came like locusts —Isaac Bashevis Singer

16. (The big racket money) comes in like water from a pipe in your bathroom, a steady stream that never stops flowing —Raymond Chandler

17. Ladled out fines like soup to breadline beggars —Bernard Malamud
    In Malamud's novel, *The Natural,* the simile refers to fines issued by a baseball coach to rule-breaking players.

18. Lush as a Flemish oil painting —Anon

19. Numerous as a bank or trust company's vice-presidents —*New York Tribune,* January 6, 1921
    With the lean-and-mean management style in vogue since the mid-eighties, this long enduring simile may well be headed for obsolescence.

20. (Children appearing here and there . . .) numerous as fireflies — Alice McDermott

21. Overdo . . . like a host who stuffs his guests with too many hors d'oeuvres —Tom Shales, Public Radio, January 10, 1986
    The simile referred to the directorial touches used in a movie, *The Color Purple.*

22. Plentiful as blackberries —William Shakespeare

23. Plentiful as New Year's Eve predictions and resolutions —Elyse Sommer

24. Plentiful as oak leaves, as plentiful as the fireflies that covered the lawn at evening —Ellen Gilchrist

25. Plentiful as tabby cats —W. S. Gilbert

26. Stuffed like a Strasbourg goose —Anon
    Strasbourg geese are over-fed and under-exercised in order to obtain the largest possible liver for making pté. Being stuffed like a Strasbourg goose is linked to any kind of excess.

27. They're like plums on a tree —H. E. Bates
    Bates compared the abundance of plums on a tree to an abundance of admirers.

28. Thick as autumnal leaves —John Milton

29. Thick as fleas —American colloquialism, attributed to New England
    Some variations from the American South: "Thick as fleas on a fat pup," or "Thick as flies on flypaper."

30. Thick as hail —William Shakespeare

31. (You have fallen into ripeness) thick as honey —Marge Piercy

32. Thick as Japanese beetles —Herman Wouk
    Wouk's simile from *Inside, Outside* refers to the behavior of people working for the president of the United States.

33. (Eyelashes) thick as June grass —Elizabeth Spencer

34. Thick as summer stars —William Blake

35. Thick as buttercups in June —Henry James

36. Thick as . . . freckles —George Garrett
    In his novel, *Death of the Fox,* Garrett refers specifically to the freckles of Sir Francis Drake.

37. Thick as the green leaves of a garden —Henry James

ACCEPTABILITY
See: BELONGING

ACCESSIBILITY
See: AVAILABILITY

ACCIDENT
See: FATE

ACCOMPLISHMENT
    See Also: ABILITY, CLEVERNESS, SUCCESS/FAILURE

1. Accomplishment and authority hang on him like a custom-tailored suit —Alvin Boretz (play-in-progress)

2. Encased in talent like a uniform —W. H. Auden

3. He uses irony as a surgeon uses a scalpel . . . with the same skill and to the same effect —Anon

4. Like a hog he does no good till he dies —Thomas Fuller
   See Also: EVIL

5. Rise to the occasion like a trout to the hook —Anon

6. Skilled and coordinated as an NFL backfield —James Mills

7. Something positive had been accomplished, like wrapping up a package in smooth paper, firm, taut, with a tight knot —Belva Plain

8. (Slowly he crept upon the heart of Manhattan, his) talent poised like a knife —Scott Spencer

9. To watch him is like watching a graceful basketball player sink shot after shot —Anon

ACCUMULATION
    See: GROWTH, SPREADING

ACCURACY
    See: CORRECTNESS

ACCUSATION
    See: CRITICISM

ACTIONS
    See Also: BEHAVIOR, CAUTION, LEAPING, JUMPING, MOVEMENT, VIOLENCE

1. Acting without thinking is like shooting without aiming —B. C. Forbes

2. The actions of men are like the index of a book; they point out what is most remarkable in them —Heinrich Heine

3. Actions of the last age are like almanacs of the last year —Sir John Denham

4. [Meaningless] actions that seemed like a charade played behind thick glass —Franz Werfel
   See Also: IMPORTANCE/UNIMPORTANCE

5. All action is involved in imperfection, like fire and smoke —*Bhagavad-Gita*

6. Driven to make a move, like a dilatory chess player prodded on by an impatient opponent —Harvey Swados

7. Evil deeds are like perfume, difficult to hide —George Herzog

8. A good deed will stick out with an inclination to spread like the tail of a peacock —Bartlett's *Dictionary of Americanisms*

9. Our deeds are like children born to us; they live and act apart from our own will —George Eliot

10. Our least deed, like the young of the land crab, wends its way to the sea of cause and effect as soon as born, and makes a drop there to eternity —Henry David Thoreau

11. Reprehensible actions are like overstrong brandies; you cannot swallow them at a draught —Victor Hugo

12. The acts of my life swarm down the street like Puerto Rican kids —William Meredith

13. Trying to shake off the sun as a dog would shake off the sea —James Dickey

14. The vilest deeds like poison weeds bloom well in prison air —Oscar Wilde

ACTIVENESS

See Also: ALERTNESS, BEHAVIOR, BUSINESS, ENERGY, ENTHUSIASM, EXCITEMENT, MOVEMENT, PERSONALITY PROFILES

1. About as active as a left-over fly in January —Anon

2. About as animated as a suit on a hanger —Elyse Sommer

3. (This region was as) active as a compost heap —Julia O'Faolain

4. Active as the sun —Isaac Watts

5. Alive as a vision of life to be —Algernon Charles Swinburne

6. (He looks) dead as a stump —Pat Conroy
   In Conroy's novel, *The Prince of Tides,* a character hearing someone described as above disagrees with another simile: "On the contrary, I think he looks as though he could rise up and whistle a John Philip Sousa march."

7. Frisky as a frisbee —Helen Hudson

8. Frisky as a colt —Geoffrey Chaucer

9. He was behaving as though the party were his: like an energetic octopus, he was shaking martinis, making introductions, manipulating the phonograph —Truman Capote

10. He is like a moving light, never still. He has the temperature and metabolism of a bird —Joy Williams

11. He [James Cagney] was like fireworks going off —Television obituary, 1986

12. Lively as a boy, kind like a fairy godfather —Robert Louis Stevenson

13. Lively as a weasel —Wallace Stegner

14. Lusty as June —Wallace Stevens

15. Mechanically animated, like the masterwork of some fiendishly inventive undertaker —Sharon Sheehe Stark

16. Pert as a sparrow —Walker Percy

17. (She had) rolled up her sleeves with all the vigor of a first-class cook confronting a brand-new kitchen —Mary McCarthy

18. She is active and strong as little lionesses —William James
    > From a letter describing the energy of women in Dresden, July 24, 1867.

19. She was like a strong head wind —Marguerite Young

20. Simmering . . . like a coal fire in the Welsh mines —Marvin Kittman about British actor Roy Marsden whose popularity thus simmers "in the collective unconscious of the American public" and bursts into flame whenever he makes an appearance in a new British import, *Newsday,* March 27, 1987

21. Small and sprightly, like a bantam hen —Truman Capote

22. Sprightly as a Walt Disney cricket —Jean Thompson

23. Tireless as a spider —Eudora Welty

24. Vibrant as an E string —Carl Van Vechten

ACTORS
See: STAGE AND SCREEN

ADAPTABILITY
See: BELONGING, FLEXIBILITY/INFLEXIBILITY

ADJUSTMENT
See: FLEXIBILITY/INFLEXIBILITY, HABIT

ADMIRATION
See: FLATTERY, WORDS OF PRAISE

ADULTERY
See: MARRIAGE

ADVANCING
See Also: ENTRANCES/EXITS, MOVEMENT

1. Advanced like armies —Anon
   > This is used to describe forward sweeps in a figurative as well as literal sense. For example, book critic Anatole Broyard used it about William Faulkner's sentences in a *New York Times Book Review,* May 17, 1987.

2. (The terrible old miser) advanced, like the hour of death to a criminal —Honor de Balzac

3. Advance like the shadow of death —John Ruskin

4. Approached . . . as stealthily as a poacher stalking a hind —Donald Seaman

5. Bearing down like a squad of tactical police —Marge Piercy

6. Bearing down like a tugboat busily dragging a fleet of barges —Frank Swinnerton

7. Came on like a last reel of a John Wayne movie —Line from "L. A. Law," television drama segment, 1987
    The simile describes a sexually aggressive woman.

8. Came [toward another person] . . . like a tidal wave running toward the coast —Isak Dinesen

9. Came with slow steps like a dog who exhibits his fidelity —Honor de Balzac

10. Come down, like a flock of hungry corbies, upon them —George Garrett
    Garret is comparing the corbies to a group of beggars.

11. Come like a rolling storm —Beryl Markham

12. Coming after me . . . like a wave —Calder Willingham

13. Coming at him like a fullback —Wallace Stegner

14. (She'd seen it) coming like a red caboose at the end of a train —Denis Johnson

15. (Cancer) coming like a train —William H. Gass

16. Coming like a truck —James Crumley
    Here the strong advance describes an aggressive woman.

17. (People) converged upon them, like a stream of ants —Hortense Calisher

18. (Faith's father) descended . . . like a storm —Charles Johnson

19. Descend on me like age —Margaret Atwood

20. Forges ahead, lashing over the wet earth like a whipcrack —T. Coraghessan Boyle

21. Glide toward them, as softly and slyly as a fly on a windowpane — Donald Seaman

22. He was upon them like a sun-flushed avalanche —Frank Swinnerton

23. Invade like weeds, everywhere, but slowly —Margaret Atwood

24. Leaned forward like a magnificent bird of prey about to swallow its victim whole —Mike Fredman

25. Like a figurehead on the prow of a foundering ship his head and torso pressed forward —John Updike

26. Like fowls in a farm-yard when barley is scattering, out came the children running —Robert Browning

27. Moved forward [towards an attractive woman] like so many iron filings to a magnet —J. B. Priestley

28. (He was) moving toward me like a carnivorous dinosaur advancing on a vegetarian sibling —Joan Hess

29. Pressing forward like the wind —Sir Walter Scott

30. Pushed forward like the nervous antennae of a large insect —Rita Mae Brown

31. [An odor] roll up . . . like fog in a valley —C.D.B. Bryan

32. Slid forward slowly as an alligator —Rudyard Kipling

33. (He could hear the roar of darkness) sweeping toward him like a fist — Jay McInerney

34. Swooped like chickens scrambling for a grain of corn —Aharon Megged

35. Went firmly on as if propelled —Stephen Crane

ADVANTAGEOUSNESS
See Also: COST

1. Beneficial . . . like water to a garden —Anon

2. Benefits, like bread, soon become stale —Caroline Forne

3. Benefits, like flowers, please most when they are fresh —George Herbert

4. Free [things] . . . free as a well to get into, but like a rat trap, not exactly free to get out of —Josh Billings
   Billings wrote in a phonetic dialect. Here's the dialect version of the above: "I hav found a grate menny things in this wurld that was free—free az a well tew git into, but like a rat trap, not ekzackly free tu git out ov."

5. A good deal . . . like trading an apple for an orchard —Anon
   The opposite of this is a German proverb: "Like trading the hen for the egg."

6. Like parenthood, you bid [at an auction,] then see what you've got — John Ciardi

7. Privileges she could list as a prisoner might count out the days of his sentence —Margaret Sutherland

ADVERSARY

1. An adversary as easily wiped out as writing on a chalkboard —Elyse Sommer

11

2. Being in the same room with the two men was like dropping in on a reunion of Capulets and Montagues —P. G. Wodehouse

3. A dead enemy is as good as a cold friend —German proverb

4. Fill me with strength against those who . . . like water held in the hands would spill me —Louis MacNeice

ADVERSITY
See: FORTUNE/MISFORTUNE

ADVERTISING
See Also: BUSINESS

1. Commercials on television are similar to sex and taxes; the more talk there is about them the less likely they are to be curbed —Jack Gould, *New York Times,* October 20, 1963

2. Doing business without advertising is like winking at a girl in the dark. You know what you are doing, but nobody else does —Stewart Henderson Britt, *New York Herald-Tribune,* October 30, 1956

3. A good ad should be like a good sermon: It must not only comfort the afflicted, it also must afflict the comfortable —Bernice Fitz-Gibbon

ADVICE
See Also: FRIENDSHIP, FUTILITY

1. Advice after an evil is done is like medicine after death —Danish proverb
   It's quite common to substitute the word 'mischief' for 'evil.'

2. Advice is like kissing: it costs nothing and is a pleasant thing to do —Josh Billings

3. Advice is like snow; the softer it falls . . . the deeper it sinks into the mind —Samuel Taylor Coleridge

4. Advice, like water, takes the form of the vessel it is poured into —*Punch,* August 1, 1857

5. The advice of old age gives light without heat, like winter sun —Marquis de Luc de Clapiers Vauvenargues

6. Advice is like castor oil, easy enough to give but dreadful uneasy to take —Josh Billings

7. Good advice is like a tight glove; it fits the circumstances, and it does not fit other circumstances —Charles Reade

8. His (Ariel Sharon's) advice on that subject (Lebanon 1984-1985) . . . was akin to a man with seven traffic accidents opening a driving school —Abba Eban, *New York Times,* February, 1986

9. It [excellent advice] is a good deal like giving a child a dictionary to learn a language with —Henry James

10. A proposal is like a flashlight. It's completely useless in the spotlight, but in the shadows it can do lots of good —Professor Steven Carvell, *Wall Street Journal,* December 11, 1986

    Professor Carvell's simile was specific to a proposal for investment research.

11. Telling a runner he can't run . . . is a bit like being advised not to breathe —Thomas Rogers on runner Fred Lebow's being so advised for medical reasons, *New York Times,* 1986

12. To heed bad advice is like eating poisoned candy —Anon

13. To listen to the advice of a treacherous friend, is like drinking poison from a golden cup —Demophilus

AFFABILITY

    See: AVAILABILITY, COURTESY, FRIENDSHIP

AFFECTION

    See Also: FRIENDSHIP, LOVE

1. Affectionate as a miser toward his money —Anon

2. (She had an) affection for her children almost like a cool governess — D. H. Lawrence

3. Affection is the youth of the heart, and thought is the heart's maturity —Kahlil Gibran

    Gibran completed the simile with "But oratory is its senility."

4. Affection, like melancholy, magnifies trifles —Leigh Hunt

5. Affection, like spring flowers, breaks through the most frozen ground at last —Jeremy Bentham

6. Affection, like the nut within the shell, wants freedom —Dion Boucicault

7. Affection or love . . . intended for someone else and spilled accidentally like a bottle of ink under a dragging sleeve —Diane Wakoski

8. Affections are like slippers; they will wear out —Edgar Saltus

9. The affections, like conscience, are rather to be led than driven — Thomas Fuller

10. Her cowlike, awkward affection surrounding him like a moist fog — Hank Searls

11. The human affections, like the solar heat, lose their intensity as they depart from the center —Alexander Hamilton

12. My affection has no bottom, like the Bay of Portugal —William Shakespeare

The shorter, more commonly used "Affection is like a bottomless well" was more than likely inspired by this comparison from *As You Like It*.

13. She was like a cat in her fondness for nearness, for stroking, touching, nestling —Katherine Anne Porter

AFFLICTIONS
See: HEALTH, PAIN

AFFLUENCE
See: RICHES

AGE
See Also: LIFE, MANKIND, YOUTH

1. Age covered her like a shawl to keep her warm —Rose Tremain
2. Age . . . indeterminate as a nun —Sharon Sheehe Stark
3. Age is a sickness, and youth is an ambush —John Donne
4. Age is like love, it cannot be hid —Thomas Dekker
5. Age, like a cage, will enclose him —Alastair Reid
6. Age, like distance, lends a double charm —Oliver Wendell Holmes, Sr.
7. Age like winter weather . . . age like winter bare —William Shakespeare
   These comparisons of age to the weather, from the poem *The Passionate Pilgrim,* are alternated with youth and the weather similes.
   See Also: YOUTH, WEATHER
8. Age, like woman, requires fit surroundings —Ralph Waldo Emerson
9. Ageless as the sun —Algernon Charles Swinburne
10. The age of man resembles a book: infancy and old age are the blank leaves; youth, the preface; and man, the body or most important portion of life's volume —Edward Parsons Day
11. (Each year in me) ages as quickly as lilac in May —F. D. Reeve
    The simile marks the opening of a poem entitled *Curriculum Vitae.*
12. Antique as the statues of the Greeks —Edward Bulwer-Lytton
13. As a white candle in a holy place, so is the beauty of an aged face — Joseph Campbell
    See Also: BEAUTY
14. At middle age the soul should be opening up like a rose, not closing up like a cabbage —John Andrew Holmes
15. At thirty-nine, the days grow shorter, and night kneels like a rapist on the edge of your bed —Richard Selzer

16. At twenty man is like a peacock, at thirty a lion, at forty a camel, at fifty a serpent, at sixty a dog, at seventy an ape, at eighty nothing at all —Valtasar Gracian

17. Awareness [of one's own age] comes . . . like a slap in the eye — Ingrid Bergman, on seeing a friend no longer young
See Also: REALIZATION

18. Being seventy-five means you sometimes get up in the morning and feel like a bent hairpin —Hume Cronyn, "Sixty Minutes" interview with Mike Wallace, April 12, 1987
See Also: PAIN, PHYSICAL FEELINGS

19. He could account for his age as a man might account for an extraordinary amount of money he finds has slipped through his fingers —John Yount
> In his novel, *Hardcastle,* Yount expands on the simile as follows: "Sure, he could think back and satisfy himself that nothing was lost, but merely spent. Yet the odd notion persists that, if he knew just how to do it, he might shake himself awake and discover that he is young after all."

20. Grow old before my eyes . . . as if time beat down on her like rain in a thunderstorm, every second a year —Erich Maria Remarque

21. He had reached the time of life when Alps and cathedrals become as transient as flowers —Edith Wharton

22. He who lives to see two or three generations is like a man who sits some time in the conjurer's booth —Arthur Schopenhauer

23. How earthy old people become . . . moldy as the gravel —Henry David Thoreau

24. Old as Methuselah —Seventeenth century proverb
> This has inspired many variations including another cliche, "As old as the hills," generally attributed to Sir Walter Scott's *The Monastery* and Dickens' *David Copperfield.*

25. I feel age like an icicle down my back —Dyson Carter

26. A man of fifty looks old as Santa Claus to a girl of 20 —William Feather

27. A man's as old as his arteries —Pierre J. G. Cabanis

28. Most old men are like old trees, past bearing themselves, will suffer no young plants to flourish beneath them —Alexander Pope

29. My age is as a lusty winter, frosty but kind —William Shakespeare

30. Old age is a tyrant which forbids the pleasures of youth on pain of death —Franois, Duc de La Rochefoucauld

31. Old age is false as Egypt is, and, like the wilderness, surprises —Babette Deutsch

32. Old age is like an opium-dream. Nothing seems real except what is unreal —Oliver Wendell Holmes, Sr.

33. Old age is like a plane flying through a storm. Once you're on board there's nothing you can do —Golda Meir, quoted on being over 70 by Oriana Fallaci, *L'Europe,* 1973

34. Old age is like being engaged in a war. All our friends are going or gone and we survive amongst the dead and dying as on a battlefield —Muriel Spark

35. Old age is like everything else. To make a success of it, you've got to start young —Fred Astaire

36. Old age is rather like fatigue, except that you cannot correct it by relaxing or taking a vacation —B. F. Skinner and M. E. Vaughan

37. Old age is rather like another country. You will enjoy it more if you have prepared yourself before you go —B. F. Skinner and M. E. Vaughan

38. Old age took her [Queen Elizabeth] by surprise, like a frost —Anon

39. Old as a garment the moths shall eat up —*The Holy Bible/Isaiah*

40. Old as a hieroglyph —John Berryman

41. Old as civilization —Morley Safer, "60 Minutes" segment on torture, November 9, 1986

42. Old as death —Elizabeth Barrett Browning

43. Old as God —Delmore Schwartz

44. Old as the sun —Slogan, Sun Insurance Co.

45. Old as history —Slogan, Anheuser-Busch beer

46. (I'm as) old as my tongue and a little older than my teeth —Jonathan Swift

47. (Made her feel) older than coal —Joseph Wambaugh

48. The old man is like a candle before the wind —Hilda Doolittle

49. An old man, like a spider, can never make love without beating his own death watch —Charles Caleb Colton

50. The old man who is loved is winter with flowers —German proverb

51. (The Jewish women were as . . .) old as nature, as round as the earth —Thomas Wolfe

52. (The problem now is as) old as realism —Max Apple

53. Old as stone —Marge Piercy

54. Old as the most ancient of cities and older —Saul Bellow

55. Old women and old men . . . huddle like misers over their bag of life —Randall Jarrell

56. Some men mellow with age, like wine; but others get still more stringent, like vinegar —Henry C. Rowland

57. The span of his seventy-five years had acted as a magic bellows—the first quarter century had blown him full with life, and the last had sucked it all back —F. Scott Fitzgerald

58. To be seventy years old is like climbing the Alps —William Wadsworth Longfellow

59. Years steal fire from the mind as vigour from the limb —Lord Byron

60. You know you're getting older when every day seems like Monday — Kitty Carlisle quoting her mother, 1985 television interview

61. Youth is like a dream; middle age, a forlorn hope; and old age a nostalgia with a pervasive flavor of newly turned earth —Gerald Kersh

AGGRESSION
See: PERSONAL TRAITS, VIOLENCE

AGILITY
See Also: MOVEMENT, SPEED, TURNING AND TWISTING, WALKING

1. (A small, shrivelled old man . . .) agile and quick like one of those whiskered little monkeys at the Zoo —Aldous Huxley

2. Agile as a fish —William Humphrey

3. Agile as a monkey —Alexandre Dumas, père

4. Agile as squirrels —Luigi Pirandello

5. (Moved) as lightly as a bubble —Hans Christian Andersen

6. As nimble as a cow in a cage —Thomas Fuller

7. Deft as spiders' catenation —C. S. Lewis

8. Frisky and graceful as young lambs at play —George Garrett

9. Graceful as joy —Babette Deutsch

10. Graceful as a panther —Raymond Chandler

11. Graceful as a premire danseuse —Natascha Wodin

12. Graceful as a Stillson wrench —Diane Wakoski

13. Graceful as the swallow's flight —Julian Grenfell

14. Graceful figure . . . which was as tough as hickory and as flexible as a whip —Thomas Wolfe

15. He could leap like a grasshopper and melt into the tree-tops like a monkey —G. K. Chesterton

16. Light-footed as a dancer waiting in the wings —Vita Sackville-West

17. (Her tiny body as) limber as a grass —Jean Stafford

18. Lithe as a swan —Richard Ford

19. Lithe as a whip —Raymond Chandler

20. Nimble as a cat —Anon

Herman Melville used this to begin chapter 68 of *Moby Dick* but it probably dates back well before that.

21. Nimble as a deer —Geoffrey Chaucer
22. Quick as a wrestler —Edward Hoagland
23. Sprang [out of his bed] like a mastiff —T. Coraghessan Boyle
24. Springy as a trampoline —Marge Piercy
25. Spry as a yearling —Eugene O'Neill
26. Step as elastic as a cat's —Jo Bannister
27. Supple as a cat —Irwin Shaw
    This is a variation of the often used "Agile as a cat" and "Agile as a cat, and just as sly."
28. Supple as a red fox —Maxine Kumin
29. Swift and light as a wild cat —D. H. Lawrence
30. There was something breath-taking in the grace of his big body which made his very entrance into a room like an abrupt physical impact — Margaret Mitchell
    Mitchell is describing Rhett Buttler, the hero of her epic *Gone With the Wind*.

AGITATION

See Also: EXCITEMENT, HEARTBEAT, NERVOUSNESS, TREMBLING

1. Agitated with delight as a waving sea —*Arabian Nights*
2. Agitation . . . like insects coming alive in the spring —William Goyen
3. Calm as a tornado —Anon
4. Composed as an egg gatherer in a rattlesnake pit —Harry Prince
5. Disturbing as decay in a carcass —Julia O'Faolain
6. Feel like he had a mouse water skiing in his stomach —Joseph Wambaugh
7. Feel my insides slipping away as if they are on a greased slide —W. P. Kinsella
8. Felt as if his heart was beating itself to death in some empty hollow — Oscar Wilde
9. Felt her heart make little leaps, as though it might creep onto her tongue and expose something —Leigh Allison Wilson
10. Felt his heart quicken, as a horse quickens at the faint warning touch of the spur —Ben Ames Williams
11. (Arrived in the library with every nerve twittering) felt like a tree full of starlings —M. J. Farrell
12. Froze my heart like a block of ice —T. Coraghessan Boyle
13. Hearts drumming like wings —Paul Horgan

14. Her heart leaped like a fish —Katherine Mansfield

15. Her heart . . . plucking inside her chest like a bird in a bag —Brian Moore

16. Her heart . . . plucking inside her chest like a bird in a bag —Brian Moore

17. His heart pumping like a boiler about to blow —Ira Wood

18. Her heart . . . thundering like ten hearts —Sharon Sheehe Stark

19. Her stomach leaped up inside her like a balloon —William Styron

20. His heart beat so hard he sometimes fondled it with his hands as though trying to calm a wild bird that wanted to fly away —Bernard Malamud

21. His heart chilled like a stone in a creek —John Farris

22. His heart . . . like a madly bouncing ball, beating the breath out of his body —Helen Hudson

23. His heart moving so fast it was like one of those motorcycles at fairs that the fellow drives around the walls of a pit —Flannery O'Connor

24. His heart racing like a quick little animal in a cage —T. Coraghessan Boyle

25. His heart sinks like a soap in a bucket —Robert Coover

26. His heart thundered like horses galloping over a wooden bridge — Gerald Kersh

27. His heart whammed like a wheezing steam engine —Bernard Malamud

28. His soul seething within him like a Welsh rabbit at the height of its fever —P. G. Wodehouse
    See Also: SOUL

29. I could hear my heart, like somebody hammering on a tree —John D. MacDonald

30. It seemed like something snapped inside of me, something like a suspender strap —John Steinbeck

31. (Scandal and chaos . . .) kicked up like chicken feathers —Pat Ellis Taylor

32. My heart behaved like a fresh-caught trout —Lael Tucker Wertenbaker

33. My heart felt like a rabbit running wildly around inside my rib cage — James Crumley

34. My heart jumped like a fox —Scott Spencer

35. My heart leaped like a big bass after a willow fly —Borden Deal

36. My heart pounded like a drowning swimmer's —Frank Conroy

37. My heart pounded . . . like the hoofbeats of a horse —Charles Johnson

38. My heart stopped as if a knife had been driven through it —Rudyard Kipling

39. My heart turned over like a dirtbike in the wrong gear —T. Coraghessan Boyle

40. My heart would flutter like a duck in a puddle, and if I tried to outdo it and speak, it would get right smack up in my throat and choke me like a cold potato —Irving Stone

41. My stomach plunged like an elevator out of control —T. Coraghessan Boyle

42. Nerves melt like jellyfish —Derek Walcott

43. Placid as a riptide —Joseph Wambaugh

44. The pressure was building in me like beer on a full bladder —T. Coraghessan Boyle

45. Seemed to smoulder like a tar-barrel on the point of explosion — Lawrence Durrell

46. The sense of horror and failure had clutched his spine like the wet, wrinkled hand of a drowned woman —William Styron

47. Set my heart to rocking like a boat in a swell —Edna St. Vincent Millay

48. She explodes like a chestnut thrown on the fire —Colette

AGREEMENT/DISAGREEMENT
See Also: COMPATIBILITY, FIGHTING

1. About as far apart as an atheist and a born-again Christian —Anon

2. Acquiesced like an old man acquiescing in death —Wilfrid Sheed

3. (Nobody can be as) agreeable as an uninvited guest —Frank McKinney
   Humorists like McKinney are notable phrase converters. This simile may be a case in point, evolving from William Wordsworth's sonnet *To a Snowdrop* which describes a flower bending its forehead "As if fearful to offend, like an unbidden guest."
   See Also: BEHAVIOR

4. Agree like a finger and a thumb —Anon

5. Agree like two cats in a gutter —John Heywood's *Proverbs*

6. Agree like cats and dogs —John Ray's *Proverbs*
   This sarcastic twist to the more commonly used "Fight like cats and dogs" dates back to the nineteenth century.

7. Agree like pickpockets in a fair —John Ray's *Proverbs*

8. Agree like the clocks of London —Richard Brinsley Sheridan

9. As coals are to burning coals, and wood to fire, so is a contentious man to kindle strife —*The Holy Bible/Proverbs*

10. As far apart as the atheists who claim there is no soul, and the Christian Scientists who declare there is no body —Anon

11. Co-operate about as much as two tomcats on a fence —Raymond Chandler

12. Far apart as the poles —Anon

13. Flock together in consent, like so many wild geese —William Shakespeare

14. Like the course of the heavenly bodies, harmony in national life is a resultant of the struggle between contending forces —Judge Louis D. Brandeis

15. Sentiments as equal as if weighed on a golden scale —Janet Flanner

16. We are made for cooperation, like feet, like hands, like eyelids, like the row of the upper and lower teeth. To act against one another is contrary to nature —Marcus Aurelius

AILMENTS
See: HEALTH, ILLNESS

AIM
See: PURPOSEFULNESS

AIMLESSNESS
See Also: BELONGING, EMPTINESS

1. Aimless as an autumn leaf borne in November's Idle Winds —Paul Hamilton Hayne

2. Chuckled aimlessly, like an old man searching for his spectacles — James Crumley

3. The crowd scurried aimlessly away like ants from a disturbed crumb — O. Henry

4. Drift about . . . aimlessly as a ghost —Lawrence Durrell

5. Drifted like winter moons —Richard Wilbur

6. Drifting like breath —Robert Penn Warren

7. Drifts like a cloud —Dante Gabriel Rossetti

8. He was without subject matter, like a tennis player in the Arctic or a skier in Sahara's sand —Delmore Schwartz

9. Kept going . . . like a car without a driver —Cornell Woolrich Woolrich's description of aimlessness is a variant of "Aimless as a ship without a rudder;" in fact, in his story, *Dawn to Dusk,* Woolrich used the two similes together.

10. Lived from day to day as if the years were circular —Alice McDermott

11. Never really taking hold of anything, he slides in and out of jobs like a wind-up toy sledding about until the inevitable slowdown —Alvin Boretz, film treatment

21

12. Ran out of motives, as a car runs out of gas —John Barth
13. Walking in aimless circles like children during a school fire drill —James Crumley
14. Wandered about at random, like dogs that have lost the scent —Voltaire

AIR

See Also: ATMOSPHERE

1. Air as clear as water —Maya Angelou
2. Air . . . as cool as water —Ethan Canin
3. The air, as in a lion's den, is close and hot —William Wordsworth
4. The air brightens as though ashes of lightning bolts had been scattered through it —Galway Kinnell
5. The air flowed like a liquid —Dan Jacobson
6. The air had a sweet, keen taste like the first bite of an apple —Phyllis Bottome
7. Air . . . hot like the air of a greenhouse —Rose Tremain
   See Also: HEAT
8. The air hovered over the city like a fine golden fog —Isak Dinesen
9. Air had lain about us like a scarf —Irving Feldman
10. The air . . . lay stifling upon the city, like a cat indifferently sprawled upon a dying mouse —Brian W. Aldiss
11. The air in the room was jumpy and stiff like it is before a big storm outside —Lee Smith
12. The air is calm as a pencil —Frank O'Hara
13. The air is pure and fresh like the kiss of a child —Mihail Lermontov
14. Air light and pleasant as children's laughter —James Crumley
15. Air like a furnace —Benjamin Disraeli, about Spain
16. Air like bad breath —T. Coraghessan Boyle
17. Air like honey —John Updike
18. The [hazy] air muffles your head and shoulders like a sweater you've got caught in —William H. Gass
19. Air pure as a theorem —Lawrence Durrell
20. The air smelled like wet clothes —Andrew Kaplan
21. The air softly began a low sibilance that covered everything, like the night expiring —Richard Ford
22. Air so thick and slow it's like swimming —Jayne Anne Phillips
23. Air streams into me like cold water —Erich Maria Remarque
24. Air sweet and fresh like milk —George Garrett

25.   Air thicker than chowder —Peter Meinke

26.   The air was like soup —Derek Lambert

27.   The air was like the silk dress Sharai wore, clean and complex and sensual —A. E. Maxwell
     Sharai is the name of a character in a novel entitled *The Frog and the Scorpion.*

28.   The air was mild and fresh, and shone with a faint unsteadiness that was exactly like the unsteadiness of colors inside a seashell —Maeve Brennan

29.   The air was smoky and mellow as if the whole earth were being burned for its fragrance like a cigar —John Braine

30.   The air was so heavy that we could feel it pressing down on us like mattresses —Jean Stafford

31.   The air was so rich and balmy it seemed that it could be scooped up with the hand —Rosine Weisbrod

32.   The air was still as if it were knotted to the zenith —Saul Bellow

33.   The cold air was like a quick shower —Paul M. Fitzsimmons

34.   The crystal air cut her like glass —Sharon Sheehe Stark

35.   (The air was moist, odorous and black; one) felt it [the air] like a soft weight —Saul Bellow

36.   The gray air in summer burned your eyes and throat like tractor exhaust trapped in a machine shed —Will Weaver

37.   There was a slow pulsation, like the quiver of invisible wings in the air —Ellen Glasgow
     In Glasgow's novel, *Barren Ground,* sets the scene for an approaching storm.

38.   The warm air and moisture . . . close in around her like a pot —Susan Neville

AIRPLANES
See: VEHICLES

ALCOHOL
See: DRINKING

ALERTNESS
See Also: ATTENTION, CLEVERNESS, SCRUTINY, WATCHFULNESS

1.   Alert as a bird in the springtime —George Moore

2.   Alert as a bloodhound at dinnertime —T. Coraghessan Boyle

3.   Bright as a bee —Julia O'Faolain

4.   Bright as a cigar band —Rita Mae Brown

5. Bright as a salesman in a car showroom —Donald Seaman

6. Bright-eyed as hawks —Walt Whitman, on the pioneer cowboys of the West

7. (It helps to have a friend at City Hall with) an ear like a redskin, always to the ground —Arthur A. Cohen

8. Ears . . . as sensitive as two microphones —Robert Culff

9. Ears quick as a cat's —Frank Swinnerton

10. His brain [when free of restraint] skips like a lambkin —Calder Willingham

11. His mind . . . was crackling like a high-tension wire —Cornell Woolrich

12. Keen as a hawk's eye —Barbara Howes

13. Keen as robins —Frank Swinnerton

14. (His alertness is nearly palpable,) keenness trembling within him like his pilot light —Philip Roth about Primo Levi, *New York Times Book Review,* October 12, 1986

15. On the watch [for recurring problem] like a captain at sea, riding the unknown forces which may produce the known disaster all over again —Paul Horgan

16. Quest about like a gun-dog —Lawrence Durrell

17. Saw like Indian scouts and heard like blind people . . . and smelt like retrievers —Wilfrid Sheed

18. Sharp-eyed as a lynx —Sir Walter Scott

19. Wait like a set trap for a mouse —Anon

20. Wide awake as a lie detector —Wallace Stegner

21. Wide awake, brain cells flashing like free-game in a pinball machine — T. Coraghessan Boyle

ALIENATION
See: ALONENESS, REMOTENESS

ALIKENESS
See: SIMILARITY

ALIMONY
See: MARRIAGE

ALLURE
See: ATTRACTION

ALONENESS
See Also: ABANDONMENT

1. Alone as a nomad —Richard Ford
2. Alone as a scarecrow —Truman Capote
3. Alone as a wanderer in the desert —Anon
4. Alone . . . like a lost bit of driftwood —Harvey Swados
5. Alone, like a planet —Richard Lourie
6. Alone . . . like bobbing corks —Jean Anouilh
     Playwright Anouilh's simile from *Thieves' Carnival* describes two characters who thus bob about because their adventures are over.
7. Alone like some deserted world —Bayard Taylor
8. Like the moon am I, that cannot shine alone —Michelangelo
9. [Building] as isolated as an offshore lighthouse —Nicholas Proffitt
10. By himself he felt cold and lifeless, like a match unlighted in a box — Stefan Zweig
     The simile, from a short story entitled *The Burning Secret,* describes a man content only in the company of others.
11. Feel lonely as a comet —Anton Chekhov, letter to his wife
12. Felt like an island —Derek Lambert
13. In your absence it is like rising every day to a sunless sky —Benjamin Disraeli
14. Isolated as if it were a fort in the sea or a log-hut in the forest —Israel Zangwill
15. Isolated like a tomb —Ian Kennedy Martin
16. Left him standing like a stump —Willa Cather
17. Loneliness became as visible as breath that turned to vapor —Tennessee Williams
18. Loneliness fell over me and covered my face like a sheet —Susan Fromberg Schaeffer
19. Loneliness overcame him like a suffocating guilt —Irving Stone
20. Loneliness . . . rises like an exhalation from the American landscape —Van Wyck Brooks
21. Loneliness surrounded Katherine like a high black fence —Tess Slesinger
22. (I wandered) lonely as a cloud —William Wordsworth
     One of the poet's most famous lines.
23. Lonely as a Hopper landscape —Brian Moore
24. Lonely as a lighthouse —Raymond Chandler
25. Lonely as a wave of the sea —Katherine Anne Porter

26. Lonely as priests —Anon
27. Lonely as Sunday —Mark Twain
28. The lonely, like the lame, are often drawn to one another —Harvey Swados
29. Lonesome as a walnut rolling in a barrel —Edna Ferber
30. Lonesome..like the A sharp way down at the left-hand end of the keyboard —O. Henry
31. Lone women, like empty houses, perish —Christopher Marlowe
32. (And I) sit by myself like a cobweb on a shelf —Oscar Hammerstein II, from lyric for *Oklahoma*
    See Also: SITTING
33. Solitary as a lonely eel —Richard Ford
34. Solitary as a tomb —Victor Hugo
35. Solitary as an explorer —Donald Hall
36. Solitary as an oyster —Charles Dickens
37. A solitary figure, like the king on a playing card —Marcel Proust
38. Solitary . . . like a swallow left behind at the migrating season of his tribe —Joseph Conrad
39. Solitude affects some people like wine; they must not take too much of it, for it flies to the head —Mary Coleridge
40. Solitude is as needful to the imagination as society is wholesome for the character —James Russell Lowell
41. Solitude . . . is like Spanish moss which finally suffocates the tree it hangs on —Anaïs Nin
42. Solitude swells the inner space like a balloon —May Sarton
43. Solitude wrapped him like a cloak —Francine du Plessix Gray
44. Stand . . . alone, like a small figure in a barren landscape in an old book —John D. MacDonald
45. Stand alone on an empty page like a period put down in a snowfall — William H. Gass
46. Survive like a lonely dinosaur —Mary McCarthy
47. (Celibate and) unattached, like a pathetic old aunt —Alice McDermott
48. Undisturbed as some old tomb —Edgar Allen Poe
49. Walk alone like one that had the pestilence —William Shakespeare
    In common usage, most generally "Like one who has the plague," or whatever contagious disease might be afoot.
50. We whirl along like leaves, and nobody knows, nobody cares where we fall —Katherine Mansfield
51. When I am alone, I feel like a day-old glass of water —Diane Wakoski

ALOOFNESS
   See: PERSONAL TRAITS, REMOTENESS, RESERVE

AMAZEMENT
   See: SURPRISE

AMBITION

1. Ambition . . . coursed like blood through her —Vita Sackville-West

2. [One woman's] ambition expanded like yeast —Rita Mae Brown

3. Ambition is as hollow as the soul of an echo —Anon

4. Ambition is a sort of work —Kahlil Gibran

5. Ambition is like a treadmill . . . you no sooner get to the end of it than you begin again —Josh Billings

6. Ambition is like hunger; it obeys no law but its appetite —Josh Billings

7. Ambition is like love, impatient both of delays and rivals —Sir John Denham

8. Ambition is like the sea wave, which the more you drink the more you thirst —Alfred, Lord Tennyson

9. Ambition, like a torrent, never looks back —Ben Jonson

10. Ambitions thin with age —James Goldman

11. Ambitious as the devil —Francis Beaumont

12. As ambitious as Lady MacBeth —James Huneker

13. Aspirations prancing like an elephant in a skirmish —Frank O'Hara

14. Good intentions . . . like very mellow and choice fruit, they are difficult to keep —G. Simmons

15. How like a mounting devil in the heart rules the unrestrained ambition! —N. P. Willis
      The word 'unrestrained' has been substituted for 'unrein'd.'

16. A man without ambition is like a woman without beauty —Frank Harris

17. Overambitious . . . like a musician trying to play every instrument in the band —Anon

18. (I think of) that ambition of his like some sort of little engine tick, tick, ticking away, and never stopping —Gore Vidal about Abraham Lincoln

19. To reach the height of ambition is like trying to reach the rainbow; as we advance it recedes —William Talbot Burke

20. Zeal without knowledge is like an expedition to a man in the dark — John Newton

ANCESTORS
    See: PAST, THE

ANGER
    See Also: EMOTIONS, IRRITABLENESS

1. Anger . . . flowing out of me like lava —Diane Wakoski

2. Anger . . . hard, like varnished wood —Lynne Sharon Schwartz

3. Anger . . . hot as sparks —Wallace Stegner

4. Anger is a short madness —Horace

5. Anger is as useless as the waves of the ocean without wind —Chinese
    proverb
    See Also: FUTILITY, USELESSNESS

6. Anger like wind is like a stone cast into a wasp's nest —Malabar
    proverb

7. Anger like a scar disfiguring his face —William Gass

8. Anger like grief, is a mark of weakness; both mean being wounded and
    wincing —Marcus Aurelius

9. Anger . . . like Mississippi thunderstorms, full of noise and lightning,
    but once it passed, the air was cleared —Gloria Norris

10. The anger of a meek man is like fire struck out of steel, hard to be got
    out, and when got out, soon gone —Matthew Henry

11. Anger spreading through me like a malignant tumor —Isabel Allende

12. Angers . . . crippling, like a fit —May Sarton

13. The anger [of a crowd of people] shot up like an explosion —H. E.
    Bates

14. Anger . . . smoldered within her like an unwholesome fire —Charles
    Dickens

15. Anger . . . spreading like a fever along my shoulders and back —
    Philip Levine

16. Anger standing there gleaming like a four-hundred-horsepower car you
    have lost your license to drive —Marge Piercy

17. Anger surged suddenly through his body like a quick pain —Beryl
    Markham

18. (His) anger was quick as a flame —Phyllis Bottome

19. Anger welled up in him like lava —Frank Ross

20. Angry as a hornet —George Garrett
    A variation by movie critic Rex Reed: "Angry as a ruptured
    hornet."

21. Angry as a wasp —John Heywood's *Proverbs*

22. Angry as a bear with a sore head —Stanley Weyman

Some variations of this popular simile are "Angry as a grizzly bear with a bad tooth" and "Cross as a bear with a sore head."

23. Angry words fan the fire like wind —Epigram

24. Bounced with indignation, as if she had robbed him of his reputation, of the esteem of honest people, of his humor, of something rare that was dearer to him than life —Guy De Maupassant

25. (He was) burning like a boiler —Saul Bellow

26. Carried on as though he had uremic poisoning —Rita Mae Brown

27. Cold, vicious rage that covered every inch of me like a rank sweat — Jonathan Valin

28. Come boiling out like bloodhounds —Richard Ford

29. Could feel her fury buzzing and burrowing into the meat under my skull like a drill bit —Stephen King

30. Die in a rage, like a poisoned rat in a hole —Jonathan Swift

31. A draft of anger and deep hurt trailing her like a cheap perfume —Paul Kuttner

32. Feel as though I had swallowed a hand grenade —Erich Maria Remarque

33. Feeling mean . . . like a bull gator —Robert Campbell

34. A feeling of rage cut him as with a sharp knife and took possession of him —Mikhaïl P. Arzybashev

35. Felt furious and helpless as if she had been insulted by a child — Flannery O'Connor
    See Also: HELPLESSNESS

36. A fit of anger is as fatal to dignity as a dose of arsenic to life —Josiah Gilbert Holland

37. Fumed like champagne that is fizzy —Bliss Carman

38. Fumes like Vesuvius —Cole Porter, from "I've Come to Wive It Wealthily in Padua," one of the lyrics from *Kiss Me Kate,* the musical adaptation of Shakespeare's *Taming of the Shrew.*
    Since Porter rarely used similes, it's natural to wonder if working on a play by as prolific a simile creator as Shakespeare inspired not just this but the several other similes in this one song.

39. Fuming anger like a toaster with crust jammed against its heating coil —Ira Wood

40. Furious . . . like a wounded bull in an arena —Dumas, Père

41. Fury pervading her like a bloat —Lynne Sharon Schwartz

42. Fury was running all through his blood and bones like an electric flood —Robert Campbell

43. Gall..like a crown of flowering thorn —W. D. Snodgrass

The poem from which this simile is extracted is about a dead marriage and the narrator's regret that his love has become a galling thing. He follows up the flowering thorn comparison with: "My love hung like a gown of lead that pulled you down."

44. Getting angry is like worshipping idols —L'Olam Midrash

45. Growling like a fox in a trap —William Diehl

46. Heaven has no rage like love to hatred turned, nor hell a fury like a woman scorned —William Congreve

47. Her rage . . . dammed up regularly as water —Louise Erdrich

48. Her resentment was like a coagulant . . . she felt sullen, dull, thick —Nancy Huddleston Packer

49. He's like a scalded cat —William Alfred

50. He was like the mule in the story that kept running into the trees; he wasn't blind, he was just so mad he didn't give a damn —Rex Stout

51. His cheeks quiver with rage —Walker Percy

52. Hissed like an angry kettle —Herbert Lieberman

53. (Barcaloo's rage took about five seconds to boil up.) It was like dropping cold water into a pot of hot iron —Robert Campbell

54. Let it [anger at wife] all come out of him, like air from a tire —Bruce Jay Friedman

55. Like ice, anger passes away in time —Anon

56. Mad as a bobcat —James Kirkwood

57. Mad as a buck —William Shakespeare

58. Mad as a bull among bumblebees —Anon

59. Mad as a cat that's lost a mouse —O. Henry

60. Mad as all wrath —Anon

61. Mad as a vexed sea —William Shakespeare
    Like many Shakespearian phrases, this one has fallen into common usage with 'vexed' usually changed to 'angry.'

62. Mad as a wet hen —American colloquialism
    A variation from George Garrett's novel, *The Finished Man:* "Mad as a doused rooster."

63. Mad as hops —American colloquialism
    In *Picturesque Expressions,* Lawrence Urdang speculates that this is a twist on being 'hopping' mad.

64. On the warpath [against world's injustices] like a materialistic Don Quixote —Clarence Day

65. Outrage which was like sediment in his stomach —Paule Marshall

66. Outrage . . . worked like acid in his temper —Frank Swinnerton

67. Puffed up with rage like a squid (my psyche let out angry ink) —Saul Bellow

68. Rage . . . as infectious as fear —Christopher Isherwood

69. Rage, as painful as a deep cut —Jean Stafford

70. Rage . . . burst in the center of my mind like a black bubble of fury — Lawrence Durrell

71. Rage sang like a coloratura doing trills —Marge Piercy

72. Rages like a chafed bull —William Shakespeare

73. Rage swells in me like gas —Marge Piercy

74. Rage whistling through him like night wind on the desert —Paige Mitchell

75. Raging back at her [an angry woman] like a typhoon —T. Coraghessan Boyle

76. Raging like some crazed Othello —Suzi Gablik describing Marc Chagall's behavior in review of *My Life With Chagall* by Virginia Haggard, *New York Times Book Review,* August 17, 1986

77. (Enemy chase me) sore as a bird —*The Holy Bible/Lamentations*

78. Sore as a boil —American colloquialism

79. Sore as a crab —John Dos Passos

80. Stammering with anger like the clucking of a hen —Émile Zola

81. Stewing hostility and mordant self-pity . . . pooled like poison almost daily in his soul —Joseph Heller

82. Tempers boil over like unwatched spaghetti —Tonita S. Gardner

83. Turned crimson with fury —Lewis Carroll

84. When he is angry he is like those creatures that lurk in hollow trees. His glare . . . causes brave men to run like scalded cats —George F. Will
    The angry man described by Will is football coach Woody Hayes.

85. Words heat up the room like an oven with the door open —Anon
    See Also: WORD(S)

86. The young man's wrath is like straw of fire, but like red hot steel is the old man's ire —Lord Byron

ANIMALS
See Also: BIRDS, INSECTS

1. The cat . . . carried his tail like a raised sword —Helen Hudson

2. The cat was sleeping on the floor like a tipped-over roller skate —Paul Theroux

3. Crows . . . circle in the sky like a flight of blackened leaves —Stephen Vincent Benét

4. Dogs . . . all snarls and teeth like knives —George Garrett

5. Dog . . . with a marking down his breast like a flowing polka-dot tie. He was like a tiny shepherd —Eudora Welty

6. Dour as a wet cat —Warren Beck

7. Fins [on fish] like scimitars —Richard Maynard

8. Frogs sparkling like wet suns —Margaret Atwood

9. He [a dog] dragged her around the block like a horse pulling a wheelless carriage —Margaret Millar

10. A herd of black and white cows moved slowly across a distant field, like pieces of torn paper adrift on a dark pond —Hilary Masters

11. His tail [a cat's] waved like a pine tree —Sheila Kaye-Smith

12. The Llama is a wooly sort of fleecy hairy goat with an indolent expression and an undulating throat. Like an unsuccessful literary man —Hilaire Belloc

13. [A cow] lying on her back like a fat old party in a bathtub —Edward Hoagland

14. [A cat] purring like a Packard engine. It worked like a lullaby —Harold Adams

15. Sheep huddled like fallen clouds —George Garrett

16. Silver whiskers . . . like rice-threads —D. H. Lawrence
    The silver whiskers described by Lawrence belong to a fox, from which his story takes its title.

17. Squirrels . . . fat as housecats —Doris Lessing

18. Swarms of bees like a buzzing cloud flew from flower to flower —Erich Maria Remarque

19. A white poodle . . . like an animated powder puff —Penelope Gilliatt

20. Wings of the swans are folded now like the sheets of a long letter — Donald Justice

ANIMATION
SEE: ACTIVENESS, ENERGY, ENTHUSIASM

ANNOYANCE
See: IRRITABLENESS

ANTICIPATION
See Also: HOPE

1. Anticipation went through me like a ripple of discordant notes —A. E. Maxwell

2. Lay in waiting like a giant crab —August Strindberg

In Strindberg's play, *The Stranger,* a character named Mrs. X thus compares the woman who wants her husband.

3. Like chill dawn waiting for sunrise, I am waiting for you —Rainer Maria Rilke

4. Wait, breathless as a bride —George Garrett

5. Waited . . . keenly as fisherman waiting for a bite —Lawrence Durrell

6. Waiting for her like a king awaiting the arrival of a courtier —Harvey Swados

7. Waiting [without thought or action] like a radio set equipped with a receiver only, for a signal from a distance which he wasn't even certain would be transmitted —Kenzaburo Oë

8. Wait . . . like a dog expecting to be taken for a walk —Rosamund Pilcher

9. Wait . . . like a pair of sea captains' wives in their widow's walks — Thomas McGuane

ANXIETY

See Also: EMOTIONS, NERVOUSNESS, TENSION

1. Anxiety flowed through the core of his bones like lava —Calder Willingham

2. (It is in those marriages and love affairs which are neither good or bad . . . that) anxiety flows like a muddy river —Norman Mailer

3. Anxiety . . . is somewhat like a blow on the head —Delmore Schwartz

4. Anxiety moved like a current through his belly —Bernard Malamud

5. Anxiety receives them like a grand hotel —W. H. Auden

6. Anxious as a law associate during his sixth year with a major law firm —Elyse Sommer

7. Anxious as an aspiring Miss Universe contestant sequestered in a soundproof booth and brought out moments later to tell what she loves most about America —Susan Barron, *New York Times*/Hers

8. Anxious as a mid-level manager in a corporate takeover—Mike Sommer

9. Anxious as an investor watching his stock go down —Anon

10. Anxious as a taxpayer with an audit notice from the IRA —Anon

11. As worried as she would have been over a lover she had cared for passionately —Sumner Locke Elliott

12. A case of the dreads so thick they seemed to whistle out the heating ducts and swarm the room like a dark mistral —Richard Ford

13. Desperation rising from him like a musk —Paule Marshall

14. A feeling of foreboding . . . like a wind stirring the tapestry, an ominous chill —Evelyn Waugh

15. A feeling of vague anxiety . . . snuffling about me like cold-nosed rodents, like reading of a favorite baseball player whose star has descended to the point where he parks cars at a restaurant or sits in a room above a delicatessen in Indianapolis, drinking vodka and waiting for his pension —W. P. Kinsella

16. Felt as if a serpent had begun to coil round his limbs —George Eliot

17. Felt as if her nerves were being stretched more tightly, like strings on violin pegs —Leo Tolstoy

18. Felt chilled as by the breath of death's head —Victor Hugo

19. Felt like a switchboard with all my nerves on Emergency Alert — Dorothy B. Francis

20. Frantic as a mouse in a trap —Anon

21. Had a chill and heavy feeling in his stomach like a lump of lead —Vicki Baum

22. Her mild, constant worries had engraved no lines in her bisque china face but had gradually cracked it like a very old plate —Lael Tucker Wertenbaker

23. His heart seemed to slide like the hook on a released pulley —Frank Swinnerton

24. I'm 'bout as worried as a pregnant fox in a forest fire —Peter Benchley

25. Over it [a face that had looked hopeful] now lay like a foreign substance a film of anxiety —Thomas Hardy

26. Second-hand cares, like second-hand clothes, come easily off and on — Charles Dickens

27. Stress is like an iceberg. We can see one-eighth of it above, but what about what's below —Patrice O'Connor

28. Suspended in his own anxiety as if in a cloudy solution of some acid — Lawrence Durrell

29. There is the same pain and panic (when your computer locks up) as when you have an attack of appendicitis —Brendan Gill quoted *New York Times,* August 2, 1986 in article by William E. Geist about a man (computer tutor Bruce Stark,) who helps people with their computer problems.
    This is typical of similes that are borrowed and modified to fit a personal sphere of interest.

30. Unease . . . it slipped out without his being able to control it, like sweat from his pores —Clive Barker

31. Worry is like a rocking chair. It gives you something to do, but it doesn't get you anywhere —Anon

APARTNESS
>See: ALONENESS

APATHY
>See: REMOTENESS

APPAREL
>See: CLOTHING

APPEARANCE
>See: PHYSICAL APPEARANCE

APPETITE
>See: HUNGER

APPLAUSE
>See: NOISE

APPRECIATION

1. Applause . . . like pebbles being rattled in a tin —Francis King
   See Also: NOISE

2. Cherish like a secret —D. H. Lawrence

3. Poorly appreciated . . . like a fine landscape in dull weather —Arthur Schopenhauer

4. She looked on him as a kind of gigantic treat, a prize won in a lottery — Anita Brookner

5. Ungrateful as children, who can never pay their debt of gratitude because they owe so much —Honoré de Balzac

6. An ungrateful man is like a hog under a tree eating acorns, but never looking up to see where they come from —Timothy Dexter

ARGUMENTS
>See Also: FIGHTING

1. Argued like a lawyer —Edith Wharton
   See Also: LAWYERS

2. Argue like geese —Ben Hecht

3. Arguing like sparring fish in a tank —Graham Swift

4. Arguing with Owen was like fencing with a bag of wool —Julia O'Faolain
   See Also: FUTILITY

5. The argument broke open, porous as cheese —Julia O'Faolain

6. Arguments are like the grinding of rusty blades —Elizabeth Hardwick

7. Can't help arguing like I can't help the man in the moon —Louise Erdrich

8. Clash like the coming and retiring wave —Alfred, Lord Tennyson

9. Clash, like waves of the sea —John Hall Wheelock

10. Contention is like fire, both burn so long as there is any exhaustible matter to contend with —Thomas Adams

11. Grabbed the argument as if it were a beachball we were tossing between us —Dorothy B. Francis

12. Her argument clung to its point like a frightened sharp-clawed animal —Edith Wharton

13. His argument is as thin as the homeopathic soup that was made by boiling the shadow of a pigeon that had been starved to death — Abraham Lincoln

14. Her arguments are like elephants. They squash you flat —Rumer Godden

15. Protesting like children at nap time —George Garrett

16. Split [in disagreement] like an egg —Paige Mitchell

17. Talking to Oscar [Levant] is like fighting a man who has three fists instead of the regulation two —Alexander Woolcott

18. True disputants are like true sportsmen, their whole delight is in the pursuit —Alexander Pope
See Also: SPORTS

19. Words..flew between them like sparks between steel striking steel — Edna Ferber

20. The words [during an argument] whipped away like weightless leaves —Lael Tucker Wertenbaker

ARITHMETIC
See: MATHEMATICS AND SCIENCE

ARM(S)
See Also: ARM MOVEMENTS, FINGERS, HAND(S)

1. Arm . . . like a fat bread roll —James Lee Burke

2. Arms and legs like tendrils —Jonathan Kellerman

3. (Her bare) arms and legs were like white vines —James Robison

4. Arms delicate as daisy stems —Sharon Sheehe Stark

5. Arms folded across his chest as primly as two blades in a Swiss Army knife —Pat Conroy

6. (An old man with) arms like driftwood scoured by salt and wind — Marge Piercy

7. Arms like gateposts —Leslie Thomas

8. Arms like logs —James Crumley

9. Arms like pythons —Nicholas Proffitt

10. Arms loose . . . like ropes dangling toward the floor —Cornell Woolrich

11. Arms . . . pink and thick as country hams —Robert B. Parker

12. Arms . . . rounded and graceful and covered with soft down, like a breath of gold —Wilbur Daniel Steele

13. Arms, soft and smooth; they must be like peeled peaches to the touch —Stefan Zweig

14. Arms spread like a crucifix —Carolyn Chute

15. Arms swinging wildly, like a great gull flapping toward the sea —Kay Boyle

16. Arms thick as firs —Paige Mitchell

17. Arms . . . thick as hickory logs —Elinor Wylie

18. Arms thick like a butcher's —Richard Maynard

19. Arms . . . very thin and pale, as though they'd been tucked away in some dark place, unused —Margaret Millar

20. Bent arms like pothooks —Erich Maria Remarque

21. Delicate wrists that moved bonelessly as snakes —Margaret Millar

22. Elbows . . . pointy, like a hard lemon —Ann Beattie

23. Forearms so hard and well-defined that the skin looked as if it had been flayed away, like drawings in an anatomy book —Jonathan Valin

24. Held their arms like bundles to their chest —William H. Gass

25. It [arm] was so thin . . . its covering didn't look like flesh but like paper wrapped around a bone to take home to a dog —Margaret Millar

26. Let her arms drop like folded wings —Julie Hayden

27. My arms fit you like a sleeve —Anne Sexton
    The descriptive frame of reference in Sexton's poem, *Unknown Girl,* is a baby.

28. My arms lie upon the desk like logs sogged with rain —David Ignatow

29. One of her arms hung down to the floor like an overfed white snake — Ross Macdonald

30. Skinny, muscular arms . . . like the twisted branches of an old apple tree —Arthur Miller

31. Swarthy arms like rolls of copper —Aharon Megged

32. Thin arms . . . ridged like braided leather —R. Wright Campbell

33. Upper arms big as legs —Will Weaver

34. Wrists like twigs —Eleanor Clark

35. Wrists . . . like two by fours —Charles Bukowski

36. Wrists . . . looked thin as a dog's foreleg —John Updike
37. Wrist . . . small like the throat of a young hen —Philip Levine
38. Wrist that looked like a lean ham —William Faulkner

ARM MOVEMENTS
See Also: HAND MOVEMENTS

1. Arms extended over his head, fists clenched, like a soccer player running mad with triumph —Daniel Curley
2. Arms spread out like wasps —James Patterson
3. Arms upraised like two giant branches —Harvey Swados
4. Arms waggled like duck wings —Martin Cruz Smith
5. Arms working like a windmill —Mike Fredman
6. Crook his arm like an usher at a wedding —Susan Neville
7. Crooking her arms like broken branches —Bernard Malamud
8. Folded her arms like hemp cord —Leigh Alison Wilson
9. Opened your arms like cupboard doors —Marge Piercy
10. Raised his arms like a fight announcer —Harvey Swados
11. Spreading their arms wide like galleons in full sail —Lawrence Durrell
12. Waving his arms like a deranged pelican —George Garrett
13. Waved . . . like a queen in a passing coach —William McIlvanney

ARMY

1. An army, like a snake, goes on its belly —Frederick the Great
2. Military intelligence has about as much to do with intelligence as military music has to do with music —John Le Carré
3. Soldiers in peace are like chimneys in summer —John Ray's *Proverbs*
   The word 'chimneys' has been modernized from 'chimnies.'

ART AND LITERATURE
See Also: BOOKS, MUSIC, POETS/POETRY, WRITERS/WRITING

1. Aesthetics is for the artist like ornithology is for the birds —Barnett Newman, *New York Times Book Review,* February 18, 1968
2. Art is a jealous mistress —Ralph Waldo Emerson
3. Art is an absolute mistress —Charlotte Cushman
4. Art is like a border of flowers along the course of civilization —Lincoln Steffens
5. Art is like baby shoes. When you coat them with gold they can no longer be worn —John Updike

6. Art is like religion. As long as you do your best to stamp it out of existence, it flourishes in spite of you, like weeds in a garden. But if you try and cultivate it, and it becomes a popular success, it goes to the dogs at once —Jane Wardle

7. Art is science in the flesh —Jean Cocteau

8. Art is wild as a cat and quite separate from civilization —Stevie Smith

9. The artist, like the neurotic, has withdrawn from an unsatisfying reality into this world of imagination; but, unlike the neurotic, he knew how to find a way back from it and once more to get a firm foothold in reality —Sigmund Freud

10. Artists . . . like bees, they must put their lives into the sting they give —Ralph Waldo Emerson

11. Art, like eros, stirs senses to full life, demands devotion —Steven Millhauser

12. Art like life is an open secret —Lawrence Durrell

13. Art, like life, should be free, since both are experimental —George Santayana

14. Art, like morality, consists of drawing the line somewhere —G. K. Chesterton

15. Art, like the microscope, reveals many things that the naked eye does not see —George Moore

16. As the sun colors flowers, so does art color life —Sir John Lubbock

17. Great art is as irrational as great music. It is mad with its own loveliness —George Jean Nathan

18. I have seen the beauty evaporate from poems and pictures, exquisite not so long ago, like hoar frost before the morning sun —W. Somerset Maugham

19. In art, as in diet, as in spiritual life, the same rules of elimination apply: the more one can do without the better —Anne Freemantle

20. In art, as in love, instinct is enough —Anatole France

21. In art, as in politics, there is no such thing as gratitude —George Bernard Shaw

22. In literature, as in love, we are astonished at what is chosen by others —André Maurois, *New York Times,* April 14, 1963

23. (Nine times out of ten,) in the arts as in life, there is actually no truth to be discovered; there is only error to be exposed —H. L. Mencken

24. Literature, like a gypsy, to be picturesque, should be a little ragged — Douglas Jerrold

25. Literature, like virtue, is its own reward —Lord Chesterfield

26. Literature's like a big railway station . . . there's a train starting every minute —Edith Wharton

In her short story, *The Angel at the Grave,* Wharton continues
the simile as follows: "People are not going to hang around the
waiting room. If they can't get to a place when they want to,
they go somewhere else."

27. It [empty white canvas] looks like an anemic nun in a snow storm —
James Rosenquist, quoted in television documentary about his work,
1987

28. Modern paintings are like women. You'll never enjoy them if you try to
understand them —Harold Coffin

29. Most works of art, like most wines, ought to be consumed in the district
of their fabrication —Rebecca West

30. Naïveté in art is like zero in a number; its importance depends on the
figure it is united with —Henry James

31. One must act in painting as in life, directly —Pablo Picasso, *Time*
interview

32. Two modern paintings . . . like Rorschach inkblots gone to seed —
Pat Conroy

33. A painting requires as much cunning as the perpetration of a crime —
Edgar Degas

34. A picture is a poem without words —Latin proverb

35. (Some of the canvases had no pictures at all, just colors,) swirls and
patches and planes of color, thickened and lumped, like hunks of
emotion —Dan Wakefield

36. Without favor art is like a windmill without wind —John Ray's
Proverbs

37. The youth of an art is, like the youth of anything else, its most
interesting period —Samuel Butler

ASTONISHMENT
See: SURPRISE

ATMOSPHERE
See Also: AIR

1. Air . . . full of unspoken words, unformulated guilts, a vicious silence,
like the moments before a bridge collapses —John Fowles

2. The atmosphere (of the room) was as vapid as a zephyr wandering over
a Vesuvian lava-bed —O. Henry

3. Evil which hung in . . . air like an odorless gas —Ross Macdonald

4. (The circle in which I moved was a self-contained world . . .) it was
like being in the treacly, supersaturated air of a hothouse filled with
luxuriant vegetation, or in an aquarium with its own special heating
unit and food supply, its own species of plankton —Natascha Wodin

5. (The whole place seemed restless and troubled and) people were crowding and flitting to and fro, like shadows in an uneasy dream — Charles Dickens

6. Sensed a wrongness around me, like an alarm clock that had gone off without being set —Maya Angelou

7. They [women who run shops in a town] have given the Square a fussy, homespun air that reminds you of life pictured in catalogs —Richard Ford

8. Thick and sultry the atmosphere steams like an island in the Pacific — T. Coraghessan Boyle

ATTENTION
See Also: ALERTNESS, SCRUTINY, WATCHFULNESS

1. (When listening he is) as focused and as still as a chipmunk spying something unknown from atop a stone wall —Philip Roth about Primo Levi, *New York Times Book Review,* October 12, 1986

2. The attention [of listeners] is like a narrow mouthed vessel; pour into it what you have to say cautiously, and, as it were, drop by drop —Joseph Joubert

3. Attention rolled down like a window shade —Sharon Sheehe Stark

4. Attention [of students] sinking . . . like sluggish iron from the cooling crust —John Updike

5. Attentive and indifferent as a croupier —George Garrett

6. Attracted about as much attention as a flea in a dog pound —Ross Thomas

7. Attracted about as much attention (in the artistic world) as the advent of another fly in a slaughter house —James L. Ford

8. Attracted as little attention as a dirty fingernail in the third grade — Ring Lardner

9. Attracted attention like the principal heads in a picture —Honoré de Balzac

10. Collected attention like twists of silver paper or small white pebbles — Elizabeth Bowen

11. Concentrates . . . like a cancer victim scanning a medical dictionary in hopes that the standard definitions have been repealed overnight in favor of good news —James Morrow

12. Curiosity, keen and cold as a steel knife —Maxim Gorky

13. Deaf as a door nail —Thomas Wilson
    This is the best known of many "Deaf as" similes. It's used in its literal sense as well as to describe inattentiveness. Popular variants include "Deaf as a post," "Deaf as a door," and "Deaf as a stone."

See Also: DEATH

14. Deaf as a piecrust —Lawrence Durrell

15. (Had honed her ability to turn) deaf as a snail —Joseph Wambaugh

16. Drinking it [information] like a bomber pilot getting ready for a mission —Harvey Swados

17. (The hoot of laughter that always made Mary) flick him off like television —Sumner Locke Elliott

18. Had taken in her every anecdote as completely as a recording machine —Louis Auchincloss

19. Heads are turning like windmills —Arthur Miller

20. Heedless as the dead —Lord Byron

21. His eyes wandered, like a mind —Penelope Gilliatt

22. His mind keeps slipping away like a fly —John Rechy

23. Inattentive, like the ear of a confessor —Mary McCarthy

24. Intent as a surgeon —Jean Stafford

25. Interest spread like a net —Nadine Gordimer

26. (She could not keep her mind on anything;) it [her mind] kept darting around like a darning needle —Jean Stafford

27. Leaned forward . . . like hounds just before they get the fox — Stephen Vincent Benét

28. Leapt from theme to theme like a water-bug —Eleanor Clark

29. Listened as intently as a blind woman —Rita Mae Brown

30. Listened, very still, like a child who is being told a fascinating and gruesome fairy tale —Isak Dinesen

31. Listen like an uncle —Herbert Gold

32. Listen . . . like snakes to a charmer's flute —Jan de Hartog

33. Mind jumps from one thing to another like drops of water bouncing off a larded pan when you test whether the griddle is hot enough to pour the pancake batter in —John Hagge

34. My mind wanders like smoke —Clifford Odets

35. Pricked up his ears like two railroad signals —Lewis Carroll

36. [Poets] receive the same care as xylophones and equestrian statues — Delmore Schwartz
    See Also: ABANDONMENT

37. Seems not to listen to her words, but rather watches her forming them . . . like some fervent anthropologist —William Boyd

38. Snaps to attention like a thumb —Irving Feldman

39. (He tried to apply his mind to the work he was doing but his) thoughts fluttered desperately, like moths in a trap —W. Somerset Maugham

40. The words bounced off Harry, like pebbles skipped on water —Paul Kuttner

41. (So scatter-brained that) words went by him like the wind —Louisa May Alcott

ATTIRE
See: CLOTHING

ATTRACTION

1. Absorbing as a love affair —Elyse Sommer

2. (A charismatic man) attracting young men to himself like filings to a magnet —Linda West Eckhardt

3. Come at him [girls to a boy] like ducks to popcorn —Max Apple

4. Drawn to as children to amusement parks —Anon

5. Drawn to as bathers to seashore —Anon

6. Drawn to as readers to a library —Anon

7. Drawn to us warily but helplessly, like a starved deer —Louise Erdrich

8. Drew . . . like pipers charming rats —Lynne Sharon Schwartz In her novel, *Disturbances in the Field,* Schwartz alludes to ideas that are attractive to the heroine and her college friends.

9. Drew (many confidences . . .) as unintentionally as a magnet draws steel filings —Vita Sackville-West

10. Enchanted . . . like a meadow full of four-leaf clovers —Mary McCarthy

11. Fascinated like sick people are fascinated by anything . . . any scrap of news about their own case —James Thurber

12. Fascinating and fantastic as toys in a shop window to a little poor boy in the street —Isak Dinesen

13. Fascinating as a burning fuse —William McGivern, about fellow writer Michael Gilbert's espionage novel, *Overdrive.*
    Whenever a simile is used to praise a book, it is invariably highlighted on the book jacket or in ads, as this one was.

14. (The salesgirls) fell on me like pigeons on breadcrumbs —Judith Rascoe

15. Had drawn her to him like a flower to the sun —John Le Carré

16. (The warm sweet center of her) had taken hold of him like a hand — John Yount

17. Held her mesmerized like a snake —Julia O'Faolain

18. He moves to you like a stable hand to a new horse —Allan Miller
    This comes from Miller's dramatization of D. H. Lawrence's short novel, *The Fox.* It did not appear in the Lawrence text.

19. Irresistible [thoughts] as intruders who force their way into your house —Dan Wakefield

20. Like children taking peeps at pantry shelves, we think we're tempted when we tempt ourselves —Arthur Guiterman

21. Men just love to buzz around me like there was a sweet smell coming from me —Pat Conroy

22. Mesmerizing as a flickering neon sign —Anon

23. (Kept watching because) something about her stayed with me. Like a cold matzo ball —Nat Hentoff

24. Take to the way a hypochondriac takes to a bed —Lorrie Moore

25. Temptation leapt on him like the stab of a knife —Edith Wharton

26. Temptations, like misfortunes, are sent to test our moral strength — Marguerite de Valois

27. Took to as an ant to a picnic —Harry Prince

28. Took to it . . . like a retriever to water-ducks —Ouida

29. Was drawn to . . . as if by strong cords —Aharon Appelfeld

ATTRACTIVENESS
See Also: BEAUTY, DESIRABILITY, PHYSICAL APPEARANCE

1. Adorable as a baby —Anon
   Babies have long been linked with adjectives that equate appealing (or peaceful) qualities. This commonly used form may have its origins in Swinburne's "Adorable as is nothing save a child."

2. Alluring as a ripe peach —Guy de Maupassant

3. Appealing as power to a politician —Anon

4. Appealing as something for nothing —Anon

5. Appealing as sunlight after a storm —Anon

6. An appeal shone from her as light from a twisted filament —John Updike

7. As likable as a jaguar —William Beechcroft

8. Charm is almost as poor a butter for parsnips as good intentions — Heywood Broun

9. Charm rolled off him like a halo off an angel —James Kirkwood
   In the television movie adaptation of Kirkwood's *There Must Be a Pony* the character played by Elizabeth Taylor uses this simile to characterize the man played by Robert Wagner.

10. Cute as a bug's ear —Bobbie Ann Mason

11. Dazzle like an impressionistic painting in which every brush stroke tells and contains something germane to the whole —V. S. Pritchett on George Meredith

12. Decorative as the scalps of an Indian brave —Frank Swinnerton

13. (The novel is often as) disarming as a work of folk art —Bethami Probst, *New York Times Book Review,* April 12, 1987

14. Have all the charm of a black widow —Pia Lindstrom, television movie review, 1986

15. Interesting, like a plot in the mystery books —Louise Erdrich

16. Inviting as a down comforter —Anon

17. Look like something that ought to be eaten for dessert —Irwin Shaw

18. More alluring than an invitation to visit rich and charming friends on the Côte d'Or —Ogden Nash

19. Seductive as Cleopatra —Louis Bromfield

20. She's like a mound of nectarines —Saul Bellow

21. Unappealing as a meringue with hardly any crust —Anon

AUTHENTICITY
See: TRUENESS/FALSENESS

AUTHORITY
See: POWER

AUTHORSHIP
See: POETS/POETRY, WRITERS/WRITING

AUTOMOBILES
See: VEHICLES

AVAILABILITY

1. About as hard to get as lion shit in Africa —Stephen Longstreet

2. Accessible as a candidate looking for another hand to shake —Mike Sommer

3. Accessible as a hooker plying her trade —Anon

4. As unattainable, as desirable, as beauty —Margaret Sutherland
See Also: DESIRABILITY

5. (Drinks here) flow like cement —John Mortimer, Public Television series, "Paradise Postponed," 1986

6. Has been handed round like snuff at a wake —Ellen Currie
The descriptive frame of reference is a promiscuous girl.

7. Inaccessible as time —Alice McDermott

In her novel, *That Night,* the author talks about old neighborhoods from which parents have moved away and now say "You can't go there anymore" as if change made a place inaccessible as time.

8. Laying around like pop-corn —Clifford Odets
   Odets follows this up with "You think good boys are laying around like pop-corn?"

9. Like an apple hanging on a tree, waiting for somebody to come along and pick it —Lee Smith

10. Like Meissen china in a glass case, the admiration [for an appealing but inaccessible woman] had to be kept at a distance —Jilly Cooper

11. Lived high up [in an apartment complex] . . . as accessible as a bald Rapunzel —William McIlvanney

12. Unobtainable as a taxi when it rains —Anon

13. Untouchable as God —Erich Maria Remarque

AVARICE
See: GREED

AWARENESS
See: REALIZATION

AWKWARDNESS
See Also: MOVEMENT

1. Awkward as a bull in a china shop —Anon
   This still popular simile endures with many substitutions for the bull such as "A blind dog," "A gorilla," "A monkey." Often, instead of a substitute comparison, a different context can lift a simile like this beyond the cliche; for example, "Like wild bulls in a china shop . . . are my awkward hands of love" from poet Delmore Schwartz's journals and notes.

2. Awkward as learning newly learned —Adrienne Rich

3. Awkward in her movements, as if she had been in solitary for years — Ross Macdonald

4. Awkward . . . like a guest at a party to whose members he carried bad news he had no right to know, no right to tell —Hortense Calisher

5. Awkward like a leaden ballet dancer lifting a fat partner —Ed McBain

6. Awoke as stiff as if I'd been spray-starched —Jonathan Kellerman

7. Blunder and fumble like a moth . . . a rabbit caught in the glare of a torch —William Faulkner

8. Bumbled up to him like a mole —Wilfrid Sheed

9. Clumsy as two kids on their first date —Anon

10. Clumsy . . . like a leaky old engine with the driving belt slipping and steam escaping from every joint —Christopher Isherwood

11. Feel awkward like a boy on a date with an older girl —Bobbie Ann Mason

12. Graceless as a pelican on the ground —George Garrett

13. Had about as much grace as a hippopotamus in a bubble bath —Harry Prince

14. Has the grace of an arthritic elephant on roller skates —Corey Sandler

15. Moved thickly, like a clumsy, good-tempered horse —William Faulkner

16. Moving stiffly like a man in a body cast —Martin Cruz Smith

17. She ran on like a clumsy goat, trampling and trespassing on land that was preserved —Daphne du Maurier

18. Stiff as a gaffer —Richard Wilbur

19. Stiff as a line in Euclid —Saul Bellow

20. Stiff as a poker grew —Wallace Irwin

21. Stumbling about like a drunken bear —James Crumley

22. Uncoordinated as a rag doll —Dorothea Straus

23. Unwieldy as a pregnant elephant —Anon

BACHELOR
See: MEN AND WOMEN

BAD LUCK
See: FORTUNE/MISFORTUNE

BADNESS
See: CRUELTY, EVIL

BALANCE
See: REGULARITY/IRREGULARITY

BALDNESS
See Also: HAIR

1. Bald as a ballpeen hammer —Thomas Lux

2. Bald as a brass knob —Beverly Farmer

3. Bald as a nun —Patrick White

4. Bald and wrinkled as a lizard —Sarah Bird
   See Also: WRINKLES

5. Bald as a balloon —Percival Wilde

6. Bald as a barefaced lie —Anon
7. Bald as a bearing —Loren D. Estleman
8. Bald as a billiard ball —Anon
   Of the many objects comparatively linked with baldness, the billiard or cue ball probably ranks at the very top.
9. Bald as a brick —Raymond Chandler
10. Bald as an egg —Anon
11. Bald as a football —William Boyd
12. Bald as an orange —Thomas Bailey Aldrich
13. Bald as a winter tree —William Morris
14. Bald as convicts —George Garrett
15. Bald as peeled onion —Margaret Laurence
16. Bald as the beach —William Diehl
17. Bald as the palm of your hand —Richard Harris Barham
18. Bald as time —Richard Prome
19. Bald head shining like a polished stone —George Garrett
20. The gleaming skull [of bald-headed man] shone like a supernatural sun —Sholem Asch
21. Had gone completely bald very young as though to get that over with as soon as possible —Helen Hudson
22. Hair beginning to recede like the polar ice cap in warm weather —Jean Thompson
23. Head as smooth as a knob —Russell Baker, *New York Times,* May 17, 1986
24. He had a bald patch on the top of his head which made him look rather like a monk —Guy De Maupassant
25. He was bald, his back hair was thick and projected like one of those large tree mushrooms that grow on the mossy side of a trunk —Saul Bellow
26. His bald head coming to a point, like an egg —Richard Llwellyn
27. His bald head shone . . . like an agitated moon —Erich Maria Remarque
28. His head [bald, with ring of grey-brown hair] was like the brown edges of a leaf in fall, a sign that the tree, however tall and green from a distance, was being eaten away at the edges, dying from the outside in —Jay Parini
29. His strong, bald head had a dull glow, like old ivory —Ivan Bunin
30. No more hair than a stone —John MacDonald
31. A semi-circular fringe of white hair surrounding his bald pate like a broken halo —Margaret Millar

BARENESS

1. Bare as the back of my hand —John Ray's *Proverbs*

2. As naked as the last leftover clap in a theatre —Joe Coomer

3. Bare as a birch at Christmas —Sir Walter Scott
   Scott used this in both *The Fortunes of Nigel* and *Quentin Durward.*

4. Bare as a bird's tail —Edward Ward

5. Bare as a newly shorn sheep —John Lydgate
   The simile has been modernized from "Bare as a sheep that is but newe shorn."

6. (There she was, on the bed beside me, as) bare-assed as Eve in Eden — George Garrett

7. Bare as shame —Algernon Charles Swinburne

8. Bare as winter trees —William Wordsworth

9. Bare like a carcass picked by crows —Jonathan Swift

10. More desolate than the wilderness —*The Holy Bible/Ezekiel*

11. Naked as an egg —F. van Wyck Mason

12. Naked as a peach pit —Helen Dudar, *Wall Street Journal,* November 26, 1986
    Even writers not given to using similes often use them as attention-grabbers at the beginning of an article, as Helen Dudar did to introduce her subject, novelist Paget Powell.

13. Naked as a stone —Angela Carter

14. Naked as a table cloth —Frank O'Hara

15. Naked as a weather report —Robert Traver

16. Naked as rain —Wallace Stevens

17. Nude as fruit on limb —George Garrett

18. (Voice wearing) raw as a rubbed heel —Sharon Sheehe Stark

19. (I'm simply against) showing girls as if they were pork chops — Germaine Greer on Playmate features in *Playboy Magazine,* January, 1972

20. Standing naked as a dead man's shadow —A. D. Winans

BARGAINS
　　See: ADVANTAGEOUSNESS

BARRENNESS
　　See: EMPTINESS

BASEBALL

See Also: SPORTS

1. The ball . . . came floating up to the plate like a generous scoop of vanilla ice cream bobbing to the top of a drugstore soda —Howard Frank Mosher

2. A ballpark at night is more like a church than a church —W. P. Kinsella

   Kinsella's novels are small treasure troves of baseball-related similes.

3. The ball . . . sailed through the light and up into the dark, like a white star seeking an old constellation —Bernard Malamud

4. The ball was coming in like a Lear jet —T. Glen Coughlin

5. Baseball games are like snowflakes and fingerprints, no two are ever alike —W. P. Kinsella

6. Baseball is like writing. You can never tell with either how it will go — Marianne Moore

   Baseball, like writing, was a Marianne Moore passion.

7. Boston hit Dwight Gooden like they were his wicked stepparents —Vin Scully, commenting on the second game of the 1986 World Series

8. The catcher is padded like an armchair —*London Times,* 1918

9. Defeat stains a pitcher's record as cabernet stains a white carpet — Marty Noble, *Newsday,* August 25, 1986

10. The dirt flew as if some great storm had descended and would have ripped up the entire [baseball] field —Craig Wolff, *New York Times,* August 3, 1986

11. Dwight Gooden [of New York Mets] pitching without his fastball was like Nureyev dancing on a broken leg or Pavarotti singing with a sore throat —Anon item, *Newsday,* October 25, 1986

12. The earth around the base is . . . soft as piecrust. Ground balls will die on the second bounce, as if they've been hit into an anthill —W. P. Kinsella

13. [Baseball] field . . . cool as a mine, soft as moss, lying there like a cashmere blanket —W. P. Kinsella

14. He bats like a lightning rod —W. P. Kinsella

15. He gets power from his bat speed . . . it's like he has cork in his arms —Pete Rose about Eric Davis, David Anderson column *New York Times,* May 7, 1987

16. He ran the bases as if he was hauling William H. Taft in a rickshaw — Heywood Broun

17.   [Dwight Gooden] his fastball crackling, his curveball dropping as suddenly as a duck shot in the air, has begun his charge for a third straight award-winning season —Ira Berkow, *New York Times*/Sports of the Times, August 3, 1986

18.   Homers are like orgasms. You run out of them after a time —Norman Keifetz
      See Also: SEX

19.   It [the patched-up Shea Stadium field] was dangerous underfoot as the Mets and the Cubs tiptoed their way though a 5-0 Met victory the way soldiers would patrol a mine field —George Vecsey, *New York Times*/Sports of the Times, September 19, 1986
      The ball players had to navigate their way through the field like soldiers because their fans had behaved so destructively the day before.

20.   Knowing all about baseball is just about as profitable as being a good whittler —Frank McKinney

21.   Outfielders ran together as if directed by poltergeists —George Vecsey, *New York Times*/Sports of the Times column on dreadful things that happen to the Mets when they play against the Houston outfielders, October 8, 1986

22.   Someone once described the pitching of a no-hit game as like catching lightning in a bottle (How about catching lightning in a bottle on two consecutive starts?) —W. P. Kinsella

23.   Sometimes I hit him like I used to hit Koufax, and that's like drinking coffee with a fork. Did you ever try that? —Willie Stargell on Steve Carlton, *Baseball Illustrated,* 1975

24.   Stepping up to the plate now like the Iron Man himself. The wind-up, the delivery, the ball hanging there like a piñata, like a birthday gift, and then the stick flashes in your hands like an archangel's sword —T. Coraghessan Boyle

25.   To be an American and unable to play baseball is comparable to being a Polynesian and unable to swim —John Cheever

26.   Trying to sneak a pitch past him is like trying to sneak the sunrise past a rooster —Amos Otis, baseball outfielder, about Rod Carew, former first baseman

27.   Twenty years ago rooting for the Yankees was like rooting for IBM — George F. Will, on the Chicago Cubs, *Washington Post,* March 20, 1974

BASKETBALL
      See: SPORTS

BEACHES
      See: OCEAN/OCEANFRONT

BEARDS

    See Also: HAIR, PHYSICAL APPEARANCE

1. Bearded as Abraham —George Garrett
2. Bearded like a black sky before a storm —George Garrett
3. Beard not clipped, but flowing like a bridal veil —Sinclair Lewis
4. Beards like Spanish moss —T. Coraghessan Boyle
5. Beard stiff and jutting like a Michelangelo prophet —Harvey Swados
6. Bristly gray beard . . . as rusted as old iron —Paige Mitchell
7. Flecks of premature gray in his beard, like the first seeds of age beginning to sprout in him —Ross Macdonald
8. Gray beard like a goat's chin tuft —Ernest Hemingway
9. A heavy black beard that grew high on his cheeks like a mask —James Crumley
10. His beard is like a bird's nest, woven with dark silks —Bobbie Ann Mason
11. His red beard looked like a toy doctor's beard stuck on a child's face — Gloria Norris
12. His sideburn, shaped like the outline of Italy, juts out onto his jaw — Bobbie Ann Mason
13. Long beard was spread out like a little blanket on his chest —Willis Johnson
14. Massive sideburns hung like stirrups on either side of his face —Ross Macdonald
15. A neat little beard, like a bird's nest, cupped his chin —Bobbie Ann Mason
16. A shadow of beard lay over his bony cheeks like soot on a chimney sweep —W. T. Tyler
17. Sideburns like brackets —Max Shulman
18. Sideburns stood like powerful bushy pillars to the beard —Saul Bellow
19. A small goatee stuck to his chin like a swab of surgical cotton — Dorothea Straus
20. A two-day growth of beard that made him look like a cactus —Sue Grafton
21. Whiskers grew like small creeper upon a scorched face —Frank Swinnerton

BEARING

    See Also: FACIAL EXPRESSIONS, MISCELLANEOUS; LYING; PERSONALITY PROFILES; PHYSICAL APPEARANCE; POSTURE; SITTING; STANDING; WALKING

1. Carried it [a bright, haggard look] . . . like a mask or a flag —William Faulkner

2. Exuded an air, almost an aroma, of justification, like a mother who has lived to see her maligned boy vindicated at last —Harvey Swados

3. Sitting up against the pillow, head back like a boxer between rounds —John Le Carré

4. Head lifted as though she carried life as lightly there as if it were a hat made of tulle —Paule Marshall
See Also: HEAD MOVEMENTS

5. Held her body with a kind of awkward pride mixed with shame, like a young girl suddenly conscious of her flesh —Ross Macdonald

6. Held herself like a daughter of the Caesars —W. Somerset Maugham

7. Held his shoulders like a man conscious of responsibility —Willa Cather

8. He leaned back and crossed his legs, as if we were settling in front of the television set to watch "Masterpiece Theater" —Joan Hess

9. Her head . . . carried well back on a short neck, like a general or a statesman sitting for his portrait —Willa Cather

10. He seemed enduringly fixed on the sofa, the one firm object in a turbulent world . . . like a lighthouse . . . the firm, majestic lighthouse that sends out its kindly light —Isak Dinesen

11. He seemed to have collapsed into himself, like a scarecrow in the rain —Christopher Isherwood

12. His chin hung on his hand like dead weight on delicate scales —Reynolds Price

13. His erect figure carrying his white hair like a flag —John Updike

14. His shoulders slumped like a man ready to take a beating —James Crumley

15. His straight black hair and craggy face gave off a presence as formidable as an Indian in a gray flannel suit —Norman Mailer

16. Holding herself forward [as she walks] like a present —Alice Adams

17. I felt that if he [man with threatening presence] were to rise violently to his feet, the whole room would collapse like paper —Margaret Drabble

18. Lay piled in her armchair like a heap of small rubber tires —Patricia Ferguson

19. Leaned forward eagerly . . . looking like a bird that hears a worm in the ground —Robert Lowry

20. A lofty bearing . . . like a man who had never cringed and never had a creditor —Herman Melville

21. Looked like a prisoner in the dock, hangdog and tentative —T. Coraghessan Boyle

22. Looking regal as a king —Gloria Norris

23. Perched on her armchair like a granite image on the edge of a cliff — Edith Wharton

24. (Sat) prim and watchful as a schoolgirl on her first field trip —Robert Traver

25. Relaxed and regal as a Siamese cat —Harold Adams

26. (They were mute, immobile, pale—as) resigned as prisoners of war — Ignazio Silone

27. Sat like a bronze statue of despair —Louisa May Alcott

28. Sat like a Greek in a tragedy, waiting for the gods to punish her for her way of life —Jonathan Valin

29. Sat helpless and miserable, like a man lashed by some elemental force of nature —Flannery O'Connor

30. Sat like a man dulled by morphine —Albert Maltz

31. (The leading members of the Ministry) sat like a range of exhausted volcanoes —Benjamin Disraeli

32. Sat on the arm of the sofa with a kind of awkward arrogance, like a workman in a large strange house —Paul Theroux

33. (Professor Tomlinson) sat up in the witness chair like a battleship raising its most powerful gun turret into position to fire —Henry Denker

34. She drew herself up with a jerk like a soldier standing easy called to stand-at-attention position —Kingsley Amis

35. She holds up her head like a hen drinking —Scottish proverb

36. She walked like a woman at her lover's funeral —Derek Lambert

37. She was still and soft in her corner [of the room] like a passive creature in its cave —D. H. Lawrence

38. She wore defeat like a piece of cheap jewelry —Pat Conroy

39. Slumped into her seat like a Pentecostal exhausted from speaking in tongues —Sarah Bird

40. Spread his arms and went springy like a tennis player —Graham Swift

41. Slumps in his chair like a badly hurt man, half life-size —Ted Hughes

42. Standing like a lost child in a nightmare country in which there was no familiar landmark to guide her —Margaret Mitchell

43. Standing . . . poised and taut as a diver —George Garrett
    See Also: PREPAREDNESS

44. Standing still alone, she seemed almost somber, like a statue to some important but unpopular virtue in a formal garden —Douglas Adams

45. Stands there like a big shepherd dog —Clifford Odets

46. Stands there like a prizefighter, like somebody who knows the score — Raymond Carver

47. Stands there vacantly, like a scared cat —Bobbie Ann Mason

48. Stately [movement] like a sailing ship —William H. Gass

49. Stood around casual as tourists —James Crumley

50. Stood before them, like a prisoner at the bar, or rather like a sick man before the physicians who were to heal him —Edith Wharton

51. Stood in one place, staring back into space and grinding fist into palm, like a bomb looking for someplace to go off —William Diehl

52. Stood looking at us like a figure of doom —Edith Wharton

53. Stood morosely apart, like a man absorbed in adding millions of pennies together, one by one —Frank Swinnerton

54. Stood stiffly as a hanged man —Leigh Allison Wilson

55. Stood . . . stiffly, like a page in some ancient court, or like a young prince expecting attention —Mary Hedin

56. Stood there like an angry bull that can't decide who to drive his horns in next —Danny Santiago

57. Walked like a man through ashes, silent and miserable —Robert Culff
    See Also: DEJECTION, WALKING

58. Went about looking as though she had had a major operation that had not proved a success —Josephine Tey

59. Wore abuse like widow's weeds —Lael Tucker Wertenbaker

60. Wore their beauty and affability like expensive clothes put on for the occasion —Edith Wharton

BEAUTY
See Also: BEAUTY, DEFINED; FACE; PHYSICAL APPEARANCE

1. (He was) all beauty, as the sun is all light —Phyllis Bottome

2. Beautiful and faded like an old opera tune played upon a harpsichord —Amy Lowell

3. Beautiful and freckled as a tiger lily —O. Henry

4. Beautiful as a feather in one's cap —Thomas Carlyle

5. (He is) beautiful as a law of chemistry —Robert Penn Warren

6. Beautiful as a motherless fawn —Bruce De Silva

7. Beautiful as an angel —William Paterson

8. Beautiful as an icon —Rachel Ingalls

9. Beautiful as an illusion —Angela Carter

10. Beautiful as a prince in a fairy story —Mary Lee Settle

11. Beautiful as a rainbow —John Dryden

12. Beautiful as a well-handled tool —Stephen Vincent Benét
13. Beautiful as a woman's blush and as evanescent too —Letitia Landon
14. (For he was) beautiful as day —Lord Byron
15. Beautiful as fire —Ambrose Bierce
16. Beautiful as honey poured from a jar —*People* book review
17. (There was a woman) beautiful as morning —Percy Bysshe Shelley
18. Beautiful as nature in the spring —O. S. Wondersford
19. Beautiful as sky and earth —John Greenleaf Whittier
20. (She was as) beautiful as the devil, and twice as dangerous —Dashiell Hammett
21. Beautiful as youth —Dollie Radford
22. Beautiful . . . like a dream of youth —Oliver Wendell Holmes, Sr.
23. Beauty . . . extraordinary, as if it were painted —Anita Brookner
24. Beauty in a woman's face, like sweetness in a woman's lips, is a matter of taste —M. W. Little
25. Beauty is as good as ready money —German proverb
26. Beauty is striking as deformity is striking —Edmund Burke
27. Beauty, like a lantern's light, will shine outward from within him — George Garrett
28. Beauty . . . like fine cutlery —John Gardner
29. Donned beauty like a robe —Iris Murdoch
30. Exquisite as the jam of the gods —Tennessee Williams
31. Fair as a lily —Diaphenia
    One of the most popular and enduring flower/beauty comparisons.
32. Fair as any rose —Christina Rossetti
33. Fair as a star —William Wordsworth
34. Fair as heaven or freedom won —Algernon Charles Swinburne
35. Fair as is the rose in May —Geoffrey Chaucer
36. Fair as marble —Percy Bysshe Shelley
37. Fairer than the morning star —Oscar Wilde
38. A fair face without a fair soul is like a glass eye that shines and sees nothing —John Stuart Blackie
39. Gorgeous as Aladdin's cave —Eleanor Mercein Kelly
40. (In the dingy park) her beauty fled as swiftly as the marmalade kitten had leapt from her grasp —William Trevor
41. Her beauty was as cool as this damp breeze, as the moist softness of her own lips —F. Scott Fitzgerald

42. He's as pretty as those long-defunct lover-gods —Charles Simic

43. (A novel that would be as) lovely as a Persian carpet, and as unreal — Oscar Wilde

44. Lovely as Spring's first rose —William Wordsworth

45. Lovely as the evening moon —Amy Lowell

46. Outstanding beauty, like outstanding gifts of any kind, tends to get in the way of normal emotional development, and thus of that particular success in life which we call happiness —Milton R. Sapirstein

47. Pretty as a diamond flush —Alfred Henry Lewis

48. (Face . . .) pretty as a greeting card —Donald E. Westlake

49. Pretty as a new-laid egg —American colloquialism, attributed to Midwest

50. (There sat Mary) pretty as a rose —Jump Rope Rhyme

51. Pretty as a spotted pony —American colloquialism, attributed to Southeast

52. Pretty as a spotted pup —Mary Hood

53. Pretty as a wax doll —Katherine Mansfield

54. Pretty as the carved face on a . . . cameo —Davis Grubb

55. Pretty like children on their birthdays —Truman Capote

56. Shed beauty like winter trees —George Garrett

57. She walks in beauty like the night —Lord Byron
    A timeless and much quoted Byron line. It continues with "Of cloudless nights and starry skies."

58. She was lovely as a flower, and, like a flower, she passed away — Richard Le Gallienne

59. There is in true beauty, as in courage, something which narrow souls cannot dare to admire —William Congreve
    In the original manuscript of *The Old Bachelor* the word 'something' was 'somewhat.'

60. A thing of beauty is a joy forever —John Keats
    A Keats classic that embodies the rule that when it comes to including or implying 'like' or 'as,' discretion is best.

BEAUTY, DEFINED

1. As fair as day —William Shakespeare

2. Beauty as definite as that of a symphony by Beethoven or a picture by Titian —W. Somerset Maugham

3. Beauty can pierce one like a pain —Thomas Mann

4. Beauty in a modest woman is like a distant fire or a sharp-edged sword: the one does not burn, the other does not cut, those who do not come near it —Miguel de Cervantes

5. Beauty is a fading flower —*The Holy Bible/Isaiah*

6. Beauty is like an almanac; if it lasts a year, it is well —Thomas Adam

7. Beauty is like summer fruits which are easy to corrupt and cannot last —Francis Bacon
   Transposed for modern style from "Beauty is as summer fruits."

8. Beauty . . . is like the morning dew —Samuel Daniel

9. Beauty is like the surf that never ceases —Struthers Burt

10. Beauty is the virtue of the body, as virtue is the beauty of the soul —Ralph Waldo Emerson

11. Beauty, like supreme dominion, is best supported by opinion —Jonathan Swift

12. Beauty, like truth and justice, lives within us —George Bancroft

13. Beauty, like wit, to judges should be shown —Lord Lyttleton

14. The beauty of a lovely woman is like music —George Eliot

15. Beauty passes like a breath —Alfred, Lord Tennyson

16. Beauty's a flower —William Shakespeare

17. Beauty vanishes like vapor —Harriet Prescott Spofford

18. Beauty without grace is the hook without the bait —Ralph Waldo Emerson

19. Beauty without modesty is like a flower broken from its stem —Anon

20. Beauty without virtue is a rose without fragrance —German and Danish proverbs

21. Glorious beauty is a fading flower —*The Holy Bible/Isaiah*

22. Women's beauty, like men's wit, is generally fatal to the owners —Lord Chesterfield
   Had Chesterfield lived to become attuned to nonsexist language he might have eliminated the gender references as follows: "Beauty, like wit, is generally fatal to the owners."

BEGINNINGS/ENDINGS
See Also: BIRTH, ENTRANCES/EXITS

1. Breaking off with a hard dry finality, like a human relationship —Lawrence Durrell

2. [A distressing event] came like a door banging on to a silent room —Hugh Walpole

3. Comes and goes like a cyclone —Marianne Hauser

4. Comes and goes like a fever —George Garrett

5. (My urge to gamble) comes and goes like hot flashes —Tallulah Bankhead

6. Come to a final end like a step climbed or a text memorized —John Cheever

7. [The ecstacies and tears of youth] die like the winds that blew the clouds from overhead —Noël Coward, lyrics for *Light Is the Heart*

8. Ebbing then flowing in again, like mud tides around a mollusc —Julia O'Faolain

9. Finished, like the flipped page of a book (this day was finished . . .) —Isaac Bashevis Singer

10. The first springs of great events, like those of great rivers, are often mean and little —Jonathan Swift

11. It was over, gone like a furious gust of black wind —William Faulkner

12. Leaving [a place to which one has become accustomed] is like tearing off skin —Larry McMurtry
    See Also: HABITS

13. Like a horse breaking from the gate, my life had begun —Scott Spencer

14. Like some low and mournful spell, we whisper that sad word, "farewell" —Park Benjamin

15. Parted [husband and wife] as an arrow from the bowstring —Amy Lowell

16. Parting is inevitably painful . . . like an amputation —Anne Morrow Lindbergh

17. (You and that money are going to be) separated like yolks and whites —Saul Bellow

18. Spent is my passion like a river dried up by the sun's fierce rays —W. Somerset Maugham

19. Things [like, popularity] come and go, like the business cycle —William Brammer

BEHAVIOR
See Also: ACTION, LIFE, MANKIND, PROPRIETY/IMPROPRIETY

1. Accepted the crisp bills with a certain famished delicacy like an aristocrat determined not to slaver at the sight of food —John Farris

2. Accumulated [information] like a nest-building bird —Louis Auchincloss

3. Act badly . . . like a man hitting a woman in the breast —George Bernard Shaw

4. Acted bored but patient, as though an enthusiastic acquaintance had just shown him the picture of a new grandchild —Joel Swerdlow

5. Allowed himself to be absorbed (into the softly palpitating life about him,) like a tired traveler sinking, at his journey's end, into a warm bath —Edith Wharton

6. Ate like Satan, and worked like a gnat —A. E. Coppard

7. Attention-getting behavior . . . like I was screaming at the universe [to fulfill my ambitions] —Mel Brooks, *Playboy,* April, 1973

8. Battled failure like the seven plagues —Anon

9. Behave . . . like a sort of love-crazed sparrow —Roald Dahl

10. Behavior is a mirror in which everyone shows his image —Johann Wolfgang von Goethe

11. Bluster like the north wind —Mrs. Centlivre

12. Butters it [the truth] over like a slice of bread —Erich Maria Remarque
   In his novel, *All Quiet on the Western Front,* Remarque uses the simile to explain that man is "Essentially a beast" but covers up this truth "With a little decorum."

13. (All he was doing was) calling attention to himself, rather like those movie stars who go around wearing dark glasses on cloudy days — Loren D. Estleman

14. Carrying on like a revivalist facing a full tent —Robert Traver

15. Charm was put forward like a piece of acting in a theatre —Hugh Walpole

16. Clutched at her throat like one stifled for want of air —Anzia Yezierska

17. Crawl into (his secret life) and nestle there, like the worm in the rose — Mary McCarthy

18. Dangled herself [before men] . . . like a drum majorette —Margaret Millar

19. Deny like a piano player in a bordello who claimed he didn't know what went on upstairs —Ed McBain

20. Flinched as if someone had thrown a baseball directly at his face — Graham Masterton

21. Flinched back like a box turtle into its shell —F. van Wyck Mason

22. Flirtatious as a Southern belle —Alice McDermott

23. For the promise of favor he will kneel down and lick boots like a spaniel —George Garrett

24. Glancing around him like a hunting dog nosing for a spoor — Kenzaburo Oë

25. Go forward like a stoic Roman —Edwin Arlington Robinson

26. Gripped life like a wrestler with a bull, impetuously —Stephen Vincent Benét

27. He had a way of . . . suddenly pouncing on something [someone says] that interested him, like a heron spearing a fish —Antonia White

28. Her not doing it was like the Baskerville hound that didn't bark — William Dieter

29. In public, they act like flat-chested old maids preaching temperance — Charles Simic

30. Intruded upon my vision like a truck on an empty road —Mary Gordon

31. I talk half the time to find out my own thoughts, as a schoolboy turns his pockets inside out to see what is in them —Oliver Wendell Holmes, Sr.

32. Jerked at the [fishing] net like a penitent —T. Coraghessan Boyle

33. Like a nun withdrawing, or a child exploring a tower, she went upstairs —Virginia Woolf

34. Lived and behaved like that sandpiper [in my poem] . . . just running along the edges of different countries, looking for something — Elizabeth Bishop, acceptance speech at University of Oklahoma, 1976 on receiving Books Abroad/Neustadt International Prize for Literature

35. Looked round . . . desperately like someone trying to find a way of crossing a muddy path without getting her shoes soiled —Franz Werfel

36. Lurking like a funeral director at a christening —W. P. Kinsella

37. Many talk like philosophers, and live like fools —H. G. Bohn's *Handbook of Proverbs*

38. Men's behavior should be like their apparel, not too straight . . . but free for exercise or motion —Francis Bacon

39. Nodded judiciously like someone making a mental note —Lynne Sharon Schwartz

40. Pedestrians in the East behave like lemmings rushing dispassionately to their deaths —W. P. Kinsella

41. People loll upon the beaches ripening like gaudy peaches —Ogden Nash

42. Play with . . . like a clever cat with a rubber mouse —Maureen Howard

43. (She) poured out feelings and thoughts that most people keep to themselves like a prodigal flinging gold pieces to a scrambling crowd — W. Somerset Maugham

44. Pushed me across [stage] like a broom —Edith Pearlman

45. Pull rank like a little red wagon (if it'd get her a place in the shade) — Tom Robbins

46. (Mary) pulled nerves like string in a blanket —Louise Erdrich

47. Pushing and jostling like a stormy sea —Stephen Vincent Benét

48. Raving, but soundlessly . . . so that she looked like a film of herself without a sound-track —Lawrence Durrell

49. Recoiled . . . like a man walking in his sleep, awakened from a frightful dream —Charles Dickens

50. Rose like a trout to the fly or a pickerel to the spoon —Mary McCarthy
    The simile as used in the short story, *Yellowstone Park,* describes a character who's an easy prey for any appeal for money to be spent for educational purposes.

51. (A day after helping the Giants to their victory over the Raiders in Los Angeles, Lional Manuel, the third-year wide receiver) sauntered through the locker room like an explorer just back from a glorious expedition —William R. Rhoden, *New York Times,* September 23, 1986

52. (She sat in bed,) sharpening her charms and her riddles like colored pencils —Yehuda Amichai

53. She went toward the sitting room seeking him like a cold animal seeking the fire —Margaret Mitchell

54. Shook himself like an angry little dog coming out of the water —Barbara Pym

55. Shrugged their shoulders as if to shake off whatever chips of responsibility might have lodged there —Helen Hudson

56. Spoke like a fool, and acted like a fiddler —Saul Bellow

57. Stuffed his own emptiness with good work like a glutton —Flannery O'Connor

58. Swallowed his temper but it left a sour taste in his stomach like heartburn —Donald McCaig

59. Swallowing hard like a stiff-necked goose —Paige Mitchell

60. Talk like a saint and behave like a fool —Jerome K. Jerome

61. Talks like a prophet and acts like a comedian —Amos Oz

62. Thought and action . . . were simultaneous in her, rather like thunder and lightning —Leigh Allison Wilson

63. Took them [spectacles] off, polished the lenses, and held them to the light like a spinster checking her crystal —Donald MacKenzie
    Were MacKenzie writing the novel from which this is culled, *Postscript to a Dead Letter,* he might well use a new bride or a proud homeowner instead of spinster, which has fallen into disfavor.

64. Toys with . . . as with a yo-yo —Benjamin Netanyahu, Israeli representative to the United Nations, *New York Times,* November 23, 1986
    This simile was used in connection with an article on Syrian terrorism. Typically, the simile was highlighted as a blurb!

65. Treat us like mushroom . . . keep us in the dark and throw shit at us —Loren D. Estleman

66. Used tranquilizing drugs . . . like the inhabitants of besieged medieval cities who, surprised by death, went back to bed, trying to fall asleep by telling themselves that the threatening flames were only a nightmare — Marguerite Yourcenar

67. Using a . . . flippant tone, as if he were talking about people in a play, or watching the ceiling at the dentist's —Ross Macdonald

68. Wore abuse like widow's weeds —Lael Tucker Wertenbaker

BELIEF

See Also: GOVERNMENT, MORALITY, POLITICS, RELIGION

1. Belief is as necessary to the soul as pleasures are necessary to the body —Elsa Schiaparelli

2. Belief, light as a drum rattle, touches us —A. R. Ammons

3. Communism is like Prohibition, it's a good idea but it won't work — Will Rogers

4. Conservatives, like embalmers, would keep intact the forms from which the vital principle has fled —John Lancaster Spalding

5. Convictions . . . the deeper you went the filmier the convictions got, until they were like an underwater picture, shifting, dreamy, out of focus —Wilfrid Sheed

6. Facism would sprout to life like a flower through a coffin's cracks, watered by the excreta of the dead —Dylan Thomas

7. Faith is like a lily lifted high and white —Christina Georgina Rossetti

8. Faith, like a jackal, feeds among the tombs, and even from these dead doubts she gathers her most vital hope —Herman Melville

9. Faith . . . stronger than a bank vault —Jimmy Breslin

10. His religious ethics fell like drowned fences —Graham Masterson

11. Ideals are like comets, revisit the earth periodically after long cycles of years—always excepting the enormous ideas that so many sublime donkeys envision of themselves —*Punch,* 1850

12. Ideals are like the stars: we never reach them, but like the mariners of the sea, we chart our course by them —Carl Schurz speech, Faneuil Hall, Boston, April 18, 1859

13. (He was fast in the clutches of his theory). It seemed to guide him like some superior being seated at the helm of his intelligence —Edith Wharton

14. (Fanatics is a pain). It's like talking to a rock trying to talk to a fanatic —Robert Campbell

15. Living up to ideals is like doing everyday work with your Sunday clothes on —Ed Howe

16. Love of country is like love of woman . . . he loves her best who seeks to bestow on her the highest good —Felix Adler

17. A man's ideal, like his horizon, is constantly receding from him as he advances toward it —W.G.T. Shedd

18. (Like many another big boss,) nationalism is largely bogus . . . like a bunch of flowers made out of plastics —J. B. Priestly

19. One by one, like leaves from a tree, all my faiths have forsaken me — Sara Teasdale

20. Our dogmas have been greatly enlarged to make them fit in with all sorts of necessities, so that they are like a patched coat, well-worn, and comfortable to wear. Our religion is as variegated as a Harlequin's dress —Anatole France

21. Patriotism is a kind of religion: it is the egg from which wars are hatched —Guy de Maupassant

22. Patriotism is as fierce as a fever, pitiless as the grave, blind as a stone and irrational as a headless man —Ambrose Bierce

23. (I think) patriotism is like charity—it begins at home —Henry James

24. Principles are like mountains; they rise very near heaven, but when they stand in our way, we drive a tunnel through them —Cardinal Rampolla

25. Skepticism [in preference to superstition] . . . it seems to be like a choice between lunacy and idiocy, -death by fire-or by water —Henry James, letter to Thomas Sergeant Perry, November 1, 1863

26. The theory towered up . . . like some high landmark by which travelers shape their course —Edith Wharton

27. We naturally lose illusions as we get older, like teeth —Sydney Smith

28. A wise conviction is like light —Sir Arthur Helps

BELIEVABILITY

1. As full of shit as a Christmas goose —American colloquialism

2. Believable as a declaration of eternal love from a call girl —Elyse Sommer

3. Believable as a forced confession —Anon

4. Believable as the testimony of a proven perjurer —Anon

5. Giving up credibility in a free society is like giving up force in a totalitarian society —Mario M. Cuomo, commenting on President's Special Review Board findings on Reagan Administration's involvement in Iran-Contra affair, *New York Times,* March 1, 1987

6. It's [my growing cold towards him] unbelievable . . . as if I had suddenly waked and found this lake dried up and sunk in the ground — Anton Chekhov
  The comparison from Chekhov's play, *The Sea Gull,* refers to the relationship between two of the characters, Nina and Trepleff.

7. Like a man who dreams he sees a friend run on him sword in hand, felt not pain so much as a wild incredulity —Dorothy Canfield Fisher

8. Shadowy and plausible as a ghost —W. D. Snodgrass

9. Some circumstantial evidence is very strong, as when you find a trout in milk —Henry David Thoreau

10. That this feeble, unintelligent old man was possessed of such power . . . seemed as impossible to believe as that he had once been a pink-and white baby —F. Scott Fitzgerald

11. To tell a soldier defending his country that "This Is the War That Will End War" is exactly like telling a workman, naturally rather reluctant to do his day's work, that "This Is the Work That Will End Work" — G. K. Chesterton
  See Also: ARMY

12. Unimaginable as hate in heaven —John Milton
  The word 'heaven' has been modernized from 'heav'n' as it appeared in *Paradise Lost.*

13. Unthinkable as an honest burglar —H. L. Mencken

14. The whole idea was fantastic, like a polar bear in the Sahara desert — Ken Follett

BELONGING

1. As much at home . . . as a fish in water —Honoré de Balzac
  An enduring comparison, as illustrated by a 1986 quote from the *New York Times:* "We belong . . . like fish in water. We're in our environment."

2. As much out of his element as an eel in a sand bag —H. G. Bohn's *Handbook of Proverbs*

3. As well adapted to the purpose as a one-pronged fork for pitching hay —Herman Melville

4. (She had) clicked into place [as teacher in school] like a well-hung door closing evenly —Barry Targan

5. Felt as well placed in the world as a fresh loaf of bread —Laurie Colwin

6. Fit [poor fit] like a breeching on a pig —Anon

7. Fit like a duck's foot in the mud —Anon

8. Fit . . . like a tongue into a groove —Jonathan Valin

In the novel, *Life's Work,* the simile refers to the way a man's body fits into a chair.

9. Fits as a hollow fits a circle —Anon

10. Fits him as easily as his skin —Thomas Hughes

11. Fits like the skin on a sausage —Anon

12. Fitted (into their scheme of life) as a well-made reel fits the butt of a good rod —Henry Van Dyke

13. Fitted in like a Marine in a parade —William Beechcroft

14. Fitted (its new home) like a coin in a slot —George Garrett

15. Fitting comfortable and heavy like a gun in a holster —George Garrett

16. Like a barber's chair, fit for everyone —Thomas Fuller

17. Like Miniver Cheevy, he had been born too late —Joseph Heller
    See Also: TIMELINESS/UNTIMELINESS

18. Looking as lost as a shipwrecked mariner —Yisrael Zarchi

19. [Feel] misplaced . . . as if she had been expelled from a dream in which she would have dearly loved to remain —Milan Kundera

20. Part of the landscape, like a tree —John Updike

21. Swam as happily in society as a fish swam in schools —Susan Fromberg Schaeffer

BENDING/BENT

1. As crooked as a corkscrew —George Kaufman and Moss Hart

2. As crooked as a dog's elbow —F. T. Elworthy

3. As crooked as a ram's horn —Charles Caleb Colton

4. Bending from the waist as if he was going to close up like a jackknife — John Dos Passos

5. Bend like a finger joint —Charles Wright

6. Bend like sheets of tin —Palmer Cox

7. Bends with her laugh . . . like a rubber stick being shaken —Alice McDermott

8. Bent as a country lane —John Wainwright

9. Bent double like a tree in a high wind —Caryl Phillips

10. Bent down like violets after rain —Thomas Bailey Aldrich

11. Bent like a birch ice-laden —James Agee

12. Bent like a bow —Aharon Megged
    A variation on the bent bow image from William McIlvanney's novel, *Laidlow:* "Arching his body like a bow."

13. Bent like a broken flower —Algernon Charles Swinburne

14. Bent like a rainbow —Robert Southey

Another way to express this image is to be "Bent like a rainbow arch."

15. Bent . . . like a soldier at the approach of an assault —Victor Hugo

16. Bent like a wishbone —William Kennedy

17. Bent slightly like a man who has been shot but continues to stand — Flannery O'Connor

18. (The headwaiter) bowed like a poppy in the breeze —Ogden Nash

19. Bows down like a willow tree in a storm —Erich Maria Remarque

20. Coiled like a fetus —William H. Gass
    A variation by Derek Lambert: "Curled up like a bulky fetus."

21. Coiled up like the letter 'S' —Damon Runyon

22. Crooked like a comma —Sharon Sheehe Stark

23. Curled himself like a comma into the waiting cab —William H. Hallhan

24. Curled like a ball —Sterling Hayden

25. Curled up in a ball like a wet puppy —Amos Oz

26. Curled up [in sleeping position] like a fist around an egg —Leonard Michaels

27. Curled up like a gun-dog —Colette

28. (Bent over your books) curled up like a porcupine with a bellyache — Marge Piercy

29. Curled up like fried bacon —Anon

30. Curling up like a small animal —Nina Bawden

31. Curling up like burning cardboard —Lawrence Durrell

32. [A cat] curls up like a dormer mouse —Jayne Anne Phillips

33. Drooped like a flower in the frost —John Greenleaf Whittier

34. Folded over like a ruler from the waist —William H. Gass

35. Folded up, like a marionette with cheap wooden hinges, and sat down —Graham Masterton

36. (Never will I be) gibbous like the moon —Diane Ackerman

37. Lean forward like firemen pulling a hose —Miller Williams

38. Tilting like a paper cutout —Susan Minot

39. Twisted as an old paint tube —Fannie Hurst

40. A very old lady, her back curved over like a snail's —Daphne Merkin

BENEFITS
See: ADVANTAGEOUSNESS

BEREAVEMENT
See: GRIEF, SADNESS

BEWILDERMENT
See Also: EMOTIONS, STRANGENESS

1. As confounding as the groom who drives into a stop sign on the way to his wedding —Amy Hempel

2. As puzzling as a page in an unknown language —Henry James
   In James' story, *The Pupil,* the personality of one of the characters serves as a frame of reference for the comparison.

3. Bewildering like a fruitless spring —Jean Garrigue

4. Confounded utterly, like an orphan in solitary confinement —Jean Stafford

5. Confused, like a mourner who has wandered into the wrong funeral parlor —James Crumley

6. He's as mixed up as the twentieth century —Clifford Odets

7. Inexplicable as the birth of a star —Stephen Vincent Benét

8. [Speaking candidly] muddled her like wine, or like a first breath of freedom —Kate Chopin

9. Mysterious as the sea —Robert Traver

10. So confused he's like a hypnotized rabbit —Derek Lambert

11. Wrinkled his long nose uncertainly, like a hound robbed of the scent by heavy rain —Donald Seaman

BIBLE
See: BOOKS

BICYCLING
See: SPORTS

BIGNESS
See Also: FATNESS, PHYSICAL APPEARANCE, TALLNESS

1. Ample as a fat man's waistline —Anon

2. As large as life —Maria Edgeworth

3. As large as life and twice as natural —Anon
   While this is most commonly attributed to Lewis Carroll, who used it in *Through the Looking Glass* in 1873, Stevenson's *Proverbs, Maxims and Famous Phrases* includes an earlier (though likely not the earliest) source, Cuthbert Bede's 1853 work, *Verdant Green.*

4. Big as a braggart's mouth —Anon

5. Big as a den bear —Richard Ford
6. Big as a draft animal —William Brammer
7. Big as all out of doors —Anon
8. [A man] big as an express train —T. Coraghessan Boyle
9. (Bombers) big as bowling alleys —Marge Piercy
10. A big man, filling the chair like a great mound of wheat —H.R.F. Keating
11. Great as man's ambition —Dame Edith Sitwell
12. Huge as a planet —Lord Byron
13. Huge as mountains —Walter Savage Landor
14. Immense as whales —Sir William Davenant
15. Large as a log of maple —Refrain from "Yankee Doodle," early American folk song
16. (My disappointment) large as capsized tugs —Richard Eberhart
17. A large business organization is like a damn big dragon. You kick it in the tail, and two years later, it feels it in the head —Frederick Kappell, *Look,* August 28, 1962
    > Kappell, chairman of American Telephone and Telegraph, began his comparison with "The Bell System is . . . " instead of the more general phrase used here.
    See Also: BUSINESS
18. A list big as a comedian's gag file —Anon
19. Over-sized like a clown's shoes —Anon
20. She's big as a damned barn and tough as knife metal —Ken Kesey
    See Also: TOUGHNESS
21. She was big as three women —Ernest Hemingway
22. Vast as water —Madeleine L'Engle
23. Vast like the inside of a Pharaoh's tomb —Arthur A. Cohen
    > In Cohen's novel, *In the Days of Simon Stern,* the comparison describes New York's Madison Square Garden.

BIGOTRY
    See: INTOLERANCE

BIOGRAPHY
    See: BOOKS, WRITERS/WRITING

BIRDS
    See Also: ANIMALS, INSECTS, SINGING
1. Bird, its little black feet tucked under its belly like miniature bombs —Peter Meinke

2. Birds afloat, like a scarf —Babette Deutsch

3. Birds . . . bobbed like clothespins on the telephone line —Elizabeth Savage

4. Birds . . . circling like black leaves —Hugh Walpole

5. Birds flew up like black gloves jerked from a line —Paul Theroux

6. Birds . . . gliding like pieces of dark paper abandoned suddenly by an erratic wind —John Rechy

7. Bird, shaped like the insides of a yawning mouth —Charles Simic

8. Birds in flight, fluid as music on a page —Anne Morrow Lindbergh

9. Birds . . . like planes stacked up over the airport, circling until they get a permission-to-land signal —Italo Calvino

10. Bird songs rang in the air like dropped coins —George Garrett

11. Birds rose into the air like blown leaves (at his approach) —Margaret Millar

12. The birds sang as if every sparkling drop were a fountain of inspiration to them —Charles Dickens

13. Birds . . . they roll like a drunken fingerprint across the sky — Richard Wilbur

14. (Birds) twitter louder than a flute —Phyllis McGinley

15. Birds . . . white as scraps of paper —Willa Cather
    See Also: WHITE

16. Crows whirled lazily in the sky like flakes of black ash rising from a fire —Guy Vanderhaeghe

17. A dove . . . glistening like a pearl —Hans Christian Andersen

18. The eagles were reveling in the air like bank robbers who had broken into the vault —Edward Hoagland

19. A flight of egrets . . . flying low, and scattered . . . like a ripple of white notes, sweet and pure and springlike, which an unseen hand drew forth, like a divine arpeggio, from an unseen harp —W. Somerset Maugham
    See Also: MUSIC

20. A flock of white swans flew like a long white veil over the water —Hans Christian Andersen

21. The fluttering, honking formation of birds was like a ship borne by the wind into the high invisible distance —Bernard Malamud

22. Geese . . . blackening the sky like a shake of pepper —Diane Ackerman

23. Gulls cry like hurt children —George Garrett

24. Gulls . . . settling and stirring like blown paper —Sylvia Plath

25. A handful of thrushes set down in an oak tree, like a flurry of leaves — Linda Bierds
    This simile marks the closing of Bierds' poem, *Mid-Plains Tornado.*

26. (That great) hawk circling like a black planet —Ellen Gilchrist

27. Hens . . . like dowager women, plump and impeccably arrayed in brown and grey —Rolf Yngve

28. His wings [Jonathan Livingston Seagull's] were smooth and perfect as sheets of polished silver —Richard Bach

29. Hummingbird . . . with a beak that looked as long as a darning needle and about as sharp —A. E. Maxwell

30. A jaybird . . . flying in a feathered flash of blue and white like a swift piece of the sky —George Garrett

31. The parrots shriek as if they were on fire —Ted Hughes
    In a poem entitled *The Jaguar,* the parrots not only shriek but "Strut like cheap tarts to attract the stroller with the nut."
    See Also: SCREAMS

32. The pigeons lolloped from illusory pediment to window-ledge like volatile, feathered madmen, chattering vile rhymes and laughing in hoarse, throaty voices —Angela Carter

33. Pigeons . . . settled into trees that shone with them like soft blue and gray fruit —Marge Piercy

34. Pigeons . . . with spreading wings like falling snow —Émile Zola

35. Soared high above the other birds, climbing like a dart —R. Wright Campbell

36. A solid line of pelicans flew . . . in graceful unison like a crew of oarsman in a racing shell —George Garrett

37. Sparrows scatter like handfuls of gravel —William H. Gass

38. Storks and pelicans flew in a line like waving ribbons —Hans Christian Andersen

39. Swans floated about like white lanterns —Lawrence Durrell

40. Swans go by like a snowy procession of Popes —George Garrett

41. Terns rise like seafoam from the breaking surf —Robert Hass

42. White gulls . . . in such close formation they were like a cloud — Phyllis Roberts

BIRTH

See Also: BEGINNINGS/ENDINGS, DEATH, ENTRANCES/EXITS, LIFE

1. Birth and death are like two ships in a harbor. There is no reason to rejoice at the ship setting out on a journey [birth] not knowing what she may encounter on the high seas, but we should rejoice at the ship returning to port [death] safely —Amora Levi

2. Into the world we come like ships launch'd from the docks, and stocks, and slips, for fortune fair or fatal! —Edward Fitzgerald

3. Once upon a time we were all born, popped out like jelly rolls —Anne Sexton

4. Passed like an envelope through a letter box [about an easy birth] —Anaïs Nin

5. The solemnity of birth, like that of death, is lost in repulsive or merely commonplace details for those who are in attendance —Marguerite Yourcenar

BITTERNESS

See Also: ANGER, FRIENDSHIP, LOVE

1. Bitter and sharp as a pulled leek with earth still clinging to it —George Garrett

2. Bitter as a broken friendship —Anon

3. Bitter as acorns —Ann Tyler

4. Bitter as a day of mourning —Joseph Conrad

5. (My youth was) bitter as a hard green fruit —Marilyn Hacker

6. Bitter as alum —Reynolds Price

7. (The air was) bitter as a stiffed hooker —Loren D. Estleman

8. Bitter as a tear —Algernon Charles Swinburne

9. Bitter as blood —Algernon Charles Swinburne

10. Bitter as coffee that's set too long —Rebecca Rule
    A variation: "Bitter as warmed up coffee."

11. (His voice was) bitter as dregs —Stephen Crane

12. Bitter as gall —John Webster

13. Bitter as self-sacrifice —Elizabeth Barrett Browning

14. Bitter as soot —Laurence Sterne

15. Bitter as the breaking down of love —Algernon Charles Swinburne

16. Bitter to me as death —William Shakespeare

17. Bitter as wormwood —*The Holy Bible/Proverbs*

18. Bitterness . . . kept coming back like a taste in the mouth after eating something bad —Rachel Ingalls

19. Embittered in mind, as a bear robbed of her whelps —*The Holy Bible/Samuel*

20. A flood of bitterness that washes over me every seven minutes like plagues visited upon a speeded-up pharaoh —William H. Gass

BLACK

See Also: COLORS; DEJECTION; FACIAL EXPRESSIONS, SERIOUS; GLOOM

1. (Hair) black and gleaming as a new galosh —Loren D. Estleman
2. (The newel post) black and shiny as a skull —W. P. Kinsella
3. Black as a black poodle's nose —Babette Deutsch
4. Black as a baker's shovel —Isaac Bashevis Singer
5. [A hall] black as a billy goat's belly —Ruth Chatterton
6. Black as a bull-moose in December —Henry Van Dyke
7. Black as a child's midnight waking —Marge Piercy
8. Black as a crow —Petronius
   An ancient simile that's still going strong, with "Black as a raven" from *The Holy* Bible the most frequently used variant.
9. Black as a funeral procession —Diane Ackerman
10. [Darkening sky] black as a giant tortoise —Stefan Zweig
11. Black as a heavy smoker's lungs —Elyse Sommer
12. Black as a manic depressive's thoughts —Elyse Sommer
13. (The room was) black as an honest politician's prospects —Dashiell Hammett
14. Black as an undertaker's hat —Donald Seaman
15. Black as a pine at night —Stephen Vincent Benét
16. (Locks) black as a raven —*The Holy Bible/Song of Solomon*
17. Black as a stack of black cats in the dark —H. W. Thompson
18. Black as a tar-barrel —Lewis Carroll
19. Black as black —W. B. Yeats
20. (Eyes . . .) black as bottomless water —Ellen du Pois Taylor
21. (Eyes) black as caverns —T. Coraghessan Boyle
22. (Black coats were) black as coffins —Rebecca West
23. Black as despair —John Phillips
24. Black as dusk —William Styron
25. Black as ebony —Oscar Wilde
26. Black like an oven (our kin was . . .) —*The Holy Bible/Lamentations*
27. Black as fate —Dame Edith Sitwell
28. Black as hell —William Shakespeare

Shakespeare, the master of so many similes, can be credited for a fair share of the best-known "Black as" comparisons. Besides this one from *Hamlet,* they include "Black as ink," "Black as ebony," and "Black as jet."

29. Black as midnight without a moon —Anon
30. Black as murder —Thomas Dekker
31. Black as perjury —Anon
32. (Our hands were) black as potatoes dug from the ground —T. Coraghessan Boyle
33. Black as some charred rafter —W. D. Snodgrass
34. Black as sorrow —Sir Philip Sidney
35. Black as the ace of spades —Anon
36. Black as the devil's hind foot —T. C. Haliburton
37. Black as the devil's heart —Ariel Dorfman
38. Black as the head of a hanged man —F. D. Reeve
39. (Black holes,) black as the moments before birth and after death —T. Coraghessan Boyle
40. Black as thunder —William Makepeace Thackeray
41. (Their visages) blacker than coal —*The Holy Bible/Lamentation*
42. (Deep and) black like an abyss —Aharon Megged
43. Black . . . like a subway tunnel —William Faulkner
44. It [a room] was black as the inside of a cat —Davis Grubb
45. The sky was as black as a monsoon —Dominique Lapierre

BLESSEDNESS
See: FORTUNE/MISFORTUNE

BLINDNESS
See Also: EYE(S); EYE EXPRESSIONS, BLANK

1. Blind as a bat —Anon
    Attribution for this enduringly popular cliche dates back to the seventeenth century and a somewhat longer old English version from John Clarke's *Paromiologia:* "Blind as a bat at noone." Less used variants are "Blind as a beetle" and "Blind as a buzzard."
2. Blind as a flame of fire —Algernon Charles Swinburne
3. Blind as a fool's heart —Robert Browning
4. Blind [about understanding love and hate] as a newborn child —Marguerite Duras
5. Blind as a newt —Leigh Allison Wilson

6.   Blind as a night fog —Daniel Berrigan

7.   Blind as a stone —Anon
     This still commonly used expression dates back to the fourteenth century, even before Chaucer used it in *Canterbury Tales:* "Blind as is a stoon."

8.   (Eyes staring,) blind as glass —Rose Tremain

9.   Blind as Hell —William Habbington

10. Blind as ignorance —Francis Beaumont and John Fletcher

11. Blind as inexperience —Victor Hugo

12. Blind as love —Percy Bysshe Shelley

13. Blind as maggots —Mark Helprin

14. Blind as night —Beryl Markham

15. (Bright and) blind as the moon in the blank mid-morning sky —F. D. Reeve

16. Blind as the waves of the sea —Eva Gore-Booth

17. Oblivious of . . . as an ant or a flea might be to the sound of the avalanche on which it rides —William Faulkner

BLOOD
     See Also: VIOLENCE

1.   Bleeding like a stuck pig —Anon

2.   Bleed, like a can of cherries —D. H. Lawrence

3.   Blood . . . hot and sticky like spilled wine —Harvey Swados

4.   Blood is like a parachute. If it's not there when you need it, you'll probably never need it again —Slogan for blood donor drive, June, 1987

5.   Blood spouting . . . as generously as water from a fountain —Jack London

6.   Blood like turpentine —George Garrett

7.   Blood spurting out of his noseholes like tomato puree —Jay Parini

8.   Bloodthirsty as a tick —Diane Ackerman

9.   Blood . . . which flows like a scream through the woods —Charles Simic

10. Bubbled blood like a little red spring —William Goyen

11. Face bloody as raw pork —Nelson Algren

12. [Man in hopes of improving world] scatters blood like a fish leaping from a lake —Janet Flanner

13. Stale, coppery smell [of blood] like the taste of pennies on the tongue —Jonathan Valin

BLOOMING
See: GROWTH

BLUE
See Also: COLORS

1. Blue and delicate as spring sky reflected in an old window —Elizabeth Spencer
2. (Eyes) blue as chicory in bloom —Ed McBain
3. (Sky . . .) blue as a robin's egg —Lee Smith
4. Blue as a brochure sea —William McIlvanney
5. Blue as a jay bird's wing —Ellen Glasgow
6. (Eyes as) blue as a peacock's neck —Flannery O'Connor
7. (Sky . . .) blue as a staring Northern eye —Elizabeth Enright
8. Blue as autumn mist —Thomas Hardy
9. (Eyes as) blue as corn-flowers —Lawrence Durrell
10. (Sea and sky are a matched set,) blue as delftware —T. Coraghessan Boyle
11. (Eyes) blue as heaven —Lord Byron
    Other famous poets to link heaven and the color blue include Christina Rossetti with "Saphires shining blue as heaven" and Percy Bysshe Shelley with "Blue as the overhanging heaven." For everyday usage there's "Blue as the sky."
12. Blue as hyacinths —Richard Ford
13. Blue as melancholy —Anon
14. (Sky) blue as the core of a match flame —George Garrett
15. Blue as the decks of the sea —Dame Edith Sitwell
16. Blue as the glimpses of sea beyond —John Greenleaf Whittier
17. Blue as the nose that graduate drunkards wear —Don Marquis
18. Blue as the sky —American colloquialism, attributed to New England
19. Blue as with the cold —Israel Zangwill
20. Blue like a corpse —Nikolai V. Gogol
21. Blue [of a repelling place] . . . like the color of the lips of an asthmatic plumber dying of lead poisoning who has put himself out of his misery with cyanide —Gerald Kersh
22. Blue like the last thundercloud of a tempest dispersed —Alexander Pushkin
23. Pale blues like old people's eyes —Edna O'Brien

BLUSHES
See Also: FACIAL COLOR, RED, SHAME, SHYNESS

1. Blood gushed crimson to her cheek . . . as though red wine had been poured into a crystal glass —Stefan Zweig

2. The blood showed clearly [on his face] like wine stains a pearly glass —Elinor Wylie

3. Blushed like a beetroot —Anatoly Rybakof

4. Blushed like a brick —Samuel Hopkins Adams

5. Blushed like a rose —Isak Dinesen

6. Blushed, like a wave of illness —Nadine Gordimer

7. Blushes rising like the tide —Lael Tucker Wertenbaker

8. Blushing like a strawberry —Marcel Proust

9. Blushing like a tomato —E. V. Lucas

10. Blushing pink as dawn —George Garrett

11. Blush like a black dog —John Ray's *Proverbs*

12. Blush like a geranium —Harry Graham

13. A blush that felt like a gasoline fire —R. V. Cassill

14. Color came to his face like blood on a galled fish —Loren D. Estleman

15. The color flew in her face like a flag —D. H. Lawrence

16. A deep flush enveloped him like darkness —Heinrich Böll

17. A delicate flush of pink . . . like the flush in the face of the bridegroom when he kissed the lips of the bride —Oscar Wilde

18. (I could feel my) face flaming as red as all the tomatoes in the world —H. C. Witwer

19. A faint blush, like the shadow of a rose in a mirror of silver came to her cheeks —Oscar Wilde

20. Felt shame flooding his cheeks like a hot geyser —Mark Helprin

21. His face went red as a peony —Julia O'Faolain

22. His neck flushing red even to his ears, like some overgrown schoolboy who had been made to recite when he didn't know his lesson —John Yount

23. Red as a barn —Susan Fromberg Schaeffer

24. Red crawling across her face like a stain —Harvey Swados

25. Ruddiness spreading across her cheeks like a wound —Joseph Koenig

26. Turned all colors—as a peacock's tail, or sunset streaming through a Gothic skylight —Lord Byron

27. Turned as red as a winter apple —American colloquialism
    The comparison of blushing cheeks to apples is common in everyday language as well as literature. An example of the latter: "Color like an apple" from Truman Capote's short story, *Children on Their Birthdays.*

28.   Turned red as . . . a nectarine, as a dahlia, as the most divinely red thing in the world —Colette

BOATS

See: SEASCAPES

BODY

See Also: AGILITY, AWKWARDNESS, BODY ORGANS, FATNESS, MUSCLES, PHYSICAL APPEARANCE, SHOULDERS, STRENGTH, STOMACH, THINNESS

1.   (A big soft) ass as wide as an axhandle —George Garrett

2.   Body and mind, like man and wife, do not always agree to die together —Charles Caleb Colton

3.   Body grown light as a shell, empty as a shell —Joyce Carol Oates

4.   The body is like a piano. It is needful to have the instrument in good order —Henry Ward Beecher

5.   The body, lady, is like a house: it don't go anywhere; but the spirit, lady, is like an automobile: always on the move —Flannery O'Connor
See Also: SOUL

6.   Body..light as milk —Philip Levine

7.   Body like a block of granite —Brian Glanville

8.   Body like a spring —Marguerite Duras

9.   (Had a) body like a stack of lumpy pillows —Robert Campbell

10. Body like dry bone —Robert Silverberg

11. Body . . . long like a weasel's —Anton Chekhov

12. Body . . . shaped like a sack half full of cement —Sterling Hayden

13. Body . . . silvery like a white rose —Isak Dinesen

14. The body turns empty as the shell of an insect, or like something inflatable but flattened —Jayne Anne Phillips

15. Body warm and flat as beer that's been standing —Marge Piercy

16. Buddha-like body still as an onyx boulder —Ralph Ellison

17. Build like a sack of angle irons —Loren D. Estleman

18. Built like a bowling pin —Clive Cussler

19. (She's hard to fit, being) built like a cement root cellar —Louise Erdrich

20. Built like a Coke machine —Joseph Wambaugh

21. Built like a crate —William Diehl

22. Built like a fire plug —Pat Conroy

23. Built like a greyhound —Miles Gibson

24. Built like a hammer —Lee K. Abbott

25. Built like a Russian weightlifter —William Diehl
26. Built like a skyscraper —Slogan, Shaw-Walker steel filing cabinets
27. Built like a snowman. A small round head atop a large round body with no neck in between —Rick Borsten
28. Built like a vault —Anon
29. Built like refrigerators —Jonathan Valin
30. Built solid, firm and square, like an unencumbered pine —Sylvia Berkman
31. Built square, like a van —William Beechcroft
32. Built with curves like the hull of a racing yacht —Ernest Hemingway
    A quick simile is about as much space as a master of conciseness like Hemingway devotes to physically describing a character. The woman with the racing yacht curves is Lady Brett from *The Sun Also Rises.*
33. Chest like a nail keg —Peter Matthiessen
34. Chest like an oak wine cask —Ira Wood
35. Chest like an oyster barrel —Ogden Nash
36. Chests and bellies like a pair of avalanches —T. Coraghessan Boyle
37. Chunky, heavy, like a Samoan swimmer —Herbert Gold
38. Corded and tough as a short piece of tallowed cable —George Foy
    The simile in Foy's novel, *Coaster,* applies to a sailor.
39. Delicate and softly rounded as a painting by Boucher —F. van Wyck Mason
40. (Against the light of the lamp,) the delicate erotic lines of her slender body came up like a photographic print in a developing tray —Brian Moore
41. Even her hipbones [like rest of angular body] jutted out as if her skirt was draped on a coathanger —Richard Maynard
42. A figure like a beer barrel —Oscar Wilde
    A variation by Charles Johnson: "Broad as a beer barrel."
43. Figure like a sack of flour —Josephine Tey
44. A figure like a two-armed Venus de Milo who had been on a sensible diet —David Niven
    Being an actor as well as a writer, Niven undoubtedly had a special appreciation for any device which would capture audience attention the minute the curtain rises; and so this simile from the first sentence of his autobiography, *The Moon's a Balloon.*
45. Figure . . . so delicate that she moved like a shadow —Inez Haynes Irwin

46. (She had) a figure that was like a swift unexpected blow to the diaphragm—that to linger on makes the beholder feel obscene — Frederick Exley

47. A fine small body, like a miniature dog bred for show —Maureen Howard

48. (He was) flat and wide as a gingerbread man —Charles Portis

49. Flat-chested and straight as a board —MacDonald Harris

50. Graceful figure, which was as tough as hickory and as flexible as a whip —Thomas Wolfe

51. Her body seemed somehow to hang on her, like somebody else's clothing —William McIlvanney

52. Her broad sexless body made her resemble a dilapidated Buddha — Ross Macdonald

53. Her firm protruding ass looked like a split peach —Steve Shagan

54. Hips like hills of sand —*Arabian Nights*

55. Hips like jugs —Eugene McNamara

56. His ancient, emaciated body looked as though it were already attacked by the corruption of the grave —W. Somerset Maugham

57. His body was covered with a dense mat of black hair. He looked like an overfed chimpanzee —Andrew Kaplan

58. His body waved like a flame in the breeze —Television obituary describing James Cagney's physical grace, 1986

59. His pectorals hung flabbily, like the breasts of an old woman —Gerald Kersh

60. It [worn body] was as if it were charred by a thunderbolt —Honoré de Balzac

61. Long body, devoid of developed muscles, was like a long, limp sash — Yukio Mishima

62. Look like a hot-air balloon with insufficient ballast —Anna Quindlen, *New York Times*/Hers, March 27, 1986
    The cause for the hot-air balloon appearance is pregnancy.

63. (A man with) a middle like a flour bag —Sharon Sheehe Stark

64. (Kaplan was examining the) midriff bulge that ballooned out over his belt like an inflated inner tube —William P. Kennedy
    The simile marks the opening of Kennedy's espionage novel, *The Masakado Lesson.*

65. (Was halfway through the process of turning from muscular to fat, so that at present he was) of uncertain consistency, like a cheap mattress —Richard Francis

66. Round and curved as a marble statue —George Garrett

67. A small boned body as easy to fragment as a young grouse's —Penelope Gilliatt

68. A small, plump woman, with her waist cinctured in sternly, like a cushion with a noose around it —John Cheever

69. Spine . . . like an iron rod —Angela Carter

70. Square as a wooden block —T. Coraghessan Boyle

71. Square like a block of stone —Willis Johnson

72. (She no longer had her slim waist or rounded bosom but was) square like a stack of firewood —Isak Dinesen

73. (A massive woman . . .) square, rather like a great piece of oak furniture —Willa Cather

74. Still had an athlete's frame . . . but the flesh had sagged on the hanger, like an old suit with change left in the pockets —Jonathan Valin

75. Straight as a mast, muscled like a gorilla —Maxwell Anderson and Laurence Stallings

76. A strong, supple body, like a tigress —Anthony Powell

77. Torso . . . thick and circular, like the bole of a tree —Madison Smartt Bell

78. (His body looked soft, his) waist puffing out like rising bread dough — Sue Grafton

79. We are bound to our bodies like an oyster to its shell —Plato

80. Weight was . . . beginning to hang like slightly inferior clothing — William McIlvanney

81. (Jill Martin was what they call a healthy lady.) Well rounded, like something out of Rubens —Mike Fredman

82. (He was) wide as a door —Andre Dubus

BODY ORGANS
See Also: SEX, TONGUE

1. A liver [from excessive drinking] like an old boot —J. B. Priestly
2. Penises as flaccid as ruined breasts —James Crumley
3. Penis . . . like a hard, live bedpost —Alice Walker
4. Penis like an upraised club —John Farris
5. Prostate like an Idaho potato —dialogue spoken by Marlon Brando in *The Last Tango in Paris,* 1972
6. Prostate . . . as round and elastic as a handball —Walker Percy
   The prostate comparison is made by the doctor-narrator of Percy's *Love in the Ruins* about an old male patient.

BOISTEROUSNESS
See: NOISE

BOLDNESS
See: COURAGE

BONDS
See: CONNECTIONS

BOOKS
See Also: READERS/READING

1. All the juice of a book is in an unpublished manuscript, and the published book is like a dead tree—just good for cutting up and building your house with —Christina Stead
2. Bad books are like intoxicating drinks; they furnish neither nourishment, nor medicine —Tryon Edwards
3. The *Bible* among books is as a diamond among precious stones —John Stoughton
4. A book is a friend whose face is constantly changing —Andrew Lang
5. A book is a mirror: if an ass peers into it, you can't expect an apostle to look out —Georg Christoph Lichtenberg
6. A book is like a garden carried in the pocket —Arab proverb
7. A book, like a child, needs time to be born —Heinrich Heine
8. A book, like a grape-vine, should have good fruit among its leaves — Edward Parsons Day
9. A book, like a landscape, is a state of consciousness varying with readers —Ernest Dimnet
10. A book may be as great a thing as a battle —Benjamin Disraeli

11. Books are like individuals; you know at once if they are going to create a sense within the sense . . . or if they will merely leave you indifferent —George Moore

12. Books . . . arranged carefully according to size, like schoolchildren lined up for recess —Helen Hudson

13. Books, like friends, should be few and well chosen —Thomas Fuller

14. Books, like men their authors, have no more than one way of coming into the world, but there are ten thousand to go out of it and return no more —Jonathan Swift

15. Books like proverbs receive their value from the stamp and esteem of ages through which they have passed —Sir William Temple

16. Books . . . as little read as tombstones —Frank Swinnerton

17. The [thick] book was just like a warm, thick eiderdown that she could pull over herself, snuggle into —Alice Munro

18. A book without an index is as incomplete as an eunuch —Theodore Stanton
    See Also: COMPLETENESS

19. A classic . . . is a successful book that has survived the reaction of the next period or generation. Then it's safe, like a style in architecture or furniture —F. Scott Fitzgerald

20. Dictionaries are like watches: the worst is better than none, and the best cannot be expected to go quite true —Samuel Johnson

21. Disliking a classic like disliking a nation one visits, it's the result of a blind spot, which goes away and leaves one embarrassed —Edward Hoagland

22. Each new book is as a ship that bears us away from the fixity of our limitations into the movement and splendor of life's infinite ocean —Helen Keller

23. Every book is like a purge, at the end of it one is empty . . . like a dry shell on the beach, waiting for the tide to come in again —Daphne du Maurier, *Ladies Home Journal,* November, 1956

24. The harmonies of bound books are like the flowers of the field —Hilaire Belloc

25. It is with books as with new acquaintances. At first we are highly delighted, if we find a general agreement . . . with closer acquaintances differences come to light; and then reasonable conduct mainly consists in not shrinking back at once —Johann Wolfgang von Goethe

26. It is with books as with men: a very small number play a great part —Voltaire

27. Like the fortune teller who sees a long journey in the cards or death by water, they [books] influence the future —Graham Greene

28. Most books, like their authors, are born to die —Joshua Swartz

29. A new book, like a young man, has a reputation to acquire —Clarence Walworth

30. A new book . . . not one of a number of similar objects, but like an individual man, unmatched —Marcel Proust

31. Novels are useful as bibles, if they teach you the secret that the best of life is conversation and the greatest success is confidence —Ralph Waldo Emerson

32. An old book, like an old man, is bound to have a good character already established, and must expect to be looked upon with suspicion if it has not —Clarence Walworth

33. The reading of good books is like a conversation with the finest men of past centuries —Rene Descartes

34. A room without books is like a body without a soul —Cicero
    A twist to this, variously attributed to Hannah More and Henry Ward Beecher, is "A house without books is like a room without windows."
    See Also: HOUSES

35. Such books are like frowzy old broads who have been handled by a thousand men —Peter De Vries
    The books being compared to frowzy old broads are telephone directories in phone booths.

36. There is no frigate like a book —Emily Dickinson
    Dickinson's simile serves as both title and first line for one of her best known poems.

37. Volumes [of books produced in America] by the dozens like doughnuts, big and soft and empty at the core —Helen Hudson

BOREDOM/BORING
See Also: DULLNESS, LIFE

1. Bored as Greta Garbo —Alice McDermott

2. Boredom enveloped her like heavy bedding —Yukio Mishima

3. Boredom . . . like a cancer in the breast —Evelyn Waugh

4. Boredom, like hookworm, is endemic —Beryl Markham

5. Boredom wafted from her like the scent of stale sweat —Anon

6. Boredom was increasing . . . like a silent animal sadly rubbing itself against the sultry grass —Yukio Mishima

7. Bore me the same as watching an industrial training film, or hearing a lecture on the physics of the three-point stance —Richard Ford

8. Boring as airline food —Anon

9. Boring as going to the toilet —Sylvia Plath

10. Boring, like reading the *Life Cycle of the Hummingbird* —Dan Wakefield

11. Could feel his boredom like an actual presence, like a big German shepherd that must be fed and restrained —Marge Piercy

12. Life's tedious as a twice-told tale —William Shakespeare
    This famous simile also appeared in Homer's *Odyssey* in the format of a question, "What's so tedious as a twice-told tale?."

13. Yawns [caused by a dull discussion] inflated in his throat like balloons —Derek Lambert

BOUNCING
See: ROCKING AND ROLLING

BOUNDLESSNESS
See: CONTINUITY

BOXING AND WRESTLING
See Also: SPORTS

1. A boxing match is like a cowboy movie. There's got to be good guys and there's got to be bad guys. What people pay for is to see the bad guys get beat —Sonny Liston, quoted from his obituary, *New York Times*

2. Fell on his face, kicking and heaving like a wounded leopard —Gerald Kersh

3. Fired himself across the ring like a stone from a catapult —Gerald Kersh

4. Got up the third time with blood like a livid splash of ripe fruit all over his face —H. E. Bates

5. He (Joe Louis) punches like he had a baseball bat in his both hands — Irwin Shaw

6. His nostrils [Joe Louis'], like the mouth of a double-barreled shotgun, took a quiet lead and let him have both barrels —Bob Considine, International News Service report on Louis-Schmeling fight, June 22, 1938

7. (Sharkey) kept coming in like the surf —Anon comment about the 1899 Jeffries-Sharkey fight

8. Their long, stiff jabs made their gloves dip and seem heavy, like big red balloons —Richard Ford

9. They clung together, spinning round and round like two twigs in a whirlpool —Gerald Kersh

10. Went down like a letter in a mail chute —Anon

11. When he (Jake La Motta) was in the ring, it was like he was in a cage fighting for his life —Ray Arcel, boxing trainer, quoted in Ira Berkow's Sports of the Times column, *New York Times*

12. Wrestled together, interlaced like snakes —Honoré de Balzac

BRAIN
See: INTELLIGENCE, MIND

BRAVERY
See: COURAGE

BREASTS
See Also: BODY, BODY ORGANS

1. Bosom like a Spanish balcony —Colette

2. Bosom like the prow of a ship —M. J. Farrell

3. Bosoms . . . large, like mounds of earth on the banks of a dug-up canal —R. K. Narayan

4. Bosoms like cheese-wheels —David Huddle

5. Bosoms like vast, half-filled hot-water bottles —M. J. Farrell

6. Bosoms set like two great prows of battleships —Brian Donleavy

7. Breasts as large and round as a bald man's head —James Crumley

8. Breasts hard as stone, project like a bulwark —Erich Maria Remarque

9. A breast divided into segments like a peeled orange, or a pair of thighs that converge into a single swollen knee —Kingsley Amis

10. Breasts heaving like a flight deck —Rita Mae Brown

11. Breasts . . . hung like water-filled balloons from her chest —Bernard Malamud

12. Breasts lie flat on her ribs like soft purses —Rose Tremain

13. Breasts, like a nursing mother's —Katherine Anne Porter

14. Breasts like a pair of piggies —Vladimir Nabokov

15. Breasts like armaments —T. Coraghessan Boyle

16. Breasts . . . like bread loaves hot from the oven —Francine du Plessix Gray

17. Breasts like . . . clusters of the vine —*The Holy Bible/Song of Solomon*

18. Breasts . . . like dried apples —Annette Sanford

19. Breasts like dunes —John D. MacDonald

20. Breasts . . . like empty purses except when they filled briefly and fed another child —H. E. Bates

21. Breasts like giant cabbages —W. Somerset Maugham

22. Breasts like overripe squash —Patricia Henley
23. Breasts like pennants —Irwin Shaw
24. Breasts like small hard apples —Francine du Plessix Gray

25. Breasts like smooth and ivory-colored hills —Marguerite Young
26. Breasts . . . sag from her chest like two plump gourds —Susan Yankowitz
27. Breasts sagging like overripe fruit —George Garrett

28. Breasts . . . shaped like crescent moons —Ira Wood
29. Breasts swaying like party balloons —Jilly Cooper
30. Breasts swelling . . . like rising bread —Marge Piercy

31. Breasts that drop, big as barrels —Dylan Thomas
32. Breasts were like long white grapes in the hot sun —D. H. Lawrence
33. Breasts, which were like apples cut in half —Colette

34. Breasts . . . whose fruits are dark as plums —C. J. Koch
35. Bursts like creamy milk-fed veal —Susan Lois
    The character who thus pronounces and describes a woman's
    breasts in a novel entitled *Personals* is a kosher butcher.
36. Chest like a promontory —Daphne Merkin

37. Cleavage deep as the jungle —T. Coraghessan Boyle
38. Enormous breasts that seemed to rise up and nearly out of her gown
    with every deep breath, defying physical laws, like a half-finished bridge
    —William Brammer
39. Full breasts soaring all over the place like billowing pennants in a
    strong wind —Joseph Heller

40. Her bosom heaved like an opera singer's —Ruth Prawer Jhabvala
41. Her breasts are tiny and hang from her chest like a pair of prunes —
    Milan Kundera
42. (An ample woman,) her breasts hung like calabashes inside her grey
    dress —Thomas Keneally

43. Her breasts looked like two five-pound flour sacks from which some of
    the contents had spilled —Sue Grafton
44. Her large heavy breasts seemed to lift like wings —James Crumley
45. Her nipples preceded her like scouts —Yehuda Amichai
46. Her small girlish breasts already sagged like little pockets on her white
    chest —Jonathan Valin

47. His bared breast glistened soft and greasy as though he had sweated out his fat in his sleep —Joseph Conrad

48. Jutting breasts like hills —Robinson Jeffers

49. Little mounds had appeared like soft marshmallows through her sweater —Carol Ascher

50. Long pointed breasts rearing like the muzzles of two Afghans —James Crumley

51. The nipple [of mother nursing child] looked like the end of a Tootsie Roll —Bobbie Ann Mason

52. Nipples . . . flat and wide as poker chips —Sue Miller

53. Nipples large as cookies —Ira Wood

54. Nipples . . . like buds of peonies —Amy Lowell

55. Nipples like two dark eyes —David Michael Kaplan

56. Nipples shaped like discs of milk chocolate —Ira Wood
    Wood's novel, *The Kitchen Man,* brims with food-related images.

57. Nipples . . . small as buttons —Miles Gibson

58. Nipples standing out like two overgrown M&Ms —T. Glen Coughlin

59. The profile of her body stood forth like the prow of a clipper ship — Calder Willingham

60. She had fenders like a GMC truck —Loren D. Estleman

61. They [breasts] were wide mounds growing like muscles across her chest —Will Weaver

62. A woman without breasts is like a bed without pillows —Anon

BREATHING

1. Alimentary canal . . . working like a derrick without a soul —Tess Slesinger

2. Breath . . . as black as funerals —Miles Gibson
   See Also: BLACK

3. (His) breath came heavily, like puffs of wind over a stormy sea — Walter De La Mare

4. Breath came like puffs from a steam locomotive —Gerald Tomlinson

5. Breath clear and sweet like a child's —Flannery O'Connor

6. Breathed as if she had a fever —Mark Helprin

7. Breathed deeply like a swimmer coming up for air —George Garrett

8. (He) breathed like a prisoner set free —Willa Cather

9. Breathe hard like a horse when you take the saddle off —O. Henry

10. Breathe like a chugging train —Tony Ardizzone

11. Breathe like a second-hand bicycle pump —O. Henry

12. Breath [from snoring] grating like bark stripped from a tree —T. Coraghessan Boyle

13. Breathing as rapidly as an exhausted dog —Derek Lambert

14. Breathing as softly as a butterfly —Ellen Glasgow

15. Breathing as though stream engines were working his lungs —Pat Conroy

16. Breathing like a hard-run horse —James Crumley

17. Breathing like almost any sort of man who has just been chased for a mile or so uphill by a bull in the pink of condition —Kingsley Amis

18. Breathing like an escape valve —Joseph C. Lincoln

19. Breathing like a tire pump —Dashiell Hammett

20. Breathing like the friction of rusted gears —T. Coraghessan Boyle

21. Breathing like two hippos with a chest cold —Jane Wagner
    This line, spoken by the character Paul (interpreted by Lily Tomlin), describes his participation at his wife's labor.

22. Breathing, quick and hoarse like a dog's panting —Albert Camus

23. Breathing . . . slow and rhythmical, like the bellows at a forge rising and falling —Henri-Pierre Roche

24. Breathing [an overweight man's] sounded like someone sitting down on a leather couch —Sue Grafton

25. Breathing with irregularity, like an overworked horse. Breathing deeply like a man asleep —George Garrett

26. Breath is like the gentle air of spring —Henry Wadsworth Longfellow

27. Breath . . . like the steam of apple-pies —Robert Greene

28. Breath popping like steam valves in old boilers —Denis Johnson

29. (Rankin's) breath rushed out like an undertow beneath the words — Richard Moran

30. Breath sweet as May —Christina Rossetti

31. The breath was pumped from their bodies as though from machines — Vicki Baum

32. Breath [of dying woman] whistled like the wind in a keyhole —Edith Wharton

33. Each breath was expelled in a puff, as if one were blowing a trumpet, Dizzy Gillespie fashion —Stephen King

34. Each breath was like a hill to climb —Barbara Reid

35. Gasped for breath like a wounded animal —Vicki Baum

36. Gasped the air deeply, like a diver escaping from a watery grave —Jan Kubicki

37. Gasping like a fish stranded on a sandbank —F. van Wyck Mason
    An extension of "Gasped like a stranded fish."

38. Gulped in air through her mouth, straining like a nearly drowned man dragged out of the water —William Moseley

39. Gulping in air like a swimmer exhausted from fighting a heavy surf — Margaret Millar

40. Hack and wheeze like an overworked horse —T. Coraghessan Boyle

41. Her breath seems to flow like the water in a frozen stream —Rochelle Ratner

42. His breath [as he kissed her hand] was between her fingers like a web on summer grass —Ellen Gilchrist

43. His breath was staccato, like obstructed sobs —Nancy Huddleston Packer

44. Holds her breath like a seal —John Berryman

45. Huff like windy giants —W. D. Snodgrass

46. Let out a long, whistling breath like a deflating tire —Cornell Woolrich

47. Lungs..blowing like leathern bellows —Frank Ross

48. (Stearn's) lungs fluttered like a sparrow's heartbeat —Z. Vance Wilson

49. (I was panting and) my breath came like fire —Louise Erdrich

50. Pant like a fat man running for a bus —Lawrence Durrell

51. Panting like a steamboat —Joyce Cary

52. Puffed like a leaky steam pipe —O. Henry

53. Puffing like a blown shire horse —Donald Seaman

54. A rasping gasp as though he were swallowing his false teeth —W. P. Kinsella

55. Sharp intake of breath, like a toy balloon suddenly deflated —Ralph Ellison

56. Snort [while asleep] like a timid locomotive —MacDonald Harris

57. Sound of breathing . . . like the soft crackle of tissue paper —Frank Swinnerton

58. Sucked air like a drowning fish —Miles Gibson

59. Took as much breath as if I'd heaved a shot put —Larry McMurtry

60. Wheezing . . . like a horse with a progressive lung disease —T. Coraghessan Boyle

BREVITY
    See Also: TIME

1. As compact as a drop of pure water —Richard E. Shepard, *New York Times,* November 3, 1986
   The simile attempts to explain the mystery of the Flamenco Puro dance troop's creative wellsprings.

2. Brief as a classified ad —Anon

3. Brief as a drop of dew —Cale Young Rice

4. Brief as a grouch's smile —Anon

5. Brief as a sinner's prayer —Anon

6. Brief as a twinge —Margaret Atwood

7. Brief as the Z column in a pocket dictionary —Irvin S. Cobb
   Or, to be even more specific, "Brief as the Z column in this dictionary."

8. Brief as youth in retrospect —Elyse Sommer

9. (Smiled) briefly, on and off like a light switch —Gavin Lyall

10. Concise as a telegram —Elyse Sommer

11. Short as any dream —William Shakespeare

12. Short, clear as a bird-note, trailing away —E. B. White

BRIGHTNESS

See Also: GLITTER AND GLOSS, LIGHTING, SHINING

1. Blazing like the windows of the city —James Dickey

2. (He possessed a brainful of information,) bright and beautiful as diamonds swaddled in midnight-blue velvet —W. P. Kinsella

3. Bright and light as the crest of a peacock —Alfred, Lord Tennyson

4. Bright and pleasing as a child's rattle —Virginia Woolf

5. Bright as a beach in the moonlight —Alfred Austin

6. (An image came to me across the years,) bright as a coin from the mint —Norman Mailer

7. Bright as a frog's eyes —Hart Crane

8. Bright as all between cloudless skies and windless streams —Percy Bysshe Shelley

9. Bright as a nettle rash —Diane Ackerman

10. (Laugh . . .) bright as a new ensign's buttons —Frederic Wakeman

11. Bright as a newly painted toy —Hugh Walpole

12. Bright as an icon —Margaret Atwood

13. Bright as any glass —Geoffrey Chaucer

14. Bright as any meteor ever bred by the North Pole —Lord Byron

15. Bright as a parakeet —Dame Edith Sitwell

16. (Every day) bright as a postcard —Karl Shapiro

17. Bright as a roomful of chrystal chandeliers —Anon
18. Bright as a splinter from a glazier's table —Beryl Markham
19. (A face) bright as a waterdrop —Padraic Fallon
20. Bright as day —Geoffrey Chaucer
21. Bright as foil —Molly Giles
22. Bright as freedom —Marge Piercy
23. Bright as joy —Hartley Coleridge
24. Bright as light —Alfred, Lord Tennyson
25. Bright as moonlight over snow —Wallace Stegner
26. Bright as Spring —Walter Savage Landor
27. (Eyes as) bright as the Dipper —Stephen Vincent Benét
28. Bright as the fullest moon in blackest air —*Arabian Nights*
29. Bright as the promises of a new administration —Elyse Sommer
30. Bright as the promise of life on commencement day —Elyse Sommer
31. Bright as the promise of a cloudless day —C. P. Wilson
32. Bright as the raindrops and roses in June —Dame Edith Sitwell
33. Bright as the world was in its infant years —John Banks
34. Bright as truth —Barry Cornwall
35. Bright like a brimming bowl of jewels —Peter De Vries
36. Bright, like a flash of sunlight —Edward Bulwer-Lytton
37. Bright (eyes) like agate —D. H. Lawrence
38. Bright like blood —Algernon Charles Swinburne
39. Brightness . . . bright as dipper —Stephen Vincent Benét
40. Brilliant as a postage stamp —Lawrence Durrell
41. (Eyes) brilliant as fire —Nadine Gordimer
42. [Oranges and grapefruits] brilliant as planets —Cynthia Ozick
43. Brilliant as the stars —Ouida
44. Brilliant as the sun —Slogan, Lustberg-Nast, Lustray shirts
45. Brilliant like a Chinese porcelain —W. Somerset Maugham
46. Brilliantly, gaudily colored as a Gypsy camp —Kate Simon
47. Dazzled the eyes like a second noonday sun —Edna Ferber
48. Growing brighter and brighter like a forest after a rain —Denis Johnson
49. Lights up like a Star Wars pinball machine —Marge Piercy
50. [Face] light up like a bonfire of joy —Carl Sandburg
51. Vivid as sun through a thin brown bottle —Reynolds Price
52. Vivid as the granules of paint in a Dubuffet —John Updike

BRITTLENESS
    See: FRAGILITY

BROWN
    See Also: COLORS
1. (Wine) as brown as November leaves —Wilbur Daniel Steele
2. [Pupils of eyes] brown and shiny like melting chocolate —Margaret Millar
3. Brown as a berry —Geoffrey Chaucer
        The old English original read "Broun as is a berye."
4. (His face was) brown as an old boot —Christopher Isherwood
    See Also: TOUGHNESS
5. Brown as an old daguerreotype fading —Robert Penn Warren
6. Brown as a nut —Henry Wadsworth Longfellow
7. (Cheeks) brown as oak-leaves —Henry Wadsworth Longfellow
8. (Hair) brown as a pecan shell —Reynolds Price
9. Brown as cinnamon —Truman Capote
10. Brown as onion soup —Saul Bellow
11. Brown as rust —George Garrett
12. (A tan) brown as seven-grain bread —Patricia Henley
13. (A girl as) brown as the ground —Cynthia Ozick
14. Brown as tobacco spit brew —Truman Capote
15. Brown . . . like the color of the basket —H. E. Bates
16. A dreggy brown, like bad coffee —Irvin S. Cobb
17. Pale brown, like canvas —Mary McCarthy

BRUTALITY
    See: CRUELTY, VIOLENCE

BUILDINGS
    SEE: HOUSES

BURST
    See Also: DISINTEGRATION, SUDDENNESS
1. (Your unexpected letter has just) burst into my existence like a meteor into the sphere of a planet —William James letter from Dresden to Oliver Wendell Holmes, Jr., May 15, 1868
2. (My poor head would) burst like a dropped watermelon —Maya Angelou
3. Burst like a raw egg —William Diehl

4. Burst like a ripe seedpod —Beryl Markham

5. Burst like a thunderbolt —Alfred, Lord Tennyson

6. (Seeds) burst like bullets —Anne Sexton

7. [Details of an event would] burst open like garbage from a bag dropped from a height —Thomas Keneally

8. Burst out like a rash —Nadine Gordimer

9. Bursting like an overdone potato —Sir Arthur Conan Doyle

10. Comes apart like a slow-ripping seam —Sharon Sheehe Stark
   The character coming apart in the author's story, *In the Surprise of Life,* is a girl who has been trying to contain her laughter.

11. Flashed [a remark] like a sheet of heat lightning —Rita Mae Brown

12. (The cursing and grumbling) flashed like a storm —Enid Bagnold

13. Like the buds let us burst —Ogden Nash

14. (He had a real gift for those flaring exclamations, those raucous) outbursts, like wounds suddenly opened —Romain Gary

15. Sputtering like a leaky valve —John Peter Toohey

16. (Our imaginations seem to have been) torn open . . . as by a charge of dynamite —Dorothy Canfield Fisher

BUSINESS

See Also: ADVERTISING, SUCCESS/FAILURE

1. As oxygen is the disintegrating principle of life, working night and day to dissolve, separate, pull apart and dissipate, so there is something in business that continually tends to scatter, destroy and shift possession from this man to that. A million mice nibble eternally at every business venture —Elbert Hubbard

2. Business is like a man rowing a boat upstream. He has no choice; he must go ahead or he will go back —Lewis E. Pierson

3. Business is like oil. It won't mix with anything but business —J. Grahame

4. Business . . . is very much like religion: it is founded on faith — William McFee

5. Business policy flows downhill from the mountain, like water —Anon

6. A business without customers is like a computer without bytes —Anon
   As the entries that follow show, this concept lends itself to many additional twists.

7. A business without customers is like a stage without light —Anon

8. A business without orders is like a room without windows —Anon

9. Buying and selling like a Rockefeller —Arthur A. Cohen

10. A corporation is just like any natural person, except that it has no pants to kick or soul to damn —Ernst and Lindley
    Playwrights Ernst and Lindley wrote this simile to be spoken by a judge in their 1930's play *Hold Your Tongue.*

11. Corporate politics is like the days of Andrew Jackson, the spoils system —Rita Mae Brown
    See Also: POLITICS

12. Customers drop away like tenpins —Anon

13. Inventory that just sits there like it's nailed to the floor —Anthony E. Stockanes

14. Nowadays almost every business is like show business, including politics, which has become more like show business than show business is —Russell Baker
    See Also: POLITICS

15. Orders fell like stones —Anon

16. (Being in the microcomputer business is) risky, like going 55 miles an hour three feet from a cliff. If you make the wrong turn you're bankrupt so fast you don't know what hit you —George Morrow, quoted in *New York Times,* March 11, 1986 when his company went bankrupt
    See Also: DANGER

17. Some businesses are like desert flowers. They bloom overnight, and they're gone —George Morrow, quoted *New York Times,* March 11, 1986
    The first two words are transposed from "Computer companies" to generalize the comparison.
    See Also: BEGINNINGS/ENDINGS

18. The tide of business, like the running stream, is sometimes high and sometimes low, a quiet ebb, or a tempestuous flow, and always in extreme —John Dryden

19. Tradespeople are just like gardeners. They take advantage of your not knowing —Agatha Christie

BUSYNESS
See Also: ACTIVENESS, WORK

1. Busier than a cat covering shit on a marble slab —American colloquialism

2. Busier than a Gulag gravedigger —Joseph Wambaugh

3. Bustled about like so many ants roused by the approach of a foe —J. Hampden Porte
    Ants rank with bees as a means to describe busyness. In modern day usage and literature the above is usually shortened; for example, "Busy as an ant" used by Ogden Nash in his poem *Children.*

4. (I've been) busy as a bartender on Saturday night —Irwin Shaw

5. Busy as a bee —Geoffrey Chaucer
   Chaucer's old English version of what has become a commonly
   used expression read "Bisy as bees ben they."

6. Busy as a dog with fleas —Anon

7. Busy as a fiddler's elbow —Harry Prince

8. Busy as a hen with one chicken —John Ray's *Proverbs*
   To strengthen the impact of the simile there's, "Busy as a hen
   with ten chickens" and "As a hen with fifteen chickens"
   attributed to James Howell and "Busy as a hen with fifteen
   chickens in a barnyard."

9. Busy as an oven at Christmas —Michael Denham

10. Busy as ants in a breadbox —Anon

11. (I am) busy as a one-armed paperhanger with the itch —American
    colloquialism
    This is often attributed to Theodore Roosevelt who used it in a
    letter to his daughter. Some extensions on the one-armed
    paperhanger image include: "Busy as a one-armed paper-
    hanger with the hives" (one of many common expressions in
    Carl Sandburg's *The People, Yes*), "Busy as a one-armed
    paperhanger with the seven-year itch" (H. W. Thompson,
    Body, Boots and Britches) and "Busy as a one-armed paper-
    hanger with the nettle rash" (O. Henry, *The Ethics of a Pig*).

12. Busy as a one-legged man in an ass-kicking contest all week long —Pat
    Conroy

13. Busy as a pair of lizards on a warm brick —James Cain

14. Busy as a ticking clock —Anon

15. (Birds shrill and musical,) busy as bullets —John Farris

16. Busy as catbirds —Hilary Masters

17. Busy as jumper cables at a Mexican funeral —Thomas Zigal

18. Busy as maggots —Marge Piercy

19. Busy as the day is long —Vincent Stuckey Lean

20. Busy as the devil in a gale of wind —Walter Scott

21. Get busy like a bomb —Erich Maria Remarque

22. Humming like a hive —John Gardner

23. Hurried..like one who had always a multiplicity of tasks on hand —
    Charlotte Brontë
    See Also: SPEED

24. [Being Secretary of Defense] is like getting a shave and having your
    appendix out at the same time —Robert Lovett, *Saturday Evening Post,*
    May 28, 1960

25. Like a squirrel in a cage, always in action —Aphra Behn
26. Like the bee, we should make our industry our amusement —Oliver Goldsmith

CALMNESS

See Also: PEACEFULNESS

1. Calm as a bathtub —George Garrett
2. Calm as a Buddhist —Elizabeth Taylor
3. Calm as a convent —Anon
4. Calm as a cud-chewing cow —Harold Adams
5. Calm as a frozen lake when ruthless winds blow fiercely —William Wordsworth
6. Calm as a gliding moon —Samuel Taylor Coleridge
7. Calm as a marble head —Eudora Welty
8. (I'm) calm as a Mediterranean sky —Frank Swinnerton
9. Calm as a mirror —Alexandre Dumas, père
10. (The sky was) calm as an aquarium —Antoine de Saint-Éxupéry
11. Calm as an iceberg —Gelett Burgess
12. Calm as a slumbering babe —Percy Bysshe Shelley
     As part of our daily language this has evolved into "Calm as a sleeping baby."
13. (Said it as) calm as a virgin discussing flower arrangement —George MacDonald Fraser
14. Calm as beauty —Robert Browning
15. Calm as dewdrops —William Wordsworth
16. Calm as fate —John Greenleaf Whittier
17. Calm as glass —Charlotte Brontë
18. Calm as ice —Nathaniel Hawthorne
19. Calm as if she were sitting for her portrait —Henry James
20. Calm as in the days when all was right —Friedrich von Schiller
21. Calm as night —Victor Hugo
22. (Voice) calm as the deepest cold —Sharon Sheehe Stark
23. Calm as the sky after a day of storm —Voltaire
24. Calm as virtue —William Shakespeare
25. Calm as water in a glass—standing water in clean cut glass —Reynolds Price

26. Calm descended (on the pool hall) as nerve shattering as if the (long barnlike) room were the ship from which Jonah had been cast into the sea —Flannery O'Connor

27. Calmed down, like a Corinthian column —John Ashbery

28. A calm . . . like the deep sleep which follows an orgy —Mark Twain

29. Cold as cucumbers —Beaumont and Fletcher
    In its original meaning this referred to sexual coldness. As currently used it means being calm, collected, or "Cool as a cucumber." Poet Stevie Smith used the simile as a title for a poem which begins with this and two other cliches to describe the subject of the poem, a girl named Mary: "Cool as a cucumber calm as a mill pond sound as a bell was Mary." (Ed: The quote from the Smith poem has no commas!)

30. Cool and collected as a dean sitting in his deanery —Ogden Nash

31. Cool and ordinary as a gallon of buttermilk —Borden Deal

32. Cool as a Buddha —Jan Epton Seale
    The simile, from a short story about a new mother entitled *Reluctant Madonna,* reads as follows in full context: "Christie intends to be cool as a Buddha about this baby. Unflappable."

33. Cool as a cop with a clipboard —Gary Gildner

34. Cool as a cube of cucumber on ice —Carl Sandburg
    This extension of the familiar "Cool as a cucumber" is particularly apt in Sandburg's epic, *The People, Yes,* which beautifully and cleverly incorporates many familiar similes.

35. Cool as a frozen daiquiri —Linda Barnes

36. Cool as an Easter lily —Erich Maria Remarque

37. Cool as a quarterback —Dan Wakefield

38. (He was) cool as a refrigerator —R.A.J. Walling

39. Cool as a veteran horse race jockey —Carl Sandburg

40. Cool as lettuce —Jay Parini

41. (He's as) cool as the other side of your pillow —Merlin Olsen, NBC-TV broadcaster, about Ken O'Brien, quarterback for the Jets, January, 1987

42. Expression . . . as calm and collected as that of a doctor by a patient's bedside —Stefan Zweig

43. Felt a certain calm fall over me like a cloak —R. Wright Campbell

44. Have kept composure, like captives who would not talk under torture —Richard Wilbur

45. His calmness was like the sureness of money in the bank —Anzia Yezierska

46. Looked as cool as a yellow diamond —Robert Campbell

47. Looking calm as an eggshell —Edith Wharton
48. (The April morning) mellow as milk —Sharon Sheehe Stark
49. Mellow as moonlight —Slogan, Vogan Candy Co.
50. Mellow as old brandy —Anon
51. Mild as cottage cheese —Stephen Vincent Benét
52. Mild as milk —Dame Edith Sitwell
53. Nonchalant as a shoplifter in the checkout line —Donald McCaig
54. The sea was calm like milk and water —Isak Dinesen
55. The sense of rest, of having arrived at the long-promised calm centre, filled him like a species of sleep —John Updike
56. Serene as a man who has just got a promotion and raise —Geoffrey Wolff
57. Stayed calm, like a hero before the battle when all the cameras are on him —Clancy Sigal
58. (Your opinion at the moment) worries me exactly as much as dandruff would a chopped-off head —William McIlvanney

CANDOR

See Also: HONESTY

1. About as sincere as the look upon the face of an undertaker conducting a nine-hundred-dollar funeral —H. L. Mencken
2. As candid as the C.I.A. —Anon
3. As devoted to candor as a high school valedictorian —Jonathan Valin
4. As forthcoming as *Pravda* —Joseph Wambaugh
5. As frank as a candid camera shot —Anon
6. As open [about revealing self] as an unsteamed clam —Elyse Sommer
7. As revealing as a locked diary —Anon
8. Candid as mirrors —Robert G. Ingersoll
9. Direct as a bullet —Flannery O'Connor
10. Phony as a laugh track —Vincent Canby, about the movie *Murphy's Romance, New York Times,* January 17, 1986
11. Sincerity is like traveling on a plain beaten road, which commonly brings a man sooner to his journey's end than by-ways in which men often lose themselves —John Tillotson
12. Took off the mask of tranquility she had worn . . . like an actress returning weary to her room after a trying fifth act and falling half-dead upon a couch, while the audience retains an image of her to which she bears not the slightest resemblance —Honoré de Balzac
13. (You get right) to the point . . . like a knife in the heart —Harvey Fierstein

Fierstein's simile is a line from *La Cage aux Folles,* the musical based on Jean Poiret's play by the same name.

14. Two-sided, like Janus —L. P. Hartley

CAPABILITY
See: ABILITY

CAREFULNESS
See: ATTENTION, CAUTION, CORRECTNESS

CARELESSNESS
1. Act with the calm forethought of a beheaded chicken —Herman Wouk
    In his novel, *Inside, Outside,* Wouk used the comparison to describe the behavior of political characters.
2. Careless as a child at play —William Winter
3. Careless as saints who live by faith alone —George Garrett
4. [Charles de Gaulle] has been abysmally careless, like a man running a bus over mountains, who forgot to equip it with good brakes —Janet Flanner
5. Ignore caution like a gambler with a hot tip —Anon

CARES
See: PROBLEMS/SOLUTIONS

CAUSE/EFFECT
1. Affect me [with revulsion] like the smell of a cheap cigar left smoldering in an ashtray —Jonathan Valin
    In Valin's novel, *Final Notice,* the descriptive frame of reference for the simile is a tattoo.
2. The certainty [of his desire] landed in the bottom of my stomach like a flatiron —Mary Gordon
3. The change [in living accommodations] would be like going from Purgatory to Paradise —Louisa May Alcott
4. The conviction that I am loved and loving affects me like a military bracing —John Cheever
5. The effort made him choke like a tiger at a bone —Robert Frost
6. Every gesture . . . aroused a beat chant like the beat of the heart of the desert —Anaïs Nin
7. (This city) exacerbates loneliness in me the same way that water makes Alka-Seltzer fizz —Pat Conroy
8. The general effect was exactly like a microscopic view of a small detachment of black beetles in search of a dead rat —John Ruskin

9. Has a disruptive effect . . . like a torpedo coming down Main Street —Anon politician on Gramm-Rudman Law, February, 1986

10. Has as little effect on me as water on a duck's back —American colloquialism, attributed to South
    A variation: "As water rolling off a duck's back."

11. Her absence felt like a presence, an electrical charge of silence in the house —John Updike

12. His death served to remind me, like a custard pie in the face, that life is sometimes like one big savage joke —Sue Grafton

13. (A blast of Prince [music] . . .) hit me like a feather boa with a length of lead pipe in it —Jonathan Valin

14. Its [melancholy] effect upon you is somewhat similar to what would probably be produced by a combined attack of toothache, indigestion and a cold in the head —Jerome K. Jerome

15. It [forcing an old priest into retirement] was just like ripping an old tree out of the ground —W. P. Kinsella

16. The kind whisper went to my heart like a dagger —Charlotte Brontë

17. Offering a flight attendant a $20 bill for a $2 drink is like spitting on an Alabama state trooper —Louis D. Wilson, *Wall Street Journal,* June 30, 1986

18. Pain and poverty and thwarted ambition . . . can break the virtues like brittle bones —George Garrett

19. Seeing her again . . . was like rediscovering a half-forgotten landmark —Ann Petry

20. [When a tired-looking woman smiles] some of the years of hard living fell away like happy tears —James Crumley

CAUTION

See Also: BEHAVIOR

1. Cagey as a feral cat —John Yount

2. Careful as a cat walking on eggshells —American colloquialism, attributed to New England

3. Carries it [a plant] as if it's made of Steuben glass —Ann Beattie

4. Carry . . . like a hot tureen —Eudora Welty

5. Caution flowed over the [telephone] wire like a wave —Robert M. Coates

6. Caution, like that of a wild beast that is fierce but feeble or like that of an insect whose little fragment of earth has given way, and made it pause in a palsy of distrust —George Eliot

7. Cautious as a burglar walking over a tin roof in cowhide boots — Wallace Irwin

8. Cautious as a good housekeeper —Honoré de Balzac

9. Cautious as a tightrope walker with a severe itch —Anon
   This is yet another perversion of the popular "Busy as a one-armed paperhanger" comparison.
   See Also: BUSYNESS

10. Cautious as his gray suit —John Dancy, NBC-TV, about Robert Gates at CIA confirmation hearings, April, 1987

11. Cautiously, like a man handling sixteenth-century lace —Roald Dahl

12. Choosy as a stud in a harem —Mike Sommer

13. Discreet . . . as if you're trying to tail yourself —William McIlvanney

14. Going as if he trod upon eggs —Robert Burton

15. Like a weight-watcher at the feast of San Gennaro, I just nibbled a bit —Lenoard M. Heine, Jr., commenting on his cautious stock purchases when others were investing freely, quoted *Wall Street Journal* column by Vartanig G. Vartan, January 19, 1987

16. Peeped out carefully like a mole from its hole —Derek Walcott

17. Picked up the pieces as carefully as if they were cuttings from the Koh-i-noor —Israel Zangwill

18. Picking his words like a man making his way through a minefield —Donald Seaman

19. Progressed like a man tracing and following a chalk line —Frank Swinnerton

20. A prudent man is like a pin; his head prevents him from going too far —Anon

21. Should be used with discretion, like cayenne pepper —Anon

22. So wary that he sleeps like a hare, with his eyes open —Thomas Fuller

23. Timid as hares —Anton Chekhov

24. To take all you want is never as good as to stop when you should —Lao Tzu

25. (We must) treat him like Dresden china —Nikolai V. Gogol

26. Wary as a blind horse —Thomas Fuller

27. Wary as a pickpocket's confidence that the policeman on the beat will stay bought —H. L. Mencken
    This is slightly changed from Mencken's original words which identified the pickpocket as an American.

28. Watched what he said as carefully as if he were in court —John Updike

CELEBRITY
See: FAME

CENSORSHIP
See: CONTROL, CRITICISM

CERTAINTY

1. Absolute as a miser's greed —Anon

2. An absolute, like the firmness of the earth —Tom Wolfe

3. Almost as predictable as the arrival of solstice and equinox —Russell Baker, *New York Times*/Observer, September 17, 1986
    Baker's comparison referred to Chief-Justice-to-be William Rehnquist's judicial opinions.

4. As certain as a gun —Samuel Butler

5. As certain as beach traffic in July —Anon

6. As certain as bodies moved with greater impulse, progress more rapidly than those moved with less —Voltaire

7. As certain as death and taxes —Daniel Defoe
    Often attributed to Benjamin Franklin, the simile continues to be popular, with many humorous twists such as "Certain as death and hay-fever," used in Philip Barry's 1923 play, *You and I.*

8. As certain as dye penetrates cotton —Daniela Gioseffi
    The simile, from a poem, continues with "The orange is a part of the living animal."

9. As certain as end-of-the season inventories —Anon

10. As certain as June graduates scanning the want ads —Anon

11. As certain as leaves falling in September —Anon

12. As certain as lines at return counters after Christmas —Anon

13. As certain as rise of taxi meter —Anon

14. As certain as that a crooked tree will have a crooked shadow —Anon

15. As certain as that bread crumbs will attract a flock of pigeons —Anon

16. As certain as that leaves will fall in autumn —Anon

17. As certain as that night succeeds the day —George Washington

18. As certain as that your shadow will follow you —Anon

19. As certain as the morning —Thomas Wolfe

20. As certain as the sunrise —Anon

21. As certain as thunderclap following lightning —Anon

22. As certain as wrinkles —Anon

23. As certainly as day follows day —Anon

24. As certainly as Segovia had been born to finger a fretboard or Willie Mays to swing a bat —T. Coraghessan Boyle

25. As inevitable as a dog at a hydrant —Anon

26. As inevitable as the turning of the earth on which you stand —Harvey Swados

27. As sure as a club —Mary Hedin

28. As sure as a goose goes barefoot —American colloquialism, attributed to Northeast

29. As sure as a tested hypothesis —Lorrie Moore

30. As sure as a wheel is round —American colloquialism

31. As sure as behave and misbehave —John Ciardi

32. As sure as day —William Shakespeare

33. As sure as death —William Shakespeare

34. As sure as death —Ben Jonson
    Jonson's use of this simile in *Every Man in His Humor* if not the first, is certainly one of the earliest encountered.

35. As sure as meat will fry —American colloquialism, attributed to Southeast

36. As sure as rain —Ben Ames Williams
    A more specific variation of this is "Sure as rain in April."

37. As sure as shooting —Anon
    This common expression probably stems from the no longer used "Sure as a gun," variously attributed to the poet John Dryden and the playwright William Congreve.

38. Sure as shooting —American colloquialism

39. As sure as snakes crawl —American colloquialism, attributed to Midwest

40. As surely as that two ends of a seesaw cannot both be elevated at the same time —Alexander Woolcott

41. As surely as the eye tends to be long-sighted in the sailor and short-sighted in the student —Herbert Spencer

42. As surely as the harvest comes after the seedtime —John Brown

43. As surely as the tree becomes bulky when it stands alone and slender if one of a group —Herbert Spencer

44. As surely as water will wet us, as surely as fire will burn —Rudyard Kipling

45. As unpreventable as blinking your eyes when a light flashes suddenly —Anon

46. Certain things will follow inevitably, just like a little trail of horseshit behind a fat old draught horse —George Garrett

47. Definite as a counter-signed contract —Anon

48. Inevitable as a comet's return —Marge Piercy

49. Inevitable as noon —Thomas Wolfe

50. Inevitable as the snick of a mouse-trap —Carl Sandburg

51. Inevitable . . . like a stone rolling down a mountain —Mary Gordon

52. Predictable as a physical law —Charles Johnson

53. (The man was as) predictable as rainwater seeking a low spot —William Beechcroft

54. Predictable as the prints left by a three-legged dog —Sharon Sheehe Stark

55. Predictable as the arrival of Monday morning —Harry Prince

56. Predictable as the menu at charity dinner —Anon

57. Predictable, like a diplomatic reception —A. Alvarez

58. Secure as an obituary in the *Times* —Marge Piercy

59. So predictable . . . just like tuning in the same radio station every night —Lee Smith
    A character in Smith's novel, *The Last Day the Dogbushes Bloomed,* uses this simile to describe a dull suitor.

60. A sweet and sure annuity; it's like taking a bath at Fort Knox —Moss Hart
    This line from *Light Up the Sky* likens a national tour for an ice show to sure-fire success.

CESSATION
See: PAUSE

CHANGE
See Also: ENTRANCES/EXITS, PERMANENCE

1. Anticipate change as though you had left it behind you —Rainer Maria Rilke

2. Any essential reform must, like charity, begin at home —John Macy
   See Also: BELIEFS, CRITICISM, PEACE, SENSE

3. Changeable as a baby's diaper —Anon

4. Changeable as the weather —American colloquialism, attributed to New England
   The variations this has sprouted typify the simple simile's extension through more particularization. Some examples: "Changeable/unpredictable as April weather or as the sky in April" and "Changeable like Midwestern weather—violent and highly volatile."

5. (Her expression would) change as quickly as a sky with clouds racing across the moon —Madeleine L'Engle

6. (Hopes) changed daily like the stock market —Margaret Millar

In her novel, *The Murder of Miranda Millar,* expands the simile as follows: "Gaining a few points here, losing a few there."

7. Changed his mind regularly, like shirts —Anon

8. Changed . . . like the shift of key in a musical score —Lawrence Durrell

9. Changed moods like a strobe of shifting lights —Alvin Boretz

10. Changeful as a creature of the tropical sea lying under a reef —Saul Bellow

11. A change, like a shift of wind, overcame the judge —Truman Capote

12. Change of attitude . . . like a fish gliding with a flick of its tail, now here, now there —Jean Rhys

13. (Life) changed like fluffy clouds —Rita Mae Brown

14. Changes . . . as breath-taking as a Celtics fast break —Larry McCoy, *Wall Street Journal* article about changes at CBS network, December 4, 1986

15. Changes his mood like a wizard —Joan Chase

16. Ever changing, like a joyless eye that finds no objects worth its constancy —Percy Bysshe Shelley

17. Everything changed . . . like the rug, the one that gets pulled — Alberto Alvaor Rios

18. Fickle as the sunlight —William Alfred

19. Fickle as the wind —Horace

20. Get used to [changes] . . . like listening to your own heart — Marguerite Duras

21. In our changes we should move like a caterpillar, part of which is stationary in every advance, not like the toad —James A. Pike
    Reverend Pike's advice was aimed at preventing anxiety.

22. [Moving from slow to fast-paced life] it was like stepping from a gondola to an ocean steamer —Edith Wharton

23. [Personality of a character] metamorphoses . . . like a butterfly bursting out of a cocoon —Frank Rich, *New York Times,* January 21, 1986

24. Mood . . . swinging like an erratic pendulum from being hurt to hurting —Ross Macdonald

25. Most reformers, like a pair of trousers on a windy clothesline, go through a vast deal of vehement motion but stay in the same place — Austin O'Malley

26. Popped out and disappeared like a heat rash —George Garrett

27. Sailing through change as effortlessly as gulls —Gail Godwin

28. (And all the shapes of this grand scenery) shifted like restless clouds before the steadfast sun —Percy Bysshe Shelley

29. (Streets) shift like dunes —Lisa Ress

30. The switch is like going from Star Wars to stagecoaches —David "Doc" Livingston, commenting on enforced job switch (from controlling air traffic to controlling commuter trains), as quoted in *New York Times* article about fired air controllers by N. R. Kleinfield, September 28, 1986

31. Up and down like mercury —May Sarton

32. (Moods may) veer as erratically as the wind —Milton R. Sapirstein

CHAOS
See: ORDER/DISORDER

CHARACTER
See Also: PERSONAL TRAITS, REPUTATION

1. As the sun is best seen at its rising and setting, so men's native dispositions are clearest seen when they are children and when they are dying —Robert Boyle

2. A character is like an acrostic . . . read it forward, backward, or across, it still spells the same thing —Ralph Waldo Emerson

3. Character is like a tree, and reputation like its shadow. The shadow is what we think of it; the tree is the real thing —Abraham Lincoln

4. Character is like white paper; if once blotted, it can hardly ever be made to appear white as before —Joel Hawes

5. A character, like a kettle, once mended always wants mending —Jean-Jacques Rousseau

6. Character, like porcelain ware, must be painted before it is glazed. There can be no change after it is burned in —Henry Ward Beecher

7. A man of words and not of deeds is like a garden full of weeds. And when the weeds begin to grow, it's like a garden full of snow —Nursery rhyme
   This dates back to the eighteenth century.

8. The reputation of a man is like his shadow, gigantic when it precedes him, and pigmy in its proportions when it follows —Alexandre de Talleyrand

9. Some people, like modern shops, hang everything in their windows and when one goes inside nothing is to be found —Berthold Auerbach

10. The soundness of his nature was like the pure paste under a fine glaze —Edith Wharton

11. A vein of iron buried inside her moral frame, like a metal armature inside a clay statue —Carlos Baker

12.   Your moral character must be not only pure, but, like Caesar's wife, unsuspected —Lord Chesterfield

CHARACTERISTICS, NATIONAL

1.   America is more a ratatouille than a melting pot —Ken Holm, *New York Times Magazine,* October 12, 1986
     The food image is particularly appropriate to Holm's article about mixing Eastern and Western ingredients when cooking.

2.   America is rather like life. You can usually find in it what you look for —E. M. Forster

3.   As American as a catcher's mit —George Jean Nathan

4.   As American as a Norman Rockwell painting —Max Shulman

5.   As American as a sawed-off shotgun —Dorothy Parker about Dashiell Hammett, *New Yorker,* April 15, 1931

6.   As American as cheesecake —Samuel Yellen

7.   As American as corn on the cob —Anon

8.   As American as jazz —Anon

9.   As American as shopping malls —Anon

10. As American as the dream of being a millionaire —Anon

11. As American as the two-car garage —Anon

12. As British as roast beef —Anon

13. As English as tea and scones —Elyse Sommer
     The variations to this are virtually limitless; to cite just a few: "As English as the changing of the guards at Buckingham Palace," "English as clotted cream," "As English as Picadilly," "As English as Trafalgar Square."

14. As in sex, the Japanese do not care for extended encounters: "in and out" is their motto in love and war —James Kirkup

15. Bullied and ordered about, the Englishman obeys like a sheep, evades like a knave, or tries to murder his oppressor —George Bernard Shaw

16. Countries are like fruit; the worms are always inside —Jean Giradoux

17. Energy in a nation is like sap in a tree, it rises from the bottom up — Woodrow Wilson, October 28, 1912 speech

18. Frenchmen are like grains of gunpowder, each by itself smutty and contemptible, but mass them together and they are terrible indeed — Samuel Taylor Coleridge

19. A French woman dips into love like a duck into water, 'tis but a shake of the feathers and wag of the tail and all is well again; but an English woman is like a heedless swan venturing into a pool who gets drowned —Washington Irving

20.   Friendship in France as impossible to be attained as orange-trees on the mountains of Scotland —Lady Mary Wortley Montague letter to Lady Pomfret, July 12, 1744

21.   (In America . . . people claim and disown 'identities') as easily as they slap on bumper stickers —Philip Roth

22.   Nations, like individuals, have to limit their objectives or take the consequences —James Reston

23.   Nations, like men, die by imperceptible disorders —Jean Giraudoux

24.   Nations, like men, have their infancy —Henry St. John, Viscount Bolingbroke

25.   A quiet Irishman is about as harmless as a powder magazine built over a match factory —James Dunne

26.   Soviet action is like a riddle wrapped inside an enigma —Winston Churchill

27.   The wheels of American foreign relations turn like the wheels of an ox cart —Clive Cussler
     See Also: POLITICS

CHARITY
See: KINDNESS

CHARM
See: ATTRACTIVENESS

CHASTITY
See: VIRTUE

CHEAPNESS
See: COST, THRIFT

CHEEKS
See Also: BLUSHES, FACIAL COLOR, SKIN

1.   Cheekbones glistening as if they'd been oiled —T. Coraghessan Boyle
See Also: SWEAT

2.   Cheekbones like bunyons —Steve Stern

3.   Cheekbones, like little gossamer-covered drums —Eudora Welty

4.   Cheeks . . . always a bright inflamed red, as if they'd been scoured — Jean Thompson

5.   Cheeks . . . big as a balloon —Njabulo Ndebele

6.   Cheeks bright as a wooden doll's —Derek Lambert

7.   Cheeks bulging like a trumpeter's —George Garrett

8. Cheeks glowing like one of those apples in an expensive fruit shop — Patrick White

9. Cheeks had turned to blotches of dull red, like some pigment which has darkened in drying —Edith Wharton

10. Cheeks had risen like puffy omelettes [from weight gain] —Phyllis Bottome

11. Cheeks . . . just tinged, like the snow apple —Helga Sandburg

12. Cheeks . . . like a raspberry patch —Truman Capote

13. Cheeks . . . like caves —John Rechy

14. Cheeks like poppies —John Galsworthy

15. Cheeks . . . pale as a winter snow upon which a few drops of blood have fallen —Arthur A. Cohen

16. Cheeks . . . round and ruddy as marzipan fruit —Sylvia Plath

17. Cheeks . . . sweet as flowers —*The Holy Bible/Song of Solomon*

18. Cheeks the luscious pink of ripening strawberries —W. P. Kinsella

19. Jowls . . . hanging like wineskins —Z. Vance Wilson

20. Red cheeks glistened like polished apples —Anon

21. Spots of rouge on her cheekbones like a couple of roses pressed into the pages of a book —George Garrett

CHEERFULNESS
See Also: BRIGHTNESS, GAIETY, HAPPINESS, SMILES

1. All smiles . . . as if ready for a thousand little curtseys —André Malraux

2. (She was) as bubbly as a magnum of champagne —Harry Prince

3. [A movie] as heart-warming as an approaching headache —Vincent Canby, *New York Times,* March 21, 1986

4. [A young girl] blithe and airy as a wind-swept leaf —Sylvia Berkman

5. Blithe as a boy —Pamela Hansford Johnson

6. [A sunlit room] bright and bouncing as a newly bathed baby —John Braine

7. Bright as a chirping bird —Stephen Longstreet

8. Buoyant as a bride —Thomas McGuane

9. Cheerful as a grove in spring —William Wordsworth

10. Cheerful as the rising sun in May —William Wordsworth

11. (Smile . . . as) cheerful as the winter solstice —William McIlvanney

12. A cheerful face is nearly as good for an invalid as healthy weather — Benjamin Franklin

13. Cheerfulness is like money well expended in charity; the more we dispense of it, the greater our possessions —Victor Hugo

14. Cheerfulness opens, like spring, all the blossoms of the inward man —Jean Paul Richter

15. Encouraging as a round of applause —Anon

16. (I am) gay as morning, light as snow —Dorothy Parker

17. Optimistic as a sweepstake ticket buyer —Anon

18. Optimistic as a company spokesperson —Anon

19. Positive as good news —G. K. Chesterton

20. Positive as the forecast in a Chinese fortune cookie —Elyse Sommer

21. Radiant like a work of art, full of strange rays —Iris Murdoch

22. (She's always happy. She) shies away from misery like a petrified horse —Carolyn Slaughter

23. Sunny and open as a May morning —Willa Cather

CHILDISHNESS
See: YOUTHFULNESS

CHILDREN
See Also: PARENTHOOD

1. A baby is like a beast, it does not think —Aeschylus

2. Childhood is like a mirror, which reflects in after life the images first presented to it —Samuel Smiles

3. Childhood . . . like so many oatmeal cookies —Frank O'Hara

4. Childhood shows the man, as the morning shows the day —John Milton

5. Children are like beggars; often coming without being called —Proverb

6. Children are like leaves on a tree —Marcus Aurelius

7. Children are like puppies: you have to keep them near you and look after them if you want to have their affection —Anna Magnani

8. Children are like pancakes: You should always throw out the first one —Peter Benchley

9. Children [in families] are like rival pretenders to a throne and their main object in life is to eliminate their competitors —Milton R. Sapirstein

10. Children in a family are like flowers in a bouquet: there's always one determined to face in an opposite direction from the way the arranger desires —Marcelene Cox

11. Children like apples . . . good enough to eat —Donald Culross

12. Children . . . like robins, pink-cheeked and rosy —Lawrence Durrell

13. Children . . . they string our joys, like jewels bright, upon the thread of years —Edward A. Guest

14. The faces of the kids . . . suddenly deprived by fear of their childhood, looked like ancient agonized adults —Herbert Gold

15. A happy childhood can't be cured. Mine'll hang around my neck like a rainbow —Hortense Calisher
    > This is the opening for the novel, *Queenie,* in which the author is much sparer with her similes than she is in her short stories.

16. Ladies touch babies like bankers touch gold —James Ferry
    > One of two similes from a little rhyme within a short story entitled *Dancing Ducks.*

17. Life without children is like a tree without leaves —Milan Kundera

18. A little girl without a doll is almost as unfortunate and quite as impossible as a woman without children —Victor Hugo

19. Maternal testimony notwithstanding, babies are like biscuits in a pan — Ellery Sedgewick

20. My childhood clings to me like wet paint —Daphne Merkin
    > In *Enchantment,* a novel about a young woman's search for self-discovery, the simile concludes: "Blotching the picture of who I am in the present."

21. With children as with plants . . . future character is indicated by their early disposition —Demophilus

CHIN

See Also: CHEEKS, FACE(S), MOUTH

1. A chin like an infant's elbow —Penelope Gilliatt

2. Chin like the butt end of a ham —Ross Macdonald

3. (A small) chin like half a rubber ball —Robert Campbell

4. Chin line . . . shaped like a persimmon —Susan Minot

5. Her chin rising and falling upon her heaving bosom like the figurehead of a vessel upon a heavy harbor swell —Arthur Train

6. Chin stood out like the knuckles in a clenched hand —Max Apple

7. Chin was blue as if it had been shot full of gunpowder —Joyce Cary

8. Jaw as rigid as a shovel —John Yount

9. A jaw like a park bench —Raymond Chandler

10. Jaw like the head of an ax slipped through at the last second like a curl of smoke —R. Wright Campbell

11. A jaw like the share of a plow —Sterling Hayden

12. Jawline like granite —William Diehl

13. Jaw set like a rock —Donald Seaman

14. (He popped a mint into his mouth and) snapped his jaws shut like a shark —Harvey Swados

15. Their shaven jowls looked like the hide of a fresh-scalded, fresh-scraped hog —William Humphrey

CHOICES

1. Alternatives faced one like knives —Hortense Calisher

2. Feel like a piece of flux caught between two magnets —William Diehl
   In Diehl's novel, *Hooligans,* the two magnets represent the choice between two life-styles.

3. Indecisive as a young boy in an ice cream parlor —Ira Berkow discussing George Steinbrenner's choices of field leaders for Yankees, *New York Times*/Sports of the Times, September 20, 1986

4. I would sooner smarm like a fart-licking spaniel than starve in a world of fat poems —Dylan Thomas

5. It [making a choice] seems like a choice between lunacy and idiocy, death by fire or by water —Henry James, letter to Thomas Sergeant Perry, November 1, 1863
   See Also: IMPOSSIBILITY

6. Like a kid jumping off the barn . . . once they decide to go, they go — John D. MacDonald

7. Sudden resolutions, like the sudden rise of the mercury in the barometer, indicate little else than the changeableness of the weather — Julius Charles Hare

8. Took all things of life for her to choose from and apportion, as though she were continually picking presents for herself from an inexhaustible counter —F. Scott Fitzgerald

CHURCHES
See: HOUSES

CITIES
See: PLACES, CITY/STREETSCAPES

CITY/STREETSCAPES
See Also: PLACES

1. Alleys open and fall around me like footsteps of a newly shod horse — Frank O'Hara

2. The ancient oaks . . . arched over the avenue like a canopy —John Kennedy Toole
   See Also: TREES

3. The asphalt shines like a silk hat —Derek Walcott

4. Bars were strung along the street like bright beads —Margaret Millar
   In her novel, *Experiment in Springtime,* Millar strings the actual names of the bars to this simile.

5. A big limestone church hangs like a gray curtain under the street lamp —John Updike

6. The black night falls like a shroud over the whole town —Lu Hsün
   See Also: NIGHT

7. A brutally ugly, utilitarian place, like a mill town without the mill —Jonathan Valin

8. The city seems to uncurl like some hibernating animal dug out of its winter earth —Lawrence Durrell

9. The city unwrinkles like an old tortoise —Lawrence Durrell

10. Far below and around lay the city like a ragged purple dream —O. Henry

11. In the distance, the city rose like a cluster of warts on the side of the mountain —Flannery O'Connor

12. The noon sun put a glaze on them [the sidewalks], so that the cement burned and glittered like glass —Carson McCullers
    See Also: SUN

13. The passing scene spread outside the windows like a plentiful, prim English tea —Dorothea Straus

14. People [on crowded sidewalk] . . . jostling along like sheep in a pen that has no end —Maeve Brennan
    See Also: CROWDS

15. The public streets, like built canals of air —David Denby

16. Raw grass sprouted from the cobbles like hair from a deafened ear —Philip Levine

17. The shadows of the palms lay like splash marks of dark liquid on the pavement —Ross Macdonald

18. The shop fronts stood along that thoroughfare with an air of invitation, like rows of smiling saleswomen —Robert Louis Stevenson

19. A steep lane, like a staircase —Émile Zola

20. The street as gray as newspapers —Marge Piercy
    See Also: GRAY

21. The street lay still as a photograph —Jack Finney

22. The street shone . . . like a fire in a forest —Robert Louis Stevenson

23. The streets looked as if they were made of silver, they were so bright and glistening —Oscar Wilde,

24. The streets (of Bethany, Massachusetts), sparkled like high-gloss picture postcards sold in drugstores of small New England villages —Susan Richards Shreve

25.   Streets tangled like old string —W. H. Auden

26.   Street . . . that neither stank or sparkled but merely had a look of having been turned, like the collar on an old shirt —Hortense Calisher

27.   The town, like an upturned sky, swollen with human lights —Albert Camus

28.   The town [seen from a distance] looked small and clean and perfect, as if it were one of those miniature plastic towns sitting beside a child's electric railroad —Ann Tyler

29.   A view (of Brewer) spread out below like a carpet —John Updike

30.   Village . . . jumbled and colorful like a postcard —George Garrett

31.   Wide, smooth, empty sidewalks looked like long canals of grey eyes — Ayn Rand

CIVILIZATION
See: SOCIETY

CLARITY

1.   (The scents of the garden descended upon him, their contours) as precise and clear as the colored bands of a rainbow —Patrick Suskind

2.   As sharp as the last daybreak —Joy Williamson
    From a book jacket blurb about Tess Gallagher's ability to portray aging people's vision of irremediable loss in novel, *The Lovers of Horses*.

3.   As unreadable as a piece of modern sculpture —Frank Swinnerton

4.   (The image) blurred . . . like something familiar seen beneath disturbed though clear water —William Faulkner

5.   (The consonants) blur together like ink on a wet page —Sue Grafton

6.   Clear and diminished like a scene cut in cameo —Edna St. Vincent Millay

7.   Clear as a bell —John Ray's *Proverbs*
    One could compile a small book of just "Clear as" similes. The bell comparison along with "Clear as a whistle" and "Clear as crystal" are probably most frequently used and familiar.

8.   [A theory synthesized from suppositions] clear as a case history written in a book —Jean Stafford

9.   Clear as a cloudless hour —Algernon Charles Swinburne

10.   Clear as a cube of solid sunshine —Anon

11.   [Eyes] clear as a fountain —Walter Savage Landor

12.   Clear as a graph —Anon

13.   Clear as a lake —Samuel Taylor Coleridge

14.   Clear as a legal confession of murder —John Cheever

15. Clear as an oboe solo —Diane Ackerman

16. Clear as A on the piano in the middle of all the tuning instruments of an orchestra —Sylvia Plath

17. Clear as a tear —Sylvia Plath

18. Clear as cold water —Mark Helprin

19. (The morning was) clear as glass —Mark Helprin

20. Clear as infant's eyes —John Keats

21. (The creek flashed) clear as quartz —Ella Leffland

22. Clear as righteousness —Algernon Charles Swinburne

23. Clear as the A, B, C —George Washington

24. Clear as the day —Miles Coverdale
    "Clear as" comparisons linked with the day, time of day, and the sun at different times of the day include "Clear as noon" (shortened from the once popular "Clear as noon-day") and "Clear as the sun" (both attributed to Roger North); "Clear as is the summer's sun" (William Shakespeare); "Clear as the mid-day sunshine" (Nathaniel Hawthorne); "Clear as day-light" (Arnold Bennett).

25. Clear as the figures at the bottom of a Profit and Loss Statement — Anon

26. Clear as the lines in a wet leaf —Charles Johnson

27. Clear as the note of doom —Lord De Tabley

28. (The men were naked and) clear as the point of a sword in the sun — George Garrett

29. (The sky is as) clear as the song of a boy —Beryl Markham

30. Clear as the twanging of a harp —Alfred, Lord Tennyson

31. Clear as wind —Alfred, Lord Tennyson

32. Clear, like accusation —Paul Horgan

33. [Voice in the "silent dead of night "] distinct as a passing footstep's fall —Henry Wadsworth Longfellow

34. Distinctly as white lace on velvet —Thomas Hardy

35. (Shouldn't the soul of a man be as) limpid and cutting as a diamond — John Cheever

36. (The air is) lucid and lonely as wind chimes —Sharon Sheehe Stark

37. (The poet's work was about as) lucid as a polygraph chart —Joseph Wambaugh

38. Lucidity is positively flowing over me like the sweet oils of Persia — Lorraine Hansberry

39. Precise as a portrait photo —Natascha Wodin

40. To read him (Descartes) was like swimming in a lake so clear that you could see the bottom —W. Somerset Maugham

41. (Lake) transparent as liquid chrysolite —T. H. White

42. Transparent as a white cloud in the moonshine —Hans Christian Anderson

43. Transparent like some holy thing —Thomas Moore

CLEANLINESS

See Also: ORDER/DISORDER

1. Clean and smooth as a peeled onion —O. Henry

2. Clean and well-kept as a cemetery —Karl Shapiro

3. (Her face) clean and white as a handkerchief —John Ashbery

4. Clean as a Band-Aid —Max Apple

5. Clean as a bleached bone —Wallace Stegner

6. Clean as a convent cell —Vita Sackville-West

7. Clean as a hound's tooth —American colloquialism, attributed to New England

8. (His heart felt) clean as a new green leaf —Stephen Vincent Benét

9. Clean as a New England kitchen —Anon

10. Clean as a newly laundered sheet —Rosamund Pilcher
Pilcher uses the "Clean as a sheet" simile to describe the smoothness and cleanliness of sand when the tide is out in a story entitled *The White Birds.*

11. Clean as a new pin of every penny of debt —Sir Walter Scott

12. Clean as a penny —William Robertson
A much used simile to describe anyone who is neatly and cleanly dressed.

13. Clean as a pig's whistle —American colloquialism, attributed to New England
Just plain "Clean as a whistle," is said to stem from the fact that it takes a clean dry whistle to produce a good sound.

14. Clean as a piglet bathed in milk —Mary Gordon

15. Clean as a rose is after rain —James Whitcomb Riley

16. Clean as a toilet bowl —Lincoln Kirstein

17. (The woman was as) clean as a white rose in the morning gauze of dew —Carl Sandburg

18. Clean as driftwood —Robert Hass

19. (Legs) clean as marble —Beryl Markham

20. Clean as new grass when the old grass burns —Carl Sandburg

21. Clean as water pouring from a silver tap —Tennessee Williams

22. Dirty as a glass roof in a train station —Leonard Cohen
23. Dust balls sail like galleons [on a carpet] on the dry sea —Robert Irwin
24. Fingernails . . . like watch crystals —Walker Percy
25. Immaculate as a laboratory —Ben Ames Williams
26. Spotless as naked innocence —John Smith
27. The water's (of swimming pool) like bouillabaisse. It's got more things in it than Macy's window —Noël Coward

CLEVERNESS
See Also: ALERTNESS

1. Adroit as a rhinoceros —Franklin P. Adams
2. Brains like the frogs, dispersed all over his body —Charles Dickens
3. Clever as a bird-dog —American colloquialism, attributed to New England
4. Clever as sin —Rudyard Kipling
5. Crafty as a new religious convert pledged to win over a sinner —Gloria Norris
6. Crafty as an exorcist —Miles Gibson
7. Crafty as the sea —W. B. Yeats
8. Cunning as a dead pig, but not half so honest —Jonathan Swift
9. Cunning is a sort of short-sightedness —Joseph Addison
10. Has as many tricks as a bear —John Ray's *Proverbs*
11. Hinted with the delicacy of a lilac bud —Sinclair Lewis
12. Ingenious as magicians —Delmore Schwartz
13. Like rats, his wits were beginning to busy themselves again —Walter De La Mare
14. Little clevernesses are like half-ripened plums, only good eating on the side that has had a glimpse of the sun —Henry James
15. Played on his misfortune as on a cello —Marguerite Yourcenar
16. Sharp and bright as a blade of sunlight —Alice Walker
17. Sharp as a cut-throat razor —Donald Seaman
18. Sharp as a knife —American colloquialism, attributed to New England
    An equally popular variation, also attributed to New England folklore: "Sharp as a razor."
19. Sharp as a needle —Anon
    Common usage has made this interchangeable with "Sharp as a pin." A variation of more recent vintage, "Sharp as a tack," has become a cliche in its own right.
20. Sharp as mustard —Ogden Nash

In Nash's poem, *The Tale of the Custard Dragon,* the descriptive frame of reference is a little dog.

21. Shrewd as a barrel-load of monkeys —Robin Sheiner

22. Shrewd as a sparrow —Janet Flanner

23. Shrewdness is often annoying, like a lamp in the bedroom —Ludwig Boerne

24. Sly and slick as a varmint —Robert Penn Warren

25. (Every move had been as stealthy and as) sly as a hungry coyote — William Humphrey

26. Smart as a whip —Anon
    Used to the point of abuse since the seventeenth century. A variation in keeping with the phrase's origin in the smarting pain caused by a whip: "Sharp as a whiplash."

27. Smart as new nails —Sharon Sheehe Stark

28. Tricky as palmistry —Karl Shapiro

29. Wily as a fox —John Clarke
    The fox continues to be a favorite link to clever, crafty behavior. Often 'cunning' is substituted for 'wiley', and the fox is not just any fox but "An old one."

CLICHE
See: ORIGINALITY, MAXIMS AND SAYINGS

CLINGING
See Also: PERSISTENCE; PEOPLE, INTERACTION; RELATIONSHIPS

1. Adhere like lint —Anon

2. Adhere like ticks to a sheep's back —Maurice Hewlett

3. Adhering . . . like shipwrecked mariners on a rock —J. M. Barrie

4. Clinging . . . like lichen to a rock —Ross Macdonald

5. Clinging like a limpet in the heaviest sea —William H. Hallhan

6. Clinging . . . like a monkey-on-a-stick —Julia O'Faolain

7. Clinging . . . stupidly, like a mule —Joseph Conrad

8. Clinging to her like chewing gum to a boot sole —Julian Gloag

9. Cling..like a wart —Tony Ardizzone
   The simile, as used in *The Heart of the Order,* describes the way a cowboy clings to the back of a bull.

10. Cling like chewing gum to a shoe sole —Anon

11. Cling like ivy —Robert Burton

12. Clings fiercely to all his titles, like an old soldier to his medals —Robert Traver

13. Clings to as a baby clings to its pacifier —Anon

14. Clings to me like a bed-bug —Maxim Gorky

15. Cling to (as to another person) as an exhausted man does to a rock —Brooks Bakeland

16. Cling to . . . like a drowning person to a piece of timber —Isak Dinesen

17. Cling to like a leech —American colloquialism, attributed to New England

18. Cling to like a vine —American colloquialism, attributed to New England
     A variation is to "Cling like ivy."

19. Cling to . . . like tenacious barnacles upon rocks —Mary Ellen Chase

20. Clung like a basket enfolding a tithe offering —Arthur A. Cohen

21. Clung [to an idea] like a shipwrecked sailor hanging on to the only solid part of his sinking universe —Marguerite Yourcenar

22. (The baby) clung like a sloth —Louise Erdrich

23. Clung . . . like a tarantula —Terry Southern

24. (Rancour) clung like curses on them —Percy Bysshe Shelley

25. Clung . . . like magnet to steel —T. Buchanan Read

26. Clung the way a tree animal clings to a branch —Rachel Ingalls

27. Clung to each other like double sweet peas —*A Broken-Hearted Gardner,* anonymous 19th century verse

28. Clung together hand in hand like men overboard —George Garrett

29. Clung to her like a man on a swaying subway car whose grip on the overhead rail keeps him from tumbling to the floor —Paul Reidinger

30. Clung to his consciousness like a membrane —John Updike

31. Clutched [at her blanket] as a faller clutches at the turf on the edge of a cliff —Virginia Woolf

32. Clutching hold of . . . with the grasp of a drowning man —Charles Dickens

33. Clutching is the surest way to murder love, as if it were a kitten, not to be squeezed so hard, or a flower to fade in a tight hand —May Sarton

34. (There she sat,) glued to the tube like a postage stamp —A. Alvarez

35. Gummed together like wet leaves —Lawrence Durrell

36. [A term to describe a problem] had stuck with him like day-old oatmeal —T. Glen Coughlin

37. Hang on like a summer cold —Anon

38. Hang on . . . like a tick —Rita Mae Brown

39. Hang on to . . . [some small, unimportant point] . . . like a dog to a bone —Barbara Greene, on her cousin Graham Greene
    > Some people like to get more specific; for example, "Hang on to . . . like a terrier" found in Iris Murdoch's novel, *The Good Apprentice.*

40. Hang over like a heavy curtain —Anon

41. Hang over like a layer of smog —Anon

42. Hang over like crepe —Anon

43. Hang over like murder on a guilty soul —Sciller

44. Hang together like burrs —John Ray's *Proverbs*

45. Hung like bees on mountain-flowers —Percy Bysshe Shelley

46. (The thought . . .) hung like incense around Francis —Dorothy Canfield Fisher

47. It [something that had been said] stuck up in the girl's consciousness like a fallen meteor —John Cheever

48. (A scar of horror, if not of guilt,) lay consciously on his breast, like the scarlet letter —George Santayana

49. Clinging . . . like starving children to a teat —Margaret Millar

50. Like swarming bees they clung —Lord Byron

51. Remained like a black cloud —Frank Swinnerton

52. She clings to me like a fly to honey —Anton Chekhov

53. She clung to him like a shadow —Margaret Mitchell

54. She's coiled around her family and her house like a python —Jane Bowles

55. She was like a sca-anemone—had only to be touched to adhere to what touched her —John Fowles

56. Sticking to [another person's side] like a melting snowbank —Marge Piercy

57. Stick like a wet leaf —Anton Chekhov

58. Sticks like a burr to a cow's tail —Edward Noyes Westcott

59. Sticks like crazy glue —Anon

60. (My touch) sticks like mud —Marge Piercy

61. Stick together like overcooked pasta —Elyse Sommer

62. Stick together like peanut butter and jelly —Ed McBain

63. Sticky as fire —Terry Bisson

64. Sticky as rubber cement —Anon

65. Stuck . . . like a barnacle to a ship's keel, or a snail to a door, or a little bunch of toadstools to the stem of a tree —Charles Dickens

66. Stuck to [him or her] like shit to a blanket —American colloquialism

67. Stuck to my side like a lung infected with pleurisy —Patrick White
68. Stuck with . . . like gas on water —Will Weaver
69. Tenacious as a Boston bull —Anon
70. They [people who cling to outmoded political concepts] are like degenerates who are color blind, except that they see something which is NOT there, instead of failing to see something which is —Janet Flanner
71. They [narrator's daughters] cling together like Hansel and Gretel — Ogden Nash
72. Tied to each other back to back [long-married people] . . . like dogs unable to disengage after coupling —Lawrence Durrell

CLOSENESS

See Also: COMPATIBILITY, FRIENDSHIP

1. Always together . . . like Siamese twins —Nina Bawden
2. [Cid and his wife Juena] are like the nail [fingernail] and the flesh —*The Lay of the Cid,* epic poem
   According to a grad student at SUNY, Stony Brook, NY, this is the only simile in this 3500-verse epic poem dating back to 1140 a.d.
3. As close to him as sticking plaster —Cornell Woolrich
4. Close as an uncracked nut —Play: *All Vows Kept,* Anon
5. Close as a dead heat —Anon
6. Close as fingers inside a pair of mittens —Anon
7. Close as flies in a bottle —Shana Alexander
8. Close as the bark to a tree —Sir Charles Sedley
   This simile is also used to describe stinginess.
   See Also: THRIFT
9. Close as the 'cu' in cucumbers —Anon
10. Close as the gum on a postage stamp —Anon
11. Close as two peas in a pod —H. I. Phillips
    Common usage has created twists such as "Close as two peas on a plate."
    See Also: SIMILARITY
12. Close like exiles from a remote and forgotten land —A. R. Guerney, Jr.
13. Close together as the two shells of an oyster —Leonard McNally
14. Get as close as an Eskimo does to a fire in his igloo in the tundra — Anon, from radio broadcast
15. His face was so close to hers that it was out of focus, like a cloud passing in front of the sun —Michael Korda
16. Inseparable as a baseball fan and a bag of peanuts —Anon

17. Inseparable as finger and thumb —George Farquhar

18. Inseparable as a shadow to a body —Robert Burton

19. Inseparable as Don Quixote and Sancho Panza —Anon

20. Inseparable like ivy, which grows beautifully so long as it twines around a tree, but is of no use when it is separated —Molière
     The original has been transcribed from "A woman is like ivy"
     for a less gender-oriented interpretation.

21. Intimate as two sardines in a can —Anon

22. Near as the end of one's nose —Anon
     See Also: OBVIOUSNESS

23. Near as twilight is to darkness —Thomas Paine

24. Stayed as close to that woman as a pimple —Charles Johnson
     See Also: CLINGING

25. They're as thick as three in a bed —Scottish saying

26. They were all standing around him thick as bees —Cornell Woolrich

27. (It is proper that families remain) thick like good soup —J. P. Donleavy

28. We were like two kernels in one almond —Sadi

29. Wrapped tight an as eggroll —Donald McCaig

CLOTHING

See Also: CLOTHING ACCESSORIES; CLOTHING, ITS FIT

1. A little-girl-type sundress that was about as sexy as a paper bag —Dan Wakefield

2. All dressed up like Christmas trees —Rosamund Pilcher

3. A baggy blue flowered housedress that looked like old slipcovers —Louise Erdrich

4. A bikini is like a barbed-wire fence. It protects the property without obstructing the view —Joey Adams

5. Blouses thin as the film of tears in your eyes —Bin Ramke

6. Clothes, pressed stiff as cardboard —Jay Parini

7. Coat like a discarded doormat —T. Coraghessan Boyle

8. A dark blue suit so rigidly correct that it looked like a uniform —Harvey Swados

9. Draped in a muumuu that covered her like a Christo curtain shrouding a California mountain —Paul Kuttner

10. Dressed all in brown, like a rabbit —Anon

11. Dressed as if she were going to a coronation —Shelby Hearon

12. Dressed in black jersey, without ornament, like a widow —Ross Macdonald

13. Dressed like a bookie —Gavin Lyall

14. Dressed like a Hollywood bit player hoping to be discovered leaning on a bar —Robert Campbell
    In his novel, *In La-La Land We Trust,* Campbell expands upon this simile for several sentences with details about the outfit.

15. Dressed up like a dog's dinner —American colloquialism
    This means to be overdressed, usually badly so.

16. Dresses conservatively as a corpse —Harvey Swados

17. (The Queen) dresses like a whistlestop town librarian —Stephen Longstreet

18. Dresses like he's got a charge at Woolworth's —Robert B. Parker
    With names of stores, companies and products constantly changing, Woolworth's may not always be synonymous with cheap; however, the simile could live on with an appropriate substitution.

19. Dress . . . gone limp in the heat, like a wilted plant —Louise Erdrich

20. A dress like ice-water —F. Scott Fitzgerald

21. Dress that was as small as scarf —Laurie Colwin

22. Fancy as a rooster up for the fair —Linda Hogan

23. Garments as weathered as an old sail —George Eliot

24. A girl who dressed like an Arabian bazaar —T. Coraghessan Boyle

25. Her white silk robe flowed over her like a milk shower —Harold Adams

26. He was dressed for this death-watch job [hotel desk clerk] as if for a lively party —Christopher Isherwood

27. In her orange fringed poncho she looked like a large teepee —Michael Malone

28. Ladies wrapped like mummies in shawls with bright flowers on them — Virginia Woolf

29. Like her husband she carried clothes, carried them as a train carries passengers —Henry James

30. Looks like she's wearing her entire wardrobe all at once and all of it hand-me-downs from someone bigger than she is —Julie Salamon, describing appearance of character played by Debra Winger in the movie, *Black Widow, Wall Street Journal,* February 6, 1987

31. A party frock sticking out all around her [a little girl's] legs like a lampshade —Joyce Cary

32. Peeled off his trousers like shucking corn —Rita Mae Brown

33. Ragged as a scarecrow —Thomas Heywood

34. Shirt [heavily patched] lays on his body like a ratty dishtowel — Carolyn Chute

35. Skirts swirling like a child's pennant caught in a stiff breeze —Tony Ardizzone

36. Slickers [worn by cops] that shone like gun barrels —Raymond Chandler
    Raymond Chandler used this simile in his early days as a pulp magazine writer, (*Killer in the Rain, Black Mask Magazine,* 1935) and later in his novel, *The Big Sleep.*

37. Starched clothes sat in the grass like white enameled teapots —Isaac Babel

38. [Formal attire] suited them the way an apron suits a grizzly bear — William McIlvanney

39. Sweater as sopped as wet sheep —Susan Minot

40. Tailored and bejeweled like a pampered gigolo —James Mills

41. Tightly wrapped in a red skirt like a Christmas present —Helen Hudson

42. Trousers pressed as sleek as a show dog's flank —R. V. Cassill

43. A wedding gown like a silver cloud —Mazo De La Roche

44. A white robe, flowing, like spilled milk —Paige Mitchell

45. Wide sleeves fluttering like wings —Marcel Proust

46. Wore his clothes as if they were an official uniform —Vernon Scannell

47. You wear your clothes as if you want to be helped out of them —W. P. Kinsella

48. Zipped and buttoned into a polyester pantsuit, she was like a Christmas stocking half-filled with fruit —Mary Ward Brown

CLOTHING ACCESSORIES
See Also: JEWELRY

1. Boots that shone like a well-rubbed table —Stephen Vincent Benét

2. A collar that looked like a pancake flapping around my head and . . . made me look like a pregnant penguin —Elizabeth Taylor

3. Glasses as thick as the bottom of a pop bottle —George Garrett

4. Handkerchief hoisted like a brave little flag from his breast pocket — Vicki Baum

5. Hat big as an Easter cake —Joyce Cary

6. A hat . . . perched right on top of her head, like a mushroom —Roald Dahl

7. Impenetrably black sunglasses like Batman's mask —John Rechy

8. Shoes gleaming like beer bottles —Loren D. Estleman

9. Shoes . . . shined up like patent leather —George Garrett

10. Shoes sticking out like tongues beneath the long black robe —Helen Hudson

11. Silk, like wrinkled skins on scalded milk —Oliver Wendell Holmes, Sr.

12. Socks which fell like a couple of woolen concertinas over his dusty shoes —John Mortimer

13. Straw hat with a bow on it like the sails of a windmill —L. P. Hartley

14. A ten-gallon hat like a walking mushroom —Truman Capote

15. Tie . . . loose and awry like a long lazy tongue . . . wore a costume as distinctive as a ballet dancer's tutu —Van Wyck Mason

16. Ties pulled loose from their collars, like weary gamblers —Graham Swift

CLOTHING, ITS FIT
See Also: CLOTHING

1. Bathing suit so tight that it seemed any moment she would burst out of it like a cooked frankfurter —George Garrett

2. A blanket wrapped around her body as tight as a cigar —Scott Spencer

3. (Clothes which) clung like refractory cobwebs —Patrick White

4. A coat which seems to fit her as her life fits, barely, inadvertently, not at all —Herbert Morris

5. Everything she wears fits like a saddle on a sow —Harold Adams

6. (Her bathing suit that) fit her like a sack —Flannery O'Connor

7. Fit like a saddle fits a sow —Anon
   An alliterative putdown for the way a person is dressed. It dates back to sixteenth century England and became an American colloquialism shortly after it crossed the ocean.

8. [A dress] fits like the skin of a grape —Charles Raddock describing Jacqueline Susann's outfit in a play, *Between the Covers.*
   Raddock's scathing review commented that the lines of the dress were the play's only good lines.

9. Fits you like flannel washed in hot suds —O. Henry

10. Fitted her like a duck's foot in the mud —American colloquialism, attributed to New England

11. Her coat fit her like a cheese box —Mary Gordon

12. Her garments seeming to flutter round her like draperies —Barbara Pym

13. Her halter top that cradled her breasts like a hammock —Phyllis Naylor

14. Her sleeves dropped like a sigh —Anaïs Nin

15. Her slip was stretched over her breast, as firmly and simply as linen over an embroidery frame —Boris Pasternak

16. Her stockings hung about her ankles like Hamlet's when he exposed himself to Ophelia and called her a whore —Leonard Michaels

17. His [shirt] collar was so tight, it felt like a string cutting his neck —Dan Wakefield

18. His jacket hung on him like a scarecrow —Ross Macdonald

19. His pants hung as full as an Arab tent from his global stomach — William Diehl

20. His shirt fit him like a sail at the back —Philip Gerard

21. His short-sleeved shirt and short pants fit him like a dirty sack —James Crumley

22. (The uniform) hung slack like a castoff on a scarecrow —Paige Mitchell

23. Jeans fit like a rubber glove —W. P. Kinsella

24. The jeans fitted like hand-me-ups from a younger, thinner sister — Margaret Millar

25. (A healthy blonde with) jeans so tight her hipbones looked like towel hooks —Erma Bombeck

26. [Pants] tight . . . like elastic bandages —Ann Petry

27. Jeans that made his legs look like tree trunks. The bright green fishnet shirt he wore made him look even more like a tree —Ann Beattie

28. Legs . . . hung straight and rigid as if she had iron shinbones and ankles —William Faulkner

29. She wears her clothes as if they were thrown on her with a pitchfork — Jonathan Swift

30. Snugger than the bark to a dead maple —Anon
    See Also: THRIFT

31. (A yellow) tee shirt that clings to her arms, breast and round belly like the skin of a sausage —Russell Banks

32. They [too-large trousers] make you look like an elephant that has lost weight —Penelope Gilliatt

33. Tight blue jeans that grip her behind like two hands —Charles Bukowski

34. Tight . . . like a lobster shell —W. S. Gilbert

35. Trousers and jacket droop like a tailor's nightmare —T. Coraghessan Boyle

36. Trousers . . . as wrinkled at the crotch as if he'd had them pressed that way —Harvey Swados

37. The trousers fitted her legs closely, but she could come out of them as though she were peeling a banana —MacDonald Harris

CLOUD(S)
See Also: CLOUD MOVEMENTS, SKY

1. A cloud like a torn shirt —Katherine Mansfield

2. Clouds are like Holy Writ, in which theologians cause the faithful or the crazy to see anything they please —Voltaire

3. Clouds . . . as white as leghorn feathers —Saul Bellow

4. The cloud showed motion within, like an old transport truck piled high with crate on crate of sleepy white chickens —Eudora Welty

5. The clouds hung above the mountains like puffs of white smoke left in the wake of a giant old-fashioned choochoo train —Sue Grafton

6. The clouds lie over the chiming sky . . . like the dustsheets over a piano —Dylan Thomas

7. Clouds like a marble frieze across the sky —Helen Hudson

8. Clouds like cruisers in the heaven —Edna O'Brien

9. Clouds like dark bruises were massing and swelling [on the horizon] — George Garrett

10. Clouds . . . like drowsy lambs around a tree —Romain Gary

11. (The sky turned sooty with) clouds like enormous thumbprints —Helen Hudson

12. Clouds like lights among great tombs —Wallace Stevens

13. Clouds like tattered fur —Jean Thompson

14. Clouds piling up like a bubble bath —Sue Grafton

15. Clouds, plump and heavy as dumplings —Anthony E. Stockanes

16. The clouds were asses' ears —Dylan Thomas

17. The clouds were huddled on the horizon like dirty sheep from the steppes —Joyce Renwick

18. The clouds were like an alabaster palace —Johnny Mercer, from his 1954 lyrics for *Midnight Sun*

19. The clouds were like old fiddles —Joyce Cary

20. A few clouds were drawn against the light like streaks of lead pencils — John Cheever

21. Fluffy white clouds, like flecks of lather, were floating across the sky — Alexander Solzhenitsyn

22. Clouds . . . wild and black and rolling like locomotives —W. P. Kinsella

23. Frail clouds like milkweed floss —John Dos Passos

24. Gleaming, white fluffy clouds peeped over the hills . . . like kittens — Stella Benson

25. High fat clouds like globs of whipped cream —William Faulkner

26. Like a grave face, lit by some last, sad thought, a cloud, tinged by the fading glow of sunset —John Hall Wheelock

27. Like blurred lenses, winter clouds cast a shade over the sun —Truman Capote

28. (Above the falling sun,) like visible winds the clouds are streaked and spun —Roy Fuller

29. Little white clouds . . . like a row of ballet-girls, dressed in white, waiting at the back of the stage, alert and merry, for the curtain to go up —W. Somerset Maugham

30. Little white clouds like flags were whipped out in the scented wind — Paul Horgan

31. Little white puffs of cloud . . . like a cat steeped in milk —W. P. Kinsella

32. A long thin cloud crossed it [the moon] slowly, drawing itself out like a name being called —Eudora Welty

33. Low clouds, drooping at the edges like felt, sailed over the woods — Boris Pasternak

34. Low on the horizon hung a fugitive wisp of cloud, spiraled and upthrust like a genie emerging from a bottle —Robert Traver

35. A massive cloud like dirty cotton —William Faulkner

36. One cloud intruded [into the blue of the sky] puffy, precise, as if piped from a pastry bag —Margaret Sutherland

37. Parcels of clouds lying against the mountainside like ghosts of dead mackerel —Paul Theroux

38. A single puff of cloud so still, it seems as if it had been painted there — Delmore Schwartz

39. Small thin clouds like puffs of frosty breath —Joyce Cary

40. Some small clouds, like rosy petals, seemed to his eyes to be dancing, gently and carefully, against the blue —Hugh Walpole

41. They [the clouds] peel the morning like a fruit —Lawrence Durrell

42. When clouds appear like rocks and towers, the earth's refreshed by frequent showers —English weather rhyme

43. White and fluffy clouds . . . one looked like a fish and one looked like a movie star, all curvy, and another looked like Santa Claus gone wrong —Lee Smith

CLOUD MOVEMENTS
See Also: RAIN

1. Black clouds lumbered off westward like ghosts of buffalo —W. P. Kinsella

2. A billow of woolly clouds . . . like milk spilt on a table, commenced to cascade down the mountain side —F. van Wyck Mason

3. Clouds floating around [in the sky] . . . like suds in a pan —Helen Hudson

4. Clouds . . . gathered like great boneless birds —Hugh Walpole

5. Clouds hastening like messengers through heaven —John Hall Wheelock

6. Clouds rising like a tide of ink just beneath the moon —John Farris

7. Clouds rose up from the meadows like soft creamy wings seeking the bodies of gigantic birds —Rita Mae Brown

8. Clouds sailing . . . like a flock of birds taking flight to distant lands — Hans Christian Andersen

9. Clouds that hung, like banners —Edgar Allan Poe

10. Clouds that swam like lonely white fish in the sky —Robie Macauley

11. Clouds would part like windows, as though to air the sky —Boris Pasternak

12. Gray clouds ballooned down like the dirty underside of a great circus tent —Brian Moore

13. Inky clouds, like funeral shrouds, sail over the midnight skies —W. S. Gilbert
    > Gilbert contributed many a simile to the famous Gilbert and Sullivan operettas, like this one from *Ruddigore.*

14. Rain clouds scudded past like big ships sailing out of harbor —Brian Moore

15. Lonely clouds were floating above, like guests strolling above the sky — Yehuda Yaari

16. A rolling cloud boiled onto the horizon like black liquid —Dorothy Francis

17. The sailing clouds went by, like ships upon the sea —Henry Wadsworth Longfellow

18. There's a feathery little cloud floatin' by like a lonely leaf on a big blue stream —Oscar Hammerstein, II, lyrics for "Two Little People" from *Carousel*

19. Troops of small feathery white clouds ranged over the sky, like grazing herds of the gods —Thomas Mann

CLUMSINESS
See: AWKWARDNESS

COLDNESS
See Also: REMOTENESS, RESERVE

1. (There was) a certain coldness, like that of a spinster about her —Boris Pasternak

2. Behave exactly like a block of ice —Noël Coward, lyrics for "I'm So In Love"

3. The chill in the air was like a constant infinitely small shudder —M. J. Farrell

4. (Some laughs are as) cold and meaningless as yesterday's buckwheat pancake —Josh Billings
    In Billings' phonetic dialect 'as' was written as 'az.'

5. Cold as a dead man's nose —William Shakespeare

6. Cold as a fish —American colloquialism, attributed to New England

7. Cold as a fish caught through the ice —F. van Wyck Mason

8. Cold as a hole in the ice —Bertold Brecht

9. (It grew as) cold as a key —Thomas Heywood

10. Cold as a lizzard —Walter Savage Landor
    In one of Landor's *Conversation* pieces, he has Fra Filippo Lippi commenting to Pope Eugenius IV that while an ordinary person could use an expression like "Cold as ice, a true poet would reach for more originality." The above is one suggestion, "Cold as a lobster" is another.

11. Cold as a miser's heart —Donald Seaman

12. [A smile] cold as a moan —Marge Piercy

13. Cold as a murder's heart —Richard Ford

14. Cold as an igloo —Reynolds Price

15. Cold as any stone —William Shakespeare

16. Cold . . . as a pane of glass —Reynolds Price

17. Cold as a snowman's dick —William H. Gass

18. (A kiss) cold as bacon —Joyce Cary

19. Cold as charity —Anon
    An English phrase in use since the seventeenth century.

20. Cold as coldest hell —Sylvia Berkman
    In a short story entitled *Who Killed Cock Robin,* the simile describes a character's personality and continues as follows: "Cruel to every fingernail, and invariably polite."

21. Cold as dew to dropping leaves —Percy Bysshe Shelley

22. Cold as fears —Algernon Charles Swinburne

23. (I felt as) cold as Finnegan's feet (the day they buried him) —Raymond Chandler

24. Cold as if I had swallowed snowballs —William Shakespeare
    A variation of this snowball simile from *The Merry Wives of Windsor* is from another Shakespeare play, *Pericles:* "She sent him away as cold as a snowball."

25. (Your heart would be as heavy and) cold as iron shackles —George Garrett

26. Cold as Monday morning's barrenness —F. D. Reeve

27. Cold as moonlight —Yvor Winters

28. (Face) cold as newsprint —Philip Levine

29. (Eyes) cold as river ice —Davis Grubb

30. Cold as snakes —American colloquialism, attributed to Northeast

31. (Men) cold as spring water —Julia O'Faolain

32. (The wet air was as . . .) cold as the ashes of love —Raymond Chandler

33. Cold as the cold between the stars —Terry Bisson

34. Cold as the north side of a grave stone in winter —Proverb

35. Cold as the snow —Lewis J. Bates

36. Cold as the tomb of Christ —Maxwell Anderson

37. Colder than a banker's heart —William Diehl

38. Colder than a dead lamb's tail —Anon

39. Colder than a lawyer's heart —George V. Higgins

40. Colder than a witch's tits —American colloquialism, attributed to the South
     Like many regional expressions that gained national currency during World War II, this one is often referred to as an Army expression.

41. (It was) colder than ice —Hans Christian Andersen
     Whether used as a pure simile "Cold as ice" or as cited above, the linking of snow and ice to cold has become as "Common as snowflakes in winter." A story in the January 23, 1987 edition of the *New York Times* about a planned freedom march in Atlanta was highlighted with a blurb stating "We are going to march if it's cold as ice . . . " proving once again that even without a new twist, a simile usually wins the spotlight.

42. Cold like a sea mist and as ungraspable —Sylvia Townsend Warner

43. Cold [in manner] like Christmas morning —Grace Paley

44. The cold was like a sleep —Wallace Stevens

45. The cold was like a thick vast sleep —Davis Grubb

46. Cool and smooth, like the breath of an air conditioner —T. Coraghessan Boyle

47. Cool as a snowbank —Louisa May Alcott

48. (Her bare arms and shoulders felt as) cool as marble —Leo Tolstoy

49. (Skin) cool as steel —Elizabeth Hardwick

50. (Voice) cool as water on shaded rocks —Beryl Markham

51. Could feel the cold climbing up his ankles like ships' rats —Penelope
     Gilliatt

52. Hardened her heart, like God had hardened Pharaoh's heart against the
     Jews —Daphne Merkin
       The simile was particularly appropriate in *Enchantment,* a
       novel about an orthodox Jewish family.

53. A heart as cold as English toast —Harry Prince

54. It [television show] was hard as fiberglass —Norman Mailer

55. My flesh was frozen for an inch below my skin, it was as if I were
     wearing icy armour —Rebecca West

56. Unresponding . . . like a wall —D. H. Lawrence

COLLAPSE

See Also: DISINTEGRATION

1.   Caved in like a sinkhole —Jonathan Valin

2.   Caving in like a mud dam —Kurt Rheinheimer

3.   (Periods in one's life that once seem important until you look back on
     them) collapsed as flat as packing cartons —Jonathan Penner
       In a short story entited *Emotion Recollected in Tranquility,* the
       author tied collapsed packing carton comparison to the
       collapse of part of one's life.

4.   Collapsed like an elephant pierced by a bullet in some vital spot —
     Kingsley Amis

5.   Collapsed like a rotten tree — Erich Maria Remarque

6.   Collapsed like a rump-shot dog —T. Coraghessan Boyle

7.   (Half a dozen career daydreams) collapsed like a telescope —Thomas
     McGuane

8.   Collapsed like a wounded soldier in the mud —Z. Vance Wilson

9.   Collapsed to the floor like a tent that has had all the guy ropes and
     poles removed at the same time —Jimmy Sangster

10. Collapsed upon the sea as if his body had telescoped into itself, like a
     picnic beaker —Joyce Cary

11. (His body) collapsed vertically like a punctured concertina —Frank
     Ross
       An older, simpler variation by Irving Cobb: "Fold up like a
       concertina."

12. (One day would) collapse like a peony —Jilly Cooper

13. Collapse like a sack of meal —Anon

The sack of meal as a comparison linked to falling, collapsing or toppling has seeded so much use and extension that one can only list some of its in-print appearances: "Went over like a sack of meal" (Frank O'Connor); "Fall heavily, like a sack of meal" (S. J. Perelman); "Went down . . . like an empty sack" (John M. Synge); "Dropped, like a flour sack falling from a loft" (Gerald Kersh). Most commonly overheard in everyday conversation is "Collapse like an empty paper bag."

14. Collapse like a snowman in the sun —Anon

15. Collapse like a tent when the pole is kicked out from under it —Loren D. Estleman

16. Collapse . . . like empty garments —Joyce Cary Collapse like sandcastles against the ocean tide —Anon

17. Collapse like a punctured blister —Mike Sommer

18. Collapse like the cheeks of a starved man —Charles Dickens

19. Collapsing like a cardboard carton thrown on a bonfire —Margaret Atwood

20. Comes apart [no longer able to control laughter] like a slow-ripping seam —Sharon Sheehe Stark

21. Crashed on the leather sofa, going down like a B-52 with a bellyful of shrapnel —Jonathan Kellerman

22. [Souvenirs of a romance] crumble like flowers pressed in dictionaries — Judith Martin

23. Crumble like tinder —Anon

24. (A small white house that was) crumbling at the corners like stale cake left out on a plate —Jonathan Valin

25. Crumbling like one of those dry sponge cakes —Francis King

26. Crumpled like caterpillars on mulberry leaves —James Purdy

27. (She) crumpled like paper crushed in a fist and began to cry —Harold Adams

28. Crumpled up as if he were a paper flower —Ruth Prawer Jhabvala

29. Crumples like a used-up piece of paper —Daphne Merkin

30. [Gulls] downed . . . like a tumbled kite —John Hall Wheelock

31. (The bird) dropped like an arrow —Leo Tolstoy

32. Dropped like an elephant's trunk —Eudora Welty

33. Dropped like one hit in the head by a stone from a sling —Eudora Welty

34. Drops like a piece of flotsam —T. Coraghessan Boyle

35. Falling as gently and slowly as a kite —Elizabeth Hardwick

36. Fall over like a frozen board —William H. Gass

37. Fall to the floor like misfired cannon balls —John Updike
38. (She's welcome to climb with man if she wishes . . . and) fall with a crash like a trayful of dishes —Amy Lowell
39. Fell as low as a toad —American colloquialism, attributed to Midwest
40. (Accents of peace and pity) fell like dew (upon my heart) —Percy Bysshe Shelley
41. Fell . . . like insects knocked off by a gardener's spray —Derek Lambert
42. Fell like one who is seized with sleep —Dante Alighieri
43. Fell slowly forward like a toppling wall —Stephen Crane
44. Fell to her knees like a nun seeking sudden forgiveness —James Crumley
45. Flopped like the ears of a dog —Edgar Allan Poe
46. Folded up like a pocket camera —George Ade
47. Fold up like a cheap camera —Anon
48. [First baseman] goes down slow as a toppling tree —W. P. Kinsella
49. Going under [dying] like shipwrecked sailors —Thomas Keneally
50. (Let life face him with a new demand on his understanding and then watch him) go soggy, like a wet meringue —D. H. Lawrence
51. He dropped like a bullock, he lay like a block —Rudyard Kipling
52. (When I tell him he must go, he suddenly) hits the floor like a toppled statue —Louise Erdrich
53. Hit the floor like an anvil —Joseph Wambaugh
54. (Slumped to the floor and) lay there like a punctured balloon —Myron Brinig
    Some variations on the balloon comparison: "I was going down . . . like a child's balloon as it gradually lets out air" (Eugene Ionesco's play, *The Stroller in the Air*) ; "Ripples to the pavement like a deflated balloon" from T. Coraghessan Boyle's novel, *Water Music, Little.*
55. Like an emptying tube, after a couple of minutes he collapses —Erich Maria Remarque
56. Over she went . . . like a little puff of milkweed —Eudora Welty
57. Pitched forward like a felled tree —Oakley Hall
58. (His heaving bulk suddenly) sagged, like a sail bereft of wind —Jan Kubicki
59. [Old man] scrunched like an old gray fetus —Grace Paley
60. Thudded like a bird against the glass wall —Ross Macdonald
61. Topple over like a doll with a round base —Wilfrid Sheed
62. Tumble down like a house of cards —George Du Maurier

The many twists on tumbling, falling or collapsing cards as comparisons include Robert Browning's "Fell like piled-up cards" and Edith Wharton's "Collapsed like a playing card."

63. Tumbled down like the Tower of Babel —Bernard Malamud

64. Tumbling dumb as a ninepin —Sharon Sheehe Stark

65. We fell to the carpet like leaves circling in a light wind —James Crumley

66. Went down like a ninepin —Edith Wharton
    This still popular simile to describe a sudden fall was probably in use before its appearance in Wharton's story, *The Pelican.*

67. Went down like a plumb line —Lawrence Durrell

68. Went down like a pole-axed steer —Donald Seaman

69. Went over [after being hit] like a paper cut-out and lay just as flat as one —Cornell Woolrich

COLORS

See Also: BLACK, BLUE, BRIGHTNESS, BROWN, GREEN, PALLOR, PINK, RED, WHITE

1. An amber mixture like autumn leaves —Francois Maspero

2. Bright gold like a diadem —Angela Carter

3. (Sky damp and) colorless as a cough —Sharon Sheehe Stark

4. Colorless as a desert —Alice McDermott

5. Colorless like the white paper streamer a Chinaman pulls out of his mouth —editor, *Dragonfly Magazine,* 1880
   This simile appeared in a rejection letter sent to Anton Chekhov when he was still a fledgling writer.

6. Colors are as soft as a Mediterranean dawn —Bryan Miller, *New York Times,* July 3, 1987
   Miller's simile pertained to the colors of a restaurant.

7. Colors as clear as notes perfectly played —A. E. Maxwell

8. Colors [of Christmas candy] . . . as piercing as the joys and sufferings of the poor . . . red like the love that was celebrated in doorways . . . yellow like the flames in a drunk man's brain — Heinrich Böll

9. Colors clear as fresh-cut flowers —Joan Chase

10. Deep colored as old rugs —Eudora Welty

11. As full of color as blood —John Logan

12. Gold as the seeds of a melon —Dame Edith Sitwell

13. A good soldier, like a good horse, cannot be of a bad color —Oliver Wendell Holmes, Sr.
    See Also: ARMY

14. Orange as the sunset —Dashiell Hammett

15. Orange bright like golden lamps in a green light —Andrew Marvell

16. [A taxi] painted in an arabesque of colors, like a psychedelic dream gone wild —Andrew Kaplan

17. (His split lip is as) purple as a nightcrawler stuck on a hook —Robert Flanagan
    This simile begins Flanagan's short story, *Naked to Naked Goes.*

18. Purple as a grape —Dashiell Hammett

19. [Cabbage] purply as cheap stained glass —Babette Deutsch

20. The reds and browns and golds of the trees seem ready to drip from their branches like wet dye —Alice McDermott
    See Also: TREES

21. Silvery as sleighbells —Diane Ackerman

22. Two-toned like a layer cake —Donald McCaig

COMFORT

1. (Feel as) comfortable as a Cossack in Kiev —Richard Ford

2. (Eugene was) comfortable as a saggy armchair —Donald McCaig

3. Comfortable as matrimony —Nathan Bailey

4. Comfortable . . . like sleeping on a cloud —Slogan, Sealy Inc.

5. Comforting as a long soak in a hot tub after a short walk in a freezing rainstorm —Elyse Sommer

6. Comforting as the Surgeon-General's statement on a pack of Lucky Strikes —Harry Prince

7. Comfort [memory of a lover] like a rosary —Sumner Locke Elliot

8. Cozy and dark as a dreary day —Sharon Sheehe Stark
   See Also: DARKNESS

9. Cozy as a cup of tea —Anon

10. Cozy as a nest —Émile Zola

11. Cozy as visiting your grandmother —Mary Lee Settle

12. Easy as an old shoe —English proverb
    New Englanders brought this from the old country as "Comfortable as an old shoe," an expression still very much in use. There's also a Ukranian proverb which incorporates a somewhat different form of this simile.
    See Also: MARRIAGE

13. Feels comfortable like in a cloud —Francois Maspero

14. Reassured . . . like a sheltering wing over a motherless bird —Louisa May Alcott

137

See Also: KINDNESS

15. Restful as one's favorite armchair —Frank Swinnerton

16. (Here Skigg lies) snug as a bug in a rug —Benjamin Franklin, letter to Georgiana Shipley, September, 1772

17. Snug as the yolk in an egg —Henrik Ibsen

18. Soothing as mother's milk —Anon

19. [Conversation] soothing, like the quiet, washing sound of an occan — Donald Justice

20. Supported [by attentive performance] as a bold swimmer by the waves —Ivan Turgenev

21. [Prospect of someone's being there] sustained him like a snug life jacket —Lynne Sharon Schwartz

22. Sustain like a stream does a trout —Andrew Dubus

23. Warm and cozy and private as a nursery —John Braine

24. Warm and old-fashioned as a potbellied stove —Anon, capsule movie review, *Newsday,* January, 1986

25. (Walls look as) warm and sturdy as a fisherman's hand-knitted sweater —Sheila Radley
See Also: PERMANENCE

26. (The whole room was as equally and agreeably) warm as a bath full of water —Anon
See Also: ROOMS

27. Warm as piss —American colloquialism

28. Warm as sunshine, light as floating clouds —Slogan, Torfeaco bedding

29. Warm like love —Sharon Sheehe Stark

COMMOMPLACE
See Also: FAMILIARITY

1. As corny as Kansas in August . . . as normal as blueberry pie —Oscar Hammerstein II, from lyric for *South Pacific.*
Another famous simile from the same score: "High as a flag on the Fourth of July."

2. As daily as bread —Thomas Lux

3. Common as adultery, and hardly less reprehensible —Lord Altringham
Societal changes have seeded "Common as divorce" and "Common as sex" before marriage.

4. Common as bag ladies on city streets —Anon

5. (Angels were as) common as birds or butterflies —Donald Justice

6. Common as dentists who molest female patients —Loren D. Estleman

7. Common as dirt —American colloquialism attributed to New England

A popular variation: "Common as mud."

8. Common as frozen dinners —Anon
    Another up-and-coming one from our fast food age: "Common as microwave dinners."

9. Common as get out —William Hazlitt This has become known and used as "Common as all get-out."

10. Common as graduation parties in June —Anon

11. Common as hot spells in July and snowflakes in winter —Elyse Sommer

12. Common as pig's tracks —H. W. Thompson
    American folklore has simplified this to "Common as dirt."

13. Common . . . as potatoes —Hugh Walpole

14. Common as the highway —John Ray's *Proverbs*

15. Common as the New York cockroach —Erik Sandberg-Diment, writing about the increased use and availability of personal computer clones of the original IBM model, *New York Times,* December 12, 1986
    New Yorkers might well argue that they have no exclusiveness when it comes to cockroaches.

16. (Charles's conversation was) commonplace as a street pavement — Gustave Flaubert

17. Commomplace as birth —Anon

18. Commonplace as slumber —Phyllis McGinley

19. Ordinary as walking a straight line —Lee K. Abbott

20. Taken for granted like a nose bob —Alistair Cooke, *New York Times* interview, referring to the television teleprompter, January 1, 1985

21. Traditional as a seven-layer wedding cake —Jonathan Valin

COMPASSION
See: KINDNESS, PITY

COMPATIBILITY
See Also: BELONGING

1. Companionable as a cat and a goldfish —Anon

2. Companionable [a mother and son] as a pair of collusive old whores — David Leitch

3. Compatible as the stars and stripes on the American flag —Elyse Sommer

4. Get on like a house on fire —Ngaio Marsh

5. Get on like salt and iron —Loren D. Estleman

6. Good taste and humor are a contradiction in terms, like a chaste whore —Malcom Muggeridge quoted in *Time,* September 14, 1953

7. Got along like Siamese twins —George Garrett

8. Go together like a computer and an abacus —Anon

9. Go together like apples and pie crust —Elyse Sommer
   These 'go-togethers' provide endless opportunity for additional twists.

10. Go together like bagels and cream cheese —Anon

11. Go together like blueberries and cream —Anon

12. Go together like coffee and danish —Anon

13. Go together like ice cream and salt —Anon

14. Go together like meatballs and spaghetti —Anon

15. Go together like paper and pencil —Anon

16. Go together like tea and lemon —Anon

17. Got on like twin souls —Edward Marsh

18. Irreconcilable as a jazz band and a symphony orchestra —Paul Mourand

19. No more affinity for each other than a robin for a goldfish —Eleanor Kirk

20. Struck [Flanner and Mike Wallace] it off together like a pair of lighted pinwheels —Janet Flanner

COMPETENCE
See: ABILITY, ACCOMPLISHMENT

COMPETITION
See Also: BUSINESS, SPORTS

1. As competitive as two dogs after a bitch in heat —Anon

2. Asking him to compete fairly is like asking a hungry lion to leave the lambs alone —Mike Sommer

3. Competition is like sugar sprinkled on cobbler pie —Elmer Kelton

4. A non-competitive businessman is like an honest crook —Elyse Sommer

5. Playing tennis without keeping score is like apple pie sans la mode — Anon

COMPLACENCY
See: CONTENTMENT

COMPLAINTS
See: ANGER, CRITICISM

COMPLETENESS

1. Fragmentary, like the text of a corrupt manuscript whose words have been effaced in the wind and rain —Arthur A. Cohen

2. Completely as hydrogen mixes with oxygen to become water . . . the orange is part of the living animal —Daniela Gioseffi

3. Incomplete as a circus without clowns —Elyse Sommer

4. Incomplete . . . like cabbage with all the flavor boiled out —Richard Brookhiser, *Wall Street Journal* book review, April 1, 1987
   The simile refers to an author's effort to serve up election information without politics.

5. Playing cards without money is like a meal without salt —Bertold Brecht

6. A store without merchandise to sell is like a library without books to read —Anon
   See Also: BUSINESS

7. (The antismoking zealots never tell you these things . . . colds, weight gain can happen to you after kicking the habit.) They [people giving incomplete information] are like Karl Malden, who is always telling you how happy American Express will be to replace your stolen traveler's checks but never bothers to tell you that if their serial numbers are stolen too, you're out of luck —Russell Baker, *New York Times Magazine,* September 21, 1986

COMPLEXION

See Also: SKIN, WRINKLES

1. A blotchy complexion like salami —Jilly Cooper

2. The cluster of red veins, like Rorschach patterns, sticking out on his cheeks —Henry Van Dyke

3. Complexion . . . as red as a boiled shrimp —Kenzaburo Oë

4. Complexion . . . as smooth as white mushrooms —Bobbie Ann Mason

5. Complexion dark as cholera —Cynthia Ozick

6. Complexion like a choir boy's —Robert Campbell

7. A complexion like the blossoms of apples —W. B. Yeats

8. A complexion like the moon at short range —Harry Prince

9. Complexion . . . like the skin on porridge —Frank Swinnerton

10. Complexion like twelve-year-old Scotch going down —Loren D. Estleman

11. Complexion the color of porridge —Christopher Isherwood

12. Complexion, which had become pale in the dimness of the house . . . shone as if it had been varnished —Guy de Maupassant

13. Face glistened as if it were covered with scar tissue from a newly healed burn —Kenzaburo Oë

14. Face . . . pock-marked like a wall against which men had stood to take the bullets of a firing squad —Penelope Gilliatt

15. Her complexion in its pallor showed clear as a lily petal —Ethel Cook Eliot

16. His face had an unnatural smoothness as though it were massaged and nourished with cold creams —W. Somerset Maugham

17. Suntan that looks like it was done on a rotisserie —Tom Wolfe Wolfe is describing actor Cary Grant.

18. The thin veins on his massive cheeks were like the engraving on gilt-edged securities —Ludwig Bemelmans

19. A tracery of red veins, distinct as mapped rivers and tributaries, showed on his cheeks —Anne Tyler

COMPLEXITY
See Also: DIFFICULTY

1. (He was) as complex as the double helix and sometimes as simple as a paramecium —Mike Sommer

2. As complicated and unavailing as a cut-out paper snowflake —Eudora Welty

3. As complicated as a full-bore, rollicking infidelity right in their own homes —Richard Ford

4. As complicated as the flush valve on a water closet —Anon

5. [A family's history] convoluted as a Greek drama —Gail Godwin

6. (Character is as) detailed, as intricately woven as the intricate Oriental carpets and brocades in Freud's office —Vincent Canby, *New York Times,* September 24, 1986
   > The Oriental carpet and brocade comparison was particularly apt for Canby's review of *Nineteen-Nineteen,* a movie about two Freud patients, with many scenes in Freud's heavily carpeted Vienna office.

7. The detail was astonishing, like the circuits on a computer chip — James Morrow

8. (By marriage she had to assume a whole new family of blood kin) elaborate as a graph —George Garrett

9. (Their relationship seemed as) intricate as a DNA blueprint —Joseph Wambaugh

10. To say Freud was complex is like saying Tolstoy could write —Anon

COMPLIMENTS
See: FLATTERY, WORDS OF PRAISE

COMPOSITION
  See: MUSIC

COMPREHENSIBLENESS
  See: CLARITY

CONCEIT
  See: VANITY

CONCENTRATION
  See: ATTENTION, SCRUTINY

CONCISENESS
  See: BREVITY

CONDEMNATION
  See: CRITICISM

CONFIDENCE
  See: SELF-CONFIDENCE, TRUST

CONFIDENTIALITY
  See: SECRECY

CONFUSION
  See: BEWILDERMENT

CONNECTIONS
  See Also: CLINGING

1. Attached [to an idea] like a slug to its shell —Paige Mitchell

2. Bonds (of family) as immutable as a tribal code —Anon

3. Bonds frail as spider webs —George Garrett
   See Also: FRAGILITY

4. The bonds which I had thought bound me . . . turned out to be as flimsy and insubstantial as a kindergartner's paper chain —Harvey Swados

5. Bound as the sun to the world's wheel —Algernon Charles Swinburne

6. Bound together as two trees with interwoven roots —Edith Wharton

7. Bound together . . . like stepsisters with completely different backgrounds forced to live together under the same roof —Margaret Millar

The comparison as used in the mystery novel, *Beyond This Point Are Monsters,* is applied to cities which are different in sight and sound but bound together by geography and economics.

8. (Different professional groups in an organization) bundled together, as carrots or sticks of asparagus are bundled together —Frank Swinnerton

9. Closely connected . . . as a mother with her baby's belly button —Bertold Brecht

10. Connect like a recurring musical leitmotif —Anon

11. Drawn together and held like snowflakes in a glass glove —Arthur A. Cohen

12. (Lives and limbs) entwined like the roots of trees —John Logan

13. Held together as backbone holds together the ribs and limbs and head to a body —H. G. Wells

14. Holds together like a quilt —James Dickey

15. Joined together as in a wedding of rivers —George Garrett

16. Linked [together] like mountain climbers —Frank Swinnerton

17. Linked together by bonds as deep and mysterious as those which tie the mother to her young —Harvey Swados

18. Lives crossing like swords —Paige Mitchell

19. Mixes like alphabet soup —Diane Ackerman

20. Roped together like climbers on a rockface —Lawrence Durrell

CONSCIENCE

See Also: REGRET

1. A bad conscience is a kind of illness, in the sense that pregnancy is an illness —Friedrich Nietzsche

2. A clear conscience is like a wall of brass —Latin proverb

3. Conscience as big as the Alps —Walter Goodman, *New York Times* movie review, May 27, 1987

4. Conscience . . . a terrifying little sprite, that bat-like winks by day and wakes by night —John Wolcott

5. Conscience is God's presence in man —Anon

6. Conscience is like a sun-dial; if you let truth shine upon it, it will put you right —Hamilton Bower
    The author expanded upon the simile as follows: "But you may cover it over so that no truth can fall upon it, or you may let false light gleam upon it and then it will lead you astray."

7. (His) conscience rose like a shining light —Honoré de Balzac

8. Conscience wide as hell —William Shakespeare

9. Gets little attacks of conscience, like hot flashes —Jonathan Valin

10. Going through life with a conscience is like driving your car with the brakes on —Budd Schulberg

11. A healthy conscience is like a wall of bronze —Erasmus

12. He that has a scrupulous conscience, is like a horse that is not well wayed [well-taught]; he starts at every bird that flies out of the hedge — John Selden
    The word 'hath' from the original simile has been modernized to 'has.'

13. The sting of conscience, like the gnawing of a dog at a bone, is mere foolishness —Friedrich Nietzsche

14. Weather-beaten conscience . . . as elastic as his heart —Arthur Train

CONSIDERATION
See: THOUGHT

CONTAGION
See: SPREADING

CONTEMPT

1. As the air to a bird or the sea to a fish, so is contempt to the contemptible —William Blake

2. Contempt is a kind of gangrene, which if it seizes one part of a character, it corrupts all the rest by degrees —Samuel Johnson

3. (His voice had turned idle,) contemptuous, uncaring, like a king throwing a handful of coppers at the feet of children —Borden Deal

4. Disdain as a gourmet disdains TV dinners —Anon

5. Disdain as a lover of literature disdains a potboiler —Anon

6. (He started) handling my exam paper like it was a turd —J. D. Salinger

7. (A waiter who) looked as if he had been cornstarched in arrogance — Pat Conroy

8. More haughty than the devil —William Shakespeare

9. Scorn will curl suddenly round silent corners like bell-less bicycles — W. R. Rodgers

10. Sneered, like a waiter in a French restaurant who has just taken an order for a Chardonnay that he disdains —Ira Berkow, *New York Times,* September 29, 1986, about Jim Rice, a baseball hitter

11. They treat me like a snakebit cowpoke just in from the range —Thomas Zigal

12. Watch . . . distastefully, as though she were a cigar being smoked in the presence of a lady without permission —Penelope Gilliatt

CONTENTMENT

See Also: HAPPINESS, JOY

1. (There she lay) as complacently feminine as a turtle-dove —Christopher Isherwood

2. Content as a Parsee priestess who had duly paid her morning devotions to the deity —Israel Zangwill

3. Content as a tick sitting quietly on a tree and living off a tiny drop of blood plundered years before —Patrick Suskind

4. (She wanted us to be as) content as trees in a rain forest —Max Apple

5. Contented as a baby on a schedule —Hollis Summers

6. Contented as a cobra full of warm milk —Rupert Hughes

7. Content . . . like a little white kitty in a basket —Eudora Welty

8. Feel rewarded, like a gardener who's cutting roots —Margaret Sutherland

9. Hummed . . . like a cook with things coming out right —William Beechcroft

10. Like jellyfish that lie beneath the warm ocean waters here [Hilton Head] there is discontent beneath the surface bonhomie (of the governors' annual conference) —David Shieman, *Wall Street Journal,* August 26, 1986

11. (She prospered and could expect to prosper more . . . but) like someone in exile, uncertain of deliverance, she was restless and dissatisfied —Robert Henson

12. Looked about as satisfied as a millionaire's mistress —William Beechcroft

13. Mood of complacency . . . like a man who, having been under dire threat of burglary, suddenly increases his insurance and changes all the locks on his house and is convinced that these emergencies will make him for ever immune —H. E. Bates

14. Pleased as a cat with two tails —American colloquialism, attributed to New England
    A common variation: "Proud as a dog with two tails."

15. Psyche . . . topped up like the tanks of the automobiles —Frank Conroy
    The simile from Conroy's novel, *Stop-Time,* refers to more than one automobile because the scene is in a gas station. Removed from this context, "Topped up like the tank of an automobile" would have the same meaning.

16. Satisfying as getting a refund on your income tax —Anon

17. Sitting pretty, like a batter with three balls and no strikes against him —James Thurber
    See Also: BASEBALL

18. Take it (killing and bloodshed) in like the sun shines and the rain falls —Eileen O'Casey

19. Wears contentment like a wreath —Barbara Howes

20. When people abhor what they cannot comprehend, they are like those burning with fever, to whom the choicest food is unpalatable —Kahlil Gibran

CONTINUITY

See Also: PERMANENCE

1. As never ending as a brook —Anon

2. Bottomless as Hell —Ben Jonson

3. Bottomless as the foundation of the Universe —Thomas Carlyle

4. Boundless as the sea —William Shakespeare

5. Boundless as the wind —Jonathan Swift

6. (Restaurants) come and go steadily as Bedouin tribesmen —Ed McBain

7. A constant figure in her life, like a white knight or a black mammy — Julia Whedon

8. Continued as on an endless escalator —Eleanor Clark

9. Continuous as an endless circle —Anon

10. Continuous as the beat of death —Amy Lowell

11. Continuous as the stars that shine and twinkle on the Milky Way — William Wordsworth
    A variation: "Infinite as the stars"

12. Endless as prairies —Margaret Atwood

13. Endless as the line around a circle —Anon

14. Eternal as mediocrity —James G. Huneker

15. (She was, for him,) eternal like the seasons —Dorothea Straus

16. Go on like an eternal flame —Lyn Lifshin

17. Had gone on like a bad sleep —Jean Stafford

18. Keeps rolling along like the Big River —John Gross

19. Lived on like names in a legend —John Hall Wheelock

20. Numberless as the sands of the desert —American colloquialism
    An equally popular variation is "Numberless as the fish in the sea."

21. Steadily as a shell secretes its beating leagues of monotone —Hart Crane

22. Timeless as a churchyard —Sharon Sheehe Stark

CONTROL

1. Abstinent as a reformed sinner —Anon

2. Censorship is like an appendix. When it is inert it is useless; when active it is extremely dangerous —Maurice Edelman

3. Censorship, like charity, should begin at home —Clare Booth Luce
   The combinations for this comparison are virtually limitless.
   See Also: BELIEFS, CHANGE, CRITICISM, PEACE, SENSE

4. Censure is like the lightning which strikes the highest mountains —Baltasar Gracian

5. Censurious . . . as a superannuated sinner —William Wycherly

6. Circumscribed like a dog chained to a tree —Beth Nugent

7. (Always trying to) confine things into the shape of a phrase, like pouring water into a sewer —Vita Sackville-West

8. (Ordered lives) contained like climbers huddled to a rock ledge —W. D. Snodgrass

9. Feel like a dog on a short leash —Joanne Kates, *New York Times*/Hers, September 18, 1986

10. He kept it [emotional feeling] rigidly at the back of his mind, like a fruit not ripe enough to eat —H. E. Bates

11. He that has no rule over his own spirit is like a city without walls —*The Holy Bible/Proverbs*
    'Hath' has been modernized to 'has.'

12. Imprison like a stone girdle —Anon

13. Irrepressible, like flame catching kindling —George Garrett

14. I wear my chains [of sexual and social roles] like ornaments, convinced they make a charming jingle —Phyllis McGinley

15. Manageable as chess pieces —George Meredith

16. [My wife's society] oppressed me like a spell —Edgar Allen Poe
    In another version of the tale *Morelia,* Poe kept the comparison but changed the frame of reference to the mystery of the wife's manner instead of her company.

17. Suffocating as the interior of a sepulchre —Anon

18. The restriction is like saying to an avid reader he can't see a book for nine months —Kent Hannon on ruling restricting basketball practice for players who don't have C average, *New York Times,* July 21, 1986

19. To be with her was like living in a room with shuttered windows —Edith Wharton

20. Uncontrollable as a swift tide with a strong undertow —Anon

21. Uncontrollable as the wind —Robert Traver

CONVERSATION

1. Conversation . . . was like trying to communicate with a ship sinking in mid-Atlantic when you're on shore —William McIlvanney

2. The American's conversation is much like his courtship . . . he gives in and watches for a reaction; if the weather looks fair, he inkles a little —Donald Lloyd, *Harper's Magazine,* September 19, 1963
    See Also: CHARACTERISTICS, NATIONAL

3. Chattering as foolishly as two slightly mad squirrels —James Crumley
    See Also: FOOLISHNESS

4. Conversation . . . as edifying as listening to a leak dropping in a tin dish-pan at the head of the bed when you want to go to sleep —O. Henry

5. A conversation between the two of you must be like listening to two pecans in a bowl —Geoffrey Wolff
    The character who utters this simile in Wolff's novel, *Providence,* follows it up with "Why don't you let him shoot 500 cc of thorazine right in your heart and get it over."

6. Conversation . . . crisp and varied as a freshly tossed salad —Anon

7. Conversation . . . it was like talk at a party, leap-frogging, sparring, showing-off —Nina Bawden

8. Conversation, like lettuce, requires a good deal of oil to avoid friction, and keep the company smooth —Charles Dudley Warner

9. Conversation . . . like dialogue from a play that had run too long and the acting had gone stale —John McGahern

10. Conversation . . . rapid and guttural as gunfire —Harvey Swados

11. The conversations . . . behaved like green logs, they fumed but would not fire —Truman Capote

12. Conversation should be like a salad, composed of various ingredients, and well stirred with salt, oil, and vinegar —Joaquin Setanti

13. Conversation . . . should flow, like waters after summer showers, not as if raised by mere mechanic powers —William Cowper

14. Conversation . . . sweet as clover —Ogden Nash

15. The conversation was just like clockwork. It recurred regularly, except that there was no need to wind anything up —Walter De La Mare

16. Conversed in whispers . . . like doctors consulting on a difficult case —Jean Stafford

17. Conversed like tennis players, back and forth, stroke for stroke —Jessamyn West

18. Converse with himself, like a prisoner alone in his cell or like a wayfarer lost in a wilderness —Joseph Conrad

19. Cutting off the small talk with an opening question like a serve — Elizabeth Spencer

20. Discourses on subjects above our comprehension . . . it's like listening to an unknown language —Henry Fielding
    See Also: BEWILDERMENT

21. A false and most unnatural kind of chatting, like fighters meeting at a weigh-in —Norman Mailer
    Mailer was describing the beginning of an interview with Mike Wallace.

22. From time to time . . . talk becomes effective, conquering like war, widening the boundaries of knowledge like an exploration —Robert Louis Stevenson

23. Gabbing like college girls with the handsomest boy on campus waiting at the curb in big convertibles —Richard Ford

24. Good communication is as stimulating as black coffee, and just as hard to sleep after —Anne Morrow Lindbergh

25. Good conversation, like any game, calls for equals in strength — Jacques Barzun

26. Good conversation unrolls itself like the spring or like the dawn —W. B. Yeats

27. A good talk is like a good dinner: one assimilates it —Jerome K. Jerome

28. Good talk is . . . like an impromptu piece of acting where each should represent himself to greatest advantage —Robert Louis Stevenson

29. Good talk is like good scenery—continuous, yet constantly varying, and full of the charm of novelty and surprise —Randolph S. Bourne

30. Had the ability to turn any conversation into an interrogation —Ann Beattie

31. He [the inveterate punster] followed conversation as a shark follows a ship, or, to shift the metaphor, he was like Jack Horner and stuck in his thumb to pull out a pun —Stephen Leacock

32. (For a person accustomed to obsequiousness and flattery) his conversation is by much too strong, like mustard in a child's mouth — Hester Lynch Thrale
    Thrale thus targeted Samuel Johnson's brusque manner.

33. (She) hit on the commonplace like a hammer driving a nail into the wall. She plunged into the obvious like a clown in a circus jumping through a hoop —W. Somerset Maugham
    Maugham's biting simile describe a dull conversationalist in his story, *Winter Cruise.*

34. In conversation . . . like playing on the harp; there is much in laying the hands on the strings to stop their vibration as in twanging them to bring out the music —Oliver Wendell Holmes, Sr.

35. In married conversation as in surgery, the knife must be used with care —Andre Maurois, February, 1955
See Also: MARRIAGE

36. The joke went on and on . . . scaring away any other kind of conversation like a schoolyard bully —William H. Gass

37. Like the alternating patches of sun and shade that fell on the windshield as the clouds skidded overhead, the conversation inside the pickup went by fits and starts —Phyllis Naylor

38. (Their habit was to engage in this) mock banter, where they slipped truths into their jokes . . . like filling cream puffs —David R. Slavitt

39. Natural talk, like ploughing, should turn up a large surface of life, rather than dig mines —Robert Louis Stevenson
Stevenson elaborated on his simile as follows: "Masses of experience, anecdote, incident, crosslights, quotation, historical instances, the whole flotsam and jetsam of two minds forced in and upon the matter at hand from every point of the compass, and from every degree of mental elevation and abasement, these are the materials with which talk is fortified, the food on which the talkers thrive."

40. (He had) practiced his portion of the conversation so many times . . . that he felt like an actor in a stock company —Herbert Gold

41. Quips flew back and forth like balls between two long-experienced jugglers in a circus ring —Natascha Wodin

42. The room seethes with talk. Always a minimum of three conversations, like crosswinds —Rosellen Brown

43. Small talk is like the air that shatters the stalactites into dust again — Anaïs Nin

44. The talk came like the spilling of grain from a sack, in bursts of fullness that were shut off in mid-sentence as if someone had closed the sack abruptly and there was more talk inside —Shirley W. Schoonover

45. Talked . . . like old friends in mourning —Nadine Gordimer

46. Talking to Bill is like opening a new bottle of ketchup; you gotta wait a while before anything comes out —Jonathan Valin
In his novel, *Life's Work,* Valin expands on this with "Sometimes you wait and nothing happens."

47. Talking to him was like playing upon an exquisite violin. He answered to every touch and thrill of the bow —Oscar Wilde

48. Talking to them is like trying to get a zeppelin off the ground — Penelope Gilliatt

See Also: DIFFICULTY

49. Talking to you is like addressing the Berlin Wall —Colin Forbes
See Also: FUTILITY

50. Talking to you is like sending out your laundry, you don't know what the hell is coming back —Neil Simon
See Also: UNCERTAINTY

51. Talking to you is like talking to my forearm —Geoffrey Wolff
See Also: ABSURDITY

52. Talking with him [George McGovern] is like eating a Chinese meal. An hour after it's over, you wonder whether you really ate anything — Eugene McCarthy
See Also: INCOMPLETENESS, INSULTS

53. Talking with you is more like boxing than talking —Larry McMurtry
The simile from *Somebody's Darling* continues as follows: "You're always hitting me with a jab."

54. Talk that warms like wine —Babette Deutsch

55. Their remarks and responses were like a Ping-Pong game with each volley clearing the net and flying back to the opposition —Maya Angelou

56. Trading talk like blows —Anne Sexton
See Also: ARGUMENT

CONVICTION
See: BELIEFS

COOKERY
See: FOOD AND DRINK

COOLNESS
See: CALMNESS

COOPERATION
See: AGREEMENT

CORPORATIONS
See: BUSINESS

CORPULENCE
See: FATNESS

CORRECTNESS
See Also: TRUENESS/FALSENESS, MANNERS, REPUTATION

1. Accurate as a hole in one —Anon

See Also: GOLF

2. Accurately as a geometrician —V. S. Pritchett

3. As scrupulous as a well-trained tailor —Robert Penn Warren

4. Exact as a blueprint —Anon

5. Exact as the technical jargon of a trade —Aldous Huxley

6. More exacting than a pasha with thirty wives —Guy de Maupassant

7. Proper as a butler —Charles Simmons

8. Respectable as Jane Austen —Marge Piercy

9. Right as a well-done sum —Sylvia Plath

CORRESPONDENCE
See Also: WRITERS/WRITING

1. Correspondences are like small clothes before the invention of suspenders; it is impossible to keep them up —Sydney Smith

2. Letters are like bodies, and their meaning like souls —Abraham Ibn Ezra

3. A letter that was like a poem. It was . . . like listening to French it was so beautiful —Philip Roth

4. A lifelong sustained correspondence like a lifelong unbroken friendship or happy marriage, requires explaining: all the cards are stacked against it —Max Lerner

5. Little letters cozy and innocent as a baby's layette —Truman Capote

6. A mess of a letter . . . it dribbles and mouths all over the place like Maurice Chevalier —Dylan Thomas

7. Printed [condolence] cards should be abolished; they're like canned music —Gwen Schwartz-Borden, director Bereavement Center, Family Service Association of Nassau County, quoted in *New York Times* article on bereavement notes, November 24, 1986

8. The time is coming when letter writing with pen and ink and sent as a personal message from one person to another will be as much of a rarity as the gold pocket watch carried on a chain —Andy Rooney

9. A woman's love letters are like her child. They belong to her more than to anybody else —Edith Wharton

10. Writing to you is like corresponding with an aching void —Groucho Marx
See Also: INSULTS

11. Your letters . . . they're like telegrams —Dorothy Parker

COST
See Also: ADVANTAGEOUSNESS, THRIFT

1. As cheap as pearls are costly —Robert Browning

2. Charge like a brain surgeon —Saul Bellow

3. Cheap as dirt —F. E. Smedley

4. Cheap as excuses —Anon

5. Cheap as lies —William Shakespeare

6. Cheap as old clothes —Horace Walpole

7. Cheap as old clothes used to be —Elyse Sommer
   An update of Horace Walpole's simile above, inspired by a change in both economic conditions and the upgraded status of old clothes.

8. Expensive as building an atomic reactor —Robert Traver

9. Expensive as Manhattan real estate —Anon

10. Expensive as sin —Anon

COURAGE

1. Adventurous as a bee —William Wordsworth

2. As brave as hell —Petronius

3. As much backbone as an eel —American colloquialism

4. As much backbone as cooked spaghetti —Harry Prince

5. (There was) a tragic daring about her, like a moth dancing around a flame —Paige Mitchell

6. (He died) bold as brass —George Parker
   Common usage has seeded modern-day modifications such as "Bold as brass balls."

7. Bold as a dying saint —Elkanah Settle

8. Bold as a lion —*The Holy Bible/Proverbs*

9. Bold as an unhunted fawn —Percy Bysshe Shelley

10. Bold as love —Edmond Gosse

11. Bold as Paul in the presence of Agrippa —William Cowper

12. Brave as a barrel full of bears —Ogden Nash

13. Brave as a tiger in a rage —Ogden Nash

14. Brave as winds that brave the sea —Algernon Charles Swinburne

15. Courage is like a disobedient dog, once it starts running away it flies all the faster for your attempts to recall it —Katherine Mansfield

16. Courage is like love; it must have hope to nourish it —Napoleon Bonaparte

17. Courage, like cowardice, is undoubtedly contagious, but some persons are not liable to catch it —Archibald Prentice

18. Courage, on nearly all occasions, inflicts as much of evil as it imparts of good —Walter Savage Landor

19. Courageous as a poker player with a royal flush —Mike Sommer

20. Courageous like firemen. The bell rings and they jump into their boots and go down the pole —Anon

21. Daring as tickling a tiger —Anon

22. Fend off pressure like a sharkhunter feeds off danger —Anon

23. Gallant as a warrior —Beryl Markham

24. Grew bold, like a general who is about to order an assault —Guy de Maupassant

25. Have the gall of a shoplifter returning an item for a refund —W.I.E. Gates

26. Indomitable as a lioness —Aharon Appelfeld

27. A man without courage is like a knife without edge —Anon

28. More guts than a gladiator —William Diehl

29. Nothing so bold as a blind horse —Greek proverb

30. Over-daring is as great a vice as over-fearing —Ben Jonson

31. Show nerve of a burglar —Anon

32. Stand my ground brave as a bear —American country ballad "If You Want to Go A-Courting"

33. Valiant as a lion —William Shakespeare
    This simile from *Henry the Fourth* has made lion comparisons part of our every day language. Another lion simile by the Bard is "Walked like one of the lions" from *The Two Gentlemen of Verona.*

34. With all the courage of an escaped convict —Honoré de Balzac

35. Valiant as Hercules —William Shakespeare

36. (I've seen plenty of great big tough guys that was as) yellow and soft as a stick of butter —George Garrett

COUNSEL
See: ADVICE

COURTESY
See: BEHAVIOR, MANNERS

COURTSHIP
See: MEN AND WOMEN

COVERTNESS
See: SECRET

COWARDICE
See: FEAR

COZINESS
See: COMFORT

CRAFTINESS
See: CLEVERNESS

CRAVING
See: DESIRE

CRAZINESS
See: MADNESS

CREDIT

1. Credit buying is much like being drunk. The buzz happens immediately . . . the hangover comes the day after —Dr. Joyce Brothers

2. Credit is like a looking glass . . . .once cracked [it] can never be repaired again —Sir Walter Scott
   An anonymous rhymed version of this is "Credit, like a looking-glass, broken once, is gone, alas!" and, from John Ray's *Proverbs* there's "Credit lost is like Venice glass broken."

3. Credit is like chastity, they can both stand temptation better than suspicion —Josh Billings

4. Creditors buzz like locusts —Anaïs Nin

5. Debts are like children: the smaller they are the more noise they make —Spanish proverb

6. The first step in debt is like the first step in falsehood, involving the necessity of going on in the same course, debt following debt, as lie follows lie —Samuel Smiles

7. It's [borrowing] like anticipating one's income, and making the future bear the expenses of the past —Bartlett's Dictionary of Americanisms

8. Just as in the relations between creditor and debtor there is always an element of the disagreeable that can never be overcome, for the very reason that the one is irrevocably committed to the role of giver and the other to that of receiver; so in a sick person, a latent feeling of resentment at every obvious sign of consideration is always ready to burst forth —Stefan Zweig

9. Lending to the feckless is like pelting a stray dog with dumplings — Arab proverb

10. No man's credit is as good as his money —Edward Watson Howe

CRIME

    See Also: DISHONESTY, EVIL

1. Crime, like virtue, has its degrees —Jean Racine

2. Crimes, like lands, are not inherited —William Shakespeare

3. Crimes, like virtues, are their own rewards —George Farquhar

4. Murder, like a snowball rolling down a slope, gathers momentum as it goes —Cornell Woolrich

5. Murder, like talent, seems occasionally to run in families —G. H. Lewes

6. Outlaws, like lovers, poets and tubercular composers who cough blood onto piano keys, do their finest work in the slippery rays of the moon — Tom Robbins

7. Passing statues creating new crimes is like printing paper money without anything back of it; in the one case there isn't really any more money than there was before and in the other there isn't really any more crime either —Arthur Train

8. Trying to find out what ultimately drove a criminal to murder is as fruitful as trying to determine what drove fate to choose its victims — Lucinda Franks, reviewing two books about a murder case, *New York Times Book Review,* March 1, 1987
    See Also: FUTILITY

CRISPNESS

    See: SHARPNESS

CRITICISM

    See Also: CRITICISM, LITERARY AND DRAMATIC

1. (They were) as critical as a fan-club —William McIlvanney

2. Blaming X [one group of an industry] for the decline of business is like blaming the iceberg for the demise of the Titanic —Bill Soutar, *Publisher's Weekly,* 1985
    Soutar was speaking specifically about poor business in his field of soft cover book distribution.

3. Criticism is like champagne: nothing more execrable if bad, nothing more excellent if good —Charles Caleb Colton

4. Criticism, like rain, should be gentle enough to nourish a man's growth without destroying his roots —Frank A. Clark, *Reader's Digest,* September, 1971

5. Criticizing, like charity, should begin at home —B. C. Forbes

6. Impersonal criticism is like an impersonal fist fight, or an impersonal marriage, and as successful —George Jean Nathan

7. Like people rummaging in boxes for a knife, everyone searched deep in his memory for a grievance —Marguerite Yourcenar

8. Long harangue [of complaints] . . . it was like a three-hour movie with no intermission —Elizabeth Spencer
   See Also: SLOWNESS

9. Muttering thin complaints like little children called from play —James Crumley

10. Rattling off her woes like mea culpas —Rita Mae Brown

11. Safe from criticsm as a stutter or a squint —Henry James

12. (Mothers) scolded in voices like amplified hens —Rumer Godden
    See Also: VOICES, HARSH

13. Shot grievances like beads across an abacus —Cynthia Ozick

14. Sounded like a cranky old man who needs a stray Airedale to kick —*New York Times* editorial criticizing New York Mayor Edward Koch for his remark about the Soviet government's arrest of an American journalist, September 17, 1986

15. Squeaking like little pigs coming out of the barn door —Congressman Dale Lotta (Ohio), April 9, 1987

CRITICISM, DRAMATIC AND LITERARY
See Also: WRITERS/WRITING, POETS/POETRY

1. Aired their grievances like the wash —Daphne Merkin

2. [Reading about Frank Sinatra's escapades] as refreshing as inhaling carbon monoxide —Barbara Grizzuiti Harrison, reviewing Kitty Kelley's unauthorized biography of Frank Sinatra, *New York Times Book Review,* November 2, 1986

3. [For author W. P. Kinsella] a baseball stadium is a window on the human heart, and his novel . . . stirs it like the refreshing crack of a bat against the ball —*Miami Herald* review of *Shoeless Joe,* a baseball novel, by W. P. Kinsella
   Like many comparisons, this one was pulled out of the review and used as an attention-getting blurb on back of the author's next novel.

4. The book is like a professor's joke. It's nothing if not erudite —Vincent Canby, review of movie adaptation of Umberto Eco's *The Name of the Rose, New York Times,* September 24, 1986

5. Book reviews . . . a kind of infant's disease to which newborn books are subject —Georg Christoph Lichtenberg

6. Critics are like brushers of other men's clothes —Benjamin Disraeli

7. Critics are like eunuchs in a harem. They see how it should be done every night. But they can't do it themselves —Brendan Behan

8. Even when he's not at his best, his books still are appetizing, much like a box of popcorn —Tom Herman, book review (*The Panic of '89* by Paul Erdman), *Wall Street Journal,* January 16, 1987

9. His [author of pamphlet] words, like cavalry horses answering the bugle, group themselves automatically into the familiar dreary pattern —George Orwell

10. It [*The House of Seven Gables*] is like a great symphony, with no touch alterable without injury to the harmony —William James, letter to brother, Henry, January 19, 1869

11. It's [*Praying for Rain,* Jerome Weidman's autobiography] . . . like a raisin-laced kugel, the noodles crammed with juicy morsels about some people, obscure and famous, who have been near and dear to him — Helen Dudar, *New York Times* Book Review, September 21, 1986

12. Language is as precise as 'hello!' and as simple as "Give me a glass of tea" —Vladimir Mayakovsky about Anton Chekhov

13. Literary criticism is an art, like the writing of tragedies or the making of love, and similarly does not pay —Clifton Fadiman

14. Much of the text reads about as joyfully as a Volkswagon manual — George F. Will

15. The novel [*A Special Destiny* by Seymour Epstein] reads like the fictionalized autobiography of a young writer exorcising frustrations and resentments —Bethamy Probst, *New York Times Book Review,* September 21, 1986

16. Novels . . . like literary knuckleballs —George F. Will, about Elmore Leonard's novels

17. One long evening of evasions, as if the playwright were taking the Fifth Amendment on advice of counsel —Frank Rich, *New York Times,* December 12, 1986
    Drama critic Rich has the gift for perfectly suiting the comparison to what it describes . . . in this case a play entitled *Dream of a Blacklisted Actor.*

18. The prose lays there like a dead corpse on the page —Anon

19. Prose rushes out like a spring-fed torrent sweeping the reader away — Chuck Morris

20. Reviewing an autobiography is the literary equivalent of passing judgment on someone's life —Richard Lourie, prefacing his review of Eric Ambler's *Autobiography, New York Times Book Review,* August 17, 1986

21. Style . . . as strong and personal as Van Gogh's brushstrokes — George F. Will, about Elmore Leonard's novels

22. (The author's) style is as crisp as if it had been quick-frozen —Max Apple, about T. Coraghessan Boyle, *New York Times Book Review,* 1979

23. They [critics] bite like fish, at anything, especially at bookes [books] — Thomas Dekker

24. They [Gorky's stories] float through the air like songs —Isaac Babel, lecture, 1934

25. Thin stuff with no meat in it, like a woman, who has starved herself to get what she thinks is a good figure —Ben Ames Williams
    This simile is used by the novelist-hero of *Leave Her to Heaven* to describe his current work.

26. To many people dramatic criticism must seem like an attempt to tattoo soap bubbles —John Mason Brown
    See Also: FUTILITY, IMPOSSIBILITY

27. The undisputed fame enjoyed by Shakespeare as a writer . . . is, like every other lie, a great evil —Leo Tolstoy

28. Watching the movie is like being on a cruise to nowhere aboard a ship with decent service and above-par fast food —Vincent Canby, *New York Times* movie review, October 2, 1983

29. [Henry James] writes fiction as if it were a painful duty —Oscar Wilde

30. (Tolstoy) writes like an ocean, in huge rolling waves, and it doesn't look like it was processed through his thinking —Mel Brook, *Playboy,* 1975

31. Writes like an angel, a fallen, hard-driving angel —A. Alvarez about Robert Stone, *New York Review of Books,* 1986

CROOKEDNESS
See: BENDING/BENT

CROWDS
See Also: CLOSENESS

1. About as much privacy as a statue in the park —Anon

2. As lacking in privacy as a goldfish —Anon

3. Bunched and jammed together as solidly as the bristles in a brush — Mark Twain

4. Came crowding like the waves of ocean, one on the other —Lord Byron

5. Clustering like a swarm of bees —Amy Lowell

6. Crowded like a view of Venice —Frank O'Hara

7. Crowded [stores] like tightly woven multi-colored carpet of people — Richard J. Meislin, *New York Times*

8. The crowd in the lobby [of a hotel] was frozen in poses like the chorus at the curtain of a musical comedy —Vicki Baum

9. The crowd scattered in all directions, like a flock of chickens among which a stone had been thrown —Aharon Megged

10. Feel like a pressed flower —Edith Wharton

11. Flocking . . . like geese —Sharon Sheehe Stark
12. (The public was) flowing in like a river —Enid Bagnold
13. Huddle together like birds in a storm —Robert Graves
14. Jostled like two steers in the stock yards —A. R. Guerney, Jr.
15. Loaded up like a garbage truck —Paige Mitchell
16. Man . . . still, like a hen, he likes his private run —W. H. Auden
17. Men milled everywhere, like cattle in a lightning storm —James Crumley
18. Mobs in their emotions are much like children, subject to the same tantrums and fits of fury —Euripides
19. No more privacy than a traffic cop —Anon
20. [People] packed as closely as herring in a barrel —Sholom Aleichem
21. Packed like a cattle pen —Paige Mitchell
22. The people bunched like cattle in a storm —James Crumley
23. People [on train] . . . hanging from straps like sides of beef on a hook —Julio Cortázar
24. People [at a party] . . . packed tight as a rugby scrum —Nadine Gordimer
    > If Gordimer's story *The Smell of Death and Flowers* had been set in America, it might have had a football lineup for the rugby scrum.
25. People streaming from the plane like busy insects on the march —Sylvia Berkman
26. Stood packed like matches in an upright box —William Faulkner
27. Swarm like bees —Anon
28. Swarm like summer flies —William Shakespeare
29. (Apartments) tenanted tight as hen-houses —Barbara Howes
30. (Surrounded by militia . . .) thick as aphids —Derek Lambert

CRUELTY

See Also: COLDNESS, EVIL

1. (He's always been) a bigger shit than two tons of manure —William McIlvanney
2. Cruel and cold as the judgment of man —Lord Byron
3. Cruel as death —James Thomson
   > This is from a double simile, the second part being "Hungry as the grave."
4. Cruel as love or life —Algernon Charles Swinburne
5. Cruel as old gravestones knocked down and scarred faceless —James Wright

6. (Nothing so) cruel as panic —Robert Louis Stevenson

7. (She knew well the virtues of her singular attractiveness, as) cruel as shears —George Garrett

8. Cruel as winter —Lewis J. Bates

9. Crueller than hell —Algernon Charles Swinburne

10. Cruel, like the ostriches in the wilderness —*The Holy Bible*
    The ostrich reference appears both in *Lamentations* and the *Book of Job*.

11. Cruelty on most occasions is like the wind, boisterous in itself, and exciting a murmur and bustle in all the things it moves among —Walter Savage Landor

12. Evil, like good, has its own heroes —Francois, Duc de La Rochefoucauld

13. Had a persoality like a black hole —Jonathan Valin
    In his novel, *Natural Causes,* from which this is taken, Valin expands upon the simile with "He sucked in everything around him and gave nothing back in return."

14. A heart like a snake —Michael V. Gazzo

15. Her coarseness, her cruelty, was like bark rough with lichen —Virginia Woolf

16. He's like a cobra. No conscience —William Diehl
    See Also: EVIL

17. Mean as a man who'd make knuckle-bones out of his aunt —Anon

18. Mean as a snake —John D. MacDonald

19. Mean as cat shit —James Kirkwood

20. Mean as cat's meat —Somerset Maugham, quoted in *New York Times Magazine* article by Thomas F. Brady, January 24, 1954

21. (That old scoundrel's) mean as ptomaine —Richard Ford

22. Mean as the man who tells his children that Santa Claus is dead —Anon

23. Merciless as ambition —Joseph Joubert

24. Merciless as bailiffs —Erich Maria Remarque

25. Ordered her about like a convict —Nicholas Monsarrat

26. Ruthless as a Gestapo thug —Raymond Chandler

27. Ruthless as any sea —Beryl Markham

28. So mean he would steal a dead fly from a blind spider —Anon

29. Spiteful as a monkey —Frank Swinnerton

30. Spiteful as the devil —Walter Savage Landor

31. Treat us like mud off the bottom of the Hudson River —Rebecca West

(E)   Use men ruthlessly like pawns —Honoré de Balzac

33.   Walk all over [another person] like a carpet —Elyse Sommer

34.   Whipping and abuse are like laudanum; you have to double the dose as the sensibilities decline —Harriet Beecher Stowe

35.   Wickedness burns like fire —*The Holy Bible/Isaiah*
      The above has been modernized from "Wickedness burneth as the fire."

36.   Would cut me down like a piece of grass —Jimmy Sangster

CRYING

See Also: GROANS AND WHISPERS, SCREAMS

1.   Bawling like sick monkeys —Henry Miller

2.   Cried naggingly, half-heartedly, like the grinding of a non-starting engine that has drained its battery —John Updike

3.   Cries out like an Arab, high wails like a dog or human in terrible pain. It rises and falls like sirens going by —Robert Campbell

4.   Cry, hopelessly and passively, like a child in a dentist's waiting room — William Faulkner

5.   Cry like a rain-water spout in a shower —Charles Dickens

6.   Crying . . . muffled, like faraway nighttime waves —Z. Vance Wilson

7.   Crying out like an abandoned infant —T. Coraghessan Boyle

8.   (Gave a) cry like a startled sea gull —Oscar Wilde

9.   Her eyes [when she wept] were like syphon bottles under pressure — Erich Maria Remarque

10. Her sob broke like a bubble on a pink geranium —John Malcolm Brinnin
      See Also: DISINTEGRATION

11. Kept on crying . . . like persistent rain —Elizabeth Spencer

12. Like a waterpot I weep —*A Broken-Hearted Gardener,* anonymous nineteenth century verse

13. A sad crying, like the birds going south for the winter to come —Ray Bradbury

14. The shrill cry of the new-born . . . like the sound of the blade of a skate on ice —Angela Carter

15. Sobbed . . . like an abandoned child —Maurice Hewlett

16. A sob broke the surface like a bubble of air from the bottom of a pond —Sue Grafton

17. Sobs . . . died off softly, like the intermittent drops that end a day of rain —Edith Wharton

18. Sobs laboring like stones from her heaving breast —James Crumley

19. Sobs rippled like convulsions through her slim body —James Crumley
20. Thin cry [of a bluebird] like a needle piercing the ear —Theodore Roethke
21. Wailed like an uneasy animal in pain —Kenneth Grahame
22. Weeping like a calf —Francois Maspero
23. Weeping raw as an open sausage —A. D. Winans
24. Wept like a fountain —Erich Maria Remarque
25. Wept like a gutter on a rainy day —Guy de Maupassant
26. Wept like a woman deceived and forsaken by a lover —George Garrett
27. Whimpers like a hurt dog —Robin McCorquodale
28. Whine, as unctuous as old bacon grease —James Crumley
29. (The twangy voice was beginning to) whine like a loosening guitar string —François Camoin

CUNNING
See: CLEVERNESS

CURIOSITY
1. Aloof curiosity like that of sixth-formers watching a sword-swallower —Frank Swinnerton
    See Also: REMOTENESS
2. Curious as a monkey —Anon
3. Curious as a two-year old —Anon
4. Curiosity . . . like thirst —Alice McDermott
5. Inquisitive as a goat —Erich Maria Remarque
6. Inquisitive as an X-ray —Anon
7. Inquisitive as a reporter smelling a scoop —Elyse Sommer
8. Pick and pry like a doctor or archeologist —Sylvia Plath
9. Poking his nose everywhere like a dog smelling out a trail —American colloquialism
10. Suppressed her curiosity as if squashing a cockroach —Marge Piercy

CURSES
See Also: WORD(S)
1. The captain broke loose [with oaths] upon the dead man like a thunderclap —Jack London
2. Cried out a Foreign Legion of four-letter words like little prayers — George Garrett
3. Cursed like a sailor's parrot —Katherine Anne Porter

4. Cursed like highwaymen —Stephen Crane

5. Curse like a drunken tinker —George Garrett

6. Curses are like young chickens, they always come home to roost — Robert Southey

7. Curses, like processions; they return to the place from which they have come —Giovanni Ruffini
   Probably taken from old Italian proverb.

8. Curses so dark they sounded like they were being fired all the way from a ghetto of hell —Ken Kesey

9. Cursing and crying like some sort of fitting had busted in her mind and this whole stream of words gushed out —Hilary Masters

10. Cursing like a jay —T. Coraghessan Boyle

11. Erupted like a volcano of profanity —Sholom Aleichem

12. Felt them [curse words] at the back of his tongue like dangerous little bombs —Thomas Williams

13. Made curses fly up like a covey of quail —George Garrett

14. Swear like men who were being branded —Stephen Crane

15. Swore like a trooper —D. M. Moir

16. To hear R curse was like hearing the Almighty tear through his own heavens and blow up the stars left and rightly —Marianne Hauser

CUSTOM
See: HABIT

DAMPNESS
See: DISCOMFORT

DANCING
See Also: AGILITY, INSULTS, WORDS OF PRAISE

1. As light on your feet as a fairy —Rita Mae Brown
   See Also: LIGHTNESS

2. As limber as a couple of Yale pass-keys (addressed to a dancer) —O. Henry

3. Danced like a faun —O. Henry
   O. Henry was well known for perverting and extending existing sayings. This one can be traced to Robert Lowell's "Dancing like naked fauns too glad for shame."

4. Danced like a wave —Dame Edith Sitwell

5. Danced like a wet dream —Martin Amis

6. Danced like sandflies —Margaret Atwood

7. Danced like something dark and slithery from the Argentine —P. G. Wodehouse

8. (People) danced, moving their bodies like thick rope —Susan Richards Shreve

9. Dancers swaying like wet washing in a high wind —Lawrence Durrell

10. Dances like a Mack truck —Cornell Woolrich

11. Dances like an angel —Joseph Addison

12. (Sometimes I think that) dancing, like youth, is wasted on the young — Max Lerner

13. Dancing with her must be a good deal like moving the piano or something —Ring Lardner

14. (Helga Danzing danced just the way she looked: big, clumsy, almost impossible to lead,) dancing with her was like pushing a weight uphill —Abraham Rothberg

15. (You've got) a foot movement like a baby hippopotamus trying to side-step a jab from a humming-bird . . . and your knees are about as limber as a couple of Yale pass-keys —O. Henry

16. Pirouetting like a Baryshnikov —T. Coraghessan Boyle

17. Sailed like a coquettish yacht convoyed by a stately cruiser —O. Henry

18. You dance like there's a stone in your shoe —John Updike

DANGER

1. (His presence was) a foreboding, or dismal signal, like drawn blinds — Elizabeth Taylor

2. Dangerous as a gift from an enemy —Anon
   A twist on the Danish proverb "Gifts from enemies are dangerous."

3. Dangerous as cocaine —Pietro Mascagni
   The danger being described is modern music.

4. (I feel so many) dangers gathering round, like shadows —Davis Grubb

5. Feel as though I'm dancing on a volcano —Rita Mae Brown

6. Felt as if they were about to dive onto a postage stamp from the top of the Eiffel Tower —Fred Taylor

7. (One's life) hangs perilously in danger, like ripe fruit on a thin branch —Stephen Longstreet

8. Hazardous as sand traps for golfers —Anon

9. It [the need to risk] was like statistics or gambling; you had to compute probabilities —Mary McCarthy

In her novel, *A Charmed Life,* McCarthy expands on her simile with this sentence: "And there was always the unforeseen, the little thing you overlooked that would catch you up in the end."

10. The menace (of insanity) is like a warder, restricting my freedom of mind —Richard Maynard

11. (His) menaces . . . idle as the wind —W. S. Gilbert

12. Menacing as a fury —Natascha Wodin

13. Ominous and dark as the hour before a storm —Gerald Kersh

14. Ominous, like waves in a gathering mid-Atlantic storm —Anon

15. Rode precariously, like high-wire artists —Ross Macdonald

16. Safe as a cow in a stockyard —Anon

17. Safe as a mouse in cheese —John Ray's *Proverbs*

18. The safe earth . . . grew narrow as a grave —Phyllis Bottome

19. There was a feeling like a concussion in the air —Eudora Welty

20. This faint shadow [of danger] lay upon his life . . . as discreetly as the shadow of cancer lies among cells —Thomas McGuane

21. Trying to maintain good relations with a Communist is like wooing a crocodile —Winston Churchill

DARING
See: COURAGE

DARKNESS

1. Dark and cool as a cave—David Huddle

2. Dark and heavy like a surface stained with ink —John Ashbery

3. (It was) dark as a closet —Niven Busch

4. Dark as a dungeon —Anon
   The simile is the title of a ballad from the American South.

5. Dark as anger —Sylvia Plath

6. Dark as a pocket —American colloquialism, attributed to Vermont

7. (All was) dark as a stack of black cats —J. S. Rioss

8. Dark as a thundercloud —Steven Vincent Benét

9. Dark as a troll —W. D. Snodgrass

10. Dark as a wolf's mouth —Miguel de Cervantes
    "Dark as" and "Black as" have been used interchangeably since the simile's appearance in *Don Quixote.*

11. Dark as a womb —T. Coraghessan Boyle

12. Dark as blackberries —Marge Piercy

13. (The room was) dark as dreamless sleep —Harry Prince
14. (Eyelashes . . .) dark as night —Lord Byron
15. Dark as sin —Mark Twain
16. Dark as the devil's mouth —Walter Scott
17. Dark as the inside of a coffin —Gavin Lyall
18. Dark as the inside of a magician's hat —Robert Campbell
19. Dark as the inside of a cow —Mark Twain
20. Dark as the river bottom —Paige Mitchell
21. Dark like wet coffee grounds —Ella Leffland
22. The darkness ahead . . . looked like Alaska —Richard North
23. Darkness as deep and cold as Siberian midnight —Gerald Kersh
24. Darkness [in a rainstorm] came closer . . . like a sodden velvet curtain —Frank Swinnerton
25. Darkness falls like a wet sponge —John Ashbery
    This is the opening line of an Ashbery poem entitled *The Picture of Little J.A. in a Prospect of Flowers.*
26. Darkness fell like a swift blow —James Crumley
27. Darkness fills her like a carbohydrate —Daniela Gioseffi
28. The darkness flew in like an unwelcome bird —Norman Garbo
29. Darkness had begun to come in like water —Alice McDermott
30. Darkness hanging over them like a blotter —T. Coraghessan Boyle
31. Darkness like a black lake —Erich Maria Remarque
32. Darkness . . . like a warm liquid poured from the throat of an enormous bird —John Hawkes
33. Darkness settling down round them like a soft bird —Rose Tremain
34. Darkness should be a private matter, like thought, like emotion — William Dieter
35. Darkness so total it seemed . . . like deep water —William Boyd
36. The darkness was like a rising tide that covered the gardens and the houses, erasing everything as a still sea erased footprints on a beach — John P. Marquand
37. Darkness was sinking down over the region like a veil —Thomas Mann
38. The darkness was thin, like some sleazy dress that has been worn and worn for many winters and always lets the cold through to the bones — Eudora Welty
39. Dim as a cave of the sea —Richard Wilbur
40. Dim as a cellar in midafternoon —Joyce Cary
41. Dim as an ill-lit railroad coach —Natascha Wodin

42. (My sun has set, I) dwell in darkness as a dead man out of sight — Christina Rossetti

43. Light . . . drained out of the windows like a sink —William H. Gass

44. So dark and murky it [a movie, *The Fugitive Kind,*] looked like everyone was drowning in chocolate syrup —Tennessee Williams, quoted in interview with Rex Reed

DAY

See Also: NIGHT, SLOWNESS, TIME

1. The afternoon droops like a hot candle —Malcolm Cowley

2. The afternoon sways like an elephant —Babette Deutsch
This begins a poem entitled *July Day.*

3. The beauty of the morning called to her like a signal bell —R. V. Cassill

4. Dawn came like a blanket of flowers —T. Coraghessan Boyle

5. The dawn came up like a Have-a-Nice-Day emblem —Tom Robbins

6. A day as fresh as spring itself —Wallace Stegner

7. (The next) day dawned like a yawning hole —Robert Barnard

8. The day drooped like a flag —Katherine Mansfield

9. The day goes by like a shadow over the heart (with sorrow where all was delight) —Stephen Foster
From Stephen Foster's famous "My Old Kentucky Home" with 'over' substituted from 'o'er' as in the original.

10. The day is flat and intense, like a photograph of itself —Marge Piercy

11. The day [Sunday] is like wide water, without sound —Wallace Stevens

12. Day like a bated breath —Sharon Sheehe Stark

13. A day like an endless empty sea —Delmore Schwartz

14. Days and nights were shuffling like lame and overweight cattle —Don Robertson

15. Days are scrolls: write on them what you want to be remembered — Bahya

16. Days . . . arrive like crows in a field of stubble corn —Robert Hass

17. The days dripped away like honey off a spoon —Wallace Stegner

18. Days . . . followed one another in an undistinguished series, growing and then fading like the leaves on a tree —Stefan Zweig

19. The days go by, like caterpillars do —Johnny Mercer, opening stanza from 1947 song, "Lazy Mood"

20. The days go by like film, like a long written scroll —Maxwell Anderson

21. Days . . . like a lengthening shadow —*The Holy Bible/Psalms*

22. The days, like the leaves, seemed to fly from the trees, as if this year was intent on its own destruction —Susan Fromberg Schaeffer

23. The day smelled like clear water —Joan Chase

24. The days pass by like a wayward tune —W. B. Yeats

25. Days pass like papers from a press —Wallace Stevens

26. The days slipped by . . . like apple parings under a knife —Stephen Vincent Benét

27. The days walking along higher and higher, like the way teachers line you up to have pictures taken —Lee Smith

28. The days were truly endless and seemed like a single black night — Barbara Reid

29. The day was dry, rather misty; like a day pictured in a Japanese print —Frank Swinnerton

30. The day was still, like a very glazed photograph —M. J. Farrell

31. Feel the pull of the long day, like a road he dragged behind him — Sharon Sheehe Stark

32. A fine morning makes you want to bust open like a pea pod —Joe Coomer

33. The gray winter morning descends like the huge lead-coated balloon — Jerry Bumpus

34. The middle of the day, like the middle of certain fruits, is good for nothing —Walter Savage Landor

35. Morning came like a stone breaking —Madison Smartt Bell

36. The morning crept out of a dark cloud like an unbidden guest uncertain of his welcome —W. Somerset Maugham

37. Morning . . . gray like a mouse —Jessamyn West

38. Morning hours of inactivity . . . like a beautiful sculpture-lined bridge across which I stroll from night into day, from dream into reality — Milan Kundera

39. (Night had died, and the) morning lay like a corpse. Like sadness, going from one end of the world to another, without a sound —Aharon Megged

40. My days are like a lengthening shadow —*The Holy Bible/Psalms*

41. One of those days that come as a surprise in the middle of winter, like a gift sent on no anniversary, so that the pleasure takes us unaware — Jean Stafford

42. Our days run as fast away as does the sun —Robert Herrick

43. Over the garden, day still hung like a pink flag —Elizabeth Bowen

44. The workday is finished, dead as the calendar page that bore its number —Beryl Markham

DEATH

See Also: ADVANCING; BEGINNINGS/ENDINGS; DEATH, DEFINED;
DEATH, FINALITY OF; ENTRANCES/EXITS; SUDDENNESS; TIMELINESS

1. As death comes on we are like trees growing in the sandy bank of a widening river —Bhartrihari

2. The body of Benjamin Franklin, Printer, like the cover of an old book, its contents torn out, and stripped of its lettering and gilding, lies here, food for worms —Benjamin Franklin
   Franklin's epitaph for himself is a fine example of appropriately suiting the comparison to what's being compared.

3. (Kill him) dead as a beef —William Faulkner

4. [Sexual feelings] dead as a burned-out cinder —Ellen Glasgow

5. Death arrives . . . sudden as a pasteboard box crushed by a foot —Marge Piercy

6. Death falling like snow on any head it chooses —Philip Levine

7. Death fell round me like a rain of steel —Herbert Read
   A simile from one of Read's many war poems, *Meditation of the Waking English Officer.*

8. Death has many times invited me: it was like the salt invisible in the waves —Pablo Neruda

9. Death lies on her, like an untimely frost —William Shakespeare

10. Death, like roulette, turning our wish to its will —George Barker

11. Death lurking up the road like a feral dog abroad in the swirling snow —Marge Piercy

12. Death, you can never tell where else it will crop up —John Hale

13. Die alone like a dog in a ditch —Aldous Huxley
    See Also: ABANDONMENT, ALONENESS

14. Died in beauty, like a rose blown from its parent stem —C.D. Sillery

15. Die like candles in a draft —Sharon Sheehe Stark
    In the short story, *The Johnstown Polka,* the simile has a literal frame of reference; specifically, a room in an old age home which is overheated because to open the windows would kill the people in it.

16. Died like flies in a sugar bowl —Rita Mae Brown

17. (I won't) drown like a rat in a trap —George Bernard Shaw

18. Like a swift-fleeting meteor, a fast flaying cloud, a flash of lightning, a break of the wave, man passes from life to his rest in the grave —William Knox

19. Dying is as natural as living —Thomas Fuller

20. Dying like flies —Anon

An even more frequently used variation is to "Drop like flies."

21. (I will) encounter darkness as a bride —William Shakespeare

22. (You couldn't) expect death to come rushing in like a skivvy because you'd rung the bell —Paul Barker

23. Feel my death rushing towards me like an express train —John Updike

24. Felt death near, like a garment she had left hanging in her closet and could not see or find, though she knew it was there —Abraham Rothberg

25. Go to their graves like flowers or creeping worms —Percy Bysshe Shelley

26. The intimations of mortality appear so gradually as to be imperceptible, like the first graying in of twilight —Richard Selzer

27. Like a clock worn out with eating time, the wheels of weary life at last stood still —John Dryden

28. Like a led victim, to my death I'll go —John Dryden

29. Like sheep they are laid in the grave —*The Holy Bible/Psalms*

30. (I now) look at death, the way we look at a house we plan to move into —William Bronk

31. Men fear death, as children fear to go in the dark; and as that natural fear in children is increased with tales, so is the other —Francis Bacon

32. Our fear of death is like our fear that summer will be short, but when we have had our swing of pleasure, our fill of fruit, and our swelter of heat, we say we have had our day —Ralph Waldo Emerson

33. Passed away, as a dry leaf passes into leaf mold —John Updike

34. [In old age] the shadow of death . . . like a sword of Damocles, may descend at any moment —Samuel Butler

35. She passed away like morning dew —Hartley Coleridge

36. Talking over the fact of his approaching death as though it were a piece of property for agreeable disposition in the family —Elizabeth Spencer

37. There are no graves that grow so green as the graves of children — Oliver Wendell Holmes, Sr.
    From a letter of condolence to W. R. Sturtevant, September 17, 1878, in which the simile continues as follows: "Their memory comes back after a time more beautiful than that of those who leave us at any other age."
    See Also: CHILDREN

38. We are all kept and fed for death, like a herd of swine to be slain without reason —Palladas

39. We end our years like a sigh . . . for it is speedily gone, and we fly away —*The Holy Bible/Psalms*

40. Wherever you go, death dogs you like a shadow —Anon, probably dating back to before Christ.

DEATH, DEFINED

1. Death is a black camel, which kneels at the gates of all —Abd-el-Kader

2. Death is like a fisherman who catches fish in his net and leaves them for a while in the water; the fish is still swimming but the net is around him, and the fisherman will draw him up when he thinks fit —Ivan Turgenev

3. Death is like thunder in two particulars: we are alarmed at the sound of it and it is formidable only from that which preceded it —Charles Caleb Colton

4. Death is simply a shedding of the physical body, like the butterfly coming out of a cocoon —Elisabeth Kuebler-Ross

5. Death, like an overflowing stream, sweeps us away —Abraham Lincoln

6. Death, like birth, is a secret of nature —Marcus Aurelius

7. Death, like life, is an affair of being more frightened than hurt — Samuel Butler

8. Dying is an art, like everything else —Sylvia Plath

9. Dying is something ghastly, as being born is something ridiculous — George Santayana

10. If a person has reached the "age of strength" [eighty years old] a sudden death is like dying from a kiss —*Babylonian Talmud*

11. Like the dew on the mountain, like the foam on the river, like the bubble on the fountain, you are gone, and for ever —Sir Walter Scott
     The above, taken from Scott's famous *The Lady of the Lake,* substitutes "You are gone" for the old English "Thou art gone."

12. The stroke of death is as a lover's pinch, which hurts, and is desired — William Shakespeare
     'Desired' has been modernized from 'desir'd.'

13. (I) think of death as a sort of deleterious fermentation, like that which goes on in a bottle of Chateau Margaux when it becomes corked —H. L. Mencken

DEATH, FINALITY OF

1. As the cloud is consumed and vanished away: so he that goes down to the grave comes up no more —*The Holy Bible/Job*
    'Goes' is a modernization of the biblical 'goeth.'

2. Dead and as far away as yesterday —W. S. Gilbert

3. Dead as a dead mackerel —C. W. Grafton

4. Dead as a dodo bird —American colloquialism, attributed to New England

5. Dead as a doornail —English phrase
Many people attribute this much used simile to Shakespeare who used it in *Henry VI* and *Henry IV.* In the first play the simile appears as follows: "If I do not leave you all as dead as a doornail, I pray God I may never eat grass more." In the second, Falstaff asks, "What, is the old king dead?" and Pistol answers, "As a nail in a door."

6. Dead as a fried oyster —S.J. Perelman
This is one of four different twists on the familiar "Dead as a doornail" from Perelman's spoof on cliches, *Somewhere a Roscoe.* The others used are "Dead as an iced catfish," "Dead as a stuffed mongoose," and "Dead as vaudeville."

7. Dead as a hammer —Scotch saying

8. Dead as a herring —Samuel Butler

9. Dead as a turd —Stephen King

10. Deader than a roast turkey on Thanksgiving —Joan Hess

11. Dead as last year's leaves —W. S. Gilbert

DEBT
See: CREDIT

DECEPTION
See: TRUENESS/FALSENESS

DECISIONS
See: CHOICES

DECORATIVENESS
See: ATTRACTIVENESS

DECREASE

1. Contract, like the pupil of an eye that confronts the sun —John Hall Wheelock

2. (My avarice) cooled like lust in the chill of the grave —Ralph Waldo Emerson

3. Decrease like a cigar: the harder you puff on it, the shorter it gets —Anon
The cigar has also been likened to an actor; e. g., "An actor decreases like a cigar; the more you puff him, the smaller he gets."
See Also: STAGE AND SCREEN

4. Decrease like a lemon drop; the more you lick it, the less it becomes —
    Anon

5. Decrease like hair after each decade —Mike Sommer

6. Devour [information] like baseball addicts devour box scores —David
    E. Sanger, *New York Times,* December 14, 1985

7. Diminished and flat, as after radical surgery —Sylvia Plath

8. (All my efforts) diminish like froth —Erich Maria Remarque

9. Drain (as a day's happenings) like water running out of a tub —Andre
    Dubus

10. Energy . . . draining out like sand —May Sarton

11. Gobble up cash the way electronic equipment gobbles up batteries —
    Anon

12. Goes down like an ebbing tide —Henry James
    James let the hero of his play, *Guy Domville,* use the ebbing
    tide comparison to explain the nature of his ignorance.

13. Go through [as bottle of pills] like a bull breaks a fence —Anon

14. Pared like a carrot —John Russell
    This is often used to mean humiliation.

15. (The conversation was already) petering out like a smoldering cigarette
    end —Stefan Zweig

16. Receding like a threatened headache which hasn't materialized —
    William McIlvanney

17. Shrinking as violets do in summer —Thomas Moore
    The original ended with "As violets do in summer's rays."

18. Shrinking like aches —Charles Wright

19. Shrivel up like the tendrils of a creeper when thrown on a bonfire —
    Francis King

20. Shrunken as a beggar's heart —Stephen Vincent Benét

21. Use up as fast as a ten dollar bill in the supermarket —Anon

22. Use up, like a cake of soap —Elyse Sommer

23. Wore off [feeling of self-confidence] quicker than champagne —Edith
    Wharton

DEDICATION
See: ATTENTION

DEEDS
See: ACTIONS

DEJECTION
See Also: EMOTIONS, GLOOM

1.   (There was about him) an air of defeat . . . as though all the rules he'd learned in life were, one by one, being reversed —Margaret Millar

2.   Dampened my mood (as automatically) as would the news of an earthquake in Cincinnati or the outbreak of the Third World War —T. Coraghessan Boyle

3.   Dejection seemed to transfix him, to reach down out of the sky and crash like a spike through his small rigid body —Niven Busch

4.   Dejection settled over her like a cloud —Louis Bromfield

5.   Depression crept like a fog into her mind —Ellen Glasgow

6.   Depression . . . is like a light turned into a room—only a light of blackness —Rudyard Kipling

7.   Depressions . . . like thick cloud covers: not a ray of light gets through —Larry McMurtry

8.   Despair howled round his inside like a wind —Elizabeth Bowen

9.   Despair is like forward children, who, when you take away one of their playthings, throw the rest into the fire for madness —Pierre Charron

10. Despair, like that of a man carrying through choice a bomb which, at a certain hour each day, may or may not explode —William Faulkner

11. Despair passed over him like cold winds and hot winds coming from places he had never visited —Margaret Millar

12. Despondency . . . lurking like a ghoul —Richard Maynard

13. Emptied, like a collapsed balloon, all the life gone out of him —Ben Ames Williams

14. Feeling of desperation . . . as if caught by a chain that was slowly winding up —Victor Hugo

15. Feel like a picnicker who has forgotten his lunch —Frank O'Hara

16. (I'm not feeling very good right now. I) feel like I've been sucking on a lot of raw eggs —Dexter Manley, of the Washington Redskins after his team lost important game, quoted in the *New York Times,* December 8, 1986

17. Feels his heart sink as if into a frozen lake —John Rechy

18. Felt depression settle on his head like a sick crow —Bernard Malamud

19. (He often) felt [suicidal] like a deep sea diver whose hose got cut on an unexpected rock —Diane Wakoski

20. Felt like Willie Loman at the end of the road —T. Coraghessan Boyle

21. Felt the future narrowing before me like a tunnel —Margaret Drabble

22. Forlorn . . . like Autumn waiting for the snow —John Greenleaf Whittier

23. (Her) heart dropped like a purse of coins falling through a ripped pocket —Joyce Reiser Kornblatt

24. His despair confronted me like a black beast —Natascha Wodin

25. His haughty self was like a robber baron fallen into the hands of rebellious slaves, stooped under a filthy load —Sinclair Lewis

26. His heart has withered in him and he has been left with the five senses, like pieces of broken wineglass —Lawrence Durrell

27. Hope and confidence . . . shattered like the pillars of Gaza —W. Somerset Maugham

28. Hope removed like a tree —*The Holy Bible/Job*

29. It was like having a part of me amputated —W. P. Kinsella
     In the novel, *Shoeless Joe,* the comparison is a character's response to being suspended from his baseball team.

30. (I was) like the old lion with a thorn in his paw, surrounded by wolves and jackals and facing his snaggle-toothed death in a political jungle — T. Coraghessan Boyle

31. Listless and wretched like a condemned man —Erich Maria Remarque

32. Live under dust covers like furniture —Michael Frayn
     Frayn's simile vividly portrays the despair of the characters in his adaptation of an untitled Checkhov play, first produced under the title *Wild Honey* in 1984.

33. Looked suddenly disconsolate, like a scarecrow with no crows to scare —Graham Masterton

34. Looking forlorn, stricken, like a little brother who, tagging along, is being deserted by the big fellows —Edna Ferber

35. Crawl back [after unanticipated defeat at golf] looking like a toad under a harrow —P. G. Wodehouse

36. Look like a dog that has lost its tail —John Ray's *Proverbs*

37. Look like the picture of ill luck —John Ray's *Proverbs*

38. Miserable, like dead men in a dream —George MacDonald

39. Miserable, lonesome as a forgotten child —F. Scott Fitzgerald

40. Misery is manifold . . . as the rainbow; its hues are as various as the hues of that arch —Edgar Allen Poe

41. Misery rose from him like a stench —Marge Piercy

42. A mood as gypsy-dark as his eyes —Robert Culff

43. My life is just an empty road and people walk on me —Tony Ardizzone

44. Must live hideously and miserably the rest of his days, like a man doomed to live forever in a state of retching and abominable nausea of heart, brain, bowels, flesh and spirit —Thomas Wolfe

45. Put away his hopes as if they were old love letters —Anon
     See Also: HOPE

46.   Relapsed into discouragement, like a votary who has watched too long for a sign from the altar —Edith Wharton

47.   Saw himself like a sparrow on the bank-top; sitting on the wherewithal for a thousand thousand meals and dropping dead from hunger the first day of winter —Christina Stead

48.   Seemed like a whipped dog on a leash —Ignazio Silone

49.   The sense of desolation and of fear became bitterer than death —William Cullen Bryant
      See Also: FEAR

50.   (I have been) so utterly and suicidally morbid that my letters would have read like an excerpt from the *Undertakers' Gazette* —Dylan Thomas
      The simile is excerpted from a November, 1933, letter to Pamela Hansford Johnson apologizing for the delay in replying to her letter.

51.   (Foster's) stomach felt like a load of wet clothes at the bottom of the dryer —Phyllis Naylor

52.   There's a state of peace following despair . . . like the aftermath of an accident —C. J. Koch

53.   Waves of black depression engulf one from time to time . . . like a rising tide —Gustave Flaubert

DELAY
See: LINGERING

DELIBERATENESS
See: PURPOSEFULNESS

DELIGHT
See: JOY

DEMOCRACY
See: FREEDOM, GOVERNMENT

DENIAL
See: BEHAVIOR

DENSITY
See: ABUNDANCE, THICKNESS

DEPARTURE
See: EXITS

DEPENDABILITY
See: RELIABILITY/UNRELIABILITY

DEPLETION
See: DECREASE

DEPRESSION
See: DEJECTION, GLOOM

DESERTION
See: ABANDONMENT

DESIRABILITY
See Also: PLEASURE

1. Beckoning . . . like summer welcoming the swallows —Ariel Dorfman

2. Cherish like a secret —D. H. Lawrence

3. Dear as a pardon —Diane Ackerman

4. Dear as a remembered kiss after death —Alfred, Lord Tennyson

5. Dear as the mother to the son —Alfred, Lord Tennyson

6. (She was . . .) desirable . . . like a dessert. Afterward you discarded the empty plate and forgot it —Derek Lambert

7. (Enigmatic remarks, as elusive and as) eagerly gobbled up as currants in a bun —Robert Culff
   See Also: ENTHUSIASM

8. Hates (publicity) the way Polly hates crackers —Arthur Baer

9. (Six years ago . . . the idea of spending an afternoon at Shea Stadium) held about as much appeal as your basic monster traffic jam —Malcom Moran, *New York Times,* October 11, 1986

10. Like a box of chocolates . . . seductive and satisfying —*Publishers Weekly* comment on a short novel
    The simile expanded on the box of chocolates appeal with "Readers will want to devour it in one sitting."

11. Welcome as a corpse is to a coroner —Mark Twain

12. Welcome as a dandelion in the bosom of winter —Josh Billings

13. Welcome as a free tickets to a hit show —Anon

14. Welcome as a letter from home —Anon

15. Welcome as a visit from an old friend —Anon

16. Welcome as happy tiding after fears —Thomas Otway

17. Welcome as sunshine after rain —Anon

A possible inspiration for this: "Love comforteth like sunshine after rain" from Shakespeare's *Venus and Adonis.*

18. Welcome as the best dish in the kitchen —H. G. Bohn's *Handbook of Proverbs*

19. Welcome as the flowers in May —John Ray's *Proverbs*

20. Welcomed it as a Bedouin in the desert welcomes the flies that are the herald of an oasis —Richard Selzer

DESIRE

See Also: SEX

1. A brief surge of sexual desire that crested and passed like a wave breaking —Paige Mitchell

2. Craves love like oxygen —Marge Piercy

3. Craving [for a man] . . . like a cigarette smoker's who knows his desire is unhealthy, knows that the next puff may set off a chain reaction of catastrophe, but nevertheless cannot by such logic tame the impulse —Paul Reidinger

4. Desire had run its course like a long and serious illness —Harvey Swados

5. Desire . . . like the hunger for a definite but hard-to-come-by food — Mary Gordon

6. Desire overtook us like a hot, breaking wave —A. E. Maxwell

7. Desires are either natural and necessary, like eating and drinking; or natural and not necessary, like intercourse with females; or neither natural or necessary —Michel de Montaigne

8. Desires..hurried like the clouds —Elizabeth Bowen

9. Desire . . . swept over her like a flame —Robin McCorquodale

10. Dying for . . . like God for a repentant sinner —Bertold Brecht

11. (She is) gasping after love like a carp after water on a kitchen table — Gustave Flaubert

12. Her needs stick out all over, like a porcupine's needles —Emily Listfield

13. His need for her was crippling . . . like a cruel blow at the back of his knees —John Cheever

14. How passionate the mating instinct is, like a giant hippo chasing his mate through the underbrush and never stopping till he finally mounts her in the muddy waters of the mighty Amazon —Daniel Asa Rose

15. Longing . . . afflicted her like a toothache —Harold Acton

16. Miss like sin —Lael Tucker Wertenbaker
    The simile in full context from the novel, *Unbidden Guests:* "I woke up missing Alex like sin."

17. Miss you like breath —Janet Flanner

18. More giddy in my desires than a monkey —William Shakespeare
19. My desire for her is so wild I feel as if I'm all liquid —W. P. Kinsella
20. A passion finer than lust, as if everything living is moist with her — Daniela Gioseffi
21. Worldly desires are like columns of sunshine radiating through a dusty window, nothing tangible, nothing there —Bratzlav Naham
22. Yearning radiating from his face like heat from an electric heater — Larry McMurtry

DESOLATION
See: ABANDONMENT

DESTITUTION
See: POVERTY

DESTRUCTION/DESTRUCTIVENESS
See Also: DISINTEGRATION

1. As killing as the canker to the rose —John Milton
2. (Bones) breaking like hearts —Bin Ramke
3. Break [a person's spirit] like a biscuit —Beaumont and Fletcher
4. Break like a bursting heart —Percy Bysshe Shelley
5. Break like dead leaves —Richard Howard
6. Cracked like parchment —Sin Ai
7. Cracked like the ice in a frozen daiquiri —Anon
8. (Her projects of happiness . . .) crackled in the wind like dead boughs —Gustave Flaubert
9. Crack like walnuts —Rita Mae Brown
10. Crack like wishbones —Diane Ackerman
11. Cracks . . . like a glass in which the contents turned to ice, and shiver it —Herman Melville
12. [Fender and hood of a car] crumpled like tinfoil —T. Coraghessan Boyle
13. Crushed like an empty beer can —Anon
14. Crushed . . . like rats in a slate fall —Davis Grubb
    In Grubb's novel, *The Barefoot Man,* the simile refers to miners who lost their lives.
15. Crushed like rotten apples —William Shakespeare
16. Crushed me like a grape —Carla Lane, British television sitcom, "Solo," broadcast, May 19, 1987
17. (And I'll be) cut up like a pie —Irish ballad

18. Destructive as moths in a woolens closet —Anon

19. [Time's malevolent effect on body] dragging him down like a bursting sack —Gerald Kersh

20. (The Communists are) eating us away like an old fruit —Janet Flanner

21. (Men) fade like leaves —Aristophanes

22. Flattened her pitiful attempt like a locomotive running on a single track full steam ahead —Cornell Woolrich

23. (Creditors ready to) gnaw him to bits . . . like maggots at work on a carcass —George Garrett

24. The grass (at Shea Stadium) looked as if it had been attacked by animals that had not grazed for ages —Alex Yannis, *New York Times,* September 18, 1986
    Yannis, in reporting on the Mets' winning the National League
    Eastern Division title, used the simile to describe the fans'
    destruction of the playing field.

25. If I do [give up] . . . I'll be like a bullfighter gone horn-shy —Loren D. Estleman

26. Like a divorce . . . goes ripping through our lives —Book jacket copy describing effect of Sharon Sheehe Stark's novel, *A Wrestling Season.*

27. Marked for annihilation like an orange scored for peeling —Yehuda Amichai

28. My heroes [Chicago Cubs] had wilted like slugs —George F. Will

29. Pollutes . . . like ratbite —William Alfred

30. Self-destructing like a third-rate situation comedy —Warren T. Brookes, on Republican party, *Wall Street Journal,* July 15, 1986

31. Shattered like a walnut shell —Charles Dickens
    In Dickens' *A Tale of Two Cities,* the comparison refers to a
    broken wine cask.

32. Shatter them like so much glass —Robert Louis Stevenson

33. Shrivel up like some old straw broom —Joyce Carol Oates

34. Snap like dry chicken bones —David Michael

35. [Taut nerves] snap like guy wires in a tornado —Nardi Reeder Campion, *New York Times*/Op-Ed, January, 5, 1987

36. (Then the illusion) snapped like a nest of threads —F. Scott Fitzgerald

37. Snapped off [due to frailness] like celery —Lawrence Durrell

38. (Who can accept that spirit can be) snuffed as finally as a flame — Barbara Lazear Ascher, *New York Times*/Hers, October 30, 1986

39. They [free-spending wife and daughter] ate holes in me like Swiss cheese —Clifford Odets

40. Wear out their lives, like old clothes —John Cheever

41.   Your destruction comes as a whirlwind —*The Holy Bible /Proverbs*

DETACHMENT
See: REMOTENESS

DETERIORATION
See: DISINTEGRATION

DETERMINATION
See: PURPOSEFULNESS

DEVOTION
See: LOYALTY/DISLOYALTY

DEW
See: NATURE

DICTION
See: SPEECH PATTERNS

DICTIONARIES
See: BOOKS

DIETS
See: EATING AND DRINKING

DIFFERENCES

1.   Alike as the gap between Little League and Major League —Anon
2.   Alike as an oil portrait and a polaroid snapshot —Anon
3.   Alike as a cliche and a sonnet —Rod MacLeish, National Public Radio, December 29, 1986
     In his obituary on mystery writer John MacDonald, MacLeish used the simile to point out the difference between MacDonald's Travis McGee character with Raymond Chandler's Philip Marlowe.
4.   Alike as a mom and pop grocery store and a multi-national corporation —Anon
5.   Alike as an abacus and a computer —Anon
6.   Alike as an elephant and a giraffe —Anon
7.   Alike as grains of sand —Anon
8.   Alike as human faces —Anon
9.   Alike as six pebbles on the beach —Eudora Welty

10. Alike as the gap between doing a gig at a neighborhood wedding and being on prime time TV —Anon

11. Alike as an apple is to a lobster —John Ray's *Proverbs*
     A variation on the same theme, also from John Ray's *Proverbs* is "As alike as an apple is to an oyster." Other entries in this section merely hint at the endless twists possible.

12. As like this as a crab's like an apple —William Shakespeare
     Here we have the above simile turned around, with the apple the comparison.

13. (In this world it is rarely possible to settle matters with an "either, or," since there are) as many gradations of emotion and conduct as there are stages between a hooked nose and one that turns up —Johann Wolfgang von Goethe

14. Different as a moonbeam from lightning, as frost from fire —Emily Brontë

15. (You and I are as) different as chalk and cheese —John Ray's *Proverbs*

16. Opposite as yea and nay —Francis Quarles

17. (Two faces) different as hot and cold —Dannie Abse

18. Different as three men singing the same chorus from three men playing three tunes on the same piano —G. K. Chesterton

19. Different as yin from yang —Harry Prince

20. Everything has in fact another side to it, like the moon —G. K. Chesterton

21. Sharply defined as salt and pepper —Anon

22. The difference between vivacity and wit is the same as the difference between the lightning-bug and lightning —Josh Billings

23. Various as the fancies of men in pursuit of a wife —James Ralph

DIFFICULTY
     See Also: FUTILITY, IMPOSSIBILITY

1. As easy as buying a pair of solid leather shoes for ten dollars —Anon

2. As easy as combing your hair with a broom —Anon

3. As easy as doing one thing at a time and never putting off anything till tomorrow that could be done today —Baron Samuel von Puffendorf

4. As easy as drawing a picture in water —Anon

5. As easy as eating soup with a fork —Anon

6. As easy as finding a two-bedroom apartment on Manhattan's east side for $400 a month —Anon
    This is the sort of topical and location-specific comparison that is adapted to the user's own locale and economic conditions.

7. As easy as getting rid of cockroaches in a New York apartment —Anon

8. As easy as making an omelet without eggs —Anon
    A simile probably inspired by the proverb "One can't expect to make an omelet without breaking eggs."

9. As easy as passing a bull in a close —William McIlvanney

10. As easy as roller skating on a collapsing sidewalk —Anon

11. As easy as running with a stitch in your side —Anon

12. As easy as trying to paint the wind —Anon

13. As easy as shaving with an axe —Anon

14. As easy as struggling through a waist-high layer of glue —Anon

15. As easy as taking a hair out of milk —*Babylonian Talmud*

16. As easy to ignore as a Salvation Army drum —William McIlvanney

17. As easy to scare Jack Cady [character in novel] as to scare an oak tree —Speer Morgan

18. As easy as trying to load a thermometer with beads of quicksilver —Bill Pronzini

19. As easy as trying to nail a glob of mercury —Anon

20. As easy as trying to open an oyster without a knife —Anon

21. As easy as trying to participate in your own funeral —Anon

22. As easy as trying to read a book on the deck of a sinking ship —Anon

23. As easy as trying to unscramble an egg —Anon
    Another proverb that has become familiar is attributed to J. P. Morgan on the dissolution of the trusts in 1905: "You can't unscramble eggs."

24. As easy as wading in tar —Anon

25. As easy as walking on one leg —Anon

26. Chasing a dream, a dream no one else can see or understand, like running after a butterfly across an endless meadow, is extremely difficult —W. P. Kinsella

27. Controlling the bureaucracy is like nailing Jell-O to the wall —John F. Kennedy

28. Dealing with him is like dealing with a porcupine in heat —Anon
    The porcupine simile made by an anonymous White House reporter in 1986 referred to deputy chief Richard G. Darmon.

29. Demanding as a Dickens novel with a cast of hundreds —Ira Wood

30. Difficult as an elephant trying to pick up a pea —H. G. Wells

31. Difficult as climbing pinnacles of ice —Elinor Wylie

32. Difficult as driving a Daimler at top speed on a slick road —Barry Tuckwell, quoted in article by Barbara Jepson, *Wall Street Journal,* July 1, 1986

33. (Getting the truth in the *New York Post* has been as) difficult as finding a good hamburger in Albania —Paul Newman, *New York Post,* October 14, 1986
    The actor's simile referred to the paper's efforts to prove that he is only 5 foot 8 inches tall.

34. Difficult as getting a concession to put a merry-go-round on the front lawn of the White House —Kenneth L. Roberts
    As true and timely a simile today as when it originated in the early part of the twentieth century.

35. Difficult as making a silk purse out of a sow's ear —Anon
    This can be traced to the German proverb "You cannot make a silk purse of a sow's ear." A less well-known French version substitutes velvet for the sow's ear.

36. Difficult as making dreams come true —Anon

37. Difficult as putting a bandage on an eel —Anon

38. Difficult as to sell a ham to a kosher caterer —Elyse Sommer

39. Difficult as sighting a rifle in the dark with rain falling —Peter Greer, "Christian Science Monitor" radio program, December 31, 1985

40. Difficult as trying to draw blood from a turnip —French proverb

41. Difficult as trying to be old and young at the same time —German proverb
    Another proverb that has evolved into simile form, in this instance from "You cannot be old and young at the same time."

42. Difficult as trying to run and sit still at the same time —Scotch proverb

43. Difficult . . . like trying to play the piano with boxing gloves — William H. Hallhan

44. Difficult . . . like swimming upstream in Jell-O —Loren D. Estleman

45. Difficult . . . like trying to grab a hold of Jell-O in quicksand —Philip K. Meyer, Eberstadt Fleming executive quoted in *New York Times,* July 25, 1986, on estimating an oilfield company's earnings

46. Difficult . . . like walking a frisky, 220-pound dog —Henry D. Jacoby, on trying to manage crude oil prices in face of changing market conditions, *New York Times,* January 26, 1986

47. Difficult to absorb . . . like trying to take a sip of water from a fire hose —Anon comment, television news program
    The comment was a response to Uranus probe, January 22, 1987.

48. Difficult to get as trying to get a pearl out of a lockjawed oyster — Robert Vinez, quoted in *Wall Street Journal* article on consumer campaign to get Ford to put air bags into all cars, July 3, 1986

The difficulty in this instance involved getting the air bag out of Ford.

49. (Satiety is as) difficult to stomach as hunger —Stefan Zweig

50. Finding a decent, affordable apartment in New York is . . . like trying to recover a contact lens from a subway platform at rush hour — Michael de Courcy Hinds, *New York Times,* January 16, 1986

51. Getting information from him was like squeezing a third cup from a tea bag —Christopher Buckley

52. Hard as building a wall of sand —Marge Piercy

53. (It was) hard to do, but quick, like a painful inoculation —Judith Rascoe

54. Hard to lift as a dead elephant —Raymond Chandler

55. It [to get woman in story to admit feelings for lover] would be rather like breaking rocks —Laurie Colwin

56. Laborious as idleness —Louis IV

57. Life is not an easy thing to embrace, like trying to hug an elephant — Diane Wakoski
    See Also: LIFE

58. Lurching up those steep stairs was like climbing through a submarine —Scott Spencer

59. Not like making instant coffee —David Brierley
    In his novel, *Skorpion's Death,* Brierly uses the comparison to describe the difficulty of learning how to fly.

60. A process that could be likened to trying to drain a swimming pool with a soda straw —Thomas J. Knudson, on project to reduce flooding of lake in Utah, *New York Times,* April 11, 1987

61. To get a cent out of this woman is like crossing the Red Sea dry-shod — Sholom Aleichem

62. Trying to define yourself is like trying to bite your own teeth —Alan Watts

63. Trying to get information out of Joe was like trying to drag a cat by its tail over a rug —F. van Wyck Mason

64. Trying to jump-start a business venture over breakfast is like working hard at going to sleep or devoting a year to falling in love —Anon participant at a business networking breakfast, *New York Times*/Column One, Michael Winerif, February 17, 1987

65. Walking [while feeling dizzy] was like a journey up the down escalator —Madison Smart Bell

66. With effort, like rising out of deep water —Elizabeth Spencer

DIGNITY
    See: PRIDE

DILEMMAS
    See: PROBLEMS/SOLUTIONS

DIPLOMACY
    See: TACT

DIRECTNESS
    See: CANDOR, STRAIGHTNESS

DISAGREEMENT
    See: AGREEMENT/DISAGREEMENT, ARGUMENT

DISAPPEARANCE
    See Also: BEGINNINGS/ENDINGS, DISPERSAL, ELUSIVENESS

1. Blown away like clouds —Henry Wadsworth Longfellow
2. Blows away like a deck of cards in a hurricane —George Garrett
3. Bobbed away like a soap-bubble —Sylvia Plath
4. (The premonition had) boiled off like a puff of bad air —Herbert Lieberman
5. Borne away like a cork on a stream —Lawrence Durrell
6. (The old worlds) died away like dew —Dame Edith Sitwell
7. Disappeared as if into fairyland —Peter Najarian
8. Disappeared . . . effortlessly, like a star into a cloud —F. van Wyck Mason
9. Disappeared like a sigh —Tom Wolfe
10. [Food being served, vegetables] disappeared like leaves before locusts — Charlotte Brontë
11. Disappeared like raindrops which fall in the ocean —John T. Morse, about the loss of many of Oliver Wendell Holmes, Sr.'s similes and other witticisms
12. Disappeared [huntsmen and hounds into a bewitched forest] like soap bubbles —Anne Sexton
13. Disappeared . . . like sparks dropped into wet grass —James Crumley
14. Disappearing like the fastest fairy who ever lived —Brian Donleavy
    See Also: SPEED
15. Disappearing, like water poured out of a wide-necked bottle —Diane Wakoski
16. Disappear like a moon entering a cloud bank —Bernard Malamud

17. Disappear like quicksilver in the cracks —Booth Tarkington
18. Disappear like socks in the laundry —Elyse Sommer
19. Disappear like the dew on the mountain —Anon
20. Drift away into infinity, like a child's balloon at a circus —Robert Penn Warren
21. Everybody peeled away like an onion —Official of a New York company on reason for his firm's bankruptcy, *New York Times,* December 12, 1986
22. (The vision of her early loveliness) faded from reality like dew licked up by the sun —Elinor Wylie
23. Faded like a cloud which has outswept its rain —Percy Bysshe Shelley
24. Faded . . . like dew upon the sea —Oliver Wendell Holmes, Sr.
25. (The restlessness in him) faded like fog before sunshine —Pearl S. Buck
26. (Light would . . .) fade like a slow gray curtain dropping —Nelson Algren
27. Fades like the lustre of an evening cloud —William Wordsworth
28. [Awareness of children] fading like old ink —Margaret Atwood
29. (The season) fading like woodwind music —George Garrett
30. Fading like young joy —Dame Edith Sitwell
31. Fall away like forgiven sins —Miller Williams
32. (All your joys start) falling like sand through a sieve —Lorenz Hart
    Hart's lyric for "A Lady Must Live" from *America's Sweetheart* omitted the letter 'g' in 'falling.'
33. Fell away like a wall —Dudley Clendinen, *New York Times,* March 31, 1985, about a publisher's declining advertising revenues
34. (Childhood and youth, friendship and love's first glow, have) fled like sweet dreams —Percy Bysshe Shelley
35. (Any thought I had for such an enterprise) fled like thunder —Richard Ford
36. Flown like a thought —John Keats
37. Fluttered away like flakes of snow —Louis Bromfield
38. [Ceremonial occasions] glide swift into shadow, like sails on the seas — John Greenleaf Whittier
39. (He was) gone again, gone like some shadow the fire had made —Davis Grubb
40. Gone and out of sight like a thought —Richard Ford
41. Gone as a dream is gone from a dreamer wakened with a shout —Lord Dunsany
    'Wakened' has been modernized from 'waked.'
42. Gone . . . as if they had evaporated —Dorothy Canfield Fisher

43. (That moment is) gone forever, like lightning that flashed and died, like a snowflake upon the river, like a sunbeam upon the tide —Percy Bysshe Shelley

44. Gone from my gaze like a beautiful dream —George Linley

45. Gone like a flushed toilet —Max Apple

46. Gone like a morning dream, or like a pile of clouds —William Wordsworth

47. Gone like a quick wind —Ursula Le Guin

48. (Our world was) gone like a scrap in the wind —Beryl Markham

49. Gone like a wild bird, like a blowing flame —Euripides

50. [Smile of a loved one] gone like dreams that we forget —William Wordsworth

51. (And all the students) gone, like last week's snow —Delmore Schwartz

52. Gone like our change at the end of the week —Palmer Cox

53. (Words) gone like sparks burned up in darkness —Jayne Anne Phillips

54. [A funeral procession] gone . . . like tears in the eyes —Karl Shapiro

55. Gone, like tenants that quit without warning —Oliver Wendell Holmes, Sr.

56. Gone, like the life from a busted balloon —Palmer Cox

57. (I am) gone like the shadow when it declines —*The Holy Bible /Psalms*
    The biblical 'declineth' has been modernized.

58. Go out . . . just like a candle —Lewis Carroll

59. (The Contessina could no longer see him;) it was as though he had slipped from her vision, and the crack had closed above him forever —Elizabeth Bowen

60. (Maybe he wanted her to) lift up, blow away somewhere, like a kite —Margaret Atwood

61. Like a match struck on a stove . . . faded and was gone —James Agee

62. Like a passing thought she fled —Robert Burns
    Burns' line has found its way into daily language as "Vanish like a passing thought."

63. Like a shadow, glided out of view —William Wordsworth

64. Like swallows in autumn they fled, and left the house silent —John Hall Wheelock

65. Lost like stars beyond dark trees —Dante Gabriel Rossetti

66. (Her patience) melted like snow before a blow-torch —Julia O'Faolain

67. (Money) melting away like butter in the sun —Bertolt Brecht

68. Off and away like a frightened fish —Ogden Nash

69. Pass as if it had never existed, like a fart in a gale of wind —Richard Russo

70. Pass away like clouds before the wind —William Wordsworth

71. Passed like a ghost from view —John Greenleaf Whittier

72. (The wild part of her had) perished like burned grass —Ellen Glasgow

73. (Life was) receding . . . as the sea abruptly withdraws, abandoning a rock it has caressed too long —Françoise Sagan

74. Receding like a bad dream —Anon

75. (He felt the distress and suspicions of the previous night) receding like a tempest —George Santayana

76. [Sounds] receding like the image of a man between two mirrors — Frank Conroy

77. Sank like lead into the sea —Brian Moore

78. Sank to the bottom as a stone —*The Holy Bible/Exodus*

79. Scuttle away . . . like moths —W. D. Snodgrass

80. (The cares that infest the day,) shall fold their tents, like the Arabs, and as silently steal away —Henry Wadsworth Longfellow

81. Shrank away like an ill-treated child —W. H. Auden

82. Shrank like an anemone —Derek Lambert

83. Slip away like water —Edna St. Vincent Millay

84. [Thoughts] slipped away . . . like bushes on the side of a sheer precipice —Edith Wharton

85. Slipping silently away like a thief in a London fog —Jack Whitaker, ABC-TV, about the Goodyear blimp disappearing in the mist above the US Open golf tournament in San Francisco, June 20, 1987

86. Slips away like a snake in a weed-tangle —Robert Penn Warren

87. Slips out of my life like sand —Diane Wakoski

88. A slow fade, like a candle or an icicle —Margaret Atwood

89. (The nights) snapped out of sight like a lizard's eyelid —Sylvia Plath

90. Suddenly disappeared with a jerk, as if somebody had given her a violent pull from behind —Charles Dickens

91. (Her voice) suddenly disappeared, like a coin in a magic trick —Scott Spencer

92. Vanish . . . as easily as an eel into sand —Arthur Conan Doyle

93. Vanish as raindrops which fall in the sea —Susan Coolidge

94. Vanish away like the ghost of breath —George Garrett

95. Vanished, ghost-like, into air —Henry Wadsworth Longfellow

96. Vanished like a puff of steam —H. G. Wells

A frequently used alternative is to vanish or leave "Like a puff of wind."

97. (The stray cat) vanished like a swift, invisible shadow —D. H. Lawrence

98. [Food being served, dessert] vanished like a vision —Charlotte Brontë

99. Vanished like a wisp of vapor —Edith Wharton

100. (He had simply) vanished, like Gaugin —Lynne Sharon Schwartz

101. Vanished like midnight ghosts —Charles Lindbergh
    Lindbergh used the simile in 1927 to describe the flight of a French plane, L'Oiseau Blanc.

102. Vanished like some little bird that has been flushed out of the shrubbery —Mikhail Lermontov

103. Vanished like the last of the buffalo hunters —George Garrett

104. Vanished [out of his mind] like the mist before the rising sun —H. G. Wells

105. [The impression made upon people by a tragedy] vanishes as quickly as a delicious fruit melts in the mouth —Honoré de Balzac

106. Vanishes as rapidly as a road runner in a cartoon —*New Yorker,* August 26, 1985
    In the "Talk of The Town" column, this referred to the speed with which a book, once finished, disappears from a writer's mental picture.

107. (Beauty) vanishing like a long sigh —George Garrett

108. Vanish like a changing mood —John Hall Wheelock

109. Vanish like a cocktail before dinner —Anon

110. Vanish like a dew-drop in a rose —Gerald Massey

111. Vanish like a ghost before the sun —P. J. Bailey

112. Vanish like an echo —Johann Wolfgang von Goethe

113. Vanish like birds in winter —George Garrett

114. Vanish like lightning —Henry Taylor

115. Vanish like plunging stars —Don Marquis

116. Vanish like raindrops which fall in the sea —Anon

117. Vanish like smoke —Percy Bysshe Shelley

118. Vanish like the Witch of the North —George Garrett

119. Vanish like white soft crowns of dandelions in the wind —George Garrett

120. Vanish like writing in the sand —Anon

121. (My awe of Cruikback) went away like a mist in a high wind —Gerald Kersh

122. Went away like a summer fly —W. B. Yeats

123. Went gloriously away, like lightning from the sky —Edgar Allen Poe

124. [Sense of peace] went out like a shooting star —Edna O'Brien

DISAPPOINTMENT
See Also: DESPAIR, FACIAL EXPRESSION

1. Disappointed as a dieter who can't lose more than an ounce —Anon

2. Disappointed as a ghost without a house to haunt —Anon

3. Disappointed . . . as if he'd seen his favorite teacher drunk —Mary Gordon

4. Disappointing as discovering the charming man you met at a party is gay —Anon

5. Disappointing, like signing up for a French gourmet cooking course and learning how to make French toast —Nina Totenberg, Public Radio

6. Disappointment . . . had fallen upon him like a blow struck by some unseen hand —Sherwood Anderson

7. Disappointment worked through me like a poison —Robertson Davies

8. Disillusioned . . . as a betrayed lover —Calder Willingham

9. Had a look of profound disappointment . . . like a child who sees a treat wafted away from him —Mary McCarthy

DISAPPROVAL
See: CONTEMPT

DISASTER
See: FORTUNE/MISFORTUNE

DISCOMFORT
See Also: PAIN

1. Comfortable as a toothache —Mark Twain

2. (Kiss) comfortless as frozen water to a starved snake —William Shakespeare

3. Comfortless as salt —Sylvia Plath

4. Damp like a vault —Maurice Hewlett

5. Felt like a door-to-door salesman, pushing unwanted sets of nature encyclopedias complete with fake walnut case —Sue Grafton

6. Indigestible as Christmas dinner —Patricia Ferguson
See Also: FOOD AND DRINK

7. I've a head like a concertina, I've a tongue like a button-stick, I've a mouth like an old potato —Rudyard Kipling

Kipling's triple simile to describe a hangover, continues as follows: "And I'm more than a little sick, but I've had my fun."

See Also: DRINKING, TASTE

8. Self-conscious as a stammer —Delmore Schwartz

9. (Joel's fingers are cold.) The apartment is like a football game in the rain —Margaret Atwood

10. Uncomfortable as running a marathon in high-heeled pumps —Anon

11. Uncomfortable as trying to sleep standing up —Elyse Sommer

12. An uncomfortable feeling, like finding oneself in the same cell, and for the same crime, as a man one repudiated on every ground —John Fowles

13. Uneasy as a dog in a vet's waiting room —Anon

14. Nothing unsettles man like a bed of stinging nettles —W. S. Gilbert

DISCONTENT

See Also: DEJECTION, GLOOM

1. Disgruntled as an under-tipped taxi driver —Anon

2. Dissatisfaction with himself had settled over him . . . as congruently as a second skin —François Camoin

3. Discontent follows ambition like a shadow —Anon

4. Discontent . . . had come over her like a blighting wind —George Eliot

5. Discontent is like ink poured into water, which fills the whole fountain full of blackness —Owen Feltham

6. Discontent like alum in the mouth —Wallace Stegner

7. His whole wounded life choked him at the throat like a death agony —Émile Zola

8. Looking as unhappy as an aging, wet and exhausted salesman whose luck had played out at last —Howard Frank Mosher

9. Men who are unhappy, like men who sleep badly, are always proud of the fact —Bertrand Russell

10. Unhappiness burns like leaves —F. D. Reeve

11. Unhappiness inhabited me as if it were another person and it had the power to pull memories from me, as if from an open file —Scott Spencer

12. Unhappiness . . . it is like climbing up a bare wall. It is like being shut up in a cellar all your life —Vicki Baum

13. Unhappy as a baseball player who can't get to third base —Anon

14. Unhappy as a character in a soap opera —Elyse Sommer

DISCORD
>See: AGREEMENT/DISAGREEMENT

DISCOURAGEMENT
>See: DEJECTION

DISCRETION
>See: CAUTION, TACT

DISCRIMINATION
>See: STYLE

DISHONESTY
>See Also: BELIEVABILITY, CRIME, LIES/LIARS

1. All frauds, like the wall daubed with untempered mortar . . . always tend to the decay of what they are devised to support —Richard Whately

2. As honest a man as any in the cards, when the kings are out —Thomas Fuller

3. At length corruption, like a general flood . . . shall deluge all — Alexander Pope

4. Borrowed thoughts, like borrowed money, only show the poverty of the borrower —Marguerite, Countess Blessington

5. Corruption is like a ball of snow . . . once set a-rolling it must increase —Charles Caleb Colton

6. Crooked as a worm writhing on a hook —Herman Wouk
    The people who are likened to worms are characters from Wouk's political novel, *Inside, Outside.*

7. (Pompous and braggadocian, he seemed to the children as flat and) false as his teeth —Ferrol Sams

8. (She was) false as water —William Shakespeare

9. Falser than vows made in wine —William Shakespeare

10. Fraudulent as falsies —Helen Hudson

11. He that builds his house with other men's money is like one that gathers himself stones for the tomb of his burial —*The Holy Bible/Apocrypha: Ecclesiasticus*
    The word 'builds' has been modernized from 'buildeth' and 'gathers' from 'gathereth.'

12. It is as difficult to appropriate the thoughts of others as it is to invent — Ralph Waldo Emerson

13. Permit memory to paint it [a long-ago life style] falsely, like the face of some old whore who could wish to be taken as young and innocent — George Garrett

14. Plays you as fair as if he'd picked your pocket —John Ray's *Proverbs*

15. Robbers are like rane, tha fall on the just and the unjust —Josh Billings
    In Billings' phonetic dialect the word 'rane' is 'rain' and 'tha' is 'they.'

16. Sneaky as a rat in a hotel kitchen —William Alfred

17. There is something in corruption which, like a jaundiced eye, transfers the color of itself to the object it looks upon —Thomas Paine

18. To rob a friend even of a penny is like taking his life —Johann B. Nappaha

DISILLUSIONMENT
See: DISAPPOINTMENT

DISINTEGRATIION
See Also: DESTRUCTION

1. (Shirley's childless marriage had) become unstuck like a piece of old and grubby sticking plaster —Gillian Tindall

2. Blown aside like thistledown —John Fowles
   Fowles used this simile once to describe the eventual collapse of a political party and another time to describe a mood. Some similes obviously transfer to different points of reference more easily than others.

3. Broke like a sea-bubble on the sand —James Montgomery

4. (Perhaps the hope will die stillborn,) broken up like wreckage by the tides of events —Lawrence Durrell

5. Come apart like wet kleenex —Anon

6. (When I hit him he) comes apart like a perfect puzzle or an old flower —Philip Levine

7. Comes apart like meat being carved —G. K. Chesterton

8. (He started) coming apart like seedpod —Sharon Sheehe Stark

9. Cracking and fading like an old photograph —George Garrett

10. Crumbled like crackers into alphabet soup —Dave Anderson, *New York Times*/Sports of the Times, November 24, 1986
    The comparison referred to disintegration of a once great heavyweight champion division.

11. Crumble like old cheese —Anon

12. Crumble like soda crackers —Dashiell Hammett

13. (Their argument) crumbles like dry rice paper —Nicholas Proffitt

196

14. (The old voice) crumpled . . . like a fragile leaf —Lawrence Durrell

15. Crumple . . . like a leaf in the fire —James Joyce

16. Crumple up like wet and falling roses —D. H. Lawrence

17. (The house was) old and decayed like the pitted trunk of a persimmon —Yasunari Kawabata

18. Disintegrate like a bubble at a touch —Anon

19. Disintegrate like a crumbling monument —Anon

20. (Words came to my lips and) dissipated like the wisps of children's breaths in the cold air outside —Kent Nelson

21. Dissolved and grew flimsy like the world after champagne —Graham Swift

22. [A committee] dissolved like a summer cloud —Edith Wharton

23. Dissolved like spit in the wind —Wallace Stevens

24. Dissolve likc vague promises —Elyse Sommer

25. (Floats on water) dissolving like a paper plate —Margaret Atwood

26. (The white sky) empties of its promise, like a cup —Sylvia Plath

27. (The shadows under the trees and bushes) evaporated like puddles after a shower —Stephen King

28. Evaporated like a drop of dew —Ruth Prawer Jhabvala

29. Evaporate . . . like hoar frost before the morning sun —W. Somerset Maugham
    Maugham's simile from *The Summing Up* refers to the way changing tastes affect perceptions of an art work's beauty.

30. Fall apart and scatter like a smashed string of beads —Yaakov Churgin

31. Falling into decay like a layer of mulch —Jean Thompson

32. (Furniture) falling to pieces like dry fruitcake —William H. Gass

33. Fizzles out like a wet firecracker —John Wainwright

34. Goes up in smoke like so much tissue paper —Elizabeth Spencer

35. Go sour [as a project] like milk abandoned in the far corner of the refrigerator —Marian Sturm

36. Melt away like salt in water —Sholom Aleichem

37. Melt away like Turkish delights —Frank O'Hara

38. Melted away like a snail —Elizabeth Spencer

39. [Members of a social set] melted away, like snow drops over a bonfire —Ayn Rand

40. Melted [in response to compliments] like butter on the Sahara —Tony Ardizzone

41. Melted like wax —*The Holy Bible*

42. (The day is) melting away like snow —Plautus

This has been used in poetry and daily language since 200 B.C., and is still going strong.

43. Melts away like moonlight in the heaven of spreading day —Percy Bysshe Shelley

44. (Your mind now) moldering like a wedding-cake —Adrienne Rich

45. Rot and shred and peel away like old wallpaper —George Garrett

46. [Resolutions] thinned away like smoke, into nothingness —Aldous Huxley (1894-1963), *The Gioconda Smile,* Harper and Brothers: New York, 1921

47. Rotted through like old shoe leather —Marge Piercy

48. Rotting like autumn leaves —Marguerite Yourcenar

49. Shredded away like leaf tobacco —Saul Bellow

50. (The snake slides again and again until all passed is left behind to) shrivel like a ghost without substance —Daniela Gioseffi

51. (The remembrance had been brought to mind so often that it was) tarnished and dull, like a trinket not worth looking at —Beryl Markham

52. (Her muscles came) undone like ribbons —Sharon Sheehe Stark

53. Wear out like a worn battery —Anon
    This makes a good update for "Wears out like a run-down gramophone record."

54. Went to pieces like a cheap umbrella in a gale —Anon
    This is updated from the original "Like a fifty cent umbrella," something today only obtainable at a rummage sale.

55. Will dissolve faster than an Alka-Seltzer under a waterfall —Barry Farber, WNYC radio, commenting on the endurance of communism.

56. Wither like the flower of the field —Miguel de Cervante

57. Withered like grass —*The Holy Bible/Psalms*

58. Wither like a blighted tree —Barbara Howes

59. Withers like the face of an aged woman —Beryl Markham

DISLOYALTY
See: LOYALTY/DISLOYALTY

DISORDER
See: ORDER/DISORDER

DISPERSAL
1. Diffused charm around like an indispensable perfume —Jules Janin, about the woman who served as the role model for *The Lady With the Camellias* by Alexandre Dumas, Fils

2. (Consciousness) disperses itself like pollen on a spring day —Carlos Fuentes

3. Dispersed like a broken family —Beryl Markham

4. Disposed of like a branch or potato sack —Graham Swift

5. Here and there like teeth in an old man's mouth —Maxim Gorky

6. Like the chaff of the summer threshing floors . . . the wind carried them away —*The Holy Bible*

7. Scatter and divide like fleecy clouds self-multiplied —William Wordsworth

8. Scattered as the seeds of wild grass —Beryl Markham

9. Scattered [audience across vacant seats in a theatre] as widely as outfielders when the champion batter steps to the plate —O. Henry

10. [Shadows of doubts and weaknesses] scattered, like a cloud in morning's breeze —John Greenleaf Whittier

11. (The rage that had been silent . . . fired and) scattered like bullets — Belva Plain

12. Scattered (across the map of the land) like carelessly dropped pennies —George Garrett

13. Scattered, like chaff in a high wind —Donald Seaman Scatter like confetti —Derek Lambert
    An extension is "To scatter like confetti at a tickertape parade."

14. Scattered like dusts and leaves, when the mighty blasts of October seize them —Henry Wadsworth Longfellow

15. Scattered like foam along the wave —George Croly

16. Scattered like foam on the torrent —Percy Bysshe Shelley

17. Scattered like mown and withered grass —Johann Wolfgang von Goethe

18. Scattered like rabbits to a gunshot —Lawrence Durrell

19. (Spite, malice and jealousy) scattered like spent foam —Iris Murdoch

20. Scatter like a bucket of water —Erich Maria Remarque

21. Scatter like balls on a billiard table —Tom Shales, movie review, WNYC Morning Edition Public Radio, March 20, 1987
    In the movie Shales reviewed, it was babies who were thus scattered about.

22. (The sparrows) scatter like handfuls of gravel —William H. Gass

23. Scatter like mist before the wind —Kenzaburo Oë
    The descriptive reference point is a feeling of contentment.

24. Scatter like pigeons across grass —Anon

25. (His foes are) scattered like chirping sparrows —Stephen Vincent Benét

26. Thrown away like used paper cups —Anon

DISPOSABILITY
See: TRANSIENCE

DISSATISFACTION
See: DISCONTENT

DISSENSION
See: AGREEMENT/DISAGREEMENT, ARGUMENT, FIGHTING

DISSIMILARITY
See: DIFFERENCES

DISTANCE
See: REMOTENESS

DISTINCTIVENESS
See: ORIGINALITY

DIVERSENESS
See Also: DIFFERENCES, PERSONAL TRAITS

1. He [Shakespeare] was as many-sided as clouds are many-formed —
Robert G. Ingersoll

2. (We had come up to the farm for our four summer weeks, and Maine
was all before us) as various and new as the flow of the heavy tides —
Barry Targan

3. As various as a Cook's tour —Delmore Schwartz

4. As various as a duck-billed platypus —Jean Stafford

5. Diverse as a smorgasbord table —Anon

6. Diverse as weather, changeful as the wind —Robert Hillyer

7. (She) had as many registers as a fine old organ —Vicki Baum

8. Like a Russian doll nesting ever smaller dolls inside of it, I house an
infinity of selves —Daphne Merkin

9. Multi-faceted like a crystal chandelier —Anon

10. Varied as the expressions of the human face —George H. Ellwanger
With this book as an example, one might add "And as varied
as the similes to describe those expressions."

DIVORCE
See: MARRIAGE

DOCILITY
    See: MEEKNESS

DOCTORS
    See Also: PROFESSIONS

1. As with eggs, there is no such thing as a poor doctor; doctors are either good or bad —Fuller Albright
   The author of this simile is a doctor.

2. A breast or a foot is examined [by doctors lacking in empathy] like a pack of cigarettes —Hildegarde Knef, quoted in interview with Rex Reed

3. Carrying his little black bag like a small sample cut from the shadow of death —Helen Hudson
   This observation from Hudson's novel, *Meyer Meyer*, is made by the main character about his doctor/brother-in-law.

4. Commonly, physicians, like beer, are best when they are old; and lawyers, like bread, when they are young and new —Thomas Fuller

5. A doctor knows the human body as a cabman knows the town; he is well acquainted with all the great thoroughfares and small turnings; he's intimate with all the principle edifices, but he cannot tell you what is going on inside of any one of them —*Punch,* 1856

6. The fame of a surgeon is like the fame of an actor; it exists only as long as they live, and their talent is no longer appreciable after they have disappeared —Honoré de Balzac

7. Physicians are like kings; they brook no contradiction —John Webster

DOGS
    See: ANIMALS

DOMINATION
    See: POWER

DOUBT
    See: TRUST/MISTRUST

DREAMS
    See Also: AMBITION, HOPE, SLEEP

1. The arc of dreams is black and streaked with gray as dead hair is — John Logan

2. Dreamed of unearned riches, like Aladdin —Phyllis McGinley

3. The dream . . . hovered about her still like a pleasant, warm fog — Lynne Sharon Schwartz

4. A dream not interpreted is like a letter not read —*Babylonian Talmud*

5. Dream safely like any child who has said prayers and to whom a lullaby has been sung —George Garrett

6. Dreams are like a microscope through which we look at the hidden occurences in our soul —Erich Fromm

7. Dreams are thoughts waiting to be thought —Jan de Hartog

8. Dreams descend like cranes on gilded, forgetful wings —John Ashbery

9. Dreams move my countenance as if it were earth being pelted by rain —Diane Wakoski

10. The dreams of idealists are like the sound of footsteps in a tornado —Melvin I. Cooperman, June 8, 1987

11. Dreams pop out like old fillings in the teeth —Diane Wakoski

12. Dreams rising from your eyes like steam —George Bradley

13. Dreams withered like flowers that are blighted by frost —Ellen Glasgow
    See Also: DISINTEGRATION

14. Dreamy as puberty —Karl Shapiro

15. Fantasy is like jam; you have to spread it on a solid slice of bread. If not, it remains a shapeless thing, like jam, out of which you can't make anything —Italo Calvino, television interview aired after his death in 1985

16. Kept it [private dream] locked in his heart and took it out only when he was alone, like a miser counting his gold —Margaret Millar

17. Like a dog, he hunts in dreams —Alfred, Lord Tennyson

18. Nightmares have seasons like hurricanes —Lorrie Moore

19. Old dreams still floated . . . like puddles of oil on the surface of a pail of water —Paige Mitchell

20. Our dreams like clouds disperse —Alfred Noyes

21. Toss wishes like a coin —George Garrett

DRINKING
See Also: EATING AND DRINKING, FOOD AND DRINK

1. Alcohol is like love. The first kiss is magic, the second is intimate, the third is routine —Raymond Chandler

2. A case of beer lying at his feet like the family dog —Jonathan Valin

3. Drank like a camel —Robert Graves

4. Drank like a fire engine —Ernest William Hornung

5. Drink like a fish —Anon

There's a whole laundry list of "Drink like" and "Drunk as" similes. Those linking drinking with fish predominate with "Drunk as a lord" and "Drunk as owls" or "Boiled as owls" following close on the fishes' fins. A nice twist by Mary Peterson Poole: "It's all right to drink like a fish, if you drink what a fish drinks."

6. (He could) drink like a suction-hose —Thomas Burke

7. Drinks cognac like soda water —Isaac Bashevis Singer

8. Drunk as a cooter brown —Richard Ford

9. Drunk as an autumn wasp —Jonathan Gash

10. Drunk as a wheelbarrow —George Garrett

11. Drunk as dancing pigs —James Crumley

12. Drunk as puffed-up pigeons —Edward Hoagland

13. Drunk like wedding guests —Charles Simic

14. Feel the vodka melting into his bloodstream, like snow —Richard Lourie

15. Half as sober as a judge —Charles Lamb

16. Lit up like a Christmas tree —Anon
    Similes linking "Lit up" with a variety of comparative references became part of the American language around 1902. Here are some offshoots of the above: "Lit up like a cathedral," "Lit up like a church," "Lit up like Main Street," "Lit up like a skyscraper," and "Lit up like Times Square."

17. Pissed as a skunk —Martin Cruz Smith

18. Pissed as a newt —American colloquialism
    This means to be very drunk.

19. Smell . . . like a tap-room —Anton Chekhov

20. Smells like a still —Cornell Woolrich

21. Some men are like musical glasses: to produce their finest tones you must keep them wet —Samuel Taylor Coleridge

22. Taught himself to drink as he would have taught himself Greek; like Greek it would be the gateway to a wealth of new sensations, new psychic states, new reactions in joy or misery —F. Scott Fitzgerald

23. (I have been) tight as a tick —Tallulah Bankhead

24. A hangover like a herd of elephants —Graham Masterton

25. (He was) so knocked out with liquor that he vomited like a whale, urinated like a dog, exposed himself like a jackass, and wallowed in his muck like a pig —St. Kitts' government newspaper, *The Democrat*, about leader of opposition, 1981

26. The stuff [liquor] was like insulin to a diabetic; he didn't need much of it at a time, but if he needed little he needed it often —Howard Nemerov
    The simile describes the drinking habits of a character in Nemerov's short story, *Unbelievable Characters.*

27. Woke up with his head like a big split millstone —John Dos Passos

28. When drunk, his color sank to a clammy white from which it rose like a thermometer as he sobered up —Mary Ward Brown

29. His head still felt like a sandbag full of maggots —Sterling Hayden

30. Whiskey . . . went through me like a rope of fire —Louise Erdrich

31. Whiskey . . . burned his stomach like hellfire —Paige Mitchell

32. The spirit of the wine was rising like smoke to his head —George Garrett

33. The bourbon was warm in her stomach . . . like a core of heat — Jayne Anne Phillips

DRIVERS/DRIVING
See: VEHICLES

DRYNESS

1. Arid as the sands of the Sahara —Joseph Conrad
   The everyday cliche is "Dry as the Sahara."

2. (I'll) drain him dry as hay —William Shakespeare

3. Dries up like snakeskin —Kate Grenville

4. (Her words were) dry as the rustle of old leaves —William Beechcroft

5. Dry and cracking like the bindings on rare books —Diane Wakoski

6. (His throat was) dry as a desert —Colin Forbes

7. (Heart) dry as an autumn leaf —Nelson Algren

8. (You'll sweat until you're as) dry as an old gourd —George Garrett

9. Dry as ashes —Fisher Ames
   Variations of this much-used cliche include "Dry as dust" as well as frame-of-reference switches such as "White as ashes."

10. (His sensitive palate as) dry as a bread crust —W. S. Gilbert

11. Dry as a spinster on a Saturday night —line from "St. Elsewhere" television drama, broadcast December 16, 1986

12. (I was) dry as a stick —Thomas Gray
    Gray used this in combination with two other similes: "I was dry as a stick, hard as a stone, and cold as a cucumber."

13. (Her voice was) dry as burned paper —Susan Fromberg Schaeffer

14. (My heart felt as) dry as dirt —Bernard Malamud

15. (Their intellectuality is as) dry as dung that's lain on a dusty road for weeks —Louis Adamic
    A shorter version seen in a poem by W. D. Snodgrass: "Parched as dung."

16. Dry as faded marigold —Stephen Vincent Benét

17. Dry as last year's crow's nest —Anon

18. Dry as poverty —John Ashbery

19. Dry as woodash —Marge Piercy

20. [Feeling of teeth against lips] dry as sandpaper —William Faulkner

21. (Hair) dry as spun glass —Elizabeth Spencer

22. (He was dry-looking, as) dry as talc —Marianne Wiggins

23. Dry as the white dunes under sunlight —Marge Piercy

24. Dry up faster than a pressed corsage —Reynolds Price

25. Parched like an open mouth —Charles Simic

DULLNESS

See Also: BOREDOM/BORING

1. About as exciting as broccoli —Fred Barnes, "McLaughlin Group" television broadcast, December 29, 1986

2. About as exciting as a ride on a stone camel —Anon

3. As much personality as a paper cup —Raymond Chandler about the city of Los Angeles
   In his essay *The Country Behind the Hill,* critic Clive James explains that this was intended as a positive simile, reflecting Chandler's fascination with the city's seediness.

4. Bland as a Bloody Mary without tabasco —Anon

5. Bland as a martini without a twist of lemon —Anon

6. Bland as hominy grits —Frederick Exley

7. Blunt as ignorance —Samuel Rowley

8. (The place was) dead as a ghost-town cemetery —Douglas Adams
   In his novel, *The Fourth Widow,* Adams extends the simile as follows: "And nowhere near as pretty."

9. (The place seemed to be as . . .) dead as a Pharaoh —Raymond Chandler

10. Dreary as an empty house —Gustave Flaubert

11. Dreary as an old dishrag —Anon, capsule movie review in *New York Times* television listings

12. Dreary as a Russian love story —William Diehl

13. Dry as the Congressional Record —James J. Montague

14. (Lies . . .) dull and senseless as a stone —Elizabeth Barrett Browning

15. Dull as a jail cell —Ira Wood

16. (A day as) dull as a lead nickel —John Wainwright

17. (A brown macramé wall hanging) dull as dirt —Patricia Henley

18. Dull as pig shit —Ethel Merman, about her friend Benay Venuta's Jewish society friends

19. Dull as brushing your teeth —Anon

20. Dull as ditch-water —Charles Dickens
    An everyday expression modernized to "Dull as dishwater."

21. (When he is gone, the world will be) dull as Mars —Lorrie Moore

22. (The road north is . . .) dull like a camel plodding through the desert —Anon

23. Dull . . . like a cookbook written by someone who doesn't like food —Pat Conroy

24. An eternal sameness, like a blank wall —Robert Silverberg

25. Flat and insipid as a pancake —Anatole France
    Anatole France loved proverbs, and so this extension of familiar wisdom.

26. [About an experience someone is relating] flat as the telling at breakfast of an ecstatic dream —Stella Benson

27. Had the personality of a dried-out fart —Anon

28. Interesting as boiled potatoes —Anon

29. Interesting as staring at a blank wall —Anon

30. Interesting as watching paint dry —Dee Weber

31. Life as humdrum as that of a country curate —W. Somerset Maugham

32. Life . . . devoid of incident as the longest of Trollope's novels —O. Henry

33. Life here is as calm as a gold-fish tank with one half-animate inmate: me —Julia O'Faolain

34. Life is as tedious as a twice-told tale —William Shakespeare

35. Looked dreary, like a theater before anybody comes —Mark Twain

36. Looked like she had the IQ of a well-mannered houseplant —A. E. Maxwell

37. Mind . . . slept and snored like a full dog by the fire —George Garrett

38. Monotonous as a sailor's chantey —Raymond Chandler

39. Monotonous like water dripping on sandstone —John MacDonald

40. My life is as flat as the table I write on —Gustave Flaubert

41. A new idea made its way into her mind with much difficulty, as if it had to traverse the meshes of a choked sieve —Stefan Zweig

42. Numb as a potato —Daniel Asa Rose

43. Obtuse as an ocelot —Gregory McDonald
44. Personality like a cup of yogurt —Pat Conroy
45. Persons without minds are like weeds that delight in good earth; they want to be amused by others, all the more because they are dull within —Honoré de Balzac
46. Seemed dull . . . as simple as a three-headed treasure-guarding troll —Anon
47. (The people who surrounded him) seemed like white bread, inexcusably bland —Phillip Lopate
48. Shadowy and uninteresting as an event in an outdated and long-unread novel —Gillian Tindall
    The frame of reference for the comparison is a brief, long-ago marriage.
49. There are some things so dull they hypnotize like the pendulum of a clock —Karl Shapiro
50. Tiresome as virtue —Edith Wharton
51. Too dull—no stir, no storm, no life about it . . . like being part dead and part alive, both at the same time —Mark Twain
    The condition thus described in Twain's story, *Captain Stormfield's Visit to Heaven,* is that of running a grocery store.
52. Unconscious as a face of stone —H. W. Hudson
53. (His friends were as) uninteresting as the dead —Rumer Godden
54. Void of life as a block of ice —Patricia Henley

DUMBNESS
See: STUPIDITY

DUTY
See: RELIABILITY/UNRELIABILITY

EAGERNESS
See: ENTHUSIASM

EARS
See: FACIAL DETAILS

EARTH
See: NATURE

EASE

1. (I meet men in the city) as easily as a finger stuck in water comes up wet —Marge Piercy

2. As easily as a hot knife cuts through butter —Ben Ames Williams
In Williams' novel, *Leave Her to Heaven,* the simile describes the ease with which flood waters penetrate a barrier. The simile has also cropped up in everyday language to show something slipping by or through easily—as a legal decision past a judge.

3. As hard to get as a haircut —Raymond Chandler

4. (Returned to normality) as smoothly as a ski jumper landing —John Braine

5. Did so without effort or exertion, like a chess champion playing a routine game —Natascha Wodin

6. Easy as a smile —Anon

7. Easy as a snake crawling over a stick —Joseph Conrad

8. Easy as breathing in and breathing out —Louise Erdrich

9. Easy as climbing a fallen tree —Danish proverb

10. Easy as drawing a child's first tooth —Johann Wolfgang von Goethe

11. Easy as falling out of a canoe —Anon

12. Easy as finding fault in someone else —Anon

13. Easy as for a cat to have twins —American colloquialism, attributed to New England

14. Easy as opening a letter —Anon

15. Easy as peeling the skin off a banana —Anon

16. Easy as pie —Anon

17. Easy as pointing a finger —Slogan, Colt Patent Fire Arms Mfg. Co.

18. Easy as pouring a glass of water —Anon

19. Easy as riding down smoothly paved road —Anon

20. Easy as rolling off a log —Mark Twain

21. Easy as running up charge account bills —Anon

22. Easy as scrambling an egg —Anon

23. Easy as shooting down a fish in a barrel —Anon

24. Easy as spitting —Anton Chekhov

25. Easy as stealing pennies from a blind man's can —Donald Seaman

26. Easy as to set dogs on sheep —William Shakespeare

27. Easy as turning on the TV set —Anon

28. Easy as turning the page in a book —Anon

29. Easy . . . like sliding into sin —Harry Prince

30. An easy thing to do, light and easy like falling in a dream —George Garrett

31. Go through . . . like so much dishwater —McKinlay Kantor

32. Stepped into his position as easily as a pair of trousers —Anon

33. Stepped into manhood, as one steps over a doorsill —Mark Twain

34. Went in . . . as easily as paper into a vacuum cleaner —Derek Lambert

35. Would happen as the turning of a light bulb on or off —John McGahern

EASE, Opposite Meaning
   See: DIFFICULTY

EATING AND DRINKING
   See Also: FOOD AND DRINK, MANNERS

1. Ate as if there were a hidden thing inside him, a creature of all jaws with an infinite trailing ribbon of gut —T. Coraghessan Boyle

2. Ate like a cart-horse —H. E. Bates

3. Ate like a famished wolf —Louisa May Alcott

4. Ate like a trucker —Jonathan Kellerman

5. Ate silently like two starving peasants —James Crumley

6. Ate slowly, thoughtfully, as if fixing the taste of each spoonful in her mind —Paule Marshall

7. Bit off an end of it [a candy bar] like a man biting off a chew from a plug —Peter De Vries

8. The bread slices collapsed like movie-set walls beneath her bite —Tom Robbins

9. Chewed..in odd little spasms, as if seeking a tooth that wouldn't hurt — Paul Horgan

10. Chews his granola like a Clydesdale —Ira Wood

11. Chomping popcorn [in a movie theatre] like their upper teeth are mad at their lower —Tonita S. Gardner, *It's All a Matter of Luck,* 1986

12. Diets, like clothes, should be tailored to you —Joan Rivers

13. Down poured the wine like oil on a blazing fire —Charles Dickens

14. Eat breakfast like a king, lunch like a prince and dinner like a pauper — Anon
    See Also: ADVICE

15. Eating [voraciously] . . . like a blowfly on a shit pile —Steve Heller

16. Eating like three men —Louis Adamic

17. Eating quickly and silently, like a bunch of taxi drivers eager to get back to the job —Daphne Merkin

18. Eating quickly and abstractedly, like a man whose habits of life have made food less an indulgence than a necessity —Elizabeth Bowen

19. Eat like wolves —William Shakespeare

20. Eats like a well man and drinks like a sick —Benjamin Franklin

21. Eats . . . like stolen fruit —Ralph Waldo Emerson

22. Gulped the tea and felt it like sleep in her body —Frank Tuohy

23. He's like a camel as far as serious liquid refreshment is concerned —Iris Murdoch
     See Also: DRINKING

24. Lap up the gravy just like pigs in a trough —Lewis Carroll

25. Mouth moving as rapidly as the treadle on Granny's sewing machine — William H. Gass

26. Nibble . . . in quick little bites like a squirrel with a nut —George Garrett

27. Sip [a drink] . . . as though he tasted martinis for a living —Sue Grafton

28. (He had) stuffed as full as an egg —Anon English ballad, "The Cork"

29. Swallowed it [a small sandwich] like a communion wafer —T. Coraghessan Boyle

ECONOMICS

1. Balancing the budget is a little like protecting your virtue—you just have to learn to say no —Ronald Reagan

2. Capital is dead labor, that, vampire-like, only lives by sucking living labor —Karl Marx

3. The Dow-Jones is floating up like a hot-air balloon —François Camoin

4. Economics is like being lost in the woods. How can you tell where you are going when you don't even know where you are? —Anon

5. Feeding more tax dollars to government is like feeding a stray pup. It just follows you home and sits on your doorstep asking for more — Ronald Reagan

6. Financial statements are like a bikini. What they reveal is interesting; what they conceal is vital —William W. Priest, Jr., Managing Director BEA Associates, "Wall Street Week" television program, January 9, 1987

7. Forecasting economic averages is like assuring the non-swimmer that he can safely walk across the river because its average depth is only four feet —Milton Friedman

8. Inflation, like DC-10s, and Three Mile Islands, and Cold Wars is bad for your mental health —Ellen Goodman

9.   It [the economy] looks more resistant to shoves and shocks than it once was. Like a clown on a roly-poly base, it swings back and forth but does not topple over —Leonard Silk, *New York Times*/Economic Scene, September 17, 1986

10. A little inflation is like a little pregnancy, it keeps on growing —Leo Henderson

11. Poverty is a temporary fault, but excessive wealth is [like] a lasting ailment —Kahlil Gibran

12. A recession is like an unfortunate love affair. It's a lot easier to talk your way in than it is to talk your way out —Bill Vaughan, *Reader's Digest,* July, 1958

13. Right now being an arbitrageur is kind of like being a fire hydrant at a dog show, you sure get a lot of attention —Anon arbitrageur, quote *Wall Street Journal,* 1987
     The fire hydrants comparison was made in connection with the image problems resulting from arbitrage scandals.

14. Signs of reviving inflation are as abundant as are skeptics who read each rise in inflationary barometers as an aberration —John C. Borland, *New York Times,* September 28, 1986

15. The stock market climbed like the horses of Apollo —Hortense Calisher

16. Takeovers on a scale that would make 19th-century pirates look like croquet players —Harry A. Jacobs (senior director of Prudential-Bache Securities), commenting on increase in company takeovers and other economic ills, as quoted in Leonard Silk's column, *New York Times*/Economic Scene, February 4, 1987

17. Tax loopholes are like parking spaces, they all seem to disappear by the time you get there —Joey Adams

18. To some economists, inflation is like those trick birthday candles, the ones that are impossible to blow out —Joel Popkin, *New York Times,* August 17, 1986

19. Turning national economic policy around is like turning the Queen Mary around in a bathtub —E. Gerald Corrigan, chairman of Federal Reserve Bank of New York, at Japan Society dinner, *New York Times,* April 17, 1987

20. The wife economy [wherein husbands assume full economic responsibility for wives] is as obsolete as the slave economy —Elizabeth Hardwick
     See Also: MARRIAGE

EDUCATION
     See Also: KNOWLEDGE

1. Alumni are like the wake of a ship; they spread out and ultimately disappear, but not until they have made a few waves —Anon

2. Colleges are like old-age homes; except for the fact that more people die in colleges —Bob Dylan

3. Education begins, like charity, at home —Susan Ferraro, *New York Times*/Hers, March 26, 1987
     The charity comparison has been effectively linked with other subjects.
    See Also: PATRIOTISM, PEACE, REFORM, SENSE

4. Education, like neurosis, begins at home —Milton R. Sapirstein

5. Education, like politics, is a rough affair, and every instructor has to shut his eyes and hold his tongue as though he were a priest —Henry Adams

6. Getting educated is like getting measles; you have to go where the measles is —Abraham Flexner

7. He was like an empty bucket waiting to be filled [with knowledge] — William Diehl

8. He who teaches a child is like one who writes on paper; but he who teaches old people is like one who writes on blotted paper —*The Talmud*

9. Human beings, like plants, can be twisted into strange shapes if their training begins early enough and is vigilantly supervised. They will accept their deformation as the natural state of affairs and even take pride in it, as Chinese women once did in their crippled feet —Milton R. Sapirstein
     Sapirstein, a psychologist, used this simile to introduce a discussion about the educational impulse and its relationship to the educational process.
    See Also: MANKIND

10. If it [learning] lights upon the mind that is dull and heavy, like a crude and undigested mass it makes it duller and heavier, and chokes it up — Michel De Montaigne

11. Learning in old age is like writing on sand; learning in youth is like engraving on stone —Solomon Ibn Gabirol

12. Learning is like rowing upstream: not to advance is to drop back — Chinese proverb

13. Learning, like money, may be of so base a coin as to be utterly void of use —William Shenstone

14. Learning without thought is labor lost —Confucius

15. Many a scholar is like a cashier: he has the key to much money, but the money is not his —Ludwig Boerne

16. Modern education is a contradiction. It's like a three-year-old kid with a computer in his hand who can multiply 10.6 per cent interest of $11,653, but doesn't know if a dime is larger or smaller than a nickel — Erma Bombeck

17. The need of a teacher to believe now and again that she fosters genius is like the writer's need to believe that he is one —Lael Tucker Wertenbaker

18. Rolling on like a great growing snowball through the vast field of medical knowledge —William James

19. A scholar is like a book written in a dead language: it is not everyone that can read in it —William Hazlitt

20. A scholar should be like a leather bottle, which admits no wind; like a deep garden bed, which retains its moisture; like a pitch-coated vessel, which preserves its wine; and like a sponge, which absorbs everything —*The Talmud*

21. Soap and education are not as sudden as a massacre, but they are more deadly in the long run —Mark Twain

22. Students are like acorns and oaks, there's a lot more bark to the oak and a lot more nuttiness in the acorn —Anon

23. Study is like the heaven's glorious sun —William Shakespeare

24. Take it in like blotting paper —Mavis Gallant
    See Also: ABSORBABILITY

25. The teacher is like the candle which lights others in consuming itself — Giovanni Ruffini

26. Teachers, like actors, must drug themselves to be at their best — Delmore Schwartz

27. Teaching a class was in a way like making love. Sometimes he did it with great enthusiasm . . . sometimes he did it because it was expected of him, and he forced himself to go through the motions — Dan Wakefield

28. Teaching a fool is like gluing together a potsherd [pottery fragment] —*The Holy Bible/Apocrypha*

29. Their learning is like bread in a besieged town; every man gets a little, but no man gets a full meal —Samuel Johnson
    Johnson's simile referred to his view of Scottish education.

30. To study and forget is like bearing children and burying them —*The Talmud*

31. To transmit wisdom to the unworthy is like throwing pearls before swine —Moses Ibn Ezra

32. Your education, like . . . carrots, is not a manufactured article, but just a seed which has grown up largely under nature's friendly influence —William J. Long

EERINESS
    See: STRANGENESS

EFFECT
    See: CAUSE AND EFFECT

EFFECTIVENESS
    See: ABILITY, CAUSE/EFFECT, SUCCESS/FAILURE,
    USEFULNESS/USELESSNESS

EFFORTLESSNESS
    See: EASE

EGO
    See: VANITY

ELASTICITY
    See: FLEXIBILITY/INFLEXIBILITY

ELEGANCE
    See: JOY

ELEGANCE
    See: CLOTHING, STYLE

ELOQUENCE
    See: PERSUASIVENESS, SPEECH MAKING

ELUSIVENESS
    See Also: DIFFICULTY

1. As slippery as an eel —Dutch proverb
    This has given rise to extensions such as, "Slippery as an eel
    dipped in butter" by F. van Wyck Mason.
2. (Love is) as slippery as greased pigskin —Delmore Schwartz
    See Also: LOVE
3. Avoided [another person] like a vampire avoids sunburn —Joseph
    Wambaugh
4. (He was) difficult as a serpent to see —D. H. Lawrence
    The elusive creature being described is a fox sliding along in
    deep grass.
5. (The feeling persisted, insidious and) difficult to trace as perfume —
    Harvey Swados
6. Elusive as a collar button —Jim Murray

Murray, sports columnist for the *Los Angeles Herald,* applied this simile to football player Mike Garrett.

7. Elusive as a dream —William Diehl
   "Fugitive as dreams," used by Tom MacIntyre in a short story *Epithalamion,* illustrates the possibility for change through word substitutions.

8. Elusive as a wet fish —Anon

9. Elusive as buried treasure —Anon

10. Elusive as the cure for cancer —Anon

11. Elusive as the cure for aging —Anon

12. Elusive as the source of a rumor —Anon

13. Elusiveness, like a thought that presents itself to consciousness and vanishes before it can be captured by words —W. Somerset Maugham

14. Evaded me, much like the myth of Tantalus —Marguerite Young

15. Evasion, like equivocation, comes generally from a cowardly or a deceiving spirit, or from both —Honoré de Balzac

16. Hard to hold as a flapping sail in a raging wind —Gerald Kersh
    The hold to which Kersh alludes is the grip of one wrestler on another in the story entitled *Ali the Terrible Turk.*

17. Intangible as a beautiful thought —W. Somerset Maugham

18. Intangible as love and fear —Andre Dubus

19. (A vision swarming through the mind as sudden and) irretrievable as smoke —William Styron

20. It [information] got away from me so easily, like the tail of a kite, when the kite's already out of your hands —Cornell Woolrich

21. It [trying to tie up a boxing opponent) was just like trying to hold onto a buzz-saw —Ernest Hemingway

22. Like fish in an aquarium, they [two girls] flashed in and out of sight — Frank Tuohy

23. Like sand from a clenched fist, he was slipping through her fingers — Ben Ames Williams

24. (She was so marvelous that, when he tried to think of her, her description) rolled away from him like a dropped coin —Mark Helprin

25. (She) seemed like a shadow within a shadow —D. H. Lawrence
    Lawrence is describing one of the two main female characters in *The Fox,* a woman the male character desires but doesn't understand.

26. She was like a rubber ball; he couldn't get a grip —Beryl Bainbridge

27. Slipped by like a mouse —Anton Chekhov

28. [Something said] slipped out of me like a cork from the deep —Reynolds Price

29. Slipped through [guards] like a fox through a barnyard —Clive Cussler

30. Slippery as shadows in day's foam —Delmore Schwartz

31. They might as well be looking for a shoe in a swamp —Clive Cussler

EMBARRASSMENT
See: SHAME, SHYNESS

EMBRACES
See Also: KISSES; MEN AND WOMEN; PEOPLE, INTERACTIONS; SEXUAL INTERACTION

1. Almost completely covered by MaButhelezi's big arms, like a blanket of flesh —Njabulo Ndebele

2. Clasped each other like a pair of abandoned children —Natascha Wodin

3. Clinch like lovers at the final fade out —George Garrett

4. Curled up together like a pair of old dogs —Jean Thompson

5. Drawing her toward him he held her and squeezed her out like a bit of old washing —Edna O'Brien

6. Drew her to him, crushing her like a pale flower to his breast —Peter De Vries

7. Drew the child to her as if she were a springing young tree —Elizabeth Taylor

8. Embraced Himiko [name of a character] like a bear hugging an enemy —Kenzaburo Oë

9. Embraced him like a hot, wet towel —William II. Hallhan

10. Embraced like bears —Madison Smartt Bell

11. Embrace like penpals —Ira Wood

12. Embraces are keen like pain —Algernon Charles Swinburne

13. Her embrace was clumsy like a bad dancer's —John Braine

14. Her long thin arms came up to wind about him and inexorably, like tight thin wires, to hold him down —H. E. Bates

15. His arm around her felt as if she'd been born with it there —William McIlvanney

16. His arms are like a cradle in which she is warm and safe —Alvin Boretz, television program, 1986

17. Hold hands like teenagers, fingers meshed like the teeth of rusty gears —Ira Wood

18. Lay locked like human vines —Charles Bukowski

216

19. Let our arms clasp like ivy —John Donne

20. Locked in a profound embrace . . . like Ahab and the whale —A. R. Guerney, Jr.
     Guerney's simile refers to the guests in his play *The Perfect Party.*

21. Marg's long tanned body entwined Fencer's like a constricting serpent —Robert Stone

22. Pressed herself upon me like someone pressing upon a bruise — Lawrence Durrell

23. She vibrated in his arms like a tuning fork —Andrew Kaplan

24. Snuggled up together like spoons in bed —Phyllis Naylor

25. They'd lie together, like a four-armed creature fearful of amputation — Julia O'Faolain

26. Was so huge and soft it was like embracing a cloud and sinking down —Lee Smith

EMINENCE
See: FAME

EMOTIONS
See Also: ANXIETY, CHEERFULNESS, DEJECTION, ENVY, GLOOM, GRIEF, HAPPINESS, HATE, LONELINESS, LOVE, SADNESS, TENSION, WEARINESS

1. Compulsion is a mirror in which he who looks for long will see his inner self endeavoring to commit suicide —Kahlil Gibran

2. Emotional antagonisms that lay in us like surly dogs at the end of a chain, ready to leap up and growl at a step —Wallace Stegner

3. Emotional . . . like a third-rate opera singer —Fred Mustard Stewart

4. Emotions buzzed and throbbed . . . like a pent-up bee —Elizabeth Bowen

5. Emotions got cut off . . . like a broken string of beads —Susan Fromberg Schaeffer

6. Emotions . . . swarm in my head like a hive of puzzled bees — Gertrude Atherton

7. Emotions to be appropriate . . . may be measuring them like potatoes, but it is better than slopping them about like water from a pail —E. M. Forster

8. Emotion akin to a physical blow —Henrietta Weigel

9. Fear and anger boiled up in my head like liquid air —Ross Macdonald

10. Feeling full of wonder and illusion—like a Columbus or a pilgrim seeing the continent of his dreams take shape in the dusk for the first time —Richard Ford

    The feelings thus described are experienced as a plane comes in for a landing.

11. Feelings bubbled in him like water from an underground spring —Paige Mitchell

12. Feelings . . . call, like a buzzing of flies in autumn air —Wallace Stevens

13. Feelings cross our flesh along nets of nerves, like a pattern of lightning flashes —Marguerite Yourcenar

14. Feelings here slice right through like speed skates —Jill Robinson

    Robinson thus described the work of poet Amy Rothholz, building on her simile with, "Racing by with fierce, original passion." The poet's publisher extracted the simile from Robinson's review to feature in an ad for the book.

15. Feelings..jumbled together like ravelled wool —Frank Swinnerton

16. Feel mushy and wet, like a pile of leaves after they have been rained on —Daphne Merkin

17. Feels herself curling up like a jaundiced leaf —Alice Munro

18. Feel the magic building like a gathering storm —W. P. Kinsella

19. Felt as small and vulnerable as a calf on its first day of life —Linda West Eckhardt

20. Felt crazy, stupid, as though, having believed a burglar was rummaging through the house, I had found only the family cat —Kent Nelson

21. Felt . . . inadequate, as if I were a new understudy taking on a role that had been played before, and much more effectively —Alice McDermott

22. Felt like a lifeline thrown out to someone —Mike Feder, *New York Times,* September 7, 1986

    Feder, a cafe story teller, thus explained how he began his career by telling stories about his day's experiences to his housebound mother.

23. Felt like a man in a Rembrandt, tinged brown with sorrow and wisdom —Laurie Colwin

24. Felt like a man reprieved from the gallows —Wilfrid Sheed

25. Felt like a man who had had a tooth out that had been hurting him for a long time —Leo Tolstoy

26. Felt like an emotional invalid, like a balloon without the helium —T. Coraghessan Boyle

27. (After my husband died I) felt like one of those spiraled shells washed up on the beach . . . no flesh, no life —Lynn Caine

28. Felt shut off like a turtle inside her skin —Laura Furman

29. Felt worry and joy flinging her about like a snowflake —Mary Hedin

30. A foul feeling, like looking over the edge of the world —Jean Rhys

31. Guilty and elated, as though I'd successfully committed a small theft — Christopher Isherwood

32. Half smiles, half tears, like rain in sun —John Greenleaf Whittier
    See Also: TEARS, SMILES

33. Heart expanded like bellows —Laurie Colwin

34. His senses nagged at him like pampered babies —Stephen Crane

35. Inhibitions gave way like an earth dam collapsing in front of a winter flood —Graham Masterson

36. Isolation, frustration and sometimes fear run like a leitmotif through our lives —Philip Taubman, *New York Times Magazine,* September 21, 1986

37. It [his emotion for a woman] struck him like sickness —H. E. Bates

38. Love and emptiness in us are like the sea's ebb and flow —Kahlil Gibran

39. My emotions flowered in me like a divine revelation —André Gide

40. My heart is like wax; it is melted in the midst of my bowels —*The Holy Bible/Psalms*

41. Old feelings gather fast upon me like vultures round their prey —Emily Brontë

42. Our feelings have edges and spines and prickles like cactus, or porcupines —Laurie Colwin
    Colwin is likening the cactus/porcupine edges and spines to the feelings of two lovers.

43. Our feelings penetrate us like a poison of undetectable nature —Anaïs Nin

44. Pride and anger seemed like overblown spent clouds of thunder —John Greenleaf Whittier

45. Profound feelings . . . swept through and racked his being like gusts of fire —George Garrett

46. (A feeling of) relief circles us like a spring breeze —Richard Ford

47. Relief courses through me like cool water —Marge Piercy

48. Relief had come in like a warm and welcome flood —Carlos Baker

49. Relieved [after things have been put right] . . . like they lifted a concrete block out of my belly —John Updike

50. Rolled in self-pity and self-hatred like a hot sulfur spring —Marge Piercy

51. Self-hatred living in him like a sick dog in a cellar —Bernard Malamud

52. Sensations gave like snowslides in him —Larry Woiwode
53. Sensations . . . whirling about him like snowflakes —Willa Cather
54. (My feelings) snapped like a glass pipette —Diane Wakoski
55. Stirred an emotion . . . like the birth of a butterfly within a cocoon —Adela Rogers St. Johns
56. Sudden relief, like a rush of tears, came to her —Nadine Gordimer
57. (Their hearts were open and) sweet sensations flowed in them like honey —Ruth Prawer Jhabvala
58. Temperament, like liberty, is important despite how many crimes are committed in its name —Louis Kronenberger
59. Temper like a bed of banked coals waiting to be fired into roaring flame by a spill of brandy —Davis Grubb
60. They [true feelings] gathered around me like a mist, whose shape can be seen as it approaches, but not when it is on you —L. P. Hartley
61. Too moved to even applaud . . . as if the air had been sucked out of the room —Samuel G. Freedman, *New York Times,* September 7, 1986
    The performer who thus moved his audience was a cafe story teller.
62. Treats his emotions . . . as vermin to be crushed in traps or poisoned with bait —Marge Piercy
63. Truth and jealousy, like a team of plow horses, came crashing into the fragile barn of his illusions —Louis Auchincloss
64. A vague uneasy stirring plagued her like some mental indigestion —Josephine Tey
65. A warm feeling like cocoa on a cold night —Jean Stafford
66. Wore his confidence like a tailored suit —Donald McCaig
67. Wore sorrow and anger like a worn-out coat and would not throw it away —Belva Plain
68. The young soldier's heart was . . . like fire in his chest —D. H. Lawrence

EMPATHY
   See: KINDNESS, PITY

EMPTINESS
   See Also: ABANDONMENT, ALONENESS
1. (I was) as hollow and empty as the spaces between the stars —Raymond Chandler
2. Barren as a fistful of rock —A. E. Maxwell
3. Barren as an iceberg of vegetation —Anon
4. Barren as crime —Algernon Charles Swinburne

5. Barren as death —John Ruskin
    William Blake voiced the same thought, using 'void' instead of 'barren.'
6. Barren as routine —G. K. Chesterton
7. Blank and bare and still as a polar wasteland —George Garrett
8. Blank as a sheet —Reynolds Price
9. Blank as a vandalized clock —Lorrie Moore
10. Blank as death —Alfred, Lord Tennyson
11. Blank as the eyeballs of the dead —Henry Wadsworth Longfellow
12. Blank as the sun after the birth of night —Percy Bysshe Shelley
13. Deserted as a park bench after a snowstorm —Anon
14. Desolate as a summer resort in midwinter —Richard Harding Davis
15. Emptied like a cup of coffee —John Ashbery
16. The emptiness inside was like an explosion —Eleanor Clark
17. Emptiness so vast it yawned like the pit of hell —George Garrett
18. The emptiness was intense, like the stillness in a great factory when the machinery stops running —Willa Cather
19. Empty-armed, empty-handed as a lone winter tree —George Garrett
20. Empty as a barn before harvest —Erich Maria Remarque
21. Empty as a broken bowl —George Garrett
22. Empty as a canyon —Elizabeth Spencer
23. Empty as a church on Monday morning —Anon
24. Empty as a diary without entries —Anon
25. Empty as a dry shell on the beach —Daphne du Maurier
26. Empty as an air balloon —Thomas G. Fessendon
27. Empty as an egg basket —Eudora Welty
28. Empty as an office building at night —Anon
29. (He was . . .) empty as an old bottle —F. Scott Fitzgerald
30. Empty as a person without a past, only present —Anon
31. (Lonely afternoons, days, evenings) empty as a rusty coffee can —Diane Wakoski
32. Empty as a waiting tomb —Louis Bromfield
33. Empty as death's head —Daniel Berrigan
34. (Eyes) empty as knotholes in a fence —Etheridge Knight
35. (The campus is as) empty as space —Babs H. Deal
36. Empty as the beach after a snowstorm —Anon
37. (The shuttle after morning rush hour is near) empty, like a littered beach after tourists have all gone home —Thomas Pynchon

38. Faceless as a masked bandit —Anon
39. Feel as dead and empty as a skeleton on a desert —Robert Traver
40. Feel as empty as a popbottle in the street —Marge Piercy
41. A feeling of emptiness, as if I had cut an artery in my wrist and all the blood had drained out —Aharon Megged
42. Flat and empty as the palm of his hand —Helen Hudson
    In Hudson's novel, *Criminal Trespass,* the comparison's frame of reference is a flat and empty field.
43. (The street below was) hollow as a bone —Peter Matthiessen
44. Hollow as a politician's head —Charles Johnson
45. Hollow as skeleton eyes —Lorrie Moore
46. A hollow feeling inside, big as a watermelon —Jay Parini
47. I'm empty . . . like a sand bag —Tina Howe
48. It's like stepping into a church in midweek: Space abounding and no one to fill it —Helen MacInnes
49. Look as hollow as a ghost —William Shakespeare
50. People, like houses, may be taken over by spirits and inhabited by ghosts when they feel they are deserted and empty —Gerald Kersh
51. So empty you could fire a canon and not hit anybody —Anon
52. Sterile as a mule —James Morrow
53. Sterile as a stone —Cynthia Ozick
54. Void as death —William Blake
55. The weight of his emptiness dragged like a dead dog chained around his neck —Bernard Malamud

ENDURANCE
See: CONTINUITY, PERMANENCE

ENEMY
See: ADVERSARY

ENERGY
See Also: ACTIVENESS, BUSYNESS, ENTHUSIASM

1. Adrenaline bubbling in my veins like grease in a deep fryer —T. Coraghessan Boyle
2. Adrenaline flooded through me like water through a storm drain —Sue Grafton
3. Adrenaline flowing like electricity —W. P. Kinsella
4. Alger-like energy —Hortense Calisher
5. As brisk as a bee in a tar-pot —Thomas Fuller

The condensed version of this, "Brisk as a bee," can be traced back to Boswell's *Life of Dr. Johnson,* where it was used to describe someone's conversational style. A variation (also from Fuller's collection of aphorisms) is, "As brisk as a body louse."

6. Bracing as an Alpine breeze —Israel Zangwill

7. (Suddenly this spring he's) bursting with energy, like the daffodils on the White House lawn —James Reston about Ronald Reagan, *New York Times,* March 30, 1986

8. Electricity dripping from me like cream —Diane Wakoski

9. Energetic and tireless . . . like a shouting insect, some kind of queen aunt —J. B. Priestly

10. Energetic . . . an explosion of vitality, rather like a teapot set not to boil over but to bubble and steam —Charles Johnson

11. (Feeling as) energetic as a licensed jester —Clarence Major

12. Energy burned off him like a light —Pat Conroy

13. (Quick, incisive) energy like quicksilver in the veins —Joan Chase

14. Energy . . . like the biblical grain of mustard-seed, will remove mountains —Hosea Ballou

15. Energy sings like a tea kettle —Marge Piercy

16. Energy . . . thin and sharp like gravy —Diane Wakoski

17. Full of pep as an electric fan —Anon

18. (Little Billie was full of piss and vinegar and) full of sap as a maple tree —Robert Penn Warren
    In Warren's long poem, *The Ballad of Billie Potts,* the maple tree comparison is followed by another simile: "And full of tricks as a lop-eared pup."

19. Full of vitality . . . like a lighted candle —Rachel Ingalls

20. Had a brisk air of bristle, like a terrier bitch —Angela Carter

21. He's like 220 pounds worth of Duracell batteries —Mike Jameson, commenting on the untiring energy of boxer Mike Tyson, quoted in *Newsday* column by Paul Ballot, December 27, 1986

22. Hum with unspent power, like a machine left to run —Mary Gordon

23. (He is) just like a blob of mercury —Alice James writing from Europe about her brother William to her father and her brother Henry in America, 1889

24. Like an old volcano, which has pretty nearly used up its fire and brimstone, but is still boiling and bubbling —Oliver Wendell Holmes, Sr.

25. Like the grass and trees and other growing things, they were quivering and glistening with vitality —Dorothy Canfield Fisher

26. Refreshing, like rain at the end of a muggy day —Jay McInerney

27. Rings with vitality, like ax-strokes on oak —Dorothy Canfield Fisher
28. Sparks and twinkles like a jarred lightning bug —Sharon Sheehe Stark
     The comparison refers to a lively four-year-old girl in a story
     entitled *The Johnstown Polka.*
29. Vigorous as a run-over cat —Marge Piercy
30. Vitality . . . like a hot flame that burnt him with an unendurable fury
     —W. Somerset Maugham
31. (She had a) vitality that warmed you like a blazing fire —W. Somerset
     Maugham
32. Warm with life as the waters of a tropic sea —Beryl Markham

ENJOYMENT
See: PLEASURE

ENTHUSIASM
See Also: ENERGY, EXCITEMENT

1. (Parisians) applaud like pugilists —Janet Flanner
2. As full of spirit as the month of May —William Shakespeare
3. Drinking in every conceivable impression and experience like wine —
     George Garrett
4. Eager as a deb waiting for the grand march —John MacDonald
5. Eager as a horse player waiting for the 6th race —John MacDonald
6. Eager as a hostess forcing leftovers on departing guests —Ira Wood
7. Eager as a leashed terrier quivering to meet every challenge —Hallie
     Burnett
8. (Looked as) eager as a morning hawk —Carlos Baker
9. Eager as an understudy —Louis Monta Bell
10. Eager as a sprinter at the starting gate —Donald McCaig
11. Eager as bears for honey —David R. Slavitt
12. Eager [to buy] . . . like a starving man at a banquet —Aaron
     Goldberg
13. Enthusiasm flows from X like light from a bulb —Anon
14. Enthusiasm is a volcano on whose top never grows the grass of
     hesitation —Kahlil Gibran
15. (About as) enthusiastic as a guy going to the chair —H. C. Witwer
16. Enthusiastic as a sommelier rhapsodizing about wine —Amal Kumar
     Naj, *Wall Street Journal,* November 25, 1986
     Naj used the sommelier simile in an article about chili to
     describe the enthusiasm of a man who grows chilis as a
     pastime.

17. Fervor, whipping around . . . like the flags in the stiff breeze — Sumner Locke Elliott

18. Follow [theatre's artistic steps] with the joy of a Mets fan checking the morning box scores —Jack Viertel, *New York Times,* June 1, 1986

19. Hearty as a friendly handshake —Anon

20. Hearty . . . like a trombone thoroughly impregnated with cheerful views of life —Charles Reade

21. Hot with haste —William Shakespeare

22. Like a racehorse in the gate; I was mad to go —Irving Feldman

23. Loved anatomy . . . as a mother her child —Dr. David W. Cheever
    The anatomy enthusiast described by Dr. Cheever is Dr. Oliver Wendell Holmes.

24. Stand like greyhounds in the slips straining upon the start —William Shakespeare

25. Talked about it [business prospects] the way a man dying of thirst might talk about a cold beer —Mike Fredman

26. With the avidity and determination of a housewife at a Macy's white sale —T. Coraghessan Boyle

27. With the fervor of castaways grasping at a smudge of smoke on the horizon —Ellery Queen

28. Zeal without humanity is like a ship without a rudder, liable to be stranded at any moment —Owen Feltham

29. Zeal without judgment is like gunpowder in the hands of a child —Ben Jonson

30. Zeal without knowledge is a runaway horse —W. G. Benham

31. Zeal without knowledge is like a fire without light —John Ray's *Proverbs*

32. Zeal without knowledge is like fire without a grate to contain it; like a sword without a hilt to wield it by; like a high-bred horse without a bridle to guide him —Julius Bate

33. Zeal without knowledge is like expedition to a man in the dark —John Newton

ENTRANCES/EXITS
See Also: BEGINNINGS/ENDINGS, DEATH, EXITS

1. (A large man in white) appeared like a cuckoo out of a clock — Madison Smartt Bell

2. (Children don't) appear and disappear like toadstools in a lawn —Miles Gibson

3. Barged in . . . like a Rugby forward —Frank Swinnerton

4. Blew in like a boisterous breeze —Cole Porter, from "You've Got That Thing," one of the lyrics for the 1929 musical *Fifty Million Frenchmen*

5. Came and went, like bees after honey —Wright Morris

6. Came as silent as the dew comes —Henry Wadsworth Longfellow

7. Came in like a swan swimming its way —Virginia Woolf

8. Came like swallows and like swallows went —W. B. Yeats

9. Came like water —Edward Fitzgerald

10. Comes and goes, like hearts —Elizabeth Bishop

11. Coming in like a kite on a string —Clive Cussler
    In his novel, *Cyclops,* Cussler used the simile to describe the entrance of a vessel.

12. Entered like a wind —Ruth Suckow
    For added emphasis there's "Come in like a high wind" as used by Aharon Megged in his novel, *Living on the Dead.*

13. Enter . . . tiptoeing like somebody trying to sneak in late to a funeral —George Garrett

14. Flitted in and out of the house like birds —Anne Tyler

15. Hopped in, light as a bird —Harvey Swados

16. Light upon the scene like a new-made butterfly —George Garrett

17. Like hoodlums come . . . with neither permits nor requests —Carl Sandburg

18. Like Santa Claus he came and went mysteriously —Frank O'Connor

19. Materialize . . . like a policeman presiding over an accident —Wilfrid Sheed

20. Plunged into it like a rabbit into its hole —Ben Ames Williams

21. Popped up here and there like bubbles in a copperful of washing — Frank Swinnerton

22. Rolling through the front door like a drunken bear —James Crumley

23. Rushed into the room like a cannon-ball —Romain Gary

24. Rush in like a gust of wind —Anon

25. Slinking in like a little ailing cat —Jean Stafford

26. Slipped in like a cat or the wind —John J. Clayton

27. Strode in like a conquering prince returning to his lands —Alice Walker

28. Sweep in here like Zeus from Olympus, with his attendant nymphs and swains —Brian Clark

29. Swept vivaciously in . . . like a champion ice-skater —Frank Swinnerton

30. Was into the living-room . . . and out again with such speed that she might have been one of the mechanical weather-people in a child's snow-globe or a figure on a medieval clock, who zooms across a lower balcony as the face shows the hands on the hour —Rachel Ingalls

ENTRAPMENT

See Also: ADVANCING; PEOPLE, INTERACTION

1. About as much chance of escape as a log that is being drawn slowly toward a buzz saw —Arthur Train

2. Captured like water in oil —John Updike

3. Caught in [as a war] like meat in a sandwich —Robert MacNeil, Public Television broadcast, December, 1986

4. Caught like a forest in a blazing fire —Delmore Schwartz

5. (What wouldn't I give to see old Cy Lambert) caught like a monkey with his fist in the bottle —Louis Auchincloss

6. (The feeling came over her that she was) caught like a mouse in the trap of life —Ellen Glasgow

7. (I went to the war; got) clapped down like a bedbug —Clifford Odets

8. [Group of people] closed in upon her, like dogs on a fox —Jean Stafford

9. [Four walls of room] close in upon you like the sides of a coffin —O. Henry

10. [Many people at a party] engulfed him like an avalanche —Robert Silverberg

11. Feel like . . . a shabby blackbird baked alive in a piecrust —George Garrett

12. Felt like a muskrat trapped in a weir —Sterling Hayden

13. Felt like a worm on a hook —Shelby Hearon

14. Gripped him like an empty belly —Cutcliffe Hyne

15. Held fast by circumstances as by invisible wires of steel —Ellen Glasgow

16. It [emotional trap] held him as with the grip of sharp murderous steel —Henry James

17. My heart chokes in me like a prison —Anzia Yezierska
     Another example of a simile used to launch a work of fiction, in this case a short story entitled *Wings.*

18. Pinned to . . . like a butterfly to a cork —F. van Wyck Mason
     The butterfly image as used by Margaret Millar: "As easily trapped as a butterfly."

19. Struggling and captive like a newborn infant —Julia O'Faolain

20. Stuck with them [undesirable companions] like falling into a barrel of blackstrap molasses —Elizabeth Spencer

21. Thrashed about . . . like a whale trying to pull free from a harpoon —William H. Hallhan

22. Trapped like a fish between two cats —Spanish proverb

23. Trapped like a peasant between two lawyers —Anon

24. Trapped [in traffic] like a fly in a spider's web —Donald Seaman

25. Felt trapped . . . like a man in a cage with a sick bear and his keeper —Ross Macdonald

26. Trapped like a rabbit on a country road —Beryl Bainbridge

ENVY

1. As a moth gnaws a garment, so does envy consume a man —Saint John Chrysostam

2. As iron is eaten by rust, so are the envious consumed by envy —Livy

3. Envy hit him . . . like lack of oxygen —William McIlvanney

4. (Fools may our scorn, not envy raise, for) envy is a kind of praise —John Gay

5. Envy is like a fly that passes all a body's sounder parts and dwells upon the sores —George Chapman

6. Envy, like fire, soars upwards —Livy

7. Envy, like the worm, never runs but to the fairest fruit; like a cunning bloodhound, it singles out the fattest deer in the flock —Francis Beaumont

8. Felt a twinge of jealousy, green as a worm, wiggling deep in my center —W. P. Kinsella

9. Intense jealousy struck him like a missile —Mark Helprin

10. It [jealousy] was like a taste in his mouth —Joyce Carol Oates

11. Jealousy . . . descended on his spirit like a choking and pestilence-laden cloud —Thomas Wolfe

12. Jealousy is a kind of civil war in the soul, where judgment and imagination are at perpetual jars —William Penn

13. Jealousy is cruel as the grave —*The Holy Bible/Song of Solomon*

14. Jealousy is like a bad toothache. It does not let a person do anything, not even sit still. It can only be walked off —Milan Kundera

15. Jealousy is like a polished glass held to the lips when life is in doubt; if there be breath, it will catch the damp and show it —John Dryden

16. Jealousy that surrounds me like a too-warm room —William H. Gass

17. Jealousy whirled inside her like a racing motor —Milan Kundera

18. Stir up jealousy like a man of war —*The Holy Bible/Isaiah*

19. A wave of jealousy floats in my stomach like a cork —Ira Wood

EPITAPHS
>   See: DEATH, PRIDE

ERECTNESS
>   See: POSTURE

ERRORS

1. A flaw . . . would surface like an aching wisdom tooth —James Lee Burke

2. The defects of the mind, like those of the face, grow worse as we grow old —Francois, Duc de La Rochefoucauld
    See Also: MIND

3. Delusions, errors and likes are like huge, gaudy vessels, the rafters of which are rotten and worm-eaten, and those who embark in them are fated to be shipwrecked —Buddha

4. Errors, like straws, upon the surface flow; he who would search for pearls must dive below —John Dryden

5. Flaunt their folly, like a washline of dirty and patched clothes —George Garrett

6. Gone astray like a lost sheep —*The Holy Bible*

7. Great blunders are often made, like large ropes, of a multitude of fibers —Victor Hugo

8. Illusion forms before us like a grove —Barbara Howes
    This simile is the first line and leitmotif in Howes' poem, *The Triumph of Death.*

9. (Is somehow) impure, as sacrilegious as a Coca-Cola machine in a cathedral —Tony Ardizzone
    See Also: INAPPROPRIATENESS

10. A mistake is like a mule, not always distinguishable from a horse in front, but known beyond doubt by acquaintance with its kicking qualities —*New York Sun,* 1918

11. Wrong as two left shoes —Arthur Baer

ETERNITY
>   See: CONTINUITY

EVENNESS
>   See: STRAIGHTNESS

EVIL
>   See Also: ACTION, CRUELTY

1. All sin is a kind of lying —St. Augustine

2. At first the evil impulse is as fragile as the thread of a spider, but eventually it becomes as tough as cart ropes —*Babylonian Talmud*

3. Bad as a rotten potato —Charlotte Brontë

4. Corruption is like a ball of snow, when once set a roll, it must increase —Charles Caleb Colton

5. The Devil . . . like influenza he walks abroad —W. H. Auden

6. Evil actions like crushed rotten eggs, stink in the nostrils of all — Bartlett's *Dictionary of Americanisms*

7. Evil . . . a quality some people are born with, like a harelip —Ross Macdonald

8. Evil as dynamiting trout —Robert Traver

9. Evil enters like a needle and spreads like an oak tree —Ethiopian proverb

10. Evil, like parental punishment, is not intended for itself —Josepiz Albo

11. Evils in the journey of life are like the hills which alarm travelers on the road. Both appear great at a distance, but when we approach them we find they are far less insurmountable than we had conceived —Charles Caleb Colton

12. Evils, like poisons, have their uses, and there are diseases which no other remedy can reach —Thomas Paine

13. He's like a fox, grey before he's good —Thomas Fuller

14. Immorality in a house is like a worm in a plant —*Babylonian Talmud*

15. Immoral, like plying an alcoholic with liquor —Anon

16. Obscene as cancer —Wilfred Owens

17. Our sins, like our shadows when day is in its glory, scarce appear; toward evening, how great and monstrous they are! —Sir John Suckling

18. (He is a man of splendid abilities, but utterly corrupt. He shines and stinks like rotten mackerel by moonlight —John Randolph

19. Sin is a sort of bog; the farther you go in the more swampy it gets — Maxim Gorky

20. Sins black as night —Robert Lowell

21. So awful [a crime] it was like an atrocity picture or one of Foxe's lives of the martyrs —Jonathan Valin

22. (You're) soft and slimy . . . like an octopus. Like a quagmire —Jean-Paul Sartre

23. Vice is like a skunk that smells awfully rank, when stirred up by the pole of misfortune —Bartlett's *Dictionary of Americanisms*

24. Vice, like virtue, grows in small steps —Jean Racine

25. Vice repeated is like the wandering wind, Blows dust in others' eyes, to spread itself —William Shakespeare

26.   Wrong as stealing from the poor box —Anon

EXACTNESS
See: CORRECTNESS

EXAMINATION
See: SCRUTINY

EXCITEMENT
See Also: AGITATION, ENERGY, ENTHUSIASM

1.   The blood burning in all his veins, like fire in all the branches and twigs of him —D. H. Lawrence

2.   The blood surged through me like a sea —R. Wright Campbell

3.   Drunk on your own high spirits, like a salesman at a convention — Dorothea Straus

4.   Excited and happy as a bride-to-be —Gloria Norris
     See Also: HAPPINESS

5.   Excited as a cop making his first pinch —H. C. Witwer

6.   Excited as a puppy at a picnic —Nicholas Proffitt

7.   Excited as a starlet, on the arm of an elderly editor —Philip Roth

8.   Excited as schoolchildren on their way to a treat —Frank Tuohy

9.   Excited . . . like a kid with his first dish of ice-cream —Louis Bromfield

10. Excitement caused his heart to thud all over his breast like some crazy and fateful drum —Frank Swinnerton
     See Also: HEARTBEAT

11. Excitement . . . had grown to become an exhausting presence within him, like the constant company of a sleepless troop of revelers —Joseph Whitehill

12. Excitement rose like a hot dry wind —Marge Piercy

13. Exhausting and exhilarating . . . it's [tracking Woody Allen's career] like mountain climbing —Vincent Canby, *New York Times,* February 9, 1986

14. Exhilarating like a swim in a rough ocean —Mary Gordon

15. Exhilarating as love —Honoré de Balzac

16. Exhilarating . . . very much like the effects of a strong dose of caffeine —Georges Simenon

17. Felt exhilarated as a young man at a romantic assignation —Louis Auchincloss

18. (Music that) fired her blood like wine —Katherine Mansfield

19. (The hate excited her . . . she was) fired up like a furnace in a blizzard night —Harold Adams

20. Flares up like a match —Sholem Aleichem

21. Flushed and voluble, like football fans on their way back from a match —Aharon Megged

22. Has about as much suspense as a loaf of bread being spread through a slicer —Scott Simon, reporting on a basketball game, "All Things Considered," WNYC, January 31, 1987

23. Her excitement strummed like wire —Marge Piercy

24. Her excitement was deep down like a desert river under the sands — Oliver La Farge

25. Life at "Nightline" [Ted Koppel television program] is like being in a popper of popcorn news —Marshal Frady, June, 1987

26. Responding like an overheated spaniel —Clancy Sigal

27. Stirring as march music —Paige Mitchell

28. Thrilled his sleepless nerves like liquor or women on a Saturday night —John Dos Passos

29. Titillated . . . like naked flesh —Paul Theroux

30. Warmed by what he'd read as if it had been draughts of rum —John Cheever

EXERCISE
See: MOVEMENT, SPORTS

EXHAUSTION
See: WEARINESS

EXITS
See Also: BEGINNINGS/ENDINGS, DISAPPEARANCE, ENTRANCES/EXITS

1. Bustled off . . . like a rolling whirlwind —Yukio Mishima

2. Crept away, after the fashion of a whipped dog —H. E. Bates

3. Fled . . . like damnmd water broken free —Z. Vance Wilson

4. Fled like quicksilver —William Shakespeare

5. Flits like a silky bat out of the room —Rose Tremain

6. Galloping out like a runaway horse —Donald Seaman

7. Go out like a candle, in a snuff —John Ray's *Proverbs*
   A commonly used version found in a short story entitled *The Beldonald Holbein* by Henry James is to "Go out like a snuffed candle."

8. I'm off like a dirty shirt —John Crier speaking in the movie *Pretty in Pink*

9. Jumped out of that house like fleas off a dead dog —Rita Mae Brown

10. Leave the room as a burglar might escape from the scene of a carefully planned crime —James Stern

11. Like a rabbit that had been fired at, bolted from the room —John Galsworthy

12. Like March, having come in like a lion, he purposed to go out (of her life) like a lamb —Charlotte Brontë
    Often a familiar simile gains freshness from the way it is applied, as illustrated by this example from *Shirley.*

13. Made like an arrow for the door —Christopher Isherwood

14. Made tracks like a jumped fawn —Thomas Zigal

15. Running away like sheep —Stephen Vincent Benét

16. Scuttled away as if he'd found a maggot in his meatball —Joseph Wambaugh

17. Slide away like a whisper down the wind —Richard Ford

18. Spook like cattle on a drive —Clinton A. Phillips, dean of faculty at Texas A & M University, quoted on departure of some academics for better opportunities, *New York Times,* December 21, 1986

19. Stumping to the door . . . like an ancient mariner who had lost his temper —Frank Swinnerton

20. Took off like a big-assed bird —American colloquialism
    Another expression spread by the American army.

21. Took off like a goosed duck —Harold Adams

22. Took off like a scalded cat —May Swenson

23. Turned and left, like a key from a lock —Desmond O'Grady

EXPANSION
See: GROWTH

EXPECTATION
See: ANTICIPATION, HOPE

EXPENSIVENESS
See: COST

EXPERIENCE
See Also: KNOWLEDGE

1. Experience is . . . a kind of huge spider-web of the finest silken threads suspended in the chamber of consciousness, and catching every air-borne particle in its tissue —Henry James

2. Experience is like medicine; some persons require larger doses of it than others, and do not like to take it pure, but a little disguised and better adapted to taste —Lord Acton

3. Experience, like a pale musician, holds a dulcimer of patience in his hand —Elizabeth Barrett Browning

4. Experience seems to be like the shining of a bright lantern. It suddenly makes clear in the mind what was already there, perhaps, but dim — Walter De La Mare

5. A new element in her experience; like a chapter in a book —Henry Van Dyke

6. The solitary and unshared experience dies of itself like the violations of love —Archibald MacLeish

7. To most men, experience is like the stern light of a ship, which illumines only the track it has passed —Samuel Taylor Coleridge

EXPLOSION
See: BURST, SUDDENNESS

EYE(S)
See Also: EYES; BRIGHT; EYEBROWS; EYE COLOR; EYE EXPRESSIONS, MISCELLANEOUS; EYELASHES; EYELIDS; EYE MOVEMENTS

1. Behind the glasses his eyes looked look like little bicycle wheels at dizzy speed —William Faulkner

2. Dull eyes set like pebbles in a puffy, unwholesome-looking face —Eric Ambler
   Eye/pebble comparisons abound, with examples throughout this section.

3. Eye-sockets deep as those of a death's head —Thomas Hardy

4. Eye-sockets . . . like dark caves —John Wainwright

5. Eyeballs like shelled hard-boiled eggs —Ivan Bunin

6. Eyes as big and as soft and as transparent as ripe gooseberries —Edna O'Brien

7. Eyes . . . as cloudy as poisoned oysters —Miles Gibson

8. Eyes . . . big and shiny, black as oil —Shirley Ann Grau

9. Eyes blackly circled like those of a raccoon —Lael Tucker Wertenbaker

10. Eyes . . . carefully painted like the eyes on Egyptian frescoes —Anaïs Nin, *Chicago Review,* Winter-Spring, 1962

11. Eyes . . . deep and dark like mountain nights —Mary Hedin

12. Eyes . . . deep as a well —Walter Savage Landor
13. Eyes flat as glass —James Lee Burke
14. Eyes . . . flat gold, like a lemur's —Sue Grafton
15. Eyes glazed and almost lightless like the little button eyes of a doll —George Garrett
16. Eyes . . . large and gray, and baleful, like glass on fire —Norman Mailer
17. Eyes large as fifty-cent pieces, but pale, like dusty stones —Ludwig Bemelmans
    Bemelmans' subject is William Randolph Hearst.
18. Eyes . . . large as saucers —E. N. Slocum, line from lyric of a song written in 1868 entitled "On the Beach at Cape May"
19. Eyes like a codfish —Frank Swinnerton
20. Eyes like a couple of wells —William Diehl
21. Eyes . . . like an Arizona sunset, and they were supported on pouches as large and shapeless as badly packed duffle bags —Jimmy Sangster
22. Eyes like a pinwheel —Ann Beattie
23. Eyes . . . like a spaniel's —Ouida
24. Eyes like a starless winter night—clear, black, bleak —A. E. Maxwell
25. Eyes . . . like chestnuts floating on twin pools of milk —William Styron
26. Eyes like cold cavities in his head —Natascha Wodin
27. Eyes . . . like crickets in daylight —Rochelle Ratner
28. Eyes like crosses burning on a lawn —Rochelle Ratner
29. Eyes like currants in a half-cooked suet pudding —Robert Graves
    A simple variation from a short story by Katherine Mansfield: "Little eyes, like currants."
30. Eyes like dark searchlights —Ross Macdonald
31. Eyes like dusty lapis lazuli —S. J. Perelman
32. Eyes like forest pools —W. Somerset Maugham
33. Eyes . . . like forget-me-nots —Mazo De La Roche
34. Eyes . . . like ground owls, deep in their burrows —Harold Adams
35. Eyes like holes burned with a cigar —William Faulkner
36. Eyes . . . like holes were poked in a snowbank —Raymond Chandler
37. Eyes like jelly —Hanoch Bartov
38. Eyes like licked stones —Virginia Woolf
39. Eyes like licorice gumdrops —Robert Campbell
40. Eyes . . . like lustrous black currants —Frank Swinnerton
41. Eyes, like marigolds, had sheathed their light —William Shakespeare

In Shakespeare's time 'sheathed' was written as 'sheath'd.'

42. Eyes like mice peeking into my pockets —Robert Campbell

43. Eyes like oiled black olives —Frank Tuohy

44. Eyes . . . like old pictures of Rachmaninoff's eyes —Henry Van Dyke

45. Eyes like onions —Donald Barthelme

46. Eyes . . . like pale marble in a field of red —Linda West Eckhardt

47. Eyes . . . like peas —T. Coraghessan Boyle

48. Eyes . . . like pebbles at the bottom of a mountain trout pool, fixed and icy —Donald MacKenzie

49. Eyes like pebbles, the kind of pebbles which kids call aggies —Ludwig Bemelmans

50. Eyes like pebbles unwashed by the sea —Kathleen Farrell

51. Eyes . . . like pools of oil —T. Coraghessan Boyle

52. Eyes . . . like punctuation marks —Geoffrey Wolff

53. Eyes . . . like rubber knobs, like they'd give to the touch —William Faulkner

54. Eyes like searchlights —Donald McCaig

55. Eyes..like shrewd marbles —Harvey Swados

56. Eyes like the brown waters of a woodland stream —Henry Van Dyke

57. Eyes like the deep, blue boundless heaven —Percy Bysshe Shelley

58. (Watery gray) eyes, like the thick edges of broken skylight glass —Willa Cather

59. Eyes . . . like those of a lobster, as if they were on stalks —William James, letter from Germany to sister Alice, January 9, 1868

60. Eyes . . . like tiny stone wedges hammer between the lids —Ross Macdonald

61. Eyes like tunnels —Arthur Miller

62. Eyes like twin daisies in a bucket of blood —Leonard Washborn, *Inter-Ocean,* Chicago newspaper, 1880s

63. Eyes . . . like two black seeds —Dashiell Hammett

64. Eyes . . . like two holes burned in a blanket —Borden Deal

65. Eyes . . . like two obeisant satellites —Cynthia Ozick

66. Eyes . . . like two pissholes in the snow —American colloquialism

67. Eyes . . . like violets by a river of pure water —Oscar Wilde

68. Eyes like washed pebbles stuck in cement (gave him a slightly aggressive look) —Donald MacKenzie

69. Eyes like white clay marbles —Randall Jarrell

70. Eyes limpid and still like pools of water —Robert Louis Stevenson

71. Eyes . . . like glass marbles —Herman Wouk
72. Eye sockets..as flat as saucers —Z. Vance Wilson
73. Eyes peering between folds of fat like almond kernels in half-split shells —Edith Wharton
74. Eyes pressed so deep in his head that they seemed . . . like billiard balls sunk in their pockets —William Styron
75. Eyes, restless, softly brown like a monkey's —F. van Wyck Mason
76. Eyes . . . round and shiny, like the glass-bead eyes of stuffed animals —Margaret Atwood
77. Eyes, round as cherries —Ignazio Silone
78. Eyes . . . round as quarters —Laurie Colwin
79. Eyes . . . round, inane as the blue pebbles of the rain —Dame Edith Sitwell
80. Eyes shaped like peach pits —Bobbie Ann Mason
81. Eyes . . . shiny and flat as mirrors —Shirley Ann Grau
82. Eyes . . . small and dark and liquid, like drops of strong coffee — Margaret Millar
83. Eyes . . . small and nacreous like painted ornaments —Jean Stafford
84. Eyes . . . small and dirty like the eyes of a potato —Ross Macdonald
85. Eyes . . . small and hard and shiny like dimes —Ross Macdonald
86. Eyes soft as a leading lady's, round as a doe's —T. Coraghessan Boyle
87. Eyes, speckled and hard as pebbles at the bottom of a stream —John Yount
88. Eyes spoked and rimmed with black, like a mourner's rosette —Edith Pearlman
    The simile is particularly appropriate as the writer is describing a character who is a widow.
89. Eyes that looked like imitation jewels —Henry James
90. Eyes the size of melons —Mary Hood
91. Eyes were small, so that with the mascara and the shadows painted on their lids they looked like flopping black butterflies —Eudora Welty
92. Her eyes looked awful [from too much liquor] as though they had been boiled —Christopher Isherwood
93. Her eyes lost in the fatty ridges of her face, looked like two small pieces of coal pressed into a lump of dough —William Faulkner
94. His eyes behind his glasses kind of all run together like broken eggs — William Faulkner
95. His eyes stood in his head like two poached eggs —Erich Maria Remarque
96. Large eyes like dark pools —Erich Maria Remarque

97. Little eyes like cigarette-ends —Charles Bukowski

98. Looked like cat's eyes do, like a big cat against the wall, watching us — William Faulkner

99. Lynx-like eyes —O. Henry

100. Our very eyes are sometimes like our judgements, blind —William Shakespeare

101. Protruding eyes that looked like two fish straining to get out of a net of red threads —Flannery O'Connor

102. The pupils of his eyes were like disks of blue fire —Oscar Wilde

103. Round eyes like blue polka dots in her crimson face —Helen Hudson

104. Sharp stains like poor coffee under her eyes —V. S. Pritchett

105. She was wearing so much eyeliner that her eyes looked as if they had been drawn in ink —Jonathan Valin

106. Small eyes, set like a pig's in shallow orbits —Francis Brett Young

107. Their eyes seemed like rings from which the gems had been dropped — Dante Alighieri

108. Two little eyes like gimlet holes —Émile Zola

109. The veins in her eyeballs twisted like a map of jungle rivers —Arthur Miller

EYES, BRIGHT

1. (Stood there . . . his) black eyes burning like anthracite —Stephen Vincent Benét

2. Burning eyes like flaming wells —Anzia Yezierska

3. Eyes as bright as sunlight on a stream —Christina Rossetti

4. Eyes blazed like molten nuggets —Robert Silverberg

5. Eyes like burning torches —*Arabian Nights*

6. Eyes like flashlights —Elizabeth Spencer

7. Eyes as glowing as the summer and as tender as the skies —James Whitcomb Riley

8. Eyes . . . blazed with a sudden burst of terror, like an explosion of the heart —Robert Campbell

9. Eyes blazing like bonfires —Miles Gibson

10. Eyes bright as dance floors —Scott Spencer

11. Eyes bright as squirrels' —John Galsworthy

12. Eyes bright as the lights in a valuable stone —Norman Mailer

13. Eyes fired up for a moment like pieces of coal. The laughter in them [eyes] was like two melting ice cubes gleaming in a dish —Alice Walker

14. Eyes gleam like those of a popular salesman about to hear an old, familiar joke —Hilary Masters

15. Eyes glittered like a wildcat's —Honoré de Balzac

16. Eyes glittered like razors —Jonathan Valin

17. Eyes . . . glittering and unsteady, like a dog's when it is looking out of a car window —Frank Tuohy

18. (His dark) eyes glowed like brandy —Rita Mae Brown

19. Eyes glowed . . . like fire in a cave —Nathaniel Hawthorne

20. Eyes glowed like two tiny electric bulbs —William Faulkner

21. Eyes . . . like black marbles lying in dust, dark and gleaming and sharp, with light —Paul Horgan

22. Eyes like chips of broken glass that catch the light —Joyce Carol Oates

23. Eyes, like cinders, all aglow —Lewis Carroll

24. Eyes like glow-worms —William Shakespeare

25. Eyes [animal] shining like wind-whipped embers on a pitch-black night —Jesse Stuart

26. Eyes shone brighter than the stars —Dante Alighieri

27. Eyes sparkled as if he'd just heard a joke or told one —Jonathan Valin

28. Eyes sparkled like rusty wet bolts —Abraham Rothberg

29. Eyes that could snap and crackle points of fire like those which sparkle from a whirling sword —Jack London

30. Eyes, they glow like tiger's eyes —James Baldwin

31. Eyes which possessed a warm, life-giving quality like the sunlight — Willa Cather

32. Ferocious eyes, much too shiny, like something boiling in a pot — Cynthia Ozick

33. Glittering eyes like rats hurrying this way and that —Louis Bromfield

34. Her eyes gave the impression of being lighted from within . . . as if she had been endowed with her own small sun —Paule Marshall

35. His eyes shone with certainty, like glints of shellac —Paul Theroux

36. The light of her eye, like a star glancing out from the blue of the sky — John Greenleaf Whittier

37. Lights shone in his eyes like travelers' fires seen far out on the river — Eudora Welty

38. Sparks burning in them [black eyes] like fire at the end of a tunnel — Paige Mitchell

EYEBROWS

1. Black eyebrows going up like a pair of swallows —V. S. Pritchett

2. A brow like a thunderclap —Peter DeVries
3. Brows and lashes smudged like charcoal across her face —Kay Boyle
4. Brows like bended bows —Thomas Campion
5. Brows . . . like charcoal arches —Aharon Megged
6. Brows like strung bows —Ruth Prawer Jhabvala
7. Brows were joined above the nose like the hilt of a large dagger —Saul Bellow
8. Dark eyebrows like sudden brushstrokes above the deep dark eyes —Sylvia Berkman
9. (Raising an) eyebrow built like a wooly worm —James Crumley
10. Eyebrows arched like skipping ropes —Henry James
11. Eyebrows as big as mustaches —Jilly Cooper
12. Eyebrows curved like big rainbows above her eyes —J. P. Donleavy
13. Eyebrows drawn so closely together that they seemed like a hedge blocking her view —Carolyn Slaughter
14. Eyebrows lifted in pink crescents upturned like the dogwood's first leaves in spring —Eudora Welty
15. Eyebrows . . . like birds of prey —T. Coraghessan Boyle
16. Eyebrows like commas —John Fowles
17. Eyebrows like frost —James Dickey
18. Eyebrows like hanging gardens —Max Shulman
19. Eyebrows like peaked black thread —Jean Stafford
20. Eyebrows like unclipped hedges —Daphne Merkin
21. Eyebrows looking like a big iron-grey caterpillar lying along the edge of a cliff —William Faulkner
22. Eyebrows overhung his eyes like mustaches —John Steinbeck
23. Eyebrows raised, like hoods on baby-carriages —Eudora Welty
24. Eyebrows rising like fans —Martin Cruz Smith
25. Eyebrows thick and full like fur frames —Paige Mitchell
26. Eyebrows were thick, tough as strips of bark —Truman Capote
27. A great deal of brow in a face is like a great deal of horizon in a view —Victor Hugo
28. His brows . . . brindled with grey and tufted like the pelt of a beast. They looked like structural beams, raised into a position that would support the weight of his knowledge and authority —John Cheever
29. His eyebrows punctuate his speech like hands —Ira Wood
30. Knitted his brows like sharply molded steel —D. H. Lawrence
    The text of *Women in Love,* where this appeared, used the English spelling 'moulded' instead of 'molded.'

31. (When she was excited she liked to) raise first one thin eyebrow and then the other so that they almost leapt off her face like antennae — Molly Giles

32. Thick, black eyebrows like the wings of a swallow —Maxim Gorky

EYE COLOR

See Also: BLACK, BLUE, BROWN, EYE(S), GRAY, GREEN

1. Black eyes like plum pits —Bernard Malamud

2. Black eyes turned shiny like the sun —Shirley Ann Grau

3. Blue eyes like transparent agate marbles, hard and polished and just about indestructible —Sylvia Plath

4. Blue eyes . . . round and open like two lakes —Aharon Megged

5. Blue eyes that sat in his lined face like a piece of sky —Erich Maria Remarque

6. Brown eyes like quicksand —Diane Ackerman

7. Eyes . . . black and burning as coal —Lord Byron
   Byron's "Black as coal" comparison from *Don Juan* has been much used, and with many new twists, several of which can be found here. The "Black as coal" comparison has also been linked with many other descriptive references.

8. Eyes . . . black as bullets and as fierce —Belva Plain

9. Eyes . . . blue and guileless as a doll's —David Brierley

10. Eyes . . . brown and irisless, like those of an old dog —William Faulkner

11. Eyes . . . deepened to the color of caramel, like sugar coming to a boil —Louise Erdrich

12. Eyes faded to a brittle, metallic gray, like chips of slate —James Crumley

13. Eyes . . . light, blue, like colorless water reflecting a blue sky — Jessamyn West
    In the short story, *The Calla Lily Cleaners & Dyers,* from which this is taken, the simile is extended as follows: "And his face being so suntanned they were more like vacancies in his head than eyes."

14. Eyes, like bitter chocolate —Margaret Millar
    A more recent example of this simile appears Ira Wood's novel *The Kitchen Man* which is as chockfull of food imagery as a refrigerator after a weekly shopping trip.

15. Eyes . . . like black buttons or raisins sunk in dough —Nina Bawden

16. Eyes . . . like blue cake-icing —Truman Capote

17. Eyes like blue-painted glass —Flannery O'Connor

18. Eyes like chocolate fudge still warm from the pan —Elizabeth Spencer

19. Eyes like the sky on a misty summer morning —Piers Anthony

20. Eyes . . . like those of a rabbit, not frightened, but utterly impenetrable —Graham Masterton

21. Eyes pale as the moon —Grace Paley

22. Eyes redder than burning coals —Gustave Flaubert

23. Eyes so pale they were like openings on the sky —Wright Morris

24. Eyes the color of water vapor —T. Coraghessan Boyle

25. Eyes . . . they didn't have much color . . . like, whoever was putting the color into them got a phone call in the middle and just quit —Lee Smith

26. Eyes . . . warmly blue as the glint of summer sunshine on an iceberg drifting in Southern seas —O. Henry

27. Gray eyes . . . watery like the winter sky —Frank Tuohy

28. Large, brown eyes like mushroom caps —Helen Hudson
    In her novel, *Meyer Meyer,* Helen Hudson returns to this simile with another: "Her dull mushroom eyes seemed to have grown smaller, as though they had been sautéed too long."

29. Light-blue eyes . . . like bits of glass —Jean Rhys

30. Pale eyes like pools of phlegm —Richard S. Prather

31. Sharp blue eyes, each like a pin —Robert Browning

32. Small green eyes, like grapes about to burst —Mary McCarthy

33. Soft brown eyes, like those of a mild-tempered dog —Frank Swinnerton

34. Toffee-colored eyes like a spaniel's —T. H. White

35. Wet blue eyes, like eyes in a clear aspic —Jonathan Valin

EYE EXPRESSIONS, MISCELLANEOUS

1. Excitement widened her eyes like periods at the end of billboard sentences —Tom Robbins

2. Expressionless blue eyes . . . like a pair of glass marbles —Frank Swinnerton

3. Eyes . . . alive, like blue tigers —Cynthia Ozick

4. Eyes . . . as cold and lacking in interest as the eyes of a tortoise —Nadine Gordimer

5. Eyes as dead as stale oysters —Raymond Chandler

6. Eyes as deep and storyless as the sea —Terry Bisson

7. Eyes as doleful and red-rimmed as an old hound's —Robert Traver

8. Eyes, as hard and cold as a frozen lake —Ellen Glasgow

9. Eyes . . . as innocent as if they had entered their sockets a half-hour ago —Ben Hecht

10. Eyes . . . as opaque as jelly beans —Joan Hess

11. Eyes . . . as shy as a wild stag's —Mary Lee Settle

12. Eyes, bland and sad as a dog's —George Garrett

13. Eyes . . . blank, clouded with anger or grief, like the sky before a snowstorm —James Crumley

14. Eyes blind as woodknots —Daniel Berrigan

15. Eyes clear and cool as rainwater —George Garrett

16. Eyes clear and candid as a winter sky at dawn —Harvey Swados

17. Eyes clear as water —John Steinbeck

18. Eyes clear as window glass —Ward Just

19. Eyes . . . cloudless as a sky in spring —George Garrett

20. Eyes . . . cold as a crocodile's —Peter Benchley

21. Eyes cold as grey agate —Margaret Mitchell

22. Eyes cool as coins —Margaret Millar

23. Eyes . . . dark and cold . . . like water under ice —Mary Hedin

24. Eyes . . . dark and empty, like open graves —Donald Seaman

25. Eyes..dead and cold, like marbles swimming in glass —Paige Mitchell

26. Eyes . . . expressionless as ice cubes —Clive Cussler

27. Eyes, fishy and staring like headlights —Harvey Swados

28. (When he is excited or amused . . . his) eyes flare like two cigarette lighters —Bryan Miller, *New York Times* story about Yves Montand, June 24, 1987

29. Eyes flat and vicious like the eyes of a mean dog crouched over a bone —George Garrett

30. Eyes frightened as if she expected any moment the stunning blow of a fist —George Garrett

31. His eyes glaze over like eggs up —Ira Wood

32. Eyes . . . grow blank as a dropped blind —Edith Wharton

33. Eyes . . . hard as almond shells with a kernel of light —Rumer Godden

34. Eyes hard as buttons —Louise Erdrich

35. (Her inky) eyes have the look of someone who has been in prison a long time and knows they can send her back —Sharon Olds

36. Eyes in which intelligence and comprehension burned like two fixed stars —Edith Wharton

37. Eyes keen as talons —T. Coraghessan Boyle

38. Eyes, like a stern judge's, seemed to pierce the heart of all questions — Honoré de Balzac

39. Eyes like flint-stones —Donald Seaman

40. Eyes like glacier lakes —Donald McCaig

41. Eyes like marbles, hard and glazed —Borden Deal

42. Eyes like needles —Lord Byron

43. Eyes like smoking tragedies —Edna O'Brien

44. Eyes . . . like the eyes in the statues blank and unseeing and serene — William Faulkner

45. Eyes . . . like the eyes of a dying man who looks everywhere for healing —James Baldwin

46. Eyes . . . like the eyes of the dead that noon has closed with love's last kiss —Johann Wolfgang von Goethe

47. (Looked back at him, his black) eyes like two drill bits —Nicholas Proffitt

48. Eyes like two steel spikes —Flannery O'Connor

49. Eyes looked like the prelude to a scream —Raymond Chandler

50. Eyes observant and curious like those of a man caught in a great catastrophe which it is his duty to record —Graham Greene

51. (Lying motionless on his back,) eyes staring up at the ceiling like a doll's —Joseph Heller

52. Eyes . . . steely as a bird's —Jean Garrigue

53. Eyes swollen with rage; they look like hard-cooked eggs —T. Coraghessan Boyle

54. Eyes that looked as if they might warm up at the right time and in the right place —Raymond Chandler

55. Eyes that looked as if they were trying to see beyond the horizon — William McIlvanney

56. Eyes went flat with terror, like a rabbit caught by a car's headlights — Andrew Kaplan

57. Eyes widened with fear, like a cat facing headlights in the night —Z. Vance Wilson

58. Eyes . . . wide open like a deer's —Colette

59. Fury flashing from her eyes like New Year's Eve sparklers —Dorothea Straus

60. Hard eyes . . . like little metal studs (pinned into the white faces of young men) —John Updike

61. His eyes [Mike Wallace's] grew flat as the eyes of a movie Apache who has just taken a rifle bullet to the stomach —Norman Mailer

The Apache comparison underscores Mailer's repeated references to Mike Wallace's resemblance to an Indian.

62. Little eyes lit up like a cat's in a room full of yarn —Thomas Zigal
63. Look in his eyes like a glutted steer in a feedlot —Mary Hood
64. Mischief crackling like static electricity in her eyes —W. P. Kinsella
65. Tired, kindly eyes, like the eyes of a monkey —Elizabeth Bowen
66. Wide amazed eyes like an expensive china doll —George Garrett
67. Wide penetrating eyes, like black raisins —Rex Reed
    The eyes Reed is comparing to black raisins belong to Sophia Loren.

EYELASHES

1. (She was an artist of the face,) drawing her long lashes out like licorice —Jay Parini
2. Eyelashes like the wicks of many extinguished candles —Frank Swinnerton
3. Eyelashes long as shish kebab —Rex Reed
   The owner of the long lashes is Carol Channing.
4. Eyelashes . . . long, like flies' legs —Aharon Megged
5. Eyelashes stiff as bird-tails —Eudora Welty
6. Eyelashes . . . thick and furry as tarantula legs —James Crumley
7. [Eyes] lash-fringed like Spanish lace —Davis Grubb
8. Lashes as thick and dark as raven feathers —Jonathan Kellerman
9. Lashes bunched together like star points —Jill Ciment
10. Lashes thick and black as if painted with a black tar-like material —Joyce Carol Oates
11. Long lashes fluttered like the feelers of a beetle on its back —Truman Capote
    The lashes thus described belong to Mae West.
12. Thick lashes, soft as paintbrushes —Louise Erdrich

EYELIDS

1. Eyelids drooped as though the lashes weighed intolerably —Truman Capote
2. Eyelids fluttering, as if assailed by gnats —Leonard Michaels
3. Eyelids heavy as if from too much dreaming. His dreaming lay like the edges of a deep slumber on the rim of his eyelids —Anaïs Nin
4. Eyelids . . . hung askew over her cloudy gray eyes [too weak to be raised or lowered] like broken blinds in the windows of a condemned house —Gerald Kersh

5. Eyelids like thin gray leather —Ken Kesey
6. Eyelids pale like a chicken's —V. S. Pritchett
7. Eyelids translucent as crepe —Jayne Anne Phillips
8. Eyelids which looked like walnut shells —Julia O'Faolain
9. Eyes . . . double-lidded like the eyes of the black bull snake —Will Weaver
10. Heavy eyelids . . . like small, brown, wrinkled egg-shells —Brian Glanville
11. Lids . . . like furrows in deeply plowed soil —Anon
12. Lower lids as straight as ruler-edges —Dashiell Hammett
13. Eyelids flutter like butterflies that children have impaled alive on pins —Erich Maria Remarque
14. The thick red-lined lids hung over the eyeballs like blinds of which the cords are broken —Edith Wharton

EYE MOVEMENTS

1. Blinked . . . as if chasing a fly away —Aharon Megged
2. Blinking like a frightened cat —Dan Wakefield
3. Blinking like a mechanical toy —Peter Benchley
4. Eyeballs bulged like a lizard's —Paige Mitchell
5. Eyes . . . beginning to bob like fishing corks on the sea —William Diehl
6. Eyes bounce like marbles —Norman Mailer
7. Eyes closed, almost as if he was silently praying —John Fowles
8. Eyes darting like astonished fish —Brian Glanville
9. Eyes dart like a shoplifter's —Hilma Wolitzer
10. Eyes dart like swallows —Marge Piercy
11. Eyes did a dance like two flies looking for a place to light —Robert Campbell
12. (He nodded his head, but his) eyes didn't move, as if they were weighted in their sockets like the eyes of a doll —Jonathan Valin
13. Eyes dilated like an animal's caught in a trap —V. S. Pritchett
14. Eyes dilate like targets on a rifle range, and each word and gesture is emphasized by a blast of cigarette smoke that makes her look like she's walking in a cumulous cloud —Rex Reed
    The actress thus profiled by Reed is Bette Davis.
15. Eyes flashed and twinkled . . . like the lamps of a lighthouse — Anthony Powell
16. Eyes flashing like magnifying glasses —H. E. Bates

17. Eyes flickered like uncertain lights —Ann Rice

18. Eyes flicker like leaves —Marge Piercy

19. Eyes fluttered around the room like moths —Donald McCaig

20. Eyes hovered about like mosquitoes —C. J. Koch

21. (Yonatan's) eyes narrowed like gunslits —Amos Oz

22. (Schwend's hurt) eyes opened like blooming peonies —Herbert Lieberman

23. Eyes opened like windows —Sharon Sheehe Stark

24. Eyes . . . opened wide like a clairvoyant's —Anaïs Nin

25. Eyes roamed about like jellyfish —H. E. Bates

26. Eyes rolled in their sockets like loose marbles —Truman Capote

27. Eyes seemed to be clambering frantically, like a pair of blatant prisoners behind her heavy glasses —V. S. Pritchett

28. (His little) eyes snapped like two sparks. Like two sparks they glowed in the smoulder of his bearded face —Katherine Mansfield
    In this example from her short story, *Ole Underwood,* Katherine Mansfield demonstrates the effectiveness of repeating a simile.

29. Eyes that kept winking and twinkling at each side of his inquisitive nose, as if they were playing a perpetual game of peep-bo with that feature —Charles Dickens

30. Eyes . . . twirling around like fruit-flies —Jane Wagner

31. Eyes were closed like a man in violent prayer —William Styron

32. Furtive little eyes kept darting around in his head like rodents — Thomas Wolfe

33. Languidly half closes his eyes, like a cat on a sofa —Anton Chekhov

34. Lowered her eyes like a nun beholding a statue —Honoré de Balzac

35. Narrowing his eyes like someone who knows there's a mouse in the soup —Peter Meinke

36. Rapidly blinking eyes, as though he were caught in a constant sandstorm —Daphne Merkin

37. Rolled his eyes like a pair of gambler's dice —Paige Mitchell

38. Tightly shutting her eyes like a shot pheasant falling out of the sky — Kenzaburo Oë

39. Wide-spaced eyes floating like sea-slivers above his cheek bones —Julia O'Faolain

FACE(S)

See Also: BLUSHES; CHEEKS; EYE(S); EYEBROWS; EYELASHES; EYELIDS; FACIAL EXPRESSION, MISCELLANEOUS; FACIAL DETAILS; HAIR; LIPS; MOUTH; MUSTACHES; PHYSICAL APPEARANCE; SKIN; WRINKLES

1. A beautiful face . . . cut as clear and sharp as a cameo —Jack London

2. Angular face, sharp as the face of the knave in a deck —George Garrett

3. A bulky white face like that of a Mother Superior —Frank Swinnerton

4. The countenance is the title page which heralds the contents of the human volume, but like other title pages it sometimes puzzles, often misleads, and often says nothing to the purpose —William Matthews

5. A desolate, cratered face, sooty with care like an abandoned mining town —Joseph Heller

6. A dry energetic face which seemed to press forward with the spring of his prominent features, as though it were the weapon with which he cleared his way through the world —Edith Wharton

7. Face . . . as broad and plain as a tin pie pan —Jean Thompson

8. A face as creased and limited as her conversation —Hortense Calisher

9. Face . . . as creased and brown as a walnut —Margaret Millar

10. Face . . . bunched up like a fist —Jonathan Valin

11. Face . . . changeable as an autumn sky —John O'Connor

12. Face . . . clean as a china plate —Dorothy Canfield Fisher

13. Face clear as a cloud —Arthur A. Cohen

14. Face crumpled as if it had been left out in the rain —Lael Tucker Wertenbaker

15. Face . . . doughy, like a fresh baking of bread just put out to rise —Paul J. Wellman

16. Face . . . dry and immobile, like a mummy's —Ignazio Silone

17. Face . . . has the compressed appearance, as though someone had squeezed his head in a vise —Woolcott Gibbs, about Thomas Dewey 1940 campaign

18. Face . . . heavy as a sack —Honoré de Balzac

19. Face . . . heavy, as if little bags of sand had been painlessly sewn into various parts of it, dragging the features away from the bones —Kingsley Amis

20. A face in many planes, as if the carver had whittled and modelled and indented to see how far he could go —Willa Cather

21. Face is like the Milky Way in the sky —Sir John Suckling

22. Face . . . its beauty fortuitous like that of a Puritan woman leaning over the washtub —Walker Percy

23. Face lean as a hatchet —William Beechcroft
24. Face like a pie . . . out of the oven too soon —William Faulkner
25. A face like a 16-oz. boxing glove —Harry Prince
26. Face . . . like a badly packed suitcase —Jimmy Sangster
27. Face like a bad orange —Joyce Cary
28. Face..like a beaked bird —James Joyce
29. Face like a benediction —Miguel de Cervantes
30. Face like a butcher's block —Frank O'Connor
31. Face . . . like a fiddle and everyone who sees him must love him — Anon Irish saying
    Carl Sandburg who had a penchant for incorporating familiar similes into his work, quoted this in his poem, *New Hampshire Again.*
32. (A pale flat woman with a) face like a fillet of flounder —Helen Hudson
33. Face like a knotty whorl in the bark of a hoary olive tree —Amos Oz
34. Face . . . like a mail-order ax —William H. Gass
35. A face like a Mediterranean Lolita —Carol Ascher
36. Face like an anemic cat's —Colette
37. Face like an old purse —Mary Hedin
38. (A little brown monkey of a man with) a face like a nut —Ruth Rendell
39. Face like a peeled beet —Hanoch Bartov
40. Face like a picture of a knight, like one of that Round Table bunch —O. Henry
41. Face . . . like a piece of the out-of-doors come indoors: as hollyberries do —D. H. Lawrence
42. Face . . . like a pillow that has been much but badly slept on — Romain Gary
43. Face . . . like a predatory bird, beaked, grim-lipped —Wallace Stegner
44. Face like a raisin cookie. Eyes set wide apart and shallow —Donald McCaig
45. A face like a rock —Thomas Carlyle
    Carlyle thus described his publisher, Frederic Henry Hedge.
46. Face like a sack of flour —T. Coraghessan Boyle
47. Face like a sallow bust on a bracket in a university library —Edith Wharton
48. Face like a shell —Ellen Gilchrist
49. Face like a slab of corned beef —Oakley Hall
50. Face like a small pale mask —William Faulkner

51. Face like a sodden pie —Edgar Lee Masters
52. A face like a very expensive cat —Josephine Tey
53. Face like a very ripe peach —Christopher Isherwood
54. Face like lean old glove leather —Richard Ford
55. Face . . . like the cement in an old cellar, rough irregular lines lying thick and lumpy along a hard white surface —Charles Johnson
56. Face like the soul's awakening —P. G. Wodehouse
57. Her big powdered face was set like an egg in a cup in the frilly high-necked blouse —John Dos Passos
58. (He had) a face like the statue of some Victorian industrialist, heavy and firm and deeply lined, giving an impression of stern willingness —John Braine
59. A face like Walt Disney's idea of a grandfather —William McIlvanney
60. Face like warm baked clay —C. J. Koch
61. Face looked like a white blown-out paper bag —V. S. Pritchett
62. Face . . . massive as a piece of sculpture —Harvey Swados
63. Face ravaged as the dimmest memories of the past . . . creased and flabby, like an old bag —Kingsley Amis
64. Face red, swollen, like an overripe fruit —Graham Swift
65. Face sagged, as if its fleshy sub-structure had dried up —McKinlay Kantor
66. Faces bunched like fists —Irving Feldman
67. Faces harder than a rock —*The Holy Bible/Jeremiah*
68. Face shimmering and flat as the moon —Diane Wakoski
69. Face . . . shines in the darkness like a thin moon —Erich Maria Remarque
70. Face short and blunt as a cat's —M. J. Farrell
71. Faces like dark boxes of secrets and desires . . . locked safely, like old-fashioned caskets for the safe conduct of jewels on a voyage —Eudora Welty
72. (Young neat unscratched boys with) faces like the bottoms of new saucers —Charles Bukowski
73. Face like flint —*The Holy Bible/Isaiah*
74. Face smooth and intent like a man listening to music —Ross Macdonald
75. Face smooth and timeless as a portrait in a darkened gallery —T. Coraghessan Boyle
76. Face . . . smooth, calculated, and precision-made, like an expensive baby doll —Ken Kesey

77. Face . . . smooth like a balmy sky where there's peace —Helga Sandburg

78. Face . . . soft and withered as an apple doll —Sue Grafton

79. Face so grimed with dirt it looked like a brown leather mask —John Dos Passos

80. Face . . . so old that it looked as if the flesh had been polished away —Ellen Glasgow

81. Face sparkles like a diamond (at mention of favorite topic-collecting) — Honoré de Balzac

82. Faces ruddy and wrinkled like old apples —Margaret Bhatty

83. Faces shimmered like they were coming out of water —Jayne Anne Phillips

84. Face . . . strong, like Greek statuary —Sue Grafton

85. Faces were like the faces of lions —*The Holy Bible/Kings*

86. A face that looked as if it had been left out on the fire escape for over half a century —Rex Stout

87. A face that resembled a diseased cauliflower —Miles Gibson

88. A face that seemed sometimes as intimidating as a clenched fist — Frank Tuohy

89. Face thin as a desert saint's —Z. Vance Wilson

90. Face thrust forward like a hatchet —Oakley Hall

91. Face twitched like a snapping rubber band —James Lee Burke

92. (The old woman's) face was like a worn rock at which all the waves of life had smashed and beaten —Thomas Wolfe

93. Face was very like a crow —Lewis Carroll

94. Face . . . wizened as an old potato —Ignazio Silone

95. (One day his) face would collapse, like that of a beautiful woman who suddenly abandons the pretense and concedes defeat —Harvey Swados

96. Face . . . wound up like a spring —Alan Sillitoe

97. Features . . . a little like a Roman emperor side-face —A. A. Milne

98. Features . . . a little like a Roman emperor side-face —A. A. Milne

99. Features . . . dark and indistinct, as if they'd been rubbed with a dirty eraser —Alice McDermott

100. A flat face like an imprint in some thick, warm tar —Robie Macauley

101. Flat white face, like a pillow with eyes —Richard Connell

102. Front face she was shapeless like poorly impressed sealing-wax —Julia O'Faolain

103. Her face had filled out into two little puffs of vanity on either side of her mouth, as if she were eating or were containing a yawn —V. S. Pritchett

104. Her face had rounded with flesh that closed in about her eyes like a dough doll's —Will Weaver

105. Her face, pinched from the cold, made her look like a young girl in the Depression of the thirties —Penelope Gilliatt

106. Her face was like an old brown bowl —Thomas Wolfe

107. His countenance was like the countenance of an angel of God, very terrible —*The Holy Bible/Judges*

108. His face was as . . . the sun —*The Holy Bible/Revelation*

109. His face, with its thick crude lines . . . and large mouth, gave him the appearance of a slightly refined monkey —H. E. Bates

110. His unkempt face hung like a bad smell over his dirty clothes —James Crumley

111. Intense aquiline profile, like the prow of a boat straining forward from too close a fastening —Ruth Suckow

112. Looked like a miniature beside a portrait in oils —Honoré de Balzac

113. Old slightly wizened face, like minor characters in novels of whom one is told that 'they might have been any age from 20 to 50' —Edward Marsh

114. A profile like a bread knife —Harvey Swados

115. A profile like a set of keys and a nose like a bicycle seat —Joey Adams

116. Profile . . . like the blade of a knife, cold and sharp —Honoré de Balzac

117. A round coarse face like a pomegranate —Frank Swinnerton

118. Round red face shone like freshly washed china —Katherine Mansfield

119. A sly, pointed face with something vixen in it, the look of a child evacuee who had lost his parents and grown up too fast —Penelope Gilliatt

120. They had long tired faces. Their yawns, snapping and unsnapping their jaws, made them look like horses —Boris Pasternak

121. A thin face, pointed as a paper knife —Helen Hudson
     The man thus described in Hudson's story, *The Tenant,* is trying to pry information out of a troubled woman. The author built upon the paper knife comparison by adding "Ready to slit her open."

122. Weather beaten face, like it was smoked and cured —George Garrett

123. Wild faces like men hopped up on dope —George Garrett

FACIAL COLOR

See Also: BLUSHES, COLOR, PALLOR, RED, WHITE

1. A face like a raw steak —John Dos Passos

2.   An extremely florid face, as if his blood pressure was about to pop — Peter Meinke

3.   A bluish pallor had spread like a shadow over his face —Walter De La Mare

4.   Carried a ruddy stain on either cheek, like a ripe apple —Robert Louis Stevenson

5.   Cheeks and bunchy lips as red as they would have been if she had fallen into a pot of jam —Frank Swinnerton

6.   Coloring as natural as a bird's egg or a leaf —Frank Tuohy

7.   Coloring . . . so like the bloom of a ripe fruit, that nature in her seemed to have rivalled art —Italo Svevo

8.   The color spread across his face like a bush fire —Mike Fredman

9.   Face . . . a curious, flat color, like the inside of a raw potato —Susan Hill

10. A face as white and almost as smooth as a bar of soap —Scott Spencer

11. Face dark with furious blood, dark as a plum —Guy Vanderhaeghe
     A variation by Gloria Norris: "Face . . . turned purple as a plum."

12. Face . . . dull red, as if baked by the heat of blazing towns —Stephen French Whitman

13. Face glows, spotty, like there's a tiny pink bulb burning behind each cheek —Sharon Sheehe Stark

14. (Marley's) face . . . had a dismal light about it, like a bad lobster in a dark cellar —Charles Dickens

15. Face like a lobster —Robert Louis Stevenson

16. Face like a raw side of beef —Robert Campbell

17. Face . . . like a strawberry —Mary Hedin
     In Hedin's short story, *The Secret,* the woman with the strawberry-like face had been bending over a stove.

18. (Passion has made his) face like pale ivory —Oscar Wilde

19. Face pale and lined like a map —Hugh Walpole

20. Face . . . pale as death and far more ghastly —Nathaniel Hawthorne

21. A face . . . puffy and sallow, the color of old piano keys —William Boyd
     In the novel, *An Ice-Cream War,* the author continues as follows: "As if he were just recovering from an illness or about to be seriously afflicted by one."

22. Face..red as a parrot's —Dame Edith Sitwell

23. Face . . . ruddy, flushed with blood, like a slaughterer's —Isaac Bashevis Singer

24. Face shone red as a cock's comb —Rita Mae Brown
25. Faces red as steak —Sharon Olds
26. Faces stained by the cool night like wine —Dame Edith Sitwell
27. Faces white like paste —Hugh Walpole
28. Face the color and texture of kangaroo hide —Frank Ross
29. Face . . . the color of cat's meat —James Thurber
30. Face turned to a dull white, like bread dough —Anon
31. Face went gray, like the mortar in the trough —Henry Van Dyke
32. Face yellow like ancient paper —Arthur A. Cohen
33. Great blushing face, like a Dutch cheese —Jilly Cooper
34. Her color had been pared away, like you pare an apple —Donald McCaig
35. Her color was high, as though she had been sitting near a fire —Geoffrey Wolff
36. Her face was . . . white-powdered like a marshmallow —Frank Tuohy
37. A medium dark face, like antique gold under a black light —Loren D. Estleman
38. Tanned as a hound's tooth —Robert Traver
39. Two spots of rouge like paper discs pasted on her cheekbones —William Faulkner
40. Unnaturally red cheeks like varnished apples —Edith Wharton

FACIAL DETAILS

1. A blemish on the ridge of his nose stood out like a connecting point between his eyebrows, like a town on a map —Bobbie Ann Mason
2. Blues under his eyes like chain links —Saul Bellow
3. The bones on his face stuck out like knobs under his skin —Gloria Norris
4. Busted blood vessels in the nose and across his cheeks look like a precinct map of the city —Robert Campbell
5. The dimple in her chin is like a tiny keyhole —Joan Chase
6. Dimples that looked as if they had been poked into her cheeks by a mischievous finger —Rex Beach
7. Ears as sharp as a fox —MacDonald Harris
   A commonly used variation: "Ears like a fox."
8. Ears like bat's wings —Aharon Megged
9. Ears like jug handles —Borden Deal
10. Ears like pointed spears —David Ignatow

11. Ears . . . pendulous scarlet ears that showed up like blobs of sealing wax on the pallor of his cheeks and were framed in wisps of silky white hair —Albert Camus

12. Ears sticking out like tabs he might be picked up and shaken by —Eudora Welty

13. (Large) ears . . . stuck out like wings —Leo Tolstoy

14. Freckled, as if she'd been sprinkled with nutmeg —Eudora Welty

15. (A mask of) freckles laid like a veil across his nose —Ben Ames Williams

16. Freckles like rust spots —Willa Cather

17. Freckles like specks of nutmeg on his cheeks —Sharon Olds

18. (Nose bridged with) freckles like splotches of huge summer rain on the sidewalk —William Faulkner

19. Freckles lingered just below the skin, like a thin wash of gold —Elizabeth Spencer

20. A gash as thick as a cigarette —T. Glen Coughlin

21. His nose was very short, just like a baby's, and he had a long blue upper lip, like a priest —Joyce Cary
    See Also: NOSES

22. A mole like a tiny cameo —Eudora Welty

23. (She brushed at the) mole that spotted her cheek like a tear —Truman Capote

24. Pimples big as candy corn —Ira Wood

25. Pimples . . . shone like the sun trying to come out —Sharon Sheehe Stark

26. Red pimples spread across her forehead like strawberry jam —Alice McDermott
    See Also: FOREHEAD

27. Scars . . . like claw marks —Louise Erdrich

28. A scar . . . that twained his face from forehead to chin, like a portrait sliced in half —Davis Grubb

29. Scratches on his face like a cat had fought him hard for every one of its lives —O. Henry

30. The shadows under my eyes were like a pair of leathery wings —Jean Thompson

FACIAL EXPRESSIONS, BLANK
See Also: EYE EXPRESSIONS, MISCELLANEOUS

1. Anonymous, like the faces one sees in a football crowd —Robert Traver

2. (Her face went as) blank as a chalkboard —Jonathan Valin

3. (The child's expression was) blank, as if her hair was drawn back and fastened so tightly that her facial muscles couldn't function —Margaret Millar

4. Countenance . . . like a still, dark day, equally beamless and breezeless —Charlotte Brontë

5. Empty look . . . like an actor without a part —John Le Carré

6. Expressionless as a smoked herring —Anon

7. Expressionless . . . like a portrait of a great beauty by a not very great painter who had caught all the listed features, but not the living stir of loveliness —Elizabeth Taylor

8. Face . . . cold and motionless, as of a man who is asleep —Mikhaïl P. Arzybashev

9. Face . . . as blank as a target after a militia shooting-match —Mark Twain

10. Face . . . as inanimate as a mask —Ellen Glasgow

11. Face as inscrutable as that of a snapping turtle —Arthur Train

12. A face as vacant as an untenanted house —Marcel Proust

13. Face, empty like that of a doll —Franz Werfel

14. Face had all the warmth, personality and individualism of an amoeba —Robert J. Serling

15. Face like a marble mask in which the lips were too rigid for speech —Edith Wharton

16. Face like one of those Easter Island stone carvings —Len Deighton

17. Face . . . locked like a vault —T. Coraghessan Boyle

18. Face set in a fixed expression of friendly interest like a mask pulled over her skull —Frank Conroy

19. Face set into a stiff mask, like that of an acroterian —John Fowles

20. Faces that were as closed, as mysterious, and as mute as the faces of the dead who are possessed of a knowledge beyond the comprehension of the living —Joseph Conrad

21. Hardly ever smiling, with no cracks showing so no one could look in . . . like an empty plate —Helen Hudson

22. Hopelessly blank, like the face of a blind man —Joseph Conrad

23. It [face] was blank, as though she no longer dwelt within her own skull, as though she had gone elsewhere —Margaret Laurence

24. His face was empty and impassive, shut tight as a graveyard gate —Nicholas Proffitt

25. Staring blankly ahead like a man with a fever —Mark Helprin

26. Wooden-faced as a cigar-store Indian —Raymond Chandler

This typifies the simile that outlives the relevancy of the comparison.

FACIAL EXPRESSIONS, MISCELLANEOUS

See Also: EYE EXPRESSIONS, MISCELLANEOUS

1. Always had a ready smile, so that her face with its round rosy cheeks was more like something you could eat or lick; she reminded me of nothing so much as an apple fritter —Edna O'Brien

2. Anger on her cheeks like rouge —Truman Capote

3. Anxiety and annoyance chasing each other like the hands of a clock around his wide, flat face —Helen Hudson

4. Blinked . . . like an owl surprised in daylight and annoyed at this interruption —John Galsworthy

5. Bright, inflamed look, as though she had just been crying or having her cheeks scrubbed by an angry nursegirl —Mary McCarthy

6. Face . . . cold as a cameo —Barbara Howes

7. His countenance was like lightning —*The Holy Bible/Matthew*

8. Expression . . . like a leopard who's just sighted a plump impala —Jilly Cooper

9. Expression like a stork that dropped a baby and broke it and is coming to explain to the parents —Mel Brooks

10. Face was wound up like a spring —Alan Sillitoe

11. Face . . . cold, as though warmth and tenderness were dead in her —Jean Rhys

12. Face . . . as calm as a mask —Ross Macdonald

13. Face . . . as hard as ice —Roberta Allen

14. Face as welcoming as an open fire —William McIlvanney

15. Face becoming creased and flabby, like an old bag, with the strain of making it smile and show interest and speak its permitted few words —Kingsley Amis

16. Face bobbing anxiously like a man bidding at an auction —Derek Lambert

17. Face changed a little . . . as if a headlight had flashed across it —Frank Tuohy

18. Face [of old man] crinkled into a laugh, so that it looked like a polished walnut —Lu Hsün

19. Face crumpled like a sheet of wadded paper —Pat M. Esslinger-Carr

20. Face . . . delicate with fear, as if it might shatter like white china —Paul Theroux

21. Face had clenched like a pale wax-paper mask, into a ball of hate —Louise Erdrich

22. Face had fallen like a waffle —Frank O'Hara

23. Face harmoniously fixed, as if for a camera —Elizabeth Hardwick

24. Face harsh and wrung and savage beneath the springing tears like sweat —William Faulkner

25. Face is still calm, as though she had a cast made and painted to just the look she wanted —Ken Kesey

26. Face laced tight as a shoe —Lorrie Moore

27. (When he came . . . her) face lighted up as if he had been sunshine —William Makepeace Thackeray

28. Face like a buttered scone, dripping complacency —Helen Hudson

29. Face lit up like a sunburst —Max Shulman

30. Face lit with a kind of radiant pain, as if she'd been bitten by a miracle —Sharon Sheehe Stark

31. (Icy anger tucked behind his) face, locked up like a store after hours —Lorrie Moore

32. Face looked all stiff, as if he were afraid the features would fall off —Helen Hudson

33. Face puckered and fierce and jowly and quizzical like a Boston bulldog —George Garrett

34. Face . . . rigid, like the face of a man in the grip of a barely controlled rage —Wallace Stegner

35. (Tiny's) face sagged like an old pillow propped against a headboard —Harold Adams

36. Faces all knotted up like burls on oaks —William Carlos Williams

37. Faces became red and swollen as from an interior fire which flamed out from the clear holes of their eyes —Émile Zola

38. Faces chipped into expressions that never change, like flint arrowheads —Ken Kesey

39. (The sheriff's) face seems to melt like a plate of butter left too close to the fire —George Garrett

40. Face shining like a great sunflower —Aharon Megged

41. Face shone with a bright glow . . . like the terrible glow of a fire on a dark night —Leo Tolstoy

42. Faces . . . lifted up like flowers in a kind of rapt and mournful ecstasy —Thomas Wolfe

43. Face squinched up like a withered apple —Robert B. Parker

44. Faces with the word 'no' stamped like a coat of arms on them —V. S. Pritchett
    The faces Pritchett describes belong to London landladies.

45. Face that looks as overworked as Gary Cooper trying to register an emotion —Wallace Stegner

46. Face twisted like a man who's accidentally swallowed a whole chili pepper —Gloria Norris

47. Face, vague like a shadow —Anatole France
See Also: VAGUENESS

48. Face . . . vigilant as some small cat's —Louise Erdrich

49. Face was set into an expression of intense attention, like a man listening to an important broadcast which might affect his course of action in some way —John Malcolm
See Also: ATTENTION

50. Face went to pieces as if by its own weight —Ross Macdonald

51. Fearful expression . . . like the fear of an animal which has been beaten and kicked for too long —Louis Bromfield

52. Features . . . softening like wax too close to the flame —George Garrett

53. Fierce and variegated countenance, appeared like war personified — Nathaniel Hawthorne
See Also: FEROCITY

54. A gentle, cowlike expression passed over her face like a cloud —Colette

55. Grimaced, like a rubber Kewpie doll being squeezed in all the wrong places —Paige Mitchell

56. The grin left his face and was replaced by the sort of amusement that rings like a coin slapped on a bar —Jonathan Valin

57. Had a face like a requiem —Honoré de Balzac

58. Had an expression on his face as if he were listening for something, so that one felt one couldn't disturb him —Ruth Prawer Jhabvala

59. (Her eyes were still red, but she) had the happy look of a child that has outslept its grief —Edith Wharton

60. Had the mankind-loving look of a convert fresh from church —Harold Adams

61. Hard, red face like a book of rules —Anthony Carson

62. Has a haunted, jumpy look, as if invisible alarm clocks were going off throughout the day, to remind him of undone duties —Christopher Isherwood

63. His fat face opened and smiled like a distorted, gold-toothed flower — John Dickson Carr

64. His mangy little face lit up like a store window going on for the night — Jonathan Valin

65. Like a peddler whose wares have been turned down all day, he waited, with a look of patient expectation —Elizabeth Hardwick

66. Lips went white, like a person who has received a stunning blow without warning and who, in the first moments of shock, does not realize what has happened —Margaret Mitchell
See Also: LIPS

67. (Every time he saw Conrad he) lit up like a fairground with hilarity and self-satisfaction —A. Alvarez

68. A lonely face, pulled in like rain off the wild stretches —Elizabeth Spencer

69. Look as startled as a hare —Joyce Cary

70. Looked smug . . . like a messenger bringing the news of a battle won —John Rechy

71. Looked wistful, like a kid who'd lost the magic penny —Robert Campbell

72. Looking as miserable as sin —Penelope Gilliatt

73. Looking puzzled and dismayed, like a baby who's learned to pull itself up on the sides of a crib, but hasn't figured out how to sit down again —Sue Grafton

74. A look of intense mirth spread over Lily's face like water released suddenly from a broken dam —Louis Bromfield

75. A look of surprise . . . as if he'd just swallowed an ice cube —T. Coraghessan Boyle
See Also: SURPRISE

76. Looks perpetually surprised, but scared and insincere, like a play actor —Jayne Anne Phillips

77. Looks puzzled and grieved, as if he can't believe his bad luck —François Camoin

78. No pity or censure in her face, it was as immovable as a fact —Margaret Millar

79. Official faces . . . like death masks —Ross Macdonald

80. Old emotions, like old scars, savaged his face —Rita Mae Brown

81. One could see thoughts crossing his face like caravans of camels lurching slowly across the seemingly endless Sahara —Delmore Schwartz
See Also: THOUGHT

82. Open-mouthed, like a fish —Anon

83. Pale astonishment in his face as if at a sudden accusation —George Eliot

84. Pleading look, a beg for help like a message from a powerless invaded country to the rest of the world —Lynne Sharon Schwartz

85. Sensuality had been eroded from his face, nibbled away, as the sea nibbles traces of meat from a shell —Julia O'Faolain

86. A set face, sad like a toy soldier's, wooden and clad with honor —Z. Vance Wilson

87. (The other diners were listening with) shocked but rather smirking expressions, like good little boys who were going to hear the bad little boy told off —Jean Rhys

88. The compassionate look of a friendly dog —André Malraux

89. Their faces seemed unusually open, like so many windows —John Cheever
See Also: CANDOR

90. Tiredness and worry chasing one another like clouds across her face — Susan Hill

91. A tremor, as quick and delicate as a pulse, passed over her features . . . so quickly it seemed a drop of rain had simply moved like a shadow across her face —Alice McDermott
See Also: TREMBLING

92. His face [as he breaks into laughter] unfolds like a peony —Erich Maria Remarque

93. Your face is a book, where men may read strange matters —William Shakespeare

FACIAL EXPRESSIONS, SERIOUS
See Also: EYE EXPRESSIONS, MISCELLANEOUS

1. Face all clouds, like a man in need of physic —George Garrett

2. A face as sad and featureless as a moon by day —George Garrett

3. Face austere as a hermit's —Lynne Sharon Schwartz

4. Face . . . gloomy as an El Greco —John Fowles
Carlos Baker makes the El Greco comparison with 'Long,' which explains the meaning to include mood as well as physical shape.
See Also: FACIAL SHAPE

5. Face grim as flu —Reynolds Price

6. Face like a clenched fist —Richard Condon

7. A face like a stomach cramp —Loren D. Estleman

8. Face like a vinegar bottle —Erich Maria Remarque

9. Face . . . somber as a churchman's —Richard Ford

10. Face tightened up like a charley-horse —Raymond Chandler

11. Face was long, like a sheep's —W. Somerset Maugham

The comparison is used to describe both sadness and a long-shaped face. To emphasize the psychological there's Daphne du Maurier's "Long and grave . . . like a complaining sheep." To combine both meanings there's this by Margaret Atwood: "Face . . . long and mournful, like a sheep's, but with the large full eyes of a dog, spaniel not terrier."

12. Grim as an ideological bigot —Frank Swinnerton

13. Had the face of a man suffering the awaited death of a loved one who's terminally ill —Mario Puzo

14. Had the look of a boy who had just lost his puppy to the county dogcatcher —Clive Cussler

15. He [Calvin Coolidge] looks as if he'd been weaned on a pickle —Alice Roosevelt Longworth

16. His long grim face, with the mouth running across its lower hem like a slipped thread in a linen sack, was as pitted as a battlefield —Cynthia Ozick

17. A long sad face like a cocker spaniel —George Garrett

18. Looked dismayed, like a child who's been used to hearing the same story with the same happy ending, and now the ending has been changed —Margaret Millar

19. Looked like a man being strapped into the electric chair while his wife French-kisses the D.A. in the hallway —T. Coraghessan Boyle

20. Looking as if the dentist had told him he'd have to have all his teeth pulled —Ross Macdonald

21. Looking as pensive as a monk in a spiritual crisis —Scott Spencer

22. Looking like a broody hen —Margaret Kennedy

23. (You) look like you just swallowed a bone —Charles Johnson

24. Sour and gray in the face, like a man who detests the food that keeps him alive; and must yet have it —Paul Horgan

25. Troubled face . . . like a gravel parking lot —Ken Follett,

26. Wore a permanently pinched look, as if he had just bitten into a piece of spoiled fish that he could neither swallow or spit out —Amos Oz

27. Worried look, like a bird dog uncertain of the scent —Elizabeth Spencer

FACIAL SHAPE

1. His flat face looked as if it were pressed against a window, except there was no window —Rebecca West

2. Big face, broad at the bottom, narrowed upward like a Dutch cheese —Saul Bellow

3. An enormous flat face like an unbaked pie —J. B. Priestly

4. Face as huge as the bowl of the sky —George Garrett

5. Face as long as his arm —Henry Van Dyke

6. Face, as round and white and incisively marked as the face of a clock — John Updike

7. Face . . . as round as a skillet —James Lee Burke

8. Face broad and oval as a meat dish —Angela Carter

9. Face flat as a dough pan —James Lee Burke

10. Face, like a large tomato, was round and very red —Kenzaburo Oë

11. Face long as a fence line in flat country —Linda West Eckhardt

12. Face long as an El Greco —Carlos Baker

13. Face round as a full moon —James Crumley

14. Face . . . round as a radar dish —John Updike

15. Faces as long as a wet week —H. E. Bates

16. Face shaped like a honeydew melon —Paige Mitchell

17. Face shaped like a shovel —Joyce Carol Oates

18. Face . . . thin as a knife —Honoré de Balzac

19. A long face like a shoe —Christina Stead

20. A long narrow face cut like a tribal mask —Miles Gibson

21. A round chubby face, like a soft beachball —John Rechy

22. Round face like the full moon —W. Somerset Maugham

23. Sharp-pointed face like a cat —Honoré de Balzac

24. A sparkling, triangular face like a cat —Pamela Frankau

25. A thin face shaped like the hatchet Lizzie Borden chopped up her mama with —Davis Dresser

FACTS

See Also: TRUTH

1. A fact is like a sack which won't stand up when it is empty —Luigi Pirandello

    In his play, *Six Characters in Search of an Author,* Pirandello expands upon the simile as follows: "In order that it may stand up, one has to put into it the reason and sentiment which have caused it to exist."

2. Facts apart from their relationships are like labels on empty bottles — Sven Halla

3. Facts fled before her like frightened forest things —Oscar Wilde

4. Statistics are like alienists, they will testify for either side —Fiorello H. La Guardia, *Liberty Magazine,* May, 1933

5. Use facts . . . the way a carpenter uses nails —R. Wright Campbell

6. Use statistics as a drunken man uses lamp posts, for support rather than illumination —Andrew Lang

FAILURE
See: COLLAPSE, DISINTEGRATION, SUCCESS/FAILURE

FAITH
See: BELIEF, RELIGION

FAITHFULNESS/FAITHLESSNESS
See: LOYALTY/DISLOYALTY

FALL
See: SEASONS

FALLING
See: COLLAPSE

FALSENESS
See: TRYENESS/FALSENESS

FAME
See Also: GREATNESS

1. Celebrities . . . get consumed just as fast as new improved soaps, new clothing fashions and new ideas —Russell Baker

2. Celebrities used to be found like pearls in oysters and with much the same defensive mechanisms —Barbara Walters

3. Celebrity is like having an extra lump of sugar in your coffee —Mikhail Baryshnikov

4. Fame always melts like ice cream in the dish —Delmore Schwartz

5. Fame grows like a tree with hidden life —Horace

6. Fame is a colored patch on a ragged garment —Alexander Pushkin

7. Fame is like a crop of Canada thistles, very easy to sow, but hard to reap —Josh Billings
   In Billings' phonetic dialect this reads: "Fame is like a crop ov kanada thissels, very eazy tew sew, but hard tew reap."

8. Fame isn't a thing. It's a feeling. Like what you get after a pill —Joyce Cary

9. Fame . . . it's like having a string of pearls given you. It's nice, but after a while, if you think of it at all, it's only to wonder if they're real or cultured —W. Somerset Maugham

10. Fame, like a river, is narrowest at its source and broadest afar off —
     Proverb

11. Fame, like a wayward girl, will still be coy to those who woo her with
     too slavish knees —John Keats

12. Fame, like man, will grow white as it grows old —Abraham Cowley

13. Fame, like water, bears up the lighter things, and lets the weighty sink
     —Sir Samuel Tuke
     > A slight variation by Francis Bacon: "Fame is like a river, that
     > bears (modernized from 'beareth') on things light and swollen,
     > and drowns things weighty and solid."

14. Fame to the ambitious, is like salt water to the thirsty, the more one
     gets the more he wants —Emil Ebers

15. Glories, like glow-worms afar off, shine bright, but looked at near have
     neither heat nor light —John Webster
     > Slightly modernized from "Afar off shine bright, but look'd too
     > near have neither heat nor light."

16. Glory is like a circle in the water, which never ceases to enlarge itself till
     by broad spreading it disperse to nought —William Shakespeare
     > Shakespeare used the old English 'ceathes.'

17. Her life had become akin to living inside a drum with the whole world
     beating on the outside —Barbara Seaman
     > In her biography of Susann, *Lovely Me,* this is how Seaman
     > describes her subject's life after she becomes a famous author.

18. Like grass that autumn yellows your fame will wither away —Phyllis
     McGinley

19. Like madness is the glory of this life —William Shakespeare

20. Men's fame is like their hair, which grows after they are dead, and with
     just as little use to them —George Villiers

21. Our glories float between the earth and heaven like clouds which seem
     pavilions of the son —Edward Bulwer-Lytton

22. Posterity is a switchboard to past, present and future —Karl Shapiro

23. The public's appetite for famous people is big as a mountain —Robert
     Motherwell, *New York Times,* January 22, 1986

24. The way to fame is like the way to heaven, through much tribulation —
     Lawrence Sterne

FAMILIARITY
See Also: COMMONPLACE

1. (The donors were as) anonymous as God —Herbert Gold

2. (Voice) as familiar as yesterday —Wallace Stegner

3. Everything reliable as the newly-wed suite in the Holiday Inn —
    Richard Ford

The simile follows a description of a never-changing, always neat apartment in Ford's novel, *The Sportswriter.*
See Also: FURNITURE AND FURNISHINGS

4. Familiar as an old mistake —Edward Arlington Robinson

5. Familiar as a town clock —Anon

6. (She became as snugly) familiar as his own armpit —Julia O'Faolain

7. Familiar . . . as household words —William Shakespeare

8. Familiar as light or dark —Wallace Stegner

9. Familiar as luggage —Richard Ford

10. Familiar as one's own front door —Anon

11. Familiar as one's own face —Anon

12. Familiar as one's own spice shelf —Anon

13. Familiar as the contents of one's own broom closet —Anon

14. Familiar as the features of the President —Dorothea Straus

15. Familiar as the stars and stripes on the American flag —Anon

16. Familiar . . . as the streets of our native town —W. H. Hudson

17. Familiar as the voice of a favorite broadcaster —Anon

18. Familiar . . . as things are familiar in dreams, like the dreams of falling to one who has never climbed —William Faulkner

19. (The agony was as) familiar . . . as waking to life —Paul Theroux

20. Familiar as warts or some birthmark —Derek Walcott

21. Familiar like an old tale —William Shakespeare

22. He knows my face. He reads it like a farmer reads the sky —Marianne Hauser

23. Knew [her children's natures] as accurately as a bugler knows the notes of réveillé —Ouida

24. Know him like a book —Charles F. Briggs
    A variation that's become a popular daily expression is attributed to mystery writer, Margaret Millar, who used it in her novel, *The Weight of the Evidence:* "I know him like I know the back of my hand."

25. Know it [Boston] as an old inhabitant of a Cheshire knows his cheese —Oliver Wendell Holmes, Sr.

26. Know . . . like a rabbit knows its warren —Frank Ross

27. (I got men that) know (these hills) like you know your wife's geography —Ross Macdonald

28. (A voice as) recognizable as a train whistle —Scott Simon about sports broadcaster, Harry Caray, National Public Radio, May 2, 1987

29. Recognized (every little curve and shadow) as he would have recognized, after half a life-time, the details of a room he had played in as a child —Edith Wharton

30. Sounds, familiar, like the roar of trees and crack of branches —Robert Frost

31. Standardized as boilerplate paragraphs in a law office —Anon

32. Standardized, as if put together with interchangeable parts —Philip Langdon, *The Atlantic,* December, 1985
   In an article entitled "Burger Shakes," Langdon used the simile to describe cities dotted with fast-food chains.

33. The stranger is like passing water in the drain —Margaret Laurence

34. Stylized as the annual report message to stockholders —Anon

FAMILY
See: PEOPLE, INTERACTION; RELATIONSHIPS

FASCINATION
See: ATTRACTIVENESS

FASHION
See: CLOTHING, STYLE

FATE
See Also: HELPLESSNESS, LIFE

1. Chase destiny like a harpoonist —Edith Pearlman

2. Fate . . . creeps like a rat —Elizabeth Bowen

3. The Fates, like an absent-minded printer, seldom allow a single line to stand perfect and unmarred —George Santayana

4. Fate treats me mercilessly, like a storm treats a small boat —Anton Chekhov

5. Like warp and woof all destinies are woven fast —John Greenleaf Whittier

6. Our lives carried us in our own dimensions, like people passing on different escalators —Mary Ladd Cavell

7. We're like dice thrown on the plains of destiny —Rita Mae Brown

FATIGUE
See: WEARINESS

FATNESS
See Also: BODY, INSULTS, PHYSICAL APPEARANCE

1. Blew up like a poisoned dog —Rita Mae Brown

    The simile refers to a character in the novel, *Southern Discomfort,* who became fat after having a child.

2. Body . . . encased in fat, like an insulated boiler —A. Alvarez

3. Body plump as a church rat's —Honoré de Balzac

4. Broad as a barn door —John Heywood's *Proverbs*
    A shorter, modern version: "Broad as a door."

5. (At the hips . . . she was) broad as a sofa —Saul Bellow

6. Corpulent as a fire plug —Samuel Shem Fine

7. Fat and sleek: a dumpling —D. H. Lawrence

8. Fat as a balloon —Mark Twain

9. Fat as a duck —John Adams
    The man Adams compared to a duck was Aaron Burr.

10. Fat as a fool —John Lyly

11. Fat as an owl —Miles Gibson

12. Fat as a pig —John Cotgrave
    This is probably the most famous and often used "Fat as" comparison. Its earliest version "Fat as a pork hog" appeared in Sir Thomas Mallory's *Morte d'Arthur.* An offshoot, "Fat as a hen in the forehead," has been variously attributed to the playwrights Beaumont and Fletcher, and Jonathan Swift.

13. (I shall grow) fat as a porpoise —Jonathan Swift

14. Fat as a whale —Geoffrey Chaucer

15. Fat as butter —William Shakespeare
    A variation which has become an American colloquialism is "Fat as a butter-ball."

16. Fat as plenty —Hugh Ward

17. The fat on her was like loose-powdered dough —Carson McCullers

18. Fat overflowed not only from her jowl to her neck, but from her ankles to her shoes . . . she looked like a pudding that had risen too high and run down the sides of the dish —Nadine Gordimer

19. (He was) fattening like a Christmas goose —Calder Willingham

20. Grew fat as a broiler —Kate Wheeler

21. He was fat, with a belly creased like a roll when he bent over —John Gunther

22. His stomach swells like a big cake baking —Carolyn Chute

23. I was square and looked like a refrigerator approaching —Jean Kerr
    Kerr likened herself to a refrigerator when she was pregnant.

24. Pudgy as a baby's hand —Jonathan Valin

25. Plump as an abbot —Robert Traver

26. Plump as a partridge —John Ray's *Proverbs*

27. She was round and plump as her favorite teapot —Peter De Vries
28. Stout as a stump —James Crumley
29. (Piglets) stout as jugs —W. D. Snodgrass
30. (A short man) wide as a door —Jessamyn West
31. A youngish plump little body, rather like a pigeon —Katherine Mansfield

FEAR

See Also: ANXIETY, EMOTIONS, NERVOUSNESS

1. Afraid, as children in the dark —Dante Gabriel Rossetti
2. An air of terrifying finality, like the clap of doom —Herbert Lieberman
3. (A vague, uncatalogued) apprehension, as cold and disquieting as a first snowflake smudging the window of a warm and complacent room — Derek Lambert
4. As courage imperils life, fear protects it —Leonardo Da Vinci
5. As easily daunted as an elephant in the presence of a mouse —Ben Ames Williams
6. Brute terrors, like the scurrying of rats in a deserted attic, filled the more remote chambers of his brain —Robert Louis Stevenson
7. Cowardice, like alcoholism, is a lifelong condition —Susan Walton, *New York Times*/Hers, June 4, 1987
     The cowardice Walton is comparing to alcoholism is that which drives the person who always does what is expected and when.
8. Cowardly as the hyena —Beryl Markham
9. His cowardice . . . fixed him like an invisible cement, or like a nail — Cynthia Ozick
10. Dreaded (her) like fire —Alexander Pushkin
11. The dread in his lungs lay heavy as cold mud —Peter Matthiessen
12. An eddy of fear swirled around her, like dust rising off the floor in some barren drafty place —Cornell Woolrich
13. Fear . . . a little like the fear of a lover who realizes that he is falling out of love —May Sarton
14. Fear . . . came and went like the throb of a nerve in an open tooth — James Warner Bellah
15. Fear . . . clutching at his heart . . . as if tigers were tearing him — Willa Cather
16. Fear . . . compressed me like a vise —Aharon Appelfeld
17. Fear fell [on crowd] like the shadow of a cloud —John Greenleaf Whittier

18. Fear . . . gnaws like pain —Dame Edith Sitwell

19. Fearing them as much . . . as a nervous child with memory filled with ghost-stories fears a dark room —W. H. Hudson

20. Fear is like a cloak which old men huddle about their love, as if to keep it warm —William Wordsworth

21. Fear . . . lay on me like a slab of stone —Norman Mailer

22. (In my body is a) fear like metal —Marilyn Hacker

23. The fear of failure . . . blew like a Siberian wind on our unprotected backs —John Le Carré

24. Fear oozed out (of the woods), as out of a cracked bottle —Dorothy Canfield Fisher

25. Fear ran through him like a sickness —Brian Moore

26. Fears . . . fell from him like dreams from a man waking up in bed — G. K. Chesterton

27. Fear . . . sat heavy in the center of his body like a ball of badly digested food —George Garrett

28. Fears came scurrying out from their hiding places like mice —Paige Mitchell

29. Fear . . . seized all his bones like water —Hugh Walpole

30. Fear shot through me like a jolt of electricity —Sue Grafton

31. Fear spread like a common chill —Paige Mitchell
    See Also: SPREADING

32. The fear [of death] . . . stood silent behind them like an inflexible and cold-eyed taskmaster —Joseph Conrad

33. Fear stuck in his throat like a cotton hook —Charles Johnson

34. Fear swelled like some terrible travail —Heinrich Böll

35. Fear tangled his legs like a barricade —Harris Downey

36. Fear tastes like a rusty knife —John Cheever

37. Fear trills like an alarm bell you cannot shut off —John Updike

38. Fear worked like yeast in my thoughts, and the fermentation brought to the surface, in great gobs of scum, the images of disaster —Evelyn Waugh

39. Fear wrapped itself around his chest like a wide leather strap tightened by a maniac —François Camoin

40. Feeling as if an ice pick had been plunged into his liver —Peter Benchley

41. (I had) a feeling in my knees like a steering wheel with a shimmy —Rex Stout

42. Feel like clammy fingers were poking at my very heart —Borden Deal

43. Feel like a tight-rope walk high over hell —Kenneth Fearing

44. Feels fear, like a water bubble in his throat —Jessie Schell

45. Felt a chill . . . like swimming into a cold pocket in a lake —Tobias Wolff

46. Felt a driblet of fear . . . like a glug of water backing up the momentarily opened drain and polluting the bath with a dead spider, three lice, a rat turd, and things he couldn't stand to name or look at — Bernard Malamud

47. Felt like a deer stepping out before the rifle of the hunter —Piers Anthony

48. Felt like a nightmare that had yet to be dreamt —Stanislaw J. Lem

49. Felt (the beginning of) panic, like a giant hand squeezing my heart — Frank Conroy

50. Felt panicky, like he was in a bad dream where he did and said all the wrong things and couldn't stop —Dan Wakefield

51. Felt the chill of mortality . . . like a toddler gifted with some scraping edge of adult comprehension —Penelope Gilliatt
    See Also: DEATH

52. Felt the sick, oppressive crush of dread, like pinpoint ashes —Sylvia Berkman

53. A foreboding, dusky and cold like the room, crept to her side —Hugh Walpole

54. Frightened as Macbeth before the ghost of Banquo —Louis Veuillot

55. Frightened as though he had suddenly found himself at the edge of a precipice —Honoré de Balzac

56. Frightened . . . like a man who is told he has a mortal illness, yet can cure it by jumping off a fifty-foot cliff into the water. "No," he says, "I'll stay in bed. I'd rather die." —Norman Mailer

57. Frightening . . . like one of those films where ghostly hands suddenly reach in and switch off all the lights —Robert E. Sherwood

58. Fright stabbed his stomach like a sliver of glass —Arthur Miller

59. Full of dread and timidness as conscripts to a firing squad doing — Richard Ford

60. Gives me the creeps . . . like petting snakes —Raymond Chandler

61. Glances round him like a lamb at a convocation of wolves —T. Coraghessan Boyle

62. (Mildred's) heart leapt with relief like a bird in her breast —Noël Coward

63. A hiss of terror, like air whistling out of a punctured tire —Cornell Woolrich

64. Horror should rise up like a clot of blood in the throat —Dylan Thomas

65. [A group of children] huddled in a corner . . . like so many wide-eyed, trembling mice —Gregory McDonald

66. I carry a scared silence with me like my smell —W. D. Snodgrass

67. I pretend that my right foot is like a bottle. I pour my fears down into the toes and cork the whole thing at the ankle, so none of my fears can escape into the rest of me —Dorothy B. Francis

68. My heart begins to pound like a thief's with the police after him —Isaac Bashevis Singer

69. My heart in my throat like a wad of sour grease —George Garrett

70. Panic, like a rabbit in front of the dogs —Peter Meinke

71. Panic rose as thick as honey in my throat —R. Wright Campbell

72. Panic shook her . . . as awful as if she had been tottering on a cliff in a roaring wind —Belva Plain

73. Panic that was like asphyxiation —Penelope Gilliatt

74. Ran terror-stricken, as if death were pursuing me —Aharon Megged

75. Scared as a piss ant —Anon

76. Scared . . . like a rabbit that spies a dog —Shelby Hearon

77. Shivered with fear like a thin dog in the cold —Stephen Vincent Benét

78. Take fear for granted like a drunken uncle —George Garrett

79. Terrifying, like a Samurai sword in motion —Robert Silverberg

80. Terrifying . . . like fingers clamped upon your throat —Beryl Markham

81. Terror ebbed like water from a basin —Julia O'Faolain

82. Terror . . . filled me as the sound of an explosion would fill a room — Scott Spencer

83. The terror inside him acted like radar —James Mitchell

84. Terror [of some hard to accomplish task] mocked, like some distant mountain peak —John Fowles

85. Terrors that brushed her like a curtain windblown against her back — Andre Dubus

86. (They) trail their fear behind them like a heavy shadow —Heinrich Böll

FEELINGS
See: EMOTIONS, PHYSICAL FEELINGS

FEET
See: LEGS

FEROCITY
See Also: SCREAMS

1. Barked like an old sergeant —Frank Swinnerton
2. Fierce as a comet —John Milton
3. Fierce as a dog with tongue lapping for action —Carl Sandburg
4. Fierce as a fever —Anon
5. Fierce as a lobster making one last lunge out of the pot —Norman Mailer
6. Fierce as hunger —Babette Deutsch
7. Fierce as vengeance —John Greenleaf Whittier
8. Fierce as young bulls —William Shakespeare
9. Fiery as tiger eyes —Jessamyn West
10. Growled . . . as a dog might do at a postman —Frank Swinnerton
11. Savage as a bear with a sore head —Frederick Marryat
12. Savage as a meat-ax —American colloquialism, attributed to Mid-south
13. (Hope) temptuous like a fire-cloud —Dante Gabriel Rossetti
14. (A fly is as) untamable as a hyena —Ralph Waldo Emerson
15. Wild as a monkey —Robert Silverberg
16. Wild as a starved cat —Elizabeth Spencer
17. Wild as the vultures' cry —Aeschylus
18. (Memories do not turn to dust. They live) wild as young colts — Elizabeth Spencer
19. (You're) wild . . . just like a sea-bird —Clifford Odets

FERTILITY
See: GROWTH

FERVOR
See: ENTHUSIASM

FICKLENESS
See: LOYAL/DISLOYALTY

FICTION
See: STORIES

FIGHT
1. Clashed like stallions —Diane Ackerman

FIGHTING
See Also: ARGUMENTS
1. Defend like a dog —Lopez Portillo

The former Mexican president's simile to describe how he would defend the peso gave his countrymen cause for anger and ridicule, often expressed by barking at him in public places.

2. (Self-dependent power can time) defy as rocks resist the billowes and the sky —Oliver Goldsmith

3. Fierce strife . . . stirs one's old Saxon fighting blood, like the tales of "knights who fought 'gainst fearful odds" that thrilled us in our schoolboy days —Jerome K. Jerome

4. Fight as one weary of his life —William Shakespeare

5. Fight [death] . . . body and breath, till my life runs out like water —Stephen Vincent Benét

6. Fighting is like champagne. It goes to the heads of cowards as quickly as heroes —Margaret Mitchell

7. Fighting like a wounded puma —George F. Will
   Will used the wounded puma simile to describe Richard Nixon's battle during the Watergate scandal.

8. Fight like devils —William Shakespeare

9. Fight . . . like lions wanting food —William Shakespeare

10. Fights fierce as duels —Anon

11. Fought like a pagan who defends his religion —Stephen Crane

12. Fought like one boxer and his punching bag . . . like mismatched twins —Erica Jong

13. Just when the opponents seem ready to slug each other into senselessness, they clinch and go into a clumsy waltz, like boxers in a comic film —Leonard Silk, *New York Times*/Economic Scene, April 22, 1987
    Silk's reference is to combatants in strained financial markets.

14. Like sailors fighting with a leak we fought mortality —Emily Dickinson

15. A quarrel between man and wife is like cutting water with a sword — Chinese proverb

FIGURE
See: BODY

FINANCE
See: ECONOMICS

FINGERS
See Also: HAND(S)

1. Fingernails . . . long as stilettos —T. Coraghessan Boyle

2. Fingernails that were long and curved and looked as tough as horn — Sue Grafton

3. Fingers are thin as ice —Marge Piercy

4. Fingers brown and hard as wood —Philip Levine

5. Fingers cool as gemstones —R. Wright Campbell

6. Fingers danced like midgets above a summer stream —O. Henry

7. Fingers fluttering . . . like butterflies —William Goyen

8. Fingers fluttering like ribbons —Sharon Sheehe Stark

9. Fingers . . . gnarled, like the roots of trees in an Arthur Rackham drawing —Antonia Fraser

10. Fingers . . . hard and inactive, like the gnarled roots of a dead tree — Frank Swinnerton

11. Fingers . . . like a bundle of broom straw, so thin and dry —Louise Erdrich

12. Fingers like long wax candles —Cynthia Ozick

13. Fingers like pliers —Donald Seaman

14. (The woman's) fingers rustled like branches against her face —Leigh Allison Wilson

15. Fingers spread apart like the talons of a predatory bird —William March

16. Fingers spreading out like fans —Pat Conroy

17. Fingers tap like a lover's fondling a girl's hard little breasts —Babette Deutsch

18. Fingers thick as sausages —James Crumley

19. Fingers tightly clenched, as if to check an involuntary gesture —Edith Wharton

20. Fingers . . . weighty as sandbags —Frank Conroy

21. Fingers were stiff as little darts —M. J. Farrell

22. Her fingers moved over his ribs gently as a harpist's —Ross Macdonald
    See Also: SEXUAL INTERACTION

23. Knuckles . . . like a row of little white onions —Roald Dahl
    The white onion look is caused by a very hard hand grip.

24. (Hands crouched on the table before her, the) knuckles like miniature snow-capped mountains —Marge Piercy

25. Knuckles [from gripping a table very hard] shone like white stones — Mary Hedin

26. Long fingers arched like grapplehooks —William Carlos Williams

27. Long inquisitive fingers thrown out like antennae —Edith Wharton

28. Long thin fingers moving like knitting needles —Liam O'Flaherty

29. Long thin nails, like splinters —Elizabeth Spencer
30. My fingers fidget like ten idle brats —Wilfred Owens
31. Opening and closing his fingers like folding and unfolding a fan — George Garrett
32. Pointed his finger like a revolver —Charles Johnson
33. Put his fingertips together thoughtfully, like a man preparing to pray — Paul Theroux
34. Snapping his fingers together like a pair of scissors —Margaret Atwood
35. Thumb like the butt of a pistol —Sterling Hayden

FIRE AND SMOKE
See Also: TOBACCO

1. Blaze like a box of matches —Joseph Conrad
2. (His house) burned like a candle —Sholom Aleichem
3. A cloud of black soot stood in it [a room] like a fairy-tale monster in a thick wood —Boris Pasternak
4. A flame as clear as a streetlight —Cynthia Ozick
5. The flame reared like the trunk of an animal —Steve Erickson
6. Flames fluttered like a school of fishes —Saul Bellow
7. (Suddenly the) flame shot up, leaping like a dancer in the air —Alix Kates Shulman
8. Oily flames curl like hair —Jean Thompson
9. Ribbons of flame slithered like orange serpents across the . . . floor — Paul Kuttner
10. The smoke ascended in a straight column, as though from a pagan altar —Isaac Bashevis Singer
11. Smoke flared through his nostrils like an old painting of a dragon — David Brierly
12. Smoke in the air like fog on the New Jersey flats —Carlos Baker
13. Smoke (from his clay pipe) lay on the air like tule fog in a marsh —Bill Pronzini
14. Smoke puffed from her nostril like a tiny exhaust —Ross Macdonald
15. Smoke rose . . . like a snake —Hugh Walpole
16. (In June when earth) smokes like slag —James Wright
17. Smoke . . . spread itself out like an infernal sort of cloud —Joseph Conrad
18. Smouldering embers of a fire blinked like red eyes —Ellen Glasgow
19. [Earth and night] smoulder like the slow, curing fire of a Javanese headshrinker —Ted Hughes

20. Sparks flew against the [fireplace] screen like imprisoned birds —Margaret Millar

FIRMNESS

See Also: FLEXIBILITY/INFLEXIBILITY

1. (Bread . . .) as hard as pumice —Mary Stewart
2. Be like a rocky head and on which the waves break incessantly, but it stands fast and the waters sink to rest —Marcus Aurelius
3. (Continue) firm and unmoved as a column —James Boswell
4. Firm as alabaster —Henry James
5. Firm as a monkey's tail —Creole expression
   Before Jean Claude Duvalier's Haitian regime toppled in 1983, he was quoted as saying, "I'm in control . . . firm as a monkey's tail."
6. [Figure] firm as an apple —H. E. Bates
7. (My heart is) firm as a stone —*The Holy Bible/Job*
8. Firm as morality —Thom Gunn
9. [A distant ridge] firm as solid crystal —William Wordsworth
10. Firm standing like a stone wall —Bernard Bee
    The term "To stonewall" comes from Bee's simile about Jackson at first battle of Bull Run.
11. Hard and dry as rustling corn —Dame Edith Sitwell
12. [A trained gangster] hard and solid, like a shark —John Malcolm
13. Hard as a billiard ball —Anon
14. (Soil) hard as a bowling alley —E. B. White
15. Hard as a bulletproof vest —Russell Baker, *New York Times,* May 21, 1986
    To put this in full context: "Americans like their fish, and fish roe too, fried hard as a bulletproof vest."
16. Hard as a heavy-duty canvas fire-hose —Sharon Olds
    In the poem from which this is taken, *Six-Year-Old Boy,* the fire-hose is used to describe a small boy waking up to urinate.
17. Hard as an egg at Easter —Michael Denham
18. (His body thin and stringy but) hard as armor plating —Clive Cussler
19. Hard as a stone pillow —Anon
    Back in the T'ang Dynasty chên or ceramic pillows were used during as well as after life as a means for keeping the eyes clear and preserving sight.
20. (The wheel of your life is . . . as) hard as caked clay which nothing can grow in —Amy Lowell
21. (Words as) hard as cannon-balls —Ralph Waldo Emerson

22. Hard as corkwood —Miguel de Cervantes
23. (Felt as) hard as dried mud —James Crumley
     The descriptive frame of reference is the face of a man who's
     been beaten up.
24. (Her breasts were small but looked) hard as green apples —Anon
25. Hard as the knots in a whip —Yehuda Amichai
26. Hard as nails —Charles Dickens
     This now commonplace simile may well precede its appearance
     in Dickens' *Oliver Twist.* Other writers who've used it since
     have modified and extended it, e.g.: "Hard and sharp as nails,"
     attributed to S. J. Weyman and "Hard as nails and sour as
     vinegar," attributed to George Beillairs.
27. Hardened and set like concrete —Karl Shapiro
28. My ass . . . was tight as a bull's in a thunderstorm —Lael Tucker
     Wertenbaker
29. (His jaw was) rigid as a horseshoe —Flannery O'Connor
30. Rigid as a starfish —Joyce Cary
31. Rigid as bamboo —Diane Ackerman
32. Rigid as iron post —Marge Piercy
33. (He went as) rigid as Lenin's mummy —Joseph Wambaugh
34. Rigid as though bound and gagged —Eudora Welty
35. She's hard as steel —William Shakespeare
36. (Heat) solid as a hickory stick —Eudora Welty
37. Solid as a hill —William Boyd
38. Stand firm as a tower, which never shakes its top, no matter what winds
     are blowing —Dante Alighieri
39. Stiff as a garden hose left out in December —Will Weaver
     In Weaver's novel, *Red Earth, White Earth,* the comparison is
     used to describe the physical condition of a man who's had a
     stroke.
40. (His head,) stiff as a scarab —Theodore Roethke
41. Stiff as chessmen —Elizabeth Bowen
42. Stiff as icicles —Anon
43. Stiff as sticks —Dan Jacobson
44. [Bed sheet] stretched tight as a drumhead —Walker Percy
45. (Backside) sturdy as baking soda biscuits —Curtis White
46. Taut as a sail —Barbara Howes
47. Taut as a tent —Karl Shapiro
48. (Neck tendons) taut as banjo strings —Derek Walcott

49. Tight as a scout's knot —Lorrie Moore

FISHING
  See: SPORTS

FITNESS
  See: HEALTH

FLATNESS
  See: SHAPE

FLATTERY
  See Also: FRIENDSHIP, WORDS OF PRAISE

1. As a wolf is like a dog, so is a flatterer like a friend —Thomas Fuller

2. Bang compliments backwards and forwards, like two asses scrubbing one another —Jonathan Swift

3. Bask in it [flattery] like a sunflower —Tennessee Williams

4. A compliment is something like a kiss through a veil —Victor Hugo

5. Compliments are like perfume, to be inhaled, not swallowed —Charles Clark Munn

6. Fawn like dogs —Percy Bysshe Shelley

7. Flattered me like a dog —William Shakespeare
  Shakespeare's simile from *King Lear* continues with, "And told me I had white hairs in my beard 'ere the black ones were there."

8. Flatterers, like cats, lick and then scratch —German proverb

9. Flatterers look like friends, as wolves like dogs —George Chapman

10. Flattering as a testimonial dinner —Anon

11. Flattery is like a cigarette; it is all right if you don't inhale —Adlai Stevenson

12. Flattery . . . is like a qualmish liqueur in the midst of a bottle of wine —Benjamin Disraeli

13. Flattery is like champagne, it soon gets into the head —William Brown

14. Flattery is like cologne water, to be smelt of, not swallowed —Josh Billings
  Paraphrased from Billings' phonetic dialect which reads: "Flattery is like Kolone water, tew be smelt of, not swallowed."

15. Flattery is like friendship in show, but not in fruit —Socrates

16. Flattery is like wine, which exhilarates a man for a moment, but usually ends up going to his head and making him act foolish —Helen Rowland

17. (Twilight was) kind as candlelight to a bad face lift —Paige Mitchell
18. An overdose of praise is like ten lumps of sugar in coffee; only a very few people can swallow it —Emily Post
19. Praise, like gold and diamonds, owes its value only to its scarcity — Samuel Johnson
20. Some folks pay a compliment like they went down in their pocket for it —Kin Hubbard

FLAVOR
See: FOOD AND DRINK, TASTE

FLAWS
See: ERRORS

FLEXIBILITY/INFLEXIBILITY
See Also: HABIT
1. Adaptable as a Norwegian wharf rat —James Mills
2. Adjustable as prices of goods sold in a flea market —Anon
3. Adjust to as your eyes adjust to darkness or sudden light —Anon
4. Be pliable like a reed, not rigid like a cedar —Rabbi Simeon ben Eleazar
5. Elastic as a criminal's conscience —Anon
6. Elastic as a steel spring —Anon
7. Flexible as a diplomat's conscience —Anon
8. Flexible as figures in the hands of the statistician —Israel Zangwill
9. Flexible as silk —Ouida
10. Has as much give as a tree trunk —Jimmy Breslin
11. Implacable an adversary as a wife suing for alimony —William Wycherly
12. (Softly, unhurriedly but) implacably, like a great river flowing on and on —Harvey Swados
13. Inflexible as a marble pillar —Anon
14. Inflexible as steel —Ouida
15. Inflexible as the rings of hell —John Cheever
16. Intractable as a driven ghost —Sylvia Plath
17. Like all weak men he laid an exaggerated stress on not changing one's mind —W. Somerset Maugham
18. (The adolescent personality is as) malleable as infant flesh —Barbara Lazear Ascher, *New York Times*/Hers, October 23, 1986
19. The man who never alters his opinion is like standing water, and breeds reptiles of the mind —William Blake

20. Mind set like concrete —George Garrett
21. Pliable as wax —James Shirley
22. Pliant as cloth —Eugene Sue
23. Pliant as flesh —Linda Pastan
24. Rigidity yielding a little, like justice swayed by mercy, is the whole beauty of the earth —G. K. Chesterton
25. Set as a piece of sculpture —Charles Dickens
26. They made their hearts as an adamant stone —*The Holy Bible/Apocrypha*
    A variation from "Hearts firm as stone" and "Cold as stone" from the *Book of Job.*
27. Uncompromising as a policeman's club —Anon
28. Uncompromising as justice —William Lloyd Garrison
29. (There he was, as) unshakable as granite —Frank Swinnerton

FLIGHT
See: DISAPPEARANCE

FLIMSINESS
See: FRAGILITY

FLOWERS
See also: NATURE
1. Primroses waving gently like lazy yellow gloves —George Garrett
2. All white scented flowers, like the perfume of love in fresh sheets — Janet Flanner
3. Blossoms covered trees like colored powder puffs —Rita Mae Brown
4. Blossoms . . . fell to the ground like confetti —Shelby Hearon
5. Bluebells like grey lace —Joan Aiken
6. Bougainvillae . . . large as basketballs —William Faulkner
7. The bud came apart . . . its layers like small velvet shells —Eudora Welty
8. Flowers burst like bombs —Vachel Lindsay
9. Forsythia . . . sprawling like yellow amoebae —A. R. Ammons
10. A host of crocuses stood up like yellow trumpets —Howard Spring
11. Irises, rising beautiful and cool on their tall stalks, like blown glass — Margaret Atwood
12. The jonquils glowed like candles —Helen Hudson
13. Lilies bunched together in a frill of green . . . like faded cauliflowers —Katherine Mansfield

14. The little red and yellow flowers were out on the grass, like floating lamps —Virginia Woolf

15. Magnolia flowers . . . like rosettes carved in alabaster —Edith Wharton

16. Oleanders with their pink flowers like something spun out of sugar — George Garrett

17. Open blooms like ballet-skirted ladies —John Steinbeck

18. Orange and yellow poppies like just-lit matches sputtering in the breeze —John Rechy

19. Out of the earth came whole troops of flowers, like motley stars —Felix Salten

20. The flowers burned on their stalks like yellow tongues of flame — Dorothy Canfield Fisher

21. Patches of tiny wildflowers . . . like luminous rugs on the grass — Gina Berriault

22. Pink roses blooming like flesh —Bin Ramke

23. The plants sprang up thick as winter grass —Annette Sanford

24. Roses, big as a man's fist and red as blood —Eudora Welty

25. Rows of white flowers . . . throwing shadows on the azure-colored ground like trails of shooting stars —Gustave Flaubert

26. Small blue flowers like points of sky —Philip Levine
    The simile launches Levine's poem, *The Voice*.

27. The tiny yellow flowers danced underfoot, like jewels in the dust — Mary Stewart

28. The tulip-beds across the road flamed like throbbing rings of fire — Oscar Wilde

29. Tulips . . . bright as the showers —Dame Edith Sitwell

30. Variations of flowers are like variations in music, often beautiful as such, but almost always inferior to the theme on which they are founded, the original air —Leigh Hunt

31. The yellow dandelions rose up like streaks of golden light —Guy De Maupassant

FOG

See Also: MIST

1. A churning mass of fog was welling up from the sea like a tidal wave — John Dos Passos

2. Fog closed in like a long sigh —George Garrett

3. Fog . . . dissolving into the sky like milk in water —Ross Macdonald

4. The fog . . . floated into the garden like gauze —Ludwig Bemelmans

5. Fog hung above the road like an alien intelligence —Charles Johnson

6. Foggy as London —Robert Traver

7. The fog rolled off the river like a woman rolling off a bed —Marianne Wiggins

8. The fog smothered sounds like an acoustical curtain —Margaret Millar

9. Fog that came like bitter smoke —Stephen Vincent Benét

10. (Pines . . . wrapped with) fog that moved like bits of cloth in the wind —Shirley Ann Grau

11. A fog wandering like a pilgrim —Patricia Hampl

12. The fog was settling in and became rapidly denser. It was like wading about in dark milk soup —Erich Maria Remarque

13. The fog was thick and strangely white. Like wet bed sheets —Bertold Brecht

14. Haze . . . like a thin smoke from slowly burning money —Ross Macdonald

15. Night fog thick as terry cloth —Maxine Kumin

16. Puffs of white fog which hung there like frozen cabbage —Donald McCaig

17. There's a fog at the waists of the trees, like a sash —William Matthews

18. Wreaths of white fog walked like ghosts in the haunted meadow —John Greenleaf Whittier

FOOD AND DRINK
See Also: EATING AND DRINKING

1. Appetizing as a boiled cocktail —H. L. Mencken

2. Blackberries big as the ball of my thumb, and dumb as eyes —Sylvia Plath

3. A bottle of wine brings as much pleasure as the acquisition of a kingdom, and not unlike it in kind: the senses in both cases are confused and perverted —Walter Savage Landor

4. The brandy went to Whit's stomach like a saber cut —John Farris

5. Cake . . . beautiful as a palace—tall, shining and pink, outlined with balconies and battlements of white frosting —Ruth Prawer Jhabvala

6. Cakes . . . iced like the rock of Gibraltar —Penelope Gilliatt

7. A chocolate [birthday] cake . . . lit up like an oil refinery —Tom Robbins

8. Coffee . . . black as the devil, hot as hell, pure as an angel, sweet as love —Charles de Talleyrand
    Talleyrand's description of good coffee once again illustrates how a simile which may sound trite by itself can gain muscle tone when appropriately combined with two or three others.

9. Coffee . . . it tasted like swamp water —William Beechcroft

10. Coffee-pots breathing wisps of steam like old men talking in winter —J. G. Farrell

11. Coffee should be black as Hell, strong as death, and sweet as love — Turkish proverb

12. Coffee . . . tasted like a third pressing —Derek Lambert

13. I consider supper as a turnpike through which one passes in order to get to bed —Oliver Edwards
    The inspiration for Edwards' simile was Samuel Johnson declaration that he never ate supper.

14. Cooking is like love. It should be entered into with abandon or not at all —Harriet Van Horn, *Vogue,* October 15, 1956

15. Croissants, light and warm as birds —Pat Conroy

16. The dining room table steamed [with hot food] like a caldron —Dan Wakefield

17. A fish without bones is like an artichoke without leaves, a coconut without a shell, a lobster without a carapace —Anon item about an Idaho company's attempt to breed boneless fish, *New York Times,* November 5, 1986

18. Food is a narcotic in a way, like alcohol —Edna Ferber

19. Good coffee is like friendship: rich and warm and strong —Slogan, Pan American Coffee Bureau, 1961

20. A good cook is like a sorceress who dispenses happiness —Elsa Schiaparelli

21. [Soup] hot as an adulterous love —Erica Jong
    This description from a poem entitled *Chinese Food* pertains to hot and sour soup. It is preceded by two other similes: "Dense as water . . . sour as death."

22. It [beer] touched his stomach like petrol on live ashes —Caryl Phillips

23. It [water] was heavy, tepid, and savorless and like castor oil —Vicki Baum

24. Lamb . . . hard as a wood chip . . . cold as Christmas —Richard Ford

25. Left their eggs up until the whites were glazed like plastic —Daniela Gioseffi

26. Lettuces like garlands of faint green roses —Cynthia Ozick

27. The liquid [broth] went down my throat like bones —Maya Angelou

28. Margaritas flow like the Colorado River in March —Bryan Miller reviewing a Mexican restaurant, *New York Times,* August 1, 1986

29. Martinis yellow as the rose and warm as summer rain —E. B. White

30. Pears . . . like too many women their beauty condemns them to uselessness —Bin Ramke

31. Pears . . . shapely as violins —Babette Deutsch

32. Rice . . . sticky as a snowball —Ira Wood

33. Roast beef, which tasted . . . like the uppers of an old pair of pumps —Shelby Hearon

34. A scrambled egg that tasted as if it had just hatched in the refrigerator —Richard S. Prather

35. Sherry . . . as thin and dry as benzine —Philip Levine

36. Slices the bread . . . into thin volumes like poetry —Sharon Sheehe Stark

37. Steam rose like incense from the bowl [of hot soup] —Joanna Higgins

38. Stick as close to that kitchen [where a gourmet cook is in residence] as the croûte to a pâté or the mayonnaise to an oeuf —Angela Carter

39. Tea . . . liquid and warm, like weeping —Margaret Drabble
    To expand upon the comparison, the author added, "It replaced the tears."

40. To drink a glass of sherry when you can get a dry martini is like taking a stagecoach when you can travel by the Orient Express —W. Somerset Maugham

41. Unripe oranges like dark-green golf balls —Ross Macdonald

42. The yolk of one of the eggs had leaked out onto the plate like a miniature pool of yellow blood —Ross Macdonald

FOOLISHNESS
See Also: ABSURDITY, FUTILITY, STUPIDITY

1. A blockhead is as ridiculous when he talks as is a goose when it flies — Lord Halifax
    The words 'talks' and 'flies' have been modernized from the old English 'talketh' and 'flieth.'

2. Comparing them [American and Oriental women] is like comparing oven broilers and banties —Bobbie Ann Mason

3. Felt foolishness drag like excess flesh on his face —Sharon Sheehe Stark

4. Foolish as to cut off the head to preserve the hair —Anon
    An alternative to the cliche, "As foolish as to cut off your nose to spite your face."

5. Foolish as to judge a horse by its harness —Anon

6. A fool is like other men as long as he is silent —Jacob Cats

7. A fool . . . says little, but that little said owes all its weight, like loaded dice, to lead —William Cowper

8. Gullible as geese —Anon

9. How foolish one would be to climb into the ring with love and try to trade blows with him, like a boxer —Sophocles

10. If all fools wore white caps, we should look like a flock of geese —Proverb

11. I'll not be a fool like the nightingale who is up till midnight without any ale —Dylan Thomas

12. Life's little suckers chirp like crickets while spending all on losing tickets —Ogden Nash

13. Lightheaded as a thistle —Mary Lavin
    See Also: LIGHTNESS

14. A man who commits suicide is like a man who longs for a gate to be opened and who cuts his throat before he reaches the gate —Dylan Thomas

15. Senseless . . . it's like wearing a bulletproof vest with a hole over the heart —Senator John Heinz, December, 1985 news item

16. Unrealistic . . . like someone who eats like a linebacker but yearns for the shape of a fashion model —Anon

FOOTBALL
See Also: SPORTS

1. The ball just skittered around in the backfield like a puck on ice —Jonathan Valin

2. The ball peeled his head like an onion —Ken Stabler and Barry Stainback

3. Both players bounce up like toys —Richard Ford

4. My teammates were cringing in the huddle, like those scurvy hounds who live off garbage at county landfill projects —Pat Conroy

5. Passes faltered and tumbled like wounded ducks —James Crumley

6. Passes swerved like a diving duck —Y. A. Tittle, New York Giants quarterback, *New York Times,* January 12, 1987
    Tittle's simile dates back to 1962 when his team won the playoff game for the National Football League championship.

7. Pro football is like nuclear warfare. There are no winners, only survivors —Frank Gifford, *Sports Illustrated,* June 4, 1960

8. [Gary Anderson of the Miami Dolphins] runs like a locomotive —Craig James, Anderson's teammate, *New York Times*/Sports of the Times, September 10, 1986

9. Some of them [professional players] always look like brooding Pillsbury Doughboys and some of them look wizened from the start, middle-aged and beaten down, as if they'd never known what it was like to be young —Jonathan Valin

10. To me football is like a day off. I grew up picking cotton on my daddy's farm and nobody asked for your autograph or put your name in the paper for that —Lee Roy Jordan

11. Treated his players as if he had bought them at auction with a ring in their noses and was trying not to notice they smelled bad —Jim Murray, about football coach Paul Brown, *Los Angeles Herald,* 1986

12. [Football] uniforms . . . heavy as mattresses —Lael Tucker Wertenbaker
    See Also: CLOTHING

13. When you hit that line, it gave like a sponge, and when you tackled that big long Swede, he went down like he'd been hit by lightning —Sinclair Lewis

14. Without a network outlet, football will disappear like cigar smoke in the wind —Harvey Meyerson, summation at NFL-USFL trial, 1986

FORCEFULNESS
See: POWER

FOREBODING
See: ANXIETY, FEAR

FOREHEAD
See Also: FACE(S)

1. The artery in his forehead bulged like a snake —Richard Ford

2. Brow like masonry —Ted Hughes

3. Forehead..as wrinkled as a washboard —Harvey Swados

4. Forehead like a bright new moon —*Arabian Nights*

5. (A slim girl with) a forehead which was shiny and protuberant, like a Bartlett pear —George Ade

6. Forehead, with wrinkles like lines drawn all over it —Ivan Turgenev

7. Her forehead shines like the gleam of morning —*Arabian Nights*

8. A high forehead with a soft vein running indirectly down the middle like an aimless trickle of water on a windowpane —John Hersey

9. His brows became contorted with thick frowns, like a bull's forehead — V. S. Pritchett

10. His brow swells out over his face like an eroded riverbank —T. Coraghessan Boyle

11. His forehead bulged [with fury] as if he were horned —Jonathan Valin
    See Also: ANGER

12. His forehead rose like a gleaming dome towards the crown of his bald head —Alexander Solzhenitsyn

13. A pair of thin horizontal lines, like furrows in a meadow of snow, appeared on her forehead —Bill Pronzini

14. The skin [on a character's forehead] was wrinkled into long horizontal lines, like lines of inquiry —Dan Jacobson

FORGETFULNESS
See: MEMORY, MIND

FORGIVENESS

1. Forgiving the unrepentant is like drawing pictures in water —Japanese proverb

2. (God) pardons like a mother who kisses away the repentant tears of her child —Henry Ward Beecher

3. Forgiving without forgetting is like loving without liking —Anon

4. Overlooked as a favorite child's failings —Anon

FORLORNNESS
See: ABANDONMENT, ALONENESS

FORMALITY
See Also: ORDER/DISORDER

1. Formal and self-conscious as a football in a photograph —George Garrett

2. Formal as a Japanese print —Ramon Delgado

3. Formal as an undertaker —William McIlvanney

4. Informal as paper napkins —Dee Weber

5. Ordered . . . like a nun's evening prayers —Charles Hanson Towne
     This simile is extracted from the first stanza of Towne's poem, *The Best Road of All,* in which he writes about the best road being that which leads to God. In full context it reads: "I like . . . a road that is an ordered road, like a nun's evening prayers."

FORTITUDE
See: COURAGE, PERSISTENCE

FORTUNE/MISFORTUNE
See Also: RICHES

1. Adversity was spreading over him like mold —Irvin S. Cobb

2. Bad moments, like good ones, tend to be grouped together —Edna O'Brien

3. Blessed as the meek who shall inherit the earth —Anon

This illustrates how a quote can be transposed into a simile.

4. The day of fortune is like a harvest day, we must be busy when the corn is ripe —Johann Wolfgang von Goethe

5. Disasters . . . rolling in the brain like pebbles —Denise Levertov

6. Fortune is as . . . brittle as glass —Publilius Syrus

7. Fortune is like glass: she breaks when she is brightest —Latin proverb

8. Fortune is like the market, where if you will bide your time, the price will fall —German proverb
   A variation by Francis Bacon begins like the above and finishes as follows: "If you can stay a little, the price will fall."

9. Fortunes made in no time are like shirts made in no time; it's ten to one if they hang long together —Douglas Jerrold

10. Fortune sits on him like a ton of shit —Irving Feldman

11. Good fortune, like ripe fruit, ought to be enjoyed while it is present —Epictetus

12. Good fortune seemed to be following me like a huge affectionate dog —John Braine

13. It's a nightmare like trying to conquer the Himalayas on roller skates or swim the English Channel lashed to a cannon —T. Coraghessan Boyle

14. Luck is like having a rice dumpling fly into your mouth —Japanese proverb

15. A luckless man . . . the kind of man who would have gotten two complimentary tickets for the Titanic —William McIlvanney
    The actual text in Scotch author McIlvanney's *Papers of Tony Veitch* reads: "The kinnaa man woulda got two complimentary tickets for the Titanic."

16. Luck shines in his face like good health —Anon

17. Misfortunes disappeared, as though swept away by a great flood of sunlight —Émile Zola

18. Misfortunes, like the owl, avoid the light —Charles Churchill

19. Misfortunes . . . passed over her like wild geese —Ellen Glasgow

20. Mishaps are like knives, that either serve us or cut us, as we grasp them by the blade or the handle —James Russell Lowell

21. The storms of adversity, like those of the ocean, rouse the faculties —Captain Frederick Marryatt

22. Sweet are the uses of adversity which, like the toad, ugly and venomous, wears yet a precious jewel in his head —William Shakespeare

23. Tried to conceal his misfortune as if it were a vice —Mihail Lermontov

24. To wait for luck is like waiting for death —Japanese proverb

FRAGILITY

See Also: WEAKNESS

1. As thin of substance as the air —William Shakespeare
2. (Laughter . . . as) delicate and frail as new ice —Frederick Barthelme
3. (She was) delicate as a pig was not —Pat Conroy
4. Bones frail as a small bird's —George Garrett
5. Brittle as a dead tree —George Garrett
6. Brittle as dry wood —Miller Williams
7. Brittle as glass that breaks with a touch —Algernon Charles Swinburne
8. Brittle as straw —Ellen Glasgow
9. Brittle as twigs —Margaret Atwood
10. (Her own body seemed) fragile and empty like blown glass —Margaret Atwood
11. Fragile and rather beautiful, like a rare kind of mosquito —Lawrence Durrell
12. Fragile as a bird's egg —George Garrett
13. Fragile as a chrysalis —John Updike
14. Fragile as a coquillage bouquet —Truman Capote
    Capote's simile refers to Isak Dinesen.
15. Fragile as a cup —Reynolds Price
16. (Shoulder) fragile as a little bit of glass —Eudora Welty
17. Fragile as ancient lace or parchment —George Garrett
18. Fragile as a reed —Cornelia Otis Skinner
19. (Her conical breasts look) fragile as birds' eggs —R. V. Cassill
20. Fragile as snowflakes —Sharon Sheehe Stark
21. (She felt very weak and her plump body seemed, somehow, flat and) fragile, like a pressed leaf between the sheets —Helen Hudson
22. Fragile . . . like a spider's web —John Fowles
23. Fragile like her good intentions —Marguerite Yourcenar
24. Fragile, like the skin on scalded milk —Sharon Sheehe Stark
25. Frail as a blade of grass —Belva Plain
26. (She felt as) frail as a cobweb —Jonathan Kellerman
27. Frail as a fading friendship —Anon
28. Frail as antique earthenware —Sylvia Plath
    Plath's simile describes the occupants of an old ladies' home.
29. Frail as April snow —Wallace Stevens
30. (Breasts rising) frail as blisters —Sharon Olds
31. Frail as flesh —Laman Blanchard

32. [School boys] frail, like thin-boned fledgling birds clamoring for food —
     Sylvia Berkman

33. I feel [fragile] like a poppy; one gust of wind and everything will blow
     away —Carla Lane, dialogue, "Solo," British sitcom, broadcast June
     23, 1987
       The reason the character in Lane's script feels so fragile is that
       she is a woman in her fifties in a relationship with a much
       younger man.

34. I felt like a moth hanging on the windowpane —Jacqueline Kennedy,
     Newsweek, January 21, 1961
       The occasion being described was her first night in the White
       House.

35. Insubstantial . . . like fake wedding cakes in a bakery window—lots of
     whipped cream rosettes and garlands surrounding a hollow middle —
     Michiko Kakutani, *New York Times*

36. Like a dry leaf closed into a book, he seemed frail and ready to crumble
     —Arthur A. Cohen

37. More frail than the shadows on glasses —Algernon Charles Swinburne

38. Promise as solid as a bundle of water —Hindu proverb

39. (Hair and garments) tenuous as gauze —W. D. Snodgrass

40. (You're so old) you're like a cup I could break in my hand —Paule
     Marshall

FRANKNESS
     See: CANDOR

FRAUD
     See: CRIME, DISHONESTY

FRECKLES
     See: FACIAL DETAILS

FREEDOM

1. Abstract liberty, like other mere abstractions, is not to be found —
    Edmund Burke

2. (They just) broke free like the water —Boris Pasternak

3. Broke free like the sun rising out of the sea —Miller Williams

4. Feels freedom like oxygen everywhere around him —John Updike

5. Felt like a volatile gas released from a bottle —Olivia Manning
    See Also: PHYSICAL FEELINGS

6. Foot-loose as a ram —Irvin S. Cobb

7. (I am) free as a breeze, free like a bird in the woodland wild, free like a gypsy, free like a child —Oscar Hammerstein, II, from lyric for *Oklahoma*

      Hammerstein used the multiple simile to paint a picture of an unattached man bemoaning the speed with which his situation can change.

8. Free as a fat bird —John D. MacDonald

9. Free as air —Alexander Pope

      The simile in full context is as follows: "Love, free as air at sight of human ties, spreads his light wings, and in a moment flies."

10. Free as a pig in a pen —Anon, from American song, "The Lane County Bachelor"

11. Free, as happens in the downfall of habit when the mind, like an unguarded flame, bows and bends and seems about to blow from its holding —Virginia Woolf

12. Free as is the wind —William Shakespeare

      A popular variation attributed to James Montgomery is, "Free as the breeze."

13. Free as Nature first made man —John Dryden

14. Free as Nature is —James Thompson

15. Free as the grace of God and twice as plentiful —Anon

16. Freed, like colored kites torn loose from their strings —Rainer Maria Rilke

17. Freedom and responsibility are like Siamese twins, they die if they are parted —Lillian Smith
      See Also: RELIABILITY

18. Freedom is like drink. If you take any at all, you might as well take enough to make you happy for a while —Finley Peter Dunne

      Several words have been changed from Dunne's dialect: any was 'nny,' 'for' was 'f'r.'

19. Free speech is like garlic. If you are perfectly sure of yourself, you enjoy it and your friends tolerate it —Lynn White, Jr., *Look,* April 17, 1956

20. Free will and determinism are like a game of cards. The hand that is dealt you represents determinism. The way you play your hand represents free will —Norman Cousins

21. Independence, like honor, is a rocky island without a beach — Napoleon Bonaparte

22. Independent as a hog on ice —American colloquialism, attributed to New England

23. Independent as a wild horse —Anon

According to Irving Stone, author of *The Passionate Journey,* this simile was used to describe the father of his fictional biography's hero, John Noble.

24. A laissez-faire policy is like spoiling a child by saying he'll turn out all right in the end. He will, if he's made to —F. Scott Fitzgerald

25. Liberty, like charity, must begin at home —James Conant
    Yet another twist on that much adopted and adapted charity comparison.
    See Also: BELIEFS, CHANGE, CRITICISM, PEACE, SENSE

26. Perfect freedom is as necessary to the health and vigor of commerce, as it is to the health and vigor of citizenship —Patrick Henry

27. There is no such thing as an achieved liberty; like electricity, there can be no substantial storage and it must be generated as it is enjoyed, or the lights go out —Robert H. Jackson

28. Unrestricted like the rain —Mark Twain

FRESHNESS

1. (She looks as) clear as morning roses newly washed with dew —William Shakespeare

2. Fresh as a daisy —Slogan, June Dairy Products Co.

3. Fresh as an unveiled statue —Henry James

4. Fresh as any rose —John Lydgate
   The natural association between freshness and flowers has made this simile and its variants a common expression. The daisy rivals the rose as a popular comparison.

5. (Looking as) fresh as apple blossoms among the tender leaves of late spring —Frank Swinnerton

6. Fresh as April grass —Karl Shapiro

7. Fresh [in the face] as a rainwashed rose —Reynolds Price

8. Fresh as a spring morning —Slogan, Little America frozen foods

9. Fresh as hope —Susan Engberg

10. Fresh as paint —Francis Edward Smedley

11. Fresh as the dawn —Anon
    An extension used as a slogan by Pacific Egg Producers: "Fresh as dewy dawn."

12. Fresh as the month of May —Geoffrey Chaucer
    The above is modernized from, "As fresh as is the month of May."

13. Fresh as salt-drenched skin —Theodore Roethke

14. Fresh as the morning —Slogan, Campbell's corn flakes

15. Fresh as the morning wind that tatters the mist —Marge Piercy

16. Fresh as thyme or parsley —W. H. Auden

17. Fresh as tomorrow —James G. Huneker

18. Fresh as yesterday —Shelby Hearon
    In Hearon's novel, *A Small Town,* what's fresh is a family feud.

19. Fresh like frilled linen clean from a laundry —Virginia Woolf

FRIENDLINESS
See: SOCIABILITY

FRIENDSHIP
See Also: LOVE, SOCIABILITY

1. An acquaintanceship, if all goes well, can linger in the memory like an appealing chord of music, while a friendship, or even a friendship that deteriorates into an enemyship, so to put it, is like a whole symphony, even if the music is frequently unacceptable, broken, loud, and in other ways painful to hear —William Saroyan

2. Became like old friends, the kind who can't leave each other on deathbeds —Thomas McGuane

3. Comradeship . . . burned and flamed like dry straw on fire —Stephen Longstreet

4. Early friends drop out, like milk teeth —Graham Greene

5. Every man is like the company he won't keep —Euripides
    An ironic twist on, "A man is known by the company he keeps" and, "Tell me the company you keep and I'll tell you who you are."

6. Friendship ought to be a gratuitous joy, like the joys recorded by art or life —Simone Weil

7. Friendship . . . should, like a well-stocked cellar, be . . . continually renewed —Samuel Johnson

8. A friendship that like love is warm; a love like friendship steady — Thomas Moore

9. Friendship with Cape was like climbing a ladder. You had to wait awhile on each rung before he invited you to climb the next —Robert Campbell

10. Friends . . . slipping from his orbit like bees from a jaded flower — Beryl Markham

11. He who helps a friend in woe is like a fur coat in the snow —Russian proverb

12. I keep my friends as misers do their treasure —Pietro Aretino
    Aretino's simile dating back to the sixteenth century, was followed by this explanation: "Because of all the things granted us by wisdom, none is greater or better than friendship."

13. Ill company is like a dog who dirts those most whom he loves best — Jonathan Swift

14. In their friendship they were like two of a litter that can never play together without leaving traces of tooth and claw, wounding each other in the most sensitive places —Colette

15. It is as foolish to make experiments upon the constancy of a friend, as upon the chastity of a wife —Samuel Johnson

16. Life without a friend is like life without sun —Spanish proverb

17. Life without a friend is death with a vengeance —Thomas Fuller

18. Life without a friend is death without a witness —John Ray's *Proverbs*

19. The light of friendship is like the light of phosphorous, seen plainest when all around is dark —Robert Crowell

20. Like old friends they wear well —Slogan, Meyer gloves

21. The loss of a friend is like that of a limb; time may heal the anguish of the wound, but the loss cannot be repaired —Robert Southey

22. My friendship [with Vita Sackwille-West] is over. Not with a quarrel, not with a bang, but as a ripe fruit falls —Virginia Woolf, March 11, 1935 diary entry
    See Also: BEGINNINGS/ENDINGS

23. A new friend is like new wine; you do not enjoy drinking it until it has matured —Ben Sira

24. A new friend is a new wine —*The Holy Bible/Apocrypha*

25. Their association together possessed a curiously unrelenting quality, like the union of partners in a business rather than the intimacy of friends —Anthony Powell

26. Went through our friendships like epsom salts, draining us, no apologies, no regrets —Rosa Guy

27. Without a friend the world is a wilderness —John Ray's *Proverbs*

FRIENDSHIP, DEFINED

1. Acquaintances . . . they're like weeds; they grow up around the real friends and choke them off —Christopher Isherwood

2. A broken friendship, like a broken cup, can be mended but it will never be perfect again —Anon
    This can be traced to the Latin proverb "A broken friendship may be soldered but will never be sound."

3. A cheerful friend is like a sunny day which spreads its brightness on all around —Sir John Lubbock

4. Choose your friends like your books, few but choice books —James Howell

5. The false friend is like the shadow of a sundial —French proverb

6. False friends, like birds, migrate in cold weather —Anon

7. The feeling of friendship is like that of being comfortably filled with roastbeef; love like being enlivened with champagne —Samuel Johnson

8. A friendless man is like a left hand without a right —Hebrew proverb

9. Friends are like fiddle strings: they must not be screwed too tight — Claude Mermet

10. Friends are like fiddle-strings, they must not be screwed too tight — John Ray's *Proverbs*

11. Friends are like melons. Shall I tell you why? To find one good, you must a hundred try —Claude Mermet

12. Friendship is a disinterested commerce between equals; love, an abject intercourse between tyrants and slaves —Oliver Goldsmith

13. Friendship is a sheltering tree —Samuel Taylor Coleridge

14. Friendship is a single soul dwelling in two bodies —Aristotle

15. Friendship is like money, easier made than kept —Samuel Butler

16. Friendship is like a treasury; you cannot take from it more than you put into it —Benjamin Mandelstamm

17. Friendship is like two clocks keeping time —Anon

18. Friendship is love without his wings —Lord Byron

19. A friendship like a soft pillow that made her feel secure and bolstered —Mary Gordon

20. Friendship, like credit, is highest where it is not used —Elbert Hubbard

21. Friendship, like love, is destroyed by long absence, though it may be increased by short intermission —Samuel Johnson

22. Friendship, like love, is but a name —John Gay

23. Friendship, like the immortality of the soul, is too good to be believed —Ralph Waldo Emerson

24. The friendship of a great man is like the shadow of a bush soon gone — French proverb

25. A group of good friends is like the relatives you wish you'd been born with —Anon
   A twist in simile form of, "You can't pick your relatives, but you can pick your friends."

26. A hollow friendship is like a hollow tooth—it's always best to have it out at once —*Punch,* 1862

27. I find friendship . . . like wine, raw when new, ripened with age, the true old man's milk and restorative cordial —Thomas Jefferson

28. An old friendship is like old wine; the longer it lasts the stronger it grows —Antonio Perez

29. Old friendships are like meats served up repeatedly, cold, comfortless and distasteful —William Hazlitt

30. Some friends are like the shadow; they follow us when our sun shines —Moses Ephraim Kuh

    A variation of this attributed to Christian Nestell Bovee is, "False friends are like our shadow, keeping close to us while we walk in the sunshine, but leaving us the instant we cross into the shadow."

31. Some friends are like a sun-dial: useless when the sun sets —Judah Jeiteles

32. An untried friend is like an uncracked nut —Russian proverb

FROWNS

See Also: FACIAL EXPRESSIONS, MISCELLANEOUS; LOOKS; STARES

1. A dark scowl playing on his face like a spotlight —Jonathan Valin

2. Face was screwed up as if he had a stomachache —Nina Bawden

3. Frowning like the Mask of Tragedy —Max Shulman

4. Frowned like a public character conscious of the interested stares of a large crowd but determined not to take notice of them —Joyce Cary

5. Frowning, as if at some infernal machine —Elizabeth Taylor

6. Frowning like a battered old bison who'd spent too many years at the zoo —Jonathan Kellerman

7. Frowning like a cat at a mouse hole —John Updike

8. The frown like serpents basking on the brow —Wallace Stevens

9. Glared at me like a wolf in a trap —Robert Traver

10. Glared slightly . . . like a judge intent upon some terrible evidence —Flannery O'Connor

11. Glares at me like a starving wolf from the forest —Bernard Malamud

12. Glares at us, his eyes like the barrels of a shotgun —T. Coraghessan Boyle

13. He was frowning, which tensed his small face up and made his deep pockmarks look like holes that went clear through his cheeks —Larry McMurtry

14. His lips curled away from his teeth like he was exposing so many switchblade knives —Donald McCaig

15. His scowl crinkled like crushed paper —F. Scott Fitzgerald

16. Like a ruffled old eagle on a high, bare rock, she scowled at the setting sun —Louis Auchincloss

17. A reddened grimace of hate and fury, like a primitive mask in a museum —Iris Murdoch

18. Scowl like a cap pulled over the brow —Peter De Vries

19. Scowl like a child about to receive an injection —Laurie Colwin
20. Scowl, like he'd turn a cold into cancer if you crossed him —J. W. Rider
    The scowler is a doctor.
    See Also: DOCTORS
21. Scowled like a junkyard dog —Jay Parini
22. Teeth bared like the rats —Eudora Welty

FRUSTRATION
See Also: DEJECTION, EMOTIONS

1. Feel so useless . . . like a still life —Margaret Drabble
2. (I'm as) frustrated as a dog on a chain —Anton Chekhov
3. Frustrated [about career] . . . as though she were peanut butter that was forced into a hypodermic syringe —Ann Jasperson
4. Frustration . . . began to creep up his neck like a hot hand — Flannery O'Connor
5. Frustration lingered between her legs like an ache —Susan Lois
6. (The writing is becoming) more and more impossible . . . I'm like a toad squashed by a paving stone, like a dog with its guts crushed out by a shit-wagon, like a clot of snot under a policeman's boot, etc. — Gustave Flaubert
7. (The reporters are still) running around like blind dogs in a meat house —James Reston, *New York Times*/The Changing Guard, February 22, 1987

FUN
See: PLEASURE

FURNITURE AND FURNISHINGS
See Also: HOUSES, ROOMS

1. Armchairs angular as choir stalls —Julia O'Faolain
2. Bed that sagged like a hammock —John D. MacDonald
3. The big oriental rug glowed like a garden of exotic flowers —George Garrett
4. (In a mirrored room) carpeted like spring grass —William Humphrey
5. The carpet . . . felt like fur laid over clouds —Alice McDermott
6. Carpeting as soft underfoot as moss —Sue Grafton
7. Carpets threadbare like ancient shrouds —Jaroslav Seifert
8. The chairs and tables looked like poor relations who had repaid their keep by a long career of grudging usefulness —Edith Wharton

9.   Chairs that looked and felt like unbaked bread dough —Jonathan Kellerman

10. Chandeliers as big as locomotives —Mark Helprin

11. Chandeliers like crystal clouds —Gavin Lyall

12. Chinese lanterns . . . hanging like fiery fruit —Babette Deutsch

13. A clock clucked like some drowsy hen on the wall —V. S. Pritchett

14. Coloured plates, like crude carnival wheels —V. S. Pritchett

15. Curtain of red velvet drawn apart like lips —Beverly Farmer

16. Curtains billow . . . as if large birds were caught in them —Charles Simic

17. Curtains billowed slightly like loose clothing —Bin Ramke

18. The curtains fluttered coyly like ladies' skirts —Margaret Millar

19. Curtains, flying out like flags from the opened, seaward window — Elizabeth Taylor

20. The curtains over the open window next to them billow suddenly like an enormous cloud —Tony Ardizzone
     This simile concludes Ardizzone's story, *The Evening News.*

21. Each time I'm inside [an apartment] all is precisely as it was the time before, as if riveted in place —Richard Ford

22. An electric night lamp that looks like a big firefly that might have come in through the half-open window —Marguerite Yourcenar

23. The furniture around me thick as elephants —Richard Ford

24. Furniture like mismatched plates —Jonathan Valin

25. Furniture with legs like those of a very fat woman planted firmly and holding her ground —Linda West Eckhardt

26. A hard bench about as comfortable as a gridiron —Emily Eden
     See Also: COMFORT

27. Huge chandeliers, like clusters of grapes —Helen Hudson

28. Lace curtains from the parlor flying like flags in the summer sky — Sharon Olds

29. Long gauze curtains flapping out the open window like ghosts waving —Dianne Benedict

30. One's chairs and tables get to be almost part of one's life, and to seem like quiet friends —Jerome K. Jerome

31. A polychromatic rug like some brilliant-flowered rectangular, tropical islet —O. Henry

32. Shadows [of flowers on window-sill] on curtains . . . waving like swans dipping their beaks in water —Jean Rhys

33. Some aura of grief and transient desperation clings to the curtains and the shabby upholstery like a sour breath —Herbert Lieberman

34. The swinging-to of a shutter was like the nervous and involuntary flicker of an eyelid —Elizabeth Bowen

35. The table [set for party] bloomed like a miracle of shining damask and silver spoons —Elinor Wylie

36. (Grandma's old long wooden dining-room) table, kept as bare and shining as an ad for spar varnish —Robert Traver

37. Table lamps with shades like extravagant hats —John Rechy

38. A threadbare carpet that looked like frayed paper —Heinrich Böll

39. The waxed (rectangular) table shone like a black lake —Alice McDermott

40. A white curtain like a wedding veil —Beverly Farmer

FURTIVENESS
See: SECRECY

FURY
See: ANGER

FUTILITY
See Also: ABSURDITY, DIFFICULTY, IMPOSSIBILITY, USEFULNESS/USELESSNESS

1. Being a producer around here is like trying to direct a Broadway show full of deaf-mutes —William Diehl

2. Charging like Don Quixote at the windmills —George Bernard Shaw

3. Cleaning your house while your kids are still growing is like shoveling the walk before it stops snowing —Phyllis Diller
   The twists on everyday life similes to describe ineffective actions are virtually without limit. A few more examples: effective "As using a sword against cobwebs," "As trying to plug a hole with Scotch tape," "As waxing a broken car."

4. Confronting Assistant Secretary of Defense Richard Perle with real arms control is like confronting Dracula with a silver cross: You expect him to make loud noises and thresh about —*Wall Street Journal* editorial, March 25, 1986

5. Convincing her [to get an abortion] is like trying to convince her the moon's a yo-yo —Ann Beattie

6. Effective as redecorating a house over a corroding plumbing system — Anon

7. Explained to, cajoled, and bullied . . . but he might as well have been boxing with a feather bolster —Lael Tucker Wertenbaker

8. Futile as an attempt to tattoo soap bubbles —Anon

9. Futile as regret —Edward Arlington Robinson

10. Futile as to attempt to dust cobwebs off the moon —Anon

11. Futile as to fight an earthquake with argument —Anon

12. Futile . . . like a lacy valentine with a red heart which contains no message of love —Louis Auchincloss

13. Futile . . . like emptying a cupful of ants into a butterfly nest for safekeeping —Beryl Bainbridge

14. Futile [to fight unfounded suspicions] . . . like fighting with air, a mock battle with blank cartridges —August Strindberg

15. Futile like Samson pulling the roof down on the Philistines —George Garrett

16. Futile, like shoveling sand into the sea —Isabel Allende

17. Futile . . . like talking to a lake, a chilled lake, no reaction, not a ripple —James Kirkwood

18. Lending to the feckless is like pelting a stray dog with dumplings — Chinese saying

19. Like a spent prisoner before the moment of execution, he knew that it was too late for protest —Dorothea Straus

20. Maintaining classical studies in 1987 is like *Cosmopolitan* magazine obstinately advertising bustles —Dennis O'Brien, *New York Times*/OpEd, February 12, 1987
    O'Brien, a university president used the comparison to support his argument that college should not be viewed as a product.

21. Might as well try to teach good manners to a wolf or a wild boar (as to bloody-minded soldiers who have lost whatever religion they may have had) —George Garrett

22. My efforts [to stir my husband out of a sense of doom] have been like so many waves, dashing against the Rock of Ages —Robert E. Sherwood
    Sherwood wrote this simile for the character of Mary Todd Lincoln in his play *Abe Lincoln in Illinois.*

23. (About as) pointless and inglorious as stepping in front of a bus —John Osborne

24. Pointless as throwing birdseed on the ground while snow still falls fast —Ann Beattie

25. The prophesying business is like writing fugues; it is fatal to everyone save the man of absolute genius —H. L. Mencken

26. Showing emotion [when with an uncommunicative father] was like having a snowball fight with a brick wall —Ann Jasperson

27. Speculating about it was like robbing last year's bee tree —Borden Deal

28. To argue with William is like arguing with Vesuvius —Delmore Schwartz
    See Also: ARGUMENT

FUTURE

See Also: TIME, SUCCESS, DESTRUCTION, ADVANCING

1. Can see about as far ahead as a goat —Harold Adams
2. Doomed like a moth —Dame Edith Sitwell
3. A dreadful prospect, like losing your potency —Harvey Swados
4. The future comes like an unwelcome guest —Edmund Gosse
5. The future grows like a scar —Philip Levine
6. The future is an opaque mirror. Anyone who tries to look into it sees nothing but the dim outlines of an old and worried face —Jim Bishop, *New York Journal-American,* October 15, 1959
7. The future is like heaven; everyone exalts it but no one wants to go there now —James Baldwin
8. The future was like a sunny road that wandered through a wide-flung, wooden plain —W. Somerset Maugham
9. The future was rushing toward her like the jaws of a trap snapping shut —A. E. Maxwell
10. Great promise [of a brilliant career] . . . faded like his imagination — Marguerite Young
11. He would fly, if he could, fly in search of a future like a sycamore seed —Louis MacNeice
12. The years stretched before her like some vast blank page spread out to receive the record of her toil —Edith Wharton

GAIETY

See Also: CHEERFULNESS, LAUGHTER

1. As merry as a grig —Frank Swinnerton
2. As merry as a mouse in malt —George Garrett
3. As merry as forty beggars —Proverb
4. As merry as notes in a tune —Dame Edith Sitwell
5. As merry as the day is long —William Shakespeare Shakespeare used this in both *Much Ado About Nothing* and *The Life and Death of King John.* In daily conversation, 'cheerful' is often substituted for 'merry.'
6. Gay as the latest statistics on cancer or crime —Elyse Sommer
7. (Yours is) a spirit like a May-day song —Dorothy Parker
8. Blithe as the air is, and as free —Henry Wadsworth Longfellow
9. Cavorted like a mule let out to pasture —Borden Deal
10. Feeling like Fourth of July —Stephen Vincent Benét
11. The gaiety of life, like the beauty and the moral worth of life, is a saving grace, which to ignore is folly, and to destroy is a crime —Agnes Repplier

12. Gay as a funeral procession —Anon
13. As merry as a condemned man eating his last meal —Elyse Sommer
14. Gay as a honey-bee humming in June —Amy Lowell
15. Gay as a parade —Hilda Conklin
16. Gay as larks —Aesop The use of "gay as" and "merry as" comparisons to larks, crickets and just about any kind of humming or buzzing bird or insect abounds throughout the annals of literature as well as in daily speech.
17. Heart . . . lighter than a flower —Elinor Wylie
18. Making merry like grasshoppers —Robinson Jeffers
19. A man without mirth is like a wagon without springs, in which one is caused disagreeably to jolt by every pebble over which it turns —Henry Ward Beecher Were Beecher alive today he might substitute "A car without shock absorbers" for "A wagon without springs."
20. (Everything went as) merrily as a marriage bell —W. Somerset Maugham
21. A merry heart does good like a medicine —*The Holy Bible /Proverbs* The word 'doeth' has been modernized to 'does,' and the simile is often shortened to "A merry heart is like medicine."
22. Mirth is like a flash of lightning, that breaks through a loom of clouds, and glitters for a moment —Joseph Addison

GAIT
See: WALKING

GARDEN SCENES
See: FLOWERS, LANDSCAPES, NATURE

GENEROSITY
See: KINDNESS

GENIUS
See: GREATNESS

GENTLENESS
See Also: KINDNESS
1. Gentle as a newborn colt —Rex Reed In Reed's novel, *Personal Effects,* the gentle behavior is that of a man making love.
2. (Looked as) gentle as a suckling dove —Arthur Train
3. Gently as a whisper —Slogan for door checks, Sargent & Co.
4. Tender as dusk —Jessamyn West

5. Tenderly as a mother —John Greenleaf Whittier
6. Tender as young love —Maxwell Anderson

GESTURES
See: HAND MOVEMENTS

GIDDINESS
See: LIGHTNESS

GIFTS
See: KINDNESS

GLANCE
See: LOOKS

GLIMMER
See: GLOSSINESS

GLITTER AND GLOSS
See Also: BRIGHTNESS, LIGHTING, SHINING

1. Aglow, like fruit when it colors —William Canton
2. All ablaze like poppies in the sun —Ouida
3. All glittering like May sunshine on May leaves —Alfred, Lord Tennyson
4. Beams like flowers —Percy Bysshe Shelley
5. (Bright faces cast a thousand) beams upon me, like the sun —William Shakespeare
6. Blazing like a jewelled sun —W. S. Gilbert
7. Blinking like a digital display —Natascha Wodin
8. A dull sheen, like the white of a hard-boiled egg —T. Coraghessan Boyle
9. (Eyes) flashed like lightning —Honoré de Balzac
10. Flashy as the slot machines in a gambling casino —Anon
11. (Evening) flickers like the midnight sun —Karl Shapiro
12. Gleam and glitter . . . like jewels in a dark velvet case —Louis Auchincloss
13. (His hair) gleamed like a freshly washed blackboard —Mavis Gallant
14. [A car] gleamed like a jewel in a box with an iridescent lining —Robin McCorquodale
15. (The Hyde Park Library, which was) gleaming like a chrome fender in the afternoon sun —Jonathan Valin

16. Gleaming like light on water —Beryl Markham
17. Gleaming like oil on water —Erica Jong
18. Gleaming like raw meat —James Crumley
19. Gleaming like water over moon-bright sand —Robert Penn Warren
20. Gleam like bone —Donald McCaig
21. Gleam like small change —Sylvia Plath
22. (The token woman) gleams like a gold molar in a toothless mouth —Marge Piercy
23. Gleams like a small coin —Philip Levine
24. Gleams like the cared-for brass of bank buildings —George Garrett
25. (The necklace) gleams, sharp as malice —Louise Erdrich
26. (Water) glimmered like a shower of diamonds in the broken moonlight —Joseph Sheridan Le Fanu
27. Glimmer . . . like glow worms twinkling through the shade —Sir Walter Scott
28. Glimmer, sparkled like a matrix of platinum sequins laid over velvet —Richard Ford The sparkling place described is Oaxaca.
29. (Eyes . . .) glinted . . . like crumpled tinfoil —Susan Neville
30. (Helmets) glinted like nailheads —Derek Walcott
31. [Shoulders] glisten as silver —D. H. Lawrence
32. Glistened, like a globe of burnished gold —Edgar Allan Poe
33. Glistened like an oiled plum —Jerzy Kosinski The descriptive frame of reference in *The Painted Bird,* the novel from which this is taken, is a snake's head.
34. (The empty pavement that) glistened like a wet leather strap —Tadeusz Borowski
35. [A dog's coat] glistened like black velvet —Roald Dahl
36. (Her neck and shoulders) glistened like liquor in a crystal bottle —Paige Mitchell
37. (Peas) glistened like medieval enamels —Mark Helprin
38. Glistened like the sun in water —Henry Wadsworth Longfellow
39. (The van) glistening like opal —MacDonald Harris
40. Glistening like satin —Ouida
41. Glisten like melted butter —Marilyn Hacker
42. [Hair] glisten like sunshine —D. H. Lawrence
43. Glistens like the scaling of a snake —Mihail Lermontov In Lermontov's *A Hero of Our Time,* the comparison refers to a river.
44. (Eyes) glittered like a string of Christmas tree icicles —Donald McCaig
45. Glittered like bracelets —Hans Christian Andersen

46. Glittered like confetti —Lawrence Durrell
47. Glittered like steel struck with a bright light —Honoré de Balzac
48. The glitter of the sea was like glass in my eyes —Steve Erickson
49. Glittering like armor —Frank O'Hara
50. [Fruit wet with mist] glowed like a globe of fire —Philip Levine
51. Glowed like painted glass —Lincoln Kirstein
52. Glowed like somebody had polished her —J. B. Priestly The narrator of Priestly's *Lost Empires* is describing a showgirl in her costume.
53. Glowed like the initials of an illuminated manuscript —Edmund L. Pearson
54. (His head) glowing like a red sun —Bernard Malamud
55. Glow like a sunbeam —Alfred, Lord Tennyson
56. Glow, like moths by light attracted and repelled —Percy Bysshe Shelley
57. (Water) glows . . . like a crystal ball —Edward Hoagland
58. Glows like a drunk's nose —Hank Searls
59. Glows like a meteor in the distant North —William Blake
60. Lights glittering like Oz —Diane Ackerman
61. Polished like new boots —John Ciardi
62. Shimmered like the wing of a dragonfly —Eudora Welty
63. Shimmer like a vision —John Gardner
64. Sparkled like stars —Percy Bysshe Shelley
65. (Four tiny black-eyed girls . . .) twinkling like Christmas trees —Hart Crane

GLOOM

See Also: BEHAVIOR; DEJECTION; FACIAL EXPRESSIONS, SERIOUS; SADNESS

1. Bleak and uninviting as an empty hotel room —Jonathan Valin
2. Bleak as a winter hillside —F. van Wyck Mason
3. Brain which had become as inhospitable to the brighter side of life as a house without windows is to cheerful lodgers —Bertold Brecht
4. Brooded over . . . misfortune, like Hamlet or a character in Ibsen — Mary McCarthy
5. Brooding . . . like a martyr —Paul Reidinger
6. Brooding like a woman unsatisfied —Joanne Selzer The comparison as used by the author in a poem entitled *Summer Heat* refers to the atmosphere after a heavy storm. The simile in its full context begins as follows: "The air hung heavy after the storm, brooding . . . "
7. Brood like a ghost —Fannie Stearns Gifford

8. Cheerful as a turkey before Thanksgiving —Anon Variants for changing seasons include: "Cheerful as a rabbit before Easter" and "Cheerful as a goose before Christmas."

9. Cold and gray . . . like the mortuary —Mike Fredman

10. Dour as a wet cat —Warren Beck

11. Felt heavy as Sunday —John Braine

12. Gloom . . . dark and stagnant like a bed of straw for sick livestock —Kenzaburo Oë

13. Gloom, like a poisonous mist, fills the car —Ira Wood

14. Gloomy and melancholy, like ghosts —Mark Twain

15. Gloomy as a beach resort on a wet Sunday in July —Anon This may be inspired by a much-used, also unattributed simile, "Gloomy as a graveyard on a wet Sunday afternoon."

16. [A house] gloomy as a crypt —Michael Korda

17. Gloomy as a tick on Sunday —Grace Paley

18. Gloomy as a wet holiday —Anon

19. Gloomy as night —Homer

20. Glum as a gumboil, as sad as despair —Don Marquis

21. Glum as a student who's fallen hopelessly behind —John Gardner

22. Glum as a tongue-tied parrot —Joseph C. Lincoln

23. Grew clouded and closed, like the dense pallid sky —Sylvia Berkman
    See Also: RESERVE

24. Ill-humor is like laziness, for it is a kind of laziness —Johann Wolfgang von Goethe

25. It was the kind of day that made suicide look like a reasonable proposition —Mike Fredman
    See Also: DAY

26. Looked like he swallowed a lemon —William Diehl

27. Melancholy as a defeated politician —Herbert V. Prochnow

28. Melancholy as a gib [castrated] cat —William Shakespeare

29. Melancholy sound . . . like the weeping of a solitary, deserted human heart —Guy de Maupassant
    See Also: NOISE

30. Moping around like a chicken with the dropsy —Babs H. Deal

31. (The men grew silent and) morose like lumps of soft coal —Richard Ford

32. A sense of melancholy had enveloped her like a sheath —Charles Johnson

33. (My grandmother had) a permanently bleak outlook . . . like one of those cartoon characters with a small cloud over their heads —Susan Walton, *New York Times*/Hers, June 25, 1987

34. Somber and unreadable as Latin —Tony Ardizzone

35. Sour as port decanted too long —Truman Capote

36. Sulked like a bear —Anon

37. We [three motorists] drove out the lane like a funeral cortege —Ross Macdonald

GLORY
See: FAME, SUCCESS/FAILURE

GLOSSINESS
See: GLITTER AND GLOSS

GLUTTONY
See: GREED, EATING AND DRINKING

GOD
See: FORGIVENESS, RELIGION

GOLD
See: COLORS, MONEY

GOLF
See Also: SPORTS

1. Addressed his ball as if he were stroking a cat —P. G. Wodehouse
   Wodehouse, known for his humorous golf stories, not surprisingly coined many funny golf similes.

2. The ball breasting the hill like some untamed jack-rabbit of the California prairie —P. G. Wodehouse

3. Before making a shot, he would inspect his enormous bag of clubs and take out one after another, slowly, as if he were playing spillikens —P. G. Wodehouse

4. Brooded over each shot like one whose heart is bowed down by bad news from home —P. G. Wodehouse

5. Drove as if he were cracking a whip —P. G. Wodehouse

6. Golf is like a love affair: if you don't take it seriously, it's no fun. If you do take it seriously, it breaks your heart —Arnold Daly, *Reader's Digest*, November, 1933

7. He stood over his ball, pawing at it with his driving-iron like a cat investigating a tortoise —P. G. Wodehouse

8. He whiffed that baby [the ball] so bad he torqued like a licorice twist
    and found his head looking straight behind him like a cockatoo —
    Joseph Wambaugh

9. I'm playing like Tarzan and scoring like Jane —Chi Chi Rodriguez
    quoted in the 1987 Masters tournament by Dick Schaap

10. A man . . . with thirty-eight golfless years behind him . . . loses all
    sense of proportion [when he takes up the game] . . . like a fly that
    happens to be sitting on the wall of the dam just when the crack comes
    —P. G. Wodehouse

11. Scooped with his mashie as if he were ladling soup —P. G. Wodehouse

12. Stood addressing his ball [to tee off] like Lot's wife just after she had
    been turned into a pillar of salt —P. G. Wodehouse

13. That poor golf ball . . . perched on the tee, as naked as a quarterback
    without a helmet —Dave Anderson, *New York Times*/Sports of the
    Times, May 11, 1987

14. Wielded his midiron like one killing snakes —P. G. Wodehouse

15. With infinite caution, like one suspecting a trap of some kind, he
    selected clubs from his bulging bag —P. G. Wodehouse

GOOD HEALTH
See: HEALTH

GOODNESS
See: KINDNESS

GOSSIP

1. [News in the computer industry] as rife with rumor as the C.I.A. or the
    National Security Council —Erik Sandberg-Diment, *New York Times,*
    January 25, 1987

2. Collected them [rumors] as a child might collect matchbooks —W. P.
    Kinsella

3. Confirmed gossips are like connoisseurs of cheese; the stuff they relish
    must be stout —Holman Day

4. Delivered more gossip than the *National Enquirer* —Joseph Wambaugh

5. Far and wide the tale was told, like a snowball growing while it rolled
    —John Greenleaf Whittier

6. Fond of gossip as an old woman —Ivan Turgenev

7. An indiscreet man is like an unsealed letter, everybody can read it —
    Sebastian Shamfort

8. Little words of speculation drone like bees in a bottle —Beryl Markham

9. News as roaring in the air like a flight of bees —Truman Capote

10. News . . . would have run like a pistol shot through Faithful House [the name of publishing business around which Swinnerton's novel, *Faithful Company*, centers] —Frank Swinnerton

11. Rumor . . . it had gone like a fire in dry grass —William Faulkner
    See Also: SPREADING

12. Rumors [on Iranian arms scandal's effect on Washington] are spreading like lava from a volcano —Senator Robert Byrd, CBS-TV news program, broadcast December 5th

13. Rumors began to thicken like a terrible blizzard —Susan Fromberg Schaeffer

14. Rumors . . . flew like birds out of the unknown —Stephen Crane

15. Rumors swirled around his name like the waters in a riptide —Peter De Vries

16. Rumors that rush around . . . inflating as they go, like giant balloons until somebody comes along to prick them —Vita Sackville-West

17. Scandal, like a kite, to fly well, depends greatly on the length of the tale it has to carry —*Punch*, 1854

18. A secret in his [the gossip's] mouth is like a wild bird put into a cage; whose door no sooner opens, but it is out —Ben Jonson

19. Spits out secrets like hot custard —Thomas Fuller

20. Stories, like dragons, are hard to kill . . . If the snake does not, the tale runs still —John Greenleaf Whittier

21. Tale-bearers are as bad as the talemakers —Richard Brinsley Sheridan

22. Tell tales out of school like a child —Honoré de Balzac

23. They come together like the coroner's inquest, to sit upon the murdered reputations of the week —William Congreve

24. They [a talkative family] fly around with news in their beaks like blue jays —Susan Fromberg Schaeffer

25. Traded in gossip the way grown-ups play the stock market —Nora Johnson This comparison by the teen-aged narrator in *The World of Henry Orient* would be equally apt without the reference to age.

26. Trumpeting it [a secret] . . . like an elephant in heat —William Alfred

27. The United States government leaks like a rusty tin can —David Brinkley, "This Week With David Brinkley," ABC-TV, November 16, 1986

28. Word gets around..it's like jungle drums —George Axelrod

29. Word of scandal spreads like a spot of oil —Marcel Proust

GOVERNMENT
   See Also: LAW, POLITICS

1. An administration, like a machine, does not create. It carries on — Antoine de Saint-Éxupéry

2. Any government, like any family, can for a year spend a little more than it earns. But . . . continuance of that habit means the poorhouse —Franklin D. Roosevelt, July 30, 1932

3. The balance of power our founding fathers so brilliantly contrived . . . has functioned like a gyroscope to keep us from plunging irretrievably into anarchy or despotism —John R. Stockwell, *New York Times*/Op-Ed, December 14, 1986 Stockwell's simile was part of his argument for open hearings on Colonel Oliver North.

4. The Constitution is an experiment, as all life is an experiment —Oliver Wendell Holmes, Jr.

5. Democracy is like a raft. It never goes down but, dammit, your feet are always wet —Fisher Ames

6. Government is like that old definition of a baby: an enormous appetite at one end and no sense of responsibility at the other —Ronald Reagan, 1986 speech

7. Government . . . like fire it is a dangerous servant and a fearful master; never for a moment should it be left to irresponsible action — George Washington

8. Governments are like men, more or less suspicious according to their temperaments —*Punch,* 1844

9. Governments, like clocks, go from the motions men give them, and as governments are made and moved by men, so by them they are ruined also —William Penn

10. A great empire, like a great cake, is most easily diminished at the edges —Benjamin Franklin

11. The life of governments is like that of man. The latter has a right to kill in case of natural defence: the former have a right to wage war for their own preservation —Charles de Secondat Montesquieu

12. Like a funeral or a marriage, an administration in the making creates disparate relationships and revives forgotten alliances —Maurice Edelman Edelman put this simile into the mind of the fictional hero of his novel, *Disraeli Rising.*

13. Like clowns, they [royalty] amuse the people, even with their funerals —Marie, Queen of Romania

14. Like knights in search of the Holy Grail, lawmakers are always looking for painless ways to raise revenues —David E. Rosenbaum, *New York Times*/Op-Ed, March 5, 1986

15. A monarchy is like a man-of-war, bad shots between wind and water hurt it exceedingly; there is danger of capsizing. But *d*emocracy is a raft. You cannot easily overturn it —Joseph Cook

16. Monarchy is like a sleek craft, it sails along well until some bumbling captain runs it into the rocks —Fisher Ames, English Tory, former monarchist, quoted *Money Magazine*

17. A nation . . . is like a body contained within a circle, having a common center, in which every radius meets; and that center is formed by representation —Thomas Paine

18. Nations are as a drop in a bucket —*The Holy Bible/Isaiah*

19. Nations are like olives. To gentle pressure they respond with sweet oil, to hard pressure with bitter oil —Ludwig Boerne

20. No nation can survive if government becomes like the man who in winter began to burn the wall boards of his house to keep warm until he had no house left —Ronald Reagan, on controlling government spending, annual address to annual conference of the International Monetary Fund and World Bank, September 30, 1986

21. States, like men, have their growth, their manhood, their decrepitude, their decay —Walter Savage Landor

22. States, like men, never protest their honor loudly unless they have a bad case to argue —Harold J. Laski

23. The superpowers often behave like two heavily armed blind men feeling their way around a room, each believing himself in mortal peril from the other whom he assumes to have perfect vision —Henry Kissinger

24. (It's all papers and forms,) the entire Civil Service is like a fortress made of papers, forms and red tape —Alexander Ostrovsky

GRACEFULNESS
See: AGILITY, BEAUTY

GRACIOUSNESS
See: BEHAVIOR, MANNERS

GRAVENESS
See: SERIOUSNESS

GRAY
See Also: COLORS, GLOOM, HAIR COLOR, SKY, WEATHER

1. An ash-gray . . . like that of the first thinning of the darkness after a rain-sodden night —Dan Jacobson

2. (His face was) faintly gray like newsprint —John Updike

3. (Eyes) gray as a goose —Geoffrey Chaucer

4. Gray as a vault —Elizabeth Spencer

5. Gray as bones —Martin Cruz Smith

6. Gray as cement —Philip Levine

7. (The weather had turned as) gray as concrete —Jean Thompson

8. Gray as flannel —Jonathan Valin In his novel, *Life's Work,* Valin thus describes what remains of a man's hair: "Bald on top, gray as flannel on the sides."

9. (Eyes) gray as glass —Geoffrey Chaucer Chaucer used the simile in *The Canterbury Tales (The Miller's Tale)* and Shakespeare used it in *Gentlemen of Verona.*

10. Gray as lava —D. H. Lawrence

11. (Skin) gray as lead —William Diehl

12. (Warships) gray as sharks —George Garrett

13. (Eyes . . .) gray as storm clouds —Margaret Millar

14. (Max was) gray as the sky —Susan Fromberg Schaeffer

15. Gray like dust —Algernon Charles Swinburne

16. Gray [hair] like the last snows of winter —John Cheever

17. Gray like washed slate —John Updike

18. (Eyes had gone) icy gray, like winter frost —Andrew Kaplan

GREATNESS

See Also: FAME, INTELLIGENCE, MIND

1. Early genius is like a cabbage: it doesn't head well —Bartlett's *Dictionary of Americanisms*

2. A fine genius, in his own country, is like gold in the mine —Ben Franklin

3. Genius, in one respect, is like gold—numbers of persons are constantly writing about both who have neither —Charles Caleb Colton

4. Genius is like a flint of many edges, but it is the edges that give the sparkle —Moritz Gottlieb Saphir

5. Genius, like humanity, rusts for want of use —William Hazlitt

6. Genius, like water, will find its level —Proverb

7. Genius must have talent as its complement and implement, just as, in like manner, imagination must have fancy —Samuel Taylor Coleridge Coleridge built on this simile as follows: "In short, the higher intellectual powers can only act through a corresponding energy of the lower."

8. Genius without education is like silver in the mine —Benjamin Franklin

9. A genius without vices is like a race horse without a good jockey — Benjamin De Casseres

10. Great men are like mountains; we do not appreciate their magnitude while we are still close to them —Joseph Chamberlain

11. Great men are like meteors; they litter and are consumed to enlighten the world —Napoleon Bonaparte

12. Great men, like great epochs, are explosive material in whom tremendous energy has been accumulated —Friedrich Nietzsche The simile is sometimes quoted with the word 'ages' substituted for 'epochs.'

13. Great men stand like solitary towers in the city of God —William Wadsworth Longfellow

14. Great minds are like eagles, and build their nest in some lofty solitude —Arthur Schopenhauer

15. It is with rivers as it is with people: the greatest are not always the most agreeable nor the best to live with —Henry Van Dyke

16. Men of genius are like eagles, that live on what they kill, while men of talents are like crows, that live on what has been killed for them —Josh Billings In Billings' special phonetic dialect this reads: "Men ov genius . . . tha live on what tha . . . while men ov . . . tha live on what haz bin killed for them."

GREED

See Also: EATING AND DRINKING, ENVY

1. (My) avarice cooled like lust in the chill grave —Ralph Waldo Emerson

2. Avarice is like a graveyard; it takes all that it can get and gives nothing back —Josh Billings

3. Avaricious . . . like a pig which seeks its food in the mud, without caring where it comes from —Jean B. M. Vianney

4. The avaricious man is like the barren sandy ground of the desert which sucks in all the rain and dew with greediness, but yields no fruitful herbs or plants for the benefit of others —Zeno

5. Covetous persons are like sponges which greedily drink in water, but return very little until they are squeezed —G. S. Bowles

6. Greedy as a colt first loosed to pasture in the spring —Ben Ames Williams

7. Greedy as a vulture —Tobias Smollett

8. He [Donald Trump] has an appetite [for property] like a Rocky Mountain vulture —Alan Greenberg, *Wall Street Journal,* April 1, 1987

9. Kings, like hyenas, will always fall upon dead carcasses, although their bellies are full, and although they are conscious that in the end they will tear one another to pieces over them —Walter Savage Landor

10. (Love surfeits not) lust like a glutton dies —William Shakespeare

11. Rapacious as a crocodile —Anon

12. Rapacious as a warlord —Sharon Sheehe Stark

13.   Sucked him dry like a raw egg —Bertold Brecht
14.   They're [the doctors] milking you like a cow —Molière

GREEN

See Also: COLORS, ENVY

1.   Bright green like a parrot's wing —Hugh Walpole
2.   (Eyes as) deeply green as an Amazonian jungle —Ed McBain
3.   Green and shiny as a frog come out of the swamp —R. Wright Campbell
4.   Green as a canker —V. S. Pritchett
5.   Green . . . as a well-watered palm —Mark Helprin
6.   Green as jealousy —Vita Sackville-West
7.   (Fields as) green as jellied mint —Malcolm Cowley
8.   (Eyes) green as leeks —William Shakespeare
9.   (The trees were) green as paper money —George Garrett
10.   Green as spring —Beryl Markham
11.   Green as St. Patrick's Day icing —Marge Piercy
12.   (Eyes) green as wings of horseflies —Erica Jong
13.   Greener than envy and money —George Garrett

GRIEF

See Also: SADNESS

1.   The eye, like a shattered mirror, multiplies the images of sorrow — Edgar Allen Poe
2.   Grief as constant as a cloud of black flies —James Crumley
3.   Grief deep as life or thought —Alfred, Lord Tennyson
4.   Grief floats off, spreading out thin like oil —Elizabeth Bishop
5.   Grief had flown away like a sparrow —Jean Stafford
6.   Grief holds him like a corset —Anon
7.   Grief is like a mine shaft, narrow and deep —Kenzaburo Oë
8.   Grief is to man as certain as the grave —George Crabbe
9.   Griefless as a rich man's funeral —Sidney Dobell
10.   Grief . . . like a mallard with clipped wings circles me summer and winter, settled for life in my lie's reedy lake —Denise Levertov The simile comes from the closing lines of Levertov's poem, *Visitant.*
11.   Grief rolled across the space between us like a wash of salt water —Sue Grafton
12.   Grief sat on his chest like a dragon —Norman Garbo
13.   Griefs . . . pain me like a lingering disease —John Milton

14. I felt as if my chest were banded, like a barrel, with iron straps of sorrow —John Hersey

15. Man sheds his grief as his skin sheds rain —Ralph Waldo Emerson

16. Mourning had lain thick in the room, like dust —Belva Plain

17. Mourn sore like doves —*The Holy Bible/Isaiah*

18. The news of his death [Byron's] came down upon my heart like a mass of lead —Thomas Carlyle

19. Our sorrows are like thunder clouds, which seem black in the distance, but grow lighter as they approach —Jean Paul Richter

20. Pure and complete sorrow is as impossible as pure and complete joy — Leo Tolstoy

21. She had borne about with her for years like an arrow sticking in her heart the grief, the anguish —Virginia Woolf

22. She wore her grief like a string of pearls —Anon

23. Sorrow as true as bread —E. E. Cummings

24. Sorrow is a kind of rust of the soul, which every new idea contributes in its passage to scour away —Samuel Johnson, *The Rambler,* August 28, 1750

25. Sorrows are like tall angels with star-crowns in their hair —Margery Eldredge Howell

26. Sorrows blurred around their edges, like a careless woman's lipstick — Jean Thompson

27. Sorrows, like rain, makes roses and mud —Austin O'Malley

28. Sorrow was like the wind. It came in gusts —Marjorie Kinnan Rawlings

29. The stains of her grief became her as raindrops to the beaten rose — Edith Wharton

30. There are peaks of anguish in life which establish themselves as peerless, like sharp ridges above a range —Davis Grubb

31. Woman's grief is like a summer storm, short as it is violent —Joanna Baille
    See Also: MEN AND WOMEN

32. Wore his broken heart like a mourning band —Lael Tucker Wertenbaker

GRINS

See Also: LAUGHTER, SMILES

1. Face . . . cut wide open by a beautiful grin . . . like pumpkins with candles shining out through their strong ivory teeth —Marge Piercy

2. Grin at each other as if we'd just completed a double steal —W. P. Kinsella

See Also: BASEBALL

3. Grinning dreamily, like a man who has just had a final fix —James Crumley

4. A grin like a flash of dental lightning —Don Marquis

5. Grin like a German Shepherd —Rick Borsten

6. Grin like a kid caught smoking behind the barn —W. P. Kinsella

7. Grin like an apple slice —Julia O'Faolain

8. Grin like a salesman —Richard Ford

9. Grin like the moon, just barely there, and like the sun, getting ready to set —Hortense Calisher

10. Grinned at her like a six-year-old boy caught doing something he must charm his way out of —Niven Busch

11. Grinned at me very engagingly, like a daddy who has just finished explaining to his little boy how the new electric train works —Harvey Swados

12. Grinned, filling his cheeks, as if he had food in his mouth —Paul Theroux

13. Grinned just like a jackass chewing briars —George Garrett

14. Grinned like a hungry tiger —Harvey Swados

15. Grinned like a pumpkin —Marge Piercy

16. Grinned like a shark —T. Coraghessan Boyle

17. Grinned like a weasel in a chicken coop —T. Coraghessan Boyle

18. Grinning like a cageful of monkeys —Erich Maria Remarque

19. Grinning like a Death's-head —Loren D. Estleman

20. Grinned like beans —Rita Mae Brown

21. Grinning like egg-sucking foxes —John D. MacDonald

22. A grin of recognition spread across Bunty's face like a burn —Harvey Swados

23. Grins like a clown with a banjo —R.H.W. Dillard

24. Grin . . . wide as a pumpkin's —Mary Hedin

25. His grin was like a big wrinkle among the small ones —Robert Campbell

26. A lop-sided grin, like he had a lemon in his mouth —Joseph C. Lincoln

GROANS AND WHISPERS
See Also: SIGHS

1. The continuous moaning was a simple irritant, like the clanking of a radiator pipe —Mary McCarthy

2. Furious whispers which sounded like the hissing of snakes roused from a summer nap in some warm garden heap —Joyce Cary

3. Gasped like a big fish —Brian Moore

4. Groaning . . . like the wind in the chimney —William Faulkner

5. Groan like a poleaxed steer —James Thurber

6. Grunted . . . like a goat hit with a sledgehammer —William Moseley

7. Grunted like a man hit with a baseball bat —James Crumley

8. Grunt like a water-buffalo —O. Henry

9. Her husky whisper, gentle as a rain breeze, was like a tender caress —Cecilia Rosas

10. Hissed . . . like the deadliest of adders —Joseph Heller

11. (Nola's) husky whisper had a thrill in it like the rattle of a snake —Wallace Stegner

12. Like the sound of water readying to boil were the whispers of his voice —Norman Mailer

13. Moan and pace like captured leopards —Diane Wakoski

14. Moaned . . . deeply, like a cello —Martin Cruz Smith

15. Moaned . . . like some baffled prowling beast —James Joyce

16. Moaning like a dumbstruck giant —Scott Spencer

17. Moans like a bedridden grandmother —T. Coraghessan Boyle

18. A moan that sounded as if it had been wrenched from her chest with a steel hook —James Crumley

19. Wail . . . like wind outside a cabin window —Charles Johnson

20. (Felt my wrinkled heart) wheeze like a dog on a leash —Jayne Anne Phillips

21. Whimpering like a puppy just yanked from its mother and thrown onto the side of the road —Gloria Norris

22. Whimper like a well-trained pet wanting to be let out —George Garrett

23. A whispering moan like the rustle of wind in trees —James Stevens

24. Whispers dramatically, as though she were telling me a state secret —Daphne Merkin

25. Whisper softly as a girl's tear —Isaac Stern

26. Wince as if somebody had driven a red-hot spike into his head —P. G. Wodehouse

GROWTH

See Also: SPREADING

1. Accumulate . . . like acorns beneath the trees of a forest —Thomas H. Huxley

2. Accumulate like a pile of dead leaves drifting onto the pavement of August —Barbara Pym

3. Accumulate like wire coat hangers in a closet —Anon

4. Blooming as a bride —Anon

5. Blooming as spring —John Dryden

6. Bloom like wildflowers in moss —George Garrett

7. [A young girl] blossomed . . . like a tree or a branch where every bud was breaking into flower —Rumer Godden

8. (Curiosity) blossomed like leprosy —Yehuda Amichai

9. (Life had) blossomed out like a flower in the sun —Ellen Glasgow

10. Blown up like a tumor —Ralph Waldo Emerson

11. Bred and nourished like a gardenia —Pat Conroy

12. Breed as quickly as cockroaches and are as difficult to stamp out —Bob Davis, in article about bugs in computer software, *Wall Street Journal,* January 28, 1987

13. Breed like cells under a microscope —Doris Lessing

14. Breeds like a rabbit —Jonathan Swift

15. (Ambassadors) cropped up like hay —W. S. Gilbert

16. (His belief . . . came to the surface and) expanded like some delicate flower —E. M. Forster

17. Expanding like the shade of a cloud on sand —Wallace Stevens

18. Fertile like the divine creation —Victor Hugo

19. (The righteous shall) flourish as a branch —*The Holy Bible/Proverbs*

20. Flourishing like a weed —Stefan Zweig

21. Flourish like a cabbage rose —John Ashbery

22. Flourish like an herb —*The Holy Bible/Isaiah*

23. Going [a criminal investigation] like a grass shack fire —Harold Adams

24. Grew . . . like a balloon being pumped full of gas —Myron Brinig

25. Grew like a larch —Emily Brontë

26. Grew like asparagus in May —W. S. Gilbert

27. [George Ade's popularity] grew like Jack's beanstalk —Lee Coyle

28. Grew like weeds in sand —Marge Piercy

29. Grow and grow like a maypole —Erica Jong

30. Grow like a summer pumpkin —W. P. Kinsella

31. (His notions) grow like a tropical forest —G. K. Chesterton

32. Grow like savages —William Shakespeare

33. (I watch our children) grow like stubborn weeds —George Garrett

34. Growth . . . as fast as the light from polar regions —John Ashbery

35. Have grown like a bug from a bug out of the garden of Eden —Dylan Thomas

36. (In earth) like a man in a woman, I'll make food out of food —Daniela Gioseffi

37. A major advance . . . it's like going from the propeller airplane to the jet —Dr. Bruce R. Baral, a dentist commenting on new cavity removal system, *New York Times*, December 31, 1986

38. (Disappointment) mounting higher every week, like a quick-growing hedge —Mazo De La Roche

39. Multiplies itself [ultimate truth about fellow men] like taxes —Ogden Nash

40. Multiplies like loaves and fishes —George Garrett

41. Multiply (thy seed) as the stars of the heaven, and as the sand which is upon the sea shore —*The Holy Bible/Genesis*

42. Multiply like fruitflies —Herbert Lieberman

43. Progress is like a merry-go-round. We get up on a speckled wooden horse . . . we think we're travelling like the devil, but the man that doesn't care about the merry-go-round knows that we come back where we were —Finley Peter Dunne In Dunne's *Observations* by Mr. Dooley some words were in dialect ('Travellin' like the divvle but th' . . . ').

44. Proliferate, like creditors at a bankruptcy —Mike Sommer

45. (Plots) ripen like fruit —O. Henry

46. Soaring like Halley's comet —Jane Wagner As used in Jane Wagner's scenario for Lily Tomlin, *The Search for Signs of Intelligent Life*, soaring refers to a sharp increase, as in the teenage suicide rate.

47. (Poems) sprout like grain from quickened seeds —George Garrett

48. [Popularity] sprung up, like a grass fire —James Thurber

49. Stockpiled . . . like grain in a grain elevator —Doug Feiden In Feiden's novel, *The Ten Million Dollar Getaway*, the people doing the stockpiling are mobsters and bodies are the frame of reference for the comparison.

50. Stretched out like a string released —Henri-Pierre Roche

51. Swelled like bullfrogs at mating time —R. V. Cassill Cassill's bullfrogs comparison is used by a character in *Hoyt's Child* to describe how policemen will fatten up their role if you let them in on your problems.

52. Swelling like a balloon —Robert Silverberg

53. Swelling up like blowfish —Peter De Vries

54. Unfolding like a tree —Philip Levine

55. We grow like a tree from the earth —Marge Piercy

GRUMBLING
See: COMPLAINTS, CRITICISM

GUILT
See Also: CONSCIENCE

1. Branded with his guilt as if he were tattooed —Henry Slesar

2. Berating himself, like an orator grading his own speech —William Diehl

3. Gather guilt like a young intern his symptoms, his certain evidence — Anne Sexton

4. Guilt is like mothers. Everyone in the world has at least one. And it's passed down like a torch to the next generation —Erma Bombeck This has been changed to the present tense from the original, which read: "I figured out long ago that guilt was like mothers. Everyone in the world had at least one. And it was passed down like a torch to the next generation."

5. Guilt, thick as ether, seeped into my body —Jonathan Valin

6. Guilt will descend on you like London fog —Walter Allen

7. The heat of shame mounted through her legs and body and sounded in her ears like the sound of sand pouring —Nadine Gordimer

8. Looked as guilty as if he'd kicked his grandmother —Raymond Chandler

9. Looking behind me . . . as guilty as a murderer whose knife drips blood —Ann Beattie

10. Looks like a hound caught slipping a chop from the table —T. Coraghessan Boyle

11. A sense of guilt like a scent —Louis MacNeice

12. Shame crowding his throat like vomit —Jean Thompson

13. The thought of the wrong she had done . . . aroused in her a feeling akin to revulsion such as a drowning man might feel who had shaken off another man who clung to him in the water —Leo Tolstoy

14. We are all like mice: one eats the cheese and all are blamed —Solomon Ibn Vega

HABIT
See Also: BEHAVIOR, FLEXIBILITY/INFLEXIBILITY

1. An annoying habit . . . like the habit of people who take nonfattening sweeteners in their coffee, and order chocolate mousse —Marilyn Sharp

2. As the snow flakes gather, so our habits are formed —Jeremy Bentham

3. A bad custom is like a good cake, better broken than kept —Randle Cotgrave

The word 'custom' is often interchanged with 'habit.'

4. Bad habits are like a comfortable bed; easy to get into, but hard to get out of —Rev. Watson C. Blake

5. The customs and fashions of men change like leaves on the bough, some of which go and others come —Alighieri Dante

6. (I like to) go tick-ticking along like a clock —Edith Wharton

7. Habit, like a crane, will bow its neck and dip its pulleyed cable, gathering me . . . into the daylight —Harold Monro

8. (All will be well, we say; it is) a habit, like the rising of the sun —Edna St. Vincent Millay

9. The habit (of command) was already fitting him like a tailored suit — Ken Follett

10. Kept on along the narrow track of habit, like a traveler; climbing a road in a fog —Edith Wharton

11. Set in his ways as a chunk of concrete —F. Hopkinson Smith

12. Set in one's way, as elderly apple trees —Allison Lurie

13. Shook my wild habits from me . . . like a worn-out cloak —O. Henry

14. Take for granted, like running water —Anon

15. Used to it, like a wart —Jonathan Kellerman

16. Using drugs like table salt —Jimmy Breslin

17. We are bagged in habit like clothes back from the cleaners —Marge Piercy

HAIR

See Also: HAIR COLOR; HAIR, CURLY; HAIR STYLES; HAIR TEXTURE

1. The abundance of his hair gives the impression that his head is not fully developed, or with time has shrunk —Wright Morris

2. Bangs down over her forehead like a sheepdog's —Margaret Atwood

3. Bangs jitter across her forehead like magnets —Susan Minot

4. Bangs . . . like overcooked bacon —Ann Beattie

5. Black hair hung like a river about her shoulders —Helga Sandburg

6. Braid of hair . . . like a thick black snake —Ann Petry

7. A crest of stiff white hair, like a prophet or a cockatoo —Ellen Currie

8. Golden hair fountaining around her shoulders like spilled beer —Paige Mitchell

9. Hair . . . as smooth and shining as a backbird's wing —John Braine

10. Hair . . . auburn and abundant, like a well-nourished orangutan's coat —James Morrow

11. Hair . . . bright and garish as brass —Margaret Millar

12.   Hair floated around my face like wet gauze —Sue Grafton

13.   Hair flying like a pennant —Paul Theroux

14.   Hair foamed around her head like a dandelion cloud —Julia O'Faolain

15.   Hair [red] . . . gleaming like the sand streaked with sunset — Marguerite Young

16.   (Gray) hair grows out of my skin like rot on an ancient tree —Anon Irish verse

17.   Hair hanging straight as nylon cord —Alfred Gillespie

18.   Hair . . . its fine smooth loops, like slabs of snow, hung low on her cheeks —Gustave Flaubert

19.   Hair like a field in bloom —T. Coraghessan Boyle

20.   Hair like dry ashes —Maureen Howard

21.   Hair like metal in the sun —Dorothy Parker

22.   Hair . . . like ripe wheat —Nelson Algren

23.   Hair like spilled barley —T. Coraghessan Boyle

24.   Hair . . . like the rumpled wig of a clown —Hallie Burnett

25.   Hair . . . moving under her comb like a muscular skin —Gary Gildner

26.   (Whitish) hair pointy and close as a burr or a sunflower when the seeds have been picked out of it —Saul Bellow

27.   (The girl's black curly) hair shone like an eclipsed sun —Carol Ascher

28.   [Blonde] hair shone like well-polished old silver —F. van Wyck Mason

29.   (White) hair smooth as a bird's breast —Raymond Chandler

30.   Hair spread out like feathers —Jayne Anne Phillips

31.   Hair . . . straight and sleek, and lay like black satin against her forehead —Vita Sackville-West

32.   Hair . . . thin and white and very short, laid over her skull like a placemat —Helen Hudson

33.   Hair tumbled about her like a veil —Jean Stafford

34.   Hair which resembled a horse's mane . . . was like filaments of the brightest gold of Araby —Miguel de Cervantes

35.   Hair which was long and smooth on either side of her face, like the shut wings of a raven —Mary Austin

36.   Heavy chestnut hair hanging like a cloak about her shoulders —Marge Piercy

37.   Heavy straight hair swinging behind like a rope —Eudora Welty

38.   Her hair fell in bright ripples like a rush of gold from the ladle of a goldsmith —Stephen French Whitman

39.   Her hair burned about her like a molten copper —Maurice Hewlett

In the original simile the hair was 'aburned.'

40. Her hair drooped round her pallid cheeks, like seaweed on a clam — Oliver Wendell Holmes, Sr.

41. Her hair fell across her shoulders like a nun's veil —Sue Grafton

42. Her hair . . . ran smooth like black water through her hands —Ross Macdonald

43. Her long, dark hair fell across her eyes like stray crayon marks —Joan Hess

44. Her long hair hung as straight as rain —Jean Stafford

45. Her wet hair lay flat as a second skin —Helen Hudson

46. His hair glittered like a skull cap of beads —Miles Gibson

47. His hair rose in an unruly swirl, like the topknot of some strange bird —John Yount

48. His hair slicks back, like a baby's or a gangster's . . . shiny as a record album —Lorrie Moore

49. His hair stood upright like porcupine quills —Boccaccio

50. His thin gray hair lay on his scalp like moulting feathers —John Cheever

51. A light fringe of hair, almost like frost —Joyce Carol Oates

52. A lock of black hair lay on his forehead like a leech —Jean Stafford

53. Nearly as hairy as a dog —John Yount

54. Peroxide hair like rope ravelings —Paul J. Wellman

55. Pomaded hair slicked back like shiny Naugahyde —Paul Kuttner

56. The thick black hair of his chest forced its way out of the opening [of his shirt] like a jungle growth seeking sunlight —Harvey Swados

57. A thick sprinkling of dandruff, like a fall of flour, on the shoulder of her blouse —Ruth Rendell

58. Thick yellow hair . . . like a palm thatch —Jean Stafford

59. Tumbling loose dark hair like a wet mop —George Garrett

60. Uncombed hair hung about her face like an old dog's —H. E. Bates

61. Untidy hair like a lion's mane —Barbara Pym

62. The wild hair of his head bloomed like fallen snow —Z. Vance Wilson

63. Wisps of hair, like sunburst grass hanging over eyes as clear as pale grey crystals —Edith Wharton

64. With his tangled mane and beard, he looked like some ridiculous lion out of a bestiary —Wallace Stegner

65. Pale brushed heads like candles burning in the summer sunlight —John Updike

HAIR COLOR

See Also: BLACK, BROWN, GRAY, RED, WHITE

1. Black [hair] with only a few gray streaks like a timid motif running through it —Helen Hudson

2. Blond as a Zulu under the bleach —Raymond Chandler

3. Blond hair . . . like long uncut grass but no color —Rosellen Brown

4. Braids, brown and shiny like a ripe hazelnut —Henry Van Dyke

5. A carroty mass of hair flaming round his cheeks and crown like a brush fire —T. Coraghessan Boyle

6. (Her long) chestnut hair was waving about like a curtain of silk — Francine du Plessix Gray

7. Gray hair . . . like meringue —James Lee Burke

8. Gray hair that looks like the head of an old worn-out wet mop left out to dry and bleach in the sun —George Garrett

9. Gray hair, which he wore like a kind of silver beret —Robert Traver

10. Hair a fading mixture of black and gray, like an afternoon storm — Laura Furman

11. Hair . . . artificially streaked, as though someone had emptied a bag of feathers over her head —Lynne Sharon Schwartz

12. Hair, as straight and red as ironed ketchup —Tom Robbins
    Redheads and their problems feature prominently in Robbins'
    Life with Woodpecker, and this is one of several similes about
    red hair.

13. Hair, black and shining like mica —Jean Garrigue

14. Hair, black as a seal's wet fur —Jean Garrigue

15. Hair..bronze and silver like pear trees in full bloom —William Alfred

16. Hair . . . dark and live as snakes —George Garrett

17. Hair . . . had gray in it like streaks of milk —William Styron

18. Hair [red] . . . like a fiery wick dipped in a well of incendiary sunlight —John Farris

19. Hair . . . like Montana wheat planted in contours on a slope of hill — John Gunther

20. Hair looks as if it had been stained with blueberries —W. P. Kinsella

21. Hair, not just blonde, but radiating gold like a candleflame behind a window in winter —Stuart Dybek

22. Hair . . . streaked like old piano keys —Reynolds Price

23. (His head and his) hair . . . white like wool —St. John

24. Hair . . . without definable color, as though it had very early begun to rehearse of its inevitable whiteness —Doris Grumbach

25. Her locks were yellow as gold —Samuel Taylor Coleridge

26. Her long hair was naturally a light brown, but the sun had bleached tawny streaks in it, like the stripes of a very old battle flag seen through imperfect glass —R. V. Cassill

27. His white hair stood out from his head like the fur of an Angora rabbit —Thomas McMahon

28. Long yellow hair like broken egg yolks spilling down all over her head —Helen Hudson

29. Pale auburn with a touch of gold . . . like butter with paprika in it —John Gunther

30. Red hair . . . all fluffed out, like her face lived in a pink cloud —Sharon Sheehe Stark

31. Red hair . . . as glossy as plum-skins —Beverly Farmer

32. Red hair like a curtain that would draw down like a shade —Shirley Ann Grau

33. White hair . . . flecked all over with little rust colored dashes, like India ink put on with a fine brush —Willa Cather

34. White hair like a cloud —Helen Hudson

35. White hair made her face look like a rose in snow —L. P. Hartley

36. White hair shone, like mountain snow —Percy Bysshe Shelley

37. White-headed as a mountain —Thomas Hardy

38. Yellow hair, like strands of gold —Anon line from early American ballad, "Locks and Bolts"

HAIR, CURLY
See Also: HAIR STYLES

1. A circlet of crisp curly gray hair like a laurel wreath —Marge Piercy

2. Curled their hair so tightly that their heads looked like bunches of black grapes —Angela Carter

3. (Her gold) curls hang like lazy springs —Ira Wood

4. Curls like those of a young hyacinth —Edgar Allen Poe

5. Curls of yellow hair like pine shavings —Peter De Vries

6. (His dark) curls were flat, plastered over his head like a wet beret —Joan Hess

7. Curly, scented, black, stiff hair, like cock feathers —Janet Flanner

8. Hair . . . as tightly curled as a poodle's —Margaret Millar
   A popular comparison with variations including the simplified as in "Hair . . . curly as a poodle," and extensions like "Hair curled like a gilded poodle's." (T. Coraghessan Boyle's *Water Music.*)

9. Hair curled as rings of iron wire —Aharon Megged

10. Hair . . . curled like the fruit on the trees —Dame Edith Sitwell
11. Hair . . . curly as moss —Marge Piercy
12. Hair . . . curly as the wool on a ram —George Garrett
13. Hair that curled naturally like very young leaves —Mollie Hardwick
14. Hair that sprang into ringlets like gold coins —Paige Mitchell
15. It [hair] covered either side of her thin face in curly muffs, like a poodle's ears —Jonathan Valin
16. Soft gray hair curled out of his skull like smoke —Miles Gibson
17. Towers of hair, curled like Indian temples —Joyce Cary

HAIR STYLES

1. Close-cropped head, cut so close to the scalp that the patches of gray are like a light stain —George Garrett
2. Hair . . . almost as if ironed in place —H. E. Bates
3. Hair . . . brushed straight back—like he was wearing a hairpiece or as though a small black beaver was lying on top of his skull —Donald McCaig
4. Hair . . . cropped so short in back that he looked like a Marine in boot camp —Jonathan Valin
5. (Her chestnut) hair, cut short, closed about her neck like a choker — Arthur A. Cohen
6. Hair hanging down, straight, as if it were cut out of wood and painted —Rumer Godden
   This is slightly modified from the dialect spoken by a character in Godden's story *No More Indians:* 'outa' and 'hangin' instead of 'out of' and 'hanging.'
7. Hair hanging . . . like a brush across his forehead —Ella Leffland
8. Hair hanging like seaweed —John Updike
9. Hair . . . hanging loose down to her shoulders, like a child's unbound for a party —Eudora Welty
10. Hair . . . lay on her forehead like a ruffled crest —James Joyce
11. Hair parted from the middle of her forehead like the two panels of a curtain —Saul Bellow
12. Hair pulled back tight as if to punish it —Marge Piercy
13. Hair . . . razor cut and blow-dried and sprayed so firmly into place that he looked like he was wearing a helmet —Robert B. Parker
14. Hair, so tightly braided it felt stitched on, showing her bare scalp like little seams all over her skull —Helen Hudson
15. Hair that grew long and thick around his face like ivy round a window —Helen Hudson

16. Hair..twisted like a pastry into a knot —Patricia Henley
17. Hair was cut close to his scalp, like freshly mowed grass —Daphne Merkin
18. (Her white) hair was so permanently waved and arranged that it looked like concrete —Noël Coward
19. Her white hair . . . stood high above her face like a chef's cap — Nancy Huddleston Packer
20. His hair . . . covered half his forehead like a bowl —Reynolds Price
21. His hair . . . cut short as that of a monk, seemed like a barber-college special —Thomas McGuane
22. His shiny brown hair was razor cut, wrapped like a scarf around his ears —Jonathan Valin
23. Pale fluffy hair whipped up beautifully on the top of her head like confectioner's cream —Elizabeth Bowen
24. Parted it [her hair] evenly, like the curtains of a neat house —Saul Bellow
25. Short-cropped hair hugging her head like a bangle bracelet —Arthur A. Cohen
26. Straight hair, cut like a little train to a point at the nape of her neck — Eudora Welty
27. Wore her hair away from her forehead, like a cloud which a little wind in May peels off finely —Elizabeth Barrett Browning
28. Wore her hair nearly to her waist, in long pastel strands like the trailing branches of a weeping willow —Harvey Swados
29. Wore it [hair] as though he'd have thought it indecent exposure to have allowed anyone to catch even a glimpse of his eyebrows, his ears, or the back of his neck —George Bagby

HAIR TEXTURE

1. Dead-looking hair..as if it had been glued on —Willa Cather
2. Frizzy brown hair like short feathers —Marianne Hauser
3. A grand shock of hair, like the best type of sheepskin rug —Phyllis Bottome
   The Point of Vantage, from which this is taken, leads off with a simile. Here it is in full context: "Teobaldo Kurt Dubrik was a large stout man with a grand shock of hair, like the best type of sheepskin rug."
4. Hair and mustache fluffy as down —Mark Helprin
   See Also: MUSTACHES
5. Hair as glossy as a blooded chestnut's coat —Elizabeth Spencer
6. Hair as sleek as a seal's fur —Sarah Bird

7. Hair . . . black and dense and glossy, like boot polish —Maeve Brennan

8. Hair . . . coarse and slightly wavy, with just a trace of oil all over it, like a well-tossed salad —Roald Dahl

9. Hair, frizzy like unravelled rope —D. H. Lawrence

10. Hair . . . like a coiled piece of copper —Laurie Colwin

11. Hair like a frizzled yellow sponge —Phyllis Bottome

12. Hair like blown-up gold and finer than gold —Joyce Carol Oates

13. Hair like dirty cotton —Loren D. Estleman

14. Hair like fuzz on a tennis ball —Jean Thompson

15. Hair like moth-eaten fur —Ellen Glasgow

16. Hair like Persian lambs' fur —Saul Bellow

17. Hair like porcupine quills —Elizabeth Tallent

18. Hair . . . like the raffia you had to soak before you could weave with it in a basket class —Saul Bellow

19. Hair . . . matted and dry, like that of a sick animal —W. P. Kinsella

20. Hair . . . tough as a rocking horse's —Penclope Gilliatt

21. Hair rich and dark, clustering thick as grapes or hyacinths —Elizabeth Spencer

22. Hair . . . rough, like a mongrel dog's —Frank Tuohy

23. (Black,) shiny hair, hard as bristles —Ivan Turgenev

24. (His curly straw) hair shone like frail golden wires on his head —James Stern

25. Hair smooth as a cat's —Jayne Anne Phillips

26. Hair . . . soft as milkweed silk —McKinlay Kantor

27. Hair . . . straight as a string —Dorothy Canfield Fisher
    In her story *Married Children,* Fisher expands on this with, "She looks like a squaw."

28. Hair . . . texture like damp thread —Anthony Powell

29. (A mane of black) hair that was as thick as a tow rope —Sumner Locke Elliott

30. Hair, thick and coarse as dune grass —Marge Piercy

31. Hair thick and glossy like fur —Martin Cruz Smith

32. Hair, thick as a cushion —Helen Hudson

33. Hair tough as a rocking horse's —Penelope Gilliatt

34. (Her pale red) hair was wispy and stuck out from her head like duckling down —Tama Janowitz

35. Her hair, after all the combing, shone like something Marco Polo might have brought back from Far Cathay to show the peasants —William Dieter

36. Her locks had been so frequently and drastically brightened and curled that to caress them . . . would be rather like running one's fingers through julienne potatoes —Dorothy Parker

37. His fine dark hair looked more like a shadow than like real hair —Katherine Mansfield

38. Long coarse hair, like a mop —Rosa Guy

39. Straight shining hair like smooth straw —James Stern

40. Thick, bulging hair, like a bear's fur —Albert Moravia

HAND(S)

See Also: ARM(S), FINGERS, HAND MOVEMENTS, HANDSHAKE

1. Big hands like the claws of a crab —Guy De Maupassant

2. The bones in her narrow wrists were small as chicken bones —Mary Hedin

3. Closed they [hands] looked like clusters of unpainted wooden balls as large as walnuts —Sherwood Anderson

4. A craftsman's hands . . . hands quick as cats —William H. Gass

5. Fist like a piece of iron —Raymond Chandler

6. Fists . . . as large as wastebaskets —Dashiell Hammett

7. Fists like knotty pine —George Garrett

8. Hand as wide as a stirrup —Richard Ford

9. Hand . . . dry, hard and cold, rather like a chicken's foot —F. van Wyck Mason

10. His hand felt like the tentacles of a sea anemone —Kate Grenville

11. Hand . . . like a fine piece of ivory carving —Rebecca West

12. A hand like a side of meat —Douglas Adams

13. Hand . . . like a baseball catcher's glove —Frank Ross

14. Hand like a boxing glove —T. Coraghessan Boyle

15. Hand like a bundle of taut wire —Oakley Hall

16. Hand like a ham —Stephen Vincent Benét

17. Hand . . . like a sharp, icy stake —Ariel Dorfman

18. Hand like a wood rasp —Raymond Chandler

19. Hand . . . limp as a tassel —Frank Swinnerton

20. Hand, quick as a bird claw —Eudora Welty

21. Hands . . . as soft as cotton-wool —Ivan Turgenev

22. Hands . . . cool, muted and frail with age like the smoothness of old yellow linen —Stephen Vincent Benét

23. Hands . . . crude and functional as if whittled out of hard wood — George Garrett

24. Hands folded like flower petals —Clare Boylan

25. Hands . . . gnarled, huge and misshapen, like chunks of wood hewn from a pale tree —James Stern

26. Hands gnarled, twisted and earth-stained like the vigorous roots of a tree —Ellen Glasgow

27. Hands, horny as a laborer's —Harvey Swados

28. Hands hung like clusters of sausages —Louis Bromfield

29. Hands . . . large and too thin, like empty gloves —Margaret Laurence

30. Hands like asbestos —Mary Hedin

31. Hands..like blocks of wood and about as gentle —Leslie Thomas

32. Hands like bunches of bananas —Frank Swinnerton

33. Hands like coal shovels —Gerald Kersh

34. Hands . . . like dangling shovels —Jonathan Gash

35. Hands . . . like elephant's ears —Arthur Baer

36. Hands . . . like great paws —Elizabeth Taylor

37. Hands like hard rubber —Helen Hudson

38. Hands like hunks of steak —Julia O'Faolain

39. Hands like lion's feet —Arthur A. Cohen

40. Hands . . . like wings of butterflies —Hart Crane

41. Hands . . . looked like roots in earth —Ram Dass and Paul Gorman

42. Hand . . . soft, like worn silk —Jayne Anne Phillips
     See Also: SOFTNESS

43. Hands ridged like topography maps —Sharon Sheehe Stark

44. Hands . . . slender and smooth as though they had lifted nothing heavier than a knife to cut corners —Helen Hudson

45. Hands . . . soft from the [dish] water, like old gum erasers —Jean Thompson

46. Hands . . . steady as steel —H. E. Bates

47. Hands that felt . . . like a scrubwoman's hands, red-knuckled and practical —Hortense Calisher

48. Hands that have thickened and calloused through the years so they look like tough paws —Louise Erdrich

49. Hands turned out flat, palms up, like a Balinese dancer —Leonard Michaels

50. Hands . . . which projected like strings upon the finger-board of a violin, and armed with claws like those on the terminations of bats' wings —Théophile Gautier

51. A hand that felt as though it was reaching for you from the grave —Harvey Swados

52. Hand that rested like a sparrow on the table —Tony Ardizzone

53. Hand . . . warm as a horn —Walker Percy

54. Hand . . . wet and cold as something fished out of a pond —T. Coraghessan Boyle

55. Her hands were stunning, like a sublime idea —Boris Pasternak

56. His hands . . . seemed large and awkward as if he was wearing invisible mittens —Stephen Crane

57. His wrists seemed to dangle from his cuffs as if they were sewn to the cloth —Jonathan Valin

58. Long hands, like pitchforks —*Arabian Nights*

59. An old man's hand, hooked and grimy with a couple of nailless fingers, like a hand in a horror film —Jonathan Valin

60. Veins [beneath skin of hands] tessellated like a blue mosaic, shining like an intricate blue design captured beneath glass —William Styron

61. Wrists like steel whips —H. E. Bates

HAND MOVEMENTS
See Also: HANDSHAKE

1. Brushed at his forehead, like an insect had landed there —Donald McCaig

2. Clapped her hands like someone shooing pigeons —Sharon Sheehe Stark

3. Clapping as loudly as if their hands were wooden slats —Louis Auchincloss

4. Clapping her hands like cymbals —Ann Beattie

5. Clasped her hands behind her back like a child embarrassed at a social function, or stuck in the middle of a recitation —Peter De Vries

6. Cradled his hand in his lap, like it was a ruined bird —Donald McCaig

7. Flapped his hand like a flag —Mary Hedin

8. Flashing the palms of both hands like two headlights —Ludwig Bemelmans

9. Folding both hands in her lap like a reprimanded schoolgirl —Ed McBain

10. (He flagged the car with . . .) gestures like hoops —Eudora Welty

11. A hand, like a leaf, fell on his shoulder —Katherine Mansfield

12. Hands clasped like the hands of an old man round a stick —Sylvia Townsend Warner

13. Hands flapping like misshapen white moths —Joan Hess

14. Hands flew off the steering wheel like a pair of startled birds —Ed McBain

15. Hands fluttered like the fins of angel-fish —Frank Swinnerton

16. (Her delicate) hands . . . flutter like birds —Phyllis McGinley

17. Hands gesticulating—flying through the air like two brown sparrows — Jonathan Kellerman

18. Hands jerked as if they were on wires —Dorothy Parker

19. Hands lifting out as if to smooth, like a sheet on a bed —John Updike

20. Hands rose and floated in the air, graceful and helpless as doves — Marge Piercy

21. Hands spread wide as calipers —Diane Ackerman

22. Hands were outspread as though he were leading an orchestra into a profound and final diminuendo —Ralph Ellison
    A plain and simple variation: "Raised his hand like an orchestra conductor."

23. Hasty, jerky gestures like a comedian in a silent movie —George Garrett

24. Held up her hand like a schoolgirl asking for permission to leave the room —Harvey Swados

25. Held up his hand like a traffic cop signaling stop —Ross Thomas

26. Kept rattling the ice in her glass, rattling her beads, rattling her bracelet like an impatient pony jingling its harness —Flannery O'Connor

27. Long thin hand . . . floated like a scarf through the air —Marge Piercy

28. Nervous, tentative gesture, like someone making up his mind to stroke a dog that has the reputation of biting —Francis King

29. Opening and closing his fingers like a neon sign flickering at night — Ariel Dorfman

30. Passed her hand over her eyes as if to dispell a cloud —Robert Graves

31. Rearranges her hair like a horse shaking away a fly —W. P. Kinsella

32. Rubbing his hands together as if working tobacco for a pipe —Patrick White

33. Spread his hands in front of him, palms up, as if he intended to read in their lines the past as well as the future —Margaret Millar

34. Using his hands like a sculptor to shape the words he throws out — George Garrett

35. Wave as regal as Henry the Eighth's —Mary Hedin

HANDSHAKE

1. A grip like a trash compactor —Jonathan Valin
2. A grip like a weightlifter —Harvey Swados
3. Grip like iron —Walker Percy
4. A grip like pincers —Gerald Kersh
5. Hand gripped like bird claws —Wallace Stegner
6. (Your) hand grips mine like a railing on an icy night —Adrienne Rich
7. Hand . . . pumping at mine as if he expected my fingertips to squirt milk or something —T. Coraghessan Boyle
8. Handshake like a bite —Leonard Michaels
9. Handshake like cold, cooked spaghetti —Mark Singer
10. Her hand was limp as a dead carp —Jay Parini
11. His fingers pressed my hand like pieces of wood —Aharon Megged
12. Shook hands . . . like competitors before a match of some kind — Ross Macdonald
13. Shook hands like strangers —John Dos Passos
14. Took it (the hand) cautiously, as if he were picking up a loathsome object preparatory to dropping it in the trash basket —Evan Hunter
15. (She) took Jim's soft fingers and held them closely, until he felt that they had been drawn into a mangle —Frank Swinnerton

HANDWRITING

1. Handwriting . . . like driven sleet —Peter De Vries
2. Handwriting looks as if a swarm of ants, escaping from an ink bottle, had walked over a sheet of paper without wiping their legs —Sydney Smith

HAPPINESS

See Also: CONTENTMENT, JOY, PLEASURE

1. All happiness is a chance encounter and at every moment presents itself to you like a beggar by the roadside —André Gide
2. The best advice on the art of being happy is about as easy to follow as advice to be well when one is sick —Madame Swetchine
   See Also: DIFFICULTY
3. Dry happiness is like dry bread. We eat, but we do not dine —Victor Hugo
   In *Les Miserables,* the hero, Jean Valjean, continues: "I wish for the superfluous, for the useless, for the extravagant, for the too much, for that which is not good for anything."

4. Ecstatic as a scientist who had just discovered the key to immortality — Susan Fromberg Schaeffer

5. Elated as though he had stumbled on a treasure —Brian Moore

6. A gay, light happiness, like bubbles in wine held up against the sun — Ben Ames Williams

7. Glowed with happiness, like a child with expectations of a birthday party —Frank Swinnerton

8. The happiest women, like the happiest nations, have no history — George Eliot

9. Happiness as wholesome as honey on the comb —John Braine

10. Happiness choked my throat like an anthem. It flowed through me like a river from the beginning of the column to its end —Aharon Megged

11. (In the midst of happiness grows a seed of unhappiness.) Happiness consumes itself like a flame. (It cannot burn forever) —August Strindberg

12. Happiness . . . descended upon her heart, like a cloud of morning dew in a dell of wild-flowers —Walter De La Mare

13. Happiness . . . filled her brain like wine —William Dean Howells

14. Happiness flits from branch to twig to branch like a hummingbird — Delmore Schwartz

15. Happiness is falling on us out of the sky . . . like a blanket of snow — Jean Giraudoux

16. Happiness is like a sunbeam, which the least shadow intercepts — Chinese proverb

17. Happiness is like manna; it is to be gathered in grains, and enjoyed every day. It will not keep; it cannot be accumulated —Tryon Edwards

18. Happiness is like time and space; we make and measure it ourselves — George Du Maurier

19. Happiness, like air, is not something you can put in a bottle —Anon
    See Also: AIR

20. Happiness, like the pink and white anemones of my childhood, is a flower that must not be picked —Andre Maurois

21. The happiness of the wicked passes away like a torrent —Jean Baptiste Racine

22. Happiness struck her like a shower of rain —Eudora Welty

23. Happiness . . . was there like light seen through moving leaves, like touching a warm stone —Sumner Locke Elliott

24. Happy and thoughtless as an apple on a tree —George Garrett

25. Happy as a butterfly in a garden full of sunshine and flowers —Louisa May Alcott

26. Happy as a clam —American colloquialism, attributed to New England
    A variation of this found in Bartlett's *Dictionary of Americanisms* is, "Happy as a clam at high water."

27. Happy as a couple of linebackers after winning a high school game — Marge Piercy

28. Happy as a couple of cherrystone clams —George Garrett

29. Happy as a dog with a bone —Anon

30. Happy as a lover —William Wordsworth

31. (I am)happy as a mother whose good baby sleeps —May Sarton

32. Happy as a pig in clover —American colloquialism
    In the American army this gave way to "Being happy as a pig in shit."

33. Happy as a robin when he trills —Anon American song "Love Letters"

34. Happy as a swallow —Richard Ford

35. Happy as a tick in a dog's ear —Jay Parini

36. Happy as trees that find a wind to sway them —Sara Teasdale

37. He loved happiness like I love tea —Eudora Welty

38. When it [happiness] comes to one, it comes as naturally as sleep — Willa Cather

39. I was high as taxes —Loren D. Estleman

40. I was like a river in flood . . . drowning in my own happiness, and buoyed up by it at the same time —Eugene Ionesco

41. Live together . . . as happily as two lobsters in a saucepan, two bugs on a muscle —Dylan Thomas
    See Also: RELATIONSHIPS

42. Looked like the sun at the zenith —Carlos Baker

43. Happy-looking as if he's just heard the foreman say, "Not guilty" — William Slavens McNutt

44. Looking for happiness is like clutching the shadow or chasing the wind —Japanese proverb
    See Also: ELUSIVENESS

45. Looks like he is a kid holding his first puppy —John Wainwright

46. Moments of happiness hang like pearls on the finest silken thread, certain to be snapped, the pearls scattered away —Joan Chase

47. On the brink of our happiness we stop like someone on a drunk starting to weep —Galway Kinnell

48. The rays of happiness, like those of light, are colorless when unbroken —Henry Wadsworth Longfellow

49. There is nothing which has yet been contrived by man, by which so much happiness is produced as by a good tavern or inn —Samuel Johnson, March 21, 1776

50. The vicissitudes of life touch him [a happy man] lightly, like the wind in the aspen-tree —Anton Chekhov

51. Wore his new happiness like an advertisement —Nancy Huddleston Packer

HARDNESS
See: FIRMNESS, TOUGHNESS

HARD-HEARTEDNESS
See: CRUELTY

HARDSHIP
See: FORTUNE/MISFORTUNE

HARD WORK
See: AMBITION, WORK

HARMLESSNESS
See Also: INNOCENCE, KINDNESS

1. As incapable of inflicting harm as a butterfly —Anon

2. Harmless and pleasant as the murmur of book and wind —Robert Buchanan

3. Harmless as a Fuller Brush salesman —Raymond Chandler
    Invariably topical or "brand name" similes either become obsolete or change when the name is no longer a household word. However, there's always a new name or catchword to take its place.

4. Harmless as a moth in a closet of Dacron —Anon

5. Harmless as an infant at play —William Cowper
    Besides other variants meaning literally harmless ("Harmless as a baby," 'Harmless as a sleeping infant'), there are also the more dramatic ones implying danger ('Harmless as an infant playing with knives/a box of pins/matches').

6. Harmless as a paper tiger —Chinese proverb

7. Harmless as doves —*The Holy Bible*
    Attribution for the simile is often given to Christina Rosetti's *Sonnet of Sonnets,* which contains this line: "She spread about her beauty for a snare, harmless as doves."

8. Harmless as leaves —Reynolds Price

9. Harmless as pigeons —Robinson Jeffers

10. Harmless as witches that have been robbed of their terror —Ellen Glasgow

HARMONY
See: AGREEMENT, COMPATIBILITY, PEACEFULNESS

HARSHNESS
See Also: VOICE, FIRMNESS

1. Austere . . . as an aging virgin —Paige Mitchell
2. Corrosive as shame —Frank Swinnerton
3. Harsh as the bitterness of death —Algernon Charles Swinburne
4. Harsh as the yelping of jackals —Gustave Flaubert
5. (I will be . . .) harsh as truth —William Lloyd
6. Rough as a cob and twice as corny —American colloquialism attributed to South
7. Shrill and active like a flight of gulls —George Garrett
   See Also: ACTIVENESS
8. Shrill as a whistling teapot with a head full of steam —Anon
9. (His nerves sang a song) shriller than a dog whistle —Douglas Adams
10. Shrill [voice] like a blade turning on a whetstone —Clifford Irving
11. Spoke sternly like a ward nurse to a familiar patient —Arthur A. Cohen
12. Strident as mustard —Marge Piercy
13. Threw orders around like lashes from a cat-o'-nine-tails —Maya Angelou

HASTE
See: SPEED

HASTINESS
See: CARELESSNESS

HATRED

1. Dislike ran round the table like electricity —Penelope Gilliatt
2. Exuded venom like a malicious old lady —Colette
3. The greatest hatred, like the greatest virtue and the worst dogs, is silent —Jean Paul Richter
4. Hate . . . flowed like electric syrup through her veins —Marge Piercy
5. Hate is ptomaine, good-will is a panacea —Elbert Hubbard
6. Hating people is like burning down your own house to get rid of a rat —Harry Emerson Fosdick

7. Hatred fills my mouth like spit —Margaret Atwood

8. Hatred is a form of subjective involvement by which one is bound to the hated object —Lao Tzu

9. Hatred like fire; it makes even light rubbish deadly —George Elliott

10. Hatreds, like chickens, come home to roost —Joseph Shearing

11. He'll (a hated individual) be getting into your beer, like prussic acid; and blotting out your eyes, like a cataract; and screaming in your ears, like a brain tumor; and boiling around your heart, like melted lead; and ramping through your guts, like a cancer —Joyce Cary

12. I hate you like all-fire —Truman Capote

13. (Lady Charlotte would swallow back her hot feeling against Cynthia.) It [hate] was like a dark web within her, a fibrous tangle like the roots of plants in too small a pot —M. J. Farrell

14. My hate is like ripe fruit —Marvin Bell

15. The pleasure of hating, like a poisonous mineral, eats into the heart of religion and turns it to rankling spleen and bigotry —William Hazlitt
    In his essay, *The Pleasures of Hating,* Hazlitt continues to describe the effects of hatred: "It makes patriotism an excuse for carrying fire, pestilence, and famine into other lands; it leaves to virtue nothing but the spirit of censoriousness."

16. Promiscuous haters get religion as promiscuous lovers get clap — Gerald Kersh

17. Spite may often see as clearly as charity —Lawrence Durrell

HEAD(S)

See Also: HEAD MOVEMENTS

1. Great head and neck rising up like a howitzer shell from out of his six-button double-breasted, after the manner of the eternal Occupation Zone commandant —Tom Wolfe
   The man being profiled by Wolfe is Otto Preminger.

2. Head like a hard apple —Hugh Walpole

3. Head stiff and to the side like the bust of a minor Roman official — Cynthia Ozick

4. A head too small for the size of his face, like an underinflated balloon —Sue Grafton

5. Held his torso like a bit of classical rubble —Cynthia Ozick

6. Her head looks as if it had worn out two bodies —American colloquialism attributed to New England

7. His skull curved like a helmet above his deep-set blue eyes —Jonathan Valin

In the novel, *Life's Work,* Valin follows this with a sentence containing another simile: "His lower face fit into that helmet like a hardwood dowel driven in by a hammer."

8. A sleek, round head like an umbrella's —Arthur Train

HEAD MOVEMENTS

1. Bowed his head . . . as if wishing to fall at her feet —Leo Tolstoy
2. Craned her head back and forth like a periscope, the way people do when they are searching for a taxi at rush hour in Manhattan —Daphne Merkin
3. Cranes his neck like a swan —Anton Chekhov
4. Drew his head into his shoulders like the bellows of an accordion — Paul Olsen
5. Ducks his head, like a man someone has menaced and who has barely gotten out of the way —Richard Ford
6. Gave a shake of his head, like a dazed boxer coming to —Peter De Vries
7. Head, bobbing like a hollow ball —John Updike
8. (She was looking at her husband) head cocked like a setter bitch (as if wondering, trying to remember who she had climbed into bed with this time) —James Crumley
9. (The old man's) head had lowered itself into his collar like a turtle's — Flannery O'Connor
10. Head moving like a prison search light —T. Glen Coughlin
11. Heads . . . bent, like flowers following the sun or thrushes listening for snails —Frank Swinnerton
12. Head sliding forward [while dozing] like an abandoned puppet —T. Alan Broughton
13. (Little Nigel's) head snaps round like a weathervane in a gale —John Le Carré
14. Head spun like a lazy susan —Jay Parini
15. Head thrust forward like a hungry hawk —Harold Adams
16. Head tilted to one side like a bib bird sitting on a branch of a tree — Harvey Swados
17. Head tilted to one side like a robin listening for worms —Jay McInerney
18. Head turning quickly from side to side, like an animal's —Eudora Welty
19. Head wagging like a mechanical toy —F. van Wyck Mason
20. Her head dropped like a soaked tea rose —Sharon Sheehe Stark

21. His head droops like a sun-flower —S. J. Perelman

22. His head hangs limp as a sock full of sand —Ira Wood

23. His head moved to and fro like a foolish kitten's after a swinging tangle of wool —Vicki Baum

24. His head rolled about his shoulders like a balloon that wanted to break its string —James Lee Burke

25. His head swung like a snake's as he talked, scanning anyone who chanced to come near —Donald MacKenzie

26. Holds up her head like a hen drinking —Scottish proverb

27. Lifted his big head like a listening deer —Zane Grey

28. Lifted up his head like a mouse sniffing the air —Isaac Babel

29. Lowered her head like a slow-witted schoolgirl trying to collect her thoughts in an effort to understand the teacher's question —Franz Werfel

30. Lowered his head to pray, like a martyr who believed the kingdom of heaven was at hand —Z. Vance Wilson

31. Made the convulsive movement of his head and neck, as if his tie were too tight —Leo Tolstoy
    See Also: NECK

32. A man with a small head is like a pin without any, very apt to get into things beyond his depth —Josh Billings

33. Nodded like a basking lizard —Derek Lambert

34. Nodded . . . like a leaf —William McIlvanney

35. Nodded smartly—like a second lieutenant's salute —Jonathan Valin

36. Nodding his head like a pecking bird —Beryl Markham

37. Nods his head like a sage old trial judge —Richard Ford

38. Pulls back his head, like a turtle sensing danger —Rick Borsten

39. Shaking her head as if to get rid of a fly —Ruth Suckow

40. Shaking her head impatiently . . . as if in a futile attempt to ease the chafing of an invisible collar —Carolyn Kizer

41. Shook his head like a wet retriever —Sharon Sheehe Stark

42. Shook his head like an overburdened professor —Martin Cruz

43. Shook my head back and forth like a silent, solid bell —Richard S. Prather

44. Tossed her head with petulant violence, like a child who doesn't want her snarls combed out —John Updike

45. Turned her head . . . cocking it a little, like a pretty canary in a cage —Harvey Swados

46. Turning his head from side to side as though his necktie were too tight (and when he did that he usually clutched at his throat) —Ivan Turgenev
    In a story entitled *Knock . . . Knock . . . Knock . . .*
    Turgenev used this simile to describe a character who always
    felt cramped in the world.

47. Turns his head from side to side, like a turtle —Margaret Atwood

48. Wagged their heads like a company of cockatoos —Katherine Mansfield

49. Waved her head here and there like a piece of wind-worried old orange-peel —F. Scott Fitzgerald

50. The way he moved his head from side to side made him seem like some sort of a little perky bird, a goldfinch, perhaps —Roald Dahl

51. Withdrew his head like a scared tortoise —Donald MacKenzie

HEALTH

See Also: PAIN

1. As clean and strong and healthy as a young tree in the sun —Hugh Walpole

2. (Has a heart) as sound as a bell —William Shakespeare

3. Drug addiction is like a light that doesn't shine —Cardinal John O'Connor, speaking at New York City ceremony to fight drug addiction, August 8, 1986

4. Felt like the symptoms on a medicine bottle —George Ade

5. (Looking) fit and taut as a fiddle —Robert Louis Stevenson

6. (I feel as) fit as a bull moose —Theodore Roosevelt to newspaper reporters

7. Fit as a fiddle —John Ray's *Proverbs*
    This is the most famous of the many "Fit as" comparisons. A
    modernized extension by novelist Geoffrey Wolff: "Fit as an
    electric fiddle."

8. (You're looking this morning as) fit as a flea —Henry James

9. Gobbled pills like a famished chicken pecking up corn —Dale Kramer

10. [Narrator's father] gradually sank as if he had a slow leak —Oliver Sacks

11. Healthy as a kayaker —Richard Ford

12. Healthy as a steer —Thomas Zigal

13. A healthy body is the guest-chamber of the soul, a sick, its prison — Francis Bacon

14. Hones himself down [to stay in top physical condition] sharper than a Gillette blade —Norman Keifetz

15. It is better to lose health like a spendthrift than to waste it like a miser —Robert Louis Stevenson

16. No neurotic is cured, he merely substitutes one set of neuroses for another. Like a man who stops biting his fingernails only to start scratching his head —Margaret Millar

17. Pent-up resentment, aggression and hostility are as bad for health as constipation —George Garrett

18. Radiate health and good will like a red-hot stove —Robertson Davies
See Also: KINDNESS

19. Sickness fell upon me like an April cloud —Edward Marsh

20. So far as ailments went, Uncle Horace was like an insatiable gardener confronted by a seedsman's catalogue. He had only to get news of an untried specimen to have a go at it —Howard Spring

21. Sound as a bell of brass —Anon
According to Larry Gottlieb, a one-time handicapper for the *New York Morning Telegraph,* this expression used to assay a thoroughbred up for sale is the most commonly used simile in racing circles. It was introduced in England during the nineteenth century.

22. Sound as a nut —Mazo De La Roche

23. Temperature as high as a tree —Mary Lee Settle

24. Unhealthy as the liver of a goose intended for pâté —Israel Zangwill

HEART(S)
See Also: AGITATION, HEARTBEAT

1. Hard hearts, and cold, like weights of icy stone —Percy Bysshe Shelley

2. The heart errs like the head —Anatole France

3. The heart (especially the Jewish heart) is a fiddle: you pull the strings, and out come songs, mostly plaintive —Sholom Aleichem

4. The heart is like the sky, a part of heaven, but changes night and day too, like the sky —Lord Byron

5. The heart is like a creeping plant, which withers unless it has something around which it can entwine —Charles James Apperley

6. The heart is like an instrument whose strings steal nobler music from Life's many frets —Gerald Massey

7. Heart like a child —Mary Hood

8. The heart of the wise, like a mirror, should reflect all objects, without being sullied by any —Confucius

9. Hearts isolated behind the bars of ribs and jumping around like monkeys —Yehuda Amichai

10. Hearts . . . mellow as well-tilled soil in which good seed flourishes —
    Valdimir G. Korolenko

11. Hearts opening like jaws —Sharon Olds

12. Heart trembling a little like the door for Elijah the Prophet —Yehuda
    Amichai

13. A heart without affection is like a purse without money —Benjamin
    Mandelstamm

14. Her heart divided like two wings —Carson McCullers

15. Her heart sank like a wounded bird —Ellen Glasgow

16. His heart ached like Niagara Falls —Frank O'Hara

17. His heart is like a viper, hissing and spitting poison at God —Jonathan
    Edwards

18. His heart . . . like the sea, ever open, brave and free —F. E.
    Weatherly

19. His heart sagged in its net of veins like a rock in a sling —George
    Garrett

20. His heart swelled up in his throat like a toad —Oakley Hall

21. His heart was open as the day —Anon ballad, "Old Grimes"

22. The human heart is like a ship on a stormy sea driven about by winds
    blowing from all four corners of heaven —Martin Luther

23. The human heart is like a millstone in a mill: when you put wheat
    under it, it turns and grinds and bruises the wheat to flour; if you put no
    wheat, it still grinds on, but then 'tis itself it grinds and wears away —
    Martin Luther

24. A man's heart is like a sponge, just soaked with emotion and sentiment
    of which he can squeeze a little bit out for every pretty woman —Helen
    Rowland

25. A man's heart, like an automobile, is always apt to skid and ditch him
    just at the psychological moment when he thinks he has it under perfect
    control —Helen Rowland

26. My heart clenched like a fist —Charles Johnson
    The fist comparison is also effective for describing a grim,
    pinched facial expression.
    See Also: FACIAL EXPRESSIONS, SERIOUS

27. My heart is like an apple-tree whose boughs are bent with thick-set fruit
    —Christina Rossetti
    The first stanza of *A Birthday,* from which this is taken,
    contains yet another heart comparison: "My heart is like a
    rainbow shell that paddles in a halcyon sea."

28. My heart is like an outbound ship that at its anchor swings —John
    Greenleaf Whittier

29. My heart is like a singing bird —Christina Rossetti
30. My little heart pops out, like springs —Diane Wakoski
    This simile is the title of a poem which begins with yet another simile: "A little spirit in me that's wound up like a clock."
31. The heart is like a creeping plant, which withers unless it has something around which it can entwine —Charles James Apperley
32. Without a loved one my heart's like a beet root choked with chickweed —A Broken-Hearted Gardener, anonymous 19th century verse

HEARTBEAT
See Also: AGITATION

1. Chest chiming like a cathedral gone berserk —Jonathan Gash
2. Feel his heart beating wildly inside his child's body, like a bird in a frail cage —Ruth Prawer Jhabvala
3. Heart banged like a drum —Katherine Mansfield
4. Heart beating like an African drum —Hugh Walpole
5. (Mrs. Arkin's) heart fluttered like a bird's wing —Gloria Norris
6. Heart jumping like a puppy —Anne Sexton
7. Heart noisy as a crockcrow —Walter de la Mare
   See Also: NOISE
8. Heart pulsing like a womb which has just given birth —Erica Jong
9. Heart . . . running like a hamster on a wheel —Diane Ackerman
10. Hearts . . . like muffled drums, are beating funeral marches to the grave —Henry Wadsworth Longfellow
11. A heart that ran up and down within the cage of ribs like a restless panther —Leonard Casper
12. Heart thumping like a June bug —Anne Sexton
13. Heart thumping like an outboard —Richard Ford
14. His heart . . . beat high and fast like the ticking of a watch under a pillow —Frank Swinnerton
15. His heart began to give off tremendous explosions like a rifle —Eudora Welty
16. His heart beating, fiercely, like a small clock —Celia Dale
17. His heart flapped like a mass of furled banners —Bernard Malamud
18. His heart fluttered like that of a small bird about to be stoned —Alice Walker
19. My heart leaps forward like a hungry dog —Karl Shapiro
20. My heart pounds away, confident as a clock —Denise Levertov
21. My heart pounds down on itself like an anvil —Richard Ford

22. My heart staggers like a drunk —George Garrett
23. My heart was beating intolerably like a held bird —Reynolds Price
24. The noise that his heart valve produced sounded like two mechanical mice making love in a spoon drawer —Tom Robbins
25. Heart like a bass drum in her chest —Susan Richards Shreve
26. Heart [of a skylark] . . . drumming like a motor —Ted Hughes
27. (In his ears his) heart sounded like jungle drums —Mary Hedin

HEARTINESS
See: EMOTIONS

HEAT
See Also: WEATHER

1. The days were like hot coals —Henry Wadsworth Longfellow
    See Also: DAY
2. A glaring, summery heat covered everything like a layer of glass —Jean Thompson
3. The heat came down on you like a leaden mantle, stifling you as it did so —Dominique Lapierre
4. [Midsummer] heat closed in like a hand over a murder victim's mouth —Truman Capote
5. Heat fell on her like a blanket —Julia O'Faolain
6. Heat gathers like fog —Angela Carter
7. Heat . . . heavy as water —Dan Jacobson
8. The heat . . . hung like a hot dust vapor —H. E. Bates
9. Heat lay on the pavement like a tired dog in the doorway of a house — Aharon Megged
    See Also: CITY/STREETSCAPES
10. Heat shimmered and bent the fields like the landscape was a reflection in an old mirror —Will Weaver
    See Also: LANDSCAPES
11. The heat thick as a swamp —Margaret Atwood
12. Heat thick as jelly —Elizabeth Enright
13. The heat was like a tyrant who hated his subjects —William H. Hallhan
14. The heat was like a wasting disease —T. Coraghessan Boyle
15. Heat waves . . . rising . . . like fumes off kerosene —Larry McMurtry
16. Heat waves rose writhing like fine wavy hair —Wallace Stegner
17. (Sun) hot as a blast furnace —Raymond Chandler
18. Hot as a blister —Sir Francis C. Burnand

19. Hot as a draft from hell —William H. Gass
20. Hot as a four-alarm fire —H. C. Witwer
21. Hot as a fox —Elizabeth Spencer
22. Hot as a jungle —T. Coraghessan Boyle
23. Hot as a mink in Africa —Reynolds Price
24. Hot as an oven —*The Holy Bible*
    Writers and speakers have long repeated and enlarged upon this simile, changing the descriptive frame of reference altogether or switching from the oven to what comes out of it. Some of these old-timers include: "Hot as hell-fire" (John Dryden), "Hot as hate" (Hamlin Garland), "Hot as hammered hell/hot as hammered lightning" (American colloquialisms) and "Hot as a basted turkey" (Will Carleton).
25. (On some nights, New York is as) hot as Bangkok —Saul Bellow
26. Hot as live ash —Beryl Markham
27. (I am as) hot as molten lead, and as heavy too —William Shakespeare
28. (I'm) hot as shit —Richard Ford
29. (Even the fog that day was) hot as soup —Marge Piercy
30. Hot as the business end of a pistol —Delmore Schwartz
31. Hot as the hinges of hell —Babs H. Deal
32. The hot days pressed people flat as irons —Susan Fromberg Schaeffer
33. Hot, like a furnace room —Frank Conroy
34. It was like being inside a radiator —David Brierley
35. It was more than hot: it was like being under a damp blanket in the tropics —Laurie Colwin
36. Scorches like nettles —Babette Deutsch
37. Steaming [from hot weather] like crabs in a soup pot —Margaret Laurence
38. (The shallow ditches were) steaming like fresh cowflap —Paul Theroux
39. [A hot bath] steams like a bowl of soup —Margaret Atwood
40. (She was) trapped between the heat of the sun and the heat rising from the earth. It was like being struck simultaneously by gusts of fire from above and from below —Margaret Millar
41. Warm as a newborn child —William Alfred
42. Warm as summer —Walter Savage Landor
43. Warm as veins —Ted Hughes
44. (The water is) warm like my blood —Marge Piercy
45. (A novel that) warms like a hug —Anon book blurb, quoted in advertisement from *San Francisco Chronicle*

HEAVINESS

1. Feel heavy . . . like a corpse —Penelope Gilliatt
2. Feel heavy like the September limbs of an apple tree —Diane Wakoski
3. The hand upon his shoulder weighed like a hand of lead —Oscar Wilde
4. Heavy and indistinct, like the consciousness of a man in a dream — Gustave Flaubert
   See Also: VAGUENESS
5. Heavy as a lecher's kiss —Sylvia Plath
6. (A cold sky) heavy as a vault —Malcolm Cowley
7. (They are) heavy as dumplings —Henry David Thoreau
   To give added emphasis and specificity, there's "Heavy as overcooked dumplings," "Heavy as matzoh balls," "Heavy as latkes," "Heavy as wontons."
8. Heavy as guilt —Anon
9. Heavy as hard luck —Philip Larkin
10. Heavy as ingots —Diane Ackerman
11. (The glass mugs were) heavy as sin —Harvey Swados
12. [A suitcase] heavy as some icon —Cynthia Ozick
13. Heavy as the weight of dreams —Henry Wadsworth Longfellow
14. Leaden like a bullet —Ted Hughes

HELPFULNESS
   See: KINDNESS

HELPLESSNESS

1. As defenseless [without a gun] as a tethered goat in a jungle —Eric Ambler
2. Brutally as on a gag in her mouth, she choked on the sense of her defenselessness —Dorothy Canfield Fisher
3. Chucked about like a cork —Nicholas Monsarrat
4. Feel like a card in a deck that is being constantly shuffled —W. P. Kinsella
5. Feel like a rookie runner caught off base by a wily pitcher, hung up in that vast area between first and second, fluttering back and forth like a wounded bird who knows he's doomed —W. P. Kinsella
   See Also: BASEBALL
6. Felt as a lost sailor on a sinking ship might feel, who throws his last rope, and no saving hands to grasp it —Stella Benson
7. Felt [as result of being moved to another home by grandparents] as if I was being kidnapped —Elizabeth Bishop

8. Felt helpless, like a rape victim —Rose Tremain

9. Felt helpless, as if he were involved in some disgraceful fraud —Katherine Anne Porter

10. Felt helpless, like a dog that's been run over —Robert Lowry

11. Felt I was nothing but a husk blown this way and that way by the winds of misfortune —Angela Carter

12. Felt like a beast in a trap, whose enemy would come upon him soon —H. G. Wells

13. Felt like a bone between dogs —Julia O'Faolain

14. Felt like a man trapped in a swamp —Donald MacKenzie

15. Felt like a marionette, as though something outside her were jerking the strings that forced her to scream and strike —Jean Rhys

16. Felt like a wounded fish who faced a larger hungry fish —William Beechcroft

17. Felt more and more like a soldier being pitched into battle without proper orders —John Fowles

18. Felt ridiculous and out of control, like an engine breaking itself apart —Mark Helprin

19. Helpless and hopeful as a blade of grass —George Garrett
    See Also: HOPE

20. Get tossed like salad —Charles Bukowski

21. Helpless . . . as a hooked fish swinging to land —Thomas Hardy

22. Helpless as a lion without teeth —F. Scott Fitzgerald

23. Helpless as an infant caterpillar in a nest of hungry ants —James Montgomery

24. Helpless as a plant without water —F. Hopkinson Smith

25. Helpless [against tide of emotions] as a swimmer swept away in a strong current —Margaret Kennedy

26. Helpless as a turtle on its back —O. Henry

27. Helpless as a writhing beetle on its back —Robert Traver

28. (I have become as) helpless as if the branch I seize and the one I stood upon both broke at the same time —Tamil

29. Helpless as shadows —Jean Garrigue

30. Helpless as the dead —W. S. Gilbert

31. Helpless as the owner of a sick goldfish —Kin Hubbard

32. Helpless . . . like a man with a rumbling volcano in his pocket, trying to hold back the eruption with his naked hand —Irving Stone

33. Impotent yet defiant . . . like a wild animal driven into a hole or fettered to a stake —Arthur Train

34. It was like being in an elevator cut loose at the top. Falling, falling, and not knowing when you will hit —Margaret Atwood

35. I was like a lamb or an ox that is brought to the slaughter —*The Holy Bible/Jeremiah*

36. Lame as a butterfly spread on a pin —Shirley Kaufman

37. Like elastic, stretched beyond its uttermost, his reason, will, faculties of calculation and resolve snapped to within him —John Galsworthy

38. Looked like sheep looking for their shepherd —W. Somerset Maugham

39. My will was a leaf in a gust of wind —Natascha Wodin

40. Powerless . . . as a stone —Elizabeth Barrett Browning

41. Powerless as before a cataract —Simone de Beauvoir

42. Powerless as the wind —Percy Bysshe Shelley

43. The sense of being trapped ran through him like fire through dry grass —Ben Ames Williams

44. Sense of helplessness . . . like a soft-shell crab that just shed its shell —Kenzaburo Oë

45. Sinking under the leaden embrace of her affection like a swimmer in a drowning clutch —Edith Wharton

46. The situation [of tumbling stock market prices] is like being caught in the Bermuda Triangle —Harvey P. Eisen, *New York Times,* January, 1986

47. Tossed about like an empty can in the sea —Romain Gary

48. Tossed about like cattle on a train —Ignazio Silone

49. Tossed about like twigs in an angry water —Willa Cather

50. Unable to do anything . . . it was like watching a big cat thrash around in a cage and being helpless to free the beast —May Sarton

51. Watching a friend fail . . . it's like a bunch of lifeguards standing and watching their friend drown —Robin Williams, "Sixty Minutes" interview, September 21, 1986
    The comedian's comparison described how comedians feel when they watch one of their own fail on stage.

52. We're all drawn by wires like puppets, and the strongest wire pulls us in the direction in which we are meant to go —Ellen Glasgow

53. Without power, like a buzzing horsefly —George Garrett

54. Worked by strings, like a Japanese marionette —W. S. Gilbert

55. Wriggling helplessly, like a butterfly impaled by a pin —Louis Bromfield

HESITANCY
　　See: UNCERTAINTY

HILLS
      See: MOUNTAINS

HISTORY
      See Also: PAST

1.   Americans treat history like a cookbook. Whenever they are uncertain what to do next, they turn to history and look up the proper recipe, invariably designated "The lesson of history" —Russell Baker
      See Also: CHARACTERISTICS, NATIONAL

2.   Carried his history with him like a tattooed sailor —Alice McDermott

3.   History is a hill or a high point of vantage, from which alone men see the town in which they live or the age in which they are —G. K. Chesterton
      Chesterton continues this simile as follows: "Without some such contrast or comparison, without some such shifting of the point of view, we should see nothing whatever of our own social surroundings. We should take them for granted, as the only possible social surroundings."

4.   History is floated like a bond issue on the fat of banks —Marge Piercy

5.   History is written to order like the Sunday funnies —Marge Piercy
      This is one of several similes pertaining to history in Piercy's poem, *For Shoshana Rihm.*

6.   History . . . like some lump of viscid porridge sliding slowly down a sink —Lawrence Durrell

7.   History passes like falling rocks in the dark —Robinson Jeffers

8.   History [in narrator's view] . . . sifting and seeping, piddling itself away as one wastes a Sunday —William H. Gass

9.   History trails its meaning like old cobwebs caught in a cellar broom —Robert Penn Warren

10.   History was a trash bag of random coincidences torn open in a wind —Joseph Heller

11.   To the scientific eye all human history is a series of collective movements, destructions or migrations, like the massacre of flies in winter or the return of birds in spring —G. K. Chesterton

12.   You can't escape history, or the needs and neuroses you've picked up like layers and layers of tartar on your teeth —Charles Johnson

HOCKEY
      See: SPORTS

HOLLOWNESS
      See: EMPTINESS

HOME
See: FURNITURE AND FURNISHINGS, HOUSES, ROOMS

HONESTY
See Also: RELIABILITY/UNRELIABILITY

1. Clean as a hound's hind leg —William Beechcroft
2. Honest as bread —Mollie Hardwick
3. Honesty is a compulsion swinging a heavy sword like loving —Marge Piercy
4. Honesty is like an icicle; if once it melts that is the end of it —Anon
5. Incorruptible as a statue —Jean Garrigue
6. Law-abiding as a cow —G. K. Chesterton
7. (I'm totally legit.) Legal as a Jesuit —Jay Parini

HONOR
See: REPUTATION

HOPE
See Also: DREAMS

1. As renewed as a baby born to middle life —Richard Ford
2. As spring flowers are promised by seed-sellers in their new catalogues, you too were once full of promise —Charles Simic
3. Carry hope like a tallow candle —Marge Piercy
4. Cold hopes swarm like worms within our living clay —Percy Bysshe Shelley
5. Every wish is like a prayer with God —Elizabeth Barrett
6. Full of inexpressible expectations, like a child running downstairs on Christmas morning, not knowing what wonderful things may be in the stocking —Harvey Swados
7. Had his hopes jerked back and forth like Pinocchio —dialogue from "Hill Street Blues," television drama, broadcast 1987
8. Hope dawned in the distance like a sail —Marguerite Yourcenar
9. Hope is like the setting of the sun. The brightness of our life is gone —William Wadsworth Longfellow
10. (Nothing in the world is as) hopeful as knowing a woman you like is somewhere thinking about only you —Richard Ford
11. Hopeful, like extras at an audition —Lawrence Durrell
12. Hope has as many lifes as a cat or a king —Henry Wadsworth Longfellow

13. Hope is a kind of cheat: in the minute of our disappointment we are angry; but upon the whole matter there is no pleasure without it —Lord Halifax

14. Hope is like the sun, which, as we journey towards it, casts the shadow of our burden behind us —Samuel Smiles

15. Hope is nearly as strong as despair, and greatly more pertinacious and enduring —Walter Savage Landor

16. Hope is to a man as a bladder to a learning swimmer; it keeps him from sinking . . . but yet many times it makes him venture beyond his height —Owen Feltham

17. Hope . . . it's like a fire in the wind; the slightest breeze will diminish it, but if I feed it the wind will make it blaze —Richard Maynard

18. Hope's as cheap as despair —H. G. Bohn's *Handbook of Proverbs*

19. Hopes like a child —Randall Jarrell

20. Hope springing like a Jack-in-the-box —Alice McDermott

21. It was as though a great eraser had swept across Stern's mind, and he was ready to start fresh again —Bruce Jay Friedman

22. Like our shadows, our wishes lengthen as our sun declines —Edward Young

23. Living on hope is like living on an 800 calorie-a-day diet —Anon
    This may have its origins in a Scottish proverb: "He who lives on hope lives on a very lean diet."

24. Look at hopefully, like a bird with its beak open waiting for a nice juicy worm —Sara Woods
    See Also: LOOKS

25. Plucked my spirits up like a hitchhiker who catches a ride when all hope was lost —Richard Ford

26. Through the sunset of hope like the shapes of a dream, what paradise islands of glory gleam —Percy Bysshe Shelley

27. Wishes, like painted landscape . . . afar off they appear beautiful; but near they show their coarse and ordinary colors —Thomas Yalden

HORROR
See: FEAR

HOSPITALITY

1. Giving a party is very much like having a baby; its conception is more fun than its completion —Anon

2. Hospitable as Welcome Wagoners —Lisa Harris
   The hospitality described in Harris' book, *The World of a Hasidic Family*, is that of the Lubavitcher women in New York's Crown Heights section.

3.   A host is like a general: it takes a mishap to reveal his genius —Horace

4.   The service was as slow as the progress of a snail and a good-humored as Rip Van Winkle —O. Henry

HOSTILITY
See: ANGER

HOUSES
See Also: FURNITURE AND FURNISHINGS, ROOMS

1.   [A modern building] all glossy undulations and shining declivities, like a razor haircut in concrete and glass —Jonathan Valin

2.   (The place was) as conspicuously unadorned as a Presbyterian church —Jonathan Valin

3.   (Tenement house with mean little) balconies pulled out one by one like drawers —Vladimir Nabokov

4.   Bricks [in path to front door of house] laid close as your hairs —Sharon Olds

5.   A building long and low like a loaf of bread —Marge Piercy

6.   Buildings as badly painted as old whores —Larry McMurtry

7.   Buildings, lined up like ships —Helen Hudson

8.   Buying a new home is like raising children; there's always room for improvement —Arlene Zalesky, *Newsday*/Viewpoints. September 27, 1986

9.   The church has a steeple like the hat of a witch —William H. Gass

10. (Church) cold, damp and smelly as a tomb —Sean O'Faolain

11. Cottages looking like something the three little pigs might have built — Sue Grafton

12. Darkened houses loomed like medieval battlements —J. W. Rider

13. Decrepit houses lay scattered around the landscape like abandoned machines on a battlefield —Peter Meinke

14. Door . . . shut like an angry face —John Updike

15. A duplex co-op that made Lenny's [Leonard Bernstein] look like a fourth-floor walkup —Tom Wolfe

16. An estate without a forest is like a house without a chimney —Sholom Aleichem

17. A first home, like the person who aroused our initial awakening to sex, holds forever strong sway over our emotions —Dorothea Straus

18. Frame houses collapsing at their centers like underdone cakes —Jean Thompson

19. A glass-and-concrete air-conditioned block of a building cantilevered from the hillside like a Swiss sanitorium —Walker Percy

20. The great glass doors . . . swished together behind him like an indrawn breath —A. Alvarez

21. Her house is like her chiffon cakes, all soft surfaces and pleasant colors —Bobbie Ann Mason

22. A home is like a reservoir equipped with a check valve: the valve permits influx but prevents outflow —E. B. White

23. A house like this is like some kinds of women, too expensive even — James Hilton

24. House narrow as a coffin —Angela Carter

25. Apartments . . . looking like giant bricks stabbed into the ground — W. P. Kinsella

26. Houses, like people, have personalities, and like the personalities of people they are partly molded by all that has happened to them —Louis Bromfield

27. Houses that aged nicely, like a handsome woman —James Crumley

28. Houses, their doors and windows open, drawing in freshness, were like old drunkards or consumptives taking a cure —Saul Bellow

29. The house stood like a huge shell, empty and desolate —H. E. Bates

30. House . . . trim and fresh as a birdcake and almost as small — William Faulkner

31. It [house] sat among ten acres of blackberry brambles, like an abandoned radio —Tom Robbins

32. [A ranch-style house] just too cute for words . . . it looked as if it had been delivered, already equipped, from a store —Christopher Isherwood

33. Kept it [an old historic house] up like a museum —Ruth Prawer Jhabvala
    See Also: ORDER/DISORDER

34. Long rows of apartment houses stood bald and desolate, like sad old prostitutes —Erich Maria Remarque

35. It [a big building
    looked as bleak as a barracks —Robert Silverberg

36. Looked as homey and inviting as the House of Usher —Sarah Bird

37. Houses (seen from belfry) looked like small caskets and boxes jumbled together —Boris Pasternak

38. A modern building made of . . . big cubes of concrete like something built by a child —Edna O'Brien

39. Modern buildings tend to look like call girls who came out of it intact except that their faces are a touch blank and the expression in their eyes is as lively as the tip of a filter cigarette —Norman Mailer

40. Paint peeled from it [an apartment house] in layers, like a bad sunburn —Paige Mitchell

41. A peculiar, suggestive heaviness, trapping the swooning buildings in a sweet, solid calm, as if preserving them in honey —Angela Carter

42. The pink stucco apartment house looked like a cake that was inhabited by hookers about to jump out of it any second —Robert Campbell

43. A pretty country retreat is like a pretty wife: one is always throwing away money decorating it —Washington Irving

44. Residences . . . of brick, whitewashed and looking faintly flushed, like a pretty girl, with the pink of the brick glowing through where the whitewash had worn off —Harvey Swados

45. Slate roofs . . . like the backs of pigeons —Don Robertson

46. Tents sprang up like strange plants. Camp fires, like red, peculiar blossoms, dotted the night —Stephen Crane

47. Victorian house . . . shaped like a wedding cake —Laurie Colwin

48. We require from buildings, as from men, two kinds of goodness: first, the doing their practical day well: then that they be graceful and pleasing in doing it —John Ruskin

HOVERING
See: LINGERING

HOWLS
See: SCREAMS

HUMANITY
See: MANKIND

HUMILITY
See: MEEKNESS

HUMOR
See Also: CLEVERNESS, LAUGHTER

1. Funny as a crutch —American colloquialism
   This typifies the ironic simile that says one thing while it means quite the opposite. A variation that takes the irony an extra step: "Funny as a rubber crutch."

2. Funny as a dirty joke at a funeral —William McIlvanney

3. Funny as your own funeral —Anon

4. Good jests bite like lambs, not like dogs —Thomas Fuller

5. Humor . . . like good cheese, mellowed and ripened by age — Dorothy Canfield Fisher

6. Humor, like history . . . repeats itself like a Gila monster —Harold Adams

7. Jokes that weren't proper and which therefore went through me like an electric shock, both pleasant and intolerable —Thomas Keneally

8. Like clothes for the needy, they [jokes] were worn, shabby and used — Henry Van Dyke

9. Sarcasm should not be like a saw, but a sword; it should cut, and not mangle —Lord Francis Jeffrey

10. A sarcastic wit is a kind of human pole-cat —Josh Billings
    In Billings' phonetic dialect this reads: "a sarkastic wit iz a kind ov human pole-cat."

11. They [poorly told jokes] just lie where they fall, plop, like dropped jellyfish —Herman Wouk

12. True sacrcasm is like a swordstick; it appears, at first sight, to be much more innocent than it really is, till, all of a sudden, there leaps something out of it, sharp and deadly and incisive, which makes you tremble and recoil —Sydney Smith

13. Wheezing out great lumps of irony like a cat spitting up fur —Wilfrid Sheed

HUNGER

See Also: EATING AND DRINKING

1. Appetite . . . as hot as a fire —Henry Fielding

2. Appetite . . . as insatiable as the sun's —Wallace Stevens

3. Had an appetite like a chain saw —Harry Prince

4. Appetite like a sparrow —Jilly Cooper

5. Ate as heartily as a hungry pike —Howard Spring

6. Ate like a gang of hungry threshers —Erich Maria Remarque

7. Belly as empty as a wind instrument —Isaac Babel

8. Hunger makes beans taste like almonds —Italian proverb

9. Hunger stirred in him like a small animal —Carlos Baker

10. Hungry as a bear —John Ray's *Proverbs*
    Of all the "Hungry as" similes, the link with bears, lions and wolves is one of the most enduring

11. (I came home) hungry as a hunter —Charles Lamb

12. Hungry as a nanny goat —Ben Hecht
    This simple and direct line from a play entitled *Winkleberg* marks a departure from Hecht's bent for far-fetched comparisons.

13. Hungry as a schoolboy —Raymond Chandler

14. Hungry as the grave —James Thomson

15. Nibbled like a minnow —Howard Spring

16. Passengers clustered around a food stall like ants trying to drag a crumb of cake back to their nest —Derek Lambert

17. Ravenous as gulls over a fishing boat —Marge Piercy

18. [A voracious eater] sits down to eat as thin as a grasshopper and gets up as big as a bug in the family way —Erich Maria Remarque

19. So hungry, it was as if there was a hand in our stomachs, like purses, rifling through them —Susan Fromberg Schaeffer

20. Stomach . . . as hollow as any trumpet —Henry Fielding

HURRYING
See Also: SPEED

ICICLES
See: SNOW

IDEALS
See: BELIEFS

IDEAS

1. As flowers grow in more tropical luxuriance in a hothouse, so do wild and frenzied ideas flourish in the darkness —Stefan Zweig

2. Every conjecture exploded like a pricked bubble —Stefan Zweig

3. The flow of ideas is broad, continuous, like a river —Gustave Flaubert
    In a letter to George Sand, Flaubert thus refers to her easy writing style. About his own style, he said, "It's a tiny trickle."

4. Get ideas like other men catch cold —Diane Ackerman

5. Getting an idea should be like sitting down on a pin; it should make you jump up and do something —E.L. Simpson

6. His fancy . . . ran along with him, like the sails of a small boat, from which the ballast is thrown overboard —Isak Dinesen

7. The history of ideas is a history of mistakes —Alfred North Whitehead
    Whitehead follows this simile with "But through all mistakes is also the history of the gradual purification of conduct."

8. The idea came . . . like a ray of light —Vladimir G. Korolenko

9. The idea danced before us as a flag —Edgar Lee Masters

10. An idea, like a ghost . . . must be spoken to a little before it will explain itself —Charles Dickens

11. The idea remained, roaming in the dark of his mind . . . like a rat in the basement, too canny to be poisoned or trapped —John Gardner

12. Ideas are free. But while the author confines them to his study, they are like birds in a cage, which none but he can have a right to let fly; for, till he thinks proper to emancipate them, they are under his own dominion —Sir Joseph Yates

13. Ideas are like beards; men do not have them until they grow up — Voltaire

14. Ideas came with explosive immediacy, like an instant birth. Human thought is like a monstrous pendulum; it keeps swinging from one extreme to the other —Eugene Field

15. Ideas come and go; they appear on the horizon as fleeting as rainbows, they rise and fall again like hemlines —Lynne Sharon Schwartz
    See Also: TRANSIENCE

16. Ideas die, like men —Marguerite Yourcenar

17. Ideas good as a fat wallet —Richard Ford
    See Also: MONEY

18. Ideas, like women's clothes and rich men's illnesses, change according to fashion —Lawrence Durrell

19. Ideas of your own are like babies. They are all right if you can keep them quiet —Anon

20. Ideas rose out of him, streamed through his hair like wildflowers —Pat Conroy
    See Also: ABUNDANCE

21. Ideas should be received like guests, in a friendly way, but with the reservation that they are not to tyrannize their host —Albert Moravia

22. Ideas that . . . in the light of day, may hide but never quite go away. Like mice in old houses, one knows they're there —David R. Slavitt
    See Also: PERSISTENCE

23. Ideas winged their way swiftly like martins round the bell at dawn — Ivan Turgenev

24. The imagination is like the drunk man who lost his watch, and must get drunk again to find it. It is as intimate as speech and custom, and to trace its ways we need to reeducate our eyes —Guy Davenport

25. Imagination is like a lofty building reared to meet the sky —Gelett Burgess

26. Imagination . . . must be immediate and direct like the gaze that kindles it —Italo Calvino

27. Lack ideas . . . as if someone had tied a tourniquet around the left side of his brain —Anon

28. Like good yeast bread, a good idea needs time to proof —Erik Sandberg-Diment, *New York Times,* August 24, 1986

29. (Olga's mind was sensuously slow: she) lingered over an idea like someone lingering in a hot tub —Wilfrid Sheed

30. Old ideas, like old clothes, put carefully away, come out again after a time almost as good as new —*Punch,* 1856

31. Picking up the idea by its corner like a soiled hanky —Rosellen Brown

32. Planted ideas . . . as a gardener will plant sticks for climbing sweet pea —Lawrence Durrell

33. A shortsighted concept . . . rather like a bankrupt saying he's invested his capital in debts —Frank Ross

34. The theory arrived neither full-blown, like an orphan on the doorstep, nor sharply defined, like a spike through a shoe; nor did it develop as would a photographic print, crisp images gradually memerging from a shadowy soup. Rather, it unwound like a turban, like mummy bandage —Tom Robbins

35. What America needs now are ideas like shafts of light —Ellen Gilchrist, National Public Radio, September 22, 1986

IDLENESS

See Also: SITTING

1. As peace is the end of war, so to be idle is the ultimate purpose of the busy —Samuel Johnson

2. Idle as a painted ship upon a painted ocean —Samuel Taylor Coleridge

3. Idle as if in hospital —Sylvia Plath

4. Idleness is a disease that must be combated —Samuel Johnson

5. Idleness is like the nightmare; the moment you begin to stir yourself you shake it off —*Punch,* 1853

6. Idleness, like kisses, to be sweet must be stolen —Jerome K. Jerome

7. An idler is a watch without both hands, as useless if it goes as when it stands —William Cowper
    This is modified from the original which reads "A watch that wants both hands."

8. Indolent and shifting as men or tides —Kenneth Patchen

9. A lazy man is like a filthy stone, everyone flees from its stench —*The Holy Bible/Apocrypha*

10. Like lambs, you do nothing but suck, and wag your tails —Thomas Fuller

11. (I've been) lying around like an old cigarette holder —Anton Chekhov
    See Also: LYING

12. A slacker is just like custard pie, yellow all through but without crust enough to go over the top —Don Marquis

13. Sloth, like rust, consumes faster than labor wears, while the used eye is always bright —H. G. Bohn's *Handbook of Proverbs*

IGNORANCE

See Also: STUPIDITY

1. The fault unknown is as a thought unacted —William Shakespeare

2. Ignorance is a form of incompetence —Natsume Sōseki

3. Ignorance is like a delicate exotic fruit; touch it and the bloom is gone —Oscar Wilde

4. Ignorance like a fire does burn —Bayard Taylor
   Modernized from "Like a fire doth burn."

5. Ignorant as dirt —Karl Shapiro

6. A man's ignorance is as much his private property, and as precious in his own eyes, as his family Bible —Oliver Wendell Holmes, Sr.

7. A man with little learning is like the frog who thinks its puddle a great sea —Burmese proverb

8. There are a great multitude of individuals who are like blind mules, anxious enough to kick, but can't tell where —Josh Billings
   Here are the words as they appear in Billing's phonetic dialect:
   "a grate multitude . . . but kant tell whare."

ILLNESSS

See Also: HEALTH

1. Afflictions are like lightning: you cannot tell where they will strike until they have fallen —Jean-Baptiste Lacordaire

2. A big pulse of sickness beat in him as if it throbbed through the whole earth —D. H. Lawrence

3. The disease and its medicine are like two factions in a besieged town; they tear one another to pieces but both unite against their common enemy . . . Nature —Lord Francis Jeffrey

4. Diseases . . . attenuate our bodies . . . shrivel them up like old apples —Robert Burton

5. His head seemed to be flying about like a pin wheel —Sherwood Anderson

6. Illness and doctors go together like priests and funerals —Armand Salacrou

7. Illness and medicines are invariable as costly as champagne and gaiety at a party —Janet Flanner

8. An illness is like a journey into a far country; it sifts all one's experience and removes it to a point so remote that it appears like a vision — Sholem Asch

9. Nausea lay like poison in his blood —Heinrich Böll

10. Our bowels were like running faucets —John Farris

11. Stricken as if an angel had landed on her bedpost —Gloria Norris

ILL TEMPER
See: ANGER

ILLUSTRIOUSNESS
See: FAME

IMAGINATION
See: IDEAS

IMITATION
See: SIMILARITY

IMMEDIACY
See: SPEED

IMMOBILITY
See Also: DEATH, LYING, POSTURE, SITTING STANDING

1. (I am) comatose like a mouse in the sun —Janet Flanner
    The simile was prompted by the writer's being heavily medicated.

2. Fixed as the garden in a wallpaper mural —Anon

3. Frozen like dogs waiting at night for a bitch in heat —Bertold Brecht

4. Immobile as a heavily sprayed coiffure —Elyse Sommer

5. Immobile as despair —Yvor Winters

6. (Lay,) immobile, like something caught, an ungainly fish —Daphne Merkin

7. Immobilized like fishes caught in a net —Dominique Lapierre

8. Immovable, emotionless, a jade Buddha serenely contemplating some quintessential episode of a TV police show —T. Coraghessan Boyle

9. (The corpse still) lay like a smashed fly —G. K. Chesterton

10. Lay motionless, as if felled by an axe —Stefan Zweig

11. Lifeless as a string of dead fish —G. K. Chesterton

12. Motionless as a dog thrown into the street —Émile Zola

13. (Clouds . . .) motionless as a ledge of rock —Willa Cather

14. Motionless as an idol and as grim —John Greenleaf Whittier

15. (Remained standing in the same place,) motionless as if he were a prisoner —Bertold Brecht

16. Motionless, in an agony of inertia, like a machine that is without power —D. H. Lawrence

17. Motionless, like a man in a nightmare —G. K. Chesterton

18. (This play has) no more action than a snake has hips —Anon

19. Remained rooted in place like an oak —Charles Johnson
20. Sat as still as a tree —Speer Morgan
21. Sat like a marble man —Margaret Millar
22. Sat . . . motionless as a drowsing man —Beryl Markham
23. Sat there like a potted plant —Delmore Schwartz
24. Sat through it all [revolution] like a slug —Rita Mae Brown
25. Sits impassive, like Rodin's *Penseur* —Frank Swinnerton
26. (I'd rather) sit still, like the pilot light inside the gas —Saul Bellow
27. Standing . . . like a hydrant —Rosellen Brown
28. Standing there like a glee-club president in granite —Erich Maria Remarque
29. Standing motionless as if turned to stone —Ivan Turgenev
30. Standing stock still . . . like George Segal plaster figures —Paul Kuttner
31. Standing there rigid as the Venus de Milo —T. Coraghessan Boyle
    In Boyle's story, *The Descent of Man,* the character voicing this simile speaks in dialect, using 'de' and 'dere' instead of 'there' and 'the' as used here.
32. Stand motionless as a pillar of the colonial portico of a mansion in a Kentucky prohibition town —O.Henry
33. Stand motionless . . . as though trying to make myself blend with the dark wood and become invisible —William Faulkner
34. Stand perfectly still, like a scarecrow —Walter De La Mare
35. Stand stone still —William Shakespeare
    The simile from *The Life and Death of King John* completes this statement: "I will not struggle; I will . . . "
36. Statue-like repose —James Aldrich
    The simile from a poem entitled *A Death-Bed* reads as follows in its full context: "Her suffering ended with the day; yet lived she at its close, and breathed the long, long night away in statue-like repose."
37. Still as a child in its first loneliness —Theodore Roethke
38. Still as a cocoon on a branch —Marge Piercy
39. Still as a folded bat —Eudora Welty
40. (Became) still as a hare caught in the light of a torch —R. Wright Campbell
41. Still as a little hare in the hollow of a furrow —Colette
42. (Sitting as) still as a lizard on a stone —Mary Stewart
43. Still as a picture —John Greenleaf Whittier
44. Still as a pillar —Reynolds Price

45. Still as a post —Fannie Stearns Gifford
    Other similes to express the same idea are to "Sit still as a fence post" and "To stand like an iron post."
46. Still as a snapshot —Anne Sexton
47. Still as a turtle on a log which is stuck in the mud near some willows — Elizabeth Spencer
48. Still as bushes —Helen Hudson
49. (The air was) still as death —MacDonald Harris
50. (The next morning was cold and clear and) still as held breath —John Yount
51. (Ray lay) still as ice —Wilbur Daniel Steele
52. Still as if a block of ice had formed around him —William McIlvanney
53. Still as a mummy in a case —Henry James
54. Still as sleeping princesses —Joyce Cary
55. Still as the wind's center —Theodore Roethke
56. Stood frozen like some sort of Mexican stone idol —Robert Silverberg
57. Stood still, petrified like the pillar of salt —Victor Hugo
58. Stood there rooted like a plant —Ellen Glasgow
59. They seemed [tired soldiers] as if they were of stone, without the strength to smile, or to swear —Boris Pasternak

IMPARTIALITY

1. Feel rather like a bridge [at being caught between problems of two friends] attached neither to one side nor the other of a tumultous river, suspended in space —May Sarton
2. Impartially welcoming as the host of a television show —Nadine Gordimer
3. Neutral as a page number —John Braine
4. (A voice) neutral as Switzerland —Anon
5. (The Yvette who assembled before me was as) objective as a police sketch —Jill Ciment

IMPATIENCE
See: RESTLESSNESS

IMPERMANENCE
See: TRANSIENCE

IMPASSIVENESS
See: COLDNESS, REMOTENESS, RESERVE

IMPOLITENESS
    See: MANNERS

IMPORTANCE/UNIMPORTANCE
    See Also: MEMORY, NECESSITY

1. Brittle and meaningless as cocktail party patter —William Brammer

2. His influence . . . it is like burning a . . . candle at Dover to show light at Calais —Samuel Johnson
    Had Johnson been an American living in America instead of an Englishman living in England, his comment on Thomas Sheridan's influence on English literature might well have illustrated with "A candle in New York to show light in Boston."

3. Hollow as the (ghastly) amiabilities of a college reunion —Raymond M. Weaver

4. Impact [of information] . . . as thin as gold —Raymond Chandler

5. (About as) important as a game of golf to an astronomer —Anon

6. Important as mathematics to an engineer —Anon

7. Inconsequential . . . like the busy work that grade school teachers devise to keep children out of mischief —Ann Petry

8. Insignifacnt as the canals of Mars —Frank Conroy

9. Its loss would be incalculable . . . like losing the Mona Lisa —Dr. Paul Parks, *New York Times,* August 23, 1986 on potential death of Florida's Lake Okeechobee

10. Meaningful as love —Kenneth Patchen

11. Meaningless, like publishing a book of your opinions with a vanity press —Scott Spencer

12. Of no more importance than a flea or a louse —Boris Pasternak
    In the novel, *Doctor Zhivago,* a character uses this simile to compare a wife to workers.

13. Seemed scarcely to concern us, like fairy tales or cautionary fables that are not to be taken literally or to heart —Joan Chase

14. Shallow as a pie pan —Anon

15. [A speech] shallow as time —Thomas Carlyle

16. Uneventful as theory —A. R. Ammons

17. Worthless as withered weeds —Emily Brontë

IMPOSSIBILITY
    See Also: ABSURDITY, DIFFICULTY, FUTILITY, OPPORTUNITY

1. About as much chance as a man with a wooden leg in a forest fire —George Broadhurst

2. About as possible as hell freezing over —Clifford Odets
3. As feasible as capturing the rain in a thimble —Jonathan Kellerman
4. As likely as a mouse falling in love with a cat —Anon
5. As likely as a talk by Doctor Ruth [Dr. Ruth Westheimer, sex therapist/media personality] in a fundamentalist church —Elyse Sommer
6. As likely as to see a hog fly —H. G. Bohn's *Handbook of Proverbs*
7. As likely to happen as hair growing on the palm of my hand —Anon
8. (Anything of a sexual sort seemed) as remote as landing on the moon or applying for French citizenship —Kingsley Amis
9. As unlikely as your car metamorphosing into a rocket ship —Elyse Sommer
10. Calling on [emotional] memory for so long a leap was like asking power of a machine wrecked by rust —Wilbur Daniel Steele
11. Getting him to join (the Federal Witness Program) was like getting the Ayatollah Khomenei to enroll in a rabbinical school —Doug Feiden
12. Has about as much chance as a cootie on Fifth Avenue —Maxwell Anderson/Laurence Stallings
13. Has about as much chance of making it into the history books as a fart in a cyclone [about fictional President] —Peter Benchley
14. Have about as much chance as a woodpecker making a nest in a concrete telephone pole —Anon sports writer, about a bad baseball team
15. Have about as much chance as a dishfaced chimpanzee in a beauty contest —Arthur Baer
    Bear's simile was part of a comment about the 1919 Willard-Dempsey fight.
16. Impossible . . . like pushing a wet noodle up a hill —Anon Washington aide, *Wall Street Journal,* July 3, 1987
    The aide made this comparison to illustrate the difficulty of trying to attract attention to economic issues and away from the Iran-Contra scandal.
17. Impossible as expecting a hook to hold soft cheese —Anon
18. Impossible as it would be to fire a joke from a cannon —Bartlett's Dictionary of Americanisms
19. Impossible as putting the genie back in the bottle —Peter Jennings, commenting on "World News Tonight" about trying to undo damage to Gary Hart's presidential campaign after release of story about his private life, May 7, 1987
20. Impossible as scratching your ear with your elbow —American colloquialism, attributed to Southwest

21. Impossible as setting a hen one morning and having chicken salad for lunch —George Humphrey
    A comment on quick economic changes during Humphrey's tenure as Secretary of the United States Treasury.

22. Impossible as to imagine a man without a head —Francisque Sarcey

23. Impossible as to pull hair from a bald man's head —Anon

24. Impossible as to rivet a nail in a custard pie —Anon

25. Impossible as to straighten a dog's tail —Anon

26. Impossible as trying to put on a laughter exhibition in a morgue —J. B. Priestly

27. Impossible as trying to blow and swallow at the same time —German proverb
    Another example of usage turning a proverbial statement, "You can't blow and swallow at the same time," into a proverbial comparison.

28. Impossible as undressing a naked man —Anon
    Another simile with proverbial origins, in this case the Greek proverb "A thousand men cannot undress a naked man."

29. Impossible as voting "maybe" —Maurine Neuberger
    Transposed from "Many times I wished I could vote 'maybe'."

30. Impossible . . . like compressing the waters of a lake into a tight, hard ball —Vita Sackville-West

31. Impossible . . . like denying a champion fighter the right to compete in the ring on the grounds that he might be hurt —Beryl Markham

32. Impossible . . . like eating chalk or trying to suck sweetness out of paving brick, or being drowned in an ocean of dishwater, or forced to gorge oneself on boiled unseasoned spinach —Thomas Wolfe
    Wolfe's writing tended towards excess. Not surprisingly, he tended to string several similes together.

33. Impossible . . . like looking for a grain of rice in a bundle of straw — Dominique Lapierre

34. Impossible . . . like me trying to wash the Empire State building with a bar of soap —Don Rickles
    The impossible situation described by Rickles is singer Eddie Fisher's ill-fated marriage to Elizabeth Taylor.

35. Impossible . . . like playing tennis with the net down —Robert B. Parker

36. Impossible . . . like selling the cow and expecting to have the milk too —Danish proverb
    Transposed from the proverbial form, "You can't expect to sell the cow and get the blood."

37. Impossible . . . like stopping a runaway horse with your pinkie — William McIlvanney

38. Impossible, like trying to get blood out of a turnip —English proverb
    Efforts to get new blood out of this cliche focus on changing the object from which to extract blood . . . anything from a stone to a corpse.

39. Impossible like trying to make cheesecake out of snow —Anon

40. Impossible like trying to write on a typewriter while riding a stagecoach —Dr. Ellington Darden

41. Impossible like trying to knock down the Great Wall with a nail file — Arty Shaw

42. Impossible [to keep a secret from my wife] like trying to sneak the dawn past the rooster —Fred Allen

43. Impossible to explain . . . like telling a religious household you had decided God was nonsense —Harvey Swados

44. It [a hard-to-beat record] was like DiMaggio's consecutive-game hitting streak: unapproachable —T. Coraghessan Boyle

45. It was like talking to a tree and expecting a reply —Clive Cussler

46. It was like trying to catch an eagle in a butterfly net —Wallace Turner, *New York Times,* February 4, 1987, reporting on efforts by Washington State game wardens to capture the large sea lions which had been destroying game fish.

47. It was like trying to write a description of how to tie shoelaces in a bow for a person who has never seen shoes —W. P. Kinsella

48. It [changing person's mind about another] was like trying to turn a mule —H. E. Bates

49. It [trying to sift through events from the past] was not unlike hunting for odd-colored stones in tidal flats —Norman Mailer

50. (Blackmailing Laidlow would be) like trying to catch a bull with a butterfly net —William McIlvanney

51. No more chance than a one-legged man in a football game —Elbert Hubbard

52. No more possible than the development of an orchid in the middle of a crowded street —W. H. Mallock

53. No more than chance than a motorist who passed a red light talking a policeman out of giving him a ticket —Anon

54. The odds were like poison —Tim O'Brien

55. To translate this situation to reality would be like trying to stuff a cloud in a suitcase —W. P. Kinsella

56. Trying to make the company [GM] competitive is like trying to teach an elephant to tap dance —Ross Perot, quoted in *Wall Street Journal* article by George Melloan, February 24, 1987

57. Unlikely as to see a stone statue walking —Anon

IMPROBABILITY
See: IMPOSSIBILITY

IMPROPRIETY
See: PROPRIETY/IMPROPRIETY

INACCURACY
See: ERRORS

INACTIVITY
See: IDLENESS, IMMOBILITY

INAPPROPRIATENESS
See Also: BELONGING

1. (I) belonged . . . like a pearl onion on a banana split —Raymond Chandler

2. Belonged . . . like a virgin in a brothel —William McIlvanney

3. Belong like a right shoe on a left foot —Elyse Sommer

4. Belong like a white poodle on a coal barge —Arthur Baer

5. Feeling like a Boston schoolteacher in Dodge City —Mary Gordon

6. (I) feel [out of place] like Babe Paley at a bar mitzvah in the Bronx — Sue Mengers, talent agent, quoted by Rex Reed

7. Felt like a gap —D. H. Lawrence

8. Fits in about as well as a bird-of-paradise among wrens —Leslie Bennetts, about character in *The Mystery of Edwin Drood, New York Times,* 1985

9. Had about as much business teaching in college as a duck has riding a bicycle —Richard Ford
See Also: ABSURDITY

10. Inappropriate as a Size 20 Cinderella —Mike Sommer

11. Inappropriate as running shoes with a cocktail dress —Anon

12. It's like a thoroughbred horse pulling a milk wagon —line from movie, *The Eagle Has Landed*

13. Looked like a greyhound puppy in a litter of collies —Michael Gilbert

14. A man without a place to be . . . that's like being alone at sea without a log to hang on —William H. Gass

15. Misplaced . . . like a dog in church —Anon

16. Misplaced . . . like a fish out of water —English phrase
    Borrowed by the English from the Greek, the simile has been much used and adapted since the fourteenth century.

17. Never fit right, like a pair of cheap shoes that sprouts a nail in the sole —Marge Piercy

18. (Looked as) out of place as a chicken in church —James Crumley

19. Out of place as matzo balls in clam chowder —Elyse Sommer

20. Out of place as a house boat on the high seas —Anon

21. Out of place as an atheist in a seminary —Anon

22. Out of place as a Presbyterian in Hell —Mark Twain

23. Out of place as some rare tropical bird —Anon

24. Out of place . . . like an old whale stranded on the beach —George Garrett

25. (Harriet always seemed a little) out of things, like somebody's mother —Mary McCarthy

26. She was like something wrecked and cast up on the wrong shore — Elizabeth Bowen

27. Sticking out like a solitary violet in a bed of primroses —Tess Slesinger

INCISIVENESS
See: SHARPNESS

INCOMPLETENESS

1. Incomplete and unfinished like an apple that has begun to shrink before it has reached maturity —Louis Bromfield

2. Incomplete as the world on the fifth day of creation —Anon

3. Incomplete like a pastrami sandwich without a pickle —Ed Mc Bain

4. Incomplete . . . like a tree without leaves, a building without a foundation, or a shadow without the body that casts it (The knight-errant without a lady is like . . .) —Miguel de Cervantes

5. Unfinished [sentence] like a plaster half of an ancient sculptured torso —Penelope Gilliatt

INCONGRUITY
See: ABSURDITY

INCORRECTNESS
See: ERRORS

INCREASE
See: GROWTH

INDECISION
See: CHOICES

INDEPENDENCE
See: FREEDOM

INDIFFERENCE
See: REMOTENESS, RESERVE

INDIGNATION
See: ANGER

INDISTINCTION
See: VAGUENESS

INDIVIDUALITY
See: ORIGINALITY

INDOLENCE
See: IDLENESS

INDUSTRIOUSNESS
See: AMBITION, WORK

INEFFECTIVENESS
See: FUTILITY, USEFULNESS/USELESSNESS

INEVITABILITY
See: CERTAINTY

INEXORABILITY
See: CERTAINTY

INFATUATION
See: LOVE

INFLATION
See: ECONOMICS

INFLUENCE
See: POWER

INGRATITUDE
See: PARENTHOOD, SHARPNESS

INHERITANCE
See: PAST, THE

INJUSTICE
See: JUSTICE

INNOCENCE
See Also: HARMLESSNESS

1. Green as apples —Sumner Locke Elliott
2. Guileless as old Huck —Richard Ford
3. Guiltless forever, like a tree —Robert Browning
4. Innocence is like an umbrella: when once we've lost it we must never hope to see it back again —*Punch*
5. (Catherine's) innocence shone like an icon —Rita Mae Brown
6. Innocent and affectionate as a child —W. H. Hudson
7. Innocent and artless, like the growth of a flower —Isak Dinesen
8. Innocent as a baby —Anon
9. Innocent as a child unborn —Anon
    Jonathan Swift who used the phrase in *Directions to Servants* is often credited as its author.
10. (I was a neophyte about as) innocent as a choirboy being asked to conduct a solemn mass at the Vatican —Alistair Cooke, *New York Times* interview, January 19, 1986
11. Innocent as a curl —Clarence Major
12. Innocent as a devil of two years old —Jonathan Swift
13. Innocent as a game —Frank Tuohy
14. Innocent as a new-laid egg —W. S. Gilbert
15. Innocent as a snowflake —Anne Sexton
16. (Gaze as) innocent as a teddy bear —Babs H. Deal
17. Innocent as a tourist's Kodak —William McIlvanney
18. Innocent, like a hornet that has been disarmed —Jean Stafford
19. (Sat there as) innocently as small boys confiding to each other the names of toy animals —Henry James
20. Innocuous as flowers afloat in a pond —John Updike
21. Perennial innocence like a chicken in a pen —William Faulkner
22. She was like a young tree whose branches had never been touched by the ruthless hand of man —Katherine Mansfield

INQUISITIVENESS
See: CURIOSITY, QUESTIONS/ANSWERS

INSECTS
See Also: ANIMALS

1. Beetles and insects with legs like grass stems —Ernest Hemingway
2. A big black ant, shaped like a dumbbell —John Gunther
3. Black beetles . . . crawled in all directions like animated ink —Harold Adams
4. Fireflies begin to rise . . . exactly like the bubbles in champagne —Elizabeth Bishop
5. Fireflies dazzle the night like red pepper —W. P. Kinsella
6. Fireflies glow like planets in the moist, silent darkness —W. P. Kinsella
7. Fleas are, like the remainder of the universe, a divine mystery —Anatole France
8. A fly is as untamable as a hyena —Ralph Waldo Emerson
9. Insects . . . crooned like old women —Stephen Crane
10. Mosquitoes . . . as big as mulberries —William Styron
11. Moths as large and white as our hands —James Crumley
12. Nothing is so like a soul as a bee. It goes from flower to flower as a soul from star to star, and it gathers honey as a soul gathers light —Victor Hugo
13. Spiders which floated like cameos in their jars —Pat Conroy
14. Yellow butterflies flickered along the shade like flecks of sun —William Faulkner

INSEPARABILITY
See: CLOSENESS, FRIENDSHIP, RELATIONSHIPS

INSIGHT
See: WISDOM

INSIGNIFICANCE
See: MEMORY, IMPORTANCE

INSTINCTIVENESS
See: NATURALNESS

INSULTS (Insult similes appear in many categories throughout)

1. (It was) an affront, like a lewd remark —Scott Spencer

2. A day away from Tallulah [Bankhead] is like a month in the country —
    Howard Dietz

3. Has a head as big as a horse, and brains as much as an ass —Thomas
    Fuller
    A more condensed version: "A head like a horse with the
    brains of an ass."

4. He's like a bagpipe, you never hear him till his belly is full —Thomas
    Fuller

5. He's like a man who sits on a stove and then complains that his
    backside is burning —W. S. Gilbert
    Gilbert's comparison was made in response to his partner's
    complaint that his (Gilbert's) words limited his desire to write
    "fine" music while the Gilbert and Sullivan work supported his
    lavish life style, quoted by Stephen Holden, *New York Times,*
    July 27, 1986

6. He [Napoleon] spoke like a concierge and said 'armistice' for 'amnesty'
    and 'section' for 'session' —Anatole France
    France compared Napoleon's speech to that of a concierge to
    emphasize that what he said unofficially was quite different
    from the sayings manufactured for him by hirelings.

7. He thinks like Nixon, talks like Eisenhower, goofs like Goldwater —
    Noel Parmentel on John V. Lindsay, *Esquire,* October, 1965

8. His arms look like a buggy whip with fingers —Fred Allen

9. If he be an infidel, he is an infidel as a dog is an infidel; that is to say, he
    has no thought upon the subject —Samuel Johnson on Samuel Foote,
    October 19, 1769

10. I missed you like Booth missed Lincoln —Elmer Rice
    This line comes from one of Rice's best known plays,
    Counsellor At Law.

11. Insults are like bad coins; we cannot help their being offered to us, but
    we need not take them —C. H. Spurgeon

12. The king [Prince Albert of England] looks like a retired butcher —
    Oliver Wendell Holmes, Sr.
    This much quoted remark originated with a letter to Holmes'
    parents, on June 13, 1834.

13. Like a sewer rat that wants to scurry into a hole —Kenzaburo Oë

14. Like so many country people who lead a natural outdoor life, his
    features had hardly any definition. He gave me the impression of an
    underdone veal cutlet —Alexander King

15. Looks as if he had never been born and could not be extinguished —
    Harriet Martineau

16. She looked like a street just before they put on the asphalt —George
    Ade

17. She looked rather like a malicious Betty Grable —Truman Capote

18. A slight (of that kind) stimulates a man's fighting power; it is like getting a supply of fresh bile —Henrik Ibsen

19. Some insults come like a blow on the head the morning after, but a few are balm —Norman Mailer

20. They're [the Kennedy men] like dogs, they have to pee on every fire hydrant —Truman Capote

21. Why don't you buy some stuffing? Your bosoms look like fried eggs — Reynolds Price

22. Why don't you get a haircut; you look like a chrysanthemum —P. G. Wodehouse

23. You are like a cuckoo, you have but one song —H. G. Bohn's *Handbook of Proverbs*
    A modern variation of this is "He has as many good features as a cuckoo has songs."
    See Also: DULLNESS

24. You look as if you'd been put through a washing machine —John Dos Passos

25. You [Harold Ross] look like a dishonest Abe Lincoln —Alexander Woolcott
    Woolcott's much quoted comparison of the *New Yorker* editor Harold Ross to a dishonest Abe Lincoln is one of many quotes seeded around the famous Algonquin Round Table, and widely circulated in the media and books ever since.

26. You look like a million dollars, green and wrinkled —Saul Bellow

27. You're funny as a boil on the ass —Harold Adams

28. Your losing one pound is like Bayonne losing one mosquito —line from the television show "The Honeymooners."
    The simile was delivered by Alice/Audrey Meadows to Ralph/Jackie Gleason.

29. You talk such convoluted crap you must have a tongue like a corkscrew —William McIlvanney

30. You've got a foot movement like a baby hippotamus trying to side-step a jab from a humming-bird . . . and your knees are about as limber as a couple of Yale pass-keys (addressed to a dancer) —O. Henry

INTELLIGENCE
See Also: MIND

1. Brain like Einstein —H. E. Bates

2. Compared with the short span of time they live, men of great intellect are like huge buildings standing on a small plot of ground —Arthur Schopenhauer

3. A country without intellectuals is like a body without a head —Ayn Rand

4. (I have) a head on my shoulders that's like a child's windmill, and I can't prevent its making foolish words —D. H. Lawrence

5. Intellect is to emotion as our clothes are to our bodies: we could not very well have civilized life without clothes, but we would be in a poor way if we had only clothes without bodies —Alfred North Whitehead

6. Intelligence is like money . . . if you don't let on how little you've got, people will treat you as though you have a lot —Anon

7. A man of active and resilient mind outwears his friendships just as certainly as he outwears his love affairs, his politics and his epistemology —H. L. Mencken

8. One good head is as good as a hundred strong hands —Thomas Fuller
   In Fuller's collection of aphorisms it's "Better than a hundred strong heads" but common usage has made "As good as" and "Like as" popular.

9. Smart as a whip —Anon
   A simile very much in the mainstream of every day usage.

10. Smart as forty crickets —American colloquialism, attributed to the South

11. Smart . . . like an idiot savant, smart enough to be dumb when he needed to —Lynne Sharon Schwartz

INTENSITY

See Also: SHARPNESS, STARES

1. Acute as the badness of no woman out in the world thinking about you —Richard Ford

2. Acute like the flow of hope —Joseph Turnley

3. As deep into . . . as a sheep is thick in wool —Anon

4. Burns like hate —George MacDonald

5. (Worries and obsessions that) come like hot rivets —Wilfrid Sheed

6. Deep as first love —Alfred, Lord Tennyson

7. Deep as earth —Madeleine L'Engle

8. Deep as hell —Beaumont and Fletcher

9. Digging in deeper and deeper, like rats in a cheese —Henry Miller

10. (Lonely and) furious as a hunt —George Garrett

11. Had a startling intensity of gaze that never wavered from its object, like that of a palmist or a seer —Mary McCarthy

12. (Curiosity) heating up like an iron —Susan Fromberg Schaeffer

13. Move through life with the intensity of one for whom each day is the last —Anon

14. Run deep, like old wounds —William Brammer
15. Sharp as a pincer —Julia O'Faolain
16. With the intensity of a cat following a rolling ball of yarn —Ira Berkow on Wade Boggs, Red Sox player's watching of a pitch, *New York Times,* October 7,1986

INTIMACY
See: CLOSENESS, RELATIONSHIPS

INTOLERANCE
1. Bigotry . . . it's like putting your elbows on the table. You know you're not supposed to. But there's that instinct —Bonnie Currie, *New York Times,* January 24, 1986
2. Closed as a bigot's mind —Anon
3. Intolerance itself is a form of egoism —George Santayana
   Santayana elaborates on his comparison of intolerance to egoism as follows: "And to condemn egoism intolerantly is to share it."
4. Intolerant as a sinner newly turned saint —Anon
5. The mind of the bigot is like the pupil of the eye; the more light you pour upon it, the more it will contract —Oliver Wendell Holmes, Jr
6. Prejudice is as a mist, which in our journey through the world often dims the brightest and obscures the best of all the good and glorious objects that meet us on our way —Anthony Ashley Cooper
7. Prejudices . . . are like rats, and men's minds are like traps; prejudices get in easily, but it is doubtful if they ever get out —Lord Francis Jeffrey

IRONY
See: HUMOR

IRREGULARITY
See: REGULARITY/IRREGULARITY

IRRITABLENESS
See Also: ANGER, NERVOUSNESS, TENSION
1. Annoying as bird droppings on your windowshield —Elyse Sommer
2. Bitter exasperation tightened like a knot in Mr. Casper's mind — William Styron
3. Bristling like a panther —Victor Hugo
4. Cross as a sitting hen —American Colloquialism, attributed to New England

5. Cross as nine highways —John Ray's *Proverbs*

6. Cross as two sticks —Sir Walter Scott

7. Cross . . . like a beautiful face upon which some one has sat down by mistake —Victor Hugo

8. Disgust like powder clotted my nose —Cynthia Ozick

9. Disturbing as a gnat trapped and mucking about in the inner chamber of his ear —John Yount

10. Disturbing as decay in a carcass —Julia O'Faolain

11. Excitable . . . like a stick of dynamite just waiting for somebody to come along and light your fuse —David Huddle

12. Feel feisty, like a galloping colt on a Mediterranean hillside —Tony Ardizzone
    > In the novel from which this is taken, *The Heart of the Order,* the narrator's irritability is caused by having his name shortened.

13. Feeling ornery as a bunkhouse cook —Richard Ford

14. Felt irritably ashamed, like a middle-aged man recalling last night's party, and his unseemly capers and his pawing of the host's wife — Wallace Stegner

15. Gnaws like a silent poison —George Santyana

16. Gruff as a billy goat —Mary Hedin

17. Her grumpiness, her irritability, her crotchets are like static that, from time to time, give way to a clear signal, just as you often hit a pure band of music on a car radio after turning the dial through a lot of chaotic squawk —Laurie Colwin

18. Irritable like a hedgehog rolled up the wrong way, tormenting himself with his own prickles —Thomas Hood
    > The prickly hedgehog is a favorite image for describing irritability. A shorter variation of the above by Tolstoy is "Bristly . . . like a hedgehog." Expanded versions include "The man who rises in the morning with his feelings all bristling like the quills of a hedge-hog, simply needs to be knocked down" (Josiah Gilbert Holland) and "An irritable man is like a hedgehog rolled up the wrong way, tormenting himself with his own prickles" (Thomas Hood).

19. Irritated as a young stag is irritated by the velvet on his antlers — Rumer Godden

20. (All the mistakes of my misspent little life came down to) irritate me like so many grains of pepper —Gerald Kersh

21. Irritating as a coughing fit during a play —Anon

22. Irritating as a fly that keeps buzzing around your head —Anon

23. Irritating as one sock or an odd glove —Helen Hudson

See Also: USELESSNESS

24. Irritating, like a dish of 'chulent' to an old man's gut —Stephen Longstreet

   'Chulent' is a Jewish dish of meat, beans, onions. Obviously this is the type of comparison that could easily be modified to be more meaningful to other groups; for example, "Irritating, like a dish of hot chili."

25. Irritating like a gun that hangs fire —Joseph Conrad

26. A minor nuisance, like having a tooth filled —Richard Connell

27. Prickly as thistles —Lawrence Durrell

28. Sizzle and splatter like batter in a pan —line from British television series "Bergerac," broadcast June 1987

29. Snappish as a junkyard dog —Robert Campbell

30. Sulk, like an old man whose son had failed to make varsity —Clancy Sigal

31. Tempers snapping like rubber bands —Anon, WNYC, Public Radio March 28, 1987

32. Troublesome as a lawsuit —Colley Cibber

ISOLATION
See: ALONENESS

JEALOUSY
See: ENVY

JEWELRY
See Also: CLOTHING

1. A pear-shaped diamond, as big as your thumb —Paige Mitchell

2. An assortment of costly [and of questionable taste] stones . . . very much like something Hansel and Gretel might well have plucked from the witch's house to eat —Henry Van Dyke

3. Bracelets seemed to grow up her arms like creeping plants —Nadine Gordimer

4. Bracelets . . . warm and heavy, alive like flesh —Elizabeth Taylor

5. A diamond as big as an Englishman's monocle —Lael Wertenbaker

6. A diamond as big as the Ritz —F. Scott Fitzgerald

   This served as the title for a famous Fitzgerald story.

7. A diamond . . . as big as your fourth fingernail —Gerald Kersch

8. Diamond pinkie rings sputtering like neon on his manicured fingers — Jonathan Valin

9. Diamonds as big as grapes —Louis Adamic

10. Diamonds as big as potatoes —Henry James
11. Diamonds flashed . . . like drops of frozen light —Paige Mitchell
12. Earrings tiny as pinheads —Richard Ford
13. A medallion that could have anchored the Queen Mary —William McIlvanney
14. Necklace . . . flashed like summer lightning —Anaïs Nin
15. Pearl . . . shaped like the full moon, and whiter than the morning star —Oscar Wilde
16. (Wedding) ring . . . pink gold like the morning light —Anon
17. Rubies as big as hen's eggs, and sapphires that were like gloves with lights inside them —F. Scott Fitzgerald
18. Rubies like cherries, sapphires like grapes —Isak Dinesen
19. Rubies like headlights —Philip Levine
20. She was encrusted with jewels like a Maharini —MacDonald Harris

JOBS

See: WORK

JOKES

See: HUMOR

JOURNALISM

See: PROFESSIONS, WRITERS/WRITING

JOY

See Also: CONTENTMENT, HAPPINESS, PLEASURE

1. Agitated with delight as a waving sea —Arabian Nights
2. Exhilaration spread through his breast like some pleasurable form of heartburn —Nadine Gordimer
3. A joyous feeling . . . shot up, like the grass in spring —Ivan Turgenev
4. (Heart is) as full of sunshine as a hay field —Josh Billings
5. Bliss . . . as though you'd suddenly swallowed a bright piece of that late afternoon sun and it burned in your bosom, sending out a little shower of sparks into every particle —Katherine Mansfield
   The simile sets the mood for one of Mansfield's best known stories, *Bliss.*
6. Ecstacy warm and rich as wine —Harvey Swados
7. Elated . . . like a lion tamer who has at last found the whip crack which will subdue the most ferocious of his big cats —John Mortimer
8. Enjoy life like a young porpoise —George Santayana
9. Gorged with joy like a pigeon too fat to fly —Marge Piercy

10. Great joys, like griefs, are silent —Shackerley Marmion
11. Gurgle like a meadowlark —W. P. Kinsella
12. Heart . . . soared like a geyser —William Peden
13. Her heart became as light as a bubble —Antonia White
14. Joy careens and smashes through them like a speeding car out of control —Irving Feldman
15. Joy . . . felt it rumbling within him like a subterranean river —André Malraux
16. Joyful as carollers —David Leavitt
17. Joy is like the ague [malaria]; one good day between two bad ones —Danish proverb
18. Joy leaping within me . . . like a trout in a brook —George Garrett
19. Joy rises in me like a summer morn —Samuel Taylor Coleridge
20. Joys are bubble-like; what makes them bursts them too —P. J. Bailey
21. Joy, simple as the wildflowers —George Garrett
22. Joys . . . like angel visits, short and bright —John Norris
    The angel visit comparison has been as effectively linked to goodness and fame.
23. Joys met by chance . . . flow for us fresh and strong, like new wine when it gushes from the press —André Gide
24. The joys we've missed in youth are like . . . lost umbrellas; we musn't spend the rest of life wondering where they are —Henry James
25. (He is) jubilant as a flag unfurled —Dorothy Parker
26. Men without joy seem like corpses —Kaethe Kolwitz
27. My heart lifted like a wave —Norman Mailer
28. Our joys are about me like a net —Iris Murdoch
29. Rose and fell, like a floating swimmer, on easygoing great waves of voluptuous joy —Christina Stead
30. A strong exhilaration ran through her like the fumes of wine —Ben Ames Williams
31. The sun in my heart comes up like a Javanese orange —Dylan Thomas
32. Their joys . . . ran into each other like water paints mingling to form delicate new colors —Sumner Locke Elliott
33. Triumphant as if I'd just hurled a shutout —W. P. Kinsella
    The term shutout was particularly appropriate in Kinsella's baseball novel, *Shoeless Joe.* Baseball expressions do, however, work well within other contexts.
34. A wonderful feeling enveloped him, as if light were being shaken about him —John Cheever

JUDGMENTS
See: OPINIONS

JUMPING
See Also: LEAPING, ROCKING AND ROLLING

1. Bouncing from foot to foot like a child in need of a potty —Joan Hess
2. Flapping and jumping like a kind of fire —Richard Wilbur
3. Hop about like mice on tiptoe —Alistair Cooke, *New York Times,* January 19, 1986
   Cooke's comparison describes how a speaker's eyes move back and forth between viewer and teleprompter.
4. Hopping about like a pea in a saucepan —Robert Graves
5. Hopping like a shot putter —Pat Conroy
6. Jogging up and down like a cheerleader —T. Coraghessan Boyle
7. Jumped about like sailors during a storm —O. Henry
8. (Mrs. Brady's mind, hopefully calculating the tip,) jumped and jumped again like a taxi meter —Katherine Bush In a short story entitled *The Night Club,* the character with the jumping mind is a rest room matron.
9. Jumped as though he'd been shot —Katherine Mansfield
10. Jumped back as if he'd been struck by a snake —T. Coraghessan Boyle
11. Jumped like a buoy —William Goyen
12. Jumped like she'd seen a vampire —Dan Wakefield
13. Jumped like small goats —Theodore Roethke
14. Jumped on him like a wild wolf —Clifford Odets
15. Jumped out of the way like an infielder avoiding a sliding runner — Howard Frank Mosher
16. Jumped sideways like a startled bird —Jay Parini
17. Jumped up as if stung by a tarantula —Sholem Asch
18. Jumped up like I was sitting on a spring —W. P. Kinsella
19. Jumping up and down like Jack-in-the-boxes —Barbara Pym
20. Jumping like a toad —Ross Macdonald
21. Jumping like Nijinsky —Saul Bellow
22. Jumping up like a squirrel from behind the log —Rudyard Kipling
23. Jump [with shock] like a flea on a frog's back —Walter Duranty
24. Jump like a chimp with a hot foot —Anon comment on radio show, about people doing Jane Fonda workout routines, December 10, 1986
25. Skipping (up the stairs) like a young ghost —Frank Swinnerton

JUSTICE

1. Even, it [justice] is as the sun on a flat plain; uneven, it strikes like the sun on a thicket —Malay proverb

2. Injustice . . . gathers like dust under everything —Rainer Maria Rilke

3. Just as a sentence meted out by a kangaroo court —Anon

4. Justice . . . inevitable as the law of cause and effect —L. P. Hartley

5. Justice is like a train that's nearly always late —Yevgeny Yevtushenko

6. Justice is like the kingdom of God; it is not without us as a fact, it is within us as a great yearning —George Eliot

7. Shed justice like paladins —Jonathan Valin

8. The tongue of the just is as choice silver —*The Holy Bible/Proverbs*

9. An unrectified case of injustice has a terrible way of lingering . . . like an unfinished equation —Mary McCarthy

10. We will not be satisfied until justice rolls down like waters and righteousness like a mighty stream —Martin Luther King Jr., speech, June 15, 1963
    This is from King's famous "I Have a Dream" speech.

11. Your righteousness is like the mighty mountains. Your judgments are like the great deep —*The Holy Bible/Psalms*
    'Your' replaces the biblical 'thy.'

KINDNESS

See Also: GENTLENESS, SWEETNESS

1. (You're) as good as an umbrella on a wet day —H. E. Bates

2. As kind as Santa Claus —Oscar Hammerstein II, from lyric for *South Pacific*

3. As much compassion as a toreador moving in for the final thrust — Marilyn Sharp

4. As occupied with worthy projects as Eleanor Roosevelt —Lisa Harris

5. Doing a favor for a bad man is quite as dangerous as doing an injury to a good one —Plautus

6. Exuding good will like a mortician's convention in a plague year — Daniel Berrigan

7. Gifts are as the gold which adorns the temple; grace is like the temple that sanctifies the gold —William Burkitt

8. Gifts are like fish hooks —Epigram, c. 65 b.c.

9. Gifts are like hooks —Martial

10. As good as gold —Charles Dickens

A simile that's become a common expression. In *A Christmas Carol*, its most frequently quoted source, it's a response to the question "And how was Tiny Tim today?" In *The Gondoliers*, W. S. Gilbert gave it a nice twist with "In the wonder-working days of old, when hearts were twice as good as gold'. In Joseph Heller's novel *Good As Gold* it serves as a play on the hero's name (Bruce Gold).

11. (He'll be) good as pie —Ring Lardner

12. A good heart . . . a heart like a house —Irwin Shaw

13. The good is, like nature, an immense landscape in which man advances through centuries of exploration —José Ortega Gassett

14. Good to the core like bananas —Marge Piercy

15. Good will . . . is like gentle sunshine in early spring. It invigorates and awakens all buds —Berthold Auerbach

16. Great minds, like heaven, are pleased in doing good, though the ungrateful subjects of their favors are barren in return —Nicholas Rowe

17. A hand as liberal as the light of day —William Cowper

18. A heart as big as a bird cage —James B. Hall

19. A heart as big as a mountain —Anon

20. Heart . . . as great as the world —Ralph Waldo Emerson
    In Emerson's essay, *Greatness,* the simile continues with "But there was no room in it to hold the memory of a wrong."

21. A heart as warm as a desert storm —Ogden Nash

22. A heart like duck soup —Jean Garrigue
    In his short story, *The Snowfall,* Garrigue elaborates on the duck soup comparison as follows: "She's the kind to want to stop a car if she hears some animal crying in the woods."

23. A heart like warm putty —Mary Stewart

24. Heart . . . soft as any melon —Franklin Pierce

25. He gives up a buck as quickly as he would a tattoo —Anon

26. A helping word to one in trouble is often like a switch on a railroad track . . . an inch between wreck and smooth-rolling prosperity — Henry Ward Beecher

27. He was like Florence Nightingale —Tennessee Williams, *Playboy,* April, 1973
    Williams used the Florence Nightingale simile to descibe his agent's devotion when he was ill.

28. (My mother is) soft as a grape —Rita Mae Brown

29. Kindness as large as a prairie wind —Stephen Vincent Benét

30. Kindness is like a baby; it grows fast —Anon

31. Kindness is like snow; it beautifies everything it covers —Anon caller on night-time radio talk show

32. Kindness, like grain, increases by sowing —H. G. Bohn's *Handbook of Proverbs*

33. A kind word is like a Spring day —Russian proverb

34. Made the Good Samaritan look like a cheap criminal —George Ade

35. Mercy among the virtues is like the moon among the stars, not so sparkling and vivid as many, but dispensing a calm radiance that hallows the whole —E. H. Chapin

36. (My mother was as) mild as any saint —Alfred, Lord Tennyson

37. My bounty is as boundless as the sea —William Shakespeare

38. Our bounty, like a drop of water, disappears when diffused too widely —Oliver Goldsmith

39. The place of charity, like that of God, is everywhere —Jaques Benigne Bossuet

40. (She was unsparing of herself, she) poured herself out like cream (into the cups of these dull people) —Sumner Locke Elliott

41. The record of a generous life runs like a vine around the memory of our dead —Robert G. Ingersoll

42. Shone [with kindness] like the best of good deeds —Frank Swinnerton

43. Solicitious as St. Peter —Norman Mailer, about David Susskind

44. A sympathetic heart is like a spring of pure water bursting forth from the mountain side —Anon

45. To do a kindness to a bad man is like sowing our seed in the sea — Phocylides

46. Unselfish as the wind —Ken Kesey

47. We are never like angels till our passion dies —Thomas Dekker
   'Never' is modernized from 'ne'er.'

KISSES

See Also: INSULTS

1. Batted them [breast nipples] over and over with my tongue like gum — Joe Coomer

2. Being kissed . . . was something done to her, like the shampoos her mother used to give her at the kitchen sink —John Updike

3. He kissed her . . . his neck arching forward, hers backward, like a pair of swans —T. H. White

4. Her lips grazed mine, cool, soft, and tremulous as the wings of a moth —Robert Traver

5. His kiss dropped on her like a cold smooth pebble —Edith Wharton

6. His [kisser's mouth] mouth was as soft as a flower and his breath as sweet —Ruth Prawer Jhabvala
See Also: SOFTNESS

7. It [kissing someone] was like putting your mouth against an automatic bank teller, where it swallows your credit card —John Updike

8. Kissed (the children) with an official air, as if she were conferring an honor, pinning on her kisses like orders —Rebecca West

9. Kisses are like confidences, one follows the other —Denis Diderot

10. Kisses are like grains of gold or silver found upon the ground, of no value themselves, but precious as showing that a mine is near —George Villiers

11. Kisses, like folks with diminutive souls, will manage to creep through the smallest of holes —J. G. Saxe

12. Kisses . . . sticky like a child's —Flannery O'Connor

13. Kisses strong like wine —Algernon Charles Swinburne

14. Kiss . . . felt like a drop of rain in the desert —John Updike

15. Kissing a person who's self-righteous and intolerant is like licking a mongoose's ass —Tom Robbins

16. Kissing a smoker is like licking an ashtray —Tom Robbins

17. Kissing her lips was like kissing warm but uncooked liver —Stephen King

18. Kissing her . . . . was like playing post office with a dead and rotting whale —Truman Capote

19. Kissing him would be like kissing razor blades —David Brierly

20. Kissing is a good deal like eating; there is not much fun when person is hungry in standing by, and seeing it done by another fellow —Josh Billings
    Portions originally in the Billings phonetic dialect: "iz hungry . . . it did bi anuther fellow."

21. A kiss without a mustache is like an egg without salt —Spanish proverb

22. Moved her head and face about under the kisses as if they were small attacking waves —Doris Lessing

23. One more such kiss and I am ready to be roasted upon a slow fire like any chicken or duckling —Delmore Schwartz

24. Pecks like chicken scratchings —Mary Morris

25. She dug her lips into my mouth like tiger's claws —Jaroslav Seifert

26. She kissed me as moistly as a little girl —John Braine

27. She took kisses like so many coats of paint —Lawrence Durrell

28. They kissed like two old people going to bed after the clock has been wound and the cat put out —Derek Lambert

29. To kiss her would be like a Becket play to a college student: She would study it, dissect it, analyze it, appraise it and inject it with the serum of significance, until at last she transformed the simple touching of four lips into a Rosetta Stone that would give meaning to her life —Peter Benchley

30. When she kissed him, he melted like a lump of milk chocolate —Marge Piercy

KNOWLEDGE
See Also: EDUCATION, MIND, INTELLIGENCE

1. A body without knowledge is like a house without a foundation — Hebrew proverb

2. The desire for knowledge, like the thirst of riches, increases ever with the acquisition of it —Laurence Sterne

3. Follow knowledge, like a sinking star, beyond the utmost bound of human thought —Alfred, Lord Tennyson

4. Gleaned bits of information like a mouse hoarding pellets of bran stolen from the feed manger —Rita Mae Brown

5. (There are no limits to his knowledge, on small subjects as well as great;) he is like a book in breeches —Sydney Smith about Macaulay

6. In knowledge, as in swimming, he who flounders and splashes on the surface, makes more noise, and attracts more attention than the pearl-diver who quietly dives in quest of treasures to the bottom — Washington Irving

7. In science, as in life, learning and knowledge are distinct, and the study of things, and not of books is the source of the latter —Thomas H. Huxley

8. It's like swimming; once you learn it, you never forget it —Miguel de Cervantes

9. Knowledgeable as a walking encyclopedia of universal knowledge — Louisa May Alcott

10. Knowledge . . . is like a fire, which must first be kindled by some external agent, but which will afterwards propagate itself —Samuel Johnson, letter to William Drummond, August 23, 1766

11. Knowledge . . . like a rough diamond . . . will never be worn or shine, if it is not polished —Lord Chesterfield

12. Knowledge, like religion, must be "experienced" in order to be known —Edwin Percy Whipple

13. The knowledge of man is like the waters, some descending from above, and some springing from beneath; the one informed by the light of nature, the other inspired by divine revelation —Francis Bacon

Paraphrased from Bacon's "Knowledge of man is as the waters."

14. Knowledge, when wisdom is too weak to guide her, is like a headstrong horse that throws the rider —Francis Quarles

15. The right to know is like the right to live. It is fundamental and unconditional in its assumption that knowledge, like life, is a desirable thing —George Bernard Shaw

16. The struggle for knowledge has a pleasure in it like that of wrestling with a fine woman —Lord Halifax
    The original simile used 'hath' instead of 'has.'

17. The understanding, like the eyes, while it makes us see and perceive all things, takes no notice of itself, and it requires art and pains to set it at a distance and make it its own subject —John Locke
    The fifth word is a modernization of the original, 'whilst.'

18. We deal our knowledge like a pack of cards —George Garrett

19. With informations we can go anywhere in the world, we are like turtles, our houses always on our backs —John Le Carré
    In his novel *A Perfect Spy,* Le Carré expands the simile as follows: "You learn to paint, you can paint anywhere. A sculptor, a musician, a painter, they need no permits. Only their heads."

LANDSCAPES

See Also: MOUNTAINS, NATURE, ROAD SCENES, PONDS AND STREAMS, TREES

1. The corn is as high as an elephant's eye and it looks like it's climbin' clear up to the sky —Oscar Hammerstein, II, from opening lyric for *Oklahoma.*

2. The country lay like an abandoned theatrical backdrop, tarnished and yellow —Beryl Markham

3. The endless fields glowed like a hearth in firelight —Eudora Welty

4. A farm . . . off the road . . . glittering like a photo in a picture book with its twin silos pointing to heaven like two fat white fingers —Harvey Swados

5. Fields like squares of a chessboard and trees and houses like dolls' furniture —Hugh Walpole

6. The fields shone and seemed to tremble like a veil in the light —Eudora Welty

7. The fields were like icing sugar —Joyce Cary

8. The fields [in March] were white as bones and dry as meal —M. J. Farrell

9. Gardens, crowded with flowers of every rich and beautiful tint, sparkled . . . like beds of glittering jewels —Charles Dickens

10. Great spots of light like white wine splash over the Jardins Publiques —Katherine Mansfield

11. Green hummocks like ancient cannon-balls sprouting grass —Elizabeth Bishop

12. The land flowed like white silk . . . flat as a bed sheet and empty as the moon —Frank Ross

13. Landscape as precise and vibrant as fine writing —Sharon Sheehe Stark

14. The landscape boiled around her like a pan of beans —Dilys Laing

15. Landscape . . . gaunt and bleak like the face of the moon —Donald Seaman

16. Landscape . . . like a gray sink —Paul Theroux

17. The landscape [when it snows] lumps like flour gravy —Lisa Ress

18. Landscapes . . . like sorrows, they require some distance —Donald Justice

19. The landscape was bleak and bereft of color . . . like a painting in grisaille with its many tints of gray —Barbara Taylor Bradford

20. The landscape was yellowish and purple, speckled like a leopard skin —Nikos Kazantzakis

21. The lawn looked as expensive as a velvet carpet woven in one piece —Edith Wharton

22. The lawns looked artificial, like green excelsior or packing material —Saul Bellow

23. The lawn, spread out like an immense green towel —Ludwig Bemelmans

24. Light hits that field, like silk being rubbed the wrong way —John Gunther

25. The long slope of the park dipped like a length of green stuff with a ceiling cloth of blue and pink smoke high above —Virginia Woolf

26. Meadows carpeted with buttercups, like slabs of gold in the somber forest —John Fowles

27. Patches of earth showed through the snow, like ink spots spreading on a sheet of white blotting paper —Edith Wharton

28. Petals . . . fell on the grass like spilled paint —Laurie Colwin

29. Populating the field in dark humps, like elephants moving across savannah, were scores of great round straw bales —Will Weaver

30. Pretty cubes and loaves of new houses are strewn among the pines, like sugar lumps —Walker Percy

31. Smooth swelling fields, like waves —Wilbur Daniel Steele

32. The stony landscape . . . is full of craters and frozen lights like a moon —Erich Maria Remarque

33. Swelling smooth fields like pale breasts —Wilbur Daniel Steele

34. The reeds and willow bushes looked like little islands swaying in the wind —Leo Tolstoy

35. Vast lawns that extend like sheets of vivid green —Washington Irving
     Irving's simile was inspired by English park scenery.

36. The wet countryside glistened and dripped as though it had been freshly scrubbed —Robert Traver

37. Wet furry fields lay like the stomachs of soft animals bared to the sky —Julia O'Faolain

38. Wet pine growth reflects the sunlight like steel knitting needles — Walker Percy

39. When you drive by them [the woods] fast, the crop rows in between spin like spokes on a turning wheel —Alec Wilkinson, *New Yorker*, August 12, 1985

40. The whole landscape loomed absolute, as the antique world was once — Sylvia Plath

41. The whole [valley] was like a broad counterpane, hued in rust and yellow and golden brown —Beryl Markham

LANGUAGE
See Also: SPEAKING, WORD(S)

1. Greek is like lace; every man gets as much as he can —Samuel Johnson

2. It is with language as with manners: they are both established by the usage of people of fashion —Lord Chesterfield
    See Also: MANNERS

3. Language, if it throws a veil over our ideas, adds a softness and refinement to them, like that which the atmosphere gives to naked objects —William Hazlitt

4. Language is a city, to the building of which every human being brings a stone —Ralph Waldo Emerson

5. Language is an art, like brewing or baking —Charles R. Darwin

6. Languages evolve like species. They can degenerate just as oysters and barnacles have lost their heads —F. L. Lucas

7. Languages, like our bodies, are in a perpetual flux, and stand in need of recruits to supply those words which are continually falling into disuse —C. C. Felton

8. Show them [Americans with a penchant for "fat" talk] a lean, plain word that cuts to the bones and watch them lard it with thick greasy syllables front and back until it wheezes and gasps for breath as it comes lumbering down upon some poor threadbare sentence like a sack of iron on a swayback horse —Russell Baker

9. Slang is English with its sleeves rolled up —Carl Sandburg, quoted by William Safire in series on English language, PBS, September, 1986

10. To write jargon is like perpetually shuffling around in the fog and cottonwool of abstract terms —Sir Arthur Quiller-Couch

LAUGHTER

See Also: GAIETY, GRINS, HUMOR, SMILES

1. As the crackling of thorns under a pot, so is the laughter of a fool —*The Holy Bible/Ecclesiastes*

2. Basically when you laugh you have to make a fool of yourself . . . it's like sex —Robin Williams, "Sixty Minutes" interview, September 21, 1986

3. Chuckle . . . it sounded like a trapped wasp —Jonathan Gash

4. Chuckles . . . empty and round, like bubbles —Dan Jacobson

5. Chuckling like a jovial insurance salesman —James Crumley

6. Contralto laughter, like a violin obligato under trills of a flute —Carlos Baker

7. A dry crackle like leaves crushed underfoot —Louise Erdrich

8. Dry laughter like the cackle of crows or the crackling of fallen leaves underfoot —Margaret Laurence

9. Giggled . . . like a naughty child which has unintentionally succeeded in amusing the grown-ups —Christopher Isherwood

10. (They kissed. And) giggled like cartoon mice —Tom Robbins

11. Giggle, like a child watching a Hollywood adventure film —Nadine Gordimer

12. A good laugh is sunshine in a house —William Makepeace Thackeray

13. Heavy, melodious laughter, like silver coins shaking in a bag —Aharon Megged

14. Her braying laugh rang out like the report of a shotgun —James Thurber

15. Her laugh broke like a dish —Cynthia Ozick

16. Her laugh crackled . . . like a leap of electricity —Richard Francis

17. Her laugh pealed out like a raven escaping into the night —Donald McCaig

18. Her laugh rang like the jangling of bracelets —Derek Walcott

19. Her laughter hung in the air like sleigh bells on a winter night —Jay Parini

20. Her laughter was a titanic, passionate thing that seemed to pass up like a wave from her toes to her mouth —Pat Conroy

21. High laugh, like a dove cry—Eudora Welty

22. A high laugh like a wicked witch —Carolyn Chute

23. His laughter thickened like a droning bell —James Wright

24. A hoarse, very small laugh, like a cat's cough —Frank Swinnerton

25. A horrifying derisive laugh, like rolling tin —Barry Hannah

26. Laugh . . . as if a demon within him were exulting with gloating scorn —Iris Murdoch

27. (Louisa's) laugh begins high and descends from there like a cascade — Daphne Merkin

28. Laughed, a little drugged giggle, like chatter —Paul Theroux

29. Laughed contemptuously like a whore being offered too little money — Gary Hart

30. Laughed, like a bowlful of jelly —Clement C. Moore

31. Laughed like a windup machine —John D. MacDonald

32. Laughed like monkeys —Richard Ford

33. Laughed like murmurs of the sea —W. B. Yeats

34. Laughed . . . like the trill of a hedge-warbler —Frank Swinnerton

35. A laugh exploded out of me like a sneeze —Scott Spencer

36. Laughing, a sound like wind in the grass —T. Coraghessan Boyle

37. A laugh is just like sunshine —Anon rhyme
    The simile is the poem's repeat motif.

38. Laugh . . . like the barking of a fox —Erich Maria Remarque

39. Laugh . . . like a bird's carol on the sunrise breeze —John Greenleaf Whittier

40. Laugh like a hyena —William Shakespeare
    This simile from *As You Like It* crops up in many a modern short story and novel.

41. Laugh . . . like a spoon tinkling against a medicine glass —Katherine Mansfield

42. Laugh . . . like a thrush singing —Oscar Wilde

43. A laugh like clapboards being ripped off the side of a house —Peter De Vries

44. Laughs [in a film] . . . come out of despair, like bits of green in a graveyard —Walter Goodman about the movie, *No Surrender, New York Times,* August 6, 1986

45. Laughs like a rhinoceros —Tom Davies
   The person Davies described was Samuel Johnson.

46. Laughs like little bells in light wind —George Garrett

47. Laughter . . . checked by small clutches of muscle, like tiny fists, at the corners of his mouth —Leonard Michaels

48. Laughter crackling like a schoolgirl who has not experienced enough of the world to fear it —Ira Wood

49. Laughter cruel as barbed wire —George Garrett

50. Laughter falls like rain or tears —Dame Edith Sitwell

51. Laughter fell like a shower of coins —George Garrett

52. Laughter . . . high and free and musical, like a happy soprano limbering up —Harvey Swados

53. Laughter hung smoke-like in the sudden stillness —Ralph Ellison

54. Laughter . . . keeps coming like a poison that must be ejected —Nora Johnson

55. Laughter leaped suddenly from her throat . . . then stopped, like something flung away and lost —Graham Swift

56. Laughter like hiccoughs —T. Coraghessan Boyle

57. Laughter, light and restrained like the clatter of rolling nuts —Yisrael Zarchi

58. Laughter lonelier than tears —Anonymous blurb preceding a humorous quote, *New York Times Book Review*/Noted With Pleasure, September 14, 1986

59. The laughter of a fool is like that of a horse —Welsh proverb
   See Also: FOOLISHNESS, STUPIDITY

60. Laughter roared through the spectators like wind through trees — Gerald Kersh

61. Laughter spilled out of his prodigious frame like gravel being unloaded from a dump truck —Pat Conroy

62. A laugh that rippled . . . like the sound of a hidden brook —O. Henry

63. A laugh that rumbles like a freight train in the night —Michael Goodwin about sports broadcaster, Steve Zabriskie, *New York Times*/TV Sports, October 2, 1986

64. A laugh that unfolds like a head of lettuce —Antler

65. Let out a cackle of a laugh, like the sound a hen might make if the hen were mad about something —Larry McMurtry

66. Men who never laugh may have good hearts, but they are deep seated; like some springs, they have their inlet and outlet from below, and show no sparkling bubble on the brim —Josh Billings
   Words originally in Billings' phonetic dialect are: 'laff' (laugh), 'hav' (have), 'sum' (some).

67. A most pleasant laugh, bubbly and controlled, like fine champagne —Margaret Millar

68. Peal of laughter like the ringing of silvery bells —Nathanial Hawthorne

69. A queer stage laugh, like the cackle of a baffled villain in a melodrama —Edith Wharton

70. (Boutin's mouth opened from ear to ear in) a roar of laughter, like the bursting of a mortar —Honoré de Balzac

71. She laughed, sounding like a small barking dog —Robert Campbell

72. She pursed her lips each time she laughed, making laughter seem a gesture of self-control —W. P. Kinsella

73. A silvery laugh, like a brook running out to meet the river —Mike Fredman

74. A slow ripple of laughter, like a scattering of autumn leaves —Robert Traver

75. A snort of a chuckle like a bull-frog —Lawrence Durrell

76. Some . . . laugh just as a rat does, who has caught a steel trap, with his tail —Josh Billings
    In the original phonetic dialect this is: "Laff just az a rat duz, who haz caught a steel trap with his tale."

77. The sound [of laughter] was like the whirring of an old grandfather clock before it strikes —Frank Swinnerton

78. Stopped laughing as suddenly as if a set ring had been broken —Loren D. Estleman

79. A sudden fizz of laughter like soda water —George Garrett

80. Tittering like a small bird —Beryl Markham

81. Twinkled like Old King Cole —Donald McCaig

82. When he laughed, a satyr-like quality suffused his face —Nathaniel Benchley

83. When she does laugh . . . it's like polished crystal, like a stream in the Alps racing over a pebbly bed here below, like . . . like another simile —Hanoch Bartov
    For anyone interested in multiple similes . . . here's the simile itself to round up a medley of comparisons.

84. When she laughed it was as if a wren sang —Frank Swinnerton

85. When she was about to laugh, her tone grew higher and melodious, easing into the laugh like a singer easing from recitative to an aria —Lynne Sharon Schwartz

86. Wrinkles of laughter leaped into sight on his face, like small friendly insects running all over it —Romain Gary

LAW

   See Also: LAWYERS

1.   Corpuses, statutes, rights and equities are passed on like congenital disease —Johann Wolfgang von Goethe

2.   Exact laws, like all the other ultimates and absolutes, are as fabulous as the crock of gold at the rainbow's end —G. N. Lewis

3.   Going to law is like skinning a new milk cow for the hide, and giving the meat to the lawyers —Josh Billings
       The original in Billings' popular dialect form reads as follows: "Going tew law iz like skinning a new milch . . . .tew the lawyers."

4.   Great cases like hard cases make bad law —Oliver Wendell Holmes, Sr.
       Justice Holmes expanded on his simile as follows: "For great cases are called great not by reason of their real importance in shaping the law of the future but because of some accident of immediate overwhelming interest which appeals to the feelings and distorts the judgment."

5.   Law is a bottomless pit —John Arbuthnot
       Arbuthnot continues as follows: "It is a cormorant, a harpy that devours everything!"

6.   Law is a form of order, and good law must necessarily mean good order —Aristotle

7.   The law is a sort of hocus-pocus science, that smiles in your face while it picks your pocket —Charles Macklin

8.   The law is like apparel which alters with the time —Sir John Doddridge

9.   Law is like pregnancy, a little of either being a dangerous thing — Robert Traver

10. The law often dances like an old fishwife in wooden shoes, with little grace and less dispatch —George Garrett
       In Garrett's historical novel, *Death of the Fox,* this simile is voiced by Sir Francis Bacon.

11. Laws and institutions . . . like clocks, they must be occasionally cleansed, and wound up, and set to true time —Henry Ward Beecher

12. (Written) laws are like spiders' webs; they hold the weak and delicate who might be caught in their meshes, but are torn in pieces by the rich and powerful —Anarchis

The spiders' web comparison to the law has been much used and modified. Here are some examples: "Laws, like cobwebs, entangle the weak, but are broken by the strong;" "Laws are like spiders' webs, so that the great buzzing bees break through, and the little feeble flies hang fast in them" (Henry Smith); "Laws are like cobwebs, which may catch small flies, but let wasps and hornets break through" (Jonathan Swift); "Laws, like cobwebs, catch small flies, great ones break through before your eyes" (Benjamin Franklin); "Laws, like the spider's web, catch the fly and let the hawk go free" (Spanish proverb).

13. Law should be like death, which spares no one —Charles de Secondat Montesquieu

14. Laws, like houses, lean on one another —Edmund Burke

15. Laws should be like clothes. They should fit the people they are meant to serve —Clarence Darrow

16. Laws wise as nature, and as fixed as fate —Alexander Pope

17. Legal as a Supreme Court decision —Anon

18. Legal studies . . . sharpen, indeed, but like a grinding stone narrow whilst they sharpen —Samuel Taylor Coleridge

19. Liked law because it was a system like a jigsaw puzzle, whose pieces, if you studied them long enough, all fell into place —Will Weaver

20. The science of legislation is like that of medicine in one respect, that it is far more easy to point out what will do harm than what will do good — Charles Caleb Colton

21. Suits at court are like winter nights, long and wearisome —Thomas Deloney

22. To try a case twice is like eating yesterday morning's oatmeal —Lloyd Paul Stryker
    See Also: REPETITION, STALENESS

23. Violations of the law, like viruses, are present all the time. Everybody does them. Whether or not they produce a disease, or a prosecution, is a function of the body politic —Anon quote, *New York Times*/Washington Talk, November 28, 1986

LAWYERS

See Also: LAW, PROFESSIONS

1. A certain criminal lawyer, like a trapeze performer, is seldom more than one step from an awful fate —Paul O'Neil, *Life,* June 22, 1959

2. A countryman between two lawyers is like a fish between two cats — Benjamin Franklin

3. The glory of lawyers, like that of men of science, is more corporate than individual —Oliver Wendell Holmes, Sr., April 15, 1890

4. If you would wax thin and savage, like a half-fed spider, be a lawyer — Oliver Wendell Holmes, Sr.
   Holmes senior gave up the law for a career in medicine and literature. His son, on the other hand, enjoyed a distinguished legal career culminated by his appointment to the Supreme Court.

5. A lawyer's face always gives warning of an ambush. Like a blockhouse. Used to conceal the artillery —Joyce Cary

6. A lawyer awaiting a decision in a big case is like a murderer waiting for the jury to come out —Robert Traver
   In the novel, *Laughing Whitefish,* this continues in both, wistful hope mingles inevitably with gloom and foreboding.

7. A lawyer deep in his case is like a man fallen in love. Whether shaving or bathing or plain old-fashioned knaving, in bed or out, always and forever he is obsessed by his goddam case —Robert Traver
   A variation of this from *People Versus Kirk* also appears in Traver's best known novel, *Anatomy of a Murder.*

8. A lawyer lacking a flock of law books is like a carpenter run out of nails —Robert Traver

9. A lawyer preparing for the trial of a difficult and complex case . . . is like a man consulting a dictionary who winds up chasing everything but the word he needs —Robert Traver

10. Lawyers are just like physicians: what one says, the other contradicts — Sholom Aleichem

11. Lawyers, like bread, are best when they are young and new —Thomas Fuller

12. Lawyers on opposite sides of a case are like the two parts of shears; they cut what comes between them, but not each other —Daniel Webster

13. Like most corporate attorneys, he sat squarely on the fence with both ears to the ground —Anon

14. Years of practice had made them sensitive to every whimsy of emotion and taught them how to play upon the psychology of the jury as the careless zephyr softly draws its melody from the aeolian harp —Arthur Train

LAZINESS
See: IDLENESS

LEAPING
See Also: JUMPING, ROCKING AND ROLLING

1. (The flashlight) leaped about like a will-o'-the-wisp —Brian Moore

2.   Leaped from his chair as a runner leaps crouching, from the mark — Frank Swinnerton
     See Also: RISING

3.   Leaped like a fawn —Pat Conroy

4.   Leaped like a high jumper —Frank Conroy

5.   (Goats) leaped . . . like arrows speeding from the bow —Willa Cather

6.   Leaped like a spring released —John Updike

7.   Leaped . . . like a startled frog —Théophile Gautier

8.   Leaped up like a little singed cat —O. Henry

9.   Leaps like a buck in air —Caroline Finkelstein

10. Leaps like a flash —Maxwell Anderson and Laurence Stallings
     This is a line from the Anderson/Stallings play, *What Price Glory.*

11. (The pulse in his palm) leapt like a trout in a brook —Eudora Welty

12. Leaping through the air like a man released from gravity —Ed Bradley, about basketball star Michael Jordan, "Sixty Minutes," February 15, 1987

LEARNING
See: EDUCATION

LEAVES
See Also: FLOWERS, NATURE, TREES

1.   Aspen and poplar leaves covered the road like yellow snow —Susan Engberg

2.   The dirty leaves were hanging down from the [rain-wet] trees like dead bats —Josephine Tey

3.   Dry leaves blew across the sidewalk like arched spiders —Joan Hess

4.   Dry leaves chatter like a children's brigade —Diane Ackerman

5.   A few leaves had fallen and lay like neglected toys on the grass — Carolyn Slaughter

6.   The forest leaves moved like small rustling animals over the moss — Hayden Carruth

7.   The last leaves of some sultry September hung stiffly, like leaves pressed between the pages of an old catechism —Nelson Algren

8.   Leaves as light and agitated as swarms of little butterflies that hovered above the clover —Willa Cather

9.   Leaves as limp as soiled money —George Garrett

10. Leaves delicately veined as a baby's hands —W. P. Kinsella

11. Leaves digest sun as men and women eat each other to love —Daniela Gioseffi

12. Leaves drooped (over white frame houses) like hands —James Reiss

13. Leaves fallen like wet rags —Bernard Malamud

14. The leaves . . . fall off the branches by the hundreds, like paratroopers from their planes —David Ignatow

15. Leaves fell like notes from a piano —Derek Walcott

16. Leaves fell like rejected brown stars —John Rechy

17. The leaves fly up like birds —Conrad Aiken

18. Leaves hanging down like tongues —Jean Thompson

19. Leaves hissing and steaming like kettles —Philip Levine

20. Leaves . . . hung lustreless, like drying tea-dregs —Julia O'Faolain

21. Leaves . . . large as a lady's apron —Caroline Finkelstein

22. Leaves . . . like a soggy blanket . . . covered gutter, sidewalk, lawn, backyard, bushes and alley —Bernard Malamud

23. Leaves like green lace —George Garrett

24. Leaves like ruffled wavelets —Sylvia Berkman

25. Leaves like scarlet hands floated on the green slow water —Truman Capote

26. The leaves of the red maples glowed like fruit —Jean Thompson

27. The leaves paled and fell from the shedding trees like old wishes — George Garrett

28. Leaves peep out so fresh and green, so pure and bright, like young lives pushing shyly out into the bustling world —Jerome K. Jerome

29. Leaves rattled dryly together, like scales of metal —Aldous Huxley

30. Leaves scatter and point to every part of the sky, like famished fingers waving —Richard Wilbur

31. (A giant tree which bore) leaves shaped like fans —Anaïs Nin

32. The leaves sift down one by one like notes in music —May Sarton

33. The leaves that a few days before had been green now dropped like heat-withered cellophane —Wallace Stegner

34. The leaves turn and twist in the wind as if quarreling with one another —David Ignatow

35. The leaves were motionless on the trees, as if they were resting in the heat —Willis Johnson

36. Leaves, wrinkled or shiny like apples —Frank O'Hara

37. Some of its [a plant's] leaves had turned black and were curled up like charred Christmas ribbons —Margaret Millar

38. Yellow leaves like lamps of gold —John Greenleaf Whittier

39. The yellow leaves swam through the air as silently as fish —Jean Thompson

40. The young leaves were still soft and slack . . . less like leaves than like petals, and drooping in the sweet forest-air like seaweeds in deep water —Isak Dinesen

LEGS

See Also: PAIN, PHYSICAL FEELINGS

1. Ankles fine as an antelope's —Josephine Edgar

2. Ankles like door knobs —Anon

3. The calves of her legs were as taut and stiff as anchor chains —Mary Ellen Chase

4. Feet heavy as anchors —Richard Ford

5. Feet large as spades —Aharon Megged

6. Feet like canoes —Herbert Wilner

7. Feet . . . swollen, driven through my shoes like devilled egg through a pastry bag —Ira Wood

8. Feet . . . tripping like the feet of a restless pony —Adela Rogers St. John

9. (The fiddler's) feet were like the black hooves of a trotting horse that never seemed to touch the ground —Will Weaver
See Also: DANCING

10. Her bony toes seemed as long and articulate as fingers —Thomas Williams

11. Her legs were shapeless . . . like a fisherwoman's —H. E. Bates

12. His legs felt like two old rusted rain gutters —Flannery O'Connor

13. (She was a vast blonde girl, with) huge limbs like a piece of modern sculpture —Barbara Pym

14. Knees tuck out . . . like two hard-boiled eggs —Anne Piper

15. Legs bowed like a wishbone —Ian MacMillan
See Also: BENDING/BENT

16. Legs . . . as heavy as sunken logs —Nolan Miller

17. Legs as shapeless and almost as thin as the lines in a child's drawing — Niven Busch

18. Legs as thick as newel posts —F. van Wyck Mason

19. Legs bent like monster springs —Richard S. Prather

20. Legs . . . bowed, rickety, like bent pipes —George Garrett

21. Legs have gone mottled, like Roquefort cheese —Nadine Gordimer
Another simile to describe the effects of cellulite is "Thighs like cottage cheese."

22. Legs in motion like the hind parts of a dog —David Ignatow
23. Legs knotted and angular as whittled wood —George Garrett
24. Legs like a baseball bat —Delmore Schwartz
25. (A large man with) legs like a billiard table —Joyce Cary
26. Legs like an emaciated monkey's —Louis-Ferdinand Celine
27. Legs like redwood trees —Pat Conroy
28. Legs . . . like two pillars —Bertold Brecht
29. Legs moving like the hammers of a grand piano —Paul Kuttner
30. Legs shaped like lion's paws —Jilly Cooper
31. Legs solid as tree trunks —Richard Deming
32. Legs . . . stiff as a wooden soldier's legs —William Kotzwinkle,
33. Legs . . . straight as a pair of poplar trees in a storm —Ariel Dorfman
    See Also: STRAIGHTNESS
34. Legs were strong as old roots —Truman Capote
35. Legs that were too long, like a colt's —Beryl Markham
36. Long, thin legs like wading birds —Elizabeth Hardwick
37. My feet feel like balloons —Anthony Powell
38. (The young lady has) a pair of ankles like chianti bottles —George Jean Nathan
    See Also: Insults
39. The pull of the tendons at his ankle like the taut ropes that control the sails of ships —Nadine Gordimer
40. She (a ballet dancer) has legs like a Fordham tackle —Irwin Shaw
41. Skinny legs, like the legs of a turkey gobbler —Ellen Glasgow
42. Swings his game leg like a gate, creaking on its hinges —Bette Howland
43. Thighs big as trees —John D. MacDonald
44. Thighs like a wild mare —Thomas Williams
45. Thighs like pillars of a temple —Peter De Vries
46. Thighs like twin portals —Paule Marshall
47. Thighs solid as poplars —Sharon Sheehe Stark
48. Thighs . . . they look like they're made of steel —Jonathan Valin
49. Varicose veins crawled like fat blue worms under her stockings —Ross Macdonald
50. Veins like big ugly worms —James Crumley

LETTER-WRITING
    See: CORRESPONDENCE

LIBERTY
   See: FREEDOM

LIES/LIARS
   See Also: DISHONESTY

1. Falsehood, like poison, will generally be rejected when administered alone; but when blended with wholesome ingredients, may be swallowed unperceived —Richard Whately

2. Falsehood, like the dry rot, flourishes the more in proportion as air and light are excluded —Richard Whately

3. A great lie is like a great fish on dry land; it may fret and fling, and make a frightful bother, but it cannot hurt you. You have only to keep still and it will die of itself —George Crabbe

4. (He's as) honest as the cat when the meat's out of reach —H. G. Bohn's *Handbook of Proverbs*

5. Lie as fast as a dog can lick a dish —John Ray's *Proverbs*

6. Lied as often and as badly as politicians —James Crumley

7. Lied like a fish —John Dos Passos

8. Lied like an Arab —Anaïs Nin

9. Lied like a rug —Anon
   In his novel, *private i,* Jimmy Sangster extends this with "Lying like a cheap carpet."

10. The lie fell as easily from his lips as a windfall apple —Donald Seaman

11. A lie is like a snowball; the longer it is rolled, the larger it is —Martin Luther

12. Lie like a trooper —American colloquialism, attributed to New England

13. Lie like fish —Saul Bellow

14. Lies are as communicative as fleas —Walter Savage Landor

15. Lies as fast as a dog trots —John Ray's *Proverbs*

16. Lies as fast as a horse can trot —Danish proverb
    The comparison tends to change with use "As fast as a dog can trot" being one of the most frequently heard variants.

17. Lies . . . buzz about the heads of some people, like flies about a horse's ears in summer —Jonathan Swift

18. Lies fall like flaxen thread from the skies —John Ashbery

19. Lies flew out of my mouth like moths —Susan Fromberg Schaeffer

20. Lies like a car-dealer —William McIlvanney

21. Lying like a book —Bertold Brecht

22. Lying like an accountant at an audit —A. E. Maxwell

23. Lying like stink —Angus Wilson

24. Lying to someone is like blindfolding him: you cannot see the other's eyes to see how he sees you and so you do not know how it stands with yourself —Walker Percy

25. The nimble lie is like the second-hand upon a clock; we see it fly, while the hour-hand of truth seems to stand still, and yet it moves unseen, and wins at last, for the clock will not strike till it has reached the goal — Henry Wadsworth Longfellow

26. (Our) one white lie sits like a little ghost (here on the threshold of our enterprise) —Alfred, Lord Tennyson

27. The prevaricator is like an idolater —Eleazar

28. The telling of a falsehood is like the cut of a sabre; for though the wound may heal, the scar of it will remain —Sadi

29. To tell a falsehood is like the cut of a sabre; for though the wound may heal, the scar of it will remain —Sadi

30. When the lie was said it had the effect of leaving her breathless, as if she had just crowned a steep rise —Nadine Gordimer

LIFE

See Also: AGE; LIFE, DEFINED; MANKIND

1. (It seemed to him that) all man's life was like a tiny spurt of flame — Thomas Wolfe

2. The art of living rightly is like all arts; it must be learned and practiced with incessant care —Johann Wolfgang von Goethe

3. The eventful life has dates; it swells and pauses like a plot —Paul Theroux

4. How ridiculous it [life] all seems . . . like a drop of water seen through a microscope, a single drop teeming with infusoria, or a speck of cheese full of mites invisible to the naked eye —Arthur Schopenhauer

5. In life as in a football game, the principle to follow is: Hit the line hard —Theodore Roosevelt

6. Let us play the game of life as sportsmen, pocketing our winnings with a smile, leaving our losings with a shrug —Jerome K. Jerome

7. Life . . . empty as statistics are —Babette Deutsch

8. Life . . . flat and stale, like an old glass of beer —Andre Dubus

9. Life folds like a fan with a click —Herbert Read

10. Life goes on forever like the gnawing of a mouse —Edna St. Vincent Millay

11. Life had been like a cloud rainbowed by the sun —Barbara Reid

12. Life imposes by brute energy, like inarticulate thunder; art catches the ear, among the far louder noises of experience, like an air artificially made by a discreet musician —Robert Louis Stevenson
See Also: ART AND LITERATURE

13. A life indifferent as a star —Randall Jarrell

14. A life is composed of a thousand frail strands, like the rainbow tangle of telphone cables. Somehow, we make connections —Jean Thompson

15. Life is shapeless as a glove —Kenneth Koch
See Also: SHAPE

16. Life . . . it slips through my hands like a fish —James Reiss
See Also: ELUSIVENESS

17. Life, like a child, laughs shaking its rattle of death as it runs — Rabindranath Tagore
See Also: DEATH

18. Life, like a good story, pursues its way from beginning to end in a firm and unbroken line —W. Somerset Maugham

19. Life, like every other blessing, derives its value from its use alone — Samuel Johnson

20. Life, like war, is a series of mistakes —F.W. Robertson

21. Life often seems like a long shipwreck, of which the debris are friendship, glory and love —Madame de Staël

22. Life's bare as a bone —Virginia Woolf

23. Life is so like a little strip of pavement over an abyss —Virginia Woolf

24. Life should be embraced like a lover —Rose Tremain

25. Life's like an inn where travelers stay, some only breakfast and away; others to dinnerstop, and are full fed; the oldest only sup and go to bed —English epitath
A variation of this, also found on a gravestone, is "Our life is nothing but a winter's day."

26. Life swings like a pendulum backward and forward between pain and boredom —Arthur Schopenhauer

27. A life that moved in spirals turned inward like the shell of a sea-snail — Malcolm Cowley

28. Life was like [motion] pictures only in that it hardly every managed to be as exciting as its preview —Larry McMurtry

29. Like a morning dream, life becomes more and more bright, the longer we live —Jean Paul Richter

30. Like following life through creatures you dissect, you lose it in the moment you detect —Alexander Pope

31. To live is like love, all reason is against it, and all healthy instincts for it —Samuel Butler

32. Man's journey through life is like that of a bee through blossoms — Yugoslav proverb

33. A man's life, like a piece of tapestry, is made up of many strands which interwoven make a pattern; to separate a single one and look at it alone, not only destroys the whole, but gives the strand itself a false value — Judge Learned Hand
    Judge Hand compared life to a piece of tapestry at the 1912 proceedings in memory of Mr. Justice Brandeis.

34. Men deal with life as children with their play, who first misuse, then cast their toys away —William Cowper

35. Moved . . . through her life, like a clumsy visitor in a museum — Susan Fromberg Schaeffer

36. Much that goes on behind Life's doors is not fixed like the pillars of a building nor preconceived like the structure of a symphony, nor calculable like the orbit of a star —Vicki Baum

37. My life felt like a fragile silk chemise —Marge Piercy

38. My life is like a stroll upon the beach, as near the ocean's edge as I can go —Henry David Thoreau

39. My life is like the autumn leaf that trembles in the moon's pale ray — Richard Henry Wilde
    This begins the second stanza of the poem, *My Life.*

40. My life is like the summer rose that opens to the morning sky, but before the shade of evening closes is scattered on the ground to die — Richard Henry Wilde
    Another simile from Wilde's *My Life,* this one the opening line.

41. My life loose as a frog's —Maxine Kumin

42. Our days on earth are as a shadow —*The Holy Bible/Job*

43. (I worry that) our lives are like soap operas. We can go for months and not tune in to them, then six months later we look in and the same stuff is still going on —Jane Wagner

44. Our lives are united like fruit in a bowl —W. H. Auden

45. Our lives run like fingers over sandpaper —Jaroslav Seifert

46. Perhaps like an ancient statue that has no arms our life, without deeds and heroes, has greater charms —Yehuda Amichai

47. Sometimes we do not become adults until we suffer a good whacking loss, and our lives in a sense catch up with us and wash over us like a wave and everything goes —Richard Ford

48. The art of life is more like the wrestler's art than the dancer's that it should stand ready and firm to meet onsets which are sudden and unexpected —Marcus Aurelius

49. There was a dimension missing from his life, as though trees were flat and rooflines painted on the sky —Margaret Sutherland

50. The vanity of human life is like a rivulet, constantly passing away, and yet constantly coming on —Alexander Pope

51. Viewed from the summit of reason, all life looks like a malignant disease and the world like a madhouse —Johann Wolfgang von Goethe

52. Wear life like an old pair of shoes that's easy on my feet —Ben Ames Williams

53. When the highest stake in the game of living, life itself, may not be risked . . . becomes as flat, as superficial as one of those American flirtations in which it is from the first understood that nothing is to happen, contrasted with a Continental love-affair in which both partners must constantly bear in mind the serious consequences — Sigmund Freud

54. Would that life were like the shadow cast by a wall or a tree, but it is like the shadow of a bird in flight —*Palestinian Talmud*

LIFE, DEFINED

1. The course of life is like the sea; men come and go; tides rise and fall; and that is all of history —Joaquin Miller

2. Each person's life is like a mountain. And each person has to climb that mountain top alone —Rosamund Pilcher
   Pilcher builds on the mountain simile by explaining that as a child you start in a warm and sunny valley, then you climb a somewhat steeper mountain with a wonderful view to make the end of the journey worthwhile.

3. A human life is like a single letter in the alphabet. It can be meaningless. Or it can be part of a great meaning —essay by National Planning Committee of Jewish Theological Seminary for Rosh Hashan, September 5, 1956

4. Human life may be regarded as a succession of frontis pieces. The way to be satisfied is never to look back —William Hazlitt

5. Life . . . a formless lump like cold tea leaves from which goodness and badness and even the last tang of bitterness have been stewed out — Gerald Kersh
   The life being compared to cold tea leaves in Kersh's novel, *The Angel and the Cuckoo,* is obviously one that is deteriorating.

6. Life is a big gambling game. Some are born lucky and some are born unlucky —Jack London

7. Life is a blister on top of a tumor, and a boil on top of that —Sholom Aleichem

8. Life is, after all, a kind of disaster through which we do what we can to keep each other's spirits up —Thomas Mallon, *New York Times Book Review,* October 12, 1986

9. Life is a kind of chess, in which we have often points to gain, and competitors or adversaries to contend with, and in which there is a vast variety of good and evil events that are, in some degree, the effect of prudence or the want of it —Benjamin Franklin

10. Life . . . is a kind of stage play, where men come forth, disguised one in one array, and one in another, each playing his part —Erasmus

11. Life is a little like disease, with its crises and periods of quiescence, the daily improvements and setbacks —Italo Svevo
   In his novel, *Confessions of Zeno,* Svevo continues the simile as follows: "But unlike other diseases life is always mortal. It admits of no cure. It would be like trying to stop up the holes in our body, thinking them to be wounds. We should die of suffocation almost before we were cured."

12. Life is . . . a long series of challenges, like hurdles in a race — Rosamund Pilcher

13. Life is a long strong twisted rope made up of a number of human relationships —Mary Borden

14. Life is an incurable disease —Abraham Cowley

15. Life is a public performance on the violin, in which you must learn the instrument as you go along —E. M. Forster

16. Life is a train constantly crossing the border from the past to the present —Susan Fromberg Schaeffer

17. Life is but a day; a fragile dew-drop on its perilous way from a tree's summit —John Keats

18. Life . . . is like a beach covered with lots of pebbles, the faster we qualify ourselves to pick these pebbles the richer we will be —Evan A. Sholl

19. Life is like a beautiful and winding lane —George Augustus Sala
   The simile continues as follows: "On either side bright flowers, beautiful butterflies, and tempting fruits which we scarcely pause to admire and taste, so eager are we to hasten to an opening which we imagine will be more beautiful still. But by degrees, as we advance, the trees grow bleak, the flowers and butterflies frail, the fruits disappear, and we find we have arrived to reach a desert waste."

20. Life is like a B-picture script. It is that corny —Kirk Douglas, *Look,* October 4, 1944
   To add emphasis to his simile, Douglas added: "If I had my life story offered to me to film, I'd turn it down."

21. Life is like a cash register, in that every account, every thought, every deed, like every sale, is registered and recorded —Fulton J. Sheen

22. Life is like a cup of tea . . . needing love to make it sweet —Edward A. Guest

To show that the same basic simile can have different meanings, there's this line from J. M. Barrie's *The Admirable Crichton:* "Life, Crichton, is like a cup of tea; the more heartily we drink, the sooner we reach the dregs."

23. Life is like a dissected map. If I could live a hundred years . . . I feel I could put the pieces together until they made a properly connected whole —Oliver Wendell Holmes, Sr.

24. Life is like a fire; it begins in smoke, and ends in ashes —Arab proverb

25. Life is like a game of dice —Alexis
    The comparison of life to the roll of the dice has been an irresistible simile throughout history. Variations include "Life is like a game of tables," the chances are not in our power but the playing is dating back to B.C., and "Life is like a game of roulette."

26. Life is like a game of cards —Edgar Watson Howe
    Howe built on the comparison as follows: "Reliability is the ace, industry the king, politeness the queen, thrift the jack. Common sense is playing to best advantage the cards you draw." A 1978 poem by Diane Wakoski used the simile for its title and theme.

27. Life . . . is like a grapefruit . . . sort of orangy-yellow and dimpled on the outside, wet and squidgy in the middle —Douglas Adams

28. Life is like a jigsaw puzzle with most of the pieces missing —Anon

29. Life is like a kiss that does not last long enough for a fellow to ascertain how good it is —Elbridge G. Dow Jr.

30. Life is like a mountain: after climbing up one side and sliding down the other, put up the sled —Josh Billings
    The word 'is' has been changed from the dialect form 'iz.'

31. Life is like an onion, which one peels crying —French proverb

32. Life is like an onion: you peel off layer after layer and then you find there is nothing in it —James G. Huneker

33. Life is like a school of gladiators, where men live and fight with one another —Seneca The Elder

34. Life is like a scrambled egg —Don Marquis

35. Life is like a stew, you have to stir it frequently, or all the scum rises to the top —Tom Robbins

36. Life is like drunkenness: the pleasure passes away, but the headache remains —Persian proverb

37. Life is like music, it must be composed by ear, feeling and instinct, not by rule —Samuel Butler

38. Life is like playing a violin solo in public and learning the instrument as one goes on —Samuel Butler

39. Life is like that, a cake-walk —Clifford Odets
   The simile is from Odets play, *Awake and Sing.*

40. Life is not a game of chess, the victory to the knowing; it is a game of cards, one's hand by skill to be made the best of —Jerome K. Jerome

41. Life is very much like an arms race, each side waiting for the other one to put his stick down first —Merle Shain

42. Life, like a dome of many-coloured glass, stains the white radiance of eternity —Percy Bysshe Shelley

43. Human life is like the petals that fall from the rose and lie soft and withering by the side of the vase —Anon Persian poem

44. The life of every man is a diary in which he means to write one story, and writes another, and his humblest hour is when he compares the volume as it is with what he vowed to make it —J. M. Barrie

45. The life of man is like a long journey with a heavy load on the back — Japanese proverb

46. Life's a library owned by an author. In it are a few books which he wrote but most of them were written for him —Harry Emerson Fosdick

47. Life seems to me like a Japanese picture which our imagination does not allow to end with the margin —Oliver Wendell Holmes, Jr.

48. Life's like a play: it's not the length but the excellence of the acting that matters —Seneca
   A variation made famous by the playwright Ben Jonson: "Our whole life is like a play."

49. Man's life is like a candle in the wind —Chinese proverb

50. The scenes of our life are like pictures done in rough mosaic . . . There is nothing beautiful to be found in them, unless we stand some distance off —Arthur Schopenhauer

51. This mundane life is like a drink of salt water, which seems to quench, but actually inflames —Gaon Elijah

52. The way of life is like a path between two forbidding roads, one of fire and one of ice —Judah
   Judah built on the simile with this advice: "The slightest bend in either direction is fatal. Let him walk in the middle."

53. A well-ordered life is like climbing a tower; the view halfway up is better than the view from the base, and it steadily becomes finer as the horizon expands —William Lyon Phelps

54. The whole of life of some people is a kind of partial death, a long lingering death-bed, so to speak, of stagnation and nonentity on which death is but the seal —Samuel Butler

LIGHTING
See Also: BRIGHTNESS, SHINING

1. All lit up like warships in a foggy port —Amos Oz

2. Everything lit up like a disco on Saturday night —Loren D. Estleman

3. A glittering neon sign like wolves' eyes —Elizabeth Bowen

4. The gray light of the winter dawn lit the bedroom like a dreary fake impressionistic painting —Jerry Bumpus

5. The house [with all lights on] blazed like a stage set —T. Coraghessan Boyle
   See Also: LIGHTING

6. Light as a paper airplane (and as elegant) —Marge Piercy

7. Lighted windows [at dawn] were scattered like yellow diamonds on black velvet —Loren D. Estleman

8. Lighting streaked the snow. Like the urine of dogs by trees —William H. Gass

9. (Offices . . . in which) light is a kind of yellow fluid, like old shellac —Scott Turow
   In his novel, *Presumed Innocent,* Scott Turow uses this comparison to paint a picture of the "Dickensenian" atmosphere in which the hero's fellow lawyers work.

10. The light seemed to be draining away like flood-water —Kenneth Grahame

11. Lights glittered . . . like a diamond necklace round the neck of a lovely signorina —Donald Seaman

12. Lights . . . pouring over us like scalding milk —Ira Wood

13. The lights (of the bridge) were like strings of pearls hanging up in the air —Cornell Woolrich

14. The light was golden like the flesh of women —Thomas Wolfe

15. Like moons around Jupiter, pale moths revolved about a lone lamp —Vladimir Nabokov

16. (The big glass window was) lit like a stage —Frank Tuohy

17. (The place was) lit up like a birthday cake —Jayne Anne Phillips

18. Lit up like a midway —Tom Robbins

19. Lit up like a paper lantern —Willis Johnson

20. Lit up like a whorehouse on Saturday night —Loren D. Estleman

21. Lit up like skyscrapers or planes taking off —Marge Piercy

22. [A truck] plastered with lights like a beer-joint —Carlos Baker

23. Streetlights cast their shadows on the wall like a sharp, white condolence —Ariel Dorfman

24. The street lights shone like tiny beads on a string —David Huddle

25. When the lamps in the house are lighted it is like the flowering of lotus on the lake —Chinese proverb

26. Windows [of a building] glowing like those of a lighted card-board house under a Christmas tree —Willa Cather

LIGHTNESSS

See Also: SOFTNESS

1. Airy as the holes in Swiss cheese —Anon

2. As giddy as a drunken man —Charles Dickens
    This is the last of a whole string of similes uttered by a reformed Scrooge in *A Christmas Carol:* I'm as light as a feather, I am as happy as an angel, I'm as merry as a schoolboy. I am as giddy as a drunken man. A merry Christmas to everybody! A happy New Year to all the world.
    See Also: GAIETY

3. As lightly as a cloud is blown —John Greenleaf Whittier

4. Flippancy, like comedy, is but a matter of visual first impressions — Joseph Conrad

5. (A light blue summer dress as) frothy as high tide —Jonathan Kellerman

6. Hands were light as moths —John MacDonald)

7. Light as a hand among blossoms —Theodore Roethke

8. (Mountains . . .) light and airy like balloons on a string —George Garrett

9. [Touch] light as a butterfly —Eleanor Farejons
    And lighter still, there's a touch that's "Light as a butterfly's kiss" from a John MacDonald novel.

10. Light as a flight of tumbling birds —C. S. Lewis

11. Light as a fly —John Ray's *Proverbs*

12. Light as a leaf —Anon
    An ancient simile which continues in use to describe lightness of heart, mind and body. "Light as" variants include "Light as a feather," "Light as wind," and "Light as air." With them all, "Lighter than" crops up as frequently as "Light as."

13. Light as a milkweed puff —Richard Wilbur

14. [A racing jockey] light as a monkey —Ernest Hemingway

15. Light as an angel —Donald McCaig

16. Light as a paper toy —Anon

17. Light as a petal falling upon stone —Theodore Roethke

18. (She is) light as a phantom —W. P. Kinsella

19. Light as a seed —Theodore Roethke

20. Light as breath —Robert Penn Warren

21. Light as cork —Henry James

22. Light as dandelion fluff —Mary Hedin

23. [Snow] light as dust —Amy Lowell

24. Light as helium —Elizabeth Bishop

25. [Snowflakes] light as milkweed —T. Coraghessan Boyle

26. [Feathers on a hat] light as mist in a breeze —Colette

27. Light as sea-foam, strong as the tide —Slogan for underwear, Paris-Hecker Co.

28. (Free and) light as the breath that clung to them like clouds —Arthur Gregor

29. Light as thistledown —John Yount

30. (We carry her indoor. She is) light as toast —Louise Erdrich

31. Lightly . . . as a child skips rope, the way a mouse waltzes —E.B. White on James Thurber's writing

32. Lightly as a wisp of air —Harvey Swados

33. Weightless as an ache —Sharon Sheehe Stark
     In Stark's novel, *A Wrestling Season,* the simile is used to answer the question of what death might be like.

34. (Her body was . . .) weightless as a strip of cane —Eudora Welty

35. Weightless as the notes rung out of bells at kindling dawn —George Garrett

LIGHTNING
See: THUNDER AND LIGHTNING

LIKELIHOOD
See: IMPOSSIBILITY

LIKENESS
See: SIMILARITY

LIMBS
See: ARM(S), LEGS

LIMPNESS
See: SOFTNESS

LINGERING

1. Brooded over . . . the way a plane caught in a fog hovers longingly over a blurred landing strip —Lynne Sharon Schwartz

2. (Haven't you got anything better to do than) hang around here like a prairie dog in heat —line from the movie, *Bronco Billy.*

3. Hang around like a rent collector or a man come to fix the faucet — Harvey Swados

4. Hang around like sullen clouds over the sun —John Ashberry

5. Hanging around like a fart in a phone box —Australian colloquialism

6. [An idea] hang over . . . like a thunderstorm reluctant to break — Gavin Lyall

7. [The smell of circus lions] hangs like August heat —Delmore Schwartz

8. Hover like a moth intoxicated with light —John Galsworthy

9. Hover like butterflies —Lee Smith

10. Hover over like an ugly bird of prey —Anon

11. Hung around . . . like a herd of sheep with no sheep dog —Ignazio Silone

12. (The Fraziers had refused to leave his mind; they had stayed on,) imposing themselves on his consciousness and his conscience like the troubling memory of a drunken evening —Elizabeth Hardwick

13. Languish like a mist at noon —Herbert Read

14. Lingered like heat, like poppy petals, like desert sand —Kay Boyle

15. Lingered, like smoke after fire —Paul Kuttner

16. Lingering like an unloved guest —Percy Bysshe Shelley

17. Lingering like second thoughts —George Bradley

18. (Light) lingers like a lover's tongue —Bin Ramke
    This simile concludes a poem entitled *What the Weather is Like.*

19. Lodged like a marble in a crack —James Crumley

20. Loitered like a school child —Jean Stafford

21. (A cold notion flew into my brain and) squatted there like a buzzard, patient, in a tree —George Garrett

22. Stalling like a Scotchman in front of a pay toilet —Harold Adams

LIPS

See Also: MOUTH

1. An upper lip shaped like a circumflex accent —Eric Ambler Drew her lips into a thin wiggly line like fish bait —Sharon Sheehe Stark

2. Full lips like a French movie star —Ira Wood

3. Her lips glistened as if she'd just eaten a pound of vaseline —Sarah Bird

4. Her lips looked . . . delicious, as though if you bit them it would be like biting into a sweetmeat, one of those candies which are filled with a pleasant warming liquid —Ben Ames Williams

5. His lips, like those of all men who work, were puckered up like a bag with the string drawn tight —Honoré de Balzac

6.   His lips were tightened in a thin line, as if he had them sewn together to keep from vomiting —Robert J. Serling

7.   His lips were too red, as if he had a hangover —Louise Erdrich

8.   His long lips tightened, as if he sought to conquer pain —Frank Swinnerton

9.   Lips always compressed as if to keep back a swarm of curses —George Garrett

10. Lips as bloodless as lips of the slain —John Greenleaf Whittier

11. Lips . . . as glossy as ripe cherries —Anton Chekhov

12. Lips delicate as peach-toned porcelain —Jayne Anne Phillips

13. Lips . . . drawn in a tight line like the lips of a child not quite ready to take a dose of bad-tasting medicine —George Garrett

14. Lips . . . dry and faint as her tea leaves —Shirley Ann Grau

15. Lips full as thighs —Lyn Lifshin

16. Lips like a thread of scarlet —*The Holy Bible/Song of Solomon*

17. Lips like lilies —*The Holy Bible/Song of Solomon*

18. Lips . . . like pale velvet —Jimmy Sangster

19. Lips like sausages —John D. MacDonald

20. Lips . . . like the petals of a red flower —Oscar Wilde

21. Lips like wet cherries —Virginia Woolf

22. Lips moved noisily, smacking like a three-day thirst —Sharon Sheehe Stark

23. Lips . . . red as two buds —Louise Erdrich

24. Lips . . . set in exasperation, as if she had just been about to say something and found out her voice was snatched in death —Louise Erdrich

25. Lips . . . shining like rain on night streets —Jayne Anne Phillips

26. Lips that, like a ventriloquist's, scarcely stirred —Katherine Bush

27. Lips that looked as if she were permanently whistling —Mike Fredman

28. Lips that shine wetly, just like a Cosmo girl —George Garrett

29. Lips that stand out from his skin like two thick weals —Aldous Huxley

30. Lips tighter than any knot —Tim O'Brien

31. Lips trembling like elastic stretched too taut —George Garrett

32. A long blue upper lip, like a priest —Joyce Cary

33. The muscles of her chapped lips were broken and loose like the snap of an old purse —Gerald Kersh

34. Pursed his lips as if he were just before receiving a terrible blow — Richard Ford

35. Set her lips as though she would never speak again —Dorothy Canfield Fisher

36. Sharp-pointed lips stretched out like a slingshot —Bobbie Ann Mason

37. She kept closing her lips over her teeth and then pursing her lips, so that she looked as though she were going to give somebody a little goodbye kiss —Maeve Brennan

38. Thick lips . . . like lozenges of hard rubber —Jonathan Valin

39. Thin lips fitted tightly together, as though they were parts of a very well-made piece of furniture —Aldous Huxley

40. An upper lip that twiched softly, like a cow's in a fly-ridden summer — Penelope Gilliatt

LITERATURE
See: ART AND LITERATURE, BOOKS, WRITERS/WRITING

LIVELINESS
See: ACTIVENESS, ENTHUSIASM, ENERGY

LOCALITIES
See: PLACES

LOGIC
See: SENSE

LONELINESS
See: ABANDONMENT, ALONENESS

LONGING
See: DESIRE

LONG-WINDEDNESS
See: TALKATIVENESS

LOOKS
See Also: FROWNS AND SCOWLS, SCRUTINY, STARES

1. Accusing look . . . as Cotton Mather might have looked at a Salem woman in the stocks —Mary Gordon

2. Always looked at you as if you had interrupted him in the performance of some slightly tedious but nonetheless necessary task —Louis Auchincloss

3. Black glance like ice —Jean Garrigue

4. Contemplate . . . with a kind of quiet premeditation, like that of a slow-witted man fondling an unaccustomed thought —Beryl Markham

5. Disdainful look like that of a coffee drinker sipping a cup of instant — Anon

6. Exchanged fidgeting looks like a pair of consternated hamsters —Sarah Bird

7. Exchanged wide-eyed looks that clinked in the air like fine glassware — Sharon Sheehe Stark

8. Eyeing me . . . like a starved hog watching the trough get filled — Harold Adams

9. Felt his eyes slide over her like a steamy wet cloak —Joseph Wambaugh

10. Gaze at me like chastened children sitting silent in a school —Thomas Hardy

11. Gazed at . . . with nudging, sympathetic smiles, like grandmothers watching babies in a play-pen —Mary McCarthy

12. Gaze . . . fixed like a snake's —Donald MacKenzie

13. Glance as vacant as the smoothness of the pond —David Ignatow

14. Glanced at one another like tigers taking measure of a menacing new rival —Erich Segal

15. Glance . . . like a needle's flash —Frank Swinnerton

16. Glowered back like a sullen watchdog —Frank Swinnerton

17. Her flat dark eyes moved down Melinda like a smudge —Jessamyn West

18. Her gaze moved like a prison searchlight —Michael Dorris

19. Her gaze was like a magnet that drew towards it my will-less secret — Jean Stafford

20. His eyes glowed on me like a warm hand —Borden Deal

21. His eyes on me as hot as a bare hand —R. Wright Campbell

22. His eyes set on Linda's open shirtfront like a cat sighting a fat bird — Gloria Norris
See Also: MEN AND WOMEN

23. His eyes slewed round to meet yours and then cannoned off again like a pool-ball —Seán Virgo

24. His glance came back across mine like saw teeth across a nail — Wallace Stegner

25. His look was like a hand in the scruff of Bruce's neck —Wallace Stegner

26. Like swallows darting about a barn her deep blue eyes flickered from one to the other —F. van Wyck Mason

27. (Gave me) a long [forgiving] look like Christ crucified —Clare Boylan

28. Look at him as if he were a lamppost —Leo Tolstoy

29. Looked about him like the fallen archangel whose only wish was for eternal enmity —Honoré de Balzac

30. Looked around her at the crowd, with eyes smarting, unseeing, and tearful as if an oculist had put caustic eye-drops into them —Boris Pasternak

31. Looked at each other like schoolboys caught masturbating —Lawrence Durrell

32. Looked at each other in a flicker fast as a snake's tongue —Rosellen Brown

33. Looked at her like she was some kind of Italian sports car and he was ready to drive her —Dialogue from "Murder She Wrote" television drama, broadcast in March 19, 1987,
    The look thus described is attributed to a jealous husband.

34. Looked at her like a bird that has been shot —D. H. Lawrence

35. Looked at him as a guinea pig looks at a big dog —Frank Swinnerton

36. Looked at him as a sergeant in the United States Marines would look at a recruit who had just called a rifle a gun —Norman MacLean

37. Looked at me as if I were a mongrel that had suddenly said, "Hi" — Harold Adams

38. Looked at me as though I had suddenly broke out with a filthy disease —M. C. Blackman

39. Looked at me expectantly as a poodle —Erich Maria Remarque

40. Looked at me intently, as if trying to recall something —Mihail Lermontov

41. Looked at me keenly, like a smart boxer stung in the first round and cagily reappraising the character of his opposition —Robert Traver

42. Looked at me like she was ready to carve my liver —Larry McMurtry

43. Looked at Whistler [character in novel] as if she'd like to crush him with her thighs or smother him with her tits —Robert Campbell

44. Looked at . . . with an awakened air, as if she were pricking up her ears like a trooper's horse at the sound of a trumpet —Honoré de Balzac

45. Looked at you without really seeing you, like a TV broadcaster reading the teleprompter —Elyse Sommer

46. Looked him up and down like a sergeant inspecting the ranks —George Garrett

47. Looked knowing and quizzical, like someone smiling with a mouthful of salts —George MacDonald Fraser

48. Looked through us like glass —Alan Williamson

49. Looked towards me as towards a jury —F. Scott Fitzgerald

50. Looking about him as if he had a score to settle —Romain Gary

51. Looking at him with something cold as dislike —Rebecca West

52. (She was) looking at us . . . like she had emptied her eyes, like she had quit using them —William Faulkner

53. Looking from face to face like he was judge —Jayne Anne Phillips

54. Looking on one another, sideways and crossways, and with lowered eyes, like guilty criminals —Anzia Yezierska

55. A look passed between them, like the silent exchange of two doctors who agree on a simple diagnosis without having to put it in words — Marilyn Sharp

56. Looks black as thunder —J. R. Planche

57. Looks . . . like the lizard watches the fly —Leslie Silko

58. A look that burned like live coals on our naked bodies —Anzia Yezierska

59. Playing his eyes over the other's face like the feelers of insects —Arthur A. Cohen

60. Regarded her with raised brows like a doctor who is considering how fully to answer a layman's question —Saul Bellow

61. Regarded me somberly but warily, as you might examine a particularly ferocious gorilla from the other side of a set of flimsy bars —Harvey Swados

62. She looked at him with that cunning which those who profess unworldliness can wield like a club of stone —Francine du Plessix Gray
See Also: CLEVERNESS

63. She took him in as if he were frozen in a block of ice or enclosed in a cage of wires —Louise Erdrich

64. That look that seemed to enter him like an enormous jolt of neat whiskey —Daniel Curley

65. The each-for-himself look in the eyes of the people about her were like stinging slaps in the face —Anzia Yezierska

66. Their eyes caromed off each other like the balls on a table —Ed McBain

67. Their eyes rolled like marbles toward one another —Mary Hedin

68. Their glances crossed like blades —Stephen Crane

69. Triumphant look, like the fallen angel restored —D. H. Lawrence

70. A true-felt look . . . laden with sweetness, white, mesmerizing, like the blossom that hangs from the cherry trees —Edna O'Brien

71. Turned to me in blank apprehension like a blind woman taken by surprise —Ross Macdonald

72. Uncomprehending gaze . . . like an anxious monkey —Mary Stewart

73. Watching me as though trying to work out a puzzle —C. J. Koch

LOOSENESS

1. (Muscle) lax as a broken shade —Diane Ackerman
2. (Face) lax as a wax work —Daniel Berrigan
3. (The gear worked) loose as a hound's shoulder —Elizabeth Spencer
4. Loose as a gossip's tongue —Anon
5. Loose as ashes —Anon
6. Loose as eggs in a nest —Walter Savage Landor
7. Loose as windblown sand —Mark Helprin
8. Slack as a toad —Barbara Howes
9. Sprawled . . . lax as a drowned man —George Garrett

LOUDNESS
    See: NOISE

LOVE
    See Also: FRIENDSHIP; LOVE, DEFINED; MEN AND WOMEN

1. Absence in love is like waters upon fire; a little quickens, but much extinguishes it —Hannah More
2. All loving emotions, like plants, shoot up most rapidly in the tempestuous atmosphere of life —Jean Paul Richter
3. Amorous as Emma Bovary —James G. Huneker
4. Could love forever run like a river —Lord Byron
5. Falling in love is something you forget, like pain —Nina Bawden
6. Felt love like a lottery prize —Geoffrey Wolff
7. First and passionate love, it stands alone, like Adam's recollection of his fall —Lord Byron
8. The force of her love . . . is bulky and hard to carry, like a package that keeps untying —Louise Erdrich
9. Going through life without love is like going through a good dinner without an appetite; everything seems flat and tasteless —Helen Rowland
10. Her love was like the swallow's, whose first thought is for its nest — Italo Svevo
11. If love were what the rose is, and I were like the leaf, our lives would grow together —Algernon Charles Swinburne
12. I love you as New Englanders love pie —Don Marquis
13. Infatuation like paralysis, is often all on one side —Helen Rowland
14. It [love] could, like grief, grow forgetful and weary and slowly wear away —Alice Mc Dermott

15. Knew as much about love as a pig knows about St. Valentine's Day — Harry Prince

16. Like the water of a deep stream, love is always too much —Wendell Berry
    This line from a poem entitled *The Country of Marriage* is followed by: "We did not make it. Though we drink till we burst we cannot have it all, or want it all."

17. Love as an old man loves money, with no stomach —William Shakespeare

18. Love burst out . . . all over our bodies, like sweat —Yehuda Amichai

19. Love can die of truth as friendship of a lie —Abel Bonard

20. Love . . . comes as a butterfly tipped with gold —Algernon Charles Swinburne

21. Love comes into your being like a tidal wave . . . sometimes it withdraws like a wave, till there isn't such a thing as a pool left, and every bit of your heart is as dry as seaweed beyond the wave's reach — Phyllis Bottome

22. Love comforts like sunshine after rain —William Shakespeare
    The original simile as used in *Venus and Adonis* had the word 'comforts' spelled as 'comforteth.'

23. Love doesn't just sit there, like a stone, it has to be made, like bread; re-made all the time, made new —Ursula K. Le Guin

24. Love . . . entered the room like a miracle —Milan Kundera

25. Love had seized her as unexpectedly as would sudden death — Elizabeth Taylor

26. (Our cook is in love.) Love hangs on the house like a mist —Phyllis McGinley

27. Love hung still as crystal over the bed —Louis MacNeice

28. Love is fierce as death —*The Holy Bible/Song of Songs*

29. Love is flower-like —Samuel Taylor Coleridge

30. Love is . . . fresh as dew when first it is new —British folk song, "The Water Is Wide" (*The Good Times Songbook,* Abingdon Press, 1974)
    The complete refrain includes yet another simile: "Oh, love is sweet and love is fair, fresh as the dew when first it is new, but love grows old and waxeth cold, and fades away like morning dew."

31. Love is like the moon; when it does not increase it decreases —Joseph Alexandre Pierre Segur

32. Love is . . . lone as the sea, and deeper blue —Dorothy Parker

33. Love . . . it makes him [the lover] fluent as a tin whistle, as limber as a boy's watch chain, and as polite as a dancing master —Josh Billings

Parts originally in the Billing phonetic dialect: 'whissel' and 'perlite' as a 'dansing.'

34. Loveless as the multiplication table —Sylvia Plath

35. Love life . . . just about as interesting as the love life of the desert horned toad —William Saroyan

36. Love, like a tear, rises in the eye and falls upon the breast —Publius Syrus

37. Love like chicken salad or restaurant hash, must be taken on blind faith or it loses all its flavor —Helen Rowland

38. Love, like death, a universal leveller of mankind —William Congreve

39. Love, like death, changes everything —Kahlil Gibran

40. Love, like fire, cannot subsist without constant impulse; it ceases to live from the moment it ceases to hope or to fear —Francois, duc de La Rochefoucauld

41. Love, like money, is probably best kept in the family —William Gaddis, *New York Times Book Review,* May 24, 1987
     Gaddis used this simile to conclude his review of Saul Bellow's novel, *More Die of Heartbreak.*

42. Love passed between them like a field of light —Ellen Gilchrist

43. Love . . . pricks like a thorn —William Shakespeare

44. Love . . . roots up the will like a leaf —Gustave Flaubert

45. Lovers are always in a hurry . . . like a racing river —Ben Ames Williams

46. Lovers fail like seasons —F. D. Reeve

47. Love's dominion, like a king's, admits of no partition —Ovid

48. Love sometimes is like the flower of the wild poppy: you can't carry it home —Jaroslav Seifert

49. Love was a treadmill, like churchgoing —Elizabeth Hardwick

50. Love washes on me like rain on a dead man's shoes —Ellen Gilchrist

51. Love without grace is like a hook without bait —Anne de Lencos

52. Love without respect is cold as a boa constrictor —Marge Piercy
     In her poem, *Witnessing a Wedding,* Piercy continues with its caresses as choking.

53. Loving someone that much younger is like taking a trip to a foreign country —Ellen Gilchrist

54. Making love to a woman too many times is like scratching a place that doesn't itch any more —Anon, *Playboy,* 1965

55. A man in love may behave like a madman but not like a dunce —Francois, duc de La Rochefoucauld

Man has been substituted for gentleman to give the simile a more modern tone.

56. The man who is not loved hovers like a vulture over the sweetheart of others —Victor Hugo

57. My heart simmered with angry love like chicken soup on grandma's stove —James Atlas

58. My love is like foliage in the woods. Time will change it as winter changes the trees —Emily Brönte
    The love described is Cathy's for Heathcliff in *Wuthering Heights.*

59. Once love is purged of vanity it is like a feeble convalescent, hardly capable of dragging itself around —Sebastien Roch Nicolas de Chamfort

60. Our love is like our life; there's no man blest in either till his end — Shackerley Marmion

61. Our love is like the misty rain that falls softly . . . but floods the river —African proverb

62. (What I want . . . is something organic . . .) potato love, natural as earth, scruffy and brown, clinging to your roots, helping you grow fit and firm —Daphne Merkin

63. Romance, like a ghost, eludes touching —G. W. Curtis

64. Romance, like alcohol, should be enjoyed but must not be swallowed to become necessary —Edgar Z. Friedenberg

65. Romantic love is ephemeral and occasionally unavoidable . . . like the viral flu —Marcia Froelke Coburn, *New York Time Book Review,* September 14, 1986

66. A rush of love swamped her heart . . . like a tide —Vita Sackville-West

67. The science of love demands delicacy, perseverance, and practice, like the piano —Anatole France

68. The simple accident of falling in love is as beneficial as it is astonishing —Robert Louis Stevenson

69. (She was long married . . . but she had recently) stepped out of the country of love; briskly, and without a backward glance, as if she had spent too much time in its steamy jungles —John Cheever

70. This was a game, like bridge, in which you said things instead of playing cards. Like bridge you had to pretend you were playing for money or playing for some stakes —Ernest Hemingway

71. Threw herself into love like a suicide into the river —Guy De Maupassant

72. To love a woman who scorns you is like licking honey from a thorn — Welsh proverb

73. To talk of honour in the mysteries of love, is like talking of Heaven or the Deity in an operation of witchcraft, just when you are employing the devil: it makes the charm impotent —William Wycherley

74. Trapped in love . . . like a great tortoise trapped in a heavy death-like shell —Joyce Carol Oates

75. It [being loved by affectionately possessive wife] was like being loved by a large moist sponge —Phyllis Bottome

76. Without love our life is . . . unprofitable as a ship without a rudder . . . like a body without a soul —Sholom Aleichem

77. With true loves as with ghosts: everyone speaks of them, but few have seen them —Francois, duc de La Rochefoucauld

78. (I) wore my heart like a wet, red stain on the breast of a velvet gown — Dorothy Parker

LOVE, DEFINED

1. Falling in love is like being thrown from a horse; if you let yourself go it doesn't hurt as badly as if you try to save yourself —Edwin L. Blanchard

2. It's [love] very like a lizard; it winds itself around your heart and penetrates your gizzard —Anon rhyme

3. A love affair is like a work of art —Laurie Colwin

4. Love is a hole in the heart —Ben Hecht

5. Love is a science where great erudition and great application are needed —Anatole France

6. Love is like a child that longs for everything that he can come by — William Shakespeare

7. Love is like a cigar, the longer it burns the less it becomes —*Punch,* 1855

8. Love is . . . like a coconut which is good while it's fresh, but you have to spit it out when the juice is gone, what's left tastes bitter —Bertold Brecht

9. Love is like a cold. Easy to catch but hard to cure —Anon

10. Love is like a dizziness —James Hogg
     This is the title and first line of a poem.

11. Love is like a dream that's too good to be true —Langston Hughes

12. Love is like a friendship caught on fire —Bruce Lee

13. Love is like a lovely rose —Christina Georgina Rossetti

14. Love is like a repeating decimal; the figure is the same but the value gets less and less —Anon

15. Love is like a wind stirring the grass beneath trees on a black night — Sherwood Anderson

16.   Love is like butter, it goes well with bread —Yiddish proverb

17.   Love is like electricity. It flares up for a second and is soon extinguished —Isaac Bashevis Singer

18.   Love is like fire . . . wounds of fire are hard to bear; harder still are those of love —Hjalmar Hjorth Boyesen

19.   Love is like growing pains; something we all have to experience for ourselves —Anon

20.   Love is like heaven, a brief possession, unsearchable, hard to reconstruct with two-by-fours and building blocks —Leonard Casper
      In Casper's story, *Sense of Direction,* the simile is in the past tense and the word building is spelled without the last letter.

21.   Love is like learning to walk; we all have to go through it —Anon

22.   Love is like linen, the more often changed, the sweeter —Phineas Fletcher
      The word 'changed' was originally 'chang'd.'

23.   Love is like malaria. You never know when you're going to catch it — Rita Mae Brown

24.   Love is like measles; you can get it only once, and the later in life it occurs the tougher it goes —Josh Billing
      The simile in Billings' dialect: "Love iz like the meazles; we kant have it bad but onst, and the later in life we have it the tuffer it goes with us." Medical science has made this much quoted comparison obsolete, though another illness, mishap, or a necessary learning experience could easily be substituted.

25.   Love is like quicksilver in the hand . . . leave the fingers open and it stays in the palm; clutch it, and it darts away —Dorothy Parker

26.   Love is like soup; it cools when the fire dies out —Anon

27.   Love is like the devil; whom it has in its clutches it surrounds with flames —Honoré de Balzac

28.   Love is like the measles; we all have to go through it —Jerome K. Jerome
      See the comment with Josh Billings love/measles simile above.

29.   Love is like a well: a good thing to drink out of, but a bad thing to fall into —Anon

30.   Love is like the wild rose-briar, friendship like the holly tree —Emily Brontë
      See Also: FRIENDSHIP

31.   Love is like those shabby hotels in which all the luxury is in the lobby —Paul Jean Toulet

32.   Love is trembling happiness —Kahlil Gibran

33.   Love is very much like a tennis match, you'll never win consistently until you learn to serve well —Dan P. Herod

34. Love is what is called the Milky Way in Heaven, a brilliant mass formed by thousands of little stars of which each perhaps is nebulous — Stendhal
    > One wonders what he might have added had he known about black holes in space and their gravity so enormous it sucks up everything surrounding itself.

35. Love . . . it's like an ocean: if you're no good, if you begin to make a bad smell in it, it just spews you up somewhere to die —William Faulkner

36. Love, like a poker game starts with a pair; with her getting a flush, him showing a diamond and both ending up together with a full house — Anon

37. Love, like death, a universal leveller of mankind —William Congreve

38. Lovers are like drunkards; once a drunkard always a drunkard, once a lover always a lover. It is simply a matter of temperament —Guy De Maupassant

39. Love's like the measles, all the worse when it comes too late —Douglas Jerrold
    > See comment following the Josh Billings love/measles simile above.

40. Love without return is like a question without an answer —Anon

41. Loving, like prayer, is a power as well a process. It's curative. It is creative —Zona Gale

42. The moods of love are like the wind —Coventry Patmore

43. My love is as a fever —William Shakespeare
    > Another famous author, Stendhal, also likened love to a fever, adding: "It comes and goes without the will having any part in the process."

44. My love is like a red red rose —Robert Burns
    > This is the first line and title of Burns' famous poem, in which love was spelled 'luv.'

45. An old man in love is like a flower in winter —Portugese proverb

46. Romance is the poetry of circumstance —Robert Louis Stevenson

47. True love is like seeing a ghost. We talk about it; few of us have seen one —Francois, Duc de La Rochefoucauld
    > Some quote La Rochefoucauld as linking the ghost comparison to perfect instead of true love.

48. A woman's love is like the dew. It falls as easily on the manure heap as on the rose —Donald McCaig

49. Young love is a flame; very pretty, often very hot and fierce, but still only light and flickering. The love of the older and disciplined heart is as coals, deep-burning, unquenchable —Henry Ward Beecher

LOYALTY/DISLOYALTY
See Also: FRIENDSHIP, LOVE

1. Always at her side like a Great Dane —Carlos Baker

2. As the rolling stone gathers no moss, so the roving heart gathers no affection —Anna Jameson

3. Devoted and caretaking as a cat with her kittens —Katherine Anne Porter

4. (In the end, people's) devotion hung like rocks around your neck —Alice Munro
See Also: CLINGING

5. Endless devotion . . . like a straitjacket —Lynne Sharon Schwartz

6. Faithful (to each other) as the Canada goose, more or less —Laurie Colwin

7. Fickle as spring sunlight —Carolyn Kizer

8. A heart true as steel —William Shakespeare
Shakespeare gave this comparison from *Midsummer Night's Dream* a slight twist in *Romeo and Juliet:* "My man's as true as steel."

9. Like a woman in her first love affair, he insisted on unconditional commitment —Ariel Dorfman

10. Loyal, like a dog —Lynne Sharon Schwartz

11. Loyalty . . . small and hard, like buckshot lodged in her stomach —Sarah Litsey

12. To say that you can love one person all your life is just like saying that one candle will continue burning as long as you live —Leo Tolstoy

13. True to her husband as the dial to the sun —Henry Fielding

LUCIDITY
See: CLARITY

LUCK
See: FORTUNE/MISFORTUNE

LUNACY
See: MADNESS

LUSHNESS
See: ABUNDANCE

LUST
See: DESIRE, SEX

LYING

See Also: BEARING, BENDING/BENT, IMMOBILITY, POSTURE, SITTING, SLEEP, STANDING

1. Lay . . . as if chloroformed —Wallace Stegner

2. Lay as still as a fallen doll —George Garrett

3. Lay in bed like a tree stump —Charles Johnson

4. Lay lifeless as if spellbound —Herman Melville

5. Lay like an aimlessly flung sack of bones —Harvey Swados

6. Lay on his back . . . rigid and ruined, like some stained window mannequin —Davis Grubb

7. Lay on the sofa like cast-off silk stockings —Delmore Schwartz
   In his journal entry Schwartz followed this with two additional comparisons: "Like fallen buildings . . . like a car over turned." Had he been writing forty years later, he would have been apt to refer to pantyhose instead of silk stockings.
   See Also: ABANDONMENT

8. Lay perfectly still, as if dead with fear —D. H. Lawrence

9. Lay . . . rigid, as if she were dead —Elizabeth Taylor

10. Lay rigidly still, as still as if he were in his coffin —Dorothy Canfield Fisher

11. Lay side by side like fish —Lawrence Durrell

12. (Fallen and helpless, he) lay there like a pine tree that has been torn up by the roots —Ellen Glasgow

13. Lay there..stretched like a corpse —Hugh Walpole

14. Lay where she was for a few minutes like a flake of foam —Vicki Baum

15. (We'd) lie . . . like two sticks in bed —Elizabeth Spencer

16. The lovers like great scissors lay —Delmore Schwartz
    See Also: MEN AND WOMEN

17. Sprawled around . . . like shepherds in a frieze —Julia O'Faolain

18. Sprawled like a man who had been threshed —Stephen Crane

19. Sprawling like an exhausted dog —Mary Hedin

MADNESS

1. As crazy as a baboon chasing shit around a tree —American colloquialism

2. As crazy as a loon —American colloquialism
   Popular variations include "Crazy as bats" and "Crazy as a bed bug," the latter said to make its first appearance in Ernest Hemingway's *For Whom the Bell Tolls*.

3. Crazy as owl shit —Pat Conroy

4. As mad as a brush —Julia O'Faolain
5. As mad as a March hare —English phrase
    Even though Lewis Carroll didn't coin the phrase as many
    people think, its appearance in *Alice in Wonderland* probably
    contributed towards its common and continued usage to
    describe irrationality. The same is true of "Mad as a hatter"
    which originally alluded to the symptoms of madness by
    workers in the hat industry caused by exposure to chemicals.
6. As mad as a serpent —Carolyn See, *New York Times*/Hers, July 3, 1986
7. As nutty as a fruitcake —American colloquialism
    In vogue since around 1935 this has seeded such twists as
    "You're as nutty as a Mars bar" (Tom Robbins) and "Nuttier
    than a Hershey bar with almonds" (Ed Mc Bain). Departing
    from the candy and cake comparisons altogether, there's "As
    nutty as a squirrel's nest" (Mike Sommer).

MANIPULATION
See: POWER

MANKIND
See Also: HELPLESSNESS, LIFE, PEOPLE

1. As the clay is in the potter's hand, to fashion at his pleasure: so man is
    in the hand of Him that made him —*The Holy Bible/Apocrypha*
2. Every man is like his affliction —André Malraux
3. Extraordinary men, like the stones that are formed in the highest
    regions of the air, fall upon the earth only to be broken and cast into the
    furnace —Walter Savage Landor
4. He [man] bolts down all events, all creeds, and beliefs, and
    persuasions . . . as an ostrich of potent digestion gobbles down bullets
    and gun flints —Herman Melville
5. Human as a kiss —Vance Thompson
6. Human beings are like timid punctuation marks sprinkled among the
    incomprehensible sentences of life —Jean Giraudoux
7. Humanity is like people packed in an automobile which is traveling
    down the highway without lights on a dark night at terrific speed and
    driven by a four-year old —Lord Dunsany
8. It is with men as with horses; those who do the most prancing make the
    least progress —Baron de Stassart
    See Also: SUCCESS
9. Like leaves on trees, the race of man is found, now green in youth, now
    withering on the ground —Homer
10. Like the hours in the day, people come in two classes: the happy and
    the sad —Bin Ramke

11. Like the irresponsible black waterbugs on summer ponds, they [people in cities] crawl and circle and hustle about idiotically, without aim or purpose —O. Henry

12. Man . . . cometh up, and is cut down, like a flower —*The Book of Common Prayer*

13. Man is a rope stretched between the animal and the Superman, a rope over an abyss —Friedrich Nietzsche

14. Man is as full of potentiality as he is of impotence —George Santayana

15. Man is like a ball tossed betwixt the wind and the billows —Friedrich von Schiller

16. A man is like a letter of the alphabet: to produce a word, it must combine with another —Benjamin Mandelstamm

17. A man is like all earth's fruit, you preserve him dry or pickled — Hayden Carruth

18. Man is like a musical box. An imperceptible jolt, and he plays a different tune —Ludwig Boerne

19. Man is like a precious stone: cut and polished by morals, adorned by wisdom —Isaac Halevi Satanov

20. Mankind is like the Red Sea: the staff has scarcely parted the waves asunder, before they flow together again —Johann Wolfgang von Goethe

21. A man like a watch is to be valued for his goings —Turkish proverb

22. Man's like a bird all the days of his breath, and pleasures are nets that allure him to death —Judah Al-Harizi

23. Man's like a candle in a candlestick made up tallow, and a little wick — John Bunyan

24. Men are like bricks, alike but placed high or low by chance —John Webster

25. Men are like ciphers: they acquire their value merely from their position —Napoleon Bonaparte

26. Men are like ears of corn: the emptier the head the more and the lower they stoop —Moritz Gottlieb Saphir

27. Men are like nuts; you can't tell what they're like till they're broken — Phyllis Bottome
     This simile marks the opening of Bottome's story, *A Lost Leader.*

28. Men are like plants; the goodness and flavor of the fruit proceeds from the peculiar soil and exposition in which they grow —Michel Guillaume Jean de Crèvecoeur

29. Men are like the herbs of the field; while some are sprouting, others are withering —*Babylonian Talmud*

30. Men are like strange dogs . . . walk right up to them, bold as life, and they're as gentle as ducks —Owen Johnson

31. Men are like the stars: some generate their own light while others reflect the brilliance they receive —José Marti

32. Men are like trees . . . each one must put forth the leaf that is created in him —Henry Ward Beecher

33. Men are like weasels: weasels drag and lay up and know not for whom, and men save and hoard and know not for whom —*Talmud*

34. Men, like peaches and pears, grow sweet a little while before they begin to decay —Oliver Wendell Holmes, Sr.

35. Others are to us like the 'characters' in fiction, eternal and incorrigible —Mary McCarthy

36. People are like planks of wood: soft until seasoned —St. John De Chevecoeur

37. People are mostly layers of violence and tenderness, wrapped like bulbs —Eudora Welty

38. People are somewhat like novels, we operate on beginnings, middles, and ends —Charles Johnson
    In Johnson's novel, *Faith and the Good Thing,* the simile includes this parenthetical comment: "Don't make too much of that simile."

39. People are very much like flagstaffs. Some flagstaffs are very tall and prominent and some are small —Harry Emerson Fosdick
    Fosdick's simile continued with the following observation: "But the glory of a flagstaff is not its size but the colors that it flies. A very small flagstaff flying the right colors is far more valuable than a very tall one with the wrong flag."

40. The race of men is like the race of leaves. As one generation flourishes another decays —Homer

41. Some individuals are like a brush heap, a helter-skelter, miscellaneous pile of twigs and branches —Harry Emerson Fosdick

42. Some men are like Einstein's theory of relativity; nobody at home understands them —Anon

43. Some men are like pyramids, which are very broad where they touch the ground, but grow narrow as they reach the sky —Henry Ward Beecher

44. Some men are like rifles with plenty of powder but no bullet . . . a great flow of language but no thought —Sylvanys Stall
    See Also: TALKATIVENESS

45. So much of a man walks about dead . . . like a pianoforte with half the notes mute —D. H. Lawrence

46. Strong men are made by opposition; like kites they go up against the wind —Frank Harris, *Reader's Digest,* June, 1936

47. The study of human nature is a good deal like the study of dissection: you find out a good many curious things, but it is a nasty job after all — Josh Billings

 Billings wrote this in dialect which read as follows: "The studdy ov huymin natur is a gooddeal like the studdy ov dessekshun, yu finde out a good menny curis things, aut it is nasty job after awl."

48. To the gods we are as flies to wanton boys —William Shakespeare

49. We are all like vessels tossed on the bottom of the deep —Pietro Mestastasio

 The simile continues: "Our passions are the winds that sweep us impetuously onward; each pleasure is a rock; the whole of life is a wide ocean."

50. We are like sun that rises and sheds light upon things, and then falls and leaves them in darkness again —William Goyen

51. We run to and fro upon the earth like frightened sheep —Robert Louis Stevenson

52. What a piece of work is a man! In action, how like an angel! In apprehension, how like a god! —William Shakespeare

MANNERS

See Also: BEHAVIOR, PROPRIETY/IMPROPRIETY

1. As chatty and polite as Rotarians —Richard Ford

2. Decorously polite as patients in a dentist's waiting room —Francis King

3. Evil manners will, like watered grass, grow up very quickly —Plautus
 While bad manners might no longer be looked upon as evil,
 Plautus' simile in relation to how any evil spreads remains true.

4. Had the manners of a disobliging steamroller . . . and he was rather less particular about his dress than a scarecrow —George Bernard Shaw

5. His speech sounds like a spoken bread-and-butter note —W. P. Kinsella
See Also: SPEAKING

6. Manners are like spices, you can't make a meal of them but they add a great deal to the meal's enjoyment —Anon

7. Manners are like the cipher in arithmetic; they may not be of much value in themselves, but they are capable of adding a great deal to the value of everything else —Anon

8. Manners . . . as soft as wool —Lorenz Hart

This is part of the refrain of a song named "Moon of My Delight" written for *Chee-Chee*.

9. Our manners, like our faces, though ever so beautiful must differ in their beauty —Lord Shaftesbury

10. The pleasure of courtesy is like the pleasure of good dancing —Alain

11. Polite as pie —F. van Wyck Mason

12. Politeness is like an air-cushion; there may be nothing to it, but it eases our jolts wonderfully —Samuel Johnson

13. Rudeness (to Mrs. Dosely) was like dropping a pat of butter on to a hot plate, it slid and melted away —Elizabeth Bowen

14. Sedate as a judge in court —Rhys Davies

15. Sit bolt upright and smile without cease like a well-bred dinner guest — Ruth Prawer Jhabvala

16. To be cordial is like roughing a man's head to jolly him up, or kissing a child that doesn't want to be kissed. You are relieved when it's over — George Santayana

17. Ungracious as a hog —Tobias Smollett

18. Ungracious . . . like a child who opens a birthday gift and barely glances at it before reaching to unwarp the next —Barbara Lazear Ascher

19. An ungracious man is like a story told at the wrong time —*The Holy Bible/Apocrypha*

MARRIAGE

See Also: MEN AND WOMEN, RELATIONSHIPS

1. Adultery in a house is like a worm in poppy seeds —*Babylonian Talmud*

2. Adultery's like the common cold, if one bedfellow contracts it, his companion automatically does —Robert Traver

3. Alimony is like buying oats for a dead horse —Arthur Baer, *New York Journal American*

4. Bridesmaids in their flowery frocks bloom round the bride like hollyhocks —Ogden Nash

5. The death of a man's wife is like cutting down an ancient oak that has long shaded the family mansion —Alphonse de Lamartine
See Also: DEATH

6. Divorced men are like marked-down clothes; you get them after the season during which they would have made a sensation, and there is less choice, but they're easier to acquire —Judith Martin

7. Divorce is like a side dish that nobody remembers having ordered — Alexander King

8. For an artist to marry his model is as fatal as for a gourmet to marry his cook: the one gets no sittings, and the other no dinners —Oscar Wilde

9. For an old man to marry a young girl is like buying a new book for somebody else to read —Anon

10. Getting married is like a healthy man going into a sickbed —Isaac Bashevis Singer

11. Getting married is serious business. It's kinda formal, like funerals or playing stud poker —line from 1940 movie, *They Knew What They Wanted*
    The actor voicing this was William Gargan.

12. He [husband of long-standing] is like an old coat, beautiful in texture, but easy and loose —Audrey Colvin, letter to *New York Times*/LI, July 17, 1986

13. A husband, like religion and medicine, must be taken with blind faith —Helen Rowland
    This has been modernized from "Like unto religion."

14. Husbands, like governments must never admit they are wrong — Honoré de Balzac

15. Husbands are like (motor) cars; all are good the first year —Channing Pollock

16. Husbands are like fires, they go out when unattended —Zsa Zsa Gabor

17. Husbands should be like Kleenex, soft, clean and disposable — Madeline Kahn, interview, television news program, December, 1985

18. A husband without ability is like a house without a roof —Spanish proverb

19. It [a second marriage] is the triumph of hope over experience —Samuel Johnson

20. It [marriage] resembles a pair of shears, so joined that they cannot be separated; often moving in opposite directions, yet always punishing any one who comes between them —Sydney Smith

21. It's [the permanence of marriage] like having siblings: you can't lose a brother or a sister. They're always there —Germaine Greer, *Playboy*, January, 1972

22. It [marriage and motherhood] was like being brainwashed, and afterward you went about numb as a slave in some private, totalitarian state —Sylvia Plath

23. Like suicide, divorce was something that had to be done on a thoughtless impulse, full speed ahead —R. V. Cassill

24. A man's wife should fit like a good, comfortable shoe —Ukrainian proverb

25. A man with a face that looks like someone had thrown it at him in anger nearly always marries before he is old enough to vote —Finley Peter Dunne

26. Many a marriage has commenced like the morning, red, and perished like a mushroom . . . because the married pair neglected to be as agreeable to each other after their union as they were before it — Frederika Bremer

27. Marriage may be compared to a cage: the birds outside frantic to get in and those inside frantic to get out —Michel de Montaigne
   > The simile also appeared in a play by a sixteenth century
   > dramatist, John Webster, beginning "Marriage is just like a
   > summer bird cage in a garden." See the French proverb below
   > for yet another twist on the same theme.

28. Marriage from love, like vinegar from wine, a sad, sour, sober beverage —Lord Byron

29. Marriage is a good deal like a circus: there is not as much in it as is represented in the advertising —Edgar Watson Howe

30. Marriage is a hand grenade with the pin out. You hold your breath waiting for the explosion —Abraham Rothberg

31. Marriage is like a three-speed gearbox: affection, friendship, love — Peter Ustinov

32. Marriage is like a beleaguered fortress; those who are without want to get in, and those within want to get out —French proverb

33. Marriage is like a dull meal with the dessert at the beginning —dialogue from the movie, *Moulin Rouge*
   > The dialogue was spoken by Jose Ferrer as Toulouse Lautrec.

34. Marriage is like a long trip in a tiny rowboat: if one passenger starts to rock the boat, the other has to steady it; otherwise they'll go to bottom together —Dr. David R. Reuben, *Reader's Digest,* January, 1973

35. Marriage is like a river; it is easier to fall in than out —Anon

36. Marriage is like a ship; sometimes you just have to ride out the storm — "L. A. Law," television drama, 1987

37. Marriage is like buying something you've been admiring for a long time in a shop window . . . you may love it when you get home but it doesn't always go with everything else in the house —Jean Kerr

38. Marriage is like life in this . . . that it is a field of battle, and not a bed of roses —Robert Louis Stevenson

39. Marriage is like panty-hose; it all depends on what you put into it — Phyllis Schlafly

40. Marriage is like twirling a baton, turning handsprings or eating with chopsticks; it looks so easy till you try it —Helen Rowland

41. Marriage like death is nothing to worry about —Don Herod

42. Marriages are like diets. They can be ruined by having a little dish on the side —Earl Wilson

43. Marriages, like houses, need constant patching —Nancy Mairs, *New York Times*/Hers, July 30, 1987

    The simile was the highlighted blurb to capture reader attention. Actually it was a capsulized paraphrase from Ms. Mairs' own concluding words: "Marriages, like houses, haven't got 'ever afters'." The stucco chips off and the cat falls through the screen and the bathroom drain runs slow. If you don't want the house falling down around your ears, you must plan to learn to wield a trowel and a hammer and a plunger.

44. Marriages were breaking up as fast as tires blowing in a long race — Norman Mailer

45. A marriage that grew like a great book, filling twenty-five years with many thousands of elaborate and subtle details —Larry McMurtry

46. A (seventeen-year) marriage that had been patched like an old rubber tire gone too many miles on a treadmill —Paige Mitchell

47. (She had decided long before that) marriage was like breathing, as soon as you noticed the process, you stopped it at peril of your life —Laura Furman

48. A married man forms married habits and becomes dependent on marriage just as a sailor becomes dependent on the sea —George Bernard Shaw

49. Married so long . . . like Siamese twins they infect each other's feelings —Mary Hedin

50. Marrying a daughter to a boor is like throwing her to a lion —*Babylonian Talmud*

51. Marrying a woman for her money is very much like setting a rat-trap, and baiting it with your own finger —Josh Billings

    In Billings' phonetic dialect: "munny is vera mutch like . . . with yure own finger."

52. Matrimony, like a dip in the sea, first stimulates, then chills. But once out of the water the call of the ocean lures the bather to another plunge —Anon

53. Middle-aged marriages in which people seem stuck like flies caught in jelly —Norma Klein

    See Also: ENTRAPMENT

54. (I am as) monogamous as the North Star —Carolyn Kizer

55. The sickening cords of their marriage drying everything like an invisible paste —John Updike

56. A successful marriage is an edifice that must be rebuilt every day — Andre Maurois

57. They [bride and groom] looked as though they belonged on top of their own enormous cake —Paul Reidinger

58. Wartime marriage . . . it's like being married on top of a volcano — H. E. Bates
     See Also: DANGER

59. Wedlock's like wine, not properly judged of till the second glass — Douglas Jerrold

60. Wife swapping is like a form of incest in which nobody's more guilty than anybody else —Germaine Greer, *Playboy,* January, 1972

MATHEMATCS AND SCIENCE

1. Arithmetic is where numbers fly like pigeons in and out of your head — Carl Sandburg

2. Every science, like a recurring decimal, has a beginning and no end — Anton Chekhov
    In his story, *On The Way,* Checkhov elaborates on this as follows: "Zoology has discovered thirty-five thousand five hundred different species of insects; chemistry can count sixty-five elements; if you were to add ten zeros to the right of each of these figures, zoology and chemistry would be no nearer the end of their labors than they are now'.

3. Science is, like virtue, its own . . . great reward —Charles Kingsley

4. Science is love with seeing eyes —Elbert Hubbard

5. The study of mathematics is like climbing up a steep and craggy mountain; when once you reach the top, it fully recompenses your trouble, by opening a fine, clear and extensive prospect —Tryon Edwards

MATRIMONY
See: MARRIAGE

MAXIMS, PROVERBS AND SAYINGS

1. Browsing through a book of proverb . . . it's like taking a turn in a garden . . . full of roses and fruit, where the bushes speak to you; and I come back rested, with smiles in my mind —Anatole France

2. Figures of speech are risky; for in art, as in arithmetic, many have no head for figures —G. K. Chesterton

3. Genuine proverbs are like good (kambrick) needles, short, sharp, and shiny —Josh Billings
    The first word was originally in Billings' phonetic dialect: 'ginowine.'

4. His sayings are generally like women's letters; all the pith is in the postscript —William Hazlitt

The man with the pith in his postscripts was Charles Lamb.

5. Like many cliches, it has the ring of truth —Anon

6. A man of maxims only is like a Cyclops with one eye, and that eye placed in the back of his head —Samuel Taylor Coleridge

7. Maxims are like lawyers who must needs see but one side of the case — Gelett Burgess

8. Proverbs, like the sacred books of each nation, are the sanctuary of the intuitions —Ralph Waldo Emerson

9. A proverb without wisdom is like a body without a foot —Moses Ibn Ezra

10. Rustic sayings which she threw, like flowers, into the conversation — Anatole France

11. A saying is like a fruit; one has first to eat it . . . before one can know its taste —Sholem Asch

12. Sayings by wise men . . . they are like burning glasses, as they collect the diffused rays of wit and learning in authors, and make them point with warmth and quickness on the reader's imagination —Jonathan Swift

13. Sayings by wise men . . . they are of great value, like the dust of gold, or the sparks of diamonds —John Tillotson

14. Similes are like songs on love: they much describe; they nothing prove —Matthew Prior

15. Similes dangle like baubles from me —William H. Gass

16. A word [that's been overused] . . . lost its identity like an old coat in a second-hand shop —Anaïs Nin

MEANINGFULNESS/MEANINGLESSNESS
See: MEMORY, IMPORTANCE/UNIMPORTANCE, NECESSITY

MEANNESS
See: CRUELTY

MEEKNESS
See Also: MODESTY

1. (Quivering and) abject . . . like some unfortunate dog abasing itself before its master —Jean Rhys
    The quivering is being done by a young woman in the embrace of a lover, in Rhys' novel, *Quartet.*

2. (Why do you sit there) apologizing to him, as if he were a fuehrer or something —Leslie A. Fieldler

3. Bowed to them like a tree in a storm —Edith Wharton

4. Complied like hostages with a gun trained on them —Louise Erdrich

5. Exist unthinkingly like a slave, like a working animal —Iris Murdoch

6. He's like a bell, that will go for everyone that pulls it —Thomas Fuller

7. Humble, friendly eyes looked up timidly, like the yes of a dog that is uncertain whether he is about to receive a pat or a blow —Ellen Glasgow
   See Also: EYE EXPRESSIONS, MISCELLANEOUS

8. Like an ox, his head bent meekly, he waited for the blow of the axe which was raised over him —Leo Tolstoy

9. Lieeke a victim, she waited: meek, like a sacrifice —Margaret Drabble

10. Looked humbly about him like a dog slipping into a strange kitchen and afraid of kicks —Honoré de Balzac

11. Meek as a hen —Fyodor Dostoevski

12. Meek as the dew —Dylan Thomas

13. Meekness takes injuries like pills, not chewing, but swallowing them down —Sir Thomas Browne

14. A meek soul without zeal, is like a ship in a calm, that moves not as fast as it ought —John M. Mason

15. Obedience simulates subordination as fear of the police simulates honesty —George Bernard Shaw

16. Obedient as a partner in a dance —Lael Tucker Wertenbaker

17. Obedient as a sheep —Robert Browning

18. Obediently as a trained seal —Anon
    The trained seal comparison has become a common cliche, with many variations such as "Obediently as a puppet on a string" and "Obediently like a trained elephant," the latter spotted in Aldous Huxley's *After Many a Summer Dies the Swan.*

19. Servility is like a golden pill which outwardly gives pleasure but inwardly is full of bitterness —Narun Tate
    The word 'gives' has been modernized from 'giveth.'

20. Waiting upon her whims like a footman —O. Henry

21. Went meekly off . . . like a repentant boy led away to reform school —Harvey Swados

22. Yield like a foolish mother —Emily Brontë

MEETINGS

See Also: BEGINNINGS/ENDINGS; PEOPLE, INTERACTION

1. Come together as inevitably as the key to the magnet —Hugh Walpole

2. Converge like pulsars —Diane Ackerman

3. Face each other [across table] like partners at bridge —Thomas Pynchon

4. Like driftwood spars, which meet and pass upon the boundless ocean-plain, so on the sea of life, alas, man meets man, meets and quits again —Matthew Arnold

5. Like mountain streams we meet and part, each living in the other's heart —Oliver Wendell Holmes, Sr

6. Like two doomed ships that pass in storm we had crossed each other's way —Oscar Wilde
   The simile, from *The Ballad of Reading Goal,* concludes as follows: "But we made no sign, we said no word, we had no word to say."

7. Met [briefly] . . . like a couple of trucks, side-swiping each other — Robert E. Sherwood

8. Meet like enemy generals, knocking your sabers against the table, bluffing each other —Scott Spencer

9. There are some meetings in life so useful, so truly wonderful, that they seem like visible interventions of Providence —Ernest Hello

MELANCHOLY
See: DEJECTION, GLOOM

MEMORY
See Also: PAST, THE

1. As bare of memories as a grain of sugar —Viña Delmar
   See Also: EMPTINESS

2. As fixed in my memory . . . as the flash of light that is followed by the thunder of pain when your shoulder is pulled out of its socket — Norman Mailer
   See Also: PERMANENCE

3. A breeze like the turning of a page brings back your face —John Ashbery
   See Also: WIND

4. [Memories] came back to run through his mind like a reel of color film —Carlos Baker

5. (I am) clean forgotten, as a dead man out of mind —*Book of Common Prayer*

6. Could be forgotten as quickly and painlessly as a doubting of Jesus or a fear of death from the measles —Peter Taylor

7. [Memory] drifted into my mind like a bit of weed carried in a current and caught there, floating but fixed, refusing to be carried away — Katherine Anne Porter

8. Eventually I thought about him [a once close friend] only once a week or so, as if he were a relative who had died years ago —Richard Burgin

9. Faded memories worn as a buffalo head a nickel —A. D. Winans

10. Felt old memories stir in him like dead leaves —Helen Hudson

11. Fettered to a pack of useless memories like a living person to a corpse —Ouida

12. Follow one after the next like cars out on the street, memories, there is just no stopping them —Tony Ardizzone

13. For a person blessed with a memory as full of holes as an Iranscam scenario, life can be a continuous state of astonishment —Donald Henahan

    Henahan uses this simile to introduce his comments about a revival of the musical, *South Pacific*. The editorial blurb writer used a simile from the musical's lyrics, "As Corny as Kansas in August" to highlight the article.

14. Forgotten as quickly as warm days in winter or cool days in summer — Ellen Glasgow

15. Forgotten like a station passed through on a train —Elizabeth Spencer

16. (Be) forgotten like spilt wine —Algernon Charles Swinburne

17. Gather memories like dry twigs, thorns and thistles —Yehuda Amichai

18. The ghosts of our remembrances throng around us like dead leaves whirled in the autumn wind —Jerome K. Jerome

19. His memory could work like the slinging of a noose to catch a wild pony —Eudora Welty

20. His memory lifted its skirts . . . and hurried convulsively, like an old lady picking her way barefoot across a shingly beach —Noël Coward

21. His memory was something like his appendix, a vestigial repository — John Cheever

22. (He never forgets a face.) His mind is like a video camera —Ilie Nastase

23. If only there could be an invention that bottled up memory, like a scent —Daphne du Maurier

24. The image [of remembered scene] . . . is like a photograph on my memory —Richard Maynard

25. An incident would suddenly crop up in her memory, like a piece in a jigsaw puzzle that seemed to have come from the wrong box —Mary McCarthy

26. It isn't a thing one forgets overnight, like losing a pencil —Mary Stewart

27. It was as though an endless series of hangars had been shaken ajar in the air base of his memory and from each, like a young wasp emerging from its cell, arose the memory of a plane —Ralph Ellison

28. Like a dull actor . . . I have forgot my part —William Shakespeare

29. Memories are like books; a few live in our hearts through life, and the rest, like the bills we pay, are read, and then forgotten —Gerald Bendall

30. Memories are like stones, time and distance erode them like acid —Ugo Betti

31. Memories . . . began to play across the surface of his mind like movies on a screen —Richard McKenna

32. Memories bursting in her mind like forsythia buds on the first warm day of the year —B. S. Johnson

33. Memories [troublesome] . . . flitted like unexplained shadows across her happier thoughts —George Eliot

34. Memories . . . floated like gossamer through her thoughts —Frank Swinnerton

35. Memories . . . like worms eating into the flesh —William Golding

36. Memories lurk like dustballs at the back of drawers —Jay McInerney

37. Memories . . . no two sets exactly the same, like fingerprints — Daphne Merkin

38. Memories of embarrassing things he had done and said, of mistakes he had made, buzzed and flitted in his mind like annoying little gnats — Dan Wakefield

39. Memories of the bad covered the good, as snow covers grass in the fall —Ann Jasperson

40. Memories . . . pierced by moments of brightness, like flashes of lightning —Yasunari Kawabata

41. Memories [when a lot of people one knows die] return to life as grass grows on graves —Lael Tucker Wertenbaker

42. Memories swept over her like a strong wind on dark waters —Carl Sandburg

43. Memories turned up like bills you thought you'd never have to pay — Hugh Leonard
    In Leonard's play, *Da,* the memories turning up like bills are evoked as a character sorts through family memorabilia.

44. Memory . . . as good as a bulldog's handshake —Loren D. Estleman
    In Estleman's mystery novel, *Every Brilliant Eye,* the character with the bulldog-like memory is a policeman.

45. Memory broke, like an old clock —Karl Shapiro

46. Memory can be like a dream, cause and effect non-existent —Gordon Weaver

47. Memory . . . crawling to the surface like a fat worm after rain — Harvey Swados

48. The memory . . . fell upon him like a weight of black water —Willa Cather

49. The memory [of a man] glimmered in her thoughts like a bright thread in the pattern of a tapestry —Mazo De La Roche

50. Memory is a rare ghost-raiser. Like a haunted house, its walls are ever echoing to unseen feet. (Through the broken casements we watch the flitting shadow of the dead, and the saddest shadows of them all are the shadows of our own dead selves) —Jerome K. Jerome

51. Memory is as full of chimerical as forgetfulness, deceptive as any other work of the imagination —Madison Smart Bell

52. Memory is like a noisy intruder being thrown out of the concert hall . . . he will hang on the door and continue to disturb the concert —Theodore Reik, *Saturday Review,* January 11, 1958

53. Memory, is like a purse, if it's too full, it can't be shut, and everything will drop out of it —Thomas Fuller

54. Memory is like the moon . . . it has its new, its full, and its wane — Duchess of Newcastle
    The word 'hath' has been modernized to 'has.'

55. The memory is salty, like sweat, like the emissions of love-making, like the sea —Lael Tucker Wertenbaker

56. Memory, like a drop that, night and day, falls cold and ceaseless, wore my heart away —Thomas Moore

57. Memory, like a horrible malady, was eating his soul away —Oscar Wilde

58. Memory, like a juggler, tosses its colored balls into the light, and again receives them into darkness —Conrad Aiken

59. Memory . . . like an old musical box it will lie silent for long years; then a mere nothing, a jerk, a tremor, will start the spring, and from beneath its decent covering of dust it will talk to us of forgotten passion and desire —Thomas Burke

60. A memory like a powerful microchip —Anon

61. A memory like a telephone directory —William McIlvanney

62. A memory like flypaper —Nora Johnson

63. Memory, like sleep, has powers which dreams obey —William Wordsworth

64. Memory, like women, is usually unfaithful —Spanish proverb
    Depending upon who's talking, the comparison would be as appropriate if attributed to men.

65. The memory of our lost friends is welcome to us like the bitter taste in wine that is very old —Michel de Montaigne

66. The memory of past favors is like a rainbow, bright, vivid, and beautiful, but it soon fades away —Thomas Chandler Haliburton

67. Memory [of something unpleasant] . . . pokes at him like a nightmare in the womb —T. Coraghessan Boyle

68. Memory returned like fire —Frank Swinnerton

69. Memory's like an athlete; keep it in training; take it for cross-country runs —James Hilton

70. The [unpleasant] memory . . . stuck like a fish-hook in her brain —Stefan Zweig

71. Memory transparent as a dream you strain to recall —Harryette Mullen

72. Memory unwound within me like a roll of film in which I played no part —Heinrich Böll

73. A memory, very beautiful and delicate like a flavor or a perfume —Ruth Prawer Jhabvala
    See Also: BEAUTY

74. Had a mind like a mainframe memory bank —William Beechcroft

75. The moment hung like crystal in Meredith's mind —Babs H. Deal

76. My memory is like camphor. It evaporates with time —Dominique Lapierre

77. My memory kicked in; one of those wonderful little mental jolts, like a quick electric shock when a plug's gone bad —Sue Grafton

78. My memory's like a policeman, never there when you want it —Ronald Harwood
    This line is spoken by the main character in Harwood's play *The Dresser.*

79. Picking over the shames and humiliations . . . like an invalid mulling over a plate of unwanted food —Harvey Swados

80. Pulled up at it [gap in memory] as if his advance had been checked by a chasm in the pavement at his feet —Edith Wharton

81. Recollections . . . collected like spit from an aging throat —Elizabeth Spencer

82. Recollections dropped over him like a noose —Laurie Colwin

83. Remembrance is a tripping stone in the path of hope —Kahlil Gibran

84. Remembrance . . . tickles the end of his nose like the fingertips of a child —Hayden Carruth

85. (I have) a retentive memory, a mind like flypaper to which facts stick —Desmond Begley

86. Shameful memories grip me like an anchor —Delmore Schwartz

87. She sank from his consciousness like one of those poor people encased in concrete who are heaved over the side and plummet to the bottom of the sea —William Styron

88. Slipped out of her mind like a newspaper dropping from the hands of a sleepy woman —Erich Maria Remarque

89. Some memories are like lucky charms, talismans, one shouldn't tell about them or they'll lose their power —Iris Murdoch

90. Stung by memories thick as wasps about a nest invaded —Edna St. Vincent Millay

91. There are many moments I cannot forget, moments like radiant flowers in all colors and hues —Jaroslav Seifert

92. Tries to remember like a deaf man remembering an opera he heard eleven years before —Lyn Lifshin
    See Also: DIFFICULTY

93. As unremembered as bird shadows on the grass —Henry Bellamann

94. Unremembered as old rain —Edna St. Vincent Millay

95. The world, like an accomplished hostess, pays most attention to those whom it will soonest forget —John Churton Collins

MEN AND WOMEN
See Also: LOVE, MARRIAGE, SEXUAL INTERACTION

1. Arm in arm . . . like a pair of loving turtle-doves —William Shakespeare

1. Court . . . as you would court a farm—for the strength of the silo and the perfection of the title —Josh Billings
    Like many Billings witticisms this one was written in phonetic dialect as follows: "As you wud court a farm—for the strength ov the sile and the parfeckshun ov the title."

2. Dating a grad student was like making hurried-up popcorn: lots of butter, high heat, instant noise —Will Weaver

3. The distance between them is like a desert, or an unswimmable body of water —Hilma Wolitzer
    In her novel, *In the Palomar Arms,* Wolitzer is describing an estranged husband and wife, lying far apart on a large bed.

4. Felt my eyes going down across her mouth, her throat like fingers — Julio Cortázar

5. Finding a man is like finding a job; its easier to find one when you already have one —Paige Mitchell

6. Girls (on the Cripple Creek 'bout half grown) jump on a boy like a dog on a bone —American folk song, "Cripple Creek"

7. Handle a small woman like she's made out of steel, and a big woman like she's made out of glass —Paige Mitchell
    See Also: ADVICE

8. The happiest women, like the happiest nations, have no history — George Eliot

9. He goes about the business of fondling you, like someone very tired at night having to put out the trash and bolt-lock the door —Lorrie Moore

10. He likes fat women the way a rat likes pumpkins —Rita Mae Brown

11. He ran through women like a child through growing hay —Louis MacNeice
    The same image from a conversation overheard on a bus describes the woman as the sexual predator: "She runs through men like a fever."

12. He regarded women in the way that little girls regard their dolls, as toys to be dressed and undressed —Frank Swinnerton

13. Her responsiveness was something that fed him as wood fed the fire — Paul Horgan

14. He swept through her like a great ragged hawk on its journey to another prey —John Le Carré

15. He thought she'd fall like a ripe apple —Rita Mae Brown

16. He was looking at me the way a butcher must size up a carcass of beef, like I was one of those drawings with the parts of the cow on it, all the choice cuts and the waste —Jonathan Valin

17. He would always feel for her that impersonal admiration which is inspired by anything very large, like the Empire State Building or the Grand Canyon of Arizona —P. G. Wodehouse

18. Holds her face in his cupped hands as carefully as a thirsty man would gather water —Hilma Wolitzer

19. I dropped her like a bad habit —James Crumley
    The simile continues with: "Put her under his arm, and all but ate ever last crust of her."

20. It's as natural for women to pride themselves in fine clothes as 'tis for a peacock to spread his tail —John Ray's *Proverbs*
    A look at fashion, both past and present, would indicate that this could well be a unisex simile.

21. I want to steep myself in you . . . as if you were a South wind — Wallace Stevens, letter to his fiancée

22. Just us two . . . like two roots joined and widening out into a flower —David Denby

23. Like an animal, he was aware of me at once —Robertson Davies

24. Like two mummies, we have been wrapped tight in love —Yehuda Amichai

25. Like two open cities in the midst of some vast plain their two minds lay open to each other —Katherine Mansfield

26. Like Ulysses tying himself to the mast to resist the song of the sirens, Jim had to brace himself to withstand the charm of Kate's voice — Henri-Pierre Roche

27. Making love to women is almost as old as chess —Robert Traver

28. A man is like a cat; chase him and he'll run . . . sit still and ignore him and he'll come purring at your feet —Helen Rowland

29. Man without woman would be as stupid a game as playing checkers alone —Josh Billings
    See Also: INCOMPLETENESS

30. Men like to pursue an elusive woman, like a cake of wet soap in a bathtub; even men who hate baths —Gelett Burgess

31. A mistress should be like a little country retreat near the town; not to dwell in constantly, but only for a night and away —William Wycherly

32. My blood is singing in her system, like whisky —Irwin Shaw

33. Paired off like the animals in the ark —Ross Macdonald

34. She drained me like a fevered moon —Edgar Lee Masters

35. She leaned easily against his shoulder . . . as if she had done herself up in a parcel, addressed to him, left on his doorstep, from now on, his responsibility —Elizabeth Taylor

36. She made the blood run round in my veins like horses on a track — Ross Macdonald

37. Sometimes being with her is like being caught in a tornado —Alvin Boretz, television drama, 1986

38. Some women learn, like slaves, to study men —Charles Johnson

39. Take them [women] away and his (man's) existence is as flat and secure as that of a moo-cow —H. L. Mencken

40. (They hugged . . .) their hearts shook them, like two people pounding at the same time on both sides of a very thin door —Eudora Welty

41. To be intimate with a foolish man's like going to bed with a razor — Ben Franklin

42. The trouble with being a woman is that you are supposed to enhance men; to add gaiety to their evening, like balloons, even if you feel heavy as stone —Daphne Merkin

43. Twenty years of romance make a woman look like a ruin; but twenty years of marriage make her something like a public building —Oscar Wilde

44. Two couples living together and talking openly for a week . . . it was like a week in a bell jar —Joanne Kates, *New York Times*/Hers, October 2, 1986

45. Very gently, as to a wild animal, I reached out my hand and made her turn her head —John Fowles

46. A woman, I always say, should be like a good suspense movie: the more left to the imagination, the more excitement there is —Alfred Hitchcock, *Reader's Digest,* July, 1963
    Hitchcock topped off his simile with this bit of advice: "This should be her aim; to create suspense, to let a man discover things about her without her having to tell him."

47. A woman is like a salad: much depends on the dressing —Anon
    There's also a saying, "Clothes make the man," to prove that this simile has no gender limitation.

48. A woman moved is like a fountain troubled, muddy, ill-seeming, thick, bereft of beauty —William Shakespeare

49. A woman's heart, like the moon, is always changing, but there is always a man in it —*Punch*

50. A woman's preaching is something like a dog's walking on his hinder legs. It is not done well; but you are not surprised to find it done at all —Samuel Johnson
    Women preachers continue to make good newspaper copy— which prompted a *Wall Street Journal* reader to use the Johnson simile in response to a December 24, 1986 story on this subject.

51. A woman without a man is like a garden without a fence —German proverb

52. A woman without a man is like a wild rose which blooms fast and . . . falls apart with the wind —Diane Wakoski

53. Women are always a touchstone . . . like litmus paper or dogs before an earthquake —Iris Murdoch

54. Women are like flowers, a little dust or squeezing makes them the more fragrant —Josh Billings
    In Billings' dialect the first part of this read as follows: "Wimmin are like flowers, a little dust ov squeezing."

55. Women are like tricks to sleight of hand. Which to admire we should not understand —William Congreve

56. Women are very much like religion; we must take them on faith or go without —F. Marion Crawford

57. Women as compared to men are like point lace to canvas —Charles H. Hoyt

58. Women follow him around like flies after garbage —Paige Mitchell

59. Women's hearts are like old china, none the worse for a break or two — W. Somer

60. You've [woman being addressed by a man] got an off-on switch like a circuit breaker —Will Weaver

MERCY
See: KINDNESS

MERIT
See: VIRTUE

MERRIMENT
See: GAIETY, JOY

METHOD
See: PURPOSEFULNESS

MIDDLE AGE
See: AGE

MIND
See Also: ATTENTION; INSULTS; MIND, DEFINED; THOUGHT

1. (You can't concentrate. You've got) a brain like a hummingbird —Jane Wagner

2. Brain as heavy as a grandfather clock —Diane Wakoski

3. A brain tooled like a twenty-jewel Swiss watch —Stephen Longstreet

4. Emptied her mind, as if emptying a bottle —Mavis Gallant

5. Her mind flickered like a lizard —Elizabeth Bowen

6. Her mind was like a one-way thoroughfare, narrow and flat, maintained in repair —Mavis Gallant

7. Her mind was like a rushing stream, tumbling downhill over rocks and boulders, eddying, bouncing, shifting direction —Ward Just

8. Her mind was strangely empty . . . an empty room through which vague memories stalked like giants —Jean Rhys

9. His brain feels like a frail but alert invalid packed inside among a lot of deep pillows —John Updike

10. His brain was like a brightly-lit factory, full of flying wheels and precision —Edith Wharton

11. His mind [Oliver Wendell Holmes, Jr.'s] resembles a stiff spring, which has to be abducted violently from it, and which every instant it is left to itself flies right back —William James, letter to brother, Harry, November 24, 1872

12. His mind's like the feet of a pre-civilized Chinese girl —Frank Swinnerton

13. The human mind should be like a good hotel, open the year round — William Lyon Phelps

14. It [his brain] felt like an immense dynamo running at top speed in an empty shed in the middle of the woods —Norman Mailer

15. Little minds, like weak liquors, are soonest soured —H. G. Bohn's *Handbook of Proverbs*

16. Mind, as clear as mountain water —Richard Wilbur
    See Also: CLARITY

17. Mind . . . blank and enclosed as a bubble of glass —Jean Thompson

18. Mind flapping like a rag on a clothesline in cold wind —Saul Bellow

19. Mind . . . fluffy as a baby's crib —Louis Auchincloss

20. (He stood for a moment outside the room, his) mind jerking spasmodically, like a severed nerve —Storm Jameson

21. Mind like a bent corkscrew —Roderic Jeffries

22. A mind like a puddle. Things fall in and float around in it and she fishes them up later when they've gotten soggy —Jean Thompson

23. A mind like a sieve —Anon

24. A mind like a sink —Agatha Christie
    Christie was thus quoted by her nephew about Miss Marple's dark view of humankind.

25. Mind . . . like a sun-dial, it records only pleasantness —Anon
    See Also: CHEERFULNESS

26. A mind like a tattered concordance —Samuel Beckett

27. A mind like a wedge of iron —Louise Erdrich

28. Mind like dead ashes —Robert Silverberg

29. Mind like moths —Anon

30. Mind . . . like some fertile garden —Edith Wharton

31. The mind, packed away like a satin wedding dress even in blue tissue, yellowing, pressing itself into permanent folds —Diane Wakoski
    The title of the poem featuring this line is also a simile: *The Mind, Like an Old Fish.*

32. Minds fossilized like lava —Isak Dinesen

33. Minds [of students] so earnest and helpless that it takes them half an hour to get from one idea to its immediately adjacent next neighbor. And when they've got the next idea, they lie down on it with their whole weight and can get no farther, like a cow on a door-mat, so that you can get neither in nor out with them —William James, letter to his wife, 1896

34. Minds stirring like poplars in a storm —Marge Piercy

35.   (Eleanor's) mind went whirling round like a wheel on the hub of this moment —Elizabeth Bowen

36.   A mind wide open to absorb all it could teach him as the flowers of the date-palm to receive the fertilizing pollen —Honoré de Balzac

37.   My brain is numb as a piece of liver —W. P. Kinsella

38.   (I seem to have read so little of late, that) my mind is like a desert, devoid of roses and leaves —Janet Flanner

39.   Our brains are like fruit stands; all the rubbish is in front and the good stuff is in the back —Carla Lane
      Dialogue from "Solo," British television sitcom, broadcast June 23, 1987

40.   Our unconscious is like a vast subterranean factory with intricate machinery that is never ideal, where work goes on all day and night from the time we are born until the moment of our death —Milton R. Sapirstein

41.   Some minds are like trunks, packed tight with knowledge, no air and plenty of moths —*Life*, January 31, 1918

42.   There is no sea as restless as my mind —Derek Walcott
      See Also: RESTLESSNESS

43.   When you have a creative mind it sometimes backs up on you like a sewer —John Farris

MIND, DEFINED

1.   The mind is a city like London, smoky and populous —Delmore Schwartz
      This simile is a follow-up to a poem's title, *The Mind Is an Ancient and Famous Capital.*

2.   As the fire-fly only shines when on the wing, so it is with the human mind; when at rest, it darkens —Letitia Landon

3.   The brain is like the hand. It grows with using —Judge Louis D. Brandeis

4.   The brain, like Rhenish wine, should be chilled, not iced to be at its best —A. J. Liebling

5.   The brain of man is filled with passageways like the contours and multiple crossroads of a labyrinth . . . in its curved folds like the imprint of thousands of images, recordings of millions of words — Anaïs Nin

6.   Brains to the sluggard are like wings to the ant, or a torch to the blind, an added load of no use or aid —Jediah Bedersi

7.   A brilliant mind without faith is like a beautiful face without eyes — Shalom Cohen

8. A child's mind is like a shallow brook which ripples and dances merrily over the stony course of its education, and reflects here a flower, there a bush and yonder a fleecy cloud —Helen Keller

9. The conscious mind may be compared to a fountain playing in the sun and falling back into the great subterranean pool of the subconscious from which it rises —Sigmund Freud

10. The cultivation of the mind is a kind of food supplied for the soul of man —Cicero

11. The human mind is kind of like . . . a piñata. When it breaks open, there's a lot of surprises inside —Jane Wagner

12. The human mind . . . is like a pendulum, which the moment it has reached the limit of its swing in one direction goes inevitably back as far as the other side and so on forever —James Russell Lowell

13. The human mind should be like a good hotel . . . open the year round —William Lyon Phelps

14. Many minds are like low-grade ores, there is gold in them, but it takes a vast deal of labor to get it out —John Alfred Spender

15. The mind is an iceberg . . . it floats with only one-seventh of its bulk above water —Sigmund Freud, quoted in *New York Times* obituary, September 24, 1939

16. The mind is like a bow, the stronger for being unbent —Ben Jonson

17. The mind is like a mechanical instrument that plays a great variety of tunes, but it must play them in succession —William Hazlitt

18. The mind is like an ocean. The surface layers of the mind function actively while the deeper levels remain silent —Maharishi Mahesh Yogi

19. The mind is like a sheet of white paper . . . the impressions it receives oftenest and retains the longest are black ones —Julius Charles and August William Hare

20. The mind is like a slate, one thing gets rubbed out for another —Sam Slick

21. The mind is like the stomach. It is not how much you put into it that counts, but how much it digests —Albert Jay Nook

22. The mind like any other organism, gradually shapes itself to what surrounds it, and resents disturbance in the form which its life has assumed —Oliver Wendell Holmes, Sr.

23. The mind of man is like a clock that is always running down, and requires to be as constantly wound up —William Hazlitt

24. The mind of the people is like mud, from which arise strange and beautiful things —Walter J. Turner

25. Minds are like parachutes . . . they only function when open —Lord Thomas Dewar

26. Minds, like bodies, will often fall into a pimpled, ill-conditioned state from mere excess of comfort —Charles Dickens

27. A mind without occupation is like a cat without a ball of yarn —Samuel Willoughby Duffield

28. Old minds are like old horses; you must exercise them if you wish to keep them in working order —John Adams

29. Our minds are like crows. They pick up everything that glitters no matter how uncomfortable our nets get with all that metal in them —Thomas Merton

30. Our minds are like our stomachs; they are whetted by the change of their food, and variety supplies both with fresh appetite —Quintilian

31. The shapes which the mind assumes are like those great forms, born of undifferentiated water, which assail or replace each other on the surface of the deep; each concept collapses, eventually, to merge with its opposite, like two waves breaking against each other only to subside into the same single line of white foam —Marguerite Yourcenar

32. Some minds are like concrete: thoroughly mixed and permanently set —Anon

33. The state of a man's mind is as much a fact as the state of his digestion —Baron Charles Synge Christopher Bowen
    The simile was used in reference to the legality of intent in an 1885 law case.

34. A weak mind is like a horoscope, which magnifies trifling things but cannot receive great ones —Lord Chesterfield
    The letter to Chesterfield's son from which this was culled addresses the question of taking a balanced view towards keeping track of expenditures. The comparison of the weak mind to a horoscope is used to underscore the author's statement that "A strong mind sees things in their true proportions."

MIRTH
See: GAIETY

MISERLINESS
See: THRIFT

MISERY
See: DEJECTION, GLOOM

MISFORTUNE
See: FORTUNE/MISFORTUNE

MIST

See Also: FOG

1. The hot mist . . . mixed with the sun like cloudy gin —David Denby

2. A light morning mist like grain on film —Clive Irving

3. Like a blanket, the mist came down —Jilly Cooper

4. Mist arose on the plain and stood round about it like a guard of honor —Vladimir G. Korolenko

5. Mist draped like ragged bits of cloth over a black line of distant hills — Alice McDermott

6. [Thinning] mist . . . drifted away like slow smoke —Howard Spring

7. The mist, like love, plays upon the heart of the hills and brings out surprise of beauty —Rabindranath Tagore

8. The mists, like flocks of trooping sheep, cloudily drifted here and there —John Hall Wheelock

9. Mist so fine it was like cigarette smoke —Paul Theroux

10. Mists, whirling and winding, like snakes —Mihail Lermontov

11. A mist that is like blown snow —W. B. Yeats

12. Mist thick as cotton batting —William Faulkner

13. A pure white mist crept over the water like breath upon a mirror —A. J. Cronin

14. A thick gray mist covered the countryside, as if to conceal the mysteries of the changes that were taking place in nature —Leo Tolstoy

MISTAKES

See: ERRORS

MISTRESS

See: MEN AND WOMEN

MIXTURE

See: CONNECTIONS

MOANS

See: GROANS AND WHISPERS

MODESTY

See Also: MEEKNESS, PERSONAL TRAITS

1. As humbly as a guest who knows himself too late —Hart Crane

2. Humility is like underwear, essential but indecent if it shows —Helen Nielsen, *Reader's Digest,* March, 1959

3.   If you really were a hero . . . you made it sound routine and unglamorous, like shrugging off a ninety-yard touchdown run as "Good luck and good blocking" —Dan Wakefield

4.   I looked as if I were trying to melt into the scenery and become invisible, like a giraffe standing motionless among sunlit leaves — Christopher Isherwood

5.   Modest as a flower —Ella Wheeler Wilcox

6.   Modest as justice —William Shakespeare

7.   Modesty is like virtue; suspected only when it is advertised —Douglas Malloch

8.   Modesty like a diver gathers pearls by keeping his head low —*Punch*

9.   Modesty's at times its own reward, like virtue —Lord Byron

MONARCHY
See: GOVERNMENT

MONEY
See Also: COST, GREED, RICHES

1.   Ate up money like Crackerjacks —Robert Campbell

2.   Bargain like a gipsy, but pay like a gentleman —Hungarian proverb

3.   (There ain't a chance of putting the bee on me . . . .I'm) flat [broke] as a ballroom floor —H. C. Witwer

4.   Getting money is like digging with a needle; spending it is like water soaking into sand —Proverb

5.   Gold, like the sun, which melts wax but hardens clay, expands great souls —Antoine Rivarol

6.   An instinct like a water diviner's where money's concerned —John Braine

7.   Loses money the way a . . . balloon loses air —Martin Cruz Smith
     In Smith's novel, *Stallion Gate,* a character is likening a great
     club's money loss to a beautiful balloon's air loss.

8.   Making money . . . is, in fact, almost as easy as losing it. Almost but not quite —H. L. Mencken

9.   A man without money is like a bird without wings; if he soars he falls to the ground and dies —Roumanian proverb

10. He that is without money is like a bird without wings —Thomas Fuller

11. A man without money is like a ship without sails —Dutch proverb

12. Money is a bottomless sea, in which honor, conscience and truth may be drowned —Ivan Kozloff

13. Money is a muscle in our society like that of a leg or arm of a man with a shovel, and both muscles must have a wage —Janet Flanner

14. Money is in some respects like fire; it is a very excellent servant —P. T. Barnum

15. Money is like an arm or a leg, use it or lose it —Henry Ford, *New York Times,* November 8, 1931

16. Money is like an eel in the hand —Welsh proverb

17. Money is like a sixth sense, and you can't make use of the other five without it —W. Somerset Maugham, *New York Times Magazine,* October 18, 1958

18. Public money is like holy water: every one helps himself to it —Italian proverb

19. Money is like promises, easier made than kept —Josh Billings
    In Billing's phonetic dialect: "Munny . . . easier maid than kept."

20. Money is like the reputation for ability, more easily made than kept — Samuel Butler

21. Money, like a boot, when it's tight is extremely trying —*Punch,* 1864

22. Money is like muck, not good except it be spread —Francis Bacon
    Variations include: "Money is like dung;" "Riches are like muck, which stink in a heap, but spread abroad, make the earth fruitful;" and "Money like manure does no good till it is spread." Two contemporary figures who have been widely quoted for perversions of the above are Clint Murchison, Jr. and J. Paul Getty. The first quoting his father's advice that, "Money is like manure. If you spread it around, it does a lot of good. But if you pile it up in one place, it stinks like hell;" the latter with "Money is like manure. You have to spread it around or it smells."

23. Money, like vodka, makes a man eccentric —Anton Chekhov

24. Money's as cold and neutral as the universe —Hortense Calisher

25. Money slips from his fingers like a watermelon seed, travels without legs, and flies without wings —Bartlett's *Dictionary of Americanisms*

26. Money . . . was exactly like sex, you thought of nothing else if you didn't have it and thought of other things if you did —James Baldwin

27. Serious money is like cancer, it breeds itself —A. Alvarez

28. Spending money like a pusher —M. S. Craig

29. Spent her money like a spoiled empress —Marjory Stoneman Douglas

30. They talk about it [money] as if it were something you got pink gums from —Ogden Nash

MONOTONY
See: DULLNESS, REPETITION

MONTHS
    See: SEASONS

MOOD CHANGES
    See: CHANGE

MOODINESS
    See: GLOOM

MOON

1. A bright moon . . . like glistening silk —Amy Lowell
2. Curled moon . . . like a feather —Dante Gabriel Rossetti
3. Everything has in fact another side to it, like the moon —G. K. Chesterton
4. A full new-risen moon like a pale medallion —Hayden Carruth
5. The moon had lost all its brilliance and looked like a little cloud in the sky —Leo Tolstoy
6. A half moon sailing like a moth up the drained blue sky —Jilly Cooper
7. It looked like a ball of paper from the back pocket of jeans that have just come out of the washing machine, which only time and ironing would tell if it was an old shopping list or a five pound note —Douglas Adams
8. Bright moonlight lay against its [house] wall like a fresh coat of paint —Raymond Chandler
9. A little slice of moon, curved like a canoe —Helen Hudson
10. The moon as beautiful as a great camellia —Max Beerbohm
11. A moonbeam . . . shimmers bright as a needle —W. P. Kinsella
12. Moon, bright as a lemon —Tom Robbins
13. The moon burned like metal —Pat Conroy
14. The moon, but half disclosed, was cut off as by a shutter —Joyce Cary
15. Moon curved like a rocker —Helen Hudson
16. The moon floats belly up like a dead goldfish —Marge Piercy
17. The moon follows the sun like a French translation of a Russian poet —Wallace Stevens
18. The moon hangs like a neon scythe over the countryside —W. P. Kinsella
19. The moon hung above the yard like a cheap earring —Isaac Babel
20. The moon hung like a pale lamp above the rim of the bay —William Styron
21. The moon is hidden by a silver cloud, fair as a halo —Christina Rossetti

22. The moon . . . is like a cake of white soap —John Phillips
23. The moon leaned low against the sky like a white-faced clown lolling against a circus wall —W. Somerset Maugham
24. Moonlight drilling in through the window like a bit into coal —Richard Wertime
25. Moonlight . . . dripped down like oil —Bernard Malamud
26. The moonlight invaded the courtyard, until it looked like a field of untrodden snow —Stefan Zweig
27. Moonlight so white that it looked like snow —Ruth Prawer Jhabvala
28. A moon like a fallen fruit reversing gravity was hoisting itself above the rooftop —Ross Macdonald
29. The moon like a flower in heaven's high bower, with silent delight sits and smiles on the night —William Blake
30. Moon like a monstrous crystal —G. K. Chesterton
31. The moon, like an eye turned up in a trance, filmed over and seemed to turn loose from its track and to float sightless —Eudora Welty
32. Moon . . . like a red-faced farmer —T. E. Hulme
    The complete line as it appears in a poem entitled *Autumn:* "I walked abroad and saw the ruddy moon lean over the hedge like a red-faced farmer."
33. The moon like a white rose shone —W. B. Yeats
34. Moon like the moving dot on sing-along lyrics —Sharon Sheehe Stark
35. The moon looked like the head of a golden bollard in a Venice lagoon —John Gunther
36. The moon, narrow and pale like a paring snipped from a snowman's toenail —Tom Robbins
37. The moon overhead tore through fierce cloud-wrack like a battered ship —Phyllis Bottome
38. Moon . . . pale, full-blown as a flower —Elizabeth Spencer
39. Moon pitted with holes, like an old brass coin —Erich Maria Remarque
40. The moon rattles like a fragment of angry candy —E. E. Cummings
41. The moon rises like a fat white god —Diane Ackerman
42. The moon . . . rode bonily in the sky, looking stark and abandoned like a decoration kids had put up for Halloween and forgotten to take down —William Dieter
43. The moon sails up out of the ocean dripping like a just washed apple — Marge Piercy
44. The moon shines like a lost button —Derek Walcott
45. The moon shone out like day —Nathanial Hawthorne
46. Moon slightly more than half full, like a tipped bowl —Patricia Henley

47. The moon stood like an arc lamp over the roofs of the houses —Erich Maria Remarque

48. The moon stuck like a wafer in the evening sky —Anon

49. The moon swelled like a plum —Philip Levine

50. Moon . . . waning, like silver that is polished so thin that it has begun to wear away —Mary Stewart

51. The moon . . . was like a slender shaving thrown up from a bar of gold —Joseph Conrad

52. The moon was like a chip of ice —Wallace Stegner

53. The moon was like a sickle —Edward Hoagland

54. The moon was out, cold and faraway as an owl's hoot —John Braine

55. The moon . . . was slowly drifting into an immense, dark and transparent hole like a lake with its depth full of stars —André Malraux

56. A pale crescent moon shaped like a woman's earring —Katharine Haake

57. A pale moon, like a claw (looked down through the claw-like branches of dead trees) —Jean Rhys

58. Quiet moonlight lay like the smile upon a dreaming face —John Hall Wheelock

59. The rising moon . . . winding like a silver thread until it was lost in the stars —Bret Harte

60. Sometimes in the afternoon sky a white moon would creep up like a little cloud, without display, suggesting an actress who does not have to "Come on" for a while and so goes "In front" in her ordinary clothes —Marcel Proust

61. The sphere hanging in the not yet darkened sky seemed like a lamp they had forgotten to turn off in the morning (a lamp that had burned all day in the room of the dead) —Milan Kundera

62. A stream of moonlight cut through the mist and hit the black water, like ink —Paige Mitchell

63. A thin moon . . . gray and marbled like a worn shell —Alice McDermott

64. A yellow moon rose like a flower blooming —Bernard Malamud

MORALITY

See Also: BELIEFS, VIRTUE

1. As moral as any elder of the church —Rumer Godden

2. Morality, like language, is an invented structure for conserving and communicating order —Jane Rule

3. Morality without religion is a tree without roots —George Bernard Shaw

4. Moral principles are like measles. They have to be caught —Aldous Huxley

5. Morals are an acquirement, like music, like a foreign language, like piety, poker, paralysis, no man is born with them —Mark Twain

6. The moral system of the universe is like a document written in alternate ciphers, which change from line to line —J. A. Froude

7. Turning the other cheek is a kind of moral jiu-jitsu —Gerald Stanley Lee

8. Wore her morality like long underwear —Delmore Schwartz
    Schwartz followed this entry in his journal with several alternative comparisons: "Fur coat, chemise, a rope of pearls."

MORTALITY
See: DEATH

MOTHERHOOD
See: CHILDREN, PARENTHOOD

MOTHERS-IN-LAW
See: PARENTHOOD

MOTIONLESSNESS
See: IMMOBILITY

MOTIVATION
See Also: AMBITION, PURPOSEFULNESS

1. Good intentions . . . like very mellow and choice fruit, they are difficult to keep —G. Simmons

2. (I simply) ran out of motives, as a car runs out of gas —John Barth

3. The true motives of our actions, like the real pipes of an organ, are usually concealed —Charles Caleb Colton

MOUNTAINS
See Also: LANDSCAPES, NATURE

1. Cropped, long-faced hills that bristled with pine like so many unshaven cheeks —T. Coraghessan Boyle

2. The hills here are long and blue, like paintings —Bobbie Ann Mason

3. Hills like breasts —Karl Shapiro

4. The hillside is dotted with white plum trees like puffs of smoke — Colette

5. Hills . . . lay there like a herd of drowsing buffalo —Yitzhak Shenhar

6. Hills . . . like a young girl's breasts —William Boyd

7. Hills rose up like bubbles —Phyllis Bottome
8. Like an enormous landscape lay the mountain —Delmore Schwartz
9. Mountains . . . like crouching camels —Milton Raison
10. Mountains like puffs of smoke —George Garrett
11. The mountains rolled like whales through the phosphorous stars —Derek Walcott
12. The mountains rose like worn, dark-skinned fists —Carlos Fuentes
13. Mountains, stretching themselves like great luxurious cats in the sunshine —Hugh Walpole
14. Mountains . . . unreal like movie props —John Rechy
15. The mountains were jagged like a page ripped out of a book —Kate Grenville
16. The mountains were just visible, dusky and black, like waves of charcoal —John Fowles
17. The mountain tops were whitened by moonlight like crests of waves —Lee Smith
18. The mountain was shining like glass in color —Paul Horgan
19. The scenery is funny little hills shaped like scoops of ice cream —Bobbie Ann Mason
20. The hills are . . . ribbed like the remains of antediluvian breasts stretched across the horizon —T. Coraghessan Boyle
21. To live in mountains is like living with someone who always talks at the top of his, or it may be her, voice —Leonard Woolf
22. Tree-covered folds in the mountains . . . lying like a gigantic crumpled velvet rug —John Fowles

MOURNING
See: GRIEF

MOUTH
See Also: CHIN; CHEEK; MOUTH, OPEN/SHUT

1. Bare his teeth like a yawning tiger —Miles Gibson
2. Cruel red mouth like a venomous flower —Algernon Charles Swinburne
3. He had his mouth all prissed up when he talked, like a man acting in a play —Iris Murdoch
4. Her mouth glistened like a wound —Jerry Bumpus
5. Her mouth hung loose like a bright ribbon —R. V. Cassill
6. Her mouth is wide and red as strawberry pie —Rex Reed
   The mouth thus described belongs to actress Carol Channing.

7. Her mouth was as little suited for smiling as a frying-pan for musical purposes —Anatole France
    See Also: FACIAL EXPRESSION, SERIOUS

8. Her peevish mouth looked like a slit cut by a knife —Stefan Zweig

9. His mouth ran like a thin dark crease between them [chin and nose] —Jonathan Valin

10. His mouth turned down like he could see death —Richard Ford

11. His open mouth was like a dark hole in his beard —Ross Macdonald

12. A loose mouth . . . slack with usage, like rubber bands —William Faulkner

13. The mouth and ear are like a bow and a fiddle; when the ear is shut, the mouth is mute —Hayyim Nahman Bialik

14. Mouth as sweet as a ripe fig —Edith Wharton

15. Mouth broad as an airstrip —Loren D. Estleman

16. Mouth . . . framed in iron-gray fluffy hair, that looked like a chin-strap of cotton wool sprinkled with coal-dust —Joseph Conrad

17. Mouth . . . clamped like a spring and right as the mouth of a witch —Borden Deal

18. (A big, pink) mouth, curled down at one corner as if he habitually smoked a pipe —Lael Tucker Wertenbaker

19. A mouth drawn in like a miser's purse —Émile Zola

20. Mouth . . . flabby like a toad's —Christopher Isherwood

21. Mouth . . . like a large wet keyhole —Roald Dahl

22. Mouth like a fireplace —Ogden Nash

23. Mouth . . . like a fold of skin over a skull, without the life —Paul Horgan

24. A mouth like an air-raid trench —Jane Wagner

25. Mouth like an arrowhead wound —Jean Cocteau about Colette

26. Mouth . . . like a scarlet wound —W. Somerset Maugham

27. Mouth like a seam —Irvin S. Cobb

28. Mouth like a slit in the sidewalk —Anon

29. Mouth like the bottom of a parrot cage —David Niven

30. A mouth like the inside of a jelly doughnut —Peter De Vries

31. Mouth open like a funnel's —Eudora Welty

32. Mouth pinched inward like a fist —Joyce Carol Oates

33. Mouth pursed up tight like a mushroom —Roald Dahl

34. Mouth . . . red and slightly swollen, as if somebody had been chewing on it —Ross Macdonald

35. Mouth . . . so wide-centred and deep-cornered, so cool and so warm, so lusciously crimson, that flaring out of the pallor of her face, it was like a blood-hot signal to the senses —Inez Haynes Irwin

36. Mouths like donuts —F. D. Reeve

37. Mouths like wet velvet —Angela Carter

38. Mouth . . . so thin that the lips seemed to hook together, like the catch of a child's purse —Frank Tuohy

39. Mouths pink as watermelon —May Sarton

40. A mouth that stretches from ear to ear when he laughs, like a mouth on a cat piggy bank —Francois Maspero

41. Mouth that was like a salmon's mouth —Roald Dahl

42. Mouth thin and straight, like a cut in his face —Honoré de Balzac

43. Mouth tight as a corset string on the preacher's wife —Harold Adams

44. Mouth tugged down on one side like a dead man's —John Updike

45. Mouth twisted like an epileptic's —Isaac Bashevis Singer

46. The old mouth closed like a zip —Julia O'Faolain

47. A quibbling mouth that would have snapped verbal errors like a lizard catching flies —Edith Wharton

48. A wide and expressionless mouth like the juncture of a casserole dish with its lid —Thomas McGuane

MOUTH, OPEN AND SHUT

1. Closed her mouth like a trap —Julia O'Faolain

2. Mouth comes open like a fish for air —Robert Penn Warren

3. Mouth slightly open, like an idiot's —D. H. Lawrence

4. (Uncle Harry's) mouth dropped open, as if either in the beginning of prayer or protest —H. E. Bates

5. Mouth gagged open . . . as if the day had stuck in his throat — William McIlvanney

6. Mouth hanging open like a stove lid —Charles Johnson

7. Mouth . . . open, black and wide as an attic —Louise Erdrich

8. Mouth opened like a dark hole —Jerry Bumpus

9. Mouth opened like a folding bed —Anon

10. Mouth round and open like a small empty cave —William Faulkner

11. Mouths came open like full moons —Will Weaver

12. (His huge brow furrowed, his gray eyes closed down to slits, his) mouth shut like a car door being slammed —Jonathan Valin

13. Mouth . . . slightly open, as though it froze in the middle of an unspellable word —Louise Erdrich

14. (Don't sit there with your) mouth sprung open like a busted letter box —William Alfred

15. Opened and closed her narrow lips once or twice, like some beached shellfish gasping for the tide —Edith Wharton

16. Opening his mouth in a kind of snarling grimace, quite without ferocity, like an old lion in a cage —Christopher Isherwood

17. Small mouth hung open birdlike (as she sang) —MacDonald Harris

18. Mouth shut abruptly, like a puppet's —Jonathan Valin

19. Yawned like a menagerie lion —Gelett Burgess

20. A yawn like an unobtrusive earthquake —G. K. Chesterton

MOVEMENT

See Also: ADVANCING, JUMPING, LEAPING, ROCKING AND ROLLING, RUNNING, TURNING AND TWISTING

1. All her movements were soft as if timed to the sleeping of children —Ada Jack Carver

2. Charged across . . . like a cat with a kerosened ass —Harold Adams

3. Crawled like a worm —Denis Diderot

4. Creep and crawl . . . stretching her fingers like a baby trying to climb the path —Eudora Welty

5. Creeping slowly toward him, like a lizard toward a bug —E. B. White

6. Crept like a man intent on crime —W. H. Auden

7. Crept . . . like a spider on an endless thread of its own spinning — George Du Maurier

8. Darted about like a hummingbird —Rita Mae Brown

9. Darted like a bird about the room —John Steinbeck

10. Darting about and banging together like bubbles in soda water —Joyce Cary

11. Darting off this way and that, like the wax of a burning candle —Anon

12. Descended the stairs like a buffalo —Joe Coomer

13. Drifted north . . . like a saddle tramp looking for a spring roundup — James Crumley

14. Floated like a weed —Mavis Gallant

15. Folded herself up like a fresh-ironed shirt —Mary Hood

16. Glided as though on little wheels —Jules Renard, drama critic, about actress Sarah Bernhardt

17. Glide, like phantoms —John Keats

18. Glides to his meeting like a lover mumbling a secret, passionate message —Wallace Stevens

19. Go as if nine men pulled you and ten men held you —John Withal

20. Going (home) stealthily and unsteadily . . . like a dissipated cat —Charles Dickens

21. Groped about like blind, cautious crabs —Ralph Ellison

22. He [a dog] dumped himself like a bag of bones —Robert Frost

23. He moved like a spring —Eudora Welty

24. He moves like a piece of darkness —Joe Coomer

25. His body waved like a flame in the breeze —TV obituary describing James Cagney's physical grace, 1986

26. Hurried with legs stretched out ahead of me like a horse —David Ignatow

27. I float like a butterfly, sting like a bee —Muhammed Ali

28. Kicking and wriggling like a retriever pup —Walter Duranty

29. Lethargically, like sloth on the move —Kenzaburo Oë
     In the novel, *A Personal Matter,* the lethargy described is that of a man pedalling his bike.

30. Like a vein of gold I darted after you —Charles Simic

31. Like shoals of fish, they all headed one way —Elizabeth Taylor

32. Lowered herself [from bus] cautiously, like a climber —Elizabeth Bowen

33. A meandering pace that makes sweet Afton look like a white water stream —Helen Dudar, *New York Times Book Review,* September 21, 1986

34. Moved as smoothly as light wind across water —James Crumley

35. Moved by as if on a treadmill —Jonathan Kellerman
     See: RESTLESSNESS

36. Moved downhill [a street that lay on an incline] like rainwater. Like the twentieth century —Tom Robbins

37. Moved like a water bug, like a skipping stone, upon the glassy tense surface of his new life —John Updike

38. Moved like benign automata —Angela Carter

39. Moved passively with her head down, like a prisoner between guards —Ross Macdonald

40. Moved with funny little steps, like a chicken with an egg wedged up its legs —William Kotzwinkle

41. Move languidly . . . like a hostess in her bathrobe emptying ashtrays on Sunday morning —Alice McDermott

42. Movement . . . quick and quiet as a fish in deep water —Gerald Kersh

43. Move mindlessly, mechanically as a toy train through a Christmas tree town —Sharon Sheehe Stark

44. (Waiters) moving as deft and soft-footed as shadows —George Garrett

45. (Hand) moving imperceptibly like a marine plant —Marguerite Yourcenar

46. Moving listlessly back and forth, like a fish in an aquarium —Jill Ciment

47. Moving quick and light as a fairy —Dame Edith Sitwell

48. Moving . . . slow and heavy as lead —Gerald Kersh

49. (The sun) moving up and down . . . like a musical note —Saul Bellow

50. Paced around . . . like a jaguar on the prowl —Jonathan Kellerman

51. Pace . . . like impatient cats —Ira Wood

52. Pace like Socrates before the court —Charles Johnson

53. Passed like a circus —Wallace Stevens

54. People moved as if groping in the dimness of the subconscious for the memory of midday warmth that lingered faintly in the skin — Kenzaburo Oë

55. Prowled around like a dog that has forgotten where he put his bone — Raymond Chandler
    See Also: AIMLESSNESS

56. Rush sideways, like an excited crab —Jerome K. Jerome

57. Scampering about like frenzied ants —Brian Burland

58. Scamper like mice —Dame Edith Sitwell

59. Scuttling around it like a mouse trying to find a hole —Cornell Woolrich

60. Settled themselves, like chickens getting ready to roost —Christopher Isherwood

61. She got up and, like a vacuum cleaner with insomnia, roamed the room —Tom Robbins

62. Shied abruptly like a startled horse —Jack London

63. Shuffled about [text of a book] like a melancholy sheep in a pen — Mavis Gallant

64. Shuffles . . . around like a deck of cards —Brian Burland

65. Slide like lizards —Anon

66. Sliding like a shadow among them —R. V. Cassill

67. The small procession moved . . . slow and spaced out like a funeral — Ivo Andric

68. (I have seen thy waters) stealing onward, like the stream of life —Henry Wadsworth Longfellow

69. Step back as though I'd stepped on a snake —Dorothy Canfield Fisher
70. Steppin' high like a rooster in deep mud —American colloquialism
71. Stirred like a rustle of leaves —Maurice Edelman
     Edelman's simile is used to draw an image of whispers stirring up around the actions of the hero of his novel, *Disraeli Rising.*
72. Stomped back to bed, trying to make my footsteps sound like angry exclamation marks —Dorothy Francis
73. Straggled on back . . . like tongue-dragging hounds —Thomas Zigal
74. Straightened up slowly, as if she were being raised —Marguerite Duras
75. Swept by like a spotlight —Donald McCaig
76. Tore through the black-and-gold town like a pair of scissors tearing through brocade —Katherine Mansfield
77. Tottering . . . like a Chinese girl with bound feet —Jayne Anne Phillips
78. Travels unsteadily, as fogs do —David Ignatow
79. Twisted himself out like an eel —Sholom Aleichem
80. Twitched her shoulders like a bird shaking off water —Laura Furman
81. Wander like Alice —Karl Shapiro
82. Weave like a dreamer —John Barth
83. [Group of children] whirling off like autumn leaves, just as gay in their bright colors, and just as elusive —Beverly Mitchell
84. Wiggled like ribbons —R. V. Cassill
85. Wiggle [a tooth] like a loose picket in a fence —William Goyen

MOVIES
See: STAGE AND SCREEN

MURDER
See: CRIME

MUSCLES
See Also: STRENGTH

1. The great muscles of his torso flickered and ran like the flank of a horse —Du Bose Heyward
2. Heavily defined pectoral muscles, on which the nipples stood out like pennies —Francis King
3. Muscled like a water buffalo —Gerald Kersh
4. Muscles [of leg] as big as a hill —Dylan Thomas
5. Muscles . . . hard and ropy like the ones on the fantastic coursing dogs in the sad stone friezes of ancient Persia —Beryl Markham

6. Muscles . . . hard as iron —Jack London

7. The muscles in his face seemed to pull together like a drawstring purse —Sue Grafton

8. The muscles in their arms bulge out like India rubber balls —Joanna M. Glass

9. Muscles in their backs rippled . . . like fretted water over a stony bed —Beryl Markham

10. Muscles like armor plates pasted on his body —John Rechy

11. Muscles . . . like blown-up balloons —François Camoin
    In his short story, *A Hunk of Burning Love,* Camoin completes the simile as follows: "Put a pipe in his mouth and he'd look like Popeye."

12. Muscles like marshmallows —Carlos Baker

13. The muscles of his arms and back stood out beneath his fair skin like the muscles of one of Rodin's bronze men —Louis Bromfield

14. Muscles of his forearms . . . moved in ridges and hollows from a knot above his elbow, like pistons working from a cylinder —L. P. Hartley

15. Muscles of strength rose like a collar from his neck —Arthur A. Cohen

16. Muscles . . . polished like metal, pure sculpture —Vita Sackville-West

17. Muscles pulled like cold rubber —Tony Ardizzone
    See Also: PAIN

18. Muscles rippled like stretching cats —Stephen Vincent Benét

19. Muscles stretched taut as cowhide stretched over a baseball —W. P. Kinsella

20. Muscles that flow like a mountain stream —Ogden Nash

21. Muscles twitching like the flesh of a horse stung by many flies —Ralph Ellison

22. Remember . . . the rippling of bright muscles like a sea —Edith Sitwell

23. The ripple of muscles goes along him, like a cat's back arching — Margaret Atwood

24. Wore faded denims through which his clumsy muscles bulged like animals in a sack —Ross Macdonald

MUSIC

See Also: SINGING

1. As music takes up the thread that language drops, so it is where Shakespeare ends that Beethoven began —Sidney Lanier

2. The band wound up the tune like a train rushing into a station — Donald McCaig

3. The cello is like a beautiful woman who has not grown older but younger with time, more slender, more supple, more graceful —Pablo Casals

4. Composing is like making love to the future —Lukas Foss

5. Composing is like organizing a meal. The different dishes must be so arranged as to rouse the appetite and renew the pleasure with each course —Moses Ibn Ezra

6. A concert is like a bullfight, the moment of truth —Artur Rubinstein

7. The conductor . . . flapped his arms like a rooster about to crow —Katherine Mansfield

8. Each musician looks like mumps from blowing umpah umpah umps —Ogden Nash

9. Fiddles tuning up like cats in pain —Harvey Swados

10. Good music, like land and machines, had no people in sight —Will Weaver
   In Weaver's novel, *Red Earth, White Earth,* this simile is used to explain a character's liking for music.

11. A great burst of music gushed up like a geyser —Mary Lavin

12. In came a fiddler, and tuned like fifty stomach aches —Charles Dickens

13. In music as in love, pleasure is the waste product of creation —Igor Stravinsky

14. It is like eating vanilla ice cream in Paradise, listening to beautiful music —Camille Lemmonnier

15. Musical as the holes of a flute without the flute —O. Henry

16. Music as loud as the roar of traffic —Marge Piercy
   See Also: NOISE

17. The music rushed from the bow [of fiddle] like water from the rock when Moses touched it —Henry Van Dyke

18. The music enchanted the air . . . like the south wind, like a warm night, like swelling sails beneath the stars —Erich Maria Remarque

19. Music is a big sublime instinct, like genius of all kinds —Ouida

20. Music is a sort of dream architecture which passes in filmy clouds and disappears in nothingness —Percy A. Scholes

21. Music is auditory intercourse without benefit of orgasm —Aldous Huxley

22. Music is essentially useless, as life is —George Santayana

23. Music is like wine . . . the less people know about it, the sweeter they like it —Robertson Davies

24. Music is like a fickle, tantalizing mistress; one is rarely happy with her, but it is sheer tormented hell ever to be long away —Robert Traver

25. Music is . . . like mathematics, very nearly a world by itself. It contains a whole gamut of experience, from sensuous elements to ultimate intellectual harmonies —George Santayana

26. Music is not water, but it moves like water; it is not fire, but it soars as warm as the sun —Delmore Schwartz

27. Music is the arithmetic of sounds as optics is the geometry of light —Claude Debussy

28. Music, like balm, eases grief's smarting wound —Samuel Pordage

29. (Drum, drum, drum, the) music like footsteps —T. Coraghessan Boyle

30. Music may be regarded as a thermometer that makes it possible to register the degree of sensibility of every people, according to the climate in which they live —André Ernest Grétry

31. Music throbbed like blood —T. Coraghessan Boyle

32. Music yearning like a god in pain —John Keats

33. Opera in English makes about as much sense as baseball in Italian —H. L. Mencken

34. The opera is like a husband with a foreign title: expensive to support, hard to understand, and therefore a supreme social challenge — Cleveland Amory

35. The orchestra sounds like fifty cats in agony —J. B. Priestly

36. Our musicians are like big canisters of gas. Light a match too close to them, and they will explode —Yevgeny Svetlanov, *New York Times,* October 20, 1986
    Svetlanov, the Moscow State Symphony conductor, thus described Russian musicians in an article by Bernard Holland.

37. The plaintive sound of saxophones moaning softly like a man who has just missed a short putt —P. G. Wodehouse

38. Playing 'bop' is like playing 'scrabble' with all the vowels missing — Duke Ellington, quoted in *New York Herald Tribune,* July 9,1961

39. Pulled music from his violin as if he were lifting silk from a dressmaker's table —Pat Conroy

40. Saxophones wailing like a litter of pigs —Lawrence Durrell

41. The string section sounded like cats in heat —Mary Hedin

42. (Wade and Beth could hear) the subterranean thudding of his rock music turned low, like a giant heart beating in a sub-cellar —John D. MacDonald

43. A symphony must be like the world, it must embrace everything — Gustav Mahler
    Mahler's comment was addressed to Jean Sibelius.

44. To some people music is like food; to others like medicines; to others like a fan —Arabian Nights

45. Tuneless and atonal, like the improvised songs of children caught up in frantic play —Robert Silverberg

46. The written note is like a strait jacket, whereas music like life itself is constant movement, continuous spontaneity, free from restriction — Pablo Casals

MUSTACHES
See Also: BEARDS, HAIR

1. Big mustaches that made him look like an animated mushroom — Arthur Train

2. A black mustache like the lowered wings of a crow —Carolyn Chute

3. A curled-up mustache, like two little rolls of barbed wire —Joyce Cary

4. A gray handlebar mustache with oiled points, like the long horns of an ox —Ira Wood

5. His mustache sags . . . like a bat —Carolyn Chute

6. His white mustache, of thin separate hairs like glass threads —Joyce Cary

7. His yellow-to-brown mustache quivered and preened over his mouth like a sparrow's wing shaking off dust —Paul Horgan

8. The insignificant mustache trembled like a twig in a storm —Jonathan Kellerman

9. A light mustache that flourished upwards as if blown that way by the breath of a constant smile —Henry James

10. A little black mustache like an eyebrow —George Du Maurier

11. Little circumflex accent mustache . . . like a black butterfly placed under his nose —Romain Gary

12. Little mustaches stiffened like a pointer's tail when he scents a bird — Arthur Train

13. A man without a mustache is like a woman with only one breast —M. M. Liberman
See Also: INCOMPLETENESS

14. Mustache . . . black as India ink and big as the switch on a cow's tail —James Crumley

15. Mustache . . . black, like a charcoal smear on his upper lip —Paige Mitchell

16. Mustache bristled like intractable gorse —Frank Swinnerton

17. Mustache curling like a sultan's —Oliver Wendell Holmes, Sr.

18. Mustache cut short like a worn-out brush —Henry James

19. Mustache hanging heavy as a pelt —Carolyn Chute

20. Mustache like a soft black mouse —Ann Tyler

21. A mustache resting like a small white cloud beneath his undistinguished nose —F. Scott Fitzgerald

22. A mustache shadowing either side of his lip with a broad sweep, like a bird's wing —William Dean Howells

23. (The faded) mustaches hung like crossed pistols above his radiant smile —Eudora Welty

24. Mustache . . . thick and neat as a bristle brush —Ira Wood

25. Mustache . . . thin and straight like it was painted on —George Garrett

26. White mustache like a Viking's —Jo Bannister

MYSTERIOUSNESS
See: STRANGENESS

NAKEDNESS
See: BARENESS

NAMES
See Also: MEMORY

1. (Alex) acquired names as other women encrust themselves with jewels —Patrick White

2. Forgotten names sang through my head like forgotten scenes in dreams —Ralph Ellison

3. Fools' names like fools' faces, are often seen in public places —Thomas Fuller

4. Handed [told it to her] her his name as though he were extending a card on a copper salver —Harvey Swados

5. His name [a politician's] has become as institutionalized as a detergent —Robert Traver

6. It is with you as with the seas: the most varied names are given to what is in the end only salt water —Johann Wolfgang von Goethe

7. Lost their names like marbles on the schoolyard —George Garrett

8. Making fun of your name is like making fun of your nose —Willie Morris

9. Names and faces eluded him like ghosts —William Diehl

10. Patients . . . they are as patient as their name —Randall Jarrell

11. Called me 'chéri' in such a way that it was a small fruit on her tongue —R. Wright Campbell

12. Some people have names like pitchforks, some people have names like cakes —Stephen Vincent Benét

13. Sounds like a name you'd see on a bracelet at Walgreen's —Richard Ford

   The character who thus expresses her discontent in the novel, *The Sportswriter,* happens to be named Vicki.

14. You carry your name forever, like a scepter alive with wings —Stephen Vincent Benét

15. Your name like a lozenge upon my tongue —Charles Wright

NARROWNESS
See: THINNESS

NATIONS
See: CHARACTERISTICS, NATIONAL; GOVERNMENTS

NATURALNESS

1. (Her tight smile returned) as automatically as a gesundheit —Loren D. Estleman

2. (The doctor . . . a man who listened to other people's hearts) as casually, as automatically, as he blew his own nose —Helen Hudson

3. As natural a part of her life as toothpaste —Julia Whedon

4. As natural as a vine grows —Babette Deutsch

5. (She was flushed, eager, and) as natural as daylight —Frank Swinnerton

6. As natural . . . as the falling of leaves —Edith Wharton

7. (A faith . . . as strong,) as natural, as irrational as the elements —Romain Gary
   See Also: Sense

8. As natural as NutraSweet —Anon

9. (Had grown up believing that overcoming handicaps was) as natural as scratching your ear —Ira Berkow, *New York Times*/Sports of the Times, September 23, 1986

   Berkow's subject is Jim Plunkett, Raider quarterback.

10. As natural . . . as the passion for air or food or drink —Stephen McKenna

11. As natural as the process of digestion —Walter De La Mare

12. He [Dr. Oliver Wendell Holmes] could no more stop it [wit flowing from him] than he could stop the blood flowing in his veins —Elizabeth Bowen

13. (His thoughts, his humor, his similes) rose as fast, as multitudinous, as irrepressible, as bubbles in the champagne, and nothing could prevent their coming to the surface —John T. Morse

The man whose wit is the subject of the comparison is Dr. Oliver Wendell Holmes.

14. Spontaneous as a child's drawing —Anon
15. Spontaneous as a six-course sit-down dinner —Anon
16. Spontaneous as the song of a bird —W. H. Hudson
17. Spontaneous as the time of day —"St. Elsewhere," TV segment, December 16, 1986
18. Unconscious as an oak tree of its growth —Anon
19. Unconscious as the loyalty of bees to their queen —Lacfadio Hearn
20. Unconscious as you grow your fingernails —George Bernard Shaw
21. Unnatural as generosity to a miser —Elyse Sommer
22. Unthinkingly as a child heaping sand on its mother at the beach — Anatole Broyard, *New York Times Book Review,* January 16, 1986

NATURE

See Also: FLOWERS, LEAVES, MOON, OCEAN/OCEANFRONT, PONDS AND STREAMS, RAIN, SEASCAPES, SKYSCAPES, SNOW, STARS, SUN, THUNDER AND LIGHTNING, TREES, WEATHER

1. Big heavy drops [of dew] . . . lie on the face of the earth like sweat — Shirley Ann Grau
2. Bushes . . . like heads; you could have sworn sometimes you saw them mounting and swaying in manly talk —Elizabeth Bowen
3. The damp stands on the long green grass as thick as morning's tears — Emily Brontë
   See Also: THICKNESS
4. The dawn clings to the river like a fog —Yvor Winters
5. Dew as thick as frost —Paul Theroux
6. Dew gleamed and sparkled like myriads of tiny mirrors —Dorothy Livesay
7. The dew is beaded like mercury on the coarsened grass —Adrienne Rich
8. Dew . . . like trembling silver leaves —Dame Edith Sitwell
9. Driftwood gnarled and knobby like old human bones —Charles Johnson
10. The earth is like the breast of a woman: useful as well as pleasing — Friedrich Nietzsche
11. Earth was like a jostling festival of seeds grown fat —Wallace Stevens
12. Flecks of ice still clung to his collar, flashing like brilliants —William H. Gass
13. Frost was like stiff icing sugar on all the roofs —H. E. Bates

14. The garden we planted and nurtured through the spring . . . fills out like an adolescent at summer camp —Ira Wood

15. The grass like a prophet's beard, thoughtful and greying —Charles Simic

16. The grass on the roadside moved under the evening wind, sounding like many pairs of hands rubbed softly together —H. E. Bates

17. Grass patches . . . like squares on a game board —Mary Hedin

18. Grass . . . thick as wind —David Ignatow

19. Hedges as solid as walls —Edith Wharton

20. Here a giant philodendron twined around a sapodilla tree and through the branches of a hibiscus bush like a green arm drawing two friends together —Dorothy Francis

21. Ice-crystals, shaped like fern-leaves —Anatole France

22. Light hung in the trees like cobwebs —Jay Parini

23. The light is in the dark river of the hot spring evening like a dry wine in a decanter —Delmore Schwartz

24. Like a great poet, Nature knows how to produce the greatest effects with the most limited means —Heinrich Heine

25. Like a slim reed of crystal, a fountain hung in the dusky air —Oscar Wilde

26. The moisture in the air seemed suspended like tiny pearls —Rita Mae Brown

27. Moss that looks and feels like felt —Brad Leithauser

28. Nature is like a beautiful woman that may be as delightfully and as truly known at a certain distance as upon a closer view —George Santayana
    > Santayana expanded on the simile as follows: "As to knowing her through and through, that is nonsense in both cases, and might not reward our pains."

29. Nature is like a revolving door: what goes out in one form comes back in another —Anon

30. Nature like life, she strips men of their pretensions and vanities, exposes the weakness of the weak and the folly of the fool —W. Macneile Dixon

31. Nature, like lives while they are being lived, is subject to laws of motion; it cannot be stopped and thereby comprehended —Margaret Sutherland

32. Pebbles [on beach] lit like eggs —Jay Parini

33. A plant is like a self-willed man, out of whom we can obtain all which we desire, if we will only treat him his own way —Johann Wolfgang von Goethe

34. A rampant twining vine of wisteria, ancient and knotted like muscles — Marge Piercy

35. Sea shells as big as melons. Others like peas —John Cheever

36. The [clam] shells shone like rainbows —Will Weaver

37. The shrubs burgeon like magic beanstalks —T. Coraghessan Boyle

38. The soil [being dug with a spade] slices off like fudge —Sharon Sheehe Stark

39. Sun-baked tomatoes . . . hung like red balloons filled with water — Anon

40. The surrounding nature is soundless as if it were under water —Shohei Ooka

41. Thistles stood looking like prophets in the Bible in Solomon's house — Eudora Welty

42. Tiny, sand-sized bits of green moss hung in slanted drifts in the water like grain dust in sunlight —Will Weaver

43. Trees and flowers that crowded to the path's edge like children —Helen Hudson

44. The tufts of moss, like piles of house dust, that hang trembling on the bare winter trees —Elizabeth Hardwick

45. The twilight seems like a canopy —Erich Maria Remarque

46. Undergrowth [of a path] spotted with moonlight like a leapord's skin — Colette

47. The water rippled like a piece of cloth —William Faulkner

48. The white of the snow and sky filled my eyes like the sheet pulled over the head of a dead man —Steve Erickson

49. A white sky made the bare branches of the elms [in March] seem like bones —Louis Auchincloss

NEARNESS
See: CLOSENESS

NEATNESS
See: CLEANLINESS, ORDER/DISORDER

NECESSITY
See Also: IMPORTANCE/UNIMPORTANCE

1. Crucial as the last game of the World Series —Anon

2. Essential as marrow —Curtis White

3. I need it like I need a hole in the head —Anon
   A Yiddish simile, typical of the colorful irony that has caused so many Jewish immigrant expressions to become integrated into American English.

4. Necessary and invisible like drafts of oxygen —Thomas Lux

5. Necessary as water to a healthy lawn —Anon
6. Necessary as a gardener to his garden —John Ray's *Proverbs*
7. Necessary as an anesthesiologist to an operation —Mary Morris
8. Necessary as applause to an actor —Anon
9. Necessary as a saw to a carpenter —Anon
10. Necessary as bytes to a computer —Anon
11. Necessary as Christmas to retailers —Anon
12. Necessary as eggs in an omelette —Anon
13. Necessary as gas to a car —Anon
14. Necessary as good lines to a play —Anon
15. Necessary as markings on a scale or a thermometer —Anon
16. Necessary as a paycheck to a worker —Anon
17. Necessary as practice to a musician —Anon
18. Necessary as quartz for a digital watch —Anon
19. Necessary as snow to a ski weekend —Anon
20. Necessary as sturdy shoes to a runner —Anon
21. Necessary as sunshine to a garden —Anon
22. Necessary as wages —John Braine
23. Necessary as workouts to an athlete —Anon
24. Necessary as work to a workaholic —Anon
25. (Men are as) necessary to her survival as water —Patricia Henley
26. Need as a dog needs a pocket handkerchief —Anon
    "Need as" similes with opposite meanings lend themselves to
    endless variations.
    See Also: USELESSNESS
27. Needed a ten minute head start like Sinatra needed singing lessons —
    John Lutz
28. Need . . . like a fish needs a bicycle —Robert B. Parker
29. Needs as a dog needs two tails —American colloquialism, attributed to
    New England
    The exact wording of this, as with anything handed down
    through common usage varies with each user; for example, a
    popular variation of the same theme is "He don't need it any
    more than a dog needs two tails."
30. Need . . . to simplify, almost like some painfully obese gourmet
    craving a stay at a health farm —John Fowles
31. Something she needs like a new navel —Richard Ford
32. As superfluous as a Gideon's Bible at the Ritz —F. Scott Fitzgerald
33. Superfluous as to light as a candle to the sun —Robert South

34. Unnecessary like rubbish —Henia Karmel-Wolfe

NECK

See Also: CHIN, CHEEKS, PHYSICAL APPEARANCE

1. Adam's apple bobbing like an eccentric toy —Robert Traver

2. Adam's apple bobbing like a fishing float —Andrew Kaplan

3. Adam's apple bobbing up and down like a prune seed in his throat —Calder Willingham

4. Adam's apple jumping up and down his throat like he got a ping-pong ball part way down and it got stuck —Carlos Baker

5. The Adam's apple of his thin, sinewy throat went up and down like a lift —Erich Maria Remarque

6. The cords in his [a man who's upset and angry] neck stick out like thumbs —Mary Hood

7. Her neck is like a stately tower —Thomas Lodge

8. Her neck rose [from folds of a shawl] like a column of slightly discolored Cararra marble —Arthur Train

9. His Adam's apple bulged so that when he drank it reminded Augustus of a snake with a frog stuck in its gullet —Larry McMurtry

10. His Adam's apple rippling up and down his skinny throat like a crazed mouse —James Crumley

11. His Adam's apple went up and down like an elevator —Cornell Woolrich

12. Limp-necked like a faded daisy —Julia O'Faolain

13. A long neck built like a tower —Colette

14. The long, pale neck rising like a beam of light from his open shirt —Helen Hudson

15. Neck . . . as a tower of ivory —*The Holy Bible/Song of Solomon*

16. Neck as thick as a telephone pole —William Diehl

17. Neck like a steel truss —Jonathan Valin

18. Neck swiveled like a lazy susan —T. Coraghessan Boyle

19. Neck . . . wrinkled like the wattles of some big bird —Anon
See Also: WRINKLES

20. The sinews of his neck . . . stood out like a cord of a hoist —Arthur Train

21. The skin of his neck, flabby and wrinkled like a turkey's cockscomb —Romain Gary

22. Thin neck like a goose —Jilly Cooper

23. Two rings of age on her neck looked like a cheap necklace —V. S. Pritchett

24.   The veins in his thin white neck stood out like cords —Leo Tolstoy

NEED
See: DESIRE

NEGLECT
See: ABANDONMENT, REJECTION

NEGLIGENCE
See: CARELESSNESS

NERVE
See: COURAGE

NERVOUSNESS
See Also: ANXIETY, TENSION, TREMBLING

1.   All nervous and jerky like a windup toy or maybe a cockroach on its back, waving its legs and trying to turn over —George Garrett

2.   Clucked nervously, like a mongoose —Romain Gary

3.   Excitable . . . like a little rooster —Irwin Shaw

4.   (Sat there open-mouthed,) feeling the nerves of his body twitter like so many sparrows perched upon his spinal column —F.Scott Fitzgerald

5.   Felt as if she were on the edge of a frozen pond, forced to go forward and not knowing how thick the ice was —Donald MacKenzie

6.   Felt as if someone had taken a vegetable peeler to my nerves —T. Coraghessan Boyle

7.   His nerves set themselves on edge like soured teeth —H. E. Bates

8.   His stomach felt like a volcano about to erupt —Andrew Kaplan

9.   It's (persistent feeling of impending insanity) like my head's in a vice and all the assholes of the world are turning the goddam handle — Thomas Williams

10.   Jumpy as a goat —James Thurber

11.   Jumpy as a greyhound —Wallace Stegner

12.   Jumpy as a jumping bean —Anon

13.   Lived like an exposed nerve —Rita Mae Brown

14.   Looked . . . like a nervous rabbit nibbling the smell of a gun barrel — Paul Theroux

15.   Nerves burned like open sores on a dog's neck —Hunter S. Thompson

16.   Nerves like a bundle of firecrackers —Amy Lowell
Lowell's poem, *Rosebud Wall-Paper,* from which this is taken was written in country dialogue, with 'of' written as 'o'.

17. Nerves like new thread —John Updike

18. Nerves tied in small, intricate knots, like embroidery stitching —Jean Thompson

19. (In rapid motion, bright,) nervous as a butterfly —Marge Piercy

20. Nervous as a cat on a hot tin roof —Anon
    In a television interview playwright Tennessee Williams stated that his father always used this phrase which became the title for one of his best known plays. It also served as a line for one of the leading characters, Maggie. During the interview Williams credited this and many other colorful phrases to Southern Blacks.

21. Nervous as a coyote in a pen —W. P. Kinsella

22. Nervous as a dog with a bone —Ben Hecht

23. Nervous as a hamster —Reynolds Price

24. Nervous as a kitten with a duck for a foster mother —Victor Canning

25. Nervous as a whore in church —American colloquialism

26. Nervous as a will o'-the-wisp —F. Scott Fitzgerald

27. On edge, like some restless night —Yasunari Kawabata

28. (They felt everything, feared everything, started back at the snapping of a twig, all their) senses strained like those of nervous explorers cautiously advancing, hand on cocked trigger, into an unknown jungle —Dorothy Canfield Fisher

29. Shuddering and wary, like horses bewildered by lightning —Ted Hughes
    Hughes' poem, *A Wind Flashes the Grass,* links the comparison of the wary horses to trees suddenly silent and motionless.

30. White and shaken, like a dry martini —P. G. Wodehouse

31. Wriggle nervously like captive fish —Margaret Millar

NEWNESS
See: FRESHNESS, TIMELINESS/UNTIMELINESS

NEWS
See Also: GOSSIP, KNOWLEDGE

1. As cold waters are to a faint soul, so is good news from a far country —*The Holy Bible/Proverbs*

2. Bad news travels fast like a bad shilling —line from British television program "Bless Me Father," 1986

3. News . . . rose like a grenade across Washington —Ellen Goodman, *Newsday,* December 2, 1986

Goodman is contrasting the normalcy with which video shopping programs are working, with the scandal over arms shipments to Iran which exploded the sense of normalcy in the capital of the nation.

4. Share information like a basket lunch —Anon

NIGHT

See Also: DARKNESS

1. The black night spread like glistening caviar —Diane Wakoski

2. The dark-blue velvet night hung like a curtain —Elizabeth Bowen

3. The darkness of night, like pain, is dumb; the darkness of dawn, like peace, is silent —Rabindranath Tagore

4. Dusk was falling like blue flakes —Truman Capote

5. The evenings and nights were like shutters opening and closing, no more than that —Dan Jacobson

6. Midnight shakes the memory as a madman shakes a dead geranium — T. S. Eliot

7. Night, bereft of dreams, is like a deserted railway station after hours — Robert Duncan

8. Night brings out stars as sorrow shows us truth —P. J. Bailey

9. Night comes like a blackout —John Rechy

10. The night dives down like one great crow —Richard Wilbur

11. Night falls like a dropped shutter —Beryl Markham

12. Night falls like fire —Algernon Charles Swinburne

13. The night feels like a gigantic Ferris wheel turning in blackness, very slowly —Margaret Laurence

14. Night had fallen like a black curtain —Colin Forbes

15. The night is as soft as milk —Albert Camus

16. The night is like flower petals, the air moist as a damp cloth —W. P. Kinsella

17. The night is soft and silent, warm as cashmere —W. P. Kinsella

18. The night roars on . . . like an express train —Erich Maria Remarque

19. The night descended on her like a benediction —Joseph Conrad

20. The nights stick together like pages in an old book —John Ashberry

21. The night stretches before me like an endless checklist —Natascha Wodin

22. The night trickles on like liquid time —Natascha Wodin

23. The still night drifted deep like snow about me —Edna St. Vincent Millay

24. The summer night is like a perfection of thought —Wallace Stevens
25. The night, like ice, seemed to harden around her —William Dieter

NIGHTMARES
See: DREAMS

NOISE
See Also: IRRITABLENESS

1. Applause . . . like pebbles being rattled in a tin —Francis King
2. Blare, like the clearing of a monstrous throat —Richard Wilbur
3. (The crowd laughing and) boo-boo-booming like frogs in a barbershop quartet —Ken Kesey
4. Boomed like a split trombone —O. Henry
5. Boom like a military band —W. H. Auden
6. A branch creaked . . . like someone turning over in bed —Jonathan Valin
7. Broke into a long roar like the falling of the walls of Jericho —Katherine Anne Porter
8. (The house-phone . . .) buzzed like an angry hornet —Cornell Woolrich
9. Cawing like a rook —Dame Edith Sitwell
10. [A dog's teeth] chattered like barbers' scissors —Frank Conroy
11. Clanged like fifty fire-engines —Herman Melville
12. Clanging [noise of truck backing out of driveway] like a half-dozen cowbells —Carolyn Chute
13. (Brake drums) clapped like cymbals —T. Coraghessan Boyle
14. Click like the snapping of a picture with an old box camera —W. P. Kinsella
15. A clopping sound . . . stung Lavinia's nerves like a box on the ears —L. P. Hartley
16. Creaked like a saddle when he shifted —Wallace Stegner
17. Creak like a rusty engine —Franz Werfel
18. A dissonant chord, as if somebody stepped on a cat —George Garrett
19. Door slam . . . like the crack of a bat when the opposition has hit a homerun to beat the Mariners in the bottom of the ninth —Tom Robbins
20. (The phone's) dull ring . . . like marbles rolling across a sheet of tin —Jean Thompson
21. Emitting throaty, explosive sounds like someone about to spit in someone else's face —Natascha Wodin

22. Fitful, hacking noise, like a dog coughing up a bone —William Styron

23. Footsteps echoing like gunfire in a well —T. Coraghessan Boyle

24. Growling away like an old mastiff with a sore throat —Charles Dickens

25. Growling like a fox in a trap —William Diehl

26. (Water) gulped and hissed like a dozen jacuzzis —T. Coraghessan Boyle

27. Heels ticking on the parquet floor like the clock of a time bomb —Margaret Millar

28. Her steps . . . made tiny, sharp pecky sounds, kind of like Mother drumming on the edge of the dinner table when Father tried to promote himself a second piece of pie —Raymond Chandler

29. The hinges and springs [of a door] screech like a woman with a hand over her mouth —Robert Campbell

30. Hissed like an adder —John D. MacDonald

31. (Tires) hissed like death —T. Coraghessan Boyle

32. (The sea) hissed like twenty thousand kettles —Joseph Conrad

33. Hisses and crackles like a doused campfire —Kate Wheeler

34. Hissing noise [as of crackling tissue paper] . . . was like a nail on glass to my nerves —Cornell Woolrich

35. Hum, like a devout crowd on its knees —Margaret Atwood

36. Like a log fire, the typewriter crackled —Delmore Schwartz
    If Delmore Schwartz were alive and keeping a diary today, instead of in 1944 when this entry was made, the crackling might well be from a computer keyboard instead of a typewriter.

37. (A beehive as) loud as an airfield —Maxine Kumin

38. Loud as gunfire —Reynolds Price

39. Loud as the last call of God —Harold Adams

40. A loud cracking sound, like a frozen river breaking up in spring —Andrew Kaplan

41. Loud . . . like a gun going off —Edith Wharton

42. Made a sound [in response to being kicked] like a sick cat —Loren D. Estleman

43. (A printer that) makes noise like a mad elephant —Edward Mendelson, reviewing computer products in *Yale Review,* 1985

44. Murmur like bees —Dame Edith Sitwell

45. (Through the audience went) a murmur, like the rustle of dead leaves —Henry Wadsworth Longfellow

46. The noise cracked like a whip in the still room —Margaret Mitchell

The noise Mitchell likened to the crack of a whip was made by Scarlett O'Hara when she slapped Ashley Wilkes' face in the famous scene from *Gone With the Wind* when he rejects her declaration of love.

47. Noise dwindling like a cut-back motor —Rosellen Brown

48. The noise level was deafening . . . like some hideous unrelenting tape-loop of trains having sex —Ben Hamper in article on changes at GM, *Mother Jones,* September, 1986

49. Noises rise and are lost in the air like balloons —Albert Camus

50. Noise [of continuous lightning] that sometimes burst like metal fireworks —Marguerite Duras

51. (The city by day was as) noisy and busy as a pack of children —Sinclair Lewis
See Also: BUSYNESS

52. (She would be as) noisy as a child at a playground —Helen Hudson

53. Noisy as a living skeleton having a fit on a hardwood floor —Leonard Washborn, reporting on 1880s baseball game for *Interocean* newspaper

54. Noisy as squirrels mating on a rooftop —Elyse Sommer

55. Noisy as the stock exchange —Augustine Bire

56. An occasional buzz [interrupting the silence] like an unheeded alarm clock —William Humphrey

57. Popping sounds, like hands clapped sharply together —W. P. Kinsella

58. [A typewriter] purrs like a seductive housecat —Tom Robbins

59. Rattling like a gong —Cynthia Ozick

60. Raucus whoop of children, spiteful and cruel like the sound of a lynch mob —Amos Oz
See Also: CRUELTY, SCREAMS

61. Resounded like a gigantic trumpet —Émile Zola

62. Ring like bells of glass —Elinor Wylie

63. Rowdy as gulls —Marge Piercy

64. Rumble . . . like a monster growl —Susan Minot

65. (The fiddle) screeched like a thing in pain —Elizabeth Bowen

66. Screeching with a noise like a buzz saw cutting through a knot — William Humphrey

67. Screech, like a car shifting gears on a dangerous uphill road —Yehuda Amichai

68. Sickening screech [of ripping metal] . . . like the scream of a wounded beast —Richard Moran

69. Slammed the door after him like a six-gun salute —Cornell Woolrich

70. The slamming of the door sounded like the last crack of doom —Jimmy Sangster

    Sangster's comparison begins the prologue to his mystery novel, *private i,* with a literal and figurative bang.

71. Snorted like a horse —Geoffrey Chaucer

72. The sound . . . filled the eardrums like wax —Wyatt Blassingame

73. Sound . . . it seemed to fill the vast room as breath fills a toy balloon —Frank Trippett

74. Sound like rhinos crashing into trees —Pauline Kael

75. The sounds [of the city] broke over her like a wave —Marguerite Yourcenar

76. Sounds came to me dully, as if people were speaking through their handkerchiefs or with their hands over their mouths —Maya Angelou

77. Sounds faded to a muffled warble, like a stream over pebbles —Curt Leviant

78. Sounds . . . grated and rumbled like a subway train —Norman Mailer

79. Sounds . . . hurt his ear like the thrust of a knife —Ambrose Bierce

80. The sound was hollow like the hammer on a coconut —Carson McCullers

81. The [baseball] stands sounded like a gigantic drawerful of voices that had suddenly been pulled open —Bernard Malamud

82. Static crackled along the line, like popcorn popping —William Diehl

83. The steady drone of the crowd, like bees humming —Anon

84. A steady murmur like the crowd noises made in a movie —Frank Conroy

85. Tapping and ticking like nervous fingers —Sylvia Plath

86. A thin plaintive sound, like a starved cat —Raymond Chandler

87. The thud of her heart in her ears like wet dirt slapped with a spade — Reynolds Price

88. Ticking [of clock] . . . sounds like a convict rhythmically pounding a rock —W. P. Kinsella

89. Twitter like bats —Angela Carter

90. Whirring, like the buzz of a giant wasp —Eddie Cohen

91. A whoop woke me up . . . as if I'd been prodded by a cattle rod —W. P. Kinsella

NONSENSE

See: ABSURDITY, FOOLISHNESS, IMPOSSIBILITY

NOSES

See Also: FACIAL DETAILS

1. A fabulous outsized nose attached to his face like a sheltering of stone —Pat Conroy

2. A flattish nose like a prizefighter —Beryl Bainbridge

3. His nose made two twists from bridge to end, like the wriggle of a snake —O. Henry

4. His nose stuck out like the first joint of a thumb —Frederick O. Brien

5. His nostrils heaved like a pair of blacksmith's bellows —Isaac Babel

6. A large nose like a trumpet —Edward Lear

7. Little snub nose, like a bulldog's —Colette

8. A long narrow nose which clung against his face as if reluctant to leave it —MacKinlay Kantor

9. A long nose flattened as if it had been tied down —Willa Cather

10. A long pink nose like a crooked beckoning finger in the middle of his face —Sue Miller

11. Nose . . . as big as an orange and the skin stretched over it was pebbled like an orange —François Camoin
   See Also: SKIN

12. Nose broad as a teacup —Carolyn Chute

13. Nose . . . crackled with tiny veins, like the nose of a hardened boozer —Gavin Lyall

14. A nose like a Bartlett pear —James Whitcomb Riley

15. A nose like a battering ram —Ross Macdonald

16. Nose like a bone —Ivan Bunin

17. A nose like a boot —Michael Gilbert

18. Nose like a butcher's thumb —Mary Hedin

19. Nose like a delicate scythe —Mary Hedin

20. Nose like a duck's bill —Ivan Turgenev

21. Nose [of a heavy drinker] like a fire ball —Erich Maria Remarque

22. Nose like a gherkin —Jonathan Valin

23. Nose like a jungle-bird's —William H. Gass

24. Nose like a knife blade —R. Wright Campbell

25. Nose like a letter opener —Jonathan Valin

26. Nose [Julius Caesar's] like an elephant's trunk —George Bernard Shaw

27. Nose like an engorged purple potato —Sarah Bird

28. Nose like a parrot's beak —Honoré de Balzac

29. Nose like a scimitar —William H. Hallhan

30. A nose like a spear in youth, in middle age becomes more like a shield, and in old age a little bit of a thing that looks like a button —William Saroyan

31. Nose like a sponge —Maxim Gorky

32. Nose like a turkey's ass —Robert Campbell

33. Nose like the beak of a bird —Anton Chekhov
     A more specific variant by Donald MacKenzie: nose like a falcon's beak.

34. Nose . . . long, like the nose in some old Italian pictures —Walter De La Mare

35. Nose . . . sharp as a pen —William Shakespeare

36. Nose small and laid back with about as much loft as a light iron —P. G. Wodehouse

37. A nose that seemed to have been bent by a tire iron —Jimmy Breslin and Dick Schaap

38. Nose was like a wooden peg —Truman Capote

39. Nose was very short, just like a baby's —Joyce Cary

40. Nostrils flaring like a colt's in winter —Charles Johnson

41. Nostrils flaring like a trotter —Joan Hess

42. Nostrils heaving like a stallion's —T. Coraghessan Boyle

43. Nostrils . . . shaped like the wings of a swallow —Oscar Wilde

44. Roman nose stuck up like the beak of a predatory bird —Carlos Baker

45. A straight nose, like a crusader modelled on a tomb —Antonia Fraser

46. An upturning nose like that of the Duchess in *Alice in Wonderland* — Frank Swinnerton

NOSTALGIA
See: MEMORY, SENTIMENT

NOURISHMENT
See: MEMORY, SENTIMENT

NOVELS
See: BOOKS

NUMBNESS
See: RESERVE

OATH
See: PROMISE

OBEDIENCE
>See: MEEKNESS

OBESITY
>See: FATNESS

OBJECTS, MISCELLANEOUS

1. Beach umbrellas, bright as lollipops . . . like flowers grown grossly out of proportion in a garden —Stanley Elkin

2. Blankets and pillows . . . like loving, hugging arms —Jean Stafford

3. (Bernard's) camera clicks like the gnashing of a lizard's tiny teeth —R. Wright Campbell

4. Canes like swords —John Dickson Carr

5. (Dangle) a long row of credit cards like the flags on the mast of a ship —George Garrett

6. Pennants steam from the twin copper peaks of the roof [of the golf course clubhouse] like a castle at tournament time —Walker Percy
   See Also: HOUSES

7. The phone goes off like a shrill alarm —Jay McInerney

8. The plow bucked and staggered like a cow with a broken back —Will Weaver

9. Refrigerator as big as a garden shed —François Camoin

10. (Sometimes I think) TVs are like dollhouses but with real, little people inside —Will Weaver
    In his novel, *Red Earth, White Earth,* Weaver expands on this image as follows: "Close your eyes sometime, and put your ear right on the side of the T.V. It's like you're listening through a wall to the neighbors."

11. Transistor radio—one of those ghetto blasters that look like assorted pie plates glued to a masonry block —Jonathan Valin

12. A [very small] watch . . . rode her bare wrist like a rubber band around a leg of lamb —Loren D. Estleman

13. Umbrellas, like faces, acquire a certain sympathy with the individual who carries them —J. W. Ferrier

OBLIVION
>See: BLINDNESS, MEMORY

OBSCURITY
>See: VAGUENESS

OBSERVATION
>   See: SCRUTINY

OBSOLESCENCE
>   See: TIMELINESS/UNTIMELINESS

OBSTINACY
>   See: PERSISTENCE

OBVIOUSNESS
>   See Also: CLARITY, VISIBILITY

1. (The magnificence of the Ambersons was) as conspicuous as a brass band at a funeral —Booth Tarkington

2. As conspicuous . . . as a butterfly among moths —George Feifer

3. As conspicuous as a second nose —Mike Sommer

4. As conspicuous as two fleas in a glass of milk, and about as welcome — Rosa Guy

5. Blatant as a slammed door —George Garrett

6. Her face was as easy to read as a crooked optometrist's chart —Loren D. Estleman

7. It was written all over him [that he was prone to trouble] in letters like headlines —William Humphrey

8. Magnificence, like the size of a fortune, is always comparative —Booth Tarkington

9. Noticeable as perfume —Wallace Stegner

10. (The film has a payoff that's as) obvious as a cream pie in the face — Gene Siskel, television review, October 13, 1986

11. Obvious as a gesture —Stephen Crane

12. Obvious as an elephant's footprint —Anon

13. (Those two guys can't move around . . . without being) obvious as turds on butcher blocks —Harold Adams

14. Obvious, like a poster forty feet high —J. B. Priestly

15. (Her thoughts and her emotions had all been) outspread . . . like jewels —Edith Wharton

16. Plain as a pig on a sofa —Flannery O'Connor

17. (The case was as) plain as a pikestaff —Arthur Train

18. Plain as graffiti on a brick wall —Elyse Sommer

19. Plain as the nose on a man's face —Rabelais
   >   A variation by Robert Burton: "As clear and as manifest as the nose on a man's face."

20. Plain as the paint on a whore's face —Stephen Longstreet

21. Stick out like a pregnant woman's stomach —Anon

22. (He was) subtle as a salvo —Jonathan Gash

23. There's no one so transparent as the person who thinks he's devilish deep —W. Somerset Maugham

24. Transparent as water in a goldfish bowl —Anon

25. Unobtrusive as the roar of a lion —Erich Maria Remarque

OCEAN/OCEANFRONTS
See Also: SEASCAPES

1. The Alvin [a ship] . . . moved through the dark sea like a robot fish —Richard Moran

2. The beach is bare as the blue bowl of the sky —John Hall Wheelock
See Also: BARENESS

3. The beach was splattered with people like bright rags —Nadine Gordimer

4. (Here in front of the summer hotel) the beach waits like an altar — Anne Sexton

5. A beach, white and slender like a young moon —Louis Bromfield

6. A breaker . . . roaring over the reef like a herd of crazed animals running before a forest fire —Clive Cussler

7. The gentle surf crested in the quick darkness with swirling phosphorous fringes of tiny animals like liquid silver —James Crumley

8. Long blue rollers coming in . . . each a neat and level line like an ironed crease —George Garrett

9. The ocean frowns like elephant hide —Karl Shapiro

10. The ocean like sleek gray stone —Robinson Jeffers

11. The ocean looked like a wide lavender ribbon stitched up against a pink-and-blue sky —Sue Grafton

12. The ocean rumbled like a train backing up —Anne Sexton

13. The ocean seemed to hover in the distance like a gray haze blending into the gray of the sky —Sue Grafton

14. The rough white crests of waves walk as if in moccasins —Diane Wakoski

15. The sea growled like a dog —John Mortimer

16. The sea has that oily sheen to it, like an empty swimming pool — William Boyd

17. The sea is like a human being . . . always moving, always something deep in itself stirring it . . . always wanting —Olive Shreiner

18. The sea [along the beach jetties] trembling among the stones like gelatin —Thomas McGuane

19. The sea whispered and hummed like a great shell held to the ear —Mary Stewart

20. The surf hisses like tambourines —Derek Walcott

21. The tide came in like ten thousand orgasms —Anne Sexton
    See Also: NOISE

22. The water ran over the sand, one wave covering another like the knitting of threads —Rachel Ingalls

23. Waves . . . black as cypresses, clear as the water of a wishing well —Denise Levertov
    See Also: BLACK, CLARITY

24. Waves crashing with the sound as of breaking biscuits —Vita Sackville-West

25. Waves . . . leaping like hounds up at the rocks —Josephine Jacobsen

26. Waves like small mountains rose with the shrieking wind into the black sky —James Stern

27. A wave like a vast castle —Arabian Nights

28. Waves, like blue animals stampeding —George Garrett

29. Waves like white feathers —George Garrett

30. The waves pulse . . . like hearts —Sylvia Plath

31. A wave suddenly raged out like a mountain cat —Stephen Crane

32. Waves that rose like mountains —D. R. MacDonald

33. The waves were skidding in like big buildings that swayed drunkenly and then toppled over on their faces and splattered all over the hard sand —Arthur Miller
    Miller, best known for his plays, has also written short stories . . . one of which, *I Don't Need You Any More,* is the source for this comparison.

34. When the surf is up its roaring fills you like a shell —Marge Piercy

35. The whole expanse of water . . . glistened like a sheet of stretched blue silk —Robie Macauley

OCCUPATIONS
See: DOCTORS, LAWYERS, PROFESSIONS

ODOR
See: SMELL

OLD
See: AGE

OPAQUENESS
    See: VAGUENESS

OPEN/SHUT

1. Closed [a newspaper] up like a surgeon closing an incision above an inoperable truth —Elizabeth Spencer

2. The door is closed like the shutter of a stalled-out camera —Thomas McGuane

3. It [a door] came [open] easy . . . like a ghost had blown it open from inside —Jay Parini

4. Locked up tighter than Dick's hatband —Richard Ford
        Ford's simile used to describe a home business that's not open, is a takeoff on the American colloquialism generally linked with stinginess.
    See Also: THRIFT

5. Open and shut as if cast from the shadow of a fallen angel's wing — Anon

6. (The elevator doors) opened suavely, like an expensive cream sliding smoothly on a flawless face —Judith Martin

7. (Let your mind) open like a clam when the waters slide back to feed it —Marge Piercy

8. Opens like a summer rose —George Garrett

9. (In love we) open wide as a house to a summer afternoon —Marge Piercy

10. (Wake up please) open yourself like a little umbrella —Donald Justice

11. (Our room was closed off and) sealed, like a grave inside a pyramid — Yehuda Amichai

12. [Emotions] sewn up tighter than a Victorian daughter's drawers — Roderic Jeffries

13. Shut down (the long Minnesota winter) like the white lid of a box —F. Scott Fitzgerald

14. Shut firmly in like a trunk locked up when the key is lost —Eibhlin Dhubh Ni Chonnaill

15. [Window-blinds] shut like an eye that sleeps —H. G. Wells

16. Shut tight as a drum —Anon

17. Shut up like a rabbit trap —Noel Streatfeild

18. (J. B's face) shut with a snap like a rat-trap —Gavin Lyall

19. (A world had opened and) was closing . . . like a curtain being silently drawn —John McGahern

OPENNESS
See: CANDOR

OPERA
See: MUSIC

OPINION
See Also: IDEAS

1.   As men grow older, their opinions, like their diseases, grow chronic — Josh Billings

   In Billings' original dialect: Az men gro older their opinuns
   like thier diseazes, grow kronick.

2.   Carried and opened this attitude like an umbrella —Delmore Schwartz

3.   Observations . . . are like children's cradles . . . sometimes empty, sometimes full of noisy imbecility, and often lulling to sleep —Sydney Smith

   Smith modestly applied this simile to his own observations.

4.   Of three minds, like a tree in which there are three blackbirds — Wallace Stevens

5.   Opinion gathered like a cloud and danced and then seemed to freeze — H. E. Bates

6.   Opinion is like a pendulum and obeys the same law. If it goes past the center of gravity on one side, it must go a like distance on the other — Arthur Schopenhauer

   Schopenhauer continued his simile like this: "And it is only
   after a certain time that it finds the true point at which it can
   remain at rest."

7.   Opinion polls: polls are like sleeping pills designed to lull the public into sleeping on election day. You might call them "sleeping polls" —Harry S. Truman

8.   Opinions, like showers, are generated in high places, but they invariably descend into lower ones, and ultimately flow down to the people, as rain unto the sea —Charles Caleb Colton

9.   Opinions, like the temperaments, fell rapidly into pre-established categories —Marguerite Yourcenar

10. Opinions richocheted through the gathering like hyperactive pheromones —Susan Ferraro, *New York Times*/Hers, Feburary 19, 1987

11. Opinions stout as oak —Phyllis McGinley

12. Passed opinions like gas —Rita Mae Brown

13. Played with our ideas like jacks, pressing our fingertips against their sharp points and round protuberances, testing how many we could scoop up at once —Lynne Sharon Schwartz

14. Public opinion in this country runs like a shower bath. We have no temperature between hot and cold —Heywood Broun
    Broun's public opinion simile is amongst the best known witticisms born at the famed Algonquin Round Table.

15. Sweeping judgments which are so common are meaningless . . . like men who salute a whole crowd of people in the mass —Michel De Montaigne

16. The man who never alters his opinion is like standing water, and breeds reptiles of the mind —William Blake

17. The pressure of public opinion is like the pressure of the atmosphere; you can't see it—but, all the same, it is sixteen pounds to the square inch —James R. Lowell, interview with Julian Hawthorne, *New York Times,* April 2, 1922

18. The public buys its opinions as it buys its meat, or takes its milk, on the principle that it is cheaper to do this than to keep a cow. So it is, but the milk is more likely to be watered —Samuel Butler

19. Tosses off insights like the spray from a speedboat —Anon comment about an author's work
    Like many such complimentary similes, this one was later featured in an ad for the work thus praised.

20. To venture an opinion is like moving a piece at chess: it may be taken, but it forms the beginning of a game that is won —Johann Wolfgang von Goethe

OPPORTUNENESS
See: TIMELINESS/UNTIMELINESS

OPPORTUNITY
See Also: FORTUNE/MISFORTUNE, IMPOSSIBILITY

1. Life was opening up . . . like an orchid in bloom —T. Coraghessan Boyle

2. Opportunities, like eggs, don't come but one at a time —Josh Billings
   In Billings' original dialect: "Oopportunitays . . . kum but one at a time."

3. Opportunity . . . it fell like a lucky coin at his feet —George Garrett

4. Possibilities rising like new mountains —Richard Ford

5. Sometimes opportunity knocks like a loud windburst; more often it arrives like a burglar and disappears before you realize it was there — Elyse Sommer

OPTIMISM
See: CHEERFULNESS

ORANGE
   See: COLORS

ORATORY
   See: SPEECHMAKING

ORDER/DISORDER
   See Also: CLEANLINESS

1. The big house ran like a Swiss clock — Rita Mae Brown

2. (The market is in absolute) chaos . . . like people running out on the field after a Mets game —Howard Farber, *New York Times,* October 5, 1986
      The chaos described by Farber refers to the x-rated video industry.

3. Chaotic as the floor of the stock exchange at the closing bell —William Diehl

4. (Chaos and) disorder is like a pebble in my shoe or loose hair under my shirt collar —Warren Miller

5. Disorder piles up like a (local California) mountain —Janet Flanner

6. Household ordered like a monastic establishment —Gustave Flaubert

7. Housekeeping, like good manners, is usually inconspicuous —Peg Bracken

8. Keeps house like a Dutch housekeeper —Anaïs Nin
      The person whose neatness is likened to that of a Dutch housekeeper is novelist Henry Miller.

9. (The whole lot was) littered like a schoolroom after a paper fight — Mary Hood

10. Neat and bare as a GI's footlocker —George Garrett
      See Also: EMPTINESS

11. (Withered little Filipino men, as) neat and brittle as whiskbrooms — Fletcher Knebel

12. Neat and dustless as a good museum —George Garrett

13. Neat and soft as a puff of smoke —George Garrett
      See Also: SOFTNESS

14. Neat as a coffin —Anon

15. Neat as a cupcake —Laurie Colwin

16. (The little one-story house was as . . .) neat as a fresh pinafore — Raymond Chandler

17. Neat as a hoop —Rosellen Brown

18. Neat as a morgue —Wilfrid Sheed

19. Neat as an employee prepared to be given a pink slip and told to clear out his desk within half an hour —Elyse Sommer

20. Neat as a pin —American colloquialism
    This has its roots in the English expression "Neat as a ninepence," and serves as continuing inspiration for catchy "Neat as" comparisons.

21. (House,) neat as a stamp collection —Marge Piercy

22. (He was) neat as a warm stone —Don Robertson

23. Neat as pie crust —Julia O'Faolain

24. (You are) rumpled like a sweater —Marge Piercy
    Another example of a simile used as an introducer, in this case a poem entitled *Nothing More Will Happen*.

25. Their rooms were neat as monk's cells —Babs H. Deal

26. (He said that) the lawn and house should be neat and pass inspection . . . like a soldier's bunk and beard —Mary Morris

27. Untidy . . . like a bird of paradise that had been out all night in the rain —Oscar Wilde

ORDINARINESS
See: COMMONPLACE

ORIGINALITY

1. As distinctive as a paper clip —Loren D. Estleman

2. As novel as teaching chickens to drive cars —Richard Ford
   See Also: ABSURDITY

3. Blowing platitudes like bubbles through air —William Styron

4. The human mind can no more produce an original thought than a tree can produce an original fruit —Jerome K. Jerome
   See Also: THOUGHT

5. Individualism is rather like innocence; there must be something unconscious about it —Louis Kronenberger

6. Original as a xeroxed letter —Elyse Sommer

7. A platitude like a bad postcard of the Parthenon —Karl Shapiro

8. Unique as the suits worn to a banker's convention —Elyse Sommer

9. Unlike the rest of the family as wine from water —J. B. Priestly

10. Unoriginal as any rabbit —Robert Frost

11. Wondrous as the butterfly's birth from the worm —Alderman

OUT OF PLACE
See: BELONGING

OUTBURST
   See: BURST

PAIN

   See Also: HEALTH

1.   Ached from head to foot, all zones of pain seemingly interdependent . . . like a Christmas tree whose lights wired in series, must all go out if even one bulb is defective —J. D. Salinger

2.   Ached like a bad tooth —Lawrence Durrell

3.   The air burning my lungs like a red-hot iron or cutting into them like a sharpened razor —Albert Camus

4.   Anguish poured out like blood from a gaping wound —Jonathan Kellerman
       In Kellerman's novel, *When the Bough Breaks,* the anguish is being poured out by a patient to the psychologist hero.

5.   Bruised like a half-back in a football game —Francis W. Crowninshield

6.   [Rash] burned like dots of acid —William Kennedy

7.   Cut like a whiplash —Ruth Chatterton

8.   (Walked out into) the dazzling sun that cut into his eyes like a knife — John Dos Passos

9.   A deadly vise of pain that clamped her head like a steel helmet — Arthur A. Cohen

10. Exposed it [pain] like a beggar used to making a show of his sores — Julia O'Faolain

11. Feel like somebody stuck thumbtacks all over my head —James Lee Burke

12. Felt as if I'd been crushed between two runaway wardrobes —J. B. Priestly
       This "similistic" comment is made by the hero of *Lost Empires* after being beaten up.

13. Felt as though his body were wrapped in layers of plaster cast — Kenzaburo Oë
       The plaster cast comparison was used by the author to describe a character who wakes up feeling stiff and achy all over.

14. Felt her head was going to break open like a coconut struck with a hammer —Marge Piercy

15. Felt pain like hot knives —Anon

16. A flash of pain darted through her, like the ripple of sheet lightning — Edith Wharton

17. For a second he remained in torture, as if some invisible flame were playing on him to reduce his bones and fuse him down —D.H. Lawrence

18. A gash . . . as wide as an open grave —Jimmy Sangster

19. Generalized racking misery that makes him feel as if his pores are bleeding and his brain is leaking out of his ears —T. Coraghessan Boyle

20. A head like a sore tooth —Anon

21. Her stomach reacted as though she'd eaten sulfuric pancakes —Rita Mae Brown

22. An hour of pain is as long as a day of pleasure —English proverb

23. The hurt had gone through her like the split in a carcass —Julia O'Faolain

24. The hurt I felt . . . was something like a thumb struck with a hammer —MacDonald Harris

25. Hurt . . . like a knot passing through an artery —Donald McCaig

26. (My brother's laugh is small, sharp, and) hurts like gravel in your shoe —Sharon Sheehe Stark

27. It [the pain of failure] was like a gnawing physical disability, an ugly mark she wanted to hide —H. E. Bates

28. A knot of pain was set like a malignant jewel in the core of his head — Truman Capote

29. (Your letter was) like a bullet straight into my heart —Sholom Aleichem

30. My back ached as if someone were holding a welding torch against my spine, turning the flame on and off at will —W. P. Kinsella

31. My breast was contracted by a pain like screws clamped on my heart — Joyce Cary

32. My insides burned like pipes in a boiler —Governeur Morris

33. My intestines felt as if they were playing host to a Bears-Raiders game —Penny Ward Moser, *Discover,* February, 1987

34. My stomach feels as if I have swallowed razor blades —W. P. Kinsella

35. My stomach feels like the crop of a hen —Katherine Mansfield

36. My whole body glows with pain as if I were being electrocuted —Iris Murdoch

37. Nausea coiled like a snake in her stomach —A. E. Maxwell

38. Pain and pleasure, like light and darkness, succeed each other — Laurence Sterne
    See Also: PLEASURE

39. The pain between his eyes seemed to be whirling about like a pinwheel —R. Wright Campbell

40. Pain comes billowing on like a full cloud of thunder —Dante Gabriel Rossetti

41. Painful . . . like cutting the heart out of her body —Phyllis Bottome

The pain described in Bottome's short story, *The Battle Field,* is that of never seeing someone again.

42. The pain goes ringing through me like alarms —Delmore Schwartz

43. Pain . . . hard as blows —John Berryman

44. The pain in his chest was like a tight breastplate —Graham Swift

45. Pain is immune to empathy . . . like love —Barbara Lazear Ascher, *New York Times*/Hers, October 16, 1986

46. Pain is like a love affair. When it's over, it's over —Elyse Sommer

47. Pain lifted like a fog that gives way to bright sunlight —Maurice Edelman

48. Pain . . . like a metal bar —Graham Swift

49. Pain (lingering) . . . like a stone pit lodged in the stomach —Anon

50. Pain rising as periodically as high water —William H. Gass

51. (The sympathy that it arouses is as) painful as charity —Mihail Lermontov

52. Pains are flinging her about like an old rag, a filthy torn rag doll —Vicki Baum

53. The pain seemed to rock inside him like a weight that would overturn him —Graham Swift

54. Pains . . . like streams of pulsating fire heating him to an intolerable temperature —Ambrose Bierce

55. Pain . . . slopped through his head like water into a sand-castle —Kingsley Amis
    See Also: TURNING AND TWISTING

56. Pains that shrieked like alarm bells —Jane Rogers

57. Pain tightens like a strip of hot metal across Martin's chest —Robert Silverberg

58. Pain . . . twisting like currents in a river —Martin Amis

59. Pain whistled through my body like splintered glass —Ross Macdonald

60. Pain would advance and recede like waves on a beach —Nathaniel Benchley
    See Also: ADVANCING

61. People in pain are like the wandering minstrels of the Renaissance. Any occupied space becomes their court. If the story's told often enough, perhaps the demons will become manifest. Made visible and mastered through words —Barbara Lazear Ascher, *New York Times*/Hers, October 16, 1986

62. A persistent jabbing in her chest that tapped back and forth like an admonishing finger —Molly Giles

63. Pierce . . . like misplaced trust —John Drury

64. (Though we love pleasure, we) play with pain like a tongue toying with a bad tooth —George Garrett

65. The pounding in his head was like ten thousand hammers —Niven Busch

66. Press like a blunt thumb —Lawrence Durrell

67. Prolonged pain is like a fire in the house, it causes you to flee and wander homeless —Barbara Lazear Ascher, *New York Times*/Hers, October 16, 1986

68. Shudder at the thrust of pain like a virgin at the thrust of love —George Garrett
See Also: TREMBLING

69. Spine ached as if it had been twisted like a cat's tail —Bernard Malamud

70. Sting you like scorn —Thomas Hardy

71. (Irony . . .) stung like squirts from a leaky hose —Geoffrey Wolff

72. Suffering is cheap as grass and free as the rain that falls on saint and sinner alike —George Garrett

73. A sweet bewildering pain, like flowers in the wind and rain —Thomas Ashe

74. [A broken ankle] swelled like a soccer ball —Clive Cussler

75. Swollen face throbbing as if it has been pumped up with a bellows —Elena Poniatowska

76. Throat . . . like sandpaper soaked in salt —H. E. Bates

77. Throat . . . like a thicket of nettles —Arthur Train

78. [The lack of respect] tormented him like a raging thirst —Marge Piercy

79. Woke up feeling as if someone had tied sandbags to my hair —Jonathan Valin

80. Writhed like a trampled snake —Oscar Wilde

81. (Sat on a bench) writhing like a woman in labor —Isaac Babel

82. Writhing . . . like the poor shell-fish set to boil alive —John Greenleaf Whittier

PAINTINGS
See: ART AND LITERATURE

PALLOR
See Also: FACIAL COLOR, GRAY, RED, WHITE

1. Pale as cardboard —Paige Mitchell

2. Pale as white wine —Sir Kenelm Digby

3. Blanch like conscious guilt personified —Charlotte Brontë

4. Bleached like the skeleton of a stranded walrus —Herman Melville

5. A face like paper —J. B. Priestly

6. Face like parchment —G. K. Chesterton

7. (His long, pendulous) face looked as if it had been dusted with white talc —Aharon Megged

8. Face . . . pale as a Chinese mandarin's —Nadine Gordimer

9. Face . . . pale as a dead man's —Ivan Turgenev

10. Face . . . pale as a fish —T. Coraghessan Boyle

11. Face, pallid and simmering like a milk pudding over a slow flame — Julia O'Faolain

12. His waxy pallor was touched along the underside of his jaw with acne, like two brush burns —John Updike

13. Look [pale] like Yom Kippur before sunset —Isaac Bashevis Singer

14. Pale as a silkfish —Diane Ackerman

15. Pale and dirty as a pulled root —George Garrett

16. Pale as a birch —Louise Erdrich

17. (A scar) pale as a fishgut —Davis Grubb

18. Pale as a ghost with pernicious anemia —Anon
    A twist on the cliche, "Pale as a ghost."

19. Pale as a hyacinth grown in a cellar —Edith Wharton

20. (Looking as) pale as a magnolia blossom —Sarah Bird

21. Pale as a primrose —William Shakespeare

22. Pale [after donating a lot of blood] as a princess after a date with Dracula —Kenzaburo Oë

23. Pale as a prisoner —Carlos Baker

24. (Always cool and) pale as a root —Jayne Anne Phillips

25. Pale as a shell —James Wright

26. Pale as a smooth-sculptured stone —John Keats

27. Pale as a white rose —Nathaniel Hawthorne

28. Pale as bleached clay —Z. Vance Wilson

29. Pale as candles —Reynolds Price
    A more specific version by McKinlay Kantor is "Pale as a tallow candle."

30. Pale as china —Sylvia Plath

31. (The desert looks) pale as death —Henry Chettle

500

According to Stevenson's *Book of Proverbs, Maxims, and Famous Phrases,* Chettle was the first to use the simile in his seventeenth century play, *Hoffman.* The earliest linkage to the complexion is variously attributed to Walter Scott's *Guy Mannering,* Thomas Hardy's *The Mayor of Casterbridge* and Henry James' *The Madonna of the Future.*

32. Pale as distemper —Miles Gibson

33. Pale as his shirt —William Shakespeare

34. Pale as ivory —Ouida

35. Pale as junket —Christina Stead

36. Pale as milk —William Shakespeare
    The similes from masters like the Bard are often used "as is" or with minor additions such as "Pale as cold milk" seen in Davis Grubb's novel, *The Golden Sickle.*

37. (Face) pale as sand —Stevie Smith

38. Pale as straw —William Evans

39. Pale as the bottom of a plate —Joseph Sheridan Le Fanu

40. Pale . . . as the mist that hangs over the river —Oscar Wilde

41. Pale as the soap in the dish —Jean Thompson

42. Pale as the tenant of a tomb —Edgar Allen Poe

43. Pale as waxworks —Maxine Kumin

44. Paler than ashes —Algernon Charles Swinburne

45. Paler than grass in summer —Algernon Charles Swinburne

46. (Thighs) pale and soft as snow —Lyn Lifshin
    See Also: SOFTNESS

47. So white she was almost transparent —Jonathan Gash

48. The transparent pallor of her skin was luminous like a sea-shell in green shadow of the pine-trees —Elinor Wylie

49. Turned white as a tablecloth —Rudyard Kipling

50. Wan as the Polar snows —Stephen Vincent Benét

PARENTAL LOVE
See: PARENTHOOD

PARENTHOOD

1. A childless person is like dead —Talmud

2. The honor due to parents is like the honor due to God —*The Holy Bible/Exodus*

3. Children, grown up, now, and moved away . . . though they had once occupied her like a house, possessing her to the fingertips —Helen Hudson

4. The ideal mother, like the ideal marriage, is a fiction —Milton R. Sapirstein

5. (Maybe I've got this secret kid. Chances are I have, 'cause) I probably got a sperm count like the national deficit —Jane Wagner

6. Love them [daughters] as sheep are loved by the shepherd —Phyllis McGinley

7. Marriage without children . . . like a garden without fruit —Phyllis Bottome
    Compare this with the German proverb below, beginning with Wedlock.
    See Also: INCOMPLETENESS

8. Mother's virtues . . . like a graft of a late fruit on an early apple or pear tree, do not ripen in her children until very late in the season — Oliver Wendell Holmes Sr.

9. A mother-in-law and a daughter-in-law in one house are like two cats in a bag —Yiddish proverb

10. A mother-in-law is like the dry rot; far easier to get into a house than to get out again —*Punch*

11. Not to bear children . . . was like a hen that did not lay eggs or a cow that was sterile or a tree that never came into blossom. —H. E. Bates

12. Raising a child is like reading a very long mystery story; you have to wait for a generation to see how it turns out —Anon

13. Realised [after giving birth] the responsibility of launching the little creature labelled by name not of its own choosing, like launching a battleship, only instead of turrets and decks and guns she had to do with the miraculous tissue of flesh and brain —Vita Sackville-West

14. Sharper than a serpent's tooth it is to have a thankless child —William Shakespeare
    This is King Lear's famous lament.
    See Also: PAIN, SHARPNESS

15. The umbilical cord stretches like a nine-hundred-and-some-mile leash —Peter De Vries

16. Wedlock without children [is like] a world without sun —German proverb

17. A woman . . . her heart is like an empty nest, if she has not a child — Henry Van Dyke

PARTING
See: BEGINNINGS/ENDINGS

PASSION

    See Also: DESIRE, LOVE, SEX

1. As passionate as shredded wheat —Lawrence Gilman

2. The echoes of passion in the emptiness of a lonely heart is like the murmurings of wind and water in the silence of the wilderness —Francois Rene de Chateaubriand

3. Genuine passion is like a mountain stream; it admits of no impediment; it cannot go backward; it must go forward —Christian Nestell Bovee

4. Hot as a forty-balled tomcat —Rita Mae Brown

5. Instant passion is like instant coffee; it's cheap and it's quick and it makes you wish you had a percolator —Carla Lane, dialogue for heroine of English television sit-com "Solo," broadcast April 7, 1987

6. Our passions are in truth, like the phoenix. The old one burns away, the new one rises out of its ashes at once —Johann Wolfgang von Goethe

7. Our passions are like convulsion fits, which, though they make us stronger for the time, leave us the weaker ever after —Jonathan Swift

8. Our world passions are like so many lawyers wrangling and brawling at a bar —Owen Feltham
       The comparison continues as follows: "Discretion is the lord-keeper of man that sits as judge, and moderation their contestations."

9. The passionate are like men standing on their heads; they see all things the wrong way —Plato

10. Passionate men, like fleet hounds, are apt to over-run the scent —H. G. Bohn's *Handbook of Proverbs*

11. Passion burned through her like a sunrise —Ellen Glasgow

12. Passion is like crime; it does not thrive on the established order —Thomas Mann

13. Passion is like genius: a miracle —Romain Rolland

14. Passionless as a clam —Gertrude Atherton

15. Passion . . . like a fire on the prairie that devours everything around it —W. Somerset Maugham

16. Passion . . . like other violent excitements . . . throws up not only what is best, but what is worst and smallest, in men's characters —Robert Louis Stevenson

17. Passions and desires, like the two twists of a rope, mutually mix one with the other, and twine inextricably round the heart —Richard E. Burton

18. Passions are like fire and water, good servants but bad masters —Alexander Pope

19. Passions are like fire, useful in a thousand ways and dangerous only in one, through their excess —Francois duc de La Rochefoucauld

20. Passions are like the trout in a pond: one devours the others until only one fat old trout is left —Otto von Bismarck

21. A passion that had moved into his body, like a stranger —Arthur Miller

22. Passion . . . went over him like an ocean wave —Jean Stafford
     At another point in her novel, *The Mountain Lion,* Stafford used the ocean waves comparison to describe the powerful smell of flowers.

PAST, THE
See Also: HISTORY, MEMORY

1. Events . . . had receded so swiftly into the near-forgotten past, like a movie seen years before and dimly remembered —Harvey Swados

2. The events [of the past] were astir in me, like the loosening phlegm in an attack of bronchitis, waiting to come up —L. P. Hartley

3. Felt himself sliding . . . back into a bumpy past where old humiliations still waited to confront him like hills grown taller with the dust of years —Helen Hudson

4. Going back is like lifting elephants with your teeth —Paul West

5. He [Sherwood Anderson] carried his childhood like a hurt warm bird held to his middle-aged breast —Herbert Gold

6. Her past years washed away like so many ridges of sand at high tide — Peter Meinke

7. Inheritance, like grace, is something you deserve —Hollis Summers
     The inheritance being compared to grace is family achievement.

8. It was like those years were just a ghost town she'd walked through and then decided to forget —Lee Smith

9. Kept coming back like a song —J. W. Rider

10. Like a ball of wool that kittens have got at . . . all the disposed-of process of my past unravelled on the floor —Louis MacNeice

11. The man who has not anything to boast of but his illustrious ancestors is like a potato . . . the only good belonging to him is under ground — Sir Thomas Overbury

12. Our past . . . clings to us like strange mystical lint —W. P. Kinsella

13. The past . . . always affected her eyes like salt water. It filled her head as if she had stayed underwater too long —Susan Fromberg Schaeffer

14. The past, as steep as stone, wider than water, like all land and ocean stretches —Archibald MacLeish

15. Past and future lie joined like a lunatic serpent —Robert Silverberg
16. The past . . . held him like a pain —Wallace Stegner
17. The past is a bucket of ashes —Carl Sandburg
18. The past is like a funeral gone by —Edmond Gosse
19. The past lies like an Alp upon the mind —Delmore Schwartz
20. Past . . . like a burnt book —Lynne Sharon Schwartz
21. The past, like an inspired rhapsodist, fills the theatre of everlasting generations with her harmony —Percy Bysshe Shelley
22. The past was drumming, like a train coming nearer and nearer, in her head —V. S. Pritchett
23. A record as long as your arm —George Garrett
    The simile is the title of a short story.
24. Rolled up his past like a carpet —Anon
25. The sense of accummulated riches of time and tradition pressed past him like a crowd moving in rank after rank, through unending centuries —G. K. Chesterton
26. Sometimes I want to go back to everything I had, as in a museum — Yehuda Amichai
27. She wears her past like other women wear perfume —Anon ambassador about Nora Astorga of Nicaragua, *New York Times Magazine,* September 28, 1986
    True to form, the simile was pulled out of the article and used as the caption for the main illustration.
28. Sloughed off my past . . . like a skin that shuns the light of day — Natascha Wodin
29. The thoughts of my past life rise like the ghosts of an unquiet dream — Percy Bysshe Shelley
30. Treated his past gingerly as if it were unfriendly to him —Jean Garrigue
31. Where she has been, she drags behind her, heavy and slurred as the speech of the deaf —Lisa Ress
32. Worrying about the past is like trying to make birth control pills retroactive —Joey Adams
    See Also: USELESSNESS

PATIENCE

1. Had the patience of a man who worked a step at a time through month-long laboratory experiments —Elizabeth Spencer
2. Mute and patient, like an old sheep waiting to be let out —Flannery O'Connor
   See Also: SILENCE

3.   Patience and diligence, like faith, remove mountains —William Penn

4.   Patience is passion tamed —Lyman Abbott

5.   Patience is so like fortitude that she seems either her sister or her daughter —Aristotle

6.   The patience of someone who finds a wounded animal in the woods and stays with it —Sharon Olds

7.   Patient as a turtle —Mary Hedin

8.   (I'll be as) patient as a gentle stream —William Shakespeare

9.   Patient as the matador —George Garrett

10.   Patient, like an old man who has just dug his grave —Sharon Olds

11.   Patiently as the spider weaves the broken web —Edward Bulwer-Lytton

12.   Patiently, like a weaver at his loom —Beryl Markham

13.   Stood as patiently as a horse being groomed —John D. MacDonald

14.   Tolerance . . . like that of a grandparent for unpredictable and troublesome children —William Faulkner

15.   Waiting patiently, in silence, as a cat does at a mousehole —Frank Swinnerton

PATRIOTISM
See: BELIEFS

PAUCHINESS
See: BODY, FATNESS, STOMACH

PAUSE
See Also: CAUTION

1.   Cease like a dropped watch —Henry James

2.   Everybody froze with expectation like an orchestra when the conductor raises his baton —George Garrett

3.   Faltered, chewing on his words sourly and fatuously, like an old cow — William Styron

4.   (We) froze [at seeing an unknown, staring man] as rabbits do —Rumer Godden

5.   Halted, suddenly trembling, like a person armed to defend himself against wild animals, but on meeting one face to face is immediately turned to stone —Jean Stafford
See Also: TREMBLING

6.   Hesitated like a cat testing an opening with its whiskers —William McIlvanney

7. A pause, barely noticeable, like a sight between one word and another —Kent Nelson

8. Shrieked to a trembling stop like a dog on a yanked leash —George Garrett

9. (Sky and earth did one last slow turn and) wobbled to a halt like a coin coming to rest on a bartop —Loren D. Estleman

10. Slowed down gradually, like a merry-go-round after a ride —Eudora Welty

11. Stalled like a whale —John Malcolm Brinnin

12. Stopped short, like a radio cut off on a crescendo —Frank Tuohy

13. Stopped speaking for a moment, like a man walking who comes to a brink —John Fowles

14. Stopped there cold, like a man raking piles of dead leaves in his yard who has turned up a severed hand —W. D. Snodgrass

15. Stops [suddenly] as though shot in the back —Erich Maria Remarque

16. Stumbled to a halt like sheep in a chute —Will Weaver

17. Suddenly there was a lull in my mind, like the détente after a retreating thunderstorm —L. P. Hartley

18. Talk died . . . as if the voices in the room were on tape and someone had pulled the plug —Will Weaver
    See Also: SPEAKING, SILENCE

PEACEFULNESS
See Also: CALMNESS

1. (There was) an ease of mind that was like being alone in a boat at sea —Wallace Stevens
    This is the first line of *Prologues to What is Possible,* a poem studded with additional similes.

2. Had a certain peace, like a stone that wouldn't roll any more —Paul Horgan

3. Inner serenity is a lot like grace under pressure except that it's all going on inside where people might not notice and give you credit —Judith Viorst

4. Like a stone thrown into the smooth water of a spring, I had disturbed their peace —Mihail Lermontov

5. Like the course of the heavenly bodies, harmony in national life is a resultant of the struggle between contending forces —Justice Louis D. Brandeis
    See Also: AGREEMENT/DISAGREEMENT

6. A peace deep as death —Daniela Gioseffi

7. Peaceful as a breast —Kenneth Patchen

507

8. Peaceful as a church —Raymond Chandler

9. Peaceful as a leaf with its superhuman silence —Daniela Gioseffi

10. Peaceful as Socrates —Anon

11. Peaceful . . . like a child asleep —Phyllis Roberts

12. Peaceful, like being in a time machine —Lee Smith

13. Peaceful like New Year's —Carlos Baker

14. Peaceful like warm Summer nights —Amy Lowell

15. Peace, like a mask, hides everything —Edwin Arlington Robinson

16. Peace, like charity, begins at home —Franklin D. Roosevelt
    See Also: COMPLAINTS, PATRIOTISM, REFORMS, SENSE

17. Peace, like war, can succeed only where there is a will to enforce it, and where there is available power to enforce it —Franklin D. Roosevelt, October 21, 1944 speech to Foreign Policy Association

18. Peacemaking is hard . . . hard almost as war —Daniel Berrigan
    The simile comprises the title and first line of a poem.
    See Also: DIFFICULTY

19. Peace was over her . . . like a mantle —Madeleine L'Engle

20. Peace will, like a broken limb united, grow stronger for the breaking — William Shakespeare

21. [A vacation] quiet and pleasant and womblike as a slow bath in a tub of warm water —Harvey Swados

22. Restful as a Rembrandt background —George Ade

23. Rest like lizards on rocks —Etheridge Knight

24. (Maybe it will emerge,) serene and smiling, like Daniel from the lion's den —Floyd K. Haskell, on tax reform, *New York Times*/Op-Ed, January 17, 1986

25. Serene as a snowman's smile —Julie Hayden

26. Serene as jade buddhas —Marge Piercy

27. Soothing . . . as waves along a shore —John Gardner

28. Still and quiet, like a good conscience —Frank Swinnerton

29. Tranquility pushed their anxieties away, like a man finding a place for himself on a crowded bench —W. Somerset Maugham

30. Tranquilizing murmur [of voice] like the music of a dream —Elinor Wylie

31. Tranquilly like the rise and fall of sand dunes —Yukio Mishima

PECULIARITY
    See: STRANGENESS

PENETRATION
See: PERVASIVENESS

PENNANTS
See: OBJECTS, MISCELLANEOUS

PENSIVENESS
See: THOUGHT

PEOPLE,INTERACTION
See Also: CROWDS, FRIENDSHIP, MEN AND WOMEN, RELATIONSHIPS

1. All her life she had looked for someone who would . . . settle her in the proper place like a cushion on a couch —Helen Hudson

2. [Different types of people] all mixed up like vegetables in soup —Flannery O'Connor

3. All the hurtful ugly things that happened between us got somehow wrapped around the sweetness like a hard rind around a delicate rare fruit. Like a flower garden completely surrounded with tangles of barbed wire —Harryette Mullen

4. (Harris) always managed to make him feel . . . like the character in the commercial who uses the wrong kind of deodorant soap —Andrew Kaplan

5. Avoid them like piranhas —Richard Ford
   See Also: ELUSIVENESS

6. Bitching patiently at each other like a couple married much too long —James Crumley
   The people doing the bitching in Crumley's novel, *The Wrong Case,* are two farmers in a bar.

7. Dealing with Valentine was like dealing with a king —Saul Bellow

8. Distance between them . . . like the Persian Gulf —Robert Anderson

9. Faced each other like scruffy bookends —Jonathan Gash

10. Groups gathered a moment like flies —Bin Ramke

11. Guided him by one elbow [to a seat] like a tugboat turning a tanker —Peter Benchley

12. Hoisted her up like a parcel —Henri-Pierre Roche

13. It was as if he could read my mind like an old tale he had learned by heart —George Garrett

14. I want to lean into her [a daughter into her mother] the way wheat leans into wind —Louise Erdrich

15. Lay side by side, like some old bronze Crusader and his lady on a sarcophagus in the crypt of some ancient church —MacDonald Harris

16. (Take her by the lily white hand and) lead her like a pigeon —Anon American dance ballad, "Weevily Heart."
    The ballad dates to the late eighteenth/early nineteenth century.

17. Leaned on [another person] . . . like a wounded man —George Garrett

18. Like the sun, his presence shone on her —Marge Piercy

19. Live together like brothers and do business like strangers —Arab proverb

20. Loneliness sifted between us, like falling snow —Judith Rascoe
    See Also: ALONENESS

21. Our heart-strings were, like warp and woof in some firm fabric, woven in and out —Edna St. Vincent Millay

22. People, like sheep, tend to follow a leader—occasionally in the right direction —Alexander Chase

23. We seemed strangers [a group of three people sitting in room] waiting in a station to take a train to another city —Henry Van Dyke

24. People sat huddled together [on street benches] like dark grapes clustered on a stalk —W. Somerset Maugham

25. Read him like a label on a beer can —William H. Hallhan

26. [Two men who don't like each other] recoiling from one another like reversed magnets —Wyatt Blassingame

27. Responded to each other nervously, like a concord of music —Lawrence Durrell

28. Sat . . . like a pair of carefully-folded kid-gloves, bound up in each other —Charles Dickens

29. She could feel the distance between them like a patch of fog —Lynne Sharon Schwartz

30. She reads my silence like a page —Robert Campbell

31. Sitting like strangers thrown together by accident —Ross Macdonald

32. Something in her face spilled over me like light through a swinging door —Sue Grafton

33. Students, their faces like stone walls around him [a college professor] —Helen Hudson

34. [Many different kinds of people] swarmed around him like startled fish —Derek Lambert

35. Tangled together like badly cast fish lines —Katherine Anne Porter

36. They [a man and woman with child between them] lay like two slices of wheat bread with a peanut-butter center —Will Weaver

37. They needed each other's assistance, like a company, who, crossing a mountain stream, are compelled to cling close together, lest the current should be too powerful for any who are not thus supported —Sir Walter Scott

38. They were . . . like two people holding on to the opposite ends of a string, each anxious to let go, or at least soon, without offending the other, yet each reluctant to drop the curling, lapsing bond between them —Hortense Calisher

39. Took me about like a roast [to make introductions] —Mark Helprin
     This spotlights the importance of using a simile within an appropriate context. The character being taken about "like a roast" in Helprin's story, *Tamar,* is the last arrival at a dinner party. If someone were being introduced in a business setting, being passed around "Like a special report or a memo" might better suit the situation.

40. Touched him on the breast as though his finger were the fine point of a small sword —Charles Dickens

41. Treated him like crows treat a scarecrow: they ignored him and avoided him —William H. Hallhan
     See Also: REJECTION

42. Wanted me to share her pain like an orgasm, like lovers in poems who slit their wrists together —Max Apple

43. Watching each other like two cats; and then, as cats do, turn away again, indifferently, as if whatever was at stake between them had somehow faded out —L. P. Hartley

44. (The Heindricks) were making me feel like a specimen in a jar — Jonathan Gash
     See Also: DISCOMFORT

45. We sat half-turned toward one another like the arms of a parenthesis — Cornell Woolrich

46. You play my heart like a concertina —Harvey Fierstein

PERCEPTIVENESS
See: ALERTNESS, SENSITIVENESS

PERMANENCE
See Also: CONTINUITY

1. As assured of longevity as the statues on Easter Island —John W. Aldridge, *New York Times Book Review,* October 26, 1986.
    The work to which Aldridge ascribes the longevity of the Easter Island statues is Joseph Heller's *Catch-22.*

2. (She was) as immutable as the hills. But not quite so green —Rudyard Kipling

3. Bonds . . . as immutable as a tribal code —Anon
4. Changeless as heaven —John Greenleaf Whittier
5. Changeless as truth —John Keats
6. Constant as the Northern Star —William Shakespeare
7. Enduring as a family feud —Anon
8. (A novelistic structure as harsh and) enduring as any tabby wall —John D. MacDonald
9. Enduring as mother love —Anon
10. Enduring as the Washington Monument —Anon
11. Enduring as the Constitution —Anon
12. Fixed as a habit or some darling sin —John Oldham
13. Fixed as a leopard's spots —Anon
14. Fixed as a tiger's stripes —Anon
15. Fixed as the cycle of life —Anon
16. Fixed as the days in the week —Anon
17. Fixed as the sun —Erasmus
18. (In two years he) had altered as little as the landscape —Ellen Glasgow
19. (My love of art seemed as) as indelible as ink —Jill Ciment
20. Invariable as a formula —Ellen Glasgow
21. Irrevocable as death —Charlotte Brontë
22. Lasts like iron —Oliver Wendell Holmes, Sr.
23. Like love we seldom keep —W. H. Auden
24. Of no more true substance than a scarecrow in a field —George Garrett
25. (The fine carnation of their skin is) perennial as sunlight —Herman Melville
26. Permanent as the bathroom fixture —Nora Johnson
        In Johnson's novel, *The World of Henry Orient,* the comparative frame of reference is a woman whom the narrator of the novel likes and trusts.
27. Settled . . . like an oil stain —Charles Johnson
28. Unalterable as the little paper flowers permanently visible inside the lumpy glass paperweights —Ezra Pound
29. Unchanging as the nation's flag —George Jean Nathan
30. (Ideas, though painfully acquired,) stick like nails in the best oak —Joyce Cary
31. (My bounded brain was as) unalterable as a ball —Jean Stafford
32. Binding as a wedding ring used to be —Elyse Sommer
33. Eternal as the sky —John Greenleaf Whittier

34. Eternity . . . like a great ring of pure and endless light —Henry Vaughan
    The simile is introduced with "I saw eternity the other night."

35. [Eyes] imperishable as diamonds —Ellen du Pois Taylor

36. (Psychology) will live long as the pyramids —Delmore Schwartz

PERPLEXITY
See: BEWILDERMENT

PERSISTENCE
See Also: CLINGING, PURPOSEFULNESS

1. As headstrong as an allegory on the banks of the Nile —Richard Brinsley Sheridan

2. (Sorrow) as nagging as envy —Karl Shapiro

3. (The name was becoming) a teasing obsession, like a tune —Wilfrid Sheed

4. Dogged as a turtle crossing a road —Marge Piercy

5. Hold on with a bulldog grip —Abraham Lincoln
   From a telegram to General Grant, August 1864.

6. I'm like a terrier pup. Somebody tells me to do something and it gets done —Sue Grafton

7. Insistent as a baby's cry at feeding time —Anon

8. Insistent as remorse —Victor Hugo

9. Jabs like a prizefighter (at their feelings about each other) —Linda Barret Osborne, reviewing a novel in *New York Times,* August 31, 1986

10. Obstinate as a Hindu woman contemplating suttee —Frank Swinnerton

11. Obstinate as death —John Dryden

12. Persistent annoyance, like the rough place on a tooth —David R. Slavitt

13. Persistent as a bulldog —Oliver Wendell Holmes, Sr.

14. Persistent as a fly on a hound's nose —Harold Adams

15. Persistent as a nagging backache —Anon

16. (Ugly and) persistent as pain —Carlos Baker

17. Persist . . . like a terrier with a rat . . . she wouldn't let go, come hell or high water —James Reeve

18. Prevail like the false pig in Aesop —G. K. Chesterton

19. Relentless as decay —Joseph Wambaugh

20. Relentless as a nagging tongue —Anon

21. Relentless as a windshield wiper —Anon

22.   Skin . . . as thick as his wallet —Jane Gross, *New York Times,* August 22, 1986
      The man with the thick skin and wallet is Abraham Hirshfeld, who ran a persistent campaign for the New York State governorship despite many insults and putdowns.

23.   Stick to it, like salmon swimming upstream —Anon

24.   Stubborn and hardy as a rubber mat —Marge Piercy

25.   (Death bugs me) as stubborn as insomnia —Anne Sexton

26.   Tenacious as remorse —Vincente Blasco-Ibâñez

27.   The thought . . . unable to move [out of his head] as a jellyfish fixed on the sand —Norman Mailer

28.   Tug at . . . like a robin with a worm —T. Coraghessan Boyle

29.   You're like a train; nothing will turn you when you get started —Joyce Cary

PERSONAL TRAITS
See Also: DULLNESS

1.   Adventurous . . . like a tropical fish. His native habitat was hot water —Anon friend about former C.I.A. director William J. Casey, *New York Times,* July 19, 1987
      The original quote began with "Bill was," implying the first word substituted here to provide a more general reference point.

2.   Dignified, like a clean-shaven Zeus: one who used plenty of after-shave —Kingsley Amis

3.   Good temper, like a sunny day, sheds a brightness over everything — Washington Irving

4.   Hears like a rabbit and strikes like an asp —William Diehl

5.   (She would be) intent and bold and willful, like a gambler —Harold Brodkey
      The author used this simile to describe a woman applying makeup.

6.   A man or woman without personality is like a tree without leaves, or a house without pictures on the wall —Anon
      See Also: INCOMPLETENESS

7.   Obstinacy and contradiction are like a paper kite; they are only kept up so long as you pull against them —John Casper

8.   Quiet and smiley and polite, like a traveling salesman —George Garrett

9.   She is like a cat, she will play with her own tail —John Ray's *Proverbs*

10.   Shines like a lighthouse over a dull sea of social tedium —Rita Mae Brown

11. Temperament . . . is permanent, like the color of a man's eyes and the shape of his ears —Mark Twain

12. A temper as explosive as a gun —Rex Beach
This is modernized from the original which read "As explosive as gun cotton."

13. A temper like a handsaw —Anon

PERSONALITY PROFILES

1. An ambitious girl . . . that looks as though she should be kneeling before a crackling fire, stroking a pussy cat, but behind it all has nerves of iron, a will of iron, and a rigid mind cast only for the search for success —Harvey Swados

2. As omnipotent and as full of faults as Jove —Wallace Stegner

3. As with an iceberg, only the craggy tip [of his personality] was revealed to the stranger's casual eye while the submerged seven eighths carried along like an unseen, irresistible force and solidity —Irvin S. Cobb

4. Barely seemed human at all: more like some Chinese figurine all ivory and silk, that should suddenly have come to life, begun to dance, to quote the poets, and to laugh at everything in this ridiculous real world —George Santayana

5. Elegant and remote . . . like a statue carved in melancholy thought — Sylvia Berkman
See Also: REMOTENESS

6. A fascinating but sometimes uneasy presence . . . as if he goes around with a black cloud over his head —Daniel Philips about fellow violinist Gidoa Kremer, *New York Times,* May 10, 1987

7. Handsome, proud, and ingrown, "like a toe-nail" —James Baldwin
The simile is an anonymous descriptions of Baldwin's father quoted in his essay, *Notes of a Native Son.*

8. He [Oliver Wendell Holmes] is a powerful battery, formed like a planting machine to gouge a deep self-beneficial groove through life — William James, letter to his brother Henry, July 5, 1876

9. He [Col. Gadhafi of Libya] is like a Bedouin in a sandstorm . . . He [the Bedouin] bends over until it passes and then stands up strong as ever —Abdel Halim Abu Ghazala, defense minister of Egypt, *Wall Street Journal,* September 9, 1986

10. He [John McEnroe] is still more like a New York cab driver, with an opinion about everything —Peter Alfano, *New York Times*/Sports of the Times, August 6, 1986
The simile is part of Alfano's speculation about the likelihood that McEnroe's will become a "laid-back Californian."

11. He [waiter upon being tipped and smiled at] looked as if he had shaken hands with God —Raymond Chandler

12. He looked as the dead do in dreams —Mavis Gallant

13. He looked businesslike, efficient, crew-cut and handsome, like a Midwestern professor just after giving a lecture on Shaw or Pinero —Harvey Swados

14. He looked hurried, as if he were catching a train or a boat —John Cheever

15. He looked like a cowboy in a cigarette ad —John D. MacDonald
     Preceding this from MacDonald's novel, *Free Fall in Crimson,* is this description: "A lean man with a deeply grooved face, an outdoor squint."

16. He [man in yellow suit, pinkish white shirt and greenish tie] looked like a friendly hound dog with light mange —Flannery O'Connor

17. He looked like a man secretly gnawed by a scarcely endurable pain — Margaret Mitchell

18. He looked like a man who had lost a penny and found a thousand pounds —Jimmy Sangster

19. He [Gordon Cooper, astronaut] looked like a man who played on a semi-pro football team because he wasn't big enough for the major leagues, and worked in a gas station the middle of the week —Norman Mailer

20. He looked like a mean mouse —Truman Capote

21. He looked like a piece of plot, standing there. An extra character, about to return to his mislaid car and his own life —Margaret Drabble

22. He looked like someone who had been long buried and then dug up again —W. Somerset Maugham

23. He somewhat resembled an owl, an angry, aging bird, recently balked of a field-mouse and looking about for another small animal to devour —Anthony Powell

24. He was a bundle of contradictions that clashed like cymbals —Irvin S. Cobb

25. He was a man around whom middle-age sat like a podium —William McIlvanney

26. He was like a monk who'd created his own order —James Mills
     Mills uses the comparison in *The Underground Empire* to describe a man who is difficult to work for.

27. His fifty-two years sat upon him like a finish which made youth appear crude —Edith Wharton

28. Horatio looked handsomely miserable, like Hamlet slipping on a piece of orange-peel —Charles Dickens

29. I am like a king of rainy country, wealthy but helpless, young and ripe with death —Charles Baudelaire

30. I am like a martini. The gin part is New York, the vermouth, Washington, and I'm not talking about the olive —Morton B. Zuckerman at party to celebrate new Washington restaurant attended by mostly Washingtonians and some New Yorkers, *New York Times* July 31, 1986

31. I look like a discouraged beetle battered by the rains of the Spring night —Colette

32. Innocent as milk and a build like a chocolate eclair —William Barry Furlon on Jack Nicklaus
See Also: INNOCENCE

33. It is as if he were in an incubator, breathing his own air —Mikhail Baryshnikov, about Fred Astaire, *Life* interview, January, 1980

34. Like people from Balzac, with their own individual characters and tastes —Janet Flanner
    Flanner's simile is from a letter to her friend Natalia Danesi Murray about some enjoyable people with whom she spent a weekend.

35. Like successful nuns, they [two older single women] had a slightly married air —Elizabeth Bowen

36. Like the [neglected] building . . . she seemed to be a victim of overuse and neglect —Margaret Millar

37. Like the hypochondriac who discovers a tumor under his arm with a surge of fatalistic joy, he has had his worst suspicions confirmed —T. Coraghessan Boyle

38. (You are a bit . . .) like the stars; happily incomprehensible, incapable of producing anxiety —Giuseppe di Lampedusa

39. Looked as if she had walked straight out of the ark —Sydney Smith

40. Looked as wholesome, stiff and unshakable as a bowl of tapioca —Rex Reed
    The stiff and unshakable man Reed describes is Robert Redford.

41. Looked . . . firm and impassable as a good privet hedge —Reynolds Price

42. Looked, if not like a duke, at least like an actor of the old school who specialized in dukes' parts —W. Somerset Maugham

43. Looked like a beautiful and highly shockable nun —David Niven
    Niven used this simile to introduce his story about actress Mary Astor's sexual life which, at the time would indeed have shocked a nun.

44. (Dorothy Parker) looked like a bird at the mercy of every beast with teeth —Norman Mailer

45. Looked like a choirboy gone to seed —Pat Conroy

46. Looked like a man who had flown three and a half thousand miles with a hot coal in his mouth —Frank Ross

47. Looked like a runaway from a whiskey bottle —Rosa Guy

48. Looked like Lazarus risen from the dead —Mavis Gallant
    A slight variation seen in Ross Macdonald's *The Underground Man:* "He looked like Lazarus coming out of the tomb."

49. Looked like someone whose spare time was devoted to calligraphy or stamp collecting —Jay McInerney

50. Looked mid-to late thirties and as if she hadn't wasted any time —William McIlvanney

51. Looked pale, mysterious, like a lily, drowned under water —Virginia Woolf
    See Also: PALLOR, STRANGENESS

52. Looked . . . something like a dissipated Robinson Crusoe —Charles Dickens

53. Looked weak, exhausted, and helpless, like a man who has been discarded by an enemy who has no further use for him —Scott Spencer

54. Looking strained and intent like a woman descending voluntarily into hell —Ross Macdonald

55. Look like a drowned mouse —John Ray's *Proverbs*

56. Look like a funeral —Clifford Odets
    Odets had a flare for pithy comparisons, like this one from *Awake and Sing.*

57. [Tennessee Williams] looks innocent-guilty, like a choirboy who has just been caught sneaking a bullfrog into the collection plate —Rex Reed

58. Looks like a demented stallion sniffling out a mare in estrus —T. Coraghessan Boyle

59. (Now he wears black horn-rims, and having lost weight and hair,) looks like an overworked insurance agent —Richard Ford
    In his novel, *The Sportswriter,* Ford profiles a character who has changed from looking "Like a grinning tractor-trailer in a plastic helmet" in his ball-playing days, to the above description.

60. Looks middle-aged and respectable like someone's favorite uncle —William Styron

61. Look strangely weary and solitary . . . like a prospector preparing a meal in the midst of the wilderness —Christopher Isherwood

62. A man like an unmade bed —Angela Carter

63. A man of shifting contrasts, like watermarks on a desert horizon —Rex Reed

The man of shifting contrasts is playwright Tennessee Williams.

64. Maturity, disappointment, decline of expectations had settled upon Palmer . . . like the wrinkles caused by smiling —Elizabeth Hardwick

65. A mind like a steel mousetrap and a heart like a twelve-minute egg — Jay McInerney
See Also: KINDNESS, MIND

66. Proceeded through life absented-mindedly, meditatively, as if considering some complex mathematical puzzle —Anne Tyler

67. She looked like a woman capable of plotting a President up from his cradle —James Patterson

68. She looks like a flower but she's as tough as a weed —Robert Campbell

69. She made Narcissus look like Mother Teresa —Peter Benchley

70. She was like a beautiful flower which though its petals had not yet begun to drop, was already faded and without fragrance —Leo Tolstoy

71. She [dimpled woman with conventional social responses] was like a musical box charged with popular airs —Edith Wharton

72. Spongy and spoiled like a child king —Wilfrid Sheed

73. Striped with good and evil like a giraffe —Delmore Schwartz
See Also: EVIL

74. That man is freckled like a trout with impropriety —Marianne Moore

75. They looked like the people you see in ticket lines, trying to get tickets for sold-out football games —Larry McMurtry

76. They looked as if they had been recruited wholesale from a Jewish nightmare —Angela Carter

77. The three of them [girls sharing an apartment] . . . all as lovely and charming and gay as if they had been turned out by some heavenly production line —Mary Ladd Cavell

78. (She was radiant; she) twinkled and glittered and dazzled like a diamond —Mary Ladd Cavell

79. The ubiquitous cigarette in its holder makes him look brittle, like a terrible actor trapped in a "Masterpiece Theatre" production —Sharon Sheehe Stark

80. Was like certain vegetables; transplant them and you stop their ripening —Honoré de Balzac
See Also: HABIT

81. With her plump torso balanced on spiked heels, she [Bette Midler] teeters ahead faster than most people run, looking like a pheasant on amphetamines —Julie Salamon, *Wall Street Journal,* January 29, 1987

PERVASIVENESS

See Also: CLINGING

1. As pervasive as a raging fever —Anon

2. (Democracy and freedom began) bouncing all over (the world) like bad checks —Ishmael Reed

3. Cover like a cold sweat —Anon

4. He's everywhere . . . like the mist, like some foul fog —William Diehl

5. He was all over him, like a cheap suit —Mark Shields

6. Penetrate [as through a barrier of complacency] . . . like the slippage of a dentist's drill through novacaine —Clare Nowell

7. Pervading [a woman's special magic] as a spilled perfume, irresistible and sweet —F. Scott Fitzgerald

8. (Egotism that seemed to) saturate them as toys are saturated with paint —O. Henry

9. (Allowed my thoughts to) sink in like a spoon in a pudding [in order to gain insight] —William H. Gass

PHYSICAL APPEARANCE

See Also: ARM(S), ATTRACTIVENESS, BEAUTY, BODY, EYE(S), FACE(S), FATNESS, HAIR, HAND(S), THINNESS, UNATTRACTIVENESS

1. As innocent of makeup as an apple he might have polished on his sleeve —John Yount

2. As straight as a stick and looked as brittle —V. S. Pritchett

3. Awful [looking] . . . like an oil filter that should have been changed five thousand miles ago —Saul Bellow

4. Began to look like the last solitary frost-touched rose on a November bush —Honoré de Balzac

5. Looked like a sparrow fallen from its nest —Dominique Lapierre

6. Belly as bright ivory overlaid with sapphires . . . legs are as pillars of marble —*The Holy Bible/Song of Solomon*

7. (He was) bowed and gnarled like an old tree —W. Somerset Maugham

8. Chorus-line figure, but with a face like a racehorse —Richard Ford

9. Dry and bony, like a handsome tree withered by blight —Louis Bromfield

10. Fragile-looking yet surprisingly voluptuous, she resembled a scaled-down ancient love goddess, the gilded plastic replica sold at museum shops —T. Gertler

11. Gnarled as a cyprus —Mary Lee Settle

12. Had a face like a barn owl. The heavy rolls of fat were covered with thick white powder and gave the appearance of a snow-covered mountain landscape. Her black eyes were like deep-set holes and she stared at Kern as though she might fly at him any moment with her claws —Erich Maria Remarque

    An example of a colorful portrait created with a string of similes, from Remarque's novel, *Flotsam.*

13. Had the aging body of a poet and the eyes of a starving panther — Ellery Queen

14. Had the rough, blowsy and somewhat old-fashioned look of a whore of the Renoir period —Thomas Wolfe

15. Had the threadbare appearance of a worn-out litigant —Sir Walter Scott

16. He'd been put together with care, his brown head and bullfighter's figure had an exactness, a perfection like an apple, an orange, something nature has made just right —Truman Capote

17. He had smooth skin and a thin moustache which made him look like the toy groom on a wedding cake —Andrew Kaplan

18. He looked like a goat. He had little raisin eyes and a string beard — Flannery O'Connor

19. (Up till then I'd assumed that "Gross" was the man's name, but it was his description.) He looked like something that had finally come up out of its cave because it has eaten the last phosphorescent little fish in the cold pool at the bottom of the cavern. He looked like something that better keep moving because if it stood still someone would drag it out back and bury it. He looked like a big white sponge with various diseases at work on the inside. He looked like something that couldn't get you if you held a crucifix up in front of you. He looked like the big fat soft white something you might find under a tomato plant leaf on a rainy day with a chill in the air —Donald E. Westlake

    A nice bit of comparative excess, something to be indulged in sparingly, which may account for the fact that Westlake's novel, *The Fugitive Pigeon,* contains few other similes.

20. He [Marvin Hamlish] looks at certain angles, like a cheeseburger with all the ingredients oozing awkwardly out of the bun —Rex Reed

21. Her anxious brown eyes and full, slightly drooping cheeks gave her the look of a worried hamster —Sheila Radley

22. Her face and hands were as white as though she had been drowned in a barrel of vinegar —O. Henry

23. Her great buttocks rolled like the swell on a heavy winter sea —Miles Gibson

24. He was handsome, in a brooding, archaic way, like a face from early Asiatic temple sculpture —Christopher Isherwood

25. He was like a piece of cinnamon bark, brown and thin and curled in on himself —David Brierley

26. He was ruddy as a ranch hand, and dressed like one —Joyce Reiser Kornblatt

27. His face and body had an evil swollen look as if they had grown stout on rotten meat —Ross Macdonald

28. His face and head had an unfinished look, like a sculpture an artist might have left under a damp cloth until he had time to work on it again —Dorothy Francis

29. (The guy didn't seem to have any neck at all.) His head rested on his shoulders like a bowling ball on a shelf —Jonathan Valin

30. (She is tall,) homely as Lincoln —Alice McDermott

31. A huge ruin of a woman with a face like a broken statue —Edith Wharton

32. In appearance she was not unlike a sea cow —Larry McMurtry

33. A little gnarled fellow like the bleached root of a tree —Zane Grey

34. Look awful, all trembling and green about the gills, like a frog with shell shock —A. Alvarez

35. Looked and moved like an elderly gentleman with bowel problems —T. Coraghessan Boyle

36. [Old people] looked dry as a locust shell stuck on a pear tree —Anthony E. Stockanes

37. Looked like a pale spectre beneath the moon —Émile Zola

38. Looked like a bat . . . had the ears and the snout and the gray pinched mouse-face, the hunched bony shoulders that were like folded wings —Paul Theroux

39. Looked like a man recuperating from a coronary or just about to have one —Jonathan Kellerman

40. Looked like a man who has stepped on the business end of a rake and given himself a good one, whack between the eyes —Stephen King

41. Looked like an animated skeleton —Jimmy Sangster

42. Looked like a pearl laid against black velvet —O. Henry

43. Looked like a seedy angel —William McIlvanney

44. Looking like a drooping and distracted hen —Patrick White

45. [Paul Newman in *The Color of Money*] looking like an only slightly worn Greek statue —Julie Salamon, *Wall Street Journal*, October 16, 1986

46. Look . . . like a fine healthy apple —Katherine Anne Porter

47. Look like someone who's spent the night in a bus station —Anon

48. Looks as if when you touch her she'd crackle like cellophane — Harryette Mullen
    See Also: FRAGILITY

49. Looks like a garage sale waiting for a place to happen —George V. Higgins

50. Looks like the side of a barn with the doors open —Ben Ames Williams

51. Managing with his mussed fair hair and mustache to look like a shopworn model for a cigarette advertisement —Derek Lambert

52. A man like a scarecrow, old and stormbeaten, with stiff, square, high shoulders, as if they were held up by a broomstick stuck through his sleeves —Vicki Baum

53. Men deteriorate without razors and clean shirts . . . like potted plants that go to weed unless they are tended daily —Beryl Markham
    Markham makes this observation in her autobiography, *West With the Night,* when she lands her plane and is met by two unshaven hunters, adding this simile about one of them (Baron Von Blixen): "Blix, looking like an unkempt bear . . . "

54. (Looks worse every time I see her, so) old and dried out, like a worn shoe —Jan Kubicki

55. Pink and glazed as a marzipan pig —Truman Capote about Henri Soule

56. A pinprick of a scarlet pimple glowed like blood against the very pale skin on the side of her nose. Her freshly washed gray hair was slightly askew, and she looked . . . like that demented figure in the painting of Pickett's charge at Gettysburg —Joseph Heller

57. Plump and sweet as a candied yam —Marge Piercy

58. Potbellied, and bearded with extra chins like a middle-aged high school gym coach —Jonathan Valin

59. A profile and neck like a pharaoh's erotic dream —Loren D. Estleman

60. Raindrops sat on his white skin like sweat —Sue Miller

61. A regular old jelly . . . sliding around like aspic on a hot plate — Joyce Cary

62. She is chipped like an old bit of china; she is frayed like a garment of last year's wearing. She is soft, crinkled like a fading rose —Amy Lowell

63. She [a woman of sixty] looked like a lovely little winter apple —Mary Lee Settle

64. She looked like a tree trunk . . . her big gnarled hands seemed to protrude from her like branches —Marguerite Yourcenar

65. She looked, with her red-cherry cheeks and wide semicircle of smile, like something that might have briskly swung out of a weather-house predicting sunshine —Peter Kemp

66. She reminded him, in her limp dust-colored garments, of last year's moth shaken out of the curtains of an empty room —Edith Wharton

67. She was gray as a wick and as thin —Patricia Hampl

68. She was heavy but not unattractive, like a German grandma —Peter Meinke

69. She was in her mid-thirties . . . faded, but still fruity, like a pear just beginning to go soft —Derek Lambert

70. She was like a fat little partridge with a mono-bosom —Kate Wilhelm

71. She [mother dancing before narrator] was like a pretty kite that floated above my head —Maya Angelou

72. She was tall like a lily, carried herself like a queen . . . was dressed like a rose —Hugh Walpole

73. A short woman, shaped nearly like a funeral urn —Flannery O'Connor

74. Slender and tall as the great Eiffel Tower —W. H. Auden

75. Small, chinless and like an emasculated Eton boy —Dylan Thomas
    The simile is a self portrait.

76. A smallish man who always looked dusty, as if he had been born and lived all his life in attics and store rooms —William Faulkner

77. Small, runty and rooty, she looks like a young edition of an old, gnarled tree —Laurie Colwin

78. Tall and flat like a paper doll —Elizabeth Bishop

79. Tan and wrinkled all over as if had been dipped and stained in walnut juice —George Garrett

80. They [an old couple] were brown and shriveled, and like two little walking peanuts —Carson McCullers

81. Thin and old-looking . . . as if the frame she was strung on had collapsed and the stuffing had shifted. Like a badly stuffed toy after a month in the nursery —Josephine Tey

82. A thin man with a collarbone like a wire coathanger —Penelope Gilliatt

83. Thin, white-whiskered . . . like a consumptive Santa Claus —Dashiell Hammett

84. With his longish head he looked like an Egyptian king —Iris Murdoch

85. With his small dark eyes and jowly cheeks he looked like an intelligent bulldog —Andrew Kaplan

PHYSICAL FEELINGS
See Also: HEALTH, PAIN

1. The cold struck him like a blow from a fist —Bernard Malamud

2. Deep down within her she felt as though a fish moved its tail —Sigrid Undset

This lyrical simile describes the first stirrings of life in a pregnant woman.

3. Disembodied feeling, like going under an anaesthetic —Gavin Lyall

4. Feeling . . . dizzy like someone who's been bound fast and is suddenly free —Cornell Woolrich

5. (John sat there open-mouthed,) feeling the nerves of his body twitter like so many sparrows perched upon his spinal column —F.Scott Fitzgerald

6. (I am beginning to live a little, and) feel less like a sick oyster at low tide —Louisa May Alcott

7. Feel my ribs and guts flattening together like leaves in a book —Dashiell Hammett

8. Feels the arch of his eyebrows like drying paste on his forehead —John Updike

9. Felt a chill like cold water at the roots of my hair —Dorothy Canfield Fisher

10. Felt a pleasurable languor running through every limb as though all the blood in his body had turned to warm milk —Joseph Conrad

11. Felt a sudden dizziness, as though, from a mad flight through the clouds and darkness, he had dropped to safety again, and the fall had stunned him —Edith Wharton

12. Felt giddy, as if I had come to the bottom of a staircase and found one more step than my feet expected —Mary Gordon

13. Felt his body . . . settling down like furniture in a house at the end of a hot day —Frank Tuohy

14. Felt like a half-digested meal eaten in a greasy-spoon joint —Raymond Chandler

15. Felt like a tree that had been struck by lightning —Richard Lourie

16. Felt like a Whoopee cushion sat on by a fat person —Peter Benchley

17. Felt like I'd eaten a pound of cold buttered popcorn and washed it down with bulk saccharin —Sue Grafton

18. A giddy feeling in his stomach, as though he were on a swing in the middle of its downward arc —John Yount

19. The great cold struck him like an icy douche —Émile Zola

20. The ground was shifting under his feet like the trick floors at sideshows —Shirley Ann Grau

21. Head [of main character] clears like a hazy morning giving way to noon —T. Coraghessan Boyle

22. Head feels like the inside of a soggy sandwich —François Camoin

23. His stomach was spinning like a stunting airplane over a cow pasture — Elizabeth Spencer

24. Joints creak like a stiff shirt —Erich Maria Remarque
25. Joints . . . stiff as dry sticks —Gloria Norris
26. Legs feel stiff, as if they are all bone —Gary Gildner
27. Legs felt like two old rusted rain gutters —Flannery O'Connor
28. Leg went to sleep . . . it feels like a bag of nails —Thomas Williams
29. (Could feel all her) muscles shrinking like severed vines in the sun — William Faulkner
30. My belly and behind were heavy as cold iron —Maya Angelou
     See Also: HEAVINESS
31. My face was sticky all over, like it wanted to sweat but it couldn't — Lee Smith
32. My throat was as dry as ginned cotton —Borden Deal
     See Also: DRYNESS
33. Put my head between my legs and feel the blood rush around like a herd of buffaloes trapped at the edge of a cliff —Tama Janowitz
34. Savoring the joy of rest as if she had twenty years' accumulation of weariness to work off —Colette
35. Shivering fits, like rows of cold wet needles up and down my spine — James Stern
     See Also: TREMBLING
36. My throat steams like a sewer —Marge Piercy
37. Stiff all over and felt like a sack of wet, chilly sand —Denis Johnson
38. The stillness soaked into her like a fine chill rain —Margaret Mitchell
39. Warmth ran through Bazely's body like a current of fire —Phyllis Bottome
40. A wonderful feeling [of relief from pain after an injection] . . . flowed through him like some wonderful, gently warmed milk —Heinrich Böll

PHYSICIANS
See: DOCTORS

PICTURES
See: ART AND LITERATURE

PINK
See Also: CHEEKS, COLORS, FACIAL COLOR
1. Pink and sweet as a magnolia —Diane Ackerman
2. Pink as a new baby —George Garrett
3. Pink as an infant's skin —Charles Wright
4. (Flesh-coloured stockings seemed) pink as blush roses —Rebecca West

5. (Rosebuds) pink as girls' first lipsticks —Marge Piercy

6. (Belly) pink as strawberry ice cream —Marge Piercy

7. (Face) pink as wild roses —W. P. Kinsella

PITY

See Also: KINDNESS

1. As fire drives out fire, so pity [drives out] pity —William Shakespeare

2. Collected sympathy like a street singer catching coins in a hat — Josephine Tey

3. Felt a positive gush of pity . . . like the rising of a warm fountain — Rebecca West

4. Felt the dull old nagging pull of other people's trouble, like a toothache you can't leave alone —Ross Macdonald

5. Pity . . . green as grain —E. E. Cummings

6. Ready sympathy that can be tapped like a vat —Sharon Sheehe Stark

7. Wanting pity like a cat wants the mange —John Farris

8. Wiped the pity away like cold sweat —James Crumley

PLACES

See Also: CITY/STREETSCAPES, INSULTS

1. American cities are like badger holes ringed with trash —John Steinbeck

2. The bargain basement [of store] where everything smelled musty and looked dull . . . as if a fine rain of dust fell constantly on the discounted merchandise —Joyce Reiser Kornblatt

3. A boarding area in an airport is a little like a waiting room in a dentist's office. Everyone tries to look unconcerned, but there's really only one thing on their minds —Jonathan Valin

4. Buckingham Palace . . . like an old prima donna facing the audience all in white —Virginia Woolf

5. The Capitol buildings look like a version of St. Peter's and the Vatican turned out by a modern firm —Shane Leslie

6. Chicago . . . living there is like being married to a woman with a broken nose; there may be lovelier lovelies, but never a lovely so real — Nelson Algren

7. (Some cities never sleep . . .) Cincinnati sleeps each night like it's drugged —Jonathan Valin
    Cincinnati may sleep each night yet Valin manages to infuse plenty of action into his Cincinnati-based mystery novels.

8. Cities, like cats, will reveal themselves at night —Rupert Brooke

9. The city [San Francisco] acted in wartime [WWII] like an intelligent woman under siege. She gave what she couldn't with safety withhold, and secured those things which lay in her reach —Maya Angelou

10. The city [New York] is like poetry; it compresses all life, all races and breeds, into a small island and adds music and the accompaniment of internal engines —E. B. White

11. The city spawned ugliness like a predatory insect spewing out blood-hungry larva —David Niven
    Niven's simile from his autobiography *The Moon's a Balloon* could probably be applied to any high-pressure place or industry.

12. [London during the day] coated with crawling life, as a blossom with blight —Jerome K. Jerome

13. Coming to New York from the muted mistiness of London . . . is like traveling from a monochrome antique shop to a Technicolor bazaar —Kenneth Tynan

14. Compared to the city, the country looks like the world without its clothes on —Douglas Jerrold

15. Comparing the Brooklyn that I know with Manhattan is like comparing a comfortable and complacent duenna to her more brilliant and neurotic sister —Carson McCullers

16. Dallas, a city that treated conspicuous consumption like an art form —Peter Applebome, *New York Times,* April 6, 1986

17. The danger and noise make it [New York or Chicago to a country person] seem like a permanent earthquake —William James

18. Detroit, city of lost industrial dreams, floats around us like a mirage of some sane and glaciated life —Richard Ford

19. Detroit lay across the river, a mile away, like a huge pincushion stuck full of lights —Eric Linklater

20. Each thought, each day, each life lies here [in Moscow] as on a laboratory table —Walter Benjamin

21. Fifth Avenue [at Christmas] shone like an enormous blue sugarplum revolving in a tutti-frutti rain of light —Hortense Calisher
    See Also: GLITTER AND GLOSS

22. The gray cloud of Denver's smog humped over the horizon like a whale's back —James Crumley

23. Hollywood without Spiegel is like Tahiti without Gauguin —Billy Wilder
    Wilder's simile was coined in 1986 when Aaron Spiegel died.
    See Also: INCOMPLETENESS

24. Ice hard as iron bands bound the streets of New York —Robert S. Silverberg

25. I'm glad to be here in Pittsburgh because I feel a sense of kinship with the Pittsburgh Pirates. Like my candidacy, they were not given much chance in the spring —John F. Kennedy, on the campaign trail

26. In great cities men are like a lot of stones thrown together in a bag; their jagged corners rubbed off till in the end they are smooth as marbles — W. Somerset Maugham

27. Ireland is something like the bottom of an aquarium, with little people in crannies like prawns —D. H. Lawrence

28. Italy is so tender, like cooked macaroni, yards and yards of soft tenderness, ravelled round everything —D. H. Lawrence

29. Japan offers as much novelty perhaps as an excursion to another planet —Isabella Bird

30. Leaving Los Angeles is like giving up heroin —David Puttnam

31. Life in Russia is like life at an English public school but with politics taking the place of sex —Isaiah Berlin

32. Like a resplendent chandelier, Paris in winter is made up of many parts —W. A. Poers

33. Like many picturesque neighborhoods, it has a chilling uniformity of character, as if the householders propped sternly in their lawn chairs or gazing out from the black space of a porch have been chosen and supplied to ornament their homes —Jonathan Valin

34. Living in England, provincial England, must be like being married to a stupid, but exquisitely beautiful wife —Margaret Halsey

35. (Looking down the wing I could see) the buildings of Manhattan, as tidy and neatly defined as an architect's model —Madison Smart Bell

36. Moscow . . . a city landscape wanting neon and city life, as if square miles of squat buildings had been abandoned at the first November snows —George Feifer

37. Most great cities (trail their own death around with them and) sleep, like John Donne, with one foot in the coffin —Jonathan Valin

38. New York . . . a haven as cosy as toast, cool as an icebox and safe as skyscrapers —Dylan Thomas

39. New York fit him [Nolan Ryan, pitcher for the Astros, formerly the Mets] like a cheap suit —Paul Daugherty, *Newsday,* October 9, 1986

40. New York . . . looked like a pagan banner planted on a Christian rampart —Douglas Reed

41. New York's like a disco, but without the music —Elaine Stritch

42. Omaha is a little like Newark, without Newark's glamour —Joan Rivers

43. Oaxaca sparkled like a matrix of platinum sequins laid over velvet — Richard Ford

44. Paris was . . . all little and bright and far away like a picture seen through the wrong end of a field glass —John Dos Passos

45. Places as magical and removed as toy towns under glass —Robert Dunn

46. A public library, like a railway station, gets all kinds. They come in groups, like packaged tours —Helen Hudson

47. Puerto Rico . . . it is a kind of lost love-child, born to the Spanish Empire and fostered by the United States —Nicholas Wollaston

48. The Statue of Liberty [as seen from the sky] tiny but distinct, like a Japanese doll of herself —Richard Ford

49. Sundays [in New York] the long asphalt looks like a dead beach — Edwin Denby

50. Texas air is so rich you can nourish off it like it was food —Edna Ferber

51. Thousands of funeral markers rise from the ground like dirty alabaster arms —Sin Ai
     The scene described in Sin Ai's poem *Two Brothers* is Arlington National Cemetery.

52. To be raised in Philadelphia is like being born with a big nose . . . you never get over it —Anon

53. To walk along Broadway is like being a ticket in a lottery, a ticket in a glass barrel, being tossed about with all the other tickets —Maeve Brennan

54. Transylvania without me will be like Bucharest on a Monday night — Dialogue in movie *Love At First Bite* by Count von Dracula

55. The United Nations looked cool and pure, like its charter —Derek Lambert

56. Venice . . . at once so stately and so materialist, like a proud ghost that has come back to remind men that he failed for a million — Rebecca West

57. Venice is like eating an entire box of chocolate liqueurs in one go — Truman Capote, November 26, 1961 news item

58. Washington, D.C . . . .at times as cold as its marble facade — Maureen Dowd, *New York Times,* March 2, 1987

59. Washington, D.C . . . .looks as if some giant had scattered a box of child's toys at random on the ground —Captain Basil Hall

60. Washington, D.C . . . .looks like a large straggling village reared in a drained swamp —George Combe

61. Writing about most American cities is like writing a life of Chester A. Arthur. It can be done, but why do it? —Clifton Fadiman

PLAINNESS
See: SIMPLICITY

PLANNING
> See: PURPOSEFULNESS

PLAYS
> See: STAGE AND SCREEN

PLEASURE
> See Also: GAIETY, HAPPINESS, JOY

1. As much fun as a newborn kitten —Mary Hood

2. As rewarding as a message from Billy Graham —Anon blurb about a romantic novel

3. A decided pleasure . . . as sweet as returning soldiers sometimes admit the act of killing to be —John Updike
   > The simile from Updike's novel, *Roger's Version,* refers to the pleasure of affronting public opinion.

4. Enjoyed [the difficulties of a job] . . . as a good fighter loves a battle —Frank Swinnerton

5. Fun is like life insurance, the older you get the more it costs —Abe Martin
   > Frank McKinney Hubbard, also known as Kin Hubbard and Abe Martin, often wrote in country dialect. In the above simile, for example, he used 'git' instead of 'get.'

6. It's (talking on the telephone) as good as a warm bath and a glass of milk —Enid Nemy, quoting Hazel Duke's telephone habits, *New York Times*/New Yorkers, August 24, 1986

7. It was marvelous, like seeing a capsized boat right itself, and knowing no serious damage had been done —John Fowles

8. Luxuriating like a fucked-out lion —John Updike

9. Pleased as a well tipped waiter —Anon

10. Pleased, like a young housewife going through her house and finding everything in good order —Isak Dinesen

11. Pleasure came like a lash —Julio Cortázar

12. Pleasure is frail like a dewdrop, while it laughs it dies —Sir Rabindranath Tagore

13. Pleasure is like a massive dose of vitamins —Anon

14. Pleasures are like poppies spread —Robert Burns

15. Pleasures are more beneficial than duties, because, like the quality of mercy, they are not strained, and they are twice blest —Robert Louis Stevenson

16. Pleasures are much like mushrooms. The right kind are fine, but you have to be on the lookout for the toadstools —*Boston Transcript,* May 21, 1921

17. Relish . . . like a robin-redbreast —William Shakespeare

18. (She was as) satisfying as the morning breeze —Frank Swinnerton

19. Savor experience as naturally as he accepts the prismatic blessing of sunshine glancing through the glass he holds —Francis X. Clines, *New York Times,* October 19, 1986
      Clines' subject is television writer John Mortimer.

20. Snarl at pleasure like a stoic —Lord Chesterfield

21. Snatches a crumb of pleasure like a dog snapping up a bone amid à host of dangers —Honoré de Balzac

PLENTY
   See: ABUNDANCE

POETS/POETRY
   See Also: WRITERS/WRITING

1. All good verses are like impromptus made at leisure —Joseph Joubert

2. Composed poetry . . . like a dancer working at the barre, continually exercising the power of imagining, like a muscle that demanded flexing and stretching —Arthur A. Cohen

3. Explaining how you write poetry . . . it's like going round explaining how you sleep with your wife —Phillip Larkin

4. He [the poet] approaches lucid ground warily, like a mariner who is determined not to scrape his bottom on anything solid. A poet's pleasure is to withhold a little of his meaning, to intensify by mystification —E. B. White

5. Like science, poetry must fix its thought in thing and symbol —Dilys Laing

6. Like a piece of ice on a hot stove the poem must ride on its own melting —Robert Frost

7. Like marijuana smoke are poet's verses —Jaroslav Seifert

8. Poems are like people . . . there are not many authentic ones around —Robert Graves

9. The poet is like the prince of the clouds who rides the tempest . . . exiled on the ground, amidst boos and insults, his giant's wings prevent his walking —Charles Baudelaire

10. Poetry is like light —Delmore Schwartz

11. Poetry is like painting; one piece takes your fancy if you stand close to it, another if you keep at some distance —Horace

12. Poetry . . . is like spray blown by some wind from a heaving sea, or like sparks blown from a smouldering fire: a cry which the violence of circumstances wrings from some poor fellow —George Santayana

13. Poets . . . are conductors of the senses of men, as teachers and preachers are the insulators —Karl Shapiro
    The simile is taken from a prose poem entitled *As You Say (not without sadness), Poets Don't See They Feel.* It contains another simile which sheds light on the poet as one who strips away insulation: "He pulls at the seams [of insulation] like a boy whose trousers are cutting him in half."

14. Poets are like baseball pitchers. Both have their moments. The intervals are the tough things —Robert Frost

15. Publishing a volume of verse is like dropping a rose petal down the Grand Canyon and waiting for the echo —Don Marquis, *The Sun Dial,* 1878

16. Rhymes you as fast as a sailor will swear —Babette Deutsch
    The simile is from a poem honoring John Skelton.

17. They [poets] are honored and ignored like famous dead Presidents — Delmore Schwartz

18. To try to read a poem with the eyes of the first reader who read it is like trying to see a landscape without the atmosphere that clothes it —W. Somerset Maugham

19. To write a lyric is like having a fit, you can't have one when you wish you could . . . and you can't help having it when it comes itself — Oliver Wendell Holmes, Sr.

20. Writing free verse is like playing tennis with the net down —Robert Frost

POISE
See: BEARING

POLITENESS
See: MANNERS

POLITICS/POLITICIANS

1. The body politic, like the human body, begins to die from its birth, and bears in itself the causes of its destruction —Jean Jacques Rousseau

2. A cannibal is a good deal like a Democrat, they are forced to live off each other —Will Rogers, weekly newspaper article, April 14, 1929

3. The Democratic party is like a man riding backward in a railroad car; it never sees anything until it has got past it —Thomas B. Reed

4. The Democratic party is like a mule, without pride of ancestry or hope of posterity —Emory Storrs

5. The Democrats are like someone at a funeral who just found out they won the lottery —Eleanor Clift, McLaughlin Group television show, December 28, 1986

The comparison was made during a discussion of the Iran Contra aid scandal.

6. Elections . . . are like mosquitoes, you can't very well fight 'em off without cussing 'em —Will Rogers, letter to *Los Angeles Times,* November 10, 1932

7. In politics as in religion, it so happens that we have less charity for those who believe the half of our creed, than for those that deny the whole —Charles Caleb Colton

8. In politics, as in womanizing, failure is decisive. It sheds its retrospective gloom on earlier endeavor which at the time seemed full of promise —Malcolm Muggeridge

9. Like American beers, presidential candidates these days are all pretty much the same, heavily watered for blandness, and too much gas — Russell Baker

10. A man running for public office is like a deceived husband; he is usually the last person to realize the true state of affairs —Robert Traver

11. A man without a vote is, in this land, like a man without a hand — Henry Ward Beecher

12. Merchandise candidates for high office like breakfast cereal . . . gather votes like box tops —Adlai Stevenson
In his August 18, 1956 speech accepting the presidential nomination, Stevenson used this double simile to verbally shake his head at the idea that politics is just like product merchanding.

13. Ministers fall like buttered bread; usually on the good side —Ludwig Boerne

14. One revolution is just like one cocktail; it just gets you organized for the next —Will Rogers

15. Patronage personnel are like a broken gun, you can't make them work, and you can't fire them —Peter Dominick, from the monthly newsletter of Senator Dominick, August, 1966

16. Political elections . . . are a good deal like marriages, there's no accounting for anyone's taste —Will Rogers, weekly newspaper article, May 10, 1925

17. Political rhetoric has become, like advertising, audible wallpaper, always there but rarely noticed —George F. Will

18. A politician is like quick-silver; if you try to put your finger on him, you find nothing under it —Austin O'Malley

19. Politicians are like drunks. We're the ones who have to clean up after them —Bryan Forbes

20. Politicians are like the bones of a horse's foreshoulder, not a straight one in it —Wendell Phillips, 1864 speech

21. Politics are almost as exciting as war, and quite as dangerous —Sir Winston Churchill
     > Churchill followed up the simile with, "In war you can only be killed once, but in politics many times."

22. Politics are like a labyrinth, from the inner intricacies of which it is even more difficult to find the way of escape than it was to find the way into them —William E. Gladstone

23. Politics is like a circus wrestling match —Nikita S. Khrushchev

24. Politics is like a race horse. A good jockey must know how to fall with the least possible damage —Edouard Herriot

25. Politics is like being a football coach. You have to be smart enough to understand the game and dumb enough to think it's important — Eugene McCarthy

26. Politics is like waking up in the morning. You never know whose head you will find on the pillow —Winston Churchill

27. Politics, like religion, hold up the torches of martyrdom to the reformers of error —Thomas Jefferson

28. Presidential appointments are left to us like bad debts after death — Janet Flanner

29. Professional politicians are like chain smokers, lighting a new campaign on the butt of the old one —Steven V. Roberts, *New York Times,* November 24, 1986
     > This was the only simile in Roberts' article. Yet, as is so often the case, it was the phrase highlighted as a boxed blurb to get reader attention.

30. The public is like a piano. You just have to know what keys to poke — John Dewey

31. The pursuit of politics is like chasing women: the expense is damnable, the position ridiculous, the pleasure fleeting —Robert Traver

32. Running for public office was not unlike suffering a heart attack; overnight one's whole way of life had abruptly to be changed —Robert Traver

33. So long as we read about revolutions in books, they all look very nice . . . like those landscapes which, as artistic engravings on white vellum, look so pure and friendly —Heinrich Heine

34. (They said) the range of political thinking is round, like the face of a clock —Tony Ardizzone

35. A voter without a ballot is like a soldier without a bullet —Dwight D. Eisenhower, *New York Times Book Review,* October 27, 1957

36.   Watching foreign affairs is sometimes like watching a magician; the eye is drawn to the hand performing the dramatic flourishes, leaving the other hand, the one doing the important job, unnoticed —David K. Shipler, *New York Times,* March 15, 1987

PONDS AND STREAMS
See Also: NATURE, SEASCAPES

1.   The black lake was shimmering like ink —Richard Russo

2.   Light spread across the river like an oil spill —Jay Parini

3.   Pond . . . covered with rain like sequins or crinkled up with wind like a watered silk —Joyce Cary

4.   River . . . like a sheet of polished metal —Boris Pasternak

5.   The river in evening like a dirty window —Delmore Schwartz

6.   The river looked like an eye which for some reason or other was growing darker and darker as happens in love at the onset of ecstacy — Bertold Brecht

7.   The river now all crinkled like tinfoil —Delmore Schwartz

8.   The river raged by like a forest fire —Edward Hoagland

9.   A river ran there as clear as the air itself, and the fish in it were like gold and silver —Hans Christian Anderson

10.   The river . . . smelled like a packing house for fish, but it looked like the melted, dark eyes of a million girls —Hortense Calisher

11.   The river was brown and bubbly . . . like cake icing —Lee Smith

12.   The stream was like a silver magnet that pulled them across the prairie —Dorothy Francis

POPULARITY

1.   Favor, like disgrace, brings trouble with it —Lao Tzu

2.   Hot as a pistol —Rex Reed
      A variant to this is to be "Hot as a two dollar pistol."

3.   (Nothing is as . . .) popular as goodness —Michel de Montaigne

4.   She looked as if her phone had been ringing continually ever since she had reached puberty —J. D. Salinger
      See Also: PERSONALITY PROFILES

POSSIBILITY
See: OPPORTUNITY

POSTURE
See Also: BEARING, BENT, STRAIGHTNESS

1. Arched like a cavalry horse getting a whiff of the battlefield — Katherine Anne Porter

2. A back like a marine drill instructor's . . . straight as a rifle shot — Loren D. Estleman

3. Bolt upright like drawn bayonets —Aharon Megged

4. Erect as a candle —Isak Dinesen
    Dinesen used this simile in a short story, *The de Cats Family*. Because many a simile is hard to establish as one writer's creative invention, it should come as no surprise that it also appeared in Ignazio Silone's novel, *The Secret of Luca*.

5. Erect as a cavalry officer —Francine du Plessis Gray

6. Erect as a Grecian pillar —Anon

7. Held his shoulders back as though they were braced, and he sucked in his stomach like a soldier —John Steinbeck

8. Her back is curved like a shell —Louise Erdrich

9. Her entire posture seemed to have bunched up like a fist —Robert B. Parker

10. Her spine droops like a dying daisy —Ira Wood

11. Huddled up like a pale misshapen piece of pastry —Hugh Walpole

12. Hunched his shoulders like a fighter tensing for a blow —Harvey Swados

13. Hunched like a cowboy that hears a rattler —Paul Theroux
    Theroux's simile was particularly apt for the photographer-heroine of his novel, *Picture Palace*.

14. Hunched, like a man made lintel-shy by too many cracks on the head through adolescence —Harold Adams

15. Hunched over like an old turtle —Louise Erdrich

16. (Sit . . .) hunched up like a crow —Elizabeth Spencer

17. Like a schoolmistress dealing with problem pupils, sat straight-backed —Dorothea Straus

18. Posture . . . like an emaciated old man who once had been an athlete —Kenzaburo Oë

19. Posture . . . rigid and stylized as a pair of bookends —George Garrett

20. Rigid as an effigy —Gavin Lambert
    See Also: FIRMNESS

21. (A sort of) savage stoop, like a bull lowering his horn —G. K. Chesterton

22. Shoulders humped like a bull's —Mary Hedin

23. Shoulders sagged like empty sacks —James Crumley

24. Shoulders . . . set like those of a man carrying a banner —Hugh Walpole

25. Sits back, relaxed, as if she were watching an invisible TV and weeping over a soap opera —John J. Clayton

26. Slumped like a chimpanzee —Mary Morris

27. Slumped there like a bag of bones —Beryl Bainbridge

28. Slump . . . like rags —Karl Shapiro

29. Slumps there like an outsized parenthesis —Marge Piercy

30. Standing to attention like a dead centurion at his post —John Le Carré

31. Stands stiff as a bobby when the Queen appears —Maxine Kumin

32. Stands tall, straight and stern as an angel —Louise Erdrich

33. Stiff-backed as a cadet —George Garrett

34. Stood like a dart —Brian Merriman

35. Stood rigid as a carving —Madison Smartt Bell

36. Stood stiff as a marble statue —Johann Wolfgang von Goethe

37. Stood up very straight like somebody in opera —Rebecca West

38. Stooped, as though half-crouching under an expected blow —Ben Ames Williams

39. Stooped like too tall visitors to an igloo —John Irving

40. Stooping like a decayed tree, he was so old —A. E. Coppard

41. Straightened like soldiers under review —Jay Parini

42. Tilted forward at the waist like a stickshift in third gear —Rick Borsten

43. Upright as a palm tree —*The Holy Bible/Proverbs*
    Variations of this biblical simile link uprightness with a variety of other trees; for example, "Upright as a pine."

44. Upright like stalks —Aharon Megged

POVERTY

See Also: ECONOMICS

1. Destitution, like a famished rat, begins by gnawing at the edges of garments —Stefan Zweig

2. Her poverty was like a huge dream-mountain on which her feet were fast rooted . . . aching with the ache of the size of the thing — Katherine Mansfield

3. (I felt as) poor as a Catholic without a sin for confession —Harry Prince

4. Poor as a church mouse —Anon

Like Job, mice (and rats) have long been, and continue to be, proverbial comparisons for poverty. The writer most frequently credited with originating the simile is William Makepeace Thackeray who used it in *Vanity Fair.*

5. Poor as a couple of shithouse spiders —Leslie Thomas

6. Poor as Job —Anon
    A simile with a history dating back to the thirteenth century, and used by many illustrious writers. In *Henry IV,* Shakespeare extended it to, "Poor as Job . . . but not so patient," while Sir Walter Scott in *The Fortunes of Nigel* made it, "Proud as Lucifer, and as poor as Job." A variation that was once a popular American colloquialism is "Poor as Job's turkey."

7. Poor as sin —F. Scott Fitzgerald

8. A poor man who oppresses the poor is like a sweeping rain which leaves no food —*The Holy Bible/Proverbs*
    The words 'oppresses' and 'leaves' have been modernized from 'oppresseth' and 'leaveth.'

9. Poverty is death in another form —Latin proverb

10. Poverty, like wealth, entails a ritual of adaptation —Arthur A. Cohen

11. Wearing squalor like a badge —Wilfrid Sheed

POWER

1. About as influential as the 'p' in pneumonia and the 'k' in knitting —Anon

2. Aggressive as an elbow in the side —Henry James

3. As omnipotent and as full of faults as Jove —Wallace Stegner

4. Authority shrivelled as muslin in a fire —Vita Sackville-West

5. Authority without wisdom is like a heavy ax without an edge, fitter to bruise than to polish —Anne Bradstreet

6. Compelling as a gun at your head —Anon

7. [Choice to do something] compelling as the sense of vocation which doctors and missionaries are supposed to experience —John Braine

8. (He is) consuming . . . like a candle —Richard Flecknoe

9. Feel like a lion in a den of Daniels —W. S. Gilbert

10. Strong [a person's pull on others] as a riptide —Reynolds Price

11. Glows with power like a successful shaman —Marge Piercy

12. Had a ring of authority, like monarchy —Barbara Lazear Ascher

13. Immoderate power, like other intemperance, leaves the progeny weaker and weaker, until Nature, as [if] in compassion, covers it with her mantle and is seen no more —Walter Savage Landor

14. Influence is like a savings account. The less you use it, the more you've got —Andrew Young

15. Influential as gnats —Susan Heller Anderson

16. It's like a Dead Sea fruit. When you achieve it, there is nothing there — Harold Macmillan, *Parade,* July 7, 1963

17. Like wealth and power, prestige tends to be cumulative: the more of it you have, the more you can get —C. Wright Mills

18. Made him fetch and carry just as if he was a great Newfoundland dog —William Makepeace Thackeray

19. (But her looks have) no power over me . . . like a tug on a tree on a limb that has lost feeling —William Getz

20. Once a man of power, always a man of power. Like being a Boy Scout —Anthony Powell

21. (Memories . . .) powerful as floods —Elizabeth Spencer

22. Power [in the Middle East] gravitates towards radicals like iron filings toward a magnet —Karen Elliott House

23. Power, like a desolating pestilence, pollutes whatever it touches —Percy Bysshe Shelley
    'Whatever' replaces the old English 'whate'er.'

24. Power, like lightning, injures before its warning —Pedro Calderon de la Barca

25. Power, like the diamond, dazzles the beholder, and also the wearer — Charles Caleb Colton

26. The right of commanding . . . like an inheritance, it is the fruit of labors, the price of courage —Voltaire

27. To rule must be a calling, it seems, like surgery or sculpture —W. H. Auden

28. Scenting power like blood —Janet Flanner

29. Seemed the personification of brute strength . . . like a gorilla dripped in peroxide —Donald Seaman

30. Strode like a colossus over the [White House] staff —Dean Rusk, *New York Times,* March 1, 1987
    Rusk used this image to compare Lyndon Johnson's control over the White House staff to Ronald Reagan's delegation of power.

31. Swept me ahead of her like a leaf —Elizabeth Bishop

32. There was authority in his attitude . . . and its heat threatened to melt Bird [name of character] like a piece of candy —Kenzaburo Oë

33. They pass him on from hand to hand, like a baton in a relay race, and he ultimately becomes a puppet manipulated by others —Vladmir Solovyou and Elena Klopikova

34. To add a little weight to his argument he put a hand like a bunch of bananas flat on my chest —Jimmy Sangster

35. Tyranny, like hell, is not easily conquered —Thomas Paine

POWERLESSNESS
See: HELPLESSNESS

PRAISE
See: FLATTERY, WORDS OF PRAISE

PRAISEWORTHINESS
See: VIRTUE

PRAYER
See: RELIGION

PRECARIOUSNESS
See: DANGER

PRECISION
See: CORRECTNESS

PREDICTABILITY
See: CERTAINTY

PREJUDICE
See: INTOLERANCE

PREPAREDNESS

1. (I was) as unprepared to meet my mother as a sinner is reluctant to meet his Maker —Maya Angelou

2. Got ready like a depression fighter going into the main bout at the Garden on Friday night —Norman Mailer, on preparing for a television appearance

3. He [the district attorney] prepares his cases as if he were laying the foundations of society —Ross Macdonald

4. In life, as in chess, forethought wins —Charles Buxton
See Also: LIFE

5. Like a basketball coach in a close game, he looked poised to spring — Fletcher Knebel

6. Poised like an acid-tipped arrow —Paige Mitchell

7. Prepare as though for a death —Katherine Mansfield, on travel preparations

8. Prepared . . . as healthy people are said to be prepared for death, in the sense of knowing it must come without in the least expecting that it will —Edith Wharton

9. Prepared for combat [in business situation] like an ambitious and hungry heavyweight boxer before a fight —Andrew M. Greeley

10. Prepared like a porcupine for cold weather —Anon

11. Stands . . . ready like a retriever —Erich Maria Remarque

12. Trained him like a race horse for academic success —Robert L. Heilbroner

    The man whose educational upbringing Heilbrone likened to training a race horse is economist John Maynard Keynes.

PRESENT, THE

1. The present, like a note in music, is nothing but as it appertains to what is past and what is to come —Walter Savage Landor

2. The word 'now' is like a bomb through the window —Arthur Miller

PRESERVATION

See: PROTECTIVENESS

PRICE

See: COST

PRETTINESS

See: BEAUTY

PREVENTION

See: PROBLEMS/SOLUTIONS

PRIDE

1. Accepts [a situation] as proudly as the mother of a Bar Mitzvah boy accepts his cracked-voice singing at the sabbath service —Ira Wood

2. Beamed pride . . . like a mother whose son has won everything on school prize day —Louis Bromfield

3. Dignified and beautiful as a Beethoven sonata —Israel Zangwill

4. Dignified as a state funeral —Anon

5. Felt as though he had feathers which had puffed up with pride — Pamela Hansford Johnson

    The pride thus described in Johnson's novel, *The Good Husband,* is caused by the admiring glances lavished upon an attractive companion.

6. Felt pride rising up through his chest like gas —Margaret Millar

7. Felt so proud, as though he had saved a life —Mary Hood

8. For a man to say all the excellent things that can be said upon one, and call that his Epitaph, is as if a painter should make the handsomest piece he can possibly make, and say 'twas my picture —John Selden

9. Like a freshly lit lamp, expanding and bright with triumph —Julia O'Faolain

10. Looking very proud like he's discovered some sort of rare bird —Hilary Masters

11. My pride stung like a slapped cheek —John Hersey

12. Pride is as loud a beggar as want —Benjamin Franklin

13. Pride is to character, like the attic to the house . . . the highest part, and generally the most empty —John Gay

14. Pride like humility, is destroyed by one's insistence that he possesses it —Kenneth P. Clark

15. Pride, like the magnet, constantly points to one object, self; but unlike the magnet, it has no attractive pole but at all points repels —Charles Caleb Colton

16. Pride steams off you like the stink of cancer —William Alfred

17. Proud as a cock on his own dunghill —Turkish proverb

18. Proud as a hen that gets a duck for a chicken —Dion Boucciault

19. (Sat there . . .) proud as an idol —Hermann Hesse

20. Proud as a peacock; all strut and show —H. G. Bohn's *Handbook of Proverbs*
    Probably the best known and most used of the many "Proud as" similes. The original used the Old English 'shew' instead of 'show.'

21. Proud as a stork —John Betjeman

22. Proud as Satan himself (and as unapproachable) —Ivan Turgenev

23. (They carefully tend to their garden and show off their vegetables like . . . .) proud new parents —Marian Thurm

24. Saw his dignity slip away like a blanket —Beryl Markham

25. Show [as success or dating a beautiful woman] off like a rose in a buttonhole —Milton R. Sapirstein

26. (The curate) sounded proud, like somebody who brushed his teeth with table salt —J. F. Powers

27. Swelled like a frog about to croak —Rita Mae Brown

28. Swelled with pride like a turkey cock —Ben Ames Williams

29. Swelling up [with pride] like a robin —Stephen Vincent Benét

30. Wear your pride like a chevron on your sleeve —George Garrett

PROBABILITY
    See: CERTAINTY

PROBLEMS/SOLUTIONS

1. As rust eats iron, so care eats the heart —Auguste Ricard

2. Being a new employee . . . it's like picking up a screenplay and starting to act your part, only it's Act Three and you have not been in Acts One or Two —Carol Clark, *New York Times,* July 28, 1986

3. Burdensome as a secret —French proverb

4. Carry your problems with you from place to place like a Santa Claus sack —George Garrett

5. Ceased to be an apparent problem . . . the way crumbs swept under a rug cease to be an apparent problem —Rick Borsten

6. Difficulties strengthen the mind, as labor does the body —Seneca, The Elder

7. (Doubt . . .) dug at his peace of mind like a broken fingernail —F. van Wyck Mason

8. (The electronics-crammed production booth is beginning to) resemble the bridge of a destroyer under air attack —Michael Cieply, writing about taping of a Bill Cosby television segment that ran into problems, *Wall Street Journal,* September 26, 1986

9. Face a problem with all the joy of a team preparing for a game it expects to lose. —Anon

10. Felt speaking about one's personal problems was rather like talking about one's surgery scars . . . a subject of consuming interest only to one's self —C.D.B. Bryan

11. Heading toward disaster, as certainly as a four-year-old behind the wheels of a Maserati —Vincent Canby, *New York Times,* February 28, 1986

12. He was like a mathematician with an abstruse problem, worrying over it, but worrying very calmly and impersonally —James Hilton

13. I am a man smothered with women and children, like a duck with onions —Sir Charles Napier
    Napier made these comparisons when he reflected on his life in England after retiring as commander of British forces in northern India.

14. An international crisis is like sex, as long as you keep talking about it, nothing happens —Harold Coffin, *Reader's Digest,* September, 1961

15. It's [being on a losing streak] like a little time box that's going to explode —John Pennywell, football player on Columbia University's Lions, *New York Times,* November 8, 1986

16. (I was) living as if I were squeezed in an iron hand —Honoré de Balzac

17. (The whole of) my life has passed like a razor . . . in hot water or a scrape —Sydney Smith

18. (My immediate) problems . . . as untouchable as a raw wound —Norman Mailer

19. The problem stayed in the front of his mind like a sheer cliff he could not begin to climb —Ken Follett

20. Pry at the mousehole of a solution like a cat with infinite patience —Bill Granger

21. Second-hand cares, like second-hand clothes, come easily on and off —Charles Dickens

22. Sign of trouble . . . like seeing a cannon muzzle poke out of the woods —James Sterngold, *New York Times,* March 22, 1986

23. The solution rushed on him like a fire storm —T. Coraghessan Boyle

24. They're [troubles] piled on my head like snows on a mountain top —Bernard Malamud

25. They would gnaw on it for days like two puppies with a rubber bone —Charles Portis

26. Troubled as a plane with one wing —Anon

27. Trouble . . . fell across her shoulders like a cloak. It was as if she had touched a single strand of a web, and felt the whole thing tremble and knew herself to be caught forever in its trembling —Ellen Gilchrist

28. Troublesome as a wasp in one's ears —Thomas Fuller

29. Troubles visited from above like tornadoes —Marge Piercy

30. Weaponless deterrence is like bodiless sex. It gets you nowhere —James Morrow

31. Women like to sit down with trouble as if it were knitting —Ellen Glasgow

32. Work like an antitoxin . . . before the complications come —Clifford Odets

PROCRASTINATION
See: LINGERING

PROFANITY
See: CURSES

PROFESSIONS
See Also: DOCTORS, LAWYERS

1. Archeologists and historians . . . they are like jewelers, examining every tiny aspect of each valuable thing, with exactness and care —Judith Martin

2. Business is a vocation. Philosophy is, or should be, an avocation — Elbert Hubbard

3. A financier is a pawnbroker with imagination —Arthur W. Pinero

4. (I guess) getting into nunhood is about as hard as pro football — Michael Malone

5. (In ordinary business, man can settle to routine. The journalist can't.) He's [the journalist] like a robin, looking in all directions at once — Frank Swinnerton

6. He who philosophizes is like a mirror that reflects objects that it cannot see, like a cave that returns the echo of voices that it does not hear — Kahlil Gibran

7. Journalism, like history, is certainy not an exact science —John Gunther

8. The Notary Public, like the domestic dog, is found everywhere —John Cadman Roper

9. The philosopher is like a mountaineer who has with difficulty climbed a mountain for the sake of the surprise, and arriving at the top finds only fog; whereupon he wanders down again —W. Somerset Maugham

10. Philosophy is like the ocean: there are pearls in its depths, but many divers find nothing for all their exertion and perish in the attempt —Ha Yevani Zerahia

11. Police business . . . it's a good deal like politics. It asks for the highest type of men, and there's nothing in it to attract the highest type of men —Raymond Chandler

12. Professors are just like actors. Actors got press agents that write things about them and they get so they believe it —Anon

13. Professors get to looking at their diplomas and get to believing what it says there —Will Rogers, radio broadcast, January 27, 1935

14. Psychoanalysis, like imagination, cannot be learned by rote —Theodor Reik

15. Psychology is like physics before Galileo's time, not a single elementary law yet caught a glimpse of —William James, letter to James Sully, 1890

16. Running a liberal paper is like feeding melted butter on the end of an awl to a wild cat —Oscar Ameringer, *Progressive,* January 17, 1942 See Also: ABSURDITY

17. Working journalists regularly chase wild geese. Like firemen, they answer alarms, many of them false —Richard Rovere

PROFICIENCY
See: ABILITY

PROFUSION
   See: ABUNDANCE

PROGRESS
   See: GROWTH

PROLIFERATION
   See: SPREADING

PROMISE
   See Also: RELIABILITY/UNRELIABILITY

1. He promises like a merchant-man and pays like a man-of-war —Italian proverb

2. His promises are lighter than the breath that utters them —John Ray's *Proverbs*

3. Lovers' oaths are thin as rain —Dorothy Parker

4. A pledge unpaid is like thunder without rain —Abraham Hasdai

5. Promise as solid as a bundle of water —Hindu proverb
      Modernized to non-sexist English from "A woman's word is like a bundle of water."

6. Promises are like pie-crusts —Danish proverb

7. The promises of authors are like the vows of lovers —Samuel Johnson
      See Also: WRITERS/WRITING

8. When a man takes an oath, he's holding his own self in his own hands. Like water. And if he opens his fingers then, he needn't hope to find himself again —Robert Bolt

PROMPTNESS

1. Arrived on time, and left on time, like a European train —Laurie Colwin
      See Also: ENTRANCES/EXITS

2. Punctual as a bride at a wedding —Honoré de Balzac

3. Punctual as a stage manager, watch in hand —Frank Swinnerton

4. Punctual as bills —Babette Deutsch

5. Punctual as death —Scott Spencer

6. Punctual as destiny —Edith Wharton

7. Punctual as lovers to the moment sworn —Edward Young

8. Punctually as a cuckoo in a Swiss clock —Edith Wharton

9. Punctually, as the tax collector —*Punch,* 1862
      Paraphrased from "Tax gatherer."

PRONUNCIATION
>   See: SPEECH PATTERNS

PROPRIETY/IMPROPRIETY
>   See Also: MANNERS

1.   About as risqué as a bed in a hospital —George Jean Nathan
2.   All wrong . . . like a priest for whom one has a great respect suddenly taking his trousers off in church —Daphne du Maurier
3.   Decorously as an old maid on the way to get her hair dyed blue —A. E. Maxwell
4.   Improper as thumbing your nose at the pope —Anon
5.   Prim as Hippolytus —Stevie Smith
6.   (Girls, at sixteen, for all our strictures, are) proper as Puritans —Phyllis McGinley
7.   Proper like the hostesses in restaurants frequented by women shoppers —Ludwig Bemelmans

PROSE
>   See: POETS/POETRY, WRITERS/WRITING

PROSPERITY
>   See: RICHES, SUCCESS/FAILURE

PROTECTIVENESS
>   See Also: WATCHFULNESS

1.   Guard [another person] like an armed sentry —Isak Dinesen
2.   Mothers him like an old mare —Jilly Cooper
3.   [Trees] preserved at all costs, like Grandpa's teeth —Elizabeth Bishop
4.   Protective [of property] as a lion in winter —Anon
      This may have been inspired by James Goldman's play, *The Lion in Winter,* a simile from which can be found under AMBITION.
5.   Protectively, like shepherd dogs —Harvey Swados
6.   [Wife] watches over my reputation like a broody hen —Luigi Pirandello

PROTRUSION
>   See Also: BELONGING, OBVIOUSNESS, VISIBILITY

1.   Bulges out like bubble gum before popping —Tom Robbins
2.   Protruding like a warning finger —Beryl Markham
3.   [A church spire] standing out conspicuously like an indicating finger — MacDonald Harris

4. Standing out unnaturally, like a male harpist in an all-girl orchestra — William Safire

5. Stand out like a blind man at a tit show —William Diehl

6. Stand out like a polar bear in the desert —Andrew Kaplan

7. Stand out like a raisin on a coconut cake —Pat Conroy

8. Stands out like a blackberry in a pan of milk —American colloquialism, attributed to Vermont

9. Stick out like a bug on a butter knife —Loren D. Estleman

10. Sticks out like the belly of a pregnant woman —Robert Lowell

PROVERBS
See: MAXIMS AND SAYINGS

PROXIMITY
See: CLOSENESS

PRUDENCE
See: CAUTION

PSYCHOLOGY
See: PROFESSIONS

PUBLIC OPINION
See: OPINION

PUBLIC, THE
See: POLITICS

PURITY
See Also: VIRTUE

1. Incapable of taint as gold of rust —Aeschylus

2. Pure and white as Rainier's snows —Slogan, Mills flour

3. Pure as a salamander in the flames or wool among the brambles — Miguel de Cervantes

4. (I'm as) pure as driven slush —Tallulah Bankhead

5. Pure as snow —William Shakespeare

6. (I had grown) pure as the dawn and the dew —Algernon Charles Swinburne

7. Pure as the mountain air —Slogan, D. L. Clark candy

8. Pure as the sun —Stephen Vincent Benét

9. Pure in thought as angels —Samuel Rogers

10.   She was as pure as snow and she drifted —Anon blurb for book, *New York Times Book Review,* November 2, 1986

11.   Unblemished as the cloudless sky —Anne Morrow Lindbergh

12.   Untouched as a nun —Wallace Stegner
      A variation on the same theme: "Pure as a nun" from Margaret Drabble's novel, *The Waterfall.*

PURPLE
      See: COLORS

PURPOSEFULNESS

1.   Came around . . . deliberately like the gun turret of a great ship —Donald McCaig

2.   Dedicated as a Japanese artist who has found the flower he must paint all his life —William McIlvanney

3.   Deliberate as a bee taking honey —Molly Kean

4.   Deliberate as a dog sniffing out a buried bone —Anon

5.   Effort as conscious and deliberate as holding his breath under water —William Peden
     From a short story entitled *Night in Funland,* this refers to a character's effort to control his emotions.

6.   Had a plan . . . simple as Cain's —Alma and Paul Ellerbe

7.   His time was organized, planned like the timetable of a battle maneuver —Arthur A. Cohen

8.   Intent as a cannibal at breakfast —T. Coraghessan Boyle

9.   Intent as a collector —W. H. Auden

10.   Men, like nails, lose their usefulness when they lose their direction and begin to bend —Walter Savage Landor

11.   Method is like packing things in a box; a good packer will get in half as much again as a bad one —Richard Cecil

12.   Moved like a steamroller, in a straight line, crushing everything that was in her way —Margaret Millar

13.   My will is like a long pencil, it must be sharpened —Delmore Schwartz

14.   (I have always envied the man who found one single role and) played it [a role or life plan], clung and grew to it like a barnacle on a ship —George Garrett
      See Also: CLINGING

15.   Rehearsed her sensuality like a summa-cum student —Francine du Plessix Gray
      See Also: SEX

16. (Somewhere in the earth is a drain of) resolution filling as a fresh teapot —Daniela Gioseffi

17. (He had) a resolution in him like an iron bar —Wallace Stegner

18. Schemed like Arabs —Thomas McGuane

19. (Ruthless and) singleminded as birds of prey —George Garrett

20. Used her charm like a tennis racket —Delmore Schwartz

21. Will without power is like children playing at soldiers —George Canning

PURSUIT

1. (He was) after her like a hound after a deer —Harriet Beecher Stowe

2. (He was) after it like a duck on a June bug —American colloquialism, attributed to the South
     A twist on the duck/bug comparison is to be after something, "Like a pet coon into the churn."

3. (He was) after it like the stink after onion —American colloquialism, attributed to the South

4. Chased him like a fox chases a turkey —Rosa Guy

5. Chased me . . . like a kid after a fire truck —Irwin Shaw

6. Follow after me like an old weasel tracing a rat —John M. Synge
     In Synge's script for *The Playboy of the Western World,* 'weasel' was spelled with the letter z.

7. Follow each other like lemmings over the cliffs of Dover —Richard Hicks, about discount book sellers, *Publishers' Weekly,* 1986

8. Follow every lead like a lawyer building a case —Anon

9. Followed her about like a little dog —William Makepeace Thackeray

10. Followed him like a trained sleuth —Shelby Hearon

11. Followed one another like insects going at dawn through the heavy grass —Eudora Welty

12. Follow you around like flies —Gavin Lyall

13. Haunted me like a passion —William Wordsworth

14. Held on his trail like an old hound after his last coon —James Crumley

15. Hounded him like bailiffs —Oakley Hall

16. Looked for . . . like a bird looking for forage in a desert —Arthur A. Cohen

17. Pursue as wolves pursue sheep —William Reese, a rare book dealer, quoted in *Wall Street Journal* article on how book collectors go after their finds, May 6, 1986

18. [A disease] pursued him like a hobgoblin —Maurice Edelman

19. Pursue as a male dog goes after a bitch in heat —Anon

20. Pursuing him like a nemesis, like an unwanted, embarrassing relative — Donald McCaig

21. Slivered after him like mercury —Wilfrid Sheed

22. Sniff out like a terrier smells a rat —Basil Blackwell

23. Tagging along [behind character in story] like an anthropologist tags along behind his Indian —Deborah Eisenberg

24. Trailing . . . like a cape before a bull —Lawrence Durrell

25. Trotting behind like a penny dog —Rita Mae Brown

26. Will run him down like a greyhound catching a hare —George Garrett

27. Would be on my back like a bad case of sunburn —Shelby Hearon

PUZZLEMENT
See: BEWILDERMENT

QUESTIONS/ANSWERS
See Also: PROBLEMS/SOLUTIONS

1. Answered me as gravely as if I had asked the meaning of life —Borden Deal

2. Answered slow, like men who wouldn't waste anything, not even language —Carl Sandburg

3. Answered with the finality of a bank vault door —Dick Francis

4. The answer was in front of him . . . like a gift-wrapped package waiting to be opened —Andrew Kaplan

5. Asked, like a man who didn't want to know —James Crumley

6. Beat back questions like a ball hitting a brick wall —Anon

7. A correct answer is like an affectionate kiss —Johann Wolfgang von Goethe

8. Curiosity . . . unrolls its question mark like a new wave on the shore —John Ashberry

9. Deflected answers like a freight train cutting through the Mississippi Delta —Les Payne on William Renquist's responses to questions about his civil rights background, *Newsday,* August 3, 1986

10. Her questions sounded unfelt as though she were speaking from a deep well of hypnosis —Geoffrey Wolff

11. His answers trickled through my head, like water through a sieve — Lewis Carroll

12. It was like the question asked by Tennyson about the flowers in the crannied wall —Saul Bellow

13. One by one, neatly, like index cards out of a machine, the little questions dropped —Roald Dahl

14. Pursued [a question] like an inquisitor in a torture chamber who was hungry and eager to get the signed statement before his supper — Christopher Isherwood

15. The question falls . . . like a bird from the sky —Aharon Megged

16. The question hangs like music in my thoughts —W. P. Kinsella

17. The question immediately bursts in the sky like a shower of fireworks —Isaiah Berlin, June, 1980

18. Question [directly] . . . like a gun —Lael Tucker Wertenbaker

19. Questions bobbed in her mind like corks on a turbulent sea —Paige Mitchell

20. Questions like ordered bricks —Mary Hedin

21. Questions like water gushed ceaselessly —Dame Edith Sitwell

22. Unpleasant and unanswerable questions flopping around in his head like a bat that had mistakenly flown in through the living room window —Laurie Colwin

23. Was like a psychiatrist, asking questions which really were not those questions at all, but deeper ones —Elizabeth Taylor

24. Worried her questions like a dog does a bone —Donald MacKenzie

25. You start a question and it's like starting a stone. You sit quietly on the top of a hill, and away the stone goes, starting others —Robert Louis Stevenson

QUICKNESS
See: RUNNING, SPEED

QUIET
See: SILENCE

RAGE
See: ANGER

RAIN
See Also: WEATHER

1. As if a mask had been peeled off, the rain ended —Tim O'Brien

2. Big soft drops splash on people's hands and cheeks, immense warm drops like melted stars —Katherine Mansfield

3. Drizzle whispered upon Joseph's umbrella like muffled applause — Rick Borsten

4. Droplets fired upon our windows like bullets of tin —Ira Wood

5. The drops like bugs stuck on the pane —F. D. Reeve

6. A dull rain, like a tap left running —Jean Thompson

7. Fall rain as fine as spray from an atomizer —Harvey Swados

8. Felt the rain like cold tears on his hot face —James Crumley

9. The good rain, like a bad preacher, does not know when to leave off —Ralph Waldo Emerson

10. The gray rain continued to fall, stubbornly and insensibly, like a frozen madness —Amos Oz

11. Hiss in the gutter [the rain] like a thousand coiled snakes —T. Coraghessan Boyle

12. It seemed as if the lowering clouds, heavy with water had burst, emptying upon the earth . . . melting it like sugar —Guy De Maupassant
    See Also: CLOUD(S)

13. Light rain fell around the big house and its trees like a veil —John McGahern

14. Light through which the slowing rain ran stitches like a sewing machine gone mad —Leslie A. Fiedler

15. The rain as thick as oil on the windows —Albert Camus

16. The rain beat down (on Paris) in endless steady sheets, straight down, like waterfalls —Sylvia Berkman
    A nice example of a simile to introduce a story and set its mood.

17. Rain . . . beating down like a stampede of horses —Paige Mitchell

18. The rain bites like a whip across a prisoner's back —Anne Morrow Lindbergh

19. The rain came down like glass bead curtains —Joyce Cary

20. The rain came like an explosion in a glass factory —T. Coraghessan Boyle

21. The rain came sifting through the air, and settled like bloom on the fields —Mary Lavin
    Another rain simile to set a fictional scene, this one for Lavin's story, *Brigid.*

22. The rain came slowly and doggedly down, as if it had not even the spirit to pour —Charles Dickens

23. Rain comes down like the sky falling in skeins and yarny drifts —Marge Piercy

24. Raindrops . . . as warm as the tears of a child not yet consoled —Marguerite Yourcenar

25. Rain drops down like worms from the trees —Anne Sexton

26. Raindrops hitting like bullets —Joyce Carol Oates

27. Raindrops, plump as Malaga grapes —Paul Kuttner

28. Raindrops pock the surface like a plague —T. Coraghessan Boyle

29. Raindrops sparkled like diamonds falling through sunshine —Rita Mae Brown

30. Raindrops tapped at our backs like insinuating fingers —T. Coraghessan Boyle

31. Raindrops that whined like bullets —Kenzaburo Oë

32. Rained like a cow pissing on a flat rock —American colloquialism

33. Rain falling just past the end of his nose like a curtain —Thomas McGuane

34. Rain . . . fell like a silver veil from the dim grey sky —Mazo De La Roche

35. Rain . . . fell like iron swords out of the black sky —Paul Theroux

36. Rain . . . flowing in streaked silver patterns down the panes of the window nearby, like tears on the smooth shining face of a child —Bill Pronzini

37. Rain . . . flying down like silver needles —Frank Swinnerton

38. Rain glimmered like silver threads being spun from the mist —Paige Mitchell

39. Rain . . . gold as the planet system —Dame Edith Sitwell

40. Rain hit the roof like pennies from heaven —T. Coraghessan Boyle

41. Rain keeps falling like a curse —Amos Oz

42. Rain knocked at the windows like a smirking voyeur —T. Coraghessan Boyle

43. Rain . . . like a river falling out of the sky —Donald Seaman

44. Rain . . . like a deluge from heaven —W. Somerset Maugham

45. Rain, like dark-ruled lines on paper —Stephen Longstreet

46. The rain like pitchforks fell —Delmore Schwartz

47. Rain plastered the land till it was shining like hammered lead —Ted Hughes

48. Rain poured down like a waterfall —Jilly Cooper

49. Rain ran from the roof like a sea —Irving Feldman

50. Rain . . . rattling hard first on one side and then on the other like someone nailing down a case —Saul Bellow

51. Rains drip like the slow beat of time —Dame Edith Sitwell

52. Rain sheeting down like a giant waterfall —Frank Swinnerton

53. The rains of summer's end were very like tears, falling warm and gradually chilling where they fell —Lael Tucker Wertenbaker

54. Rain, so loud, like horses weeping —F. Scott Fitzgerald

55. Rainstorms that blacken like a headache —Amy Clampitt

56. The rain struck you so hard that it was like a warm gag in your mouth —Louis-Ferdinand Celine

57. The rain stung like whips, and from underfoot the mud oozed up over shoes and ankles like a live thing —Hugh Walpole

58. Rain . . . swept the deck in angry gusts, like a nagging woman who cannot leave a subject alone —W. Somerset Maugham

59. Rain thudded against the car like rotten fruit —Jean Thompson

60. The rain was blowing down the window glass like silk —Paul Horgan

61. Showers . . . drifting like scarves of gauze across the landscape — Jules Romains

62. A slanted sheet of rain swept like a scythe across Placid Cove Trailer Park —John Lutz
    The scene being set with this simile is for a mystery story entitled *Ride the Lightning.*

63. The sound of rain seemed . . . like the repeated attentions of a lover —John Cheever

64. A squall of rain driven around us in gusts like a wet veil —Erich Maria Remarque

65. Through the mist it was as if fine threads of rain were being teased down slowly —John McGahern

66. Torrents of rain streamed through the darkness, like incessant floods of tears which threatened to devour the earth and drown it in a deluge of unquenchable grief —Vladimir G. Korolenko

67. The [rain] water was loud as a crowd hissing —Susan Minot

68. When it rains, there's a wonderful lush wooden wetness in the air, and you feel as refreshed as if you were the earth itself, drinking in the water —Christopher Isherwood

69. The wind-blown rain was smeared like jam on the glass [of the window] —Jonathan Valin

RANTING
See: ROARS

RAPIDITY
See: SPEED

RARITY
See Also: ORIGINALITY

1. Exclusive as a mail box —Raymond Chandler

2. He's unusual all right . . . like the last of the orange flamingos —Saul Bellow

3. A miracle as great as art —Charles Bukowski

4. (And what is so) rare as a day in June —James Russell Lowell
    One of Lowell's most memorable lines!

5. (To think of nothing benign to memorize is as) rare as feeling no personal blemish —W. H. Auden

6. Rare as a man without self-pity —Stephen Vincent Benét

7. Rare and wonderful feeling, like the first moments of love —George Garrett

8. Rare as a black swan —Anon
    This probably evolved from "Rare to be found as black swans" featured in Daniel Rogers' seventeenth century *Matrimonial Honors.*

9. Rare as a Cockney accent at Eton —Anon

10. Rare as a man without self-pity —Stephen Vincent Benét

11. Rare as an Emperor moth —Lawrence Durrell

12. Rare as a New York City subway train without graffiti —Elyse Sommer

13. Rare as a nine dollar bill —Anon

14. Rare as a politician on the stump who doesn't make promises —Anon
    A partner to this one: "Rare as a politician who lives up to his campaign promises."

15. Rare as a well-spent life -Anon

16. (A lucky man is) rare as a white crow —Juvenal

17. Rare as a winter swallow —Honoré de Balzac

18. Rare as discretion in a gossip —Anon

19. Rare as humility in a grizzly bear —Julian Ralph

20. (Movies like Paul Mayersberg's *Captive* are as) rare as peacocks' teeth —Vincent Canby, *New York Times,* April 3, 1987

21. Rare as rocking horse manure —Anon

22. Rare as snow in July —Anon
    Another modern simile which can be traced to an earlier form: "Like snow at Midsummer, exceeding rare."

23. Rare in life as black lightning on a blue sky —Fitz-Greene Halleck

24. (The liberal "effete snobs" that Spiro T. Agnew railed against are as) rare today as Republicans on the welfare rolls —Barbara Ehrenreich

25. Scarce as below par golf scores —Anon

26. Scarce as fat men in a long-distance marathon —Anon

27. Scarce as a six figure advance for a first novel by an unknown author — Elyse Sommer

28. [Money . . . was as] scarce as frogs' teeth, crabs' tails or eunuchs' whiskers —Pat Barr

Barr's colorful multiple simile refers to the scarcity of money in Korea during the late nineteenth century when the heroine of her book, *Curious Life For a Lady*, was there.

29. Scarce as ice cream vendors on a snowy day in January —Anon
     The comparative twists on this are endless, for example: "Scarce as lemonade stands in the desert," or "Scarce as women in fur coats in ninety degree weather."

30. Scarce as low-cost, high profit ideas for an untapped market —Anon

31. Scarce as squirrels at a busy city street crossing —Elyse Sommer

32. Scarce as the buffalo that once roamed the prairie —Enid Nemy, *New York Times*, July 6, 1986
     Nemy likened the buffalo scarcity to newsy letters.

33. Scarce as the cardinal virtues —Ross Macdonald

34. Scarce as two dollar gourmet lunches —Anon

35. (One of the kindest-natured persons that I ever knew on this earth, where kind people are) as rare as black eagles or red deer —Ouida

RASHNESS
See: SPEED

READERS/READING
See Also: BOOKS

1. Deprive him [the habitual reader] of printed matter and he grows nervous, moody and restless; then, like the alcoholic bereft of brandy who will drink shellac or methylated spirit, he will make do with the advertisements of a paper five years old; he will make do with a telephone directory —W. Somerset Maugham

2. A person who cannot read is something like a blind man walking through a pleasant meadow, where there are flowers and fruit trees; there are many pleasant things and many wise and good things printed in books, but we cannot get them unless we read —Timothy Dwight

3. Reading is to the mind what exercise is to the body —Sir Richard Steele

4. The reading of detective stories is an addiction like tobacco or alcohol —W. H. Auden

5. Reading that is only whimful and desultory amounts to a kind of cultural vagrancy. It neither wets nor fortifies the mind. It merely distracts and tires it like traffic noises on an overcrowded street —John Mason Brown

6. Reading the same book over and over again is a mechanical exercise like the Tibetan turning of a prayer-wheel —Clifton Fadiman
    See Also: REPETITION

7. Reads like some people wrestle; she gets involved —François Camoin

READINESS
> See: PREPAREDNESS

REALIZATION
> See Also: TRUTH

1. Awareness of failure plagued at him like a sword, twisting in his consciousness cruelly as though it had been lying in wait to murder his self-respect —Noël Coward

2. Began to see herself from the outside, as if she was a moving target in someone else's binoculars —Margaret Atwood

3. Flash of insight as pitiless as the late-autumn light —Sharon Sheehe Stark

4. Horror . . . burst upon him like an electric storm that throws a vivid light into the darkest shadow —Mazo De La Roche

5. It [realization] came to her slowly as a negative being developed — Elizabeth Spencer

6. Knowledge penetrated my consciousness like a red-hot knife —Stefan Zweig

7. Light burst on me as if a window of my memory had been suddenly flung open on a street in the city —Joseph Conrad

8. Like a lover or lecher, the awareness came to her at night. Every perception rejoices in itself like a fire catching fire through itself — Delmore Schwartz

9. Like French women who can tell if a bottle of Cognac has been opened in the next room, Guido could tell what was happening at home as soon as he put his key in the lock —Laurie Colwin

10. Realization . . . dawned . . . like the sunrise —Donald Seaman

11. Realization came . . . like a fist knocking the wind out of her —David Leavitt

12. Realization grips them like a seizure —T. Coraghessan Boyle

13. The realization . . . made the nape of my neck feel like I'd just applied an ice pack —Sue Grafton

14. Saw as one sees a landscape in a flash of lightning —Virginia Woolf

15. Saw it like a thunderbolt —Clifford Odets

16. See it all like a chart unrolled —John Greenleaf Whittier

17. Suddenly, as if a wet sheet had been thrown over her, the truth of the matter strikes her —T. Coraghessan Boyle

18. The knowledge sank like a plummet —Jean Stafford

19. A thousand things . . . suddenly added up like a column of figures in her mind —William Humphrey

20. (Trifles . . . like a spark falling upon tinder, can) throw a flame of light into the abyss of a mind —Stefan Zweig

21. The truth flared in his head like a marron —Miles Gibson

22. The truth popped out like a jack-in-the-box —George Garrett

23. Trying to find it [self-knowledge] in the bosom of a Mississippi family was like trying to find some object lost in a gigantic attic, when you really didn't know what you were looking for —Elizabeth Spencer
     See Also: IMPOSSIBILITY

24. An uncomfortable truth had come to settle like a shroud over the . . . investigation —Doug Feiden
     The comparison in Feiden's novel, *The $10,000,000 Getaway,* pertains to the investigation of a Lufthansa airline robbery.

25. Understanding fell across me like a velvet curtain —Russell Banks

REALNESS/UNREALNESS

1. Artificial like a piece of water in a French garden —W. Somerset Maugham

2. Abstract and decorative as a snowstorm in a glass paperweight — George Garrett

3. Artificial as a false mustache —Dorothea Straus

4. Blurred, unreal, like a picture in the newspaper —Katherine Mansfield

5. Distorted as the view through the wrong end of a telescope —Anon

6. False as waxworks —Karl Shapiro

7. (Sometimes I) feel like a figment of my own imagination —Lily Tomlin

8. Genuine as rain —J. B. Priestly

9. Had a squinty close view of the truth like a jeweler studying facets and flaws, like a man at a microscope —George Garrett

10. He could block out reality as easily as exposing a roll of film — Jonathan Kellerman

11. Real and insistent as a wound in one's body —Milovan Djilas

12. (The pain returned) real as a toothache —John Braine

13. Real as hunger —Anon

14. Real as several grain sacks thrown on top of each other —Flannery O'Connor

15. Real as the passing of time —Anon

16. (You and I are as) real at least as the people upstairs —James Merrill

17. Reality met him like a swung shovel —Sharon Sheehe Stark

18. (The room seemed as) unreal as a stage set —William McIlvanney

19. Real, like a punch on the nose —Stephen Longstreet

20. Unreal, as ghostly as the brushing of a leaf against his face —Katherine Anne Porter

21. Unreal as the emptiness of the air —Leonid Andreyev

22. Unreal, like a poorly-played drama on the stage —Ben Ames Williams

23. Unreal like mid-summer sunshine remembered at Christmas — Elizabeth Bowen

REAPPEARANCE

1. Always came back to me like a dog to his kennel —Nathan Shaham

2. (The day) began all over again, like a toothache, in her memory — Frank Swinnerton

3. [Kisses can . . .] come back like ghosts —Carl Sandburg
     Sandburg used this simile to open and close a poem, as well as for its title. In between are several additional similes to illustrate that love does come to an end to be put away "Like a clock," "Like a violin," or "Like a summer day near fall time."

4. Double back like a fox eluding his pursuing hounds —Robert Traver

5. Keeps cropping up, like toadstools after a flood —Jonathan Kellerman

6. Like a repentant lover, I returned to that previous way of life —John Rechy

7. Recur like wind from a returning storm —Hallie Burnett

8. (Questions about her parentage) recurred like malaria —Rita Mae Brown

9. Recurring like a motif in music —G. K. Chesterton

10. (They were) returning again, like birds to their roosts —Graham Swift

11. Return like a bad penny —Anon

12. Return like a homing pigeon —Anon

13. Rolled like a stone back to where he'd started —Martin Cruz Smith

14. Turn up like an old arrest record —Marge Piercy

15. Turn up like a single boot after I finally threw the other away —Marge Piercy

16. [A deep-seated flaw] would surface like an aching wisdom tooth — James Lee Burke

REASON
     See: SENSE

RECOLLECTION
     See: MEMORY

RED

See Also: BLUSHES, CHEEKS, COLORS, HAIR, LIPS, MOUTH

1. As red as any rose —William Shakespeare

2. Red as a matchtip —James Reiss

3. (Tongue) red as a pomegranate —Miles Gibson

4. Red as a radish —Anon

5. Red as a robin's breast —Anon

6. Red as a rooster's comb —Dorothy Canfield Fisher
   The simile from Canfield's *Sex Education* describes a face
   turned red with embarrassment.

7. Red as a strong man's heart —Robert Tristram Coffin
   The objects being compared are Vermont barns.

8. (Lips) red as a sun rising on the Atlantic and setting on the Pacific —
   Mary Morris

9. Red as a wound —Jon Silkin

10. [A cloak] red as blood —William Shakespeare
    Similes linking the color red with blood abound throughout
    literature as well as everyday speech.

11. (Hair) red as chili powder —Saul Bellow

12. Red as fire —William Shakespeare

13. (Lips) red as hell —Dame Edith Sitwell

14. (Fingernails) red as satin ribbons —Diane Ackerman

15. [Leather seats of a showy car] red as spilt blood —Saul Bellow

16. Red like poppies —Charlotte Brontë

17. Thin streaks of red, like veins in marble showed on his chalky teeth —
    Wright Morris

REDUCTION

See: DECREASE, DISAPPEARANCE

REFLECTION

See: THOUGHT

REFORM

See: CHANGE

REGRET

See Also: CONSCIENCE

1. Remorse is as the heart in which it grows —Samuel Taylor Coleridge

Coleridge's poem, *Remorse,* continues as follows: "If that be gentle, it drops balmy dews of true repentance; but if proud and gloomy, it is the poison tree, that pierces to the inmost."

2. Repentance, like the sea, is always open to the ventures —Shimoni Yalkut

3. Repentance, without amendment, is like continually pumping without mending the leak —Lewis W. Dilwyn

4. Repentance follows crime . . . as changes follow time —Percy Bysshe Shelley

5. Regret is like a mountaintop from which we survey our dead life, a mountaintop on which we pause and ponder, and very often looking into the twilight we ask ourselves whether it would be well to send a letter or some token —George Moore

6. The pang of regret, sharp as a sword thrust —L. P. Hartley

7. Regret is like tears seeping through closed eyelids —Galway Kinnell

8. (When I fall) let me fall without regret like a leaf —Wendell Berry

9. Remorseless as an alarm clock —Anon

REGULARITY/IRREGULARITY

1. Balance as a tail balances a kite —Anon

2. Balanced as the scales of justice —Anon

3. [A cat's purring] intermittent as a walkie-talkie —Lorrie Moore

4. Irregular as French verbs —Anon

5. Random, like love's choices —Patricia Hampl

6. Regular as a clock —Slogan for Serutan laxative, Healthaids, Inc.

7. Regular as a heartbeat —Mary Hedin

8. Regular as a metronome —Edward Hoagland

9. Regular as a motor boat —Lee Smith
   A more specific variation: "Regular as the chug-chug of a motor boat."

10. Regular as sun and tide —Wallace Stegner

11. Regular as the moon makes the tides —Henry James

12. Rhythmic as water —Amy Hempel
    In Hempel's story, *Beg, sl tog, Inc, Cont, Rep,* it's the sliding knitting needles that are likened to water.

13. Scattered like applause during a bad act —Anon

14. Steadily as a shell secretes its beating leagues of monotone —Hart Crane

15. Symmetrical as a doily —Betsy Wade, *New York Times,* May 2, 1986
    The descriptive frame of reference is a tree.

REJECTION

See Also: ABANDONMENT

1. Cast away [anger] like spoiled milk —Marge Piercy

2. Discarded like outmoded customs —Elyse Sommer

3. Discarded (me) like yesterday's underpants —Sue Grafton

4. Dropped . . . like a dead fish —T. Glen Coughlin

5. Dropped [from a list] . . . like a hot rivet —Loren D. Estleman

6. He shook them [young women] off his back like a young stallion shaking off an unskilled rider —Russell Banks

7. Keep at a distance, like someone with an infectious disease —Anon
   The many twists on this usually refer to a specific diseases, whatever is most feared. Like so many phrases that have been mainstreamed into our language, this can be traced back to a line from Shakespeare, in this case: "Barred, like one infectious."

8. Push her away like a clinging dog —Daphne du Maurier

9. Push me aside like a kitchen chair —Philip Levine

10. Put (such thoughts) aside like chewed-up grapeskins —Bertold Brecht

11. Rejected [bad news] . . . like a transplanted organ —Pat Conroy

12. Rejected [praise] like counterfeit money —William McIlvanney

13. Shoved aside like a row boat nosed away by a tanker —Mary Gordon

14. Shun him like the plague —Charles Dickens

15. Some men, like spaniels, will only fawn the more when repulsed, but will pay little heed to a friendly caress —Abd-el-Kader

16. Spurn my passion like a worm —Jean Racine

17. Swept her aside as if she were a cobweb —Susan Kelly

18. They just dropped me . . . like a bag of potatoes —Njabulo Ndebele

19. Threw aside everything . . . like a contemptible burden —Heinrich Böll

RELATIONSHIPS

See Also: MARRIAGE; MEN AND WOMEN; PARENTHOOD; PEOPLE, INTERACTION

1. Charted his moods like a cartographer —Pat Conroy
   Conroy's simile from *The Great Santini* refers to the main character's understanding of and adjustment to his father's temperament.

2. Families are a kind of closed system; like locked trunks, they are hard to penetrate from the outside —Daphne Merkin

3. Families are like wine. You get the old vintage that goes right off: goes weak as coloured water or old scent —Julia O'Faolain

4. A family, if it is large and well-connected, is like a religion —Paul Theroux
   In the novel, *Picture Palace,* from which this is taken, the author follows up the simile with the following explanation: "It serves the same purpose, to bewitch the believer with joy and offer him salvation; it consoles, it enchants, it purifies."

5. Getting to know someone is like opening a safe: you have to learn the unique combination of numbers —Delmore Schwartz
   Schwartz followed this entry into his journal with "No, this is not really true."

6. Her life was hung upon this relationship, like the cloth of a tent that would collapse into loose folds without the central post that supported it —Tennessee Williams

7. Human relations just aren't fixed in their orbits like the planets; they're more like galaxies, changing all the time, exploding into light for years, then dying away —May Sarton

8. The idea of a step-father is like a substitute host on a talk show — Bobbie Ann Mason

9. In the beginning of a relationship, if you're lucky enough to find wit at the right moments, it's like getting a cab in the rain —Steve Post, WNYC/FM, December 22, 1986

10. (There were Ben and his father, eye to eye, as) intimate as lovers —Pat Conroy

11. I was there for you, like an Eye-Beam . . . any other beam would do —John Updike

12. Know each other's thoughts. Without words, as if traveling on connected bloodstreams —Mary Hedin

13. Know each other, crack and flaw, like two irregular stones that fit together —Adrienne Rich

14. Like the slowly tumbling arabesque of little cloud shapes drifting across the sand cliffs on a summer wind, neither [of two close sisters] was anything without the other —Wilbur Daniel Steele

15. Never got on . . . like a couple of dogs not liking each other's smells —Frank Swinnerton

16. Relationship . . . as fragile as spindly bridges —David Leavitt, *New York Times Book Review,* 1986
    See Also: FRAGILITY

17. The relationship bumps along like a car with three tires —Ira Wood

18. Relationship . . . like two engines running at variance —D. H. Lawrence

565

19. The relationship waxed, billowed like scenery on the breeze —John Ashberry

20. Spread herself out like a cloak for the king to walk on —Suzi Gablik, *New York Times Book Review,* 1986
    The simile is used to explain the relationship between the author of *My Life with Chagall* and the artist.

21. The string between you wore out . . . like old elastic —Tess Slesinger

22. The sweet sorrow of loving a parent is as pure as the taste of a sourball when you are five —Norman Mailer

23. Their (a mother and daughter) connection had built-in tension and resiliency. Like the coiled telephone cord through which they communicated —Ellen Goodman

24. There was room for improvement [in relationship between two men] . . . a sort of gap, like the Grand Canyon —J. F. Powers

25. Torn between them [warring parents] like a plot of land they both wanted to lay claim to —Ann Jasperson

26. Treated her like a twenty-carat diamond —Rita Mae Brown

27. Understand one another like thieves at a fair —Anatole France

28. (After half an hour . . .) we were as familiar with one another as if we had unbosomed our whole life histories —Erich Maria Remarque

RELENTLESSNESS
See: PERSISTENCE

RELIABILITY/UNRELIABILITY
See Also: FIRMNESS, STEADINESS

1. (I found the almond trees as) dependable as the swallows of Capistrano, announcing another spring —Wallace Stegner

2. As reliable as the day following the night —Dorothea Straus

3. [A collection of art works] as spotty as a Dalmation and not half as beautiful —Manuela Hoelterhoff, on the new Wallace wing at the Metropolitan Museum of Art, *Wall Street Journal,* March 17, 1987

4. Consistent and productive as machines —Gay Gaer Luce

5. Dealing with Owen Roe was like walking across a bog. You never knew when the ground might give way under your feet —Julia O'Faolain

6. Dependable as a floating crap game —Harry Prince

7. Dependable as clockwork . . .   —Anon

8. Dependable as daylight —Beryl Markham

9. A duty dodged is like a debt unpaid; it is only deferred, and we must come back and settle the account at last —Joseph Fort

10. Duty without responsibility is like pomp without power —Edward, Duke of Windsor

11. Fickle as a changeful dream —Sir Walter Scott

12. It [buying a house] was like joining a church because it committed me to spending every weekend I could get . . . to working on the place — George V. Higgins

13. (You've got) no more responsibility than a one-eyed jack rabbit — Elmer Kelton

14. Reliability's like a string we can only see the middle of —William McFee

15. (About as) reliable as a Pravda editorial —Joseph Wambaugh

16. Reliable as a salary —Frank R. Stockton

17. Reliable as crystal balls, goat innards, and prayer —Harold Adams

18. Reliable as he was eccentric —Mark Twain

19. Reliable as reading tea leaves or the bumps on one's head —Peter J. Bonacich, letter to editor of *Discover,* April, 1986

20. Responsibility rested upon him as lightly as the freckles on his nose — Alice Caldwell Hegan

21. Solid as tombstones —Helen Hudson

22. Wore, like a garment, an air of wholesome reliability —Mazo De La Roche

23. Would always be there . . . like some familiar landmark —Barbara Pym, *The Sweet Dove Died*

RELIEF
See: EMOTIONS

RELIGION
See Also: BELIEFS

1. As men's prayers are a disease of the will, so are their creeds a disease of the intellect —Ralph Waldo Emerson

2. As religious as any man who prays daily and hangs a rabbit's foot on his windshield —Harry Prince

3. Beautiful women without religion are like flowers without perfume — Heinrich Heine

4. Catholicism's a little too much like the gold standard: a fixed weight of piety translatable into a fixed exchange rate of grace —Michael M. Thomas

5. The Christian is like the ripening corn; the riper he grows, the more lowly he bends his head —Thomas Guthrie

6. Christianity is like electricity. It cannot enter a person unless it can pass through —Bishop Richard C. Raines

7. The church is a sort of hospital for men's souls, and as full of quackery as the hospitals for those bodies —Henry David Thoreau

8. A consistently godless world is like a picture without perspective — Franz Werfel

9. Faith . . . a stiffening process, a sort of mental starch, which ought to be applied as sparingly as possible —E. M. Forster

10. Faith is like love: it cannot be forced —Arthur Schopenhauer

11. Faith without works is like a bird without wings —Francis Beaumont

12. Folded into his religion like a razor into its case —Anon

13. God's like a kid with too many toys to take care of —Sharon Sheehe Stark

14. People are born churchy or unchurchy, just as they are born with a tendency to arteriosclerosis, cancer or consumption —Anatole France

15. In religion, as in friendship, they who profess most are the least sincere —Richard Brinsley Sheridan

16. In religion as in politics it so happens that we have less charity for those who believe half our creed than for those who deny the whole of it — Charles Caleb Colton

17. Living without faith is like driving in a fog —Anon

18. The majority takes the creed [Calvinism] as a horse takes his collar; it slips by his ears, over his neck, he hardly knows how, but he finds himself in harness and jogs along as his fathers and forefathers before him —Oliver Wendell Holmes, Sr.

19. A man who writes of himself without speaking of God is like one who identifies himself without giving his address —Ben Hecht

20. Men's anger about religion is as if two men should quarrel for a lady they neither of them care for —Lord Halifax

21. Our faith . . . runs as fast as feeling to embrace —William Alfred

22. Our faith is too often like the mercury in the weather-glass; it gets up high in fine weather; in rough weather it sinks proportionally low — Anon

23. Piety, like aristocracy, has its nobility —Johann Wolfgang von Goethe

24. Prayed like an orphan —Wendell Berry

25. Prayer is a force as real as terrestrial gravity —Alexis Carrel

26. Priestly mannerisms clung to him like the smell of candle-wax and incense —Peter Kemp

27. Religion is comparable to a childhood neurosis —Sigmund Freud

28. Religion is like love; it plays the devil with clear thinking —Rose Macaulay

29. Religion is like the breath of heaven; if it goes abroad in the open air, it scatters and dissolves —Jeremy Taylor

30. Religion, like water, may be free, but when they pipe it to you, you've got to help pay for the piping. And the piper —Muriel Spark

31. Religious as a lizard on a rock —Anon

32. Religious sense is like an esthetic sense. You're born with it or you aren't —P. D. James, *New York Times Magazine,* October 5, 1986

33. Sects and creeds of religion are like pocket compasses, good enough to point you in the direction, but the nearer the pole you get the worse they work —Josh Billings
    In Billings' phonetic dialect: "Sekts and creeds of religion are like pocket compesses, good enuff tu point you inte the right direction, but the nearer the pole yu git the wuss tha wurk."

34. She fought off God like an unwelcome suitor —Nancy Evans about Emily Dickinson, "First Editions"/WNYC February 18, 1987

35. Some Christians are like soiled bank notes: while we acknowledge their value we wish them changed —William Lewis

36. Sometimes the curse of God comes like the caress of a woman's hand, and sometimes His blessing comes like a knife in the flesh —Amos Oz

37. The soul united to God is like a leaf united to the tree —Ignazio Silone

38. They treated their God like a desk clerk with whom they lodged requests and complaints —Helen Hudson

39. Without dogma a religion is like a body without skeleton. It can't stand —James G. Huneker

REMEDY
See: PROBLEMS/SOLUTIONS

REMORSE
See: REGRET

REMOTENESS
See Also: RESERVE

1. Acting like an absentee landlord who was either unaware of or indifferent to the tenants smashing the windows or breaking up the furniture —Senator William S. Cohen commenting on President Ronald Reagan's leadership during Iran-contra affair, *New York Times,* March 1, 1987

2. Alienated as Camus —Richard Ford

3. As far apart as the sound of waves on the shore —John Updike

4.   (Fury) as unpersonal as disease —David Denby

5.   Behaved like a dowager queen at a funeral, acknowledging everyone's politenesses but keeping her own majestic feelings isolated —Judith Martin

6.   Detached [from an excited crowd] as a droplet of oil —Stefan Zweig

7.   Detached [mind from body] . . . like a kite whose string snaps on a windy day —Julia O'Faolain

8.   Detached, passive, still as a golden lily in a lily-pond —Ellen Glasgow

9.   Distant as an ocean —Reynolds Price

10. Distant as heart-parted lovers are —Babette Deutsch

11. (She was as silent and) distant as the moon —Kate Wheeler

12. Feeling impersonal and fragile as a piece of china waiting on a serving table —F. Scott Fitzgerald
     See Also: FRAGILITY

13. He speaks to me as if I were a public monument —Queen Victoria about her prime minister, Gladstone

14. Impassive as an apple —Laurie Colwin

15. Impassive as a tank —Seamus Heaney

16. Impersonal as a cyclone —Anon

17. Impersonal as the justice of God —Victor Hugo

18. Incurious as a stone —Robert Hass

19. (Until that minute she had been as) impersonal to me as a doll in a well-stocked toy department —R. V. Cassill
     See Also: SOCIABILITY

20. Indifferent as a blizzard —Anon

21. Like the hermit crab, he ventured out of his shell only on the rarest occasions —A. J. Cronin

22. Looked disinterested, like a customs inspector —Julia Whedon

23. A look of remoteness . . . like cathedrals, like long gleaming conference tables, like the crackling, hissing recordings of the voices of famous men long dead —John D. MacDonald
     An example to illustrate that several distinctly different similes can be effectively linked to a single reference base.

24. Look through 'em all like windows —Edith Wharton

25. Otherworldly like a monk —F. Scott Fitzgerald

26. Personal as a letter addressed to 'Occupant' —Anon

27. (His father had always been) remote . . . as a figure in a pageant —Hortense Calisher

28. Remote as a nightmare —Walter De La Mare

29. [Sky scrapers] remote as castles in a fairy tale —Bobbie Ann Mason

30. (Bomb shelters are as) remote as the covered wagon —Edward R. Murrow broadcast from European front during World War II

31. Remote, unapproachable, like the expression of an animal that man has forced into sullen submission —Ellen Glasgow

32. Seemed like a perpetual visitor —Henry Van Dyke

33. (They get together and tell each other what women are like, but they never listen to find out.) Shut up in their heads like clams —Nancy Price

34. Stiff and remote, rather like a sleep-walker —Alice Munro

35. Stolid as ledgers —Julia O'Falain

36. (He sat there, heavy and massive, suddenly) sunk back into himself and his drunkenness, like a lonely hill of unassailable melancholy —Erich Maria Remarque
    See Also: BEARING

37. To ask Henrietta was like asking the door knob —Sholom Aleichem
    See Also: FUTILITY

38. As unreachable as all the landscapes beyond the limits of my eye — John Fowles
    See Also: IMPOSSIBILITY

39. (Face,) withdrawn as a castle —Nadine Gordimer

RENOWN

See: FAME

REPETITION

See Also: CONTINUITY, DULLNESS

1. Continue unceasingly like a drip from a leaking faucet —Anon

2. Iteration, like friction, is likely to generate heat instead of progress — George Eliot

3. Kept on repeating the words like a talisman —Edith Wharton

4. Life as repetitive as the seasons —J. B. Priestly

5. Like warmed-up cabbage served at each repast the repetition kills the wretch at last —Juvenal

6. Monotonous . . . like a tap with a worn-out washer dripping . . . in a kitchen sink —Gerald Kersch
    In Kersh's novel, *Repetition,* the dripping faucet image describes a character's voice.

7. Recited tirelessly as a language record —Marge Piercy
    In Piercy's poem, *A Cold and Married War,* the narrator is reciting her sins and errors.

8. (Rages . . . which seemed to) recur in cycles, like menstruation — Ursule Molinaro

9. (Thought) repeated like a lesson —William H. Gass

10. Repeated like a rhyme —Amy Lowell

11. Repeats . . . like an advertisement in neon —Marge Piercy

12. Repetitive as hieroglyphs —Derek Walcott

13. (Disembodied and) repetitive as the sea in a shell —Elizabeth Spencer

14. [The sweep hand of a clock] went around and around like a door-to-door salesman —Raymond Chandler

REPUTATION

1. As for taking a good man's name from him, you might as well undertake to pull goose-quills from the wings of an angel —Elbridge G. Dow, Jr.

2. A bad reputation in a woman allures like the signs of heat in a bitch — Aldous Huxley
   Huxley wrote *Point Counter Point* from which this is taken long before the women's movement raised our consciousness to gender-biased characterization.

3. Disgraces are like cherries: one draws another —George Herbert

4. A good name, like good will, is got by many actions and lost by one — Lord Francis Jeffrey

5. A good reputation is like the cypress; once cut, it never puts forth leaf again —Francesco Guicciardini

6. His record's as clean as a vestal virgin's —Dialogue from a 1967 movie, *The Deadly Affair.*

7. Honor is like a rocky island without a landing place; once we leave it we can't get it back —Nicolas Boileau

8. Honor is like the eye, which cannot suffer the least injury without damage; it is [like] a precious stone, the price of which is lessened by the least flaw —Jaques Bénigne Boussuet

9. Honor, like freedom, is a luxury for those with independent incomes — John Braine

10. Honors trailing away behind him like the tail of a comet —Vita Sackville-West

11. In scandal, as in robbery, the receiver is always as bad as the thief — Lord Chesterfield

12. A liar's reputation . . . stuck with him like a cockleburr —Carlos Baker

13. A person's reputation is as fragile and vulnerable as human life itself — Robert Traver

14. To steal it [a person's honor] is like stealing your soul —William Diehl

RESENTMENT
See: ANGER

RESERVE
See Also: EMOTIONS, PERSONALITY TRAITS, REMOTENESS

1. Animated as a department store mannequin —Anon

2. Apathy dropped from her like a garment —Edna Ferber

3. As excited as a mortician at a cheap funeral —Raymond Chandler

4. As much feeling as a sphinx —Maureen Dowd, *New York Times,* 1985

5. (My father was) born without emotions like some people are born without little fingers —Pat Conroy

6. Buries her feelings as a dog buries a bone —Anon

7. Closed himself like a shellfish under attack —Kenzaburo Oë

8. Detached as a funeral director —Stanley Elkin

9. Detach oneself [as from a situation] like a zipout lining —Anon

10. (The sun is as) dispassionate as the hand of a man who greets you with his mind on other things —Beryl Markham

11. Drew a circle around herself, like the safe zone in a children's game where no pursuers may enter and no prisoners may leave —David Michael Kaplan

12. (I could) feel the armor, like a steel skin, slipping around me —William Diehl

13. The habit of reserve was like an iron mould —Ellen Glasgow
See Also: HABIT

14. Keep them [emotions] tucked away, and only produce them very occasionally, like special little pots of jam, when the people whom I love come to tea —Katherine Mansfield

15. Like a toothpaste . . . gave only a little at a time —Donald Seaman

16. Lived inside herself as precisely as a walnut in its shell, nothing rattling, nothing wasting —Jessamyn West

17. (She had withdrawn into herself and) no longer projected anything, like an actor reaching the wings, the character falling like a cape to reveal the person beneath, innocuous —Lynne Sharon Schwartz

18. Numb as a broomstick —William Alfred

19. Persons extremely reserved are like old enamelled watches, which had painted covers that hindered your seeing what o'clock it was —Horace Walpole

20. A prudent reserve [about being open with other people] is as necessary as a seeming openness is prudent —Lord Chesterfield

21. Retreated into himself like a turtle —Carlos Fuentes

22. She was reserved . . . like a picture so hung that it can be seen only at a certain angle; an angle known to no one but its possessor —Edith Wharton

23. Shrunk into herself as though she had been touched by something coarse —Anton Chekhov

24. Sit inside themselves like honey in a jar and just be —Elizabeth Janeway

25. Spiritless as corked champagne —James G. Huneker

26. Taught herself to control feelings . . . the way an Indian fakir controls pain —Shana Alexander

RESIGNATION
See: MEEKNESS

RESPONSE
See: QUESTIONS/ANSWERS, WORD(S)

RESPONSIBILITY
See: RELIABILITY/UNRELIABILITY

RESTLESSNESS

1. Always fidgeting around to go, like a horse in an antbed —Elmer Kelton

2. Fidgeted as though the skin on her back were as a plucked fowl's in a poulterer's shop window —Virginia Woolf

3. Fidgety as a child —Richard Wilbur

4. Fidgety, like a rabbit's nose—or a commuter —Don Marquis

5. Fitful as a cautery —Diane Ackerman

6. I'm as restless as a willow in a windstorm, I'm as jumpy as a puppet on a string —Oscar Hammerstein II, opening lines for "It Might As Well Be Spring" from *State Fair*
   "It Might As Well Be Spring" is a particularly outstanding example of Hammerstein's mastery of the light-hearted simile. The lyrics also compare a nightingale without a song to a feeling of discontentment, a spider to busyness and a baby on a swing to a feeling of giddiness.

7. As impatient as a wedding dick —American colloquialism

8. (It is a night like many another with the sky now a bit) impatient for today to be over like a bored salesgirl shifting from foot to stockinged foot —John Ashberry

9. Pacing up and down like an animal in a cage —Elizabeth Taylor

10. (Walking around) restless as a big animal in the lowering weather — Elizabeth Spencer

11. Restless as a rolling stone —Anon

12. Restless as sharp desire —Arthur C. Benson

13. Restless as Ulysses —William Makepeace Thackeray

14. Restless like a man running downhill who cannot keep on his legs unless he runs on, and will inevitably fall if he stops —Arthur Schopenhauer

15. A restless mind, like a rolling stone, gathers nothing but dirt and mire —John Balguy
    See Also: MIND

16. Seemed always looking for a place, like one who goes to choose a grave —Stephen Crane

17. (Settled on the couch,) shifting and fluttering like birds in a nest — Peter Meinke

18. Squirming as though bitten by bugs —Bernard Malamud

19. Squirm like a country mule hitched beside the railroad track — American colloquialism, attributed to South

20. Tossed all night like a man running from himself —Paige Mitchell

21. Wriggling in her place, as if her chair was hot —Frank Swinnerton

RESTRAINT
See: CONFINEMENT, EMOTIONS

RESULTS
See: CAUSE/EFFECT

RETREAT
See: DISAPPEARANCE, EXITS

RETURN
See: PAST, THE; REAPPEARANCE

REVELRY
See: GAIETY

REVENGE
See Also: BITTERNESS

1. Revenge is a kind of wild justice, which the more a man's nature runs to, the more ought law to weed it out —Francis Bacon

2. Revenge is like a boomerang. Although for a time it flies in the direction in which it is hurled, it takes a sudden curve, and, returning, hits your own head the heaviest blow of all —John M. Mason

3. Revenge is often like biting a dog because the dog bit you —Austin O'Malley

REVOLUTIONS
See: POLITICS

RHETORIC
See: SPEECHMAKING, WORD(S)

RICHES
See Also: ABUNDANCE, FORTUNE/MISFORTUNE, MONEY, SUCCESS/FAILURE

1. Appearance of wealth will draw wealth to it. As honey draws hungry flies —George Garrett

2. Have money like sand —Louis MacNeice

3. His bank account swelled like a puff ball —Christina Stead

4. Inherited wealth is as certain death to ambition as cocaine is to morality —William K. Vanderbilt

5. Like our other passions, the desire for riches is more sharpened by their use than by their lack —Michel de Montaigne

6. A man that keeps riches but doesn't enjoy them is like an ass that carries gold and eats thistles —Thomas Fuller
   "Doesn't enjoy them" has been modernized from "And enjoys them not."

7. More money than the telephone company's got wrong numbers —Sam Hellman

8. (The auction was attended by collectors with) pockets as deep as wells —Anon

9. Property, like liberty, thought immune under the Constitution from destruction, is not immune from regulation essential for the common good —Benjamin Cardozo

10. Prosperity is like a tender mother, but blind, who spoils her children — English proverb

11. Prosperity is like perfume, it often makes the head ache —Duchess of Newcastle

12. The rich are driven by wealth as beggars by the itch —W. B. Yeats

13. Rich as a congressman —Carson McCullers

14. Riches, like insects, when concealed they lie, wait but for wings, and in their season fly —Alexander Pope

Pope spelled the fifth word "conceal'd."

15. The way to wealth is as plain as the way to market. It depends chiefly on two words, industry and frugality —Benjamin Franklin

16. Wealth is an engine that can be used for power if you are an engineer; but to be tied to the flywheel of an engine is rather a misfortune —Elbert Hubbard

17. Wealth is like a viper, which is harmless if a man knows how to take hold of it; but if he does not, it will twine round his hand and bite him —Saint Clement

18. Wealth like rheumatism falls on the weakest parts —John Ray's *Proverbs*

19. Worldly riches are like nuts; many clothes are torn in getting them, many a tooth broke in cracking them, but never a belly filled with eating them —Ralph Venning

RICHNESS

1. Rich as apricots in brandy —Robert D. McFadden

2. (Vellum) rich as country cream —Oliver Wendell Holmes, Sr.

3. Rich as memory —Marge Piercy

4. Rich as velvet brocade —Morris Philipson, describing the rich texture of language in a book, *New York Times Book Review,* April 12, 1987

RIDICULE
See: INSULTS

RIGHTEOUSNESS
See: JUSTICE, VIRTUE

RIGHTNESS
See: CORRECTNESS, TRUENESS/FALSENESS

RISING
See Also: BEARING, STANDING

1. Everything undulates like water weed —John Berger
   Berger's simile appeared in his afterword for the published script of the movie, *Nineteen-Nineteen.*

2. Got up clumsily, cautiously, like one standing in a stalled Ferris wheel —Stanley Elkin

3. Lifts like a starting gate —Daniel Berrigan

4. Popped up . . . like a released spring —Elizabeth Spencer

5. Raising himself in his seat like a panelist answering a question from the audience —Kingsley Amis

6. Reared like a seal —Erich Maria Remarque
7. (He felt his cock) rearing up like a kite —Jilly Cooper
8. Rise (from sleep) like driftwood out of surf —Karl Shapiro
9. (Smoke that) rises like birds —D. H. Lawrence
10. Rising gawkily like a tame goose trying to fly —Margaret Laurence
11. Rising like a north wind —Lawrence Durrell
12. Rising like a salmon against the bullnecked river —Louis MacNeice
13. Rising like cakes —Thomas Lux
14. Rising uncomfortably, like a schoolboy in the presence of a censuring teacher —Jan Kubicki
15. Rose like bubbles to the surface —Ivo Andric
16. Rose, like royalty —Edna Ferber
17. Rose . . . slowly, like a statue coming reluctantly to life —James Crumley
18. Rose to go . . . like a business man who has wasted a valuable twenty minutes on a prospective customer —Christopher Isherwood
19. Rose up like a flying swan —Stevie Smith
20. Scrambled back out of his chair like a foot soldier ducking a grenade —Robert Lewis Taylor
21. Stood [up to go], like Cinderella hearing the stroke of midnight —Eric Knight
22. Stood up, tawny and twinkling like a mobile in a breeze —Dick Francis
23. Surfaced like a nugget on sinking soil —Derek Lambert
24. Surfaced like a trout that had spotted a dragonfly just above the water —Joan Hess
    What surfaces in Hess' novel, *Strangled Prose,* is a character's alter ego.

RISK

See Also: DANGER

1. About as risky as selling the farm to buy up blocks of Xerox in the early '60s —John Stravinsky about horse syndicate investments, *Wall Street Journal,* August 15, 1986
2. The art of gambling is like the art of painting. You've got to know when to stop —Maurice Edelman
3. Betting on Martin was like betting on an aging horse that lived on sourmash whiskey —Will Weaver
4. (Politics with a mass of people is as) chancy and fickle as a whore's heart —Robert Traver

5. Chancy as trying to catch a fish in the open hand —Elizabeth Hardwick

6. It [the need to risk] was like statistics or gambling; you had to compute probabilities. And there was always the unforseen, the little thing you overlooked that would catch you up in the end —Mary McCarthy

7. Precarious as wheat farming —Larry McMurtry
   The profession McMurtry is likening to wheat farming is film making. He builds on the simile as follows: "He might raise a great crop of films . . . then watch them all wither in the theater."

8. Risky . . . It's like playing with a chemistry set without reading the directions —Vincent Canby, *New York Times,* January 22, 1986
   The risky activity described is movie making by the inexperienced.

9. To remove the element of risk is like playing cards with a stacked deck —Stephen Gillers, *New York Times*/Op Ed, November 23, 1986
   Gillers, a law professor, used this simile to discuss the exposé of people in the financial world who had been taking the risk out of arbitrage by dealing on specially garnered or insider information.

RIVERS
   See: PONDS AND STREAMS

ROAD SCENES
   See Also: NOISE, VEHICLES

1. The cars come down them [London streets] like rats —V. S. Pritchett

2. Cars nestled around the place like puppies feeding off a giant tit —Dan Wakefield

3. Cars . . . run along together like sticks on a stream —John Updike

4. Cars were flashing by [on highway] like toucans, bright red, hot pink and high yellow —Hortense Calisher

5. A dirt road that ran like string through some nearby woods —Wilfrid Sheed

6. The divided road looked like a striped gray snake curving across the brown landscape —A. E. Maxwell

7. Far off the highway . . . lone lights signalled like boats anchored far at sea —Louise Erdrich

8. Gradually the landscape on either side of the road became like an embrace —Susan Engberg

9. Grunting taxicabs . . . wallowing yellowly in the bright sun like panting porkers —Harvey Swados

10. The headlights of the cars in the deepening dusk were like a continuous stream of tracer-bullets aimed at anyone with temerity enough to cross their trajectory —Cornell Woolrich

11. The highway shimmers like a polished stove top —Mary Hedin

12. The interstate highway was like the ocean. It seemed to go on forever and was a similar color. Mirages of heat were shining in the distance like whitecaps —Bobbie Ann Mason

13. The lighted road seemed to shift like snow —Martin Cruz Smith

14. The motorway opened out before them like a black river, roaring — MacDonald Harris

15. The road, black as a ravine —Helen Hudson

16. The road dipped and rippled like a ribbon —Phyllis Naylor

17. The road lay straight as a spear —Terry Bisson

18. The road like a cat flattening its ears went into a straightaway —John Updike

19. Roads that never stopped . . . but looped and turned with exquisite abandon, like a ball of yarn given infinite slack —Sharon Sheehe Stark

20. Road that looked as smooth as a tablecloth —Wallace Stegner

21. The road was tree-lined, the oaks arching over the roadway from either embankment like a canopy —Jonathan Valin
    See Also: TREES

22. The road wound like a twisted snake —Stephen Vincent Benét

23. Saw the train pulled like a string of black beads over the horizon — Louise Erdrich

24. The searchlights [of cars on the highway] coursed ahead like elongated greyhounds —Erich Maria Remarque

25. The sound of the traffic is as faint as the roaring of a shell —John Cheever

26. Steely [railway] tracks . . . like clean penstrokes —Dorothy Canfield Fisher

27. Traffic moved like flies through a sieve —Tom Robbins

ROARS

See Also: SCREAMS

1. Ranting like a mad prophet —Amos Oz

2. Roar as loud as a howitzer —Norman Mailer

3. (The tiger) roaring like the sea —Dame Edith Sitwell

4. Roar like a jetport —T. Coraghessan Boyle

5. Roared like a tiger —Eudora Welty

6. Roar [of laughter] . . . like a tractor backfiring —Raymond Chandler

7. Roar like a winter breeze —Cole Porter, from "I've Come to Wive It Wealthily In Padua," one of the lyrics for the musical, *Kiss Me Kate,* an adaptation of Shakespeare's *Taming of the Shrew.*

8. Roar like bears —*The Holy Bible/Isaiah*

9. Roars like a rhino (as she comes and comes) —Carolyn Kizer

10. We roar all like bears —*The Holy Bible/Isaiah*

11. A whoop like Yale making a touchdown against Princeton —Raymond Chandler

ROBBERY
See: DISHONESTY

ROCKING AND ROLLING
See Also: MOVEMENTS, UNSTEADINESS, VIBRATION

1. Bobbed like a duck —F. van Wyck Mason

2. Bobbed like a ten-cent toy —John Updike
    Like the nickel pickle and cigar, the ten-cent toy is an endangered species, but fond remembrances are likely to have comparisons like this show up for a bit longer.

3. Bobbing like milkweed —W. D. Snodgrass

4. Bobbing up and down like a barometer on an April morning —Clifford Mills

5. Bobbing up and down . . . like an apple in a bowl of toddy —Edgar Allan Poe

6. [Stomach from laughing hard] bounced like a cat in a sack —Gerald Kersh

7. Bounce . . . like a basketball —Raymond Chandler

8. Bounces like an india-rubber ball —G. K. Chesterton

9. (I was) bouncing around (in my seat) like a pellet of quicksilver in a nervous man's palm —Dashiell Hammett

10. (Testicles) bouncing . . . like peas in a colander —Richard Ford

11. The bus rocked like a cradle —Carson McCullers
    See Also: VEHICLES

12. Rocking back and forth like Jews praying —Irwin Shaw

13. (Franklin stood) rocking from side to side like a man on the deck of a ship in an angry sea —Wilbur Daniel Steele

14. Roll about . . . like a pea —Frank Swinnerton

15. Rolled down the hills like marbles —Boris Pasternak

16. Rolled like a stone in a riverbed —Muriel Rukeyser

17. Rolled like tropic storms along —Edgar Allen Poe

In Poe's poem 'rolled' was spelled 'roll'd.'

18. Rolled off the bed like a rolling pin off a kitchen table —Rita Mae Brown

19. Rolled over and over like a shot rabbit —P. G. Wodehouse

20. [A drunk] rolling about like a ball-bearing —Mark Helprin

21. Rolling around like a cannon ball in a high sea —Hank Searls

22. [Baby in pregnant woman's body] rolling around like a basketball — Lynne Sharon Schwartz

23. (The words) roll on like bells —Alastair Reid

24. Rolls over . . . like surf —Lawrence Durrell

25. Swayed like a bird on a twig —Arnold Bennett

26. (A tipsy fellow,) swaying like a wind-rocked palm —Beryl Markham

27. Swaying like cobras about to strike —Robert Silverberg

28. Sways as a wafer of light —Carl Sandburg

ROMANCE
See: LOVE, MEN AND WOMEN

ROOMS
See Also: FURNITURE AND FURNISHINGS, HOUSES

1. [An office] almost as severe as the cell of some medieval monk —J. D. McClatchy

2. Bathroom, mirrored like a discotheque —Diane Ackerman

3. Bedroom . . . large as a football field and as cold —John Le Carré

4. Black bedroom with mirrors . . . looks like a wet dream from Walt Disney —Richard North Patterson

5. The blue and white room was . . . cold and hollow as an October mist —M. J. Farrell

6. The cramped space of the vestibule felt like the inside of a hooded cage —Kenzaburo Oë

7. [Small room] done up in moist red velvet, like the interior of a womb — Angela Carter

8. Dusty [a windowsill] as a literal Sahara —Tom Robbins

9. Entry hall . . . as impersonal as a hotel lounge —John Braine

10. Everything in the room was yellow . . . it was a bit like having been swallowed by a butterfly —Pat M. Esslinger-Carr

11. [Wooden] floors as blonde as a movie star's hair —William Hamilton, National Public Radio, "Morning Edition," April 15, 1987

12. The floor [of room set aside for dancing] gleamed like egg yolk —Susan Fromberg Schaeffer

13. A hall that was cool and vaulted like a cloister —Ross Macdonald

14. (The little den was now) hideous as a torture-chamber —Stephen Crane

15. It [a room] is like a monastic cell —V. S. Pritchett

16. The living room was spacious and divided like Gaul into three parts — John Cheever

17. Oak floors shone like brown glass —Rebecca West

18. On the ceiling the reflection of the waves of the bay outside flickered on and on like conversation —Kate Grenville

19. The paint [on ceiling of room] peeling like the surface of the moon — Jilly Cooper

20. (In my gray) room, bare as a barn —Randall Jarrell

21. Room [small and narrow] . . . friendly as Death Row —Gavin Lyall

22. The room glows like a field of forget-me-nots in the high country — Patricia Henley

23. A room is like a cast-off shoe, which holds the shape of its owner's unique foot —Paul Theroux

24. Room . . . like a cell, except that there were no bars over the one small window —Dashiell Hammett

25. Room like a cupboard —Katherine Mansfield

26. The room [at a Howard Johnson's motel] . . . sat like a young bride . . . wanting only to please you —Max Apple

27. The room was as hot as the inside of a pig's stomach —Madison Smartt Bell
See Also: HEAT

28. The room was as quiet and empty as a chapel —Wallace Stegner
See Also: SILENCE

29. The room was filled like a pool with darkness —Josephine Jacobson

30. The [empty] room was like a fowl plucked clean —Jean Stafford

31. Room . . . with nothing actually matching anything else but everything living happily together, like the random sowing of flowers — Rosamund Pilcher

32. Study . . . like the returned-letter department of a post office, with stacks of paper everywhere, bills paid and unpaid, letters answered and unanswered, tax returns, pamphlets, leaflets. If by mistake we left the door open on a windy day, we came back to find papers flapping through the air like frightened birds —Mary Lavin

33. Twilight came drifting into the room like a shimmering cloud of powdered glass —Natascha Wodin

34. Walls white like a physician's consultation room —W. D. Snodgrass

ROUNDNESS
See: SHAPE

ROWDINESS
See: NOISE

RUDENESS
See: MANNERS

RUMOR
See: GOSSIP

RUNNING
See Also: MOVEMENT, SPEED

1. Came running like a race —Lee Smith
2. A queer little hustling run, like a puppet jerked by wires —Ross Macdonald
3. Raced around . . . like a migrant bird —Elizabeth Hardwick
4. Ran across the lawn towards us crookedly, like someone in an egg-and-spoon race —Kate Grenville
5. Ran after . . . like a dog after its master —Isaac Babel
   See Also: PURSUIT
6. Ran down the steps as if the Devil was behind her —Donald Seaman
7. Ran in and out . . . like a squirrel —Henry Van Dyke
8. Ran like a blind man —Stephen Crane
9. Ran like a stag —Jonathan Gash
10. Ran like a whirlwind —Thomas Macaulay
    Another simile that has outlived its source, "The Battle of Lake Regillu," as a commonly used phrase.
11. Run . . . like a blind sheep in a snowstorm —Borden Deal
12. (A man comes up to them with a gun, they) run like antelopes —Irwin Shaw
13. Run like a scalded dog —Rita Mae Brown
14. (Engineers and executives were) running around like ants in a burning mound —Speer Morgan
15. Running around in circles like crazy sheepdogs —George Garrett
16. Running as if on fire —Bernard Malamud
17. Running . . . like a leaf driven by the wind —Joseph Conrad
18. Running like a man who has jumped up in the dark and runs listening between his footfalls for the reason of his still running —Ted Hughes
19. [A rabbit] runs like a faucet —Marge Piercy

20. They [joggers] looked like an organized death march as they ran by gasping, perspiring, stumbling, their faces contorted with pain —Erma Bombeck

21. Trotted beside him like a frightened puppy beside an elephant —Thomas Wolfe

RUTHLESSNESS
   See: CRUELTY

SADNESS
   See Also: DEJECTION, EMOTIONS, GLOOM

1. As full of sorrow as the sea of sands —William Shakespeare

2. Could feel it [the sadness] pierce him like a foreign body in his heart —Amos Oz

3. Crest-fallen as a dried pear —William Shakespeare

4. Crest-fallen as a spy who had been caught by a thief —Victor Hugo

5. Depressing as the last day of fishing —Robert Traver

6. A feeling of sadness that is not akin to pain, resembles sorrow only as the mist resembles rain —Henry Wadsworth Longfellow

7. (Scarlett) felt bereft, as though she had sold one of her children —Margaret Mitchell
    The sadness which inspired the comparison was that experienced by the heroine of *Gone With the Wind* when she sold her lumber business.

8. Felt melancholy grip him, like a pain in the heart —Mary McCarthy

9. (I felt depressed,) filled to the neck with sadness like a carafe with bad wine —T. Coraghessan Boyle

10. His heart throbbed like a bruise in the sigh —Norman Mailer

11. His heart would sink down to his bowels like lead —Thomas Wolfe

12. Looked and acted like a man who had just driven home from a couple of heart-rending funerals —George Ade
     See Also: FACIAL EXPRESSIONS, SERIOUS

13. Melancholy as a discarded statesman —William Mountford

14. Melancholy as a fiddle with one string —Thomas Holcroft

15. My heart is within me as an ash in the fire —Algernon Charles Swinburne

16. My heart was as lead —Jack London

17. Pathetic as all final efforts —Alice McDermott

18. Pathetic as an autumn leaf —George Moore

19. (A low call,) plaintive as a shepherd calling to sheep who need no strident invocation —Arthur A. Cohen

20. Sad as an eagle without wings, sad as a violin with only one string —
    Jean Rhys

21. Sad as night —William Shakespeare

22. Sad as professional mourners —F. Scott Fitzgerald

23. Sad as twilight —George Eliot

24. Saddening as a forest fire —Robert Traver

25. Sad like graveyards —Terry Bisson

26. Sad . . . like somebody who's pilot light got blown out a long time ago
    —Susan Kelly

27. Sadness . . . gnawed like a rat at his mind —Roderic Jeffries

28. Sadness, like that inspired by a grave strain of music —Joseph Conrad

29. Sadness that, over the years, had gathered in his chest like matter in a
    clogged drain —Joyce Reiser Kornblatt

30. There would come, like water washing over a sunken buoy, the little
    knell of sadness —Hortense Calisher
    Just as similes are used to give dramatic beginning to literary
    works, they can also be used to wind things up, as
    demonstrated by this final sentence from Calisher's novel,
    Point of Departure.

SAFETY

See Also: DANGER, RISK

1. Feel as safe as a lone subway rider at 2 a.m. —Anon

2. Feel as safe as guarded by a charm —Elizabeth Barrett Browning

3. Looked as dangerous as a squirrel and much less nervous —Raymond
   Chandler

4. The man who looks for security, even in the mind, is like a man who
   would chop off his limbs in order to have artifical ones which will give
   him no pain or trouble —Henry Miller

5. Nothing as safe as simplicity —Edith Wharton

6. Safe and more or less invulnerable like sulky Achilles among Trojans —
   George Garrett

7. (I thought I was) safe as a good new boat —Reynolds Price

8. (They think they're) safe as angels —Dashiell Hammet

9. Safe as a nun in a roomful of eunuchs —Donald Seaman

10. Safe as a tank town —W. R. Burnett

11. Safe as houses —Mary Gordon

12. Safe as in a cradle —William Wordsworth

13. Safe as in God's pocket —American colloquialism, attributed to New
    England

14. Safe as sunshine —Slogan R. E. Dietz Co.

15. Security . . . tighter than the skin on a snake —William H. Hallhan

16. She's safe as a vault —Raymond Chandler

17. Squatting in safety like the yolk in an egg —Bertold Brecht

SALES
See: SUCCESS/FAILURE

SARCASM
See: HUMOR

SATISFACTION
See: CONTENTMENT

SAYINGS
See: MAXIMS AND SAYINGS

SCANDAL
See: REPUTATION, SHAME

SCARCITY
See: RARITY

SCARS
See: FACIAL DETAILS

SCATTERING
See: DISPERSAL

SCIENCE
See: MATHEMATICS AND SCIENCE

SCREAMS
See Also: NOISE

1. Bellowed like a locomotive —Marge Piercy

2. Bellowing like a wounded whale —William Diehl

3. Bellow, like an animal in pain —Jean Rhys

4. A broken shriek like a viola gone sour —T. Coraghessan Boyle

5. Cried out hoarsely like a bird warning the forest that a predator is on the loose —Derek Lambert

6. Cries . . . shrill, like a pig having his throat cut —W. Somerset Maugham

7. Gave a short roar like a lion keeping in voice —Kingsley Amis
8. Gave a shriek like an engine —Joyce Cary
9. Gave a shrill scream like a wrung hen —Hugh Walpole
10. He bellered like a bull calf —William A. Owens
11. A high-pitched wail like a cat on fire —Peter Benchley
12. His scream sliced the night like a hatchet —William Diehl
13. Howled . . . like a savage beast being goaded to death with knives and spears —Emily Brontë
14. Howling (through the streets) like an outcast dog —Erich Maria Remarque
15. Howl like dogs —Dante Alighieri
16. Howl like stabled wolves, or tigers at their prey —John Milton
17. A loud yell which rang through the lonely fields like the howl of an evil spirit —Charles Dickens
18. Screamed like a door creaking —Hugh Walpole
19. (Laughed and) screamed like herring gulls —Joan Aiken
20. Screamed like a horse in a fire —Gerald Kersh
21. Screamed . . . like an eight-legged wildcat having a fit —Harold Adams
22. Screamed like gulls on stormy water —Saul Bellow
23. Screaming at the top of her lungs like a railroad whistle —Paige Mitchell
24. Screaming filled the air like an icy mist —Bertold Brecht
25. Screaming like a hawk making a long dive at a rabbit —W. P. Kinsella
26. Screaming . . . like a saint sent to hell by mistake —Rosellen Brown
27. Scream like a peacock in heat —Tennessee Williams
28. Scream like a village of raped virgins —Clive Cussler
    In Cussler's novel, *Cyclops,* the simile refers to protests in Washington about a space shuttle in Russian hands.
29. Scream like sandstorms in the desert, like the death of the universe —T. Coraghessan Boyle
30. Scream . . . like the death rattle of a slaughtered animal —Ignazio Silone
31. A scream of rage . . . like a blast from hell —Fred Mustard Stewart
32. The scream rose like an aria —Larry McMurtry
33. Screams as if ice water is rippling down her back —Ira Wood
34. Screeched like a cage of mynas —Tony Ardizzone
35. Screeched like a dying pullet —Frank Ross
36. Screeched like a nighttime cat —Cynthia Ozick

37. (The women) screeching like bony parrots —H. E. Bates
38. Shout as demonstrative as a lizard —George Foy
39. Shrieked like an old screen door —Carolyn Kizer
40. Shrieking . . . like she was at a fireman's picnic —John Dos Passos
41. Shriek like a knife in the heart —T. Coraghessan Boyle
42. A shriek like a needle-point —Elizabeth Bowen
43. Shriek like infuriated switch engines —Irvin S. Cobb
44. Shriek . . . louder than the loud ocean —Lord Byron
45. Stormed and screamed like some shrill, wet hurricane about the house —Anita Desai
46. Talked and shouted for hours on end like a preacher —Ignazio Silone
47. Yelled . . . as if I were being roasted alive —Natascha Wodin
48. Yelling and growling like savage but cowardly dogs —Lawrence Durrell
49. Yelping (at captain of waiters) like a terrier who had cornered some small defenseless animal —Ross Macdonald
50. Yowl like a tortured cat —Madison Smartt Bell

SCRUPULOUSNESS
See: CORRECTNESS

SCRUTINY
See Also: INTENSITY

1. Approach [society section of Sunday paper] like a lapidopterist advances on butterflies —Shana Alexander
2. [A maitre d'] bent over (his guest list) like a conductor studying a score —Jonathan Valin
3. Carefully surveyed the living room and, like an auctioneer brought in for appraisal, every object it contained —Richard Russo
4. Examine [a face] as though it were a portrait in a public gallery —Ella Leffland
5. Examine like a customs inspector —Anon
6. Examine like a job hunter finecombs the employment ads or a New York apartment hunter finecombs the real estate ads —Anon
7. Examine like a monkey picking fleas —Mike Sommer
8. Examine with care, like a horse player eyeing the "Racing Form" — Shana Alexander
9. Examine with care of diamond dealer examining a rare stone —Anon
10. Explore [feelings] . . . like someone trying to locate a hollow tooth — Lawrence Durrell

11. His scrutiny was like a well that pulled on you, making you eager to find your own face in the depths down there —Hortense Calisher

12. Investigate . . . like a burglar twirling the dial of a well-constructed safe, listening for the locks to click and reveal the combination —Mary McCarthy

13. Like a traveller in unfamiliar regions she began to store for future guidance the minutest natural signs —Edith Wharton

14. Look at as does an experienced fish at a purchased fly —Gregory McDonald

15. Looking at it [a letter] as if it were a code in need of breaking — Graham Swift

16. (Should be) noted with care like the names of places passed on an important journey —John McGahern

17. Peered around [the room] like a hungry toad —Harold Adams

18. Pore over . . . like a Little-Leaguer entranced by a pack of baseball cards —Jill Ciment

19. Pore over like possessed students of cabalist text —Joseph Weizenbaum
    Weizenbaum's simile referred to the computer enthusiast's intense absorption.

20. Prodding [in search of something] like a great bird rummaging for seed —Edith Wharton

21. Read their faces like texts and their gestures like punctuation marks — Helen Hudson
    The character thus studying faces in the novel, *Criminal Trespass,* is not surprisingly, a librarian. The description of the gestures the librarian studies includes another simile: "The way they . . . yank down the volumes and riffle the contents like the *Yellow Pages.* "

22. Scrutinize as if he were a new character in a soap opera —Bobbie Ann Mason

23. Scrutinized . . . with the air of an epicure examining a fly in his vichyssoise —T. Coraghessan Boyle

24. Studied Barksdale's face, openly, like a man taking inventory —Paige Mitchell

25. Studies me like a teacher trying to decide how to discipline an unruly student —W. P. Kinsella

26. Study [a trip schedule] as though it were a pack of Tarot cards in some tricky configuration —Sue Grafton

27. Studying him like a culture —William McIlvanney

28. Surveyed [books] like a guard with his flashlight making the midnight rounds —Elizabeth Hardwick

29. Being watched like a rabbit in a laboratory —Willa Cather

30. Watching people, probing like a dentist into their innermost thoughts —Ivan Turgenev

31. Went through everything . . . like detectives after fingerprints [describing antiques dealers] —Edith Wharton

SEASCAPES

See Also: NATURE, OCEAN/OCEANFRONT, PONDS AND STREAMS

1. The boat sails away, like a bird on the wing —Kate Greenaway

2. Fishing boats sleep by the docks like men beside their wives —Donald Justice

3. The great ships dipped low down in the water, like floating swans — Hans Christian Andersen

4. The lights on the canals [of Holland] like gold caterpillars —Jean Rhys

5. Little masted boats thick on the water, like blown leaves —Donald Justice

6. Sailboats moved gently in the water like large white butterflies that had dipped down to drink —Margaret Millar

7. The sea crinkled like foil —Derek Walcott

8. The sea is like a pale green fabric, stretched but not entirely smooth — Richard Maynard

9. The sea is sparkling like joy itself —Christopher Isherwood

10. The sea, like a crinkled chart, spread to the horizon —Daphne du Maurier

11. The sea was as smooth as a duck-pond —Rudyard Kipling

12. The sea [on a windless day] was like a sheet of steel —Fred Mustard Stewart

13. The sea was quite calm, like milk-and-water —Isak Dinesen

14. The sea was silver, wrinkled like a snake's skin —Sir Hugh Walpole

15. The sea, wrinkling with light, was stretched taut like a piece of silk — Elizabeth Taylor

16. Smaller vessels bobbing like petals on the glass of the harbor — Francine du Plessix Gray

17. There was a shimmer on the sea as though a loitering breeze passed playful fingers over its surface —W. Somerset Maugham

18. The town seems to lean against the cliffs like a rusting ocean liner, thrown to shore by a storm —Miles Gibson

19. Water like glass —Joseph Conrad

20. The water looked flat and impervious, as if a dead membrane had been stretched over it —Cynthia Ozick

21. Water . . . pebbly-surfaced by the insistent breeze that kept sweeping it like the strokes of invisible broomstraws, and mottled with gold flecks that were like floating freckles in the nine o'clock September sunshine —Cornell Woolrich

22. Water . . . rippled like stretched grey silk in the wind —Gavin Lyall

23. The water that shone smoothly like a band of metal —Joseph Conrad

SEASONS

1. August steamed in like the first slow day of creation —Shelby Hearon

2. The autumnal radiance fluttered like a blown shawl over the changeless structure of the landscape —Ellen Glasgow

3. Autumn felt as dark with life as spring —M. J. Farrell

4. The autumn frosts will lie upon the grass like bloom on grapes of purple-brown and gold —Elinor Wylie

5. In the spring . . . life, like the landscape around us, seems bigger and wider and freer, a rainbow road leading to unknown ends —Jerome K. Jerome

6. The long gray winter settles in like a wolf feeding on a carcass —Marge Piercy

7. March . . . comes in like a lion and goes out like a lamb —John Ray's *Proverbs*
   See Also: ENTRANCES/EXITS

8. Now that it's spring and the blossoms fall like sighs —Louis MacNeice

9. October had come in like a lamb chop, breaded in golden crumbs and gently sautéed in a splash of blue oil —Tom Robbins

10. October morning . . . sallow as a faded suntan —Jessamyn West

11. One of those honey-warm fall days that brought out summer habits like chilled bees —Hortense Calisher

12. The seasons shine like new coins —George Garrett
    See Also: SHINING

13. Sleepy winter, like the sleep of death —Elinor Wylie

14. The specter of winter hovering like a pale-winged bird —W. P. Kinsella

15. Spring, animating and affecting us all . . . like a drug, a pleasant poison of annual mortal gaiety —Janet Flanner

16. Spring arose on the garden fair, like the spirit of love felt everywhere —Percy Bysshe Shelley

17. Spring comes like a life raft —George Starbuck

18. Spring sunlight flowed in the streets like good news —William H. Hallhan
    See Also: SUN

19. Spring came that year like a triumph and like a prophecy —Thomas Wolfe

20. Summer . . . dropping from the sky like a blanket of steam —John Rechy

21. Summer is like a fat beast —Wallace Stevens

22. Winter came down like a hammer —Lawrence Durrell

23. Winter [in Madison Square] . . . was tamed, like a polar bear led on a leash by a beautiful lady —Willa Cather

SECRECY

1. About as loose-lipped as a Swiss banker —Harold Adams

2. Another person's secret is like another person's money: you are not so careful with it as you are with your own —Edgar Watson Howe

3. As secret as the grave —Miguel de Cervantes

4. Close up like a cabbage —John Andrew Holmes

5. Close up like a fist —Anon

6. Covert as a brass band —George F. Will

7. Fondles his secrets like a case of tools —Karl Shapiro

8. Furtive as a chipmunk —R. V. Cassill

9. Hide . . . like a disgrace —George Gissing

10. In the mind and nature of a man a secret is an ugly thing, like a hidden physical defect —Isak Dinesen

11. Lurking like a pilot fish among sharks —Speer Morgan

12. Move . . . like a rodent, furtively —John Phillips

13. Peered out (into the corridor) as stealthily as a mouse leaving its subterranean hole —Donald Seaman

14. (My face is an open secret but in my letters I) perform like a true diplomat, cunning and sly —Delmore Schwartz
     See Also: CLEVERNESS

15. Private and tight as a bank vault —Marge Piercy

16. Secrecy as tight as a bull's ass in fly time —Stephen Longstreet

17. Secret as silence —Babette Deutsch

18. A secret at home is like rocks under tide —D. M. Mulock

19. Secret operations [by a government] are like sin; unless you're good at sinning, you shouldn't do it —George Kennan, CBS/TV, March 31, 1987

20. Secrets are like measles: they take easy and spread easy —Bartlett's *Dictionary of Americanisms*

Now that measles is controlled by vaccine, a virus or the common cold would probably be a more appropriate point of reference.

21. She has a mouth like a padlock —Graham Greene

22. Sneak away [for an acceptable, honorable activity] . . . as furtively as if he were stealing to a lover's tryst —Edith Wharton

23. Stealthy and slow as a hidden sin —Stephen Vincent Benét
    See Also: SLOWNESS

SEDATENESS
See: SERIOUSNESS

SELF-CONFIDENCE
See Also: PRIDE, VANITY

1. The acceptance of oneself . . . is like falling heir to the house one was born in and has lived in all one's life but to which, until now, one did not own the title —Jean Stafford

2. (Sit there with) all the quiet certainty of a marauding chimp —Carla Lane, line from British television sitcom, "Solo"

3. As cocksure as if he had a fistful of aces —Honoré de Balzac

4. Confidence leaking like gas all over the room —Wilfrid Sheed

5. Confidence, like the soul, never returns whence it has once departed — Publius Syrus

6. Confident as a man dialing his own telephone number —Jack Bell

7. (He would be as) confident as a married man of how the evening would turn out —Alice McDermott

8. Confident as a master baker with a cake in the oven —Elizabeth Irvin Ross

9. Feel his title hang loose about him, like a giant's robe upon a dwarfish thief —William Shakespeare
   See Also: NAMES

10. Feeling power and confidence rise strongly up in her like wine filling a glass —Celia Dale

11. Felt like the cock of the walk —John Dos Passos

12. He displayed like an aura the lordly demeanor of a man who not only had dined on success throughout his lifetime but also had been born to it —Joseph Heller

13. I feel like a dime among pennies —Fiorello H. La Guardia, *Village Voice*, November 21, 1968
    The former New York City mayor responded thus when asked how it felt to be smallest man in a group.
    See Also: SMALLNESS

594

14. I'm like a cat. Throw me up in the air and I'll always land on my feet — Bette Davis, quoted in Rex Reed interview
   See Also: SUCCESS/FAILURE

15. Pitching is a rollercoaster ride through the land of confidence —Ron Darling, New York Mets pitcher, *New York Times*/Sports of the Times, August 3, 1986
   See Also: BASEBALL

16. (The children) roamed through the neighborhood like confident landlords —Alice Mc Dermott

17. Self-confidence like an iron bar —Stephen Vincent Benét

18. Self-confidence surrounds him like force field —William Boyd

19. She was a human duck off whose back even the most seering of words flowed like harmless rain —H. E. Bates
   A twist on the timeworn "Rolled off him/her like water off a duck's back."

20. Very pleased with herself . . . like a boa constrictor that had just enjoyed a rather large lunch —Mike Fredman

21. Walked the lane between the indifferently rowed cabins like he owned them, striding from shade into half-light as if he could halve the setting sun —Sherley Anne Williams

SELF-CONSCIOUSNESS
See: DISCOMFORT, NATURALNESS

SELFISHNESS

1. The force of selfishness is as inevitable and as calculable as the force of gravitation —Anon

2. A man is a lion in his own cause —Henry G. Bohn's *Handbook of Proverbs*

3. The private life of the narcissist, like the private parts of the exhibitionist, ought not to be hung out uninvited in the public space — Willard Gaylin

4. Self-love . . . leaped back into her like a perpetually coiled snake — Anaïs Nin

5. Wound up in his own concerns like thread on a spool —Anon

SENSATIONS
See: EMOTIONS

SENSE
See Also: INTELLIGENCE

1. As reasonable as Latin —Anne Sexton

2. Beyond rationality . . . like stepping out into deep space, or going to the center of the world, or both at once —Susan Engberg

3. Common sense is as rare as genius —Ralph Waldo Emerson
   See Also: RARITY

4. Human reason is like a drunken man on horseback; set it up on one side, and it tumbles over on the other —Martin Luther

5. Like precious stones, his sensible remarks derive their value from their scarcity —W. S. Gilbert

6. Logic, like whisky, loses its beneficial effect when taken in too large quantities —Lord Dunsany

7. A mind all logic is like a knife all blade. It makes the hand bleed that uses it —Rabindranath Tagore

8. Reason in man is rather like God in the world —St. Thomas Aquinas

9. Reason is a bladder on which you may paddle like a child as you swim in summer waters; but, when the winds rise and the waves roughen, it slips from under you, and you sink —Walter Savage Landor

10. Reason is like the sun, of which the light is constant, uniform, and lasting —Samuel Johnson

11. Sense, like charity, begins at home —Alexander Pope
    Pope's *Moral Essays* can be credited with the first of many "Charity begins at home" comparisons.
    See Also: CHANGE, EDUCATION, PEACEFULNESS, SENSE

12. Tried to size up the situation reasonably, to tote odds like a paramutual —Jonathan Valin

SENSELESSNESS
See: ABSURDITY

SENSITIVENESS
See Also: KINDNESS

1. Bruise easily like a ripe pear —A. C. Greene

2. Ego . . . as delicate as tissue paper —Christopher Buckley

3. Exposed as if on a raft —Joseph Conrad

4. Felt like a shell-fish that had lost its shell —Olivia Manning

5. Felt like a vegetable without its skin: raw and vulnerable —Laurie Colwin

6. Felt myself exposed . . . as sharply as in a photograph —John Updike

7. Gentle as milk —Sylvia Berkman

8. Inherited sensibilities like jewels as red as rubies and blood —Janet Flanner

9. Interpreted the episode as sensitively as an unleashed bull would —Z. Vance Wilson

10. My sensibility begins to screech like chalk upon the blackboard scrawled —Delmore Schwartz

11. A person who is always having her feelings hurt is about as pleasant a companion as a pebble in a shoe —Elbert Hubbard
    A non-gender specific paraphrased from the original which began with "The woman."

12. Sensitive as a barometer —Thomas Bailey Aldrich

13. Sensitive as a stick of dynamite or a hand grenade —Mike Sommer

14. [An alert horse, with ears turning and twitching to catch all sounds] sensitive as radar —Jilly Cooper

15. Sensitive as the leaves of a silver birch —Joseph Hergesheimer

16. Sensitive as the money market —Thomas Hardy

17. (Taste buds as) sensitive as the skin on a mailman's feet —Ira Wood

18. Thick-skinned as a brontosaurus —Francis Goldwin, quoted on his sensitiveness to anything but imitations of his company's toy dinosaurs, *Wall Street Journal,* June 15, 1987

19. Touchy as a second degree burn —Harry Prince

20. Vulnerable as one of those primitive creatures between two skins or two shells, like a lobster or a crab —David R. Slavitt

21. (You are) vulnerable as the first buds of the maple —Marge Piercy

22. With all her stubbornness and punch, she could be sliced like scrapple —Sharon Sheehe Stark

SENTIMENT

1. Like most sentimentalists, his heart's as chilly as the Pole —Frank Swinnerton

2. Nostalgia . . . like a lover's pain in the chest —John Hersey

3. Nostalgic . . . like a letter from home —Mahalia Jackson
   Jackson's frame of reference, gospel music, is particularly appropriate.

4. Sentimental as flowers pressed between the pages of a diary —Anon

5. (I've been) talking sentiment like a turtledove —Oliver Wendell Holmes, Sr.

SEPARATION
See: BEGINNINGS AND ENDINGS

SERENITY
See: PEACEFULNESS

SERIOUSNESS

1. Bearing his earnestness like an emblem —Donald MacKenzie

2. Every man will have his hours of seriousness; but like the hours of rest, they often are ill-chosen and unwholesome —Walter Savage Landor

3. Grave as a judge that's giving charge —Samuel Wesley

4. Grave as an old cat —Anon

5. Grave as an owl in a barn —George Farquhar

6. Sedate as a committeeman —William McIlvanney

7. Serious as a doctor —Eudora Welty

8. Serious as an overdue mortgage —Alexander King

9. Serious as a pig pissin' —C. J. Koch

10. (You are so) serious, as if a glacier spoke in your ear —Frank O'Hara

11. Serious as if at church —Émile Zola

12. Serious as the Ten Commandments —W. B. Yeats

13. Serious like a hyacinth . . . which has had no sun —Virginia Woolf

14. Sober as a bone —Erich Maria Remarque

15. Sober as a coroner inspecting a corpse —Amelie Rives

16. Sober as a judge —Anon
    According to Stevenson's *Book of Proverbs, Maxims and Famous Sayings,* John Arbuthnot used the simile in *John Bull* in 1712, and 22 years later, Henry Fielding used it in *Don Quixote In England.* Since then, it has become common usage; its meaning more frequently tied to a serious manner than sobriety. In one of his *Tutt and Tutt* legal stories, Arthur Train added an interesting note of specificity with "Sober as a Kansas judge."

17. Solemn as a child in shock —C. J. Koch

18. Solemn as a clergyman —Nina Bawden

19. Solemn as a lawyer at a will reading —J. B. Priestley

20. Solemn as a nun —R. Wright Campbell

21. Solemn as a soldier going to the front —Norman Mailer

22. Solemn as kewpie dolls —Diane Ackerman

23. Solemnly agreed, as though pledging allegiance to the flag —Robert Traver
    See Also: AGREEMENT/DISAGREEMENT

24. Stern as a Tartar —Lorenz Hart
    The Tartar described is Queen Elizabeth. This is also the title of a song from Hart's lyrics for *The Garried Gaities of 1926.*

598

SERMONS
        See: SPEECHMAKING

SERVILITY
        See: MEEKNESS

SEX
        See Also: ATTRACTIVENESS, BODY ORGANS, BREASTS, MEN AND
        WOMEN, SEXUAL INTERACTION, RELATIONSHIPS

1. (To me they are) as as sexual as money; and, like money, unless they can engender passion, they are useless to me —W. P. Kinsella
   The frame of reference for Kinsella's double simile is the other woman.

2. Batten's [character in a novel] sex had wilted like a flag in the rain — George Garrett

3. Celibate, like the fly in the heart of an apple —Jeremy Taylor

4. An erection like a steeple —Jilly Cooper

5. Erotic as an ape —Karl Shapiro

6. I felt an abrupt rush of my semen, racing through me like twin rivers — Scott Spencer

7. Her climax came . . . suddenly, like an accident —Scott Spencer

8. Her sex power . . . hid in her eyes like a Sicilian bandit —Saul Bellow

9. His sex beat about like the cane of a furious blind man —Amos Oz

10. Horny as a tomcat —T. Coraghessan Boyle

11. In her passional life she was direct—like an axe falling —Lawrence Durrell

12. It's rather like a sneeze —Truman Capote, responding to television interviewer's question as to his feelings about sex

13. It [a first sexual encounter] was best when it was finished . . . like having a cup of really good coffee and a Havana after an indifferently cooked but urgently needed meal —John Braine

14. Just whispering "teenage sex" is like yelling fire in a crowded theatre — Ellen Goodman

15. A lack of sexuality so total that her smart clothes and too heavy-make-up made her pathetic; like an unsuccessful geisha —John Fowles

16. Like flowers groping toward the sun, millions of Americans are groping towards sexual nirvana —Anon
     See Also: CHARACTERISTICS, NATIONAL

17. Like hatred, sex must be articulated or, like hatred, it will produce a disturbing internal malaise —George Jean Nathan

18. (Her husband complained she) made love like an eager, clumsy cellist —J. D. McClatchy

19. My sex life . . . it'd make Moll Flanders look like she needed hormone therapy —Sue Miller

20. The only sex we were exposed to was with dreadful old whores..like diseased orchids —Tennesse Williams, *Playboy,* April, 1973

21. Orgasm is like a slight attack of apoplexy —Democritus

22. Orgasm is like the tickling feeling you get inside your nose before you sneeze —Children's 1972 sex education manual

23. Pornography is like peanut butter—a little goes a long way —Arthur Morowitz, *New York Times,* October 5, 1986

24. [Sexual] restraints fell from her like mere rags, or rather, like that dead skin which is scraped off in a steam bath —Marguerite Yourcenar

25. Sensual as a ripe, thick-veined scarlet fruit —John Logan

26. Sex becomes as routine as tying one's shoes —Deborah Phillips, *New York Times*/Personal Health, October 8, 1986
     See Also: COMMONPLACE

27. Sex is a subject like every other subject. Every bit as interesting as agriculture —Muriel Spark

28. Sex . . . it's great stuff, like chocolate sundaes —Raymond Chandler

29. Sexless as a machine —Ellen Glasgow

30. Sexless as an anemic nun —Sinclair Lewis

31. (Some men have a) sexual disposition as vigorous, indiscriminate, and as demanding, as a digestive tract —John Cheever

32. Sexual pleasure, like rending pain, represents the stunning triumph of the immediate —Simone de Beauvoir

33. She seems to regard sex as a wholesome, slightly silly indulgence, like dancing and nice dinners —Alice Munro

34. Sometimes I feel like a public utility —Charles Johnson
     The character who makes this comparison about herself in
     Johnson's novel, *Oxherding Tale,* is a woman who has had "an
     army" of lovers.

35. There were people . . . for whom love and sex came easy, without active solicitation, like a strong wind to which they had only to turn their faces —David Leavitt

36. Virility . . . was like a gloss on him —Barbara Taylor Bradford

37. Wears her sex like an expensive perfume —Lawrence Durrell

38. (Lucille's aunt had) wrapped her own dank virginity round her like someone sharing a mackintosh —Elizabeth Bowen

SEXUAL INTERACTION
See Also: INSULTS

1. Attacked her with a loose and greedy mouth, like a man sucking at a torn fruit —Miles Gibson

2. Even when they made love . . . it was perfunctory, as if he were listening for something else, a phone call, a footfall. He was like a man scratching himself. She was like his hand —Margaret Atwood

3. (She could only remember the times that he had lain with her,) fleeing into her body as if it were a refuge from his daily wage of fear and frustration —Davis Grubb

4. Gave her whole body to me, like something without a bone —Winston Graham

5. Gobbled her like a ripe peach —Peter De Vries

6. He aroused her so excrutiatingly that she wanted to lie down right now for him in the middle of the muddy road and let him plough through her like a car —Julia O'Faolain

7. He fell into her with the ease and velocity of a stone dropping into the sea —MacDonald Harris

8. He fell on me like a wave. But like a wave he washed away, leaving no sign he'd been there —Louise Erdrich

9. He had never before made love like this . . . as if he had found a twin whose body had been cast in the matching mold of his own —Amos Oz

10. He pulled up my clothes like a man unwrapping a parcel —Graham Swift

11. Her touch moving over my body like pebbles in a stream —Arthur A. Cohen

12. He slips into her like a thief entering a doorway —Hilma Wolitzer

13. He was like something washed ashore on her —Flannery O'Connor
    This observation is prompted by an unsuccessful sexual
    encounter.

14. His love making felt like having a tooth stopped by a singularly
    incompetent dentist —Vicki Baum

15. It [sexual intercourse] was as if we'd been fused together, melting into
    each other like amoebae but violently, like cars crashing head on —
    John Braine

16. The lovemaking wasn't exactly by the numbers, but she did order
    everything on the menu, like a teenage kid trying to impress his date —
    Jonathan Valin

17. Made love like monkeys —Charles Johnson

18. Making love with Charlie was like being taken into a big warm machine
    —Sue Grafton

19. (Harry) maneuvered her around like a load of wet wash —R. Wright
    Campbell

20. Our body warmth flowed back and forth, coursing between us like some
    underground hot spring —Harvey Swados

21. Our two bodies met like a thunderclap —Carolyn Kizer

22. Places her gently upon the bed like a newly pressed suit —Roger
    McGough

23. She gave herself up to me like a condemned criminal —John Hagge

24. She snuggled into him like a kitten at the breast of its mother —Rita
    Mae Brown

25. She stiffened on penetration and clung to him, relaxing as if unlocked
    with his blunt key —Paul Theroux

26. Spills him off her body like a pile of sand —John Updike
    See Also: REJECTION

27. Their touch together was like a miniature jolt of electricity —Paul
    Horgan

28. Undressed deliberately, slowly, as if she were unwrapping a gift —
    Graham Swift

29. We crashed against one another like waves on a breakwater —Sue
    Grafton

30. We ended up in bed together, sort of, spastic and looped, doomed for
    failure, like two senile inventors in an upstairs room, lonely as spoons
    —Lorrie Moore

31. We flowed together again like a stream that for an instant an island had
    separated —Truman Capote

32.   We half walked half stumbled towards the bed, like uncertain dancers learning a new step —Peter De Vries

SHADOW

1.   His shadow dragging like a photographer's cloth behind him —Elizabeth Bishop

2.   Long shadows deep as oil —Philip Levine

3.   My shadow spilled over the grass like great leaks of ink —Henry Van Dyke

4.   Shadows black as parts of dreams —David Denby

5.   Shadows deep as caves —Jerry Bumpus

6.   Shadows [of elm trees] falling all over her head and shoulder like a web —Ellen Gilchrist

7.   Shadows lay like broad hurdles across my path —Beryl Markham

8.   The whole shadow of Man is only as big as his hat —Elizabeth Bishop

SHALLOWNESS
See: IMPORTANCE/UNIMPORTANCE

SHAME
See Also: BLUSHES

1.   As sheepish as a fowl —La Fontaine

2.   Embarrassing, like showing up for a party on the wrong date and finding the host and hostess in the middle of a family squabble —Elyse Sommer

3.   Embarrassment lay like a cloak over everyone's shoulders —Belva Plain

4.   Embarrassment thickened in his throat like phlegm —Ross Macdonald

5.   Embarrassing as a rich man without admirers —David Denby

6.   Embarrassed as a nudist caught with his clothes on —Anon

7.   He felt a drench of shame like a hot liquid over his neck and shoulders —Saul Bellow

8.   In scandal, as in robbery, the receiver is always thought as bad as the thief —Lord Chesterfield

9.   Looked embarrassed, as if he were a spy whose cover had been blown —Robert Barnard

10. Red-faced . . . like a puppy caught in his own piss —R. Wright Campbell

11. Scandal will rub out like dirt when it is dry —John Ray's *Proverbs*

12. Shame came over me like a blanket of steam —Mary Gordon

13. Shame . . . it came in twenty-eight delicious flavors, like Howard Johnson's ice cream —Harvey Swados

14. Uncomfortable as if she had tumbled out of a warm bed into a cold room and there was no time to dress before a crowd came to view her discomfort —Henrietta Weigel

15. Waves of shame ran through her, like savage internal blushes —Mary McCarthy

SHAPE

1. (Breasts) flat as paper —William Trevor

2. As two-dimensional as a household weather vane —Saul Bellow

3. Flat and pale as an empty sheet of nonerasable bond —Lyn Lifshin
See Also: PALLOR

4. (The back of his head) flat as a book —T. Coraghessan Boyle

5. (Suit lapels as) flat as a cardboard —Derek Lambert

6. Flat as a carpet —Anon
To be more specific, there's "Flat as Oriental rugs."

7. Flat as a fashion model's breasts —Anon

8. Flat as a flounder —Anon
In his novel, *Death of the Fox,* George Garrett found a new application for this commonly used simile: "I am panting and my body twitches and heaves. Like a man with a woman, flat as a flounder, beneath him."

9. [A cleft in a rock] flat as a fresco —John Farris

10. Flat as an empty wallet —Anon

11. Flat as a pancake —American colloquialism, attributed to New England
The comparison which has been with us since the fifteenth century applies most often to very flat persons and objects.

12. (A blue sea as) flat as a table top —Jean Stafford

13. Flat as a tracer bullet —Frank Conroy

14. Flat as a waiter's feet —Arthur Baer

15. Flat as melted iron —Joyce Cary

16. Flat as paper dolls —Elyse Sommer

17. Flat as the palm of one's hand —American colloquialism, attributed to New England
A shorter version, "Flat as my hand," was used by Robert Louis Stevenson in *Will O' the Will.*

18. (I lie on my single bed,) flat, like a piece of toast —Margaret Atwood

19. (Her talk is) formless as a dream —Henry Miller

20. [A field of July corn] level as a mat —H. E. Bates
21. Long and slender like a cat's elbow —H. G. Bohn's *Handbook of Proverbs*
22. Pressed myself flat as a tick against the wood of the wall —Davis Grubb
23. (Pebbles . . .) round and white as pearls —John Cheever
24. Round as a ball —Alexander Hamilton
25. Round as a melon —Anon
26. Round as a pillow —William Wordsworth
27. (The Jewish women were as . . .) round as the earth —Thomas Wolfe
28. Round as the world —Dame Edith Sitwell
29. (Eyes as) shapeless as a kneecap —Charles Johnson
30. Shapeless as fear —Beryl Markham
31. (The neighbors lounged on each other's steps, big and) shapeless as worn cushions —Helen Hudson
32. Shapeless like a slug —Heinrich Böll
33. (Born) a shapeless lump, like anarchy —William Drummond
34. They [passing lovers] are flat as shadows —Sylvia Plath

SHARPNESS
See Also: PAIN, PARENTHOOD

1. (A whippet head,) barbed like a hunting arrow —Ted Hughes
2. Bite . . . as deadly as a camel's —Wallace Stegner
3. Biting [language used in a book] as a chain saw —Bruce De Silva
4. (Her voice was) crisp as a freshly starched and ironed doily —Maya Angelou
5. Crisp as a handclap —Maxine Kumin
    From a poem entitled *A New England Gardener Gets Personal*, the simile describes how kale comes to the salad bowl.
6. Crisp as frost —Babette Deutsch
7. Crisp as new bank notes —Charles Dickens
8. (A voice that) cut like a blade of ice —G. K. Chesterton
9. Cut like a knife —Rudyard Kipling Kipling's simile links the knife's sharpness to the wind.
10. [Cat's fangs . . .] fine as a lady's needle —Ted Hughes
11. Incisively as an acid (a yell bit into the situation) —F. van Wyck Mason
12. Peppery as curry —Marge Piercy
13. Sharp as a bird's painted bill —Dame Edith Sitwell
14. Sharp as an assassin's dagger —Mike Sommer

15. (Face as) sharp as an ice pick —Graham Masterton
16. (The longing for lovely things . . . became as) sharp as a pang —Ellen Glasgow
17. Sharp as a scorpion —Dame Edith Sitwell
18. Sharp as a two-edged sword —*The Holy Bible/Proverbs*
19. (The smell of smoke was) sharp as brimstone —John Gardner
20. (My ideas fade, yours come out) sharp as cameos —Joseph Conrad, letter to Stephen Crane
21. (Eyes) sharp as mica —R. Wright Campbell
22. (All these things fell on her) sharp as reproach —Lord Alfred Tennyson
23. Sharp as the teeth of a saw —Marge Piercy
24. Sharp as truth —John Greenleaf Whittier
25. Sharp as white paint in the January sun —Wallace Stevens
26. Sharper than birth —Madeleine L'Engle
27. Sharper than ingratitude —Anon
    This may be inspired by King Lear's famous lament about a child's ingratitude being "Sharper than a serpent's tooth" in the PARENTHOOD category.
28. Sharp like joy —Sharon Sheehe Stark
29. Sharp-tongued, like a sadistic dentist —Neil Gabler Gabler, a television movie commentator, thus described a colleague, Pauline Kael.
30. A tongue like a cat o' nine tails —Ben Hecht

SHINING
See Also: BRIGHTNESS, GLITTER AND GLOSS
1. Gleamed like dogs' eyes in a car's headlights —Frank Swinnerton
2. [A ballroom] polished like a skull —Lawrence Durrell
3. (Her face could) shine as a sack of apples —Wallace Whatley
4. Shine like a tear —Yocheved Bat-Miriam
5. [Hands] shine like old wood —Philip Levine
6. (A pool) shines, like a bracelet shaken in a dance —Wallace Stevens
7. Shines like a glowworm —Robert Penn Warren
8. Shines like a rhinestone in a trashcan —Nora Ephron reviewing a Jaqueline Susann novel within its context as a roman à clef
9. (Say to the court it glows and) shines like rotten wood —Sir Walter Raleigh
10. Shining and clear as white stones in a brook —George Garrett
11. [A table] shining like a pair of shoes —Shelby Hearon
12. [A room] shining like holiness —Jessamyn West

13. (Eyes) shining like the icing on a cake —Scott Spencer
14. Shone [the city in the light] as dazzling bright and pretty as money that you find in a dream of finding money —Edna St. Vincent Millay
15. Shone darkly, like water before a storm —Donald Seaman
16. Shone like a brand-new quarter —Karl Shapiro
17. Shone . . . like a cloud of lightning bugs —Eudora Welty
18. Shone like a meteor streaming in the wind —John Milton
19. Shone like patent leather —Rita Mae Brown
20. (The rails) shone like quicksilver —John Yount
21. (Her black, oiled hair) shone like a river under the moon —Colette
22. (Porch-slats) shone like sculpture —Alan Williamson
23. Sparkle like wedding cakes —Graham Swift
     In Swift's novel, *The Sweet-Shop Owner,* the comparison refers the effects of the sun's rays on graves.

SHOCK

See Also: CAUSE/EFFECT, SURPRISE

1. As dazed as a man who has just been told he hasn't long to live — Françoise Sagan
2. Felt amazed, as if the clouds had blown away, as if the bare bones were finally visible —Louise Erdrich
     In Erdrich's novel, *The Beet Queen,* the amazed feeling stems from a character's realization that he is homosexual
3. Felt as if I was being hit by a blast from a giant hair drier —Dominique Lapierre
4. The first shock [of English society] is like a cold plunge —Robert Louis Stevenson
5. He was white and shaken, like a dry martini —P. G. Wodehouse
6. (Then the familiarity of the name . . .) hit him like a contract cancellation —William Beechcroft
7. [A brutal murder] shocked me and held onto me as if I'd shaken hands with a live wire —Jonathan Valin
8. The shock . . . held everybody as in a still photo —Ray Bradbury
9. The shock hit me like a fist under the ribs —David Brierly
10. [Time awareness] shocking a douche of cold water —P. G. Wodehouse
11. Shocking as the realization that you're not invincible —Elyse Sommer
12. Shocking realization . . . like a fist knocking the wind out of her — David Leavitt
13. Shock [went through room] like the twang of a bow string —Iris Murdoch

14.   The shock numbed him out like a drug —George Garrett

15.   (She can) shock you like a lightning bolt at high noon —Aharon Megged

16.   Stunned . . . as if a good boxer had just caught me with a startling left hook and a stultifying right —Norman Mailer

17.   The sudden shock striking somewhere inside her chest like an electric bolt —William Styron

SHOULDERS
See Also: BODY

1.   Bony shoulders . . . like wings —Richard Ford

2.   Protruding shoulder blades that pushed out the back of his shirt like hidden wings —Harvey Swados

3.   Shoulder blades . . . almost as soft and small as a bird's wings — Penelope Gilliatt

4.   Shoulder blades jutted like a twin hump —Harvey Swados

5.   [Protruding] shoulder blades . . . like wedges —Jay Parini

6.   Shoulders like a buffalo —Willa Cather

7.   Shoulders like a five-barred gate —Donald Seaman

8.   Shoulders like a pair of walking beams —H. C. Witwer

9.   Shoulders like a wall —Paul J. Wellman

10.   Shoulders like the ram of a battleship —P. G. Wodehouse

11.   Shoulders like the Parthenon —H. L. Mencken

12.   Shoulders protruding like a Swiss chalet —Rufus Shapley

13.   Shoulders rounded like a question mark —T. Coraghessan Boyle

14.   Sunburned shoulders like the knobs of well-polished furniture —Nadine Gordimer

SHOUTS
See: SCREAMS

SHREWDNESS
See: CLEVERNESS

SHRIEKS
See: SCREAMS

SHUT
See: OPEN/SHUT

SHYNESS
See Also: MEEKNESS, PERSONAL TRAITS

1. Bashful as an egg at Easter —Sir John Denham
   This has expanded with the seasons to include "Bashful as a turkey at Thanksgiving or Christmas."

2. Demure as an African violet —Maya Angelou

3. Demure as an old whore at a christening —Thomas Fuller

4. Demure as if butter wouldn't melt in his mouth —Thomas Fuller

5. Shy as a squirrel —George Meredith

6. Shy as infants —Alice McDermott

7. Shy as rabbits —Anon

8. Shy, like a hospitable country hostess anxious to give pleasure, but afraid that she has not much to offer citizens of a larger world —Phyllis Bottome

9. A shy man men is as a lonely man . . . between him and his fellow-men there runs an impossible barrier . . . a strong invisible wall — Jerome K. Jerome

SICKNESS
See: ILLNESS

SIDEBURNS
See: BEARDS

SIGHS
See Also: GROANS AND WHISPERS

1. A collective sigh, like an escaping jet of steam —Robert Traver

2. Gave a deep sigh, like pain was a habit —Cornell Woolrich

3. Releasing a muffled sigh like a baby animal with a full belly — Kenzaburo Oë

4. Sighed, a rustling sound like wandering autumn leaves —Derek Lambert

5. Sighed like a long-suffering teacher —Ramsey Campbell

6. Sighed like a pair of bellows —William McIlvanney

7. Sighed like a poet in love —Beryl Markham

8. Sighed once with relief . . . like a low note on a bagpipe —Sue Grafton

9. Sighed with pain, as if a knife had twisted deep inside —Louise Erdrich

10. Sighing, like a bagpipe's dying breath —Patrick White

11. Sighing like a punctured tire —Guy Bolton

12.   Sighing like the night wind and sobbing like the rain —Stephen Foster
      This is a line from the song, "Jeanie with the Light Brown
      Hair," which begins with yet another simile: "I dream of Jeanie
      with the light brown hair, borne like a vapor on the summer
      air."

13.   Sigh like some sweet plaintive melody —William Motherwell

14.   A sigh of relief escaped his lips like a long-needed crap —John Lennon

15.   Sighs as if a mountain lay on her chest —Cora Sandel

16.   Sigh . . . tender and enchanting, like the wind outside a wood in the
      evening —Virginia Woolf

17.   A sigh that was like a gust of sand raised and dropped suddenly by the
      wind —Flannery O'Connor

SIGNIFICANCE
      See: IMPORTANCE/UNIMPORTANCE

SILENCE
      See Also: SECRECY

1.   Behaved a little like a stuffed frog with laryngitis —P. G. Wodehouse

2.   A brief silence, like an indrawn breath —Sylvia Plath

3.   A brittle silence stretched like iced cords through the kitchen —
      Anthony E. Stockanes

4.   Dole out his words like federal grants —Shelby Hearon

5.   Dumb as a drum with a hole in it —Charles Dickens

6.   Dumb as a yearning brute —Martin Cruz Smith

7.   The enfolding silence was like an echo —William Styron

8.   Fall silently, like dew on roses —John Dryden

9.   A great painful silence came down, as after the ringing of a church bell
      —Loren D. Estleman

10.   Grew still, like a congregation in silent prayer —Edgar Lee Masters

11.   Hears the silence . . . like a heart that has ceased to beat —Joyce
      Carol Oates

12.   (The room was suddenly full of . . .) heavy silence, like a fallen cake
      —Raymond Chandler

13.   Her silence bore down on him like a tombstone —Heinrich Böll

14.   Her silence had a frequency all its own . . . like one of those dog
      whistles that make a sound only dogs can hear—a sound that cracked
      eggs, or something —Larry McMurtry

15.   He tried to say something but his tongue hung in his mouth like a dried
      fruit on a tree —Bernard Malamud

16. (The crowded courtroom grew as) hushed and still as a deserted church —Robert Traver

17. Hushed like a holy place —Lynn Sharon Schwartz

18. A hush prevailed like that in an art gallery —Jean Stafford

19. A hush rose like a noisy fog —Bernard Malamud

20. I'll be like an oyster —Ivan Turgenev
    The character making this statement in *A Month in the Country* underscores it with not another syllable.

21. Men fear silence as they fear solitude, because both give them a glimpse of the terror of life's nothingness —André Maurois

22. Moving as silently as fish under water —Ross Macdonald

23. Mute like a faded tapestry —Louis MacNeice

24. Mute as a fish —John Melton

25. Mute as a gargoyle —Sharon Sheehe Stark

26. My tongue lay like a stone in my mouth —Pat Conroy

27. Noiseless as fear in a wilderness —John Keats

28. Quiet as the visible murmur is their vaporizing breath —William Faulkner

29. Quiet and meaningless as wind in dry grass —T. S. Eliot

30. Quiet as a lady's fart —Harold Adams

31. Quiet as a lamb —William Langland

32. Quiet as a mouse —Anon

33. Quiet as an eel swimming in oil —Arthur Baer

34. Quiet as a nun —William Wordsworth
    English novelist Antonia Fraser borrowed Wordsworth's simile for a mystery novel about a nun.

35. (It was) quiet as a prayer —Mary Lee Settle

36. (The whole immense room . . . was) quiet as a sepulchre —Walter De La Mare

37. Quiet as a stone —John Keats

38. Quiet as a street at night —Rupert Brooke

39. Quiet as a street of tombs in a buried city —John Ruskin

40. Quiet as a wasp in one's nose —John Ray's *Proverbs*

41. Quiet as a wooden-legged man on a tin roof —Anon
    This is one of many American folk similes incorporated by Carl Sandburg into his unique long poem, *The People, Yes.*

42. (The house was as) quiet as death, as the inside of a skull —John Fowles

43. Quiet as dust —Ken Kesey

44. (Her mind was) quiet, as if a needle had been lifted from a phonograph record —Ellen Gilchrist

45. (The town was all as) quiet as the hills —A. E. Coppard

46. Quiet as two tombs —Robert B. Parker

47. Quietly as a moth —Louis Bromfield

48. Quietly as smoke rising —Loren D. Estleman

49. Quiet . . . pressed on her eardrums like a weight —Hortense Calisher

50. Quiet settled in the room like snow —Rumer Godden

51. Significant silences like fingers that point —William Bronk

52. The silence seemed to come drifting down like flakes of snow — Katherine Mansfield

53. Silence fell like a guillotine in the middle of raw, bleeding conversations —Susan Fromberg Schaeffer

54. The silence around them, like the silence inside a mouth, squirms with colors —James Dickey

55. Silence as absolute as death —Robert Penn Warren

56. Silence as deep as held breath —John Yount

57. (It was Sunday, and there was a feeling of quietness,) a silence as though nature were at rest —W. Somerset Maugham

58. Silence beat about them like waves —Mavis Gallant

59. The silence between us . . . it lay coiled like a sleeping cat, graceful in its way but liable to claw if stroked indelicately —Scott Spencer
    See Also: PEOPLE, INTERACTION

60. Silence descending over the room like a blackwinged bird —John Rechy

61. Silence drifting in . . . settling like dust —Helen Hudson

62. The silence [at the other end of telephone] . . . felt absolute, as if he had been trying to telephone God —William McIlvanney

63. Silence filled the space [of empty room] like water in a lock —Julia Whedon

64. Silence filled the sunlit room like gas —Harvey Swados

65. Silence grand as Versailles —Lorrie Moore

66. Silence heavy in the air like a threat —William Boyd

67. Silence . . . hung in the air like a dead pheasant —Penelope Gilliatt

68. Silence is deep as eternity —Thomas Carlyle

69. Silence is his delight and instruction now . . . as if a blessed quiet came to him like water made into music —George Garrett

70. Silence . . . like a great hand pressed across a mouth struggling to give vent to a scream —Stephen French Whitman

71. Silence . . . like an explosion —John Fowles

72. The silence like an ocean rolled, and broke against my ear —Emily Dickinson

73. The silence of the place was like a sleep, so full of rest it seemed — Henry Wadsworth Longfellow

74. Silence . . . poured in between them like a drifting dune —Lawrence Durrell

75. The silence ran between them like a fuse —William McIlvanney

76. Silence, rather like somebody had died —Elizabeth Spencer

77. Silence . . . rich and winey, like a rest in music —Zona Gale

78. Silence rose like a mountain —Arthur A. Cohen

79. Silence settled on him like a mist —Frank Ross

80. Silence . . . so intense that it was like a third presence in the room — Antonia White

81. Silence so thick that he imagined he could cut a slice out of it, like a succulent melon —Ella Leffland

82. Silence . . . steadily filling up the bare white room, like water rising in a tank —Christopher Isherwood

83. Silence stretched out like membrane on the point of tearing —Ross Macdonald

84. Silence [in tension-filled room] stretched like a wire vibrating with impulses that were never heard —Hortense Calisher

85. Silence that falls between them . . . like deep snow —Donald Justice

86. Silence that fell upon her like a restraining hand —Nadine Gordimer

87. Silence that made his own breathing seem like the breaking of distant surf —Mark Helprin

88. Silence walked beside them like the ghost of a dead man —W. Somerset Maugham

89. The silence [in the room] was like an invasion, a possession by the great silent mountains —Gina Berriault

90. The silence was like a tranquilizer —Mignon F. Ballard

91. Silent as a burglar behind a curtain —Raymond Chandler

92. Silent as a cat on velvet —Reynolds Price

93. Silent as a country churchyard —Thomas Babington Macaulay

94. Silent as a ghost —Percy Bysshe Shelley

95. (Rooms) silent as a lantern —Daniela Gioseffi

96. Silent as a midnight thought —Anne Finch

97. Silent as a prisoner —Richard Ford

98. Silent as a snowflake settled on the ground —Donald Seaman

99. Silent as a standing pool —William Wordsworth

100. Silent as a stuffed sausage —Helen Hudson

101. Silent as a white shark —Diane Ackerman

102. Silent as despair —John Greenleaf Whittier

103. Silent as despairing love —William Blake
     A modern variant: "Silent as a breaking heart."

104. Silent as flight —Wendell Berry

105. (An object) silent as pillows —Diane Wakoski

106. Silent as rain or fleece —Lawrence Durrell

107. [Thoughts] silent . . . as space —Lord George Byron
     Here is the complete simile as it appeared in *Don Juan:* "There
     was a depth of feeling to embrace . . . thoughts, boundless,
     deep, but silent too as space."

108. Silent as the moon —John Milton
     Many writers continue to link the moon with silence, with
     frequent twists and extensions. Some examples from
     contemporary literature include: "She was as silent and distant
     as the moon" from a short story by Kate Wheeler and "Silent
     as the dark side of the moon" from *Water Music* by T.
     Coraghessan Boyle.

109. Silent as the pictures on the wall —Henry Wadsworth Longfellow

110. Silent as the rays of the sun —Slogan, Silent Glow Oil Burner
     Corporation

111. Silent as thought —Sir William Davenant

112. Silent as your shadow —Colley Cibber

113. Silent . . . like an empty room —Carlos Baker

114. Silent like a stockpiled bomb —C.D.B. Bryan

115. Silently as a dream —William Cowper
     "Silent as a dream" variations include: "Dumb as a dream" by
     Algernon Charles Swinburne and "Mute as any dream" by
     Elizabeth Barrett Browning.

116. (Made his way through the yard as) silently as a tom-cat on the prowl
     —Donald Seaman

117. Silently as a turtle —John Hersey

118. Silent men, like still waters, are deep and dangerous —H. G. Bohn's
     Handbook of Proverbs

119. (The crowd was) silent . . . totally, in a hush like the air in the
     treetops —Paul Horgan

120. A small silence came between us, as precise as a picture hanging on a
     wall —Jean Stafford

121. So quiet . . . it felt like Sunday without church —Elizabeth Spencer

122. (You were) so silent it was like playing with a snowman —Martin Cruz Smith

123. Soundless as a gong before it's struck —Donald Justice

124. Soundless as any breeze —Dame Edith Sitwell

125. The sound of the silence was like the hum of her own nerves stretched taut —William Humphrey

126. Speechless as an anchorite —Lawrence Durrell

127. Speechless as though his tongue were paralyzed —Ouida

128. Stealthy silence as of a neatly executed crime —Joseph Conrad

129. (The house was) still as a bottomless well —Hugh Walpole

130. Still as a desert —Anon

131. Still as a mouse —Richard Flecknoe
    An extension of this by Sir Walter Scott: "Quiet as a mouse in a hole."

132. Still as a stone —*The Holy Bible/Exodus*

133. Still as mourners —Mark Strand

134. Still as the grave —William Shakespeare

135. Still like gulls —W. H. Auden

136. Stillness struck like a stopped guitar —Sharon Sheehe Stark

137. A sudden silence . . . shook them like an inaudible explosion —Frank Tuohy

138. There seemed to be a lot of silence in the house, like something deep and sticky you had to wade through —Jane Rogers

139. There was absolute silence. It said as plainly as if silence were a language itself, "Go back." —Flannery O'Connor

140. (They walk close together,) silent as painted people —Julie Hayden

141. Tight-lipped as a Sioux —Charles Johnson

142. Tongues tight as immigrants —Daniel Berrigan

143. Untalkative as native Vermonters —Max Lerner on commuters

144. Unheard like dog whistles pitched too high for human ears —George Garrett

145. Uses silence like a blackjack —Tim O'Brien

146. Vocal chords seem glued together like two uncut pages in a book — Elyse Sommer

147. Withdraw behind a wall of silence like children confronted with the disapproval of an authority figure —Margaret Millar

SILLINESS
    See: ABSURDITY, FOOLISHNESS, IMPOSSIBILITY, STUPIDITY

SIMILARITY
    See Also: DISSIMILARITIES

1. As alike as buttons on a shirt —Anon

2. (We're almost) as alike as eggs —William Shakespeare
    Similes about things which tend to be uniform have and
    continue to inspire many "As alike as" comparisons. The other
    famous author most frequently credited for the "Alike as eggs"
    simile is Miguel de Cervantes with "As alike . . . as one egg is
    like another" from *Don Quixote.*

3. As alike . . . as grapes in a cluster —Edna Ferber

4. As alike as my finger is to my finger —William Shakespeare

5. As alike as two drops of water —James Miller
    This simile has become so common that no "As alike"
    introduction is needed, as illustrated by, "Just like two drops of
    water," used by Isaac Bashevis Singer in *The Family Moskat* to
    describe the resemblance between a mother and son.

6. As alike as two peas in a pod —Jack London
    Even in an age where more peas make their way to the dinner
    table from frozen food packages than pods, this now
    commonplace expression shows no sign of diminishing use.
    The form shown here has supplanted older and now little used
    versions such as, "Alike as two peas to one another" and, "As
    like each other as two peas."

7. As like a hand to another hand —Robert Browning

8. As like as like can be —William Wordsworth

9. As like as rain to water —William Shakespeare

10. As undifferentiable . . . as ballots in a ballot box —Richard Ford
    The simile as used by Ford in *The Sportswriter* describes
    modern parents whose lives are so lacking in mystery and
    difference that they are undifferentiated from their children.

11. [Pencilled doodles] identical as tracings —Margaret Millar

12. [TV commentators] looked alike as bowling pins —T. Coraghessan
    Boyle

13. Looked as alike . . . as hair pins —Loren D. Estleman

14. Looked as much alike as blackbirds on a fence —John Yount

15. Resembled each other like waves —Gustave Flaubert

16. They're like as a row of pins —Rudyard Kipling

SIMILES
>   See: MAXIMS AND SAYINGS

SIMPLICITY
>   See Also: EASE

1.   As devoid of any taste for luxury as a stone-deaf person of the sense of hearing —Isak Dinesen

2.   Crude as life among farming people —Daniel Berrigan

3.   Great men, like nature, use simple language —Marquis de Luc de Clappiers Vauvenargues
>   See Also: WORD(S), SPEAKING

4.   I am simple . . . just like that broken bottle. I have no secrets —John Updike

5.   Physically as plain as a pike —Charles Johnson
>   A variation is to be "Plain as a pikestaff."

6.   [Body as] plain as a cheap clothes-rack —Brian Moore

7.   Plain as a pine door —Sumner Locke Elliott

8.   Plain as black and white —Karl Shapiro

9.   (Hands) plain as blank pages —Gerald A. Browne

10.   Plain as English mutton —E. B. White

11.   Simple as a bucket —Paul Theroux

12.   Simple as a Hopper painting —Anon

13.   Simple as chessboards —George Bernard Shaw

14.   Simple as children's cradle songs —Adrienne Rich

15.   (Words) simple as potatoes —Marge Piercy

16.   Simple as rain —Theodore Dreiser

17.   (Would that life were as) simple as sport —Rita Mae Brown

18.   Simple as the golden rule —Anon

19.   A very simple man . . . like a tree that has not many roots, but one tap-root that goes down deep —Willa Cather

SIN
>   See: EVIL

SINCERITY
>   See: CANDOR

SINGING
>   See Also: MUSIC

1. As anxious about his voice as a Don Juan about his sexual equipment: a roughness was the equivalent of a dose of clap, laryngitis of impotence —Francis King
    See Also: ANXIETY

2. Carry a tune as well as a mouse carries an elephant —Anon

3. His care for his voice was like that of a parent for a sickly and therefore abnormally cherished child —Francis King

4. Melody . . . sweetened the air like raindrops —Paul Theroux

5. Most of them [sopranos] sound like they live on seaweed —Sir Thomas Beecham

6. Sang in a drone like a far-away tractor —Mary Ward Brown

7. Sang without passion, like a conscientious schoolgirl —Antonia White

8. Singing is as natural and common to all men as it is to speak high when they threaten in anger, or to speak low when they are dejected — William Law

9. Singing voice . . . like a bee in a bottle, a melodious slightly adenoidal whine, wavering, full of sobs and breaks, and of a pitch like a boy's before the change of voice —William Humphrey
    See Also: VOICE(S)

10. Sing like a lark —William Makepeace Thackeray

11. Sings as sweetly as a nightingale —William Shakespeare

12. Song . . . old as air, and dark as doom —Mark Van Doren

13. Sopranos trilling loudly as if terrorized —Harvey Swados

14. (I tried to sing along but) the notes themselves kept sliding away from me like water drops dancing across a hot skillet —A. E. Maxwell
    See Also: ELUSIVENESS

15. [A whistled] tune . . . seemed to be pouring out of him as though he were a bird —James Baldwin

16. Tune . . . that climbed and plummeted like a kite in the wind — Lynne Sharon Schwartz

SITTING

See Also: BEARING, IMMOBILITY

1. Carefully lowered himself into the chair like someone entering a steaming hot bath —Andrew Kaplan

2. Grandly sitting like a great rock —John Ashbery

3. Hit his chair like a large rock —Rita Mae Brown

4. Hunkered down on our haunches like Indians —Stephen King

5. Just sits there . . . like a sick cat —Niven Busch

6. Perched [on a stool] like a night owl —Jonathan Valin

7. [Eight matrons] perched like pigeons around two identical card tables —Leigh Allison Wilson

8. Sank back [into chair] . . . like a weighted diver into water —Richard Moran
   > The diver comparison is particularly apt within the context of Moran's novel, *Cold Sea Rising,* with its many ocean scenes.

9. Sank into a chair like a stone sinking into water —Lael Tucker Wertenbaker

10. Sat as still as a bird sleeping on a limb —James Crumley

11. Sat bolt upright, like a character in a work of cheap fiction —Peter De Vries

12. Sat down heavily, like a farmer getting ready for Sunday dinner — Harvey Swados

13. Sat like a bronze figure —William Brammer
    > The variations on sitting, standing or being "Still as a statue" are virtually limitless.

14. Sat like a humped stone —Flannery O'Connor

15. Sat like a lump of lead —Erich Maria Remarque

16. Sat like granite —Walter Stone

17. Sat like half-folded shirts, arms out of the way and knees close together —Mary Ward Brown

18. Sat [silently] like someone who can't remember the punch-line — William McIlvanney

19. Sat like some portent against the skies of the evening —E. M. Forster

20. Sat like wood —Leslie Thomas

21. Sat silent, motionless, like guests waiting to be welcomed —Helen Hudson

22. Sat stiff as a cockroach, waiting to spring to life —Miles Gibson

23. Sat stolidly, like an egg flattened on its bottom —David Ignatow

24. Sat there like a mountain —Eudora Welty

25. Sat up abruptly like a clockwork figure released by a spring —Joyce Cary

26. Sat up and crossed his legs like a tailor. Like a tailor with no needle — Sterling Hayden

27. Sat up as if she'd been shot from a cannon —Jonathan Valin

28. Sat up—like a soldier at reveille —Jonathan Valin

29. Sat up like Lazarus —Ray Bradbury

30. She is dumped on the seat like a barrel of ashes —Malcolm Cowley

31. Sitting [on the floor] like a sack —Ivan Turgenev

32. Sit like a frog on a chopping block —John Ray's *Proverbs*

33. Sit like an umbrella —Bertold Brecht
34. Sit like fixed candlesticks —William Shakespeare
35. Stood there like a mannequin —T. Coraghessan Boyle
36. Sit silent and still as if they were in a photograph, slightly out of focus —George Garrett
37. Sits like a pile of dough —Lee Smith
38. Sits quietly with her hands in her lap, like a pregnant woman being driven to the delivery rooom —Alice McDermott
39. Sits up high like a job applicant —Richard Ford
40. Sitting like somebody found at Pompeii —William McIlvanney
41. Sitting motionless . . . like a mother who affects not to notice the rude or awkward conduct of her children —Marcel Proust
42. (She straightened up,) sitting stiff and small, like a small mast against a storm —Elizabeth Spencer
43. Sitting there pop-eyed as a ventriloquist's dummy —Antonia White
44. You sit with your head like a carving in space —Wallace Stevens

SKEPTICISM
See: TRUST/MISTRUST

SKILLS
See: ABILITY, ACCOMPLISHMENT

SKIN
See Also: BALDNESS, COMPLEXION, FACIAL COLOR, FACIAL DETAILS, PALLOR, WRINKLES

1. The blue of her veins . . . on her breasts, under the clear white skin, like some gorgeous secret —Joe Coomer
2. Each summer his skin becomes like brown velvet —John Rechy
3. Flesh . . . as chill as that of a mermaid —Angela Carter
4. The flesh drooping like wattles beneath the jawbone —Nina Bawden
5. (Miss Quigg's) flesh looks as if it's been steeping in brine for years — Sharon Sheehe Stark
6. Flesh . . . luminous as though coated with milk —Cynthia Ozick
7. Flesh . . . soft and boneless as apple pulp —Margaret Millar
8. Flesh was as firm and clean as wood —Kay Boyle
9. Flesh, white as the moon —Charles Johnson
10. Freckles all over . . . like a speckled egg —Phyllis Naylor
11. Grained like wood (where the sweat had trickled) —Willa Cather
12. Hairless as a statue —Harvey Swados

13. Hands and forehead were deeply spotted like a seagull's egg —Frank Tuohy

14. Her skin cracked like skim milk —Arthur Miller

15. Her skin felt like plaster of Paris —Nancy Huddleston Packer

16. Her skin had a startlingly fine texture, like flour when you dip your hand into it —John Updike

17. Her skin had the bad, stretched look of the white cotton hand towels they give you in poor hotels —Maeve Brennan

18. Her skin was as pink as sugar icing —Georges Simenon
    The simile underscores Simenon's characterization of a woman like a 'bonbon.'
    See Also: PINK

19. Her skin was the color of smoked honey —R. V. Cassill

20. Her toadstool skin drapes her bones like cloth worn thin —William Hoffman
    The simile is taken from a scene in a short story describing a dying woman.

21. His skin hung on his bones like an old suit much too large for him —W. Somerset Maugham

22. His skin is pale and looks unwholesomely tender, like the skin under a scab —Margaret Atwood

23. His skin was tea-colored, like a farm boy's —Ella Leffland

24. My skin hangs about me like an old lady's loose gown —William Shakespeare

25. Pimpled like a brand-new basketball —M. Garrett Bauman
    The skin described in Bauman's short story *Out from Narragansett* belongs to a blowfish.

26. She had pale skin with the kind of texture that looked as if a pinch would crumble it —Jonathan Kellerman

27. Skin brown as a saddle —Linda West Eckhardt
    See Also: BROWN

28. (The waitress . . . has) skin dark as garden earth —Leslie Garis, *New York Times Magazine,* February 8, 1987
    See Also: DARKNESS

29. Skin . . . (slack, sallow and) draped like upholstery fabric over her short, boardlike bones —Louise Erdrich

30. Skin felt like a series of damp veils, like the wet paper you fold over the wires when you are making papier-mâché —Elizabeth Tallent

31. Skin felt like rawhide which hasn't been soaked —Niven Busch

32. Skin . . . flushed as if by a fresh breeze —Franz Werfel

33. Skin freckled like a mango leaf —Derek Walcott

34. Skin, freckled like a lawn full of clover —Rosellen Brown
35. Skin glowed like a golden peach —Lillian de la Torre
36. Skin . . . gray and rough like dirty milk —Heinrich Böll
37. Skin . . . hard and leathery . . . as though you could strike a kitchen match on it —Pat Conroy
38. Skin, hairless and white as bird droppings —Harvey Swados
39. Skin [when you're old and thin] hangs like trousers on a circus elephant —Penelope Gilliatt
40. The skin . . . hung from her bones like a quilt on the line —Suzanne Brown
41. Skin like a baby's behind —François Camoin
42. (One of those lovely, ageless women, with) skin like an Oil of Olay ad —Tony Ardizzone
43. Skin like an overwashed towel —Jean Thompson
44. Skin like dark flames —Margaret Atwood
45. Skin like flan —Scott Spencer
46. Skin like ice cream, like toasted-almond ice cream —T. Coraghessan Boyle
47. Skin like polished stone —Richard Wilbur
48. (He was pale, his) skin like sausage casing —Paul Theroux
49. Skin like shells and peaches —M. J. Farrell
50. Skin . . . like silk —*Arabian Nights*
51. Skin like the skin of fruit protected by shade —Paul Horgan
52. Skin like the underpetals of newly-opened June rosebuds —Cornell Woolrich
53. Skin like wax paper —Frank Tuohy
54. Skin like wood —Elizabeth Harris
55. The skin merely hung at her neck like a patient animal waiting for the rest of her to join in the decline —Max Apple
56. The skin of her neck was like a piece of chamois leather that had been wrung out and left to dry in brownish, uncomfortable, awkward folds —H. E. Bates
57. Skin pale as a snowdrop —Jaroslav Seifert
    This is both the first line and title of a poem.
58. Skin . . . pale as glossy paper —Geoffrey Wolff
59. Skin [around neck] . . . sagging like a turkey's —John Braine
60. Skin seemed as sheer as rubber, pulled over her hands like surgical gloves —Sue Grafton
61. Skin shines in dull gray translucence, like wax —Ira Wood

62. Skin shines like polished mahogany —R. Wright Campbell

63. Skin smelled like fresh cotton —John Updike

64. Skin . . . smooth, as if dampened and then stretched on his skull — Wright Morris

65. Skin smooth as Pratesi sheets . . . eyes that shimmer like Baccarat at the bottom of a Bel Air hot tub . . . earrings sparkling like all the chandeliers at Lincoln Center, in Malcolm Forbes yacht and maybe even in all of Donald Trump's Tower —Stephanie Mansfield, *Washington Post,* June 21, 1986

> Mansfield's string of similes sets the mood for a profile of Judith Krantz, renowned for her best sellers about glamorous people.

66. Skin . . . soft and flabby as used elastic —Jean Rhys

67. Skin so unwholesomely deficient in the natural tinge, that he looked as though, if he were cut, he would bleed white —Charles Dickens

68. Skin . . . stretched over his bones like a piece of old shining oilcloth —Dominique Lapierre

69. Skin stretched tight like a rubber ball —Margaret Atwood

70. Skin supple and moist like fine leather that had been expertly treated — Elizabeth Spencer

71. Skin, the color of creamed tea —W. P. Kinsella

72. Skin the color of ripe grapefruit —T. Coraghessan Boyle

73. Skin . . . the texture like the pit of a peach —Stanley Elkin

74. Skin tight and rugged as a mountain climber's —Ward Just

75. The skin under the eyes was gray, as though she had stayed up every night since puberty —Ella Leffland

76. Skin [a baby's] was delicious to touch, fine-grained and blemishless, like silk without the worminess —John Updike

77. Skin was pale and drawn, her bones lay like shadows under it — William H. Gass

78. Skin was reddish brown like that of an overbaked apple —Jerzy Kosinski

79. Skin [of bald scalp] was sunburned, and ridged like dried leather — Cornell Woolrich

80. Skin . . . weathering toward sunset like cracked glaze on porcelain — Dick Francis

81. The startling whiteness of her skin, lush and vulnerable, was like the petal of a gardenia —Kaatje Hurlbut

82. The texture of her skin was round and hard like the rind of winter fruit —Ellen Glasgow

83. The texture of his skin, like coffee grounds —Charles Johnson

84. White skin that looks like thin paper —John Cheever

SKY

See Also: CLOUD(S), MOON, SKY COLOR

1. Bleak [sky] . . . as if the sun had just slipped off the edge of the world —Susan Welch

2. A blue, cloudless sky spread like a field of young violets —Hugh Walpole

3. The cloudless sky was like an inverted bowl that hemmed it in —W. Somerset Maugham

4. The clouds formed like a beach and the stars were strewn among them like shells and moraine —John Cheever

5. A cloudy grey sky through which the sun shone opaque like an Alka Seltzer —Jilly Cooper

6. The evening sky, with its head dark and its scarves of color, looked like an Italian woman with an orange in her hand —Christina Stead

7. The expanse of the sky was like an infinite canvas on which human beings were incapable of projecting images from their human life because they would seem out of scale and absurd —Anaïs Nin

8. The gray (Seattle) sky lies around her, filmy and thick, like you could eat it —Barry Hannah

9. The grey, soft, muffled sky moved like the sea on a silent day —Nadine Gordimer

10. The horizon was like an open mouth —David Ignatow

11. Lifeless sky . . . like the first day of creation —Edith Wharton

12. Light spread across the horizon like putty —T. Coraghessan Boyle

13. Skies like inverted cups —John Rechy

14. Sky . . . as clear as a window —Beryl Markham

15. Sky as clear, as firm-looking, as blue marble —David Ignatow

16. Sky as drab as a cast-iron skillet —Jessamyn West

17. Sky . . . as soft as clouds of blue and white hyacinths —Ellen Glasgow

18. The sky bloomed like a dark rose —James Reiss

19. The sky covered with stars . . . like dots in a child's puzzle —Helen Hudson

20. Sky . . . flat and unreal as a glimpse of distant ocean —Sharon Sheehe Stark

21. The sky . . . flung itself over the earth like a bolt of blue cloth — Dianne Benedict

22. (Over the city) the sky hangs like a giant silken tent —Erich Maria Remarque

23. The sky hangs like lead —Erich Maria Remarque

24. The sky hisses and bubbles like a cauldron —W. P. Kinsella

25. The sky hovering overhead like a soundless dirigible that was about to crash —Heinrich Böll

26. The sky hung over the valley . . . like a slack white sheet —Elizabeth Bowen

27. The sky is darkening like a stain —W. H. Auden

28. The sky is like a heavy lid —Ridgely Torrence

29. The sky is like a human mind, with uncountable shifting pictures and caverns and heights and misty places, and lakes of blue, and big sheets of forgetting, and rainbows, illusions, thunderheads, mysteries —John Hersey

30. The sky is like a page from a book that hasn't been written —François Camoin

31. The sky is like a peach-colored sheet drawn taut at the horizon — Russell Banks

32. A sky like a dirty old slate —M. J. Farrell

33. A sky like a dustbin-lid —William McIlvanney

34. Sky like a forget-me-not —Joyce Cary

35. Sky like a great glass eye —George Garrett

36. Sky like an immense blue gentian —Henry Van Dyke

37. Sky like a pig's backside —Sylvia Plath

38. A sky like a tinted shell —Helen Hudson

39. The sky looked billowy, as if you could catch the corners of it and toss the stars around as in a net —Ada Jack Carver

40. Sky, pale and unreal as a photographer's background screen — Katherine Mansfield

41. The sky seemed to be spread like a bottomless lake above them — William Styron

42. The sky shone like enamel —John Cheever

43. The sky swayed like a blue balloon on a string —Ross Macdonald

44. A sky that looked like water, broad, blue, its clouds rolling like great, feathery waves —Charles Johnson

45. The sky was full of little puffs of white clouds, like the ships we saw sailing far out to sea —Wilbur Daniel Steele

46. The sky [on a windy day] was like an unmade bed —Helen Hudson

47. The sky was like glass —James Reiss

48. The sky was like muslin —John Ashbery

49. The sky was like new-cleaned window glass full of its own shine — Joyce Cary

50. The sky was . . . like wet gray paper —Paul Horgan

51. The sky was overcast, monotone, as if it were made of pale gray rubber —Jean Thompson

52. The sky was pale and smudged like a dirty sheet —George Garrett

53. Smoke drifted across the sky looking like a gigantic horse's mane blowing in the wind —Boris Pasternak

54. A starless sky as dark and thick as ink —Émile Zola

55. The sun bubbled in the sky, giving off clouds like puffs of steam — Helen Hudson

56. Winter skies hover over Iowa like a gray dome —W. P. Kinsella

SKY COLOR

1. The colors hanging suspended in midair like huge, floating ostrich plumes —Paul Kuttner

2. The edges of the sky had a yellowish tinge like cheap paper darkening in the sunlight —Ross Macdonald

3. Pale blue sky like some Stuka dive-bomber —Donald Seaman

4. A redness in the sky, like the flame at the back of a vast baker's oven — Saul Bellow

5. Skies are gray as tarn —Richard Ford

6. Sky blue as winter milk —Joyce Cary

7. The sky changed through several colors and became a soft crumbled gray. It was like walking under the roof of an enormous cave where hidden fires burned low —Ross Macdonald

8. Sky [at dusk] . . . green as unripe apples —Erich Maria Remarque

9. The sky is gilded with red, as if intoxicated —Cora Sandel

10. Sky . . . like terra cotta —Saul Bellow

11. Sky so pale blue and clear as a baby's eye —Joyce Cary

12. Sky the color of oiled steel —T. Coraghessan Boyle

13. The sky was a dome of gray, stretched evenly like parachute silk at full billow —Lael Tucker Wertenbaker

14. The sky was gray as a battleship —Mike Fredman

15. The sky was hard blue, like bright ink —James Stern

16. The sky was the color of dishwater —T. Coraghessan Boyle

17. The sky was yellow as brass —Erich Maria Remarque

SLANDER

1. Slanderers are like flies; they leap over all a man's good parts to light upon his sores —John Tillotson

2. Slander is like a hornet; if you cannot kill it dead at the first blow, better not strike at it —Josh Billings

3. Slander, like coal, will either dirty your hand or burn it —Russian proverb

SLEEP

See Also: DREAMS, SNORES

1. Asleep and dreaming, like bees in cells of honey —Thomas McGuane
   The simile completed McGuane's novel, *The Sporting Club.*

2. As near to sleep as a runner waiting for the starter's pistol —J. B. Priestley

3. As sound asleep as a coon in a hollow log —Borden Deal

4. Awoke . . . like some diver emerging from the depths of ocean — Francis King

5. (Paul lay in his berth) between wakefulness and sleep, like a partially anesthetized patient —John Cheever

6. (Mr. Samuel Pickwick) burst like another sun from his slumbers — Charles Dickens

7. Came out of a deep sleep slowly, like a diver pausing at each successive level —Norman Garbo

8. Come from sleep as if returning from a far country —Mary Hedin
   The simile which begins the story, *Blue Transfer,* continues with, "A stranger to myself, a stranger to my life."

9. Doze and dream like a lazy snake —George Garrett

10. Drowsy as an audience for a heavy speech after an even heavier dinner —Anon

11. Emerges from slumber like some deep-sea creature hurled floundering and gasping up into the light of day by a depth-charge —Francis King

12. Fell into a sleep as blank as paving-stone —Patrick White

13. Felt himself falling asleep like gliding down a long slide, like slipping from a float into deep water —Oakley Hall

14. Heavy with sleep, like faltering, lisping tongues —Boris Pasternak

15. I shall sleep like a top —Sir William Davenant
    This simile has outlived the play from which it is taken, *The Rivals,* as a colloquial expression. A somewhat different version, "Slept like any top" appeared in the German children's story, *Struwelpeter,* by Heinrich Hoffman.

16. I want sleep to water me like begonias —Diane Wakoski

17. Kept falling in and out of it [sleep] like out of a boat or a tipping hammock —Rose Tremain

18. Lies asleep as softly as a girl dreaming of lovers she cannot keep —F. D. Reeve
    Reeves, a poet, is describing a river.

19. Lying awake like a worried parent —Robert Silverberg

20. Nodding, like a tramp on a park bench —Robert Traver

21. Not sleeping but dozing awake like a snake on stone —Malcolm Cowley

22. Sleep as smooth as banana skins —Diane Wakoski
    See Also: SMOOTHNESS

23. Sleep came over my head like a gunny sack —Ross Macdonald

24. Sleep covered him like a breaker —Harris Downey

25. Sleep fell on her like a blow —Hortense Calisher

26. Sleeping like a lake —Theodore Roethke

27. Sleeping like a stone in an empty alcove of the cathedral —Clive Cussler

28. Sleep like a dark flood suspended in its course —Percy Bysshe Shelley

29. Sleep like a kitten, arrive fresh as a daisy —Slogan, Chesapeake & Ohio Railroad

30. Slept like a cocked pistol —Émile Zola

31. Slept a great deal, as if years of fatigue had overtaken him —Peter Matthiessen

32. Slept almost smiling, as if she had a secret —William McIlvanney

33. (He usually) slept like a corpse —Ring Lardner

34. (While the Weary Blues echoed through his head, he) slept like a rock or a man that's dead —Langston Hughes

35. Slept like he'd gone twelve rounds with a pro —Geoffrey Wolff
    See Also: WEARINESS

36. Slumber fell on their tired eyelids like the light rain of spring upon the fresh-turned earth —W. Somerset Maugham

37. Sunk into sleep like a stone dropped in a well —John Yount

38. Wake abruptly, with an alarm clock which breaks up their sleep like the blow of an ax —Milan Kundera

SLIGHTNESS
   See: WEAKNESS

SLIMNESS
   See: THINNESS

SLOPPINESS
See: CARELESSNESS, ORDER/DISORDER

SLOWNESS
See Also: MOVEMENT

1. Agonizingly slow like the gradual ripening of a peach on a limb —Sue Grafton

2. By degrees, as lawyers go to heaven —Anon

3. [A locomotive] came slowly, like a bison —Saul Bellow

4. (An hour) crawled by like a sick cockroach —Raymond Chandler

5. Creeping like a snail —William Shakespeare

6. Dragged around . . . like a dog with three legs —Shelby Hearon

7. [An endless journey] like crossing the Sahara by pogo stick —Robert Silverberg

8. Gather slowly, like a storm that swirls at sea —Anon

9. Gradually, like a man entering a swimming pool slowly —Michael Korda
   The gradual process being compared to entering a pool is a return to work.

10. Grew with such infinite slowness, like a stalactite —Lawrence Durrell

11. Happening in slow motion like a baseball replay —Maxine Kumin

12. Have all the speed and liquidity of a slug skating across salt —Erik Sandberg-Diment, *New York Times,* January 18, 1987
    Diment's comparison refers to a word processing program.

13. It [the movie *Kangaroo]* moves like a slug climbing a cornstalk —Rex Reed, 1987

14. It takes time . . . like getting your hair curled —Carlos Baker

15. Leisurely as the drift of continents —T. Coraghessan Boyle

16. Life passed him as slowly as traffic on a main artery during the evening rush hour —Anon

17. Moved as slow as paste —Paul Theroux

18. (My feet seemed deep in sand. I) moved like some heat-weary animal — Theodore Roethke

19. Moved slowly, like a diver with heavy boots —Graham Swift

20. Moved slowly through her days, like a mermaid floating in a translucent sea where all was calm, shadowy, and ambiguous —Peter Meinke

21. (Here and there a herd of stray cows) moves as slowly as old men on their way to the graveyard —A. D. Winans

22. (The government) moves like a huge blob of molasses on a two-degree slope —John D. MacDonald
An extension of the cliche, "Slow as molasses."

23. Moving about, slow as earthquake survivors —Brian Moore

24. A process about as slow and arduous as the building of the pyramids — Edith Wharton
The process Wharton is describing is character building.

25. Pushes ahead; slow as a weight —Delmore Schwartz

26. Slow and silent, like old movies —Sharon Sheehe Stark
See Also: SILENCE

27. Slow as a dream —Robert Penn Warren

28. Slow as a hog on ice with his tail frozen —American colloquialism, attributed to Vermont
The way Vermonters say it: "With his tail froze."

29. Slow as a tortoise —American colloquialism
To add emphasis there's, "As old as an old tortoise."

30. Slow as dough —Sharon Sheehe Stark
In a story entitled *The Horsehair,* the simile is used to draw a portrait of a dull, unambitious man.

31. Slow as molasses going uphill —Jamaican expression
A variant of, "Slow as molasses."

32. Slow as the hands of a schoolroom clock —W. D. Snodgrass

33. Slow as the oak's growth —John Greenleaf Whittier

34. Slow-blooded, like a lizard in winter —Mary Hood

35. Slowly, like bodies being dragged —Ross Macdonald

36. Slowly, like turtles cooking in the sun, we rotated our heads —T. Coraghessan Boyle
See Also: HEAD MOVEMENTS

37. Slow-moving like an old woman with a walker —Anon

38. Slow reluctant process [a city's morning stirrings], like the waking of a heavy sleeper —Edith Wharton

39. (Opened the case) with deliberate ceremonial slowness, as if breaking bread at a wedding banquet —Richard Lourie

SMALLNESS

1. As tiny as the glint of a silver dime in a mountain of trash —Elizabeth Spencer

2. Big as a broom closet —Anon
This modern colloquialism usually applies to a small living or working space. A common variation often used with "No bigger than" is "As big as a shoe box."

3. Big as your thumbnail —Julian Gloag

4. He [a very short man] with his chin up, gazing about as though searching for his missing inches —Helen Hudson

5. Small and undistinguishable, like far-off mountains turned into clouds —William Shakespeare

6. Small as a breadcrumb —Anon

7. Small as a fly in the fair enormity of a night sky —Elizabeth Spencer

8. Small as a garden pea —Lawrence Durrell

9. Small as a snail —Babette Deutsch
   The comparison describes the subject of a poem entitled *The Mermaid.*

10. Small as grain of rice —Anon

11. Small as sesame seed —Anon

12. Small as snowflake —Anon

13. Tight as a gnat's cock —English expression used by engineers to describe an extremely small space

14. (Paper ripped into pieces,) tiny as confetti —Ann Beattie

15. (Jewelled chips) tiny as grass seed —Jayne Anne Phillips

SMELL

See Also: AIR, SWEAT

1. The air smelled like damp flannel —Jonathan Kellerman

2. The air smelled . . . like the interior of the Bastille in 1760 —Carlos Baker

3. As malodorous as a badly ventilated lion house in a zoo —John Cheever

4. A close antiseptic odor like an empty schoolroom —George Garrett

5. A dark wet smell like a cave —Pat Conroy

6. He smelled like something that spent the winter in a cave —Sue Grafton

7. It [a hotel lobby] smelled like fifty million dead cigars —J. D. Salinger

8. A kitchen odor hung about like a bad mood —Tom MacIntyre

9. The lingering odor of sweat like sour wheat —Louise Erdrich

10. (He gave off an) odor like a neglected gym locker —Wallace Stegner

11. The odor of her body, like salted flowers —Bernard Malamud

12. The odor (of newly turned earth) steamed up around him like incense —Dorothy Canfield Fisher

13. The office smelled like hot coffee —Richard Ford

14. An old man smells old . . . like old clothes that need an airing —Saul
     Bellow

15. The place smells like a wrestler's armpit —Jilly Cooper

16. Pleasantly pungent, like the smell of one's own body —John Updike

17. Reek like last week's fish —Mike Sommer

18. The scent [from garden] rises like heat from a body —Margaret
     Atwood

19. Scent rising like incense (from the cleavage of her splendid bosom) —
     Jilly Cooper

20. The sea smelled like a sail whose billows had caught up water, salt, and
     a cold sun —Robert Goddard

21. Sexual smells, like the odor of an excellent cheese, are considered foul
     by those who experienced them without their appetites being involved
     —Judith Martin

22. A smell [of cheap cologne] like rotten bananas in a straw basket —
     Jonathan Valin

23. [Hallway of a hotel] smelled like hot bread and clean laundry —
     Richard Ford

24. Smelled like something the cat dragged in —American colloquialism

25. (Mrs. Lamb) smelled like spoiled lilacs —Richard Ford

26. [A boy] smelled like the bottom of a calf pen where the piss settled and
     burned the yellow straw red and when you turned the straw over with a
     fork the ammonia smell made your eyes water —Will Weaver

27. Smell fresh as apples —John Braine

28. (Soft-spoken women) smelling like washed babies —Philip Levine

29. Smell like an open drain —Louis MacNeice

30. Smell like a sick skunk —Elmer Kelton

31. The smell of moist earth and lilacs hung in the air like wisps of the past
     and hints of the future —Margaret Millar

32. Smells like the underneath of a car —Carolyn Chute

33. Smells badly like things that have been too long dead —Donald McCaig

34. Smells fresh as melting snow —W. P. Kinsella

35. Smell stronger than a ton of rotten mangoes —Hunter S. Thompson

36. Smell (of carnations) . . . thick as smoke in the sun —Mary Stewart

37. [Honeysuckle smell] smothering, like an anesthetic —Lynne Sharon
     Schwartz

38. A stale smell like a bad embalming job —Jimmy Sangster

39. (The married man is grateful for) the stuffy room that smells of his wife
     like a bar smells of beer —David Denby

40. There was a foul reek of something fecund and feline, like the stench of old lion spore upon the veldt —Tama Janowitz

41. Wet fields reek like some long empty church —John Betjeman

SMILES

See Also: BRIGHTNESS; FACIAL EXPRESSION, MISCELLANEOUS; GRINS; LAUGHTER

1. Adjusted her smile like a cardboard mask —Vicki Baum

2. An attempt at a smile creased Willie's face like old tissue —Paige Mitchell

3. Beamed like a child that stops crying the moment you return his favorite toy and promise never to confiscate it again —Natascha Wodin

4. Beamed like a lighthouse —Clive Cussler

5. Beamed like an August moon —F. van Wyck Mason

6. Beamed like a small boy uncrating his first bicycle —Robert Traver

7. Beamed like the sun —Mikhail Lermontov
The sunshine-like smile in Lermontov's *A Hero of Our Time* is in response to a nod from a young woman at a dance.

8. Beams like a politician —Dilys Laing

9. The faint, slow smile clung like an edge of light to her lips —Ellen Glasgow

10. Flashed her smile [and] bit it off like a thread —John Cheever

11. A flashing smile, like a knife gleaming briefly from concealment —Ross Macdonald

12. Had a smile for every occasion, like Hallmark cards —Andrew Kaplan

13. Her vivid smile was like a light held up to dazzle me —Edith Wharton

14. His smile drops from his face like a mask with a broken cord —Erich Maria Remarque

15. His smile lit up the world like a strobe light —Herbert Gold

16. His smile spread across his bearded face in crooked jerks . . . like a crack spreading across a dam —Rick Borsten

17. An indestructible smile cracked forever across the front of his face like the brim of a black ten-gallon hat —Joseph Heller
The comparison is particularly apt as it applies to a character who's a Texan.

18. Kept smiling, as if the corners of his mouth were strung up on invisible wires —Sylvia Plath

19. The lines of a smile split his jaw like a field furrow —Leigh Allison Wilson

20. Looked like a lizard regarding a fly —John Irving

21. A lovely smile, like a shining seal upon a contract —Graham Swift

22. On-and-off smile . . . like a light-switch —Eleanor Clark

23. Pinched-lip smile that dug deep grooves like chisel strokes in her cheeks —Anthony E. Stockanes

24. A pure and radiant smile suddenly shone out under her beautiful wet eyelashes, like sunshine among branches after a summer shower — Anatole France

25. Quick smile like somebody with a fever —George Garrett

26. Quick smiles that were like small coins thrown without fuss to someone who has done a service —Graham Swift

27. She smiled like a belle —Jonathan Valin

28. (Smile more widely and) show his teeth like a politician visiting a high school —James Reiss

29. Simpering like a wolf —Dylan Thomas

30. A slight smile, like a knife mark in fresh dough —James Crumley

31. Sly, satisfied smile . . . like a wink, a nudge in the ribs —Ann Petry

32. A small puckered-up smile like an old scar —Helen Hudson

33. Smile as spare as the décor along Death Row —Loren D. Estleman

34. Smile . . . warm and steady as summer sun —Mary Hedin

35. Smile . . . like a crack in old plaster —Rita Mae Brown

36. A smile, as artificial as the last touch of makeup —Marguerite Yourcenar

37. Smile as cold as a polar bear's feet —Eugene O'Neill

38. A smile as guileless as that of a serpent —R. Wright Campbell
    See Also: INNOCENCE

39. The smile, as it went from her face, reminded me of a flame turned off by a tap —H. E. Bates

40. Smile as phony as that of a trained horse —James Crumley

41. Smile as sharp as a blade —Ellen Glasgow

42. Smile broke apart like a cheap tumbler shattering —Geoffrey Wolff

43. A smile broke over his face like the sunrise over Monadnock —Steven Vincent Benét

44. Smile . . . cool as clean linen, friendly as beer —John Braine

45. Smiled as broad as a Halloween pumpkin —Charles Johnson

46. (Blinked and) smiled like a lizard on a rock —John D. MacDonald

47. Smiled like a submissive wife —Herbert Gold

48. Smiled like a wolf at the thought of the next meal —Mike Fredman

49. Smiled like a woman resigned to a fate worse than death —James Crumley

50. Smiled like La Gioconda —Gerald Kersh

51. Smiled [upon being introduced] like people who had been introduced years before and had flirted and were now hiding their acquaintance — Christina Stead

52. Smiled like she had just discovered a cure for the common cold — Arnold Sawislak

53. Smiled off and on, like a neon sign —Clancy Sigal

54. Smiled with all the charm and cunning of the dangerously insane — Miles Gibson

55. Smile, fixed like that of a ventriloquist's doll —Eric Ambler

56. A smile . . . flashed like an inspired thought across her face —O. Henry

57. A smile had widened her lips, spreading like oil —Hortense Calisher

58. Smile . . . it refreshes, like a shower from a watering pot —*A Broken-Hearted Gardener,* anonymous nineteenth century verse

59. Smile like a cocktail gone flat —Malcolm Cowley

60. Smile . . . like a crack in an eggshell —Leslie Thomas

61. A smile like a cunning little flame came over his face, suddenly and involuntarily —D. H. Lawrence

62. Smile . . . like a fresh saber scar —R. V. Cassill

63. A smile like a large plaster ornament —Marge Piercy

64. Smile . . . like all the lights of a Christmas tree going on at once — George Garrett

65. Smile . . . like an invitation —Flannery O'Connor

66. Smile like a plastic daisy —Marge Piercy

67. Smile like a razor-cut before the blood comes —John Dickson Carr

68. Smile . . . like a white flower flung on an open wound —Adela Rogers St. Johns

69. A smile like Christmas morning —Harry Prince

70. Smile like heaven —Edith Wharton

71. Smile . . . like holiday sunshine —John Le Carré

72. Smile . . . like that of the boa constrictor about to swallow the rabbit —Arthur Train

73. Smile . . . like the crêpe on a coffin —Lawrence Durrell

74. A smile like the first scratch on a new car —Tom Robbins

75. Smile . . . like the smile of a chipmunk sucking on a toothpick —Don Robertson

76. Smile like transparent water stirred by a light breeze —Italo Svevo

77. (Flashes his eyes in) a smile like triumph —D. H. Lawrence

78. Smile of a man with a terminal headache —T. Coraghessan Boyle

79. A smile passed over his big face like a soundless storm —Erich Maria Remarque

80. A smile passed over her lined face like sunlight on a plowed field —Ross Macdonald

81. The smile she gave him was like a white flower flung on an open wound —Adela Rogers St. Johns

82. Smiles stolidly flickered like home movies —Stephen Sandy

83. Smiles tossed like fanciful flowers —Joan Chase

84. Smiles wanly . . . like an actor with no conviction —Rosellen Brown

85. Smile sweet as cake —Lorrie Moore
    See Also: SWEETNESS

86. A smile that came and went as quickly as a facial tic —John D. MacDonald

87. Smile that stretches like a rubber band —Daphne Merkin

88. Smile . . . vacant and faint like the smile fading on an old photograph —V. S. Pritchett

89. A smile wide as a mousetrap —David Brierly

90. A smile with closed lips which was at once sorrowful and comic, very like a clown's —Storm Jameson

91. Smiling encouragingly but rather distantly, like friends saying good-bye in a hospital to a patient who is not expected, except by some miracle, to recover —John Mortimer

92. Smiling like a bailiff —Sumner Locke Elliott

93. Smiling like a birthday child —John Gardner

94. Smiling . . . like a fat yellow cat —J. B. Priestley

95. Smiling like a winking shudder —Robert Campbell

96. Smiling secretly as cats do in the midst of mouse dreams —Sue Grafton

97. Smiling to himself like a mysterious Buddha —Margaret Landon

98. A soft silky smile [of mother] slipped over her [young daughter] like a new dress, making her feel beautiful —Helen Hudson

99. Stretching a smile across her face like a rubber band —Susan Ferraro, *New York Times*/Hers, March 12, 1987

100. Suddenly, like a crocus bursting out of winter earth, she [a child] looked up at Alison and smiled —John Fowles

101. The suggestion of an ironic smile rippled about her face like a breeze on a pond —James Crumley

102. (She smiled at me, and) the smile broke against my face like a cool wave —L. P. Hartley

103. The way you smile, with your whole face, with your eyes, it's like a certificate of trust —T. Coraghessan Boyle

104. When Henry smiled, showing his newly crowned front teeth, he looked like a male lead in an old silent film —Kathleen Farrell

105. When she smiled her eyes and mouth lighted up as if a lamp shone within —Ellen Glasgow

106. A wide smile, glamorous and trembly, like a movie star's —Molly Giles

SMOKE
See: FIRE AND SMOKE

SMOKING
See: TOBACCO

SMOOTHNESS

1. (The syllables) flow like wind on water —T. Coraghessan Boyle

2. Glib as an auctioneer —James Crumley

3. Go down like milk and molasses —Russell Baker

4. Goes down like chopped hay —John Ray's *Proverbs*

5. It [a drink] was about as smooth as a rusty hacksaw —Harold Adams

6. (Cold,) polished as a marble column —Honoré de Balzac
   Balzac's description deftly characterizes Gosbeck, the main character in a short novel by that name.

7. Sleek and pretty as a new dime —Borden Deal
   See Also: BEAUTY

8. (Her breasts protruded from the suds wet and) sleek as seals —Jean Thompson

9. Slick as a button —American colloquialism
   Unlike "Smooth as glass" or "Smooth as alabaster" which usually describe texture, this generally applies to something easily done. Other widely used variations to describe a glib, shrewd person are "Slick as an eel" and "Slick as grease."

10. Slick as a cake of soap —Charles Wright

11. Slick as a pig —R. Wright Campbell

12. (Would make my life as) slick as a sonnet —Tallulah Bankhead

13. Slick as spit —James Lee Burke

14. Slick as a water snake —George Garrett

15. [Wet streets] slick as black satin —Paige Mitchell

16. Slick as black marble —Donald McCaig

17. [An icy roof] slick as cake icing —Davis Grubb

18. Slick as nail polish —Rosellen Brown

19. Slick as snot —Jonathan Kellerman

20. Slick as water —Terry Bisson

21. (Her glasses were) slippery as icicles —Cynthia Ozick

22. Smooth as a carpet —John Ray's *Proverbs*
    Still widely used . . . or as one might say "Popular and enduring as a John Ray proverb."

23. Smooth as a kitten's ear —Slogan, Hammond Cedar Company

24. Smooth as a phantom —John Betjeman

25. (His movement was as) smooth as a ripple of water —Raymond Chandler

26. Smooth as a sage —Lawrence Durrell

27. (Her mind, clear and as) smooth as a sea stone beaten by the waves and elements for a millenium —Charles Johnson

28. Smooth as a suburbanized television professor —Harvey Swados

29. Smooth as corn syrup —Helen Hudson

30. (Her skin was as) smooth as glass —English ballad
    Probably one of the most frequently used "Smooth as" comparisons, with 'slick' and 'smooth' often used interchangeably, as in "The frozen lake was slick as a mirror," found in Mark Helprin's short story, *Ellis Island*.

31. Smooth as marbles —Anon

32. (Voice) smooth as mink oil —Linda Barnes

33. Smooth as monumental alabaster —William Shakespeare

34. Smooth as oil —William Shakespeare

35. (The sea was) smooth as pewter plate —Mazo De La Roche

36. Smooth as pine-nuts —Suzanne E. Berger

37. (Works as) smooth as sand running through an hour glass —William Diehl

38. (Glasses) smooth as sea-washed stones —Ann Beattie

39. (Cheeks) smooth as silk —Juvenal
    Though first used to describe complexion, the simile was expanded to broader use by O. Henry when he wrote "Everything goes smooth as silk."

40. Smooth as skin in oil —Reynolds Price

41. (The fellow was) smooth as soap —Jessamyn West

42. (Skin) smooth as stones on the shore —Mary Morris

43. Smooth as the inner lips of a shell —Sharon Olds
    The shell comparison is used by poet Olds to describe the reddened, sun-swollen lips of the author's daughter.

44. Smooth as the nose of a moth —Karl Shapiro
45. Smooth as the road to ruin —Anon
46. (He shrugged and rolled up his sleeves. Both forearms were as) unmarked as a baby's bottom —Jonathan Valin
47. Worn smooth and slick as a chewed bone —George Garrett
48. Worn smooth as a tiger's eye —Sharon Sheehe Stark

SNORES

See Also: SLEEP

1. Snored as if all the frogs of spring were inside him —Eudora Welty
2. (Punctuated the air with a periodic) snore like the honk of geese — Paige Mitchell
3. Snores go up and down like a zipper —Brad Leithauser
4. Snores like a diesel truck —Ira Wood
5. (Hoffman's) snores . . . like muffled lamentations —Ross Macdonald
6. Snores . . . like stones dropped on a polished surface —T. Coraghessan Boyle
7. Snoring like a snare drum —John D. MacDonald
8. Snoring like a steamroller —Brian Burland

SNOW

See Also: NATURE, WEATHER

1. Big flakes . . . floating like parachutes in the still air —Frank Ross
2. Drifts [of snow] heaping themselves like scaling-ladders against the walls —O. Henry
3. (Those) drifts of soft snow looked like featherbeds —Scott Spencer
4. A dry pellety snow hitting the sidewalk like uncooked grains of rice — Marge Piercy
5. Falling snow . . . sinking into the ground as slowly as breadcrumbs thrown to fishes sink through water —Boris Pasternak
6. The fine snow had melted (on his hair and his eyelashes) and sparkled now like raindrops in a sunshower —Harvey Swados
7. Flakes . . . bob and sail like moths across the driveway —Anon
8. The flakes fall like asterisks —James Reiss
9. Flakes of snow . . . falling like feathers from the sky —Grimm Brothers
10. The flakes . . . seemed thick as tarts —Peter De Vries
11. Flakes swarming around the streetlamps like soft, huge moths — George Garrett
12. The flakes were as large as an hour's circular tatting —O. Henry

The comparison is a vivid one but with tatting no longer a familiar pastime, a brief explanation would be needed for any but needlework aficionados.

13. Flakes were like feathers —Frank Swinnerton

14. (The sundial was) heaped with a foot-high frosting of snow like a tall, fantastic cake —Davis Grubb

15. (Snow was still falling,) heavy flakes like goose feathers —Jilly Cooper

16. (A row of) icicles like the crystal drops of a chandelier hung from the roof —H. E. Bates

17. Icicles like the teeth of fish —Saul Bellow

18. Icicles sparkling at the eaves like pendant blades of glass —William Styron

19. It [snow] fell like a great armistice, bringing all simple struggles to an end —Elizabeth Hardwick

20. It looks pretty in the garden [in the snow], like a living Christmas — Janet Flanner

21. A light fringe of snow lay like a cape on the shoulders of his overcoat and like toecaps on the toes of his galoshes —James Joyce

22. Lightly and whitely as wheat from the grain, thickly and quickly as thoughts through the brain, so fast and so dumb do the snowflakes come —Grace Denio Lichtfield

23. Like an army defeated, the snow has retreated —William Wordsworth

24. Long icicles, like crystal daggers —Oscar Wilde

25. (I looked down at the street . . . at the) masses of snow like dirty suds —Saul Bellow

26. Melted [snow], leaving the gray grass like a pallet, closely pressed — Wallace Stevens

27. One of those brilliant, glittery snows that ought to emit some glorious sound with each crystal falling to earth, something transcendent like a Bach cantata —Lynne Sharon Schwartz
    The musical comparison is particularly appropriate to the novel, *Disturbances in the Field,* in which it appeared, as its main character is a classical musician.

28. The pilings of snow were like the white waves of a white sea —Truman Capote

29. (Her feet disperse the) powdery snow, that rises up like smoke — William Wordsworth

30. Snow as smooth to see as cake frosting and as light as powder —Ernest Hemingway

31. The snow at the roadside full of bubbles like white of egg beaten up — Joyce Cary

32. The snow began to spill down like quiet feathers —H. E. Bates
33. The snow came down last night like moths —Richard Wilbur
   A simile to begin a poem entitled *First Snow in Alsace.*
34. Snow . . . came in thick tufts like new wool, washed before the weaver spins it —Leslie Silko
35. Snow . . . comes down like lace —Marge Piercy
36. Snow . . . decking the fields and trees with white as for a fairy wedding —Jerome K. Jerome
37. Snow . . . driving him like a fusillade of frozen needles —T. Coraghessan Boyle
38. Snow fell in swift spirals, floating like gulls into the tree branches — Jean Stafford
39. Snowflakes dove at our window like fat moths —Donald McCaig
40. Snowflakes grew bigger and bigger, till at last they looked like big white chickens —Hans Christian Andersen
41. Snowflakes . . . large as white carnations —Janet Flanner
42. Snow flakes shone like silver —Hugh Walpole
43. Snowflakes sifting like crumbs into the yard —Paul Theroux
44. The [blindingly thick] snowflakes tormented him like a swarm of silver bees —G. K. Chesterton
45. The snow [during snow storm] flapped like an endless white blanket — Scott Spencer
46. Snow flying quick as thought —Adrienne Rich
47. Snow had begun to fall. It made the sidewalk a spotted hide, like leopard skin —Rosellen Brown
48. Snow had fallen like a fine dust —Martin Cruz Smith
49. The snow is now coming like dollar-sized confetti —John Wainwright
50. Snow . . . it's like inebriation because it's very pleasing when it's coming, but very unpleasant when it's going —Ogden Nash
51. The snow lay soft like a down pillow —Thomas Mann
52. Snow lies like a down mattress over the earth —Lu Hsün
53. Snow . . . lighted the streets like moonlight —Jean Stafford
54. Snow, like sheep's wool, only whiter —Gillian Tindall
55. The snow like the fuzz the morning after too much Stolichnaya — Derek Lambert
   Lambert's suspense novel, *The Red House,* is set in Russia and so the reference to a Russian drink.
56. Snow poured down like salt —Helen Hudson
57. Snow . . . settling like wool on the unmown grass —H. E. Bates

58. Snow smooth as the sky can shed —William Wordsworth
59. Snow . . . soft as froth and easy as ashes —W. R. Rodgers
60. Snow sparkles like eyesight falling to earth —Wallace Stevens
61. Snow was falling in larger flakes, like a multitude of frozen moths — Ellen Glasgow
62. The snow was yellow . . . with orange seeping into its honey color like an aftertaste at sunset —Boris Pasternak
63. Snow will settle like a sheet over all live color —Frank O'Hara

SOAP OPERA
See: STAGE AND SCREEN

SOCIABILITY/UNSOCIABILITY
See Also: BEHAVIOR

1. Antisocial as death —Mary McCarthy
2. (About as) chummy as a pair of panthers —James Forbes
3. Flung himself upon Arthur like a young bear —Christopher Isherwood
4. Friendly as a letter from home —Slogan, wine advisory board
5. (He insisted on being) friendly, like a man running for sheriff —Jay Parini
6. Greeted me like the morning sun that had deserted the skies —Mike Fredman
7. The greeting I received (from Phoebe) was as damp as the weather outside —Mike Fredman
8. He was never alone. He wore other people like armour —William McIlvanney
9. (The knocking was) hostile as a kick in the balls —Harold Adams
    Similes can provide attention-getting openings for a story, as this one did for Adams' mystery novel, *The Fourth Widow.*
10. Pleasant as a smile —Anon
11. Snarled like a racoon (whenever she was pushed) —Miles Gibson
12. Unresponsive as a bag of wet laundry —David Leavitt
13. Affable as a wet dog —Alfred Henry Lewis

SOCIETY

1. Civilization, like beauty, is in the eyes of the beholder —Anon
2. A good civilization spreads over us freely like a tree, varying and yielding because it is alive. A bad civilization stands up and sticks out above us like an umbrella —G. K. Chesterton

3. A community is like a ship; every one ought to be prepared to take the helm —Henrik Ibsen

4. Modern society is like a Calder mobile: disturb it here and it jiggles over there, too —George F. Will

5. Social life is a form of do-it-yourself theater —Muriel Oxenberg Murphy, *New York Times* interview

6. Societies, like individuals, have their moral crises and their spiritual revolutions —Richard H. Tawney

7. Society is a kind of parent to its members. If it, and they, are to thrive, its values must be clear, coherent and generally acceptable —Milton R. Sapirstein

8. Society is a masked ball, where everyone hides his real character, and reveals it in hiding —Ralph Waldo Emerson

9. Society is like air; very high up, it is sublimated, too low down, a perfect choke-damp —Anon

10. Society is like a lawn, where every roughness is smoothed, every bramble eradicated, and where the eye is delighted by the smiling verdure of a velvet surface —Washington Irving

11. Society is like a wave. The wave moves onward, but the water of which it is composed does not —Ralph Waldo Emerson

12. Society is like the air, necessary to breathe, but insufficient to live on —George Santayana

SOFTNESS

1. Feels like walking on velvet —Slogan, Clinton Carpet Co.

2. Flabby as an empty sack —Luigi Pirandello

3. Flabby as a sponge —Guy de Maupassant

4. (Arm . . .) flabby as butter —Katherine Mansfield

5. Fluffy as thistledown —William Humphrey

6. (When I reached out to touch it, it) gave like a rubber duck —T. Coraghessan Boyle

7. Gentle as a pigeon's sound —Stephen Vincent Benét

8. (Squeezed the trigger as) gently as a bee touching down to drink from a cowslip —Donald Seaman

9. Gone limp as a bath towel —T. Coraghessan Boyle

10. Graceful as Venetian quill strokes —Clarence Major

11. Lank as a ghost —William Wordsworth

12. [A chocolate bar] limp as a slab of bacon —Margaret Atwood

13. Limp as calamari —Ira Wood

14. (Paper bags as) limp as cloth —Alice McDermott

15. (Arms) limp as old carrots —Anne Sexton

16. (The potted palms were) limp as old money —George Garrett

17. Looks soft as darkness folded on itself —Babette Deutsch

18. Soft and scented as a damask rose —Vita Sackville-West

19. Soft and silky as a kitten's purr —Slogan, Alfred Decker Society Brand clothes

20. (You are) soft as a bean curd —John Hersey

21. (The rock was as white and as) soft as a bed —Vladimir Nabokov

22. Soft as a bowl of jello —Anon

23. [A distant ridge] soft as a cloud —William Wordsworth

24. (Love's twilight hours) soft . . . as a fairy's moan —John Greenleaf Whittier

25. Soft as a fat woman without a girdle —Anon

26. (Humble love in me would look for no return) soft as a guiding star that cheers, but cannot burn —William Wordsworth

27. (Cheeks) soft as a hound's ear —Theodore Roethke

28. Soft as a kitten's ear —Slogan used for both Hews & Potter belts and Spiegel Neckwear ties

29. Soft as a marshmallow —Anon
    Used primarily to imply a kind nature. "Soft as mush" is a common variation.

30. (His touch was) soft as an airbrush —Molly Giles

31. Soft as angel hair —Susan Richards Shreve

32. (Snow) soft as a young girl's skin —F. D. Reeve

33. (Waves looked) soft as carded wool —Henry Wadsworth Longfellow

34. Soft as fleece —Stephen Vincent Benét

35. Soft as linen —Hayden Carruth
    The simile, which describes a stone, continues with another: "And flows like wax." A slight twist gave Scott tissues its "Soft as old linen" slogan.

36. Soft as lips that laugh —Algernon Charles Swinburne

37. Soft as love —Hallie Burnett

38. (Heartbeat) soft as snow on high snow falling —Daniel Berrigan

39. (Her cheeks were . . .) soft as suet —Raymond Chandler

40. Soft as the thighs of women —W. D. Snodgrass

41. Soft as the west-wind's sigh —W. S. Gilbert
    This form of the west-wind comparison comes from *Ruddigore*. Using the qualitative comparison form, "Softer than it" dates back to the poet Shelley.

42. Soft as yesterday's ice cream —James Lee Burke

43. Soft as young down —William Shakespeare

44. Softening like pats of butter —John Updike
   In Updike's story *Made in Heaven,* the comparison refers to the softening light in windows he describes as golden.

45. (You are) soft like a shower of water —William H. Gass

46. Soft, like a strokable cat —Beryl Markham

47. Soft to the touch as a handful of yarn —Jessamyn West

48. [Bodies] wobbly as custard —Alice Munro

SOLIDITY
See: FIRMNESS, STEADINESS, STRENGTH

SOLITUDE
See: ALONENESS

SORROW
See: GRIEF

SOUL

1. Feel my soul rolling as if it were inside an empty barrel —Yehuda Amichai

2. The human soul is like a bird that is born in a cage. Nothing can deprive it of its natural longings or obliterate the mysterious remembrance of its heritage —Epes Sargent

3. The inner chambers of the soul are like the photographer's darkroom. Like a laboratory. One cannot stay there all the time or it becomes the solitary cell of the neurotic —Anaïs Nin

4. I thought that the soul went round like a Gladstone bag, never caring a damn for any particular station-rack or hotel cloakroom —Dylan Thomas

5. My soul is like a desert and the wind blows in its silent barren spaces — W. Somerset Maugham

6. My soul is like the oar that momentarily dies in a desperate stress beneath the wave, then glitters out again and sweeps the sea —Sidney Lanier

7. Some souls are like sponges. You cannot squeeze anything out of them except what they have sucked from you —Kahlil Gibran

8. Soul . . . as disheveled as your apartment —Jay McInerney

9. A soul as white as heaven —Beaumont and Fletcher

10. The soul dwells in the body like a spider in its web —Anon Greek philosopher

> A variation from the same source: "The soul resides in the body like a sailor in a ship."

11. Soulless as apes. Spineless as mosquitoes or dandelions —Rick Borsten

12. The soul, like fire, abhors what it consumes —Derek Walcott

13. The soul of man is larger than the sky —Hartley Coleridge

14. A soul that, like an ample shield, can take in all, and verge enough for more —John Dryden

15. A soul through which the morning shines as through a leaf —Rainer Maria Rilke

16. Strong souls live like fire-hearted suns, to spend their strength in further striving action —George Eliot

17. The sweetest souls, like the sweetest flowers, soon canker in cities — Walter Savage Landor

18. Your soul was like a star, and dwelt apart —William Wordsworth

> In Wordsworth's sonnet the first word was 'Thy.'

19. (Even if you're racked by troubles, and sick and poor and ugly,) you've got your soul to carry through life like a treasure on a platter —Alice Munro

SOUNDNESS
See: HEALTH

SOUNDS
See: NOISE

SPEAKING
See Also: CONVERSATION, SPEECH PATTERNS, TALKATIVENESS

1. [A statement] came out flat as a sheet of onion-skin paper —Cornell Woolrich

2. Can speak as flashy as water runs —R. Wright Campbell

3. Cut short his speech, like a pang of pain —Joseph Conrad

4. The few sentences she uttered were like eternal judgments —Larry McMurtry

5. Had a habit . . . of making a narrow remark which, like a plumber's snake, could work its way through the ear down the artery, half-way to my heart —Grace Paley

6. He [Peter O'Toole] doesn't just talk, he offers his words like presents, gift-wrapped —Robert Goldberg, *Wall Street Journal,* April 21, 1987

7. He was gathering toward speech, like a man about to rhumba, waiting to feel the beat —Leonard Michaels

8.   His tongue [is] as a devouring fire —*The Holy Bible/Isaiah*

9.   His rhetoric falls like a freight train over a bridge —David Brinkley about John L. Lewis

10. His talk was like a stream which runs with rapid changes from rock to roses —Winthrop Mackworth Praed
     To illustrate the simile, the poem in which it appears continues with "It slipped from politics to puns; it passed from Mahomet to Moses."

11. If I open my mouth it's like pebbles rattling together —Albert Camus

12. Phrases . . . looping out of her mouth like a backward spaghetti-eating process —Elizabeth Spencer

13. A remark thrown off like an idle dart —Sylvia Berkman

14. Said grimly . . . like a man announcing that X-rated movies had been shown at the deacons' party —Stephen King

15. Said it flatly, like a tour guide reading from a Baedeker —Jonathan Valin

16. Sentences came . . . fluently enough, even though they did sound rather like quotations from a phrase book —Christopher Isherwood

17. Sharpened their tongues like a serpent —*The Holy Bible/Psalms*

18. [Words] slipped out of me in a spasm of candor, like a sneeze —Paul Reidinger

19. Some men are like bagpipes, they can't speak till their belly's filled — Seumas MacManus

20. Speaking without thinking is like shooting without aiming —English proverb

21. Speak pleasantly . . . like a stewardess in an airliner with only one wing and two engines, one of which is on fire —Douglas Adams

22. Spoke to them mildly as mid-May weather —Stephen Vincent Benét

23. Talked like birds, with a gentle malice —Dame Edith Sitwell

24. Talked like her eyes looked, like her eyes watching us and her voice talking to us did not belong to her. Like she was living somewhere else, waiting somewhere else —William Faulkner

25. Talking is like playing on the harp; there is as much in laying the hands on the strings to stop their vibrations as in twanging them to bring out the music —Oliver Wendell Holmes, Sr.

26. Talks like his tongue is in a cramp . . . like he has adenoids as big as footballs . . . and muscles to match —John Wainwright

27. Tough talk . . . like whistling in a haunted house —John Wainwright

28. Voice stopped, like words written off the edge of a page —Elizabeth Spencer

SPEECHLESSNESS
See: SILENCE

SPEECHMAKING

1. An after-dinner speech is like a love letter. Ideally, you should begin by not knowing what you are going to say, and end by not knowing what you've said —Lord Jowitt

2. Eloquence must flow like a stream that is fed by an abundant spring —Henry St. John, Viscount Bolinbroke

3. A good speech is like a pencil; it has to have a point like a breathless messenger's report —James Atlas

4. Great eloquence, like a flame, must have fuel to feed it, motion to excite it, and brightens by burning —Tacitus
   William Pitt the Younger is often credited with coining this simile, which was in fact a paraphrase from an unknown source: "It is with eloquence as with a flame; it requires fuel to feed it, motion to excite it, and brightens as it burns."

5. His speech was like a tangled chain; nothing impaired, but all disordered —William Shakespeare

6. Human speech is like a cracked tin kettle, on which we hammer out tunes to make tears dance when we long to move the stars —Gustave Flaubert

7. Make a speech that's like a long-horned steer, with a point here and there and a lot of bull in between —Norman Mailer

8. Oratory, like the drama, abhors lengthiness; like the drama, it must keep doing —Edward Bulwer-Lytton

9. Pompous words and long pauses which lie like a leaden pain over fever —Norman Mailer
   The pompous words and pauses were heard by Mailer at the 1960 Democratic convention.

10. Rhetoric without logic is like a tree with leaves and blossoms, but no root —John Selden

11. Sermons are like pie crusts, the shorter the better —Austin O'Malley

12. Speeches are like babies: easy to conceive, hard to deliver —Pat O'Malley

13. Speeches forgotten, like a maiden speech, which all men praise, but none remember —Winthrop Mackworth Praed

14. A speech is like a love affair. Any fool can start it, but to end it requires considerable skill —Lord Mancroft, *Reader's Digest,* February, 1967

15. A speech is like an airplane engine. It may sound like hell but you've got to go on —William Thomas Piper

Piper's involvement with airplanes makes this particularly appropriate.

16. Speech is shallow as time —Thomas Carlyle

17. Speech is silver; silence is golden —Thomas Carlyle

18. The speech of men is like embroidered tapestries, since, like them, it must be extended in order to display its patterns; but, when it is rolled up, it conceals and distorts them —Plutarch

19. The speech . . . took shape in his head as clearly and precisely as if it were an official report —Leo Tolstoy

SPEECH PATTERNS

1. Accent . . . almost as authentic as that of the white-jacketed medico peddling hand cream to the TV millions —Harvey Swados

2. Accent . . . thick as porridge —W. P. Kinsella

3. Diction . . . each word distinct and unslurred, as if he were a linguistics professor moderating a panel discussion on the future of the language —T. Coraghessan Boyle

4. The doctor's English was perfect, pure Martha's Vineyard; he sounded like Ted Kennedy's insurance salesman —T. Coraghessan Boyle

5. Dragging his words along like reluctant dogs on a string —Edith Wharton

6. Had spoken the lines without expression, running them past, uninspired, one behind the other like passing freight cars —William Brammer

7. He [Edmund Wilson] spoke in a curiously strangled voice, with gaps between his sentences, as if ideas jostled and thrashed about inside him, getting in one another's way as they struggled to emerge, which made for short bursts —Isaiah Berlin, *New York Times Book Review,* April 12, 1987

8. His facile elocution . . . which had so long charmed them, was now treated like warm gruel made to put cowards to sleep —Émile Zola

9. His statements are often preceded by stretches of silence as painful as the space between a stutterer's syllables, as he tries to translate his images into words —Ira Wood

10. Inflections that rise and fall with a tidal surge equal to that of the Bay of Fundy —Richard F. Shepard about comedian Jackie Mason, *New York Times*

11. Intoned monotonously like a sleep-walker —MacDonald Harris

12. Mouthing the words and nodding to himself like an actor memorizing his lines —Donald Seaman

13. Repeated slowly, as if he were sounding out syllables in a book — Jonathan Valin

See Also: REPETITION

14. The rest of it [a remark] was delivered at a clipped, furious pace, like Morse code —Jonathan Valin

15. Said one word, carefully pursed in his mouth, spat out like a grape pip —John Fowles

16. The sentences were spoken like sentences from a judge summing up, bit by bit —V. S. Pritchett

17. Short brief staccato sentences like slaps —William Faulkner

18. Spaces her adjectives like little whiplashes —John Fowles

19. Spacing his words as if for a particularly stupid and stubborn person — Nancy Huddleston Packer

20. Spat out the words like orange seeds —Dorothy Francis

21. Speak falteringly, like an unrehearsed actor —Anon

22. Speaking [in a heavy tone] . . . as if he were dropping words like molten lead —G. K. Chesterton

23. Speak like a death's head —William Shakespeare

24. Speak . . . like a telegram —Dashiell Hammett

25. Spitting the word from her mouth . . . as if it were a poisonous seed —Flannery O'Connor

26. Splutter and splash like a pig in a puddle —W. S. Gilbert

27. Spoke clearly, but in a low and hesitant voice, as if he were translating from Spanish as he went along —Norman Mailer

28. Spoke like a radio program —Ludwig Bemelmans

29. Spoke more slowly than ever before and with difficulty, like someone who fears a stammer —Dan Jacobson

30. Spoke slowly, with a kind of uniformity of emphasis that made his words stand out like the raised type for the blind —Edith Wharton

31. Spoke very slowly and deliberately, like a man reading aloud from a difficult text —Jonathan Valin

32. Sputtered out [words] like a wet fuse —Richard Moran

33. Stutter like a new-clipped crow —George Garrett

34. Talked flowingly like a medium —Anaïs Nin

35. Talked like she had bugs in her mouth —Madison Smartt Bell

36. Talked with commas, like a heavy novel —Raymond Chandler

37. (He had developed an unfortunate habit of) talking like a Chinese fortune cookie —John Cheever

38. (Tendency to) talk like a Sten gun —George F. Will about Hubert Humphrey

39. Used the English language with dictionary precision . . . almost as if it were a foreign tongue he had learned perfectly —Lael Tucker Wertenbaker

40. Use her words cautiously, like weapons that might slip and inflict a wound —Edith Wharton

41. Words . . . dragging out like words in an anthem —G. K. Chesterton

42. Words, each distinct and separate, like multicolored marbles —Francis King

43. Words leaped out of his mouth like machine-gun bullets —Frank Conroy

44. Words were being mouthed like signal flags —Norman Mailer

SPEED

See Also: RUNNING

1. (Poems have become) as instant as coffee or onion soup mix —Donald Hall

2. (They'll whip her back . . .) as quick as shit through a goose —Derek Lambert

3. As swift as meditation, or the thoughts of love —William Shakespeare

4. As swiftly as a reach of still water is crisped by the wind —Rudyard Kipling

5. Be not in a hurry, like the almond, first to blossom and last to ripen. Be rather like the mulberry, last to blossom and first to ripen —*The Holy Bible/Apocrypha*

6. The crowd was moving fast . . . like a big spread ravelling, and the separate threads disappeared down the dark street —Flannery O'Connor

7. Drive [a car] like the hounds of hell —Rosamund Pilcher

8. Fast as a bird on the wing —Anon

9. Fast as a cat scurrying up a tree at the approach of a strange dog — Anon

10. Fast as a cook cracks eggs —Thomas Nash

11. Fast as a heartbeat —John D. MacDonald

12. Fast as a jet —Mark Helprin

13. Fast as a pickpocket —Anon

14. Fast as a propeller —Bertold Brecht

15. (Scrambles into the room,) fast as a spider —Robert Silverberg

16. Fast as greased lightning —American colloquialism

17. Fast as the blink of an eye —Anon

18. Fast-moving as the gray fox that climbs trees after squirrels —Marge Piercy

19. (Little and) fleet as a terrier running beside a bloodhound —Erich Maria Remarque

20. (To vanish,) fleet as days and months and years, fleet as the generations of mankind —William Wordsworth

21. Flying like ice in a sleet storm —Ben Ames Williams

22. Fly like a donkey with pepper up its behind —Aharon Megged

23. Galloped through [religious mass] like a man with witches after him —Edith Wharton

24. Goes like a ship-lash flicked across a horse's neck —Rudyard Kipling

25. Going like flames —Samuel Beckett

26. Going like sixty —F. D. Reeve

27. Go like a house afire —Anon
    One of many "Go like" similes that have worked their way into the American language mainstream since the late 1830s. Some other examples: "Go like a shot," "Go like hell" and "Go like mad."

28. Go through like a dose of salts —American colloquialism
    While purgative salts are pretty much a thing of the past, the simile endures as a way to describe a very rapid pace. With the penchant for brand names, "Go through like Ex-Lax" has become a common alternative.

29. Go through them [reading materials] like a kid through potato chips —James Crumley

30. He rushed past her like a football tackle —James Thurber

31. (Wedding plans were) hurtling along like a train on tracks —Paul Reidinger

32. Insectlike swiftness —Saul Bellow

33. It must be done like lightning —Ben Jonson

34. Just a glance, like passing your eyes over the spines of books without being able to read the title . . . that quick —Arthur A. Cohen
    See Also: LOOKS

35. (Scurried off, his) legs going like a windmill —Paige Mitchell
    See Also: MOVEMENT

36. Like a sunbeam, swift and bright —Sir Walter Scott

37. Move with the speed of a Grand Prix Racer —Anon

38. Moving fast as a train —Anon

39. My days are swifter than a weaver's shuttle —*The Holy Bible/Job*
    While this simile is not much used these days, it is the one that has seeded the many contemporary variations.

40. Quick and nimble, more like a bear than a squirrel —Henry G. Bohn's *Handbook of Proverbs*

41. Quick as a lizard —Anthony Trollope

42. Quick as an attack dog —Gloria Norris

43. (Acted) quick as a knife —Penelope Gilliatt

44. (The wolf . . . ate her up as) quick as a slap —Anne Sexton

45. Quick as a striking snake —George Garrett

46. Quick as a weasel —Robert B. Parker

47. Quick as a wink —Anon
    While variations such as "Quick as dust" and "Quick as scat" have faded from the American vocabulary, "Quick as a wink" endures to the point of overuse.

48. (Goes) quick as light —Noël Coward, lyrics for "Chase Me Charlie"

49. Quick as lightning —Frances Sheridan
    The American adaption of the simile first used by Sheridan in a play named *Discovery* is "Quick as greased lightning."

50. Quick as mercury —Marguerite Yourcenar

51. (Slipped down) quick as minnows —Marge Piercy

52. (Barry's eye was as) quick as sound —Frank Swinnerton

53. Quicker than a crab underwater —John Updike

54. Quicker than boiling asparagus —Caesar Augustus
    According to Stevenson's *Proverbs, Maxims and Famous Sayings,* Augustus used this expression whenever he wanted anything to be done fast.

55. Quick on his feet as a running deer —Stephen Vincent Benét

56. (Lavella's brain) raced like a trapped rabbit —William Beechcroft

57. (Feet) rapid as the river —Henry Wadsworth Longfellow

58. Rash as fire —William Shakespeare

59. (Raleigh) rushed through (these hypotheses) like rosary beads — Michael Malone

60. (Men) rushing like they were bolt out of a cannon —Richard Ford

61. Rushing wildly from room to room like a flustered hen —Christopher Isherwood

62. Scurried like a crab —Michael Malone

63. She was so swift . . . it was like having a small cute dog with you — Isak Dinesen

64. Some people are too fast for their own good, like Asahel in the Book of Samuel —Saul Bellow

65. Sped around like intergalactic missiles —Lisa Harris

Harris's simile describes the activity of the Lubavitcher women in Crown Heights, the subject of her book *The World of a Hasidic Family.*

66. (The game) speeds along like a fast freight —W. P. Kinsella
    The game speeding along is baseball, the background for *The Iowa Baseball Confederacy* and other Kinsella novels.

67. Speedy as a steam roller —George Ade

68. Started for me (as to attack) like a streak of lightning —Rex Stout

69. Swift as a cloud between sea and sky —Percy Bysshe Shelley

70. Swift as a greyhound —Ouida

71. Swift as a mugger —David Leavitt

72. Swift as an arrow —Anon
    This has been attributed to numerous sources dating back to the early seventeenth century.

73. Swift as a plunging knife —Rudyard Kipling

74. Swift as a shadow —William Shakespeare

75. Swift as desire —Mary Pix

76. Swift as fear —Thomas Parnell

77. Swift as the eagle (flieth) —*The Holy Bible/Deuteronomy*

78. Swift as the waters —*The Holy Bible/Job*

79. Swift as thought —William Shakespeare

80. Swift as unbridled rage —Henry Abbey

81. Swifter than the wind —William Shakespeare

82. Swift in motion as a ball —William Shakespeare

83. (Fluttering her bristly black lashes as) swiftly as butterflies' wings — Margaret Mitchell
    The girl fluttering her lashes is Scarlett O'Hara of *Gone with the Wind* fame.

84. Travelling fast as a wish —Elizabeth Bishop

85. (The race) went by like an express train —Enid Bagnold

86. (She dressed and) went off like a top with the whip behind it —Vicki Baum

87. Went past . . . like lightning past a hill —Jessamyn West

88. Went through it like a clown through a paper hoop —Temole Scott

89. Went through like shit through a tin horn —American colloquialism

SPIRIT

See: COURAGE

SPOILAGE
    See: DISINTEGRATION

SPONTANEITY
    See: NATURALNESS

SPORTS
    See Also: BASEBALL, BOXING AND WRESTLING, FOOTBALL, GOLF

1. Batted the [tennis] ball away like an irritating gnat —Rita Mae Brown

2. An American winning the French bicycle race is like a Frenchman winning most valuable baseball player —Chris Wallace commenting on Greg Le Mond's winning of Tour De France race, NBC-TV, July 26, 1986

3. Angling may be said to be so like the mathematics that it can never be fully learned —Izaak Walton

4. The [tennis] ball knifes right onto the face of the strings and stays there like a piece of cheese —Ron Carlson

5. Basketball is like poetry in motion —Jim Valvano, North Carolina State coach, 1987

6. Bathers hop across the waves agilely, aimlessly, like fleas —Malcolm Cowley

7. Coaching is like a monkey on a stick. You pass the same fellows on the way down as you pass on the way up —Steve Owen, New York Giants football coach

8. [A swimmer] floated on her back [in water] like a pink air mattress — Will Weaver

9. Having the America's Cup yacht race in San Diego instead of Newport is like going to Mardi Gras in Pittsburgh —Rhode Island Representative St. Germaine, *Wall Street Journal,* February 5, 1987

10. Hockey players are like mules. They have no fear of punishment and no hope of rewards —Emory Jones, general manager of the St. Louis Arena, *St. Louis Post-Dispatch,* December 26, 1963

11. Holds a siren yellow tennis ball up in front of her, like the torch on the Statue of Liberty, and hits it with a combination of force and grace — Daphne Merkin

12. If a tie is like kissing your sister, losing is like kissing your grandmother with her teeth out —George Brett, Cincinnati Royals third baseman, *Sports Illustrated,* June 23, 1986

13. I saw more sails biting the wind than I've ever seen before; it was like sailing through the mouth of a shark —Jean Lamuniere, September 15, 1986

14. Legs [bicycling] pumping like wheels —Murray Bail

15. Little Pat played [tennis] . . . like a weekly wound up machine —John Updike

16. Records fell like ripe apples on a windy day —E. B. White

17. The reel was screaming . . . humming like a telegraph wire in a sixty-mile gale —Arthur Train

18. The skaters [on the Ranger hockey team] . . . perform like an electrocardiogram readout —Craig Wolff, *New York Times,* September 8, 1986

     Wolff's simile alluded to the team's impersonal performance.

19. Sports is like a war without killing —Ted Turner, baseball team owner

20. Swim like a cannonball —Tony Ardizzone

21. (I can) swim like a duck —William Shakespeare

22. Swimming the English Channel, it was like swimming in dishwater — Sandra Blewett, long distance swimmer, *The Evening Standard,* August 21, 1979

23. Tearing through the water like a seal —Rosamond Lehmann

24. Tennis is like a lawsuit; you can always be surprised by what happens on the other side of the court —Anon

25. Their arms were so high on the follow-through it looked like a mass ascension of Mount Everest —Archie Oldham

     The simile, taken from a basketball story, *The Zealots of Cranston Tech,* describes a team of players all shooting for basket together.

26. The undulant fly line coiled out over the pond like a fleeing serpent — Robert Traver

27. Violent exercise is like a cold bath. You think it does you good because you feel better when you stop it —Robert Quillen

28. (Bicycling children) wheeled like swallows through luminous, lemon-coloured air —Julia O'Faolain

29. Working out the [fishing] line at his feet, like a cowboy coiling a rope — Robert Traver

30. You will find angling to be like the virtue of humility, which has a calmness of spirit and a world of other blessings attending upon it — Izaak Walton

SPREADING

See Also: GROWTH, PERVASIVENESS

1. (Anxiety was) as contagious as a yawn —Barbara Lazear Ascher, *New York Times*/Hers, October 23, 1986

2. Blown up [with fever] like a tire —Elena Poniatowska

3. (Excuses) breaking out like pimples —Marge Piercy

4. Breed like guinea pigs —Raymond Chandler
5. Catch happiness as quickly as others catch colds —Storm Jameson
6. Catching like fire in dry grass —William Dean Howells
7. Contagious like the gladness of a happy child —Edward Bulwer-Lytton
8. Excitement swept through Jalna [the estate which is the setting for a series of De La Roche novels] like a forest fire —Mazo De La Roche
9. Expand like air in a pressure chamber —Penelope Gilliatt
10. Gather like dust on a windowsill —Anon
11. Multiply like troubles —Marge Piercy
12. Passed around [German measles] like a dish of cool figs at the first rehearsal —Reynolds Price
13. (Houses) popping up everywhere like the heat rash. Like pimples — George Garrett
14. Spread a thought . . . like butter on toast —Carlos Fuentes
15. (Feel her pleasure deepening and) spreading like a chord struck in all octaves at once, sustained, played, and then held and held till it slowly faded into its overtones —Marge Piercy
16. (She looked at me, recognition) spreading like a rash —Sharon Sheehe Stark
17. (Pain) spreading like lava —John Braine
18. Spreading [throughout her system] . . . like poison dye —Margaret Millar
    In the mystery novel, *The Fiend,* the author uses the simile to describe a key character's growing alertness to a dangerous situation.
19. (Affection . . .) spread like an epidemic through the room —Jean Stafford
20. Spread like an unconfirmed rumor —Elyse Sommer
21. Spread like a quenchless fire —Percy Bysshe Shelley
22. Spread . . . like a tiny spray of ink on a piece of blotting paper — Franz Werfel
23. Spread like butter under a knife —Lawrence Durrell
24. Spread like dandelions after spring rain —Marilyn Ross about growth of directories, *Publishers Weekly,* June 5, 1987
25. (But they cling and) spread like lichen —Elizabeth Bishop
26. Spread like mushrooms after a fresh spring rain —Anon
    Mushrooms have long lent themselves to quick growth comparisons. A variation: "Grow like toadstools."
27. Spread like mushrooms across an unsuspecting garden —Tom Robbins
28. Spread like pancake batter on a hot griddle —Elyse Sommer

29. Spread like the desert —Henry James

30. (Silence) spread . . . like water that a pebble stirs —Dante Gabriel Rossetti

31. Spread out like a doily —Alma Stone

32. Spread out (the sun) like a jellyfish —John Steinbeck

33. (I saw the vineyards) spread out like wings —Eudora Welty

34. Spreads faster than panic in a plane —Donald Seaman

35. Spreads like a sigh —Anon

36. (Love that) spreads like a stain of ink in absorbent cloth —Diane Wakoski
    As poet Wakoski links the spreading stain with love in her poem, *My Little Heart Pops Out,* so W. H. Auden uses "Ruin spreading like a stain" in *Something Is Bound to Happen.*

37. Spreads like good news —Slogan for Satinwax, Economic Laboratory

38. Spread through like a clumsy, uninvited guest who is obese and eats too much —Lorrie Moore
    The descriptive frame of reference in Moore's novel, *Self-Help,* is cancer.

39. (Enemies . . . are) sprouting (around me) like tulips —Peter Benchley

SPRIGHTLINESS
See: ACTIVENESS

SPRING
See: SEASONS

STAGE AND SCREEN

1. An actor is a sculptor who carves in snow —Edwin Booth

2. An actor is like a cigar; the more you puff him, the smaller he gets — Anon

3. Actors are like burglars: they always change their names for business purposes —Frank Richardson

4. An actor's soul must be like a diamond. The more facets its got, the more shining his name —Grace Paley

5. Every film is launched like a squid in an obscuring cloud of spectacular publicity —Dudley Nichols

6. [Danny Kaye] feels about an audience the way most men feel about a date. He woos them. He wants to make them happy —Sylvia Fine, quoted in husband Kaye's obituary, *New York Times,* March 4, 1987

7. The movie actor, like the sacred king of primitive tribes, is a god in captivity —Alexander Chase

8. A movie is like a person. Either you trust it or you don't —Mike Nichols

9. Movie stars are like race horses. Everybody knows their name, but they have to obey the stable boys —MacDonald Harris

10. Not to go to the theater is like making one's toilet without a mirror —Arthur Schopenhauer

11. A play, like a bill, is of no value till it is accepted —Henry Fielding

12. Prologues, like compliments, are a loss of time —David Garrick

13. Sex percolates merrily through all of the daytime soaps like grounds in a coffee pot —Carin Rubenstein, *Channels Magazine,* March, 1986
    See Also: SEX

14. Soap opera is like sex outside marriage: many have tried it, but most are ashamed of being caught —Peter Buckham

15. Television is like the little girl who had a little curl. When it is good, it is very, very good, and when it is bad, it is horrid —Melvin I. Cooperman, discussing quality of playwriting for stage, screen and television writers, *Word Wrap* (electronic bulletin board for writers), May 8, 1987

16. The theater is a communal event, like church —Marcia Norman, *New York Times Book Review* interview, May 24, 1987

17. Theater is like baseball; it depends on hits and runs —Anon

STALENESS

See Also: TIMELINESS/UNTIMELINESS

1. As trite as the lyrics to a fifties hit —Hilma Wolitzer
    In her novel, *In the Palomar Arms,* Wolitzer compares the triteness of old song lyrics to what happens to the words spoken by someone once loved passionately.

2. Felt about as fresh as an old piece of chewing gum —Mike Fredman

3. Flat and cold as the muffins of this morning's breakfast —Henry James
    In James' play, *Pyramus and Thisbe,* this describes personality traits grown stale with overuse and familiarity.

4. Flat as last night's beer —Louis Untermeyer

5. Stale as an old cigar —Wilfrid Sheed

6. Stale as yesterday's bread —Arthur A. Cohen

7. (But it was all unmeaningful to us, and all the proverbs seemed stiff and) stale, like dusty labels on neglected antiquities —G. K. Chesterton

8. Stale, like the butt of a dead cigar —Rudyard Kipling

9. Tired as a much-told joke —Anon

STANDING

See Also: BEARING, IMMOBILITY, PERSONAL PROFILES, POSTURE

1. He was standing there with his arms at his sides like a wooden soldier —Ann Beattie

2. (Mrs. Snow was) standing framed in the doorway like a faded vestal virgin guarding a shrine —Ross Macdonald

3. Standing . . . like a painted statue —Iris Murdoch

4. Stand like clockwork toys —W. S. Gilbert

5. Stands like the figurehead at a ship's prow —Stevie Smith
   A variation on the same theme: "Stood, like a carving on the prow of a ship."

6. Stood around like shadows —Maya Angelou

7. Stood as if thunderstruck —Joseph Conrad

8. Stood before us, huge and dark like a colossus —Margaret Drabble

9. Stood like a private before his colonel —Frank Swinnerton

10. Stood like lead —Wallace Irwin

11. Stood like stocks —Dorothy Canfield Fisher

12. Stood stiffly as a hanged man —Leigh Allison Wilson

13. Stood up and stretched like a sleepy cat —Gloria Norris

STARES

See Also: FROWNS, LOOKS

1. Dug his blue eyes into me, like nails —Jay Parini

2. (I've been feeling your) eyes boring into me like a pair of yellow jackets. She had a curiously intense stare, like a greedy child waiting for sweets —Beryl Bainbridge

3. Stared at each other quietly, like enemies —Robert Campbell

4. Stared at him, holding him, like the high point on a compass —Richard Ford

5. Stared at [a question] keenly as if it were a fly that he was waiting to swat when it came round again —V.S. Pritchett
   See Also: SCRUTINY

6. Stared at me like blocks of wood —Donald Justice

7. Stared blankly at me like a dead fish —Joe Coomer

8. (Had no expression in his gray eyes. He) stared like a cat at an empty window —Bill Granger

9. Stared . . . with the intensity of a man having a private audience with an angel —James Morrow

10. Stares at me like I'm dirt he intends to one day wipe off his shoes — Robert Campbell

See Also: CONTEMPT

11. Stares at my idea like a crystal vase suspended in his mind's rare ether —Richard Ford

12. (Powell's) stare seemed to pinch her like a pair of tongs —Flannery O'Connor

13. (Stood there) staring at him like a stunned ox —Oakley Hall

14. Staring at me with a studied air, as though measuring me —Kent Nelson

15. Staring into his face like a devotee before an idol —Elizabeth Spencer

16. Staring like rustics at a fair —Henry James

17. A way . . . of staring at the wall or at the window like a detective at a murder scene, desperate for clues —Clive Barker

STARS

1. The dipper burned like a strand of diamonds on a sable cloak —Joseph Wambaugh

2. The divisions between the rings [of Saturn] are furrows in which the satellites rotate . . . like sheepdogs running around the flock to keep it compact —Italo Calvino

3. The evening star flickered like a lamp just lit —Willa Cather

4. In the dark vault of the sky, the stars hung like muted dots of leaden silver —Heinrich Böll
   This lovely simile is the first sentence of Böll's short story, *The Ration Runners.*

5. Jupiter displays two equatorial stripes like a scarf decorated with interwoven embroideries —Italo Calvino

6. A lovely star . . . large as the full moon —Jaroslav Seifert

7. The Milky Way stands out so clearly that it looks as if it had been polished and rubbed over for the holidays —Anton Chekhov

8. A star as bright as day —Anon Christmas ballad, probably dating to Middle Ages

9. Starlight fell like rain —F. Scott Fitzgerald

10. Stars are dropping thick as stones —Sylvia Plath

11. (Tonight) the stars are like a crowd of faces moving round the sky —Wallace Stevens

12. The stars burned steadily, like the lights of far-off ships —Marjory Stoneman Douglas

13. The stars clung like snow crystals in the black sky —Ross Macdonald

14. Stars . . . cold, like pieces of ice —Paige Mitchell

15. Stars . . . dissolved like bubbles —Katherine Mansfield

The simile in full context: "In the sky some tiny stars floated for a moment and then they were gone—they were dissolved like bubbles."

See Also: DISINTEGRATION

16. Stars gleamed and winked like searching fireflies —Robert Traver

17. Stars . . . huge, like daisies —May Sarton

18. Stars large as asters —Mary Stewart

19. Stars . . . like countless diamond lamps —Hans Christian Andersen

20. (At night) stars rise like the bubbles of the drowned —Yehuda Amichai

21. The stars seemed to look down like a thousand winking eyes —William Humphrey

22. The stars which at midnight looked like a spillway of broken pearls, did not shine at this hour; they were holes of light, like eye squints in black masks —Paul Theroux

23. Twinkle, twinkle, little star how I wonder what you are, up above the world so high, like a diamond in the sky —Anne Taylor

STARTING AND STOPPING
See: BEGINNINGS/ENDINGS, PAUSE

STATELINESS
See: BEARING

STATISTICS
See: FACTS

STEADINESS
See Also: FIRMNESS

1. (Believe in justice) inexorable as the decay of an isotope —Marge Piercy

2. Solid as earthenware —Anne Sexton

3. Solid as the continent —Slogan, North American Life Insurance

4. Stayed steady as a castle —John Le Carré

5. (His touch is quick, sure,) steady as a laser —T. Coraghessan Boyle

6. Steady as the moonlight —Saul Bellow

7. (Hands as) steady as the murder rate —Loren D. Estleman

8. Steady as the stare of a glass eye —Arthur Baer

9. Steady as the water flowing from a hydrant —James G. Huneker

STEALTH
See: SECRECY

STERILITY
> See: BARRENNESS

STICKINESS
> See: CLINGING

STILLNESS
> See: IMMOBILITY, PEACEFULNESS, SILENCE

STINGINESS
> See: THRIFT

STOMACH
> See Also: BODY, FATNESS, SHAPE, THINNESS

1. A beer gut like a beach ball —Rick Borsten
2. A belly like a huge alabaster bowl —Paule Marshall
3. Belly like a meadow —John D. MacDonald
4. Belly . . . round as a tub —Will Weaver
5. Belly stuck out like a full moon —Carlos Baker
6. (My soft) belly that hangs over my shorts like the cap of a mushroom —Ira Wood
7. Belly tight as a drumhead —George Garrett
8. Big belly all puffed out in front like he took a tube in the morning and blew it up as far as it would go —George Garrett
9. A big belly that hung over his pants like a melon —Gloria Norris
10. Carried his paunch like something stolen and badly hidden beneath his shirt —John Irving
11. Her belly looked like a balloon —Tony Ardizzone
12. Her [pregnant] belly rises, tight as a beach ball —François Camoin
13. Her belly split like a backside by her caesarian scar —Alice McDermott
14. His abdomen looked like the carapace of a lobster, all rock-hard, etched, and segmented musculature —Jonathan Valin
15. His gut protruded like a basketball pumped to maximum pressure per square inch —Sue Grafton
16. The jowls of his belly crawl and swell like the sea —Karl Shapiro
    This vivid simile is the opening line of a poem entitled *The Glutton.*
17. Stomach . . . hard as a cord of wood —Richard Ford
18. Stomach hard as a washboard —Cynthia Ozick
19. Stomach [of pregnant woman] like a globe —Ruth McLaughlin

20.   Tight potbelly like a swallowed ball —Peter Matthiessen

STOP
See: PAUSE

STORIES
See Also: BOOKS, WRITERS/WRITING

1.   All circumstances in a tale answer one another like notes in music —Robert Louis Stevenson

2.   Fiction is like a spider's web, attached ever so slightly perhaps, but still attached to life at all four corners —Virginia Woolf

3.   A good story compels you like sexual hunger but the pace is more leisurely —Robert Hass

4.   A good story is like a bitter pill with the sugar coating inside of it —O. Henry

5.   A poor story is a good deal like a grist, the oftener it is told, the less there is of it —Josh Billings
   In Billings' dialect this reads: "The oftner it iz told, the less thare iz ov it."

6.   Stories are like snapshots . . . pictures snatched out of time with clean, hard edges —James Crumley

7.   Stories, like whiskey, must be allowed to mature in the cask —Sean O'Faolain, *Atlantic Monthly,* December 1956

8.   Stories that meandered along like lazy streams —George Garrett

9.   A storyteller is like a ship's captain. He takes the passengers places where they might laugh or cry, but they always feel safe —Michael Parent, storyteller, *New York Times,* May 19, 1986

10.   A story with a moral appended is like the bill of a mosquito. It bores you, and then injects a stinging drop to irritate your conscience —O. Henry

11.   A tale without love is like beef without mustard —Anatole France
    See Also: INCOMPLETENESS

STRAIGHTNESS
See Also: POSTURE

1.   Direct, like a guided torpedo —William Humphrey

2.   Erect as compass in its curve —Anne Morrow Lindbergh

3.   Even as a row of West Point cadets on parade —Arthur Baer

4.   Even as a set of false teeth —Arthur Baer

5.   (Noses . . .) even as buttons on a tape —Beryl Markham

6.   Straight as a column —Louis Adamic

7. Straight as a gun barrel (she carried her lengthy shadow up and down the golden sand) —Jean Stafford
8. (Walks) straight as a hoe —T. Coraghessan Boyle
9. (A woman) straight as a hunting knife —Stephen Vincent Benét
10. Straight as a line —Geoffrey Chaucer
    This is transcribed from Chaucer's Old English: "Streight as any lyne." An American folk variant said to originate in Maine is the much-used "Straight as a ramrod."
11. Straight as an arrow —Aphra Behn
    A simile much in use, both to describe physical and moral erectness. To emphasize the latter meaning there's "Straight as your sister" attributed to Jerome Barry.
12. (Teeth . . .) straight as a picket fence —Susan Fromberg Schaeffer
13. Straight as a plumb line —Mike Sommer
14. Straight as a stick and looked as brittle —V. S. Pritchett
15. (I felt her to be) straight as a die —Colette
16. Straight as a fir tree —Henry Van Dyke
17. (The country road is wide, light gray,) straight as a ruler —Cora Sandel
18. [Lower eyelids] straight as ruler edges —Dashiell Hammett
19. Straight as the backbone of a herring —John Ray's *Proverbs*
20. Straight like a pine —Joseph Conrad
21. Straight . . . like long rows of soldiers —Oscar Wilde
22. Straight, thin as a pencil —Miller Williams
    This marks the opening of a poem entitled *The Writer.*
    See Also: THINNESS
23. (His two rifles as) upright as umbrellas —Edward Hoagland

STRANGENESS

1. Alien and mysterious and uncanny, like sleeping out in the jungle alone —Christopher Isherwood
2. Eerie as a man carving his own epitaph —William McIlvanney
3. Miraculous as fire in the snow —Sam Shepard
4. Mysterious as an Agatha Christie story with the last page torn out — James Brooke
5. Mysterious as cells seen under a microscope —Ann Beattie
    In Beattie's story, *Janus,* the comparison refers to the bits of color in a ceramic bowl.
6. Mysterious as tea leaves —Vincent Canby
7. Mystery emanated from her like a fire alarm —Richard Ford
8. Peculiar as a middle-aged man undressed —David Denby

9. Queer as a green kielbasa —Petter Meinke
    A colloquialism on the same theme: "Queer as a three dollar bill."

10. Queer as a jaybird —Anon

11. The scenes and incidents had the strangeness of the transcendental, as if they were snatches torn from lives on other planets that had somehow drifted to the earth —Boris Pasternak

12. Strange as a wedding without a bridegroom —Anon

13. Strange, eerie: like something out of a fairy tale —T. Coraghessan Boyle

STREETSCAPES
See: CITY/STREETSCAPES

STRENGTH
See Also: BODY, COURAGE, MUSCLES, TOUGHNESS

1. Air of impregnability that he carried with him like a briefcase full of secrets —Derek Lambert

2. As indestructible as a bride's first set of biscuits —Jim Murray, about football player Mike Garrett, *Los Angeles Herald*

3. Bones . . . like bars of iron —*The Holy Bible/Job*

4. Built like a bouncer in a clip joint —Saul Bellow

5. Built like a brick shit-house —American colloquialism, popularized in American army.
    With slight alterations some of the more colorful army and country similes can be cleaned up with the original meaning still implicit. For example, in her novel, *Love Medicine,* Louise Erdrich describes a character as being "Built like a brick outhouse."

6. Built like a toolbox —Lee K. Abbott

7. A cobweb is as good as the mightiest cable when there is no strain upon it —Henry Ward Beecher

8. Gave off a sense of virility almost as positive as an odor —Samuel Yellen

9. Get the upper hand . . . like a strong sun —Albert Camus

10. Grew strong, as if doubt never touched his heart —Wallace Stevens

11. (Our meaning together is) hardy as an onion (and layered) —Marge Piercy

12. I am as strong as a bull moose —Theodore Roosevelt

13. I am like a forest that has once been razed; the new shoots are stronger and brisker —Victor Hugo

14. Looked as durable and tough as a tree growing on a stony hillside —Mazo De La Roche

15. Solid and strong, like a little bull —Frank Tuohy

16. Solid as a temple —Louis MacNeice

17. Strong and hard as a tree —Vicki Baum
Some other strength/tree comparisons include: "Strong as an old apple tree" (Eudora Welty) and "Sturdy as an oak trunk" (Ignazio Silone).

18. Strong as a door —Reynolds Price

19. Strong as a giant —Erich Maria Remarque

20. (A soul) strong as a mountain river —William Wordsworth

21. (An alibi as) strong as a twenty-foot wall —Jimmy Sangster

22. (And the muscles of his brawny arms are) strong as iron bands —Henry Wadsworth Longfellow

23. Strong as jealousy —William Blake

24. Strong as money —Philip Levine
What poet Levine is comparing to the strength of money is work.

25. (Somone wakens to a life as) strong as the smell of urine —Philip Levine

26. Strong as the summer sun —Anon

27. (Had grown) strong as the sun or the sea —Algernon Charles Swinburne

28. (This old woman is dangerous: she is as) strong as three men —George Bernard Shaw

29. Strong as the young, and as uncontrolled —Henry Wadsworth Longfellow

30. Stronger than mahogany —Anne Sexton

31. Strong, like a tower —Nina Bawden

32. (Vemish and his wife were) strong, like rocks, not like rivers. Their strength was more in remaining than in doing —Barry Targan

33. (Your blunderer is as) sturdy as a rock —William Cowper

34. Takes brute strength, like pushing a cow uphill —Anne Sexton

35. Using his fist the way a carpenter uses a hammer —Irwin Shaw

36. You're [Alais addressing King Henry in *The Lion in Winter*] like the rocks at Stonehenge; nothing knocks you down —James Goldman

STRUGGLE
See Also: BEHAVIOR, FUTILITY, LIFE

1. (In his efforts with the numbing pain,) he was like a man wrestling with a creature of the air —Stephen Crane

2. Like the tiny coral insect, working deep under the dark waters, we strive and struggle, each for our own little ends —Jerome K. Jerome

3. Struggle along . . . stopping and starting like a blown newspaper —J. G. Farrell

4. (The coalition Israeli government) struggled like two cats in a bag — Ebra Ames

5. Struggle like a fish —Leo Tolstoy

6. Struggling like a fly trapped in a glass of water —Anon

7. Struggling like a moth to break its chrysalis —Rumer Godden

8. Struggling through life like a wearied swimmer trying to touch the horizon —Israel Zangwill

STUBBORNNESS
See: PERSISTENCE

STUDENTS
See: EDUCATION

STUPIDITY
See Also: ABSURDITY, DULLNESS, FOOLISHNESS, INSULTS, MIND

1. Assholes are like weeds, a bitch to get rid of and when you do, another one grows back in the same place —Jonathan Kellerman

2. Brains like mashed potatoes —Anon

3. Dumb as a beetle —Anon
   The beetle has been linked to dullness and stupidity since the sixteenth century.

4. Dumb as a stick of wood —Anon

5. Dumb as pure white lead —John Updike

6. Had the brains of a Playboy bunny and fucked like one —Jonathan Valin

7. He'd be sharper than a serpent's tooth, if he wasn't as dull as ditch water —Charles Dickens
   A Dickensian twist on King Lear's lament about an ungrateful child.

8. He's like the man who thinks it's raining when you pee in his eyes — Anon

9. His head was as empty as a politician's speech —Anon

10. I'm as thick as a plank —Princess Diana excusing herself from playing a game with a patient during a hospital visit, quoted, Public Radio

11. (About as) intelligent as a bundle of shawls —Henry James

12. Isn't very intelligent . . . he's like a hound that simply follows the scent. He crumples his nose up, looking for his fleas —Henri-Pierre Roche

13. Like dogs, that meeting with nobody else, bit one another —John Ray's *Proverbs*

14. (He) looked as if he'd stood in line twice when the brains were being handed out —Christopher Hale

15. Look stupid as a poet in search of a simile —Thomas Holcroft

16. A man with a small head is like a pin without any, very apt to get into things beyond his depth —Josh Billings

17. (A snail's about as) smart as mud —CBS-TV news story about snails being grown for escargot lovers, November 5, 1986

18. (That man is) so stupid it sits on him like a halo —Emlyn Williams

19. (The free press in Israel has belatedly awakened to the meaning of this act, which was as) stupid as cracking the safe of your own bank — William Safire, *New York Times*/Op-ed, March 9, 1987
    Safire's simile refers to Israel's recruitment of an American as a spy.

20. Stupid as jugs without handles —Honoré de Balzac

21. Stupid as oysters —August E. F. Von Kotzbue

22. To serve an unintelligent man is like crying in the wilderness, massaging the body of a dead man, planting water-lilies on dry land, whispering in the ear of the deaf —Panchatantra

23. While he was not dumber than an ox, he was not any smarter either — James Thurber

STURDINESS
See: FIRMNESS, STRENGTH

STYLE
See Also: CLOTHING

1. Dress as if having been born in a clothing store —David Ignatow

2. Elegance stamped on her as by a die —Henry James

3. Elegant as a Cole Porter lyric —Eric Pace, *New York Times,* December 1, 1986
   Pace made this comparison about actor Cary Grant at the time of his death.

4. Elegant as a fifty-dollar whore —Raymond Chandler

5. Fashion is like a shadow: fly from it and it follows you; follow it and it flies from you —Anon

6. Had that elusive style some older women carry like blossom —Jonathan Gash

7. A man's style is intrinsic and private with him like his voice or his gesture, partly a matter of inheritance, partly of cultivation —Maurice Valency

8. Style, like the human body, is specially beautiful when the veins are not prominent and the bones cannot be counted —Tacitus

9. You can't get high aesthetic tastes, like trousers, ready-made —W. S. Gilbert

SUBSERVIENCE
See: MEEKNESS

SUBTLETY
See: TACT

SUCCESS/FAILURE
See Also: BUSINESS; GROWTH; PAST, THE

1. The anatomy of the first major success is like the young human body, a miracle only the owner can fully savor —John Fowles

2. As he rose like a rocket, he fell like a stick —Thomas Paine

3. A certain prosperity coats these people like scent or the layer of buttery light in a painting by Rubens —Jean Thompson

4. A conqueror, like a cannon ball, must go on; if he rebounds, his career is over —The Duke of Wellington

5. (The midlist author is) dogged by his past sales record, like a utility infielder with a .228 lifetime batting average —Phillip Lopate, *New York Times Book Review,* May 24, 1987

6. Failed . . . like an old hanging bridge —Marge Piercy

7. Fail like a five-year plan —Derek Lambert

8. Failure grabs a man like an old and shabby suit —Derek Lambert

9. (A great beauty) flourishing like a rose —Isak Dinesen

10. Flourishing like a weed in a hot house —Susan Fromberg Schaeffer

11. Flourishing like trees —Hilma Wolitzer

12. Had risen to his great height like a man lifted to the ceiling by a sort of slow explosion —G. K. Chesterton

13. High office is like a pyramid; only two kinds of animals reach the summit, reptiles and eagles —Jean Le Rond d'Alembert

14. His life, day after day, was failing like an unreplenished stream —Percy Bysshe Shelley

15. Moving up hand over hand . . . like a champion —Tom Wolfe

16. Pursued success as a knight the Holy Grail —Anon
    See Also: PERSISTENCE

17. Sailed through the world like a white yacht jubilant with flags —John Gardner

18. Selling like lemonade at a track meet —T. Coraghessan Boyle

19. Sell like hotcakes —Anon
    Different industries have coined many phrases for things which sell well. This American simile which came into use in the middle of the nineteenth century is still the most widely used. For a twist in meaning there's "Selling like cold hot cakes" from *The Last Good Kiss* by James Crumley.

20. Sold [books by nineteenth century author Karl May] like pancakes topped by wild blueberries and heavy cream —Vincent Canby, *New York Times,* June 25, 1986

21. Sold like picks and pans in a gold rush —Robert Guenther, *Wall Street Journal,* August 6, 1986

22. Success is as ice cold and lonely as the North Pole —Vicki Baum
    See Also: ALONENESS

23. Success is feminine and like a woman, if you cringe before her, she will override you —William Faulkner
    Faulkner expanded on this simile still further: "So the way to treat her is to show her the back of your hand. Then maybe she will do the crawling."

24. Success on some men looks like a borrowed coat; it sits on you as though it had been made to order —Edith Wharton

25. Triumphs like a trumpet —Wallace Stevens

26. Wanted his success acknowledged . . . like the high school loser who dreams of driving to the class reunion in a custom-made sports car — Jean Thompson

27. Winning an Oscar . . . it's like getting thirty thousand red roses at one time —Louise Fletcher, from Rex Reed interview

28. Wore his success like his health —George Garrett

SUDDENNESS
See Also: ENTRANCES/EXITS, SHOCK, SURPRISE

1. Abrupt as a sultry little thunder shower —Amy Leslie

2. Abruptly as string that snaps beneath the bow —Ernest William Hornung

3. Abruptly, like a summer rainstorm —Derek Lambert

4. Abrupt, startling shock, like the slap of a wet towel —Norman Mailer

5. All at once, like the wind dispersing storm clouds at a single puff — Lawrence Durrell

6. Appear suddenly as if out of a fold of the air —Iris Murdoch

7. Arbitrary as a cyclone —Anon

8. Burst into the room like a bullet crashing through a window —Guy De Maupassant
   See Also: BURST

9. Didn't expect it . . . like a storm on a very fine day —Ivan Turgenev

10. He was with them as suddenly as a gift, as if an arm had thrust in a bunch of roses or a telegram —Eudora Welty

11. (A reflex as) immediate as a sneeze —Leigh Allison Wilson
    A common variation: "Sudden as a sneeze."

12. Steep as a broom handle —Elizabeth Spencer

13. Steep as hell's half acre —George MacDonald Fraser

14. Stopped all of a sudden, as if he had been shot —William Makepeace Thackeray

15. Sudden and foolish as that almost silent fart —George Garrett
    See Also: FOOLISHNESS

16. Sudden as a burst of hiccuping —Anon
    This and the entries that follow typify the simile that develops new twists from conversation to conversation, writer to writer.

17. Sudden as a dislocated joint slipping back into place —Anon

18. Sudden as a massacre —Anon

19. Sudden as a meteor shooting across the sky —Anon

20. Sudden as an epileptic seizure —Anon

21. Sudden as a stitch in your side —Anon

22. Sudden as a summer shower —Anon

23. Sudden as a tornado swooping down on a small town —Alistair Cooke, Public Television, March 8, 1987
    The comparison referring to the suddenness of the first World War was made during an introduction to an episode in the "Lost Empire" series.

24. [Call of a jaybird] sudden as conscience —Robert Penn Warren

25. Sudden as the stopping of breath —Mary Lee Settle

26. (The end was) sudden, like a foolish play —Karl Shapiro

27. Suddenly, as a train comes out of a tunnel —Virginia Woolf

28. Suddenly, like a pair of obscene words, (there appeared on the path two boys) —Truman Capote

29. Sudden resolutions, like the sudden rise of the mercury in the barometer, indicate little else than the changeableness of the weather — Julius Charles Hare and Augustus William Hare

30. Sudden, surprising . . . it is like encountering a pun in a telephone directory —Karl E. Meyer

31. Too sudden . . . like the lightning —William Shakespeare

SUMMER
See: SEASONS

SUN
See Also: MOON, SKY, SUNSET

1. The afternoon sunlight was like gold embroidery on the grass —Paul Horgan

2. Autumn sunlight poured out over the rock [of Quebec] like a heavy southern wine —Willa Cather

3. Bars of sunlight crossed the backyard like the bars of a bright strange cell —Carson McCullers

4. Bits of sunlight bright as butterflies —Eudora Welty

5. The citronade of the pale morning sun shimmered like a multitude of violins —Angela Carter

6. The daylight-saving sunshine lay like custard on the oaks and mistletoe —Wallace Stegner

7. The fast-setting sun lighted the tops of the trees like flames of candles —Z. Vance Wilson

8. The heat from the scorching [California] sun hit them like a knock-out punch —Jilly Cooper

9. The high sun fell like balm on her body —Mary Hedin

10. The huge sun light flamed like a monstrous dahlia with petals of yellow fire —Oscar Wilde

11. It [sunlight] licks thick as a tongue at my skin —Sharon Sheehe Stark

12. The last of the sun [at dusk] like a great splash of blood on the sky — George Garrett

13. The muffled sunlight gleamed like gold tissue through grey gauze — Edith Wharton

14. The new morning sun shone like a pink rose in the heavens —Kenneth Koch

15. A pale sun appeared over the clouds like an invalid sitting up in bed — John Mortimer

16. A red sun as flat and still against the sky as moonlight on pond water —Charles Johnson

17. The red sun was pasted on the sky like a wafer —Anon

18. The rising sun is like a ball of blood —Robert W. Service

19. A scarlet sun, round and brilliant as a blooded egg yolk —Cynthia Ozick

20. A sharp-as-needle sun sat high over Virginia . . . like a heathen god, sure of itself —Thomas Keneally

21. The sinking sun hung like a red balloon over the Hudson River —Belva Plain

22. The strong sun (of late April) pours down as though a gigantic golden basin full of light and wind were being emptied on us —Erich Maria Remarque

23. The sun advanced on the city and lit the topmost spines of the hill, painting the olive drab slopes in crazy new colors, like the drawing of a spangled veil —William Brammer

24. Sun . . . as light and dry as old sherry —Raymond Chandler
     See Also: DRYNESS, LIGHTNESS

25. The sun, as red as a furnace on the edge of the horizon —Émile Zola

26. The sun blazed like a flaming bronze mirror —Bernard Malamud

27. The sun breaks [over the land] like a cracked egg —T. Coraghessan Boyle

28. The sun breaks through the cloud like revelation —Delmore Schwartz

29. The sun burned feebly through the mist like a circle cut from Christmas paper —MacDonald Harris

30. The sun dazzled off the asphalt in fragments like breaking glass — George Garrett

31. The sun drew strength from them like a giant sponge —Caryl Phillips

32. The sun . . . drops on our heads like a stone —Marge Piercy

33. The sun, dull, like the face of an old man —Maxim Gorky
     See Also: DULLNESS

34. The sun fades like the spreading of a peacock's tail —John Ashbery

35. The sun fell thick as a blanket —Lee Smith

36. The sun flared in the sky, fat and red as a tangerine —T. Coraghessan Boyle
     A variation by Marge Piercy: "The sun hangs like a tangerine."

37. The sun flashed like a torrent of warm white wine —Du Bose Heyward

38. The sun floats up above the horizon, like a shimmering white blimp — Margaret Atwood

39. The sun hangs overhead like a lantern —T. Coraghessan Boyle

40. The sun hits him like a slap in the face —T. Coraghessan Boyle

41. The sun . . . shone like a polished brass knob —Helen Hudson

42. The sun hung in the cloudless sky like an unblinking yellow eye — Harvey Swados

674

43. (It was a misty autumn morning,) the sun just struggling through like a great chrysanthemum —Pamela Hansford Johnson

44. The sun lay like a friendly arm across her shoulder —Marjorie Kinnan Rawlings

45. The sun . . . lay on the horizon like a dissolving orange suffused with blood —John Hawkes

46. The sunlight dripped over the house like golden paint over an art jar — F. Scott Fitzgerald

47. Sunlight dropped into it (the dark foliage) like a drizzle of gold —Isak Dinesen

48. Sunlight fell like a shower of gold through the leaves of the chestnut trees —Silvia Tennenbaum

49. The sunlight hit her like a boxing glove —Jilly Cooper

50. The sunlight . . . plunged like tiny knives into my already bleary eyes —James Crumley

51. Sunlight splashed through the trees, the beams hazy like shafts of light filtered through stained glass —Robert J. Serling

52. Sunlight that was like a bright driving summer rain —Paule Marshall

53. Sun (is sitting atop the trees) like a big round cheddar —T. Coraghessan Boyle

54. The sun looks, through the mist, like a plum on the tree of heaven, or a bruise on the slope of your belly —William H. Gass

55. The sun lulled in the sky like a mule —Larry McMurtry

56. The sun overhead beat the surface of the pool like a drum —James B. Hall

57. The sun peeping above the trees, looked like a giant golf ball —P. G. Wodehouse
    Wodehouse was known for his golf stories so this is a particularly apt comparison for him.
    See Also: GOLF

58. The sun . . . poised like a ball of fire on the very edge of the mountains —Henry Van Dyke

59. The sun popped over the edge of the prairie like a broad smiling face — Willa Cather

60. The sun poured down like fire —Isaac Bashevis Singer

61. Sun . . . reflected back to me like a shiny bedspread whose design is hundreds of wind-driven roller coasters —Richard Brautigan

62. The sun rested like a warm palm on the back of her neck —Francis King

63. The sun rolled over the horizon like the red rim of a wagon wheel — Rita Mae Brown

64. The sun . . . rose swiftly and flashed like a torch with dazzling rays —Felix Salten

65. The sunshine burned the pasture like fire —Rudyard Kipling

66. The sunshine [of January day] cut like icicles —Edith Wharton

67. The sunshine made spots before your eyes . . . as though a thousand weddings were to be held that day —Boris Pasternak

68. Sunshine spread like butter over the fields —Lael Tucker Wertenbaker

69. Sunshine that stretched like cloth of gold all up and down Fifth Avenue —Helen Hudson

70. The sun shone as if there were no death —Saul Bellow

71. The sun shone like a million dollars —Larry McMurtry

72. The sun shone like Mr. Happy Face himself —Tom Robbins

73. The sun shone with such violence that in an illumination like a long-prolonged glare of lightning the heavens looked black and white —Eudora Welty

74. The sun shot upward and began to spin like a red cup on the point of a spear —Isaac Babel

75. Sun sizzling like a skillet in the sky —Helen Hudson

76. Sun slanting like a blade —Bin Ramke

77. The sun's rays like sheaves of wheat are gold and dry —Dame Edith Sitwell

78. The sun stood still like a great shining altar —Hans Christian Andersen

79. The sun swerves silently like a cyclist round the bend —Herbert Read

80. The sun throbbed like a fever —William Plomer

81. Sun . . . huge as a mountain of diamonds —Dame Edith Sitwell

82. The sun up in the towering sky turns like a spinning ball —Edwin Muir

83. The sun was high enough to sit on the roofs of buildings like a great open fire warming everything —Mark Helprin

84. The sun was like a burning-glass —William Plomer
    This comparison from a poem entitled *In the Snake Park* refers to a lens used to focus the sun's rays to start a fire.

85. The sun was like a good cup of tea, strong and hot —Mike Fredman

86. The sun was like a hot iron on their backs —Paul Horgan

87. The sun was like a whip —T. Coraghessan Boyle

88. The sun was pouring in like maple syrup into a green bowl —Carlos Baker

89. The sun was shining like a congratulation —Margaret Millar

90. The sun was streaking the sky with strips of red and white, like a slab of bacon —Jean Thompson

91. [Sun] swung . . . like a faded shabby orange —Hugh Walpole

92. (While they embraced,) the sun vanished as if it had been switched off —W. P. Kinsella

93. The white sun twinking like the dawn under a speckled cloud —Percy Bysshe Shelley

94. The yellow sun was ugly, like a raw egg on a plate —Elizabeth Bishop

SUNSET

1. A huge sunset that drained away in the west like blood —William Styron

2. The sun . . . drops like an angry brick at nightfall —Raymond Chandler

3. A sunset as thick as jam simmered in the sky —Isaac Babel

4. Sunset cast its colors through the leafless trees . . . like panes of stained glass —Madison Smartt Bell

5. The (Montana) sunset lay between two mountains like a gigantic bruise from which dark arteries spread themselves over a poisoned sky —F. Scott Fitzgerald

6. The sunset looked like the fires of Hell were consuming it —Harry Prince

7. The sun was moving down slowly as if it were descending a ladder — Flannery O'Connor

8. The sun went down lopsided and wide as a rose on a stem —Eudora Welty

SURPRISE

See Also: SHOCK, SUDDENNESS

1. Crops up when you least expect it, like dandruff —Robin Worthington

2. (I read the note over several times with a kind of stupid) incredulity, like an unbelieving prisoner reading the formal sentence of his own execution —Robert Traver

3. Started [at sound of a sudden call] like a horse at the sound of the bugle —Stefan Zweig

4. (She) started like a quiet, lovely insect into which someone had suddenly stabbed a pin —Elizabeth Spencer

5. Startling as curves in a mountain road —Lorrie Moore

6. (The idea was as) startling . . . as if in a blank wall before her a door had opened —Dorothy Canfield Fisher

7. (Perception as) startling as watching a feeling cross a face on Mount Rushmore —Paige Mitchell

8. Startling, like a face changing in front of you, from young to old, well to ill —Wilfrid Sheed

9. Surprised and shocked as if she had heard an explosion and seen her own shattered legs go flying across the floor —Rachel Ingalls

10. Surprised as a sardine that went to sleep in the ocean and woke up in a delicatessen store —Arthur Baer

11. Surprised [physical reaction] me as much as if I were a baby suddenly popped from the womb —Angela Carter

12. Surprise made me look like a goldfish —Rebecca West

13. Surprises keep us living: as when the first light surprised our infant eyes —Louis MacNeice

14. Surprising as a child's laugh rising higher, higher, higher —Babette Deutsch

15. (Sharp pain pierced his chest, as quick and) unexpected as the materialization of a hairline crack in bone —Paige Mitchell

16. Unexpected as aluminum siding in Buckingham Palace —Anon

17. Unexpected as best seller status for a book of Latin quotations —Anon

18. Unexpected as a heart attack —Anon

19. Unexpected as a heat wave in February —Anon

20. Unexpected as gourmet food in a second rate hotel —Anon

21. Unexpected as snow in July —Anon

22. Unexpectedly wonderful treat, like blue skies and warmth in a chilly spring —Janet Flanner

23. You never know what somebody's got in him: like the man with germs, suddenly he's down in bed with a crisis —Clifford Odets

SURVIVAL
See: IMPOSSIBILITY, SUCCESS/FAILURE

SUSPENSE
See: EXCITEMENT

SUSPICION
See: TRUST/MISTRUST

SWEARING
See: CURSES, WORD(S)

SWEAT
See Also: SMELLS

1. Beads of perspiration, like seed pearls —Dorothea Straus

2.   Beads of sweat gathered on his brow like tiny blisters —William Styron

3.   Beads of sweat . . . popped on his forehead like tiny, glistening prairie dogs —Joan Hess

4.   Beads of sweat, tiny as dewdrops —Leigh Allison Wilson

5.   (My forehead) bubbled sweat like a burning plastic bag —Ira Wood

6.   Cold sweat burst from his pores, trickling down his back like ice water —Dorothy Canfield Fisher

7.   A drop of it [sweat] hung like a Christmas tree ornament from the tip of his nose —Jonathan Valin

8.   Feel the sweat like needles at my hair-roots —Randall Jarrell

9.   Fine beads of sweat glistened [on a man's mustache] like little brilliants —Jessamyn West

10. Glistening with sweat like a circus seal —Ralph Ellison

11. Little pears of sweat had popped out like a corona around his shiny skull —Harvey Swados

12. Looked as if it would cost a thousand dollars to shake hands with him —Raymond Chandler

13. Small beads of sweat adorn his bald head like pearls on a bright dress — Erich Maria Remarque
     See Also: BALDNESS

14. Sweat clings like a crystal fixture to his receding brow —Mary Morris

15. Sweat collects in pores like ink does on fingerprints —Noel Behn

16. The sweat coming out on his face like somebody had squeezed it — Ernest Hemingway

17. Sweat crawling, like a procession of spiders and ants —George Garrett

18. Sweated like a coolie —Richard Wilbur

19. Sweated with self-consciousness and the effort to be suave, like a teenager dancing with a haughty girl —Derek Lambert

20. Sweating freely . . . like a squeezed sponge —Ben Ames Williams

21. Sweating like a swamp rat —Norman Mailer

22. Sweating like a very fat man in a Turkish bath —Kingsley Amis

23. Sweating like Judas —Samuel Beckett

24. Sweat like black plates under his arms —Ian Kennedy Martin

25. Sweat poured out . . . like a sprinkler —Andrew Kaplan

26. Sweat poured like rain —Ken Stabler, football quarterback and Berry Stainback, writer

27. Sweat ran down like water down a hill —American negro ballad "John Henry"
     In the original of this famous ballad 'water' was spelled 'watah.'

28. The sweat ran over my back and down my arms and legs, branching, like an upside-down tree —Eudora Welty

29. Sweats like a mother of six, preparing lunch —Ira Wood

30. Sweat was pouring from his body like water coming out of a showerhead —Ann Petry

31. Sweat was running down behind his ears and under his collar like cold, restless worms —Margaret Millar

32. Under each arm of his striped shirt there was a dark semicircle like a stain of secret guilt —Margaret Millar

SWEETNESS
See Also: PLEASURE, TASTE

1. Sweet as a chaplain —Elizabeth Hardwick
   'Sweet' as a comparison dates way back probably beginning with Chaucer's "Sweet as the root of licorice" and Henry Buttes' "Sweet as a nut." Variations continue to develop, or, to coin another simile, "Grow like the taste for sweet things."

2. Sweet as a first love affair —Isak Dinesen

3. (My tongue was) sweet as a fresh plum —George Garrett

4. Sweet as a kiss —Isak Dinesen

5. Sweet as a mountain lilac —Raymond Chandler

6. Sweet as apple cider —Eddie Cantor
   This simile was immortalized by singer-vaudevillian Eddie Cantor in his musical ode to his wife Ida: "Ida . . . sweet as apple cidah!"

7. (The words) sweet as a reprieve —Delmore Schwartz

8. (We bit into life and life was) sweet as a ripe apple —George Garrett

9. Sweet as cream —Marge Piercy

10. Sweet as love, or the remembrance of a generous deed —William Wordsworth

11. Sweet as love songs —Slogan, Kerr butterscotch candy

12. Sweet as melancholy —Robert Burton

13. Sweet as new-mown hay —W. S. Gilbert

14. Sweet as pie —Anon
    The "Sweet as pie" continues in use, both in its literal sense and to describe someone's personality.

15. (Kisses as) sweet as sweet mountain dew —Langston Hughes

16. Sweet as the hope of Paradise —F. van Wyck Mason

17. Sweeter than honey from a rock —Christina Rossetti

18. Sweeter than perfume —William Shakespeare

19. Sweet like pineapple —Marge Piercy

SWIMMING
See: SPORTS

SYMMETRY
See: REGULARITY/IRREGULARITY

SYMPATHY
See: KINDNESS, PITY

TACT
See Also: INSULTS

1. Diplomacy, like politics, is the art of the possible —George W. Ball

2. A diplomatic note is like an anonymous letter. You can call a fellow anything you want, for nobody can find out exactly whose name was signed to it —Will Rogers

3. Discretion like a good priest —George Garrett

4. Had about as much finesse as a trained elephant doing the gavotte among ninepins —Cornell Woolrich

5. Subtle as fanfare —William McIlvanney

6. Subtle as snakes —Christina Rossetti

7. Subtle as the London blitz —T. Coraghessan Boyle

8. A tactless man is like an axe on an embroidery frame —Malay proverb

TALENT
See: ABILITY, ACCOMPLISHMENT

TALKATIVENESS
See Also: CONVERSATION

1. As full of words as a hen salmon of eggs —Ben Ames Williams

2. Babble as one mad with wine —Algernon Charles Swinburne

3. Chattered like a shipload of monkeys in a storm —Anon

4. Chattered like squirrels —Larry McMurtry

5. Chattered on like a lunatic chimpanzee —Truman Capote

6. Chattered on like a chickadee in a feed trough —Donald McCaig

7. Chattering . . . like a flock of starlings —Jimmy Sangster

8. Chattering like magpies —Christina Rossetti

9. Chattering like one to whom speech was a new accomplishment — Calder Willingham

10. Chatter like a bluejay —Eleanor Clark

11. Chatter like a mob of sparrows —Jerome K. Jerome

12. Chatter like sick flies —Algernon Charles Swinburne

13. Gabbled on like machines set in motion —Charlotte Brontë

14. Gabbling at one another like so many turkeys —Harvey Swados

15. Great talkers are like leaky pitchers, everything runs out of them —H. G. Bohn's *Handbook of Proverbs*

16. Had a tongue that flapped like a banner in a fair wind —George Garrett

17. He was like a man who'd just emerged from six months in solitary, like the sole survivor of a shipwreck, Crusoe with a captive audience: he could not shut up —T. Coraghessan Boyle

18. Jabbered on like a drunk old uncle —Richard Ford

19. Like a book in breeches . . . he [Macaulay] has occasional flashes of silence, that make his conversation perfectly delightful —Sydney Smith

20. Like a crane or a swallow, so did I chatter —*The Holy Bible/Isaiah*

21. Long-winded as a writer who gets paid by the word —Anon

22. Open [up, with information] like a wet envelope —Harold Adams

23. [Coleridge] speaks incessantly, not thinking or imagining or remembering, but combining all these processes into one; as a rich and lazy housewife might mingle her soup and fish, beef and custard into one unspeakable mass —Thomas Carlyle

24. Talkative persons are like barrels; the less there is in them, the more noise they make —John Gideon Mulligan

25. Talked and talked like a man in a high fever —Erich Maria Remarque

26. Talked on and on as if he was rehearsing for a speech —John Dos Passos

27. A tremendous talker and like a greedy eater at an ordinary dinner, keeping to himself an entire dish of which everyone present would like to have partaken —*Punch,* 1857

28. Went into detail . . . like an obstetrician describing how he got two fingers in to turn the baby's head out of breech, or, yes, like an old fisherman taking you along step by step on how to bait a hook so that the wriggler stays alive —Norman Mailer

29. The words came out of his throat like a cataract —Carson McCullers

30. Words came tumbling out of me like coins from a change dispenser — Natascha Wodin

31. Words flowed from him like oil from a gusher —O. Henry

32. Wordy like somebody with a fever —George Garrett

33. The world to him is a vast lecture-platform . . . as one long after-dinner, with himself as the principal speaker of the evening —P. G. Wodehouse

TALLNESS

1. I'm about as tall as a shotgun and just as noisy —Truman Capote
2. I towered over my parents like some big-footed freak of another species, like a cuckoo raised by sparrows —T. Coraghessan Boyle
3. Long and tall as a scarecrow —John Yount
4. Tall and gaunt as a hangman —Angela Carter
   See Also: THINNESS
5. Tall as a building —Louise Erdrich
6. Tall as a crane —Dame Edith Sitwell
   This is part of the opening and closing refrain of Dame Edith's *Aubade,* the full stanza reading, "Jane, Jane, tall as a crane, the morning light creaks down again." In the United States the "Tall as a crane" comparison can be traced back to an Arkansas railroad song in which the simile is used as follows: "He was six feet seven in his stocking feet and taller than any crane."
7. Tall as a stork —Angela Carter
8. Tall as a thunderstorm —Miles Gibson
9. (He was) tall as a tree in the middle of the night —Wallace Stevens
10. (Poppies as) tall as buildings —Arthur A. Cohen
11. Tall men are like houses of four stories, wherein commonly the uppermost room is worst furnished —James Howell
12. Tower over . . . like the Washington Monument —James Thurber

TASTE

1. A mouth on me like a Turkish wrestler's jock-strap —M. C. Beaton
2. As pleasingly prickly as a kitten's tongue —Slogan for Gevrey-Chamertin wine
3. A fastidious taste is like a squeamish appetite; the one has its origin in some disease of the mind, as the other has in some ailment of the stomach —Robert Southey
4. Full of rich flavor as a piece torn off an old shirt —Raymond Chandler
5. His mouth felt as if it had been to a party without him —Peter DeVries
6. His mouth was tastelessly dry, as though he had been eating dust —Joseph Conrad
7. My mouth [from smoking a cigarette] tasted like a cross between charred sticks and spoiled eggs —Sue Grafton

8. My mouth was dry and tasty as a hen-coop floor —Harold Adams

9. My mouth tasted like an old penny —Robert B. Parker

10. My tongue felt like a slice of ham in my mouth, salty and pink —Jay Parini

11. Palates like shoe leather —Angela Carter

12. (Melons . . . as) sweet to the tongue as gold is to the mind —Borden Deal

13. Tasted like a fart —Reynolds Price

14. Tasted like it had been fried in tar —Larry McMurtry

15. Taste is the luxury of abeyant claims and occurs, like Wordsworth's poetry, in a kind of tranquillity —Stanley Elkin

16. Taste like a cup of lukewarm consommé at a spinsterish tearoom —Raymond Chandler, on mystery writing

17. (The crap still in his mouth made everything) taste like feathers —William McIlvanney

18. Taste like the Volga at low tide —Line from movie *Love At First Bite.* The character making this comparison is Count Von Dracula.

19. Tastes like cool, wet sand under pearly seaside light —Slogan for Château Guiraud's Château "G" wine

20. Tastes like the wrath to come —Irvin S. Cobb
    Cobb used the comparison to describe the taste of corn liquor.

21. Tastes rather like an old attic —J. B. Priestly

22. Tasty as summer's first peach —Elyse Sommer

23. Tasty, like an angel pissing on your tongue —Anon
    This was used throughout the galleys of Great Lakes steamships to describe good-tasting liquid or solid food.

TEACHERS/TEACHING
See: EDUCATION

TEARS
See Also: CRYING

1. Could feel the tears, like fire, coming up —James Baldwin

2. Feel the tears brimming and sloshing in me like water in a glass that is unsteady and too full —Sylvia Plath

3. Generally men's tears, like the droppings of certain springs, only harden and petrify what they fall on —Walter Savage Landor

4. He [a weeping man] was like a sponge saturated with water, and then squeezed —Leonid Andreyev

5. Like a summer tempest came her tears —Lord Alfred Tennyson

This also appears as a chapter title in Kenneth Grahame's contemporary children's classic, *The Wind in the Willows.*

6. My tears like berries fell down —W. B. Yeats

7. Produce tears freely like a great actor —Erich Maria Remarque

8. Slow as the winter snow the tears have drifted to mine eyes —Elizabeth Barrett Browning

9. Suspended like shimmering icicles on Maxell's cheeks were tears —Arthur A. Cohen

10. A teardrop hung out of each blue eye, like a fat woman leaning out of a tenement window —Tom Robbins

11. Teardrops come a-splashin' down his cheeks like summer rain —Edward A. Guest

12. A tear had slipped down to dangle like sweat at the tip of a nostril —Truman Capote

13. A tear ran down her cheek, turning white with powder, like a tiny ball of snow —Jonathan Valin

14. Tears . . . brightened her eyes and made them glitter like dark stars in a stormy sky —Frank Swinnerton

15. Tears died as laughter dies away —Dante Gabriel Rossetti

16. Tears fall like soft fruit juice —Rose Tremain

17. Tears fell like a plot —Stevie Smith

18. Tears fill up her eyes like a cup —Jessie Schell

19. Tears . . . flailing my face like the torn ends of shattered rope —John Updike

20. Tears flooded out of his eyes like the floodwater over a levee —Pat Conroy

21. Tears . . . flowed down upon him like a bower of willows —Arthur A. Cohen

22. Tears . . . flowed like fountains —William Wordsworth
     A twist by Guy De Maupassant: "Wept like a fountain."

23. Tears flow . . . like a swollen gutter gushing through the streets —Henry Fielding

24. Tears gathered like small pools in the declivation of his eye cups —Arthur A. Cohen

25. Tears glittered in her eyes, deep down, like the sinking reflection of a well —Louise Erdrich

26. Tears glittered like rhinestones on her lashes —Ross Macdonald

27. Tears, like a stream, like a ceaselessly flowing fountain, flowed and flowed —Nikolai V. Gogol

28. Tears like bits of glass formed in his eyes —Leonard Michaels

29. Tears like molten lead surged in her eyes —Ruth Prawer Jhabvala

30. Tears . . . like two little brooks —Carson McCullers

31. Tears . . . made patterns on his cheeks, like wax trickling down a candle —Julia O'Faolain

32. Tears on his lashes, like silver drops of dew —Ruth Prawer Jhabvala

33. Tears rolled down like rain —Elizabeth Spencer

34. Tears . . . roll one from each eye, like droplets on wax fruit —Ira Wood

35. Tears running down like lemonade —Anne Sexton

36. Tears rushed forth . . . like mountain mists at length dissolved in rain —Lord Byron

    This simile from Byron's famous *Don Juan* has been slightly modernized and shortened. The original first line begins "The tears rush'd forth from her o'erclouded brain, like . . . "

37. The tears seemed to cause the features of her face to melt and soften like hot wax —George Garrett

38. Tears, silent as a china egg —Marge Piercy

39. Tears, small as sequins, glinting in her narrowed eyes —Miles Gibson

40. Tears streamed down her cheeks, soft and bland like the sides of a Guernsey —John Updike

41. Tears that slipped like melting pellets of sleet down their grieved and angered cheeks —Alice Walker

42. Tears that streamed ceaselessly like a veil to keep her from seeing too clearly —Paul Horgan

43. Tears . . . they deluge my heart like the rain —Emily Brontë

44. Tears welled up as freely as water from a drinking fountain —Jean Stafford

45. Though the tears had no healing power, they took off the edge of it [pain], like cold water on a burn —Margaret Drabble

46. A woman's tears, like a dog's limping, are seldom real —Russian proverb

TEDIUM
See: BOREDOM, DULLNESS, REPETITION

TEETH

1. Beautiful teeth, like china plates —Rosellen Brown

2. Big teeth . . . like chunks of solidified milk —Frank Swinnerton

3. Front teeth showed like those of a squirrel —George Ade

4. (When she opened her mouth) gaps like broken window panes could be seen in her teeth —Sholem Asch

5. Her front teeth overlapped each other like dealt cards —Alice McDermott

6. His teeth looked like a picket fence in a slum neighborhood —Stephen King

7. His [false] teeth moved slightly, like the keyboards of a piano —Pamela Hansford Johnson

8. His teeth stood out like scored corks set in a jagged row —Sterling Hayden

9. Lower teeth crooked, as if some giant had taken his face and squeezed them loose from his jaw —Larry McMurtry

10. My teeth felt like they had little sweaters on them —Anon
    See Also: TASTE

11. Sharp-worn teeth like slivers of rock —Ella Leffland

12. The shiny new false teeth gave him the peculiar look of someone who smiles for a living —Andrew Kaplan

13. Small pointed teeth, like a squirrel's —Willa Cather

14. Teeth all awry and at all angles like an old fence —George Garrett

15. Teeth, as yellow as old ivory —Frank Swinnerton

16. Teeth . . . big and even as piano keys —Helen Hudson

17. Teeth . . . channelled and stained like the teeth of an old horse —R. Wright Campbell

18. Teeth . . . chattering like castanets —Maurice Edelman

19. Teeth clatter like ice cubes in a blender —Ira Wood

20. Teeth clicking like dice —T. Coraghessan Boyle

21. Teeth like cream —Willa Cather

22. Teeth like a row of alabaster Britannicas —Joe Coomer

23. Teeth like pearls —Robert Browning

24. Teeth like piano keys —Elizabeth Spencer

25. Teeth like white mosaics shone —Herbert Read

26. Teeth . . . tapping together like typewriter keys —Cornell Woolrich

27. White teeth, the kind that look like cheap dentures even when they are not —Eric Ambler

TEMPER
See: ANGER

TEMPERAMENT
See: PERSONAL TRAITS

TEMPTATION
See: ATTRACTION

TENACITY
See Also: PERSISTENCE

TENDERNESS
See: AFFECTION, GENTLENESS, KINDNESS, LOVE

TENNIS
See: SPORTS

TENSION
See Also: ANXIETY, NERVOUSNESS

1. Back . . . tense as a tiger's —D. H. Lawrence
2. Body rigid from shoulder to belly as though he had been stricken with elphantiasis —Kenzaburo Oë
3. (There continued to be) a certain strain, like dangerously stretched rubber bands —Thalia Selz
4. Feel tension rising off me like a fever —Richard Ford
5. Feel the tension coming out of Justin like a fever —Paige Mitchell
6. Felt his insides drawn together like the lips of a wound —Helen Hudson
7. Felt like a swimmer about to dive —Marguerite Yourcenar
8. His solar plexus knotted up like a sea anemone —Ursula Le Guin
9. In times of stress I enter into a semicomatose state like an instinct-driven opossum —Leigh Allison Wilson
10. My back became like a stick —Natsume Sōseki
11. My stomach drops as if I'm in a balky elevator —W. P. Kinsella
12. (Looked about as) relaxed as a safecracker —Joseph Wambaugh
13. Spines . . . stiffened like pulled twine —Louise Erdrich
14. Stiffen like a cat that's been hit by something —Shirley Ann Grau
15. (When I approach you) stiffen like an egg white —Diane Ackerman
16. Stiffen like a stump —David Wagoner
17. Strung up like a piano wire —Elizabeth Spencer
18. (Body) taut like wire —Anaïs Nin
19. Tense and careful as a man handling a bomb —Dorothy Canfield Fisher
    See Also: CAUTION
20. Tense and fluttering like a fish out of water —George Garrett

See Also: TREMBLING

21. Tense and still like a figure in a frieze —Ross Macdonald
    See Also: IMMOBILITY

22. Tense as an animal in fear, ready to snap or go limp beneath its keeper's grasp —Louise Erdrich

23. (I lay) tense as a piano wire —W. P. Kinsella

24. Tense as a player on the bench —Maureen Howard, *New York Times Magazine,* May 25, 1986

25. Tense as a thoroughbred at the starting gate —Anon television feature on New York marathoners, November 1, 1986

26. Tense as a wound spring —Joseph Heller

27. (Voices) tense as barks —Edward Hoagland

28. (People were as) tense as fiddle strings —Dorothy Canfield Fisher

29. Tense as if my neck were tipped back, my mouth agape, and I was preparing for the dentist's needle —W. P. Kinsella

30. Tense as rectitude —Norman Mailer

31. Tension broke like heat after a thunderstorm in a nervous burst of laughter —Lael Tucker Wertenbaker

32. Tension ran like a red-hot wire through the men —Marjory Stoneman Douglas

33. Tension stretching like taut wires across the room —Ross Macdonald

34. Tension . . . vibrates like a melancholy bell —David K. Shipler, *New York Times Book Review,* March 1, 1987

35. Tight as a duck —Graham Masterton
    The simile was found as part of a sex scene. In full context it reads: "With her own fingers, she slipped him inside her, and although she was as tight as a duck, she was also warm and wet and irresistible."

36. (His hand was) tight as a knot —Ann Beattie

37. Tight as a man going to the electric chair —Norman Mailer
    Mailer before being interviewed by Mike Wallace.

38. Tight as a quivering string —David Nevin

39. Tight as a sheet on a hospital bed —Anon

40. (Throats were) tight as tourniquets —Karl Shapiro

41. Tightly controlled . . . as if he was tied down to his desk by leather straps —Anon White House colleague about Robert McFarlane during the Iran-Contra scandal, quoted in New York Times, March 2, 1987

42. (He always came back from the ballfield) turned tighter than the bolts on an automobile tire —Norman Keifetz

The simile from a novel about a baseball player (*The Sensation*) continues as follows: "By that jack-handle known as 'being a pro'."

TENTATIVENESS
See: UNCERTAINTY

TERROR
See: FEAR

THEATER
See: STAGE AND SCREEN

THEORIES
See: IDEAS

THICKNESS
See Also: ABUNDANCE

1. Newspaper . . . thick as a folded bath towel —W. P. Kinsella
2. Richly covered . . . as a hen is with feathers —Anon
3. Thick . . . as a brier patch with briers —Ellen Glasgow
4. Thick as a mist —Percy Bysshe Shelley
5. Thick as autumnal leaves —John Milton
6. Thick as blood —Anon
   This is used with many different reference points. To cite two examples from current fiction: "An aroma thick as blood" from Frank Conroy's *Stop-Time* and "Automobile traffic thick as blood" from the story, *White Gardens,* by Mark Helprin.
7. Thick as elephant trunks —Kay Boyle
8. Thick as foreign coffee —Sylvia Plath
9. (The atmosphere of sex is) thick as the dark —John Rechy
10. (Exudes self-disgust) thick as the smell of a slept-in undershirt — Rosellen Brown
11. (Fog) thick as night —Gertrude Atherton

THIGHS
See: LEGS

THINNESS
See Also: BODY

1. Body . . . as meager as a pole —Leslie Thomas
2. Lean and thin as a fallen leaf —George Garrett

3. Lean as a bird dying in the snow —Émile Zola

4. Lean as a herring —Irwin Shaw

5. Lean as a shadow or ghost —George Garrett

6. Lean as a snake —John Berryman

7. Lean as a whipcord —Norman Mailer

8. Lean as El Greco's Saint Andres —Harry Prince

9. Lean as the dead branch of a tree —Frank Swinnerton

10. Lean as Ugulino —Dylan Thomas
    The comparison refers to Count Ugolino of Pisa, imprisoned and starved to death in Dante's *Inferno.*

11. Leaner than wasps —Phyllis McGinley
    McGinley's comparison referred to the stone lions at the doors of the New York Hispanic Society building.

12. Looked beaky and thin, like a bird —Mavis Gallant

13. Looking as skinny and blue as a jailhouse tattoo —Tom Robbins

14. Looks as if he's been carved from a shadow —T. Coraghessan Boyle

15. [A red line in the sky at dawn] narrow as a needle —John D. MacDonald

16. Skinny as a fence post —George Garrett

17. Slender as a flower's stem —Arthur Sherburne Hardy

18. Slim and evasive as a needle's eye —Paige Mitchell
    See Also: ELUSIVENESS

19. Slim as a cat —Sue Grafton

20. Slim as a little serpent —Anton Chekhov

21. Slim as a mast —Geoffrey Chaucer

22. Slim . . . like a twig stripped of bark —John Updike

23. So skinny he looked as though, if you shook him, his bones would sound like one of those Javanese musicians who play on coconut shells —Leslie Hanscomb, *Newsday,* September 11, 1986
    The thin man so described is Frank Sinatra in his early days.

24. So skinny he looked like he'd been pulled through a keyhole —Fred Allen

25. So skinny you clack like a floating crap game when you walk down the street —Russell Baker

26. So thin that he was like a clothed skeleton —Jean Rhys

27. So thin that if you touch her back you can feel the ribs, like ridges on a roll-top desk —Leslie Garis, *New York Times Magazine,* February 8, 1987
    The person thus described is author Joan Didion.

28. (She remained) thin as a baseball contract —Norman Keifetz

29. Thin and clear as green leaves in April —Elinor Wylie

30. Thin and quiet as shadows —George Garrett
    See Also: SILENCE

31. Thin as a bean pole —Anon

32. Thin as a cobweb —Jean Garrigue

33. Thin as a dime —American colloquialism, attributed to New England

34. Thin as a file —Reynolds Price

35. Thin as a moonbeam —Max Apple

36. Thin as an empty dress —Marge Piercy

37. Thin as an exclamation mark —Anon

38. Thin as an onion shoot —Gloria Norris

39. Thin as a pauper's wallet —Anon

40. Thin as a pencil line —Mary Lee Settle

41. Thin as a rail —American colloquialism, attributed to New England

42. [A heron] thin as a safety pin —Susan Minot

43. Thin as a scythe —Donald Justice

44. Thin as a sheet (his mother came to him) —John Berryman

45. Thin as a sheeted ghost —Stevie Smith

46. Thin as a thread —William H. Hallhan

47. Thin as a switch —Mark Helprin

48. Thin as a thermometer —Albert L. Weeks

49. Thin as a walking stick —Doris Grumback

50. (The steering wheel is . . .) thin as a whip —John Updike

51. Thin as a whisper —Anon

52. Thin as a wire —Raymond Chandler

53. Thin as breath —Sharon Sheehe Stark

54. Thin as chop-sticks —Rumer Godden

55. [Partitions] thin as crackers —Tom Robbins

56. Thin as linguini —Anon

57. [Children] thin as little white-haired ghosts —Carson McCullers

58. (The old man looked) thin as paper —Richard Ford
    An extension made popular in New England is: "Thin as the paper on the wall."

59. Thin as pared soap —Sharon Olds
    In the poem in which this appears, the simile is extended to include breasts "As opalescent as soap bubbles."

60. Thin as phantoms —Thomas Hardy

61. (Her face, without make-up, was an oval of white that looked as) thin as porcelain —Paul Theroux

62. [TV antennas] thin as skeletons —Italo Calvino

63. Thin as tapers —T. Coraghessan Boyle

64. Thin as the edge of the moon —Stephen Vincent Benét

65. Thin as the girl who didn't have enough to her to itch —Anon

66. Thin as the girl who swallowed the pit of an olive and was rushed to a maternity ward —Anon

67. Thin as the homeopathic soup that was made by boiling the shadow of a pigeon that had starved to death —Abraham Lincoln, October 13, 1852 speech

68. Thin as the line between self-confidence and conceit —Anon

69. Thin as the skin seaming a scar —Sylvia Plath

70. Thin as tissue —H. E. Bates

71. (Skin) thin as tracing paper —John Updike

72. Thin . . . like a skeleton —Ann Petry

THREATS
See: VIOLENCE

THOUGHTS
See Also: IDEAS, INTELLIGENCE

1. Common thoughts on common things, which time is shaking, day by day, like feathers from his wings —John Greenleaf Whittier

2. Each was in his own thoughts, like a sleeping-bag —William McIlvanney

3. Every thought is like dough; you have only to knead it well; you can make anything you like out of it —Ivan Turgenev

4. Exceptions [to theories] would crowd into her mind like a mob of unruly children —Peter Meinke

5. (He succeeded in starting) a familiar train of thought . . . like a brackish taste in his mouth —Dorothy Canfield Fisher

6. Great thoughts, like great deeds, need no trumpet —P. J. Bailey

7. Heavy on my mind, like a lump of soggy yeast dough, expanding, suffocating, blotting out all other thoughts —Mignon F. Ballard

8. Her thought ran like a barge along a river —Marianne Wiggins

9. Her thoughts ran round and round like dogs trapped behind a fence — Marge Piercy

10. Her thoughts rose as a veil before her vision —Charles Johnson

11. Her thoughts seemed to lead backwards and forwards like a shuttle weaving the moments, hours, days together in a pattern —Rumer Godden

12. (Booksellers were like dope-pushers to him.) He was like a junkie on thought —Saul Bellow
    Bellow's simile describes an avid reader.

13. His thoughts like wild animals fed upon themselves —Charles Johnson

14. His thoughts went round and round like rats in a cage —Stephen Vincent Benét

15. Human thought is not a firework, ever shooting off fresh forms and shapes as it burns; it is a tree growing very slowly —Jerome K. Jerome

16. Human thought, like God, makes the world in its own image —Adam Clayton Powell

17. I have thought about you until I feel like a bee —William Diehl

18. I will not go so far as to say that to construct a history of thought without profound study of the mathematical ideas of successive epochs is like omitting Hamlet from the play which (was) named after him . . . but it is certainly analogous to cutting out the part of Ophelia —Alfred North Whitehead

19. Meditative . . . like the chirping of a solitary little bird —Eudora Welty

20. Meditative, like a girl trying to decide which dress to wear to a party — O. Henry

21. Men's thoughts are thin and flimsy like lace; they are themselves pitiable like the lacemakers —Soren Kierkegaard

22. My mind paddles away like a wooden spoon in a bowl of dough — Richard Maynard

23. My thoughts are like sprouts, like sprouts on the branch of your brain —Edna O'Brien

24. My thoughts are whirled like a potter's wheel —William Shakespeare
    A variation in common use: "My head is spinning like a merry-go-round."

25. My thoughts turn over like a patchwork quilt —Diane Wakoski

26. Our thoughts are always happening . . . like leaves floating down a stream or clouds crossing the sky, they just keep coming —Ram Dass and Paul Gorman

27. Preoccupied in following his own thought, like someone out to net a butterfly —William McIlvanney

28. Reasoning comes as naturally to man as flying to birds —Quintilian

29. Reflective as an old sextant —Richard Ford

30. Ripe in her thought like a fresh apple fallen from the limb —Karl Shapiro

31. Sudden a thought came like a full-blown rose —John Keats

32. Thinking is like loving and dying. Each of us must do it for himself — Josiah Royce

33. Thinking was like a fountain. Once it gets going at a certain pressure, well, it is almost impossible to turn it off —Walter De La Mare

34. Thought ascends, and buds from the brain, as the fruit from the root — Victor Hugo

35. A thought as neat and final as though a ticker tape had fed it into his brain and left off with a row of dots —Kaatje Hurlbut

36. The thought . . . clanged like pipes in my mind —Scott Spencer

37. The thought kept beating in her like her heart —Wallace Stevens
    The World as Meditation, from which this is taken, follows the simile with this sentence: "The two kept beating together."

38. The thought [of women] . . . once it came it usually tended to stay for several hours, filling his noggin like a cloud of gnats —Larry McMurtry

39. Thoughts buzzing in his head like crazy flies —H. E. Bates

40. (His) thoughts drove in like a night-cloud —Stevie Smith

41. Thoughts . . . fall from him like chantering from an abundant poet — Wallace Stevens

42. Thoughts flickering like heat lightning —F. van Wyck Mason

43. Thoughts floating like light clouds through the upper air of his mind — George Santayana

44. Thoughts . . . flowing in unison, like a mountain-stream and a lake-stream meeting, but not yet merging, in a single river —George Santayana

45. Thoughts ground each other as millstones grind when there is no corn in between —Rudyard Kipling

46. Thoughts like fleas jump from man to man, but they don't bite everybody —Anon

47. The thought . . . slipped through his mind like a dot of quicksilver — Stanley Elkin

48. (Foolish) thoughts play in her mind like firelight and shadow in a dim room —George Garrett

49. Thoughts ran like squirrels in the boy's head —Conrad Richter

50. Thoughts rising like fish to the fluid surface of his mind —Ellen Glasgow

51. (Lying awake with her) thoughts running round and round inside her skull like trapped mice —Josephine Tey

52. Thoughts spinning and tumbling like a week's wash —Julia Whedon
53. Thoughts that peel off and fly away at breathless speeds like the last stubborn leaves ripped from wet branches —John Ashbery
54. Thoughts . . . tied up in knots like snakes, squeezing and suffocating them —V. S. Pritchett
55. Thoughts . . . twisting like snakes through his brain —Alice Walker
56. Thoughts . . . untidily stacked like dishes slanting (in) a full sink — Lincoln Kirstein
57. Thoughts . . . vague and pale, like ghosts —Jean Rhys
58. Thoughts veering through her like a flight of birds —Anon
59. Thoughts went on, coming and going like leaves blown in the wind — Ellen Glasgow
60. Thoughts wheeled like a flight of bats in her mind —Ellen Glasgow
61. Thoughts which moved, like the clouds, slowly, shedding dim yet vivid light —Iris Murdoch
62. Thoughts . . . whirling around on themselves, like the apocryphal snake seizing its own tail and then devouring itself —Stanley Elkin
63. Unusable and contradictory thoughts filled Quinn's mind with almost physical duress as though his poor head were a golf ball which, slashed open, shows its severed rubber filaments snapping and racing about in confusion —Thomas McGuane
64. When thought grows old and worn with usage it should, like current coin, be called in, and from the mint of genius, reissued fresh and new —Alexander Smith

THREATS
See: VIOLENCE

THRIFT

1. Act like they are bargaining with some Arab street trader . . . like they are buying lemons —John Wainwright
2. False economy is like stopping one hole in a sieve —Samuel Johnson, April 17, 1788
3. Frugal as a poor farmer's wife —George Garrett
4. Generous as someone who would give you the sleeves out of his vest — Anon
5. His money comes from him like drops of blood —John Ray's *Proverbs*
6. Kept his wallet shut tight as an accordion —Anon
7. Pinches a penny like money is going out of style —George Garrett
8. Soliciting a miser is like fishing in the desert —Solomon Ibn Gabirol

9. Thrifty as a French peasant —G. K. Chesterton

10. Tight as a miser's wallet —Anon

11. Tight as a scout knot —Geoffrey Wolff
In his novel, *Providence,* Wolff expands upon the simile with "Wouldn't pay a nickel to watch an earthquake."

12. Tight as a tic —Anon

13. Tight as Dick's headband —American colloquialism
This was coined by and is still used by Texas ranchers.

14. Tight as the bark to a tree —American colloquialism
This still popular simile originated in New Hampshire. A variation from Indiana, "Tight as a wad," has pretty much given way to the jargon word 'tightwad.' There's also Ulysses S. Grant's literal application to describe the pantaloons he had to wear as a West Point cadet as being, "Tight to my skin as the bark to a tree."

15. Tight as the paper on the wall —Mignon Eberhart

16. Watch pennies like a streetcar conductor —Irwin Shaw

THROAT
See: NECK

THUNDER AND LIGHTNING
See Also: NATURE, WEATHER

1. (There was the low boom of) distant thunder echoing like cannon — Barbara Taylor Bradford

2. Heard the heat thunder roll . . . like a hard apple rattling in the bottom of a barrel —James Lee Burke

3. Lightning plays over the horizon like the flicker of ideas —T. Coraghessan Boyle

4. Lightning and thunder spat and roared like a wounded tiger —Robert Traver

5. Lightning falls like silent saber blows —Erich Maria Remarque

6. Lightning flickers like a genie inside the bottle-shaped cloud —Walker Percy

7. Lightning flutters . . . like a wing—like a broken bird —Katherine Mansfield

8. Lightning . . . letting down thick drips of thunder like pig iron from the heart of a white-hot furnace —F. Scott Fitzgerald

9. Lightning snapped at the world like a whip —John Rechy

10. Lightning winked across the eastern sky like fitful fireflies —Fletcher Knebel

11. Thunder beating like tribal drums —T. Coraghessan Boyle
12. Thunder like great stones falling —Stephen Longstreet
13. Thunder rolled like a cannon —Anon
14. Thunder rustling like water down the sky's eaves —A. R. Ammons
15. Thunder sounded like a far-off cracking of the earth —Martin Cruz Smith
16. Thunder steps down like a giant walking the earth —T. Coraghessan Boyle
17. A thunderstorm came rushing down . . . roaring like a brontosaur — Carlos Baker

TIDINESS
See: ORDER/DISORDER

TIGHTNESS
See: FIRMNESS, TENSION, THRIFT

TIME
See Also: DAY, DEATH, LIFE

1. About as much time left as an ice cube in a frying pan —William Diehl
2. Any decent church service lasts forty-five minutes, like the sex act — Heinrich Böll
3. As the waves make toward the pebbled shore, so do our minutes hasten to their end —William Shakespeare
4. As the years go by me, my life keeps filling up with names like abandoned cemeteries —Yehuda Amichai
5. The day runs through me as water through a sieve —Samuel Butler
6. The days chase one another like kittens chasing their tails —H. L. Mencken
7. The days slipped by . . . like apple-parings under a knife —Stephen Vincent Benét
8. A decade falling like snow on top of another —Elizabeth Hardwick
9. Each class seemed endless to him, as if the hour were stuck to his back like his damp shirt —Helen Hudson
10. Each year is like a snake that swallows its tail —Robert Penn Warren
    This line is the curtain raiser for Warren's poem, *Paradigm*.
11. Every day yawned like a week —Donald Seaman
12. Forty-five minutes passed, like a very slow cloud —Dylan Thomas
13. Here [at a country inn] time swings idly as a toy balloon —Phyllis McGinley

14. The hours weighed like centuries on his heart —Lawrence Durrell

15. If time seems to pass so quickly, this is because there are no landmarks. Like the moon when it is at its heights on the horizon —Albert Camus

16. The hours [with nothing to do] hunted him like a pack of bloodhounds —Edith Wharton

17. If you let slip time, like a neglected rose it withers on the stalk with languished head —John Milton

18. The lagging hours of the day went by like windless clouds over a tender sky —Percy Bysshe Shelley
    The word 'over' is spelled 'o'er' in the original.

19. Leisure is like a beautiful garment that will not do for constant wear — Anon

20. Life goes like the river —Clifford Odets

21. Like a run in a stocking. It [lost time] always got worse —Anne Morrow Lindbergh

22. Like January weather, the years will bite and smart —Dorothy Parker

23. Like sand poured in a careful measure from the hand, the weeks flowed down —Paule Marshall

24. Like the swell of some sweet tune, morning rises into noon, May glides onward into June —Henry Wadsworth Longfellow

25. Like the waves make towards the pebbled shore, so do our minutes hasten to their end —William Shakespeare

26. The minutes crawl like last year's flies —Ridgely Torrence

27. The minutes ticked off like separate eternities —Dan Wakefield

28. The moment hung in time like a miner's hat on an oaken peg in a saloon abandoned ninety years ago —Loren D. Estleman

29. The moment shimmered like a glass of full-bodied wine —Marge Piercy

30. The moments [between two people] were stretching longer and longer, like so many rubber bands —Elizabeth Spencer

31. My days are consumed like smoke —*The Holy Bible/Psalms*

32. The passing years are like a mist sweeping up from the sea of time so that my memories acquire new aspects —W. Somerset Maugham

33. Saw the days of the year stretching ahead like a series of bright, white boxes, and separating one box from another was sleep, like a black shade —Sylvia Plath

34. She was forever saving time, like bits of string —Helen Hudson

35. Slowly the generations pass, like sand through heaven's blue hour-glass —Vachel Lindsay
    Lindsay used this simile as a repeated refrain for his poem *Shantung.*

36. The summer was melting away like the unfinished ice cream Sonny left on his plate —Dan Wakefield

37. That night and the next day swept past like the waters of a rapids — James Crumley

38. (Time seems thin, one-dimensional,) the hours long and slender, stretched like a wire —Dan Wakefield

39. There is a rhythm inside a year of time, like a great mainspring that keeps it ticking from spring to summer to fall to winter —Borden Deal

40. Time . . . a substance of some sort which existence burned up like a fire —Susan Fromberg Schaeffer

41. Time can be nibbled away as completely as a tray of canapés in an irresolute fat man's reach, or grandly lost in victory like the great marlin in *The Old Man and the Sea* [by Hemingway] —Charles Poore

42. Time crawled like ants —Marge Piercy

43. Time crouched, like a great cat, motionless but for tail's twitch — Robert Penn Warren

44. Time dripped like drops of blood —Yukio Mishima

45. Time drops sail like a ketch in a lagoon —Diane Ackerman

46. Time fled past us like a startled bird —James Crumley

47. Time flies . . . like an arrow —Amy Hempel

48. Time goes cooly through the funnel of his fingers . . . like water over stones —William H. Gass

49. Time has moved on like a great flock of geese —Stephen Minot

50. Time is a storm in which we are all lost —William Carlos Williams

51. Time is like an enterprising manager always bent on staging some new and surprising production, without knowing very well what it will be — George Santayana

52. Time is like a river made up of the events which happen, and its current is strong. No sooner does anything appear than it is swept away and another comes in its place, and will be swept away too —Marcus Aurelius

53. Time is like money; the less we have of it to spare the further we make it go —Josh Billings

54. Time is like some balked monster, waiting outside the valley, to pounce on the slackers who have managed to evade him longer than they should —James Hilton

55. Time, like a flurry of wild rain, shall drift across the darkened pane — Charles G. D. Roberts

56. Time like an ever-rolling stream bears all its sons away —Isaac Watts

57. Time, like a pulse, shakes fierce through all the worlds —Dante Gabriel Rossetti

58. Time looked like snow dropping silently into a black room or . . . like a silent film in an ancient theatre, one hundred billion faces falling like those New Year balloons, down and down into nothing —Ray Bradbury

59. Time moves . . . like a treacle —Hortense Calisher

60. Time passes as on a fast day —Anon

61. Time pleated like a fan —Julia O'Faolain

62. Time pulses from the afternoon like blood from a serious wound — Hilma Wolitzer

63. Time roared in his ears like wind —John Barth
    See Also: NOISE

64. Time roars in my ears like a river —Derek Walcott

65. Time rushes past us like the snowflake on the river —Gore Vidal

66. Time seemed to have slowed down, dividing itself into innumerable fractions, like Zeno's space or marijuana hours —Ross Macdonald

67. Time . . . sounded like water running in a dark cave and voices crying and dirt dropping down upon hollow box lids, and rain —Ray Bradbury

68. Time sticking to her like cold grease —Marge Piercy

69. Time swells like a wave at a wall and bursts to eternity —George Barker

70. Time went on like an unchanging ribbon drawn across a turbulent background —Heinrich Böll

71. Upon his silver hairs, time, like a Panama hat, sits at a tilt and smiles — Karl Shapiro
    In his poem, *Boy-Man,* Shapiro expands on the simile as follows: " . . . and smiles. To him the world has just begun. And every city waiting to be built."

72. The week is dealt out like a hand —Randall Jarrell

73. The week passed slowly . . . like a prolonged Sunday —Edith Wharton

74. When a man sits with a pretty girl for an hour, it seems like a minute. When he sits on a hot stove for a minute, then it's longer than any hour —Albert Einstein

75. When you're deeply absorbed in what you're doing, time gives itself to you like a warm and willing lover —Brendan Francis

76. The years are crawling over him like wee red ants —Ogden Nash

77. The years come close around me like a crowd of the strangers I knew once —Randall Jarrell

78. The years dropped from Randstable [character in novel] like a heavy overcoat —James Morrow

79. The years like great black oxen tread the world, and God the herdsman goads them on behind —W. B. Yeats

80. The years peeled back like the skin of an onion, layer on top of layer — T. Coraghessan Boyle

81. The years rolled in against one another like a rush of water —Frieda Arkin

82. The years shall run like rabbits —W. H. Auden

83. The years ticked past like crabs —Randall Jarrell

84. Years which rushed over her like weathered leaves in a storm —Ellen Glasgow

85. A year that dragged like a terminal illness —Rosellen Brown

TIMELINESS/UNTIMELINESS
See Also: STALENESS

1. As modern as tomorrow —Slogan, Royal Worcester Corset Co.

2. As out of date as the black stockings and high shoes worn by inmates of asylums that used to take up city blocks and loom large in the countryside —Eileen Simpson, *New York Times*/Op-Ed, May 1, 1987

3. As seasonable as snow in summer —John Ray's *Proverbs*

4. By the time they take place [dinner parties] the original impulse is lost . . . like sending a Christmas card into space and hoping an alien finds it on the right date —Maxine Chernoff

5. Dated as a dodo, but who cares —Anon capsule review, television movie listings, *New York Times,* April, 1987

6. Dead as a failed product launch —Anon
   For other "Dead as" similes which apply to obsolescence,
   See Also: DEATH

7. Dead as an unsuccessful book —Henry James

8. Dead as Greek —Karl Shapiro

9. Dead as Sunday's paper on Tuesday morning —Anon
   Commonly used variations are "Dead as yesterday's front page news" and "Dead as last week's ticker tape."

10. Extinction, like a thing of beauty, is forever —Brad Leithauser, *New York Times Book Review,* June 7, 1987
    Another simile that was extracted from an article and featured as an attention-getting blurb.

11. Gone like the carriage-horse —Louis MacNeice

Poet MacNeice precedes the simile with this question: "What's become of the squadron of butlers, valets, grooms and second housemaids?" Clearly, appropriate substitutions for the carriage-horse could give rise to as many similes beginning with "Gone like" as there are obsolete customs and objects. "Gone . . . like five-cent candy and the drainboard on the sink" from a novel by Babs H. Deal offers just one possibility.

12. Good that comes too late is as good as nothing —Thomas Fuller

13. It's a little like being given the captaincy of the *Titanic* after it hit the ice floe —Senator Lawton Chiles of Florida, quoted in many newspapers on prospect of heading Senate budget committee, after November, 1986, Democratic victory
    See Also: FUTILITY

14. Like a punchline of a bad joke, the moment passed —T. Coraghessan Boyle

15. (Conflicts as) new as each generation —Anon, jacket copy
    Because similes are so often pulled out from book jacket copy, the more one can appropriately include, the better; and so, this and the "Old as literature" comparison below were both featured on one book jacket.

16. New as tomorrow —Slogan, dictaphone company

17. (Passions and conflicts as) old as literature —Anon book jacket copy

18. No day is so dead as the day before yesterday —W. Somerset Maugham

19. Obsolete as books in leather bindings —Louis MacNeice

20. Outdated like a last year's almanac —John Greenleaf Whittier

21. Timing . . . as elegant as that of the Budapest String Quartet —Karl Shapiro

22. (The reference library is quite) unfrequented . . . like the mausoleum of a once-proud family that has died out —Robert Barnard

TIREDNESS
See: WEARINESS

TOBACCO
See Also: SMELLS

1. An acrid cigar held tightly in your teeth, you look like a banker or a psychiatrist or both —Daniela Gioseffi

2. Ash flows like a breaking thundercloud from his clenched cigar —Harvey Swados

3. Ashtray . . . crammed with smoked cigarettes like dead bugs —John Rechy

4. Blowing a cloud of coarse smoke [from pipe], like a steam roller —
    Frank Swinnerton

5. (I lit) a cigar, a cheap twisted black thing like half a pepperoni —T.
    Coraghessan Boyle

6. Cigarette coals dotted the room like watchfires —Thomas Pynchon

7. Cigarettes . . . dangle from his lips like a second tongue —Jonathan
    Valin

8. Cigarettes tasted like hot ashes —Anthony E. Stockanes

9. Cigars . . . when lit, they exuded an overwhelming odor, like burning
    manure from constipated giraffes —Richard S. Prather

10. A dead cigar which was always in his hand, seemed to belong there, like
    a thumb or finger —Willa Cather

11. The glow in the bowl of his pipe went on and off like a firefly —Jean
    Stafford

12. A good cigar is as great a comfort to a man as a good cry is to a woman
    —Edward Bulwer-Lytton

13. His cheeks puffed [from smoking a cigar] like a bellows —Jay Parini

14. His cigar . . . had become a natural appendage . . . like a pipe stuck
    in the face of a snowman —Robert Traver

15. It [tobacco] smells like Saturday, and consequently puts me in a chronic
    holiday mood —Robert Benchley

16. It [cigarette] tasted like burning rope —F. Van Wyck Mason

17. Lit his stogy, which flared up like a burning bush —Arthur Train

18. My psyche felt as different without cigarettes as my body felt in moving
    from air to water —Norman Mailer

19. Removed his water-logged cigar, like a man calmly unscrewing his nose
    —Robert Traver

20. The smell of good tobacco . . . heavy as incense in a church —
    Howard Spring

21. Smoked like a chimney —Richard Harris Barham

22. The smoke of cigars and cigarettes like curtains before the lights —R.
    Wright Campbell

23. Smoking his clay pipe with the elegance of an Indian chief —André
    Malraux

24. Stubbed out the cigarette as if he were squashing a cockroach —Derek
    Lambert

25. The tip of his narrow cigarette danced like a tiny ballerina in the dark
    —Nelson Algren

26. Took another deep drag of his cigarette, letting the smoke curl up out of
    his mouth and around his head like ectoplasm —Margaret Millar

27. To smoke a cigar through a mouthpiece is the equivalent of kissing a lady through a respirator —Anon

TONGUE

See Also: MOUTH, SHARPNESS

1. Her tongue felt like a freshly painted shingle —Edwin L. Sabin

2. Her tongue hung out like a yard of red hall carpet —Wilson Mizener

3. Her tongue [as she kissed him] was like a kitten's, soft and rough, tasting of milk —Shirley W. Schoonover

4. His tongue darted in and out when he talked, as if he were keeping count of the words —Shelby Hearon

5. (A large dog lay panting,) his tongue unrolled like a carpet —Peter Meinke

6. My tongue is big as a liverwurst —Marge Piercy

7. The tongue is like a race horse: the less weight it carries, the faster it runs —Joseph Addison

This has been modernized from the original. "The tongue is like a race-horse, which runs the faster the lesser weight it carries."

8. Tongue like a pink dart —Joseph Conrad

9. The tongue . . . like a stream, could run smooth music from the roughest stone —Elizabeth Barrett Browning

10. Your tongue curls up in your mouth like a cat lapping up cream —R. Wright Campbell

TOUGHNESS

1. Babies you about as much as Perry White babies Clark Kent —Peter H. Lewis describing a tough-to-master computer program, *New York Times,* 1985

2. (The man is as) hard as a cash register —Dialogue, "Miami Vice" television drama, broadcast January 7, 1986

3. (She can be) hard as a mineral —Philip Roth

The "Hard as a mineral" lady is the mother of Nathan Zuckerman, hero of several Roth novels.

4. Hard as flint —Larry McMurtry

5. Hard as my fist —Tennessee Williams

6. Hard as a tortoise-shell —John Galsworthy

7. Hardboiled as a picnic egg —Edward E. Paramore

8. Resilient and tenacious as an amoeba —Natascha Wodin

9. She's [Genevieve Bujold] tough as a little green apple —Rex Reed

10. Tough and leathery as a jockey —John Mortimer

11. Tough and shrill as an old bird —H.E. Bates

12. Tough and hard-boiled as an Easter egg —Anon

13. Tough as a black oak —Dee Brown

14. Tough as a bone —W. S. Gilbert

15. Tough as a fast food steak —Tim McCarver, describing baseball player Dave Parker on television, January, 1987

16. Tough as a kibbutz woman —T. Coraghessan Boyle

17. (She was short and fat,) tough as a monkey —Rudolf Nassauer

18. Tough as an elephant's hide —Calder Willingham

19. (He was as) tough as a resistant bacterium —Patrick Suskind

20. Tough as a stale bagel —Anon

21. (Memories as) tough as a thorn —Babette Deutsch

22. Tough as boiled owls —Hubert H. Humphrey on his opponent for presidential election

23. (She's big as a damned barn and) tough as knife metal —Ken Kesey

24. Tough as marshmallows —Anon, *Forbes,* March 23, 1987
     The simile was used as a blurb to introduce an article about the government sounding tough but not following through.

25. (She was) a tough lady, like a military jeep rolling from place to place on thick tires —Harvey Jacobs

26. (She's as) tough as old boots —Mary Bridgman
     Around since 1870. A popular variant: "Tough as old shoe leather."

27. Tough as seaweed —Linda Pastan

28. Tough as teak —Bryan Forbes

29. Tough as tire treads —Lynn Haney
     The person being compared to tire treads is the late Edith Piaf.

TRADING
See: ADVANTAGEOUSNESS, SUCCESS/FAILURE

TRAFFIC
See: ROAD SCENES, VEHICLES

TRAIL
See: PURSUIT

TRANQUILITY
See: PEACEFULNESS

TRANSIENCE

See Also: BREVITY, DEATH, LIFE

1. About as fixed as liquid mercury —Leslie Bennetts, *New York Times,* June 8, 1986

2. The brilliant passes like the dew at dawn —Johann Wolfgang von Goethe
   In *Faust,* from which this is taken, Goethe continues by presenting the other side of the coin: "The true endures for ages yet unborn."

3. Burnt like a faggot in a tempest —Willa Cather

4. Changed them like underwear —Paige Mitchell
   In Mitchell's novel, *The Covenant,* law clerks are what are being so changed.

5. (His smile) comes and goes as quickly as snow —Robert Goldberg about film maker Alain Renais, *Wall Street Journal,* March 24, 1987
   See Also: ENTRANCES/EXITS

6. Disposable as extra income —Anon

7. Disposable as razor blades —Anon

8. Disposable as TV dinner containers —Anon

9. Enduring as a summer shower —Anon

10. Ephemeral as butterflies —Susan Heller Anderson on literary magazines, *New York Times*/Column One, October 24, 1986

11. Ephemeral things, like movement, are manifestations of immortality —Joanne Selzer
    This is the closing line for a poem entitled *Prima Ballerina.*

12. Flare briefly like the candles upon a cake —Donald Justice

13. (Embrace . . .) fleeting as a bird's poise —Edith Wharton

14. Fleeting as a dream of night lost in the garish day —Aeschylus

15. Fleeting as a raspberry season —Line from television drama, "St. Elsewhere," broadcast December 16, 1986

16. Fleeting as the estate of man —Marcus Aurelius

17. A fleeting gratification . . . like alms thrown to the beggar, that keeps him alive today that his misery may be prolonged till the morrow —Lynne Sharon Schwartz

18. How fading are the joys we dote upon! Like apparitions seen and gone —John Norris

19. Like a rainbow, spectacular but short-lived —Anon
    A variation: "Like a shooting star—spectacular but short-lived."

20. Like water thrown on the sand: it [media campaign about energy crisis] left little trace —George F. Will

21. Mortality weights heavily on me like unwilling sleep —John Keats

22. (The moment of agitation) passed (from his gaze) like a cloud, leaving a clear blue sky —Christopher Isherwood

23. Passing through a certain stage, something rather like an illness —Thomas Mann

24. Permanent as a temporary price increase —Anon

25. Temporary as an idea in an empty head —Anon

26. Temporary as a wave —Anon

27. (Beauty is as) temporary as flowers —Anon

28. Transience (His self-possession was) temporary, like a reflection in water that may be wiped out at the first swell —Saul Bellow

29. (His love was as) transient as the first golden streaks of dawn —Harry Prince

30. Transitory as childhood —Lawrence Durrell

31. Will last about as long as a snowball in hell —Anon

TRANSPORTATION
See: VEHICLES

TRAVEL

1. Like a chastity belt, the package tour keeps you out of mischief but a bit restive for wondering what you missed —Peg Bracken

2. Like film critics, the guidebooks don't always see eye to eye —Peg Bracken

3. Like gin or plum pudding, travel is filling —Peg Bracken

4. One's travel life is basically as incommunicable as his sex life is —Peg Bracken

5. A traveller without knowledge is a bird without wings —Sadi

6. Travel light, like the prayers of Jews —Yehuda Amichai

7. Travelling is almost like talking with men of three other centuries —Rene Descartes

TREES
See Also: LEAVES, NATURE

1. Apple-trees on which the apples looked like great shining soap bubbles —Hans Christian Andersen

2. The bark hung in ribbons from the trunks like the flayed skins of living creatures —R. Wright Campbell

3. Beeches . . . their beautiful bare green trunks like limbs —Elizabeth Bowen

4. The big pine was like greenish bronze against the October sky —Ellen Glasgow

5. (In the moonlight) the big trees around us looked as bare as gallows —John Braine

6. The birches bend like women —Caroline Finkelstein

7. The birches stand out . . . like gay banners on white poles —Erich Maria Remarque

8. The birch trees wavered their stark shadows across it [snow] like supplicating arms —Leo Tolstoy

9. Boughs . . . as rough and hornily buckled as the hands of old farmers —Margaret Laurence

10. [Tree] branches . . . looked like the powerful contorted fingers of a gigantic hand —Sholem Asch

11. The branches [of a weeping willow] were thin, like the bleached bones of a skeleton —Daphne du Maurier

12. Cedars . . . black and pointed on the sky like a paper silhouette —William Faulkner

13. Chestnut trees . . . their clusters of white blossoms like candelabras —Dorothea Straus

14. Copses of hazel and alder stood like a low, petrified forest —H. E. Bates

15. Cypresses rose like cathedral spires —Jilly Cooper

16. Elms rich like cucumbers —Joyce Cary

17. Evergreens as big as tents —Julia O'Faolain

18. Evergreens . . . out of place [amid the other trees that change their foliage in Autumn] . . . like poor relations at a rich man's feast —Jerome K. Jerome

19. Huge hardwood trees draped with clusters of Spanish moss guarded the house from the afternoon heat like overdressed sentinels —Paul Kuttner

20. Magnolia . . . its chalices of flowers like superb classical emblems —H. E. Bates

21. Maples, burning like bonfires, pure yellow and pure red —Pamela Hansford Johnson

22. My poplars are . . . like two old neighbors met to chat —Theodosia Garrison

23. The oaks stood silent and tired, like old, worn-out seekers after pleasure, unable to keep up in this grimy, mechanized world of ours —Anthony Powell

24. Palms . . . like Spanish exclamation points —Sue Grafton

25. A pear tree glistened in bloom like a graceful drift of snow —George Garrett

26. The pear tree lets its petals drop like dandruff on a tabletop —W. D. Snodgrass

27. Pines . . . moaning like the sea —John Greenleaf Whittier

28. Pines tossing their green manes like frightened horses —George Garrett

29. The pines were packed like a quiver of arrows —John Farris

30. The pine-trees roared like waves in their topmost branches, their stems creaked like the timber of ships —Katherine Mansfield

31. A poplar covered with snow looked, in the bluish mist, like a giant in a winding sheet —Anton Chekhov

32. Poplars like dark feathers against the green and gold sunset —Sharon Sheehe Stark

33. The poplars stood like tall guards, attentive, at attention —Delmore Schwartz
    A week after the poet entered this in his diary as a fragment he incorporated it into a poem as follows: "The poplar stood like a rifle."

34. Poplars that rose above the mist were like a beach stirred by the wind —Gustave Flaubert

35. Red maples and orange oaks, shaped like hands —Jonathan Valin

36. The redwoods let sink their branches like arms that try to hold buckets filling slowly with diamonds —James Dickey

37. Rows of bay trees like children's green lollipops —Graham Masterton

38. Saw the bare branches of a tree, like fine lace, against the blackness [of garden] —Jean Rhys

39. The scarlet of the maples can shake me like a cry —Bliss Carman

40. The shadows hung from the oak trees to the road like curtains — Eudora Welty

41. Tall trees like towers —Carlos Baker

42. A thick low-hanging branch sags like a wounded arm —John Rechy

43. The tops of pines moonlit, like floating Christmas trees —Frank Conroy

44. The tree, in full bloom, was like a huge mountain lit with candles — Alice Walker

45. Trees against walls, flattened like spies in old movies —Lisa Ress

46. The trees and the shrubbery seemed well-groomed and sociable, like pleasant people —Willa Cather

47. The tree sat like a party umbrella (trunk sturdy, branches gently arching) —W. P. Kinsella

48. Trees bent like arches —Graham Swift

49. The trees cast still shadows like intricate black laces —H. G. Wells

50. Trees darkening like clusters of frightened wrens —Philip Levine
51. The trees dimmed the whiteness [of snow] like a sparse coat of hair — John Cheever
52. The trees drooped like old men with back problems —T. Coraghessan Boyle
53. Trees grew close and spread out like bouquets —Stephen Crane
54. The trees have a look as if they bore sad names —Wallace Stevens
55. Trees . . . hunched against the dawn sky like shaggy dark animals, like buffalo —Alice Munro
56. A tree slender as life, and as tall —Kenneth Patchen
57. Trees . . . like burnt-out torches —Oscar Wilde
58. Trees . . . like fresh-painted green —Danny Santiago
59. Trees . . . like prophet's fingers —Dylan Thomas
60. Trees like tall ships —Sharon Sheehe Stark
61. Trees [planted 40 years ago] . . . now stately, like patriarchs whose wisdom lives in their mere physical presence, after all sight and mind have been feebled —Paul Horgan
62. Trees spaced out in ordered formality . . . like a ballet of spinsters — W. Somerset Maugham
63. Trees spread like green lather —F. Scott Fitzgerald
64. Trees . . . spread their scant shade upon the ground like fine strands of hair —Yitzhak Shenhar
65. The trees stood motionless and white like figures in a marble frieze — Helen Keller
66. (In the park) the trees stood reticent as old men —Helen Hudson
67. Trees . . . tall and straight as the masts of ships —Donald Hall
68. Trees tall as mythical giants —David Ignatow
69. Trees . . . vibrating headily like coins shaken in a dark money-box — Robert Culff
    See Also: VIBRATIONS
70. The trees were beginning to put out buds like tiny wings —Helen Hudson
71. The trees were plucked like iron bars —Wallace Stevens
72. Trees whose branches spread like hugging, possessive arms —John Rechy
73. Trees with branches like the groping fingers of men long dead —Loren D. Estleman
74. Trunks like thick skirts hanging in folds —Paul Theroux
75. Twigs grasped for the sky like frayed electrical wires —Z. Vance Wilson

76. Willow trees . . . their trailing leaves hung like waterfalls in the morning air —Eudora Welty

TREMBLING
     See Also: ROCKING AND ROLLING, VIBRATION

1.   Body quivers like a dancing animal's —Maureen Howard

2.   Felt a tremor . . . like an earthquake in a swamp —William Getz
     The tremor described is the shiver that goes through a person.

3.   (The handkerchief) flapped like a jib in a crosswind —T. Coraghessan Boyle

4.   (Ali's brain) flickered and wavered like a candle flame in a draft — Gerald Kersh

5.   (My tongue) fluttered like a dead leaf —George Garrett

6.   Fluttered like paper in the wind —Gertrude Atherton

7.   Fluttering around like birds in a thicket —Ariel Dorfman

8.   Fluttering around . . . like a yardful of hens —Harvey Swados

9.   Fluttering in the wind, like a schooner in full rig —Anatole France
     This referred to a feather fluttering on a hat, and while feathered hats have not been in style for many years, the comparison is not limited to this descriptive reference point.

10. Fluttering like a white moth —O. Henry

11. Fluttering like pigeons —Christina Rossetti

12. Flutter like large butterflies —Oscar Wilde

13. Her hands and face shook like Jell-O —Joseph Heller
     Trembling flesh and pudding make for vivid similes. Some variants: "Quivering all over . . . like a dish of jelly on a rickety table" (Nikolay Leskov); "The whole huge torso, the shoulders, arms and breast and the great heaving belly, would shake and tremble like a hogshead full of jelly." (Thomas Wolfe)

14. His whole body was shaking and the more he tried to control it, the more violently it shook, as though the lines of communications between his brain and his muscles had been cut —Margaret Millar

15. (Nostrils) pulse like a heart on fire —Gertrude Atherton

16. Quake like mice when the cat is mentioned —Honoré de Balzac

17. (His whole face) quivered convulsively as if pricked by pins and needles —Luigi Pirandello

18. [An evening gown] Quivered like a butterfly about to take wing — Dorothea Straus

19. Quivered like a pointer dog —Jonathan Gash

20. Quivered like a sob —Conrad Aiken

21. Quivered like forest-leaves —Dante Gabriel Rossetti
22. Quivering . . . like a wounded bird —Leo Tolstoy
23. Quiver like a twig in a gale —L. P. Hartley
24. Quiver like tuning forks —Peter De Vries
25. (The Saab) rattled like a trayful of china —Scott Spencer
26. Shaking all over like someone attached to an electric reducing belt — Cornell Woolrich
27. Shaking like a dog shittin' peach pits —Ken Kesey
28. Shaking like a drunk the morning-after —Clarence Major
29. Shaking like a lamb led to slaughter —Sholom Aleichem
30. Shaking like an ague-fit —William Faulkner
31. Shaking like a piece of grass —Louise Erdrich
32. Shaking like a treed raccoon —Harvey Swados
33. Shaking like a wet spaniel —T. Coraghessan Boyle
34. (Her breath) shaking like turning leaves —Mary Hedin
35. Shiver as at the sight of a bug or a repulsively dirty man in the street — Colette
36. Shivered, like a swimmer who has tested the water with a toe and found it exceeding chill —Stefan Zweig
37. Shivering like a puppy —Ross Macdonald
38. Shivering like a whippet on a cold day —Jilly Cooper
39. Shiver like a flame —George Garrett
40. Shiver like ostriches in a zoo —Marge Piercy
41. Shivers like a fish in a net —George Garrett
42. Shook like a harpstring —Beryl Markham
43. [A hand that had been beaten] shook like a loose leaf in the air —James Joyce
44. Shook like an autumn leaf —Dante Gabriel Rossetti
    To "shake like an aspen leaf" is a familiar variant. "I shook like a leaf . . . like a little leaf in a big storm" from a short story, *The Actor,* by Nunally Johnson exemplifies the simile extended.
45. (His whole body) shook like a thunder-stricken tree —Yisrael Zarchi
46. (His face was gray and) shook like a torn sail —Malcolm Cowley
47. Shook like a wet mutt [describing a dynamited building] —Tom Robbins
48. Shudder as if she were passing a cemetery —Elsa Schiaparelli
49. Shuddered all over, like a dog that recognizes the vet and smells its oncoming death —Frank Tuohy

50. Shuddered like a broken doll —Louise Erdrich
51. Shudders like an epileptic —T. Coraghessan Boyle
52. Shudders . . . like a woman gently coming —Diane Ackerman
53. Shuddery like a hooked fish or a stallion —W. D. Snodgrass
54. Silently quivering like the waters of a lake when the wind blows off-shore —Yitzhak Shenhar
55. Swayed like the tail of a dog attempting to be friendly —F. van Wyck Mason
56. Sways like a broken stalk —Elizabeth Bishop
57. (Her body) sways like a willow in spring wind —Robert Penn Warren
58. Sways like tropical seaweed —Lawrence Durrell
59. Trembled like an adolescent —Robert Silverberg
60. Trembled tensely like a released harp-string —Joseph Conrad
61. Tremble like an aspirin —Ogden Nash
62. Trembling as if something were shaking him —Ben Hecht
63. Trembling like a colt —Lawrence Durrell
64. Trembling like an invalid —Mavis Gallant
65. Trembling like a string —Ivan Turgenev
66. (Knees) trembly like water —Peggy Bennett
67. Shudder as if she were passing a cemetery —Elsa Schiaparelli
68. Tremulous as a plant in a stream —Vita Sackville-West
69. Twitching like a hooked fish —Gerald Kersh
70. Twitching like a skate [fish] in a frying pan —Lawrence Durrell
71. An unexpected shudder rippled over her body, like a cold wind moving across water —Madeleine L'Engle
72. Wobble like a skittle —Graham Swift

TRIUMPH
See: SUCCESS/FAILURE

TRITENESS
See: STALENESS

TROUBLES
See: PROBLEMS/SOLUTIONS

TROUBLESOMENESS
See: DIFFICULTY

TRUENESS/FALSENESS

1. Deceptive as a cat's fur —Margaret Atwood
2. Deceptive as a Venus flytrap —Vivian Raynor, *New York Times,* February 27, 1987
    Ms. Raynor's simile refers to the fleeting and misleading resemblance of one artist's work to another's.
3. Deceptive as new paint on a second-hand car —Herbert V. Prochnow
4. False as a lead coin —George Garrett
5. Falser than a weeping crocodile —John Dryden
6. Falser than malice in the mouth of envy —Mary Pin
7. Good and true as morning —Babs H. Deal
8. Right as rain —William Raymond
    An older, less commonly used version from Shakespeare's *Richard III:* "Right as snow in harvest."
9. Ring as true as chapel bells on a windless morning —Anon
10. Ring true, like good china —Sylvia Plath
11. True as life itself —Louis Bromfield
12. True as the dial to the sun —Barton Booth
13. (I found him large as life and) true as the needle to the pole —Henry James
14. True as the sky is blue —James Reiss
15. True as truth —Louis Bromfield
16. The true is stripped from the false like bone from meat —George Garrett

TRUST/MISTRUST

See Also: UNCERTAINTY

1. Finding paranoia in your heart is like discovering a lump in your breast—just knowing it's there won't make it go away —Jerry Bumpus
2. As confiding as a doe peeping between the tree trunks —Vita Sackville-West
3. As suspicious of me as Hamlet was of his mother —Daphne Merkin
4. Carried years of suspicion strapped to her hip like a gun —Ann Jasperson
5. Confidence in an unfaithful man in time of trouble is like a broken tooth, and a foot out of joint —*The Holy Bible/Proverbs*
6. Confidence (in their amorous destinies) like that of birds in their wings —William Faulkner
7. Confidence, like the soul, never returns, once it is gone —Publius Syrus
8. Doubt . . . secret and gnawing like a worm —Joseph Conrad

9. Doubts seemed to steam like wet flies inside his own head —Julia O'Faolain

10. Head . . . awhirl with doubts like a sky full of starlings —George Garrett

11. He was like a suspicion-caked old prospector —Ellery Queen

12. It [the thought that something was not right] was on the edge of her mind like a speck at the corner of your eye or fluff in your nostril —Julia O'Faolain

13. Lean on . . . like a man on crutches —Ross Macdonald

14. Mistrust swells like a prune —Marge Piercy

15. No more to be trusted (with news) than a cat with a saucer of milk —Christopher Isherwood

16. Suspicion amongst thoughts are like bats amongst birds, they ever fly by twilight —Francis Bacon

17. Suspicion developed like a muscle —F. Scott Fitzgerald

18. Suspicious . . . as a rat near strange bread —Patrick Kavanagh

19. Suspicious as a wild cat —Frank Swinnerton

20. Trust as I'd trust a rattlesnake —Anon

21. A trust, fierce and passionate, burning in her like a prayer —F. Scott Fitzgerald

22. Trust flourishes like a potato plant, mostly underground —Marge Piercy

23. As trusting to the future as a blind sky-diver —Richard Ford

24. Trust is like an egg and it's not like an egg. If you want to break an egg you have to do it from the outside. The only way to break up a trust is from the inside —O. Henry

25. Trustworthy as advice given by a cat to a mouse —Anon
    A simile with clear links to an Arabic proverb: "He gives advice such as a cat gives to a mouse."

26. Wearing doubt like a raincoat —Carlos Baker

TRUTH

See Also: CANDOR, HONESTY

1. All the durable truths that have come into the world within historic times have been opposed as bitterly as if they were so many waves of smallpox —H. L. Mencken

2. As with the pursuit of happiness, the pursuit of truth is itself gratifying whereas the consummation often turns out to be elusive —Richard Hofstadter

3. Honest as the skin between his brows —William Shakespeare

4. Plain truths, like plain dishes, are commended by everybody, and everybody leaves them whole —Walter Savage Landor

5. Pure truth, like pure gold, has been found unfit for circulation, because men have discovered that it is far more convenient to adulterate the truth than to refine themselves —Charles Caleb Colton

6. Random truths are all I find stuck like burrs about my mind —Phyllis McGinley

7. Rich honesty dwells like a miser . . . in a poor house; as your pearl in your foul oyster —William Shakespeare

8. Speaking the truth is like writing well, and only comes with practice — John Ruskin
    This has been modernized from "The truth is like writing"

9. Truth . . . drag it out and beat it like a carpet —Hortense Calisher

10. Truth is a cow which will yield such people no more milk, and so they are gone to milk the bull —Samuel Johnson

11. Truth is as difficult to lay hold on as air —Walter Savage Landor
    See Also: ELUSIVENESS

12. Truth is as old as God —Emily Dickinson

13. The truth is cold, as a giant's knee will seem cold —John Ashbery

14. Truth is impossible to be soiled by any outward touch as the sunbeam —John Milton

15. Truth . . . is not a thing to be thrown about loosely, like small change; it is something to be cherished and hoarded and disbursed only when absolutely necessary —H. L. Mencken

16. The truth is tough. It will not break, like a bubble, at a touch . . . you may kick it about all day, like a football, and it will be round and full at evening —Oliver Wendell Holmes, Sr.

17. The truth kept wandering in and out of her mind like a lost child, never pausing long enough to be identified —Margaret Millar

18. Truth, like a bird, is ever poised for flight at man's approach —Jean Brown

19. Truth, like a gentle shower, soaks through the ears and moistens the intellect —Anon

20. Truth, like a point or line, requires an acuteness and intention to its discovery —Joseph Glanville

21. Truth, like a suit of armor, stubbornly resists all attempts to penetrate it —Robert Traver
    In his novel, *People Versus Kirk,* Traver continues the simile with " . . . while the lie, under probing, almost invariably reveals some chinks and cracks."

22. Truth is like a torch, the more it is shook, the more it shines —Sir William Hamilton

Modernized from "The more 'tis shook, it shines."

23. Truth, like gold, is not less so for being newly brought out of the mine —John Locke

24. Truth, like light, blinds —Albert Camus
    Camus prefaces his simile from *The Fall* as follows: "Sometimes it is easier to see clearly into the liar than into the man who tells the truth."

25. Truth, like the juice of the poppy, in small quantities, calms men; in larger, heats and irritates them, and is attended by fatal consequences in its excess —Walter Savage Landor

26. Truth's like a fire, and will burn through and be seen —Maxwell Anderson

27. A truth's prosperity is like a jest's; it lies in the ear of him that hears it —Samuel Butler

28. The way of truth is like a great highway. It is not hard to find —Mencius

TURNING AND TWISTING

1. Circling like polishing rags —Diane Ackerman

2. (His brain) spinning around and around like a ship's propeller —Graham Masterton

3. Spinning like a wind vane —William Faulkner

4. Spun like someone caught in a revolving door —William McIlvanney

5. (My whole house) spun around me like a crazy carnival ride —George Garrett

6. Swerving like a bird in mid-air —Lawrence Durrell

7. Swirling about like boiling milk —H. G. Wells

8. Sway like an elephant's trunk —Anon

9. (My senses) swivel like guns in their fixed sockets —Margaret Atwood

10. (We caught him red-handed and he) turned as easily as a trout in the pan —Bryan Forbes

11. Turned as a bucket turns in a well —Dante Gabriel Rossetti

12. Turning . . . like a chicken on a spit —Enid Bagnold

13. Turning like a ghost across the road —Eudora Welty

14. Turning like a hand in water —Philip Levine

15. Turns and turns like a dog making a place to lie down —Maxine Kumin

16. Twisted like a caterpillar —Cornell Woolrich

17. Twisted like a desperate fish —Peter S. Beagle

18. (Ryan's mouth) twisted, like a key in a lock —Julia O'Faolain

19. Twisting his whole body as if his bones were made of rubber — Alexander Solzhenitsyn

20. Went around and around like the policeman and Charlie Chaplin, both intending to fall down —Eudora Welty

21. Wheeled like an ambushed cat —Nelson Algren

22. Whipped round like a steel spring —John Fowles

23. Whisking about like a swallow into its nest —O. Henry

24. (She was always) whisking about like a clean starched napkin —H. E. Bates

25. Wriggle . . . like a snake —Mary Stewart

26. Writhing like a baited worm —Countee Cullen

TYRANNY
See: POWER

UMBRELLAS
See: OBJECTS, MISCELLANEOUS

UNATTRACTIVENESS
See Also: UNDESIRABILITY

1. Disgusting, like moving cheese, like hills of ants or of flies —Ralph Waldo Emerson

2. (Furniture) emanating bad taste like a cold draft —Milan Kundera

3. Lurid as a porcelain souvenier —Derek Walcott

4. (It sounded) obscene, like a rarely glimpsed body part —Lorrie Moore

5. Plain as cement sidewalks. Plain as bread crust —Jean Thompson

6. Ugly and fat as a maggot —Miles Gibson

7. Ugly and indesctructible as the aluminum beer can —Stephen Minot
See Also: PERMANENCE

8. Ugly as a hairless monkey —Margaret Mitchell

9. Ugly as a hatful of assholes —Geoffrey Wolff

10. Ugly as a mud fence —American colloquialism, attributed to Southeast
Southerners often elaborated on this as follows: "Ugly as a mud fence daubed with tadpoles."

11. (He was like most new babies as) ugly as an artichoke —Anne Sexton

12. Ugly as sin —Maria Edgeworth

13. Ugly . . . like a great black spider —Rosamund Pilcher

14. Unappealing as a meringue with hardly any crust —Anon

15. As erotically stimulating as a mouthful of sardines —Ira Wood

UNAWARENESS
See: BLINDNESS

UNCERTAINTY
See Also: FATE

1. Accidental as life —Lord Shaftesbury

2. I am rather like a mosquito in a nudist camp; I know what I ought to do but I don't know where to begin —Stephen Bayne
   Mr. Bayne's comment was made in 1986 upon assuming a newly created job.

3. Indecision is like the stepchild: if he doesn't wash his hands, he is called dirty; if he does, he is wasting the water —Madagascan proverb
   Modern day psychologists have adopted this as a neurosis and labeled it a "double bind."

4. Indecision sent me forward and back, as if I were propelled by a piston in my back —Joan Hess

5. Indecisive as a fellow who pulls back one leg as he moves forward with the other —Anon
   Probably inspired by this Arabic proverb: "He advances one leg and draws back the other."

6. Like children with a piece of ice . . . neither able to hold it nor willing to let it go —Plutarch

7. Not quite sure of herself, like a new kitten in a house where they don't care much about kittens —Raymond Chandler

8. An obscure doubt brushed her, like a dove that wavers to a perch and is gone again without lighting —Marjorie Kinnan Rawlings

9. (He'd become about as) predictable as a Chinese earthquake —Joseph Wambaugh

10. Predictable as a Tijuana dog race —Joseph Wambaugh

11. Swing [uncertainly] like a hammock in the breeze —Anon

12. Tentative as first taste of hot soup —Anon

13. Tentative as a schoolgirl —Richard Ford

14. Uncertain as the glory of an April day —William Shakespeare

15. Uncertain . . . like a golf ball hit by a new golfer, continually getting close to the hole-in-one, but only getting into it by a fluke —Anon

16. Uncertainty . . . as vertiginous as a lift descending down a bottomless shaft —Graham Masterton

17. Up in the air, like jugglers in a freeze-frame —John Updike

UNCOMFORTABLENESS
See: DISCOMFORT

UNCONSCIOUSNESS
See: NATURALNESS

UNDEMONSTRATIVENESS
See: COLDNESS

UNDERSTANDABILITY
See: CLARITY

UNDERSTANDING
See: KNOWLEDGE

UNDESIRABILITY

1. About as inviting as Lenin's tomb —Manuela Hoelterhoff, reporting on a large wall surrounding a new museum complex in Los Angeles, *Wall Street Journal,* December 15, 1986

2. About as pleasant as to have an umbrella jammed down your throat, and opened there, and pulled out open, so that the broken ribs lacerate your lungs, and beaten over the head with the handle —Don Marquis

3. About as thrilling as swimming lessons would be to a middle-aged goldfish —H. C. Witwer

4. As bad as marrying the devil's daughter and living with the old folks — G. L. Apperson

5. As bad as offering Satan a lost soul —Emily Brontë

6. As desirable as meeting a former lover during a honeymoon —Elyse Sommer

7. As much fun as a month in Gdansk —Joseph Wambaugh

8. (John Singer Sargent liked to make painting portraits sound) attractive as catching toads for a living —Manuela Hoeltershoff, introducing review of John Singer Sargent show at Whitney Museum, *Wall Street Journal,* October 15, 1986

9. Come like ill weather, unsent for —Brian Melbancke

10. (She was . . .) desirable . . . like a whore on a street corner —Derek Lambert

11. Disagreeable . . . like a scent which raises fine hair on animals —John Updike

12. Gave him no pleasure . . . it was like being invited to stretch himself out to be amputated, without an anesthetic —Storm Jameson

13. (Haggling about military bases) has all the joys of arm-wrestling on a sinking raft —*New York Times* editorial, March 23, 1987

14. Have about as much pleasure ahead of us as a pig in a butcher shop — George Garrett

15. Jumped at the chance like a sardine leaps for the can —Anon

16. Liked . . . about as much as I liked snakes or trunk murders —T. Coraghessan Boyle

17. Like foul weather, you come unsent for, and troublesome when you come —H. G. Bohn's *Handbook of Proverbs*

18. To love as a cat loves mustard —John Ray's *Proverbs*

19. Needed [an unpleasant scene] like a cover girl needs acne —Loren D. Estleman

20. Position as enviable as that of a catcher on a javelin team —George V. Higgins, on Rolland Smith's interaction with Mariette Hartley on CBS-TV program, *Wall Street Journal,* January 19, 1987

21. To love as the devil loves holy water —John Ray's *Proverbs*

22. To love it as a dog loves a whip —John Ray's *Proverbs*

23. A trifle less welcome than something you would scrape off the bottom of your shoe —C. W. Grafton

24. An unpleasant guest is as welcome as salt to a sore eye —Danish proverb

25. Unsatisfying as a set compliment —Heywood Broun

26. Unwelcome as a mouse in your shoe —Elyse Sommer

27. Wanted (to play baseball) like he wanted a third nostril —Max Shulman

28. Welcome as a guest with sneakers at a Palm Beach party —Tom Brokaw

29. Welcome as a mugger —Anon

30. Welcome as a painful and chronic disease —Elyse Sommer

31. Welcome as a storm —Thomas Fuller

32. Welcome as a tree falling across your Volkswagon —"PM-TV Magazine"

33. Welcome as Satan —Alfred, Lord Tennyson

34. Welcome as snow at harvest time —John Ray's *Proverbs*

35. Welcome as the season's first snowstorm —Anon
    A skier or ski resort operator might look for this under the Desirability category.

36. (In the rarefied upper echelons of Japanese sumo wrestling, foreigners have been about as) welcome as Visigoths were at the gates of Rome — Clyde Haberman, about wrestler from Hawaii, *New York Times,* May 28, 1987

37. Welcome as water in a leaking ship —John Ray's *Proverbs*
    To tone down the image of disaster to common distress, there's another Ray proverb: "As welcome as water in one's shoes."

38. Welcomed . . . the way a cardiac case does chest pains —William McIlvanney

UNEMPLOYMENT
> See: WORK

UNEXPECTEDNESS
> See: SUDDENNESS, SURPRISE

UNFAIRNESS
> See: INTOLERANCE

UNFRIENDLINESS
> See: SOCIABILITY

UNGRACIOUSNESS
> See: MANNERS

UNHAPPINESS
> See: DEJECTION, DISCONTENT, GLOOM

UNHELPFULNESS
> See: USEFULNESS/USELESSNESS

UNIQUENESS
> See: ORIGINALITY

UNKINDNESS
> See: CRUELTY

UNLIKELIHOOD
> See: IMPOSSIBILITY

UNNATURALNESS
> See: NATURALNESS

UNPLEASANTNESS
> See: UNDESIRABILITY

UNPREDICTABILITY
> See: SURPRISES, UNCERTAINTY

UNPROFITABILITY
> See: ADVANTAGEOUSNESS

UNREALITY
　　See: REALNESS/UNREALNESS

UNRELIABILITY
　　See: RELIABILITY/UNRELIABILITY

UNRESPONSIVENESS
　　See: COLDNESS, REMOTENESS, RESERVE

UNSTEADINESS
　　See Also: MOVEMENT

　1. Flounder around like a fish on the beach —Anon
　　A commonly used variation: "Flounder around like a beached whale."

　2. Floundered like a waterlogged ship —James Hilton

　3. Floundered like insects in yogurt —George F. Will, about those involved in Watergate crimes

　4. Floundering like someone running in deep sand, blind without glasses, burdened with books —George Garrett

　5. Flounder like a compass that's lost its needle —Anon
　　A variation: "Flounder like a windup watch without a dial."

　6. (Was solidly built but) gave the impression of not being very stable, like a building with imperfect foundations —MacDonald Harris

　7. Reel like a leaf that's drawn to a water-wheel —Dante Gabriel Rossetti

　8. Stagger like a drunken man —*The Holy Bible/The Psalms*

　9. Staggers slightly . . . like a carnival clown —Hilary Masters

　10. Staggers to his feet like a battered middleweight coming out for the fifteenth round —T. Coraghessan Boyle

　11. Stumbled . . . like an old woman leaning on a cane that wasn't there —Ross Macdonald

　12. Stumbled like fat sheep —Stephen Crane

　13. Stumbling a little over his own feet like an adolescent not accustomed to his new growth —Margaret Millar

　14. Tumbling . . . like a moth blinded by sudden brightness —Jerzy Kosinski

　15. Unconstant as the wind; as wavering as the weathercock —William Walker

　16. Unstable as water —*The Holy Bible/Genesis*

　17. (She seemed volatile right now,) unstable, like a vial of nitroglycerin — Sue Grafton

18. Unsteady like a pole balanced on the tip of one's finger —Arthur Schopenhauer

19. Wavering as the wind —John Heywood's *Proverbs*
    Modernized from the Old English: "Waueryng as the wynde."

20. Wobbled like an overfed penguin —Len Deighton

21. (His new English) wobbles like a first bicycle —Diane Ackerman

UNTIDINESS
See: ORDER/DISORDER

UNTIMELINESS
See: TIMELINESS/UNTIMELINESS

UNTRUSTWORTHINESS
See: TRUST/MISTRUST

UNTRUTH
See: LIES/LIARS

UNWELCOMENESS
See: UNDESIRABILITY

UPRIGHTNESS
See: POSTURE, STRAIGHTNESS

UP-TO-DATENESS
See: TIMELINESS/UNTIMELINESS

URGENCY
See: IMPORTANCE/UNIMPORTANCE

USEFULNESS/USELESSNESS
See Also: FUTILITY, NECESSITY

1. As much use as a life preserver to a duck —Anon

2. Effective as a bullet —Edgar Saltus

3. Effective as an umbrella in a hurricane —Anon

4. Effective as bailing out a boat with a sieve —Anon

5. Effective as chicken soup. It can't hurt —Anon

6. Effective as dousing a fire with a dixie cup full of water —Anon

7. Effective as fixing a broken leg with a bandaid —Anon

8. Feel like an old clerk on a high stool —Wilfrid Sheed

9. Handy as a pocket in a shirt —Bartlett's Dictionary of Americanisms

10. Helpful as a bathing suit in a blizzard —Ed McBain

11. (The information was probably as) helpful as a wooden compass — William McIlvanney

12. Helpful as throwing a drowning man both ends of a rope —Arthur Baer

13. Ineffective as breaking into a bank vault and taking a bag of pennies — Anon

14. Ineffective like putting the steak on the fire and the skillet on top of the steak —Norman Mailer

15. Ineffective, like sending flies in pursuit of fly paper —Elliot Janeway, *Barron's,* January 20, 1986

16. (Lonely and) ineffectual as two left-handed gloves —Helen Rowland

17. Ineffectually as a firefly in Hell —Stephen Vincent Benét

18. It [Medicare's health-care coverage] is like walking around in a bulletproof vest with a hole over the heart —Senator John Heinz, *Wall Street Journal,* October 15, 1986

19. It's [everything valued by others] like so much fluff —Anton Chekhov

20. A lot of useless barging around, like a man with his sleeve in a thresher —Richard Ford

21. Making lists is like taking too many notes at school; you feel you've achieved something when you haven't —Dodie Smith

22. Pointless . . . like you'd give caviar to an elephant —William Faulkner

23. (Educating you would be about as) redundant as teaching a lion to like red meat —line from movie *Victor-Victoria,* spoken by Julie Andrews

24. Sending a teacher into a classroom with no cane is like sending a boxer into the ring with one hand tied behind his back —Philip Squire

25. Some men are like a clock on a roof . . . useful only to the neighbors —Austin O'Malley

26. Some people are like wheelbarrows, only useful when pushed, and very easily upset —Jack Hebert

27. Unhelpful . . . like someone running round with black-currant lozenges to the victims of an earthquake —Josephine Tey

28. Unnecessary as another designer label —Anon

29. Useful as a bale of hay in a garage —Anon

30. Useful as a bicycle without tires —Anon

31. Useful as a buttonhole without buttons —Anon

32. Useful as a comb to a bald man —Anon

33. Useful as a defective parachute —Anon

34. Useful as an annuity —Anon

35. Useful as an umbrella to a fish —Anon

36. Useful as a pocket with a big hole in it —Anon
37. Useful as a sixth finger —Anon
38. Useful as a Swiss army knife —Anon
39. Useful as a thermometer or a scale without markings —Anon
40. Useful as a third nostril —Peter Benchley
41. Useful as hayfever when the pollen count is high —Mike Fredman
42. Useful as information trying to convey the locality and intentions of a cloud —Joseph Conrad
43. Useful as teats on a boar hog —American colloquialism
44. Useful as the marketable skill mom told you to acquire —Anon
45. Useless as a bell that doesn't ring —Anon
46. Useless as putting a bandaid on a gunshot wound —Anon
47. Useless as a broken feather —Anon
48. Useless as a bump on a log —Anon
     A variation on this familiar simile from *The Last Good Kiss* by James Crumley: "Stood around like a knot on a log."
49. Useless as a car without gasoline —Anon
50. Useless as a glass eye at a keyhole —Louis Monta Bell
51. Useless . . . as a half-built bridge —William H. Hallhan
52. Useless as an expectant lover —Ellen Glasgow
53. Useless as a single glove —Anon
54. Useless as a torn sock —Marianne Hauser
55. Useless as a twisted arm —Desmond O'Grady
56. Useless as Ronald Reagan's right ear —Joseph Wambaugh
57. Useless . . . like buying an air conditioner for a building without electricity —Anon
58. Useless . . . like the cow that gives a good pail of milk, and then kicks it over —H. G. Bohn's *Handbook of Proverbs*

VAGUENESS

1. (The image) blurred . . . like something familiar seen beneath disturbed though clear water —William Faulkner
2. (The consonants) blur together like ink on a wet page —Sue Grafton
3. Clear as mud —Richard Harris Barham
    This typifies the quick, humorous similes that were most often imported by New Englanders to add color to American speech.
4. Obscure as a bureaucrat's memorandum —Anon
5. Obscure as modesty —Sidney Lanier
6. (Eye . . .) opaque as a muddy pool —F. Scott Fitzgerald

7.   Opaque as a milk-glass bowl —Linda West Eckhardt

VALOR
   See: COURAGE

VALUE
   See: IMPORTANCE/UNIMPORTANCE

VANITY
   See Also: PRIDE

1.   An aura of self-love clung to him like a cloak —Robert Traver
2.   Arrogance . . . was escaping from him like steam —Cornell Woolrich
3.   Arrogant as a hummingbird with a full feeder —A. E. Maxwell
4.   As careful about his looks as a young girl getting ready for her first dance —Carlos Fuentes
5.   Conceit grows as natural as hair on one's head; but it is longer in coming out —Bartlett's Dictionary of Americanisms
6.   Conceit like a high gloss varnish smeared over him —Rosa Guy
7.   Conceit that plays itself in an elevated nose . . . that is only playing at being conceited; like children play at being kings and queens and go strutting around with feathers and trains —Jerome K. Jerome
8.   The ego blows up like a big balloon —Delmore Schwartz
9.   Flaunt my knowledges, like a woman will flaunt her pretty body — Borden Deal
10. He was like a cock who thought the sun had risen to hear him crow — George Eliot
11. He [a man without vanity] would be a very admirable man, a man to be put under a glass case, and shown round as a specimen, a man to be stuck upon a pedestal, and copied like a school exercise —Jerome K. Jerome
       Jerome concluded his comparison as follows: "A man to be reverenced, but not a man to be loved, not a human brother whose hand we should care to grip."
12. (Ed Koch) is like the rooster who takes credit for the sunrise —Jack Newfield, *Village Voice,* October 7, 1986
13. Looks at herself in the mirror like she was the first woman in the world —George Garrett
14. A man is inseparable from his congenital vanities and stupidities, as a dog is inseparable from its fleas —H. L. Mencken
15. A man who shows me his wealth is like the beggar who shows me his poverty; they are both looking for alms . . . the rich for the alms of envy, the poor man for the alms of my pity —Ben Hecht

16. My vanity [after hurtful remark] like a newly-felled tree, lies prone and bleeding —Carolyn Kizer

17. Preening himself like a courting rooster —Robert Traver

18. Preening like a politician after a landslide victory —Elyse Sommer

19. Puffed himself up like a ship in full sail —Hans Christian Andersen

20. Self-love is a cup without any bottom; you might pour all the great lakes into it, and never fill it up —Oliver Wendell Holmes, Sr.

21. Sleek and smug as a full-bellied shark —T. Coraghessan Boyle

22. Strutting . . . like a pouter pigeon —Jerome K. Jerome
    The pigeon named for its propensity for puffing out its distensible crops provides a novel alternative of the more commonly used "Strutting like a peacock."

23. Vanity is as ill at ease under indifference as tenderness is under a love which it cannot return —George Eliot

24. Vanity, like murder, will out —Hannah Parkhouse Cowley

25. Vanity, like sexual impulse, gives rise to needless self-reproach — Charles Horton Cooley
    Cooley followed up on his simile with "Why be ashamed of anything so human? What, indeed should we be without it."

26. Vanity may be likened to the smooth-skinned and velvet-footed mouse, nibbling about forever in expectation of a crumb —William Gilmore Simms

VARIETY
See: DIVERSENESS

VEHICLES
See Also: ROAD SCENES

1. Beechcraft Twin [airplane] . . . its wings flapping hectically like a fat squawking goose unable to get itself aloft —Herbert Lieberman

2. Brakes squawk like Donald Duck —Joyce Cary

3. The bus rode on the highway, like a ship upon the sea, rising and falling on hills that were like waves —Nathan Asch

4. Buzz of traffic . . . like the hum of bees working a field of newly blossomed clover —James Crumley

5. Car accelerated silently like a lioness which has sighted the prey — Elizabeth Spencer

6. A car is just like a gun. In the wrong hands it is nothing less than an instrument of death —Charles Portis

7. Car . . . ran as if lubricated with peanut butter —Peter De Vries

8. Cars shot by like large bees —Cynthia Ozick

9. Cars . . . their taillights like cigarette embers —Daphne Merkin

10. The cloud of exhaust [from car] rose like a sail behind them —Alice Mc Dermott

11. The engines [of a Mercedes] ticking like wizard-made toy millipedes — Saul Bellow

12. The exhaust [of car] bloomed in the air like a bizarre, blue-white flower —William Dieter

13. Felt about cars the way Casanova felt about women —Mike Fredman

14. Guzzles gas the way computers gobble up bytes —Anon

15. Headlights [of cars on highway] flash by like a procession of candles — Stuart Dybek

16. Like a wasp rising from a rose, a helicopter chut-chut-chutted toward them —Will Weaver

17. The limousine slid to the curb and nestled there, sleek as a wet otter stretched out in the noonday sun —Paige Mitchell

18. The . . . limousine slid up to the curb, like a great, rolling onyx — Hortense Calisher

19. The motor [of car engine] sounded like a polishing drum with a dozen new agates turning inside —Will Weaver

20. Parked cars . . . stretched like a file of shiny beetles —Donald MacKenzie

21. Planes humming across the sky like bees —H. E. Bates

22. [A car] polished until light glanced off it like a knife —Jayne Anne Phillips

23. The power of the big tractor drew the plow through the damp earth like a potter's knife through wet clay —Will Weaver

24. A Rolls Royce glittering like a silver tureen —Saul Bellow

25. The rumbles of the big diesel engine were like ocean surf —Will Weaver

26. A ship . . . its masts jabbing the sky like upended toothpicks — Francis King

27. (The bus) spews out fumes black and substantial as octopus oil —W. P. Kinsella

28. Square black automobiles . . . like glossy black beetles —Robert Silverberg

29. Taillights [of car] gleaming like malevolent eyes —Stanley Elkin

30. Taillights red as smudged roses —Richard Ford

31. Tires humming like inflated snakes —John Hawkes

32. Tractors [at night] . . . like neon tetras drifting in the dark tank of the fields —Will Weaver

33. Train . . . wriggling like some long snake —Natsume Sōseki

34. The windshield wipers [of the car] kicked like a weary dance team —
Elizabeth Spencer

VEHICLES, OPERATION OF

1. Drive like a nursemaid with a pramful of kids —Calder Willingham

2. Drove as if he were handling a hearse —Lael Tucker Wertenbaker

3. Drove silently, like a silent wind —Elizabeth Spencer

4. (Pulled out into traffic, his) engine cooking like grease on a cheap
griddle —Loren D. Estleman

5. He [driver of car] took the curves like a bird —Erich Maria Remarque

6. Keeps that engine purrin' like a whore on a hundred-dollar date —John
Farris

7. Touchdown [of airplane] was as smooth as arriving at the ground floor
in a lift —Donald Seaman

VERBOSENESS
See: TALKATIVENES

VEXATION
See: ANGER, IRRITABLENESS

VIBRATION
See Also: TREMBLING

1. Body jerking like a fish —David Mamet, dialogue from "Hill Street
Blues" television show, broadcast January 13, 1987

2. (Light . . . came at him) throbbing like a drum —Mark Helprin

3. Jerking like a decked shark —Denis Johnson

4. A little ripple (went through her) like the commmotion set up in a
weeping willow by a puff of wind —O. Henry

5. Oscillate like a blancmange in an earthquake —John Wainwright

6. (Thoughts) rattle about . . . like dried seeds in a pod —Ellen Glasgow

7. Rattle about [a large apartment] like dried peas in a pod —Janet
Hobhouse

8. Rattled like a dicer's cup —Davis Grubb

9. (The King's heart) rattled like spook chains in a horror show —Tom
Robbins

10. Rattling like a crockery shop in an earthquake —Arthur Baer

11. [A cough] shook me like a coconut tree in a tornado —Dominique
Lapierre

12. Throbbing like a heart —Marguerite Yourcenar

731

13. Throb like the heart of a coffee drinker —O. Henry
14. Vibrating like a dog's tail —Norman Mailer
15. Vibrating . . . like a man with a high fever —Anon

VICE
See: EVIL

VICTORY
See: SUCCESS/FAILURE

VIGILANCE
See: ALERTNESS, WATCHFULNESS

VIGOR
See: ENTHUSIASM, STRENGTH

VIOLENCE
See Also: ADVANCING, BEHAVIOR

1. Battered to and fro as a rat is shaken by a dog —Rudyard Kipling
2. Came after him like an antelope —William Diehl
3. Came at him like a kamikaze —T. Coraghessan Boyle
4. Cored him like an apple —John Yount
5. Dealt out blows with the precision of a punch press —Natascha Wodin
6. Drove his fist straight in like a saber thrust —Joseph Wambaugh
7. Grabbed hold of me, as a cat grabs a mouse —George Garrett
8. Hit it [a man's chin] as if I was driving the last spike on the first transcontinental railroad —Raymond Chandler
9. Hit like a tank —Ken Stabler and Berry Stainback
10. Howling and clawing at each other like wild beasts in heat —Hunter S. Thompson
11. I can flatten him out like a crépe in a frying-pan —Henry Van Dyke
12. I could slice you down like cold meat before you could whisper Mercy —Davis Grubb
    In Grubb's novel, *The Golden Sickle,* the man making this threat is wielding a knife.
13. I'll crush his ribs in like a rotten hazelnut —Emily Brontë
14. I'm gonna pop your eyes like busted eggs —William Kennedy
15. Knocked to the ground like a winged partridge —T. Coraghessan Boyle
16. Lunged [into the midst of group of people] like a whirlwind on a summer's day —Flannery O'Connor

17. [Mobster Sam Giancana, who) ordered killings as easily as he ordered linguini —Kitty Kelley

18. The propensity for violence exists like a layer of buried molten magma underlying all human topography —Robert Ardrey

19. Put me in an arm lock as easily as he might twist a soft pretzel —James Crumley

20. Showered her blows . . . with the force and rapidity of a drummer beating his drum —Guy De Maupassant

21. Slapped her like a volleyball —Rochelle Ratner

22. Terorism is a natural by-product of modern life. Like air pollution, family breakdown, excessively casual sexual promiscuity and exaltation of greed —Russell Baker, *New York Times,* 1986

23. Threw themselves at him like dogs at a bear —Mikhail Bulgakov

24. Violence and wrong are as a dream which rolls from steadfast truth, an unreturning stream —Percy Bysshe Shelley

25. Violence (was an inescapable factor of the heart . . .) an ineradicable thing . . . like a bad seed —William March

26. Violence in a house is like a worm on vegetables —Hebrew proverb

27. Violence is as American as cherry pie —Eldridge Cleaver

28. The violence of my impulses [to harm another person] was still within me, like the sharp end of a splinter improperly removed —Scott Spencer

29. Violence weighed him down like a pack —Harris Downey

30. Violent and ruthless as a puppy —James Mills

31. Violent death is like a monster. The closer you get to it, the more damage you sustain —Sue Grafton

32. Violent death leaves an aura, like an energy field that repels the observer —Sue Grafton

33. Was on him like a falling tree —Jerry Bumpus

34. A wound like a burst fruit —Jean Stafford

VIRTUE

See Also: ACCOMPLISHMENT, MORALITY, PURITY

1. Admirable as the rabbit that lets a tortoise win the race —Mike Sommer

2. Chaste as ice —William Shakespeare

3. Chastity consists, like an onion, of a series of coats —Nathaniel Hawthorne

4. Good as a mother —Vicki Baum

5. Hanging on to his virtue like a thief to his loot —Paige Mitchell

6. Like gentle streams beneath our feet innocence and virtue meet — William Blake
   See Also: INNOCENCE

7. Many individuals have, like uncut diamonds, shining qualities beneath a rough exterior —Juvenal

8. Piety is like garlic. A little goes a long way —Rita Mae Brown

9. Rare virtues are like rare plants or animals, things that have not been able to hold their own in the world —Samuel Butler
   Butler's comparison continues as follows: "A virtue to be serviceable must, like gold, be alloyed with some commoner but more durable metal."

10. Rich in virtue, like an infant —Lao Tzu

11. True merit, like a river, the deeper it is, the less noise it makes —Lord Halifax

12. Virginal as Eve before she knew Adam —Anon

13. Virgins are bores . . . like people with overpriced houses —Thomas McGuane

14. Virtue and learning, like gold, have their intrinsic value; but if they are not polished, they certainly lose a great deal of their luster; and even polished brass will pass upon more people than rough gold —Lord Chesterfield
    See Also: EDUCATION

15. Virtue is a kind of health, beauty and good habit of the soul —Plato

16. A virtue is like a city set upon a hill, it cannot be hid —Robert Hichens

17. Virtue is like an enemy avoided —Dante Alighieri

18. Virtue is like a polar star, which keeps its place, and all stars turn towards it —Confucius

19. Virtue is like a rich stone, best plain set —Francis Bacon

20. Virtue is like health: the harmony of the whole man —Thomas Carlyle

21. Virtue is like precious odors—most fragrant when they are incensed or crushed —Francis Bacon

22. Virtue lies like the gold in quartz; there is not very much of it and much pain has to be spent on the extracting of it —Jerome K. Jerome

23. Virtue, like a strong and hardy plant, takes root in any place, if she finds there a generous nature and a spirit that shuns no labor — Plutarch

24. Virtues, like essences, lose their fragrance when exposed —William Shenstone

25. Virtuous as convict in the death house —H. L. Mencken

VISIBILITY

See Also: CLARITY, OBVIOUSNESS, PROTRUSION

1. Conspicuous, like giraffes —Karl Shapiro

2. (A trail as) faint as a whisp —Edward Hoagland

3. (The writing was as) faint as sparrow tracks in sand —Will Weaver

4. Hidden from view, like undeveloped negatives —Anon

5. Hide . . . as a boat finds a cove until the storm passes —Mary Lee Settle

6. Hiding like tumors —Charles Johnson

7. Imperceptible as a spring breeze —Susan Richards Shreve

8. Imperceptible as grief —Emily Dickinson
   This is both the title and the first line of a poem.

9. Invisible as a city sparrow —Marge Piercy

10. Invisible as the web in a spider's belly —Marge Piercy

11. Invisible, like a bad odor —Stephen Longstreet

12. Just out of sight like stars in the noon sky —John Farris

13. Lurking beneath the surface like a nest of snakes —Anon article on drugs as the X factor in National Football League violence, *New York Times,* November 30, 1986

14. Noticeable as a fart in a hail storm —American colloquialism

15. Prominent as a fried egg stain on the front of a full dress vest —Arthur Baer

16. Protrude like hairs from an old man's nose —F. D. Reeve

17. (The scene in front of him remained) unclear, like a painting so encrusted with dirt and varnish its depths refuse the investigating eye —Clive Barker

18. Unnoticeable as a pore —Karl Shapiro

19. Unobtrusive as a thief —Paul Theroux

20. Unseen like our shadows —Margaret Atwood

21. Visible . . . like a goldfish in a bowl —Cornell Woolrich

VIVIDNESS

See: BRIGHTNESS

VOCATION

See: PROFESSIONS

VOICE(S)

See Also: CRYING; GROANS AND WHISPERS; SINGING; VOICE, EFFECT OF; VOICE, HARSH; VOICE, MONOTONOUS; VOICE, MUSIC-RELATED; VOICE, SOFT

1. (Voice . . .) artificial, like paper flowers or the cheapest kind of greasepaint —Heinrich Böll
   See Also: REALNESS/UNREALNESS

2. Bitterness had come through into her voice, buzzing like a wasp —Ross Macdonald

3. A cold voice . . . like a big freezer that whines slowly and precisely —Ariel Dorfman

4. A deep quiet voice like wrapped thunder —Loren D. Estleman

5. A disagreeable voice like the grating of broken glass —Aharon Megged

6. A frank, vaguely rural voice more or less like a used car salesman —Richard Ford

7. A frosty sparkle in his voice that presupposed opposition—like the feint of a boxer getting ready —Willa Cather

8. A grand rolling voice, like the sound of an underground train in the distance —Frank Swinnerton

9. Her tone clicked like pennies —Ross Macdonald

10. Her voice bristled like a black cat's fur —John Updike

11. Her voice burst from her like a bubble of blood from her mouth —Marge Piercy

12. Her voice was like the mirrored wind chimes in a lost lake house of long ago —John MacDonald

13. Her voice was rich and dark like good brandy, yet somehow lively too, like the very best champagne —George Garrett

14. High chirpy voice like a cricket —Marge Piercy

15. His voice was somehow familiar, yet . . . it had a quality that made it unrecognizable, like one's own dress worn by someone else —L. P. Hartley

16. (Skinner was ready to melt with sweetness;) his tone sounded like Romeo in the balcony scene —Rex Stout

17. His voice rumbled like a bumblebee in a dry gourd —Nelson Algren

18. In old age her voice had become thin as a bird's —Pauline Smith

19. His voice tremored defiantly, like that of a man presenting doubtful credentials at a bank —Hortense Calisher

20. It [her voice] sprang from her mouth like water from a spring —Guy De Maupassant

21. Loud enthusiastic voices like the Amens said in country churches —Flannery O'Connor

22. A loud, hurrying voice, like the bell of a steamboat —Henry James
23. Muffled voices sobbed like foghorns —Kay Boyle
24. Official-sounding, something like a radio announcer —Bobbie Ann Mason
25. Raised his voice like an auctioneer's —Truman Capote
26. Talked like she had a Jew's harp struck in her throat —Will Weaver
27. A terrible edge to her voice like a line of force holding back a flood —R. Wright Campbell
28. Urgent tone, like a buzzer —Daphne Merkin
29. Voice . . . like a ship lost at sea —Mike Fredman
30. Voice . . . whining and self-pitying, like some teenage-tragedy song — Bobbie Ann Mason
31. Voice and lecturing style . . . like a chilled aperitif: enticing you to the main course —Robert Goddard
32. Voice as confidential as that of a family doctor —Donald MacKenzie
33. Voice as freshly perked as morning coffee —Patricia Leigh Brown, *New York Times,* June 12, 1986
34. Voice as intimate as the rustle of sheets —Dorothy Parker
35. Voice as lonely as the stars —Justin Scott
36. A voice as warm and tender as a wound —Julian Symons
37. Voice . . . blunt as a blow —Ben Ames Williams
38. Voice . . . both jarring and vulnerable: like a bloodshot eye —Tom Robbins
39. Voice burst up and broke like boiling water —Cynthia Ozick
40. Voice clear as a bell, yet slithery with innuendo, it leaped like a deer, slipped like a snake —Norman Mailer
41. Voice . . . clear-pitched like an actor's —Christopher Isherwood
42. Voice . . . clenched like a fist —Borden Deal
43. Voice . . . controlled, chilly, beautiful, like a hillside spring on an August afternoon —F. van Wyck Mason
44. Voice . . . flavored with a stout sweetness as though her words were sopped in rich, old wine —Jean Stafford
45. Voice . . . high and clear as running water over a settled stream bed —Sherley Anne Williams
46. Voice . . . jaggedly precise . . . as if every word emitted a quick white thread of great purity, like hard silk, which she was then obliged to bite clearly off —Cynthia Ozick
47. A voice light and soaring, like a lark's —Joseph Conrad
48. A voice like a bird —Marge Piercy

49. Voice . . . like a dull whip —Ayn Rand
50. Voice like a gurgling water pipe —Hugh Walpole
51. Voice like an iron bell —Peter Meinke
52. Voice like a parrot's scream —Robert Campbell
53. Voice . . . like a wind chime rattling —Louise Erdrich
54. A voice like blowing down an empty straw —Helen Hudson
55. Voice like butter when he wanted something from you and poison if you got in the way (of story character's 15% commission) —Victor Canning
56. Voice . . . like gravel spread with honey —Jay McInerney
57. Voice like ice —Raymond Chandler
58. Voice . . . like saw grass when the edges duel in the wind blowing over swampland —Lael Tucker Wertenbaker
59. (Ask weakly. His) voice like that of a child being squeezed in wrestling and asking for mercy —John Updike
60. Voice . . . like that of a helpless orphan —Ignazio Silone
61. Voice . . . like the tolling of a funeral bell —Paule Marshall
62. A voice like the stuff they use to line summer clouds with —Raymond Chandler
63. Voice . . . like the uncanny, unhuman gibber of new wine fermenting in a vat —W. Somerset Maugham
64. Voice . . . like thin ice breaking —James Thurber
65. Voice . . . opulent and vast like an actor's —Arthur A. Cohen
66. A voice queerly pitched, like a parrot's —Mary McCarthy
67. A voice rich as chocolate —David Tuller, *New York Times,* August 24, 1986
68. Voice roaring like the inside of a shell —Susan Neville
69. Voice . . . rough-smooth, like velvet dragged over fine sandpaper — Loren D. Estleman
70. (Our dried) voices (when we whisper together) are quiet and meaningless as wind in dry grass —T. S. Eliot
71. Voices [of ball field vendors] like crows crowing —W. P. Kinsella
72. Voices like gongs reverberate in the mind —C. S. Lewis
73. Voices [of children] . . . like the fluttering of wings —Anon
74. Voices like uniforms, tinny, meaningless . . . voices that they brandish like weapons —Jean Rhys
75. Voice . . . smooth as cheesecake, sweet and proper —Patricia Henley
76. Voice smooth as whipping cream —Harvey Swados
77. Voice . . . so low it sounded like a roll of thunder —Maya Angelou

78. (He had spoken with taut control, and his) voice sounding like the steady firmness of a cello muted in the minor mode —Arthur A. Cohen

79. Voices . . . went mad, like a chorus of frogs on a spring evening —D. H. Lawrence

80. A voice that boomed and echoed, like a man standing under a bridge, ankle-deep in rushing water —Paige Mitchell

81. Voice thin and distinct as a distant owl's call —John Updike

82. Voice . . . very sweetly piercing, like the sight of the moon in winter —Angela Carter

83. A warm voice . . . quivering like corn in a light summer wind —Aharon Megged

84. Worry remained suspended in her voice like a fly in amber —Jonathan Kellerman

VOICE, EFFECT OF

1. Accent which tortured me as much as a fiddle with a soft G string or a clarinet reed blown through bubbles of saliva —Harvey Swados

2. Her low voice soothed him like honey in whiskey —Rita Mae Brown

3. Her voice curled around Melinda like a damp tongue —Jessamyn West

4. His father's voice entered Ben's ear like an icepick —Pat Conroy

5. His loud clear voice fell on her ears soft as snow —Margaret Millar

6. Loud voice that scrapes over our nerves like a brush —Erich Maria Remarque

7. The shrill voices stung her eardrums like sharp pebbles —Paul Kuttner

8. The sound of her voice drove itself into his senses like a spike —Kaatje Hurlbut

9. Voice . . . irritating to the nerves like the pitiless clamour of the pneumatic drill —W. Somerset Maugham

10. Voices hitting the wall like stones —Maya Angelou

11. The voices were unnerving, like the dark come to life —Martin Cruz Smith

12. The voice (of a platoon leader) would buzz against his ear like a passing insect, undefined and rather annoying —Norman Mailer

VOICE, HARSH

See Also: HARSHNESS

1. A hard, crushing voice like stones smashing against each other —Aharon Megged

2. Her voice . . . creaked like the hinges of a rusty iron gate —Stefan Zweig

3. Her voice flew around like pots and pans —Leonard Michaels

4. Her voice sounded as brittle and sharp as a broken sliver of glass — Graham Masterton

5. High, irritating voice, like a razor blade —Caryl Phillips

6. His voice was harsh, like a great whirring mill saw —T. Coraghessan Boyle

7. Hoarse bass voice like an echo in an empty house —Amos Oz

8. A hoarse voice . . . like something broken —Romain Gary

9. A retching voice like a tin shovel scooping water off a concrete barn floor —Leonard Casper

10. A roughness in her voice like a grasshopper's —Virginia Woolf

11. [Voice] sounded like two shards of pottery being rubbed together — Norman Mailer

12. Their voices slash like reeds —William Meredith

13. A thick, husky voice that sounded as if he'd swallowed too many years of fog —Margaret Millar

14. A voice as hard as the blade of a shovel —Raymond Chandler

15. Voice . . . brittle as the first ice of autumn —Michael Gilbert

16. Voice . . . brittle, like overdone candy cracking on a plate —Pat M. Esslinger-Carr

17. Voice cracking like a trunk lid unopened for years —Patricia Henley

18. Voice . . . croaky and tense and faintly honking, as if a metal tube were involved in its production —John Updike

19. Voice, cruel as a new knife —George Garrett

20. Voice . . . deep, like crusted port wine —Donald Seaman

21. Voice flat and hard as a stove lid —James Crumley

22. Voice . . . fringed and sharp like the edge of a saw —Carson McCullers

23. Voice . . . hard as a nail on glass —William Beechcroft

24. Voice harsh and light as the scratching of dry leaves over the hard ground —Edna St. Vincent Millay

25. Voice harsh like tin and without heat like tin —William Faulkner

26. Voice . . . hoarse as a rooster —John Farris

27. Voice like a chair scraping across a tiled floor —Roderic Jeffries

28. Voice like a fingernail scraping down a dry blackboard —Reynolds Price
    Modern usage favors 'chalkboard.'

29. Voice . . . like a foghorn in foul weather —George Garrett

30. A voice like a howitzer —Thomas Carlyle about his publisher Frederic Henry Hedge

31. Voice . . . like a pointer moving sharply on a map or blackboard — Mary McCarthy
    McCarthy's *Charmed Life* was written in the forties. As indicated in entry #28, the currently preferred word for 'blackboard' is 'chalkboard.'

32. Voice, like a rusty hinge —Margaret Mitchell

33. Voice like a slate-pencil squeak —Paul J. Wellman

34. Voice like a spoon scraping a cooking pot —Annette Sanford

35. Voice like a tight squeak —Anon, about Marilyn Monroe by Columbia Pictures when they fired her in 1948

36. Voice, like barbed wire —Helen Hudson

37. A voice like cracking glaciers —Elinor Wylie

38. A voice like frosted trees in the wind —Rolaine Hochstein

39. A voice like hot ashes —James Agee

40. Voice . . . like sand —T. Coraghessan Boyle

41. Voice like scruffed gravel —Hortense Calisher

42. Voice like the cracked shriek of a desert wind —Phyllis Bottome

43. Voice . . . reedy like a tall-legged, tall-necked bird —Carolyn Chute

44. Voice . . . scratchily metallic as though it were being raked across miles of rusted roofing tin —Sharon Sheehe Stark

45. Voice . . . sharp as a snowflake on a sunburned nose —Rex Reed, about Tennessee Williams

46. Voice . . . sharp as porcupine quills —John Updike

47. Voice . . . sharp, splintering, like dry kindling split by an ax. Voice like pebbles in a bucket —Carlos Baker

48. Voice so ruined it sounded like a wood rasp —John Yount

49. Voice sounded like a crow with a cold —Harold Adams

50. Voice . . . sounds as if her throat is swollen shut —John Updike

51. Voices shrill as children's whistles —Marge Piercy

52. Voice that sounded like tires on a wet road —Richard Maynard

53. Voice . . . with a hardness in it like struck steel —John Yount

54. Voice . . . with an alluring crack in it, like some magisterial old woman who has smoked all her life —Lynne Sharon Schwartz

VOICE, MONOTONOUS

1. Drone on like a dull wind at night —James Stern

2. Voices grind on, like machines boring their way through tunnels —
    John Updike

3. Low monotonous voice like an absent-minded child haltingly reciting a
    lesson —Edith Wharton

4. No more inflection than a traffic light —John Updike

5. A noncommitable noplace voice like a computer salesman, or somebody
    taking a poll, or an anchorman on TV —Lee Smith

6. Voice . . . low and monotonous, like a voice that had never expressed
    any human passions —Henry James

7. Voices, fixed like leeches to their solitary subject —Jean Stafford

8. The voice went on, like the steady pressure of a surgeon's hand on a
    shrieking nerve —Edith Wharton

VOICE, MUSIC RELATED

1. Chimed in . . . like a cracked bell —Angela Carter

2. Deep voice like a jovial bassoon —Willa Cather

3. His voice resonated like the bass in a barbershop quartet —Peter
    Meinke

4. Scratches in her soft voice like an old phonograph record —Wilfrid
    Sheed

5. Voice . . . with a monotonous beat of syllables, like the rhythm of a
    wide and shallow drum pounding in the heart of a jungle night —
    Wilbur Daniel Steele

6. Voice . . . clear and brassy, like a bugle —O. Henry

7. Voice . . . deep as a gong —Rosamund Pilcher

8. Voice . . . delicate and pleasant, like a reed pipe —Yuri Kazkov

9. A voice like a bassoon —Gerald Kersh

10. Voice like a cello solo —O. Henry

11. Voice like a church bell —George MacDonald Fraser

12. Voice like an aging church-choir soprano —Z. Vance Wilson

13. A voice like an old-fashioned wind instrument —Henry James

14. Voice like a sexual cello —Angela Carter

15. (Lift up thine) voice like a trumpet —*The Holy Bible/Isaiah*

16. Voice like a tuba —Charles Johnson

17. Voice . . . like clarinets all ebony and silver —George Garrett

18. Voice like quiet music —Carlos Baker

19. Voice . . . like someone relentlessly playing the kazoo during one of
    the more somber passages of a war requiem —Douglas Adams

20. Voice like the "D" string in a cello —Henry Van Dyke

21. Voice like the deepest woodwind —George Garrett

22. Voice . . . off-key, like a neglected piano —Paige Mitchell

23. Voice rang like a great silver bell —O. Henry

24. Voice roared like an organ pipe —Joyce Cary

25. Voices like French horns —Margaret Millar

26. Voice soft, like the voice of a violin —Isak Dinesen

27. Voice sounds like an accordion played down at the end of a dark tunnel —Charles Baxter

28. Voice . . . thin as a flute —Ross Macdonald

29. Voice . . . vibrant as the tones of a crystal bell —Théophile Gautier

30. Voice . . . refined and finicky, like a tenor's in a cathedral choir — Frank Tuohy

31. What a little piccolo voice she had, like a living character from a Walt Disney Cartoon —Tama Janowitz

VOICE, SOFT

1. A gentle, circling voice, as a warm hand is gentle circling the wrist — Kaatje Hurlbut

2. Her voice is a caress which strokes you like fingers —Jules Lemaître
   Lemaître, a critic, was describing actress Sarah Bernhardt's voice.

3. His voice died in a frail wistful sigh, like wind through a shutter — William Styron

4. That beautiful voice which made everything she said sound like a caress —Virginia Woolf

5. Voice . . . like a page of music —Pat Conroy

6. Voice like dark brown velvet —Josephine Tey

7. Voice like down feathers —William Diehl

8. Voice . . . like liquid —Mark Helprin

9. Voice . . . like melting honey —Jimmy Sangster

10. Voice like thick soup —Edith Wharton

11. Voices as soft and murmurous as wings —George Garrett

12. Voice soft and cool as a prison yard —Joseph Wambaugh

13. Voice soft and rich as that of a counselling angel —Henry James, letter to Thomas Sergeant Perry, November 1, 1863

14. Voice soft as maple syrup running into a glass container —F. Scott Fitzgerald

15. Voice . . . soothing as running water —Dorothy Parker

16. When we spoke, it was softly, like TV cowboys expecting an ambush —
     Deborah Eisenberg

VOICE, WEAK

1. Forced little voice, wavering like a puff of smoke —Ivan Turgenev

2. Her voice came soft and faint, as though another person had said the
    words first and she was merely passing them on —Harvey Swados

3. Her voice was small, as if she had to squeeze it up from the depths —
    Laura Furman

4. Little voice, that wavered like a thread of smoke —Ivan Turgenev

5. Voice as faint as the buzzing of a bee's wings —Kenzaburo Oë

6. Voice . . . faded, thin away. Like a river diminishing to a stream and
    then to a trickle —Maya Angelou

7. Voice no bigger than a starling's —R. Wright Campbell

8. Voice . . . thin as a sheet of Zig Zag —Arnold Sawislak

9. His voice [Tennessee Williams,] wavers unsteadily like old gray cigar
    smoke in a room with no ventilation, rising to a mad cackle like a
    wounded macaw, settling finally in a cross somewhere between Tallulah
    Bankhead and Everett Dirksen —Rex Reed

VOTERS
See: POLITICS

VULGARITY
See: TASTE

VULNERABILITY
See: SENSITIVENESS

WALKING
See Also: AWKWARDNESS, CAUTION, MOVEMENT, RUNNING

1. As fond of long walks as hairdressers are of fishing —Colette
    See Also: PLEASURE

2. As she walked she lifted her knees high, her feet far out in front of her,
    like a drum majorette on parade —Nancy Huddleston Packer

3. A curiously modest gait, like a preoccupied steer —Cynthia Ozick

4. A heavy man who walked as though he was still a lean one —Pat
    Conroy
    See Also: FATNESS

5. His feet strike at the trembling earth like a bailiff pounding a door with
    an iron bar —Angela Carter

6. His stride was a sort of ambulatory Rorschach test. One could project anything one fancied into it —James Morrow

7. His stride was light and long, like that of a man on the moon —Mark Helprin

8. Light rapid steps . . . like the hops of a bird —Paul Horgan

9. The men walked like scissors; the women trod like cats —Katherine Mansfield

10. My steps became extravagantly buoyant, like those of a high-wire artist walking on a hidden trampoline —Robert Traver

11. Paced [from room to room] . . . like a marathon runner cooling down —Gerald A. Kersh

12. Paced the room like proctors at a college board examination —Scott Spencer

13. Picked his way as if he were walking on an iceberg —Peggy Bennett

14. A shambling gait like a trained bear —William Faulkner

15. Stalked over . . . like a traffic cop —James Thurber

16. Step as light as summer air —John Greenleaf Whittier
    A popular variation: "Trod as lightly as if he were walking on air."

17. Stiffly, like a man walking the trunk of a tree that bridges a chasm, he began to walk —Anon

18. Strut like a crow in a gutter —John Ray's *Proverbs*

19. Strut like a fighting cock —George Garrett

20. Struts like a bandit —Diane Ackerman

21. Strutting . . . like an Olympic shot putter —T. Coraghessan Boyle

22. (I still have) a trotting bounce to my walk, like a middle-aged coyote who lopes along avoiding the cougars and hedgehogs, though still feeling quite capable of snapping up rabbits and fawns —Edward Hoagland

23. Unsteady but purposeful walk, as if she were on a wheel that misguided her —Eudora Welty

24. Up and down he went, like a sailor with a limp —Wright Morris

25. Walked as a man might show off a garden, stopping here and there to pluck a flower —Lawrence Durrell

26. Walked as if a puppet master dangled her from a set of strings —Jay Parini

27. Walked as if he were completely alone, like an abdicated king —Beryl Markham

28. Walked high on his feet, like his shoes were hurting him —Donald McCaig

29. Walked like a man with a pain in his gut —William H. Hallhan
30. Walked like two snakes —Maeve Brennan
31. Walked neither fast nor slow, like a man going to work at a job he didn't enjoy —Harold Adams
32. Walked sedately, as though he were being watched —Helen Hudson
33. Walked very quickly, moving his arms as he walked like a tall thin bird flapping its wings —Jean Rhys
34. Walk . . . like an invalid just liberated from the sedentary months of his sickbed —Frederick Exley
35. Walking sedately back and forth, like a plump abbot who has just found exquisite confirmation of his long-cherished view of paradise —Robert Traver
36. Walks like a stately yacht listing disconcertingly to starboard —Frank Rich, about Robert Mitchum's performance in television mini-series, *New York Times,* 1986
37. Walk slowly, like one accustomed to be alone —Karl Shapiro
38. Walk together, like prisoners out for exercise —W. D. Snodgrass
39. Wandering around like a tit in a trance —Carolyn Slaughter
40. When he walks, he moves like an engine —William Shakespeare
41. With those long strides he looks like an antelope when he runs —Gary Thorn

WAR

See Also: ARMY

1. The art of war is like the art of the courtesan; indeed, they might be called sisters, since both are the slaves of desperation —Pietro Aretino
2. The beginning of war is like the first days of peace: neither the world nor our hearts know they are there —Jane Wagner
3. Being a soldier [in war time] was like being on a team in a sport that drew no crowds, except for the players' own parents and friends —Dan Wakefield
4. Great warriors, like great earthquakes, are principally remembered for the mischief they have done —Christian Nestell Bovee
5. Marrying in wartime is like sowing among thorns —Ignazio Silone
   See Also: MARRIAGE
6. Success in war, like charity in religion, covers a multitude of sins — Lord Napier
7. War is like an aging actress; more and more dangerous, and less and less photogenic —Robert Capa
8. War will disappear, like the dinosaur, when changes in world conditions have destroyed its survival value —Robert A. Millikan

9. Went to war with an air, as if they went to a ball —Stephen Vincent Benét

WARMTH
See: COMFORT, HEAT

WASTE
1. In delay we waste our lights in vain, like lamps by day —William Shakespeare
2. Wasted his wealth like spittle —Stephen Vincent Benét
3. Wasted more money in a day than a Boeing 747 full of proverbial welfare queens could have squandered in a century —Hodding Carter III, *Wall Street Journal,* March 30, 1986
   Carter's simile referred to new defense spending policies.
4. Wasteful as drunkenness at undue times —Robert Browning
5. Wasteful as regrets —Anon

WATCHFULNESS
See Also: ATTENTION, PROTECTIVENESS, SCRUTINY
1. Followed [by keeping eyes fixed on other person] . . . like someone studying a historical figure —Lawrence Durrell
2. Had a way of looking around . . . as if hidden cameras were photographing her —Ann Beattie
3. He watched her as a cat does a mouse —James Howell
   Of all the comparisons linked to watchfulness this is probably the most famous and enduring, dating back to 1624. In Robert Louis Stevenson's *Kidnapped* it appears as "We sat at table like a cat and a mouse, each stealthily observing the other."
4. Hovering like an old bird over one egg —Eudora Welty
5. (Each evening I) peered surreptitiously through the kitchen curtains, like a spinster keeping tab on her neighbors —W. P. Kinsella
6. Vigilant as cat to steal cream —William Shakespeare
7. Watched as if from a cat's distance —Martin Cruz Smith
8. Watched him like musicians watching the conductor —Wilfrid Sheed
9. Watched . . . like a warden —Anon
   The warden comparison has gained considerable currency in the last decade or so. Two recent novels in which it appeared are *Disturbances in the Field,* by Lynne Sharon Schwartz: "Kept watch like a warden" and *Riders,* by Jilly Cooper: "Watching him like a warden."
10. Watched, like Indians at a corral —Etheridge Knight
11. Watched me like a fish hawk —James Crumley

12. Watched . . . tensely, like a spider lying in wait for the fly's last drop of blood —Heinrich Böll

13. (My mother) watches me for signs of bloom and decay, like a plant —Daphne Merkin

14. Watchful as a ferret —R. Wright Campbell

15. Watching me like a bloodhound after a convict —Shelby Hearon

16. Watching [someone's looks and moves] . . . with an attention as intense as if an ordeal involving my life depended on them —Joseph Sheridan Le Fanu

17. Watch (tensely) like a cat stationed near a bird feeder —Bobbie Ann Mason

18. Watch . . . like a dead white moon —Ross Macdonald

19. Watch . . . like a nursemaid —Nicholas Monsarrat

20. Watch like one who fears robbing —William Shakespeare

21. Watch like ravens on a tree branch —R. Wright Campbell

WATER
See: OCEAN/OCEANFRONT, PONDS AND STREAMS, SEASCAPES

WEAKNESS
See Also: HELPLESSNESS, INSULTS, PERSONAL TRAITS, SOFTNESS

1. Arms felt like spaghetti —Dan Wakefield

2. As much strength as a seaweed —Ann Beattie

3. (A poor weak rag of a man with a) backbone like a piece of string —Dorothy Canfield Fisher

4. Boneless as poured water —George Garrett

5. Diminished and flat, as after radical surgery —Sylvia Plath

6. (The great white sails of the ships were) drooping like weary wings —Mazo De La Roche

7. Feeble as a babe —Ted Hughes

8. Feel as if I'm strung together by threads that pop and snap —Rosellen Brown

9. Feel diluted, like watered-down stew —Susan Minot

10. Felt a faintness stunning her senses as though someone had cut open the arteries of her wrists and all the blood rushed out of her body —Anzia Yezierska

11. Felt as if my legs had turned to warm lead —Stephen King

12. Forceful as a wet noodle —Anon

13. Forceless as a child —Aeschylus

14. The program has been like an elderly turtle on its back: it twitches feebly every now and then, but gets nowhere —Jack D. Kirwan, *Wall Street Journal,* March 19, 1987
     The turtle comparison referred to the tragedy-weakened Challenger space program.

15. Knees like liquid —Elizabeth Spencer

16. (The man sprawls . . . spent, empty) limp as a drowned man tossed on the sand —George Garrett

17. (He was) limp as laundry —W. P. Kinsella

18. (I must have been worked up even more than I'd thought those past weeks, for now that it was all over I was) limp as a rag —Wilbur Daniel Steele

19. Looking like an advertisement for jelly —Mike Fredman

20. My legs felt as if . . . made of two lengths of rope —George Garrett

21. No more backbone than a chocolate eclair —Theodore Roosevelt
     Roosevelt coined this simile about President McKinley when he was Secretary of the Navy.

22. She was like an overstretched bow, almost breaking —Stephen French Whitman

23. Softened and weakened, like a wax doll left too near the flame —George Garrett

24. Strength running out of him like sawdust —Vicki Baum

25. Was washed out like a disemboweled sack —Aharon Megged

26. Weak as a broken arm —Raymond Chandler

27. Weak as air —Ann Bradstreet
     By contrast, you could also say "Strong as air," especially if you've ever seen a ship in dry dock.

28. Weak as an nonagenarian —T. Coraghessan Boyle

29. (He's as) weak as a stick —Mary Lee Settle
     In Settle's novel, *Celebration,* the simile relates to emotional weakness.

30. Weak as water —*The Holy Bible/Ezkiel*

31. Weak . . . like a cream puff with the cream squeezed out —Tom Robbins

32. Weak, like a moth newly broken out from its chrysalis —E. F. Benson

WEALTH
See: RICHES

WEARINESS

1. Adrenalin . . . seeps out of us like sawdust seeping from a stuffed toy —W. P. Kinsella

2. An atmosphere of luxurious exhaustion, like a ripened shedding rose — Truman Capote

3. Eyelids feel as if they are being held open by taxidermy needles —Jay McInerney

4. Fatiguing as the eternal hanging on of an uncompleted task —William James

5. Feel . . . as is if my machine has temporarily run down —Janet Flanner

6. Feel like a sneaker that's been through a ringer —Nicholas S. Daniloff, television interview, September 14, 1986
    Daniloff's simile expressed his feelings after two weeks in Russian captivity.

7. Felt like an old soldier exhausted by a long retreat from battle — Kenzaburo Oë

8. Felt like Sisyphus taking a five-minute break, like Muhammad Ali at the end of the fourteenth round in Manila —T. Coraghessan Boyle

9. Felt perpetually tired, as though she were bleeding —Francis King

10. Felt tired as though she had spent the day on a hot beach —Mary Hedin

11. A flurry of fatigue swept over us like a tropical rainstorm, dropping us like sodden flies —James Crumley

12. Growing drowsier . . . as if he had been counting a flock of pedigree Southdowns —Sylvia Townsend Warner

13. Had the look of an overworked nag —Sholom Aleichem

14. His state [from working all day] was like a flabby orange whose crushed skin is thin with pulling, and all dented in —Amy Lowell

15. I could lie down like a tired child, and weep away the life of care — Percy Bysshe Shelley

16. Looked haggard . . . like a child after too much carnival —John D. MacDonald

17. (My time is past,) my blood is dry as my bones —Grace Paley

18. My fingers and back feel like I'm Quasimodo —Ray Schmidt
    Schmidt's weariness was caused by a long session of entering data into his computer, September 24, 1986

19. Squeezed out like an old paint-tube —Lawrence Durrell

20. Tired as an old coal miner —Reynolds Price

21. Tired as a preacher in a border town —Thomas Zigal

22. Tired-eyed as a diplomat —Frank Swinnerton
23. A wave of sleepiness knocked me over like an ocean breaker —Gloria Norris
24. Weariness . . . like a crushing weight —Kaatje Hurlbut
25. (Shrugs) weary and eloquent as an ox under a yoke —George Garrett
26. Weary and exhausted as though I had travelled along an unending road —Stefan Zweig
27. Wearying as a holiday to a workaholic —Elyse Sommer
28. Wore me out like a fever —Sholom Aleichem

WEATHER
See Also: CLOUD(S), COLDNESS, ENTRANCES/EXITS, FOG, HEAT, MIST, RAIN, SUN, THUNDER AND LIGHTNING, WIND

1. The chilly, drizzly June day smelled like a basement —Marge Piercy
2. The elements are but as qualities that change forever, like all things that have known generation —Dame Edith Sitwell
3. Frost made the sunny air seem like a bright keen knife —Howard Spring
4. Humidity . . . dropped down over the city like a damp serge cloak — Carlos Baker
5. The humidity . . . slapped me in the face like a mugger's glove — Loren D. Estleman
6. Rain and thaw took its [snow's] place, and now the world looks about as pleasing as a wet cat —John Wainwright
7. The storm crashes like god-wars —Hayden Carruth
8. The [hot] weather clings, like a low fever you cannot shake off — Angela Carter
9. Weather . . . cool and gray as wash water —George Garrett
10. Weather in towns is like a skylark in a counting-house, out of place and in the way —Jerome K. Jerome
11. The weather was like a waiter with a tray —Wallace Stevens
12. The whine of wind and rattle of rain and the thunder rolling terribly loud and near overhead like a thousand beer trucks roaring over the bridge —John Dos Passos

WEDDINGS
See: MARRIAGE

WEIGHT
See: HEAVINESS, LIGHTNESS

WELCOMENESS
See: DESIRABILITY

WELL-BEING
See: HEALTH

WHISPERS
See: GROANS AND WHISPERS

WHITE
See Also: COLORS, COMPLEXION, PALLOR

1. (Face) more white than sin —Dame Edith Sitwell
2. Pure white as china door knobs —Reynolds Price
3. White and bare as a winter moon —George Garrett
4. White and clean as driftwood —George Garrett
   See Also: CLEANLINESS
5. (A yacht) white and pretty as a birthday cake —George Garrett
   See Also: BEAUTY
6. White and wan, like the head and skin of a dying man —Percy Bysshe Shelley
7. (The desert is) white as a blind man's eye —Sylvia Plath
8. (He's as) white as a chicken —Honoré de Balzac
9. (Face) white as a bandage —Helen Hudson
10. White as a dog's bone —Anne Sexton
11. White as a foam-flower —Henry Van Dyke
12. (Ball) white as a leghorn egg —W. P. Kinsella
13. White as a lily —William Shakespeare
14. (In marble halls as) white as milk —Anon old English riddle
    Some variations to intensify the image: "White as new milk" by Dorothy Canfield Fisher and "Snow white as white milk from a white cow" by Eleanor Wylie.
15. White as a milk tooth —Charles Simic
16. (Body) white as an aspirin —Richard Ford
17. White as any bough that blooms in May —Geoffrey Chaucer
18. White as a peeled stick —Helen Hudson
19. (Moon) white as a sand dollar —Diane Ackerman
20. White as blanched almonds —Charles Cotton
21. (Teeth) white as detergent —Margaret Atwood
22. White as ermine —Dame Edith Sitwell
23. (Her neck and temples were) white as flour —T. Coraghessan Boyle

24. White as frost —G. K. Chesterton
    An extension of this opening line of Chesterton's poem, *The Mirror of Madmen,* is "White as hoarfrost."

25. White as ivory —Oscar Wilde
    An extension by a contemporary short story writer, Barry Targan: "White as polished ivory."

26. White as lightning —Cynthia Ozick
    The comparison is being used to describe the look of a woman in a nurse's uniform.

27. (The air blew white in my face,) white as my daughter's communion dress, white as a bridal veil —Elizabeth Spencer

28. (The little space between earth and sky was filled by a broken veil of drifting flakes as) white as pear blossoms —Phyllis Bottome

29. (Teeth,) white as peeled almonds —Gerald Kersh

30. (Veins) white as porkfat —Sylvia Plath

31. White as pulverized bone —T. Coraghessan Boyle

32. White as rice —Reynolds Price

33. White as sheets and blizzards —T. Coraghessan Boyle

34. White as snow —*The Holy Bible*
    Similes comparing the whiteness of complexions, hair and miscellaneous objects to snow can be found throughout literature as well as in our everyday language. Some well-known variations include: "White as driven snow" by William Shakespeare, "White as new-fallen snow" by William Wordsworth, "White as dead snow" by Algernon Charles Swinburne and "White as the snow on high hills" by Elizabeth Barrett Browning.

35. (Teeth) white as sun-cured bone —Beryl Markham

36. (Hand) white as talcum —Mavis Gallant

37. (Teeth) white as the petals of a daisy —Dan Jacobson

38. White as the sun —Henry Chettle

39. White as the surf —Oscar Wilde

40. (Face is) white as the wall —Daphne du Maurier

41. (Chest . . .) white as wax —Patricia Henley

42. (Hair) white as whipped cream —W. P. Kinsella

43. (Face) white like a whitewashed fence —William Faulkner

44. White like May-blossom —Charlotte Brontë

45. White like salt —Aharon Megged

46. White like sea foam —Joan Chase

WICKEDNESS
>   See: EVIL

WILDNESS
>   See: FEROCITY

WIND
>   See Also: WEATHER

1. Breeze [after a very hot day] . . . as torrid as the air from an oven —Ellen Glasgow

2. The breeze flowed down on me, passing like a light hand —Louise Erdrich

3. The breeze . . . sent little waves curling like lazy whips along the shingle [of a house] —John Fowles

4. A breeze which came like a breath —Paul Horgan

5. A draft . . . struck through his drenched clothes like ice cold needles —Cornell Woolrich

6. A gathering wind sent the willows tossing like a jungle of buggy whips —William Styron

7. High wind . . . like invisible icicles —Rebecca West

8. Level winds as flat as ribbons —M. J. Farrell

9. A northeaster roared down on us like a herd of drunken whales —T. Coraghessan Boyle

10. A northeast wind which cut like a thousand razors —Frank Swinnerton
    See Also: PAIN

11. A sandy wind blowing rough as an elephant —Truman Capote

12. The sound of wind is like a flame —Yvor Winters

13. The sunless evening wind slid down the mountain like an invisible river —Dorothy Canfield Fisher

14. The night wind rushed like a thief along the streets —Brian Moore

15. There came a wind like a bugle —Emily Dickinson
    This is both title and first line of a poem.

16. The warm spring wind fluttered against his face like an old kiss —Michael Malone

17. Wind . . . beat like a fist against his face —Vicki Baum

18. The wind blew gusts of wind into his face that were much like a shower-bath —Honoré de Balzac

19. The wind blew him like a sail up against a lifeboat —F. Scott Fitzgerald

20. Wind . . . blowing down from a flat black sky like painted cardboard —Marge Piercy

21. Wind . . . driving the dry snow along with it like a mist of powdered diamonds —Henry Van Dyke

22. The wind drove against him like a granite cliff —Edith Wharton

23. Wind . . . dry and faint, like the breath of some old woman —Joe Coomer

24. Wind . . . dry and fresh as ice —Frank Ross

25. The wind filled his shirt like a white sail —Yitzhak Shenhar

26. The wind flicked about a little like the tail of a horse that's trying to decide what sort of mood it's in tonight —Douglas Adams

27. The wind howls like a chained beast in pain —Delmore Schwartz

28. The wind howls like air inside a shell —Tracy Daugherty

29. The wind is like a dog that runs away —Wallace Stevens

30. The wind is like a hand on my forehead, in caress —John Hall Wheelock

31. Wind like a hungry coyote's cry —Patricia Henley

32. Wind like a perfumed woman in heat —Clive Irving

33. The wind like a razor —Miles Gibson

34. The wind like a saw-edged knife —Paul J. Wellman

35. The wind [in autumn] moves like a cripple among the leaves —Wallace Stevens

36. The wind plunged like a hawk from the swollen clouds —Ellen Glasgow

37. (The gray winter) wind prowling like a hungry wolf just beyond the windows —George Garrett

38. The wind ran in the street like a thin dog —Katherine Mansfield

39. Wind ringing in their ears like well-known old songs —Hans Christian Andersen

40. The wind rose out of the depth below them, sounding as if it were pushing boulders uphill —Martin Cruz Smith

41. Wind . . . rustling the . . . child's hair like grass —Marguerite Duras

42. The wind screamed like a huge, injured thing —Scott Spencer

43. Wind . . . surges into your ear like breath coming and going —Philip Levine

44. The wind swept the snow aside, ever faster and thicker, as if it were trying to catch up with something —Boris Pasternak

45. The wind whistled . . . like a pack of coyotes —Paige Mitchell

46. A wind will . . . knock like a rifle-butt against the door —Wallace Stevens

The comparison appears in Stevens' poem, *The Auroras of Autumn*. The full line from which the rifle-butt comparison is taken includes "A wind will spread its windy grandeurs round and . . . "

WINNING
See: SPORTS, SUCCESS/FAILURE

WINTER
See: SEASONS

WISDOM
See Also: EDUCATION, KNOWLEDGE

1. Chewing over their combined worldly wisdom like so many puppies with a shoe —Mary Ladd Cavell
   The wisdom in Cavell's story, *The Rotifer,* is being shared by three apartment mates.

2. The heart of the wise man lies quiet like limpid water —Cameroonian proverb

3. The heart of the wise, like a mirror, should reflect all objects, without being sullied —Confucius

4. If a man is as wise as a serpent, he can afford to be as harmless as a dove —Josh Billings
   This is an elaboration of "Harmless as a dove" which dates back to the Bible. In Billings' phonetic dialect this reads, "Iz az wize az a serpent."

5. Insight as keen as frosty star —William Wordsworth

6. A learned man is a tank; a wise man is a spring —William R. Alger

7. String of wise jests . . . like gold links —Penelope Gilliatt

8. To learn a person's life . . . like learning a language, you must start with the little things, the little pictures —Susan Fromberg Schaeffer

9. Wisdom and virtue are like two wheels of a cart —Japanese proverb
   See Also: VIRTUE

10. Wisdom in a poor man is like a diamond set in lead —H. G. Bohn's *Handbook of Proverbs*

11. Wisdom is like fire: a little enlightens, much burns —Moses Ibn Ezra

12. Wisdom is like gold ore, mixed with stones and dust —Moses Ibn Ezra

13. Wisdom, like life itself, appeared to me to be comprised of continuing progress, of starting over again, of patience —Marguerite Yourcenar

14. Wisdom, like perfume, rises out of its own essence —Norman Mailer

15. Wisdom shook itself like a drop off a dog (and he lost it) —Cynthia Ozick

16. Wise as a wisp —George Garrett

17. Wise as heaven —Algernon Charles Swinburne

WISH

See: DESIRE

WIT

See Also: CLEVERNESS, HUMOR, WISDOM

1. As much wit as three folks, two fools and a madman —Thomas Fuller

2. One wit, like a knuckle of ham in soup, gives a zest and flavor to the dish, but more than one serves only to spoil the pottage —Tobias Smollett

3. Satire is a sort of glass, wherein beholders do generally discover everybody's face but their own —Jonathan Swift

4. Sharp wits, like sharp knives, do often cut their owner's fingers — Aaron Arrowsmith

5. Wit and wisdom are like the seven stars, seldom seen together — Thomas Fuller

6. Wit is as infinite as love —Agnes Repplier
   Repplier built on her simile with "And a deal more lasting in its qualities."

7. Wit . . . like a quick-flashing blade —Henry James

8. Wit . . . like champagne, not only sparkles, but is sweet —Benjamin Disraeli

9. Wit, like money, bears an extra value when rung down as soon as it's wanted —Douglas Jerrold

10. Wit must grow like fingers —John Selden

11. Wit . . . penetrates through the coldness and awkwardness of society, gradually bringing men nearer together, and, like the combined force of wine and oil, giving every man a glad heart and a shining countenance —Sydney Smith

12. Wit, without learning, is like a tree which bears no fruit —Aristippus

13. Wit, without wisdom, is like a song without sense; it does not please long —Josh Billings

WIVES

See: MARRIAGE

WOMEN

See: HEART(S), MEN AND WOMEN

WORD(S)

See Also: SPEAKING; WORDS, DEFINED; WORDS, EFFECT OF; WORDS OF PRAISE; WRITERS/WRITING

1. Applying words like bandages —William McIlvanney

2. Words should be scattered like seed; no matter how small the seed may be, if it has once found favorable ground, it unfolds its strength —Seneca

3. Words, like Nature, half reveal and half conceal the Soul within —Alfred, Lord Tennyson

4. Her words still hung in the air between us like a whisp of tobacco smoke —Evelyn Waugh

5. It is with words as with sunbeams, the more they are condensed, the deeper they burn —Robert Southey

6. Words, like men, grow an individuality; their character changes with years and with use —Anon

7. Words, like fine flowers, have their color too —Ernest Rhys

8. Words, like clothes, get old-fashioned, or mean and ridiculous, when they have been for some time laid aside —William Hazlitt

9. Words, like fashions, disappear and recur throughout English history —Virginia Graham

10. The word seemed to linger in the air, to throb in the air like the note of a violin —Katherine Mansfield

11. Her words at first seemed fitful like the talking of the trees —Dante Gabriel Rossetti

12. (She spoke to them slowly,) dropping the words like ping pong balls —Helen Hudson

13. Every word hanging like the sack of cement on a murdered body at the bottom of the river —Diane Wakoski

14. Her words fell like rain on a waterproof umbrella; they made a noise, but they could not reach the head which they seemed destined to deluge —Frances Trollope

15. His words were smoother than oil (and yet be they swords) —*The Book of Common Prayer*

16. It is as easy to draw back a stone thrown from the hand, as to recall a word once spoken —Menander

17. Like blood from a cut vein, words flowed —James Morrow

18. My words slipped from me like broken weapons —Edith Wharton

19. An old sentence . . . ran through her mind like a frightened mouse in a maze —Babs H. Deal

20. The rest [words meant to remain unspoken] rolled out like string from a hidden ball of twine —Lynne Sharon Schwartz

21. The sentence rang over and over again in his mind like a dirge — Margaret Millar

22. Stiff as frozen rope words poke out —Marge Piercy

23. They [a group at a party] flung them [words] like weapons, handled them like jewels, tossed them on air with reckless abandon as though they scattered confetti —Mary Hedin

24. The word hissed like steam escaping from an overloaded pressure system —Ross Macdonald

25. A word once spoken, like an arrow shot, can never be retracted —Anon
    This simile was first used by Talmudic rabbis

26. Words as meaningless and wonderful as wind chimes —Sharon Sheehe Stark

27. The words came out like bullets —H. E. Bates

28. Words came out . . . tumbling like a litter of puppies from a kennel — F. van Wyck Mason

29. The words crumbled in his mouth like ashes —William Diehl

30. Words . . . danced in my mind like wild ponies that moved only to my command —Hortense Calisher

31. Words falling softly as rose petals —Mary Hedin

32. Words, frothy and toneless like a chain of bursting bubbles —L. P. Hartley

33. Words gushing and tumbling as if a hose had been turned on —Rose Tremain

34. Words gush like toothpaste —Margaret Atwood

35. The words [just spoken] hung like smoke in the air —Doris Grumbach

36. Words . . . like bits of cold wind —Mary Hedin

37. (She dealt her) words like blades —Emily Dickinson

38. Words, like butterflies, stagger from his lips —John Updike

39. Words, like glass, obscure when they do not aid vision —Joseph Joubet

40. Words . . . limp and clear like a jellyfish . . . hard and mean and secretive like a horned snail . . . austere and comical as top hats, or smooth and lively and flattering as ribbons —Alice Munro
    The narrator of Munro's story, *Spelling,* contemplates the meaning of words while visiting an old woman.

41. The word spiralled through the silence like a worm in wood —Harris Downey

42. The words (out) of his mouth were smoother than butter, but war was in his heart; his words were softer than oil, yet they were drawn swords —*The Holy Bible/Psalms*

43. Words . . . plunked down with a click like chessmen —Yehuda Amichai

44. Words . . . poured wetly from her red lips as from a pitcher —Lynne Sharon Schwartz

45. The words rang in the silence like the sound of a great cash register —Kingsley Amis

46. Words ran together too quickly, like rapid water —Joanna Wojewski Higgins

47. Words roll around in Benna's mouth [heroine of novel, *Anagrams*, by Lorrie Moore] like Life Savers on a tongue —Carol Hills, *New York Times Book Review*, November 2, 1986

48. Words that string and creep like insects —Conrad Aiken

49. Words . . . tumbling out and tripping over each other like mice — Susan Fromberg Schaeffer

50. The words went by like flights of moths under the star-soaked sky — Adrienne Rich

51. Words . . . white and anonymous as a snowball —Donald McCaig
    See Also: WHITE

52. (If he once . . . let loose . . . the) words would come like a great flood, like vomiting —George Garrett

53. Your words to the end, hard as a pair of new cowboy boots —A. D. Winans
    See Also: TOUGHNESS

WORDS, DEFINED

1. The English language is like an enormous bank account —Robert Claiborne

2. The great man's word is like the elephant's tusk [i.e. not to be concealed or withdrawn] —Hindu saying

3. Long words, like long beards, are often the badge of charlatans —F. L. Lucas

4. Pithy sentences are like sharp nails which force the truth upon our memories —Denis Diderot

5. Technical terms . . . are like red, white and blue poker chips. They stand for whatever the players agree upon —John B. Kerfoot

6. A word fitly spoken is like apples of gold in a setting of silver —*The Holy Bible/Proverbs*

7. A word is not a crystal transparent and unchanged; it is the skin of a living thought and may vary greatly in color and content according to the circumstances and the time in which it is used —Oliver Wendell Holmes, Sr.

8. Words are like bodies, and meanings like souls —Abraham Ibn Ezra

9. Words are like labels, or coins, or better, like swarming bees —Anne Sexton

10. Words are like leaves, some wither every year —Horace
    Alexander Pope's variation of this reads as follows: "Words are like leaves and where they most abound, much fruit of sense beneath is rarely found."

11. Words are like money, not the worse for being common, but . . . it is the stamp of custom alone that gives them circulation or value — William Hazlitt

12. Words are like money; there is nothing so useless, unless when in actual use —Samuel Butler

13. Words are like money, a medium of exchange; and the sureness with which they can be used varies not only with the character of the coins themselves, but also with the character of the things they buy, and that of the men who tender and receive them —Allen Upward

14. Words are like money; and when the current value of them is generally understood, no man is cheated by them —Sir Richard Steele
    This and the next three entries rely on what follows the basic simile for individuality.

15. Words are loaded pistols —Jean-Paul Sartre

16. Words . . . a syllable which sounds like a bumblebee breaking wind — Hortense Calisher

17. Words, like cavalry horses answering the bugle, group themselves automatically into familiar dreary patterns —George Orwell
    Orwell's simile was used to urge against re-using any phrase once it appears in print. Anyone following his advice would use this book strictly as a guide to phrase elimination.

18. The words of a man's mouth are as deep waters, and the wellsprings of wisdom as a flowing brook —*The Holy Bible /Proverbs*

19. A word without thought is like a foot without sinew —Moses Ibn Ezra

WORDS, EFFECT OF

1. Epithets, like pepper, give zest to what you write —Lewis Carroll
    Carroll expanded on the simile as follows: "And if you strew them sparely, they whet the appetite; but if you lay them on too thick, you spoil the matter quite!"

2. Everything you say is just like scraping a wound with a knife —Iris Murdoch

3. Hearing a word break like a wave on the shells of my ears —John Hersey

4. Her words pelted me like hail —Edith Wharton

5.   Her words showered down upon us like little glass pellets —Saul Bellow

6.   His words dropped in Spandarian's ear like pellets of ice —Derek Lambert

7.   Like heavy hostile fists the words pounded on Andrew's incredulous ears —F. van Wyck Mason

8.   Listening to The Weasel [an unpleasant person] was like having a dirty hand paw through your personal belongings, leaving them in confusion and so soiled that after the first look you were disgusted and tempted to throw them away, for they had changed —Ann Petry

9.   The sentences . . . like toy life-buoys made of paper, they carried no weight or conviction —James Stern

10. That terrible word caused Flora's heart to slide like frozen snow — Frank Swinnerton

11. The word . . . went through Morgan's heart like a poisoned spear — Noël Coward

12. The word pierced her side like a sharp horn —Z. Vance Wilson

13. The words beat on Gerty's brain like the sound of a language which had seemed familiar at a distance but on approaching is found to be unintelligible —Edith Wharton

14. Words cutting like diamonds —Frank Swinnerton

15. Words dig at her like fingers in clay —T. Coraghessan Boyle

16. The words drive home like separate blows from a mallet —T. Coraghessan Boyle

17. The words felt like a medicine ball to the stomach —T. Glen Coughlin

18. Words, like daggers, enter in my ears —William Shakespeare
     In *Hamlet* the words enter into 'mine' not "my ears." Another Shakespearean dagger image from *Titus Andronicus:* "These words are razors to my wounded heart."

19. Words . . . rattle and roll like dice —George Garrett

20. The words shook her like a tempest —Edith Wharton

21. The words slid over her like water poured on stones —Ellen Gilchrist

22. Words that sting and creep like insects —Karl Shapiro

23. Words were like nails. Like little knives. —George Garrett

24. The words trickled through his mind like a warm and friendly brook, or a leak in a boat which filled it only slowly —MacDonald Harris

25. The word went home. It hit on his heart like a tennis ball in fast play — Vicki Baum

WORDS OF PRAISE

1.   For you, words are like birds. They sing. They fly —Helen Hudson

The character who thus praises a friend's gift with words describes himself as someone for whom "Words are worms."

2. (My wife . . . always) looks like a barrel full of stardust —Moss Hart

3. My doll is as dainty as a sparrow —Oscar Hammerstein II, from lyric for *South Pacific*
   The lyric heaps simile upon simile with "Where she's narrow, she's as narrow as an arrow."

4. My sister, my spouse, is a secret spring —John Hall Wheelock
   This is the first line and leitmotif of a poem entitled *An Old Song.*

5. She seemed like a yellow sunrise on mountain tops —O. Henry

6. She shines against the backdrop of this provincial place like a jewel on a beggar's coat. She is like the moon forgotten by the pale sky of the day. She is like a butterfly over a plain of snow —Milan Kundera

7. When I walk with you I feel as if I had a flower in my buttonhole —William Makepeace Thackeray

8. When she passed it seemed like the ceasing of exquisite music —Henry Wadsworth Longfellow

9. When you came, you were like red wine and honey . . . now you are like morning bread, smooth and pleasant —Amy Lowell

10. When you get up, it's like the flag being raised. I want to pledge allegiance —John Updike

11. You're a girl like candy —Clifford Odets

12. You're beautiful, like a May fly —Ernest Hemingway to Mary Welsh before she became Mrs. Hemingway

13. You're perfect as a textbook example —Sharon Olds
    Poet Olds uses the simile in a poem dedicated to her father and aptly entitled *The Ideal Father.*

14. Your lips taste like paradise —Isaac Bashevis Singer

WORK

See Also: ATTENTION, BOREDOM, DOCTORS, LAWYERS, PROFESSIONS

1. All the romance had been scuffed off it [playing professional baseball against small-town teams] like the gloss on a brand-new baseball after nine innings of hard use —Howard Frank Mosher

2. All work is as seed sown; it grows and spreads, and sows itself anew —Thomas Carlyle

3. The back-breaking sixteen-hour day, like a heavy hand slapping —Bernard Malamud

4. Being a president is like riding a tiger. A man has to keep on riding or be swallowed —Harry S. Truman

5.   (Reagan's nostalgic wit was contributing to the feeling that he) dropped in and out of his job, like a cameo star on "The Love Boat" —Gerald Gardner

6.   (My mom) getting paid for giving advice is like the Cookie Monster getting paid for eating cookies —Glenn Sapadin, upon hearing that his mother, Linda Sapadin, was finalist in contest to select a replacement for advice columnist Ann Landers, *New York Times*/About New York, April 11, 1987

7.   This job [being a prize fighter] needs gorgeous concentration . . . it's like being a priest; our work comes first —Clifford Odets

8.   The job [dean at a university] is like being pecked to death by ducks — John Roche, lecture at Ohio State University, 1962.

9.   Jobs are like lobster pots, harder to get out of them than into —Hugh Leonard

10. Labor like Hercules —William H. Gass

11. The only time some people work like a horse is when the boss rides them —Gabriel Heatter

12. Toiled like movers trying to get a refrigerator into a fifth-floor walk-up —Russell Baker

13. Toiling like a bee in a hive —Noël Coward, lyrics for "World Weary"

14. (Fifty-two Sundays a year . . . for three hours my mother was) unemployed in her own house. Like a queen —Philip Roth
        Roth's comparison of a mother to an unemployed queen comes from his novel, *The Ghost Writer.*

15. Unemployed people (i.e. actors between plays) like ghosts looking for bodies to inhabit —Gail Godwin

16. Work drives you like a motor —Janet Flanner

17. Working the rivet line [at auto factory] is like being paid to flunk high school the rest of your life —Ben Hamper in article on changes at General Motors, *Mother Jones,* September 1986

18. Work is as much a necessity to man as eating and sleeping —Karl Wilhelm Humboldt

19. Work like a beaver —American colloquialism
        This expression was popularized by the fur trappers who roamed the Rockies during the nineteenth century. Like many such terms it has gained much wider currency and seeded off-shoots like "Eager as a beaver" and "Busy as a beaver."

20. Work like a Trojan —Anon
        A still popular simile that had its origins in the Greek classics which portrayed the Trojans as hard workers.

21. The work was getting to be like licking stamps eight hours a day — Loren D. Estleman

WORLD

See Also: LIFE

1. Our world is only a practical joke of God, like a bad day —Franz Kafka

2. This world is like Noah's Ark in which few men but many beasts embark —Samuel Butler

3. The universe is like a safe to which there is a combination, but the combination is locked up in the safe —Peter de Vries

4. The world is a gaming table so arranged that all who enter the casino must play and all must lose more or less heavily in the long run, though they win occasionally by the way —Samuel Butler

5. The world is a looking glass, and gives back to every man the reflection of his own face —William Makepeace Thackeray
    The looking glass comparison from *Vanity Fair* continues as follows: "Frown at it and it will in turn look sourly upon you; laugh at it and with it, and it is a jolly kind companion."

6. The world is a mirror: what looks in looks out. It returns only what you lend it —Ludwig Boerne

7. The world is an expensive hotel; you pay dearly for each pleasure —Israel Salanter Lipkin

8. The world is like a beautiful book, but of little use to anyone who cannot read it —Carolo Goldon
    The original simile used the word 'him' instead of 'anyone.'

9. The world is like a board with holes in it, and the square men have got into the round holes, and the round into the square —Bishop George Berkeley

10. The world is like a cucumber, today it's in your hand, tomorrow up your arse —Arabic proverb

11. The world is like a drunken peasant. If you lift him into the saddle on one side, he will fall off on the other. One can't help him, no matter how one tries —Martin Luther

12. The world is like a fair: people gather for a while, then part; some profit and rejoice, others lose and grieve —Bahya

13. The world is like a fountain-wheel: the buckets ascend full and descend empty —*The Holy Bible/Exodus*
    The biblical passage concludes with "Who's rich today may not be so tomorrow."

14. The world is like a foyer leading to the world to come —Rabbi Jacob
    In the *Mishna,* this continues with "Prepare yourself in the foyer, so that you may enter into the inner chamber." Another version of this reads: "The world is like an antechamber to the next. Prepare yourself here that you may be admitted to the banquet hall there."

15. The world is like a great staircase, some go up and others go down — Hipponax

16. The world is like a house, with the sky as a ceiling, the earth spread out like a carpet, the stars arrayed like lamps . . . and man its master — Bahya

17. The world is like a ladder: one goes up, another goes down —Immanuel of Rome

18. The world is like a map of antipathies . . . in which everyone picks the symbolic color of his difference —Juan Ramón Jiménez

19. The world is like an enormous spider web and if you touch it, however lightly, at any point, the vibration ripples to the remotest perimeter — Robert Penn Warren

20. The world is like an old coquette who conceals her age —Voltaire

21. The world is like a pump-wheel, through which the full is emptied and the empty filled —Naham Bratzlav

22. The world like a cradle rises and falls on a wave of confetti and funerals —Louis MacNeice

23. The world waits to be made over by each man who inhabits it, and it is made over every morning like a bed —William Saroyan

24. A world where cliches fit like a gown by Edith Head —Tom Nolan, *New York Times Book Review,* November 9, 1986
    The comparison to a Hollywood designer's gowns was most appropriate as the book being reviewed had a Hollywood background.

WORRY
See: AGITATION, ANXIETY

WOUND
See: PAIN

WRINKLES
See Also: COMPLEXION, FOREHEAD, SKIN

1. All the flesh of him that showed, had creases like miniature gullies in the skin —Paul Horgan

2. Deep lines that looked like dark parentheses around her lips —Alice McDermott

3. Face as creased as his trousers —Sumner Locke Elliott

4. Face as lined as an Indian squaw's —John Fowles

5. Face creased up like a fine soft handkerchief —Lawrence Durrell

6. A face crisscrossed with lines like an old paper bag —Margaret Millar

7. Face . . . delicately wrinkled like a fine thin notepaper —Louise Erdrich

8. The face grows lined and wrinkled like a chart —Karl Shapiro

9. Face like a withered walnut —Edith Wharton

10. Face lined as soft leather —Sue Grafton

11. Face, lined like a much-folded map —Mollie Hardwick

12. Face lined like a river delta —T. Coraghessan Boyle

13. Face . . . marked by a little cross-hatching of fine lines, as though his cheek had lain on corduroy —Harvey Swados

14. Face marked with gossamer lines like the craze of enamel —Samuel Yellen

15. Face . . . savagely gouged, like the land after the passage of a fast-running rain that makes temporary rivers which plow the ground and leave sunbaked veins of rut afterward —Paul Horgan

16. Face so wrinkled that it was like a parchment loaded with hieroglyphics —G. K. Chesterton

17. Faces . . . wrinkled by wind and sun like cured meat —George Garrett

18. Face wrinkled in deep furrows like the fissures in a red clay road after rain —Ellen Glasgow

19. Face . . . wrinkled like the bark of the pine trees —Susan Fromberg Schaeffer

20. Face . . . wrinkling like a bent leather glove —Harvey Swados

21. Grooves like gashes ran from his nostrils to his mouth-corners — Dashiell Hammett

22. Had a thousand wrinkles on her face, so that she looked most like an aging Barbie doll —Shelby Hearon

23. Her face is etched all over with fine lines, as though her skin has been caught under a butterfly net —Daphne Merkin

24. Her face was wrinkled like a roll-top desk —Arthur Baer

25. Her skin had a pattern all its own of numberless branching wrinkles and as though a whole little tree stood in the middle of her forehead — Eudora Welty

26. His neck all in wrinkles resembling cracks, criss-crossing one another, as though his neck were made of cork —Ivan Bunin

27. His skin wrinkled up like crumpled butcher paper —Jonathan Valin

28. Jagged lines around his eyes, lines like scars from a broken bottle — Richard Lourie

29. The lines deep graven in the soft skin about her eyes and mouth were like rivers in a black-and-white map —Frank Swinnerton

30. Lines etched by age, like frost patterns on a windowpane —Dorothea Straus

31. The lines on her forehead and neck were as if scored with a knife —John Braine

32. Pink skin scored with wrinkles like the furrows of a corn field —Carlos Fuentes

33. Shriveling like an overbaked potato —Ira Wood

34. Skin . . . wrinkled like a wine-skin —W. Somerset Maugham

35. Skin wrinkled like an old paper bag —Margaret Millar

36. Skin wrinkles like paint —Derek Walcott

37. Stretch marks . . . looked like streaky bacon held up to the light —David Niven

38. (On my skin) the wrinkles branch out, overlapping like hair or feathers —Margaret Atwood

39. Thin long lines like the lines in cracked glass or within a cake of ice —Saul Bellow

40. A sheaf of fine wrinkles spread [from corners of eyes] like a fan —L. P. Hartley

41. Wary lines around the corners of his eyes, like sparrow's claws —Derek Lambert

42. Wrinkled as an iguana —Richard Ford

43. Wrinkled as a dry plum —Anon
    A much-used variation: "Wrinkled as a prune."

44. [A newborn baby] wrinkled as a head of lettuce —Charles Johnson

45. Wrinkled as a walnut —Dominique Lapierre

46. A wrinkled, wizened face, like that of an aged monkey —William Styron

47. Wrinkle like an apple left uneaten too long —Anon
    Simile makers are greatly drawn to comparisons between apples and wrinkled skin. Some examples from current literature: "Wrinkled as a roasted apple" (Desmond O'Grady); "Wrinkled like a stale apple" (Graham Greene); "Wrinkled like a winter apple" (Isak Dinesen); "Wrinkled like the skin of a winter-kept apple" (Wallace Stegner); "Wrinkles crept into it [a woman's face] like worms" (Erich Maria Remarque).

48. The wrinkles in her skin shone like a bright net —Eudora Welty

49. Wrinkles of delight appearing on the leathery skin like cracks in a shattered safety glass —Robert J. Serling

50. Wrinkles [in forehead] . . . rush together like sentinels —Irving Stone

51. Wrinkling like a potato —W. D. Snodgrass

WRITERS/WRITING
See Also: POETS/POETRY

1. The act of writing itself is done in secret, like masturbation —Stephen King

2. Alliteration is like ivy, some of it is poison —Delmore Schwartz

3. As a baker bakes more bread than brown; or as a tumbler tumbles up and down; so does our author, rummaging his brain, by various methods try to entertain —Henry Fielding

4. An author at work is like an oyster, clam-quiet and busy —Rumer Godden

5. An author introduced to people who have read, or who say they have read his books, always feels like a man taken for the first time to be shown to his future wife's relations —Jerome K. Jerome

6. An author is like a baker; it is for him to make the sweets, and others to buy and enjoy them —Leigh Hunt

7. Authors are like cattle going to a fair: those of the same field can never move on without butting one another —Walter Savage Landor

8. Authors, like coins, grow dear as they grow old; it is the rust we value, not the gold —Alexander Pope

9. An author who speaks of his own books is almost as bad as a mother who talks about her own children —Benjamin Disraeli

10. Being an author is like treading water in the middle of the ocean; you can never stop, you can never stop treading water —Delmore Schwartz

11. Being a writer in a library is rather like being a eunuch in a harem — John Braine, *New York Times,* Oct. 7, 1961

12. A biographer is like a contractor who builds roads: it's terribly messy, mud everywhere, and when you get done, people travel over the road at a fast clip —Arthur Wilson

13. Churn out books as though his days were numbered —Michiko Kakutani, *New York Times,* February 14, 1987
    In reviewing Anthony Burgess' autobiography, *Little Wilson and Big God,* Kakutani uses this simile to introduce her recounting the story of how Burgess began writing when he thought that his days were in fact numbered.

14. Clear writers, like fountains, do not seem so deep as they are —Walter Savage Landor
    The simile is followed by this about the less-than-clear: "The turbid look the most profound."

15. A collection of essays is a collection of variations —Elizabeth Hardwick

16. The essayist is kind of poet in prose —Alexander Smith

17. Every author, however modest, keeps a most outrageous vanity chained like a madman in the padded cell of his breast —Logan Pearsall Smith

18. For the blocked or hesitant, the advent of the computer is like the advent of spring: the frozen river surges, the hard earth flowers — Edward Mendelson reporting on computers for writers, *Yale Review,* 1985

19. Getting a book published without a literary agent is like swimming dangerous waters without a shark repellent —Rae Lawrence, *New York Times Magazine,* July 5, 1987
    Lawrence's simile serves to introduce her experience in finding and choosing a literary agent for her first novel.

20. Good writing is a kind of skating which carries off the performer where he would not go —Ralph Waldo Emerson

21. Grammar is an art. Style is a gift. You are born with your style, just as you are born with your voice —Anatole France

22. The great writer finds style as the mystic finds God, in his own soul — Havelock Ellis

23. Hiring someone to write your autobiography is like hiring someone to take a bath for you —Mae West, quoted in *Bookviews,* February 11, 1977

24. I can get a kind of tension when I'm writing a short story [as compared to a novel], like I'm pulling on a rope and know where the rope is attached —Alice Munro, quoted *New York Times Book Review,* September 14, 1986

25. I get a thing I call sentence-fever that must be like buck-fever; it's a sort of intense literary self-consciousness that comes when I try to force myself —F. Scott Fitzgerald

26. (I enjoy the hell out of writing because) it's [writing] like an Easter egg hunt. Here's 50 pages and you say, "Oh, Christ, where is it? Then on the 51st page, it'll work" —John D. MacDonald

27. Like thrifty French cooks, waste nothing —Leslie Garis, *New York Times Magazine,* February 8, 1987
    Garis used the simile to describe Joan Didion and John Gregory Dunne's extensive note taking.

28. A long preface to a short treatise is like a high hat crowning a low brow —Zevi Hirsh Somerhausen
    Paraphrased for more modern English usage from "Like a high hat crowning a low brow is a long preface to a short treatise."

29. Long sentences in a short composition are like large rooms in little houses —William Shenstone

30. Method in writing is like ceremony in living too often used to supply the want of better things —Thomas Killigrew

31. Minor characters [in scripts] are rather like knights in chess: limited in movement, but handy in their capacity for quick turns, for fixing situations —John Fowles

32. A narrative is like a room on whose walls a number of false doors have been painted; while within the narrative, we have many apparent choices of exit, but when the author leads us to one particular door, we know it is the right one because the door opens —John Updike

33. Nobody can write a real drama who hasn't smelled the grease paint; it's like somebody composing who's never played an instrument —Mary McCarthy

34. Novels, like human beings, usually have their beginnings in the dark — Rita Mae Brown

35. People who write books take as much punishment as prizefighters — Norman Mailer

36. A pin has as much head as some authors and a great deal more point — George D. Prentice

37. The profession of book-writing makes horse racing seem like a solid, stable business —John Steinbeck

38. The profession of writing is wrong, like smoking cigarettes, bad for your health, a diminisher of life expectancy —William Saroyan

39. Prose as smooth and burnished as well-oiled furniture —A. R. Gurney Jr., *New York Times Book Review,* 1985
    The author of this smooth prose is Louis Auchincloss.

40. Prose consists of . . . phrases tacked together like the sections of a prefabricated hen-house —George Orwell

41. Prose is like music, every word must be placed for sound, color and nuance —James G. Huneker

42. A sentence should read as if its author, had he held a plough instead of a pen, could have drawn a furrow deep and straight to the end —Henry David Thoreau

43. Sometimes writing a recipe takes me a whole day . . . to communicate it correctly. It's like writing a little short story —Julia Childs

44. To inclose him (a fictional character) as irradiantly as amber does the fly and yet the while to preserve every detail of his being has, of all tasks, ever been the dearest to me —Stefan Zweig
    In his foreword to a collection of stories and novelettes, Zweig used this simile to explain that he considers his short fiction as much an accomplishment as his more "spacious" works.

45. Typing your own manuscript for submission is a lot like dressing to see that old lover who left you five years ago —Ira Wood

In his novel, *The Kitchen Man,* Wood expands the simile as follows: "Ready to walk out the door you stop one last time at the mirror, just to be sure they're going to regret what they walked out on. Well, maybe the belt is wrong, you think, throwing it on the bed, pulling out another. No, these old shoes won't do, too dowdy. After an hour, you're stripped to your socks and in tears, absolutely sure now that you are the perfect mess they said you were. And so your manuscript will be if you don't fight every urge to better every sentence."

46.   A well-written life is almost as rare as a well-spent one —Thomas Carlyle

47.   Words flowed from his pen like sparkling spring water —Yoko Ono, about husband John Lennon's writing

48.   A writer may take to long words, as young men to beards, to impress — F. L. Lucas

49.   Writers, like teeth, are divided into incisors and grinders —Walter Bagehot

50.   The writer's work is a little like handwriting. It comes out to be you no matter what you do —John Updike, *New York Times,* January 18, 1987

51.   The writer who draws his material from a book is like one who borrows money only to lend it —Kahlil Gibran

52.   Writes like a comrade, the kind of friend with whom it is a pleasure to dispute —Jacques Barzun about H. W. Fowler, the author of *Modern English Usage, New York Times Book Review,* December 12, 1986
      Reviewer John Gross in his turn applied the simile to Barzun's book, *A Word Or Two Before You Go.*

53.   Writing a first draft is like groping one's way into a pitch dark room, or overhearing a faint conversation, or telling a joke whose punchline you've forgotten —Ted Solotaroff

54.   Writing for a newspaper is like running a revolutionary war; you go into battle not when you are ready but when action offers itself —Norman Mailer

55.   Writing for him was as hard work as catching fleas —Ivan Turgenev

56.   Writing is akin to fortunetelling . . . you look into someone's life, read where they have been and predict what will happen to them —Marcia Norman, quoted *New York Times Book Review,* May 24, 1987

57.   Writing is like building a house —Ellen Gilchrist

58.   Writing is like pulling the trigger of a gun: if you are not loaded, nothing happens —Henry Seidel

59.   Writing is like religion. Every man who feels the call must work out his own salvation —George Horace Lorimer

60. Writing is like serving a jail sentence, you're not free until you've done time on the rock-heap —Paul Theroux

61. Writing is like writing a check . . . it's easy to write a check if you have enough money in the bank, and writing comes more easily if you have something to say —Sholem Asch

62. Writing . . . it is rather like building a house, every separate word is another brick laid into place, cemented to its fellows, and gradually you begin to see the wall beginning to rise, and you know that the rooms inside will take their shape as you intended —Vita Sackville-West

63. Writing without publishing gets to be like loving someone from afar, delicious for fantasies but thin gruel for a living —Ted Solotaroff

64. Wrote not without puzzlements and travail, nevertheless as naturally as birds —Cynthia Ozick

65. You become a good writer just as you become a good joiner: by planing down your sentences —Anatole France

66. Your article should be like a lady's skirt: long enough to cover the essentials, and short enough to be interesting —editorial advice to free lancers, *PhotoGraphic*, January 1987

YEARNING
See: DESIRE

YELLS
See: SCREAMS

YELLOW
See Also: COLORS, HAIR

1. Dun-yellow color, a color like that of old lions in the zoo —Harold Brodkey

2. Yellow and solid as lemons —Joyce Cary

3. (Hair) yellow as a dandelion —Anne Sexton

4. (Hair) yellow as a full moon —George Garrett

5. Yellow as a marsh-marigold —Henry Van Dyke

6. Yellow as an old tooth —Howard Spring

7. (Dandelions . . .) yellow as butter —Cynthia Ozick

8. (The field is) yellow as egg-bread dough —Randall Jarrell

9. (Hair) yellow as hay —Henry Wadsworth Longfellow

10. Yellow as mustard —Edna St. Vincent Millay

11. Yellow as the yolk of eggs —Marcel Proust

12. (Eyes) Yellow like amber —Isaac Bashevis Singer

13. Yellow like moldy linen —Sinclair Lewis

14. Yellow like ripe corn —Dante Gabriel Rossetti
    The point of reference is to the golden hair of the subject of
    Rossetti's famous poem, *The Blessed Damozel.*

15. Yellow like unburnished gold —Honoré de Balzac

YOUTH

See Also: AGE

1. As young as truth —Dante Gabriel Rossetti

2. At sixty-eight, he is as pink and fat as a baby, ingenuous as a teenager
   —T. Coraghessan Boyle

3. Between eighteen and twenty, life is like an exchange where one buys
   stocks, not with money, but with actions —André Malraux

4. Childish, like believing in Beauty and the Beast —Janet Flanner

5. Each youth is like a child born in the night who sees the sun rise and
   thinks that yesterday never existed —W. Somerset Maugham

6. He is like one of those young-old engineers at Boeing, who at seventy
   wear bow ties and tinker in their workshops —Walker Percy

7. It is like a long hopeless homesickness . . . missing those young days
   —Grace Paley

8. Like the tongue that seeks the missing tooth I yearned for my extracted
   youth —Ogden Nash

9. Looked about sixteen and as defenseless as a babe at a Mafia convention
   —Jimmy Sangster

10. Midway between youth and age like a man who has missed his train:
    too late for the last and too early for the next —George Bernard Shaw

11. Seemed as perpetually youthful as movie stars —Donald Justice

12. She was just eighteen, rich and warm as one eagerly waiting for the play
    to begin —Arthur Schopenhauer

13. Their [young people's] impulses are keen but not deep-rooted . . . like
    sick people's attacks of hunger —Aristotle

14. The young leading the young is like the blind leading the blind —Lord
    Chesterfield

15. Youth . . . flashing like a star out of the twilight —Willa Cather
    The simile is from an introductory poem to Cather's novel, *O
    Pioneer.*

16. Youthful rashness skips like a hare over the meshes of good counsel —
    William Shakespeare

17. Youth is like spring, an overpraised season: delightful if it happen to be
    a favored one, but in practice very rarely favored and more remarkable,
    as a general rule, for biting east winds than genial breezes —Samuel
    Butler

18. Youth . . . it did not go by me like a flitting dream. Tuesdays and Wednesdays were as gay as Saturday nights —Grace Paley

19. Youth like summer morn . . . youth like summer brave —William Shakespeare

    Shakespeare used these similes in his poem, *The Passionate Pilgrim,* to describe the pleasures of youth, alternating them with comparisons about age and the weather.

    See Also: AGE

20. (My) youth passed like a sleep —Dame Edith Sitwell

ZEAL

See: ENTHUSIASM

Bibliography

Anthologies that encompass the work of one author are alphabetized by the author's name. Multiple author anthologies are alphabetized according to the editor's name and by title if there is no editor or if the anthology is an annual with rotating editors, e.g., *The Best American Short Stories* series.

Ackerman, Diane. *Lady Faustus.* William Morrow & Co., Inc., 1983.

Adams, A. K. *The Home Book of Humorous Quotations.* Dodd, Mead & Co., 1942.

Adams, Douglas. *The Hitchiker's Guide to the Galaxy.* Harmony Books, 1979.

Adams, Douglas. *So Long, And Thanks for All the Fish.* Harmony Books, 1984.

Adams, Harold. *The Fourth Widow.* Mysterious Press, 1985.

Adams, Harold. *The Naked Liar.* Mysterious Press, 1985.

Adams, Joey. *Strictly for Laughs.* A & W. Publishers, Inc., 1981.

Ade, George. *Fables In Slang.* Herbert S. Stone & Co., 1899.

Adler, Mortimer J. and Van Doren, Charles. *Great Treasury of Western Thought.* R.R. Bowker Co., 1977.

Agee, James. *A Death in the Family.* McDowell & Obolensky, 1938, 1956.

Agee, James. *The Collected Poems of James Agee.* Robert Fitzgerald, ed. Houghton Mifflin Co., 1968.

Ai, Sin. *Poems by Sin Ai.* Houghton Mifflin Co., 1986.

Aiken, Joan. *The Girl From Paris.* Doubleday & Co., Inc., 1982.

Alcott, Louisa May. *Glimpses of Louisa.* Cornelia Meigs, ed. Little, Brown & Co., 1968.

Alcott, Louisa May. *Little Women.* Grosset & Dunlap, 1947, 1981.

Alcott, Louisa May. *Little Men.* J. M. Dent & Sons, Ltd., 1957.

Aldiss, Brian W. *Helliconia Summer.* Atheneum Publishers, 1983.

Aleichem, Sholom. *Wandering Star.* Crown Publishers, Inc., 1952.

Aleichem, Sholom. *The Adventures of Menahem-Mendl.* G.P. Putnam's Sons, 1969.

Aleichem, Sholom. *The Old Country.* Crown Publishers, Inc., 1946.

Alexander, Shana. *The Nutcracker.* Doubleday & Co., Inc., 1985.

Alfred, William. "Hogan's Goat." *Best American Plays Sixth Series 1963-1967,* John Gassner and Clive Barnes, eds. Crown Publishers, Inc., 1971.

Algren, Nelson. *The Man With the Golden Arm.* Doubleday & Co., Inc., 1949.

Algren, Nelson. *A Walk On the Wild Side.* Farrar, Straus & Cudahy, 1956.

Allen, Fred. *Treadmill to Oblivion.* Little, Brown & Co., 1954.

Allen, Roberta. *The Traveling Woman.* Vehicle Editions/Talman, 1986.

Allende, Isabel. *The House of the Spirits.* Alfred A. Knopf, Inc., 1985.

Alvarez, A. *Hunt.* Simon & Schuster, 1978.

Ambler, Eric. *Journey Into Fear.* Alfred A. Knopf, Inc., 1940.

Ambler, Eric. *The Siege of the Villa Lipp.* Random House, Inc., 1977.

Amichai, Yehuda. *The Selected Poetry of Yehuda Amichai.* Chana Bloch and Stephen Mitchell, eds. Harper & Row, Publishers, 1986.

Amis, Kingsley, *Lucky Jim.* Penguin Books, 1953, 1976.

Amis, Kingsley. *I Want It Now.* Harcourt, Brace & World, 1968.

Amis, Kingsley. *The Green Man,* Harcourt, Brace & World, Inc., 1969.

Amis, Kingsley. *The Old Devils.* Summit Books/Simon & Schuster, Inc., 1987.

Amis, Martin. *Money.* Viking Penguin, Inc., 1985.

Ammons, A. R. *Collected Poems.* W. W. Norton & Co., Inc., 1971.

Andersen, Hans Christian. *Andersen's Fairy Tales.* Macmillan Publishing Co., Inc., 1963.

Anderson, Maxwell. "Winterset." *Twenty Best Plays of the Modern American Theatre,* John Gassner, ed. Crown Publishers, Inc., 1939.

Anderson, Maxwell and Stallings, Laurence. "What Price Glory." *Famous American Plays of the 1920s.* Dell Books, 1959.

Anderson, Sherwood. *Winesburg, Ohio.* Viking Press, 1919.

Angelou, Maya. *I Know Why the Caged Bird Sings.* Random House, Inc., 1970.

Anouilh, Jean. "Thieves' Carnival." *The Modern Theatre.* Eric Bentley, ed., Vol. 3. Hill & Wang, 1958, 1967.

Anthony, Piers. *With a Tangled Skein.* Del Rey/Ballantine Books, 1985.

Appelfeld, Aharon. *To the Land of the Cattails.* Weidenfeld & Nicolson, 1986.

Apple, Max. *The Oranging of America and Other Stories.* Grossman Publishers/Viking Press, 1976.

Apple, Max. *Free Agents.* Harper & Row, Publishers, 1984.

Arabian Nights, Stories from The Thousand and One Nights. Charles W. Eliot, ed. P. F. Collier & Son, Corp., 1937.

Ardizzone., Tony. *The Evening News.* University of Georgia Press, 1986.

Ardizzone, Tony. *The Heart of the Order.* Henry Holt & Co., 1986.

Asch, Sholem. *Three Cities.* G.P. Putnam's Sons, 1933.

Ashberry, John. *Selected Poems.* Elisabeth Sifton Books/Viking Penguin, Inc., 1985.

Atwood, Margaret. *Selected Poems.* Simon & Schuster, 1976.

Atwood, Margaret. *Bodily Harm.* Simon & Schuster, 1982.

Atwood, Margaret. *Bluebeard's Egg and Other Stories.* Houghton Mifflin Co., 1986.

Atwood, Margaret. *The Handmaid's Tale.* Houghton Mifflin Co., 1986.

Auchincloss, Louis. *Powers of Attorney.* Houghton Mifflin Co., 1963.

Auchincloss, Louis. *The Country Cousin.* Houghton Mifflin Co., 1978.

Auchincloss, Louis. *Honorable Men.* Houghton Mifflin Co., 1985.

Auden, W. H. *W. H. Auden Collected Poems.* Edward Mendelson, ed. Random House, Inc., 1976.

Available Press/Pen Short Story Collection. Ballantine Books, 1985.

Axelrod, George. "The Seven Year Itch." *Best American Plays 1951-1957.* John Gassner, ed. Crown Publishers, Inc., 1958.

Babel, Isaac. *You Must Know Everything.* Farrar, Straus & Giroux, Inc., 1969.

Bach, Bob and Mercer, Ginger, eds. *Our Huckleberry Friend . . . The Life, Times and Lyrics of Johnny Mercer.* Lyle Stuart, Inc., 1982.

Bagby, George. *Mugger's Day.* Doubleday & Co., Inc., 1979.

Bainbridge, Beryl. *A Quiet Life.* George Braziller, Inc., 1976.

Bainbridge, Beryl. *Sweet William.* George Braziller,Inc., 1976.

Baker, Carlos. *A Friend in Power.* Charles Scribner's Sons, 1958.

Baker, Carlos. *The Land of Rumbelow.* Charles Scribner's Sons, 1963.

Baker, Carlos. *The Talismans and Other Stories.* Charles Scribner's Sons, 1976.

Baker, Russell. *So This Is Depravity.* Congdon & Lattès, Inc., 1980.

Baldwin, James. *Giovanni's Room.* Dial Press, 1956.

Baldwin, Robert and Paris, Ruth. *The Book of Similes.* Routledge & Kegan Paul Ltd., 1982.

Ballard, Mignon F. *Raven Rock.* Dodd, Mead & Co., 1986.

Balzac, Honoré de. *Short Stories.* Carleton House, n.d.

Balzac, Honoré de. *The Short Novels of Balzac.* Dial Press, 1948.

Balzac, Honoré de. *Old Goriot.* Modern Library/Random House, Inc., 1950.

Bankhead, Tallulah. *Tallulah.* Harper & Brothers, Publishers, 1952.

Banks, Russell. *Searching for Survivors.* Fiction Collective, 1975.

Bannister, Jo. *Mosaic.* Doubleday & Co., Inc., 1987.

Barker, Clive. *In the Flesh.* Poseidon Press, 1986.

Barker, Paul. *The Century's Daughter.* G. P. Putnam's Sons, 1986.

Barnard, Robert. *Fête Fatale.* Charles Sribner's Sons, 1985.

Baron, Joseph L. *A Treasury of Jewish Quotations.* Crown Publishers, Inc., 1956.

Barthelme, Frederick. *Tracer.* Simon & Schuster, 1985.

Bartlett, John, ed. *Familiar Quotations.* Little, Brown & Co., 1937, 1948, 1955.

Bartlett, John Russell. *Dictionary of Americanisms: A Glossary of Words and Phrases/Addenda or Proverbs and Similes,* 4th Edition. Little, Brown & Co., 1877.

Bartov, Hanoch. *The Brigade.* Holt, Rinehart & Winston, Inc., 1968.

Barzun, Jacques. *The House of Intellect.* Harper & Brothers, 1959.

Bates, H. E. *Spella Ho.* Little, Brown & Co., 1938.

Bates, H. E. *The Nature of Love.* Little, Brown & Co., 1953.

Bates, H. E. *The Watercress Girl.* Little, Brown & Co., 1959.

Bates, H. E. *The Daffodil Sky.* Little, Brown & Co., n.d.

Bates, H. E. *A Moment in Time.* Farrar, Straus & Co., 1964.

Baum, Vicki. *Grand Hotel* Doubleday, Doran & Co., Inc., 1931.

Baum, Vicki. *Hotel Berlin '43.* Doubleday, Doran & Co., Inc., 1944.

Baum, Vicki. *The Mustard Seed.* Dial Press, 1953.

Bawden, Nina. *The Grain of Truth.* Harper & Row, Publishers, 1968.

Baxter, Charles. *Through the Safety Net Stories.* Viking Penguin, Inc., 1985.

Beaton, M. C. *Death of a Cad.* St. Martin's Press, 1987.

Beattie, Ann. *The Burning House.* Random House, Inc., 1982.

Beattie, Ann. *Love Always.* Random House, Inc., 1985.

Beattie, Ann. *Where You'll Find Me and Other Stories.* Linden Press/Simon & Schuster, 1986.

Beauvoir, Simone de. *The Second Sex.* Alfred A. Knopf, Inc., 1953.

Beechcroft, William. *Image of Evil.* Dodd, Mead & Co., 1985.

Beechcroft, William. *Chain of Vengeance.* Dodd, Mead & Co., 1986

Behn, Noel. *The Kremlin Letter.* Simon & Schuster, 1966.

Bell, Madison Smartt. *Waiting For the End of the World.* Ticknor & Fields, 1985.

Bell, Madison Smartt. *Straight Cut.* Ticknor & Fields, 1986.

Bell, Marvin. *A Probable Volume of Dreams.* Atheneum Publishers, 1969.

Bellow, Saul. *The Victim.* Vanguard Press, 1947.

Bellow, Saul. *The Adventure of Augie March.* Viking Press, 1953.

Bellow, Saul. *Henderson, the Rain King.* Viking Press, 1959.

Bellow, Saul. *Herzog.* Viking Press, 1961, 1963, 1964.

Bellow, Saul. *Mr. Sammler's Planet.* The Viking Press, 1970.

Bellow, Saul. "The Last Analysis." *Best American Plays Sixth Series 1963-1967.* John Gassner and Clive Barnes, eds., Crown Publishers, Inc., 1971.

Bellow, Saul. *Humboldt's Gift.* Viking Press, 1975.

Bellow, Saul. *The Dean's December.* Harper & Row Publishers, Inc., 1982.

Bemelmans, Ludwig. *I Love You, I Love You, I Love You.* Viking Press., 1942.

Bemelmans, Ludwig. *Tell Them It Was Wonderful.* Madeleine Bemelmans, ed. Viking Penguin, Inc., 1985.

Benchley, Nathaniel. *Lassiter's Folly.* Atheneum Publishers, 1971.

Benchley, Peter. Q. *Clearance.* Random House, Inc., 1986.

Benét, Stephen Vincent. *Thirteen O'Clock.* Farrar & Rinheart, Inc,. 1925, 1928, 1930, 1935, 1937.

Benét, Stephen Vincent. *Selected Works of Stephen Vincent Benét,* Vol. 1. Farrar & Rinehart, Inc., 1942.

Benét, William Rose, ed. *The Reader's Encyclopedia.* 2nd Edition, Volume One A-L and Volume Two M-Z. Thomas Y. Crowell, 1965.

Benson, Stella. "The Man Who Missed the Bus." *Reading Modern Fiction,* 4th Edition. Charles Scribner's Sons, 1968.

Berkman, Sylvia. *Blackberry Wilderness.* Doubleday & Co., Inc., 1959.

Berrigan, Daniel. *Selected and New Poems.* Doubleday & Co., Inc., 1973.

Berry, Wendell. *Collected Poems 1957-1981.* North Point Press, 1985.

Berryman, John. *The Dream Songs.* Farrar, Straus & Giroux, Inc., 1969.

The Best American Short Stories 1951. Martha Foley, ed. Houghton Mifflin Co., 1951.

The Best American Short Stories 1958. Martha Foley and David Burnett, eds. Houghton Mifflin Co., 1958.

The Best American Short Stories 1960. Martha Foley and David Burnett, eds. Houghton Mifflin Co., 1960.

The Best American Short Stories 1961. Martha Foley and David Burnett, eds. Houghton Mifflin Co., 1961.

The Best American Short Stories 1966. Martha Foley and David Burnett, eds. Houghton Mifflin Co., 1966.

The Best American Short Stories 1968. Martha Foley and David Burnett, eds. Houghton Mifflin Co., 1968.

The Best American Short Stories 1974. Martha Foley, ed. Houghton Mifflin Co., 1974.

The Best American Short Stories 1975. Martha Foley, ed. Houghton Mifflin Co., 1975.

The Best American Short Stories 1976. Martha Foley, ed. Houghton Mifflin Co., 1976.

The Best American Short Stories 1977. Martha Foley, ed. Houghton Mifflin Co., 1977.

The Best American Short Stories 1979. Joyce Carol Oates, ed. Houghton Mifflin Co., 1979.

The Best American Short Stories 1980. Stanley Elkin ed., with Shannon Ravenel. Houghton Mifflin Co., 1980.

The Best American Short Stories 1981. Hortense Calisher ed., with Shannon Ravenel. Houghton Mifflin Co., 1981.

The Best American Short Stories 1982. John Gardner ed., with Shannon Ravenel. Houghton Mifflin Co., 1982.

The Best American Short Stories 1983. Anne Tyler, ed., with Shannon Ravenel. Houghton Mifflin Co., 1983.

The Best American Short Stories 1984. John Updike ed., with Shannon Ravenel. Houghton Mifflin Co., 1984.

The Best American Short Stories 1986. Raymond Carver ed., with Shannon Ravenel. Houghton Mifflin Co., 1986.

The Best of Winter. A.D. MacLean ed. St. Martin's Press, Inc., 1979. (See also *Winter's Tales*) .

The Best Short Stories of World War II. Viking Press, 1957.

Bierce, Ambrose. *The Collected Writing of Ambrose Bierce.* Citadel Press, 1946.

Billings, Josh. *Josh Billings: His Book.* G. W. Carleton, 1865.

Billings, Josh. *Josh Billings: His Sayings.* G. W. Carleton, 1866.

Bird, Sarah. *Alamo House.* W. W. Norton & Co., 1986.

Bishop, Elizabeth. *The Complete Poems 1927-1979.* Farrar, Straus & Giroux, Inc., 1983.

Bisson, Terry. *Talking Man.* Arbor House, 1986.

Blake, William. *The Portable Blake,* selected and arranged by Alfred Kazin. Viking Press, 1946, 1968.

Bohn, Henry George. *A Hand-book of Proverbs, Comprising Republication of Ray's [John Ray] Collection of English Proverbs.* Reprint Bohn's 1855 ed., AMS Press 1968.

Böll, Heinrich. *The Stories of Heinrich Böll.* Alfred A. Knopf, Inc., 1986.

Bombeck, Erma. *Four of a Kind.* McGraw-Hill Book Co., 1985.

Borsten, Rick. *The Great Equalizer.* Permanent Press, 1986.

Botkin, B. A., ed. *A Treasury of American Folklore.* Crown Publishers, Inc., 1944.

Botkin, B. A., ed. *A Treasury of New England Folklore.* Crown Publishers, Inc., 1947.

Botkin, B. A., ed. *A Treasury of Southern Folklore.* Crown Publishers, Inc., 1949.

Bottome, Phyllis. *The Mortal Storm.* Little, Brown and Co., 1938.

Bottome, Phyllis. *The Best Stories of Phyllis Bottom* e, chosen by Daphne du Maurier. Faber & Faber, 1963.

Bowen, Elizabeth. *Yankee from Olympus.* Little, Brown & Co., 1945.

Bowen, Elizabeth. *The Death of the Heart.* Alfred A. Knopf, 1963.

Bowen, Elizabeth. *The Collected Stories of Elizabeth Bowen.* Alfred A. Knopf, Inc., 1981.

Bowles, Jane. *My Sister's Hand In Mine.* Ecco Press, 1978.

Boyd, William. *An Ice-Cream War.* William Morrow & Co., Inc., 1983.

Boyd, William. *On the Yankee Station.* William Morrow & Co., Inc., 1984.

Boyle, Kay. *Generation Without Farewell.* Alfred A. Knopf, Inc., 1960.

Boyle, Kay. *The Wild Horses.* Doubleday & Co., 1966.

Boyle, T. Coraghessan. *Water Music.* Little, Brown & Co., 1980-1981.

Boyle, T. Coraghessan. *Budding Prospects.* Viking Press, 1984.

Boyle, T. Coraghessan. *Greasy Lake & Other Stories.* Viking Press, 1958.

Boyle, T. Coraghessan. *The Descent of Man.* Atlantic Monthly Press Book/Little, Brown & Co., 1974, 1976, 1977, 1978, 1979.

Bracken, Peg. *But I Wouldn't Have Missed It for the World!.* Harcourt Brace Jovanovich, Inc., 1973.

Bradford, Barbara Taylor. *Act of Will.* Doubleday & Co., Inc., 1986.

Bradley, George. *Terms to Be Met.* Yale University Press, 1986.

Braine, John. *Room at the Top.* Houghton Mifflin Co., 1957.

Brammer, William. *The Gay Place.* Houghton Mifflin Co., 1961.

Braude, Jacob M. *The Speaker's Desk Book of Quips, Quotes and Anecdotes.* Prentice-Hall, Inc., 1963.

Brautigan, Richard. *So the Wind Won't Blow It All Away.* Seymour Lawrence/ Delacorte Press, 1982.

Brecht, Bertold. *Bertolt Brecht Short Stories 1921-1946.* John Willett and Ralph Manheim, eds. Metuhen, Inc., 1983.

Brennan, Maeve. *The Long-Winded Lady.* William Morrow & Co., Inc., 1969.

Breslin, Jimmy. *Table Money.* Ticknor & Fields, 1986.

Breslin, Jimmy and Schaap, Dick. *.44.* Viking Press, 1978.

Brierley, David. *Cold War.* Summit Books/Simon & Schuster, 1979.

Brierley, David. *Skorpion's Death.* Summit Books/Simon & Schuster, 1985.

Brinig, Myron. *The Sisters.* Farrar & Rinehart, Inc., 1937.

Brinnin, John Malcolm. *Skin Diving in the Virgins and Other Poems.* A Seymour Lawrence Book/Delacorte Press, 1943, 1944, 1949-53, 1956, 1958, 1960, 1962, 1963, 1970.

Bromfield, Louis. *The Green Bay Tree.* Grosset & Dunlap Publishers, c. Frederick A. Stokes Co., 1924.

Bromfield, Louis. *Here Today and Gone Tomorrow.* P. F. Collier & Son Corp., 1934.

Bromfield, Louis. *It Takes All Kinds.* Harper & Brothers, Publishers, 1939.

Bronk, William. *Life Supports, New and Collected Poems.* North Point Press, 1981.

Brontë, Charlotte. *Jane Eyre.* E. P. Dutton, Inc., 1963.

Brontë, Charlotte. *Shirley.* Everyman's Library/J. M. Dent & Sons, Ltd., 1908, 1974.

Brontë. Charlotte. *Emma.* Everest House, 1980.

Brontë, Emily. *Wuthering Heights.* Dodd, Mead & Co., 1942.

Brookner, Anita. *The Misalliance.* Pantheon Books, 1986.

Brown, Dee. *Conspiracy of Knaves.* Henry Holt & Co., 1987.

Brown, Rita Mae. *Southern Discomfort.* Harper & Row, Publishers, Inc., 1982.

Brown, Rita Mae. *Sudden Death.* Bantam Books, 1983.

Brown, Rita Mae. *High Hearts.* Bantam Books, 1986.

Brown, Rosellen. *Street Games.* Doubleday & Co., Inc., 1974.

Browne, Gerald A. *19 Purchase Street.* Arbor House, 1982.

Browning, Elizabeth Barrett. *The Complete Poetical Works of Elizabeth Barrett Browning.* Harriet Waters Preston, ed. Scholarly Press, Inc., 1978.

Browning, Robert. *The Poetry of Robert Browning.* Jacob Korg ed. Bobbs-Merrill Co., Inc., 1971.

Brussell, Eugene E. *Dictionary of Quotable Definitions.* Prentice-Hall, Inc., 1970.

Bryan, C.D.B. *Beautiful Women; Ugly Scenes.* Doubleday & Co., Inc., 1983.

Bukowski, Charles. *Love Is a Dog From Hell Poems 1974-1977.* Black Sparrow Press, 1977.

Bulgakov, Mikhail. *The Master and Margarita.* Harper & Row, Publishers, 1967.

Burke, James Lee. *The Lost Get-Back Boogie.* Louisiana State University Press, 1986.

Burnet, Whit, ed. *The Story Pocket Book.* Pocket Books/Simon & Schuster, 1944.

Busch, Niven. *Duel in the Sun.* William Morrow & Co., 1944.

Butler, Samuel. *The Way of All Flesh.* James Cochrane, ed. English Library Series, 1966.

Cain, James. *Career in C Major and Other Fiction.* Roy Hoopes, ed. McGraw-Hill Book Co., 1986.

Caine, Lynn. *Widow.* William Morrow & Co., Inc., 1974.

Calisher, Hortense. *Queenie.* Arbor House, 1971.

Calisher, Hortense. *The Bobby-Soxer.* Doubleday & Co., Inc., 1986.

Calisher, Hortense. *The Collected Stories of Hortense Calisher.* Arbor House Publishing Co., 1948-52, 1954-57, 1960, 1962, 1968, 1975.

Calvino, Italo. Harcourt Brace Jovanovich, 1985.

Camoin, François. *Why Men Are Afraid of Women.* University of Georgia Press, 1984.

Campbell, R. Wright. *Circus Couronne.* G. P. Putnam's Sons, 1977.

Campbell, R. Wright. *Where Pigeons Go to Die.* Rawson Associates Publishers, Inc., 1978.

Campbell, R. Wright. *Malloy's Subway.* Atheneum Publishers, 1981.

Campbell, R. Wright. *Fat Tuesday.* Ticknor & Fields, 1983.

Campbell, Ramsey. *The Hungry Moon.* Macmillan Publishing Co., Inc., 1986.

Campbell, Robert. *The Junkyard Dog.* New American Library, 1986.

Campbell, Robert. *In La-La Land We Trust.* Mysterious Press, 1986.

Camus, Albert. *The Stranger.* Random House, Inc., 1942.

Camus, Albert. *Notebooks 1935-1942.* Modern Library/Random House, Inc., 1963.

Capote, Truman. *The Dogs Bark: Private Places and Public People.* Random House, Inc., 1973.

Carlyle, Thomas. *Early Letters of Thomas Carlyle.* Charles E. Norton, ed. Longwood Publishing, 1977.

Carr, John Dickson. *All But Impossible.* Ticknor & Fields, 1981.

Carroll, Lewis. *Through the Looking Glass.* Clarkson N. Potter, Inc., n.d.

Carruth, Hayden. *The Selected Poetry of Hayden Carruth.* Macmillan Publishing Co., Inc., 1985.

Carter, Angela. *The War of Dreams.* Harcourt Brace Jovanovich, 1972.

Carter, Angela. *Nights At the Circus.* Viking Penguin, Inc., 1984.

Carter, Angela. *Saints and Sinners.* Viking Penguin, Inc., 1986.

Cary, Joyce. *Herself Surprised.* Harper & Row, Publishers, Inc., 1941.

Cary, Joyce. *The Horse's Mouth.* Harper & Row, Publishers, Inc., 1945.

Cary, Joyce. *Spring Song and Other Stories.* Harper & Brothers, 1951-1958, 1960.

Cassill, R. V. *Doctor Cobb's Game,* Bernard Geis Associates, 1970.

Cassill, R. V. *Hoyt's Child,* Doubleday & Co., Inc., 1976.

Cassill, R. V. *Labors of Love.* Arbor House, 1980.

Cather, Willa. *One of Ours.* Alfred A. Knopf, Inc., 1922.

Cather, Willa. *Youth and the Bright Medusa.* Alfred A. Knopf, Inc., 1929.

Cather, Willa. *Shadows on the Rock.* Alfred A. Knopf, Inc., 1931.

Cather, Willa. *My Antonia.* Houghton Mifflin Co., Inc., 1954.

Cather, Willa. *Death Comes to the Archbishop.* Alfred A. Knopf, Inc., 1962.

Cather, Willa. *Obscure Destinies.* Vintage Books/Random House, Inc., 1974.

Celine, Louis-Ferdinand. *Journey to the End of the Night.* New Directions Books, 1934.

Cerf, Bennett and Hornblow, Leonora eds. *Bennett Cerf's Take Along Treasury.* Doubleday & Co., Inc., 1963.

Cervantes, Miguel de. *Don Quixote.* Viking Press, 1949.

Chandler, Raymond. *The Midnight Raymond Chandler.* Houghton Mifflin Co., 1971.

Chandler, Raymond. *The Big Sleep.* Vintage Books/Random House, Inc., 1976.

Chandler, Raymond. *Lady in the Lake.* Random House, Inc., 1976.

Chase, Joan. *During the Reign of the Queen of Persia.* Harper & Row Publishers, 1983.

Chase, Mary Ellen. *The Edge of Darkness.* W. W. Norton & Co., Inc., 1957.

Chatterton, Ruth. *The Southern Wind.* Doubleday & Co., Inc., 1958.

Cheever, John. *The Wapshot Scandal.* Harper & Row, Publishers, Inc., 1959, 1961, 1961, 1963, 1964.

Cheever, John. *The Housebreaker of Shady Hill and Other Stories.* Harper & Brothers, 1953-1958.

Cheever, John. *The Stories of John Cheever.* Alfred A. Knopf, Inc., 1978.

Chekhov, Anton. "The Cherry Orchard." *Best Plays.* The Modern Library/Random House, Inc., 1956.

Chekhov, Anton. "The Sea Gull." *The Twenty Best European Plays on the American Stage.* John Gassner ed. Crown Publishers, Inc., 1974.

Chekov, Anton. *Stories of Russian Life.* Charles Scribner's Sons, 1915.

Chesterfield, Lord. *Lord Chesterfield's Letters to his Son and Others.* J. M. Dent & Sons Ltd., 1929, 1957.

Chesterton, G. K. *The Innocence of Father Brown.* Dodd, Mead & Co., 1911.

Chesterton, G. K. *The Secret of Father Brown.* Dodd, Mead & Co., 1927, 1954.

Chesterton, G. K. *All Is Grist.* Books For Libraries Press, Inc., 1932, 1967.

Chesterton, G. K. *The Man Who Was Thursday.* Dodd, Mead & Co., 1935.

Chesterton, G. K. *As I Was Saying.* Robert Knille ed. William B. Eerdmans Publishing Co., 1955.

Chesterton, G. K. *Father Brown Mystery Stories.* Raymond T. Bond, ed. Dodd, Mead & Co., 1974.

Chitham, Edward and Winnifrith, Tom, eds. *Selected Brontë Poems.* Basil Blackwell, Ltd., 1985.

Christy, Robert, ed. *Proverbs Maxims and Phrases of All Ages.* G.P. Putnam's Sons, 1887.

Churgin, Yaakov. *A Whole Loaf.* Sholom J.Kahn, ed. Vanguard Press, Inc., 1957.

Chute, Carolyn. *The Beans of Egypt, Maine.* Ticknor & Fields, 1985.

Ciardi, John. *Selected Poems John Ciardi.* University of Arkansas Press, 1984.

Ciment, Jill. *Small Claims.* Weidenfeld & Nicolson, 1986.

Claiborne, Robert. *Our Marvelous Native Tongue.* Times Books,1987.

Clark, Brian. "Whose Life Is Is It Anyway." *The Best Plays of the Seventies.* Stanley Richards, ed. Doubleday & Co., Inc., 1980.

Clark, Eleanor. *Gloria Mundi.* Pantheon Books, 1979.

Cobb, Irvin S. *Ladies and Gentlemen.* Books for Libraries Press, 1927, 1970.

Cohen, Arthur A. *In the Days of Simon Stern.* Random House, Inc., 1972, 1973.

Cohen, Arthur A. *Acts of Theft.* A Helen and Kurt Wolff Book/Harcourt Brace Jovanovich, 1980.

Cohen, J.M and M.J., eds. *The Penguin Dictionary of Quotations.* Penguin Books, 1960.

Cole, William ed. *The Fireside Book of Humorous Poetry.* Simon & Schuster 1959.

Coleman, Elliott, ed. *Poems of Byron, Keats and Shelley.* Doubleday & Co., Inc., 1967.

Colette. *Three Short Novels by Colette.* Farrar, Straus & Young, 1952.

Colette. *The Collected Stories of Colette.* Farrar, Straus & Giroux, Inc., 1983.

Colwin, Laurie. *Passion and Affect.* Viking Press, 1974.

Colwin, Laurie. *Happy All the Time.* Alfred A. Knopf, Inc., 1978.

Colwin, Laurie. *Another Marvelous Thing.* Alfred A. Knopf, Inc., 1986.

Condon, Richard. *Prizzi's Family.* G. P. Putnam's Sons, 1986.

Connolly, Cyril, ed. *Great English Short Novels.* Dial Press, 1953.

Conrad, Joseph. *Tales of Unrest.* Doubleday, Page & Co., 1920.

Conrad, Joseph. *Typhoon and Other Stories.* Doubleday, Page & Co., 1925.

Conrad, Joseph. *Lord Jim.* Doubleday & Co., 1927.

Conroy, Frank. *Stop-Time.* Viking Press, 1965.

Conroy, Pat. *The Great Santini.* Houghton Mifflin Co., 1976.

Conroy, Pat. *The Lords of Discipline.* Houghton Mifflin Co., 1980.

Conroy, Pat. *The Prince of Tides.* Houghton Mifflin Co., 1986.

Coomer, Joe. *Kentucky Love.* Richard Marek/St. Martin's, 1985.

Cooper, Jilly. *Riders.* Ballantine Books, 1985.

Coppard, A. E. *Collected Tales of A. E. Coppard.* Alfred A. Knopf, Inc., 1948.

Cortázar, Julio. *We Love Glenda So Much.* Alfred A. Knopf, Inc., 1983.

Coughlin, T. Glen. *The Hero of New York.* W. W. Norton & Co., Inc., 1986.

Coward, Noël. *To Step Aside.* Doubleday, Doran & Co., Inc., 1939.

Coward,, Noël. *The Lyrics of Noël Coward.* Doubleday & Co., Inc., 1967.

Bibliography

Cowley, Malcolm. *Blue Juniata: A Life Collected and New Poems.* Elisabeth Sifton Books/Viking Penguin, Inc., 1968.

Coyle, Lee. *George Ade.* Twayne Publishers, Inc., 1964.

Craig, M. S. *Flash Point.* Dodd, Mead & Co., 1987.

Crane, Hart. *The Complete Poems and Selected Letters and Prose of Hart Crane.* Brom Weber, ed. Anchor Books/Doubleday & Co., Inc., 1966.

Crane, Stephen. *The Red Badge of Courage.* D. Appleton & Co., 1894.

Crofton, Ian and Fraser, Donald, eds. *A Dictionary of Musical Quotations.* Schirmer Books/Macmillan Publishing Co., Inc., 1985.

Cronin, A. J. *Shannon's Way.* Little, Brown & Co., 1948.

Crumley, James. *One To Count Cadence.* Random House, Inc., 1969.

Crumley, James. *The Wrong Case.* Random House, Inc., 1975.

Crumley, James. *The Last Good Kiss.* Random House, Inc., 1978.

Crumley, James. *Dancing Bear.* Random House, Inc., 1983.

Curley, Daniel. *Living with Snakes.* University of Georgia Press, 1985.

Currie, Ellen. *Available Light.* Summit Books/Simon & Schuster, 1986.

Cussler, Clive. *Cyclops.* Simon & Schuster, 1986.

Dahl, Roald. *Someone Like You.* Alfred A. Knopf, Inc., 1966.

Dass, Ram and Gorman, Paul. *How Can I Help?* Alfred A. Knopf, Inc., 1985.

David, Rhys. *The Chosen One and Other Stories.* Dodd, Mead & Co., 1960, 1962, 1964, 1966, 1967.

Davidoff, Henry. *The Pocket Book of Quotations.* Pocket Books/Simon & Schuster, 1942, 1952.

Davies, Robertson. *A Mixture of Frailties.* Charles Scribner's Sons, 1958.

Davies, Robertson. *The Rebel Angels.* Viking Press, 1981.

Davies, Tom. *The Life of Johnson.* Christopher Hibbert, ed. Penguin Books, 1979.

Deal, Borden. *The Other Room.* Doubleday & Co., Inc., 1974.

Deal, Babs H. *The Walls Came Tumbling Down.* Doubleday & Co., Inc., 1968.

Deal, Babs H. *The Crystal Mouse.* Doubleday & Co., Inc., 1973.

De Hartog, Jan. *The Call of the Sea.* Atheneum Publishers, 1966.

De La Mare, Walter. *The Riddle and Other Tales.* Alfred A. Knopf, Inc., 1930.

De La Roche, Mazo. *The Building of Jalna.* Little, Brown & Co., 1944.

De La Roche, Mazo. *Renny's Daughter.* Little, Brown & Co., 1951.

De La Roche, Mazo. *Morning at Jalna.* Little, Brown & Co., 1960.

Delmar, Viña. *The Big Family.* Harcourt, Brace & Co., 1961.

Denby, David. *The Complete Poems.* Ron Padgett ed. Random House, Inc., 1986.

Deutsch, Babette. *The Collected Poems of Babette Deutsch.* Doubleday & Co., Inc., 1969.

De Vries, Peter. *Reuben, Reuben.* Little, Brown & Co., 1956, 1962, 1964.

De Vries, Peter. *Consenting Adults.* Little, Brown & Co., 1980.

De Vries, Peter. *Slouching Towards Kalamazoo.* Little, Brown & Co., 1983.

De Vries, Peter. *Mrs. Wallop.* Little, Brown and Co., 1983.

De Vries, Peter. *Peckham's Marbles.* G. P. Putnam's Sons, 1986.

De Witt, Henry, ed. *The Ploughshares Reader: New Fiction For the Eighties.* Pushcart Press, 1985.

Dickens, Charles. *The Posthumous Papers of The Pickwick Club.* Charles Scribner's Sons, 1910.

Dickens, Charles. *The Best Short Stories of Charles Dickens.* Edwin Valentine Mitchell, ed. Charles Scribner's Sons, 1947.

Dickens, Charles. *A Tale of Two Cities.* Grosset & Dunlap Publishers, 1948.

Dickens, Charles. *Hard Times.* New American Library, Inc., 1964.

Dickens, Charles. *Our Mutual Friend.* Penguin Books, 1971.

Dickens, Charles. *Oliver Twist.* Oxford University Press. 1966.

Dickey, James. *James Dickey Poems 1957-1967.* Wesleyan University Press, 1958-1967.

Dickinson, Emily. *Bolts of Melody.* Mabel Loomis Todd and Millicent Todd Bingham eds. Harper & Brothers, Publishers, 1945.

Diehl, William. *Sharky's Machine.* Delacorte Press, 1978.

Diehl, William. *Chamelon.* Random House, Inc., 1981.

Diehl, William. *Hooligans.* Villard Books, 1984.

Dieter, William. *The Cactus Garden.* Atheneum Publishers, 1986.

Dinesen, Isak. *Winter's Tales.* Random House, Inc., 1942.

Dinesen, Isak. *Anecdotes of Destiny.* Random House, Inc., 1958.

Dinesen, Isak. *Carnival.* The University of Chicago Press, 1977.

Disraeli, Benjamin. *The Letters of Disraeli to Lady Chesterfield and Lady Bradford.* Marquis of Zetland ed., Volume I. D. Appleton & Co., 1929.

Djilas, Milovan. *The Leper and Other Stories.* Harcourt, Brace & World, Inc., 1964.

Donleavy, J. P. *The Beastly Beatitudes of Balthazar.* Seymour Lawrence/Delacorte Press, 1968.

Donleavy, J. P. *The Destinies of Darcy Cancer, Gentleman.* Seymour Lawrence/Delacorte Press, 1977.

Donne, John. *John Donne, Complete Poetry and Selected Prose.* John Hayward, ed. Random House, Inc., 1936.

Dorfman, Ariel. *The Last Song of Manuel Sendero.* Viking Penguin, Inc., 1987.

Dos Passos, John. *U.S.A.* Houghton Mifflin Co. 1930, 1932, 1933, 1934, 1935, 1936, 1937.

Downes, Olin and Siegmeister, Eli. *A Treasury of American Song.* Alfred A. Knopf, Inc., 1940, 1943.

Drabble, Margaret. *A Summer Bird-Cage.* William Morrow & Co., 1964.

Drabble, Margaret. *The Waterfall.* Alfred A. Knopf, Inc., 1969.

Drabble, Margaret. *The Realms of Gold.* Alfred A. Knopf, Inc., 1975.

Drennan, Robert E., ed. *The Algonquin Wits.* Citadel Press. 1968.

du Maurier, Daphne. *The Parasites.* Doubleday & Co., Inc., 1950.

du Maurier, Daphne. *Rebecca.* Doubleday & Co., Inc., 1938.

Du Maurier, George. *Peter Ibbetson.* Harper & Brothers, 1891.

Dubus, Andre. *The Times Are Never So Bad.* David R. Godine, 1983.

Duncan, Robert. *Ground Work-Before the War.* A New Directions Book 1968-1972, 1974-1977, 1981, 1984.

Duras, Marguerite. *Ten-Thirty On a Summer Night.* Grove Press, Inc., 1960.

Duras, Marguerite. *Montorato Cantabile.* Grove Press, Inc., 1960.

Duras, Marguerite. *The Lover.* Random House, Inc./William Collins Sons & Co., Ltd., 1985.

Durrell, Lawrence. *Justine* E. P. Dutton & Co., Inc., 1957.

Durrell, Lawrence. *Balthazar.* E. P. Dutton & Co., Inc., 1958.

Durrell, Lawrence. *Mountolive.* E. P. Dutton & Co., Inc., 1959.

Durrell, Lawrence. *Tunc.* E. P. Dutton & Co., Inc., 1968.

Durrell, Lawrence. *Livia.* Viking Press, 1978.

Edelman, Maurice. *Disraeli Rising.* Stein & Day Publishers, 1975.

Eden, Emily. *The Semi-Detached House.* Dial Press, 1979.

Edgar, Josephine. *Bright Young Things.* St. Martin's Press, 1986.

Edwards, Tryon, original compiler; Catrevas, C.N. and Edwards, Jonathan, eds. rev. ed., *The New Dictionary of Thoughts.* Standard Book Co., 1955.

Eisenberg, Deborah. *Transitions in a Foreign Currency.* Alfred A. Knopf, Inc., 1986.

Eliot, Charles W., ed. *The Harvard Classics,* Volumes 1-50. P. F. Collier & Son Corp., 1909, 1910, 1937.

Eliot, George. *Romola.* J. M. Dent & Sons Ltd., 1948.

Eliot, George. *Adam Bede.* Washington Square Press, 1971.

Eliot, George. *The Mill On the Floss.* Gordon, Haight, ed. Oxford University Press, 1982.

Eliot, T. S. *T. S. Elliot Collected Poems 1909-1962.* Harcourt, Brace & World, Inc., 1963.

Elkin, Stanley. *Criers and Kibitzers, Kibitzers and Criers.* Random House, Inc., 1959-1965.

Elkin, Stanley. *The Specialty of the House and Other Stories.* Mysterious Press, 1979.

Elliott, Sumner Locke. *Signs of Life.* Ticknor & Fields, 1981.

Ellison, Ralph. *The Invisible Man.* Random House, Inc. 1963.

Ellman, Richard and O'Clair, Robert, eds. *The Norton Anthology of Modern Poetry.* W. W. Norton & Co., Inc., 1973.

Emerson, Ralph Waldo. *Ralph Waldo Emerson Selected Prose and Poetry.* Holt, Rinehart & Winston, 1963.

Émile Zola. *A Love Episode.* Sociéte des Beaux-Arts, n.d.

Engberg, Susan. *A Stay By the River.* Viking Penguin, Inc., 1985.

Erdrich, Louise. *Love Medicine.* Holt, Rinehart & Winston, 1984.

Erdrich, Louise. *The Beet Queen.* Henry Holt & Co., 1986.

Erickson, Steve. *Rubicon Beach.* Poseidon Press, 1986.

Esar, Evan, ed. *Dictionary of Humorous Quotations.* Paperback Library, 1949.

Estleman, Loren D. *Motor City Blues.* Houghton Mifflin Co., 1980.

Estleman, Loren D. *The Midnight Man.* Houghton Mifflin Co., 1982.

Estleman, Loren D. *Every Brilliant Eye.* Houghton Mifflin Co., 1986.

Estleman, Loren D. *Lady Yesterday.* Houghton Mifflin Co., 1987.

Evans, Bergen, ed. *Dictionary of Quotations.* Delacorte Press, 1968.

Exley, Frederick. *A Fan's Notes.* Harper & Row, Publishers, 1968.

Fadiman, Clifton. *Party of One: The Selected Writings of Clifton Fadiman.* World Publishing Co., 1955.

Fadiman, Clifton, ed. *The American Treasury 1455-1955.* Harper & Row Publishers, 1955.

Fadiman, Clifton ed. *The World of the Short Story.* Houghton Mifflin Co., 1986.

Farmer, Beverly. *Home Time.* McPhee Gribble/Penguin Books, 1985.

Farrell, G. J. *Troubles.* Alfred A. Knopf, Inc., 1971.

Farrell, M. J. (Molly Keane). *The Rising Tide.* Virago Press/Viking Penguin, Inc. 1985.

Farris, John. *Wildwood.* Tom Doherty Associates/A Tor Book, 1986.

Faulkner, William. *Sanctuary.* Random House, Inc., 1931.

Faulkner, William. *Absalom, Absalom.* Random House, Inc., 1936.

Faulkner, William. *Wild Palms.* Random House, Inc., 1939.

Faulkner, William. *A Rose for Emily.* Ronald Press Co., 1962.

Faulkner, William. *The Collected Stories of William Faulkner/Fox Hunt.* Random House, Inc., 1934, 1950.

Faulkner, William. *The Faulkner Reader.* Random House, Inc., 1929-1932, 1934, 1938, 1939, 1951, 1954.

Feiden, Doug. *The Ten Million Dollar Getaway.* Jove Books, 1980.

Feifer, George. *The Girl From Petrovka.* Viking Press. 1971

Feldman, Irving. *New and Selected Poems.* Viking Press, 1979.

Ferber, Edna. *One Basket.* Doubleday & Co., Inc., 1957.

Ferber, Edna. *Ice Palace.* Doubleday & Co., Inc., 1958.

Ferber, Edna. *Show Boat.* G. K. Hall & Co., 1981.

Ferguson, Patricia. *Family Myths and Legends.* Andre Deutsch Ltd., 1985.

Fielding, Henry. *Joseph Andrews.* W. W. Norton & Co., Inc., 1958.

Finkelstein, Caroline. *Windows Facing East.* Dragon Gate, Inc., 1986.

Finney, Jack. *The Night People.* Doubleday & Co., Inc., 1977.

First-Prize Stories 1919-1954 from the O. Henry Memorial Awards. Doubleday & Co., Inc., 1954. (See Also *Prize Stories of . . . . O. Henry Awards)*

Fisher, Dorothy Canfield. *A Harvest of Stories.* Harcourt, Brace & Co., 1927, 1943-1947, 1949, 1955.

Fitzgerald, Edward. *The Rubáiyát of Omar Khayám.* Heritage Books, Inc., 1946.

Fitzgerald, F. Scott. *This Side of Paradise.* Charles Scribner's Sons, 1920.

Fitzgerald, F. Scott. *The Beautiful and Damned.* Charles Scribner's Sons, 1922, 1950.

Fitzgerald, F.Scott. *All The Sad Young Men.* Charles Scribner & Sons, 1926.

Fitzgerald, F. Scott. *The Stories of F. Scott Fitzgerald.* Charles Scribner's Sons, 1951.

Flanagan, Robert. *Naked to Naked Goes.* Charles Scribner's Sons, 1986.

Flanner, Janet. *Darlinghissima: Letters to a Friend.* Natalia Danesi Murray, editor and commentator. Random House, Inc., 1985.

Flaubert, Gustave. *Salammbô.* Marvin Press, 1931.

Flaubert, Gustave. *Madame Bovary.* Holt, Rinehart & Winston, 1948.

Flaubert, Gustave. *The Selected Letters of Gustave Flaubert.* Francis Steegmuller ed. Farrar, Straus & Cudahy, 1953.

Flexner, Stuart Berg, ed. *I Hear America Talking.* Van Nostrand Reinhold Co., 1976.

Follett, Ken. *Triple.* Arbor House, 1979.

Forbes, Bryan. *The Endless Game.* Random House, Inc., 1986.

Forbes, Colin. *Cover Story.* Atheneum Publishers, 1986.

Forbes Scrapbook, Thoughts On the Business of Life. Forbes, Inc., 1950, 1967, 1968, 1976.

Ford, Richard. *A Piece of My Heart.* Harper & Row, Publishers, 1976.

Ford, Richard. *The Ultimate Good Luck.* Houghton Mifflin Co., 1980.

Ford, Richard. *The Sportswriter.* Vintage Books/Random House, Inc., 1986.

Forster, E. M. *A Room With a View.* Alfred A. Knopf, Inc., 1925.

Forster, E. M. *Two Cheers for Democracy.* Harcourt, Brace & World, Inc., 1947.

Fowles, John. *The Magus,* rev. ed. Little, Brown & Co., 1977.

Fowles, John. *Daniel Martin.* Little, Brown & Co., 1977.

Foy, George. *Coaster.* Viking, 1986.

France, Anatole. *Anatole France Himself.* Jean Jacques Brousson, ed. Wm. H. Wise & Co., 1925.

France, Anatole. *The Crime of Sylvestre Bonnard.* Dodd, Mead & Co., 1931.

Francis, Dick. *Break In.* G. P. Putnam's Sons, 1986.

Francis, Dorothy B. *The Flint Hills Foal.* Abingdon Press, 1976.

Francis, Dorothy B. *Run of the Sea Witch.* Abingdon Press, 1978.

Francis, Dorothy B. *Captain Morgana Mason.* Lodestar, 1981.

Francis, Richard. *Swansong.* Atheneum Publishers, 1986.

Franklin, Ben. *Poor Richard's Almanac.* Peter Pauper Press, 1936.

Fraser, Antonia. *Quiet As a Nun.* Viking Press, 1977.

Fraser, George MacDonald. *Flashman at the Charge.* Alfred A. Knopf, Inc., 1973.

Fredman, Mike. *Kisses Leave No Fingerprints.* St. Martin's Press, 1979.

Fredman, Mike. *You Can Always Blame the Rain.* St. Martin's Press, 1980.

Friedman, Bruce Jay. *Stern and A Mother's Kisses.* Simon & Schuster, 1966.

Fuentes, Carlos. *The Old Gringo.* Farrar, Straus & Giroux, 1985.

Fuller, Thomas. *Aphorisms of Wisdoms or, A Complete Collection of the Most Celebrated Proverbs in the English, Scotch, French, Spanish, Italian and Other Languages.* R & D. Malcolm, 1814.

Furman, Laura. *Tuxedo Park.* Summit Books/Simon & Schuster, 1986.

Gallant, Mavis. *A Fairly Good Time.* Random House, Inc., 1970.

Galsworthy, John. *Caravan: The Assembled Tales of John Galsworthy.* Charles Scribner's Sons, 1925.

Garbo, Norman. *Gaynor's Passion.* Houghton Mifflin, 1985.

Gardner, Gerald. *All the Presidents' Wits.* Beech Tree Books/William Morrow & Co., Inc., 1986.

Gardner, John. *The Art of Living and Other Stories.* Alfred A. Knopf, Inc., 1981.

Garrett, George. *King of the Mountain.* Charles Scribner. Sons, 1957.

Garrett, George. *The Finished Man.* Charles Scribner's Sons, 1959.

Garrett, George. *Which Ones Are the Enemy?* Little, Brown & Co., 1961.

Garrett, George. *Cold Ground Was My Bed Last Night.* University of Missouri Press, 1964.

Garrett, George. *Do, Lord Remember Me.* Doubleday & Co., Inc., 1965.

Garrett, George. *Death of the Fox.* Doubleday & Co., Inc., 1971.

Garrett, George. *The Magic Striptease.* Doubleday & Co., Inc., 1973.

Garrett, George. *The Succession.* Doubleday & Co., Inc., 1983.

Garrett, George. *The Collected Poems of George Garrett.* University of Arkansas Press, 1984.

Garrett, George. *An Evening Performance.* Doubleday & Co., Inc., 1985.

Garrigue, Jean. *Studies for an Actress and Other Poems.* Macmillan Publishing Co., Inc., 1973.

Gary, Romain. *The Company of Men.* Simon & Schuster, 1950.

Gary, Romain. *The Roots of Heaven.* Simon & Schuster, 1958.

Gash, Jonathan. *The Sleepers of Erin.* Joan Kahn Book/E. P. Dutton, Inc., 1983.

Gash, Jonathan. *Pearlhanger.* Joan Kahn Book/St. Martin's Press, 1985.

Gass, William H. *In the Heart of the Heart of the Country.* Harper & Row, Publishers, 1958, 1961, 1962, 1967, 1968.

Gass, William H. *Omensetter's Luck.* The New American Library 1966.

Gazzo, Michael V. "A Hatful of Rain." *Best American Plays 1951-1957.* John Gassner ed. Crown Publishers, Inc., 1958.

Geoffrey, Chaucer. *The Canterbury Tales.* Random House, Inc., 1965.

Gerard, Philip. *Hatteras Light.* Charles Scribner's Sons, 1986

Gibran, Kahlil. *The Spiritual Sayings of Kahlil Gibran.* Citadel Press, 1962.

Gibson, Miles. *Dancing With Mermaids.* E. P. Dutton, 1985.

Gidé, Andre. *The Fruits of the Earth.* Alfred A. Knopf, Inc., 1981.

Gilbert, Micheal. *The Country-House Burglar.* Harper & Brothers, 1955.

Gilbert, Michael. *Overdrive.* Harper & Row, Publishers, 1967.

Gilbert, W. S. *The Complete Plays of Gilbert and Sullivan.* Random House, Inc., n.d.

Gilchrist, Ellen. *Victory Over Japan.* Little, Brown & Co., Inc., 1983.

Gilchrist, Ellen. *The Annunciation.* Little, Brown & Co., 1983.

Gilchrist, Ellen. *With Love.* Little, Brown & Co., 1985.

Gildner, Gary. *The Second Bridge.* Algonquin Books, 1987.

Giles, Molly. *Rough Translations.* University of Georgia Press, 1984.

Gilliatt, Penelope. *22 Stories.* Dodd, Mead & Co., 1965, 1967-1968, 1970-1974, 1976, 1979-1984, 1986.

Gilliatt, Penelope. *Spendid Lives.* Coward, McCann & Geohegan, Inc., 1978.

Gilliatt, Penelope. *The Cutting Edge.* Coward, McCann & Geoghegan, Inc., 1979.

Gioseffi, Daniela. *Eggs in the Lake.* BOA Editions, 1979.

Gioseffi, Daniela. *Animal Intimacies: A Book of poems in mss. 1968-1975,* 1977-1983.

Giraudoux, Jean. "Tiger at the Gates." *The Twenty Best European Plays on the American Stage.* John Gassner ed. Crown Publishers, Inc., 1974.

Glanville, Brian. *The Survivor from The Bad Streak.* Martin Secker & Warburg Ltd., 1961.

Glasgow, Ellen. *They Stooped to Folly.* The Literary Guild/Country Life Press, 1929.

Glasgow, Ellen. *The Sheltered Life.* Doubleday, Doran & Co., 1932.

Glasgow, Ellen. *Barren Ground.* Harcourt Brace Jovanovich, 1925, 1933.

Glasgow, Ellen. *Vein of Iron.* Harcourt, Brace & Co., 1955.

Gloag, Julian. *Blood for Blood.* Holt, Rinehart & Winston, 1985.

Gloria, Norris. *Looking for Bobby.* Alfred A. Knopf, Inc., 1985.

Godden, Rumer. *The Greengage Summer.* Viking Press, 1957,1958.

Godden, Rumer. *The Battle of the Villa Fiorita.* Viking Press 1963.

Godden, Rumer. *Gone A Thread of Stories.* Viking Press, 1968.

Godwin, Gail. *Dream Children.* Alfred A. Knopf, Inc., 1976.

Goethe, Johann Wolfgang von. *The Permanent Goethe.* Thomas Mann, ed. Dial Press, 1953.

Goethe, Johann Wolfgang von. *Maxims and Reflections of Goethe.* Macmillan Publishing Co., Inc., 1892.

Gold, Herbert. *The Age Of Happy Problems.* Dial Press, 1962.

Gold, Herbert. *Slave.* Arbor House, 1979.

Gold, Herbert. *Family.* Arbor House, 1981.

Gold, Herbert. *A Girl of Forty.* Donald F. Fine, Inc., 1986.

Golding, William. *The Paper Men.* Farrar, Straus & Giroux, Inc., 1984.

Goldman, James. "The Lion in Winter." *Best American Plays Sixth Series 1963-1967.* John Gassner and Clive Barnes eds. Crown Publishers, Inc., 1971.

Goldsmith, Oliver. *Goldsmith's Poems and Plays.* J. M. Dent & Sons, Ltd., 1910.

Golson, Barry G., ed. *The Playboy Interview.* Wideview Books, 1981.

Goodman, Ellen. *At Large.* Summit Books/Simon & Schuster,1981.

Gordimer, Nadine. *Burger's Daughter.* Viking Press, 1979.

Gordimer, Nadine. *Friday's Footprint and Other Stories.* Viking Press, 1960.

Gordimer, Nadine. *Selected Stories.* Viking Press, 1976.

Gordon, Mary. *Final Payments.* Random House, Inc., 1978

Gordon, Mary. *Company of Women.* Random House, Inc., 1981.

Gorky, Maxim. *A Treasury of the Theatre.* Volume II. John Gassner ed. Simon & Schuster, 1963, 1967.

Gornick, Vivian. *Fierce Attachments.* Farrar, Straus & Giroux, Inc., 1987.

Goyen, William. *The Fair Sisters.* Doubleday & Co., Inc., 1972.

Goyen, William. *The Collected Stories of William Goyen.* Doubleday & Co., Inc., 1975.

Grafton, Suc. *"A" Is For Alibi.* Holt, Rinehart & Winston, 1982.

Grafton, Sue. *"B" Is For Burglar.* Holt, Rinehart & Winston, 1985

Grafton, Sue. *"C" is for Corpse.* Henry Holt & Co., 1986.

Graham, Winston. *The Merciless Ladies.* Doubleday & Co., Inc., 1980.

Graham, Don, ed. *South By Southwest.* University of Texas Press, 1986.

Grahame, Kenneth. *The Wind in the Willows.* Charles Scribner's Sons, 1908, 1933, 1953.

Granger, Bill. *Hemingway's Notebook.* Crown Publishers, Inc., 1986.

Grau, Shirley Ann. *The Black Prince and Other Stories.* Alred A. Knopf, Inc., 1955.

Graves, Robert. *Collected Short Stories.* Doubleday & Co., Inc., 1964.

Gray, Francine du Plessix. *World Without End.* Simon & Schuster, 1981.

Greeley, Andrew M. *Ascent Into Hell.* Warner Books, Inc., 1983.

Greenaway, Kate. *The Kate Greenaway Treasury.* Edward Ernest, ed. World Publishing Co., 1967.

Greene, Graham. *Collected Stories.* Viking Press, 1973.

Grenville, Kate. *Lilian's Story.* Viking Press, Inc., 1985, 1986.

Grey, Zane. *The Thundering Herd.* Harper & Row, Publishers, Inc., 1924, 1925, 1952, 1953.

Grigson, Geoffrey. *The Gambit Book of Popular Verse.* Gambit, Inc., 1971.

Grubb, Davis. *The Golden Sickle.* World Publishing Co., 1968.

Grubb, Davis. *The Barefoot Man.* Simon & Schuster, 1971.

Grumbach, Doris. *Chamber Music.* E. P. Dutton/A Henry Robbins Book, 1979.

Grumback, Doris. *The Ladies.* E. P. Dutton, 1984.

Guest, Edward A. *Collected Verse of Edgar A. Guest.* Reilly & Lee Co., 1934.

Gunther, John. *The Lost City.* Harper & Row, Publishers, 1964.

Guy, Rosa. *A Measure of Time.* Holt, Rinehart & Winston, 1983.

Hacker, Marilyn. *Separations.* Alfred A. Knopf, Inc., 1976.

Hale, John. *The Whistle Blower.* Atheneum Publishers, 1985.

Hall, James B. *The Short Hall.* Stonehenge Books, 1980

Hall, Oakley. *The Bad Lands.* Atheneum Publishers, 1978.

Hallhan, William H. *Catch Me: Kill Me.* Bobbs-Merrill Co., Inc., 1977.

Hallhan, William H. *Foxcatcher.* William Morrow & Co., Inc., 1986.

Halliday, Brett, ed. *Best Detective Stories of the Year.* E. P. Dutton Co., Inc., 1962.

Hamalian, Leo and Volpe, Edmond L., eds. *International Short Novels: A Contemporary Anthology.* John Wiley & Sons, Inc., 1974.

Hammerstein, Oscar II. *6 Plays by Richard Rodgers and Oscar Hammerstein.* Random House, Inc., n.d.

Hammett, Dashiell. *The Big Knockover.* Lillian Hellman ed. Random House, Inc., 1962, 1965, 1966.

Hammett, Dashiell. *Trial and Error.* Houghton Mifflin, 1973.

Hammett, Dashiell. *The Continental Op.* Steven Marcus ed. Random House, Inc., 1974.

Hampl, Patricia. *Resort and Other Poems.* Houghton Mifflin Co., 1983.

Hannah, Barry. *Captain Maximus. Getting Ready.* Alfred A. Knopf, Inc., 1985.

Hansberry, Lorraine. "The Sign in Sidney Brustein's Window." *Best American Plays Sixth Series 1963-1967.* John Gassner and Clive Barnes, eds. Crown Publishers, Inc., 1971.

Hardwick, Elizabeth. *Bartleby in Manhattan and Other Essays.* Random House, Inc., 1962-1968, 1970, 1974-1976, 1978-1983.

Hardwick, Elizabeth. *Sleepless Nights.* Random House, Inc., 1979.

Hardwick, Mollie. *Malice Domestic.* St. Martin's Press, 1986.

Hardy, Thomas. *The Return of the Native.* Harper & Brothers, 1922.

Harré, Everett, ed. *The Bedside Treasury of Love,* Sheridan House, 1945.

Harré, Everett. *The Pearls of Loreto.* Herald Publishing Co./Sheridan House, Inc., 1945.

Harré, Everett. *Alaskan Romance.* Herald Publishing Co./Sheridan House, Inc., 1945.

Harris, Lisa. *The World of a Hasidic Family.* Summit Books/Simon & Schuster, 1986.

Harris, MacDonald. *Screenplay.* Atheneum Publishers, 1982.

Harris, MacDonald. *The Little People.* William Morrow & Co., Inc., 1986.

Hart, Gary. *The Strategies of Zeus.* William Morrow & Co., Inc., 1987.

Hart, Lorenz. *Thou Swell, Thou Witty, The Life and Lyrics of Lorenz Hart,* Dorothy Hart ed. Harper & Row, Publishers, 1976.

Hart, Moss. *Light Up the Sky.* Random House, Inc., 1949.

Hartley, L. P. *The Go-Between.* Stein and Day Publishers, 1967.

Hartley, L. P. *The Complete Short Stories of L. P. Hartley.* Beaufort Books, 1973.

Harwood, Ronald. *The Dresser.* Grove Press, Inc., 1980.

Hass, Robert. *Praise.* Ecco Press, 1974-1979.

Hass, Robert. *Field Guide.* Yale University Press, 1973.

Hassall, Christopher. Harcourt, Brace & World, Inc., 1964.

Hauser, Marianne. *The Memoirs of the Late Mr. Ashley.* Sun & Moon Press, 1986.

Hawkes, John. *Blood Oranges.* New Directions Books, 1970, 1971.

Hawthorne, Nathanial. *My Kinsman, Major Molineux.* Ronald Press Co., 1962.

Hayden, Julie. *The List of the Past.* Viking Press, 1976.

Hayden, Sterling. *Voyage.* G. P. Putnam's Sons, 1976.

Hearon, Shelby. *A Small Town.* Atheneum Publishers, 1985.

Hecht, Ben. *A Treasury of Ben Hecht by Ben Hecht.* Crown Publishers, Inc., 1959.

Hedin, Mary. *Fly Away Home.* University of Iowa Press, 1980.

Heller, Joseph. *Catch-22.* Simon & Schuster, Inc., 1955.

Heller, Joseph. *Good As Gold.* Simon & Schuster, 1976, 1979.

Helprin, Mark. *Ellis Island & Other Stories.* Seymour Lawrence/Delacorte Press, 1976, 1977, 1979, 1980, 1981.

Helprin , Mark. *Winter's Tale.* Harcourt Brace Jovanovich, 1983.

Hemingway, Ernest. *A Farewell to Arms.* Charles Scribner's Sons, 1919.

Hemingway, Ernest. *The Sun Also Rises.* Charles Scribner's Sons, 1926, 1954.

Hemingway, Ernest. *The Short Stories of Ernest Hemingway.* Charles Scribner's Sons, 1925, 1953.

Hemingway, Ernest. *The Nick Adams Stories.* Charles Scribner's Sons. 1972.

Hempel, Amy. *Reasons to Live.* Alfred A. Knopf, Inc., 1985.

Henderson, Bill, ed. *The Pushcart Prize,IX: Best of the Small Presses.* Pushcart Press, 1984-1985.

Henderson, Bill, ed. *The Pushcart Prize X: Best of the Small Presses.* Pushcart Press, 1985-1986.

Henderson, Bill, ed. *The Pushcart Prize XI: Best of the Small Presses.* Pushcart Press, 1986-1987.

Henley, Patricia. *Friday Night at the Silver Star.* Graywolf Press, 1986.

Henry, Lewis C., ed. *5000 Quotations for All Occasions.* Doubleday & Co., Inc., 1945.

Hentoff, Nat. *The Man From Internal Affairs.* Mysterious Press, 1985.

Hersey, John. *The War Lover.* Alfred A. Knopf, Inc., 1959.

Hersey, John. *A Single Pebble.* Alfred A. Knopf, Inc., 1956.

Hess, Joan. *Strangled Prose.* St. Martin's Press, 1986.

Hibbert, Christopher, ed. *The Life of Johnson.* Penguin Books, 1979.

Higgins, George V. *The Imposters.* Henry Holt & Co., 1986.

Hill, Susan. *A Bit of Singing and Dancing.* Hamish Hamilton, 1973-1984.

Hills, Rust. *Great Esquire Fiction, The Finest Stories From the First Fifty Years.* Viking Press. 1983.

Hilton, James. *Good-Bye Mr. Chips.* Little, Brown & Co., 1934.

Hilton, James. *Random Harvest.* Little, Brown & Co., 1941.

Hoagland, Edward. *Seven Rivers West.* Summit Books/Simon & Schuster, Inc., 1986.

Hoagland, Edward. *The Edward Hoagland Reader.* Geoffrey Wolff ed. Random House, Inc., 1968-1976.

Hobhouse, Janet. *Nellie Without Hugo.* Viking Press, 1982.

Hoch, Edward D., ed. *The Year's Best Mystery & Suspense Stories.* Walker & Co., 1986.

Holmes, Oliver Wendell, Sr. *Poems.* W. B. Conkey Co., n.d.

Holmes, Oliver Wendell, Sr. *Over the Teacups.* Houghton, Mifflin & Co., 1890, 1891.

Homer. *The Odyssey.* Doubleday & Co., Inc., 1974.

Hood, Mary. *And Venus Is Blue.* Ticknor & Fields, 1986.

Horgan, Paul. *Mountain Standard Time.* Farrar, Straus & Cudahy, 1962.

Hornung, E. W. *Raffles, the Amateur Cracksman.* St. Martin's Press, 1984.

Howard, Maureen ed. *The Penguin Book of Contemporary American Essays.* Viking Penguin, Inc., 1984.

Howard, Maureen. *Grace Abounding.* Little, Brown & Co., 1982.

Howells, William Dean. *Selected Writings of William Dean Howells.* Henry Steele Commager ed. Random House, Inc., 1950.

Howes, Barbara. *Light and Dark.* Wesleyan University Press, 1958.

Hubbard, Elbert. *An American Bible.* Roycrofters, 1918.

Huddle, David. *Only the Little Bone.* David R. Godine, 1986.

Hudson, W. H. *Green Mansions.* Three Sirens Press, n.d.

Hudson, Helen. *Meyer Meyer.* E. P. Dutton, 1967.

Hudson, Helen. *The Listener and Other Stories.* E. P. Dutton, 1968.

Hudson, Helen. *Criminal Trespass.* G. P. Putnam's Sons, 1985.

Hughes, Langston. *Five Plays by Langston Hughes,* Webster Smalley, ed. Indiana University Press, 1963.

Hughes, Ted. *Ted Hughes Selected Poems 1957-1967.* Harper & Row, Publishers 1972, 1973.

Hugo, Victor. *Les Miserables.* Vols. I and II. D. W. Mc Devitt Publishers, n.d.

Hugo, Victor. *The Hunchback of Notre Dame.* New American Library, 1965.

Humphrey, William. *Home from the Hill.* Alfred A. Knopf, Inc., 1958.

Huxley, Aldous. *The Gioconda Smile.* Harper & Brothers, 1921.

Huxley, Aldous. *Those Barren Leaves.* George H. Doran Co., 1925.

Huxley, Aldous. *Point Counter Point.* Harper & Row, Publishers, 1928.

Hyman, Robin, ed. *A Quotation Dictionary.* Macmillan Publishing Co., Inc., 1962.

Jackman, Michael. *Crown's Book of Political Quotations.* Crown Publishers, Inc., 1982.

Ibsen, Henrik. "An Enemy of the People." *Nine Great Plays.* Leonard F. Dean ed. Harcourt, Brace & World, Inc., 1950, 1956.

Ignatow, David. *Poems 1934-1969.* Wesleyan University Press, 1946, 1948, 1953-1970.

Ignatow, David. *New and Collected Poems, 1970-1985.* Wesleyan University Press, 1975, 1978, 1981, 1984, 1985.

Ingalls, Rachel. *Mediterranean Cruise.* Gambit, Inc., 1971.

Ingalls, Rachel. *Mrs. Caliban.* Gambit, Inc., 1983.

Irving, Clive. *Comrades.* Villard Books/Random House, Inc., 1986.

Irving, John. *The Cider House Rules.* William Morrow & Co., 1985.

Irving, Washington. *The Sketch Book.* New American Library, 1961.

Isherwood, Christopher. *The World in the Evening.* Random House, Inc., 1952, 1954.

Isherwood, Christopher. *The Berlin Stories.* New Directions Publishing Co., 1945, 1954.

Jacobson, Dan. *The Zulu and the Zeide.* Little, Brown & Co., 1953, 1954, 1956, 1958, 1959.

James, Clive. *First Reactions, Criticial Essays 1968-1979.* Alfred A. Knopf, Inc., 1980.

James, Henry. *The Wings of the Dove.* Charles Scribner's Sons, 1909, 1937.

James, Henry. *The Complete Plays of Henry James.* Leon Edel, ed. J. B. Lippincott, 1949.

James, Henry. *The Ambassadors.* Harper & Brothers, 1948.

James, Henry. *The Portable Henry James.* Morton Dauwen Zabel ed. Viking Press, 1951.

James, Henry. *Ten Short Stories of Henry James.* Michael Swan ed. John Lehmann, Ltd., 1958.

James, Henry. *The Europeans.* Penguin Books, 1964.

James, Henry. *Henry James Letters.* Vol I. Leon Edel ed. Harvard University Press, 1974.

Jameson, Storm. *A Cup of Tea for Mr. Thorgill.* Harper & Brothers Publishers, 1957.

Janeway, Elizabeth. *The Writer's World.* McGraw-Hill Book Co., 1969.

Janowitz, Tama. *Slaves of New York.* Crown Publishers, Inc., 1986.

Jarrell, Randall. *The Complete Poems.* Farrar, Straus & Giroux, Inc., 1968, 1969.

Jeffers, Robinson. *The Women at Point Sur and Other Poems.* Liveright, 1977.

Jeffries, Roderic. *Just Deserts.* St. Martin's Press, 1981.

Jerome, Jerome K. *The Humorous World of Jerome K. Jerome.* Robert Hutchinson ed. Dover Publications, 1962.

Jerome, Jerome K. *Idle Thoughts of an Idle Fellow.* A. L. Burt Co. Publishers, 1859.

Jhabvala, Ruth Prawer. *In Search of Love and Beauty.* William Morrow & Co., Inc.,1983.

Jhabvala,Ruth Prawer. *Out of India, Selected Stories.* William Morrow & Co., Inc., 1957, 1963, 1966, 1968, 1971-1973, 1975, 1976, 1986.

Johnson, B. S. *Christie Malry's Own Double-Entry.* Richard Seaver Book/Viking Press, 1973.

Johnson, Charles. *Faith and the Good Thing.* Viking Press, 1974.

Johnson, Charles. *Oxherding Tale.* Indiana University Press, 1982.

Johnson, Denis. *Angels.* Alfred A. Knopf, Inc., 1983.

Johnson, Nora. *Love Letter in the Dead-Letter Office.* Seymour Law-rence/Delacorte Press, 1966.

Johnson, Nora. *The World of Henry Orient.* Little, Brown & Co., 1985.

Johnson, Pamela Hansford. *The Good Husband.* Charles Scribner's Sons, 1978.

Johnson, Samuel. *The Rambler.* J. M. Dent & Sons, Ltd., 1953.

Jong, Erica. *Half-Lives.* Holt, Rinehart & Winston, 1971-1973.

Joyce, James. *The Dubliners.* B. W. Huebach, Inc., 1916.

Joyce, James. *Portrait of the Artist as a Young Man.* Viking Press, 1964.

Just, Ward. *The American Ambassador.* Houghton Mifflin Co., Inc., 1988.

Justice, Donald. *The Summer Anniversaries.* Wesleyan University Press, 1952-1960.

Justice, Donald. *Departures.* Atheneum Publishers, 1973.

Justice, Donald. *Night Light.* Wesleyan University Press, 1961-1967.

Kahn, Joan, ed. *Trial and Error.* Houghton Mifflin, 1973.

Kahn, Joan, ed. *Chilling and Killing.* Houghton Mifflin Co., 1978.

Kantor, MacKinlay. *The Voice of Bugle Ann.* Coward, McCann, Inc., 1935.

Kantor, MacKinlay. *Spirit Lake.* World Publishing Co., 1961.

Kaplan, Andrew. *Scorpion.* Macmillan Publishing Co., Inc., 1985.

Kaplan, David Michael. *Comfort.* Viking Penguin, Inc., 1987.

Kawabata, Yasunari. *The Snow Country.* Alfred A. Knopf, Inc., 1936.

Kawabata, Yasunari. *The Sound of the Mountain.* Alfred A. Knopf, Inc., 1970.

Kaye-Smith, Sheila. *Joanna Godden Married.* Andrew Dakers Ltd., n.d.

Kazantzakis, Nikos. *Freedom or Death.* Simon & Schuster, 1956.

Keats, John. *The Complete Poetry and Selected Prose of John Keats.* Harold Edgar Briggs ed. Random House, Inc., 1951.

Keifetz, Norman. *The Sensation.* Atheneum Publishers, 1975.

Kellerman, Jonathan. *When the Bough Breaks.* Atheneum Publishers, 1985.

Kellerman, Jonathan. *Blood Test.* Atheneum Publishers, 1986.

Kelley, Kitty. *His Way.* Bantam Books, 1986.

Kelly, Susan. *The Summertime Soldiers.* Walker & Co., 1986.

Kelton, Elmer. *The Good Old Boys.* Doubleday & Co., Inc., 1978.

Keneally, Thomas. *Confederates.* Harper & Row, Publishers, 1979.

Keneally, Thomas. *Passenger.* Harcourt Brace Jovanovich, 1979.

Keneally, Thomas. *Family Madness.* Simon & Schuster, 1986.

Kennedy, Margaret. *The Constant Nymph.* Doubleday, Page & Co., 1925.

Kennedy, William P. *Legs.* Coward, McCann & Geoghegan, Inc., 1975.

Kennedy, William P. *The Masakado Lesson.* St. Martin's Press, 1986.

Kerr, Jean. *Please Don't Eat The Daisies.* Crest/Fawcett Books, 1979.

Kersh, Gerald. *Fowlers End.* Simon & Schuster, 1957.

Kersh, Gerald. *The Thousand Deaths of Mr. Small.* Doubleday & Co., Inc. 1959.

Kersh, Gerald. *The Angel and the Cuckoo.* New American Library, 1966.

Kesey, Ken. *One Flew Over the Cuckoo's Nest.* New American Library. 1975.

Kesey, Ken. *Demon Box.* Viking Penguin, Inc., 1986.

Kimball, Robert, ed. *Cole.* Holt, Rinehart & Winston, 1971.

Kin, David. *Dictionary of American Maxims.* Philosophical Library, 1955.

King, Alexander. *Mine Enemy Grows Older.* Simon & Schuster, 1959

King, Alexander. *I Should Have Kissed Her More.* Simon & Schuster, 1961.

King, Francis. *One Is a Wanderer.* Little, Brown & Co., 1985.

King, Stephen. *Different Seasons.* Viking Press, 1982.

King, Stephen. *The Mist.* G. P. Putnam's Sons, 1985.

Kinnell, Galway. *Selected Poems.* Houghton Mifflin Co., 1982.

Kinsella, Thomas. *Assumption.* Oxford University Press, 1986.

Kinsella, Thomas, ed. *The New Oxford Book of Irish Verse.* Oxford University Press. 1986.

Kinsella, W. P. *Shoeless Joe.* Houghton Mifflin Co., 1982.

Kinsella, W. P. *The Iowa Baseball Confederacy.* Houghton Mifflin Co., 1986.

Kipling, Rudyard. *Kipling, A Selection of His Stories and Poems.* Vol. III. John Beecroft ed. Doubleday & Co., Inc., 1892-1912, 1913, 1919, 1924, 1932.

Kirkwood, James. *Some Kind of Hero.* Thomas Y. Crowell Co., 1975.

Kirstein, Lincoln. *Rhymes and More Rhymes of a PFC.* New Directions, 1964, 1966.

Kizer, Carolyn. *The Poet's Story.* Howard Moss, ed. Macmillan Publishing Co., Inc., 1973.

Kizer, Carolyn. *Mermaids in the Basement.* Copper Canyon Press, 1984.

Kizer, Carolyn. *Yin.* Boa Editions, Ltd., 1984.

Klein, Norma. *American Dreams.* E. P. Dutton, 1987.

Klopikova, Solovyou and Vladmir, Lena. *Behind the High Kremlin Walls.* Dodd, Mead & Co., 1986.

Knebel, Fletcher. *Sabotage.* Doubleday & Co., Inc., 1986.

Knille, Robert, ed. *As I Was Saying.* William B. Eerdmans Publishing Co., 1955.

Koch, C. J. *The Doubleman.* McGraw Hill Book Co., 1986.

Koenig, Joseph. *Floater.* Mysterious Press, 1986.

Korda, Michael. *Queenie.* Simon & Schuster, 1985.

Kornblatt, Joyce Reiser. *Breaking Bread.* A William Abrahams Book/E. P. Dutton, 1987.

Kosinski, Jerzy. *The Painted Bird.* Houghton Mifflin Co., Inc., 1965.

Kronenberger, Louis. *The Last Word, Portraits of Fourteen Master Aphorists.* Macmillan Publishing Co., Inc., 1972.

Kubicki, Jan. *Breaker Boys.* Atlantic Monthly Press, 1986.

Kumin, Maxine. *Up Country.* Harper & Row, Publishers,1972.

Kumin, Maxine. *The Long Approach.* Viking Press, 1985.

Kundera, Milan. *The Farewell Party.* Alfred A. Knopf, Inc., 1976.

Kundera, Milan. *The Unbearable Lightness of Being.* Harper & Row, Publishers, 1984.

Kuttner, Paul. *The Man Who Had Everything.* Sterling Publishing Co., Inc., 1977.

Kuttner, Paul. *Condemned.* Dawnwood Press, 1983.

Kuttner, Paul. *Absolute Proof.* Dawnwood Press, 1986.

Kuttner, Paul. *The Iron Virgin.* Dawnwood Press, 1987.

La Farge, Oliver. *Laughing Boy.* Houghton Mifflin Co., 1929.

Laing, Dilys. *The Collected Poems of Dilys Laing.* Press of Case Western Reserve University, 1967.

Lambert, Derek. *The Red House.* Coward, McCann & Geoghegan, Inc., 1972.

Lambert, Derek. *The Yermakov Transfer.* E. P. Dutton & Co., Inc., 1974.

Lambert, Derek. *The Man Who Was Saturday.* Stein & Day, 1985.

Landon, Margaret. *Anna and the King of Siam.* Pocket Books, 1949.

Landor, Walter Savage. *Imaginary Conversations and Poems, A Selection.* J. M. Dent & Sons, Ltd., 1933.

Lanier, Sidney. *Poems of Sidney Lanier.* Mrs. Lanier, ed. Middle Georgia Historical Society, Inc., Reprint edition, 1967.

Lapierre, Dominique. *The City of Joy.* Doubleday & Co., Inc., 1985.

Lardner, Ring. *The Best Short Stories of Ring Lardner.* Charles Scribner's Sons. 1957.

Laurence, Margaret. *A Jest of God.* Alfred A. Knopf, Inc., 1966.

Laurence, Margaret. *A Bird in the House.* Alfred A. Knopf, Inc., 1970.

Lawrence, D. H. *The Complete Short Stories.* Vols. I and II. Viking Penguin, Inc., 1934, 1962.

Lawrence, D. H. *Four Short Novels.* Viking Press, 1923.

Lawrence, D. H. *A Modern Lover.* Viking Press, 1932.

Leavitt, David. *Counting Months.* Alfred A. Knopf, Inc., 1983.

Leavitt, David. *The Lost Language of Cranes.* Alfred A. Knopf, Inc., 1986.

Le Baron, Joseph L., ed. *A Treasury of Jewish Quotations.* Crown Publishers, Inc., 1956.

Le Carré, John. *A Perfect Spy.* Alfred A. Knopf, Inc., 1986.

Leffland, Ella. *Rumors of Peace.* Harper & Row, Publishers, 1979.

Leffland, Ella. *Last Courtesies and Other Stories.* Harper & Row, Publishers, 1980.

Le Guin, Ursula. *The Wind's Twelve Quarters.* Harper & Row, Publishers, 1975.

Lehmann, Rosamond. *A Sea-Grape Tree.* Harcourt Brace Jovanovich, 1976.

Leitch, David. *Family Secrets.* Delacorte Press, 1986.

Leithauser, Brad. *Cats of the Temple.* Alfred A. Knopf, Inc., 1986.

Lennon, John. *Skywriting by Word of Mouth.* Harper & Row, Publishers, 1986.

Leonard, Hugh. "Da." *The Best Plays of the Seventies.* Stanley Richards, ed. Doubleday & Co., Inc., 1980.

Lermontov, Mihail. *A Hero of Our Time.* Doubleday, Anchor Books, 1958.

Lessing, Doris. *A Man and Two Women.* Simon & Schuster, 1958, 1962, 1963.

Lessing, Doris. *The Golden Notebook.* Simon & Schuster, 1962.

Levenson, Leonard Louis. *Bartlett's Unfamiliar Quotations.* Cowles Book Co., Inc., 1971.

Levertov, Denise. *The Freeing of the Dust.* New Directions Press, 1972-1975.

Levertov, Denise. *Candles in Babylon.* New Directions Press, 1978-1983.

Levertov, Denise. *Collected Earlier Poems 1940-1960.* New Directions Press, 1957-1961, 1979.

Levine, Philip. *Not This Pig.* Wesleyan University Press, 1963-1968.

Levine, Philip. *Ashes.* Atheneum Publishers, 1979.

Levine, Philip. *One For the Rose.* Atheneum Publishers, 1981.

Levine, Philip. *Sweet Will.* Atheneum Publishers, 1985.

Levine, Philip. *Selected Poems.* Atheneum Publishers, 1984.

Lewis, Sinclair. *Lewis At Zenith.* Harcourt, Brace & World, Inc., 1920, 1922, 1925.

Levine, Philip. *The Names of the Lost.* Atheneum Publishers, 1976.

Lewis, Alfred, ed. *The Quotable Quotations Book.* Cornerstone Library/Simon & Schuster, Inc., 1980.

Lewis, C. S. *Poems.* Walter Hooper, ed. Harcourt, Brace & World, Inc., 1964.

Lewis, Sinclair. *Lewis at Zenith.* Harcourt, Brace & World, Inc., 1920, 1922, 1925.

Lewis, Sinclair. *It Can't Happen Here.* Doubleday, Doran & Co., Inc., 1935.

Lewis, Sinclair. *Elmer Gantry.* Harcourt, Brace & Co., Inc., 1927.

Leyner, Mark; White, Curtis; and Glynn, Thomas, eds. *American Made.* Fiction Collective, 1986.

Lieberman, Herbert. *The Climate of Hell.* Simon & Schuster, 1978.

Lifshin, Lyn. *Kiss the Skin Off.* Cherry Valley Editions, 1985.

Lindbergh, Anne Morrow. *The Unicorn and Other Poems 1935-1955.* Pantheon Books, 1956.

Lindbergh, Anne Morrow. *Gift From the Sea.* Pantheon Books, 1955.

Logan, John. *The Anonymous Lover.* Liveright, 1969-1973.

Logan, John. *Only the Dreamer Can Change the Dream.* Ecco Press, 1981.

Lois, Susan. *Personals.* Dell Books, 1986.

London, Jack. *The Sea-Wolf.* Macmillan Publishing Co., Inc., 1904.

Longfellow, Henry Wadsworth. *The Poems of Henry Wadsworth.* Random House, Inc., n.d.

Longstreet, Stephen. *Ambassador.* Avon Books, 1978.

Longstreet, Stephen. *Our Father's House.* G. P. Putnam's Sons, 1985.

Lourie, Richard. *First Loyalty.* Harcourt Brace Jovanovich, 1985.

Lowell, Amy. *The Complete Poetical Works of Amy Lowell.* Houghton Mifflin Co., 1917, 1922, 1925, 1926, 1927, 1955.

Lowell, Robert. "Benito Cereno." *Best American Plays Sixth Series 1963-1967,* John Gassner and Clive Barnes eds. Crown Publishers, Inc., 1971.

Lux, Thomas. *Half Promised Land.* Houghton Mifflin Co., 1986.

Lyall, Gavin. *Shooting Script.* Charles Scribner's Sons, 1966.

Lyall, Gavin. *The Secret Servant.* Viking Press, 1980.

Bibliography

Lyall, Gavin. *The Crocus List.* Viking Penguin, Inc., 1985, 1986.

Lynskey, Winifred, ed. *Reading Modern Fiction,* 4th Edition. Charles Scribner's Sons, 1968.

Macdonald, Ross. *The Moving Target.* Alfred A. Knopf, Inc., 1949.

Macdonald, Ross. *The Way Some People Die.* Alfred A. Knopf, Inc., 1951.

Macdonald, Ross. *The Barbarous Coast.* Alfred A. Knopf, Inc., 1956.

MacDonald, Ross. *Archer at Large.* Alfred A. Knopf, Inc., 1970.

Macdonald, Ross. *The Underground Man.* Alfred A. Knopf, Inc., 1971.

Macdonald, Ross. *Sleeping Beauty.* Alfred A. Knopf, Inc., 1973.

MacDonald, John D. *The End of the Night.* Simon & Schuster, 1960.

MacDonald, John D. *The Last One Left.* Doubleday & Co., Inc., 1967.

MacDonald, John D. *The Lonely Silver Rain.* Alfred A. Knopf, Inc., 1985.

MacDonald, John D. *Barrier Island.* Alfred A. Knopf, Inc., 1986.

MacKenzie, Donald. *The Quiet Killer.* Houghton Mifflin Co., 1968.

MacKenzie, Donald. *Postscript to a Dead Letter.* Houghton Mifflin Co., 1973.

MacKenzie, Donald. *Raven's Longest Night.* Doubleday & Co., Inc., 1983.

MacLeish, Archibald. *New & Collected Poems, 1917-1976.* Houghton Mifflin Co., 1976.

MacNeice, Louis. *The Collected Poems of Louis MacNeice.* E. R. Dodds, ed. Oxford University Press, 1967.

Magill, Frank N., ed. *Magill's Quotations in Context.* Harper & Row, Publishers, 1969.

Mailer, Norman. *The Naked and the Dead.* Rinehart & Co., Inc., 1948.

Mailer, Norman. *Of A Fire On the Moon.* Little, Brown & Co., 1970.

Mailer, Norman. *Pieces & Pontifications.* Little, Brown & Co., 1982.

Mailer, Norman. *Ancient Evenings.* Little, Brown & Co., 1983.

Mailer, Norman. *Tough Guys Don't Dance.* Random House, Inc., 1984.

Major, Clarence. *My Amputations.* Fiction Collective, 1986.

Malamud, Bernard. *Idiots First.* Farrar, Straus & Giroux, Inc., 1950, 1959, 1961, 1962, 1963.

Malamud, Bernard. *The Natural.* Farrar, Straus & Giroux, Inc., 1952.

Malamud, Bernard. *The Assistant.* Farrar, Straus & Giroux, Inc., 1957.

Malamud, Bernard. *Pictures of Fidelman.* Farrar, Straus & Giroux, Inc., 1958, 1962, 1963, 1968, 1969.

Malamud, Bernard. *A New Life.* Farrar, Straus & Giroux, Inc., 1961.

Malamud, Bernard. *The Fixer.* Farrar, Straus & Giroux, Inc., 1966.

Malamud, Bernard. *The Tenants.* Farrar, Straus & Giroux, Inc., 1971.

Malcolm, John. *The Gwen John Sculpture.* Charles Scribner's Sons, 1986.

Malone, Michael. *Handling Sin.* Little, Brown & Co., 1986.

Malraux, André. *Man's Fate.* Random House, Inc., 1934.

Mann, Thomas. *Death in Venice.* Alfred A. Knopf, Inc., 1915.

Mann, Thomas. *The Magic Mountain.* Alfred A. Knopf, Inc., 1927.

Mann, Thomas. *Stories of Three Decades.* Alfred A. Knopf, Inc., 1931, 1959.

Mansfield, Katherine. *The Daughters of the Late Colonel.* Ronald Press Co., 1962.

Mansfield, Katherine. *The Short Stories of Katherine Mansfield.* Alfred A. Knopf, Inc., 1967.

March, William. *The Bad Seed.* Holt, Rinehart & Winston, Inc., 1954.

Markham, Beryl. *West With the Night.* North Point Press, 1983.

Marquand, John P. *Sincerely, Willis Wayde.* Little, Brown & Co., Inc., 1955.

Marquis, Don. *When the Turtles Sing.* Doubleday Co., Inc., Books for Libraries Press, 1970.

Marquis, Don. *The Best of Don Marquis.* Doubleday & Co., Inc., 1946.

Marsh, Ngaio. *Death in Ecstacy.* Ameron Ltd., 1976.

Marsh, Edward. *Ambrosia and Small Beer.* Harcourt, Brace & World, Inc., 1964.

Marshall, Paule. *Reena and Other Stories.* Feminist Press, 1983.

Martin, Judith. *Style and Substance.* Atheneum Publishers, 1986.

Martin, Ian Kennedy. *The Juggler.* William Heinemann Ltd., 1985.

Mason, Bobbie Ann. *Shiloh and Other Stories.* Harper & Row, Publishers, 1982.

Mason, Bobbie Ann. *In Country.* Harper & Row, Publishers, 1985.

Mason, Van Wyck. *Zanzibar Intrigue.* Doubleday & Co., Inc., 1963.

Maspero, Francois. *Cat's Grin.* Alfred A. Knopf, Inc., 1986.

Masters, Edgar Lee. *Spoon River Anthology.* Macmillan Publishing Co., Inc., 1959.

Masters, Hilary. *Hammertown Tales.* Stuart Wright, 1986.

Masterson, Graham. *Solitaire.* William Morrow & Co., Inc., 1982.

Masterson, Graham. *Maiden Voyage.* St. Martin's Press, 1984.

Mathews, M. M., ed. *A Dictionary of Americanisms.* Vols. 1 and 2. University of Chicago Press, 1951.

Matthews, William. *A Happy Childhood.* Little, Brown & Co., 1984.

Matthiesen, F. O., ed. *The Oxford Book of American Verse.* Oxford University Press, 1950.

Matthiessen, Peter. *At Play in the Fields of the Lord.* Random House, Inc., 1965.

Maugham, W. Somerset. *Of Human Bondage.* Doubleday & Co., Inc., 1936.

Maugham, W. Somerset. *The Razor's Edge.* Penguin Books, 1944.

Maugham, W. Somerset. *A Writer's Notebook.* Doubleday & Co., Inc., 1949.

Maugham, W. Somerset. *The Complete Short Stories of W. Somerset Maugham.* Volume I, East and West. Doubleday & Co., Inc., 1921, 1934.

Maugham, W. Somerset. *The Complete Short Stories of W. Somerset Maugham.* Volume II, The World Over. Doubleday & Co., Inc., 1921, 1934.

Maupassant, Guy de. *The Portable Maupassant.* Viking Press 1947.

Maurois, André. *The Kingdom of God.* Alfred A. Knopf, Inc., 1948.

Maxwell, A. E. *Steal the Sun.* Richard Marek Publishers, 1981.

Maxwell, A. E. *The Frog and the Scorpion.* Doubleday & Co., Inc., 1986.

Maynard, Richard. *The Coconut Book.* Grove Press, Inc., 1985.

McBain, Ed. *Cinderella.* Henry Holt & Co., 1986.

McBain, Ed. *Heat.* Viking Press, 1981.

McCahern, John. *High Ground.* Viking Penguin, Inc., 1987.

McCaig, Donald. *The Butte Polka.* Rawson Wade Publishers, 1980.

McCaig, Donald. *Nop's Trials.* Crown Publishers, Inc., 1984.

McCaig, Donald. *The Man Who Made the Devil Glad.* Crown Publishers, Inc., 1986.

McCarthy, Mary. *On The Contrary.* Farrar, Straus & Giroux, Inc., 1953.

McCarthy, Mary. *Cast A Cold Eye.* Harcourt, Brace & World, Inc., 1940-1950.

McCarthy, Mary. *The Groves of Academe.* Harcourt, Brace & Co., 1951, 1952.

McCarthy, Mary. *A Charmed Life.* Harcourt, Brace & World, Inc., 1954-1955.

McCorquodale, Robin. *Dansville.* Harper & Row, Publishers, 1986.

McCullers, Carson. *The Member of the Wedding.* Houghton Mifflin Co., 1946.

McCullers, Carson. *The Ballad of the Sad Cafe. The Novels and Stories of Carson McCullers.* Houghton Mifflin Co., 1951.

McCullough, David Willis, ed. *Great Detectives: A Century of the Best Mysteries from England and America.* Pantheon Books, 1984.

McDermott, Alice. *A Bigamist's Daughter.* Random House, Inc., 1982.

McDermott, Alice. *That Night.* Farrar, Straus & Giroux, 1987.

McDonald, Gregory. *Flynn's In.* Mysterious Press, 1984.

McDonald, Gregory, ed. *The 1986 Mystery Writers of America Anthology.* Mysterious Press, 1986.

McGahern, John. *Getting Through.* Harper & Row Publishers, 1980.

McGinley, Phyllis. *Times Three.* Viking Press, 1960.

McGuane, Thomas. *The Bushwacked Piano.* Simon & Schuster, 1971.

McGuane, Thomas. *Ninety-Two In the Shade.* Farrar, Straus & Giroux, 1972, 1973.

McGuane, Thomas. *Something To Be Desired.* Random House, Inc., 1984.

McGuane, Thomas. *To Skin a Cat.* Seymour Lawrence/E. P. Dutton, 1986.

McIlvanney, William. *Laidlaw.* Pantheon Books, 1977.

McIlvanney, William. *The Papers of Tony Veitch.* Pantheon Books, 1983.

McIlvanney, William. *The Big Man.* William Morrow & Co., Inc., 1985.

McInerney, Jay. *Bright Lights, Big City.* Vintage Books/Random House, Inc., 1984.

McInerney, Jay. *Ransom.* Vintage Books/Random House, Inc., 1985.

McMahon, Thomas. *Loving Little Egypt.* Viking Penguin, Inc., 1987.

McMurtry, Larry. *Somebody's Darling.* Simon & Schuster, 1978.

McMurtry, Larry. *Lonesome Dove.* Simon & Schuster, 1985.

McNamara, M. Frances, ed. *2000 Famous Legal Quotations.* Aqueduct Books/Lawyers Co-operative Publishing Co., 1967.

McPhee, Nancy. *The Book of Insults.* St. Martin's Press, 1978.

Megged, Aharon. *Living on the Dead.* McCall Publishing Co., 1965.

Megged, Aharon. *Asahel.* Taplinger Publishing Co., 1982.

Meinke, Peter. *The Piano Tuner.* University of Georgia Press, 1986.

Melville, Herman. *Great Short Works of Herman Melville.* Warner Berthoff, ed. Harper & Row, Publishers, 1969.

Mencken, H. L. *A Mencken Chrestomathy.* Alfred A. Knopf, Inc., 1953.

Mencken, H. L., ed. *A New Dictionary of Quotations Mencken.* Alfred A. Knopf, Inc., 1942.

Merkin, Daphne. *Enchantment.* Harcourt Brace Jovanovich, 1984, 1986.

Michaels, Leonard. *Going Places.* Farrar, Straus & Giroux, Inc., 1966, 1969.

Michaels, Leonard. *The Men's Club.* Farrar, Straus & Giroux, Inc., 1978.

Millar, Margaret. *Experiment in Springtime.* Random House, Inc., 1947.

Millar, Margaret. *How Like an Angel.* Random House, Inc., 1962.

Millar, Margaret. *The Fiend.* Random House, Inc., 1964.

Millar, Margaret. *Beyond This Point Are Monsters.* Random House, Inc., 1970.

Millar, Margaret. *The Murder of Miranda.* Random House, Inc., 1979.

Millar, Margaret. *Spider Webs.* William Morrow & Co., Inc., 1986.

Millay, Edna St. Vincent. *Collected Poems Edna St. Vincent Millay.* Norma Millay ed. Harper & Row, Publishers, 1917, 1921-1923, 1928, 1931, 1933, 1934, 1936-1944, 1950.

Miller, Arthur. "A View From the Bridge." *Best American Plays 1951-1957.* John Gassner ed. Crown Publishers, Inc., 1958.

Miller, Henry. *Tropic of Capricorn.* Grove Press, Inc., 1961.

Miller, Sue. *The Good Mother.* Harper & Row, Publishers, 1986.

Mills, C. Wright. *The Power Elite.* Oxford University Press, 1956.

Mills, James. *The Underground Empire.* Doubleday & Co., Inc., 1986.

Milton, John. *The Portable Milton.* Douglas Bush, ed. Viking Press, 1949.

Minot, Susan. *Monkeys. Hiding.* E. P. Dutton, 1986.

Mishima, Yukio. *The Sea of Fertility.* Alfred A. Knopf, Inc., 1973.

Mitchell, James. *Russian Roulette.* William Morrow & Co., 1973.

Mitchell, Margaret. *Gone With the Wind.* Macmillan Publishing Co., Inc., 1936.

Mitchell, Paige. *The Covenant.* Atheneum Publishers, 1973.

Mitchell, Paige. *Wild Seed.* Doubleday & Co., Inc., 1982.

Molière. "The Would-Be Invalid." *Nine Great Plays.* Leonard F. Dean, ed. Harcourt, Brace & World, Inc., 1950, 1956.

Monsarrat, Nicholas. *The Cruel Sea.* Alfred A. Knopf, Inc., 1951.

Montaigne, Michel Equem de. *The Essays of Montaigne.* Heritage Press, 1947.

Moore, Brian. *The Lonely Passion of Judith Hearne.* Atlantic-Little, Brown & Co., 1955.

Moore, Brian. *The Mangan Inheritance.* Farrar, Straus & Giroux, Inc., 1979.

Moore, Lorrie. *Self-Help.* Alfred A. Knopf, Inc., 1985.

Moore, Lorrie. *Anagrams.* Alfred A. Knopf, Inc., 1986.

Moore, Marianne. *The Complete Poems of Marianne Moore.* Macmillan Publishing Co., Inc./ Viking Press, 1967.

Moran, Richard. *Cold Sea Rising.* Arbor House, 1986.

Moravia, Albert. *Two.* Farrar, Straus & Giroux, Inc., 1971.

Morgan, Speer. *The Assemblers.* E. P. Dutton, 1986.

Morris, Herbert. *Dream Palace.* Harper & Row, Publishers, 1986.

Morris, Mary. *The Bus of Dreams.* Houghton Mifflin Co., 1985.

Morris, Willie. *The Last of the Southern Girls.* Alfred A. Knopf, Inc., 1973.

Morris, Wright. *Collected Stories 1948-1986.* Harper & Row, Publishers, 1951, 1958, 1981-1986.

Morrow, James. *This Is the Way the World Ends.* Henry Holt & Co., 1986.

Morse, John T. *Life and Letters of Olvier Wendell Holmes.* Volume I. Houghton, Mifflin Co., 1897.

Mortimer, John. *Paradise Postponed.* Viking Penguin, Inc., 1985.

Mortimer, John. *Charade.* Viking Penguin, Inc., 1986.

Moss, Howard, ed. *The Poet's Story.* Macmillan Publishing Co., Inc., 1973.

Munro, Alice. *The Moons of Jupiter.* Alfred A. Knopf, Inc., 1983.

Munro, Alice. *The Progress of Love.* Alfred A. Knopf, Inc., 1986.

Murdoch, Iris. *The Good Apprentice.* Viking Penguin, Inc., 1986.

Murphy, George E., Jr., ed. *Editors' Choice: New American Stories.* Vol. 1. Bantam Books, 1985.

Murphy, Edward F. *The Crown Treasury of Relevant Quotations.* Crown Publishers, Inc., 1978.

Nabokov, Vladimir. *A Russian Beauty and Other Stories.* McGraw-Hill Book Co., 1973.

Nash, Ogden. *I'm a Stranger Here Myself.* Little, Brown & Co., 1945.

Nash, Ogden. *Many Long Years Ago.* Little, Brown & Co., 1945.

Navas, Deborah, ed. *New Fiction from New England.* Yankee Books, 1986.

Naylor, Phyllis. *Unexpected Pleasures.* G. P. Putnam's Sons, 1986.

Ndebele, Njabulo. *Fools and Other Stories.* Readers International, Inc., 1986.

Neider, Charles, ed. *Great Short Stories.* Holt, Rinehart & Winston, 1966.

Neruda, Pablo. *The Heights of Macchu Picchu.* Farrar, Straus & Giroux, 1947.

Neville, Susan. *The Invention of Flight.* University of Georgia Press, 1984.

Nevins, Francis, Jr. and Greenberg, Martin Harry, eds. *Hitchcock Prime Time.* Avon Books-Hearst Corp., 1985.

The New Yorker Book of Poems. Editors of *The New Yorker.* Viking Press, 1969,

Nin, Anaïs. *Winter of Artifice.* Swallow Press, 1945-1946, 1948.

Nin, Anaïs. *House of Incest.* Swallow Press, 1958.

Nin, Anaïs. *Children of the Albatross.* Swallow Press, 1959.

Nin, Anaïs. *Seduction of the Minotaur.* Swallow Press, 1961.

Nin, Anaïs. *The Diary of Anaïs Nin.* Volume Four. Harcourt Brace Jovanovich, 1971.

Niven, David. *The Moon's a Balloon.* G. P. Putnman's Sons, 1972.

Norris, Gloria. *Looking for Bobby.* Alfred A. Knopf, Inc., 1985.

Oates, Joyce Carol. *The Wheel of Love.* Vanguard Press, 1965-1970.

Oates, Joyce Carol. *The Silver Dish.* Houghton Mifflin Co., 1979.

Oates, Joyce Carol. *Raven's Wing.* William Abrahams/E. P. Dutton, 1986.

O'Brien, Edna. *The Love Object.* Alfred A. Knopf, Inc., 1969.

O'Brien, Edna. *A Scandalous Woman and Other Stories.* Harcourt Brace Jovanovich, 1972, 1973, 1974.

O'Brien, Edward J., ed. *The Best Short Stories of 1931.* Dodd, Mead and Co., 1931.

O'Clair, Robert and Ellmann, Richard, eds. *The Norton Anthology of Modern Poet.* W. W. Norton & Co., Inc., 1973.

O'Connor, Flannery. *The Complete Stories of Flannery O'Connor.* Farrar, Straus & Giroux, 1971.

O'Connor, Frank. *The Collected Stories of Frank O'Connor.* Alfred A. Knopf, Inc., 1965.

Odets, Clifford. *Six Plays of Clifford Odets.* Modern Library/Random House, Inc., 1933, 1935, 1936, 1937, 1939.

Oë, Kenzaburo. *A Personal Matter.* Grove Press, Inc., 1968.

O'Faolain, Julia. *No Country for Young Men.* Carroll & Graf Publishers, Inc., 1980.

O'Faolain, Julia. *The Irish Signorina.* Adler & Adler, Publishers, Inc., 1985.

O'Hara, Frank. *The Collected Poems of Frank O'Hara.* Donald Allen, ed. Alfred A. Knopf, Inc., 1971.

O. Henry. *The Complete Works of O. Henry.* Doubleday & Co., Inc., 1899-1953.

O. Henry. *Strictly Business.* Doubleday, Doran & Co., Inc., 1910, 1938.

Olds, Sharon. *The Dead and the Living. The Elder Sister.* Alfred A. Knopf, Inc., 1984.

O'Neill, Eugene. "A Moon For the Misbegotten." *Best American Plays 1951-1957.* John Gassner, ed. Crown Publishers, Inc., 1958.

Orwell, George. *Shooting An Elephant and Other Essays.* Harcourt, Brace & World, Inc., 1945, 1946, 1949, 1950.

Ouida. *Cecil Castlemaine's Rage and Other Stories.* Books for Libraries Press, 1868, 1970.

Ouida. *Under Two Flags.* L. Burt Co., n.d.

The Oxford Dictionary of Quotations. Oxford University Press, 2nd ed., 1953.

Oz, Amos. *Unto Death.* A Helen and Kurt Wolff Book/Harcourt Brace Jovanovich, 1971.

Oz, Amos. *A Perfect Peace.* Harcourt Brace Jovanovich, 1982.

Ozick, Cynthia. *Levitation-Five Fictions.* Alfred A. Knopf, Inc., 1982.

Ozick, Cynthia. *The Pagan Rabbi and Other Stories.* E. P. Dutton, Inc., 1983.

Ozick, Cynthia. *The Cannibal Galaxy.* Alfred A. Knopf, Inc., 1983.

Paley, Grace. *Enormous Changes At the Last Minute.* Farrar, Straus & Giroux, Inc., 1974.

Paley, Grace. *The Little Disturbances of Man.* Doubleday & Co., Inc., 1959.

Parini, Jay. *The Patch Boys* . Henry Holt & Co., 1986.

Parker, Dorothy. *The Portable Dorothy Parker.* Viking Press, 1944.

Parker, Dorothy. *The Collected Poetry of Dorothy Parker.* Modern Library/Random House, Inc., n.d.

Parker, Robert B. *Ceremony.* Seymour Lawrence/Delacorte Press, 1981.

Parker, Robert B. *A Savage Place.* Seymour Lawrence/Delacorte Press, 1981.

Parker, Robert B. *A Catskill Eagle.* Seymour Lawrence/Delacorte Press, 1985.

Partisan Review Reader 1934-1944. Dial Press, 1946.

Partnow, Elaine, ed. *The Quotable Woman.* Anchor Press/Doubleday Co., Inc., 1978.

Pasternak, Boris. *Doctor Zhivago.* Pantheon Books, Inc., 1958.

Patchen, Kenneth. *The Collected Poems of Kenneth Patchen.* New Directions Publishing Corp., 1939, 1942, 1949, 1954, 1967.

Pattern, William, ed. *Short Story Classics.* Vol. 4. P. F. Collier & Sons, 1907.

Patterson, Richard North. *Private Screening.* Villard Books, 1985.

Percy, Walker. *Love in the Ruins.* Farrar, Straus & Giroux, Inc., 1971.

Perelman, S. J. *The Best of S. J. Perelman.* Random House, Inc., 1947.

Perry, Ralph Barton. James, William. *The Thought and Character of William James.* Ralph Barton Perry. Harvard University Press, 1935.

Peter, Laurence J. *Peter's Quotations.* William Morrow & Co., Inc., 1977.

Peterson, Houston, ed. *50 Great Essays.* Pocket Books/Simon & Schuster, Inc., 1954.

Petry, Ann. *County Place.* Houghton Mifflin Co., 1947.

Petry, Ann. *Miss Muriel and Other Stories.* Houghton Mifflin Co., 1971.

Phillips, Caryl. *A State of Independence.* Farrar, Straus & Giroux, Inc., 1986.

Phillips, Jayne Anne. *Black Tickets.* Seymour Lawrence Book/Delacorte Press, 1975-1979.

Phillips, Jayne Anne. *Machine Dreams.* E. P. Dutton, 1984.

Piercy, Marge. *Breaking Camp.* Wesleyan University Press, 1963-1968.

Piercy, Marge. *Living in the Open.* Alfred A. Knopf, Inc., 1976.

Piercy, Marge. *Woman on the Edge of Time.* Alfred A. Knopf, Inc., 1976.

Piercy, Marge. *Vida.* Summit Books/Simon & Schuster, 1979.

Piercy, Marge. *Braided Lives.* Summit Books/Simon & Schuster, 1982.

Piercy, Marge. *Circles On the Water.* Alfred A. Knopf, Inc., 1982.

Piercy, Marge. *My Mother's Body.* Alfred A. Knopf, Inc., 1985

Pilcher, Rosamund. *The Blue Bedroom and Other Stories.* St. Martin's Press, 1985.

Pirandello, Luigi. *Better Think Twice About It.* E. P. Dutton & Co., Inc., 1934.

Plain, Belva. *The Golden Cup.* Delacorte Press, 1986.

Plath, Sylvia. *The Bell Jar.* Harper & Row Publishers, 1971.

Plath, Sylvia. *The Collected Poems.* Ted Hughes ed. Harper & Row, Publishers, 1960, 1965, 1971, 1981.

Poe, Edgar Allen. *The Complete Stories and Poems of Edgar Allan Poe.* Doubleday & Co., Inc., 1966.

Porter, Katherine Anne. *Flowering Judas and Other Stories.* Harcourt Brace & Co., Inc., 1930, 1935.

Porter, Katherine Anne. *Ship of Fools.* Little, Brown & Co., 1945, 1946, 1947, 1950, 1956, 1958, 1959, 1969.

Portis, Charles. *Norwood.* Simon & Schuster, 1966.

Powell, Anthony. *A Dance to the Music of Time.* Little, Brown & Co., 1951, 1955.

Powell, Anthony. *The Fisher King.* W. W. Norton & Co., 1986.

Powers, J. F. *Look How the Fish Live.* Alfred A. Knopf, Inc., 1975.

Prather, Richard S. *The Amber Effect.* Tom Doherty Associates Book/Tor, 1986.

Priestley, J. B. *Saturn Over the Water.* Doubleday & Co., Inc., 1961.

Priestly, J. B. *Found, Lost, Found.* Stein & Day Publishers, 1976.

Pritchett, V. S. *Collected Stories.* Random House, Inc., 1947, 1949, 1953, 1956, 1959, 1960, 1961, 1962, 1966, 1967, 1969, 1973.

Pritchett, V. S. *The Oxford Book of Short Stories.* Oxford University Press, 1981.

Prize Stories of 1920: O. Henry Memorial Award Prizes. Doubleday, Page & Co., 1921.

Prize Stories of 1925: The O. Henry Memorial Awards. Doubleday, Page & Co., 1926.

Prize Stories of 1927: The O. Henry Memorial Awards. Doubleday, Doran & Co., Inc., 1928.

Prize Stories of 1928: The O. Henry Memorial Awards. Doubleday, Doran & Co., Inc., 1928.

Prize Stories of 1957: The O. Henry Awards. Paul Engle, ed. Doubleday & Co., Inc., 1957.

Prize Stories of 1959: The O. Henry Awards. Paul Engle, ed. Doubleday & Co., Inc., 1959.

Prize Stories of 1965: The O. Henry Awards. Richard Poirier and William Abrahams, eds. Doubleday & Co., Inc., 1965.

Prize Stories of 1972: The O. Henry Awards. William Abrahams, ed. Doubleday & Co., Inc., 1972.

Prize Stories of 1978: The O. Henry Awards. William Abrahams, ed. Doubleday & Co., Inc., 1978.

Prize Stories of 1981: The O. Henry Awards. William Abrahams, ed. Doubleday & Co., Inc., 1981.

Prize Stories of 1986: The O. Henry Awards, William Abrahams, ed. Doubleday & Co., Inc., 1986.

Proffitt, Nicholas. *The Embassy House.* Bantam Books, 1986.

Pronzini, Bill. *The Vanished.* Random House, Inc., 1973.

Pronzini, Bill. *Quicksilver.* St. Martin's Press, 1984.

Proust, Marcel. *Swann's Way.* Random House, Inc., 1928.

Purdy, James. *In the Hollow of His Hand.* Weidenfeld & Nicolson, 1986.

Pushkin, A. S. *The Complete Prose Tales of Alexandre Sergeyevitch Pushkin.* W. W. Norton & Co., Inc., 1966.

Pym, Barbara. *Excellent Women.* E. P. Dutton, 1952.

Pym, Barbara. *Less Than Angels.* Jonathan Cape Ltd., 1955.

Pym, Barbara. *An Academic Question.* E. P. Dutton, 1986.

Pynchon, Thomas. *V.* J.B. Lippincott Co., 1961.

Quiller-Couch, Sir Arthur, ed., *The Oxford Book of English Verse 1250-1980.* Oxford University Press, 1900.

Radley, Sheila. *Fate Worse Than Death.* Charles Scribner's Sons, 1985, 1986.

Ramke, Bin. *The Language Student.* Louisiana State University Press, 1986.

Rand, Ayn. *The Living.* Random House, Inc., 1963, 1959.

Ratner, Rochelle. *Practicing to be a Woman: New & Selected Poems.* Scarecrow Press, 1982.

Ratner, Rochelle. *Bobby's Girl.* Coffee House Press, 1986.

Raun, Barry. *The Movie Quote Book.* Lippincott & Crowell, 1980.

Ravenel, Shannon, ed. *New Stories from the South: The Year's Best, 1986.* Algonquin Books, 1986.

Read, Herbert. *Collected Poems.* Horizon Press, 1966.

The Reader's Digest Treasury of Modern Quotations. Reader's Digest Press, 1975.

Rechy, John. *City of Night.* Grove Press, Inc., 1963.

Rechy, John. *Numbers.* Grove Press, Inc., 1967.

Reed, Rex. *People Are Crazy Here.* Delacorte Press, 1974.

Reed, Rex. *Valentines & Vitriol.* Dell Publishing Co., Inc./Stet, Inc., 1977.

Reed, Rex. *Personal Effects.* Arbor House, 1986.

Reeve, F. D. *In the Silent Stones.* William Morrow & Co., Inc., 1968.

Reidinger, Paul. *The Best Man.* A William Abrahams Book/E. P. Dutton, 1986.

Reiss, James. *The Breathers.* Ecco Press, 1974.

Reiss, James. *Express.* University of Pittsburgh Press, 1983.

Remarque, Erich Maria. *All Quiet on the Western Front.* Little, Brown & Co., 1928.

Remarque, Erich Maria. *The Road Back.* Little, Brown & Co., 1931.

Remarque, Erich Maria. *Three Comrades.* Little, Brown & Co., 1936, 1937.

Remarque, Erich Maria. *Flotsam.* Little, Brown & Co., 1941.

Remarque, Erich Maria. *A Time To Love and a Time To Die.* Harcourt, Brace & Co., 1954.

Remarque, Erich Maria. *The Black Obelisk.* Harcourt, Brace & Co., 1957-1958.

Rendell, Ruth. *An Unkindness of Ravens.* Pantheon Books, 1985.

Ress, Lisa. *Flight Patterns.* University Press of Virginia, 1985.

Reynolds, Price. *A Long and Happy Life.* Atheneum Publishers, 1962.

Reynolds, Price. *The Names and Faces of Heroes.* Atheneum Publishers, 1963.

Reynolds, Price. *Kate Vaiden.* Atheneum Publishers, 1986.

Rhys, Jean. *Quartet.* Harper & Row, Publishers, 1929, 1957.

Rhys, Jean. *After Leaving Mr. MacKenzie.* Harper & Row, Publishers, 1931.

Rhys, Jean. *Good Morning, Midnight.* Harper & Row, Publishers, 1939.

Rice, Ann. *Cry to Heaven.* Alfred A. Knopf, Inc., 1981.

Rich, Adrienne. *Poems Selected and New 1950-1974.* W. W. Norton & Co., Inc., 1975, 1973, 1971, 1969, 1966.

Richardson, Joan. *Wallace Stevens: the Early Years, 1879-1923.* Beech Tree/William Morrow Co., Inc., 1986.

Richter, Conrad. *The Light in the Forest.* Alfred A. Knopf, Inc., 1966.

Rider, J. W. *Jersey Tomatoes.* Arbor House/A Belvedere Book, 1986.

Rilke, Rainer Maria. *Poems 1906 to 1926.* Hogarth Press, 1959.

Rilke, Rainer Maria. *The Sonnets to Orpheus.* Simon & Schuster, 1986.

Robbins, Tom. *Another Roadside Attraction.* Random House, Inc., 1971.

Robbins, Tom. *Even Cowgirls Get the Blues.* Houghton Mifflin Co., Inc., 1976.

Robbins, Tom. *Still Life With Woodpecker.* Bantam Books, 1980.

Robert Irwin. *The Limits of Vision.* Dedalus/Viking Press, 1986.

Roberts, Kate Louise, ed. *Hoyt's New Encyclopedia of Practical Quotations.* Funk & Wagnalls Co., 1922, 1927, 1940.

Robertson, Don. *Make a Wish.* G. P. Putnam's Sons, 1975, 1977, 1978.

Robison, James. *Rumor and Other Stories.* Summit Books/Simon & Schuster, 1985.

Roethke, Theodore. *The Collected Poems of Theodore Roethke.* Doubleday & Co., Inc., 1966.

Rogers, Jane. *Her Living Image.* Doubleday & Co., Inc., 1986.

Romains, Jules. *The Seventh of October.* Alfred A. Knopf, Inc., 1946.

Rooney, Andy. *And More by Andy Rooney.* Atheneum Publishers, 1982. Rose, Daniel Asa. *Flipping For It.* St. Martin's Press, 1987.

Rosenberg, M. R. *Quotations for the New Age.* Citadel Press, 1978.

Ross, Frank. *Dead Runner.* Atheneum Publishers, 1977.

Rossetti, Christina. *Selected Poems of Christina Rossetti.* Marya Zaturenska, ed. Macmillan Publishing Co., Inc., 1970.

Rossetti, Dante Gabriel. *The Poetical Works Dante Gabriel Rossetti.* William M. Rossetti, ed. Ellis & Elvey, 1900.

Roth, Philip. *The Ghost Writer.* Farrar, Straus & Giroux, Inc., 1979.

Roth, Philip. *The Counter Life.* Farrar, Straus & Giroux, Inc., 1986.

Rovere, Richard. *Final Reports.* Doubleday & Co., Inc., 1984.

Rowes, Barbara. *The Book of Quotes.* E. P. Dutton, 1979.

Rukeyser, Muriel. *The Collected Poems Muriel Rukeyser.* McGraw-Hill Book Co., 1978.

Russo, Richard. *Mohawk.* Vintage Books/Random House, Inc., 1986.

Sackville-West, Vita. *The Edwardians.* Doubleday, Doran & Co., Inc., 1930.

Sackville-West, Vita. *All Passion Spent.* Hogarth Press, 1931.

Sackville-West, Vita. *The Easter Party.* Doubleday & Co., Inc., 1953.

Sackville-West, Vita. *No Signposts In the Sea.* Doubleday & Co., Inc., 1961.

Sagan, Françoise. *A Few Hours of Sunlight.* Harper & Row, Publishers, 1971.

Saint-Éxupéry, Antoine de. *Night Flight.* Century Co., 1932.

St. Johns, Adela Rogers. *Never Again and Other Stories.* Doubleday & Co., 1949.

Salacrou, Armand. "Marguerite." *Best Short Plays of the World Theatre 1968-1973.* Stanley Richards, ed. Crown Publishers, Inc., 1973.

Salinger, J. D. *Nine Stories.* Little, Brown & Co., 1948-1953.

Salinger, J. D. *The Catcher in the Rye.* Little, Brown & Co., 1951.

Salten, Felix. *Bambi.* Nelson Doubleday, Inc., 1929.

Sams, Ferrol. *Run With the Horsemen.* Peachtree Publishers, Ltd., 1982.

Sandburg, Carl. *The Complete Poems of Carl Sandburg.* Harcourt Brace Jovanovich, 1969, 1970.

Sandel, Cora. *Cora Sandel: Selected Short Stories.* Seal Press, 1960, 1973.

Sangster, Jimmy. *Private i,* W. W. Norton & Co., Inc., 1967.

Sangster, Jimmy. *Foreign Exchange.* W. W. Norton & Co., Inc., 1968.

Sangster, Jimmy. *Your Friendly Neighbourhood Death Pedlar.* Dodd, Mead & Co., 1971.

Santayana, George. *The Last Puritan.* Charles Scribner's Sons, 1947.

Santiago, Danny. *Famous All Over Town.* Simon & Schuster, 1983.

Sapirstein, Milton R. with De Sola, Alis. *Paradoxes of Everyday Life.* Random House, Inc., 1955.

Saroyan, William. *The Human Comedy.* Harcourt, Brace & World, Inc., 1943.

Sarton, May. *Journal of Solitude.* W. W. Norton & Co., Inc., 1973.

Sarton, May. *Crucial Conversations.* W. W. Norton & Co., Inc., 1975.

Sartre, Jean-Paul. "No Exit." *The Twenty Best European Plays on the American Stage.* John Gassner, ed. Crown Publishers, Inc., 1974.

Scannell, Vernon. *Ring of Truth.* Robson Books, 1983.

Schaeffer, Susan Fromberg. *Anya.* Macmillan Publishing Co., Inc., 1974.

Schaeffer, Susan Fromberg. *Time In Its Flight.* Doubleday & Co., Inc., 1978.

Schiaparelli, Elsa. *A Schocking Life.* E. P. Dutton & Co., 1954.

Schulberg, Budd. *What Makes Sammy Run.* Random House, Inc., 1941.

Schwartz, Delmore. *Portrait of Delmore, Journals and Notes of Delmore Schwartz 1939-1959,* Elizabeth Pollet, ed. Farrar, Straus & Giroux, Inc., 1986.

Schwartz, Lynne Sharon. *Rough Strife.* Harper & Row, Publishers, 1978.

Schwartz, Lynne Sharon. *Disturbances In the Field.* Harper & Row, Publishers, 1983.

Schwartz, Lynne Sharon. *Acquainted With the Night and Other Stories.* Harper & Row, Publishers, 1984.

Schwed, Peter and Herbert Warren Wind, eds. *Great Stories from the World of Sport.* Vols. 1, 2 and 3. Simon & Schuster, 1958.

Scott, Sir Walter. *The Heart of Mid-Lothian.* J. M. Dent & Sons, Ltd., n.d.

Scott, Sir Walter. *The Lady of the Lake.* Christopher Sower Co., 1915.

Seaman, Barbara. *Lovely Me.* William Morrow & Co., Inc., 1987.

Seaman, Donald. *The Bomb That Could Lip-Read.* Stein & Day Publishers, 1974.

Seaman, Donald. *The Committee.* Atheneum Publishers, 1978.

Seaman, Donald. *The Duel.* Doubleday & Co., Inc., 1979.

Seaman, Donald. *The Wilderness of Mirrors.* St. Martin's Press, 1984.

Searls, Hank. *The Big X.* Harper & Brothers, 1959.

Seifert, Jaroslav. *The Selected Poetry of Jaroslav Seifert.* George Gibian ed. Macmillan Publishing Co., Inc., 1986.

Seldes, George, ed. *The Great Quotations.* Pocket Books/Simon & Schuster, 1967.

Selzer, Joanne. *Summer Heat.* California State Poetry Society, Spring, 1978.

Selzer, Richard. *Confessions of a Knife.* Simon & Schuster, 1979.

Settle, Mary Lee. *Blood Tie.* Houghton Mifflin Co., 1977.

Sexton, Anne. *The Complete Poems Anne Sexton.* Houghton Mifflin Co., 1981.

Shagan, Steve. *Save the Tiger.* Dial Press, 1972.

Shain, Merle. *When Lovers Are Friends.* J. P. Lippincott Co., 1978.

Shakespeare, William. *The Annotated Shakespeare.* A. L. Rowse, ed. Vols. I, II, III. Clarkson Potter, 1978.

Shapiro, Karl. *Shapiro Selected Poems.* Random House, Inc., 1940-1955 1956-1958, 1961-1964, 1967-1968.

Shapiro, Nat, ed. *Encyclopedia of Quotations About Music.* Doubleday & Co., 1978.

Sharp, Marilyn. *Sunflower.* Richard Marek Publishers, 1979.

Shaw, Irwin. *Irwin Shaw Short Stories: Five Decades.* Delacorte Press, 1937-1947, 1949-1958, 1961-1964, 1967-1969, 1972, 1973, 1977-1980.

Shaw, Irwin. *Welcome to the City.* Random House, Inc., 1941.

Shaw, George Bernard. *Seven Plays by Bernard Shaw.* Dodd, Mead & Co., 1951.

Sheed, Wilfrid. *Office Politics.* Farrar, Straus & Giroux, Inc., 1966.

Shelley, Percy Bysshe. *The Complete Poetical Works of Percy Bysshe Shelley.* Thomas Hutchinson, ed. Oxford University Press, 1905.

Shenhar, Yitzhak. *A Whole Loaf.* Sholom J. Kahn, ed. Vanguard Press, Inc., 1957.

Sherwood, Robert Emmet. "Idiot's Delight." *Twenty Best Plays of the Modern American Theatre.* John Gassner, ed. Crown Publishers, Inc., 1939.

Shreve, Susan Richards. *Queen of Hearts.* Simon & Schuster, Inc., 1986.

Shulman, Alix Kates. *On the Stroll.* Alfred A. Knopf, Inc., 1981.

Shulman, Max. *Rally Round the Flag, Boys!.* Doubleday & Co., Inc., 1957.

Sigal, Clancy. *Going Away.* Houghton Mifflin Co., 1962.

Sillitoe, Alan. *Guzman, Go Home and Other Stories.* Simon & Schuster, 1964.

Silone, Ignazio. *The Secret of Luca.* Harper & Brothers, 1958.

Silone, Ignazio. *Fontamara.* Atheneum Publishers, 1960.

Silone, Ignazio. *Bread and Wine.* Signet/New American Library Inc., 1982.

Silverberg, Robert. *Beyond the Safe Zone, Collected Stories of Robert Silverberg.* Donald I. Fine, 1986.

Simenon, Georges. *The Murderer.* A Helen and Kurt Wolff Book/Harcourt Brace Jovanovich, 1986, c. 1937 Editions Gallimard.

Simic, Charles. *Return to a Place Lit by a Glass of Milk.* George Braziller, 1974.

Simic, Charles. *Charon's Cosmology.* George Braziller, 1977.

Simmons, Charles. *The Belles Lettres Papers.* William Morrow & Co., Inc., 1987.

Simon, Kate. *A Wider World: Portraits in an Adolescence.* Harper & Row, Publishers, 1986.

Simpson, James P., ed. *Contemporary Quotations.* Thomas Y. Crowell Co., 1964.

Singer, Isaac Bashevis. *The Collected Stories of Isaac Bashevis Singer/The Letter Writer.* Farrar, Straus & Giroux, Inc., 1982.

Sitwell, Dame Edith. *The Collected Poems of Edith Sitwell.* Vanguard Press, Inc., 1968.

Skinner, B. F. and Vaughan, M. E. *Enjoy Old Age.* W. W. Norton Co., Inc., 1983.

Skinner, Cornelia Otis. *Madame Sarah.* Houghton Mifflin Co., 1967.

Slaughter, Carolyn. *A Perfect Woman.* Ticknor & Fields, 1985.

Slavitt, David R. *Alice at 80.* Doubleday & Co., Inc., 1984.

Slesinger, Tess. *On Being Told That Her Second Husband Has Taken His First Lover and Other Stories.* Quadrangle/New York Times Book Co., 1935.

Smart, William, ed. *Eight Modern Essays.* St. Martin's Press, 1973.

Smith, Lee. *The Last Day the Dogbushes Bloomed.* Harper & Row, Publishers, 1968.

Smith, Lee. *Oral History.* G. P. Putnam's Sons, 1983.

Smith, Lee. *Family Linen.* G. P. Putnam's Sons, 1985.

Smith, Martin Cruz. *Stallion Gate.* Random House, Inc., 1986.

Smith, Pauline. *The Little Karoo.* Vanguard Press, Inc., 1956.

Smith, Stevie. *The Collected Poems of Stevie Smith.* Oxford University Press, 1976.

Smollett, Tobias. *The Expedition of Humphrey Clinker.* Oxford University Press, 1966.

Snodgrass, W. D. *After Experience.* Harper & Row, Publishers, 1958-1969.

Snodgrass, W. D. *Heart's Needle.* Harper & Row, Publishers, 1958-1969.

Solzhenitsyn, Alexander. *Stories and Prose Poems.* Farrar, Straus & Giroux, Inc., 1970, 1972.

Sōseki, Natsume. *Ten Nights of Dream, Hearing Things, The Heredity of Taste.* Charles E. Tuttle Co., 1974.

Spaeth, Sigmund. *Weep Some More, My Lady.* Doubleday, Page & Co., 1927.

Spark, Debra, ed. *20 Under 30.* Charles Scribner's Sons, 1986.

Spark, Muriel. *Memento Mori.* Perigree/Putnam Group, 1959.

Spencer, Elizabeth. *The Snare* . McGraw-Hill Book Co., 1972.

Spencer, Elizabeth. *The Voice at the Back Door.* McGraw-Hill Book Co., 1956.

Spencer, Elizabeth. *The Stories of Elizabeth Spencer.* Doubleday & Co., Inc., 1981.

Spencer, Scott. *Preservation Hall.* Alfred A. Knopf, Inc., 1976.

Spencer, Scott. *Endless Love.* Alfred A. Knopf, Inc., 1979.

Spinrad, Leonard and Thelma. *Speaker's Lifetime Library.* Parker Publishing Co., 1979.

Spring, Howard. *Hard Facts.* Viking Press, 1944.

Spring, Howard. *Time and the Hour.* Harper & Brothers, 1958.

Stafford, Jean. *Boston Adventure.* Harcourt, Brace & World, Inc., 1944.

Stafford, Jean. *The Mountain Lion.* Farrar, Straus & Giroux, Inc., 1947, 1972.

Stafford, Jean. *The Collected Stories of Jean Stafford.* Farrar, Straus & Giroux, Inc., 1945-1953, 1956.

Stafford, Jean. *The Catherine Wheel.* Harcourt, Brace & Co., 1951, 1952.

Stallman, R. W. and Watter, R. E., eds. *The Creative Reader, An Anthology of Fiction, Drama, Poetry.* Ronald Press Co., 1954.

Stannard, David E. *Shrinking History: On Freud and the Failure of Psychiatry.* Oxford University Press, 1980.

Stark, Sharon Sheehe. *A Wrestler's Tale.* William Morrow, Co., Inc., 1985.

Stark, Sharon Sheehe. *The Dealers' Yard And Other Stories.* William Morrow Co., Inc., 1985.

Stead, Christina. *The Christina Stead Reader, Selected by Jean B. Read.* Random House, Inc., 1976.

Stead, Christina. *Ocean of Story.* Viking Penguin Books, 1985.

Steele, Wilbur Daniel. *The Best Stories of Wilbur Daniel Steele.* Doubleday & Co., Inc., 1946.

Stegner, Wallace. *The Women on the Wall.* Houghton Mifflin Co., Inc., 1940-1948.

Stegner, Wallace. *The City of the Living and Other Stories.* Houghton Mifflin Co., 1956.

Stegner, Wallace. *All the Little Live Things.* Viking Press, 1967.

Stegner, Wallace. *Recapitulation.* Doubleday & Co., Inc., 1979.

Steinbeck, John. *The Long Valley.* Viking Press, 1939.

Stern, James. *The Man Who Was Loved. The Woman Who Was Loved.* Harcourt, Brace & Co., 1940, 1945, 1951.

Stevens, Wallace. *The Collected Poems of Wallace Stevens.* Alfred A. Knopf, Inc., 1961.

Stevenson, Burton, ed. *The Macmillan Publishing Co., Inc., Book of Proverbs, Maxims and Famous Phrases.* Macmillan Publishing Co., Inc., 1948.

Stevenson, Burton, ed. *The Home Book of Bible Quotations.* Harper & Brothers, 1949.

Stevenson, Burton, ed. *The Home Book of Quotations.* 9th Edition. Dodd, Mead Co., 1958.

Stevenson, Robert Louis. *The Strange Case of Dr. Jekyll and Mr. Hyde.* E. P. Dutton, 1925.

Stevenson, Robert Louis. *Treasure Island.* Macmillan Publishing Co., Inc., 1962.

Stevenson, Robert Louis. *The Travels and Essays of Robert Louis Stevenson.* Charles Scribner's Sons, 1903.

Stevenson, Burton Egbert, ed. *The Home Book of Modern Verse.* Holt, Rinehart & Winston, 1925, 1953.

Stewart, Fred Mustard. *The Titan.* Simon & Schuster, Inc., 1985.

Stewart, Mary. *My Brother Michael.* William Morrow & Co., 1960.

Stewart, Mary. *The Moon-Spinners.* William Morrow & Co., 1963.

Stockanes, Anthony E. *Ladies Who Knit for a Living.* University of Illinois Press, 1981.

Stone, Irving. *The Irving Stone Reader.* Doubleday & Co., Inc., 1963.

Stories from the New Yorker 1950-1960. Simon & Schuster, 1960.

Stout, Rex. *Five of A Kind.* Viking Press, 1961.

Straus, Dorothea. *The Birthmark.* George Braziller, 1987.

Streatfeild, Noel. *Thursday's Child.* Random House, Inc., 1971.

Strindberg, August. *Six Plays of Strindberg.* Doubleday, Anchor Books, 1955.

Sturm, Marian. *Floating.* Viking Press, 1984.

Styron, William. *Lie Down in Darkness.* Bobbs-Merrill Co., Inc., 1951.

Suckow, Ruth. *Some Others and Myself.* Rinehart & Co., Inc., 1932, 1935, 1952.

Summers, Hollis. *Standing Room.* Louisiana State University Press, 1984.

Suskind, Patrick. *Perfumey.* Alfred A. Knopf, Inc., 1986.

Sutherland, Margaret. *Dark Places, Deep Regions and Other Stories.* Stemmer House Publishers, Inc., 1980.

Svevo, Italo. *Confessions of Zeno.* Vintage Books/Random House, Inc., 1923.

Swados, Harvey. *Nights in the Gardens of Brooklyn.* Viking Penguin, Inc., 1951, 1952, 1958-1965.

Swados, Harvey. *Out Went the Candle.* Viking Press, 1955.

Swados, Harvey. *False Coin.* Atlantic-Little, Brown Books, 1959.

Swenson, May. *The Poet's Story.* Howard Moss, ed. Macmillan Publishing Co., Inc., 1973.

Swift, Graham. *The Sweet-Shop Owner.* Washington Square Press/Simon & Schuster, Inc., 1980.

Swift, Graham. *Waterland.* Poseidon Press, 1983.

Swinburne, Algernon Charles. *Algernon Charles Swinburne Poems and Ballads.* Morse Peckham ed. Bobbs-Merrill Co., Inc., 1970.

Swinnerton, Frank. *Faithful Company.* Doubleday & Co., Inc., 1948.

Swinnerton, Frank. *An Affair of Love.* Doubleday & Co., Inc., 1953.

Swinnerton, Frank. *A Month in Gordon Square.* Doubleday & Co., Inc., 1954.

Swinnerton, Frank. *Quadrille.* Doubleday & Co., Inc., 1965.

Swinnerton, Frank. *Nor All Thy Tears.* Doubeday & Co., Inc., 1972.

Swinnerton, Frank. *Some Achieve Greatness.* Doubleday & Co., Inc., 1976.

Synge, John M. *The Complete Works of John M. Synge.* Random House, Inc., 1935.

Tallent, Elizabeth. *Museum Pieces.* Alfred A. Knopf, Inc., 1985.

Tarkington, Booth. *Magnificent Ambersons.* Charles Scribner's Sons, 1919.

Taylor, Archer and Whiting, Bartlett Jere. *A Dictionary of American Proverbs and Proverbial Phrases.* Harvard University Press, 1958.

Taylor, Elizabeth. *Hester Lilly.* Viking Press, 1954.

Taylor, Fred. *Walking Shadows.* St. Martin's Press, 1984.

Taylor, Peter. *The Collected Stories of Peter Taylor.* Farrar, Straus & Giroux, Inc., 1961.

Tennyson, Lord Alfred. *The Poetical Works of Tennyson.* G. Robert Stange, ed. Houghton Mifflin Co., 1974.

Tey, Josephine. *Three by Tey.* Macmillan Publishing Co., Inc., 1947, 1948, 1954.

Theroux, Paul. *The Family Arsenal.* Houghton Mifflin Co., 1976.

Theroux, Paul. *Picture Palace.* Houghton Mifflin Co., 1978.

Theroux, Paul. *The Mosquito Coast.* Houghton Mifflin Co., 1982.

Thomas, Dylan. *Dylan Thomas, The Collected Letters.* Paul Ferris ed. Macmillan Publishing Co., Inc., 1957, 1966, 1985.

Thomas, Leslie. *Bare Nell.* St. Martin's Press, 1978.

Thomas, Ross. *The Cold War Swap.* William Morrow & Co., Inc., 1966.

Thompson, Hunter S. *Fear and Loathing on the Campaign Trail '71.* Straight Arrow Books, 1973.

Thompson, Jean. *The Gasoline Wars.* University of Illinois Press, 1979.

Thompson, Jean. *Little Face and Other Stories.* Franklin Watts, 1984.

Thornton, James, ed. *Table Talk From Ben Jonson to Leigh Hunt.* J. M. Dent & Sons, Ltd., 1934.

Thurber, James. *You Could Look It Up.* Curtis Publishing Co., 1941.

Thurber, James. *The Secret Life of Walter Mitty.* Harcourt Brace & World, Inc., 1942.

Thurber, James. *The Thurber Carnival.* Harper & Row, Publishers, 1945.

Tindall, Gillian. *Dances of Death.* Walker & Co., 1973.

Tolstoy, Leo. *War and Peace.* Modern Library/Random House, Inc., 1931.

Tolstoy, Leo. *Anna Karenina.* Bantam Books, Inc., 1977.

Tolstoy, Leo. "Redemption." *The Twenty Best European Plays on the American Stage,* John Gassner, ed. Crown Publishers, Inc., 1974.

Toole, John Kennedy. *Confederacy of Dunces.* Louisiana State University Press, 1980.

Train, Arthur. *Tutt and Mr. Tutt.* Charles Scribner's Sons, 1920.

Train, Arthur. *Mr. Tutt Takes the Stand.* Charles Scribner's Sons, 1936.

Train, Arthur. *Mr. Tutt At His Best.* Charles Scribner's Sons, 1961. Traver, Robert. *Anatomy of a Murder.* St. Martin's Press, 1958.

Traver, Robert. *Hornstein's Boy.* St. Martin's Press, 1962.

Traver, Robert. *Laughing Whitefish.* McGraw-Hill Book Co., 1965.

Traver, Robert. *People Versus Kirk.* St. Martin's Press, 1981.

Tremain, Rose. *Letter to Sister Benedicta.* St. Martin's Press, 1978.

Tremain, Rose. *The Swimming Pool Season.* Summit Books/Simon & Schuster, Inc., 1985

Tripp, Rhoda Thomas. *The International Thesaurus of Quotations.* Harper & Row, Publishers, 1970.

Bibliography

Tuohy, Frank. *The Collected Stories.* Holt, Rinehart & Winston, 1984.

Turgenev, Ivan. *First Love and Other Tales.* W. W. Norton & Co., 1960.

Turow, Scott. *Presumed Innocent.* Farrar, Straus & Giroux, Inc., 1987.

Twain, Mark. *The Family Mark Twain.* Harper & Row, Publishers, 1896-1899, 1901-1903, 1906, 1908, 1910, 1935.

Twain, Mark. *The Mysterious Stranger and Other Stories.* Harper & Row, Publishers, 1922, 1950.

Twain, Mark. *The Complete Essays of Mark Twain.* Charles Neider, ed. Doubleday & Co., Inc., 1963.

Tyler, Anne. *If Morning Ever Comes.* Alfred A. Knopf, Inc., 1964.

Tyler, Anne. *Dinner at the Homesick Restaurant,* Alfred A. Knopf, Inc., 1982.

Tzu, Lao. *The Way of Life.* Signet/New American Library, 1955.

Untermeyer, Louis, ed. *A Treasury of Great Poems.* Simon & Schuster, Inc., 1942.

Untermeyer, Louis, ed. *Treasury of Great Humor.* McGraw-Hill Book Co., 1972.

Updike, John. *Rabbit Run.* Alfred A. Knopf, Inc., 1960.

Updike, John. *Pigeon Feathers.* Alfred A. Knopf, Inc., 1959-1962.

Updike, John. *The Centaur.* Alfred A. Knopf, Inc., 1976

Updike, John. *The Poorhouse Fair.* Alfred A. Knopf, Inc., 1977.

Updike, John. *Marry Me.* Penguin Books, 1977.

Updike, John. *The Witches of Eastwick.* Alfred A. Knopf, Inc., 1984.

Updike, John. *Roger's Version.* Alfred A. Knopf, Inc., 1986.

Updike, John. *Trust Me.* Alfred A. Knopf, Inc., 1987.

Urdang, Laurence; Hunsinger, Walter J.; and La Roche, Nancy. *Picturesque Expressions: A Thematic Dictionary.* Gale Research Co., 1985.

Urdang, Laurence and Robbins, Ceila Dame. *Slogans.* Gale Research Co., 1984.

Valin, Jonathan. *Final Notice.* Dodd, Mead & Co., 1980.

Valin, Jonathan. *The Lime Pit.* Dodd, Mead & Co., 1980.

Valin, Jonathan. *Day of Wrath.* Congdon & Lattès, Inc., 1982.

Valin, Jonathan. *Natural Causes.* St. Martin's Press, 1983.

Valin, Jonathan. *Life's Work.* Delacorte Press, 1986.

Van Dyke, Henry. *The Ruling Passion.* Charles Scribner's Sons, 1901.

Van Dyke, Henry. *Ladies of the Rachmaninoff Eyes.* Farrar, Straus & Giroux, Inc., 1965.

Vidal, Gore. *Burr.* Harper & Row, Publishers, 1973.

Viorst, Judith. *Yes, Married.* Saturday Review Press, 1972.

Vogue's First Reader. Julian Messner, 1943.

Wagner, Jane. *The Search for Signs of Intelligent Life in the Universe.* Harper & Row, Publishers, 1986.

Wagoner, David. *Collected Poems 1956-1976 David Wagoner.* Indiana University Press, 1976.

Wainwright, John. *The Hard Hit.* St. Martin's Press, 1974.

Wakefield, Dan. *Going All the Way.* Seymour Lawrence/Delacorte Press, 1970.

Wakeman, Frederic. *The Hucksters.* Rinehart & Co., Inc., 1946.

Wakoski, Diane. *The George Washington Poems.* Riverrun Press, 1967.

Wakoski, Diane. *Inside the Blood Factory.* Doubleday & Co., Inc., 1968.

Wakoski, Diane. *Smudging.* Black Sparrow Press, 1972.

Wakoski, Diane. *Motorcycle Betrayal Poems.* Simon & Schuster, Inc., 1972.

Wakoski, Diane. *Dancing On the Grave of a Son of a Bitch.* Black Sparrow Press, 1973.

Walcott, Derek. *Derek Walcott Collected Poems 1948-1984.* Farrar, Straus & Giroux, Inc., 1986.

Walker, Alice. *Meridian.* Harcourt Brace Jovanovich, 1976.

Walling, R. A. J. *A Corpse by Any Other Name.* William Morrow & Co., Inc., 1943. Walpole, Hugh. *The Fortress.* Doubleday, Doran & Co., Inc., 1932.

Walpole, Hugh. *Vanessa.* Doubleday, Doran & Co., Inc., 1933.

Walpole, Hugh. *The Bright Pavilions.* Doubleday, Doran & Co., Inc., 1940.

Walpole, Hugh. *Katherine Christian.* Doubleday, Doran & Co., Inc., 1943.

Wambaugh, Joseph. *The Secrets of Harry Bright.* William Morrow & Co., Inc., 1985.

Wambaugh. Joseph. *Echoes in the Darkness.* A Perigord Press Book/William Morrow & Co., Inc., 1987.

Warner, Sylvia Townsend. *Sylvia Townsend Warner, One Thing Leading to Another and Other Stories.* Susanna Pinney ed. Viking Penguin, Inc., 1984.

Warren, Robert Penn. *All the King's Men.* Random House, Inc., 1960.

Warren, Robert Penn. *New and Selected Poems 1923-1985.* Random House, Inc., 1985.

Waugh, Evelyn. *Brideshead Revisited.* Little, Brown & Co., 1946.

Weaver, Will. *Red Earth, White Earth.* Simon & Schuster, Inc., 1986.

Wellman, Paul J. *The Walls of Jericho.* J. B. Lippincott Co., 1947.

Wells, H. G. *The Complete Short Stories of H. G. Wells.* A Ernest Benn, Ltd., 1927.

Welty, Eudora. *Delta Wedding.* Harcourt, Brace & Co., 1945, 1946.

Welty, Eudora. *The Collected Stories of Eudora Welty.* Harcourt Brace Jovanovich, Publishers, 1936-1939, 1941-1943, 1947-1949, 1951, 1954, 1955, 1963, 1966, 1980.

Welty, Eudora. *Losing Battles.* Random House, Inc., 1970.

Werfel, Franz. *Embezzled Heaven.* Viking Press, 1940.

Wertenbaker, Lael Tucker. *Unbidden Guests.* Little, Brown & Co., 1970.

Wertenbaker, Lael Tucker. *The Afternoon Women.* Little, Brown & Co., 1966.

West, Jessamyn. *The Life I Really Lived.* Harcourt Brace Jovanovich, 1979.

West, Jessamyn. *Collected Stories of Jessamyn West.* Harcourt Brace Jovanovich, 1986.

West, Rebecca. *The Harsh Voice.* Doubleday, Doran, 1937.

West, Rebecca. *The Birds Fall Down.* Viking Press, 1966.

West, Rebecca. *Cousin Rosamund.* Viking Penguin, Inc., 1986.

Westcott, Edward Noyes. *David Harum.* D. Appleton & Co., 1939.

Wharton, Edith. *The House of Mirth.* Charles Scribner's Sons, 1905.

Wharton, Edith. *The Reef.* D. Appleton & Co., 1912.

Wharton, Edith. *The Collected Short Stories of Edith Wharton.* R. W. B. Lewis, ed. Vols. I and II. Charles Scribner's Sons, 1968.

Whedon, Julia. *Two & Two Together.* Congdon & Weed, Inc., 1983.

Wheeler, Kate. *20 Under 30.* Charles Scribner's Sons, 1986.

Wheelock, John Hall. *The Gardner and other Poems.* Charles Scribner's Sons, 1961.

Wheelock, John Hall. *By Daylight and In Dream, New and Collected Poems, 1904-1970.* Charles Scribner's Sons, 1970.

White, Antonia. *The Sugar House.* Dial Press, 1979.

White, E. B. *Poems and Sketches of E. B. White.* Harper & Row, Publishers, 1925-1926, 1928-1952, 1954-1959, 1957, 1969-1970, 1976, 1981.

White, Patrick. *The Twyborn Affair.* Viking Press, 1979.

White, Patrick. *Memoirs of Many in One.* Viking Penguin, Inc., 1986.

White, T. H. *The Maharajah & Other Stories.* Kurth Sprague, ed. G. P. Putnam's Sons, 1981.

White, Thomas Glynn. *The Seersucker Suit.* Fiction Collective, 1986.

Whitehead, Alfred North. *The Wit and Wisdom of Alfred North Whitehead,* A. H. Johnson, ed. Beacon Press, 1947.

Whitehead, Frank, ed. *Modern Short Stories Book One.* Chatto & Windus, 1965.

Whittier, John Greenleaf. *The Complete Poetical Works of Whittier.* Houghton Mifflin Co., 1894.

Wiggins, Marianne. *Went South.* Delacorte Press, 1980.

Wiggins, Marianne. *Separate Checks.* Random House, Inc., 1984.

Wilbur, Richard. *The Poems of Richard Wilbur.* Harcourt, Brace & World, Inc., 1956.

Wilbur, Richard. *Walking To Sleep.* Harcourt, Brace & World, Inc., 1963-1965, 1967, 1968, 1969.

Wilde, Oscar. "The Importance of Being Earnest." *Sixteen Famous British Plays.* Bennett A. Cerf and Van H. Cartmell, eds. Random House, Inc., 1942.

Wilde, Oscar. *The Poems and Fairy Tales of Oscar Wilde.* Modern Library/Random House, Inc., n.d.

Wilde, Oscar. *The Picture of Dorian Gray.* Random House, Inc., 1880.

Will, George F. W. *The Pursuit of Happiness and Other Sobering Thoughts.* Harper & Row, Publishers, 1978.

Williams, Ben Ames. *The Strange Woman.* Houghton Mifflin Co., 1941.

Williams, Ben Ames. *Leave Her to Heaven.* Houghton Mifflin Co., 1944.

Williams, Miller. *So Long At the Fair.* E. P. Dutton & Co., Inc., 1968.

Williams, Miller. *The Only World There Is.* E. P. Dutton & Co., Inc., 1971.

Williams, Oscar, ed. *A Little Treasury of Modern Poetry.* Charles Scribner's Sons, 1952.

Williams, Sherley Anne. *Dessa Rose.* William Morrow & Co., Inc., 1986.

Williams, Tennessee. *The Roman Spring of Mrs. Stone.* New Directions Books, 1950.

Williams, Tennessee. *The Knightly Quest.* New Directions Book, 1966.

Williams, Tennessee. *Eight Mortal Ladies Possessed.* New Directions Book, 1971.

Williams, Thomas. *The Hair of Harold Roux.* Random House, Inc., 1966.

Williams, William Carlos. *The Collected Earlier Poems of William Carlos Williams.* New Directions Publishing Co., 1966.

Williamson, Alan. *Presence.* Alfred A. Knopf, Inc., 1983.

Willingham, Calder. *The Big Nickel.* Dial Press, 1975.

Wilson, Angus. *No Laughing Matter.* Viking Press, 1967.

Wilson, Leigh Allison. *From the Bottom Up.* University of Georgia Press, 1983.

Wilson, Z. Vance. *The Quick and the Dead.* Arbor House, 1986.

Wilstach, Frank J. *Dictionary of Similes.* Harrap, 1917.

Winans, A. D. *North Beach Poems.* Second Coming Press, 1977.

Winans, A. D. Vergin Press, 1987.

Winter's Tales. A. D. MacLean, ed. Vols. 8, 12, 26, 28. St. Martin's Press, 1962, 1966, 1980, 1982.

Winter's Tales. James Wright, ed. Vol. 22. St. Martin's Press, 1976.

Winter's Tales. Caroline Hobhouse, ed. Vol. 25. St. Martin's Press, 1979.

Winters, Yvor. *The Collected Poems of Yvor Winters.* Swallow Press, Inc., 1932, 1934, 1940, 1943, 1950, 1952, 1960, 1966.

Wodehouse, P. G. *Cocktail Time.* Simon & Schuster, 1958.

Wodehouse, P. G. *The Golf Omnibus.* Simon & Schuster, 1973.

Wodehouse, P. G. *Fore! The Best of Wodehouse on Golf.* D. R. Bensen ed. Ticknor & Fields, 1983.

Wodehouse, P. G. *The Eighteen-Carat Kid and Other Stories.* David A. Jasen, ed. Continuum Publishing Corp., 1980.

Wodin, Natascha. *The Interpreter.* Harcourt Brace Jovanoovich, 1986.

Wolfe, Thomas. *Of Time and The River.* Charles Scribner's Sons, 1935.

Wolfe, Thomas. *You Can't Go Home Again.* Harper & Brothers, Publishers, 1940.

Wolfe, Tom. *The Kandy-Kolored Tangerine-Flake Streamline Baby.* Farrar, Straus & Giroux, Inc., 1965.

Wolfe, Tom. *The Right Stuff.* Farrar, Straus & Giroux, Inc., 1980.

Wolfe, Tom. *Radical Chic & Mau-Mauing the Flak Catchers.* Farrar, Straus & Giroux, Inc., 1970.

Wolff, Tobias. *Back in the World.* Houghton Mifflin Co., 1985.

Wolff, Geoffrey. *Inklings.* Random House, Inc., 1977.

Wolff, Geoffrey. *Providence.* Elisabeth Sifton Books/Viking Penguin, Inc., 1986.

Wolitzer, Hilma. *In the Palomar Arms.* Farrar, Straus & Giroux, Inc., 1983.

Wood, Ira. *The Kitchen Man.* Crossing Press, 1985.

Woods, Ralph L. *The Family Reader of American Masterpieces.* Thomas Y. Crowell Co., 1959.

Woods, Ralph L. *A Second Treasury of the Familiar.* Macmillan Publishing Co., Inc., 1959.

Woods, Ralph L. *A Third Treasury of the Familiar.* Macmillan Publishing Co., Inc., 1970.

Woods, Sara *Most Deadly Hate.* St. Martin's Press, 1986.

Woolf, Virginia. *Mrs. Dalloway.* Harcourt, Brace & Co, 1925.

Woolf, Virginia. *To the Lighthouse.* Harcourt, Brace & Co., 1927.

Woolf, Virginia. *The Complete Shorter Fiction of Virginia Woolf.* Susan Dick ed. Harcourt Brace Jovanovich, 1985.

Woolrich, Cornell. *Nightwebs.* Francis M. Nevins, Jr. ed. Harper & Row, Publishers, 1971.

Woolrich, Cornell. *Angels of Darkness.* Harper & Row, Publishers, 1971.

Wordsworth, William. *Wordsworth Poetical Works.* Thomas Hutchinson ed. Oxford University Press, 1904, 1936.

World's Great Humorous Stories. World Publishing Co.,1944.

Wouk, Herman. *Inside, Outside.* Little, Brown & Co., Inc., 1985.

Wright, Charles. *Country Music.* Wesleyan University Press, 1963-1977, 1982.

Wright, James. *This Journey. To the Cicada.* Random House, Inc., 1977-1982.

Wylie, Elinor. *Collected Prose of Elinor Wylie.* Alfred A. Knopf, Inc., 1946.

Yaari, Yehuda. *A Whole Loaf.* Sholom J.Kahn, ed. Vanguard Press, Inc., 1957.

Yankowitz, Susan. *Silent Witness.* Alfred A. Knopf, Inc., 1976.

Yapp, Peter, ed. *The Travellers' Dictionary of Quotation.* Routledge & Kegan Paul, 1983.

Yarmolinsky, Avrahm, ed. *A Treasury of Great Russian Short Stories.* Macmillan Publishing Co., Inc., 1944.

Yeats, W. B. *The Collected Poems of W. B. Yeats.* Macmillan Publishing Co., Inc., 1956.

Yellen, Samuel. *The Passionate Sepherd.* Alfred A. Knopf, Inc., 1957.

Yezierska, Anzia. *Hungry Hearts and Other Stories.* Persea Books/ Houghton Mifflin Co., 1920.

Young, Marguerite. *Miss MacIntosh, My Darling.* Charles Scribner's Sons, 1965.

Yount, John. *Hardcastle.* Richard Marek Publishers, 1980.

Yount, John. *Toots in Solitude.* Richard Marek Publishers, 1984.

Yourcenar, Marguerite. *The Abyss.* Farrar, Straus & Giroux, Inc., 1976.

Yourcenar, Marguerite. *A Coin In Nine Hands.* Farrar, Straus & Giroux, Inc., 1982.

Yourcenar, Marguerite. *Alexis.* Farrar, Straus & Giroux, Inc., 1984.

Zarchi, Yisrael. *A Whole Loaf.* Sholom J. Kahn, ed. Vanguard Press, Inc., 1957.

Zola, Emile. *Germinal.* New American Library, 1970.

Zweig, Stefan. *Kaleidoscope.* Viking Press, 1934.

Zweig, Stefan. *Beware of Pity.* Harmony Books, 1982.

Newspapers and Periodicals (current and back-dated editions)
Dialect Notes
Esquire
Harper's Magazine
Holiday Magazine
Ladies' World
New Yorker
New York Post
New York Times
Newsday
North American Review
North American Mentor Magazine
Parade

Publishers' Weekly
Punch
Reader's Digest
Redbook
St. Nicholas Magazine
USA Today
Wall Street Journal
Washington Post
Woman's Home Companion
Writer's Digest

Author Index

All references are to entry numbers in the listed categories. A -c (e.g., CLARITY: 24-c) indicates that the entry does not have its own number but is incorporated into a comment following the listed number.

Andreyev, Leonid
REALNESS/UNREALNESS: 21;
TEARS: 4

Andric, Ivo
MOVEMENT: 67; RISING: 15

Angelou, Maya
AIR: 1; ATMOSPHERE: 6; BURST:
2; CONVERSATION: 55; FOOD
AND DRINK: 27; HARSHNESS: 13;
NOISE: 76; PHYSICAL
APPEARANCE: 71; PHYSICAL
FEELINGS: 30; PLACES: 9;
PREPAREDNESS: 1; SHARPNESS: 4;
SHYNESS: 2; STANDING: 6;
VOICE(S): 77; VOICE, EFFECT OF:
10; VOICE, WEAK: 6

Anouilh, Jean
ABILITY: 21; ALONENESS: 6

Anthony, Piers
EYE COLOR: 19; FEAR: 47

Antler
LAUGHTER: 64

Appelfeld, Aharon
ATTRACTION: 29; COURAGE: 26;
FEAR: 16

Apperley, Charles James
HEART(S): 5, 31

Apperson, G.L.
UNDESIRABILITY: 4

Apple, Max
ATTRACTION: 3; CHIN: 6;
CLEANLINESS: 4; CONTENTMENT:
4; CRITICISM, DRAMATIC AND
LITERARY: 22; DISAPPEARANCE:
45; PEOPLE, INTERACTION: 42;
ROOMS: 26; SKIN: 55; THINNESS:
35

Applebome, Peter
PLACES: 16

Aquinas, St. Thomas
SENSE: 8

Arabian Nights
AGITATION: 1; BODY: 54;
BRIGHTNESS: 28; EYES, BRIGHT:

5; FOREHEAD: 4, 7; HAND(S): 58;
JOY: 1; OCEANS/OCEANFRONTS:
27; SKIN: 50

Arbuthnot, John
LAW: 5; SERIOUSNESS: 16-c

Arcel, Ray
BOXING AND WRESTLING: 11

Ardizzone, Tony
BREATHING: 10; CLINGING: 9;
CLOTHING: 35; DEJECTION: 43;
DISINTEGRATION: 40; ERRORS: 9;
FURNITURE AND FURNISHINGS:
20; GLOOM: 34; HAND(S): 52;
IRRITABLENESS: 12; MEMORY:
12; MUSCLES: 17;
POLITICS/POLITICIANS: 34;
SCREAMS: 34; SKIN: 42; SPEED:
20; STOMACH: 11

Ardrey, Robert
VIOLENCE: 18

Aretino, Pietro
FRIENDSHIP: 12; WAR: 1

Aristippus
ABILITY: 16; WIT: 12

Aristophanes
DESTRUCTION: 21

Aristotle
FRIENDSHIP, DEFINED: 14; LAWS:
6; PATIENCE: 5; YOUTH: 13

Arkin, Frieda
TIME: 81

Arnold, Matthew
MEETINGS: 4

Arrowsmith, Aaron
WIT: 4

Arzybashev, Mikhail P.
ANGER: 34; FACIAL
EXPRESSIONS, BLANK: 8

Asch, Nathan
VEHICLES: 3

Asch, Sholem
BALDNESS: 20; ILLNESS: 8;
JUMPING: 17; MAXIMS,
PROVERBS AND SAYINGS: 11;
TEETH: 4; TREES: 10;
WRITERS/WRITING: 6

Author Index

FORTUNE/MISFORTUNE: 8-c;
KNOWLEDGE: 13; MONEY: 22;
REVENGE: 1; TRUST/MISTRUST:
16; VIRTUE: 19, 21

Baer, Arthur
DESIRABILITY: 8; ERRORS: 11;
HAND(S): 35; IMPOSSIBILITY: 15;
INAPPROPRIATENESS: 4;
MARRIAGE: 3; SHAPE: 14;
STEADINESS: 8; STRAIGHTNESS:
3, 4; SURPRISE: 10;
USEFULNESS/USELESSNESS: 12;
VIBRATION: 10; VISIBILITY: 15;
WRINKLES: 24

Bagby, George
HAIR STYLES: 29

Bagehot, Walter
WRITERS/WRITING: 49

Bagnold, Enid
BURST: 12; CROWDS: 12; SPEED:
85; TURNING AND TWISTING: 12

Bahya
DAY: 15; WORLD: 12, 16

Bail, Murray
SPORTS: 2

Bailey, Nathan
COMFORT: 3

Bailey, P.J.
JOY: 20; NIGHT: 8; THOUGHTS: 6

Baille, Joanna
GRIEF: 31

Bainbridge, Beryl
FUTILITY: 13; NOSES: 2;
POSTURE: 27; STARES: 2

Bakeland, Brooks
CLINGING: 15

Baker, Carlos
CHARACTER: 11; EMOTIONS: 48;
ENTHUSIASM: 8; FACIAL SHAPE:
12; FIRE AND SMOKE: 12;
HAPPINESS: 42; HUNGER: 9;
LAUGHTER: 6; LIGHTING: 22;
LOYALTY/DISLOYALTY: 1;
MEMORY: 4; MUSCLES: 12; NECK:
4; NOSES: 44; PALLOR: 23;
PEACEFULNESS: 13; PERSISTENCE:

16; REPUTATION: 12; SLOWNESS:
14; SMELL: 2; STOMACH: 5; SUN:
88; THUNDER AND LIGHTNING:
17; TREES: 41; TRUST/MISTRUST:
26; VOICE, HARSH: 47; VOICE,
MUSIC RELATED: 18; WEATHER:
4

Baker, Russell
BALDNESS: 23; CERTAINTY: 3;
COMPLETENESS: 7; FAME: 1;
FIRMNESS: 15; HISTORY: 1;
LANGUAGE: 8;
POLITICS/POLITICIANS: 9;
SMOOTHNESS: 3; THINNESS: 25;
VIOLENCE: 22; WORK: 12

Baldwin, James
EYES, BRIGHT: 31; EYE
EXPRESSIONS, MISCELLANEOUS:
45; FUTURE: 7; MONEY: 26;
PERSONALITY PROFILES: 7;
SINGING: 15; TEARS: 1

Balguy, John
RESTLESSNESS: 15

Ball, George W.
TACT: 1

Ballard, Mignon F.
THOUGHTS: 7

Ballou, Hosea
ENERGY: 14

Balzac, Honoré de
ADVANCING: 2; ADVANCING: 9;
APPRECIATION: 5; BELONGING:
1; BODY: 60; BOXING AND
WRESTLING: 12; CANDOR: 12;
CAUTION: 8; CONSCIENCE: 7;
COURAGE: 34; CRUELTY: 32;
DOCTORS: 6; DULLNESS: 45;
ELUSIVENESS: 15; EXCITEMENT:
14; EYES, BRIGHT: 15; EYE
EXPRESSIONS, MISCELLANEOUS:
38, 34; FACE(S): 18, 81, 112,
116; FACIAL EXPRESSIONS,
MISCELLANEOUS: 57; FACIAL
SHAPE: 18, 23; FATNESS: 3;
FEAR: 55; GLITTER AND GLOSS:
9, 46; GOSSIP: 22; LAUGHTER:

Benedict, Dianne
  FURNITURE AND FURNISHINGS:
  29; SKY: 21
Benét, Stephen Vincent
  ANIMALS: 3; BEAUTY: 12;
  BEHAVIOR: 26, 47;
  BEWILDERMENT: 7; BLACK: 15;
  BRIGHTNESS: 27, 39; CALMNESS:
  53; CLEANLINESS: 8; CLOTHING
  ACCESSORIES: 1; DARKNESS: 8;
  DECREASE: 20; DISPERSAL: 25;
  DRYNESS: 16; EYES, BRIGHT: 1;
  FEAR: 77; FIGHTING: 5; FOG: 9;
  GAIETY: 10; HAND(S): 16, 22;
  KINDNESS: 29; MUSCLES: 18;
  NAMES: 12, 14; PALLOR: 50;
  PRIDE: 29; PURITY: 8; RARITY:
  6, 10; ROAD SCENES: 22;
  SECRECY: 23; SELF-CONFIDENCE:
  17; SMILES: 43; SOFTNESS: 7, 34;
  SPEAKING: 22; SPEED: 55;
  STRAIGHTNESS: 9; THINNESS: 64;
  THOUGHTS: 14; TIME: 7;
  USEFULNESS/USELESSNESS: 17;
  WAR: 9; WASTE: 2
Benham, W.G.
  ENTHUSIASM: 30
Benjamin, Park
  BEGINNINGS/ENDINGS: 14
Benjamin, Walter
  PLACES: 20
Bennett, Arnold
  CLARITY: 24-c; ROCKING AND
  ROLLING: 26
Bennett, Peggy
  TREMBLING: 66; WALKING: 13
Bennetts, Leslie
  INAPPROPRIATENESS: 8;
  TRANSIENCE: 1
Benson, Arthur C.
  RESTLESSNESS: 12
Benson, E. F.
  WEAKNESS: 32
Benson, Stella
  CLOUD(S): 24; DULLNESS: 25;
  HELPLESSNESS: 6

Bentham, Jeremy
  AFFECTION: 5; HABIT: 1
Berger, John
  RISING: 1
Berger, Suzanne E.
  SMOOTHNESS: 36
Bergman, Ingrid
  AGE: 17
Berkeley, Bishop George
  WORLD: 9
Berkman, Sylvia
  BODY: 30; CHEERFULNESS: 4;
  COLDNESS: 20; CROWDS: 25;
  EYEBROWS: 8; FEAR: 52;
  FRAGILITY: 32; GLOOM: 23;
  LEAVES: 24; PERSONALITY
  PROFILES: 5; RAIN: 16;
  SENSITIVENESS: 7; SPEAKING: 13
Berkow, Ira
  BASEBALL: 17; CHOICES: 3;
  CONTEMPT: 10; INTENSITY: 16;
  NATURALNESS: 9
Berlin, Isaiah
  PLACES: 31;
  QUESTIONS/ANSWERS: 17;
  SPEECH PATTERNS: 7
Berriault, Gina
  FLOWERS: 21
Berrigan, Daniel
  BLINDNESS: 6; EMPTINESS: 33;
  EYE EXPRESSIONS,
  MISCELLANEOUS: 13; KINDNESS:
  6; LOOSENESS: 2; PEACEFULNESS:
  18; RISING: 3; SIMPLICITY: 2;
  SOFTNESS: 38
Berry, Wendell
  LOVE: 16; REGRET: 8; RELIGION:
  24
Berryman, John
  AGE: 40; BREATHING: 44; PAIN:
  43; THINNESS: 6, 44
Betjeman, John
  PRIDE: 21; SMELL: 41;
  SMOOTHNESS: 24
Betti, Ugo
  MEMORY: 30

Author Index

POSTURE: 21; REAPPEARANCE: 9;
ROCKING AND ROLLING: 9;
SHARPNESS: 8; SNOW: 44;
SOCIETY: 2; SPEECH PATTERNS:
22, 41; STALENESS: 7;
SUCCESS/FAILURE: 12; THRIFT: 9;
WHITE: 24

Chettle, Henry
PALLOR: 31; WHITE: 38

Chevecoeur, St. John De
MANKIND: 36

Childs, Julia
WRITERS/WRITING: 4

Chiles, Senator Lawton
TIMELINESS/UNTIMELINESS: 13

Chonnaill, Eibhlin Dhubh Ni
OPEN/SHUT: 14

Chopin, Kate
BEWILDERMENT: 8

Chrysostam, Saint John
ENVY: 1

Christie, Agatha
BUSINESS: 20; MIND: 24

Churchill, Charles
FORTUNE/MISFORTUNE: 28

Churchill, Winston
CHARACTERISTICS, NATIONAL:
26; DANGER: 21;
POLITICS/POLITICIANS: 21, 26

Churgin, Yaakov
DISINTEGRATION: 30

Chute, Carolyn
ARM(S): 14; CLOTHING: 34;
FATNESS: 22; LAUGHTER: 22;
MUSTACHES: 2, 5, 19; NOISE: 12;
NOSES: 12; SMELL: 32; VOICE,
HARSH: 43

Ciardi, John
ADVANTAGEOUSNESS: 6;
CERTAINTY: 31; GLITTER AND
GLOSS: 59

Cibber, Colley
IRRITABLENESS: 32; SILENCE: 112

Cicero
BOOKS: 34; MIND, DEFINED: 10

Cieply, Michael
PROBLEMS/SOLUTIONS: 8

Ciment, Jill
EYELASHES: 9; IMPARTIALITY: 5;
MOVEMENT: 46; PERMANENCE:
19; SCRUTINY: 18

Claiborne, Robert
WORDS, DEFINED: 1

Clampitt, Amy
RAIN: 55

Clark, Brian
ENTRANCES/EXITS: 28

Clark, Carol
PROBLEMS/SOLUTIONS: 2

Clark, Eleanor
ARM(S): 34; ATTENTION: 28;
PERMANENCE: 8; EMPTINESS: 16;
SMILES: 22; TALKATIVENESS: 10

Clark, Frank A.
CRITICISM: 4

Clarke, John
BLINDNESS: 1-c; CLEVERNESS: 29;
PRIDE: 14

Clayton, John J.
ENTRANCES/EXITS: 26; POSTURE:
25

Cleaver, Eldridge
VIOLENCE: 27

Clement, Saint
RICHES: 18

Clendinen, Dudley
DISAPPEARANCE: 33

Clift, Eleanor
POLITICS/POLITICIANS: 5

Clines, Francis X.
PLEASURE: 19

Coates, Robert M.
CAUTION: 5

Cobb, Irvin S.
ABILITY: 3; BREVITY: 7; BROWN:
15; COLLAPSE: 11-c;
FORTUNE/MISFORTUNE: 1;
FREEDOM: 6; MOUTH: 27;
PERSONALITY PROFILES: 3, 24;
SCREAMS: 43; TASTE: 20

Author Index

GROWTH: 11; INSECTS: 13;
JUMPING: 5; LAUGHTER: 20, 61;
LEAPING: 3; LEGS: 27; MADNESS:
3; MOON: 13; MUSIC: 39;
PERSONALITY PROFILES: 45;
PROTRUSION: 6; REJECTION: 11;
RELATIONSHIPS: 1, 10; RESERVE:
5; SHAPE: 13; SKIN: 37; SMELL:
5; SPEECH PATTERNS: 43; TEARS:
20; VOICE, EFFECT OF: 4; VOICE,
SOFT: 5; WALKING: 4

Considine, Bob
BOXING AND WRESTLING: 7;
FRAGILITY: 3

Cook, Joseph
GOVERNMENT: 15

Cooke, Alistair
COMMONPLACE: 20; INNOCENCE:
10; JUMPING: 3; SUDDENNESS: 23

Cooley, Charles Horton
VANITY: 25

Coolidge, Susan
DISAPPEARANCE: 93

Coomer, Joe
BARENESS: 2; KISSES: 1;
MOVEMENT: 12, 24; SKIN: 1;
STARES: 7; TEETH: 22; WIND: 23

Cooper, Jilly
AVAILABILITY: 10; BREASTS: 29;
COLLAPSE: 12; COMPLEXION: 1;
EYEBROWS: 11; FACIAL COLOR:
33; FACIAL EXPRESSIONS,
MISCELLANEOUS: 8; HUNGER: 4;
LEGS: 30; MIST: 3; MOON: 6;
NECK: 22; PROTECTIVENESS: 2;
RAIN: 48; RISING: 7; ROOMS: 19;
SENSITIVENESS: 14; SEX: 4
SKY: 5;
SMELL: 15, 19; SNOW: 56; SUN:
8, 49; TREES: 15; TREMBLING:
38; WATCHFULNESS: 9-c

Cooperman, Melvin I.
DREAMS: 10; STAGE AND
SCREEN: 15

Coover, Robert
AGITATION: 25

Coppard, A. E.
BEHAVIOR: 6; POSTURE: 40

Cornwall, Barry
BRIGHTNESS: 34

Corrigan, E. Gerald
ECONOMICS: 19

Cortázar, Julio
CROWDS: 23; MEN AND WOMEN:
5; PLEASURE: 11

Cotgrave, John
FATNESS: 12

Cotgrave, Randle
HABIT: 3

Cotton, Charles
WHITE: 20

Coughlin, T. Glen
BASEBALL: 4; BREASTS: 58;
CLINGING: 36; FACIAL DETAILS:
20; HEAD MOVEMENTS: 10;
REJECTION: 4; WORDS, EFFECT
OF: 17

Cousins, Norman
FREEDOM: 20

Coverdale, Miles
CLARITY: 24

Coward, Noël
BEGINNINGS/ENDINGS: 7;
CLEANLINESS: 27; COLDNESS: 2;
FEAR: 62; HAIR STYLES: 18;
MEMORY: 20; REALIZATION: 1;
SPEED: 48; WORDS, EFFECT OF:
11; WORK: 13

Cowley, Abraham
FAME: 12; LIFE, DEFINED: 14

Cowley, Hanna Parkhouse
VANITY: 24

Cowley, Malcolm
DAY: 1; GREEN: 7; HEAVINESS:
6; LIFE: 27; SITTING: 30; SLEEP:
21; SMILES: 59; TREMBLING: 46

Cowper, William
ABUNDANCE: 12;
CONVERSATION: 13; COURAGE:
11; FOOLISHNESS: 7;

HARMLESSNESS: 5; IDLENESS: 7;
KINDNESS: 17; LIFE: 34; SPORTS:
6; STRENGTH: 33

Cox, Marcelene
CHILDREN: 10

Cox, Palmer
BENDING/BENT: 6;
DISAPPEARANCE: 52, 56

Crabbe, George
DISHONESTY: 13; GRIEF: 8;
LIES/LIARS: 3

Craig, M. S.
MONEY: 28

Crane, Hart
BRIGHTNESS: 7; PERMANENCE:
21; GLITTER AND GLOSS: 63;
GOSSIP: 14; HAND(S): 40, 56;
MODESTY: 1;
REGULARITY/IRREGULARITY: 14

Crane, Stephen
ADVANCING: 35; BITTERNESS: 11;
COLLAPSE: 43; CURSES: 4, 14;
EMOTIONS: 34; FIGHTING: 11;
INSECTS: 9; LOOKS: 68; LYING:
18; OBVIOUSNESS: 11;
OCEANS/OCEANFRONTS: 31;
RESTLESSNESS: 16; ROOMS: 14;
RUNNING: 8; STRUGGLE: 1;
TREES: 53; UNSTEADINESS: 12

Crawford, F. Marion
MEN AND WOMEN: 57

**Crèvecoeur, Michel Guillaume
Jean de**
MANKIND: 28

Crier, John
EXITS: 8

Crockett, David
ABILITY: 13

Croly, George
DISPERSAL: 15

Cronin, A. J.
MIST: 13; REMOTENESS: 21

Cronyn, Hume
AGE: 18

Crowell, Robert
FRIENDSHIP: 19

Crowninshield, Francis W.
PAIN: 5

Crumley, James
ADVANCING: 16; AGITATION: 33;
AIMLESSNESS: 2; AIR: 14; ARM(S):
8; AWKWARDNESS: 21; BEARDS:
9; BEARING: 14, 49;
BEWILDERMENT: 5; BODY
ORGANS: 2; BREASTS: 7, 44,
50; BREATHING: 16;
CAUSE/EFFECT: 20; CLOTHING,
ITS FIT: 21; COLLAPSE: 44, 65;
CRITICISM: 9; CONVERSATION: 3;
CROWDS: 17; CRYING: 18, 19,
28; DARKNESS: 26;
DISAPPEARANCE: 13; DRINKING:
11; EATING AND DRINKING: 5;
ENTRANCES/EXITS: 22;
EYEBROWS: 9; EYE COLOR: 12;
EYE EXPRESSIONS,
MISCELLANEOUS: 13; EYELASHES:
6; FACE(S): 110; FACIAL SHAPE:
13; FATNESS: 28; FINGERS: 18;
FIRMNESS: 23; FOOTBALL: 3;
GLITTER AND GLOSS: 18; GRIEF:
2; GROANS AND WHISPERS: 7,
18; HEAD MOVEMENTS: 8;
HOUSES: 27;
INAPPROPRIATENESS: 18;
INSECTS: 11; LAUGHTER: 5;
LEGS: 50; LIES/LIARS: 6;
LINGERING: 19; MEN AND
WOMEN: 20; MOVEMENT: 13, 34;
MUSTACHES: 14; NECK: 10;
OCEANS/OCEANFRONTS: 7;
PEOPLE, INTERACTION: 6; PITY:
8; PLACES: 27; POSTURE: 23;
PURSUIT: 14;
QUESTIONS/ANSWERS: 5; RAIN: 8;
RISING: 17; SMILES: 30, 40, 49,
101; SMOOTHNESS: 21; SPEED:
29; STORIES: 6;
SUCCESS/FAILURE: 19-c; SUN: 50;
TIME: 37, 46;
USEFULNESS/USELESSNESS: 48-c;
VEHICLES: 4; VIOLENCE: 19;

Deutsch, Babette
AGE: 31; AGILITY: 9; BIRDS: 2; BLACK: 3; COLORS: 19; CONVERSATION: 54; FEROCITY: 6; FINGERS: 17; FOOD AND DRINK: 31; FURNITURE AND FURNISHINGS: 12; HEAT: 36; LIFE: 7; NATURALNESS: 4; POETS/POETRY: 16; PROMPTNESS: 4; REMOTENESS: 10; SECRECY: 17; SHARPNESS: 6; SMALLNESS: 9; SOFTNESS: 17; SURPRISE: 14; TOUGHNESS: 21

De Vries, Peter
BOOKS: 35; BRIGHTNESS: 35; EATING AND DRINKING: 7; EMBRACES: 6; EYEBROWS: 2; FATNESS: 27; FROWNS: 18; GOSSIP: 15; GROWTH: 53; HAIR COLOR: 5; HAIR, CURLY: 5; HAND MOVEMENTS: 5; HANDWRITING: 1; LAUGHTER: 43; LEGS: 45; MOUTH: 30; PARENTHOOD: 15; SEXUAL INTERACTION: 5, 32; SITTING: 11; SNOW: 10; TASTE: 6; TREMBLING: 24; VEHICLES: 7; WORLD: 3

Dewar, Lord Thomas
MIND, DEFINED: 25

Dewey, John
POLITICS/POLITICIANS: 30

Dexter, Timothy
APPRECIATION: 6

Diana, Princess of Wales
STUPIDITY: 10

Diaphenia
BEAUTY: 32

Dickens, Charles
AGE: 24-c; ALONENESS: 36; ANGER: 14; ANXIETY: 26; ATMOSPHERE: 5; BEHAVIOR: 49; BIRDS: 12; CLEVERNESS: 2; CLINGING: 32, 65; COLLAPSE: 18; CRYING: 5; DESTRUCTION: 31; DISAPPEARANCE: 90; DULLNESS:

19; EATING AND DRINKING: 13; EYE MOVEMENTS: 29; FLEXIBILITY/INFLEXIBILITY: 25; IDEAS: 10; KINDNESS: 10; LANDSCAPES: 9; LIGHTNESS: 2; MIND, UDEFINED: 26; MOVEMENT: 20; MUSIC: 12; NOISE: 24; PEOPLE, INTERACTION: 28, 40; PERSONALITY PROFILES: 28, 52; PROBLEMS/SOLUTIONS: 21; RAIN: 22; REJECTION: 14; SCREAMS: 17; SHARPNESS: 7; SKIN: 67; SLEEP: 6; STUPIDITY: 7

Dickey, James
ACTIONS: 13; BRIGHTNESS: 1; CONNECTIONS: 14; EYEBROWS: 17; FACIAL COLOR: 14; SILENCE: 54; TREES: 36

Dickinson, Emily
BOOKS: 36; FIGHTING: 14; TRUTH: 12; VISIBILITY: 8; WIND: 15; WORD(S): 37

Diderot, Denis
KISSES: 9; MOVEMENT: 3; VAGUENESS: 16; WORDS, DEFINED: 4

Diehl, William
ABSURDITY: 24; ANGER: 45; BALDNESSNESS: 16; BEARING: 51; BODY: 21; BURST: 3; CHIN: 12; CHOICES: 2; CLOTHING, ITS FIT: 19; COLDNESS: 37; COURAGE: 28; CRUELTY: 16; DULLNESS: 12; EDUCATION: 7; ELUSIVENESS: 7; EYE(S): 20; EYE MOVEMENTS: 5; FUTILITY: 1; GLOOM: 26; GRAY: 11; GUILT: 2; NAMES: 9; NECK: 16; NOISE: 25, 82; ORDER/DISORDER: 3

Dieter, William
BEHAVIOR: 28; DARKNESS: 34; HAIR TEXTURE: 35; MOON: 42; NIGHT: 25; VEHICLES: 12

Dietz, Howard
INSULTS: 2

Digby, Sir Kenelm
PALLOR: 2
Dillard, R. H. W
GRINS: 23
Diller, Phyllis
FUTILITY: 3
Dilwyn, Lewis W.
REGRET: 3
Dimnet, Ernest
BOOKS: 9
Dinesen, Isak
ADVANCING: 8; AIR: 8;
ATTENTION: 30; ATTRACTION:
12; BEARING: 10; BLUSHES: 5;
BODY: 13, 72; CALMNESS: 56;
CLINGING: 16; IDEAS: 6;
INNOCENCE: 7; JEWELRY: 18;
LEAVES: 40; MIND: 32;
PLEASURE: 10; POSTURE: 4;
PROTECTIVENESS: 1; SEASCAPES:
13; SECRECY: 10; SIMPLICITY: 1;
SPEED: 63; SUCCESS/FAILURE: 9;
SUN: 49; SWEETNESS: 2, 4;
VOICE, MUSIC RELATED: 26;
WRINKLES: 47-c
Disraeli, Benjamin
AIR: 15; ALONENESS: 13;
BEARING: 31; BOOKS: 10;
CRITICISM, DRAMATIC AND
LITERARY: 6; WIT: 8;
WRITERS/WRITING: 9
Dixon, W. Macneile
NATURE: 30
Djilas, Milovan
REALNESS/UNREALNESS: 11
Dobell, Sidney
GRIEF: 9
Doddridge, Sir John
LAWS: 8
Dominick, Peter
POLITICS/POLITICIANS: 15
Donleavy, Brian
BREASTS: 6; CLOSENESS: 27;
DESTRUCTION: 14; EYEBROWS: 12
Donne, John
AGE: 3; EMBRACES: 19

Dorfman, Ariel
BLACK: 37; DESIRABILITY: 1;
HAND(S): 17; HAND MOVEMENTS:
29; LEGS: 33; LIGHTING: 23;
LOYALTY/DISLOYALTY: 9;
TREMBLING: 7; VOICE(S): 3
Dorris, Michael
LOOKS: 18
Dos Passos, John
ANGER: 79; BENDING/BENT: 4;
CLOUD(S): 23; DISHONESTY: 18;
DRINKING: 27; EXCITEMENT: 28;
FACE(S): 57, 79; FACIAL COLOR:
1; FOG: 1; HANDSHAKE: 13;
INSULTS: 24; LIES/LIARS: 7;
PAIN: 8; PLACES: 44; SCREAMS:
40; SELF-CONFIDENCE: 11;
TALKATIVENESS: 26; VAGUENESS:
7; WEATHER: 12
Dostoevski, Fyodor
MEEKNESS: 11
Douglas, Kirk
LIFE, DEFINED: 20
Douglas, Marjory Stoneman
ABILITY: 17; STARS: 12;
TENSION: 32
Dow, Elbridge G. Jr.
LIFE, DEFINED: 29; REPUTATION:
1
Dowd, Maureen
PLACES: 58; RESERVE: 4
Downey, Harris
FEAR: 35; SLEEP: 24; VIOLENCE:
29; WORD(S): 41
Doyle, Arthur Conan
BURST: 9; DISAPPEARANCE: 92
Drabble, Margaret
BEARING: 17; DEJECTION: 21;
FOOD AND DRINK: 39;
FRUSTRATION: 1; MEEKNESS: 9;
PERSONALITY PROFILES: 21;
PURITY: 12-c; STANDING: 8;
TEARS: 45
Dreiser, Theodore
SIMPLICITY: 16

PHYSICAL APPEARANCE: 76;
PHYSICAL FEELINGS: 29;
SPEAKING: 24; SPEECH
PATTERNS: 17; SUCCESS/FAILURE:
23; TREES: 12; TREMBLING: 30;
TRUST/MISTRUST: 6; TURNING
AND TWISTING: 3;
USEFULNESS/USELESSNESS: 22;
VAGUENESS: 1; VOICE, HARSH:
25; WALKING: 14; WHITE: 43
Fearing, Kenneth
FEAR: 43
Feather, William
AGE: 26
Feder, Mike
EMOTIONS: 22
Feiden, Doug
GROWTH: 49; IMPOSSIBILITY: 11;
REALIZATION: 24
Feifer, George
OBVIOUSNESS: 2; PLACES: 36
Feldman, Irving
AIR: 9; ATTENTION: 38;
ENTHUSIASM: 22; FACE(S): 66;
FORTUNE/MISFORTUNE: 10; JOY:
14; RAIN: 49
Feltham, Owen
DISCONTENT: 5; ENTHUSIASM:
28; HOPE: 16; PASSION: 8
Felton, C. C.
LANGUAGE: 7
Ferber, Edna
ALONENESS: 29; ARGUMENTS: 19;
BRIGHTNESS: 47; DEJECTION: 34;
; FOOD AND DRINK: 18; PLACES:
50; RESERVE: 2; RISING: 161;
SIMILARITY: 3
Ferguson, Patricia
BEARING: 18; DISCOMFORT: 6
Ferraro, Susan
EDUCATION: 3; OPINIONS: 10;
SMILES: 99
Ferrier, J.W.
OBJECTS, MISCELLANEOUS: 13
Ferry, James
CHILDREN: 16

Fessendon, Thomas G.
EMPTINESS: 26
Fiedler, Leslie A.
MEEKNESS: 2; RAIN: 14
Field, Eugene
IDEAS: 14
Fielding, Henry
CONVERSATION: 20; HUNGER: 1,
20; LOYALTY/DISLOYALTY: 13;
SERIOUSNESS: 16-c; STAGE AND
SCREEN: 11; TEARS: 23;
WRITER/WRITING: 3
Fierstein, Harvey
CANDOR: 13; PEOPLE,
INTERACTION: 46
Fine, Samuel Shem
FATNESS: 6
Fine, Sylvia
STAGE AND SCREEN: 6
Finkelstein, Caroline
LEAPING: 9; LEAVES: 21; TREES:
6
Finney, Jack
CITY/STREETSCAPES: 21
Fisher, Dorothy Canfield
BELIEVABILITY: 7; BURST: 16;
CLINGING: 46; DISAPPEARANCE:
42; ENERGY: 25, 27; FACE(S): 12;
FEAR: 24; FLOWERS: 20; HAIR
TEXTURE: 27; HELPLESSNESS: 2;
HUMOR: 5; LIPS: 35; LYING: 10;
MOVEMENT: 69; NERVOUSNESS:
28; RED: 6; ROAD SCENES: 26;
SMELL: 12; STANDING: 11;
SURPRISE: 6; SWEAT: 6; TENSION:
19, 28; THOUGHTS: 5;
WEAKNESS: 3; WHITE: 14-c;
WIND: 13
Fitzgerald, Edward
BIRTH: 2; ENTRANCES/EXITS: 9
Fitzgerald, F. Scott
AGE: 57; BEAUTY: 41;
BELIEVABILITY: 10; BOOKS: 19;
CHOICES: 8; CLOTHING: 20;
DEJECTION: 39; DESTRUCTION:
36; DRINKING: 22; EMPTINESS:

DRINKING: 8; EXITS: 17;
EMOTIONS: 10; FACIAL
EXPRESSIONS, SERIOUS: 9;
FACE(S): 54; FAMILIARITY: 3, 9;
FEAR: 59; FOOD AND DRINK: 24;
FOOTBALL: 1; FOREHEAD: 1;
FURNITURE AND FURNISHINGS:
21, 23; GLITTER AND GLOSS: 28;
GLOOM: 31; GRINS: 8; HAND(S):
8; HAPPINESS: 34; HEAD
MOVEMENTS: 5, 37; HEALTH: 11;
HEARTBEAT: 13, 21; HEAT: 28;
HOPE: 1, 10, 25; IDEAS: 17;
INAPPROPRIATENESS: 9;
INNOCENCE: 2; IRRITABLENESS:
13; JEWELRY: 12; LAUGHTER:
32; LEGS: 4; LIFE: 47; LIPS: 34;
MANNERS: 1; MOUTH: 10;
NAMES: 13; NECESSITY: 31;
OPEN/SHUT: 4; OPPORTUNITY: 4;
ORIGINALITY: 2; PEOPLE,
INTERACTION: 5; PERSONALITY
PROFILES: 59; PHYSICAL
APPEARANCE: 8; PLACES: 18, 43,
48; REMOTENESS: 2; ROCKING
AND ROLLING: 11; SHOULDERS:
1; SIMILARITY: 10; SITTING: 39;
SKY COLOR: 5; SMELL: 13, 23,
25; SPEED: 60; STARES: 4, 11;
STOMACH: 17; STRANGENESS: 7;
TALKATIVENESS: 19; TENSION: 4;
THINNESS: 58; THOUGHTS: 29;
TRUST/MISTRUST: 23;
UNCERTAINTY: 13;
USEFULNESS/USELESSNESS: 20;
VEHICLES: 30; VOICE(S): 6;
WHITE: 16; WRINKLES: 42

Forne, Caroline
ADVANTAGEOUSNESS: 2

Forster, E. M.
EMOTIONS: 7; GROWTH: 16; LIFE,
DEFINED: 15; RELIGION: 9;
SITTING: 19

Fort, Joseph
RELIABILITY/UNRELIABILITY: 9

Foss, Lukas
MUSIC: 4

Fosdick, Harry Emerson
DEATH: 32; HATRED: 6;
MANKIND: 39, 41

Foster, E. M.
CHARACTERISTICS, NATIONAL: 2

Foster, Stephen
DAY: 9

Fowles, John
CLINGING: 55; DISINTEGRATION:
2; EYEBROWS: 16; EYE
MOVEMENTS: 7; FACIAL
EXPRESSIONS, BLANK: 19;
FACIAL EXPRESSIONS, SERIOUS:
4; FEAR: 84; FRAGILITY: 22;
HELPLESSNESS: 17; LANDSCAPES:
26; MEN AND WOMEN: 46;
MOUNTAINS: 16, 22; NECESSITY:
31; PAUSE: 13; PLEASURE: 7;
REMOTENESS: 38; SEX: 15
SMILES: 100; SPEECH PATTERNS:
18; SUCCESS/FAILURE: 1;
TURNING AND TWISTING: 22;
WIND: 3; WRINKLES: 4;
WRITERS/WRITING: 3

Foy, George
BODY: 38; SCREAMS: 38

Frady, Marshal
EXCITEMENT: 25

France, Anatole
ART AND LITERATURE: 20;
BELIEF: 20; DULLNESS: 24;
FACIAL EXPRESSIONS,
MISCELLANEOUS: 47; INSECTS: 7;
INSULTS: 6; LOVE: 67; LOVE,
DEFINED: 5; MAXIMS, PROVERBS
AND SAYINGS: 1; MOUTH: 8;
NATURE: 21; RELATIONSHIPS: 27;
RELIGION: 14; SMILES: 24;
STORIES: 11; TREMBLING: 9;
WRITERS/WRITING: 2, 65

Francis, Brendan
TIME: 75

Francis, Dick
QUESTIONS/ANSWERS: 3; RISING: 22; SKIN: 80

Francis, Dorothy B.
ANXIETY: 19; ARGUMENTS: 11; CLOUD MOVEMENTS: 16; FEAR: 67; MOVEMENT: 72; NATURE: 20; PONDS AND STREAMS: 12; SPEECH PATTERNS: 20

Francis, Richard
BODY: 65

Frankau, Pamela
FACIAL SHAPE: 24

Frankfurter, Justice Felix
ABILITY: 18

Franklin, Benjamin
CHEERFULNESS: 12; COMFORT: 16; EATING AND DRINKING: 20; GREATNESS: 8; LAWYERS: 2; LIFE, DEFINED: 9; MEN AND WOMEN: 42; PRIDE: 12; RICHES: 16

Franks, Lucinda
CRIME: 8

Fraser, Antonia
FACIAL COLOR: 9; NOSES: 45; SILENCE: 34-c

Fraser, George MacDonald
CALMNESS: 14; LOOKS: 47; SUDDENNESS: 13; VOICE, MUSIC RELATED: 11

Frayn, Michael
DEJECTION: 32

Frederick the Great
ARMY: 1

Fredman, Mike
ADVANCING: 24; ARM MOVEMENTS: 5; BODY: 81; ENTHUSIASM: 25; GLOOM: 25; LAUGHTER: 73; LIPS: 27; FACIAL COLOR: 8; SELF-CONFIDENCE: 20; SKY COLOR: 14; SMILES: 48; SOCIABILITY/UNSOCIABILITY: 7; STALENESS: 2; SUN: 85;

USEFULNESS/USELESSNESS: 41; VEHICLES: 13; VOICE(S): 29; WEAKNESS: 19

Freedman, Samuel G.
EMOTIONS: 6

Freemantle, Anne
ART AND LITERATURE: 19

Freud, Sigmund
ART AND LITERATURE: 9; LIFE: 53; MIND, DEFINED: 9, 15; RELIGION: 27

Friedenberg, Edgar Z.
LOVE: 64

Friedman, Bruce Jay
ANGER: 54; HOPE: 21

Friedman, Milton
ECONOMICS: 7

Fromm, Erich
DREAMS: 6

Frost, Robert
CAUSE/EFFECT : 5; FAMILIARITY: 30; MOVEMENT: 22; ORIGINALITY: 10; POETS/POETRY: 6, 14, 20

Froude, J.A.
MORALITY: 6

Fuentes, Carlos
DISPERSAL: 2; MOUNTAINS: 12; RESERVE: 22; SPREADING: 14; VANITY: 4; WRINKLES: 32

Fuller, Roy
CLOUD(S): 28

Fuller, Thomas
ACCOMPLISHMENT: 4; AFFECTION: 9; AGILITY: 6; BELONGING: 16; BOOKS: 13; CAUTION: 22, 26; DEATH: 19; DISHONESTY: 2; DOCTORS: 4; ENERGY: 5; EVIL: 13; FLATTERY: 1; FRIENDSHIP: 17; GOSSIP: 19; HUMOR: 4; IDLENESS: 10; INSULTS: 3, 4; INTELLIGENCE: 8; LAWYERS: 112; MEEKNESS: 6; MEMORY: 53; MONEY: 10; NAMES: 3; PROBLEMS/SOLUTIONS:

EYE(S): 15; EYE EXPRESSIONS, MISCELLANEOUS: 12, 15, 19, 30, 66; FACE(S): 2, 3, 122, 123; FACIAL EXPRESSIONS, MISCELLANEOUS: 39, 52; FACIAL EXPRESSIONS, SERIOUS: 1, 2, 17; FACIAL SHAPE: 4; FEAR: 27, 69, 78; FINGERS: 31; FLOWERS: 16; FLEXIBILITY/INFLEXIBILITY: 20; FLOWERS: 1; FOG: 2; FORMALITY: 1; FRAGILITY 4, 5; FURNITURE AND FURNISHINGS: 3; FUTILITY: 15, 21; GAIETY: 2; GRAY: 12; GREEN: 9, 13; GRINS: 13; GROANS AND WHISPERS: 22; GROWTH: 6, 33, 40; HAIR: 59; HAIR COLOR: 8, 16, 12; HAIR, CURLY: 12; HAIR STYLES: 1; HAND(S): 7, 23; HAND MOVEMENTS: 23, 34; HAPPINESS: 24, 28; HARSHNESS: 7; HEALTH: 17; HEART(S): 19; HEARTBEAT: 22; HELPLESSNESS: 19, 53; INAPPROPRIATENESS: 24; INTENSITY: 10; JOY: 18, 21; KNOWLEDGE: 18; LAUGHTER: 46, 49, 79; LAWS: 10; LEAVES: 9, 23, 27; LEAVES: 20; LEGS: 23; LIGHTNESS: 8, 35; LINGERING: 21; LIPS: 9, 13, 28, 31; LOOKS: 46; LOOSENESS: 9; LYING: 2; MOUNTAINS: 10; MOVEMENT: 44; MUSTACHES: 25; NAMES: 7; NOISE: 18, 5; OBVIOUSNESS: 5; OCEANS/OCEANFRONTS: 8, 28, 29; OPEN/SHUT: 8; OPPORTUNITY: 3; ORDER/DISORDER: 10, 13; PAIN: 64, 68, 72; PALLOR: 15; PAST, THE: 23; PATIENCE: 9; PAUSE: 2, 7; PEOPLE, INTERACTION: 13, 17; PERMANENCE: 24; PERSONALITY TRAITS: 8; PHYSICAL APPEARANCE: 79; PINK: 2; POSTURE: 19, 33; PRIDE: 30; PROBLEMS/SOLUTIONS: 4;

PURPOSEFULNESS: 14, 19; PURSUIT: 26; RARITY: 8; SPEED: 45; REALIZATION: 22; REALNESS/UNREALNESS: 2, 9; RICHES: 1; RUNNING: 15; SAFETY: 6; SEASONS: 12; SEX: 2; SHAPE: 8; SHOCK: 14; SITTING: 36; SKY: 35, 52; SLEEP: 9; SMELL: 4; SMILES: 25, 64; SMOOTHNESS: 14, 47; SNOW: 11; SOFTNESS: 16; SPEECH PATTERNS: 33; SPREADING: 13; STOMACH: 7, 8; STORIES: 8; SUCCESS/FAILURE: 28; SUDDENNESS: 15; SUN: 12, 30; SWEAT: 17; SWEETNESS: 3, 8; TACT: 3; TALKATIVENESS: 16, 32; TEARS: 37; TEETH: 14; TENSION: 20; THINNESS: 2, 5, 16, 30; THOUGHTS: 48; THRIFT: 3, 7; TREES: 25, 28; TREMBLING: 39, 41; TRUENESS/FALSENESS: 4, 16; TRUST/MISTRUST: 10; UNDESIRABILITY: 14; UNSTEADINESS: 4; VAGUENESS: 18; VANITY: 13; VIOLENCE: 7; VOICE(S): 13; VOICE, HARSH: 19, 29; VOICE, MUSIC RELATED: 17, 21; VOICE, SOFT: 11; WALKING: 19; WEAKNESS: 4, 16, 20, 23; WEARINESS: 25; WEATHER: 9; WHITE: 3, 4, 5; WIND: 37; WISDOM: 16; WORD(S): 52; WORDS, EFFECT OF: 19, 23; YELLOW: 4

Garrigue, Jean
BEWILDERMENT: 3; EYE EXPRESSIONS, MISCELLANEOUS: 52; HAIR COLOR: 13, 13; HELPLESSNESS: 29; HONESTY: 5; KINDNESS: 22; LOOKS: 3; PAST, THE: 30; THINNESS: 32; TREMBLING: 5; TURNING AND TWISTING: 5

Garrison, Theodosia
TREES: 22

ENERGY: 22; EXCITEMENT: 14;
FRIENDSHIP, DEFINED: 19;
INAPPROPRIATENESS: 5; LOOKS:
1; PHYSICAL FEELINGS: 12;
REJECTION: 13; SAFETY: 11;
SHAME: 12

Gore-Booth, Eva
BLINDNESS: 16

Gorky, Maxim
ATTENTION: 12; CLINGING: 14;
DISPERSAL: 5; EVIL: 19;
EYEBROWS: 32; NOSES: 31; SUN:
33

Gorman, Paul
HAND(S): 41; THOUGHTS: 26

Gornick, Vivian
ABSORBABIITY: 1

Gosse, Edmond
COURAGE: 10; FUTURE: 4; PAST,
THE: 18

Gould, Jack
ADVERTISING: 1

Goyen, William
AGITATION: 2; BLOOD: 10;
FINGERS: 7; JUMPING: 11;
MANKIND: 50; MOVEMENT: 85

Gracian, Valtasar
AGE: 16; CONTROL: 4

Grafton, Sue
BEARDS: 20; BODY: 78;
BREASTS: 43;
CAUSE/EFFECT : 12; CLARITY: 5;
CLOUD(S): 5, 14; CRYING: 16;
DEATH, FINALITY OF: 3;
DISCOMFORT: 5; EATING AND
DRINKING: 27; ENERGY: 2;
EYE(S): 14; FACE(S): 78, 84;
FACIAL EXPRESSIONS,
MISCELLANEOUS: 73; FEAR: 30;
FINGERS: 2; FURNITURE AND
FURNISHINGS: 6; GRIEF: 11;
HAIR: 12, 41; HEAD(S): 4;
HOUSES: 11; MEMORY: 77;
MUSCLES: 7;
OCEANS/OCEANFRONTS: 11, 13;
PEOPLE, INTERACTION: 32;

PERSISTENCE: 6; PHYSICAL
FEELINGS: 17; REALIZATION: 13;
REJECTION: 3; SCRUTINY: 26;
SEXUAL INTERACTION: 18, 29
SKIN: 60; SLOWNESS: 1; SMELL:
6; SMILES: 96; STOMACH: 15;
TASTE: 7; THINNESS: 19; TREES:
24; UNDESIRABILITY: 23;
UNSTEADINESS: 17; VAGUENESS:
2; VIOLENCE: 31, 32; WRINKLES:
10

Graham, Harry
BLUSHES: 12

Graham, Virginia
WORD(S): 9

Graham, Winston
SEXUAL INTERACTION: 4

Grahame, J.
BUSINESS: 3

Grahame, Kenneth
CRYING: 21; LIGHTING: 10;
TEARS: 5-c

Granger, Bill
PROBLEMS/SOLUTIONS: 20;
STARES: 8

Grant, Ulysses S.
THRIFT: 14-c

Grau, Shirley Ann
EYE(S): 8, 81; EYE COLOR: 2;
FOG: 10; HAIR COLOR: 32; LIPS:
14; NATURE: 1; PHYSICAL
FEELINGS: 20; TENSION: 14

Graves, Robert
CROWDS: 13; DRINKING: 3;
EYE(S): 29; HAND MOVEMENTS:
30; JUMPING: 4; POETS/POETRY:
8

Gray, Francine du Plessix
ALONENESS: 43; BREASTS: 16, 24;
HAIR COLOR: 6; POSTURE: 5;
PURPOSEFULNESS: 15;
SEASCAPES: 16

Gray, Thomas
DRYNESS: 12

Greeley, Andrew M.
PREPAREDNESS: 9

Hazlitt, William
COMMONPLACE: 9; EDUCATION:
19; FRIENDSHIP, DEFINED: 29;
GREATNESS: 5; HATRED: 15;
LANGUAGE: 3; MAXIMS,
PROVERBS AND SAYINGS: 4;
MIND, DEFINED: 17, 23;
WORD(S): 8; WORDS, DEFINED: 11

Heaney, Seamus
REMOTENESS: 15

Hearn, Lacfadio
NATURALNESS: 19

Hearon, Shelby
CLOTHING: 11; ENTRAPMENT:
13; FEAR: 76; FLOWERS: 4; FOOD
AND DRINK: 33; FRESHNESS: 18;
PURSUIT: 10, 27; SEASONS: 1;
SHARPNESS: 11; SILENCE: 4;
SLOWNESS: 6; TONGUE: 4;
WATCHFULNESS: 15; WRINKLES:
22

Heatter, Gabriel
WORK: 11

Hebert, Jack
USEFULNESS/USELESSNESS: 26

Hecht, Ben
ARGUMENTS: 2; EYE
EXPRESSIONS, MISCELLANEOUS:
9; HUMOR: 12; LOVE, DEFINED:
4; NERVOUSNESS: 22; RELIGION:
19; SHARPNESS: 30; TREMBLING:
62; VANITY: 15

Hedin, Mary
BEARING: 55; CERTAINTY: 27;
EMOTIONS: 29; EYE(S): 11; EYE
EXPRESSIONS, MISCELLANEOUS:
23; FACE(S): 37; FACIAL COLOR:
17; FINGERS: 25; GRINS: 24;
HAND(S): 2, 30; HAND
MOVEMENTS: 7, 35; HEARTBEAT:
27; IRRITABLENESS: 16;
LIGHTNESS: 22; LOOKS: 67;
LYING: 19; MARRIAGE: 49;
NATURE: 17; NOSES: 18, 19;
PATIENCE: 7; POSTURE: 22;
ROAD SCENES: 11;

QUESTIONS/ANSWERS: 20;
REGULARITY/IRREGULARITY: 7;
RELATIONSHIPS: 12; SLEEP: 8;
SMILES: 34; SUN: 9; TREMBLING:
34; WEARINESS: 10; WORD(S): 23,
31, 36

Hedge, Frederic Henry
VOICE, HARSH: 30

Hegan, Alice Caldwell
RELIABILITY/UNRELIABILITY: 20

Heilbroner, Robert L.
PREPAREDNESS: 12

Heine, Heinrich
ACTIONS: 2; BOOKS: 7; NATURE:
24; POLITICS/POLITICIANS: 33;
RELIGION: 3

Heine, Lenoard M.
CAUTION: 15

Heinz, Senator John
FOOLISHNESS: 15;
USEFULNESS/USELESSNESS: 18

Heller, Joseph
ANGER: 81; BELONGING: 17;
BREASTS: 39; EYE EXPRESSIONS,
MISCELLANEOUS: 52; FACE(S): 5;
GROANS AND WHISPERS: 10;
HISTORY: 10; PHYSICAL
APPEARANCE: 56; SELF-
CONFIDENCE: 12; SMILES: 17;
TENSION: 26; TREMBLING: 13

Heller, Steve
EATING AND DRINKING: 15

Hellman, Sam
RICHES: 7

Hello, Ernest
MEETINGS: 9

Helps, Sir Arthur
BELIEF: 28

Helprin, Mark
BLINDNESS: 13; BLUSHES: 20;
BREATHING: 6; CLARITY: 18, 19;
ELUSIVENESS: 24; ENVY: 9;
FACIAL EXPRESSIONS, BLANK:
25; FURNITURE AND
FURNISHINGS: 10; GLITTER AND
GLOSS: 39; GREEN: 5; HAIR

Higgins, Joanna Wojewski
  WORD(S): 46
Hill, Susan
  FACIAL COLOR: 9; FACIAL
  EXPRESSIONS, MISCELLANEOUS:
  90
Hills, Carol
  WORD(S): 47
Hillyer, Robert
  DIVERSENESS: 6
Hilton, James
  HOUSES: 24; MEMORY: 69;
  PROBLEMS/SOLUTIONS: 12; TIME:
  54; UNSTEADINESS: 2
Hinds, Michael de Courcy
  DIFFICULTY: 50
Hipponax
  WORLD: 15
Hitchcock, Alfred
  MEN AND WOMEN: 47
Hoagland, Edward
  AGILITY: 22; ANIMALS: 13;
  BIRDS: 18; BOOKS: 21;
  DRINKING: 12; GLITTER AND
  GLOSS: 57; MOON: 53; PONDS
  AND STREAMS: 8;
  REGULARITY/IRREGULARITY: 8;
  STRAIGHTNESS: 23; TENSION: 27;
  VISIBILITY: 2; WALKING: 22
Hobhouse, Janet
  VIBRATION: 7
Hochstein, Rolaine
  VOICE, HARSH: 38
Hoelterhoff, Manuela
  RELIABILITY/UNRELIABILITY: 3;
  UNDESIRABILITY: 1, 8
Hoffman, Heinrich
  SLEEP: 15-c
Hoffman, William
  SKIN: 20
Hofstadter, Richard
  TRUTH: 2
Hogan, Linda
  CLOTHING: 22
Hogg, James
  LOVE, DEFINED: 10

Holcroft, Thomas
  SADNESS: 14; STUPIDITY: 15
Holland, Josiah Gilbert
  ANGER: 36; IRRITABLENESS: 18-c
Holm, Ken
  CHARACTERISTICS, NATIONAL: 1
Holmes, John Andrew
  AGE: 14; SECRECY: 4
Holmes, Oliver Wendell Jr.,
  GOVERNMENT: 4
Holmes, Oliver Wendell, Sr.
  AGE: 6, 32; BEAUTY: 22;
  BEHAVIOR: 31; CLOTHING
  ACCESSORIES: 11; COLORS: 13;
  CONVERSATION: 34; DEATH: 37;
  DISAPPEARANCE: 55; ENERGY:
  24; FAMILIARITY: 25;
  GOVERNMENT: 4; HAIR: 40;
  IGNORANCE: 6; INSULTS: 12;
  INTOLERANCE: 5; LAWS: 4;
  LAWYERS: 3, 4; LIFE, DEFINED:
  23, 47; MANKIND: 34;
  MEETINGS: 5; MIND, DEFINED:
  22; MUSTACHES: 17;
  PARENTHOOD: 8; PERMANENCE:
  22; PERSISTENCE: 13;
  POETS/POETRY: 19; RELIGION:
  18; RICHNESS: 2; SENTIMENT: 5;
  SPEAKING: 25; TRUTH: 16;
  VANITY: 20
Homer
  GLOOM: 19; MANKIND: 9, 40
Hood, Mary
  EYE(S): 90; EYE EXPRESSIONS,
  MISCELLANEOUS: 64; HEART(S):
  7; IRRITABLENESS: 18;
  MOVEMENT: 15; NECK: 6;
  ORDER/DISORDER: 9; PLEASURE:
  1; PRIDE: 8
Hood, Thomas
  IRRITABLENESS: 18-c
Horace
  ANGER: 4; CHANGE: 19; FAME:
  5; HOSPITALITY: 3;
  POETS/POETRY: 11; WORDS,
  DEFINED: 10

Author Index

Ibn Ezra, Moses
EDUCATION: 31; MAXIMS,
PROVERBS AND SAYINGS: 9;
MUSIC: 5; WISDOM: 11, 12;
WORDS, DEFINED: 19

Ibn Gabirol, Solomon
EDUCATION: 11; THRIFT: 8

Ibn Vega, Solomon
GUILT: 14

Ibsen, Henrik
COMFORT: 17; INSULTS: 18;
SOCIETY: 3

Ignatow, David
ARM(S): 28; FACIAL DETAILS: 10;
LEAVES: 14, 34; LEGS: 22;
LOOKS: 13; MOVEMENT: 26, 78;
NATURE: 18; SITTING: 23; SKY:
10, 15; STYLE: 1; TREES: 68

Immanuel of Rome
WORLD: 17

Ingalls, Rachel
BEAUTY: 8; BITTERNESS: 18;
CLINGING: 26; ENERGY: 19;
ENTRANCES/EXITS: 30;
OCEANS/OCEANFRONTS: 22;
SURPRISE: 9

Ingersoll, Robert, G.
DIVERSENESS: 1; KINDNESS: 41

Ionesco, Eugene
COLLAPSE: 54-c; HAPPINESS: 40

Irving, Clive
MIST: 2; WIND: 32

Irving, John
POSTURE: 39; SMILES: 20;
STOMACH: 10

Irving, Washington
CHARACTERISTICS, NATIONAL:
19; HOUSES: 44; KNOWLEDGE: 6;
LANDSCAPES: 35; PERSONALITY
TRAITS: 3; SOCIETY: 10

Irwin, Inez Haynes
BODY: 45; MOUTH: 35

Irwin, Robert
CLEANLINESS: 23

Irwin, Wallace
AWKWARDNESS: 20; CAUTION: 7;
STANDING: 10

Isherwood, Christopher
ABSURDITY: 19; ANGER: 68;
AWKWARDNESS: 10; BEARING:
11; BROWN: 4; CLOTHING: 26;
COMPLEXION: 11;
CONTENTMENT: 1; EMOTIONS:
31; EXITS: 13; EYE(S): 92;
FACE(S): 53; FACIAL
EXPRESSIONS, MISCELLANEOUS:
62; FRIENDSHIP, DEFINED: 1;
LAUGHTER: 9; MODESTY: 4;
MOUTH: 20; MOUTH, OPEN/SHUT:
16; MOVEMENT: 60;
PERSONALITY PROFILES: 61;
PHYSICAL APPEARANCE: 24;
QUESTIONS/ANSWERS: 14; RAIN:
68; RISING: 18; SILENCE: 82;
SOCIABILITY/UNSOCIABILITY: 3;
SPEAKING: 16; SPEED: 61;
STRANGENESS: 1; TRANSIENCE:
22; TRUST/MISTRUST: 15;
VOICE(S): 41

Jackson, Mahalia
SENTIMENT: 3

Jackson, Robert H.
FREEDOM: 27

Jacobs, Harry A.
ECONOMICS: 16

Jacob, Rabbi
WORLD: 14

Jacobs, Harvey
TOUGHNESS: 25

Jacobson, Dan
AIR: 5; FOREHEAD: 14; GRAY: 1;
HEAT: 7; LAUGHTER: 4; NIGHT:
5; SPEECH PATTERNS: 29; WHITE:
37

Jacobsen, Josephine
FIRMNESS: 43;
OCEANS/OCEANFRONTS: 25;
ROOMS: 29

Jacoby, Henry D.
DIFFICULTY: 46

Author Index

DEFINED: 40; LOVE, DEFINED: 29; MEMORY: 18, 50; MOVEMENT: 56; ORIGINALITY: 4; PLACES: 12; SEASONS: 5; SHYNESS: 9; SNOW: 36; STRUGGLE: 2; TALKATIVENESS: 11; THOUGHTS: 115; TREES: 18; VANITY: 7, 11, 22; VIRTUE: 22; WEARINESS: 10; WRITERS/WRITING: 5

Jhabvala, Ruth Prawer
BREASTS: 40; COLLAPSE: 29; DISINTEGRATION: 28; EMOTIONS: 57; EYEBROWS: 6; FACIAL EXPRESSIONS, MISCELLANEOUS: 58; FOOD AND DRINK: 5; HEARTBEAT: 2; HOUSES: 34; KISSES: 6; MANNERS: 14; MEMORY: 73; MOON: 27; TEARS: 29, 32

Jiménez, Juan Ramón
WORLD: 18

Jonson, Ben
AMBITION: 9; CERTAINTY: 34; PERMANENCE: 2; COURAGE: 30; ENTHUSIASM: 29; GOSSIP: 18; MIND, DEFINED: 16; SPEED: 33

Johnson, B. S.
MEMORY: 32

Johnson, Charles
AGITATION: 37; CERTAINTY: 52; CLARITY: 26; CLOSENESS: 24; EMPTINESS: 44; ENERGY: 10; FACE(S): 55; FACIAL EXPRESSIONS, SERIOUS: 23; FEAR: 33; FINGERS: 32; FOG: 5; GLOOM: 32; GROANS AND WHISPERS: 19; HEART(S): 26; HISTORY: 12; IMMOBILITY: 19; LYING: 3; MANKIND: 38; MEN AND WOMEN: 39; MOUTH, OPEN/SHUT: 6; MOVEMENT: 52; NATURE: 9; NOSES: 40; PERMANENCE: 27; SEX: 34; SEXUAL INTERACTION: 17; SHAPE: 29; SILENCE: 141;

SIMPLICITY: 5; SKIN: 9, 83; SKY: 44; SMILES: 45; SMOOTHNESS: 27; SUN: 16; THOUGHTS: 10, 13; VISIBILITY: 6; VOICE, MUSIC RELATED: 16

Johnson, Denis
ADVANCING: 14; ADVANCING: 18; BRIGHTNESS: 48; PHYSICAL FEELINGS: 37; VIBRATION: 3

Johnson, Nora
GOSSIP: 25; LAUGHTER: 54; MEMORY: 62; PERMANENCE: 26

Johnson, Nunally
TREMBLING: 44-c

Johnson, Owen
MANKIND: 30

Johnson, Pamela Hansford
CHEERFULNESS: 5; PRIDE: 5; SUN: 43; TEETH: 7; TREES: 21

Johnson, Samuel
BOOKS: 20; CONTEMPT: 2; EDUCATION: 29; FLATTERY: 20; FOOD AND DRINK: 13; FRIENDSHIP: 7, 15; FRIENDSHIP, DEFINED: 7, 21; GRIEF: 24; HAPPINESS: 49; IDLENESS: 1; IDLENESS: 4; IMPORTANCE/UNIMPORTANCE: 2; INSULTS: 9; KNOWLEDGE: 10; LANGUAGE: 1; LIFE: 19; MANNERS: 11; MARRIAGE: 19; MEN AND WOMEN: 51; PROMISE: 7; SENSE: 10; THRIFT: 2; TRUTH: 10

Johnson, Willis
BEARDS: 13; BODY: 71; LEAVES: 35; LIGHTING: 19

Jones, Emory
SPORTS: 10

Jong, Erica
FIGHTING: 12; FOOD AND DRINK: 21; GLITTER AND GLOSS: 17; GREEN: 12; GROWTH: 29; HEARTBEAT: 8

Jordan, Lee Roy
FOOTBALL: 8

Lambert, Derek
  AIR: 26; ALONENESS: 12;
  BEARING: 36; BEWILDERMENT:
  10; BOREDOM/BORING: 13;
  BREATHING: 13; CHEEKS: 6;
  COLLAPSE: 41; CROWDS: 30;
  DESIRABILITY: 6;
  DISAPPEARANCE: 82; DISPERSAL:
  13; EASE: 34; FACIAL
  EXPRESSIONS, MISCELLANEOUS:
  16; FEAR: 3; FOOD AND DRINK:
  12; HEAD MOVEMENTS: 33;
  HUNGER: 16; KISSES: 28; PEOPLE,
  INTERACTION: 34; PHYSICAL
  APPEARANCE: 51, 69; PLACES:
  55; POSTURE: 20; RISING: 23;
  SCREAMS: 5; SHAPE: 5; SIGHS: 4;
  SNOW: 55; SPEED: 2; STRENGTH:
  1; SUCCESS/FAILURE: 7, 8;
  SUDDENNESS: 3; SWEAT: 19;
  TOBACCO: 24; UNDESIRABILITY:
  10; WORDS, EFFECT OF: 6;
  WRINKLES: 41
Lampedusa, Giuseppe di
  PERSONALITY PROFILES: 38
Lamuniere, Jean
  SPORTS: 13
Landon, Letitia
  BEAUTY: 13; MIND, DEFINED: 2;
  SMILES: 97
Landor, Walter Savage
  BIGNESS: 13; BRIGHTNESS: 26;
  CLARITY: 11; COLDNESS: 10;
  COURAGE: 18; CRUELTY: 11, 30;
  DAY: 34; EYE(S): 12; FOOD AND
  DRINK: 3; GOVERNMENT: 21;
  GREED: 9; HEAT: 43; HOPE: 15;
  LIES/LIARS: 14; LOOSENESS: 6;
  POWER: 13; PRESENT, THE: 1;
  PURPOSEFULNESS: 10; SENSE: 9;
  SERIOUSNESS: 2; SOUL: 17;
  TASTE: 3; TRUTH: 4, 11, 25;
  WRITERS/WRITING: 7, 14
Lane, Carla
  DESTRUCTION: 16; MANKIND: 3;
  MIND: 39; PASSION: 5; SELF-
  CONFIDENCE: 2

Lang, Andrew
  BOOKS: 4; FACTS: 65
Langdon, Philip
  FAMILIARITY: 32
Langland, William
  SILENCE: 31
Lanier, Sidney
  MUSIC: 1; SOUL: 6; VAGUENESS:
  11
Lapierre, Dominique
  BLACK: 45; HEAT: 3;
  IMMOBILITY: 7; IMPOSSIBILITY:
  33; MEMORY: 76; PHYSICAL
  APPEARANCE: 5; SHOCK: 3;
  SKIN: 68; VEHICLES: 12;
  WRINKLES: 45
Lardner, Ring
  ATTENTION: 8; DANCING: 13;
  KINDNESS: 11; SLEEP: 33
Larkin, Philip
  HEAVINESS: 9; POETS/POETRY: 3
Laski, Harold J.
  GOVERNMENT: 22
Laurence, Margaret
  BALDNESS: 15; FACIAL
  EXPRESSIONS, BLANK: 23;
  FAMILIARITY: 33; HEAT: 37;
  LAUGHTER: 8; NIGHT: 13;
  RISING: 101; TREES: 9
Lavin, Mary
  FOOLISHNESS: 13; MUSIC: 11;
  RAIN: 21; ROOMS: 32
Law, William
  SINGING: 8
Lawrence, D. H.
  AFFECTION: 2; AGILITY: 29;
  ANIMALS: 16; APPRECIATION: 2;
  ATTRACTION: 19; BEARING: 37;
  BLOOD: 2; BLUSHES: 15;
  BREASTS: 32; BRIGHTNESS: 37;
  COLDNESS: 56; COLLAPSE: 50;
  DESIRABILITY: 2;
  DISAPPEARANCE: 97;
  DISINTEGRATION: 16;
  ELUSIVENESS: 4, 25; EMOTIONS:
  68; EXCITEMENT: 1; EYEBROWS:

Long, William J.
EDUCATION: 32

Longfellow, Henry Wadsworth
AGE: 58; BREATHING: 26;
BROWN: 6, 7; CLARITY: 33;
CLOUD MOVEMENTS: 17;
DISAPPEARANCE: 80, 95;
DISPERSAL: 14; EMPTINESS: 11;
ENTRANCES/EXITS: 6; GAIETY: 8;
GLITTER AND GLOSS: 39;
GREATNESS: 13; HAPPINESS: 48;
HEARTBEAT: 10; HEAT: 1;
HEAVINESS: 13; HOPE: 9, 12;
LIES/LIARS: 25; MOVEMENT: 68;
NOISE: 45; SADNESS: 6; SILENCE:
73; SPEED: 57; STRENGTH: 22,
29; TIME: 24; WORDS OF PRAISE:
8; YELLOW: 9

Longstreet, Stephen
ABILITY: 7; AVAILABILITY: 1;
CHEERFULNESS: 7; CLOTHING:
17; DANGER: 7;
DISAPPEARANCE: 1; FRIENDSHIP:
3; IRRITABLENESS: 24; MIND: 3;
OBVIOUSNESS: 20; RAIN: 45;
SECRECY: 16; THUNDER AND
LIGHTNING: 12; VISIBILITY: 11

Longworth, Alice Roosevelt
FACIAL EXPRESSIONS, SERIOUS:
15

Lopate, Phillip
DULLNESS: 48; STYLE: 5

Lorimer, George Horace
WRITERS/WRITING: 5

Lotta, Congressman Dale
CRITICISM: 15

Louis IV
DIFFICULTY: 56

Lourie, Richard
ALONENESS: 5; CRITICISM,
DRAMATIC AND LITERARY: 20;
DRINKING: 14; PHYSICAL
FEELINGS: 15; SLOWNESS: 39

Lovett, Robert
BUSYNESS: 24

Lowell, Amy
BEAUTY: 2, 45;
BEGINNINGS/ENDINGS: 15;
BREASTS: 54; COLLAPSE: 38;
PERMANENCE: 10; CROWDS: 5;
FIRMNESS: 20; GAIETY: 14;
LIGHTNESS: 23; MOON: 1;
NERVOUSNESS: 16;
PEACEFULNESS: 14; PHYSICAL
APPEARANCE: 62; REPETITION:
10; WEARINESS: 14; WORDS OF
PRAISE: 9

Lowell, James Russell
ALONENESS: 40;
FORTUNE/MISFORTUNE: 20;
LANGUAGE: 12; OPINIONS: 17;
RARITY: 4

Lowell, Robert
EVIL: 20; PROTRUSION: 9

Lowry, Robert
BEARING: 19; HELPLESSNESS: 10

Lubbock, Sir John
ART AND LITERATURE: 16;
FRIENDSHIP, DEFINED: 3

Lucas, E. V. (Edward Verrall)
BLUSHES: 9

Lucas, F. L.
LANGUAGE: 6; WORDS, DEFINED:
3; WRITERS/WRITING: 4

Luce, Clare Booth
ABSURDITY: 14; CONTROL: 3

Luce, Gay Gaer
RELIABILITY/UNRELIABILITY: 4

Lurie, Allison
HABIT: 12

Luther, Martin
HEART(S): 22, 23; LIES/LIARS: 11;
SENSE: 4; WORLD: 11

Lutz, John
NECESSITY: 27; RAIN: 62

Lux, Thomas
BALDNESS: 1; COMMONPLACE: 2;
NECESSITY: 4; RISING: 13

Lyall, Gavin
BREVITY: 9; CLOTHING: 12;
FURNITURE AND FURNISHINGS:

MacLeish, Rod
DIFFERENCES: 3
MacMahon, Thomas
HAIR COLOR: 27
Macmanus, Seumas
SPEAKING: 19
Macmillan, Harold
POWER: 16
MacMillan, Ian
LEGS: 15
Macneice, Louis
ABANDONMENT: 12; ADVERSARY:
4; FUTILITY: 11; GUILT: 11;
LOVE: 27; MEN AND WOMEN: 12;
PAST, THE: 10; RICHES: 2;
RISING: 12; SEASONS: 8; SILENCE:
23; SMELL: 29; STRENGTH: 16;
SURPRISE: 13;
TIMELINESS/UNTIMELINESS: 11,
19; WORLD: 22
**MacNeil, Robert, Public
Television**
ENTRAPMENT: 3
Macy, John
CHANGE: 2
Magnani, Anna
CHILDREN: 7
Mahler, Gustav
MUSIC: 43
Mailer, Norman
ANXIETY: 2; BEARING: 15;
BRIGHTNESS: 6; COLDNESS: 54;
CONVERSATION: 21; EYE(S): 16;
EYES, BRIGHT: 12; EYE
EXPRESSIONS, MISCELLANEOUS:
62; EYE MOVEMENTS: 6; FEAR:
21, 56; FEROCITY: 5; GROANS
AND WHISPERS: 12; HOUSES: 40;
IMPOSSIBILITY: 49; INSULTS: 19;
JOY: 27; KINDNESS: 43;
MARRIAGE: 44; MEMORY: 2;
MIND: 14; NOISE: 78;
PERSISTENCE: 27; PERSONALITY
PROFILES: 19, 44;
PREPAREDNESS: 2;
PROBLEMS/SOLUTIONS: 18;

RELATIONSHIPS: 22; ROARS: 2;
SADNESS: 10; SERIOUSNESS: 21;
SHOCK: 16; SPEECHMAKING: 7,
9; SPEECH PATTERNS: 37, 44;
SUDDENNESS: 4; SWEAT: 21;
TALKATIVENESS: 28; TENSION:
30, 37; THINNESS: 8; TOBACCO:
18; USEFULNESS/USELESSNESS:
14; VIBRATION: 14; VOICE(S): 40;
VOICE, EFFECT OF: 12; VOICE,
HARSH: 11; WISDOM: 14;
WRITERS/WRITING: 35, 54
Mairs, Nancy
MARRIAGE: 43
Major, Clarence
INNOCENCE: 11; SOFTNESS: 10;
TREMBLING: 28
Malamud, Bernard
ABUNDANCE: 17; AGITATION: 20,
27; ANXIETY: 4; ARM
MOVEMENTS: 7; BASEBALL: 3;
BIRDS: 21; BREASTS: 11;
DEJECTION: 18; DISAPPEARANCE:
16; DRYNESS: 14; EMOTIONS: 51;
EMPTINESS: 55; EYE COLOR: 1;
FEAR: 46; FROWNS: 11; GLITTER
AND GLOSS: 55; HEARTBEAT: 17;
LEAVES: 13, 22; MOON: 25, 64;
NOISE: 81; PAIN: 69;
PROBLEMS/SOLUTIONS: 24;
RESTLESSNESS: 18; RUNNING: 16;
SILENCE: 19; SMELL: 11; SUN: 26;
WORK: 3
Malcolm, John
ABANDONMENT: 17; COLLAPSE:
63; FACIAL EXPRESSIONS,
MISCELLANEOUS: 49; FIRMNESS:
12
Malloch, Douglas
MODESTY: 7
Mallock, W. H.
IMPOSSIBILITY: 52
Malone, Michael
CLOTHING: 27; PROFESSIONS: 4;
SPEED: 59, 62; WIND: 16

Malraux, André
FACIAL EXPRESSIONS,
MISCELLANEOUS: 88; JOY: 15;
MANKIND: 2; MOON: 55;
TOBACCO: 23; YOUTH: 3

Maltz, Albert
BEARING: 30

Mamet, David
VIBRATION: 1

Mancrft, Lord
SPEECHMAKING: 14

Mandelstamm, Benjamin
FRIENDSHIP, DEFINED: 16;
HEART(S): 13; MANKIND: 16

Manley, Dexter, of the
DEJECTION: 16

Mann, Thomas
BEAUTY, DEFINED: 3; CLOUD
MOVEMENTS: 19; DARKNESS: 37;
PASSION: 12; SNOW: 51;
TRANSIENCE: 12

Manning, Olivia
FREEDOM: 5; SENSITIVENESS: 4

Mansfield, Katherine
AGITATION: 14; ALONENESS: 50;
BEAUTY: 53; CLOUD(S): 1;
COURAGE: 15; DAY: 8;
EXCITEMENT: 18; EYE(S): 29-c;
EYE MOVEMENTS: 28; FACE(S):
118; FLOWERS: 13; HAIR
TEXTURE: 37; HAND
MOVEMENTS: 11; HEAD
MOVEMENTS: 48; HEARTBEAT: 3;
INNOCENCE: 22; JOY: 5;
JUMPING: 9; LANDSCAPES: 10;
LAUGHTER: 41; MEN AND
WOMEN: 26; MOVEMENT: 76;
MUSIC: 7; PAIN: 35; POSTURE: 2;
PREPAREDNESS: 7; RAIN: 2;
REALIZATION: 4; RESERVE: 15;
ROOMS: 25; SILENCE: 52; SKY:
40; SOFTNESS: 4; STARS: 15;
THUNDER AND LIGHTNING: 7;
TREES: 30; WALKING: 9; WIND:
38; WORD(S): 10

Mansfield, Stephanie
SKIN: 65

March, William
FINGERS: 15; VIOLENCE: 25

Marie, Queen of Romania
GOVERNMENT: 13

Markham, Beryl
ADVANCING: 11; ANGER: 17;
BLINDNESS: 14;
BOREDOM/BORING: 4;
BRIGHTNESS: 18; BURST: 4;
CLARITY: 29; CLEANLINESS: 19;
COLDNESS: 50; COURAGE: 12;
CRUELTY: 27; DAY: 44;
DISAPPEARANCE: 48;
DISINTEGRATION: 51; DISPERSAL:
3, 8; ENERGY: 32; FEAR: 8, 80;
FRIENDSHIP: 10; GLITTER AND
GLOSS: 17; GOSSIP: 8; GREEN: 10;
HEAD MOVEMENTS: 36; HEAT:
26; IMMOBILITY: 22;
IMPOSSIBILITY: 31; LANDSCAPES:
2, 41; LAUGHTER: 80; LEGS: 35;
LOOKS: 4; MUSCLES: 5, 9;
NIGHT: 11; PATIENCE: 12;
PHYSICAL APPEARANCE: 53;
PRIDE: 24; PROTRUSION: 1;
RELIABILITY/UNRELIABILITY: 8;
RESERVE: 10; ROCKING AND
ROLLING: 26; SHADOW: 5;
SHAPE: 30; SIGHS: 7; SKY: 14;
SOFTNESS: 46; STRAIGHTNESS: 5;
TREMBLING: 43; WALKING: 27;
WHITE: 35

Marlow, Christopher
ALONENESS: 31

Marmion, Shackerley
JOY: 10; LOVE: 60

Marquand, John P.
DARKNESS: 36

Marquis, Don
BLUE: 16; DISAPPEARANCE: 115;
GLOOM: 20; GRINS: 4; IDLENESS:
12; LIFE, DEFINED: 34; LOVE: 12;

15; TENSION: 35; TREES: 37;
TURNING AND TWISTING: 2;
UNCERTAINTY: 16; VOICE,
HARSH: 4

Matthews, William
FACE(S): 4; FOG: 17

Matthiessen, Peter
BODY: 33; EMPTINESS: 43; FEAR:
11; SLEEP: 31; STOMACH: 20

Maucaulay, Thomas Babington
SILENCE: 93

Maugham, W. Somerset
ABANDONMENT: 7, 22; ART AND
LITERATURE: 18; ATTENTION: 39;
BEARING: 6;
BEGINNINGS/ENDINGS: 18;
BEHAVIOR: 43; BIRDS: 19; BODY:
56; BREASTS: 21; BRIGHTNESS:
45; CLARITY: 40; CLOUD(S): 29;
COMPLEXION: 16;
CONVERSATION: 33; CRUELTY:
20; DAY: 36; DEJECTION: 27;
DISINTEGRATION: 29; DULLNESS:
31; ELUSIVENESS: 17; ENERGY:
30, 31; EYE(S): 32; FACIAL
EXPRESSIONS, SERIOUS: 11;
FACIAL SHAPE: 22; FAME: 9;
FLEXIBILITY/INFLEXIBILITY: 17;
FOOD AND DRINK: 40; FUTILITY:
8; GAIETY: 20; HELPLESSNESS:
38; MONEY: 17; MOON: 23;
MOUTH: 26; OBVIOUSNESS: 23;
PASSION: 15; PEACEFULNESS: 29;
PEOPLE, INTERACTION: 2;
PERSONALITY PROFILES: 22, 42;
PHYSICAL APPEARANCE: 7;
PLACES: 26; POETS/POETRY: 18;
PROFESSIONS: 9; RAIN: 44, 58;
READERS/READING: 1;
REALNESS/UNREALNESS: 1;
SCREAMS: 6; SEASCAPES: 17;
SILENCE: 57, 88; SKIN: 21; SKY:
3; SLEEP: 36; SOUL: 5; TIME: 32;
WRINKLES: 34;

TIMELINESS/UNTIMELINESS: 18;
TREES: 62; VOICE(S): 63; VOICE,
EFFECT OF: 9; YOUTH: 5

Maupassant, Guy de
ANGER: 24; ATTRACTIVENESS: 2;
BALDNESS: 24; BELIEF: 21;
COMPLEXION: 12; CORRECTNESS:
6; CRYING: 25; FLOWERS: 31;
GLOOM: 29; HAND(S): 1; LIFE:
18; LOVE: 71; LOVE, DEFINED:
39; RAIN: 12; SOFTNESS: 3;
SUDDENNESS: 8; TASTE: 22-c;
VIOLENCE: 20; VOICE(S): 20

Maurois, André
ART AND LITERATURE: 22;
CONVERSATION: 35; COURAGE:
25; MARRIAGE: 56; SILENCE: 21

Maxwell, A. E.
AIR: 27; ANTICIPATION: 1;
BIRDS: 29; COLORS: 7; DESIRE: 6;
DULLNESS: 36; EMPTINESS: 2;
EYE(S): 24; FUTILITY: 9;
LIES/LIARS: 22; PAIN: 37;
PROPRIETY/IMPROPRIETY: 3;
ROAD SCENES: 6; SINGING: 14;
VANITY: 3

Mayakovsk, Vladimir
CRITICISM, DRAMATIC AND
LITERARY: 12

Maynard, Richard
ANIMALS: 7; ARM(S): 18; BODY:
41; DANGER: 10; DEJECTION:
126; HOPE: 17; MEMORY: 24;
SEASCAPES: 8; THOUGHTS: 22;
VOICE, HARSH: 52

McBain, Ed
AWKWARDNESS: 5; BEHAVIOR:
19; BLUE: 1; CLINGING: 62;
PERMANENCE: 6; GREEN: 2;
HAND MOVEMENTS: 9;
INCOMPLETENESS: 3; LOOKS: 66;
MADNESS: 7-c;
USEFULNESS/USELESSNESS: 10;
VAGUENESS: 17

McCaig, Donald
BEHAVIOR: 58; CALMNESS: 55;
CLOSENESS: 29; COLORS: 22;
COMFORT: 2; EMOTIONS: 66;
ENTHUSIASM: 10; EYE(S): 54; EYE
EXPRESSIONS, MISCELLANEOUS:
40; EYE MOVEMENTS: 19;
FACE(S): 44; FACIAL COLOR: 34;
FOG: 16; FROWNS: 14; GLITTER
AND GLOSS: 20, 44; HAIR
STYLES: 3; HAND MOVEMENTS: 6,
14; LAUGHTER: 17, 81;
LIGHTNESS: 15; LOVE, DEFINED:
49; MOVEMENT: 75; MUSIC: 2;
PAIN: 25; PURPOSEFULNESS: 1;
PURSUIT: 20; SMELL: 33;
SMOOTHNESS: 16; SNOW: 39;
TALKATIVENESS: 6; WORD(S): 51

McCarthy, Eugene
CONVERSATION: 52;
POLITICS/POLITICIANS: 25

McCarthy, Mary
ACTIVENESS: 17; ALONENESS: 46;
ATTENTION: 23; ATTRACTION:
10; BEHAVIOR: 17, 50; BROWN:
17; DANGER: 9;
DISAPPOINTMENT: 9; EYE COLOR:
31; GLOOM: 4; GROANS AND
WHISPERS: 1;
INAPPROPRIATENESS: 25;
INTENSITY: 11; LOOKS: 11;
MANKIND: 35; MEMORY: 25;
RISK: 6; SADNESS: 8; SCRUTINY:
12; SHAME: 15;
SOCIABILITY/UNSOCIABILITY: 1;
VOICE(S): 66; VOICE, HARSH: 31;
WALKING: 28;
WRITERS/WRITING: 3

McCarver, Tim
TOUGHNESS: 15

McClatchy, J. D.
ROOMS: 1; SEX: 18

McCorquodale, Robin
CRYING: 27; DESIRE: 9; GLITTER
AND GLOSS: 14

McCoy, Larry
CHANGE: 14

McCullers, Carson
CITY/STREETSCAPES: 12;
HEART(S): 14; NOISE: 80;
PHYSICAL APPEARANCE: 80;
RICHES: 13; ROCKING AND
ROLLING: 11; SUN: 3;
TALKATIVENESS: 29; TEARS: 30

McDermott, Alice
AIMLESSNESS: 9; ALONENESS: 47;
BEHAVIOR: 22; AVAILABILITY: 7;
BENDING/BENT: 7;
BOREDOM/BORING: 1; COLORS: 4,
20; CURIOSITY: 4; DANGER: 29;
EMOTIONS: 21; FACE(S): 99;
FACIAL DETAILS: 26; FACIAL
EXPRESSIONS, MISCELLANEOUS:
91; FURNITURE AND
FURNISHINGS: 5, 39; HISTORY: 2;
HOPE: 20; LOVE: 14; MIST: 5;
MOON: 63; MOVEMENT: 41;
PHYSICAL APPEARANCE: 30;
SADNESS: 17; SELF-CONFIDENCE:
7, 16; SHYNESS: 6; SITTING: 38;
SOFTNESS: 14; STOMACH: 13;
TEETH: 5; VEHICLES: 10; VOICE,
HARSH: 22; WRINKLES: 2;
WRITERS/WRITING: 2

McDonald, Gregory
DULLNESS: 43; FEAR: 65;
SCRUTINY: 16

McFadden, Robert D.
RICHNESS: 1

McFee, William
BUSINESS: 4

McGahern, John
CONVERSATION: 9; EASE: 35;
OPEN/SHUT: 19; RAIN: 13, 65;
SCRUTINY: 16

McGinley, Phyllis
BIRDS: 14; COMMONPLACE: 18;
CONTROL: 14; DREAMS: 2; FAME:
18; HAND MOVEMENTS: 16;
LOVE: 26; OPINIONS: 11;
PARENTHOOD: 6;

McNutt, William Slavens
HAPPINESS: 43

Megged, Aharon
ADVANCING: 34; ARM(S): 31;
BENDING/BENT: 12; BLACK: 42;
CROWDS: 9; DAY: 39; EMPTINESS:
41; EXCITEMENT: 21; EYEBROWS:
53; EYE COLOR: 4; EYELASHES:
4; EYE MOVEMENTS: 1; FACIAL
DETAILS: 8; FACIAL
EXPRESSIONS, MISCELLANEOUS:
40; FEAR: 74; HAIR, CURLY: 9;
HANDSHAKE: 11; HAPPINESS: 10;
HEAT: 9; LAUGHTER: 13; LEGS:
5; PALLOR: 7; POSTURE: 3;
POVERTY: 44;
QUESTIONS/ANSWERS: 15; SHOCK:
15; SPEED: 22; VOICE(S): 5, 83;
VOICE, HARSH: 1; WEAKNESS: 25;
WHITE: 45

Meinke, Peter
AIR: 25; BIRDS: 1; EYE
MOVEMENTS: 35; FACIAL COLOR:
2; FEAR: 70; HOUSES: 13; PAST,
THE: 6; PHYSICAL APPEARANCE:
68; RESTLESSNESS: 17;
STRAIGHTNESS: 9; THOUGHTS: 4;
TONGUE: 5; VOICE(S): 51; VOICE,
MUSIC RELATED: 3

Meir, Golda
AGE: 33

Meislin, Richard J.
CROWDS: 7

Melbancke, Brian
UNDESIRABILITY: 9

Melton, John
SILENCE: 24

Melville, Herman
BEARING: 20; BELIEF: 8;
BELONGING: 3; DESTRUCTION:
11; LYING: 4; MANKIND: 4;
NOISE: 11; PALLOR: 4;
PERMANENCE: 25

Menander
WORD(S): 16

Mencius
TRUTH: 28

Mencken, H. L.
ABSURDITY: 8; ART AND
LITERATURE: 23; BELIEVABILITY:
13; CANDOR: 1; CAUTION: 27;
DEATH DEFINED: 13; FOOD AND
DRINK: 1; FUTILITY: 25;
INTELLIGENCE: 7; MEN AND
WOMEN: 40; MONEY: 8; MUSIC:
33; SHOCK: 11; TIME: 6; TRUTH:
1, 15; VANITY: 14; VIRTUE: 25

Mendelson, Edward
NOISE: 43; WRITERS/WRITING: 1

Mengers, Sue
INAPPROPRIATENESS: 6

Mercer, Johnny
CLOUD(S): 18; DAY: 19

Meredith, George
CONTROL: 15; SHYNESS: 5

Meredith, William
ACTIONS: 12; VOICE, HARSH: 12

Merkin, Daphne
BENDING/BENT: 40; CHILDREN:
20; COLDNESS: 52; COLLAPSE:
29; CRITICISM, DRAMATIC AND
LITERARY: 1; DIVERSENESS: 8;
EATING AND DRINKING: 17;
EMOTIONS: 16; EYEBROWS: 20;
EYE MOVEMENTS: 36; GROANS
AND WHISPERS: 24; HAIR
STYLES: 17; HEAD MOVEMENTS:
2; IMMOBILITY: 6; LAUGHTER:
27; LOVE: 62; MEMORY: 37; MEN
AND WOMEN: 43;
RELATIONSHIPS: 2; SMILES: 87;
SPORTS: 11; TRUST/MISTRUST: 3;
VEHICLES: 9; VOICE(S): 28;
WATCHFULNESS: 13; WRINKLES:
23

Merman, Ethel
DULLNESS: 18

Mermet, Claude
FRIENDSHIP, DEFINED: 9, 11

Merriman, Brian
POSTURE: 34

Merrill, James
REALNESS/UNREALNESS: 16
Merton, Thomas
MIND, DEFINED: 29
Mestastasio, Pietro
MANKIND: 49
Meyer, Karl E.
SUDDENNESS: 30
Meyer, Philip K.
DIFFICULTY: 45
Meyerson, Harvey
FOOTBALL: 12
Michael, David
DESTRUCTION: 34
Michaels, Leonard
BENDING/BENT: 26; CLOTHING,
ITS FIT: 16; EYELIDS: 2; HAND(S):
49; HANDSHAKE: 8; LAUGHTER:
47; SPEAKING: 8; TEARS: 28;
VOICE, HARSH: 3
Michelangelo
ALONENESS: 8
Midrash, L'Olam
ANGER: 44
Millar, Margaret
ANIMALS: 9; ARM(S): 19, 41, 45;
BALDNESS: 31; BEHAVIOR: 18;
BIRDS: 11; BREATHING: 39;
BROWN: 3; CHANGE: 6;
CITY/STREETSCAPES: 4;
CLINGING: 49; CLOTHING, ITS
FIT: 24; CONNECTIONS: 7;
DEJECTION: 1, 11; DREAMS: 16;
ENTRAPMENT: 18-c; EYE(S): 82;
EYE COLOR: 14; EYE
EXPRESSIONS, MISCELLANEOUS:
22; FACE(S): 9; FACIAL
EXPRESSIONS, BLANK: 3; FACIAL
EXPRESSIONS, MISCELLANEOUS:
78; FACIAL EXPRESSIONS,
SERIOUS: 18; FAMILIARITY: 20-c;
FIRE AND SMOKE: 20; FOG: 8;
FURNITURE AND FURNISHINGS:
18; GRAY: 13; HAIR: 11; HAIR,
CURLY: 8; HAND MOVEMENTS:
33; HEALTH: 16; HEAT: 40;

IMMOBILITY: 21; LAUGHTER: 68;
LEAVES: 37; NERVOUSNESS: 31;
NOISE: 27; PERSONALITY
PROFILES: 26; PRIDE: 6;
PURPOSEFULNESS: 12;
SEASCAPES: 16; SILENCE: 147;
SIMILARITY: 11; SKIN: 7; SMELL:
31; SPREADING: 18; SUN: 89;
SWEAT: 31, 32; TOBACCO: 26;
TREMBLING: 14; TRUTH: 17;
UNSTEADINESS: 13; VOICE,
EFFECT OF: 5, 13; VOICE, MUSIC
RELATED: 25; WORD(S): 21;
WRINKLES: 6; WRINKLES: 35
Millay, Edna St. Vincent
CLARITY: 6; DISAPPEARANCE:
83; HABIT: 8; LIFE: 10; MEMORY:
90, 94; NIGHT: 23; PEOPLE,
INTERACTION: 21; SHINING: 14;
VOICE, HARSH: 24; YELLOW: 10
Miller, Allan
ATTRACTION: 18
Miller, Arthur
ARM(S): 30; ATTENTION: 19;
EYE(S): 61, 109; FEAR: 58;
OCEANS/OCEANFRONTS: 33;
PASSION: 21; PRESENT, THE: 2;
SKIN: 14
Miller, Bryan
COLORS: 6; EYE EXPRESSIONS,
MISCELLANEOUS: 28; FOOD AND
DRINK: 28
Miller, Henry
CRYING: 1; INTENSITY: 9;
SAFETY: 4; SHAPE: 19
Miller, James
SIMILARITY: 5
Miller, Joaquin
LIFE, DEFINED: 1
Miller, Nolan
LEGS: 16
Miller, Sue
BREASTS: 52; NOSES: 10
PHYSICAL APPEARANCE: 60; SEX:
19

Author Index

SNOW: 2, 12; STORIES: 4;
STORIES: 10; TALKATIVENESS: 31;
THOUGHTS: 20; TREMBLING: 10;
TRUST/MISTRUST: 24; TURNING
AND TWISTING: 23; VIBRATION:
4, 13; VOICE, MUSIC RELATED:
6, 10, 23; WORDS OF PRAISE: 5

Oldham, Archie
SPORTS: 25

Oldham, John
PERMANENCE: 12

Olds, Sharon
EYE EXPRESSIONS,
MISCELLANEOUS: 35; FACIAL
COLOR: 25; FACIAL DETAILS: 17;
FINGERS: 6; FIRMNESS: 16;
FRAGILITY: 30; FURNITURE AND
FURNISHINGS: 28; HABIT: 13;
HEART(S): 11; HELPLESSNESS: 26;
HOUSES: 4; IMMOBILITY: 32;
INSULTS: 30; JUMPING: 7;
PATIENCE: 6, 10; SMOOTHNESS:
43; THINNESS: 59; WORDS OF
PRAISE: 13

Olsen, Merlin
CALMNESS: 43

Olsen, Paul
HEAD MOVEMENTS: 4

O'Malley, Austin
CHANGE: 25; GRIEF: 27;
POLITICS/POLITICIANS: 18;
REVENGE: 3;
USEFULNESS/USELESSNESS: 25

O'Malley, Pat
SPEECHMAKING: 12

O'Neill, Eugene
AGILITY: 25; SMILES: 37

O'Neil, Paul
LAWYERS: 1

Ooka, Shohei
NATURE: 40

Orwell, George
CRITICISM, DRAMATIC AND
LITERARY: 9; WORDS, DEFINED:
17; WRITERS/WRITING: 41

Osborn, Linda Barret
PERSISTENCE: 9

Osborne, John
FUTILITY: 23

Ostrovsky, Alexander
GOVERNMENT: 24

Otis, Amos
BASEBALL: 26

Otway, Thomas
DESIRABILITY: 16

Ouida
ATTRACTION: 28; BRIGHTNESS:
43; EYE(S): 23; FAMILIARITY: 23;
FLEXIBILITY/INFLEXIBILITY: 9;
GLITTER AND GLOSS: 2, 40;
MEMORY: 11; MUSIC: 19;
PALLOR: 34; RARITY: 35;
SILENCE: 127

Overbury, Sir Thomas
PAST, THE: 11

Ovid
LOVE: 47

Owens, Wilfred
EVIL: 16; FINGERS: 30

Owens, William A.
SCREAMS: 10

Oz, Amos
BEHAVIOR: 61; BENDING/BENT:
25; EYE MOVEMENTS: 21;
FACE(S): 33; FACIAL
EXPRESSIONS, SERIOUS: 26;
LIGHTING: 1; NOISE: 60; RAIN:
10, 41; RELIGION: 36; SADNESS:
2; VOICE, HARSH: 7

Ozick, Cynthia
BRIGHTNESS: 42; BROWN: 12;
COMPLEXION: 5; CRITICISM: 13;
EMPTINESS: 53; EYE(S): 65; EYES,
BRIGHT: 33; EYE EXPRESSIONS,
MISCELLANEOUS: 3; FACIAL
EXPRESSIONS, SERIOUS: 16; FEAR:
9; FINGERS: 12; FIRE AND
SMOKE: 4; FOOD AND DRINK:
26; HEAD(S): 3, 5; HEAVINESS:
12; IRRITABLENESS: 8;
LANGUAGE: 15; NOISE: 59;

SMILES: 88; SPEECH PATTERNS: 16; STARES: 5; STRAIGHTNESS: 14; THOUGHTS: 54

Probst, Bethamy
ATTRACTIVENESS: 13; CRITICISM, DRAMATIC AND LITERARY: 15

Prochnow, Herbert V.
GLOOM: 27; TRUENESS/FALSENESS: 3

Proffitt, Nicholas
ALONENESS: 9; ARM(S): 9; DISINTEGRATION: 13; EXCITEMENT: 6; EYE EXPRESSIONS, MISCELLANEOUS: 48; FACIAL EXPRESSIONS, BLANK: 24

Prome , Richard
BALDNESS: 18

Pronzini, Bill
DIFFICULTY: 18; FIRE AND SMOKE: 13; FOREHEAD: 13; RAIN: 36

Proust, Marcel
ALONENESS: 37; BLUSHES: 8; BOOKS: 30; CLOTHING: 45; FACIAL EXPRESSIONS, BLANK: 12; GOSSIP: 29; MOON: 60; SITTING: 41; YELLOW: 11

Proverbs, Misc.
ABSURDITY: 3, 5, 9, 10, 11, 12, 13; ANGER: 5, 6; ADVANTAGEOUSNESS: 5; ADVERSARY: 3; ADVICE: 1; AGE: 24, 50; ART AND LITERATURE: 34; BEARING: 35; BEAUTY: 25; BEAUTY, DEFINED: 20; BOOKS: 7; CHILDREN: 5; CLOSENESS: 25; COLDNESS: 34; CONSCIENCE: 2; COURAGE: 29; CREDIT: 5, 9; DIFFICULTY: 40, 41, 42; EASE: 9; EDUCATION: 12; ELUSIVENESS: 1; ENTRAPMENT: 22; EVIL: 9; FAME: 10; FIGHTING: 15; FLATTERY: 8; FOOD AND DRINK: 11; FOOLISHNESS: 10; FORGIVENESS: 1;

FORTUNE/MISFORTUNE: 7, 8, 14, 24; FRAGILITY: 38; FRIENDSHIP: 11, 16; FRIENDSHIP, DEFINED: 5, 8, 24, 32; FUTILITY: 18; GAIETY: 3; GREATNESS: 6; HAPPINESS: 16, 44; HARMLESSNESS: 6; HEAD MOVEMENTS: 26; HOPE: 23-c; HUNGER: 8; IGNORANCE: 7; IMPOSSIBILITY: 27, 36, 38; JOY: 17; JUSTICE: 1; KISSES: 21; KNOWLEDGE: 1; LAUGHTER: 59; LAWS: 12-c; LIES/LIARS: 16; LIFE: 32; LIFE, DEFINED: 24, 31, 36, 45, 49; LIGHTING: 25; LOVE: 61, 72; LOVE, DEFINED: 16, 46; MANKIND: 21; MARRIAGE: 18, 24; MARRIAGE: 32; MEMORY: 64; MEN AND WOMEN: 1, 52; PAIN: 22; PARENTHOOD: 9, 16; PEOPLE, INTERACTION: 19; POSTURE: 9; PRIDE: 17; PROBLEMS/SOLUTIONS: 3; PROMISE: 1, 5, 6; RICHES: 10; SLANDER: 3; SPEAKING: 20; TACT: 8; TEARS: 46; UNCERTAINTY: 3, 5-c; UNDESIRABILITY: 24; VIOLENCE: 26; WISDOM: 2, 9, 18; WORDS, DEFINED: 2; WORLD: 10

Puffendorf, Baron Samuel von
DIFFICULTY: 3

Purdy, James
COLLAPSE: 26

Pushkin, Alexander
BLUE: 21; FAME: 6; FEAR: 10

Puttnam, David
PLACES: 30

Puzo, Mario
FACIAL EXPRESSIONS, SERIOUS: 13

Pym, Barbara
BEHAVIOR: 54; CLOTHING, ITS FIT: 12; GROWTH: 2; HAIR: 61; JUMPING: 19; LEGS: 13; RELIABILITY/UNRELIABILITY: 23

Read, T. Buchanan
CLINGING: 25
Read, Herbert
DEATH: 7; LIFE: 9; LINGERING:
13; SUN: 79; TEETH: 25
Reade, Charles
ADVICE: 7; ENTHUSIASM: 20
Reagan, Ronald
ECONOMICS: 1, 5; GOVERNMENT:
6, 20
Rechy, John
BIRDS: 6; CHEEKS: 13; CLOTHING
ACCESSORIES: 7; DEJECTION: 17;
FACIAL EXPRESSIONS,
MISCELLANEOUS: 70; FACIAL
EXPRESSIONS, SERIOUS: 21;
FLOWERS: 18; FURNITURE AND
FURNISHINGS: 37; LEAVES: 16;
MOUNTAINS: 14; MUSCLES: 10;
NIGHT: 9; REAPPEARANCE: 6;
SILENCE: 60; SKIN: 2; SKY: 12;
THICKNESS: 9; THUNDER AND
LIGHTNING: 9; TOBACCO: 3;
TREES: 42, 72
Reed, Douglas
PLACES: 40
Reed, Ishmael
PERVASIVENESS: 2
Reed, Rex
EYE EXPRESSIONS,
MISCELLANEOUS: 67; EYELASHES:
3; EYE MOVEMENTS: 14;
GENTLENESS: 1; MOUTH: 6;
PERSONALITY PROFILES: 40;
PERSONALITY PROFILES: 57, 63;
PHYSICAL APPEARANCE: 20;
POPULARITY: 2; TOUGHNESS: 9;
VOICE, HARSH: 45; VOICE, WEAK:
9
Reed, Thomas B.
POLITICS/POLITICIANS: 3
Reese, William
PURSUIT: 17
Reeve, F. D.
AGE: 11; BLACK: 38; BLINDNESS:
15; COLDNESS: 26; DISCONTENT:

10; MOUTH: 36; RAIN: 5; SLEEP:
18; SOFTNESS: 32; SPEED: 26;
VISIBILITY: 16
Reeve, James
PERSISTENCE: 17
Reid, Alastair
AGE: 5; ROCKING AND ROLLING:
23
Reid, Barbara
BREATHING: 34; DAY: 28; LIFE:
11
Reidinger, Paul
CLINGING: 29; DESIRE: 3;
GLOOM: 5; MARRIAGE: 57;
SPEAKING: 18; SPEED: 31
Reik, Theodore
MEMORY: 52; PROFESSIONS: 14
Reiss, James
LEAVES: 12; LIFE: 16; RED: 2;
SKY: 18, 47; SMILES: 28; SNOW:
8; TRUENESS/FALSENESS: 14
Remarque, Erich Maria
AGE: 20; ANGER: 32; ANIMALS:
18; ARM(S): 20; AVAILABILITY:
13; BALDNESS: 27; BEHAVIOR:
12; BENDING/BENT: 19; BREASTS:
8; BUSYNESS: 21; CALMNESS: 38;
COLLAPSE: 5, 55; CRUELTY: 24;
CRYING: 9, 24; CURIOSITY: 5;
DARKNESS: 31; DECREASE: 8;
DEJECTION: 31; DISPERSAL: 20;
EMPTINESS: 20; EYE(S): 95, 96;
EYE COLOR: 5; EYELIDS: 13;
FACE(S): 69; FACIAL
EXPRESSIONS, MISCELLANEOUS:
92; FACIAL EXPRESSIONS,
SERIOUS: 8; FOG: 12; GRINS: 18;
HOUSES: 34; HUNGER: 6, 18;
LANDSCAPES: 32; LAUGHTER: 38;
LOOKS: 39; MEMORY: 88; MOON:
39, 47; MUSIC: 18; NATURE: 45;
NECK: 5; NIGHT: 18;
OBVIOUSNESS: 25; PAUSE: 15;
PHYSICAL APPEARANCE: 12;
PHYSICAL FEELINGS: 24;
PREPAREDNESS: 11; RAIN: 54;

Rives, Amelie
SERIOUSNESS: 15

Robbins, Tom
BEHAVIOR: 46; CRIME: 6; DAY:
5; EATING AND DRINKING: 8;
EYE EXPRESSIONS,
MISCELLANEOUS: 1; FOOD AND
DRINK: 7; HAIR COLOR: 12;
HEARTBEAT: 24; HOUSES: 31;
IDEAS: 34; KISSES: 15, 16;
LAUGHTER: 10; LIFE, DEFINED:
35; LIGHTING: 18; MADNESS: 7-c;
MOON: 12, 36; MOVEMENT: 36,
61; NOISE: 19, 58; PROTRUSION:
1; ROAD SCENES: 27; ROOMS: 8;
SMILES: 74; SPREADING: 16; SUN:
72; TEARS: 10; THINNESS: 13,
55; TREMBLING: 47; VAGUENESS:
8; VIBRATION: 9; VOICE(S): 38;
WEAKNESS: 31

Roberts, Charles G. D.
TIME: 55

Roberts, Kenneth L.
DIFFICULTY: 34

Roberts, Phyllis
BIRDS: 42; PEACEFULNESS: 11

Roberts, Steven V.
POLITICS/POLITICIANS: 29

Robertson, Don
DAY: 14; ORDER/DISORDER: 22;
SMILES: 75

Robertson, F.W.
LIFE: 20

Robertson, William
CLEANLINESS: 12

Robinson, Edward Arlington
FUTILITY: 9; PEACEFULNESS: 15

Robinson, Jill
EMOTIONS: 14

Robinson, Edwin Arlington
BEHAVIOR: 25

Robison, James
ARM(S): 3

Roche, Henri-Pierre
BREATHING: 23; GROWTH: 50;
MEN AND WOMEN: 27; PEOPLE,
INTERACTION: 12; STUPIDITY: 12

Roche, John
WORK: 8

**Rochefoucauld, François, duc de
La**
AGE: 30; CRUELTY: 12; ERRORS:
2; LOVE: 40, 55, 77, 48;
PASSION: 19

Rodgers, W. R.
CONTEMPT: 9; SNOW: 59

Rodrigue, Chi Chi
GOLF: 9

Roethke, Theodore
CRYING: 20; FIRMNESS: 40;
FRESHNESS: 13; IMMOBILITY: 37,
55; JUMPING: 13; LIGHTNESS: 7,
17, 19; SLEEP: 26; SLEEP: 18;
SOFTNESS: 27

Rogers, Jane
PAIN: 56

Rogers, Samuel
PURITY: 9

Rogers, Thomas
ADVICE: 11

Rogers, Will
BELIEF: 3; POLITICS/POLITICIANS:
2, 6, 14, 16; PROFESSIONS: 13;
TACT: 2

Rogers, Jane
SILENCE: 138

Rolland, Romain
PASSION: 13

Romains, Jules
RAIN: 61

Rooney, Andy
CORRESPONDENCE: 8

Roosevelt, Franklin D.
GOVERNMENT: 2; PEACEFULNESS:
16, 17

Roosevelt, Theodore
HEALTH: 6; LIFE: 5; STRENGTH:
12; WEAKNESS: 21

Russell, John
DECREASE: 14
Russo, Richard
DISAPPEARANCE: 69; PONDS
AND STREAMS: 1
Rybako, Anatoly
BLUSHES: 3
Sabin, Edwin L .
TONGUE: 1
Sacks, Oliver
HEALTH: 10
Sackville-West, Vita
AGILITY: 16; AMBITION: 1;
ATTRACTION: 9; CLEANLINESS: 6;
CONTROL: 7; GOSSIP: 16; GREEN:
6; HAIR: 31; IMPOSSIBILITY: 30;
LOVE: 66; MUSCLES: 16;
OCEANS/OCEANFRONTS: 24;
PARENTHOOD: 13; POVERTY: 4;
REPUTATION: 10; SOFTNESS: 18;
TREMBLING: 68;
TRUST/MISTRUST: 2;
WRITERS/WRITING: 62
Sadi
CLOSENESS: 28; LIES/LIARS: 28,
29; TRAVEL: 5
Safer, Morley
AGE: 41
Safire, William
PROTRUSION: 3; STUPIDITY: 19
Sagan, Françoise
DISAPPEARANCE: 73
St. Augustine
EVIL: 1
Saint Clement
RICHES: 17
Saint-Éxupéry, Antoine de
CALMNESS: 10; GOSSIP: 1
St. Germaine, Representative
SPORTS: 9
St. John
HAIR COLOR: 23
St. John, Henry, (Viscount Bolinbroke)
CHARACTERISTICS, NATIONAL: 24

St. Johns, Adela Rogers
EMOTIONS: 55; LEGS: 8; SMILES:
68
Sala, George Augustus
LIFE, DEFINED: 19
Salacrou, Armand
ILLNESS: 6
Salamon, Julie
CLOTHING: 30; PERSONALITY
PROFILES: 81; PHYSICAL
APPEARANCE: 45
Salinger, J. D.
CONTEMPT: 6; PAIN: 1;
POPULARITY: 4; SMELL: 7
Salten, Felix
FLOWERS: 19; SUN: 64
Saltus, Edgar
AFFECTION: 8;
USEFULNESS/USELESSNESS: 2
Sams, Ferrol
DISHONESTY: 7
Sandberg-Diment, Erik
COMMONPLACE: 15; GOSSIP: 1;
IDEAS: 28
Sandburg, Carl
BRIGHTNESS: 50; BUSYNESS: 11-c;
CALMNESS: 36, 41; CERTAINTY:
50; CLEANLINESS: 17, 20;
ENTRANCES/EXITS: 17;
FEROCITY: 3; LANGUAGE: 9;
MATHEMATICS AND SCIENCE: 1;
MEMORY: 42; PAST, THE: 17;
QUESTIONS/ANSWERS: 2;
REAPPEARANCE: 3; ROCKING
AND ROLLING: 28; SILENCE: 41-
c; SLOWNESS: 12
Sandburg, Helga
CHEEKS: 11; FACE(S): 77; HAIR: 5
Sandel, Cora
SIGHS: 15; SKY COLOR: 9;
STRAIGHTNESS: 17
Sandler, Corey
AWKWARDNESS: 14
Sandy, Stephen
SMILES: 82

Schiller, Friedrich von
CALMNESS: 21; MANKIND: 15
Schlafly, Phyllis
MARRIAGE: 39
Schmidt, Ray n.d.
WEARINESS: 18
Scholes, Percy A.
MUSIC: 20
Schoonover, Shirley, W.
CONVERSATION: 44; TONGUE: 3
Schopenhauer, Arthur
AGE: 22; APPRECIATION: 32;
GREATNESS: 14; LIFE: 4, 26;
OPINIONS: 6; RELIGION: 10;
RESTLESSNESS: 14; STAGE AND
SCREEN: 10; UNSTEADINESS: 18;
YOUTH: 12
Schulberg, Budd
CONSCIENCE: 10
Schurz, Carl
BELIEF: 12
Schwartz, Delmore
ABSURDITY: 25; AGE: 43;
AIMLESSNESS: 8; ANXIETY: 3;
AWKWARDNESS: 1-c;
CLEVERNESS: 12; CLOUD(S): 38;
DAY: 13; DISAPPEARANCE: 51;
DISCOMFORT: 8; DIVERSENESS: 3;
ELUSIVENESS: 2, 30;
ENTRAPMENT: 4; FACIAL
EXPRESSIONS, MISCELLANEOUS:
81; FAME: 4; FUTILITY: 28;
HAPPINESS: 14; IMMOBILITY: 23;
KISSES: 23; LEGS: 24;
LINGERING: 7; LYING: 7, 16;
MEMORY: 86; MIND, DEFINED: 1;
MORALITY: 8; MOUNTAINS: 8;
MUSIC: 26; NATURE: 23; NOISE:
36; OPINIONS: 2; PAIN: 42; PAST,
THE: 19; PERMANENCE: 36;
PERSONALITY PROFILES: 73;
POETS/POETRY: 10, 17; PONDS
AND STREAMS: 5, 7;
PURPOSEFULNESS: 13, 20; RAIN:
46; REALIZATION: 8;
RELATIONSHIPS: 5; SLOWNESS:

25; SUN: 28; SWEETNESS: 7;
TREES: 33; VANITY: 8; WIND: 27;
WRITERS/WRITING: 10
Schwartz, Lynne Sharon
ABSURDITY: 15; ANGER: 2;
ANGER: 41; ATTRACTION: 8;
BEHAVIOR: 39; COMFORT: 21;
DISAPPEARANCE: 100; DREAMS:
3; EDUCATION: 26; FACIAL
EXPRESSIONS, MISCELLANEOUS:
84; FACIAL EXPRESSIONS,
SERIOUS: 3; HEAT: 30; IDEAS: 15;
INTELLIGENCE: 11; LAUGHTER:
85; LINGERING: 1;
LOYALTY/DISLOYALTY: 5, 10;
OPINIONS: 13; PAST, THE: 20;
PEOPLE, INTERACTION: 29;
RESERVE: 18; ROCKING AND
ROLLING: 22; SILENCE: 17;
SINGING: 16; SMELL: 38; SNOW:
27; TRANSIENCE: 6; VOICE,
HARSH: 54; WATCHFULNESS: 9-c;
WORD(S): 20
Schwartz-Borden, Gwen
CORRESPONDENCE: 7
Sciller
CLINGING: 43
Scott, Justin
VOICE(S): 35
Scott, Sir Walter
ADVANCING: 29; AGE: 24-c;
ALERTNESS: 18; BARENESS: 3;
BUSYNESS: 20; CLEANLINESS: 11;
CREDIT: 2; DARKNESS: 16;
GLITTER AND GLOSS: 27;
IRRITABLENESS: 6; PALLOR: 31-c;
PEOPLE, INTERACTION: 37;
PHYSICAL APPEARANCE: 15;
POVERTY: 6-c;
RELIABILITY/UNRELIABILITY: 11;
SILENCE: 131-c; SPEED: 36
Scott, Temole
SPEED: 88
Scully, Vin
BASEBALL: 7

Seale, Jan Epton
CALMNESS: 34

Seaman, Barbara
FAME: 17

Seaman, Donald
ADVANCING: 4; ADVANCING: 21;
ALERTNESS: 5; BEWILDERMENT:
11; BLACK: 14; BREATHING: 52;
CAUTION: 18; CHIN: 13;
CLEVERNESS: 17; ADVANCING: 4,
21; ALERTNESS: 5;
BEWILDERMENT: 11; BLACK: 14;
BREATHING: 52; CAUTION: 18;
CHIN: 13; CLEVERNESS: 17;
COLDNESS: 11; COLLAPSE: 68;
DISPERSAL: 13; EASE: 25;
ENTRAPMENT: 24; EXITS: 6; EYE
EXPRESSIONS, MISCELLANEOUS:
24, 39; FINGERS: 13;
LANDSCAPES: 15; LIES/LIARS: 10;
LIGHTING: 11; POWER: 29; RAIN:
43; REALIZATION: 10;
REPUTATION: 16; RESERVE: 16;
RUNNING: 6; SILENCE: 98, 116;
SKY COLOR: 3; SOFTNESS: 8;
SPEECH PATTERNS: 12;
SPREADING: 34; TIME: 11;
VEHICLES: 7; VOICE, HARSH: 20

Searls, Hank
AFFECTION: 10; GLITTER AND
GLOSS: 58; ROCKING AND
ROLLING: 21

Sedgewick, Ellery
CHILDREN: 19

Sedley, Sir Charles
CLOSENESS: 8

See, Carolyn
MADNESS: 6

Segal, Erich
LOOKS: 14

Segur, Joseph Alexandre Pierre
LOVE: 31

Seidel, Henry
WRITERS/WRITING: 5

Seifert, Jaroslav
FURNITURE AND FURNISHINGS:
7; KISSES: 25; LIFE: 45; LOVE:
48; MEMORY: 91; POETS/POETRY:
7; SKIN: 57; STARS: 6

Selden, John
CONSCIENCE: 12; PRIDE: 8;
SPEECHMAKING: 1

Selz, Thalia
TENSION: 3

Selzer, Joanne
GLOOM: 6; TRANSIENCE: 11

Selzer, Richard
AGE: 15; DEATH: 26;
DESIRABILITY: 20

Seneca
LIFE, DEFINED: 48; WORD(S): 2

Seneca The Elder
LIFE, DEFINED: 33;
PROBLEMS/SOLUTIONS: 6

Serling, Robert J.
FACIAL EXPRESSIONS, BLANK:
14; LIPS: 6; SUN: 51; WRINKLES:
49

Service, Robert W.
SUN: 18

Setanti, Joaquin
CONVERSATION: 12

Settle, Elkanah
COURAGE: 7

Settle, Mary Lee
BEAUTY: 10; COMFORT: 11; EYE
EXPRESSIONS, MISCELLANEOUS:
11; HEALTH: 23; PHYSICAL
APPEARANCE: 11, 63; SILENCE:
35; SUDDENNESS: 25; VISIBILITY:
5; WEAKNESS: 29

Sexton, Anne
ARM(S): 27; BIRTH: 1; BURST: 6;
CONVERSATION: 56;
DISAPPEARANCE: 12; GUILT: 3;
HEARTBEAT: 6; IMMOBILITY: 46;
INNOCENCE: 15;
OCEANS/OCEANFRONTS: 4, 12,
21; PERSISTENCE: 25; RAIN: 25;
SOFTNESS: 15; SPEED: 44;

Smith, Logan Pearsall
WRITERS/WRITING: 1

Smith, Martin Cruz
ARM MOVEMENTS: 4;
AWKWARDNESS: 16; DRINKING:
17; EYEBROWS: 24; GROANS AND
WHISPERS: 14; HAIR TEXTURE:
31; HEAD MOVEMENTS: 42;
MONEY: 7; REAPPEARANCE: 13;
ROAD SCENES: 13; SILENCE: 6,
122; SNOW: 48; THUNDER AND
LIGHTNING: 15; VOICE, EFFECT
OF: 11; WATCHFULNESS: 7;
WIND: 40

Smith, Pauline
VOICE(S): 18

Smith, Stevie
ART AND LITERATURE: 8;
CALMNESS: 30-c; PALLOR: 37;
PROPRIETY/IMPROPRIETY: 5;
RISING: 19; TEARS: 17;
THINNESS: 45; THOUGHTS: 40

Smith, Sydney
BELIEF: 27; CORRESPONDENCE:
1; HANDWRITING: 2; HUMOR:
12; KNOWLEDGE: 5; MARRIAGE:
20; OPINIONS: 3; PERSONALITY
PROFILES: 39;
PROBLEMS/SOLUTIONS: 17;
STANDING: 5; TALKATIVENESS:
19; WIT: 11

Smollett, Tobias
GREED: 7; MANNERS: 16; WIT: 2

Snodgrass, W. D.
ABUNDANCE: 14; ANGER: 43;
BELIEVABILITY: 8; BLACK: 33;
BREATHING: 45; CONTROL: 8;
DARKNESS: 9; DISAPPEARANCE:
79; DRYNESS: 15-c; FATNESS: 29;
FEAR: 66; FRAGILITY: 39; PAUSE:
14; ROCKING AND ROLLING: 3;
ROOMS: 34; SLOWNESS: 32;
SOFTNESS: 40; TREES: 26;
TREMBLING: 53; WALKING: 38;
WRINKLES: 51

Socrates
FLATTERY: 16

Solotaroff, Ted
WRITERS/WRITING: 5, 63

Solovyou, Vladmir and Elena
POWER: 33

Solzhenitsyn, Alexander
CLOUD(S): 21; FOREHEAD: 12;
TURNING AND TWISTING: 19

Somer, W.
MEN AND WOMEN: 60

Somerhausen, Zevi Hirsch
WRITERS/WRITING: 2

Sommer, Elyse
ABUNDANCE: 23; ACTIVENESS: 2;
ADVERSARY: 1; ANXIETY: 6;
ATTRACTION: 1; BELIEVABILITY:
2; BLACK: 11, 12; BREVITY: 8,
10; BRIGHTNESS: 29, 30;
CHEERFULNESS: 20; CLINGING:
61; COMFORT: 5;
COMMONPLACE: 11;
COMPATIBILITY: 3, 9;
COMPETITION: 4; COMPLETENESS:
31; COST: 7; CRUELTY: 33;
CURIOSITY: 7; DECREASE: 22;
DISAPPEARANCE: 18;
DISCOMFORT: 11; DISCONTENT:
14; DISINTEGRATION: 24;
GAIETY: 6, 13; IMMOBILITY: 4;
IMPOSSIBILITY: 5, 9;
INAPPROPRIATENESS: 3;
INAPPROPRIATENESS: 19;
IRRITABLENESS: 1; LOOKS: 45;
NATURALNESS: 21; NOISE: 54;
OBVIOUSNESS: 18; OPINIONS: 5;
ORDER/DISORDER: 19;
ORIGINALITY: 6, 8; PAIN: 46;
PERMANENCE: 32; RARITY: 12,
27, 31; REJECTION: 2; SILENCE:
146; SPREADING: 20, 29; TASTE:
22; UNDESIRABILITY: 6, 26, 30;
VANITY: 18; WEARINESS: 27

Sommer, Mike
ABSURDITY: 20; ANXIETY: 8;
AVAILABILITY: 2; CANDOR: 3;

Author Index

Steffens, Lincoln
ART AND LITERATURE: 4

Stegner, Wallace
ACTIVENESS: 14; ADVANCING: 13; ALERTNESS: 20; ANGER: 3; BRIGHTNESS: 25; CLEANLINESS: 5; DAY: 6, 17; DISCONTENT: 6; EMOTIONS: 2; FACE(S): 43; FACIAL EXPRESSIONS, MISCELLANEOUS: 34, 45; FAMILIARITY: 2; GROANS AND WHISPERS: 11; HAIR: 64; HANDSHAKE: 5; HEAT: 16; LEAVES: 33; LOOKS: 24, 25; MOON: 52; NERVOUSNESS: 11; NOISE: 16; PAST, THE: 16; PERSISTENCE: 2; POVERTY: 3; PURITY: 12; PURPOSEFULNESS: 17; REGULARITY/IRREGULARITY: 10; RELIABILITY/UNRELIABILITY: 1; ROAD SCENES: 20; ROOMS: 28; SMELL: 10; SUN: 6; VAGUENESS: 6; VOICE, MUSIC RELATED: 5; WRINKLES: 47-c

Steinbeck, John
AGITATION: 30; EYEBROWS: 22; EYE EXPRESSIONS, MISCELLANEOUS: 17; FLOWERS: 17; MOVEMENT: 9; PLACES: 1; POSTURE: 7; SPREADING: 32; WRITERS/WRITING: 37

Stendhal
LOVE, DEFINED: 35, 44-c

Stern, Isaac
GROANS AND WHISPERS: 25

Stern, James
EXITS: 10; HAIR TEXTURE: 24, 39; HAND(S): 25; OCEANS/OCEANFRONTS: 26; PHYSICAL FEELINGS: 35; SKY COLOR: 15; VOICE, MONOTONOUS: 1; WORDS, EFFECT OF: 9

Stern, Steve
CHEEKS: 2

Sterne, Laurence
BITTERNESS: 14; FAME: 24; PAIN: 38

Sterngold, James
PROBLEMS/SOLUTIONS: 22

Stevens, James
GROANS AND WHISPERS: 23

Stevens, Wallace
ACTIVENESS: 14; BARENESS: 16; CLOUD(S): 12; COLDNESS: 44; DAY: 11, 25; DISINTEGRATION: 23; EMOTIONS: 12; FRAGILITY: 29; FROWNS: 8; GROWTH: 17; HUNGER: 2; MEN AND WOMEN: 22; MOON: 17; MOVEMENT: 18, 52; NATURE: 11; NIGHT: 24; OPINIONS: 3; PEACEFULNESS: 1; SITTING: 44; SNOW: 26, 60; STARS: 11; STRENGTH: 10; SUCCESS/FAILURE: 25; TALLNESS: 9; THOUGHTS: 37, 41; TREES: 54, 71; WEATHER: 11; WIND: 29, 46

Stevenson, Adlai
FLATTERY: 12; POLITICS/POLITICIANS: 12

Stevenson, Robert Louis
ACTIVENESS: 12; CITY/STREETSCAPES: 18, 22; CONVERSATION: 22, 28, 39; CRUELTY: 6; DESTRUCTION: 32; EYE(S): 70; FACE(S): 4; FACIAL COLOR: 15; FEAR: 6; HEALTH: 5; HEALTH: 15; LIFE: 12; LOVE: 68; LOVE, DEFINED: 47; MANKIND: 51; MARRIAGE: 38; PASSION: 16; PLEASURE: 15; QUESTIONS/ANSWERS: 25; STORIES: 1; WATCHFULNESS: 3-c

Stewart, Fred Mustard
EMOTIONS: 3

Stewart, Mary
FLOWERS: 27; IMMOBILITY: 42; KINDNESS: 23; LOOKS: 72; MEMORY: 27; MOON: 50;

Author Index